THE SOCIOLOGY PROJECT

Introducing the Sociological Imagination

THE SOCIOLOGY PROJECT

Introducing the Sociological Imagination

FROM THE

NEW YORK UNIVERSITY DEPARTMENT OF SOCIOLOGY

JEFF MANZA	COLIN JEROLMACK
RICHARD ARUM	ERIC KLINENBERG
LYNNE HANEY	STEVEN LUKES
VIVEK CHIBBER	GERALD MARWELL
TROY DUSTER	HARVEY MOLOTCH
PAULA ENGLAND	ANN MORNING
KATHLEEN GERSON	CAROLINE H. PERSELL
JEFF GOODWIN	PATRICK SHARKEY
GUILLERMINA JASSO	FLORENCIA TORCHE
JENNIFER L. JENNINGS	LAWRENCE L. WU

Boston   Columbus   Indianapolis   New York   San Francisco   Upper Saddle River   Amsterdam
Cape Town   Dubai   London   Madrid   Milan   Munich   Paris   Montréal   Toronto   Delhi
Mexico City   São Paulo   Sydney   Hong Kong   Seoul   Singapore   Taipei   Tokyo

Editorial Director: Craig Campanella
Editor in Chief: Dickson Musslewhite
Acquisitions Editor: Brita Mess
Assistant Editor: Seanna Breen
Editorial Assistant: Joseph Jantas
Director of Development: Sharon Geary
Senior Development Editor: Lisa McLellan
Senior Development Editor: Deb Hartwell
Director of Marketing: Brandy Dawson
Marketing Manager: Jessica Lasda
Marketing Assistant: Frank Alarcon
Managing Editor: Denise Forlow
Production Liaison: Barbara Reilly
Senior Manufacturing and Operations Manager for Arts and Sciences: Mary Fischer
Operations Specialist: Alan Fischer
Interior and Cover Design / Design Manager: John Christiana
Cover Illustrator: Max-o-matic/Máximo Truja

Cover Photo: Background wall: Jon Helgason/Alamy; Sidewalk background: Mary Rice/Shutterstock; Soccer player: Aflo Foto Agency/Alamy; Man with cane: Paul Maguire/Alamy; Tai Chi man: Robert Harding Picture Library Ltd./Alamy; Young rockers: rgbstudio/Alamy; Asian couple: TongRo Images/Alamy; Doctors: Image Source/Glow Images; Yoga woman: Edvard March/Corbis/Glow Images; Woman in striped shirt: Bill Sykes/Cultura/Glow Images; Male couple: Kablonk/Glow Images
Digital Acquisitions Editor: Debbie Coniglio
Digital Media Director: Brian Hyland
Digital Media Editor: Rachel Comerford
Digital Media Project Manager: Nikhil Bramhavar
Full-Service Project Management: PreMediaGlobal
Printer/Binder: RR Donnelley & Sons Company
Cover Printer: Lehigh-Phoenix Color
Text Font: Adobe Caslon Pro 10.5/13

Credits and acknowledgments borrowed from other sources and reproduced, with permission, in this textbook appear on appropriate page within text (or on page A-27).

Library of Congress Cataloging-in-Publication Data

Manza, Jeff.
  The Sociology Project : Introducing the Sociological Imagination / From the New York University
    Department of Sociology ; Jeff Manza [and nineteen others].—1st edition.
      pages cm
  Includes bibliographical references and index.
  ISBN-13: 978-0-205-09382-3
  ISBN-10: 0-205-09382-5
  1. Sociology.   I. New York University. Dept. of Sociology.   II. Title.
  HM585.M3456 2013
  301—dc23   2012026698

10 9 8 7 6 5 4 3 2

Student Edition ISBN 10: 0-205-09382-5
ISBN 13: 978-0-205-09382-3

Books à la Carte Edition ISBN 10: 0-205-09428-7
ISBN 13: 978-0-205-09428-8

BRIEF CONTENTS

CONTENTS

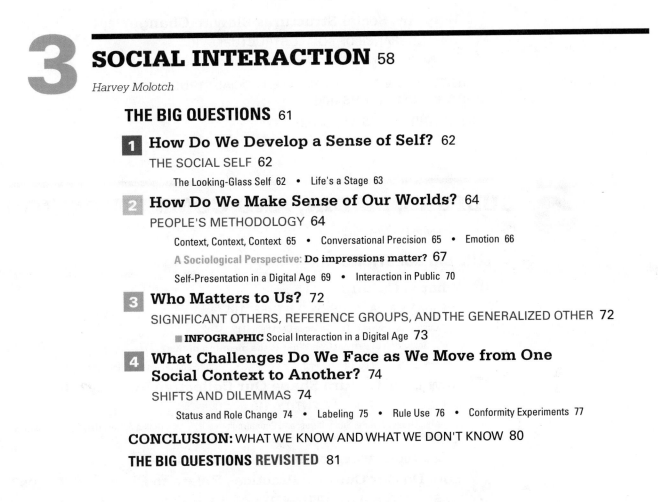

3 SOCIAL INTERACTION 58

Harvey Molotch

4 SOCIAL STRUCTURE 84

Jeff Manza with Harel Shapira

5 CULTURE, MEDIA, AND COMMUNICATION 110

Eric Klinenberg with David Wachsmuth

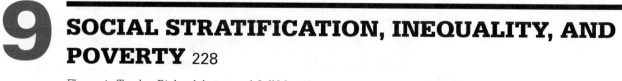

RACE AND ETHNICITY 260

Ann Morning, with Nandi E. Dill, Rachel Garver, and John Halushka

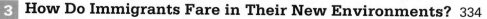

13 FAMILIES AND FAMILY LIFE 348

Kathleen Gerson with Stacy Torres

16 CRIME, DEVIANCE, AND SOCIAL CONTROL 442

Troy Duster and Jeff Manza

19 POPULATION, AGING, AND HEALTH 536

Lawrence L. Wu and Jennifer L. Jennings

PREFACE

In *The Structure of Scientific Revolutions*, his famous study of the history of science, Thomas Kuhn argued that introductory textbooks are inevitably the most backward part of any scientific field. He suggested that because they seek to appeal to the lowest common denominator to maximize their audience, they reproduce out-of-date ideas and findings far removed from the cutting-edge of knowledge. Even worse, Kuhn argued, they tend to reinforce popular but out-of-date dogmas that stand in the way of progress. Worst of all, they provide beginning students an entirely misleading view of the discipline. When it comes to sociology textbooks, Kuhn's claim is reinforced because of the simple fact that sociology is such a wide-ranging discipline, with many rich subfields of scholarship and knowledge. No one author (or small team of authors), however well-meaning and determined, can possibly attain mastery of the whole discipline and convey that knowledge to students.

We created this new introductory book in the hopes of overcoming the problem Kuhn so famously identified, and offer up to our beginning students a new kind of textbook. Our aim is nothing less than to reinvent the introductory sociology textbook. We envision an entirely new kind of introduction to the discipline, one that draws on the collective wisdom of a large, successful sociology department and its faculty to bring to our students and readers the real excitement of each of the main subfields of sociology. Rather than reproducing what is said in existing textbooks, as so often happens, the chapters in this book are freshly authored by one or more faculty members from the New York University sociology department who write and teach in the area. In this way, we seek to bring together the best of sociology as a discipline with the challenge of reaching our students.

At the center of this book is a set of tools for learning how to ask hard questions about the world around us. These tools are what we call, following C. Wright Mills, the "sociological imagination." In every chapter, we draw upon contemporary research findngs, those of our colleagues and in many cases our own, to puzzle through how individuals are shaped by the contexts in which they live and act. We treat social norms, organizations, institutions, and global dynamics as a linked set of puzzles to explore. Rather than simply giving answers, we suggest a set of questions that sociological research poses. We do not suggest that all of the answers are at hand, but we show how and in what ways sociologists and other social scientists struggle to answer them. If nothing else, we hope that our readers will take away from this book a new determination to question things.

The proceeds from this book will be reinvested in the graduate and undergraduate sociology programs at NYU, and used to support minority graduate student fellowships. We have deliberately entitled the book *The Sociology Project Project* both to reflect our commitment to a collective agenda of our field as an evolving project, and to signal our intention to continue to develop the book in future editions as sociology itself evolves. New findings, theories, and ideas are constantly being developed. Our book will evolve as that research develops in new directions, and we look forward to revising our ideas and questions as the evidence suggests we should. But perhaps most importantly, we think of *The Sociology Project* as a dialogue with our readers – including both our students and our colleagues around the country. We invite you to engage and challenge us where we come up short, tell us what we are doing wrong, and share ideas you have for the presentation of sociology as a field.

Jeff Manza for the NYU Sociology Department
New York City
August 2012

Acknowledgements

Writing a textbook takes a village, as they say, and we have been blessed with a strong and committed team of colleagues, friends, graduate students and editors to pull the book together. Our first and most important debt is to the truly wonderful team at Pearson Education, who have thrown themselves into a new and untested project with conviction and determination. Our image of corporate publishers has been completely transformed by this experience. In particular, Dickson Musslewhite and Brita Mess, the Editor-in-Chief and Acquisitions Editor for Sociology at Pearson, respectively, embraced our project from the beginning, got if off the ground, and stayed in good spirits as we progressed, unevenly, towards completion. They were wonderfully supportive and helpful at every stage. Our development editors Lisa McLellan and Deb Hartwell have done a masterful job, wrestling 20 different chapters written by different authors, into a coherent whole. Often working under considerable time pressure, they kept track of and resolved an endless array of problems and issues as we moved along. The rest of the Pearson team also deserves our gratitude: Sharon Geary, Seanna Breen, Rachel Comerford, Kelly May, Jessica Lasda, Denise Forlow, Barbara Reilly, Blair Brown, John Christiana, Kathie Foot, Karen Noferi, Ben Ferrini, Martha Shethar, and Joe Jantas. We are also thankful for the help of Melissa Sacco, Jen Nonenmacher, Liz Kincaid, and the rest of the team at PreMediaGlobal.

At NYU, we have a number of debts to acknowledge. Joe Juliano, formerly the Dean of Business Affairs at the College of Arts and Sciences, now the Vice Provost for Strategic Planning, connected us to Pearson through a personal relationship with Tim Bozik, the CEO of Pearson US Higher Ed. Joe also provided early advice on the project in a number of ways. In the Sociology Department, several wonderful staff members played key roles in the book. The extraordinary Chloe Anderson served as the Managing Editor of the project and ran it to perfection, turning the impossible to the possible with hard work and subtle organizational acumen. As we were nearing completion, Chloe left for graduate school at Columbia, but we had the good fortune to be able to replace her with the brilliant Poulami Roychowdhury, a PhD student in Sociology who will soon make her own mark on the discipline. In addition to co-authoring a couple of chapters, Harel Shapira provided critical help and advice on many of the chapters while managing to finish his own important book on immigration politics. Writing a book in the way that we did, with the full involvement of the faculty of the Sociology Department, allowed us to draw on the great wealth of intellectual resources of a first-rate group of undergraduate and graduate students. A number of them co-authored chapters and are identified there. Others did critical work behind the scenes, and we can only thank them here: Jonah Birch, Mark Cohen, Nandi E. Dill, Francesco Findeison, Jennifer Heerwig, Julian Jurgenmeyer, Noah McClain, Joshua Musoulf, Ihsan Sadi, Harel Shapira, David Wachsmuth, Christine Baker-Smith, Abby Larson, Michael McCarthy, Max Besbris, Rachel Garver, John Halushka, Leslie-Ann Bolden, Carse Ramos, Stacy Torres, Abigail Weitzman, Shelly Ronen, Adam Murphree, Julia Mendoza, Rene Rojas, Catherine G. Cochran, Emily Rauscher, Eyal Press, Albert Yin, and Madhavi Cherian.

As drafts of the book began to appear, we received exceptional help and guidance from an editorial board assembled by Pearson. Most authors find the "advice" of external reviewers to be more of a pain in the neck than useful feedback, but in this case the final book was genuinely and often critically improved by the generous help we received from our anonymous editors. Often working on short deadlines, every chapter benefitted from their feedback, and we thank them all of them for their help: Angie Beeman, Borough of Manhattan Community College; Karen Bradley, University of Central Missouri; Jim Castleberry, University of South Dakota; Karen Done, Coahoma Community College; Richard Jones, Marquette University; Hence Parson, Hutchinson Community College; Janice Purk, Mansfield University; Rachel Schneider, University of Akron; David Townsend, Ivy Tech Community College; and Thomas Waller, Tallahassee Community College.

How can MySocLab help me succeed in this course?

MySocLab for *The Sociology Project* provides all the tools you need to engage each student's sociological imagination before, during, and after class. An assignment calendar and gradebook allow you to assign specific activities with deadlines and to measure your students' progress throughout the semester.

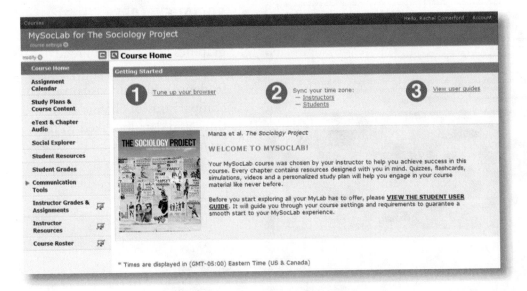

- The **PEARSON eTEXT** lets students access their textbook anytime, anywhere, and any way they want, including listening online.

- A **PERSONALIZED STUDY PLAN** for each student, based on Bloom's Taxonomy, arranges content from less complex thinking—like remembering and understanding—to more complex critical thinking—like applying and analyzing. This layered approach promotes better critical-thinking skills, and helps students succeed in the course and beyond.

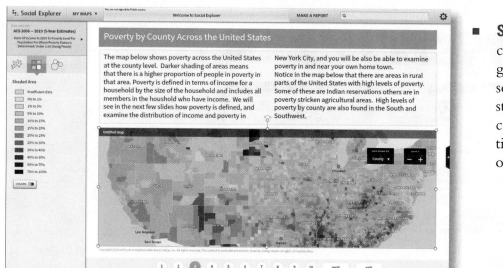

- **SOCIAL EXPLORER** activities connect to the chapter infographics as well as to broad sociological topics, engaging students with data visualizations, comparisons of change over time, and data localized to their own communities.

- **INSPIRING YOUR SOCIOLOGICAL IMAGINATION, APPLYING YOUR SOCIOLOGICAL IMAGINATION,** and **BIG QUESTIONS VIDEO ACTIVITIES** quiz students on the concepts covered in each video and provide opportunities for students to upload and share their own videos.

How can I interact with sociological data to see what's happening in the world, the nation, and in my own community?

The new Social Explorer allows students to easily engage with sociological data to see concepts in action, change over time, and local statistics.

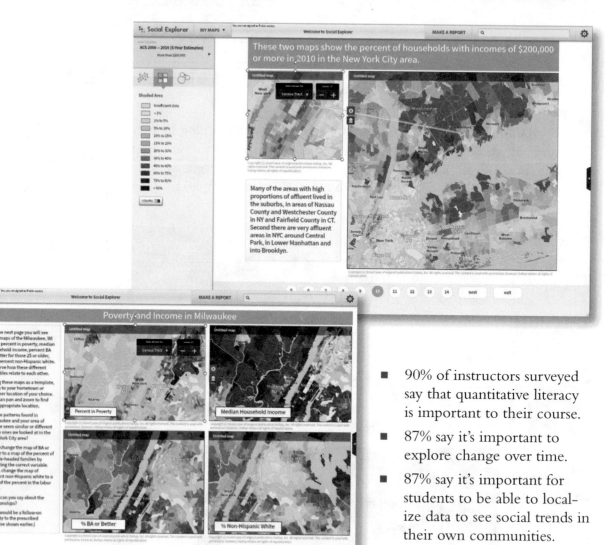

- 90% of instructors surveyed say that quantitative literacy is important to their course.
- 87% say it's important to explore change over time.
- 87% say it's important for students to be able to localize data to see social trends in their own communities.

Working with data starting in 1790 up until today, Social Explorer employs information from the U.S. Census, American Community Survey, General Social Survey, CIA World Factbook, and more.

Students are just as excited about the new Social Explorer as instructors:

"It's fantastic that it's all in one spot. I think it will be huge for citing in papers... it's awesome."

"The fact that we don't have to extrapolate all of the Census data, that that's compiled for us, that's amazing."

Useful as a presentation tool in the classroom and a homework tool after class, Social Explorer includes a number of assignments that introduce students to important concepts in sociology using real-world data.

THE SOCIOLOGY PROJECT includes 40 assignments unique to this program that draw from The Big Questions and infographics in each chapter.

Instructors and students can build their own presentations in Social Explorer utilizing interactive maps, charts, and graphs. Full presentations as well as individual maps and graphs can be exported to PowerPoint or image files.

1

THE SOCIOLOGICAL IMAGINATION

((•)) **Listen** to the **Chapter Audio** in **MySocLab**

by JEFF MANZA, LYNNE HANEY, and RICHARD ARUM

 ho are we? When we are asked to describe ourselves, we tend to think in terms of our individuality: our likes and dislikes, our interests and skills. But what about the time and place we live in or the family we were born into? We are also products of these contexts, as well as of the relationships we had growing up, our neighborhoods and communities, the schools we attended, the jobs we've had, the organizations we belong to, and so forth. We are individuals, but we are also *social* individuals, connected to other people in a variety of different ways.

The social nature of our lives is becoming increasingly clear in recent years. In 2004, Harvard undergraduate Marc Zuckerberg created a website originally intended for students at Harvard to make such social connections with each other. The idea caught on like wildfire, and the social networking site Facebook was born. Facebook is a worldwide phenomenon with hundreds of millions of registered users that allows us to link to and communicate with "friends" (actual or "virtual" friends) and create or join communities of users. Through these networks, individuals become linked together.

Facebook is extremely popular in part because of its wide variety of uses. As the TV show *Entertainment Weekly* jokingly put it, "How on earth did we stalk our exes, remember our co-workers' birthdays, bug our friends, and play a rousing game of Scrabulous before Facebook?" But Facebook is much more than that. Although the Facebook founders were not

MY SOCIOLOGICAL IMAGINATION
Richard Arum

I grew up as a white privileged Jewish kid in the suburbs of New York, but in a manner a little different than the norm. While my friends were surrounded with adult role models who were in professional fields such as law and medicine, I grew up connected to a broader set of individuals, including cultural icons and civil rights heroes such as Muhammad Ali. This early personal exposure shaped who I was and the choices I would end up later making as an adult.

In the years following, I received a teaching certificate from Harvard University and subsequently worked as a teacher in a segregated public high school in Oakland, California. In that institutional setting, in order to make sense of the dysfunction of the school as an organization as well as the impact that the school was having on the lives of the students, I increasingly was drawn to asking sociological questions of the world. In order to move beyond simply asking these questions, I enrolled at the University of California, Berkeley—coincidentally joining my coauthors on this chapter, Lynne and Jeff, who were also training in the Department of Sociology there—with the objective of developing sociological tools and skills to better understand the problems around schooling in America. Developing a sociological imagination for me was an attempt to develop a set of analytical competencies to participate actively in policy discussions that could substantively improve the outcomes of youth.

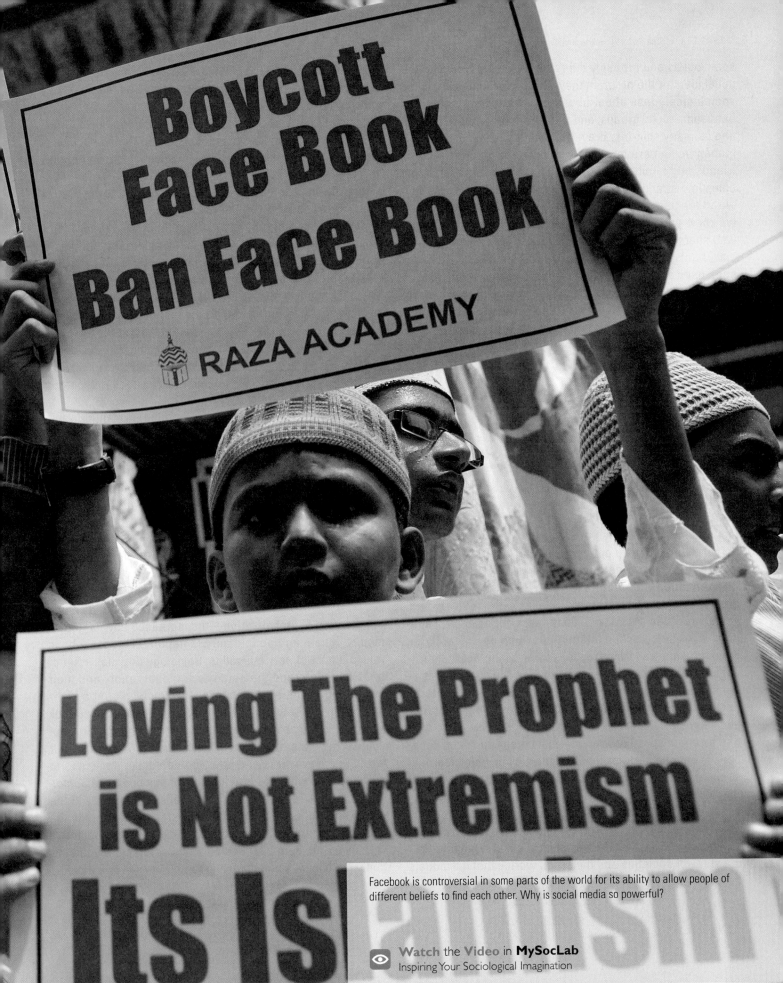

Boycott Face Book Ban Face Book

RAZA ACADEMY

Loving The Prophet is Not Extremism Its Islamism

Facebook is controversial in some parts of the world for its ability to allow people of different beliefs to find each other. Why is social media so powerful?

Watch the Video in **MySocLab**
Inspiring Your Sociological Imagination

sociologists and probably didn't realize it, in developing the initial idea for the program they drew upon some very basic sociological ideas about how **social networks**, or the ties between people, groups, and organizations, work. Facebook and its many spin-offs draw from the sociological idea that human beings are not simply individuals with a few close friends and family members who otherwise only randomly bump into strangers in the course of their daily lives. Rather, we all are part of otherwise hidden social networks in which we know people who know other people we don't know but who share some important traits with us (like common interests, backgrounds, areas of expertise, and so forth). Facebook uses an algorithm that makes these normally hidden connections between people suddenly visible. Your friends' friends can now become your "friends" as well. If you identify a particular interest, say in an obscure band, religion, TV show, or political group, you will be prompted to connect to other individuals with similar interests.

Facebook's success in connecting networks of like-minded people has been sufficiently powerful that some governments and citizens around the world have attempted to curtail its use out of fear that it can help people create and spread antigovernment ideas or mobilize groups of citizens to protest in the streets. In the last couple of years, for example, Facebook has been blocked in countries such as China, Syria, Pakistan, and Iran. In other, less threatening but still critical ways, Facebook appears to change the nature of relationships, making it much easier to develop new contacts as well as to keep in touch with old friendships even after people geographically drift apart.

The entire social networking phenomena, of which Facebook is but one part, exemplifies one way in which learning sociological ideas can help us better understand some of the ways that our own existence is dependent on our relationships with others. Hidden in our individual biographies is a story about **society**, a large group of people who live in the same area and participate in a common culture. **Sociology**—the study of societies and the social worlds that individuals inhabit within them—faces the specific challenge of trying to uncover and analyze the patterns that lie beneath the surface of these social worlds for individual lives.

Sociologists are keen to explore phenomena like Facebook, which raises fundamental issues about the social aspect of our lives, but the insights of sociologists do not end there. Sociologists are also asking hard questions about the future of social networking and its implications for how individuals and societies relate to one another. These include: How has new technology changed the form, content, and character of friendship? How has the emergence of online dating changed the nature of intimate relationships? How has technology changed the way work is organized, how we find employment, and what kinds of jobs are likely to be available in the future? Is the new technology helping governments spy on their citizens or helping citizens better monitor their governments and exercise their democratic rights?

The digital revolution has facilitated and deepened long-standing patterns of global interaction. In recent decades, sociologists have begun to think about how what happens in any one society is influenced by the rest of the world. Sociology has always drawn upon cross-national comparisons and explored how societies differ, but theories of **globalization**—the increased flow of goods, money, ideas, and people across national borders—have raised a host of new questions. Sociology provides a set of tools to understand the patterns of globalization, and their impact, on societies and individuals. You won't get a high-paying job in international finance simply because you took a course in introductory sociology (or read this book!), but you *will* have the tools to think hard about how and why our world is the way it is and how you can make decisions to navigate its challenges. We have titled this book *The Sociology Project* to reflect the idea that constant changes in the world around us make life, and the study of sociology, an ongoing project. We invite you to explore sociological ideas with us in this book, to develop your sociological imagination, and to join us and others in participating in this project.

> # The entire social networking phenomena exemplifies one way in which learning sociological ideas can help us better understand some of the ways that our own existence is dependent on our relationships with others.

THE BIG QUESTIONS

👁 **Watch** the **Big Question Videos** in **MySocLab**

Each chapter in this book identifies a set of questions that have defined the research and teaching puzzles of that topic. These questions organize each chapter and provide a lens for exploring sociological thinking about each topic we cover. In starting from questions, not answers, and puzzling together in the search for answers, you will learn to think sociologically. In this first chapter, we will explore the following questions:

How can a sociological imagination help you better understand your world? In this section we introduce the concept of the sociological imagination and explore how it helps us learn to ask hard questions.

Why do social contexts matter? Sociology is fundamentally concerned with how we are influenced by society. All of us are situated in an array of social contexts. How do these influence us and our behavior?

Where did sociology come from, and how is it different from the other social sciences? Here we examine the context in which sociology began to develop and explore the question of how sociology "fits" into, and relates to, the other social sciences.

How can this book help you develop a sociological imagination? Our goal for this book is to provide enough background on the key areas and findings of sociological research in foundation for you to develop your own sociological imagination.

1 How Can a Sociological Imagination Help You Better Understand Your World?

THE SOCIOLOGICAL IMAGINATION

◉ **Watch** the **Big Question Video** in **MySocLab**

Sociology since its inception has puzzled over how we are connected to each other in the world. These relationships shape not only how our individual lives unfold but also how we come to understand them. This book aims to assist you in developing a sociological imagination that will provide you with a scientifically informed understanding of the social aspects of your life. A **sociological imagination** is the capacity to think systematically about how many things we experience as *personal* problems—for example, debt from student loans, competing demands from divorced parents, or an inability to form a rewarding romantic relationship at college—are really *social* issues that are widely shared by others born in a similar time and social location as us. The sociologist C. Wright Mills (1916–1962), who coined the term in 1959, wrote that "the sociological imagination enables us to grasp history and biography and the relations between the two within society" (Mills 1959:6) To understand the world around us, and to begin to think in a deep way about how to improve it, is to recognize the extent to which our individual lives are strongly shaped by where, when, and to whom we were born and the range of experiences we have as a child, an adolescent, and later as an adult. At each stage, we are both individuals and are members of a social world. Our opportunities and potentials are always influenced by the inequalities and injustices we encounter, but understanding these requires that we think about them sociologically. In short, the sociological imagination helps us to ask hard questions and seek answers about the social worlds we inhabit.

☐ Looking through a Sociological Lens

A sociological imagination challenges some very basic impulses all of us have. The human mind wants to make sense of the world around us by seeing aspects of it, and differences in it, as somehow inevitable or natural. If we have grown up in a social context where marriage is defined as a life-long commitment between a man and a woman, we might be quick to conclude that such an arrangement was

The sociologist C. Wright Mills on his motorcycle in a famous photo. Mills coined the phrase "the sociological imagination."

People watching is an enjoyable activity and a way of beginning to exercise our sociological imagination to make guesses about people we don't know. But we may also be tempted to draw on stereotypes in making those guesses.

the way that intimate relationships were meant to be. Observing those relationships across societies and over time shows, however, that marriage is only sometimes a lifetime commitment between a man and a woman. In some contexts, intimate relationships may be between two men, or two women, or among a man and multiple women, or among a changing carousel of romantic partners. A sociological imagination helps us see the diversity of intimate relationships and question our assumptions about a particular form of marriage being natural as opposed to social in its origins.

In a similar fashion, we are also often quick to identify differences across groups of people—men and women, rich and poor, whites and other races—as inherent to characteristics of these groups. When we attach such differences to real people, it is all too easy to develop faulty generalizations, or what are known as stereotypes. **Stereotypes** are beliefs about members of a group that are usually false, or at least exaggerated, but are the basis of assumptions made about individual members of the group. For instance, some people think that older individuals are not good workers. It *is* true that at some point most of us will become too old to perform jobs that they we may have done for many years. But older workers often face active **discrimination**—which refers to any behavior, practice, or policy that harms, excludes, or disadvantages individuals on the basis of their group membership—because of their age long before they are too old to do their jobs. Many employers and fellow employees generalize from conclusions based on *some* older people (who may have reached a point where they can no longer do a certain kind of work) to *all* older workers. This example will apply to almost everyone at some point, even if it seems a long way off for many of us. But if we are reasonable lucky, we're going to get older, and when we do, we may run headlong into stereotypes about aging.

A sociological imagination also challenges such stereotypes by raising questions about where they come from, what they are based on, who stands to benefit from them, and why they are harmful. Sociology not only produces important theories and ideas, it *also* gives us tools to understand and think critically and creatively about our own lives, the times we are living in, and why we are the way we are. Possessed of a sociological imagination, we are able to be more active and effective participants in the world around us.

How can a sociological imagination help us to challenge stereotypes?

▯ Engaging Our Sociological Imaginations: Learning to Ask Good Questions

Everyone has some degree of a sociological imagination. We exercise our sociological imaginations every time we try to make sense of something in the social worlds around us. Walking through a shopping mall or going to a concert or sporting event, we observe lots of people. If we look closely, it is not hard to make educated guesses about many of these people. We can identify their gender and perhaps their age, race or ethnicity, and maybe even their religion (for example, if they are wearing some kind of identifying clothing). The way they dress may also convey something about their income (look closely, for example, at whether someone's jeans are expensive and high-fashion, or cheap knock-offs). If you hear them speak, it is not too difficult to gather even more information about them. Are they well-educated or not? Are they from a particular region of the United States, or from a foreign country, that is suggested by their accent?

When we "people watch" in this way, we are, without necessarily realizing it, beginning to engage our sociological imaginations. We are using information we know about our society to make educated guesses about the individuals we encounter. But how good are these guesses? That depends, in part, on how well we've trained our sociological imagination to look beyond our assumptions and stereotypes to search for deeper understandings. A good sociological imagination goes much further than just making broad generalizations about individuals. The well-developed sociological imagination is rich with ideas and theories about the endless complexity of the very categories in which we assign individuals. Knowing that someone is white or African American or Asian does not necessarily tell us very much about their annual income, the type of job they have, what they like to do in their spare time, whether they are hardworking or lazy, or in fact much else about them. In this sense, then, just looking at people or groups around us and making generalizations is not in and of itself an example of the use of our sociological imaginations. A sociological imagination instead requires one to ask deeper and more meaningful questions. It does not allow us to settle for simple answers in understanding human beings and the worlds they inhabit. *It is our ability to ask hard questions instead of just accepting easily available answers that is the hallmark of a good sociological imagination.*

From Personal Puzzles to Sociological Questions

All professional sociologists, including the authors of this book, have had experiences in their lives, before they began doing sociological research, where a light bulb first went off that ignited their sociological imaginations. For some it was triggered by a particular event, while for others it may have developed more slowly—a combination of things that inspired them to develop a sociological imagination. One situation that often triggers our sociological imaginations occurs when we see some kind of conventional wisdom, or widely shared assumption, as incorrect. That can literally happen at any moment, but when it does and we start to question what we observe around us, we are taking the first step towards developing a sociological imagination.

Forming Sociological Questions What are these questions? They can range from what is right before us to questions about entire societies. Here are a few examples. Consider eating at a restaurant or school cafeteria. If you look around, you probably will notice that there are relatively few, if any, groups that include both whites and blacks. Or visit a bunch of churches; you will rarely find large numbers of blacks and whites worshipping together. Why is it

FIGURE 1.1   THE RICH ARE GETTING RICHER   Income inequality is particularly great in the United States, and the divide between rich and poor is growing. While the rich are getting richer, the majority of Americans are not. In 2010, as the United States continued to recover from an economic recession, a remarkable 93 percent of the additional income created in the country that year went to the top 1 percent of taxpayers, those with at least $352,000 in income, while the bottom 99 percent received a minuscule $80 increase in pay per person.

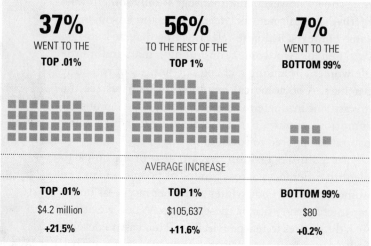

Of Total Income Increase in 2010 …

37% WENT TO THE **TOP .01%**	**56%** TO THE REST OF THE **TOP 1%**	**7%** WENT TO THE **BOTTOM 99%**
AVERAGE INCREASE		
TOP .01% $4.2 million +21.5%	**TOP 1%** $105,637 +11.6%	**BOTTOM 99%** $80 +0.2%

Source: The New York Times (2012).

that, long after major civil rights legislation has ended legal discrimination, friendship networks so rarely cross the racial divide? Or think about two-parent families you know (your own or others): How much more housework does the female member of a heterosexual couple perform? Or think about the United States. Why is it that the richest country in the world has so many people living in poverty—far more than other, less wealthy countries (see Figure 1.1)?

Thinking more generally about such questions, it is not a great leap to turn simple observations like these into broader and more profound questions for research. Sociologists have developed a set of **social theories**, or overarching frameworks that suggest certain assumptions and assertions about the way the world works, for posing such questions and evaluating evidence related to those questions. They also have developed **research methods**—ways of systematically studying these questions—in order to develop new evidence that allows new answers to be generated. While we do not just pose questions in our research, learning to ask questions about received wisdom is a key part of learning to think seriously about the world around us.

Asking questions can be dangerous. Governments often do not like it when their citizens begin to ask questions about topics government officials would prefer to keep secret. Large corporations or other organizations often do not like it when workers or members start to ask questions rather than doing what they are told. School authorities often do not like it when students, parents, or outside observers raise questions about the character and quality of student learning. It is true that questioning everything without any foundation for the questions is counterproductive; when a small child starts asking the same question over and over (Why? Why? Why?), it is a game meant to fluster adults, not produce useful knowledge. But hard questions are important, and oftentimes the world becomes a better place only when the authorities are forced to address such questions.

Sociological Questions: An Example

Sociologist Richard Arum, one of the authors of this chapter, has been carrying out a project tracking more than 2,000 young adults as they progressed through 24 diverse colleges and universities and then left college to work, live with friends, move in with romantic partners, or return to live with their parents (Arum and Roksa 2011). The students in the study had quite different college experiences and fared very differently in terms of learning outcomes. Some of these students were in college settings where they were exposed to challenging coursework and successfully moved into well-paying jobs immediately following graduation. Yet many more students did not enjoy such fates. In fact, two years out of college, 24 percent of college graduates in the study were back living at home with their parents or relatives (see Figure 1.2). What explains such differences in outcomes?

Consider the following two students tracked in the project. Maria attended a highly selective, residential liberal arts college in a small Midwestern town. She had come to college with a high SAT score and three high school Advanced Placement course credits. In college, she quickly decided on becoming a social science major after taking a small freshman seminar with a sociologist who did her research on urban youth culture. She spent a semester of her junior year abroad in Europe, and during her semesters at college she reported that she met frequently with her instructors outside of class to discuss her work and that faculty at the school had high expectations for students like her. She also reported that her classmates—many of whom she had come to know well as the college had integrated her academic program with her residential dorm—were equally encouraging of her focus on academic work; on average, she estimated devoting 20 hours per week preparing for classes, many of which in her social science major had significant reading and writing requirements. When we measured her performance on tasks that required critical thinking, complex reasoning, and written communication, her score moved up dramatically from freshman to senior year. Two years out of college, she was living with a friend she had met at college and was working at a job where she made slightly more than $38,000 per year. Although she had assumed a great deal of student debt, she was on a path to adult success.

Contrast Maria's college experiences with Robert's. Robert attended a high school that was predominantly

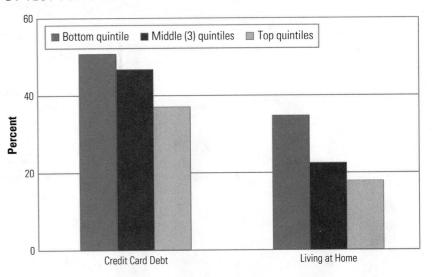

FIGURE 1.2 FORMS OF SUPPORT TWO YEARS AFTER COLLEGE BY TEST PERFORMANCE AT TIME OF GRADUATION

nonwhite before enrolling in a nonselective large public university in his state. Like many of his classmates, he entered college without any Advanced Placement coursework completed and did not score particularly well on the SAT. In college, he reported rarely meeting with his instructors outside of class. When asked about whether faculty had high expectations for students like him, he reported that they largely did not. He muddled through coursework with passing grades but did not finding his coursework either interesting or challenging; he found himself increasingly focused on socializing with his friends and earning spending money to support himself at school. Like many of his peers, he only studied about eight hours per week; when he did prepare for his classes, he often found himself doing so with his friends, who ended up frequently distracting him from really focusing on his work. During his senior year, when we tested his performance on the same tasks that Maria completed, we found no improvement in his performance after attending college for four years. He was not alone. We found slightly more than a third of students in our study demonstrating no significant improvement on a test of general skills. If he had learned subject-specific skills that were not captured well by our assessment indicator, they were not ones that were rewarded in the labor market when he graduated in 2009. Two years after graduation, he was about $30,000 in debt, unemployed, and living back at home with his parents (see Figure 1.3).

How can we understand why these two students had such different college experiences and ended up on such different postcollege paths? There are many ways in which the ideas and research of sociologists give us the tools to understand how Maria's and Robert's lives are unfolding. A sociological view of student experiences in college poses a range of questions about how individuals, institutions, and societies vary. Some of the questions sociologists might ask include: Do Maria and Robert and others like them spend less time

FIGURE 1.3 THE RISE OF STUDENT DEBT   Student Debt is on the rise. According to the Project on Student Debt, in 2009, average debt levels for graduating seniors with student loans rose to $24,000, just about double what they were in 1996.

Average Debt of Graduating Seniors at 4-Year Universities, 1996-2009

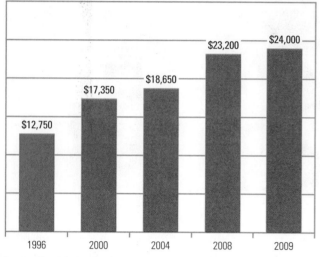

Source: The John William Pope Center for Higher Education Policy (2011).

rewire our brains and cause us to think differently. While these studies are at the cutting edge of research on education and technology, they address questions about how *individuals* think—which does not necessarily tell the whole story. What about the broader *social* factors shaping academic performance and thinking? How do our relationships with each other, as well as our participation in groups and organizations, affect how we learn and experience education? What about the even broader effects of government social policies, regulations, and laws—and the ways they can make education inaccessible or unappealing to certain social groups?

These are the questions that sociologists are particularly well equipped to explore. Because research on higher education is abundant and crosses many fields of study, new discoveries happen all the time. But some of the things that sociologists of higher education conduct research on include:

■ How do students' lives *before* college shape their experiences *in* college? We all know that freshmen enter college with quite different backgrounds. But how do those backgrounds shape students' paths through college? For instance, how does your family influence your educational experience? How does your parents' educational background influence your own education—how would being the first in your family to go to college hurt or help? What about your parents' educational expectations for you—do parents expect more from their female or male children, or from their firstborn? To return to Maria and Robert: Might Maria's parents have had particularly high expectations for her because she was the first in the family to go to college? Or might Robert have learned to value his friends over his studies well before he stepped onto a college campus—perhaps because his parents expected less from him than from his siblings?

on their studies now than students did a generation ago? And if so, why? Why are certain colleges more focused on academic learning than others? Why do some schools become known as "party schools"? And how has the nature of campus life changed in the past few decades? Are students more or less likely to join organizations or to interact with each other collectively during their college years than at other points in their life? As the ratio of male to female students on college campuses changes, how have dating and courtship patterns been altered? And is the United States alone in these changes in higher education, or are there global shifts underway to change the meaning and experience of college across national borders?

What types of questions are sociologists particularly well equipped to explore?

Our sociological questions are different from the questions asked by researchers in other academic disciplines. Psychologists who study cognition, for example, are also interested in what shapes academic achievement. Among other things, they are interested in what affects our ability to concentrate and focus for a sustained amount of time. These interests have led some to study the wiring of our brains—and how things like online media, e-mail, text messages, and Twitter updates can

The use of new technologies in everyday life raises different issues for psychologists (who are interested in how they are rewiring our brains) than sociologists, who are studying how social media is changing our connections to each other and society as a whole.

How does the social organization of college life shape students' experiences? Universities are organizations. Like other organizations, universities have their own structures, logics, and informal rules. Yet we are only beginning to understand how those structures and rules put students onto different academic paths. College is a time when students form a variety of social, cultural, and political identities. And universities play an important role in those formations—through things like class size, faculty accessibility, and study abroad programs, all of which can give students more opportunity to form academic bonds and support academic focus. Even the physical layout of campus can help or hinder the development of group interaction and identification. Back to Maria and Robert: Perhaps Maria's engagement with professors and other students had less to do with her own internal motivation and more to do with the college context that encouraged such engagement? Perhaps Robert's lackluster academic performance had less to do with his own laziness and more with the lack of supportive academic contexts at his university?

- Does the experience of college benefit everyone equally? We know that the social hierarchies of class, race, and gender shape who goes to what kind of college. But what about students' experiences in college? Are those students with more resources (money, connections, and confidence) better able to take advantage of university opportunities? Does this give them an advantage over other students? Does college life offer more privileges to those who came to school privileged? Or is college the great equalizer, as is often promised? Consider again Maria and Robert: Did their college paths simply reflect advantages they came to college with? Or did those advantages get reversed through their decisions about how to spend time while in college?

- How are students' college paths shaped by the larger labor markets awaiting students upon graduation? The U.S. economy is undergoing massive restructuring as its manufacturing sector continues to transform into service and high-tech sectors. Yet even in these expanding economic sectors, there are changes: Many jobs that once required skilled human intervention have been automated, leading to drastic reductions in the amount of human labor required. There is an international component to this. New information technology now means that many jobs can be performed anywhere in the world, even if their company headquarters remain in rich countries. How have all of these changes affected students' experiences in college? Have they made students more or less motivated in their studies? More or less optimistic about their future? Have they influenced what students major in? The kinds of clubs and organizations they join? The amount of student

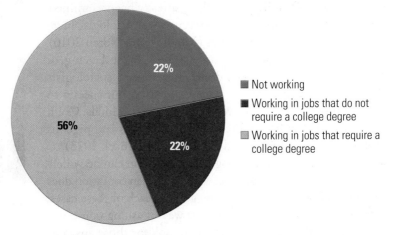

FIGURE 1.4 EMPLOYMENT STATUS OF RECENT COLLEGE GRADUATES What kind of jobs are recent college graduates getting? Fifty-six percent are working in fields that require a college degree, but 22 percent are working in fields that don't require a college degree, apparently taking jobs they are overqualified for. And the bad news is that another 22 percent are out of work altogether.

Source: John J. Heldrich Center for Workforce Development at Rutgers University (2011).

loans they are willing to take out? And once more with respect to Maria and Robert: Has the world of work changed in ways that help explain Maria's ability to secure well-paying work and Robert's postcollege unemployment? See Figure 1.4 for more information about the employment status of recent college graduates.

As these four examples suggest, sociological questions are concerned with a broad canvas of the modern world. Our questions range widely from the basic units of human life—or individuals' relationships with others—to the groups and organizations we are a part of, all the way up to a now rapidly changing global economy that is impacting all of our social relationships.

In short, the project of this book is to outline the big questions in many of the most important topics sociologists investigate. We will also suggest how sociologists and other social scientists are thinking about these but at the same time learning about the world around us. But our first big point is this: Learning how to ask the important questions, and to think hard about how to probe for answers, is the heart of the sociology project.

The Endless Reach of the Sociological Imagination

There are very few areas of life that cannot be studied sociologically. The smallest of particles, say our DNA, would appear to fall outside the sociological imagination. Not so: Sociologists like Troy Duster have studied the discovery of DNA and its political and economic ramifications, such as the idea that there is a genetic foundation to race (Duster 1990). Sociology might appear ill equipped to address the really big issues, like how world economic systems developed across time and space. That, too, has been done—40 years ago by sociologist Immanuel Wallerstein, who created an influential area of research to map the development of a world economy. What about the seemingly frivolous aspects of popular culture, like daytime talk shows? They have been studied. Or toilets? They have already been examined, although in this case only very recently by sociologist Harvey Molotch and his colleagues (Molotch and Noren 2010). Or senior proms, gay and lesbian families, ballet dancing, or street gangs? All have been done. In fact, some sociologists have even moved beyond a narrow focus on our species to study human interactions with the world of animals. Colin Jerolmack has written a book on how humans and pigeons relate to one another around the world (Jerolmack 2013).

The fact that the sociological imagination can be widely stretched to explore many aspects of the human condition does not mean, however, that anything goes. In each of these cases, sociologists draw upon a particular way of asking questions, and a set of theories about where to look for those answers, that have evolved over the past hundred years. Sociologists also deploy a common set of tools for studying those questions. In one way or another, those questions build off a common starting point: How and in what ways do social contexts matter?

Exposure to violence is another topic that has been explored by sociologists: Living in a high-crime neighborhood increases stress levels and is harmful to children in many ways.

Read the **Document** *Invitation to Sociology* in **MySocLab**.

2 Why Do Social Contexts Matter?

SOCIAL CONTEXTS: FROM INDIVIDUALS TO SOCIETY

Watch the **Big Question Video** in **MySocLab**

Sociology is fundamentally concerned with how individuals are influenced by society. The story of college students Maria and Robert provide one example. We refer to this influence of society on individuals as the **social context**. What is that context? What do we mean when we refer to it?

One way of thinking about the diverse kinds of contexts individuals face is through the following thought experiment. Imagine you are in the maternity ward of a large hospital, looking at a group of newborn babies. They are all helpless and adorable, with a full life ahead of them. In some perfect world, they would all have an equal opportunity to develop their many talents and abilities and succeed in life. In fact, we might look at those cute little creatures and think to ourselves something like "any one of these babies could one day be the president of the United States." But we know that is not really realistic. Why not?

At the core the sociological imagination is the idea that individual lives unfold in contexts—in this case, the social environments, including economic and cultural conditions, that each of these infants will live in. If we could know something about the contexts each of these infants will grow up in, we would be able to make much better-educated guesses about their prospects. What are these contexts? We can immediately identify a variety of factors that are going to influence each baby's life:

How do our families and communities shape our social development?

- the child's immediate family (past and present) and parents' education level, wealth, and income;
- the neighborhood and community the child will grow up in or will live in as an adult;
- the education the child will get (including the quality of the schools he or she will attend);
- the types of organizations (churches, clubs, or groups) the child will join or have access to and the people he or she will meet in these settings; and
- the type of employment he or she will find.

Other contexts of the birth are also important to keep in mind, such as:

- the country he or she is born into (a rich country, a poor country, or a rapidly developing country); and
- the period of history in which he or she is born.

That cute little baby will, in fact, enter a social world that will have a huge impact on where he or she ends up. Let's review these in more detail.

☐ Families and Communities as Context

We are born into families, and generations of sociological research have stressed the importance of family situation as a key to understanding how individuals develop. Our families shape who we are in a variety of ways: by giving us racial, ethnic, and religious identities; by teaching us the basic rules of society and how to behave in society or in particular social settings; through the networks parents provide us and where they have chosen to live (and thus where we grow up); by the financial resources that our parents can invest in our education as well as the emotional and cognitive capacities they have developed in us through life-long interactions; and (possibly) in the extent to which they are willing and able to help out later in life as we become adults and perhaps even attempt to raise a new generation of children of our own.

This brings a second important context into view: the neighborhood and community in which we grow up. Living in a safe neighborhood with good schools, surrounded by families who encourage their children to do well in school and to be ambitious and confident, creates a different set of pathways than that experienced by a child living in an impoverished, high-crime neighborhood with poor schools. The latter environment can have many negative consequences, including not just obvious things like the continual risk of being a victim of crime and the lack of people who can provide positive social networks, but also more subtle things like increased stress levels that may reduce sleep and school performance. Explore *A Sociological Perspective* on page 14.

For instance, in groundbreaking recent research, New York University sociologist Pat Sharkey has discovered a link between neighborhood violence and children's school performance (Sharkey 2010). He discovered that within the week following a homicide in their neighborhood, children in Chicago scored significantly lower on reading and vocabulary tests than they had in the week prior to the homicide. Amazingly, this drop occurred regardless of whether or not the children had actually witnessed or heard about the violence directly. Among other things, Sharkey's research teaches us how violence can be absorbed by and transmitted through neighborhood contexts—and how children, who are perhaps the most vulnerable to such exposure, experience their effects at school as well as home. Aside from our interest in reducing violent crime, Sharkey's work suggests we need to also think about the consequences of neighborhood violence on innocent children.

☐ Organizations and Institutions

From the families that raise us to the neighborhoods we are raised in, contexts then flow outward to the schools we attend, the occupations we enter, and the organizations where we become members. What church, synagogue, or mosque do we go to? What unions or professional associations do we join (or do we have a chance to join a union or professional association in the first place)? What clubs and political groups do we participate in? What bowling leagues, knitting circles, book clubs, or fraternities or sororities do we belong to? The doors to special opportunities that may (or may not) open for us down the road hinge partly on what kinds of groups we place ourselves in and what kinds of contacts we forge—as well as how valuable those contacts become. The same is true of the identities we form for ourselves—both our public identities, like political and religious affiliations, and our personal identities, like our sexual, gender, ethnic, or racial identifications. The organizations we are a part of shape what identities are available to us, how we value them, and why we gravitate to some and not others.

A SOCIOLOGICAL PERSPECTIVE

When you see someone begging for money on the street, what do you think?

One way to think about this particular unemployed person might be to consider his situation a personal one: He is poor and unemployed, possibly because he is lazy and didn't work hard in school. Maybe he has a bad attitude and his situation is a reflection of his personality. But putting our sociological imaginations into action requires us to look at this situation differently. It asks us to look beyond the individual and uncover this person's larger social situation.

If we use our sociological imagination to think about this person not as an individual but as part of society, we consider poverty not an individual problem but a social one. Doing so allows us to reframe the question so we no longer just ask, why is this person in this situation, but why are so many individuals in this situation? And to do this, the sociological imagination asks us to take account of context. Where is this happening? When is this happening?

How does a lack of jobs for all who need them lead to poverty and homelessness?

Where in the U.S. has the housing crisis most affected homeowners and what is the impact on those communities?

What factors cause businesses to lay off workers, or go out of business?

HUNGRY
HOMELESS
PLEASE HELP
THANK YOU
GOD BLES

How has globalization affected the U.S. economy and an individual's opportunities to find work?

⊙➤ **Explore** A Sociological Perspective in **MySocLab** and then ...

◼ **Think About It**

Unemployment rises in economic recessions, as do the numbers of families living in poverty, and many people will remain unemployed far longer than normal as a result. Is this a valid reason to support increasing the amount of unemployment insurance the government provides to those in need?

◼ **Inspire Your Sociological Imagination**

How does the knowledge that being unemployed is frequently due to forces beyond a person's control impact how we view those who live in unemployment and poverty? Why is this alternative view not mentioned in the media? How does its absence influence the way Americans think about poverty and homelessness?

Being in prison can change the way we think of ourselves, including our racial identities.

Sociologists have found that something as fundamental as our racial identity can change according to the kind of institutions where we are connected. For example, serving time in prison (where African Americans are significantly overrepresented) can actually prompt a change in one's racial identification. Sociologists recently discovered that male prisoners were more likely to identity as African American after doing time in prison or jail than before (Saperstein and Penner 2010). What's more, the researchers who interviewed these men were also more likely to define them as African American after learning they had served time—again, even when these same men had earlier been categorized as white prior to incarceration. This is a dramatic case of how deeply our sense of self is tied to the institutions in which we are a part (or, in the case of prison, the institutions from which we cannot escape).

Social and Economic Contexts

Beyond specific organizations and institutions lie the social, economic, and historical contexts of our lives. The state of the world we are born into shapes the opportunities available to us, either limiting or enabling us to pursue different goals and aspirations. An African American male born in the South in 1910 faced a very different environment than the same man would today. A child growing up in a working-class family in Detroit in the 1940s would experience a different set of economic opportunities than the same child growing up in contemporary Detroit (once the center of the automobile industry and home to a large number of high-paying working-class jobs, today the Detroit area has been hard hit by a devastating decline in the U.S. manufacturing sector). Women entering adulthood in the 1950s faced a different set of choices and cultural expectations than women currently entering adulthood. Finally, all of these contexts are influenced by a global environment. We live in an era where events in regions and countries around the world deeply influence the lives of Americans—and vice versa. In particular, many types of jobs once done in the U.S. are now performed by workers in other countries. As jobs, ideas, and technology move around the globe at an unprecedented pace, it is increasingly clear that we are connected to people and places far away. Examples like these highlight how C. Wright Mills' (1959) notion of sociology as the study of where history and biography meet comes to life.

How do the organizations and institutions we are a part of help us form our identities?

Sociology as the Study of Social Contexts

We can now define more fully and clearly what we mean by *sociology:* Sociology is the study of the diverse contexts within which society influences individuals. In order to understand those contexts, sociology ranges widely from how individual attributes (like race, class, gender, education, religion, and so on) are associated with differences in life course outcomes, all the way up to the world of politics, government policies, technology, and the global economy and environment.

At the core of social contexts is a distinction between social interaction and social structure. **Social interaction** refers to the way people act together, including how they modify and alter their behavior in response to the presence of others. Social interaction is governed by a set of **norms**, which are the basic rules of society that help us know what is and is not appropriate to do in any situation. The violation of norms of behavior will cause us all kinds of problems. As we interact with others, we engage in a process of working within those rules and norms to try to present a pleasing version of ourselves to others. Examples include our Facebook and professional website profiles, our business cards, and the different ways we characterize ourselves in social settings when we meet new people or introduce ourselves to a group. For example, the authors of this chapter are sometimes sociologists, sometimes professors, sometimes parents, sometimes politically active citizens, and sometimes various other things depending on the situation. In choosing among these identities, we are engaging with the social world. We always occupy the same body, but who exactly we are (or how we characterize ourselves) depends on the context we are in.

The importance of the "social" part of social interaction becomes most clear to us when we violate societal rules of acceptable behavior (or when we imagine the social sanctions that would follow if we did violate the rules). Consider this example. What would happen if a student in a college classroom were to suddenly stand up on her or his desk and shout profanities at the instructor or fellow students? Even if any of us might occasionally feel like doing this, there are powerful constraints that discourage such action. Without anyone saying anything, we understand that if we did this our classmates might shun us; the instructor might lower our grade or, perhaps, call campus security to escort us out of the class. So even when we are annoyed or frustrated or bored in our classes, or in similar situations like being in seemingly endless meetings or standing in long lines, we generally know to keep our true feelings to ourselves.

But even if you think there is no chance of any significant consequences, you still "know" it is wrong to be disruptive in that way. How? Sociologists argue that we censor ourselves because of our concern for the social consequences of our action. Societies develop a set of norms that typically govern our behavior. Norms gives us guidelines for our behavior; while they are generally not written down anywhere, we learn and absorb them from our interactions with important others (such as parents, friends, teachers, ministers, or mentors). Knowing what the norms of a situation are is important for avoiding embarrassment and acting appropriately in different contexts, and because most of the time we want to "fit in" wherever we find ourselves. Not knowing, or failing to act in accordance with, the norms governing the situation can be costly in either sense. Something as simple as messing up a handshake or a kiss-on-the-cheek greeting can violate norms. We have various funny phrases for when that happens—we might call it a gaffe, a mishap, a misstep, a *faux pas,* and many others—but whatever name we might use to call it, when we violate social norms we will be embarrassed and possibly sanctioned for our failures.

The complexity of the rules of social interaction has perhaps been most clearly revealed by the limits of artificial intelligence. It was the dream of a generation of computer scientists to build robots that could think and perform like human beings. But trying to program all of the rules and thought processes humans experience, even when doing the simplest of tasks or having relatively simple conversations, proved too difficult. While robots could do some tasks some of the time, they would always and inevitably make some catastrophic misjudgment. So the ambitions of the first generation of artificial intelligence (AI) researchers failed. Later, however, AI research moved on to approaches that have proved remarkably valuable, such as Internet search engines that can predict what we are looking pretty effectively and lead us to information that in the precomputer age was extremely difficult to obtain.

What is the distinction between social interaction and social structure?

Social structure, the flip side of social interaction, refers to the external forces, most notably in the social hierarchies and institutions of society. A **social hierarchy** is a set of important social relationships that provide individuals and groups with different kinds of status, in which some individuals and groups are elevated above others. The **institutions** of society—those longstanding and important practices (like marriage, family, education, and economic markets) as well as the organizations that regulate those practices (such as the government, the military, schools, and religion)—provide the frameworks for our daily lives. These external forces confront us in our daily lives and require that we work within them. These social structures are both limiting but also enabling; without them, chaos ensues. Social structures provide both order and organization, but they are often invisible. They are most obvious to us when they are absent or when they break down. In the aftermath of a catastrophic natural disaster—think of a major hurricane, tsunami, or earthquake—social structures can, at least for a period of time, disappear. There are no authorities around to tell people what to do, no police to enforce order. Rules are unclear, and everyone has to improvise. To be sure, some parts of the social structure may be visible in the ways that the poor have a much more difficult time either getting away from danger or surviving after it strikes. But it is in these moments of their absence that the power of social structures becomes most clear.

What exactly, then, is this mysterious thing called social structure? Two distinct components of social structure are, as we noted, hierarchies and institutions. Every society has at its core a set of inequalities (such as those along class, race, or gender lines), and where we stand in those hierarchies impacts who we are and what we can accomplish. Our **roles** in life—our positions within an institution or organization that come with specific rules or expectations about how to behave—are partly determined by our social standing. Institutions matter as well. Because they are not easily changed, institutions are difficult to avoid, and we frequently must answer to them. This is fairly obvious in the case of laws and the legal system but perhaps less so when we think about institutions like economic markets. But even if we try to avoid the formal institutions of the economy (such as a paid job working for a company), we will find that even the underground economy operates according to a set of rules and norms that are often not that different than those of the regular economy. Just because you sell drugs or other illegal goods does not mean that you can escape basic social rules about contracts (for example, in which buyers and sellers each make a promise to the other). Violate the implicit terms of a contract with a conventional business and you may face a lawsuit. Violate the implicit terms of a contract with an underground business and you may face a different (and possibly more dangerous) type of threat. But in either case, contract violations tend to be subject to social enforcement.

3 Where Did Sociology Come From, and How Is It Different from the Other Social Sciences?

THE SOCIOLOGY OF THE SOCIAL SCIENCES

Watch **the Big Question Video** in **MySocLab**

We can apply the sociological imagination to study many topics, including the development of sociology and the **social sciences**. To do so, we need to ask questions such as: In what context did sociology begin to develop? How does sociology "fit" into, and relate to, the other social sciences?

☐ Sociology and the Industrial Revolution

In general, sociology and other social sciences began to develop when growing numbers of people began to turn from abstract ideas or debates (like "democracy is good" or "racism is bad") to thinking about how things work in the real world and how that world could be systematically investigated. But the sociological imagination was not built overnight. In fact, traces of sociological thinking can be found everywhere people talk or think about their communities or institutions. The desire to answer hard questions about the world with something other than pure speculation lies at the heart of the modern sociological enterprise. This is the point where philosophy crosses over into sociology and social science.

The development of a new way of questioning and seeking answers to issues and problems of the modern world unfolded in fits and starts throughout the nineteenth century, but the idea that the social world could be studied with rigor and scientific methods akin to those that had been applied to nature and the natural world took hold from the 1880s onward.

What was the historical context in which sociology began to develop?

The term *sociology* is typically credited to Auguste Comte (1798–1859), who first used it in 1839. Comte thought that sociology would eventually become the ultimate science of the social world and would include both what he called "social statics" (the study of societies as they are) and "social dynamics" (the processes of social change) (Comte [1839–1853] 2009).

As time went by, a variety of different ways of studying the social world began to emerge. The lines between these social scientific disciplines were very fuzzy at first. Early social scientists often identified with several disciplines. For example, two of the most famous and influential early economists, Thorstein Veblen (1857–1929) and John Commons (1862–1945), held chairs in sociology at one point in their long and storied careers. Similarly, some of the social theorists that later influenced sociology, most notably those of philosophers Adam Smith (1723–1790) and Karl Marx (1818–1883), spent much of their time writing and thinking about the economy and economic relations. As one study of the rise of the social sciences has put it, these early years were characterized by the "chaos of the disciplines" (Abbott 2001). But between 1880 and 1910, however, the social sciences began to settle down into organized bodies of knowledge and distinctive professional profiles.

For sociology, this settling down first occurred in Europe. Indeed, the "father of sociology," Emile Durkheim (1858–1917), founded the first European Sociology Department at the University of Bordeaux in 1895 and the first major European journal of sociology in 1898. On the other side of the

The Chicago School developed many important ideas about society based on detailed studies in the city of Chicago.

Atlantic, a distinctively American tradition of sociology also emerged around this time, centered around the Sociology Department at the University of Chicago, founded in 1895 as the first such department in America. Frequently taking the city of Chicago as its laboratory, the so-called Chicago School intensively studied the problems of cities and the groups of people living in them, developing a body of knowledge that remains influential to this day.

But great thinkers and schools alone cannot explain what makes a set of ideas take off. It is instructive that most of the earliest thinkers we now call sociologists did not train to be sociologists. So what was the social context that made people interested in this new kind of knowledge? Two critical developments spurred the social sciences in general and sociology in particular. The very rapid period of **industrialization**—the growth of factories and large-scale goods production—and **urbanization**—the growth of cities—in the late nineteenth century in the United States, Europe, and elsewhere was especially important. This was a period when new technologies and innovations made possible the growth of large-scale manufacturing of consumer products—transforming economies based primarily in agriculture to those based in the manufacturing of goods. The spread of factory labor in this period of industrialization created jobs that were concentrated in **urban**

areas, which are commonly defined as those with a population density of at least 1,000 people per square mile and all surrounding areas that have an overall density of at least 500 people per square miles). This period of urbanization was marked by growth in the proportion of the population living in urban areas and cities—which grew rapidly in size between 1850 and 1920 (see Figure 1.5). Chicago grew from a population of 29,963 in 1850 to 2.7 million people in 1920. Detroit went from 21,019 in 1850 to just under 1 million in 1920. Philadelphia, the fourth largest city in America in 1850, with 121,000 people, reached 1.8 million inhabitants by 1920. Figure 1.5 summarizes the growth of cities and surrounding metropolitan areas throughout American history. The jobs driving this growth pulled people away from farms and rural communities and provided economic opportunities for wave after wave of immigrants from other countries who arrived in steadily increasing numbers from the 1870s until the early 1920s, but continuing into the 1960s.

The social changes enabled by industrialization were immense. The contexts of both individual lives as well as whole communities were changing rapidly. And it was clear that the natural and biological sciences seemed unable to explain fully what was occurring. While chemistry and physics proved enormously useful in providing the basis for new industrial processes and could be drawn upon to explain the physical effects of the pollution spewing from the newly constructed industrial landscape, they could offer little insight into how working for wages in factories was changing the most basic human relations and group identifications. Similarly, while biology might have been able to predict some of the physical challenges that people faced once they moved to crowded cities,

FIGURE 1.5 GROWTH OF THE URBAN POPULATION IN THE UNITED STATES

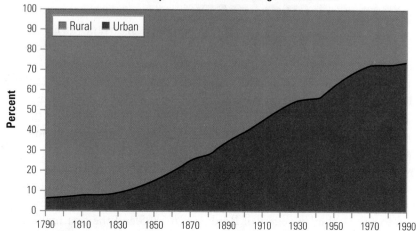

Urban Population as a Percentage of U.S. Total

■ Rural ■ Urban

Source: U.S. Geological Survey (2004).

it could provide little clue as to how city life was altering how politics was practiced, how work was done, or how families were organized. For these kinds of issues, different approaches to the emerging world were needed.

The exploding cities that developed in the United States and Europe from the middle of the nineteenth century onward were teeming with deep problems that were markedly different from the agricultural economies of previous centuries. To begin with, these cities were rife with high levels of poverty. The early factories paid poorly, and living in the expanding cities was often expensive as the housing supply struggled to keep up with the demand. Cities were dirty places—this was before public health and public sanitation measures had become widely implemented—and they were breeding grounds for disease, infant mortality, and early death. They were also places where crime and violence were much more common than in rural communities. Finally, they were places where people could organize themselves to protest unpleasant conditions of life. Instead of tolerating misery alone on one's farm, now it was possible to meet and discuss problems with dozens or hundreds of people in close proximity. This created a new type of political challenge, especially as organized associations of workers (created in order to protect and fight for their rights) called **unions** began to form. Also on the rise during this period were **social movements**, which are marked by collective action aimed at bringing about some kind of change in society.

In the face of these challenges and conditions, sociology found its place in beginning to seek to understand the sources of these emerging social problems. Of course, sociology was not the only academic discipline to emerge from this period of social change; a diverse group of disciplines also emerged right around the same time, in the late nineteenth and early twentieth centuries, concurrent with the rise of the modern research university. It was really quite remarkable how all of the traditional social science disciplines consolidated into coherent, organized, and increasingly distinct fields of study at a similar historical moment. In large part, this was due to important expansions in higher education in both Europe and America in the period. The dates of the founding of the major social science professional associations give some idea of how compacted the rise of the social sciences was (displayed in Table 1.1). In a span of just 20 years, then, a whole battery of social sciences would come to establish an institutional presence in the United States.

☐ Sociology's Family: Siblings

While all the social sciences were born from a similar impulse to understand the emerging social worlds spawned by industrialization and urban growth, there was considerable disagreement over where to go from that common starting point. So how did sociology come to differ from other social sciences? We would point to two fundamental distinctions:

TABLE 1.1 DATES OF THE FOUNDING OF MAJOR SOCIAL SCIENCE PROFESSIONAL ASSOCIATIONS

American Economics Association: 1885

American Psychological Association: 1892

American Anthropological Association: 1902

American Political Science Association: 1903

American Sociological Association: 1905

1. Our concepts and theories cover a wider range of topics than other disciplines—we are promiscuous in what we study.
2. Our explanations of how the external world shapes behaviors of individuals and social outcomes are broader than those of other disciplines and encompass different units of analysis. Sociologists move *from individuals to groups to institutions to global society*. Sociology is the social science discipline that is most concerned about how different units of analysis link up to and mutually influence one another.

Of course, the danger in working with such a broad spectrum of topics is that it can be hard to define the parameters of sociology. As professional sociologists we are often asked, what exactly *is* sociology? Sometimes we struggle to give a short, simple answer. Unlike other social scientists, sociologists don't define ourselves according to a specific institution or area of life. We don't claim one piece of the external world as our sole area of expertise. For the most part, other social scientists do precisely this: Political scientists are primarily concerned with topics that involve governments and the policies they produce. Economists are mainly concerned with individuals' economic behavior (microeconomics) and the performance of the national or global economy (macroeconomics). Psychologists are interested in understanding the workings of the mind and the dynamics of the psyche. And anthropologists claim expertise in the practices of diverse cultures and how they vary across time and place.

Sociology cannot easily be pigeonholed in this way. Sociologists can and do move into all the areas that are the "home turf" of the other social sciences. But we do so just as systematically and rigorously as other social scientists. As our name indicates, we claim scientific expertise over those parts of life we call the "social" and in topics with "social" significance. But the "social" is a bit fuzzier of an area than those studied by our counterparts. That is, most people know exactly what a political scientist means when he or she studies "government"—or what an economist does when researching the "economy." But sociologists often get perplexed looks when we say we study the "social world." It took one of our grandmothers 20 years to stop telling the women she lunches with that her granddaughter was a professor of "socialism" or "social work." For her, this was a concrete way to make sense of the social and to translate it into something meaningful (albeit a bit scary, as

How we see a community or social setting is shaped by what vantage point we use. Viewed from space, social life doesn't appear very different, but the closer we get the greater the differences we can see.

she was a staunch Republican). So while sociologists' refusal to break up the world into small, narrow slices and proclaim expertise over them does cause confusion, most of us would have it no other way.

To make sociology even messier (but, in some ways, more exciting), there is enormous flexibility in how sociologists approach our topics of study. We have considerable leeway to decide what to analyze in our research. As we outlined earlier, sociology consists of the many contexts shaping our lives—from the small to the large, from the local to the global. This means that we focus on many different levels of analysis when examining a given topic; we can choose to highlight one or more surrounding contexts. And we have more freedom to make these choices than most of our social scientific siblings.

Another way to say this is that sociology works with different **units of analysis**. These are the pieces of a topic that a researcher bites off when she or he studies it. They are akin to the camera lens settings you use when taking a picture—say of a family. A narrow lens might zoom in on only the individual members of the family. This would allow a sociologist to capture the interpersonal dynamics of family members with great detail and nuance, but not the larger context in which the photo was taken. An alternative is to pull back a bit and try to capture the environment the family is posing in—perhaps revealing the neighborhood around them or the surrounding natural environment. Or even further, use a wide-angle lens to place each family member in the organizations they are part of, from the places they work to the schools they attend, to the clubs they participate in, to the friendship networks they value. Or even more dramatically, replace the camera with a camcorder to draw into view all the ways in which families can change over time. And all of these devices can be used to study different types of families and to compare them historically or in different societies.

Sociologists have all of these techniques at our disposal. And unlike our social scientific siblings, we use them all. In doing so, we offer multifaceted perspectives on similar social phenomenon. Continuing with our example of how sociologists study the family, like psychologists many sociologists are interested in the emotional life of families. In fact, a classic

What units of analysis do sociologists work with, and how do these differ from those of other disciplines?

sociological study addresses this: Nancy Chodorow's best-selling 1978 book *The Reproduction of Mothering*. Yet unlike the classic psychological studies of family life, which tend to isolate the family unit to study patterns of interaction and their psychological effects, Chodorow places family life and the dynamics between family members in a larger context. She asks, why is it that women are the ones to parent offspring? How does women's exclusion from the world of work shape the kind of parenting they do? Does it lead them to treat boys and girls differently? And does that lead boys and girls to develop different senses of self and emotional needs? All of these questions then push Chodorow to yet another unit of analysis: What happens to family life when these traditional patterns of caretaking break down? Historically, as more women work outside the home, do they parent differently? And do families then have to change the emotional ties that bind them? In effect, Chodorow's sociological approach uses multiple lenses to zoom in and zoom out on her topic—and thus to gain different perspectives on the complexities of contemporary family life (Chodorow 1978).

Units of analysis are important not only because they affect what aspects of our topics we can see—they also shape the explanations sociologists provide. Precisely because sociologists work on different levels, with different units of analysis, they typically address a wider range of connections than other social sciences. Consider again the difference between sociology and psychology. Psychology is centered on the study of the mind, the psyche, and the physical brain. Sociologists have much to learn from psychological findings, some of which we've already mentioned in this chapter. At the same time, sociologists part company with psychologists in insisting that individuals must also always be located in larger social contexts. For sociologists,

Why are some occupations typically "female" and others "male"? What kinds of changes have to take place for that to change?

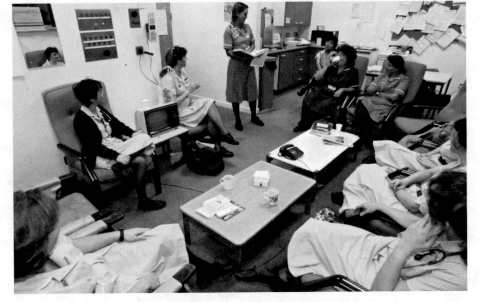

it is not enough to explain individual behavior by simply understanding the intricacies of the psyche. Going back to the family example, most individuals are embedded in families (of some sort), which are themselves embedded in communities, which are themselves embedded in cultural, economic, and political environments. To explain individual action, these other contexts must also come into view.

A similar gap separates sociology from economics. Economists pride themselves on building and testing models of economic behavior using clear and simple assumptions about human nature (e.g., that everything being equal, we will always act in ways that we think will enhance our self-interest and financial well-being). Their ideas and mathematical models of human behavior are often elegant and lead to clear predictions that can be tested by researchers. Sociologists, by contrast, tend to believe that for all of their impressive advances, economists sometimes miss important outcomes because they don't consider a wide enough range of factors and forces affecting human behavior. Sociologists argue that there are many things motivating individuals—altruism as well as self-interest, reputations and status as well as money. And in a different context, the same person might behave differently. So while sociological theories tend to be messier and more difficult to test than economic theories, they can also produce a wider range of possible explanations that, when successful, can produce genuinely new understandings.

All of this sibling rivalry aside, most social scientists today end up drawing on the ideas and insights of other fields and disciplines. After more than a century of building their own disciplines and professional associations, there is now increasingly a move to blur the boundaries. **Interdisciplinary research**, as it is known, is an increasingly central part of learning about any topic in the social sciences. Few students and scholars in the social sciences would be foolish enough not to draw on ideas in the neighboring social sciences. And sociology is perhaps the most likely to do so—it is the most interdisciplinary of all the traditional social science disciplines. Depending on the question at hand, sociologists will need to know something about the research and theories developed by economists, political scientists, psychologists, or anthropologists. We also often draw on the work of historians—a discipline that is in the humanities but is closely related to the

social sciences. Although our main interest in this book is introducing you to sociological insights and approaches, and indeed it is impossible to start thinking interdisciplinarily until you have at least some grasp of disciplinary knowledge, we would certainly *not* want to leave the impression that sociology by itself has all the answers to all the questions that social scientists raise. It does not.

☐ Sociology's Children

One interesting side note on the relationship between sociology and the other social sciences is the way in which sociology has mothered a number of new areas of study into existence. In most universities today, there is a large group of spin-off majors and programs that have developed out of one of the social sciences, more often than not sociology. This list includes such fields as criminology, gender studies, African American Studies, Latino/a studies, organizational or management studies, industrial relations or labor studies, demography, and others. There was once a time when much of the research and scholarship on these topics was done within the discipline of sociology. But for various reasons, these subfields would eventually split off from sociology to became independent fields of study and develop their own knowledge bases and professional associations. Indeed, it is remarkable just how many spin-off fields originally started (at least in part) in sociology. Explore the Infographic on page 22.

Looking at this list of these other fields of study, it is clear that sociology has long served as an important *incubator* for new arenas of investigation. Even today, there are exciting new areas of study in sociology that may eventually grow into disciplines of their own. In this sense, learning the basics of sociology is an essential foundation for any one of these newer fields. At its core, sociology will remains a foundational discipline for many of the interdisciplinary social sciences.

What are some of the spin-off fields that originally started in sociology?

Sociology in America

Today, there are 816 sociology departments in the United States.
And compared with 1930 when only 40 people received PhDs in Sociology, in 2010 that number increased to 638 people.

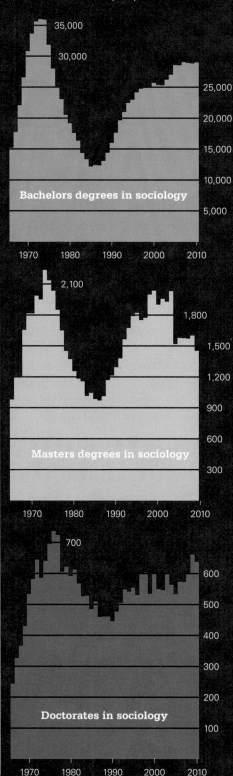

Bachelors degrees in sociology

35,000
30,000
25,000
20,000
15,000
10,000
5,000

1970 1980 1990 2000 2010

2,100
1,800
1,500
1,200
900
600
300

Masters degrees in sociology

1970 1980 1990 2000 2010

700
600
500
400
300
200
100

Doctorates in sociology

1970 1980 1990 2000 2010

Sociology has come a long way. Unlike long standing academic fields such as physics, history, or philosophy, which were established centuries ago, sociology emerged relatively recently. This is particularly true of sociology in America. In fact, the first sociology department in America wasn't established until 1892 at the University of Chicago, and it was not until around the 1940s that a large number of American universities had a department of sociology. Up until then, if and when sociology was taught, it was done as part of an economics, history, or philosophy curriculum.

Sources: Based on data from the American Sociological Association

Explore the **Data** on Sociology in America in **MySocLab** and then ...

■ Think About It

What is a possible explanation for the decline in sociology students from the mid-1970s to the mid-1980s, and then the subsequent increase?

■ Inspire Your Sociological Imagination

After reviewing the list of areas in sociology, what new areas do you see emerging in the twenty-first century?

Sociology is a dynamic field. As the world changes what sociologists study changes. One of the powerful aspects of the sociological imagination is that it can be applied to a diverse set of issues and problems.

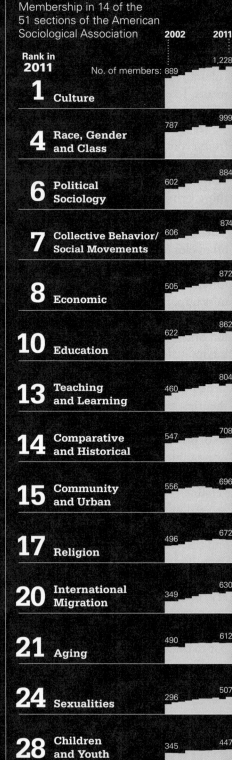

Membership in 14 of the 51 sections of the American Sociological Association

Rank in 2011		2002	2011
	No. of members:	889	1,228
1	Culture		
4	Race, Gender and Class	787	999
6	Political Sociology	602	884
7	Collective Behavior/ Social Movements	606	874
8	Economic	505	872
10	Education	622	862
13	Teaching and Learning	460	804
14	Comparative and Historical	547	708
15	Community and Urban	556	696
17	Religion	496	672
20	International Migration	349	630
21	Aging	490	612
24	Sexualities	296	507
28	Children and Youth	345	447

4 How Can This Book Help You Develop a Sociological Imagination?

LOOKING AHEAD

👁 Watch the **Big Question Video** in **MySocLab**

Our goal for this book is to provide enough background on the key areas and findings of sociological research to provide our readers with the foundation for developing your own sociological imagination. By understanding how individuals' lives are embedded in particular social contexts that are not always of their own choosing, we hope that you will learn to appreciate how personal issues that individuals face often can also be understood as larger social problems facing society.

This book is organized into five sections, each containing four chapters. The first section discusses foundational issues to the discipline, such as research methods, social interaction, and social systems. The second section of the book provides the "building blocks" for applying sociology to understand the individual and society. Topics covered include culture, politics and power, organizations and markets, and cities and communities. The next section covers processes of social inequality, with chapters on class, race and ethnicity, gender and sexuality, and immigration. Next are chapters exploring four main social institutions that individuals face in their lives—the family, religion, education, and the criminal justice system. We conclude with a section on different dimensions of large-scale social change, including social movements, environmental change, health and population change, and globalization.

The authors of each of the chapters in this book are writing about the topics that they do research in and teach courses on. We believe that a collective approach to presenting the discipline of sociology provides a better way of unearthing and exciting our readers' sociological imaginations. In the course of thinking about (and teaching) the topics we are writing about, we have developed deep appreciation for the complexities, but also the excitement, of our respective topics.

In order to create a unified text, we've taken a number of steps to make it easier for our readers to move from chapter to chapter. Each chapter opens with a puzzle or story that highlights one or more of the key sociological problems that will be tackled in the chapter. Following this, each chapter identifies a set of big questions that have defined the research and teaching puzzles of the field. These questions organize what follows as the authors explore how sociological thinking about each question has developed. At all points, some basic facts and data are helpful to have in hand, but at the same time we want our readers to learn to think sociologically through learning how to ask hard questions and where to look for answers.

> ## What does it mean to describe this book and sociology as a whole as a *project?*

In short, we want to stress that this book—and indeed sociology as a discipline—truly is a *project:* something we are collectively engaged in building and something for which there are relatively few completely settled answers. The problems confronted by sociologists are hard questions because there are so many things that influence individuals and group life. This is what makes sociology endlessly interesting and a sociological imagination very much worth acquiring.

👁 **Watch** the **Video** Applying Your Sociological Imagination in MySocLab

1 How Can a Sociological Imagination Help You Better Understand Your World? (p. 6)

◉ **Watch** the **Big Question Video** in **MySocLab** to review the key concepts for this section.

This section introduced the concept of the sociological imagination and explored how it helps us learn to ask hard questions.

THE SOCIOLOGICAL IMAGINATION (p. 6)

Looking through a Sociological Lens (p. 6)

- **How can a sociological imagination help us to challenge stereotypes?**

Engaging our Sociological Imaginations: Learning to Ask Good Questions (p. 7)

From Personal Puzzles to Sociological Questions (p. 8)

- **What types of questions are sociologists particularly well equipped to explore?**

The Endless Reach of the Sociological Imagination (p. 11)

📖 **Read** the **Document** *Invitation to Sociology* by Peter L. Berger in **MySocLab.** In this reading, Berger invites readers to discover their passion while they observe the world around them.

2 Why Do Social Contexts Matter? (p. 12)

◉ **Watch** the **Big Question Video** in **MySocLab** to review the key concepts for this section.

Sociology is fundamentally concerned with how we are influenced by society. All of us are situated in an array of social contexts. This section explored how these influence us and our behavior.

SOCIAL CONTEXTS: FROM INDIVIDUALS TO SOCIETY (p. 12)

Families and Communities as Context (p. 13)

- **How do our families and communities shape our social development?**

◉ **Explore** A Sociological Perspective in **MySocLab**

Organizations and Institutions (p. 13)

- **How do the organizations and institutions we are a part of help us form our identities?**

Social and Economic Contexts (p. 15)

Sociology as the Study of Social Contexts (p. 15)

- **What is the distinction between social interaction and social structure?**

3

Where Did Sociology Come From, and How Is It Different from the Other Social Sciences? (p. 17)

Watch the **Big Question Video** in **MySocLab** to review the key concepts for this section.

This section examined the context in which sociology began to develop and explored the question of how sociology fits into, and relates to, the other social sciences.

THE SOCIOLOGY OF THE SOCIAL SCIENCES (p. 17)

Sociology and the Industrial Revolution (p. 17)

- **What was the historical context in which sociology began to develop?**

Sociology's Family: Siblings (p. 19)

- **What units of analysis do sociologists work with, and how do these differ from those of other disciplines?**

Sociology's Children (p. 21)

- **What are some of the spin-off fields that originally started in sociology?**

Explore the **Data** on Sociology in America in **MySocLab**

4

How Can This Book Help You Develop a Sociological Imagination? (p. 23)

Watch the **Big Question Video** in **MySocLab** to review the key concepts for this section.

Our goal for this book is to provide enough background on the key areas and findings of sociological research in foundation for you to develop your own sociological imagination.

LOOKING AHEAD (p. 23)

- **What does it mean to describe this book and sociology as a whole as a *project*?**

Watch the **Video** Applying Your Sociological Imagination in **MySocLab** to see these concepts at work in the real world

2
STUDYING the SOCIAL WORLD

by LYNNE HANEY

 Listen to the **Chapter Audio** in **MySocLab**

ost of us have a clear idea about what prisons look like: located in a far-off locale, enclosed by wire fencing and concrete watch towers, and filled with scary-looking men spending their days in tiny cells. When I entered my first prison, located in a large, dilapidated mansion on an inner-city street in northern California, in 1992, as a young researcher eager to understand how women were "socialized" by the penal state, a very different image confronted me. The residents were young women, all official wards of the state of California, who had been sent to this prison to serve their time with their children. In place of small, dark prison cells were nicely decorated bedrooms; in place of the prison mess hall was an open, well-stocked kitchen; and in place of the barren prison recreation room was a cozy living room. Then there was daily life. It was comprised not of big, burly men sitting in cells but of small children running around, chased by their mothers. The only fights I ever saw were between hungry, sleepy kids and their exasperated mothers—over what the kids should eat or when they should go to bed—hardly the stuff of *Prison Break* or *OZ*.

One of the most common mistakes young researchers make is to assume that our own research "a-ha" moments are shared by others. I made just such a mistake in this prison study—while I had been shocked by the

MY SOCIOLOGICAL IMAGINATION
Lynne Haney

Sometimes I think I was born with a sociological imagination—although that would be thoroughly unsociological of me to say. I grew up in the California Bay Area in the 1970s, when the feminist, civil rights, and gay-rights movements were at their peak—and all kinds of identities and relationships were being questioned. As a result, thinking sociologically seemed to be in the air; everyone was asking the big questions about why the world was the way it was. But then the context changed and morphed into the 1980s of Ronald Reagan and social conservatism (as well as bad hair and bad fashion). And much of the social and cultural questioning I grew up with began to wane as more rigid and limiting assumptions about the world and our places within it became acceptable. This shift left me wondering how people come to accept or reject received wisdom: Was it just a matter of who had the power and resources to impress their version of reality on others? Or was there some way to discern fact from fiction, myth from reality?

It was around this time that I discovered social science research. As a young college student, sociology appealed to me because it seemed to offer the empirical tools to resolve many political and social conflicts. It offered the possibility that not everything was relative, a matter of opinion, or open to ideological debate. In this way, although I've had a sociological imagination for a long time, it was not until I learned to conduct social research that I could use my imagination productively—as a way of teaching myself and others how to learn from and be surprised by the social world.

There are over 200,000 women in prison in the U.S.; over 70 percent of them have minor children. Many gave birth to their children while in prison, which often involved being shackled to a hospital bed during childbirth—as this woman is.

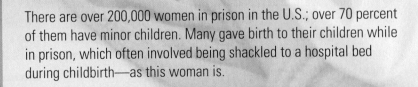

Watch the **Video** in **MySocLab**
Inspiring Your Sociological Imagination

existence of "mommy/baby" prisons, other sociologists had been writing about them for years. And whereas I was unnerved by even the idea of small children being raised in prison, other researchers seemed hopeful and optimistic about the practice. These other researchers often insisted that one way to end the pains of incarceration and to stop the familial cycle of imprisonment was to keep women and children together—even if it meant bringing kids to prison. Of all these studies, the most seemingly definitive was a statistical study by the California Department of Corrections. It tracked rearrest records of thousands of women who had done time in these prisons and found they had slightly lower repeat arrest rates than those who had served time in traditional facilities. Although the effects were small, researchers found mommy/baby prisons to be a success—and a real alternative to traditional incarceration.

All of this left me wondering: Perhaps raising children in prison wasn't such a bad idea. So I returned to prison to do a more extensive study. This time I chose my sample carefully. After meeting with prison officials at all the mommy/baby prisons in California, I located my work in the state's model facility and joined prison life. This is what **ethnographers** do: We enter the everyday lives of those we study in hopes of understanding how they navigate and give meaning to their worlds. For over three years, I observed as hundreds of women and children passed through the prison's steel doors. I went to group sessions; I attended mothering classes; I taught inmates creative writing; and I went to staff meetings and strategy sessions. By the end of the research, I was so integrated that I had keys to the prison.

Yet the more integrated into prison life I got, the more convinced I became that these were brutal, punishing places—but not in the way one might expect. The children, whom I thought would suffer most from the loss of freedom, seemed okay. With three meals a day, good childcare and education, healthcare, and lots of other kids to play with, they were surviving life in prison fairly well. It was their mothers who were suffering. They suffered from a prison environment that stripped them of all parental power—how could they gain any maternal authority when they were ordered around, told where to go and what to do? They suffered from the loss of privacy—how could they parent when unsupervised, one-on-one time with children was not even allowed? In the end, some women became extremely anxious about their mothering; others simply collapsed under the pressure. But no one experienced the hope and optimism promised in those other research accounts.

Research methods are tools. They are a means to an end—not an end in and of themselves.

So were other researchers wrong? Not necessarily. Although we studied similar criminal justice facilities, we had different research questions and used different research methods. Other researchers were interested in examining whether serving time with kids made it less likely for women to reoffend, so it made sense for them to track rearrest data and interview women who had reoffended. Had I been interested in this, I would have used a similar approach. But I wasn't. My research questions revolved around how the women and children did time together—the practice of mothering behind bars and its implications for the mother/child bond. For this, ethnographic observation made the most sense because it gave me access to the data I needed to answer my research questions. All of this led me to paint a very different picture of these prisons—and to draw very different conclusions about their possibilities and limitations.

Our **sociological imaginations**, the way we take into account how our individual lives are impacted by social context, prompt us to ask particular kinds of questions of the world—which then lead us to specific research methods. The order here is critical: Sociologists first decide what we want to ask, and then we figure out the best way to go about answering our questions. Research methods are tools. They are a means to an end—not an end in and of themselves.

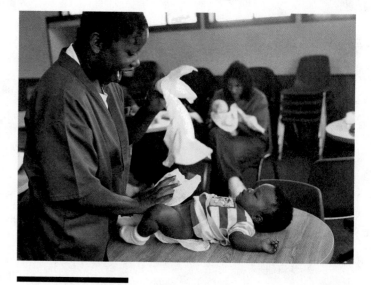

Sociologists have only recently begun to research the familial effects of maternal imprisonment.

THE BIG QUESTIONS

◉ **Watch** the **Big Question Videos** in **MySocLab**

This chapter examines how sociologists study the social world by addressing the following big questions.

Where do sociological questions come from? We begin with the basic stages of sociological research, discussing the issues that often come up as researchers practice sociology for the first time, such as how sociologists turn their research interests into workable questions and how we know what to study.

What is the best method to research a sociological question? Once sociologists have a working research question, they need to decide the best way to go about answering it. In this section we examine the process sociologists use to determine the best research method and design. We also consider the question of why choosing the right research method to study motivations and behaviors is often a complex process.

How is data collected? Here we examine not only the different types of methods that sociologists use in their research but also how they adhere to a scientific method.

How do sociologists make sense of their findings? Finally we consider how sociologists make sure their findings are reliable and trustworthy and how they decide what kind of general claims to draw from their research.

1 Where Do Sociological Questions Come From?

THE BUILDING BLOCKS OF SOCIOLOGICAL RESEARCH

👁 Watch the **Big Question Video** in **MySocLab**

Most discussions of research methods make a clear distinction between **quantitative research** and **qualitative research**—or research that relies on statistical analysis of data (quantitative) and research that relies on words, observations, or pictures as data (qualitative). And in many ways they are very different. But all sociological research shares a series of basic building blocks—ways of asking questions, approaching data collection, and making generalizations. Whether done quantitatively or qualitatively, all good research is attentive to the particular issues that arise at these stages of the research process. Because of this, I emphasize the common phases of the research enterprise, noting the important differences in how sociologists approach them when necessary.

Why is it essential to review existing research on a topic before asking a new research question?

 Moving from Research Topics to Research Questions

Few of us are ever at a loss for good topics to study. If you've found your way to a sociology course, chances are there is at least one sociological topic you feel strongly about—if not many more. The challenge is not usually to find an interesting subject to investigate. The hard part is carving out a researchable question from that topic. Most often, this involves narrowing and focusing. It implies breaking the topic down into several parts and deciding which one to begin researching. This doesn't mean dumbing down our research interests. This is something new sociologists often struggle with, especially those conducting research for the first time. They sometimes feel like focusing their research questions drains them of their larger significance. Nothing could be further from the truth: Narrowing is a way of creating a manageable bite of a larger topic so that you can more readily transmit its significance to others.

There is no recipe for turning an interesting topic into a good research question. In general, good questions are both feasible and sociologically relevant. They are feasible in the sense that they lead us to think more specifically about a topic and to turn our ideas about that topic into a working **hypothesis**, which is the tentative prediction we have about what we are going to discover before we begin the research. In this way, good research questions also imply a critical role for what others have already found and written about our topic. Conducting a good review of the literature before formulating a research question is essential. This not only helps with the narrowing down of interests to questions, but it helps to know if the ground to be covered is already charted territory. There is nothing worse than thinking we have an original sociological question, only to discover late in the research process that others have already asked it—and have published volumes of articles and shelves of books debating it.

The Complexities of Research Questions

Although there is no easy-to-follow recipe for turning a research topic into a question, there are at least six questions sociologists should ask about a potential research question to determine its merit and feasibility.

1. Do I Already Know the Answer? If so, find another research question. The goal of social research is not to confirm what we already know; it is not to shore up support for a position you already have. Rather, it is to ask something new and interesting about the world—and then to go out and answer that question systematically. For instance, if statistical studies consistently show that 50 percent of marriages end in divorce, it would not be very meaningful for a sociologist to conduct research simply on the prevalence on divorce—unless there was some reason to believe this trend was changing. Instead, this sociologist would be better off focusing on some aspect of divorce that we know far less about, such as its effects on children or its relationship to poverty. In this way, our objective as researchers is to gain new insight into social life; it is to be surprised and informed by the world. Of course, this doesn't mean that you cannot or should not have a hunch about what you may find, or that you should be clueless about the findings you'll come up with. Instead, it means that your question strives to produce new knowledge and not simply to confirm what you think you already know.

2. Is the Question Researchable? Put another way, we make sure we are asking a question that can actually be answered. This may seem obvious, but often it is not. Some questions are clearly unanswerable. Not even the best social researcher can answer what the meaning of life is or when there will be world peace. Other questions may seem researchable but require data that we could never get access to, such as asking why governments make particular choices or why corporations do what they do. Indeed, many of the most unresearchable questions imply a kind of **causality**, the belief that one factor or phenomenon is leading to changes in another, that can't be substantiated with the data accessible to us. For instance, although many of us might want to know why young boys and girls seem to act so differently,

Although we might like to design a research project to provide a definitive answer to why boys and girls seem to act so differently, this is not really a researchable question. Instead, sociologists have amassed lots of data on the particular ways gender differences (and similarities) surface in everyday life, as well as the cultural meanings we give to those differences

few of us are able to answer that definitely. Because "why" questions like this are very hard, if not impossible, for new researchers to answer properly, I usually advise them to stay clear of such ambitions.

3. Is the Question Clear? Clear questions come from clear thinking. So if a question is unclear, it probably means the thinking underlying it isn't clear. The problem might be that the question includes concepts that are not defined—or have yet to be defined. For example, say you are curious about how social class affects students' educational outcomes. This may seem like a good start, but how do you define "social class" or "educational outcomes"? This requires some additional work to clarify exactly what you mean.

Connected to this, as sociologists clarify their research questions, we make sure to flesh out any hidden assumptions implied in them. Such assumptions can be definitional, including terms or concepts we draw on without being clear about their meanings. They can also be assumptions of causality, such as a question that takes for granted the relationship between two things rather than interrogating that relationship. For instance, let's say you want to understand how parents' occupations shape their kids' academic interests—asking the question in this way assumes that parents' occupations do affect what their kids are interested in. And that relationship is exactly what needs to be researched. One way to uncover any hidden assumptions is to look closely at each word in the question and to make sure each one can be defined, even provisionally. Then step back and ask whether any assumptions are being made about the relationships among those words. Doing this at an early stage in the research process can save a lot of grief later when those hidden assumptions can surface to subvert even the best research plan.

This is precisely what happened to me in the first study I did in graduate school. The assignment was to conduct a small survey on a topic of interest to us, and I thought I had come up with a winner: Having just moved to Berkeley from San Diego, I was stunned by all of the homeless men and women who approached people for money on the streets. While that might not stun us today, this was the early 1990s, when panhandling was not as common. Yet walking from my apartment to the Berkeley Sociology Department, I was hit up countless times for money. So I asked: How do people decide which panhandlers to give money to? How do their larger sensibilities enter into the decision? How do they define "worthiness"? And how does the gender, race, and age of the person asking for money shape who received it?

I spent weeks coming up with a complicated survey that asked about all of the factors shaping the decision to give money to panhandlers. But then, after having administered only one or two surveys, I realized I had made two assumptions: First, I assumed that people actually gave money when asked. Second, I assumed that they considered the characteristics of the person asking when deciding to give money. Both assumptions were faulty. Many people never gave money to panhandlers. Those who did considered only one factor: If they had change in their pocket. Nothing else seemed to matter. Had I interrogated the hidden assumptions in my project, I would have detected the problem earlier and saved myself a lot of time.

4. Does the Question Have a Connection to Social Scientific Scholarship?
I would have saved time if I had subjected my research question on panhandling to this fourth

What six questions should a sociologist ask to determine the merit of a research question?

question. As noted earlier, sociologists decide what to research and what questions to ask once they are familiar with what others have already discovered. My questions about panhandling had been formulated without a clear sense of what others already knew about the phenomenon. So while the rise in homelessness and panhandling may have been news to me in the early 1990s, it was hardly news to social scientists. By then, sociologists had done a lot of work on the topic—research that should have informed my own survey about it. Without knowledge of what others had already found, I asked a question that was misguided and full of hidden assumptions.

Sociologists connect their questions to the existing literature in many ways. Research is like a conversation. Just like entering a conversation, there are many modes of contributing to the existing scholarship. Some sociologists read other scholarship for specific debates that interest them and then construct research questions and design research projects to resolve some aspect of those debates. Others look to scholarship to uncover questions other sociologists have ignored and then create research to fill the void. While sociologists don't have to read everything before they form their research question, they need to have at least general idea about the debates in the area as well as the concepts and frameworks that structure those debates.

5. Does the Question Balance the General and the Specific?
Using the existing literature to help construct a research question allows sociologists to grapple with this fifth question. Is the question too broad? Too specific? Clearly, our questions should not be so broad that they can't be grasped in a meaningful way. Questions like "How does contemporary capitalism operate?" or "Why do men and women differ?" are overly abstract and too general, making it impossible to draw boundaries around them or figure out what kind of evidence a researcher would need to answer them.

At the same time, our research questions should not be so narrow and specific that they only appeal to us or to a very small group of people like us. I once had a student propose a research question about how college students who recently emigrated from Thailand to the Bronx made sense of their parents' work in service-sector jobs. Needless to say, this student wanted to understand her own immigration experience and constructed a question specific to it. So she had to step back and think about what was interesting about her experience for others. She then had to reformulate her question, taking it up a level of abstraction and asking about the implications of downward mobility for recent immigrants.

6. Do I Care about the Answer? This final question is perhaps the most important question to ask of a research question. Sociologists aren't in the business of producing knowledge that no one cares about. If we don't care about our research, chances are that others won't either. If we don't care about our work, we won't be as willing to put the necessary time and energy into it—and research takes a lot of time and energy. The danger here is in producing competent but lifeless research results. The more interest you demonstrate in your research, the more you'll get in return. Of course, there are real dangers in caring too much about our research. This can lead us to lose our distance from a topic and to become an advocate as opposed to a scientist. But there are also dangers of ignoring the passion we have for our research. Denying how strongly we may feel about a research topic or question can actually leave us unprepared to manage this passion if needed. It can leave our biases unchecked, thus allowing them to seep into our research in undetected ways. The goal is to maintain a critical distance from what we study while remaining passionate about and committed to the questions we ask.

☐ How Do We Know What to Study?

If you ask practicing sociologists why they study what they study, you will likely get a long response about all of the scholarly debates that motivate them. Such explanations are surely accurate. But probe a little deeper and other influences may also come to the surface. There are endless scholarly debates for us to choose from—and we gravitate toward some areas for particular reasons. For many, the pull is personal: We find ourselves asking sociological questions that have personal significance. That significance may be direct—as when a sociologist researches something he or she has experienced first-hand, like racial inequality, religious discrimination, divorce, or educational stratification. Indeed, many sociologists have looked to their biographies to enhance their sociological imaginations and used those imaginations to inform their research agendas. But personal influences can also be more indirect, as when a sociologist forms a research interest by observing others' experiences. For instance, people often ask me why I study incarceration. While I have never been imprisoned myself, other parts of my background shaped the interest, including many friends who got tangled up in the justice system as juveniles and adults.

For others, the pull to certain sociological questions may be less personal and more political. For instance, many sociologists are interested in questions of power and privilege because of their understandings of the causes of social inequality and because of their sense that research and knowledge can help point to better policies to address that inequality. Others grew up in periods of intense social and civil unrest, which left them with an understanding of the

importance of collective mobilization and an interest in studying how and when it emerges. It is not by chance that the study of social movements really took off in the 1970s, when the antiwar, civil rights, and feminist movements were at their peak, or that sociological interest in the environment has surged in recent years as more political and media attention has been devoted to issues of climate change and environmental racism.

Indeed, there are many factors that shape sociologists' choices about what to research (see Figure 2.1). They range from the implicit, like epistemological leanings, to the explicit, like theory, values, and ethics.

Let's start with most abstract: Although **epistemology** is a big word that sounds complicated, it actually encompasses a quite simple idea. It refers to what we think we can know about the world. Indeed, sociologists do differ here. For instance, some insist that, as good scientists, we can figure out what causes our world to look like it does—what causes poverty, inequality, or violence. Yet other sociologists are more skeptical about our ability to discern cause and effect in such a complex world. This is an epistemological difference, reflective of divergent ideas about what is an answerable question or a knowable inquiry. Similarly, sociologists differ in terms of how they actually claim to know something and what counts as evidence. This variation surfaces in how sociologists substantiate our ideas and make claims to the "truth." Must these claims always be anchored in rigorous scientific findings? What role should experience—and people's interpretations of their lives—play in sociological claims to knowledge?

FIGURE 2.1 WHAT INFLUENCES SOCIAL RESEARCH?

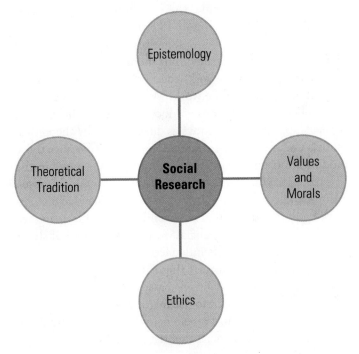

Of course, sociologists are not the only ones who confront epistemological issues. Indeed, all people employ epistemological stances. When we have discussions or arguments in our everyday lives, we make epistemological decisions. If we want to convince someone of something, we must make decisions about the kind of evidence to draw on. Do we cite statistics? Do we refer to scientific research to bolster our case? Or do we draw on our experiences? Or the experiences of others we know or observed? These are essentially epistemological decisions—reflective of what we think we can know about the world and what counts as knowledge about it.

What factors shape sociologists' choices about what to research?

In sociology, we make a distinction between positivist and interpretivist epistemologies. On the one hand, many sociologists believe that the only true way to gain knowledge about the world is to use the logic of the natural sciences—by distancing ourselves from what we study, using universal standards to advance truth claims, determining cause and effect, and generalizing from part to whole. We call this approach **positivism**. Then there are those who insist that the social sciences cannot follow the logic of the natural sciences because our object of investigation is too different. For them, the goal is to understand how people give meaning to social life, objects, and processes—how they make sense of social reality and navigate social interaction. We call this approach **interpretivism**: They see social scientists as the interpreters of people's interpretations. Importantly, these approaches to research are not always fixed—some sociologists merge them in their work, while others fluctuate between them depending on the research question guiding a particular study.

Few sociologists make their epistemological orientations obvious—they are more like the hidden pushes and pulls that guide us toward some research questions and methods. The same is true of our **theoretical traditions**, or those conceptual frameworks that sociologists use to imagine and make sense of the world. While sociologists are usually explicit about how our work contributes to the existing scholarship, we are not always as direct about the theoretical models underlying our research. In part this is because those models are often meant to remain implicit—they are the lens through which we see the world and the main processes, groups, and categories in it. For instance, many sociologists working in the tradition of nineteenth-century German theorist Max Weber see the social world as comprised of status groups; those sociologists influenced by work of nineteenth-century social and political theorist Karl Marx would be more likely to see the divisions based on social classes. And whereas a Marxian sociologist might search the world for examples of revolution, a researcher working in the tradition of twentieth-century social theorist Michel Foucault might

set out to document everyday forms of resistance. Theoretical traditions thus play a critical role in shaping the questions sociologists find interesting and intriguing about the social world.

Values—or the belief systems that shape sociologists' views of and perspectives on the world we study—also play a critical role in shaping the questions sociologists find interesting and intriguing about the social world. To say that our values influence our research questions is not the same as saying that they determine our findings. Like all scientists, sociologists remain open to all kinds of answers to our research questions—even those we may not like. Indeed, it is all the more imperative that sociologists remain open to being surprised by the social world through our research. That said, the values we bring to our research clearly motivate us to work on specific themes. For instance, if a sociologist values the democratic process, she might orient her research to questions about the factors enhancing or inhibiting it in organizations. Or if a sociologist places high value on equality of opportunity, he might be most intrigued by research questions that focus on the policies enacted by different societies to level the playing field. Do such influences make sociologists less objective? Not if we keep our commitment to scientific inquiry and remain insistent on not letting our values cloud our scientific judgment.

This leads to a final area of influence on social research: the **code of ethics**—which is a set of guidelines that outline what is considered moral and acceptable behavior—that all scientists share. This code is especially essential when the objects of investigation are real people. Perhaps even more than those working in the natural sciences, social scientists must commit to protecting those we study and to not doing them any harm. Among other things, this requires us to disclose our identity as researchers and to obtain **informed consent** from our subjects by making their participation voluntary and based on a full understanding of possible risks and benefits involved. We also maintain confidentiality, guaranteeing that we will not reveal the true identities our subjects. These commitments then shape the kind of questions sociologists can ask in our research. While we could dream up all sorts of questions we'd love to be able to research, we must consider the ethics involved in exploring them. So while a sociologist might want to ask questions about how and when people acquiesce to authority—as social psychologist Stanley Milgram did in a classic 1950s study that pretended to have his subjects administer electric shocks to others when ordered to do so—this might be considered harmful and detrimental for research subjects today. Or if a sociologist wanted to study the experience of prison—as Craig Haney and Philip Zimbardo did in their 1970s Stanford Prison Experiment that turned young students into guards and prisoners—this would most likely be considered out of bounds and dangerous for participants today.

Of course, researchers are not always aware when their questions could jeopardize their subjects' well-being. When both the Milgram and the Haney-Zimbardo studies were conducted, the researchers did not anticipate how much harm their studies would inflict on participants. Moreover, what constitutes "harm" can and has changed over time—in both cases, researchers worked within the acceptable protocols of their universities. Today, to help researchers foresee any potential dangers and to safeguard the ethical standards of their work, **institutional review boards (IRBs)** operate at most universities and are required at all universities that receive research funds from the federal government (see Table 2.1). These boards review researchers' proposals before any work can begin in order to assess their potential harm and benefits of the research for participants. They also evaluate whether ethical procedures will be in place and followed by researchers. Needless to say, such reviews have influenced the questions sociologists ask. Consciously and unconsciously, sociologists end up steering themselves away from those areas they know will encounter problems in these boards, like electroshock studies of authority and simulated prison experiments.

TABLE 2.1 ETHICAL STANDARDS FOR SOCIOLOGICAL RESEARCH Academic organizations and institutions, such as the American Sociological Association (ASA), have created ethical standards to guide sociologists' professional and research responsibilities and conduct. The major focus of these standards falls into the following categories.

Professional and Scientific Standards

There is a standard set of guidelines for use in sociological research that aims to reduce bias, dishonesty, and deception and to ensure that sociological research reflects the highest commitment to the discipline's academic and scientific principles.

Competence

Sociologists must attain both academic and professional credentials and complete specialized training to reach competency in the discipline. Sociologists can choose to research and/or to teach, and to do so in public or private institutions, yet sociology is an expertise that spans all areas of our lives.

Conflicts of Interest

There are many opportunities for sociologists to conduct research. However, many of these opportunities present potential sources of conflict, bias, and influence. These might include incentives offered by research funding entities or governmental agencies in pursuit of specific research outcomes. Or they might include sociologists who conduct research with the sole purpose of obtaining financially for themselves, their associates, or colleagues. All of these factors must be addressed so they do not taint sociological work. In their personal, academic, or business lives, sociologists must maintain the highest level of integrity.

Research Planning, Implementation, and Dissemination

Sociological research is meant to be seen by the public. Before this happens, research is usually subjected to peer review, a process by which others working in similar fields comment on and review the work conducted by other sociologists. The practice of peer review helps to maintain research integrity and ensures that the standards of research are upheld. Many sociologists also ensure such integrity by sharing their findings with the people and institutions they have studied.

Informed Consent

All colleges and universities where research is conducted have Institutional Review Boards (IRBs) that oversee research involving human subjects. The board, working independently of a researcher's influence and pressure, reviews research projects and assesses researchers' goals, methods, sampling procedures, and approach to data collection. The IRB evaluates the legal issues involved in the research, including the rights of research subjects and any potential researcher bias. These boards can then require changes to the research plan. One of the most important things IRBs look for is that the rights of research subjects are respected at all points in the research process. Subjects must receive verbal and/or oral explanation of the project; they also must sign an informed consent document stating that they agree to participate in the study, although they retain the right to stop or leave the research project at any time they want.

Confidentiality

There are many ways in which sociologists conducting research ensure confidentiality of their subjects before, during, and after the research is conducted. Subjects are often given pseudonyms or identifiers throughout the research process. This prevents even the researchers from knowing which participant is involved in which aspect of the research—or from associating their research results with any particular person. Confidentiality follows through to any presentation, publication, or discussion of the research results.

Based on American Sociological Association (2008).

2 # What Is the Best Method to Research a Sociological Question?

MOVING FROM RESEARCH QUESTIONS TO RESEARCH METHODS

👁 Watch the Big Question Video in **MySocLab**

Once we have worked through all of these questions and have at least a working version of a research question, we need to decide on the best way to go about answering it. This implies deciding on a research method and a research design. This is the "who, what, where, when, and how" stage of the research process. It's when we decide what or who to study. It's when we decide exactly how many people, places, or things to sample—to include in our research project. It's when we decide where to locate our research, both in terms of time and place. It's when we decide when to conduct the research and for how long. It's when we decide if we will do a comparison and, if so, what it will consist of. It's when we determine how to **operationalize** what we are studying, or when we spell out the operations and techniques to be used to assess our key concepts. And it's when we decide how to measure our variables—those factors, attributes, or phenomenon to be studied. To measure these, researchers often separate the **dependent variable(s)** from the **independent variable(s)**—that is, those aspects of our research that we predict will fluctuate in relation to other variables (dependent) or that we predict exist separate from them (independent). All of these decisions imply particular research methods (see Figure 2.2).

Sociology is unique within the social sciences in that it encompasses a range of acceptable research methods. Some sociologists conduct **surveys** that ask standardized questions of large groups of people. Others carry out in-depth, one-on-one **interviews** with their respondents. Others do ethnographic research by observing or participating in people's everyday lives and interactions, like the research I conducted in the mommy/baby prisons discussed at the beginning of this chapter. Others conduct social **experiments** by creating artificial situations that enable them to watch how people respond to them. Others still carry out **historical research** on records and documents to understand how people, places, or things worked in the past. Sometimes sociologists combine these research methods, using different ones to obtain evidence related to different parts of the research question.

As noted at the start of this chapter, the decision about which method to use is based on the research

FIGURE 2.2 A HYPOTHESIS ABOUT CRIME An increase in the level of inequality in society will result in an increase in the crime rate in that society. In this hypothesis, we are claiming that our independent variable, inequality, impacts our dependent variable, crime.

An increase in the (level of inequality) in society   →   *Causal Claim*   an increase in the (crime rate)

Independent Variable   *Dependent Variable*

Survey research can be done in person or over the telephone. Yet with the rise of cell phones and internet communication, survey researchers are confronting new obstacles to obtaining diverse, representative samples.

question—methods are means to an end, not an end themselves. So we must figure out what kind of evidence we need to answer the question we have posed. Can the question be answered by surveying people large numbers of people and perhaps comparing the responses of different groups? Or it is best addressed by talking directly to a subsample of these people, perhaps in more depth and for a longer period of time? Or is it best addressed by observing them and watching them interact? Or can the question be captured by looking at similar or different groups of people in other times and places?

Sometimes the choice here is obvious: When a research question centers on patterns of behavior among large groups of people, surveys methods are usually the best bet. For instance, if you wanted to know how crime affects communities, you might use statistical methods to chart inhabitants' well-being in high-crime neighborhoods, as sociologist Pat Sharkey did in his study of the school performance of kids living in areas marked by violence. But when the question is about the thought processes that lead people to have certain opinions or engage in certain behaviors, those questions usually require in-depth interviews, like the questions asked by sociologist Kathleen Gerson in her study of how young people negotiate their relationship ideals and expectations in a world of changing gender roles. But if the question has more to do with how people interact and less with how they say they interact—like my questions about how women and children do time together in prison—then ethnographic observation is often the way to go.

Other times, the decision about which research method to employ is less obvious. Indeed, many studies go wrong here: They ask a good, clear research question grounded in the existing scholarship, but they end up collecting data that don't help them answer it. For example, whenever I teach research methods, several students want to study gender differences in romantic relationships. Usually, they want to know something about how men and women act differently in their relationships—whether men are more distant and withdrawn (from Mars) and women more open and

Which types of research questions are best investigated using surveys, and when are in-depth interviews required?

connected (from Venus). And usually these students start off planning to use interview methods, largely because those seem most familiar to them.

Then they inevitably encounter problems with the question/method choice: First and foremost, asking interview questions about motivation rarely gets at actual behavior. What people say about what they do in relationships may have nothing to do with how they really act in them. For instance, research shows that, when interviewed, married men almost always overestimate how much housework they do, while married women exhibit the opposite reporting error, claiming to do less housework than they actually do. And this is not because either group is being consciously deceptive. We all have powerful scripts we tell ourselves about how and why we act like we do, especially when it comes to emotionally laden things like romantic relationships. So interviews are a great way to capture those scripts and opinions but not the best way to learn about what men and women actually do in their relationships—much less the invisible influences that shape those behaviors.

The reverse problem can also surface—that is, when a researcher wants to study individuals' opinions about something and tries to do so by observing behavior. Over the years, I have also had many students interested in knowing what young people think about interracial dating. Their hypothesis is usually that attitudes toward interracial dating have changed, and thus they want to test their hunch. So they propose observing women and men as they date. I've had students propose to do ethnographic work in college parties, campus groups and clubs, and bars (if they are 21, of course)—all with the intention of observing young people's dating interactions to see if they approve or disapprove of interracial romantic relationships and encounters.

What's the problem with this? Quite simply, looking at behavior doesn't allow them to say much about opinions or motivation. People are complicated—they often act in ways that are not consistent with their ideas and opinions. This is especially true when it comes to dating and sexuality, as studies of abstinence groups have shown. So let's say these students saw people of different races talking and flirting. Would that tell them anything reliable about their views of interracial dating? Not really. Just like we can't assume that opinions lead clearly to behavior, there's a danger in reading motivation from actions. If we want to study opinions, we need to ask respondents about them; if it's motivations we are after, we need to go out and observe real behaviors and interactions.

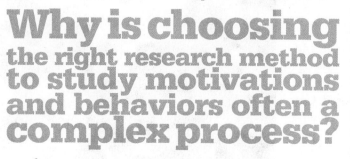
Why is choosing the right research method to study motivations and behaviors often a complex process?

Hence, choosing a research method is a complicated and complex process; it requires considerable thought. It requires good logic and analytical skills to foresee what kind of evidence is needed to answer a research question. And it requires an honest assessment of what kind of person the researcher is. Extremely shy sociologists (they do exist) are perhaps best advised not to carry out in-depth, face-to-face interviews. Socially awkward sociologists (they definitely exist) would perhaps not make the best ethnographers because that method requires lots of social interaction and rapport building. And those researchers who are allergic to math might want to stay clear of statistical work with large surveys and data sets.

Read the Document *Sense and Nonsense about Surveys* in **MySocLab**.

3 How Is Data Collected?

VARIETIES OF RESEARCH METHODS IN SOCIOLOGY

 Watch the **Big Question Video** in **MySocLab**

Once our questions are narrowed and research methods chosen, sociologists are in the position to begin collecting data. This is when we go out and get the information needed to answer our questions. It is when we deal with the nuts and bolts, the nitty gritty, of research. It is when we discover things about the social world. Of course, the process of discovery looks different depending on the method used in the research. Sociologists who rely on survey data must conduct those surveys or clean up the data already collected in large data sets like the General Social Survey (GSS), a general survey which is done twice a year to cover a range of topics of interest to social scientists. The same is true of those who use already-collected administrative data or information collected by other large institutions, like schools, the criminal justice system, the police, welfare agencies, or other governmental bodies. These sociologists must make sure the administrative data is complete, inclusive, and comprehensive—particularly because those data have usually been compiled by administrators as opposed to social scientists. Other sociologists recruit respondents and conduct in-depth interviews with them. Still others set off to work and live among those being studied for participant observation. And others still head off to the archives to analyze past events and to unearth their contemporary relevance.

Scientific Methods of Collecting Data

In addition to differences in concrete research practices, the logic underlying data collection can vary. Some sociologists stay true to the classic steps of the **scientific method**: They formulate research hypotheses based on the existing scholarship; they operationalize the variables key to their hypothesis and predict relationships among those variables; they collect data on the variables using a random sample; they hold those other variables constant so they can determine if the relationship they hypothesized between their key variables held up; and they draw empirical and conceptual generalizations from their data.

Other sociologists take a looser approach to this process of discovery. They may work according to different research stages or cover those same stages in a different order. While some sociologists may have clear hypotheses, others may prefer to work with hunches based on observation or experience and bold guesses about what they think they might find. While some sociologists may be able to operationalize the key factors to be studied, others find it impossible to arrange the social world in such a way that they can focus on a particular subset of variables or a relationship among them. So they may opt to remain more flexible about what they are looking for, allowing the people they observe and interview to help define key issues and problems. Or they may begin by collecting information on several issues until they decide which they want to focus on. And this looser approach to data collection might even prompt researchers to return to their questions for refinement and specification once the research is underway.

Despite these differences, there is a common set of practical issues that can surface in all kinds of data collection. First, when collecting data, all sociologists, regardless of the specific method they use, tend to obsess over issues

related to the reliability and validity of the information they gather. While these two concepts are related, sociologists tend to think of them in distinct ways. When sociologists talk about **reliability** in measurement, they want to know whether, if they used the same measurement technique in an additional study, they would end up with similar results. If the results can indeed be replicated by them, we say that the results are reliable. However, reliability does not necessarily mean that the measurement correctly reflects what the researcher is trying to uncover. One can get the same measurement again and again, but the results might not mean what the researcher thinks they mean. For instance, we might know people who are always 10 minutes late to class or appointments—they are reliably late in their arrival time. But they are still late, consistently inaccurate in their timing. **Validity** captures this—namely, whether the measurement a researcher uses is actually accurate. If the measurement reflects what the researcher is hoping to understand about the social world, we say the results are valid.

Second, regardless of method used, all sociologists grapple with **sampling** issues: They must decide whom or what to include in their study. We are rarely able to study everything and everybody we are interested in. So we make choices: What groups will be examined? What documents will be included? Which settings will be observed? Sampling also involves decisions about numbers—how many people should be surveyed? How many respondents should be interviewed? How many documents should be collected? How often should observations be made? There are no standard answers to any of these questions, but fortunately with some reasonable care we can learn a lot about an entire population by only studying a much smaller subset. The logic of sampling is, in this way, like the way a doctor takes only a test tube of our blood to examine for a whole range of possible problems, or the way a chef tests soup by tasting a small amount. Other types of sampling problems—where we don't actually know the full population we are trying to study—are more challenging. The way we answer them depends largely on what we want to know and who we want to know about—that is, our research questions.

For instance, many sociologists use some form of **probability sampling**, which means they select their samples to mirror a larger population and to reflect its characteristics or dynamics. For some, this is achieved through **random sampling**, through which everyone or everything being studied has an equal chance of being selected for study. This only works, however, when a researcher has a list of the entire population he or she wants to sample. At that point, flipping a coin or taking every third name (or fifth, or tenth, or some other fraction) is the most common form of random

Why are issues of reliability and validity so important to sociological researchers?

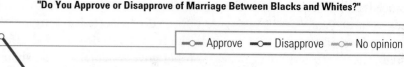

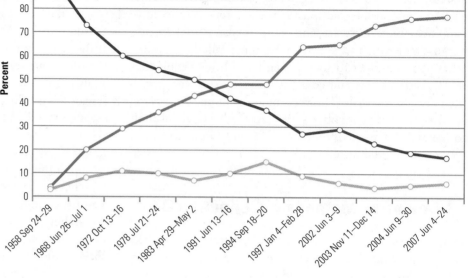

FIGURE 2.3 SURVEYING AMERICA

In 1936, George Gallup, a little-known statistician from Iowa, conducted a survey regarding the upcoming presidential election between Franklin Roosevelt and Alf Landon. Unlike most of the other surveys that were taken by leading magazines and newspapers, Gallup's survey correctly predicted that Franklin Roosevelt would win. Following this success, Gallup grew to prominence, and the Gallup Poll would soon become the most utilized tool for measuring the U.S. public's attitudes concerning virtually every political, social, and economic issue. One of the most remarkable features of the Gallup Poll is that it has allowed us to track significant changes and trends in U.S. public opinion over time. Consider this example, in which Americans were asked if they "approve or disapprove of marriages between blacks and whites," a question Gallup first asked over 50 years ago.

Source: Gallup (2007).

selection, because the chance of getting a head or a tail is the same with each flip. Of course, social scientists use far more sophisticated methods for securing random assignment, many of which involve assigning numbers to potential participants and drawing a subsample of them through computer programs. If and when sampling randomly is not possible, sociologists frequently rely on **representative sampling**, in which they make sure that the characteristics of their sample reflect those of the total population they are studying. In effect, the researchers craft a smaller sample to represent the larger population in ways that are relevant to the study. So if a sociologist is interested in understanding college students' dating practices, and 60 percent of college students are female, this should be reflected in the sample because gender is surely relevant to a study of dating practices. If, however, the initial sample of college students is only 50 percent female, the researcher has undersampled women.

Once a proper sample is drawn, it is then possible to administer a survey (or poll), in which each **respondent**, or person participating in the study, can be asked a large number of questions covering anything of interest to the investigator. A survey might ask questions about each respondent's life, job, family, friends, or community. Surveys that focus on collecting **demographic data**, or information on the size, structure, or distribution of the population, are useful in understanding a wide range of social phenomena. Another kind of survey asks respondents about their attitudes across one or more

issues, for example whether or not they favor gun control or the right of women to have an abortion, or whether they think the president is doing a good job. Some of these kinds of questions are asked on a regular basis in polls conducted by pollsters who work for the media (such as CNN, Fox, or the *New York Times*), although academic social scientists also explore these questions as well (see Figure 2.3).

Of course, decisions about sampling also hinge on the issue of **access**. Do we have access to a survey large and diverse enough? To documents that are complete and representative enough? To interview respondents with the characteristics we are looking for? Or to settings that encapsulate the processes we are most interested in? Sociologists can dream up the perfect population or setting from which to address our research questions, but that population and setting might be completely inaccessible to us. This is why so few observational studies are done about the very rich and influential—it is close to impossible to get them to give researchers unfettered access to their lives. The same is true of interview studies of them—just try to get Donald Trump or Bill Gates to sit down for an interview with you! Even historical studies of the rich and famous are few and far between because they often have the ability to protect and control what is written about them long after they were alive.

So sociologists work with what we can get. For survey researchers, this might mean settling for a data set that only approximates the target population or consists of survey

What sampling issues do sociologists grapple with when they begin their research?

questions covering only some of the relevant issues. For historical sociologists, it might mean working with documents that only indirectly relate to the events or actors being studied. And for an ethnographer, it might mean working in a setting where some, but not all, of the processes to be analyzed are at play. Even then, gaining access to sociological data can be quite a challenge and requires some good negotiating skills on the part of researchers. This is because most social research implies imposing on others' lives and asking them to tolerate disruptions caused by us, whether for the hour it takes to complete a survey or the afternoon it takes to give an in-depth interview or the months and years of being observed.

In this way, good researchers spend a significant amount of time on their data collection. This is particularly true of those who collect their own data (as opposed to using data sets collected and compiled by others). Those who conduct interviews can spend months, even years, putting together their sample and carrying out their interviews; because in-depth interviews can be exhausting for both the interviewer and interviewee, most researchers spread them out over time. Similarly, historical and archival research can be extremely time consuming as sociologists must locate the appropriate documents, gain approval to review them, and weed their way through hundreds or thousands of pages of documents, some of which are hardly decipherable and have not weathered the test of time very well.

Yet arguably the most time-intensive form of data collection is ethnographic research. Not only can it take a long time to find an appropriate field site, but it can take months of negotiating and establishing rapport before gaining the (in)formal approvals to study it. Then comes the research itself: Ethnographers who embed themselves in their subjects' everyday lives often do so for so long that they have a hard time ending the research and exiting those lives. It is not uncommon for ethnographic research to go on for several years. In fact, some of the most famous contemporary ethnographies have approached a decade of data collection.

Given the issue of time, sociologists learn to pace ourselves and not to assume we can collect our data as fast as others might like us to. We make detailed research schedules and try to stick to them. We foresee any problems that could, and probably will, surface because studying real people with real lives and real responsibilities can mean delays, postponements, and cancellations. Most of all, we remember to step back and enjoy the process of learning about the social world, and we remind ourselves that collecting new insights about that world is one of the most powerful and rewarding activities sociologists engage in.

Conducting archival research can be a lonely experience, as sociologists spend hours on end alone with their documents. The payoff is uncovering new and surprising things about the past as well as figuring out what those findings can teach us about the present.

☐ Sociological Methods and Challenges

Just as the choice of a research question leads to a specific research method, the choice of a method implies specific research challenges. So while all research has its dilemmas, different methods highlight different dilemmas. To provide a concrete sense of this as well as a feel for what each of the main sociological methods actually involves in practice, in this section we discuss one of the main issues confronting sociologists using each method—including examples of how they grappled with it. How hard is it for historical sociologists to select their cases? How difficult is it for quantitative researchers to establish causality? How tricky is it for interviewers to draw their samples? And how difficult is it for ethnographers to theorize and generalize from their work?

What types of sociological questions are best studied from a comparative-historical perspective?

Comparative-Historical Methods and the Complexity of Comparison Some of the questions sociologists want to study have an important time dimension to them, that is, they involve history and historical processes in one way or another. For example, questions involving social structure in the most general sense, including institutions (among them governments), public policies (that is, those policies made by governments), culture, or social inequalities can often be profitably studied from a **comparative-historical perspective**, a method of analysis examining a social phenomenon over time or in different places (across time and place). While comparisons are implicit in most social research, some kinds of questions are particularly well suited to studying from a historical perspective as well. History provides a remarkably vast laboratory to study large-scale processes of social change. Not surprisingly, sociologists have found in that vast laboratory ways of testing theories of social, cultural, and political change. Historical research has always been an important part of the sociological tradition.

Sociologists who study history do so in ways that are often quite different than those of historians. Historians are typically experts in a particular time and place—nineteenth-century England, czarist Russia, Nazi Germany, and so forth—and most of their research centers on issues in their area of specialization. By virtue of their deep immersion in a particular context, historians are able to capture nuance and detail in ways that most historical sociologists would not. Historians conduct most of their research in archives, where they evaluate the written record left behind by important historical figures and ordinary citizens. By contrast, sociologists who study history typically do so to make *comparisons* over time and context. They are not necessarily experts in any one time period or place (although if they are to do good research, they will have to become deeply knowledgeable about their cases), but rather they take advantage of the variations in time and place to make sense of larger patterns that the study of history affords.

Comparative-historical sociologists may examine archival materials, but they typically do not do so to nearly the same extent as historians (something that historians frequently criticize them for). They will draw on the findings of historians, often as much or more than the archival record, to develop their conclusions. But historical sociologists have also been very innovative in constructing new sources of data that allow for surveys and comparisons over time. For example, the influential work of Charles Tilly (1929–2008) developed a method for reconstructing the history of protest movements by ordinary citizens over long historical periods in countries like France and Britain by coding newspaper reports (including small, obscure, local papers). Matching these records to other social and economic data, Tilly was able to develop a theory of the cycles of protest over time that showed that protests were not random or irrational eruptions but rather developed in particular contexts such as food shortages, wars, and periods of political turmoil.

Several different kinds of historical comparisons are possible. Research within a single country—say, for example, comparing neighborhoods, cities, or states within the United States, or specific organizations or institutions in different historical periods—is one common type of comparative-historical investigation. By contrast, **cross-national comparisons** typically have as their goal explaining the differences between countries, such as understanding why some outcome is observed in one country and not another.

In order to explore how comparative-historical research is conducted, let's examine one classical piece of scholarship,

Max Weber's *The Protestant Ethic and the Spirit of Capitalism* (Weber [1904] 1976), and a modern classic, Theda Skocpol's study *States and Social Revolutions* (Skocpol 1979). Weber's *Protestant Ethic* is one of the true classics of the social sciences. Weber's starting puzzle was that he wanted to know why it was that capitalism as an economic system was thriving in some parts of Europe but not others. He noted, for example, that in his native Germany some parts of the country were much more economically advanced than others. How could he study this phenomenon, and what might provide an answer to his puzzle?

Weber noticed one important difference between the regions of Europe that were the most economically successful and those that were further behind: The advanced regions tended to be areas where Protestants were dominant (see Figure 2.4). In the long history of religion in European history, the struggle between Catholics and Protestants had produced an uneven map of religious influence. Catholicism retained its historic influence in many parts of southern Europe, such as Spain, France, and Italy, whereas Protestantism was the dominant religion in most parts of Northern Europe. A few countries, like Germany, were divided regionally, with Protestants controlling some areas and Catholics others. The United States was another country where Protestants were numerically dominant (indeed, some of the early settlers in America practiced a kind of extreme form of Protestantism that faced persecution in Europe).

Having made this discovery, Weber then had to try to account for why Protestantism might have been associated with the early rise of capitalism. This led him to dig deeply into the relationship between the views of key figures in the history of Protestantism (especially Martin Luther and John Calvin) and their more modern followers (including Benjamin Franklin in the United States), whom Weber saw as a great popularizer of economic doctrines that connected Protestant religious beliefs to the promotion of individual virtues like thrift and saving that were beneficial for capitalism as an economic system. Weber concluded that a critical aspect of Calvin's form of Protestantism was this: Being economically successful was a way of demonstrating your worthiness to God, whereas consuming whatever you have is a sign that you were not one of the select who would be sent to Heaven.

If Weber's puzzle seemed to have a single answer, most contemporary historical sociologists would be skeptical that religious beliefs alone could solve such a huge question. Theda Skocpol's work on revolutions provides an example of how historical sociologists now tend to think that a wider range of factors are needed to account for particular outcomes. Skocpol asks why there were revolutions from below that brought into existence new kinds of governments in France (in 1789), Russia (in 1917), and China (from 1911 to 1949) but not in other cases that appeared similar in various ways. Skocpol reasoned that if she could

FIGURE 2.4 RELIGIOUS DIVIDES IN EUROPE Max Weber noted that the regions of Europe in the early 1900s that were the most economically successful tended to be areas where Protestants were dominant. How did Protestantism associate with an early rise of capitalism?

Source: Courtesy of the Perry Castaneda Library.

identify those factors that were present in some cases but not others, she would have pinned down the social conditions necessary for revolutions to occur. Her reconstruction of the cases of France, Russia, and China pointed to three factors that were present in each case: a crisis in governing institutions, further international pressures on the government caused by either failed wars or financial problems, and widespread peasant revolts. Each of these factors, she argues, were present in the cases of France, Russia, and China, but one or more was missing in similar cases where attempted revolutions failed (such as in Meiji Japan or nineteenth-century Prussia).

Scholars have been debating the arguments and evidence that Weber and Skocpol presented ever since their books first appeared. For example, Weber wrote before Western scholars had a better understanding of the Muslim world (which included pockets of early capitalism), and he may have missed some important religious differences even in Europe. Skocpol's analysis of the three revolutions may have overlooked some important additional factors in each case, and her focus on the centrality of peasant revolts and government crisis may or may not be useful for understanding most twentieth-century revolutions (which have tended to be rooted in urban areas and not always preceded by crises

in government circles). Nevertheless, in using historical variation to test theories about the importance of religion and states, Weber and Skocpol respectively show how sociologists can draw upon history to test important propositions about society.

Statistical Methods and the Complications of Causality
One of the biggest worries for sociologists conducting statistical analysis is developing techniques to improve their ability to make *causal inferences*. Sociologists interested in understanding the world or informing social policy often want to go beyond simply documenting that two social phenomenon appear together—in other words, that they "co-vary" with each other. This is what sociologists call **correlation**. The most obvious example of this is income and education—they are correlated in that higher income is associated with higher education. Put another way, those who are richer tend to be better educated. These social attributes vary together; a change in one is linked to a change in the other (see Figure 2.5).

But how are they linked? What is motivating the changes? To answer this, sociologists often need to know if it is likely that one thing is caused by another. That's what **causal inference** is all about. And it's not easily done. To

FIGURE 2.5 CORRELATION, BUT NOT CAUSATION It is easy to confuse correlation with causation. But while two variables may be correlated, this does not mean that one necessarily causes the other. Things can be correlated in different ways. A positive correlation means that as one variable increases (or decreases), the other variable follows suit, while a negative correlation means that while one variable increases (or decreases), the other does the opposite. But while correlation simply expresses a relationship between two variables, causation means that one variable is directly responsible for the changes in the other variable. There are many things that may correlate with each other, but that does not mean that they cause each other. Consider these graphs showing the relationship between the number of countries in the United Nations and global warming. We can see a positive correlation between the two variables: As the average world temperature has increased, so too have the number of countries in the United Nations. But while these two have a positive correlation, it would obviously be incorrect to say that global warming has been the cause of more countries being admitted to the United Nations.

Source: About.com (2009); GISS/NASA (2012).

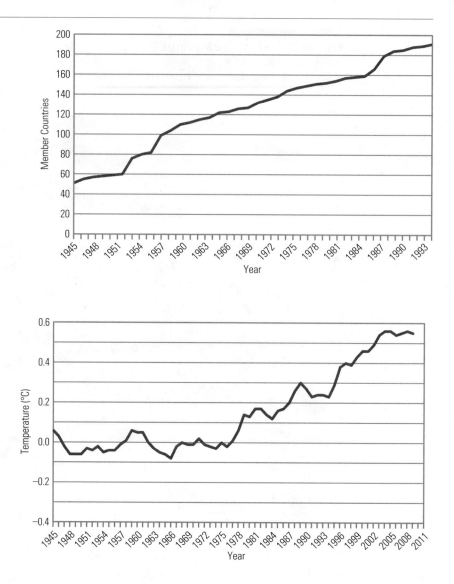

illustrate the challenges, we will take one area of research that not only has been a prominent focus of sociological attention but also is familiar to all twenty-first-century students: educational achievement as measured by standardized test scores. Sociologists have a long tradition of attempting to understand variation in student test scores.

While schools and the U.S. government began widely using test scores to assess individuals and schools early in the twentieth century, the most important contributions of sociologists were made in the past half century. With the Civil Rights Act of 1964, Congress explicitly required the government to "conduct a survey and make a report to the President and Congress, within two years of the enactment of this title, concerning the lack of availability of equal educational opportunities for individuals by reason of race, color, religion or national origin in public educational institutions at all levels in the United States." A prominent sociologist, James Coleman, was put in charge of

How does the Coleman Report illustrate the challenges of making causal inferences?

the effort. Researchers in the fall of 1965 collected and processed 639,650 surveys and, remarkably, by the summer of 1966 completed and distributed a report of approximately 1,000 pages, which came to be known as the Coleman Report (Coleman et al. [1966] 1974).

Coleman and his associates had student surveys that included test score items. Based on this information, they explored how student background and school characteristics were related to test score performance. At the time, many individuals assumed that differences in test score results were likely the product of inequalities in school resources—that is, many members of Congress and the public worried that African American students were often placed in schools with inadequate science labs, libraries, and other resources that inhibited their academic achievement. If you looked simply at test score results in poor or wealthy schools, you would find just that pattern. Test scores were higher in schools with more resources.

However, analysis in the Coleman Report demonstrated that this relationship between school resources and student test scores was largely a spurious relationship. When two factors seem to move in the same direction but both are themselves caused by something else (i.e., a third factor), sociologists refer to the apparent relationship between the first two factors as a **spurious relationship**. Coleman and his colleagues showed that such was exactly the case with the relationship between educational resources and student test scores. Specifically, Coleman demonstrated that while it looked like one caused the other, in fact other factors—namely, family background and the racial composition of schools—were behind the relationship. If you wanted to reduce inequality in student outcomes, equalizing funding would not do much. Instead, one would have to begin to better racially integrate U.S. public schools so that the school peers of African American students more closely resembled those that a typical white student encountered in schools.

The Coleman Report, however, was based on data with a serious limitation: It was **cross-sectional**—that is, it was all collected at one point in time. How could one hope to get at what caused what, when both things examined were being measured simultaneously? By 1980, Coleman and other social scientists had convinced the government that one needed **longitudinal** data, which is collected over a long period of time, to address these questions more productively. A new data set called "High School and Beyond" was collected that followed a random sample of 10th graders as they grew older. With students followed over time, sociologists were able to calculate "value-added test scores" by measuring how much individual test scores improved between 10th and 12th grade.

This change in methods allowed researchers to more accurately identify the effects of school on student academic achievement. Rather than trying simply to adjust test scores for social background as had been done in the Coleman Report, social scientists were now able to see how much growth in test scores occurred in different school settings. In analyzing this new longitudinal data, Coleman and his colleagues found that students in Catholic schools learned more than similar students in public schools (Coleman et al. 1987). Coleman thought that this was most likely due to better discipline in Catholic schools that emerged from the fact that parents and students in these schools were part of closely knit social communities with shared agreement on appropriate student behavior. Whereas findings from the Coleman Report were used to support busing students for racial integration, this new set of findings was used by many to argue in favor of school vouchers, which are government-issued certificates parents can use to send their children to private schools instead of the public schools they were zoned for.

Since the 1980s, sociologists have continued to improve quantitative methods for examining student academic achievement as measured by test scores. For example,

Schools vary a great deal in the kind of facilities and resources available to students. How are those differences related to student performance? It turns out that there is no simple answer to this question—and sociologists have been working hard to answer it for decades.

researchers have devised techniques that better account for the fact that students are clustered in particular classrooms and schools. Sociologists have also studied how academic achievement differs after students have been assigned randomly to alternative types of classrooms or schools (even though students and families often end up not staying in or complying with these random assignments). Alternatively, if students are sorted into classrooms based on particular cutoffs, for example their date of birth or standardized test score, researchers have narrowed in on individuals right before or after those arbitrary cutoff points to see if outcomes end up being notably different on either side of the line. None of these techniques are able to allow sociologists definitively to establish causation. However, they have helped researchers more accurately infer causality than earlier methods. With these improvements in methods, is it any surprise that students increasingly find themselves tested in schools?

Interview Methods and the Dilemmas of Sampling

Interviews come in many shapes and sizes. There are survey

interviews, which are closed-ended exchanges that form the basis of most quantitative data. The U.S. census is a good example of this kind of interview. There are in-depth interviews, which can be highly structured or unstructured in terms of the precise order and wording of questions and seek to get at people's perspectives on some aspect of social life. And then there are life history and oral history interviews, which take respondents through different events and stages in their lives to elicit memories of the past and views of specific experiences.

As a sociological method, all interviews share some key strengths and weaknesses. Their main strength is their ability to get at how people make sense of their worlds. This is particularly true of in-depth interviews. There is no better way to determine how people understand their lives and experiences than by asking them. And there is no better way to ask them than face to face because interview exchanges allow sociologists to probe for nuance and to follow up directly and immediately on unexpected findings. Interviews also allow sociologists to give voice to groups who are often silenced by others and to bring their experiences to bear on social scientific concepts and theories. Of course, with these strengths come challenges. It is enormously difficult to turn a research question into a series of focused interview questions. This kind of work takes great skill. It is also challenging to conduct interviews—sitting down with someone you do not know and asking them lots of questions, often about sensitive issues, can be tricky. And then there are the complexities of making sense of and analyzing all the data from these interviews, which can often yield hundreds of pages of transcripts and quotes from respondents.

Of the many challenges facing interviewers, one of the most complicated comes at the beginning of the research: drawing the interview sample. This is when researchers decide who and how many people to talk to. It is an enormously consequential decision—samples can make or break interview studies because they shape what kind of things researchers find and what they can conclude from their study. The possibilities here are endless: Researchers could interview a few to several hundred people. They could interview men or women, old or young, tall or short, married or single—not to mention all the variations in occupation, education, income, religion, geographical location, identity, and other characteristics they could include in or exclude from their sample. Obviously, not all of these characteristics will be relevant to every interview study, so the first thing an interviewer must figure out is which ones are relevant. Those then become the attributes to be represented in the sample. But they should not be reflected too closely—with too limited a pool of people to sample from, the researcher could be accused of "stacking the deck," or sampling in order

to get a particular outcome, as well as of only interviewing those with a narrow set of views or experiences.

In this way, interviewers follow the sampling approaches discussed earlier in this chapter. But they often do so with a twist because sociologists usually use interviews to elicit people's ideas about a particular issue or aspect of social life. So the "universe" they sample from is rarely the U.S. population in general (as in statistical probability sampling) but rather subgroups with the information they want to know about. This may seem obvious, but it often confuses young interviewers: If you want to examine how an issue is experienced, you need to draw your sample from people who have actually had that experience. If you want to know about people's perceptions of a social or cultural phenomenon, you should talk to people who are likely to have views on those things. And it is not always clear exactly who those people are, not to mention how you should go about accessing them.

What are the key strengths and weaknesses of interview methods?

If all of this sounds tricky in the abstract, it is even trickier in practice. Again, how well interviewers negotiate these challenges largely determines the strength of their study and the kind of generalizations they can make from their research. Here is an example of a successful approach to sampling: In the early 1990s, a team of sociologists set out to study how low-income single mothers viewed marriage (Edin 1997). It was an issue that both scholars and policymakers had been grappling with for decades, even centuries: Do poor single mothers stay unmarried by choice or by force? Are they unmarried because they can be or because they want to be? These questions had become specially timely in the 1990s, in light of the massive overhaul of the U.S. welfare system in 1996—an overhaul that seemed to increase the costs of being a single parent by decreasing the benefits one could claim from the state. The assumption underlying the policy was that single mothers would begin to marry more if other financial options were not available to them (i.e., public assistance). Yet this, the researchers reasoned, begged the question of how these mothers thought about marriage in the first place because no one had really asked them.

So the researchers went out to ask them. But whom to ask? Given their focus, the authors obviously needed to draw their sample from the larger universe of single mothers. That was the easy part. But how to decide which single mothers to include? Here the researchers confronted several complications. First, they wanted to make the findings to say something in general about low-income single mothers and marriage in the United States. So they needed the sample to be representative of those women. But in what ways? They had to decide what relevant attributes and characteristics to represent in the sample. And this took some thinking about the research question and an understanding

Why do some mothers remain unmarried? Is it by choice or by force? These questions have preoccupied social scientists and policymakers for a long time.

of the possible pushes and pulls affecting poor women's marital decisions. On the one hand, because so many policymakers assumed that welfare benefits competed with marriage for women's loyalty, it made sense to include women with access to different kinds of benefits. But there are 50 welfare states in the United States, with each state determining the form and focus of its specific welfare program. How to decide which to sample among them? Along the same lines, women's employment options are often thought to affect their views of marriage—with more labor-market options thought to allow for women to opt out of marriage if they so decide. But there are far more than 50 local labor markets in the United States. How to decide which to draw respondents from?

In the end, the researchers conducted in-depth interviews with close to 300 low-income single mothers from four cities: Chicago, Illinois; Charleston, South Carolina; San Antonio, Texas; and Philadelphia, Pennsylvania. They decided to sample single mothers from these cities because of the kind of welfare benefits they offered as well as their labor-market conditions. In this way, they compared benefit levels and labor markets across the United States to come up with representatives of different patterns: a city with average benefits and labor markets (Chicago), a city with modest welfare benefits and tight labor markets (Charleston), a city with good labor markets but modest benefits (San Antonio), and a city with higher benefits and better labor markets (Philadelphia). They also opted to do a lot of interviews—close to 80 in each city—because the sample also had to vary by race, work history, and marital history. For instance, if they had not interviewed equal numbers of African American and white respondents in each city, their findings could have been an artifact of racial differences in marital ideas more than anything else. Hence, while the researchers did not randomly sample low-income single mothers across the United States, they used what they knew about poverty and parenthood to draw a representative sample that was theoretically motivated.

The result is a sophisticated analysis that continues to influence both social scientists and policymakers. These findings not only complicate stereotypical ideas about poor mothers and marriage, but they suggest a far more nuanced picture of the role marriage plays in their lives—with these women assessing the affordability, respectability, control, and trust that comes with marriage as opposed to simple cost-benefit calculations of the resources they can get through it. Had the authors not been careful to make sure that the women in the sample had access to different kinds of welfare benefits and work options, their conclusions about how they factored into women's views would have been less convincing. The same is true of racial differences—without equal numbers of African American and white respondents, the researchers would not have been able to differentiate what marital views applied to all single mothers from those that might have been race-specific. These kinds of nuanced findings are the payoffs of good interviewing research that uses good sampling procedures: They allow sociologists to paint a complex picture of how people perceive their lives and the decisions they make in them. Explore *A Sociological Perspective* on the politics of motherhood in America on page 48.

Ethnographic Methods and the Challenge of Theory If deciding who to focus on is an issue plaguing interviewers, the frameworks through which those people are viewed and analyzed are a key preoccupation of ethnographers. It is not that ethnographers don't worry about sampling—they also have to decide where to locate their observations, that is, in what "site" they think the phenomenon they are interested in can be found. So they pick a site they believe will help answer their sociological puzzle. Then, once "in the field," ethnographers need to decide who, where, and what to observe. Ethnography is an ongoing project of sampling as researchers are always asking themselves if they should include different kinds of observations or if they should

A SOCIOLOGICAL PERSPECTIVE

Who is a good mother and who is not?

What does a good mother look like to you? Does it depend on her age, financial status, clothing, or whether or not she has a job? The politics of motherhood has been a source of major social conflict in the United States as well as a hot topic for sociological researchers. In an effort to challenge assumptions that women who are poor, young, single, and lack social supports are not good mothers, Ricki Solinger wrote a book based on her research (*Beggars and Choosers*, 2002), in which she focused on stereotypically "unfit" mothers and recast them as nurturing, attentive mothers.

According to Solinger's research, the politics of motherhood takes on particular significance when it comes to the issue of abortion. Although we like to think that every woman has an equal opportunity to be a mother, Solinger shows this is not the reality for all. We talk about abortion in terms of "being a choice" rather than a right granted to every woman. But the truth is that when we say "choice" in a world where some women have access to more resources than others, we are in danger of making motherhood a privilege granted to some but not others.

Are there differences in access to healthcare and social services for women at all economic levels?

Why have resources such as Planned Parenthood become such a controversial topic in today's political debates and what is the impact of that debate on the availability of these services to women?

Regina and Stanley. Marcy Houses. Brooklyn, NY, 1996. Photograph © Regina Monfort

Are Americans' perceptions of good or bad mothers based on stereotypes?

Is there a formula that guarantees one will be a good mother?

expand the kind of people and interactions they are focusing on. Yet one of the major challenges of ethnographic work comes later in the process as researchers try to make sense of their data and figure out how to generalize from them.

As with interviews, there are many types of ethnographic research. As sociologist Kristen Luker (2010) puts it, ethnography is a continuum. On one end are delineated observations in contexts researchers are fairly familiar with and on questions that are clearly defined, such as an ethnographer who goes out to study how men interact in a local barbershop in Philadelphia or an ethnographer who studies how women negotiate the dynamics of power and beauty in nearby nail salons in New York City. On the other end is total immersion in another culture or subculture for long periods of time, such as an ethnographer who heads off to Rwanda to study postgenocidal society or an ethnographer who observes the religious practices of Muslim women in Eastern Europe. Most ethnographic work in sociology falls someplace in the middle, with researchers documenting the patterns, processes, and practices of everyday life both of those they may be familiar and unfamiliar with. Unlike anthropologists, who often carry out their research in foreign cultures—called **fieldwork** among ethnographers—for years at a time, sociologists are more apt to study their own cultural settings for a fixed amount of time.

The real strength of ethnographic analysis is that it can produce some of the richest, most nuanced accounts of social life in sociology. If done well, ethnography transports us to places and spaces we don't normally have access to, from to the inside of prison cells to the dealings of street gangs to the struggles of homeless heroin addicts to the trials and tribulations of fashion models. It can provide **thick descriptions** of the people living in those spaces—that is, rich and detailed descriptions of the ways they make sense of their lives, written from the perspective of those people themselves. And it is the ideal method to use for getting at "practice"—the point where words and actions collide, and frequently diverge. Instead of taking people's words at face value, ethnographers are able to link them to the way people act, a connection that

In what way is the main strength of ethnography its central weakness?

frequently leads to fascinating examples of inconsistency—which can themselves tell us an enormous amount about social life.

A great example of this inconsistency between what people say about their actions and their actual behavior is Arlie Hochschild's (1989) account in *Second Shift*. Researched and written in the late 1980s, the book remains unusual for its combination of interviews with and observations of couples, focusing on how they manage the tensions between work and family. What she finds is fascinating: The way couples represent what goes on in their homes almost always differs from what Hochschild sees in their homes. In some cases the couple claims to be "traditional"—with the husband taking care of the world of paid work and the wife the domestic arena of unpaid labor—but then in everyday life, Hochschild watches as these men do most of the cleaning, shopping, and household organizing. In other cases, she finds the opposite: Couples claim to have an equal division of labor outside and inside the home, yet their lives revealed something else. Their interview proclamations were contradicted by sound of the pitter-patter of the wives' feet as they ran around the house cooking, cleaning, and caring for the kids while their husbands watched television or worked on their cars. Faced with the differences between words and action, Hochschild was able to analyze the complex ways couples smooth over what they would like from their relationship and what they actually get from them, what she calls "family myths." Now decades old, the account still provides an amazingly insightful analysis of the

Some ethnographers immerse themselves deep into the culture or subculture they are studying. Others observe people in contexts they are fairly familiar with, such as an ethnographer who studies how people interact in a barbershop.

workings of these myths and still shows off the importance of observing what people do and not only what they say.

The irony is that ethnography's main strength can also be its central weakness. In the process of producing thick descriptions of interesting aspects of social life, ethnography can sometimes lack analytical focus or theoretical relevance. Some ethnographers seem reluctant to conceptualize or theorize from their data. While this was not true in Hochschild's case—in part because her empirical findings about the discrepancies between words and actions had such clear conceptual relevance—other ethnographies are plagued with an inability to generalize beyond their specific fields. Indeed, generalizing from ethnographic data can be particularly thorny. Ethnographers can find it hard, if not impossible, to claim that their cases are representative of a larger trend or issue. They can find it hard, if not impossible, to move beyond the everyday lives they are embedded in and to analyze them in terms that would seem foreign to those lives. And they can find it hard, if not impossible, to make broad points from the small, local contexts ethnographers tend to research. All of this can leave ethnographers wary of using their work to engage in the larger theoretical and conceptual debates of sociology.

Of course, the ethnographic tendency toward thick description is not considered a weakness by everyone. In fact, some embrace and celebrate this aspect of ethnographic work. Clifford Geertz, the famous anthropologist who came up with the term *thick description* to describe what ethnographers do, saw it as an asset of the method—a way for social scientists to render an "understanding of understanding." More contemporarily, there are some ethnographic studies that set their goal as offering new and different descriptions of social life. One of the best, most prominent examples of this is an ethnographic account of homeless street vendors and magazine sellers in New York City, a study that provided a *tour de force* of detail and insight into what everyday life on the street looks and feels like for these men: The indignities they suffer, the meanings they make, the ways they attempt to protect their sense of self, and the strategies they use to maintain a "moral order" on the street (Duneier 1999). And while no one can look at this study and not learn an enormous amount about how men like this live and survive, there is not much in the way of explanation or theory in the account. There is not even very much about what others have found in studies of similar topics. In fact, the researcher almost explicitly rejects using theory even to organize his account, opting instead to divide up his story according to the different types of men on the street and the different labor they engage in. Hence, ethnographies in the tradition of studies like these are so engaging and so captivating that they reveal the power of good thick description. Yet they can also leave readers without a sense of what these men's lives tell us about broader sociological concepts and theory.

For this kind of analysis, there are other ethnographic traditions. There are those ethnographers who try to move beyond descriptive accounts of specific locales to connect their ethnographic insights to larger sociological debates and theoretical questions. For instance, one sociologist oriented his career to debunking the idea that ethnography must be atheoretical and ahistorical. To do this, he has developed what he calls the **extended case method**, a way of doing ethnography that emphasizes its contribution to social theory (Burawoy 2009). As he points out, an ethnographic site need not be representative of a large social process to extend the reach of theory. It need not cover lots of randomly sampled cases for an ethnographic account to contribute to the making of better social theory. Instead, he insists that ethnographers can and should be theoretically focused from the start of their research: When they head out into the field, they should go armed with concepts and theories they want to hold up to the social world. Because the real world is almost always more complex than our theories of it, ethnographers' job is to revise social theory in light of what they observed in that world. So rather than striving for thick description, these ethnographic accounts aim for theoretical reconstruction. The books and articles done in this ethnographic mode reveal its payoffs. From Burawoy's own work on how factories work in the United States and Eastern Europe to his students' work (often published in collections he coauthors with his students) on everything from HIV activists to housekeepers to welfare workers to Chinese assembly-line workers, many theoretical breakthroughs have emerged from their ethnographic research (see Burawoy 1979; Burawoy et al. 1991; Burawoy et al. 2000).

The two different ethnographies just described are located at two ends of the ethnographic continuum. For many, the goal is to combine the benefits of both, finding a way to embed their rich empirical observations in theoretical debates and dialogues. Indeed, this is a goal most social researchers strive for, regardless of the questions they ask or the methods they use. Much of this chapter has stressed the differences among methods—how different questions imply different methods and how different methods involve different challenges and dilemmas. Yet the project of social research unites more than it divides: All sociologists want to ask innovative questions and develop new puzzles about the social world. We want to solve those puzzles in ways that are convincing, intriguing, and provocative. And we want our solutions to prompt others to carry on, to ask better questions in their own research, and to add to the development of the sociological imagination.

4 How Do Sociologists Make Sense of Their Findings?

ANALYZING DATA AND REACHING CONCLUSIONS

👁 **Watch** the **Big Question** Video in **MySocLab**

With our questions asked and data collected, sociologists are finally in the position to make sense of what we have found. This is called **data analysis**—when we interpret the information we've collected and look for patterns across it. Some sociologists wait until this stage before they do any interpretive work. Those who work with survey data, for instance, rarely stop midway to analyze only a subsample of their subjects. Instead, they tend to wait until all the data are in to begin analyzing them and drawing conclusions from them. Yet for others it is essential that analysis occur while the data are being gathered. For ethnographers—especially those who spend years in the field—it would be a disaster to wait until all observations are made before analyzing them. Facing hundreds of pages of unanalyzed field notes would overwhelm even the most experienced researcher. The same is true of historical sociologists who spend months or even years in the archives, so waiting until they are confronted with thousands of index cards of unanalyzed data would be a disaster. Thus, along-the-way analysis is critical for many social researchers.

In this way, the amount of work involved in data analysis varies quite a bit, and not only by the research method used. Sociologists often differ in the timing and location of the analysis. Sometimes their research is "front heavy," with a great deal of its work occurring before data are collected as researchers frame their questions around existing theoretical and scholarly debates, extract hypotheses, decide how to conceptualize the relevant categories or variables, and define precise ways to measure them. Hence, once the data are collected, the analysis begins. Other times the reverse is true: Some research tends to be "back heavy," with a lot of the analytical work saved for the post–data collection phase, once researchers have collected their observations, carried out their interviews, or studied their historical records. Only then do they put together a picture of what emerged from the research, thus building their arguments from the specific to the general. And that building process can take a considerable amount of time and energy.

How Do the Puzzle Pieces Fit Together?

Whichever logic a sociologist uses, the goal is the same: to figure out how the pieces of the empirical puzzle fit together and what the completed puzzle tells us about the social world. Indeed, we can think about data as pieces of a larger puzzle—and the job of the researcher is to put them together into patterns and make research conclusions. But for anyone who has struggled with a thousand-piece puzzle, it is clear that the process of making it whole can be very difficult. Sociologists have many strategies to aid them here. First, most of us engage in some form of **data coding**—that is, organizing the data

How do sociologists use data coding to help them reach conclusions?

Representing Data

There are not only **different ways to collect data**, but also **different ways to represent data**. Indeed, while we often think of data as an objective thing, in fact, the meaning of data can change dramatically depending on how we chose to visually represent it. And because data carries so much weight when it comes to making arguments, the decision of how to represent the data visually is often very strategic.

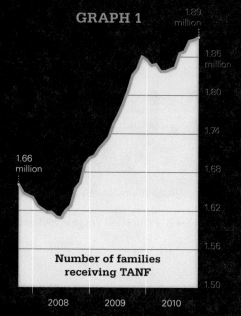

GRAPH 1

1.89 million

1.66 million

1.86 million
1.80
1.74
1.68
1.62
1.56
1.50

Number of families receiving TANF

2008   2009   2010

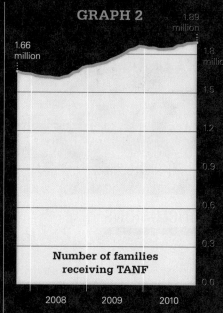

GRAPH 2

1.89 million

1.66 million

1.8 million
1.5
1.2
0.9
0.6
0.3
0.0

Number of families receiving TANF

2008   2009   2010

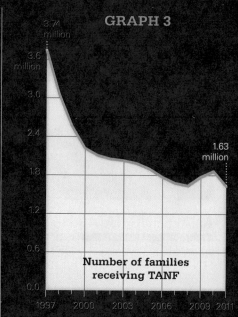

GRAPH 3

3.74 million

3.6 million

1.63 million

3.0
2.4
1.8
1.2
0.6
0.0

Number of families receiving TANF

1997   2000   2003   2006   2009 2011

The chart above shows the number of families receiving TANF (Temporary Assistance to Needy Families) between October 2007 and December 2009. The graph gives the appearance that the number of families receiving TANF has jumped dramatically. And if you're a politician who was wants to show that this is the trend because you made a campaign promise to increase welfare, then this is a good graph for you.

 Explore the **Data** on Representing Data in **MySocLab** and then ...

■ **Think About It**

What other ways could these data be represented to create additional images of the rise and fall of welfare in the U.S. (by region, recipients' race, family status, etc)?

■ **Inspire Your Sociological Imagination**

If you wanted to study the reasons behind these changes in TANF over time, what would you focus on?

But suppose you're a politician who wants to argue that in fact, the number of families receiving TANF has not increased? We might think that there is nothing you could do because the data simply says the opposite. But consider the graph above, showing the exact same data. Suddenly it looks like there was little change in the number of families receiving welfare. The data didn't change, but how we represented them did. The big difference was the scale we used on the x-axis which indicates the number of families. Whereas in Graph 1 the number of families begins at 1,500,00, in Graph 2 it begins at 0.00. And in Graph 1 we increased by increments of 25,000, while in Graph 2, we showed increments of 250,000. The result is dramatic.

Now suppose you're a politician wanting to argue that in fact, the number of welfare recipients has neither increased nor stayed the same, but actually gone down? Once again, you don't need different data, just a different way of showing it.

In Graph 3 we have changed the scales again, and in so doing changed the meaning of the data. This time we've done it on the x-axis, which shows increments of time. While in Graphs 1 and 2, our x-axis proceeded by months, starting in October of 2007 and ending with 2009, this time it proceeds by year beginning in 1996 and ending in 2011. So, have the number of families receiving this form of welfare increased or decreased over time?

Source: Based on data from the Administration for Children and Families, U.S. Department of Health and Human Services

according to key categories and concepts. For those doing statistical analysis, this means putting the data into a form that is computer useable—standardizing the raw data, usually by assigning numbers to them. Sometimes coding has already been done for researchers, especially if they are using secondary survey data from data sets. In this case, researchers can use precoded data that come ready for statistical manipulation.

Because most interviewers, ethnographers, and historical sociologists collect primary-source data, or their own data, they must do their own coding. On the one hand, this involves assigning a specific code to classify a specific piece of data. Those codes then becomes the mechanism through which the data are sorted, systematized, and arranged. It is the way data are categorized across cases.

Once our data are coded, sociologists usually do more analytical work before making research conclusions. This work involves making sense of the data and breaking them down to see emergent patterns. For those who think visually, **data displays** can be a useful way to go about this. These are visual images of the patterns forming in the data. They are ways to represent the data; they are visuals summaries of what has been found. Such displays include diagrams, flowcharts, typologies, tables, and matrices. Even if these visuals never make it into the final research product, their importance lies in the process of constructing them and in drawing out the connections being made across the data as well as the patterns that still need to be fleshed out. For those who tend to think verbally, **research memos** can serve a similar purpose. These are extended versions of research notes, usually organized analytically, that allow researchers work through their findings and the evidence they have to support them, as well as to make sure the analytical forest is not lost amid all the trees of data. Explore the Infographic *Representing Data* on page 52 to learn more about data displays.

What Do Our Conclusions Tell Us about the Social World?

In the end, the goal of all of this work is to make reliable research conclusions. In this final step, sociologists go back to the research questions we began with and figure out how the empirical patterns that we uncovered help to answer them. Put another way, we strive to make general claims about the issues posed by our research question. Yet this **generalization**

is a tricky thing in much sociological research. On the one hand, sociologists don't want to limit our conclusions only to the specific sample of people, places, or things we studied directly; we also want to form conclusions from those samples to say something overall about the broad patterns they are associated with. But we need to make sure we don't overextend our claims; we must be careful that the conclusions we draw from our data are reliable and valid.

So sociologists proceed with caution here. Some have conducted their research in a way that allows them to claim **empirical generalizability**—they apply conclusions from their findings to a larger population. So if the sample was big enough and drawn randomly, these sociologists feel confident generalizing from a part to the whole. Other sociologists who did not work with a big national data set, and who were unable (or unwilling) to sample randomly, cannot make those kind of empirical claims. So they tend toward **theoretical generalizability**—they apply conclusions from their findings to larger sociological processes. To use one sociologist's phrasing, they "bump up a level of generality" to bring their findings to bear on a broader concept or theory (Luker 2010). Whatever level a sociologist decides to generalize to, we all strive to address the "big questions" in the social sciences —questions that we will outline and discuss throughout this text.

How do sociologists decide what kind of general claims to draw from their research?

CONCLUSION THINKING CRITICALLY ABOUT RESEARCH

Now that you are armed with new methodological knowledge, I invite you to bring those critical insights to bear on all of the research you will read about in this text. Whether the research is on the family, popular culture, the government, race relations, religion, or the environment, you are equipped to ask the big methodological questions of the work: What was the research question? Was the method used appropriate for addressing the question? Were the data collected systematically? Were the findings reliable and trustworthy? And what's the larger take-away from the work? What does it teach us about the larger world we live in?

Watch the Video in **MySocLab**
Applying Your Sociological Imagination

Study and **Review** in **MySocLab**   **Watch** the **Video** Inspiring Your Sociological Imagination in **MySocLab**

1 Where Do Sociological Questions Come From? *(p. 30)*

 Watch the **Big Question Video** in **MySocLab** to review the key concepts for this section.

This section began the chapter by discussing the basic stages of sociological research and issues that often come up as researchers practice sociology for the first time, such as how sociologists turn their research interests into workable questions and how we know what to study.

THE BUILDING BLOCKS OF SOCIOLOGICAL RESEARCH (p. 30)

Moving from Research Topics to Research Questions (p. 30)

- **Why is it essential to review existing research on a topic before asking a new research question?**

The Complexities of Research Questions (p. 31)

- **What six questions should a sociologist ask to determine the merit of a research question?**

How Do We Know What to Study? (p. 33)

- **What factors shape sociologists' choices about what to research?**

KEY TERMS

ethnographer *(p. 28)*

sociological imagination *(p. 28)*

quantitative research *(p. 30)*

qualitative research *(p. 30)*

hypothesis *(p. 30)*

causality *(p. 31)*

epistemology *(p. 33)*

positivism *(p. 34)*

interpretivism *(p. 34)*

theoretical tradition *(p. 34)*

value *(p. 34)*

code of ethics *(p. 34)*

informed consent *(p. 34)*

institutional review board *(IRB)* *(p. 35)*

What Is the Best Method to Research a Sociological Question? *(p. 36)*

 Watch the **Big Question Video** in **MySocLab** to review the key concepts for this section.

Once sociologists have a working research question, they need to decide the best way to go about answering it. In this section we examined the process sociologists use to determine the best research method and design. We also considered the question of why choosing the right research method to study motivations and behaviors is often a complex process.

MOVING FROM RESEARCH QUESTIONS TO RESEARCH METHODS (p. 36)

- **Which types of research questions are best investigated using surveys, and when are in-depth interviews required?**
- **Why is choosing the right research method to study motivations and behaviors often a complex process?**

Read the **Document** *Sense and Nonsense about Surveys* by Howard Schuman in **MySocLab.** This reading examines the complicated nature of surveys and how many things can affect the results and quality of the data collected.

3 How Is Data Collected? *(p. 38)*

 Watch the **Big Question Video** in **MySocLab** to review the key concepts for this section.

In this section, we examined the different types of methods that sociologists use and how they adhere to a scientific method.

VARIETIES OF RESEARCH METHODS IN SOCIOLOGY (p. 38)

Scientific Methods of Collecting Data (p. 39)

- **Why are issues of reliability and validity so important to sociological researchers?**
- **What sampling issues do sociologists grapple with when they begin their research?**

Sociological Methods and Challenges (p. 41)

- **What types of sociological questions are best studied from a comparative-historical perspective?**
- **How does the Coleman Report illustrate the challenges of making causal inferences?**
- **What are the key strengths and weaknesses of interview methods?**

Explore A Sociological Perspective: Who is a good mother and who is not? in MySocLab

- **In what way is the main strength of ethnography its central weakness?**

4 How Do Sociologists Make Sense of Their Findings? (p. 51)

 Watch the **Big Question Video** in **MySocLab** to review the key concepts for this section.

This section examined how sociologists make sure their findings are reliable and trustworthy and how they decide what kinds of general claims to draw from their research.

ANALYZING DATA AND REACHING CONCLUSIONS (p. 51)

How Do the Puzzle Pieces Fit Together? (p. 51)

- **How do sociologists use data coding to help them reach conclusions?**

Explore the **Data** on Representing Data in **MySocLab**

What Do Our Conclusions Tell Us about the Social World? (p. 53)

- **How do sociologists decide what kind of general claims to draw from their research?**

Watch the **Video** Applying Your Sociological Imagination in **MySocLab** to see these concepts at work in the real world.

3
SOCIAL INTERACTION

 **Listen** to the **Chapter Audio** in **MySocLab**

by HARVEY MOLOTCH

 he public restroom might be the last place you would expect to learn about the ways people think and interact with others. We spend our days carefully managing how we present ourselves and interact with others in all different kinds of social situations. But nowhere is the presence of others felt more strongly than in a public restroom, making it an interesting place to learn about social interaction. What happens in the public restroom provides clues about how we achieve and safeguard our own identity, always in ways appropriate to the context we are in. The public restroom shows the intensity of the stakes in getting things right, and maybe this justifies, even invites, bringing it up as an academic topic. The specific restroom predicament is that we humans need to eliminate our own body waste, but that process is somewhat animalistic. It conflicts with our efforts to show ourselves as civilized. We must do it, but unlike other creatures in the animal kingdom, our culture intervenes to shape what it means to perform this so-called natural act. We notice who is present and where and how they look—at themselves and at us. We manage in tiny, moment-by-moment ways what others see and hear, looking inward and outward at the same time. A casual touch or accidental bump registers immediately, just as we acutely pick up on gestures, sounds, and movements.

Among the reasons the stakes are so high is that, in sociologist Erving Goffman's famous terms, the bathroom is part of our "backstage" where we set

MY SOCIOLOGICAL IMAGINATION
Harvey Molotch

My work over the years has explored power, social interactions, and culture. I have written extensively on cities and urban spaces, demonstrating how social interests coalesce into "local growth machines" that promote development aligned with their self-interests. My work on understanding media includes research on how news is socially constructed. When I was teaching at the University of California–Santa Barbara, I observed and wrote about the historic Santa Barbara oil spill of 1969 and how the media represented the events. More recently, I have been writing about objects and how social meanings and values are associated with them. I came to sociology through a philosophy professor who put me on to C. Wright Mills and his various books, including *The Sociological Imagination*. Mills tells us that anything like a meaningful community cannot happen when some people have so little power compared to others. I became convinced that Mills shows us a way out. The trick is to link up with others situated as we are and see our problems as common ones, caused by the same types of external forces.

58

While it may seem to be an unusual setting to study sociology, we can learn a lot about social interaction in the public restroom.

Watch the Video in **MySocLab**
Inspiring Your Sociological Imagination

up our "presentation of self" (Goffman 1959). More usually, we are in the privacy of our own home when we do these core personal activities. In contrast, the public restroom is not private. So besides avoiding the usual public embarrassments—slipping on the floor, crying out loud, wearing mismatched socks—we take on other worries of giving away something so private: There should be no suspicious soiling or water splash on our clothes. Indeed there should be no evidence at all of where we've been or what we've done. And while on task inside the restroom, we must carefully monitor what we expose and to exactly whom. To mess up in any of these regards would risk spoiling our identity, maybe implying we were not decent or competent in other regards as well.

One way we avoid such labels is through our specific cultural knowledge of what to do and when. This includes smoothly working the hardware and equipment at hand: sinks, toilets, toilet paper, and stall doors, as well as the social aspect. We ordinarily do not fumble with doorknobs or shout approval at the sound of another person's defecation. We follow the rule of respecting separate rooms for women and men without being told by a police officer to do so. Men choose a urinal, if available, not adjacent to one being used by a stranger.

But imagine the problems for visitors from a part of the world where things are different. In other countries, people may squat over an opening—in fact a superior arrangement both in sanitary and physiological terms compared to the chair-sit of the Western world. They may cleanse themselves not with toilet paper but by using water piped into the stall that they can spray at fouled body parts. Women and men may share facilities by using them at different *times* instead of having different *places*. And what a contrast all of it is with the practices in the Roman Empire, where citizens did their business with as many as 80 to 90 individuals sitting adjacent along a room's perimeter, open to one another and apparently speaking about issues of the day. Speaking for myself, I would be culturally lost and quite disturbed to be so exposed.

Besides worry about germs, something common among restroom users, there is concern about social contamination. So the very presence of the wrong kind of person, one imagined as inappropriate for social interaction, is a pollutant. In India this means avoiding persons of the lowest caste (whose role is, among other lowly tasks, cleaning toilets); in countries like the United States, those who appear unkempt or disorderly may generate worries about their being too nearby. Some people will not enter a restroom with a homeless person inside and avoid sharing one with any of those too far below their own social standing.

Our behavior in public restrooms is heavily influenced by gender. In their respective restrooms, men and women behave differently, much beyond constraints imposed by biological variation. Men, for example, virtually never have conversation from stall to stall (women apparently do so on occasion) and converse only in very constrained ways at the urinals. They take pains to keep their eyes straight ahead, never looking at the exposed anatomy of another man *and not looking like they are trying not to look* at another man's anatomy. Yet women are more at ease. They report that restrooms are where they go to chat. It is where, they sometimes say, they learned as girls how to groom themselves, hold their bodies, use menstrual products, and adjust their clothes—with pals and relatives fussing around them with help and suggestions (Saurez 2008). Whether male or female, in choosing the "right" room to go in and then engaging in practices appropriate to that room, users reinforce their unique identity as a particular kind of person, namely a man or woman, and one who grooms him- or herself and handles the presence of others in a specific way. Precisely because of the actions we take, guided as we are by the watchful judgments of those who matter to us, we form our very identities. This chapter examines how we can each be distinctive yet subject to the influence of others. How can there be, sociologists ask, both individual identity yet also conformity? And just how does all this get accomplished in human interaction?

The answers, as it turns out, come not from thinking of "individual" and "society" as opposite or even separate things at all. Instead, an individual and her or his society influence one another continuously through history and constantly from moment to moment. It happens—and this is a fundamental starting point for understanding human beings—through how we interact and how we think. Here is the key: We introspect, and we do it with the help of other people.

> **Precisely because of the actions we take, guided as we are by the watchful judgments of those who matter to us, we form our very identities.**

THE BIG QUESTIONS

◉ **Watch** the **Big Question Videos** in **MySocLab**

In examining how humans develop a sense of self through social interaction, our discussion is guided by exploring the following big questions:

How do we develop a sense of self? Each one of us has a unique identity. But is this sense of self a single thing, or is it a process of interaction? In this section, we examine how we know ourselves through the reflections of ourselves that mirror back from others' opinions of us—the "looking glass" of others.

How do we make sense of our worlds? Human beings have specific methods for demonstrating competence as interacting members of society. In this section, we explore how the sociological field of ethnomethodology examines these methods.

Who matters to us? Not everyone we encounter has the same capacity to influence our sense of self or shape our identity—some people matter to us more than others. In this section, we examine the relative influence of significant others, reference groups, and the generalized other.

What challenges do we face as we move from one social context to another? The social self is not fixed but is always changing, which can sometimes bring challenges. Here we examine what happens when individuals experience role conflict and how informal rules and our keen awareness guide our behavior. We also look at how and why people conform and what consequences conformity has on how people live together.

1   "How Do We Develop a Sense of Self?"

THE SOCIAL SELF

👁 **Watch** the **Big Question Video** in **MySocLab**

e have the ability to think not just about objects before us, like a banana or a mate, but about our very selves. Not even smart and sensitive French poodles can do that. Like other nonhumans, intelligent dogs are driven by instinct rather than introspection, which is why they pee all over town even when they will get the same amount of food and love by going only once or twice and only in one spot. The remarkable human capacity for consciousness of **self**—that is, individual reflection on one's own identity and social position, which is made and reformulated through interaction—becomes the vehicle through which we take our actions, interpreting and evaluating everything that comes our way, including other people. As a man once said to me while he was sitting on a locker-room bench pondering the world with his head in his hands, "I may not be much, but I'm all I ever think about."

The social self is the only kind of self there can be: *The self is not a thing, but a process of interaction*. This important school of thought in sociology, based in the thinking of the early twentieth-century philosopher George Herbert Mead, is called symbolic interaction, or just **interactionism**, and it guides ideas for this chapter. Central to this line of thinking is the idea that an individual's personality, preferences, ideas, and so forth are constructed and shaped by and through communication with both others and his or her self.

Why is social interaction vital to the development of self?

☐ The Looking-Glass Self

The concept of the social self or social identity is so basic that, if it becomes too hard to achieve, even the physical self becomes problematic. We know from studies of orphanages that babies have a hard time surviving biologically without social stimuli. The psychoanalyst René Spitz learned this when he compared, in a classic 1945 study, the babies and small children in an orphanage to a nursery for the children of incarcerated mothers. Caring professionals staffed both facilities, which were clean, warm environments where the babies received good medical attention and nutritious food. But there were differences. In the nursery, the infants were surrounded by the bustle of attendants and visitors going about their business. They could see everything and each other right through the bars of their cribs. The biggest medical problem in the nursery was the common cold, and the infants were otherwise healthy and happy.

Meanwhile, in the orphanage, the babies were separated from the staff most of the time and only had human contact when being fed or changed. They lived in cubicles, making it impossible to see each other, and their cribs had solid sides so they could not even see out of them. The result, wrote Spitz, was that "each baby lies in solitary confinement up to the time he is able to stand up in his bed" (Spitz 1945). Unlike

Why do we put on make up? Even at a young age, other people's impressions of us matter to us. Whether it is eye liner or a baseball cap, we all put on some kind of make up to try to impact the image people have of us.

the nursery, the orphanage infants suffered emotionally and physically. They became progressively more withdrawn and more susceptible to hosts of chronic maladies as they grew. Forty percent actually died within two years of Spitz's first observations. He concluded that the poor emotional and physical health of the orphanage babies was caused by a lack of social contact with others. When the orphanage switched cribs and caregivers started interacting with children, mortality sharply declined.

Adults do not fare much better in solitary confinement. In U.S. prisons, it is common to discipline inmates by sending them "to the hole" for weeks, months, and even years for breaking rules. In windowless cells, prisoners' food may be delivered through a slot in the door, and if they are allowed visitors at all, these may be held via videoconference, in what University of California–Santa Cruz psychologist Craig Haney dubbed the supermax prison. According to Haney, without real contact with others, prisoners' health falls apart. The minds of some begin to grind to a halt with confusion, lethargy, and inability to concentrate. The minds of others go wild with hallucinations, paranoia, and intense anxiety. That's why, in search of basic social contact, some may resort to tapping on the pipes and air ducts running through their cells just to be acknowledged by someone else who might tap back (Haney 2003). Or they commit suicide.

So where does this need for social contact come from that looms so large and can be a matter of life or death itself? We really only know ourselves through the eyes of other people. The actions that we take, the expressions that we use, the gestures we give off enlist evaluations from those around us. Those others tell us, not necessarily with explicit words, what we are—and we interpret their evaluations as representing our being. It starts, of course, with our parents or other caregivers who can't help but notice our early babbling and silly movements. Their smiles and frowns becomes the stuff that gives us an early sense that we even exist. From then on feedback comes about what *type* of person we are, including how good or bad.

The judgments accumulate throughout our lives as we gather playmates, siblings, friends, teachers (sometimes psychiatrists and police)—a stream of judges and judgments that fill in our sense of our own being. Are we clever? Pretty? Short or tall? Nice or selfish? We are, in effect, asking all these things all the time, and others are providing the answers. We know ourselves through the "looking glass" of others that mirror back to us the impressions we create. The **looking-glass self** was a term coined by sociologist Charles Horton Cooley in 1902 to emphasize the extent to which our own self-understandings are dependent on how others view us. We see ourselves as others see us. Interaction makes our world go round.

Looking for approval becomes truly motivating. If there is a fundamental human instinct, this is it. Because we want to belong and make connections with others, we try to anticipate what will be made of what we do. We have the ability to, in the lingo of sociology, "take the role of the other." This gives us the tool to conform to others' expectations because we can imagine how they will receive what we do or say. And those others shape their behaviors in light of their expectations of how we will receive them. It becomes a complicated system of interactions across a wildly complicated array of people in direct and indirect communication. This is where, sociologically speaking, conscience and guilt come from. We don't want to let others down. We really do want to satisfy their expectations for us because that is also the way to create a positive sense of one's own being and to socially belong and be connected in positive ways with others. Even if it is only indirect contact through things we have read, seen on television, or picked up on Facebook, we take note and gain some understanding of what we need to do to please, and fit into social behavior expected by, others.

How do the opinions and judgments of others shape our identities?

📖 **Read** the **Document** *The Looking-Glass Self* in **MySocLab**.

☐ Life's a Stage

We are always, in a sense, on stage—performing the self in the spotlight of others. We need approval not just as some kind of bonus for a nicer life. We need it to *be*. The show must go on, and the show is our life.

Evidence of how carefully we consider which parts of ourselves to share can be found by examining the stuff we carry around each day. Ethnographer Christena Nippert-Eng (2010) discovered our wallets and pocket books are toolkits for managing the multiple faces we show to others. Business cards, if we have them, are meant for just about anyone we might meet. They are props on our most public stage. But more personal things in the same wallet, such as a drug prescription, may be kept secret from our closest friends yet shared with any random employee of a pharmacy. While we all conduct life through these multiple faces, Nippert-Eng found different people think differently about what they are willing to share. Some would be horrified to let others see the receipts in their wallets, but others do not worry about what these slips of paper might reveal. We think differently about what aspects of our identities we are willing to show, and exactly how.

While we all share the fact that we live as if on stage, we are not all the same. Whereas a geneticist might think we are each unique because of our biological codes, a sociologist views each of us as different because no one has had the same set of social interactions. Each of us bounces, searches, lurches, and passes through particular settings, interacting with a different array of individuals and expectations. There are overlaps for sure, especially among those with common origins and similarities of gender, class, or ethnicity, but never in a way that creates identical individuals.

It also follows that we are always changing. Because the process never stops and our circumstances keep shifting, we constantly alter identity over time, even if only in tiny ways, from minute to minute. Sometimes we are American; sometimes we are Irish American or African American. Sometimes we identify ourselves by our occupation ("I am a lawyer"), other times by hobbies or passions ("I am an activist," or "I am a Giants fan"). As we act in the world and the world responds to us, we become different selves—including how "good" or "bad" we take ourselves to be and in just what ways. That means we each bring at least a slightly different self to any new circumstance—different from anybody else's and different from what we were at all prior times.

2 How Do We Make Sense of Our Worlds?

PEOPLE'S METHODOLOGY

Watch the **Big Question Video** in **MySocLab**

So now we know that social interaction forms the individual. But then what? What underlies the capacity to make this happen? At the most basic level: how do individuals demonstrate competence as interacting members of society? How do we show that we are safe to be around and capable of sharing in social life? Some sociologists, influenced by interactionism but branching out in some new directions from it, study this problem with precise observations and experiments. It turns out that human beings have specific methods for interacting with others, and people all over the world, regardless of culture or historical moment, use these same methods. That at least is the perspective of the influential sociologist Harold Garfinkel, the inventor of the sociological field, called **ethnomethodology**—the study of people's methods.

Context, Context, Context

And what do those methods look like? Well, one of them—a kind of master method—is that people persistently and intensively take context into account. So even a word that may seem straightforward, such as *kill,* gets its meaning from context. When we hear a phrase like "I'll kill you," it matters whether it is a child tickling her brother, a teenager whose sister ruined her new sweater, or an interrogator in a secret prison. The participants in "I'll kill you" draw on context to figure out what it really means—at the particular moment. The setting doesn't just adjust the meaning of the word *kill;* it can radically alter it—teasing a laughing child versus threatening an arch nemesis, for example. There is no freestanding meaning; people always construct meaning by drawing on social context.

There are other methods that follow from taking context into account, like not demanding that people provide absolutely complete responses to the questions we ask them. Instead, drawing on context, we have a sense of how much there should be and let it go at that. Otherwise, those answers could go on infinitely. So when we ask people "how are you?" we ordinarily don't want to know their body temperature, for example. Given the context, we let it pass, maybe with just "fine" or "okay." Of course, what is or is not the appropriate answer varies by who is asking and under just what circumstances: Our doctor might really want to know our body temperature, and our best pal may want to know how we are getting along with our boyfriend or girlfriend. It all depends, and in pretty exact ways, on who is doing the asking, who is doing the answering, their relationship, and the specific occasion. And we know that at least tacitly and act accordingly; it is our method.

How do we use context and conversation patterns to know what's going on?

the fundamental basis of conversation, can occur, and how people use careful tactics to allow it to happen.

We notice the slightest forward nod of the head as signaling that somebody wants a turn—and we often defer to it by becoming silent ourselves. We pick up on silence. It only takes three-tenths of a second before a conversationalist notices that nothing is happening and thus there is an opportunity to come in, like the way a jazz performer can "feel" a signal to come in on a beat. Or make that three-tenths of a second of silence to notice that something *is* happening. The UCLA sociologist Emanuel Schegloff learned that even very brief silences are in fact information (Schegloff 1996). So if you ask somebody on a date, if the answer is going to be "yes," the yes happens immediately—within a split second of the request or even overlapping the end of it. But if the answer is going to be "no," the answer comes with a delay, indeed *through* the delay. A tiny silence serves notice of the bad news that's coming. Or the "no" can be detected in little words and utterances that sort of waste time, like "uh" or "well" or "gee" or even a string of all of them—a turn-down in process.

Here is an actual example (it might be helpful to read it out loud with someone else) (from Davidson 1984):

> EDNA: Wanna come down and have a bite of lunch with me? I got some beer and stuff.
>
> NANCY: Well, your real sweet, hon. Uhm. Let—I have—
>
> EDNA (coming in on Nancy's 'Let'):
> Or do you have something else t—
>
> NANCY (coming in at the middle of Edna's 'else'): No, I have … to uh call … Bob's mother.

In fact, in this exchange the substance of the bad news comes long after the invitation. Nancy gives a hint with her "well …" and then gives Edna a second warning with her "uhm." Edna picks up on the signals and offers them both an escape route ("or do you have something else t—") from

Conversational Precision

We can see people's methods in action in a conversation—any conversation. Without being fully aware that they do so, people fit each utterance in a precise way to the ongoing flow of what the other is saying. Sociologists who study such ordinary talk learn exactly how turn taking,

What kinds of messages do we send with our bodies? Even without hearing people talk, we can tell a lot about an interaction just from people's body language.

the situation by the time Edna finishes her "uhm." Nancy joins Edna in the escape route and takes the route Edna offered her: She *does* have something else to do, something she *has* to do. Whether or not Nancy *wants* to have lunch with Edna is set aside. And all is well.

One of the nice things about saying "no" in such a convoluted way is that the questioner can reframe the request, maybe adding something like "or do you have something else to … ," as Edna does. One of the things it accomplishes is that it takes some of the sting out of rejection. We do this for each other all the time. It, and many other arrangements like it that analysts have found, helps us build a sense of safety and solidarity even when we can't agree to one another's requests. We help each other "save face," as we sometimes say, and retain a more positive sense of self. And it can only happen because of the remarkable capacity we have for sensing the very small moves we all make. Even when we argue with others, we tend to maintain these types of "practical ethics." It builds a sense of safety and solidarity with other human beings even when we can't agree on the substance.

A very simple conversational device, one that lets us see how the process gets managed, and sometimes not in an equal way, is turn taking. People take turns because simultaneous talk is almost impossible to maintain (try it with a friend and you'll see). Somebody has to bow out, and they almost always do within seconds of the start of an overlap. Sociologists refer to this kind of response to conversation disruption as a *repair*, a way one of the speakers helpfully acts to safeguard the interaction (Schegloff 2000). It turns out we are all active in doing such repairs, but some of us are more ready to do it than others.

Sociologists have discovered some patterns to who gives in. Allowing of course for some frequent exceptions, men, quite counter to the stereotype of being "strong and silent," interrupt women more than the reverse. Should both be speaking simultaneously, it is the women who most often relent. Doctors interrupt patients more than patients interrupt doctors—except when the doctor is a woman; then the pattern becomes more equal (West 1984). Adults interrupt children more than children interrupt adults, something that goes against the common assumptions (certainly that of parents) (West and Zimmerman 1977).

So the process is not necessarily democratic. Besides the gender and age difference, bosses—it will not be a surprise to learn—show their power in talk, something employees may pick up on in sensing their employer has "talked down" to them. Conversational inequalities, precisely because of the subtleties involved, are sometimes hard to notice or at least describe by those taking part. But they are important not just because being interrupted, for example, is insulting. When someone lacks access to a conversational turn, they miss the opportunity for their opinions to count. They have less capacity to help create the reality that they and others live by.

The way we greet others matters, too. Explore *A Sociological Perspective* on page 67 to see how important it is for a President to get greetings right.

☐ Emotion

Another method people use in social interaction is emotion. Emotions are not, as the stereotype might imply, utterly beyond our control. Sometimes we speak of emotions as "outbursts"—laughs and cries that break out contrary to anyone's intentions. But for sociologists, emotions are also performances we arrange for specific purposes, although the specific content of the displays varies by context.

Who should cry differs from society to society. In some cultures and some situations, people who fail to cry are thought to be inappropriate; they "should" do so at the death of a loved one. Certainly, they should not laugh on such an occasion, although in some settings of the world (New Orleans or Bali), it can certainly be appropriate to *dance* at funerals. At football (what Americans call soccer) matches in Europe and South America, disorderly mayhem and interpersonal belligerence occur with some frequency; in the United States such behavior is much less frequent. Yet rates

> # How do individuals manipulate emotion in social interaction?

At the funeral for North Korea's ruler Kim Jong-il, people wailed with grief. How do societies differ in the way individuals express emotion? How do specific occasions call out particular ways of expressing emotion?

A SOCIOLOGICAL PERSPECTIVE

Do impressions matter?

Different greetings and behaviors in specific situations give off different impressions, and because our greeting or behavior can set the tone for the rest of the interaction, we'd better get it right. But what's right? When the greeting or behavior in question concerns heads of state on a world stage, the answer can have enormous ramifications. Consider the photos below of a) President Barack Obama greeting Japanese Emperor Akihito and Empress Michiko as he arrived to the Imperial Palace in Tokyo; and b) President Obama bowing at a military funeral.

Consider another example where greetings and behavior are adapted depending upon the situation or the person being greeted. Hillary Clinton is the United States Secretary of State and is married to former President Bill Clinton. In the photos below, c) President Obama greets the Secretary of State with a hug and a kiss on the cheek and she responds in kind; and d) the President greets Bill Clinton with a handshake and arm pat.

Although it is customary to bow upon greeting in Japan as a sign of respect, why were some people in the United States outraged that Obama followed this custom?

a)

Is it a sign of warmth and affection for Obama to greet Hillary Clinton in this manner even though they work together?

c)

Why is the President's greeting to Bill Clinton different from his greeting to Hillary Clinton?

What is the difference, if any, between the President's bow in these two photos?

b)

d)

◎→ **Explore** A Sociological Perspective in **MySocLab** and then ...

▪ Think About It

We make adjustments to our behavior depending on where we are and who we are with. How is your behavior different from when you are in a church versus at a friend's house?

▪ Inspire Your Sociological Imagination

Which people do you hug, and which people do you just shake hands with? Have you ever been in a foreign place where you didn't know what was considered appropriate or inappropriate?

of violent crimes in the United States, including "crimes of passion," are higher than in most parts of the world. Somehow there are conventions of time and place for exhibiting aggression and emotional breakdown toward others.

At a more micro level, sociologists studying fights and conflict notice how contestants carefully fit their threats and gestures into a script of calls and countercalls that all parties understand ("oh yeah," "says who"). University of Pennsylvania sociologist Randall Collins calls such strings of events "interaction ritual chains." By looking systematically at confrontations among people on the street or in other settings, Collins saw how seldom individuals come to blows. It is because, in the great majority of instances, the participants know their own bluster and rant, as well as that of their opponent, is theatrical. And besides, most people have no idea how to fight physically; we are afraid of one another. So we look for ways to end the argument without resorting to violence—and socially talented as we all are, we find them. People only *appear* to be out of control (Collins 2008).

Bursts of laughter alongside others are, as UCLA ethnographer Jack Katz argues, also displays of how context affects emotion and its display. By studying families looking at each other in funhouse mirrors, Katz discovered that unlike conversation, where turn taking is the rule, in laughter everyone can get in on the action all at once. Others may invite us into laughter with a chuckle, but when we all laugh together, we laugh also in collective agreement that something warrants abandoning our façades of emotional reserve. Together, our laughter affirms one another's emotion, our togetherness in feeling that emotion, and that it is safe to express that emotion with loud yelps and unconventional bodily movement (Katz 1999). In contrast to conversation turn taking, it would be considered odd, even disruptive, to hold off one's laugh until the prior laugher was finished.

One way to understand the social nature of emotion is to study how audiences interact with those who perform on stage. We excite each other. Appreciating a performance with others of like mind and spirit is *rousing*. After going to a concert, we sometimes remark not just about the performer but also about the audience. And indeed performers acknowledge that they feed off the audience in front of them just as the audience feeds off the performer. It becomes a cycle of mutual reinforcement.

Again, people fit their response to the conditions at hand. One does not hoot and holler at a Catholic Church mass, and one does not remain somber and still at a rock concert. To do either would be an offense not just to those on the stage but also to one's compatriots in the audience. We need each other to build a common experience, and the greater the mutual appreciation, the greater the show. We like it when someone knows how to rouse us in the crowd. If nothing like this happens, it is disappointing. There is a "collective effervescence" as audience members egg each other on. As in a frequent sociological dynamic, people change the situation that changes them.

The British sociologist Max Atkinson (1984) studied a version of all of this in a very precise way. Atkinson recorded speeches being made by British politicians at party rallies, paying close attention, split second by split second, to what the speakers were doing and how their audiences responded. Using a decibel meter, he measured the volume of audience applause and how long each round of applause lasted, including the clapping interruptions during the speech itself. Atkinson learned that applause happens in bursts, quickly rising to a crescendo in about one second before gently leveling off (see Figure 3.1). We all know the embarrassment of applauding alone, of not knowing, for example, that a symphony has a series of movements and that one should wait until the end of the last one before clapping. Regular symphony goers learn the ropes and avoid the stigma. But in other situations, such as being at a political speech, knowing when to let loose can be more ambiguous.

So Atkinson learned that the talented speechmaker provides audience members with cues that tell when to

When we argue with someone we will often show lots of emotion and aggression, but only rarely get physical in the confrontation.

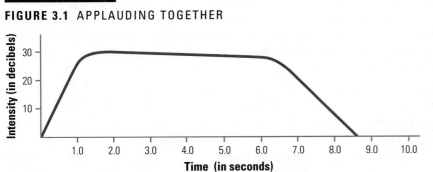

FIGURE 3.1 APPLAUDING TOGETHER

Note: Sociologist Max Atkinson used a decibel meter and sound recordings to measure the volume and timing of an outburst of applause. He found that applause started very fast (reaching its full crescendo in about a second) and remained level for about 5.5 seconds before trailing off fairly fast. This suggests how strongly people work to coordinate their applause with one another, careful to start clapping at the "right" time and careful to stop when it seems others are stopping as well.

Source: Atkinson (1984).

applaud—moments when they can presume others will be applauding with them. As one example, Atkinson learned that effective orators speak in threes—"of the people, by the people, for the people." Aligned with the right kind of intonations, audience members will respond appropriately and clap at just the right moment and together. Sometimes we say people who can generate such a response are charismatic. We think that there is some trait deep within them that causes others to respond with obedience or enthusiasm—as if they have magic or some kind of spiritual gift not found in ordinary human beings.

But in fact, argues Atkinson, the ability to work a crowd comes from knowing what people need to act together. It is a social skill. A successful speech involves mastering the interaction system of individuals with one another by the speaker who is trying to get through to them. And by extension, people are popular when they can do something

What impact have new communication technologies and social media had on our methods of self-presentation?

similar in ordinary life. They are effective with those among whom they live and perform—at a party or just meeting up in hallways. We all, to one degree of success or another, "work the crowd," and the crowd indeed wants to be worked.

☐ Self-Presentation in a Digital Age

We strive to use the same techniques as communication moves to other media, including print and now electronic communication. The new social media, like texting and Facebook, of course change some of the details of the patterns of interaction, but they have many of the same features. When we fret over our Facebook profiles, arranging and rearranging the details, we are manipulating our presentation of self in ways that Goffman would immediately recognize. Based on others' responses or lack of responses, we alter our pages accordingly. We can see, in this e-version,

once again how much people yearn for the approval of others and work social media to bring it about.

We also know that much of the texting, Tweeting, and Facebooking is designed to bring about "copresence"—such as scheduling a date, a reunion, or a business meeting. Sociologist Deirdre Boden, an early researcher of the Internet, learned that a great deal of e-mail and text messaging, just as with the use of telephone in a prior time, involves arranging face-to-face get-togethers. When business people come to an impasse in their electronic communication, they try to set up a face-to-face meeting. Corporate leaders as well as heads of nation-states live intensely social lives, with copresence providing the most crucial elements of coordinating and making decisions. There is a compulsion for proximity. One of the reasons we want to be together is the richness of nonverbal information we give off, like those nods of the head, hesitations, and real smiles that only copresence can provide (Boden and Molotch 1994). And no matter what the ostensible topic, part of the information we gain is about our selves.

This goes on even as we figure out some rudimentary ways of compensating for a lack of face-to-face interaction. Sociologists studying a group of other researchers communicating mostly by e-mail found, indeed, the participants often got confused about one another's meanings (Menchik and Tian 2008). They didn't catch each other's tone and spent a great deal of time clarifying how they intended their words to be heard. One round of e-mails got particularly heated when one of the participants seemed to imply another had engaged in plagiaristic behavior (a very hot charge for these academics), giving rise to offense. The person who sent that e-mail then wrote to all:

I wrote "I think it would appear plagiaristic" (though I failed to put the word 'plagiaristic' in quotes as I had intended). A careful reading of this, I believe, is that I am not absolutely certain and I am not calling Victor a plagiarist as he seems to imply....

The sociologists who conducted the study noticed how the e-mailers often responded to their difficulties by incorporating little signs to clarify how they wanted their words to be understood. Sometimes, this meant words in all capital letters to show emphasis or quotation marks to show some qualification; other times it meant a smiley face, " :-)", or another kind of emoticon, as we now call them. They might sign off saying what city they were in as a signal that they were traveling (so maybe were less available), in a different time zone, busy with something unusual, or about to get on a plane. So the e-mailers were creative in figuring out ways to adjust to the technology, increasing their clarity and lessening the likelihood of being misunderstood (Menchik and Tian 2008). As we see, changes in how we communicate stimulate new ways to send social signals. But they are not a complete substitute for the real person-to-person thing and indeed show us what we are missing when we make the switch from being there to relying on media technology.

☐ Interaction in Public

Another set of special conditions comes about when people are interacting not with people they know but in public spaces among strangers. This alters our interaction strategies somewhat: We become wary about dealing with those with whom we may lack prior experience and whose intentions are less routinely known to us. The public restroom is extreme in the careful monitoring that goes on, but we use the same basic techniques most everywhere in public places. For example, in dealing with strangers pretty much anywhere, we glance at faces, but only for a fleeting moment. To do otherwise implies we have some special business with them or may even be attracted to them. If that is not plausible, we may be perceived as a threat or as weird or crazy. So in Goffman's terms, the parties solve the problem by mutually "dimming the lights" as their paths cross. They engage in **civil inattention**—ignoring each another to an appropriate degree although noticing that the other is present. In this way, dozens and dozens, maybe even hundreds and hundreds on city streets and crowded campus walks, see and hear each other without being a needless bother or stirring up anxiety. According to one of the great social thinkers, German theorist Georg Simmel, *inattention*, especially in dense places, makes social life possible (Simmel 1950).

The next time you enter an empty bus or movie theater, or another place where strangers sit together, you are likely to see civil inattention in action. As people search for a seat, they look at the empty chairs, not the faces of others already sitting. Everyone may be drawn toward a particular region of the space, like the middle rows of the theater, but as more people file in one at a time or in groups, they are likely to take seats that are not directly next to strangers. If they did, it would be considered odd—almost as bad as a man choosing the adjacent urinal when others are available. The person the newcomer sat next to might be alarmed. So without any sign we are paying any attention to those around us, we navigate to a place where others have a bit of space from us, and we from

them. But when there are not so many open spaces, the seats next to strangers become fair game. Even then, however, we usually do not pay obvious attention to those strangers right next to us. Like when we ride the bus, we try hard not to stare at their newspapers or, worse, their faces.

Sometimes our public performances are imperfect—but we have remedies. If I am standing in the library and inadvertently knock a group of books over onto the floor, others who saw or heard the books fall might become anxious. For all they know, I have dropped out of my role as professor—or just as a rational human being—and gone berserk. Nobody wants to create such a scene. We can see how people use special techniques to repair potential damage. One famous and simple method is to just say, "oops." Goffman made a big deal out of *oops*. By blurting out this one syllable, not even really a word at all, I can signal that all is okay, the world is functioning in a more or less reasonable way, and I have not gone out of role or out of my mind (Goffman 1978). Our capacity to say "oops" (or "darn" or a more pungent expletive we can't print in this book) at just the right instant, at just the right volume, with just the right intonation, is only one tiny example of a vast number of techniques that each of us calls on to help get out of a bind.

But just as there are rude interrupters, sometimes people are not very nice in how they deploy their demeanor, and it is not due to being clumsy or socially unskilled. Individuals may deliberately not avert their glance. Schoolyard bullies may stare down their victims as a form of intimidation. If a stranger sits next to me on an empty bus and proceeds to

How is interaction in public unique?

It is not always rude to ignore someone. If you see a friend it might be rude not say hello. But it might also be rude to start talking to random strangers. By engaging in civil inattention, we can politely ignore others in public places.

stare at my face, all the right alarms go off because something is going very wrong.

Ethnographer Mitchell Duneier and I analyzed troubles that happen between street people and those they bother with requests for small change or call out to for other reasons. Most of us know the experience of being asked for money by strangers. Often those who ask do not observe the fine points of conversation. They approach us even when we do not signal we want to talk. In that regard, they pay us no mind. They may blurt out their request and do not seem to register the fact we are not showing any interest. They do not modify their question to avoid us having to give a flat-out "no." They may force the issue and require us to be rude. And that is something people do not like to do to one another. We are upset precisely because we are forced to behave in an uncivil way.

Duneier and I noticed problems in particular with women passersby. The men on the street routinely remark on their bodies and how they look and try to entangle them with questions. Duneier recorded one such set of interactions in New York in the year 1999, between a man named Mudrick and a woman passerby.

Have you ever been approached by someone begging for money? What did you do? What kinds of signs do we give off to people in order to show that we either do or don't want to engage in conversation?

> MUDRICK: Hey pretty. (8/10th of a second goes by)
>
> WOMAN (flatly): Hi how you doin.
>
> MUDRICK (coming in on 'doin'): You alright? (2.2 seconds go by)
>
> MUDRICK: You look very nice you know. I like how you have your hair pinned. (8/10th of a second goes by)
>
> MUDRICK: You married?
>
> WOMAN: Yeah.
>
> MUDRICK: Huh?
>
> WOMAN: Yeah.
>
> MUDRICK (interrupting): Where the rings at?
>
> WOMAN: I have it home.
>
> MUDRICK: Y' have it home?
>
> WOMAN: Yeah.
>
> MUDRICK: Can I get your name?
>
> MUDRICK: My name is Mudrick, what's yours?

We see the tactics at work that many of us find so difficult. Timing is everything. The woman responds to Mudrick's initial greeting, but only after what is, in conversational terms, a lengthy silence of nearly a second. If you listened to the recording of the conversation, you would hear that her "how you doin" is said as a statement, not a question. Both are signs that she wants the conversation to stop there. Mudrick ignores the signals as he delivers a follow-up attempt at further conversation (line 3) before she even finishes her response. The woman does not respond as more than two seconds pass—an eternity. Mudrick tries again with another compliment, followed by yet another barrage of questions: Are you married? What? Where's the evidence? Really? What's your name? What's your name? The woman gives some responses, but each signals a desire to end the conversation. Mudrick is still asking questions as the woman walks away.

When people make a compliment or ask a question, they almost always get a response, and get one pretty quickly if they have a willing conversation partner. But people may signal they don't want to talk through pauses and nonresponses, what conversation analysts call disaffiliative gestures. Mudrick not only ignores those signals the woman gives, he ups the ante with even more intrusive questions. The woman's disaffiliative gestures escalate until she does something rude by not responding at all to repeat questions—just as she was a bit rude in the first place by not really taking up Mudrick's efforts to converse.

The way Mudrick forces the woman to be really rude by ignoring her signals to end the conversation is what Duneier and I call interactional vandalism (Duneier and Molotch 1999). An offense takes place, but one that is very subtle. When it happens to us we are aware of a problem, but without the kind of painstaking sociological observations carried out by Duneier, it is hard to pin down. We see from the start that Mudrick does not count for much to the woman, and this had something to do with the bad footing on which the whole thing began. If it had been the mayor of New York or a movie star being abrupt, she might have gone along even if she was spoken to in the same way. This tells us that besides the intricacies of conversational technique, people put up with more from others depending on the kinds of statuses in play and how individual identities are socially categorized, with street people way down on the totem pole.

3 Who Matters to Us?

SIGNIFICANT OTHERS, REFERENCE GROUPS, AND THE GENERALIZED OTHER

👁 Watch the **Big Question** Video in **MySocLab**

So far we've examined the methods we use for interacting with others, but do all *others* matter to us equally? Sociologists try to determine how other people, by virtue of their social location, do or do not matter to us. We take some people and types of people more seriously than others, which is evident in the ways we defer to them and seek their approval. Homeless street people do not count for as much as those able to present themselves in a higher-status way. At the individual level, sociologists, following in the footsteps of George Herbert Mead, use the term **significant other** to denote individuals close enough to us to have a strong capacity to motivate our behavior. Many people now use the term *significant other* to refer to a spouse or lover, but sociologists invented the term for relationships like parent-child or other close family members, as well as somebody you always bring to parties.

Sometimes individuals have a more or less similar level of significance because of their common membership in a relevant social category. Doctors are alert to the opinions of other doctors. They are not as dependent for their sense of self on the viewpoints of say, the custodial staff. College students are likely more interested in the opinions of their fellow students than those they once knew who left high school without going on to higher education. In figuring out how we are doing, we *reference* others whose social positions and preferences makes them especially relevant to our own sense of worth.

How do reference groups guide our behavior?

Sociologists call these groups that influence our behavior **reference groups**. Each of us has our own set of these groups, and we tend to stick with our reference groups in part because, once we are in, we spend our time doing things that people like us do alongside other people who do them. We model our behavior on such individuals, and sometimes there are particular individuals in the group, "stars" in a way, who may function as **role models**. They have disproportionate influence as we imitate how they move, dress, and carry out life.

We are each associated with a number of reference groups, even at the same time. For some of us this is made vivid through online social networking sites: We are located in webs of groups that are themselves clustered around commonalities of age, taste, or status. Others we know share some of the same linkages; our list of groups and their list have high overlap. Those we friend, they friend. Clubs we join, they join. Their influence on us is likely to be particularly strong compared to, say, an acquaintance who hardly knows anyone else we know or does any of the things we do. While we may of course develop bonds to such outsiders, sociologists who study social networks found that these relationships tend to be few in number and dissolve more quickly than with those in groups having multiple links into our own social circles and interests (McPherson, Smith-Lovin, and Cook 2001). Birds of a feather do stick together and keep at it; if they go off, it is an unstable departure.

Social Interaction in a Digital Age

Who matters to us, and how much time do we devote to maintaining our social contacts? Earlier in the chapter we talked about how social media has changed some of the details of our patterns of interaction. But just how much of our daily social interaction has moved online? And what are our motivations for using social networking sites?

Face-to-Face Social Interaction

Of the **4.66 hours** spent on relaxing and leisure activities. Americans reported spending **less than one hour per day** socializing and communicating (40.8 minutes for or men; 43.8 minutes for women).

Online Social Interaction

Kids 8-18 spend over **7½ hours per day online** (with over 11 hours of media content)

In 2010, **the average American spent 32 hours per month on the internet** The graph at right breaks this out by age group.

66% of adults use social media platforms such as **Facebook** and **Twitter** These survey respondents say that connecting with family and friends are the key reason they use these sites.

 Explore the **Data** on Social Interaction in a Digital Age in **MySocLab** and then . . .

◼ Think About It

When people use the internet are they doing it as a substitute for socializing with friends and family or as a way to increase those connections — like sending them messages or maybe using the internet to arrange face-to-face get-togethers?

◼ Inspire Your Sociological Imagination

What would a graph look like that showed not differences in age in online use, but differences in social class? In gender? Across regions of the world?

Average Monthly Hours Spent Online by Age Group, 2010

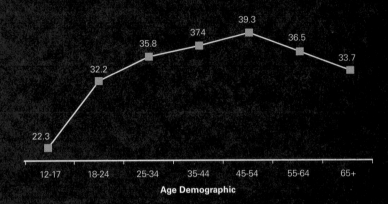

Age Demographic	12-17	18-24	25-34	35-44	45-54	55-64	65+
Hours	22.3	32.2	35.8	37.4	39.3	36.5	33.7

Key Reasons for Using Social Media

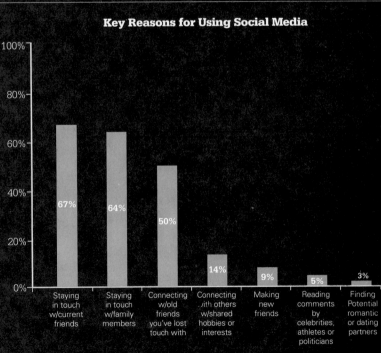

	%
Staying in touch w/current friends	67%
Staying in touch w/family members	64%
Connecting w/old friends you've lost touch with	50%
Connecting with others w/shared hobbies or interests	14%
Making new friends	9%
Reading comments by celebrities, athletes or politicians	5%
Finding Potential romantic or dating partners	3%

Sources: Based on data from American Time Use Survey (2010); Kaiser Family Foundation (2010); ComScore (2011); Pew Research Center (2011).

Some of our ties are far more general than our immediate social networks, whether face-to-face or electronic (review the Infographic on page 73). Grounded in the larger cultures in which each of us participates, people have a sense of what everyone knows to be appropriate as proper behavior. For example, in the United States no one goes about her or his business in public while naked. Wearing clothes is so commonly understood that there generally does not need to be a rule about it. Also, we do not eat dogs or insects. We all know these things and risk making a severely bad impression if we betray them. Sociologists call this social control exercised by common-sense understandings of what is appropriate in a specific time and place the **generalized other**. We walk around with all kinds of unspoken knowledge of do's and don'ts without much understanding or need to consult where we got them. We just do it. Virtually all the significant others do it; all the role models do it, and the reference groups too.

What role does the voice of the generalized other play in shaping our sense of self?

Through the various machinations already described in this chapter, we grow from the babbling, spitting creatures we are at birth to become socialized as competent adults. Through **socialization**—the process by which we come to understand the expectations and norms of our groups, as well as the various roles we transition into over the life course—we come to understand the expectations of how to behave in the larger society or in particular social settings. Sometimes sociologists use the word **culture** to refer to the substance—the systems of beliefs and knowledge—of the taken-for-granted world that together we have been socialized into, sometimes coinciding with the country boundaries where we live—although not necessarily, given all the variations possible in worlds made fluid by immigration and shifts of borders. There is thus always the possibility of splits into **subcultures**, sets of individuals who share common preferences or understandings of specific aspects of the social world but remain part of a larger group that is tied together on a more basic level.

4 What Challenges Do We Face as We Move from One Social Context to Another?

SHIFTS AND DILEMMAS

◉ Watch the Big Question Video in **MySocLab**

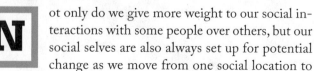

Not only do we give more weight to our social interactions with some people over others, but our social selves are also always set up for potential change as we move from one social location to another. And as we move between these social contexts, we sometimes encounter difficulties in deciding how to act.

☐ Status and Role Change

One type of challenge comes from the fact that we enter into different life statuses as we age or just change our life situation. A **status** is a distinct social category that is set off from others and has associated with it a set of expected behaviors and roles for individuals to assume. Each of the status changes brings different types of groups, and the expectations they have for us, into play. So in terms of educational status, we move from elementary school to being high school and then college students; on the personal front, we become girlfriends or boyfriends, husbands or wives, parents, business managers, professionals, or employees (of course, many of these statuses overlap). What interests sociologists is that these different statuses each come with a set of roles *others* expect us to perform. Think of there being a menu of statuses, each with accompanying expectations arising from society.

So the readers of this book are students, and students are supposed to fulfill certain expectations, or **role sets**, attached to the student role: respect the teacher, show up for lecture, keep hands to one's self while sitting in the classroom, complete assigned papers, and take exams. Because students do generally conform, life in the college classroom is pretty stable and looks a lot different than life in a mosh pit. And so it goes: What is appropriate for a funeral director differs from that for a lawyer, for a teenager from that for a husband, for a restaurant chef compared to a physician. If the doctor really made us the chicken soup she suggests we drink, we would find it to be creepy.

Sometimes we will experience **role conflict**—fulfilling the expectations of one of our roles conflicts with meeting the expectations of another. Most of us have experienced this uncomfortable situation when our role as son or daughter conflicts with fulfilling the expectations of a friend. As a son or daughter, we want to fulfill our parents' expectation that we come home for a grandmother's birthday, but our best friend needs our help during a move to a new apartment. Which role are we supposed to fulfill? We are damned if we do and damned if we don't. Severe instances can create enough psychological stress to put some of us on the therapist's couch or push others into escape with drugs or alcohol.

Inconsistent demands arise in patterned ways based on the variety of reference groups exerting influence. So it may be important for certain types of working-class youths, for example, to satisfy peer-group expectations that are not consistent with those of school authorities. Sociologists who study delinquency, for example, have found exactly this kind of conformity dilemma. It is not that these so-called rule breakers are nonconformists; rather, they are conforming to groups who are devalued by those with authority. This type of conflict can then be intensified as police or other officials try to assert control.

☐ Labeling

However similar people are in the fact that they conform, they are made different depending on other's opinions of the groups with which they identify. Sociologists have long been concerned with people regarded as a problem by dominant members of society, often referred to as **deviants** by those who make the rules and express opinions about behaviors they find troubling. According to the sociological school of thought called labeling theory, so-called deviants come about because there is a person or group that can serve as the object of the label "deviant" and an individual or institution that can put the label on and make it stick. Sociologists long ago stopped believing it was useful to think of people like criminals or most of the so-called insane as essentially different from others. Indeed, it was once common to regard people like divorced women and gay and lesbian individuals as deviant, even criminal or diseased in the case of homosexuals. We no longer think this way, at least in the United States, and we understand these labels to have been conventions of their time and place but not as corresponding to the nature of the individuals involved. In sociology, and now across the academic disciplines, in what has more grandly become known as the **social construction of reality**—or the interactive process by which knowledge is produced and codified, making it specific to a certain group or society—the goal has become to understand the larger interaction systems that create such classifications, keep them alive, or cause them to erode.

One consequence of being labeled (no matter whether it makes sense or doesn't), some versions of the theory say, is that the individuals so identified in fact change their conduct and embrace the very behavior that led them into the deviant category in the first place. So the kid who is told he is no good links up with others told the same thing. Whatever their common bonds before, they now at least share a label—presto, a gang. Their networks may start to overlap, especially if they are put in the same detention centers or programs. The boys provide mutual social support and clear the way for, even value, the disapproved behavior. Just as the nice kids evolve into virtual saints, so it is that others fulfill the expectations of delinquents, rebels, or bad girls. This is an example of what the sociologist Robert Merton called a **self-fulfilling prophecy** (Merton 1949). Something becomes true because people say it is true.

University of California–Santa Barbara professor Thomas Scheff studied how this works in a mental hospital. Some people fight against the label of "crazy" but may face an uphill battle as everyone around them pressures them to accept it (Scheff 1999). Their diagnosis, after all, rests on a whole set of labeling institutions, largely held to be legitimate, of doctors, nurses, and the institution. They learn, according to Scheff, that the best route to being released from treatment is to acknowledge the judgments of others that they are crazy.

But quite apart from the labeling apparatus, people inside a mental institution may indeed be about as normal as

What causes role conflict?

anyone else. To test this idea, psychologist David Rosenhan sent his research assistants, all with no history of mental health issues, to present themselves to different psychiatric hospitals and tell a single lie: that they were hearing voices in their heads. The people on duty diagnosed all of them as having psychiatric disorders and admitted them to the hospital. Once in the hospital, the undercover assistants told everyone, doctors and nurses included, that they had no more symptoms and continued acting normally. Some of the researchers were held for months (this is research commitment!), and none were released by the hospital until they agreed that they, indeed, had a mental illness (Rosenhan 1973). Sometimes even our freedom depends on agreeing to the labels placed on us.

The Rosenhan study did lead to some reform. Published under the title "Being Sane in Insane Places," many took to heart the dangerous power of labeling in psychiatric

How does a self-fulfilling prophecy influence label formation?

(and other) institutions. In an example of how social research can lead to policy change, it (along with the writings of Scheff and some by Goffman) became part of the deinstitutionalization movement that led to the closing of many psychiatric hospitals and their replacement (alas, often not fulfilled) by community-based treatment facilities.

☐ Rule Use

Even for those of us not in mental institutions, we are surrounded by organizations we have to answer to, and they all have their rules. These rules often are explicit (such as laws or institutional regulations), but they can also be informal and include norms and expectations for individual behaviors. We must enact our various statuses and roles within the businesses, government agencies, and schools where we make our living, buy our stuff, and get our housing. In doing so, we also have some tricky maneuvering to do.

Consider, for example, the way we understand and deal with rules that are supposed to determine how we relate to each other. Let's get back to *kill*. The Bible is explicit: Don't do it. The law says the same. But only a jerk would reprimand somebody who swats a mosquito or shoots a rattlesnake about to bite the baby. We might have to kill the person getting ready to throw a bomb in a theater. If we are on active duty in the military, it is not acceptable to denounce someone (at least someone on your side) who is prepared to kill others. So even this most important of rules requires human interpretation. And that is just what happens, whether in everyday life or in a large-scale organization: interpretation, interpretation, interpretation.

Here's an example quite common to ordinary life, one that we witness all the time in places like restaurants or the Department of Motor Vehicles: "first come, first served." But if a huge celebrity like Lady Gaga or Michelle Obama wants some service, any competent receptionist would not have them wait in line before being served. The sociologist Don Zimmerman, who studied how receptionists handle clients in a welfare agency, found that they continuously modified the rule in order to keep the overall operation running smoothly (Zimmerman 1970). If there are screaming children, they and their parents get taken ahead of others to curtail the deafening noise that would inhibit anyone from getting work done. If somebody came in who was visibly ill, disorderly, or injured, they would get early attention, even if it was to call in help from the outside, like police or an ambulance.

Similarly, although there may be no official rule that instructs the doctors in busy emergency rooms to make drunken alcoholics wait longer for care (even risking their lives), they will likely give preference to a more innocent

What do "deviants" look like? And who gets to decide who a deviant is?

individual, maybe an elderly person hit by a car or a suffering child (Sudnow 1967). Each of us judges the context and uses the amazing human capacity to scan organizational and individual needs to come up with the appropriate behavior.

Sometimes we invoke what sociologists have called informal rules that exist alongside the official ones, notions like "respect the needs of children," perhaps. We may use some informal rules to explain to others (or even to ourselves) after the fact that we "really" were not breaking a rule, just following a different one. For example, as I learned in researching the New York subways, the train conductors and other workers explain they rarely report suspicious packages to their supervisors, as they are supposed to do, because that would slow down the system, and that, in turn, would defeat the more informal rule that it is their job to keep the trains running on time.

What really makes us competent members of society is not so much knowing all the rules (formal or informal) but rather knowing what to do on particular occasions given what is expected of us. We don't so much follow rules as use them to make what we did appear both to ourselves and to others as a rational and appropriate action. We act to maintain the normalness of the world so we can all move forward. It's kind of like saying "oops" so people will know things are pretty much OK.

There are people who seem unable to function in this way; they have trouble taking context into account. They insist on "going by the book." When we meet them in real life, they strike us as silly or severely incompetent. We have all come across such extremely annoying people. They seem to lack proper discretion. Garfinkel referred to such individuals as "judgmental dopes" (Garfinkel 1967, chap. 2). This makes them difficult as coworkers, as neighbors, or even as friends. They may literally live in communities, but they are more like ants in the anthill than humans who interpret and know, as we often say, "it all depends."

So true is it that when people do not ordinarily follow the rules in literal ways, when they actually do so it screws everything up. For example, to cause disruptions, labor unions sometimes call on the rank and file to "work to rule." It is a call to go by the book—exactly. This means not taking the kind of shortcuts that allow the work to actually get done. It is a good union tactic because the only response for employers is to insist workers go back to their old ways of *not* strictly following procedures, an awkward stance for management to take. In one recent study of an Idaho sawmill, an employee in a work-to-rule action left a fire burning in an expensive piece of machinery and

walked away to make it to a "mandatory" safety meeting on time (Richardson 2009). After the protest period, workers return to the ordinary ways of working, acknowledging that a fire is a good exception to the "mandatory" requirement, to get it all done.

☐ Conformity Experiments

Just how people conform to their social circumstance has fundamental consequences for how people live together. Social scientists sometimes set up laboratory experiments to see how people interact under one condition or another, in particular the way they do or do not go along with social pressure. It is almost like a laboratory for rats, except that the experimenter watches people instead of some other kind of animal. But unlike in dealing with other animals, we get to see how interpretation works—how people press each other into one kind of action as opposed to another. The stakes can be high.

What does it take, an experimenter asks, to get people to give an obviously wrong answer to an obvious and factual question? Not much, as it turns out. A social scientist named Solomon Asch, in a classic midcentury study, presented individuals (127 males) with a line drawn on a card and asked them to choose among three lines drawn on another card the one that matched it most closely in length (see Figure 3.2). It was pretty simple to do because one of the lines indeed matched perfectly. But the other individuals (varying from five to seven) sitting with the experimental subject were working with the professor running the experiment.

> **In what types of social interactions is it acceptable to invoke informal rules?**

FIGURE 3.2 THE ASCH CONFORMITY EXPERIMENT

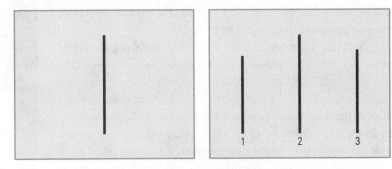

Solomon Asch showed groups of research subjects two cards like these. He asked them to match the line on card 1 with the one of the same size on card 2. Asch's research collaborators were secretly mixed in with the research subjects and sometimes agreed that the wrong lines matched. Asch found that the naïve subjects went along with the research collaborators about one-third of the time, and approximately 75 percent conformed to the research collaborators' wrong answer at least once.

Source: Asch (1955).

After a few warm-up runs, where everyone provided the same correct answer, the clued-in participants gave consistently wrong answers. Conformity started happening, with naïve subjects agreeing to a wrong answer *37 percent of the time.* Three-quarters of them conformed at least once, 5 percent conformed every time, but about 25 percent never did (Asch 1955). So there we have it: People do differ, but social context changes what happens in many, many instances.

In various versions of this experiment, some conducted by other researchers following in Asch's footsteps, it was possible to change the specific conditions to see what causes conformity to rise or fall. One striking finding is that a single ally strongly influences results. If the experiment permitted one person to join the naïve subject in reporting an accurate result, the impact of a majority opinion to the contrary lost much of its power. This implies the importance of people having even just one other person in support. It is much easier to "go against the world" if you have a companion, whether it is a companion in love, or crime, or truth.

What makes people conform, and how does conformity impact how we live together?

These kinds of experiments have their critics. Real life might be different, say the skeptics. And we do not know if those taking part in the experiment really believed that the group was right, only that they *reported* wrong answers to the experimenter. Even so, saying things you don't believe is also conforming and has effects: If nobody says the emperor has no clothes, it makes it easier for the emperor to continue to rule even though he is naked. And the experimental results, it could be argued, are especially impressive given that the research subjects had no good reason to lie other than the pressure to conform. In real life, we really are trying to gain other people's favor. We may not want to go against significant others and reference group members who could fire us from our jobs, flunk us in our courses, or put us in prison. That people will go along to get along when nothing is at stake explains why they do so when there are strong reasons for compromising the truth.

An even more severe lesson from the social science laboratory is that when conditions are right, people—ordinary people—will harm other ordinary people, perhaps even kill them. Inspired indeed by concerns about major real-life situations, the Yale social psychologist Stanley Milgram wanted to learn the conditions that might cause otherwise respectable individuals to harm one another, merely because they were asked to do so. Milgram conducted his experiments in the post–World War II period when the Holocaust was fresh in people's minds. Some were speculating that the Germans blindly followed Hitler because of some peculiar attribute of the German personality, or at least particular patterns distinct to German culture. Repeated in various settings besides the original version at Yale University, Milgram's so-called obedience studies revealed the Germans to be not so special in these regards.

In his experiment, Milgram (1963) induced his subjects (sometimes college undergraduates) to deliver what they thought were painful, even fatal, electrical shocks to a stranger who had given a wrong answer in what they were told was some kind of learning training. In fact no such learning training was taking place; the whole thing was just a ruse to see how much harm subjects would deliver when instructed to do so. Even with the "learner" (who actually was an employee of the professor) letting out painful screams and the experimenter indicating the learner had a heart condition, over 60 percent of subjects eventually delivered, three times in a row, the last-stage shock of 450 volts (see Table 3.1). The learner went silent to imply there was in fact a fatal dose, but the shocking continued after that point in all these cases (Blass 1999).

Under some conditions, people were less likely to shock an innocent victim than under others. So when the experimenter caused the subject to actually place the victim's hand on the shocking grid (thus making full physical contact), the rate of shocking went down. In real life, of course, much violence occurs only in indirect ways. Legislators say it's okay to bomb another country, assassinate another person, or close a

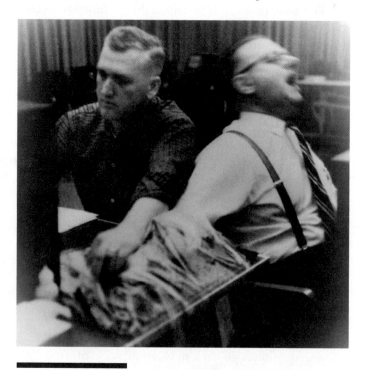

When a person in charge tells us to do something, we tend to do it without thinking about the consequences. We're just following order. Milgram's experiment showed that obedience to rules can often lead people to do some awful things.

TABLE 3.1 MILGRAM'S SHOCKING FINDINGS

Verbal designation and voltage indication	Number of subjects for whom this was maximum shock
"Slight Shock"	
15	0
30	0
45	0
60	0
"Moderate Shock"	
75	0
90	0
105	0
120	0
"Strong Shock"	
135	0
150	0
165	0
180	0
"Very Strong Shock"	
195	0
210	0
225	0
240	0
"Intense Shock"	
255	0
270	0
285	0
300	5
"Extreme Intensity Shock"	
315	4
330	2
345	1
360	1
"Danger: Severe Shock"	
375	1
390	0
405	0
420	0
XXX	
435	0
450	26

When Stanley Milgram asked 40 research subjects to issue "shocks" at ever-increasing levels of intensity to others, he found that even while most hesitated, almost all delivered an "Extreme Intensity" shock when told to do so by an authority figure. This table shows the point at which subjects stopped giving shocks. Fourteen people refused to go further at some point, while 26 gave the maximum shock allowed in the experiment.

Source: Milgram (1963).

health clinic down—without ever getting close to the bodies or being on the scene. Those situations, like the extreme case of the Nazis, do not involve direct aggression but only indirect bureaucratic action. Many conclude from the Milgram results that it could happen here and in our own time.

Another famous study followed up on the problem of obedience a few years later in 1971. Twenty-four Stanford undergraduate men were recruited by Professor Philip Zimbardo to live in a mock prison. They were randomly assigned roles either as prisoners or guards. Psychologists had selected them out of a total of 75 volunteers because they were deemed the most psychologically stable and healthy. The amazing outcome was that despite the fact that the participants knew nothing was real about their incarceration, they conformed only too well to their assigned roles. In many cases, the guards became intensely sadistic, humiliating their prisoners, forcing them to go naked, and limiting their capacities to urinate or defecate. Early on the prisoners rebelled but then, after their rebellion failed, submitted to gross abuse. Several had emotional breakdowns, and about a third were judged to have had strongly negative psychological effects. Despite the fact that it was all make believe, the prisoners became radically dependent on their guards' attitude toward them. Some became supplicants, weeping and trembling in the face of those on whom they bestowed authority.

The consequences of the experiment were so intense that Zimbardo had to shut it down after only the sixth day of what was supposed to be a two-week run. Five students had quit rather than go through with even the six days. It became apparent that Zimbardo was risking the mental health and perhaps long-term well-being of others. That people would so readily accept a social role and so fervently conform to the expectations surrounding it provides sobering information about how far people will go to conform to their role set, with perhaps catastrophic consequence. Zimbardo was later to note, in connection with U.S. guards' sadistic treatment of Iraqi prisoners at Abu Ghraib, that his experiments were only too relevant to real life and the extremes to which otherwise normal people will go if supported by role expectations and the right (that is, wrong) kind of social context (Zimbardo 2007).

We can start to understand how face-to-face interactional systems can build up group loyalties, which can follow along ethnic, racial, or national lines. Unlike among the Stanford students, these demarcations are not randomly assigned, and as is the case with race for example, individuals have little choice in how they start the process. People really are born into particular groups and have to deal with how others react to those identities.

However we get into one identity classification or another, those who surround us give meanings to self and personal identity. I act out to satisfy my reference group, and this puts me in opposition to yours. People link up and cast others away as deviant or different in some lesser or dangerous way. But like fish that live in the same school and never even get out of the water, sometimes they do not know that another world is possible—where people have different beliefs and judgments that, in their context, make sense. Our deviance is their normal and vice versa. Not seeing this possibility is the root of what sociologists call **ethnocentrism**—the inability to understand, accept, or reference patterns of behavior or belief different from one's own. My ethos is the one and true way; my way or the highway. Other peoples' ways of life, if known at all, are inferior or maybe even evil—in part just because they are different. Those who belong to groups at the top of the structure have special capacity to demean and punish those below, whether within their same community or in societies farther afield.

CONCLUSION WHAT WE KNOW AND WHAT WE DON'T KNOW

Interactionism provides us the tools for understanding the social self. To understand what an individual is, it introduces the presence of others. For each of us, those relevant others differ, and this helps create uniqueness. At the same time, these unique individuals must gain approval from at least some people and groups to have a positive sense of self and be able to function in the world. To achieve these ends, people have all sorts of artful techniques to know exactly what to do and under what conditions. We read contexts, we use exacting precision as we converse, and we play our emotions to fit the conditions at hand. We do not simply obey rules but creatively interpret them to make them work for ourselves and the organizations that, for better or worse, we come to serve.

This creates not only distinctiveness but also conformity. At the individual level we can get in a double bind of having to conform to inconsistent demands coming from opposing parties. It can mean trouble for whole groups who get labeled as deviant because of the relevant others and reference groups that shape their identity and destiny. At the macro level, terrible danger can arise when people conform in ways that create harm and havoc on a mass scale. Building a society that gives people a sense of their own dignity while at the same time doing the least harm to others is a huge challenge. Many of the important dramas of world history reveal instances when we did not get it right.

Sociology still has some explaining to do; while we have concepts that explain the overall order, we have trouble with the exceptions. So although most people conform to society's laws and accepted codes, some are renegades. One-fourth of Asch's subjects would not conform; five of Zimbardo's dropped out. In the Milgram experiment, there were people who would not only refrain from giving the fatal shock (about one-third), there was a scattering of subjects who walked out early on. Given

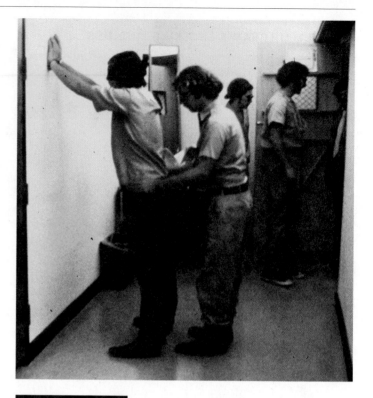

The Stanford Prison Experiment showed that people alter their behavior according to the position they occupy. What are the different behavioral expectations of the positions in society – from student to teacher to son to father – which we occupy?

how much people usually conform to the social circumstances at hand, we do not have a strong explanation for those who do not go with the flow. We don't know why some Germans risked their lives to hide Jewish families from the Nazis nor, at a different part of the moral spectrum, what produces an individual who would mow down strangers at a shopping mall.

Nor do we have a firm understanding of why some individuals, of whatever background and circumstance, seem more interactionally creative than others. They can work a room, work an audience, and work their lives in ways that overwhelm others of similar sociological location. Labels, especially negative ones, may come their way, but they do not so often stick. Some of us survive double binds much better than others.

Maybe having such strengths could enable people to lead beneficial social and political movements as well as more satisfying personal lives. If we could find ways to "bottle it," maybe working with like-minded scholars from psychology, we could conceivably encourage, through child rearing and education, more of these people into being.

Watch the **Video** in **MySocLab**
Applying Your Sociological Imagination

Study and **Review** in **MySocLab**   **Watch** the **Video** Inspiring Your Sociological Imagination in **MySocLab**

1

How Do We Develop a Sense of Self? *(p. 62)*

 Watch the **Big Question Video** in **MySocLab** to review the key concepts for this section.

KEY TERMS

self *(p. 62)*

interactionism *(p. 62)*

looking-glass self *(p. 63)*

Each one of us has a unique identity. But is this sense of self a single thing, or is it a process of interaction? In this section, we explored how we know ourselves through the reflections of ourselves that mirror back from others' opinions of us—the "looking glass" of others.

THE SOCIAL SELF (p. 62)

- **Why is social interaction vital to the development of self?**

The Looking-Glass Self (p. 63)

- **How do the opinions and judgments of others shape our identities?**

 Read the **Document** *The Looking-Glass Self* by Charles Horton Cooley in **MySocLab**. This reading examines Cooley's belief that the self does not exist without society.

Life's a Stage (p. 63)

- **How is interaction in public unique?**

2

How Do We Make Sense of Our Worlds? *(p. 64)*

 Watch the **Big Question Video** in **MySocLab** to review the key concepts for this section.

KEY TERMS

ethnomethodology *(p. 65)*

civil inattention *(p. 70)*

We all have specific methods for demonstrating competence as interacting members of society. In this section, we explored how the sociological field of ethnomethodology examines these methods.

PEOPLE'S METHODOLOGY (p. 64)

Context, Context, Context (p. 65)

Conversational Precision (p. 65)

- **How do we use context and conversation patterns to know what's going on?**

Emotion (p. 66)

● **How do individuals manipulate emotion in social interaction?**

 Explore A Sociological Perspective: Do impressions matter? in **MySocLab**

Self-Presentation in a Digital Age (p. 69)

● **What impact have new communication technologies and social media had on our methods of self-presentation?**

Interaction in Public (p. 70)

 3

Who Matters To Us? *(p. 72)*

 Watch the **Big Question Video** in **MySocLab** to review the key concepts for this section.

Not everyone we encounter has the same capacity to influence our sense of self or shape our identity—some people matter to us more than others. In this section, we examined the relative influence of significant others, reference groups, and the generalized other— and how each influences our sense of self.

SIGNIFICANT OTHERS, REFERENCE GROUPS, AND THE GENERALIZED OTHER (p. 72)

● **How do reference groups guide our behavior?**

 Explore the **Data** on Social Interaction in a Digital Age in **MySocLab**

● **What role does the voice of the generalized other play in shaping our sense of self?**

KEY TERMS

significant other *(p. 72)*

reference group *(p. 72)*

role model *(p. 72)*

generalized other *(p. 74)*

socialization *(p. 74)*

culture *(p. 74)*

subculture *(p. 74)*

4 What Challenges Do We Face as We Move from One Social Context to Another? *(p. 74)*

👁 **Watch** the **Big Question Video** in **MySocLab** to review the key concepts for this section.

KEY TERMS

status *(p. 74)*

role set *(p. 75)*

role conflict *(p. 75)*

deviant *(p. 75)*

social construction of reality *(p. 75)*

self-fulfilling prophecy *(p. 75)*

ethnocentrism *(p. 80)*

The social self is not fixed but is always changing, which can sometimes bring challenges. This section examined what happens when we experience role conflict and how informal rules and our keen awareness guide our behavior. We also looked at how and why people conform and what consequences conformity has on how people live together.

SHIFTS AND DILEMMAS (p. 74)

Status and Role Change (p. 74)

- **What causes role conflict?**

Labeling (p. 75)

- **How does a self-fulfilling prophecy influence label formation?**

Rule Use (p. 76)

- **In what types of social interactions is it acceptable to invoke informal rules?**

Conformity Experiments (p. 77)

- **What makes people conform, and how does conformity impact how we live together?**

👁 **Watch** the **Video** Applying Your Sociological Imagination in **MySocLab** to see these concepts at work in the real world

4
SOCIAL STRUCTURE

((Listen to the **Chapter Audio** in **MySocLab**

by JEFF MANZA
with HAREL SHAPIRA

Inge Deutschkron was born in 1922 and grew up in a socially mixed neighborhood in the north of the German capital of Berlin. Her father, Dr. Martin Deutschkron, belonged to a high-status group in Germany because he held a doctoral degree and taught at an elite secondary school. Despite his social standing, Inge's father was a socialist, believing that modern society could best be understood as shaped by a struggle between two classes, the owners of capital—the bourgeoisie—and the workers they exploited—the proletariat. Martin and his wife sympathized with the proletariat and labored tirelessly for the Marx-inspired German Social Democratic Party, taking young Inge along to meetings and demonstrations.

In January 1933, Adolf Hitler's Nazis came to power in Germany. Shortly thereafter, Inge's father was dismissed from his teaching position as an enemy of the Nazi regime for his political views. But there were worse things to come for the family. On March 31, 1933, Inge's mother sat the 10-year-old down and revealed to her something she could barely comprehend: The country's new rulers considered her Jewish, and she could expect to be persecuted for this. This news came as a surprise to the young girl as religion had played no part whatsoever in her upbringing. Had she lived in a different time or place, it is likely that her Jewishness would have played little or no role in her life. Yet for the Nazi government, Jewishness was a matter of ethnic (or, in their terminology, "racial") identity that would eventually lead to a death sentence in the Holocaust. Because Inge's grandparents were Jewish, she was considered Jewish as well. It had nothing to do with how she felt as an individual; Hitler and his followers, despite her birth and upbringing in Germany, viewed her as a member of an

MY SOCIOLOGICAL IMAGINATION
Jeff Manza

Growing up in the college town of Berkeley, CA, my family was neither elite (my parents worked for the local university, but not as professors) nor unprivileged. I experienced the differences between these various worlds, and in particular the inequalities they represented, as an endlessly fascinating puzzle. I was also always interested in politics and occasionally participated in political protests and movements. My intellectual interest in sociology began to develop while I was an undergraduate student because it seemed to me to provide a way of connecting my emerging concerns about inequality and injustice with a set of theories and ways of studying how those inequalities persist. Since then, I have been exploring various ways that social inequalities influence political life. More recently I have become interested in how public opinion does or does not shape government policies and how and when public attitudes can be manipulated or misused by political elites. I hope that my work can contribute, in some small way, to making American democracy more representative and egalitarian than it currently is.

Nazism is an extreme example of how external forces beyond our control shape our lives, but what about America? What external forces shape the lives of Americans?

Watch the Video in **MySocLab**
Inspiring Your Sociological Imagination

alien people locked in an eternal struggle with German "Aryans." Although her father would flee in 1939 to England, Inge and her mother remained trapped in Berlin, threatened after 1941—like all other people classified as Jewish—with deportation to concentration camps and a near-certain death. With the help of a network of sympathetic fellow citizens, however, she and her mother miraculously survived underground in Berlin—the heart of Hitler's Third Reich—until the end of the war. In February 1945, they took advantage of the destruction and occupation of many cities in Germany to pass themselves off as refugees who had lost their identity papers. Yet even this return to a "legal" German identity nearly proved fatal when Russian soldiers reached greater Berlin in April 1945 and could only see Inge and her mother as members of a hated nationality (German). Only after they could produce Nazi documents attesting to their Jewishness were they protected and granted the privileged status of "victims of fascism" (Deutschkron 1989).

The story of Inge Deutschkron illustrates in a particularly graphic way the importance of society, or more precisely, of social structure, for individual lives. But not everyone agrees that social structure does, in fact, exist. The former British prime minister Margaret Thatcher once famously declared that "There is no such thing as society." By this she meant that the notion of "society" used in both everyday conversations and in the research and writings of sociologists and other social scientists was a myth, a vague idea that could be used as a way of making excuses for disappointing outcomes. For example, to say that criminals are "made," not "born," suggests that society, not the individual offender, is responsible for their criminal behavior. Thatcher preferred the idea that it is always individuals who are entirely responsible for their own behaviors and their successes and failures in life. In the history of sociology, there have also been prominent figures who adopted a similar view. The German sociologist Georg Simmel (1858–1918), one of the founding figures in sociology, once declared that "Society is merely the name for a number of individuals connected by interaction" (Simmel [1902] 1950, p. 10).

Yet the way Inge's family members saw themselves, and were seen by others, was not simply their own choice but rather was shaped by social and political factors beyond their control (in this case, the Nazi government's theory of race

that classified them as Jewish). For millions in 1940s Europe, this act of classification would prove to be a matter of life and death. Of course, most people have not been subjected to arbitrary racial laws or the whims and injustices of a dictatorial state like the victims of the National Socialism era in Germany. But in many other everyday ways, societies and social structures exert influence over individuals: It sets limits on our choices and opportunities, it enables and motivates us to do some things and not others, and it makes some outcomes more likely than others. Social structures are sometimes mysterious and hard to see, but they are also truly very powerful. As we will explore in this chapter, understanding the social worlds humans inhabit requires us to go far beyond Thatcher's image of a world defined by a bunch of individuals acting freely and without societal constraints to consider the impact of social structure on the lives of individuals.

> ## Social structures are sometimes mysterious and hard to see, but they are also truly very powerful.

Born in 1922, Inge Deutschkron and her mother of Jewish ancestry miraculously survived living underground in Berlin at the heart of Hitler's Third Reich until the end of the war.

THE BIG QUESTIONS

◉ **Watch** the **Big Question Videos** in **MySocLab**

In this chapter we explore the concept and importance of social structure by examining five central questions:

1 What is social structure? Does society exist at all, or is the world made up of a collection of individuals all of whom shape their own lives and fates? In this section, we introduce the concept of social structure and we explore how it is very much like the structure of a tall building—normally hidden from view, but essential to what is possible to build.

How do social hierarchies shape our life choices and relationships?

The social structure of any society consists in part of the social divisions between groups. In this section, we will explore where these social divisions come from and why they matter.

3 Why do institutions influence social life? The other key part of a society's social structure is its basic institutions. In this section, we will explore where institutions come from and why they influence our behavior.

How is social structure linked to social interaction? Where do the identities and roles that are so important for social interaction come from? How do changes in social structure influence social interaction? Does acknowledging the existence of social structure mean that we have limited free will?

5 Why are social structures slow to change? Why and how do they change? What are the forces that hold societies, and social structures, together? Why is change in social structure relatively slow?

1 What Is Social Structure?

SOCIAL STRUCTURE
AS THE CONTEXT OF HUMAN ACTION

Watch the Big Question Video in MySocLab

Social structure is fundamental to the entire way sociologists understand the human world. Let's start with a straightforward example. If you are born into a poor family, it is much more likely that you will be poor as an adult than if you are born into a rich family. Why? Margaret Thatcher's answer is that it comes down to the personalities and actions of these individuals: The rich adult has a better work ethic and simply worked harder or took advantage of opportunities better than the poor adult. For sociologists, however, the answer is more complicated: A bundle of forces, collectively known as **social structure**, also contribute to helping the rich child become a rich adult, and also make it much more difficult for the poor child to become a rich adult. That does not mean that individuals and their actions and behavior do not matter, but there is more to the story. Rich children are more likely than not to have opportunities for growth (i.e., travel to foreign countries, attending very good private schools, having tutors and other forms of special help along the way), people who will help them find their place in the world (private school counselors who help place students in the best possible college or university, family friends who may help find a good job), and benefit in many other ways from being born into rich families. The poor child, by contrast, is likely to enjoy few or

How are social structures similar to the physical structure of a building?

none of these resources. The rich child benefits by her place in the social structure, while the poor child suffers.

We can think of social structure as very much like the structure of a tall building. The structural foundation of a building is what keeps it upright. When the building is completed, you can't usually see the underlying structure that holds it up as it is adorned with lots of architectural details that obscure it. But it is still there. Undermine a building's structural foundation and the entire thing can come down (as Americans witnessed on 9/11 when the two main buildings at the World Trade Center collapsed in a matter of minutes after being struck by airplanes piloted by terrorists). Hidden in the background of everyday life are these forces, or structures, that shape, constrain, and enable everything that we do. Without social structure, everyday life as we know it would be impossible.

Like anything that is normally hidden from view, it is only when structure is *absent* that its importance becomes clear. We've all seen movies or read novels about situations where social structures completely break down—for example, in the aftermath of a nuclear war, a mammoth plague, or a shattering natural disaster, or even in horror films where zombie-like creatures have taken over the world—where all of sudden the characters have to make do without the rules of social structure. These fictional renderings play off a very real idea: that

When social structures break down, so does social order. A powerful recent example of this was during Hurricane Katrina, when lootings and crime skyrocketed in New Orleans. Have you ever been in a situation when you felt like the social structure was weak or falling apart?

underneath everyday social life is a foundation that makes social order possible.

Moving from the realm of fiction to real experiences, one good way to understand what the absence of social structure means is to think about the importance of structure for group activities. Take meetings: A well-run meeting requires having some rules (for example, how long people can speak and how often), some organization (someone has to set the agenda for the meeting), and an appropriate way of managing time (meetings have to begin and end at a certain time; some system for allocating time to different activities has to be devised). Meetings that lack one or more of these structural components will not be very successful. Participants will quickly start to grumble that the meeting lacks purpose, direction, or, in a word, structure. Social structure is essential to everything we do, but we are most likely to notice its importance when it is not there.

One of the most important points about any structure, physical or social, is that it endures over time, even as other things change all around it. Buildings again provide good examples. Architects and builders can dramatically change a building's look by altering the façade or interior of the building. But the underlying structure of the building—the foundation, the supporting beams that hold it up, the location of load-bearing walls— are much more difficult to alter without tearing the building down completely. While working with the existing structure is often cheaper than a complete tear-down, the existing structure will have a huge impact on what is possible in any renovation. This is also true with social structures. Social structures tend to persist over time, giving social life a regularity that it might not otherwise have. Historical changes do occur, but most of the time they happen slowly and modestly, more like a renovation than a complete rebuilding. The very persistence of structures—and their durability—is an important part of what gives them their power. We will explore this idea in much more detail later in the chapter.

Although the concept of social structure may seem a bit challenging to define, we all know about social structures in one way or another. Poor people know that the world is stacked up against them, and the rich know they have a lot of advantages (even if they sometimes prefer to think that isn't true). We all know that we are supposed to show respect to our teachers,

What are the two key components of social structure?

doctors, judges, ministers, and the president. We all know that states with a higher percentage of evangelical Christians are more likely to favor Republican candidates for political office than Democrats. And we are all sensitive to the ways social structures are slowly changing—just think about the types of jobs and careers that will be opening up in the future versus the kinds of jobs and careers that were common 50 or 100 years ago.

But just because we know these things doesn't mean we necessarily understand them. Social structures are mysterious because they have multiple interlocking parts and because many of these components are not usually directly observable. In fact, much of the research of contemporary sociology involves examining small pieces of social structure, not the entire thing. Trying to study the entire social structure of the United States, or any other country, would be a daunting task indeed! It is only through our collective efforts that a fuller picture of social structure emerges. Nevertheless, the overarching concept of social structure is essential to the sociological imagination because it is through social structure that society imposes its will on individuals and groups.

We can begin to understand social structures in a general way by breaking the concept down to two key but distinct components:

1. The *social hierarchies* that can be found in any society, in which some groups or individuals are elevated above others
2. The *institutional environments* made up of laws, rules, organizations, and the government in which individuals navigate

Both of these components make up what sociologists mean by social structure, and we need to consider them separately in the next two sections before exploring how they are connected in their impact on social interaction.

2 How Do Social Hierarchies Shape Our Life Choices and Relationships?

THE FIRST DIMENSION OF SOCIAL STRUCTURE: SOCIAL HIERARCHIES

👁 Watch the **Big Question** Video in **MySocLab**

Social structures contain within them a set of important social relationships, or a **social hierarchy**, that provides individuals and groups with different kinds of status. Every society in the world today contains many such hierarchies. They can be based on almost any way that people divide themselves into groups, although some are obviously more important than others. Social hierarchies are a critical source of what gives social structure its meaning and often motivate people who benefit from them to try to maintain the existing social structure in most or all of its dimensions (or to try to delay change as much as possible).

Social hierarchies arise and persist in any situation in which members of one group are able to use their possession of some *asset* as the basis for claiming special advantages over others who do not have that asset. The asset in question can vary widely. It might be something individuals are born with (like skin color or gender), something they are usually born into but can change in adulthood (such as membership in a particular religious denomination), or something they may either acquire at birth or attain later in life (such as the possession of enough resources to start a business and hire others). The most common social hierarchies found around the world today are those based on class, race, ethnicity, religion, education, region, and gender,

but others can be found as well. Most societies have hierarchies along each of these dimensions as well as a few others. One of the central tasks of all of sociology is the study of **inequality**, that is, the differences in endowments and valued goods held by individuals or families, such as income, wealth, status, or well-being. In the rest of this book we will be exploring each of these types of social divisions and how they manifest themselves in the United States and elsewhere. For now, let us just sketch some basic ideas.

What two critical reasons make social hierarchies an important component of a society's structure?

Social hierarchies are important components of any society's social structure for two critical reasons: (1) Where we stand in key social hierarchies will have a huge bearing on our lives and life chances, and (2) hierarchies shape our social lives and relationships in many different ways.

Let's start from the impact of social hierarchies on **life chances**, by which we mean individuals' long-term possibilities and potential. Generations of research about social hierarchies have reached one key conclusion: Where you stand in relation to the important social hierarchies in society will have a major impact on your chances in life. As we noted above, if you are born into a rich family or have well-educated parents, you are much more likely to do well in school and eventually find a good job. If you are a male, you are more likely to be employed in an occupation, or in that

History is filled with examples of the power imbalance within social structure. It can be seen in the capacity of the powerful to influence the behavior of others, including establishing laws that will exclude subordinate groups and reproduce the power inequality.

part of an occupation, that pays higher wages than if you are a female, even though the men and women in that occupation might be doing similarly demanding jobs and be equally well educated. Similarly, white people have advantages over minorities, and so forth. The bottom line is that if you are a member of a more powerful group, you have advantages over others; those advantages, and not just your own hard work, help determine where you will end up in life. Three generations of research on **intergenerational social mobility**, the movement of individuals from the social position of their parents into their own social position as adults, have widely documented these conclusions (Blau and Duncan 1967; DiPrete 2002).

Society as a whole is impacted by social hierarchies because they generate tensions and conflicts between dominant and subordinate groups. The general requirement of having to defer to or respect higher-status people, and the disgust that may sometimes entail, is an example we are all familiar with. More generally, when social hierarchies allow dominant groups to get more of something that is valued than subordinate groups, it is hardly surprising to find subordinate groups wanting to challenge their exclusion. Examples are everywhere. Gender has long been one basis for exclusion from the opportunity to compete for management positions and positions of power and authority. The so-called **glass ceiling** is a metaphor used to describe the lack of progress women have made moving into valued executive positions. Corporations now willingly hire women to work in the lower rungs of management, but when it comes time to promote, women remain disadvantaged. Currently, only 12 of the Fortune 500 companies are run by women, nearly four decades after the principle of gender equality was fully established, as male executives continually find ways to frustrate the desires of women in large corporations. This fact is a critical source of gender tension in the workplace, and one that impacts the lives of all women who seek entrance to managerial positions.

We want to turn now to two key issues—power and demography (or more specifically, the size of key groups)—that these aspects of hierarchies raise.

Power and Privilege in Social Hierarchies

The case of the glass ceiling highlights the ways in which social hierarchies involve **power**—the ability to influence the behavior of others—and **privilege**—the ability or right to have special access to opportunities or claims on rewards—by which a dominant group seeks to monopolize opportunities and control rewards or at least prevent its existing privileges from eroding. Subordinate groups, by contrast, are subjected to inferior status and limited opportunities. The most common mechanism through which privilege is maintained is **discrimination**, where a dominant group uses either legal or informal means to control opportunities and reduce or eliminate challenges from subordinate groups. Legal means of exclusion—where one group is prevented by law from attaining certain kinds of valued positions—are blunt and powerful. The rules of social hierarchies become most visible and have their biggest impact when they are explicit and clear to everyone and when the sanctions for violating them are most clear. Consider this example. Imagine that it's the 1950s and you're somewhere in the South, let's say Alabama. And let's say you are African American. And you need to go to the bathroom. Your choices are limited. And they are limited because of certain features of the social structure—in this case, race and racism—that are in place. These rules are features that exist outside of you as an individual and outside of the walls of the bathroom itself, but they organize your options.

But such laws and rules are also blatantly unfair in ways that violate fundamental ideas about equality in modern democratic societies. Not surprisingly, they are subject

In what ways do social hierarchies involve power and privilege?

to powerful challenges by subordinate groups for precisely that reason. Challenges have come both from **social movement** protests—collective action aimed at bringing about some kind of change, like the civil rights movement and the women's movement—as well as legal and political challenges. Laws passed by the government (such as the Civil Rights Act of 1964 and the Voting Rights Act of 1965) and rulings adopted by courts of law have in most cases thrown out explicit barriers. For example, legal barriers preventing racial, ethnic, or religious minorities and women from voting, competing on equal terms in admission to college and universities, entering professional occupations, or serving in the armed forces—all of which once provided a secure basis for dominant groups to monopolize opportunities—have been overturned in the past 50 years. Today, in most democratic countries around the world there are few, if any, explicit legal barriers to equal opportunity based solely on group membership. (One of the few remaining exceptions is the U.S. military's restrictions on placing women in combat roles; such discrimination has been upheld by military and federal courts even though the lack of combat-role opportunities hurts women officers in winning promotions.)

However, just because explicit legal restrictions on subordinate groups disappear does not mean that social hierarchies and the inequalities associated with them suddenly cease to exist. The persistence of the glass ceiling in business is but one of many examples. Dominant groups can still assert their power through a variety of informal means that do not rely on formal legal advantages. One of the most important of these is the development and deployment of negative **stereotypes**, or faulty generalizations about a subordinate group applied to all members of the group. Examples of classic negative stereotypes include that some groups are lazy, unintelligent, prone to criminal activity, better suited for caring work than high-paying professional employment, have bad attitudes, or lack ambition. Any of these stereotypes, if widely held by members of the dominant group and others in society, justify continuing discrimination against subordinate groups *even if* formal legal equality is achieved. For example, laws can be passed that require employers to consider all applicants for jobs equally. But if employers hold negative stereotypes about subordinate groups, research suggests that they will consistently favor members of the dominant group in making decisions about who to hire.

☐ Demography and Social Hierarchies

One of the most important aspects of the social hierarchies of any society is the relative size of key social groups and how these change over time. The study of population size, or **demography**, becomes particularly important for examining the ways in which the groups within a social hierarchy relate to one another. Changes in the overall size of different social roles—such as the mix of jobs and occupations, but also including the size of various social groups such as those divided along racial and ethnic lines—can become a critical source of overall social change and impact individual lives. But as with other aspects of social structure, these often occur in ways that individual citizens may not notice until these changes reach a **critical mass**, a point where everyone becomes aware of them and they are large enough to sustain some kind of important activity.

The most common way populations change over time is the result of **immigration**, when individuals and families move to take up residence in a new country. At first, the flow of immigrants from a particular country or region of the world to a new place may be just a trickle, and hardly anyone notices their presence. But as members from a foreign land settle in their new country, they often encourage other family members and friends to join them, and over time people from these new places have become more numerous and perhaps even threatening to those who had lived there before. Competition for jobs, housing, places in schools, and other forms of conflict may begin to occur. All of sudden, the native group may feel that the presence of immigrants has reached a critical mass, decide that the immigrants are posing a threat to their way of life, and seek to exclude them from opportunities by employing stereotypes and active discrimination. In some cases, changes in the relative size of the native and immigrant populations may continue to evolve over time such that eventually the immigrants may be as numerous as the native group, although more commonly the immigrant population will remain a minority in the community. However the situation of immigrants evolves over time, the key point is that changing population size can itself generate important social conflicts.

Changes in the mix of racial and ethnic groups have been a constant challenge throughout American history, largely as the result of immigration. There have been two periods of high immigration from foreign countries that have had particular impact. The first of these waves of immigration occurred between the 1880s and the 1920s as the United States became the destination for large numbers of immigrants from Central and Southern Europe. These immigrants were drawn to America as exploding economic growth meant the availability of job opportunities, especially in manufacturing industries in large cities in the Northeast and Midwest. A second, more recent wave of immigration into the United States started in 1965, coming primarily from Mexico and other countries in Central America and Asia. The current immigration wave shows few signs of slowing down any time soon, although high unemployment since 2007 has at least temporarily reduced the flow of migrants; it is expected to surge again in the near future.

In what ways does population change matter?

The other major population shift that had a dramatic impact on social structure in America was the movement of different groups of Americans within the United States, most notably the "Great Migration" of African Americans from the South to the North from the 1910s through the 1960s. During the Great Migration, millions of black families moved to northern cities in search of better opportunities for jobs and education for their children. In the process, they changed the racial composition of the cities where they moved: Chicago, Detroit, New York, Pittsburgh, Cleveland, and many others. As the population composition of these cities shifted, tensions and conflicts over race grew as well.

Another important example of how population changes can impact the life chances of individuals and generate important social conflicts can be seen in the overall mix of jobs in the economy and how those change over time. These changes in the economy heavily influence the patterns of immigration as well. A wide variety of data sources provide a good statistical portrait of the overall, or macrosocial, structure of a given country, region, or locality. We can draw on census and other survey data to determine the distribution of employment across sectors—in other words, how many people work in agriculture, various branches of industry, and services like wholesaling and retailing, transportation and communication, finance and insurance, and education and healthcare. We can also divide up these numbers a different way and distinguish between those who are self-employed, those who have jobs in the private sector, and those who work for the government.

Such evidence allows us to trace two critical long-term trends that have fundamentally transformed societies around the world, including the United States. The first of these trends—the long-term decline in agricultural production and employment—happened in the late nineteenth and early twentieth centuries in the United States and Europe, and later in other parts of the world (and is just beginning in still others). The second key trend—the dramatic rise in employment in white-collar, knowledge-based occupations, began in the second half of the twentieth century and is now ongoing in the early part of the twenty-first century. Let's start with the shift from agriculture to manufacturing. The social structure of early- to mid-nineteenth-century America, and indeed that of much of the rest of the world, was dominated by the central role of agriculture in the economy. Farm work was dominated by manual labor and was by today's standards very inefficient. Once upon a time, American politicians and party leaders used to actively appeal to the "farm vote," trying to outdo each other in presenting

FIGURE 4.1 DECLINING FARM EMPLOYMENT IN THE UNITED STATES

Source: Marron (2009).

policies (like government payments to support farms) that would appeal to farmers. By the early part of the twenty-first century, however, with the exception of a few mostly smaller states that still have large farming populations, the farm vote is now almost completely forgotten (see Figure 4.1). The overall shift away from farming was driven by enormous improvements in the technologies of farming, including the introduction of machines to replace things that were once done by people, and also (and much more controversially) the use of a wide range of pesticides and other techniques to reduce crop losses.

The second big demographic shift in the American economy is one that it is currently ongoing. Manufacturing jobs were the primary source of job growth in the American economy between the end of the Civil War and the 1960s. If the typical American worker in 1850 was a farmer, in 1950 he (and full-time workers were mostly men) was a factory worker. Employment in manufacturing skyrocketed in the early decades of the twentieth century, and entire communities were built around large factories or manufacturing industries. Opportunities for employment in America's rapidly growing manufacturing sector were important factors encouraging Europeans to move to America up until the mid-1920s. The most famous of these industrial centers dominated by manufacturing was the concentration of the automobile industry in Detroit, but there were many others as well (e.g., steel in Pittsburgh and Gary, Indiana; meatpacking in Chicago; rubber in Akron; grain milling in Buffalo; and transportation hubs for manufacturing companies in places like New Orleans). All of these places prospered as demand for manufactured products grew both in America and around the world. But beginning in the 1970s,

FIGURE 4.2 MANUFACTURING EMPLOYMENT IN THE UNITED STATES

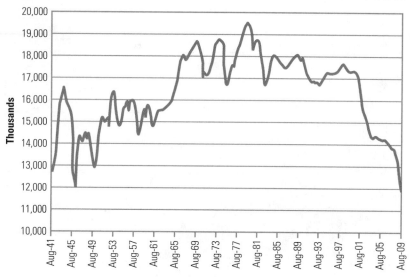

Source: Business Insider (2009).

employment in manufacturing began a steep and seemingly irreversible decline (see Figure 4.2). The many causes of this decline have been widely debated, but one key factor that all analysts agree on is that major technological advances both displaced human workers and made it possible for manufacturing companies to produce efficiently in countries where wages were far lower than in the United States. Manufacturing in countries like China, India, and Vietnam is playing a similar role in leading a transition away from agriculture towards cities, and most of the consumer goods we buy today are largely assembled outside the United States.

What has replaced those manufacturing jobs? The total number of Americans working continued to climb into the early 2000s, although it has since leveled off. The new jobs that were being created were primarily in the so-called service sector, a term used to describe a wide range of industries that include finance, real estate, professional and personal service of all kinds (ranging from expensive lawyers and doctors to child- and elder-care workers), sales jobs of one kind or another, and emerging knowledge-based occupations in computing and the Internet (including software and hardware design). These shifts also include a growing number of "bad" jobs such service and maintenance work, janitorial services, farm labor, and fast-food restaurant work. As a result of these shifts, immigration to America today is dominated by two very different kinds of migrants: those with limited skills who come to occupy some of the "bad" jobs that few Americans want, and those with very high-level skills that are in short supply in fields like computing, engineering, and science.

These changes did not happen overnight (although the decline of manufacturing jobs in America in the late 1970s and 1980s did happen very rapidly). But the consequences for individuals and families were immense. As these changes

accumulate in key historical periods, having the wrong set of skills becomes increasingly a problem for individuals, and entire communities can be affected as well. For example, someone born in a working-class community in 1940, growing up with the expectation of working in factory, could expect to find a decent job in his or her late teens or early 20s (say around 1960). But 20 to 25 years later, in middle age, those factory jobs were disappearing rapidly. Millions and millions of factory workers lost employment in this period and struggled to find similar paying jobs. But what alternative would you have if you were in your 40s and 50s and had spent a lifetime acquiring the knowledge to be a skilled factory worker? Explore the Infographic *The Rise and Fall of Detroit* on page 95 to learn about how this happened to the city of Detroit.

For individuals, the decline of manufacturing jobs meant, among other things, that higher education was an increasingly important dimension of employment. When manufacturing employment was abundant, a high school education was frequently adequate. Today, an individual with only a high school education is at a severe disadvantage in competition for better-paying jobs in the service sector, where knowledge and credentials are increasingly important.

Why do such changes in group size matter for individual life chances? The types of jobs and employment available to individuals is one answer. But the size of different population groups is also important for individuals' chances in life. When competing but unequal groups become more equal in size, competition between them (for many kinds of things including jobs, housing, relationship partners, etc.) will grow. By contrast, if a subordinate or immigrant group is very small, it may pose less of a threat to a dominant group, and laws explicitly limiting a subordinate group may be rarer. When a subordinate group grows large, by contrast, it can threaten a dominant group in many ways. If members of a subordinate group with a large membership have the right to vote, for example, they may be able to use political means to change their subordinate status.

The size of competing groups within social hierarchies can vary widely, and almost any possible combination can be found once we look at history or around the world. Dominant groups can be made up of majorities of a population (such as, say, whites in America for most of the twentieth century) or minorities (such as, for example, whites in South Africa during the long period of **apartheid** in that country, in which explicit racial laws and rules relegated the large African majority to second-class citizenship until they were undone in peaceful revolution in the early 1990s). Under apartheid, South African blacks (who made up over 80 percent of the population in the country) were required to live in certain areas, known as townships; were denied the right to vote or to organize politically or even speak freely in

The Rise and Fall of Detroit

Peak Growth Period by Community in Southeast Michigan

1900-30	1930-50	1950-70	1970-90	1990-2000
Manufacturing boom draws migrants	Depression and war years	Suburbanization and post-war boom	Suburbanization spreads out	Newest high-growth areas

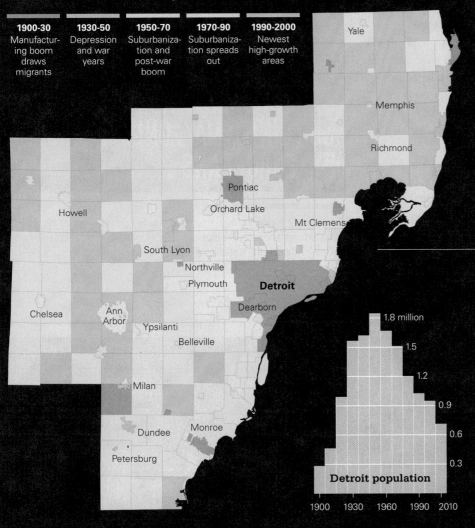

Detroit population

1900   1930   1960   1990   2010

1.8 million
1.5
1.2
0.9
0.6
0.3

If you were to visit Detroit in the 1950s you would find a thriving city. Henry Ford had just built a new addition to his already gigantic auto factory, and the Detroit train station had more people coming through it than nearly any other train station in the world. But visit the train station today and you will find an abandoned building. The last train left in 1988. Vacant lots fill the city, its population having plummeted to less than half of what it used to be.

Population Growth, Decline

What happened? **The rise and fall of Detroit is directly connected to economic change**. Communities that rely on one kind of industry can be severely hurt when the winds of change move in another direction. Big centers of manufacturing such as Detroit have gone through wrenching changes in the latter half of the 20th Century, hemorrhaging jobs and crippling neighborhoods.

⊙→ **Explore** the **Data** on The Rise and Fall of Detroit in **MySocLab** and then ...

■ Think About It

Was there anything that local leaders in Detroit—the mayor, the city council, civic leaders—might have been able to do to prevent the city from going into severe decline? If so, what might that have been?

■ Inspire Your Sociological Imagination

One of the most important insights of the sociological imagination is how personal troubles relate to public problems. How would your life be changed if you were a resident of Detroit during the period in which the rapid decline in manufacturing jobs was occurring?

A City Without Jobs and a People Without Work

Today the city of Detroit has only a handful of automobile manufacturing jobs left. While a new economy based on service sector work has grown, it remains very small in comparison to what once was, and many people whose lives were built on working in the auto factories are simply unable to transition into these different jobs which require different skills. Once an emblem of economic strength, Detroit now symbolizes the impact of the changing economic system.

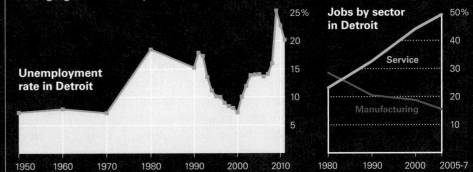

Unemployment rate in Detroit

25%
20
15
10
5

1950   1960   1970   1980   1990   2000   2010

Jobs by sector in Detroit

50%
40
30
20
10

Service

Manufacturing

1980   1990   2000   2005-7

Sources: Based on data from Southeast Michigan Council of Governments; U.S. Bureau of Labor Statistics; U.S. Census Bureau

opposition to apartheid; faced many legal restrictions on the kinds of jobs they could obtain and businesses they could operate; and were subject to frequent harassment by the police. The case of apartheid is extreme, but in the United States today there are some cases where a very small group can exert dominance over much larger groups. Many analysts of economic inequality, for example, emphasize that people at the very top have gained or maintained advantages over everyone else. For example, many top earners are able to take advantage of tax loopholes and preferential treatment that no one else, even the merely affluent, has the resources to take advantage of. In this way, they can pay lower taxes than everyone else. Finally, in many other cases dominant groups can be very large, or a dominant group can be the same size as a subordinate group. Throughout most of the twentieth century, European whites constituted a very large proportion of the total population in the United States, while racially disadvantaged groups were much smaller in size. In the case of gender, the key groups (men and women) are approximately equal in size.

DIE WASGERIEWE IN HIERDIE GEBOU MAG ALLEENLIK DEUR BLANKES GEBRUIK WORD.

THE WASHING FACILITIES IN THIS BUILDING MAY ONLY BE USED BY EUROPEANS.

The majority does not always have more power in society. Rather, history is filled with instances like Apartheid in South Africa where a minority (whites in South Africa) is the dominant group.

3 Why Do Institutions Influence Social Life?

THE SECOND DIMENSION OF SOCIAL STRUCTURE: THE POWERS OF INSTITUTIONS

👁 **Watch the Big Question Video in MySocLab**

The second dimension of social structure involves the ways in which institutions influence social life. **Institutions** are enduring customs of social life, like religion or the "institution of marriage," as well as longstanding formal organizations, like government agencies or schools. Whether we are discussing institutions in terms of enduring customs or concrete organizations, they are critical to how the social world is organized. Individuals not only are members of social groups, they

also are involved (voluntarily or involuntarily) with a wide range of social and political institutions.

☐ Enduring Customs as Institutions

Institutions emerge whenever groups of people begin to try to formalize social relationships and ensure their continuity over time. A classic example would be organized religion. For vast stretches of human history people would gaze at the sky and wonder what it all meant. At different moments in different places, however, some people began to develop more systematic ways of thinking about the wonders of nature and the place of human beings in the world. They began to develop ideas and theories about how the world began, and the possibility of a higher being. As they began to pass these ideas down from one generation to another, the ideas began to solidify, become accepted, and then become **institutionalized**, or formalized, when beliefs became systematically spread. Eventually, people started writing down some of these ideas and then electing specific people to teach them and building specific places where they could be read and studied. As formal roles and rules were introduced, from one generation to the next or from one group of people to another (sometimes by wars), religion came to be organized.

In this way religion became institutionalized, through both religious texts and places of worship, and was organized into religious traditions, denominations, and individual places of worship (such as churches or temples).

Another important example of the process of institutionalization can be seen in the development of schools and educational systems. Teaching and learning have existed from the beginning of human civilization in some form. Parents would educate their children as best they could to do whatever was necessary to survive, such as hunting, food gathering, or agriculture. Even small nomadic tribes or the very earliest human settlements developed ways of passing knowledge from one generation to the next. But that kind of teaching and learning is rather different than what we think of when we talk about education today. At some point, these civilizations got the idea that learning could be facilitated by bringing children together in groups. Eventually, the first schools appeared and began to establish a concrete **curriculum**, which is the structure of coursework and content of a sequence of courses making up a program of study in a school or school system. It was at this point that learning truly began to become institutionalized. Interestingly, many of the earliest schools were founded by religious orders wanting to train future religious leaders. Only later did members of elite families begin to see schools as places that could effectively teach their children the arts and knowledge of upper-class life, and it was still much later that, with the rise of mass universal schooling, formal education spread to all children.

We explore the details and workings of many important social institutions elsewhere in this book, but one key point about institutions in relation to social structure and social hierarchies should be made here. Institutions are the creations of human beings, and they can be, and often are, reinvented over

What are some examples of enduring customs that have been institutionalized?

time. The current struggle over the institution of marriage is a good example; if gays and lesbians are allowed the same rights to marry as heterosexuals, as is slowly happening in many countries around the world the potential impact on our entire conception of marriage, intimate relationships, and the status of same-sex unions will change. Institutions can be designed to foster more or less equality between members of different groups in a social hierarchy, and their change has far-reaching consequences. Continuing with the marriage example, for much of human history, the law and practice of marriage provided definite advantages to men. In many societies, including the United States until the latter part of the nineteenth century, married women could not own property in their own name, and in many cases unmarried women could not either. Until the twentieth century, physical violence inside a marriage was rarely, if ever, treated as criminal by courts of law. Today marriage and divorce laws are far more egalitarian, or equal, although most research finds that men on average fare better financially after divorce than women.

Read the **Document** *Through a Sociological Lens: Social Structures and Family Violence* in **MySocLab**.

Organizations and Governments as Institutions

Large formal **organizations**—social networks that are unified by a common purpose, including government agencies—are important elements of the overall institutional context in any society. Among the most important of these organizations are schools, the economic institutions of society (and all of its various components), the government (and all of its many bureaucracies and agencies, including the military), religion (including all of the major religious denominations and forms of organized religion individuals practice), and many others. Also among the most important institutions are those of the legal system (including the courts, prisons, and jails). Laws specify what we can and cannot do and also include a set of formal penalties when we fail to follow them.

Why are the institutions of the government critically important to the overall social structure?

The institutions of the government are critically important in determining the overall social structure because government policy can influence many other institutions in a number of ways. The government stands above the institutional structure of any society and is the ultimate expression of the powers of institutions. Sociologists refer to the government, in this sense, as the **state**, which refers to all of the agencies and offices of government, the legal system, the military, and the constitution that provides the basis for their respective roles. The power of the state to change social life is easy to see when we think about extreme cases like Hitler's Nazi government in Germany in the 1930s and 1940s, which Inge Deutschkron lived under. Brutal dictatorships often literally choose who gets to live and who must die. Joseph Stalin, the dictator of the Soviet Union at the same time that Hitler ruled Germany, sometimes had as his bedtime reading a list of Communist Party members marked for death; he would go through the list and mark off those who were to be executed and those who would be sent to prisons in the outer reaches of the Soviet Union.

Dictatorships are extreme, but all states have some capacity to determine how wide the gap between individuals is, how many people will live in poverty, and how well advantages can be passed on to children. The governments in richer countries have, not surprisingly, more resources to influence outcomes, but all governments do so to some extent.

Government policies, particularly those associated with the bundle of policies and programs that provide social insurance and social assistance known as the **welfare state**, can reduce the amount of poverty and inequality in society or allow high levels of poverty and inequality (Garfinkel, Rainwater, and Smeeding 2010). Countries with large welfare states typically impose higher taxes on affluent citizens and set some limits on how wealthy individuals or families can become. Welfare states also provide benefits to poor families and children that reduce some of the harshest aspects of poverty, as well as benefits for people who are too old to continue working. Most welfare states also provide health insurance for all citizens, although historically the American welfare state has not done so for everyone (only for those over 65 through the Medicare program and for poor families through Medicaid). In this way, the welfare state changes the very conditions of social life, as our lives would be very different in a world without such programs.

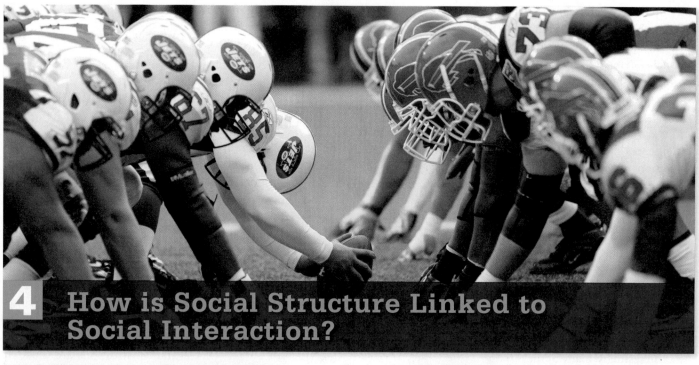

4 How is Social Structure Linked to Social Interaction?

THE CONTEXT OF SOCIAL INTERACTION

👁 Watch the Big Question Video in MySocLab

Sociologist Harvey Molotch has explored how, in the setting of the public toilet and in the different ways people behave in them, we can see social interaction occurring. In fact, Molotch suggests, individuals define themselves through the identities required for such social interaction (Molotch and Noren 2010). But how do we acquire those identities in the first place? In order to answer this question, sociologists have to

consider some of the broader structures of society, like hierarchies and institutions, but also point to some specific processes that influence our social identities and forms of interaction. Social structures are in many ways the flip side of the coin from social interaction.

One way to begin to think about how social structure and social interaction are linked is to think about organized group activities. Consider American football. There is a set of rules that governs play; these rules are established by the governing body of the sport (the National Football League, in this case), which can be thought of as playing a similar role to a society's government. Within those rules, teams (organizations) and their coaches (leaders) have developed a handful of ways to organize play. On the field, a football team consists of different players assigned different responsibilities based on the positions that they play. There's the quarterback, the wide receivers, the running backs, the linebackers, the cornerbacks, and so forth. Each of these players, as a result of the position he occupies and the team he plays for, has a specific **role** to play. That is, each of them is expected to do certain things: If you're the quarterback you better throw the ball (and not to the other team!), and if you're a wide receiver you better try to catch the ball. Workplaces are often organized in similar ways. Some people sort the mail, some people answer the phones, some people go out and get clients, some people do things that the clients want to have done, and so forth.

Organizations establish roles because it is generally an efficient way to organize things. By having assigned roles, people know what they are supposed to do at any given time. In an ideal world, roles complement rather than interfere with each other. Ironically, in the real world, roles often overlap—indeed, on a good football team the wide receivers will not only catch passes but also block and run with the ball when they get the chance. Research in organizational efficiency finds that the most efficient workplaces are often those where the divisions between tasks are reduced such that people do lots of different things and share responsibilities. Still, roles are powerful aspects of the broader social order.

The power of these roles can perhaps be seen most easily in the ways that occupying a particular role changes our behavior over the course of our lives. As we shift from one stage of what sociologists call the **life course** to another, we are supposed to transition as we age through our lives. In other words, we are expected to "grow up." By growing up, we are in many cases expected to alter our behavior to fit new roles. Thus, as we shift from toddler

to kindergarten age, from student to employee, from dating to entering a long-term relationship, from being a worker to becoming a supervisor, or from being in the workforce to being retired, the different roles entail different kinds of expectations. And people typically adopt these roles in appropriate ways that change them and their behavior. The worker who becomes a supervisor has to adopt a different persona, going from a coworker to someone who has to begin to think about larger issues and sometimes make hard decisions about the workers he or she supervises.

If social roles create one type of instructions or set of clues for individuals, there is a broader set of constraints that are known as social **norms**. These are the basic rules of society that help us know what is and is not appropriate to do in any situation. Norms are related to formal rules of behavior, like laws and written guidelines, but norms are generally not written down anywhere. Rules are straightforward, explicit guidelines for behavior. Norms, by contrast, are somewhat more ambiguous. They are things we just know. We know that picking our nose or shouting at strangers or urinating are not appropriate kinds of public behavior. We know that we are supposed to be polite to strangers, respectful to our supervisors at work, and helpful to our family members when they are in need. These are all examples of beliefs that can be traced to behavioral norms that are pervasive in the United States and most other countries around the world today.

How does socialization contribute to the creation of roles and norms?

From a young age we are taught what the proper norms for behavior in the classroom are, and by the time we are in college, they have become second nature and we just "know" how we are supposed to behave without even being told.

Norms and even formal rules and laws are important, but they are also often violated. Who among us has not committed acts that were, or could under certain circumstances, be considered inappropriate or even criminal? Most of the time we can get away with petty violations of rules and norms; but there are costs to such violations. When rules are formalized into law, their violation can carry severe sanctions (including even jail or prison sentences). When that happens, and you are caught, there is a formal sanction to follow. But even violating routine norms can be consequential. Those who do not act in accordance with basic norms may be thought of by others as "weird" or abnormal and be shunned from social interactions and gatherings. To see that this is true, just try doing some small thing that violates a basic norm, like getting too close to someone when you talk to them, refusing to stop shaking someone's hand, or talking loudly in the movie theatre. Because there are consequences that follow even from routine violations of social norms, we all have powerful incentives to follow the basic rules and norms almost all (or even all) of the time.

How Does Social Structure Create Roles and Norms?

If roles and norms are so important in shaping identities and social interaction, where do they come from? The short answer is that social structures provide processes, or mechanisms, that reinforce roles and norms. Social hierarchies themselves provide important clues to appropriate behavior. But it is through our participation in various institutional settings throughout our lives that we more or less learn about, and accept, the basic norms and rules of the broader society.

At the heart of the transmission of ideas about rules, norms, and roles in institutions is the process of socialization. **Socialization** is the process through which we are taught and trained to behave in society or in particular social settings. It is how we come to understand the expectations and norms of our groups. Throughout our lives, we are constantly being socialized to behave in certain ways (or to not behave in others). The process begins in families, where parents attempt to teach their children a wide range of different rules and norms. But socialization continues at every stage of the life course and involves learning from many different people: in schools from our classmates and teachers; in workplaces from our colleagues and bosses; in churches from priests, rabbis, imams, and our fellow congregants; in political, cultural, and civic organizations, where we are socialized by any array of people ranging from a camp counselor to a piano teacher; and even through the mass media, where we learn about behavior by reading magazines, listening to the radio, and watching TV shows. Explore *A Sociological Perspective* to learn more about the process of socialization on page 101.

Analysts of socialization processes have identified a number of universal features of the ways in which society imposes itself on us as we grow up. Children play games, and these games often involve role playing of one kind or another. Developmental psychologists find that these games are important because they teach children the importance of subscribing to an assigned role, even if only for the purposes of the game at hand. As they get older, children move from play to structured learning environments. Here, among other things, they learn about rules and the need to conform to rules in places like daycares, schools, and in the various activities (including sports) that they participate in. Eventually, children begin to socialize with other children and learn things like how to get along and interact with others. As they move through school, they learn how to do things that will be rewarded—like how to take a test or how to write a paper—and their success in mastering these activities goes a long way toward determining their outcomes in life.

However, socialization is not simply something learned in childhood. Learning and adapting to new situations is something that everyone has to do throughout their lives. Taking a new job, participating in a new activity or hobby, making new friends and entering a new circle of people, or joining a new kind of organization, require the acquisition of new skills and ways of handling ourselves. We are always learning, or adapting to new situations as they arise. And when we take on new roles, we have to learn new guidelines and rules.

A simple, but nearly universal, example of how individuals adapt to new situations occurs when we learn how to drive. Driving is not at all the simple process many think it is—cognitive psychologists have shown that learning to drive is mentally challenging in many ways—but it is a skill that almost everyone can eventually master with enough practice. Driving requires us to learn a large set of rules and to be able to apply them in making split-second decisions

From knowing when to use the blinkers, to what the different road signs mean, learning how to drive is fundamentally about learning rules.

A SOCIOLOGICAL PERSPECTIVE
How responsible are you for your own behavior?

From our ability to ride a bicycle to the way we know how to be quiet in a library, behavior is something that is learned. Sociologists refer to the process of learning how to behave as socialization, and it is a key element of how social structures reproduce themselves. Schools are one of the most important institutions when it comes to socialization. In addition to learning basic things like algebra or science, we also learn how to interact with each other, and we learn about things like authority figures and manners. But different schools are organized differently and seek to socialize people in different ways. Students who wear uniforms and attend an all-girl Catholic school will be socialized differently than students who attend a mixed-gender public school.

Socialization continues throughout the life course. When we enter a new job or become involved in any organization, new forms of learning occur as we learn about the basic ins and outs of our new activity or group. Other important institutions of society also socialize us in a variety of ways. The many formal rules and sanctions of the legal system remind us of what we can and cannot do in many situations. But the formal socialization provided by law has its limits; we may obey without actively believing that everything the legal system tells us is correct. Churches and religious institutions, by contrast, socialize through ritual and repetition, attempting to teach moral values and behaviors to followers.

How and in what ways do work organizations have to socialize their workers? How different are the rules and norms of the workplace different from everyday life?

How might the patterns of socialization differ for female students in all-girl schools versus coed schools?

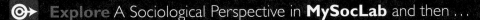

Are the benefits or pitfalls of socialization always transparent to us as we make decisions in our lives?

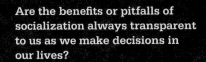 Explore A Sociological Perspective in **MySocLab** and then . . .

■ Think About It
Sociologists argue that behaviors are first and foremost learned. How have you been socialized as a college student? How has the social structure in your sociology course, for example, reinforced a specific role or norm?

■ Inspire Your Sociological Imagination
A great deal of socialization is about learning rules. It's about learning to do things the way other people do them. But how then does change happen? How is it that people can be creative? Can we be socialized into being creative?

101

where mistakes can have large consequences. Our ability to learn those rules and apply them correctly (at least most of the time) is critical to what makes car travel as (relatively) safe as it is. Learning how to date is another common new situation that almost everyone must pass through. If learning how to drive is something that almost everyone masters, dating is such a complicated ritual, with so many subtle and hard-to-grasp mechanics, that evidently many people never learn to do it very well. Still, it is something that virtually everyone learns how to do and, as the permanence of the institution of marriage declines, for many it is something they will do their entire lives (Klinenberg 2012).

Some of the most exciting ideas about socialization were developed by the French sociologist Pierre Bourdieu (1930–2002). Bourdieu argued that socialization works most powerfully through the development of a set of specific habits, or what he called our **habitus**. We develop, Bourdieu argued, a set of understandings about rules and norms that become so ingrained that they become routine, taken for granted in ways that we do not even reflect upon as we act. Our habitus guides how we act in the world and respond to situations, and includes our tastes, preferences, skills, and dispositions. Our habitus represents the outcome of the various socialization processes we have been through in our lives, and because people go through different socialization processes, they acquire different habituses. These differences depend on family background and the particular kinds of institutions (most notably schools, but also cultural institutions and products like museums, theater, films, and books) that we are exposed to and absorb as we grow up.

We will have more to say about Bourdieu's important concept of habitus shortly. The key point is that our habitus is developed over time through our upbringing and socialization experiences. As we spend more time being educated about how to do certain things or how to think about the world around us, our routine behavior comes to be second nature to us. Think, for example, of tying a shoelace. When we are young and first learning how to do it, we go through the motions of doing the loops and thinking step by step of the exact procedure. But once we're older, it's so ingrained in us that our fingers sort of move by themselves and just do it for us.

Bourdieu's research and theories about the growth of habitus specifically examined how different economic and social groups—or **classes**—teach their members different kinds of ways of living. Children born into poor families, with parents who have little education, will grow up with one kind of habitus. Middle-class children, and very rich and privileged children, will grow up with yet different kinds of habituses. In this way, Bourdieu enlarged the meaning of class differences to include more than just how much money people have. In other words, the differences between the middle and upper classes also include all those things contained in the habitus, including tastes, dispositions, and ways

of carrying yourself. To be a middle-class person is not only to have less money than an upper-class person but also to think and act in the world differently. From this perspective, your habitus shows that you "belong" to a particular group by acting in specific ways. Imagine attending a fancy dinner party. Are you able to speak knowledgeably about which wine goes well with which food? Do you know which is the salad fork? People who grow up in wealthy families that place emphasis on these things acquire this knowledge while growing up, just as someone who grows up on a farm might know how to milk a cow or track the footprints of cattle.

Differences in habitus become especially important when we try to move from one social location to another. By the time we reach adulthood, we have developed a set of habits of acting that are hard to undo or remake. The rich and well-educated child is often right at home with "high culture" products and ideas and can comfortably interact with similar kinds of people. The less economically advantaged child, by contrast, even one who has worked very hard to acquire a good education and learn something about the ways of the world, might still struggle to appear at home with these same people. Old habits, as they say, die hard.

Social Structure and Individual Free Will

Social structures are powerful. Indeed, sometimes when social scientists write about the power of structures, it almost appears as if they are *too* powerful. Individuals seem to become robots, fulfilling roles and acting according to scripts handed down in the rules and norms guiding their behavior. They fill positions in the society but are largely replaceable by other individuals and have little control over the worlds they inhabit. It almost makes it sound like individuals have no free will of their own, no capacity to choose how to act. If this were the case, society would just reproduce itself in the same shape over and over, creativity would not exist, and nothing would ever change. But we know from our own experiences that this is not true. Of course we have some choices about what we can do, about how we behave and what course of action we might take. And, surely, things can change as a result of human action. Just think of the civil rights movement or the more recent uprisings in support of democracy in the Middle East; revolutions happen, new laws are passed, old ones are overturned, and social hierarchies change shape.

These are dramatic examples of how structures are not all-powerful, but there are also plenty of everyday examples from our own lives we can consider. For example, we can readily observe that two people will often behave very differently if they find themselves in the same situation. This will be true even if they live in the same society and face the same rules and norms governing their behavior. Take two people who hear someone cry out for help: One may intervene, while another may simply ignore it. Take two investment bankers facing a shortfall in a large investment fund: One may try to raise more money from other investors, the other may illegally move funds from other accounts to cover the losses. A huge body of research makes this point over and over again: People are not robots. They will respond in different and occasionally unpredictable ways, depending on the choices and opportunities confronting them. Such examples and evidence from experiments suggest that people do indeed have some significant measure of individual choice. Philosophers of free will can rest easy; the sociological account of social structure does not mean that all individual choice is irrelevant.

The critical question becomes how to weigh the relative impact of social structure versus individual choice. This is a truly important debate within both sociology and the contemporary social sciences as a whole (Kahneman 2011). Examining this debate is important in part because it reveals some of the different ways that sociologists define social structures and understand their role in shaping society. But it is also important because thinking about the relative impact of social structure versus individual choice can impact the moral judgments we make about people and their position in our society.

At the beginning of this chapter we talked about Margaret Thatcher's claim that there is no such thing as society. When she said this, she was basically saying that everyone in society is responsible for their position because everyone has freedom to act and make of their life what they want. No one, or, as she would put it, nothing in society ever prevents people from making different choices. In other words, your life is what you make of it, and you are free to make of it what you want. Sociologists rarely take the stance that Thatcher took. While most accept a certain level of free will and choice, they tend to consider how we act in the world as being limited by structures. The debate revolves around a question of how much and to what degree. Another way to pose this question is as follows: How much do individuals impact the world, and how much does the world impact individuals?

On the one side of the debate are those scholars who more strongly emphasize the ways in which social structure primarily determines our individual lives and behavior, a view called **structuralism**. They believe that individuals have little **agency**, or capacity to make free choices and exert their own wills. In this way, while structure is connected with constraints, agency is connected with freedom. While agency places power in the hands of the individual, structure places power in the hands of the larger society.

Very often, those sociologists who strongly emphasize the power of structures to determine how we think and act

in the world tend to focus on one particular part of social structure or feature of the social structure that they believe is extremely powerful. One of the most famous social theorists, Karl Marx (1818–1883), for example, believed that the most important social structure was the economy, and individual behavior was largely determined by one's place within the economic structure. If you are a worker you will act and think one way, and if you own a company that employs workers you will think and act a different way. For Marx and other structuralists, being in different locations in the social structure means having different interests, and these different interests are the basis for a lot of social conflict.

There have been many other influential sociologists who have held very structuralist views. Not surprisingly, however, these positions have also been criticized on various grounds. While for Marx the primary determining structure was the economy, others emphasize that our lives are not so neatly organized, and we belong to many different groups, play different roles, and are affected by multiple structures all exerting influence on us at once. For example, in some settings race may be far more important an influence than class. This is a point that the first prominent African American sociologist, W. E. B. Du Bois (1869–1963), made in the early twentieth century. In *The Souls of Black Folks*, using the case of African Americans Du Bois argued that people inhabit multiple roles and are located in different hierarchies. Du Bois was particularly concerned with analyzing how black Americans both had to be members of white society and yet were excluded from it in ways that required them to create their own culture. In this way, Du Bois suggested that identities—in his case that of black Americans, but the idea readily extends to many other groups—are actually very complex things with multiple strands, and there is no simple way to categorize someone. In some sense, we are all different. The political scientist Adam Przeworski (1985, p. 94) once put the point like this:

> We encounter a Mrs. Jones. She works as a salesperson in a department store, is an owner of a piece of land inherited from her farmer father, is married to a machinist, has a son who is studying to be an accountant, and is white and Catholic. We hesitate on how to classify her ... to classify is to homogenize.

If this is true, it becomes very difficult to pinpoint, as the structuralists often want to, exactly which single structure we are responding to when we think and act. We have, instead, a blur of pressures that may pull us in very different directions.

Not surprisingly, most contemporary sociologists are uncomfortable with excessively structuralist approaches, on the one hand, but also with approaches that leave society and social structure out altogether. One of the principle ways that they have tried to reconcile these two positions is by

What is at issue in the debate over the relative impact of social structure versus individual choice?

considering structures as not just constraints on action but also things that *enable* action. Workplace hierarchies, for example, while they certainly place limits on what people can do, also give individuals a sense of identity from which their behavior stems. In football, the rules of the game tell the players what they cannot do, but they also help outline what they *can* do. Moreover, without these rules the game would be in utter chaos and no one could do anything, or especially do things together. In this way, structures give order to society, and without this order action would be impossible.

This leads to a second aspect of the debate, one that takes on the question of how and why change happens in society. Those sociologists who place too heavy an emphasis on the power of structure are criticized for being unable to account for how change happens. If structures determine how we behave, how is it that anything ever changes? On the flip side, those social scientists who place too heavy an emphasis on individual agency and the power of free will are criticized for being unable to account for the fact that most things tend to stay the same or change very slowly. Hierarchies and inequalities, not to mention the basic structure of groups like families, tend to persist over generations. What makes the structures of our society endure? This is our next big question.

5 Why Are Social Structures Slow to Change?

THE ENDURANCE OF SOCIAL STRUCTURES

👁 Watch the Big Question Video in **MySocLab**

One of the hallmark features of social structures is their endurance. People come and go, but social structures continue to exist. The economist and social theorist Joseph Schumpeter (1883–1955) once likened this process to a hotel with a few fancy rooms on the top floors for the very rich, more modest rooms in the middle, and a lot of cheap rooms at the bottom for the poor (Schumpeter 1955). The rooms of this hotel, Schumpeter argued, remain while the specific occupants change. This metaphor is useful because it underscores one of the key ideas of social structure: the separation of individuals (like any of us) from the various positions that exist. It applies widely to almost any kind of institution we can think of. Take for example a university. In any given year at a university, a group of professors will retire. But the role of professor does not end with their retirement. Similarly, a class of students graduates, but their graduation does not mean the end of students as one of the key features of the education system. And even if this particular university were to go bankrupt, the larger educational system will continue.

This raises an important question: Why are these social structures so persistent? Or to put the point more bluntly, why do those parts of the social structure that the majority of people think are unfair persist? There are a number of answers to these questions that we will explore in this section, beginning with the processes known as path dependency.

☐ Path Dependency

Social structures persist in part because earlier developments and institutionalization make it much easier for individual to work within them than to try to rip them apart. This process is commonly known as **path dependency**, or more specifically the ways in which outcomes of the past impact actors and organizations in the present, making some choices or outcomes logical and others illogical. A classical example of this is the QWERTY keyboard. Nobody in their right mind today would invent a keyboard laid out the way the keys are, with many of the most commonly used letters placed in hard-to-reach locations. Yet attempts to replace the QWERTY keyboard have always failed. Why? One answer is simply that in order to use a computer, more or less everyone learns to navigate the QWERTY keyboard. Switching to a better-designed keyboard will be initially time consuming and costly, and even if you were willing to master the other keyboard, every time you use a friend's computer or a public computer, you will have to go back to the QWERTY layout. And if you practice enough on the new machine your fingers will develop a different kind of muscle memory that will make it hard to go back and forth. So instead of switching to a new keyboard, we struggle with the one we are used to.

Path dependency, as the QWERTY example suggests, rests on the idea that paths, once adopted, are extraordinarily difficult to reverse (Pierson 2000). What has happened in the past sets limits on what is possible today or in the future. Path dependency is a deeply historical process and is tied up with how, why, and when particular institutions take root. Sometimes particular paths are established for accidental reasons, while in other cases they emerge in specific historical moments. Sometimes elements of social structure are created deliberately by a specific individual or groups of individuals, although more commonly social structures develop slowly over time as people stumble on better and better ways to do things.

The United States Constitution provides an example of how a particular pathway to modern social structure and society was influenced by a single key event. The Constitution was created by a group of men, meeting in 1787, who eventually (after many dramatic twists and turns) would settle on a document that has continuously provided the foundation for modern American governance. The Constitution was in many ways a remarkable document, envisioning an entirely new form of democratic government. It also contains a number of features that have shaped American politics ever since. For example, the Constitution sets up institutions of democracy that make it very difficult for more than two political parties to win elections to Congress. That is because, unlike later innovations in electoral systems where the seats are divided up among parties based on the percentage of votes each party receives at each election, in the United States elections

Change is difficult, as August Dvorak learned in 1936 when he created the DVORAK keyboard. Although its layout is more efficient and easier to use than the standard QWERTY keyboard, very few people use it.

for Congress take place in either districts (House elections) or in individual states (Senate elections). Each district or state elects the person who gets the most votes. A small party trying to build up support cannot start slowly, electing a few representatives at first and then more over time. The existing major parties (the Democratic and Republican parties since the Civil War) simply prove too powerful in this kind of electoral system. Efforts to change this system have always failed. The Constitution had, of course, many other important impacts as well: It granted unusual powers to the legal system and the courts, and it gave exceptional power to state governments (which declined over time, but to this day there remains far more power in the hands of state and local governments than in most other democratic countries).

Why are path-dependent processes so powerful?

If the Constitution provides an example of how a single decision at one point in time by a distinct group shaped one important set of institutions in American society, many other key institutions and hierarchies have evolved slowly over longer periods of time. But even without a single "big bang" moment that creates an institution, path dependence still operates. Consider the racial hierarchy in America. In the late nineteenth century, the dominant white racial category was limited to European whites from Northern European Protestant countries (they would eventually come to be known as WASPs—white Anglo-Saxon Protestants). Immigrants from Catholic countries like Ireland and Italy, as well as Jews and growing numbers of immigrant from Eastern Europe, had light skin tone but were subject to many of the same negative stereotypes as African Americans and indeed were in many cases referred to as black (Jacobson 1998). Eventually, however, the racial hierarchy proved flexible enough to expand the definition of *white* to include all of these groups (but not African Americans). The process by which, for example, "the Irish became white" (Ignatiev 1995) is a remarkable story of how hierarchies can adapt while retaining their importance (in this case, by maintaining a black/nonblack distinction that has remained powerful right up to the present). Immigrant Europeans excluded from the category of whiteness choose to struggle, in ways large and small, to be included in the dominant racial category rather than trying to eliminate race altogether.

☐ Why Social Structures Are Sticky

The idea of path dependence is important, but we also need to know exactly why it is so powerful. Social structures tend to persist over time for a number of concrete reasons. One reason is political: Once a particular element of social structure comes to be established, it often will generate its own **interest groups**, that is, organizations established to promote the concerns of a group or business corporation. These interest groups will fight to protect and extend existing social arrangements when they are viewed as beneficial to their members. We've already discussed how this works in the case of social hierarchies, where members of a dominant group have strong incentives to maintain their privileges. Similar dynamics exist in social institutions. For example, institutions create jobs, and the workers in those jobs have incentives to try to maintain the institution. When proposals to cut the budget for any institution—schools, the military, prisons, and so forth—are routinely met with strong opposition from those who have jobs and currently draw an income from the institution. Similarly, even people who do not work for the institution but benefit from it in some way will often resist any changes to it. Not just police officers will oppose cuts to the police force; citizens who fear an increase in crime can often be mobilized to fight police budget cuts as well. When a local church is threatened with closure, members of the church, not just the clergy, can be counted to rally in support.

Social structures also persist because there is often broad public support for existing hierarchies and institutions or fears the consequences of completely starting over. We are frequently more comfortable living within the worlds we know and trying to make them better, however much they may make us grumble and complain, than opting for something radically new. The expression "you are better off with the devil you know than the one you don't" is the commonsense version of this idea, and it expresses a powerful reality. Of course not everyone feels completely averse to change all the time, and under extreme or unusual conditions people can and do opt to try to tear down parts of the social structure rather than reform it. But more often than not, individuals and groups reinforce social structure by reforming the parts that are not working rather than tearing it down completely.

CONCLUSION THE LINK BETWEEN SOCIAL STRUCTURE AND SOCIAL PROBLEMS

Social structures are everywhere, and they matter deeply. Writing about the social and political upheavals in France in the middle of the nineteenth century, Karl Marx opened a little book (called *The Eighteenth Brumaire*) by declaring that "Men make their own history, but not under circumstances of their own choosing." Setting aside the sexist language (typical for Marx's day), few clearer expressions of the importance of social structures can be found.

When he wrote that sentence, Marx was thinking about nineteenth-century France, but his idea applies to all of us. Our ability to act, and the choices we make, is always limited by the circumstances in which we find ourselves. We noted in the chapter's introduction that Inge Deutschkron would not have been Jewish but for the rise of Adolph Hitler and the Nazi government's anti-Jewish racial laws. She did not become Jewish because she suddenly discovered religion. Rather, she was forced to completely alter her life and her self-understanding and identity because of an arbitrary and external decision imposed upon her. There are many similar examples all around us that we can point to once we begin to understand the logic and language of social structure, as we have highlighted throughout this chapter. Throughout our lives, we are continually making choices shaped by the hierarchies and institutions in our world.

Social structures have positive but also negative features. In the positive sense, social life as we know it would be impossible without at least some overarching social structures. Under conditions of extreme social disorder, such as during a brutal war or in the immediate aftermath of a natural disaster like an earthquake or tsunami, social structures can break down in ways that make their everyday reality visible. When people begin rioting and looting in such situations, society itself appears threatened, even if only briefly. In the normal course of things, however, social structures provide some order and rhythm to daily life. Left to our own devices, freed of all constraints, we would be in trouble; but with social structures to guide us, we manage to get by.

Yet social structures, especially when they fail to respond to changes in society, have the potential to be harmful. This is particularly true in the case of the social hierarchies that form such a central part of the overall social structure of any society. When these social hierarchies are rigid and allow some groups to exploit or dominate others, the possibility of true equality of opportunity (not to mention basic fairness) is undermined. When some groups enjoy advantages not shared by others, they can use the slow-to-change structures of society to resist challenges from other, weaker groups. When social institutions fail to adapt to changing external conditions they can threaten our well-being. There is no clearer example of that in the world today than the difficulty that economic and political institutions around the world are having in adapting to the threat of global warming. Modern economic systems have thrived on ever-growing levels of production and consumption, and governments work very hard to try to maximize both. But in the race to produce we may be destroying the ecological foundations of human existence.

Understanding social structures is central to the larger project of the sociological imagination. Sociologists pay so much attention to trying to understand the different elements of social structure, and where and why they limit the possibilities for improving the human condition, out of a recognition that only by understanding these underlying structures can we make meaningful progress on the social problems we care about.

⊙ **Watch** the Video in **MySocLab**
Applying Your Sociological Imagination

 1

What Is Social Structure? *(p. 88)*

 **Watch** the **Big Question Video** in **MySocLab** to review the key concepts for this section.

Does society exist at all, or is the world made up of a collection of individuals all of whom shape their own lives and fates? This section examined exactly what social structure is and how it can best be understood.

SOCIAL STRUCTURE AS THE CONTEXT OF HUMAN ACTION (p. 88)

- **How are social structures similar to the physical structure of a building?**
- **What are the two key components of social structure?**

2

How Do Social Hierarchies Shape Our Life Choices and Relationships? *(p. 90)*

 **Watch** the **Big Question Video** in **MySocLab** to review the key concepts for this section.

The social structure of any society consists in part of the social divisions between groups. In this section, we examined where social divisions between groups come from and why they matter.

THE FIRST DIMENSION OF SOCIAL STRUCTURE: SOCIAL HIERARCHIES (p. 90)

- **What two critical reasons make social hierarchies an important component of a society's structure?**

Power and Privilege in Social Hierarchies (p. 91)

- **In what ways do social hierarchies involve power and privilege?**

Demography and Social Hierarchies (p. 92)

- **In what ways does population change matter?**

 Explore the **Data** on The Rise and Fall of Detroit in **MySocLab**

3 Why Do Institutions Influence Social Life? *(p. 96)*

👁 **Watch** the **Big Question Video** in **MySocLab** to review the key concepts for this section.

Another key part of a society's social structure is its basic institutions. This section explored where institutions come from and why they influence our behavior.

THE SECOND DIMENSION OF SOCIAL STRUCTURE: THE POWERS OF INSTITUTIONS (p. 96)

Enduring Customs as Institutions (p. 96)

● **What are some examples of enduring customs that have been institutionalized?**

📖 **Read** the **Document** *Through a Sociological Lens: Social Structures and Family Violence* by Richard J. Gelles in **MySocLab**. This reading explores the broader structural influences on violent behavior in families.

Organizations and Governments as Institutions (p. 97)

● **Why are the institutions of the government critically important to the overall social structure?**

KEY TERMS

institution *(p. 96)*
institutionalized *(p. 97)*
curriculum *(p. 97)*
organization *(p. 97)*
state *(p. 97)*
welfare state *(p. 98)*

4 How is Social Structure Linked to Social Interaction? *(p. 98)*

👁 **Watch** the **Big Question Video** in **MySocLab** to review the key concepts for this section.

Where do the identities and roles that are so important for social interaction come from? In this section, we explored how changes in social structure influence social interaction. We also examined if acknowledging the existence of social structure means that we have limited free will.

THE CONTEXT OF SOCIAL INTERACTION (p. 98)

● **How does socialization contribute to the creation of roles and norms?**

How Does Social Structure Create Roles and Norms? (p. 100)

⊙ **Explore** A Sociological Perspective: How responsible are you for your own behavior? in **MySocLab**

Social Structure and Individual Free Will (p. 102)

● **What is at issue in the debate over the relative impact of social structure versus individual choice?**

KEY TERMS

role *(p. 99)*
life course *(p. 99)*
norm *(p. 99)*
socialization *(p. 100)*
habitus *(p. 102)*
class *(p. 102)*
structuralism *(p. 103)*
agency *(p. 103)*

5 Why Are Social Structures Slow to Change? *(p. 104)*

👁 **Watch** the **Big Question Video** in **MySocLab** to review the key concepts for this section.

KEY TERMS

path dependency *(p. 105)*
interest group *(p. 106)*

Why and how do social structures change? In this section, we explored the forces that hold societies and social structures together and why change in social structure is relatively slow.

THE ENDURANCE OF SOCIAL STRUCTURES (p. 104)

Path Dependency (p. 105)

- **Why are path-dependent processes so powerful?**

Why Social Structures are Sticky (p. 106)

👁 **Watch** the **Video** Applying Your Sociological Imagination in **MySocLab** to see these concepts at work in the real world

5

CULTURE, MEDIA, and COMMUNICATION

 **Listen** to the **Chapter Audio** in **MySocLab**

by ERIC KLINENBERG
with DAVID WACHSMUTH

 ore people live alone now than at any other time in history. In prosperous American cities—Atlanta, Denver, Seattle, San Francisco, and Minneapolis—40 percent or more of all households contain a single occupant. In Manhattan and in Washington, nearly one in two households is occupied by a single person. In Paris, the city of lovers, more than half of all households contain single people, and in Stockholm, Sweden, the rate tops 60 percent. The decision to live alone is increasingly common in diverse cultures whenever it is economically feasible.

The mere thought of living alone once sparked anxiety, dread, and visions of loneliness. But those images are dated. Now the most privileged people on earth use their resources to separate from one another, to buy privacy and personal space.

How has this happened? At first glance, living alone by choice seems to contradict entrenched cultural values—so long defined by groups and by the nuclear family. But after interviewing more than 300 "singletons" (my term for people who live alone) during nearly a decade of research, it appears that living alone fits well with modern values (Klinenberg 2012). It promotes freedom, personal control, and self-realization—all prized aspects of contemporary life. It is less feared, too, than it once might have been, for the crucial reason that living alone no longer suggests an isolated or less-social life.

Our species has been able to embark on this experiment in solo living because global societies have become so interdependent. Dynamic markets, flourishing cities, and open communications systems make modern autonomy more appealing; they give us

MY SOCIOLOGICAL IMAGINATION
Eric Klinenberg

I grew up in the center of Chicago, and my interest in the sociology of culture and cities grew out of my experiences there. I lived in a bohemian but rapidly gentrifying neighborhood called Old Town, a place that was long famous for its vibrant street life and for its blues clubs, jazz bars, cafés, and counterculture scenes. Chicago is a segregated city, and Old Town is wedged between two of the city's most affluent areas, the Gold Coast and Lincoln Park, and Cabrini Green, a housing project (recently demolished) where most of the residents were African American and poor. I was always puzzled by this arrangement, and trying to understand it as a child was the beginning of my sociology career.

My research examines cities, culture, climate, and communications. My first book, *Heat Wave: A Social Autopsy of Disaster in Chicago*, explores the two questions, Why did so many people die during a short heat spell in 1995? And why was this disastrous event so easy to deny, overlook, and forget? My second book, *Fighting for Air: The Battle to Control America's Media*, examines how media consolidation has affected newspapers, radio stations, television news, and the Internet and tracks the emergence of the global media reform movement. My latest book, *Going Solo: The Extraordinary Rise and Surprising Appeal of Living Alone*, analyzes the incredible social experiment in solo living that began in the 1950s and is now ubiquitous in developed nations throughout the world.

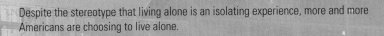

Despite the stereotype that living alone is an isolating experience, more and more Americans are choosing to live alone.

Watch the **Video** in **MySocLab**
Inspiring Your Sociological Imagination

111

the capacity to live alone but to engage with others when and how we want and on our own terms. In fact, living alone can make it easier to be social because single people have more free time, absent family obligations, to engage in social and cultural activities.

Compared with their married counterparts, single people are more likely to spend time with friends and neighbors, go to restaurants, and attend art classes and lectures. Surveys, some by market research companies that study behavior for clients developing products and services, also indicate that married people with children are more likely than single people to hunker down at home. Those in large suburban homes often splinter into private rooms to be alone. The image of a modern family in a room together, each plugged into a separate reality—be it a smartphone, computer, video game, or TV show—has become a cultural cliché. New communications technologies make living alone a social experience, so being home alone does not feel involuntary or like solitary confinement. The person alone at home can digitally navigate through a world of people, information, and ideas. Internet use does not seem to cut people off from real friendships and connections.

Yet some pundits have predicted that rates of living alone would plummet because of the challenging economy: Young people would move into their parents' basements; middle-aged adults would put off divorce or separation for financial reasons; the elderly would move in with their children rather than hold on to places of their own. Thus far, however, there's little evidence that this has happened. True, more young adults have moved in with their parents because they cannot find good jobs, but the proportion of those between 20 and 29 who live alone decreased only slightly, from 11.97 percent in 2007 to 10.94 percent in 2011. In the general population, living alone has become more common in both absolute and proportional terms. The latest census report estimates that more than 32 million Americans live alone today, up from 27.2 million in 2000 and 31 million in 2010.

All signs suggest that living alone will become even more common in the future, at every stage of adulthood and in every place where people can afford a place of their own. Modern culture has shifted in ways that have made this dramatic change in the way we live possible. In this chapter, we will explore the sociology of culture and look more carefully at how these changes in culture and communication are changing the way we live our lives. One important part of the sociology of culture involves studying people's daily routines and practices. Another involves examining the values, social norms, and collective beliefs that make some behaviors acceptable and others suspect. Fortunately, the search for this kind of information is as rewarding as its discovery, which explains why the sociology of culture is one of the fastest-growing parts of the field today.

> # Modern culture has shifted in ways that have made this dramatic change in the way we live possible.

The United States isn't the only place where more people are choosing to live alone. Here, Dai Haifei, 24, reads a book in his egg-shaped cabin in Beijing, China.

THE BIG QUESTIONS

👁 **Watch** the **Big Question Videos** in **MySocLab**

What is culture? When sociologists talk about culture, they refer to systems of collective meaning making as well as the ways people use those systems in their lives.

How does culture shape our collective identity?
Cultural practices both reflect and define group identities, whether the group is a small subculture, a nation, or a global community.

How do our cultural practices relate to class and status?
People's cultural habits help define and reproduce the boundaries between high status and low status, upper class and lower class.

Who produces culture, and why? The cultural field is the place for creativity and meaning making. But it is also a battlefield: Who controls the media and popular culture, and what messages they communicate, are central to how social life is organized and how power operates.

What is the relationship between media and democracy? The media are arguably the most important form of cultural production in our society. The news is vital to democracy, and new ways of participating in the media are changing how democracy works.

1   What Is Culture?

THE MANY MEANINGS OF CULTURE

Watch the Big Question Video in MySocLab

he latest song by Beyoncé, a performance of the opera, our assumptions about monogamy, a series of posts on Twitter, a headline in the newspaper, the reason one person sleeps in and another wakes up early: These are all examples of culture. People use the word *culture* to refer to all sorts of things, from art to traditions to individual learned behavior. In everyday language, culture is often a synonym for art or artistic activities, as indicated by the expression "getting some culture," or a synonym for refined taste, as when we call a person "cultured." These are certainly two of the ways that sociologists use the word, but there are a number of others. In fact, as one writer puts it, "culture is one of the two or three most complicated words in the English language" (Williams 1976:87).

The modern Western history of the concept of culture begins with the rise of world travel in the eighteenth and nineteenth centuries, when merchants from Europe came into contact with non-Europeans for the first time. These merchants were struck not only by the physical differences between themselves and the non-Europeans but also by the differences in how they behaved. This included everything from how they dressed to the way their families were organized. In an attempt to make sense of these differences, scientists in the nineteenth century connected the physical differences with the behavioral differences, arguing that people's biology—and particularly their race—determined how their societies were organized.

Toward the end of the nineteenth century, anthropologists began to criticize this idea and instead argued that it was not race that was responsible for these differences but

something else—something that was not hereditary but rather learned; something that was not natural and biological but rather socially produced. That something was culture. These days, the argument that the differences between groups of people are more than just biological, and that we learn how to behave, seems obvious. But at the time, it was an important discovery.

From this early research came three basic conclusions about culture, which continue to influence cultural sociology today. First, culture is a characteristic not of individuals but of groups. Second, culture is a way of understanding differences between groups and similarities within groups. Last, culture is an aspect of social life that is different from nature or biology. Indeed, what makes culture a social phenomenon is precisely that it is not natural. While it's difficult in practice to draw a line between nature and culture, sociologists now recognize that certain biological things about humans are relatively constant throughout history (for example, everyone gets hungry), while cultural things are not (for example, the kind of food we eat and how we eat it).

In the early twentieth century, sociologists and anthropologists generally used these insights to define culture as the entire way of life of a people. If you were transported back to ancient Rome, what kinds of things would you need to fit in? You would certainly need language and information about art, customs, and traditions. But you would also need all sorts of material objects, including clothing, tools, and a house. This was all considered part of a society's culture. Today, when sociologists talk about **culture**, however, they are usually referring to one of two things: either a shared system of beliefs and knowledge (which is often called a system of meaning) shared among a group and transmitted to individuals through social interactions; or a set of tools for social action—a "tool kit" of assumptions and behaviors for daily life. In other words, culture is a system and culture is a practice (Sewell 2005).

Culture as a System: The Balinese Cockfight

Every society is full of **symbols** that communicate an idea while being distinct from the idea itself. Some are straightforward: For example, in contemporary American society, a red heart implies love and a green traffic light tells you that you are allowed to drive. Other symbols are less obvious: When a car commercial shows a car driving off-road at high speeds, it is likely that the advertiser is trying to make you think about freedom and excitement and associate those ideas with the car. A national flag might have a number of different meanings for different people. Symbols, whether simple or complex, are things that communicate implicit meaning about an idea. Taken together, a group's symbols can be considered its culture. Explore *A Sociological Perspective* on page 116 and consider how culture and context are related.

The anthropologist Clifford Geertz demonstrated the idea that culture is a system of collective meaning by analyzing a Balinese cockfight in 1950s Indonesia (Geertz 1972). Cockfights—boxing matches between roosters—were outlawed by the national government but were still important events in local communities. Multiple pairs of birds would fight over the course of an afternoon, and hundreds of residents would watch, cheer, and place bets. Geertz studied the cockfight the way a student of literature might study a novel, as an object full of symbols needing to be interpreted. For example, Geertz found that participants in the cockfights often gambled far more money than seemed to be rational from an economic perspective. He concluded that the betting wasn't just about winning or losing money; it was a way of indicating and reworking

What are some collective symbols of contemporary U.S. culture?

status hierarchies (those who bet aggressively and were successful were simultaneously securing and displaying high status in the eyes of other participants). The cockfights allowed the Balinese to collectively interpret their own status hierarchies: "a story they tell themselves about themselves" (Geertz 1972:26).

Symbols always exist in specific social contexts—a green traffic light would be mysterious to someone raised in a society without cars, for example, while you would probably find the rituals of a Balinese cockfight equally mysterious. For this reason, studying symbols helps us understand things about society that are not often discussed, such as distinctions of honor, inequality, and competition. For instance, if Geertz had asked them directly, the Balinese cockfighters would not have told him that betting was more a status issue than a financial one. That was something that he could only perceive through careful observation of a place where he had moved and a group that he had gotten to know well. This research method, based on lengthy and intimate observation of a group, is called **ethnography**.

How could we use Geertz's insights to interpret the collective symbols of the contemporary United States? In the place of a cockfight, we could study the Super Bowl—the most-watched cultural event in the country, which features familiar rituals and symbols such as betting on the outcome, Super Bowl parties with friends and family, an elaborate half-time show, and blockbuster television ads. These rituals demonstrate common **values**—or judgments about what is intrinsically important or meaningful—such as patriotism, competitiveness, and consumerism. And the uproar that followed Justin Timberlake exposing Janet Jackson's breast during their half-time performance in 2004 demonstrates

The collective rituals we display in our cultural events, such as this cockfight in modern Indonesia, can demonstrate shared values. What cultural events could reveal shared American values?

A SOCIOLOGICAL PERSPECTIVE

What is the meaning of this?

We've all experienced moments when we see something happening, perhaps when visiting a country other than our own, and have been confused by what exactly we are witnessing. For many sociologists, "What is the meaning of this?" is at the heart of understanding culture. To understand culture is to uncover the meaning of things.

In order to uncover culture, Clifford Geertz argued the need for "thick descriptions," or detailed accounts of the context that allow us to understand the meaning behind behaviors. As he put it, sometimes a wink may mean one thing (flirting with someone), and sometimes it may mean another (sharing a secret with someone) – it depends on the cultural context. When we are trying to not only act in but also explain the world, it is important to have a good grasp of the cultural context.

How could the similar looking gestures in these photos potentially be confused by a person unfamiliar with sporting events or Nazi Germany?

Consider similar behaviors such as children raising their hands in class or a person hailing a taxi. What cues in these and other gestures you've encountered help differentiate the cultural context of each?

Explore A Sociological Perspective in **MySocLab** and then . . .

Think About It

The same symbol can mean very different things in different cultural contexts. What is another common behavior or gesture that people from different cultural backgrounds would interpret differently?

Inspire Your Sociological Imagination

Some hand gestures can elicit strong reactions; a raised middle finger and the "V" peace sign are two examples. What gives some hand gestures their importance or cultural power? Can you think of examples of gestures that have switched from a positive to a negative meaning, or vice versa?

values that are *not* commonly associated with the event. But collective symbols don't have to be massive spectacles to be meaningful. Nowadays we might focus on different cultural events, such as popular videos on YouTube, which would uncover a different America. From music videos to people filming their cats to back-and-forth video debates about politics or technology, sites such as YouTube display our new collective symbols by allowing people to share and interpret culture together (Burgess and Green 2009).

Culture as Practice: Habitus and Tool Kit

For Geertz, culture was out there in the world, expressed through the collective meaning given to objects and events. But how does such collective meaning help to shape our social behavior? Is culture just a set of values and ideas, or does it actually influence how we live our lives? In other words, how is culture actually practiced? The answer is that culture influences the kinds of decisions we make in our lives, whether or not we are aware of it.

How is culture actually practiced?

Some sociologists see culture as guiding our behavior by establishing goals for us. The values we develop in the course of our lives may lead us to want to earn a lot of money, make a positive difference in the world, raise a family, travel, or countless other possibilities. But in recent decades, this approach has become much less common. Instead, now sociologists usually study culture's effect not on the goals or *ends* of our behavior but rather on the *means* of our behavior: in other words, less the "why" and more the "how" of social life.

The French sociologist Pierre Bourdieu argued that we all develop certain sets of assumptions about the world and our place in it: our tastes, preferences, and skills. We develop these habits—what Bourdieu called **habitus**—in the course of growing up and socializing with others, and they become so routine that we don't even realize we are following them (Bourdieu 1992). The kind of habitus we develop depends upon our upbringing. Poor Americans are much less likely to have bank accounts than middle-class and rich Americans, and a large part of the explanation for this fact is their different habituses. If you are born into a poor family, not only will you have less money than someone born into a rich family, but you'll have a different education and assumptions about how to handle money, and these differences will become harder and harder to change as you grow older. If you didn't observe your parents and peers using bank accounts, you won't take for granted that you should have your own account the way that a middle-class or rich child would.

Bourdieu's concept of habitus helps explain how our future choices and opinions are always guided by our past experiences. Someone raised in a wealthy family on the Upper West Side of Manhattan will have no trouble fitting in at a fancy dinner party but probably quite a bit of trouble fitting in on a farm, while someone raised on a farm will have the opposite experience. But people are exposed to all sorts of different cultural systems and forms of meaning, after all. So how is it that you choose to act one way at one time and a different way at another? One way to answer this question is to think of culture as a **tool kit**—a set of symbolic skills or devices that we learn through the cultural environment we live in and apply to practical situations in our own lives (Swidler 1986). If a friend introduces you to someone, how do you behave? If you're single and interested in flirting, you'll draw on one set of cultural tools you've developed; if you're just trying to be polite, you'll draw on a different set of tools. Just as a car mechanic has a box of tools at her disposal for fixing a variety of problems, people have a kind of tool kit of behaviors and opinions that they apply to different situations they find themselves in. Some people will have better tools for certain situations, and some people will have better tools for others. What's more, even though people immersed in the same cultural environments will tend to have similar cultural tools in their tool kit, they probably will have quite different levels of expertise and familiarity with the tools. So two people who hang out in similar social circles might have the same basic set of conversational tools in their cultural tool kits, but the one who keeps to himself will be less comfortable using them than the one who frequently chats with people she doesn't know very well.

One researcher studying love in contemporary America found that the two most important cultural tools are love as a voluntary choice and love as a commitment (Swidler 2003). Most Americans have both of these tools available to them, but their personal backgrounds will affect which one they tend to rely on and which one they are more competent with. Your own past experiences with love might make you leery of thinking of it in terms of commitment, so this will change how you navigate future romantic encounters. Or you may not have had much experience with commitment, such that when you try to use that cultural tool you don't do a good job of it. From this perspective, culture does not just establish differences in how we interpret the world and give it meaning but rather influences what kinds of strategies and actions are practically available to us.

Culture and Communication

Both culture as a system and culture as practice describe forms of *communication*, which is the sharing of meaningful information between people. One important way this occurs is through language. **Language** refers to any comprehensive system of words or symbols representing concepts, and it does not necessarily need to be spoken, as the hundreds of different sign languages in use around the world suggest. Culture and language are closely related. The ancient Greeks called the supposedly uncultured peoples they encountered "barbarians," which literally means people who babble—who have no language.

Researchers have disagreed over the years as to the importance of language for culture. At a basic level, language is a **cultural universal**, a cultural trait common to all humans: As far as we know, all human groups throughout history have used language to communicate with each other. Some linguists have even argued that language is the fundamental building block of thought—that if you don't have a word for something, you literally can't think it. The implication of this view is that a group's language is directly responsible for many of its cultural symbols and practices. A simple example is the distinction between two different words for "you" in French: an informal *tu* and a more formal *vous*. English used to have a similar distinction (*thou* versus *you*), but it died out over time. As a result, English speakers would possibly place less emphasis on formality in their communication with each other and hence in their group culture.

But just because people speak the same language does not mean they share the same culture. Canadians and Americans both speak English, but of course there are many cultural differences between (and within) the two countries. Now most linguists and cultural sociologists believe that language *influences* culture without completely determining it. So while English no longer has an informal *you* and a formal *you*, this doesn't mean that all our conversations are informal. Instead, we have developed different ways of communicating those concepts, such as the frequent use in the South of *ma'am* and *sir* when speaking to an elder.

Communication can occur between individuals, or it can occur at large within society—what is normally called **mass communication**. In recent history, mass communication has occurred primarily through the mass media: television, radio, and newspapers. Prior to the emergence of the mass media, meaning was still communicated on a large scale, just not quite as large or as quickly; the Balinese cockfight could be considered a form of mass communication at a smaller scale, for example, as could a minister giving a sermon to a large congregation.

In recent years the Internet has emerged as the main medium for mass communication. People increasingly access traditional media sources online via newspaper websites or video sources such as Hulu and YouTube. In so doing, they also transform formerly passive

media consumption into something they can participate in by writing comments, reposting stories, and creating their own mashups. Old media and new media now blur together (Jenkins 2006). But the Internet has also created a whole new set of communication possibilities only loosely tied to previous forms of mass communication, most notably through social networks and instant messaging.

Social media have altered the way children, adults, and (increasingly) the elderly engage with each other, both online and in person and at distances near and far. They have changed the ways corporations as well as anticorporate activists operate, the ways that charitable organizations raise funds (especially after a catastrophe), the ways that political officials campaign and govern, and the ways that social movements organize. They have affected the ways we get, and sometimes even make, news and entertainment. Cultural sociologists are curious about how and to what extent social media have transformed everyday life for people at different ages and in different places, as well as about how the rising use of social media will affect our interest in other kinds of media, from newspapers to telephones and radios to books.

The social theorist Manuel Castells argues that we are participating in a new form of Internet-centered communication that he calls mass self-communication because it can potentially reach a global audience but its content is self-generated and self-directed (Castells 2009:58). In other words, the Internet offers both the large scale and ever-present nature of the mass media and the individualized content of interpersonal communication. Facebook, for example, has exploded in size such that it rivals the scope of the largest of the traditional media. As Figure 5.1 shows, there were 145 million active Facebook users by the end of 2008, 350 million by the end of 2009, and fully 800 million users by the end of 2011. That's more than 10 percent of

In what ways is culture a form of communication?

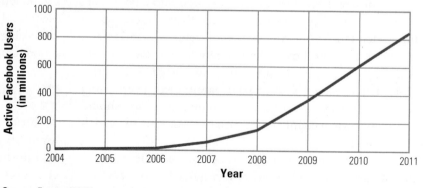

FIGURE 5.1 THE FACEBOOK EXPLOSION By the end of 2011, more than 10 percent of the entire world's population was logging into Facebook on a regular basis.

Source: Fromer (2012).

the entire world's population logging into Facebook on a regular basis.

How are the Internet and mass self-communication changing cultural systems and practices? If the constant flow of communications, information, and entertainment online makes it difficult to focus, does this also mean that our work and our relationships will suffer? Will our accumulation of Facebook friends be offset by a loss in deep friendship, or does connecting through social media make us more likely to spend time with others offline? Will our ideas become more superficial because we'll lack the attention span necessary to develop them? Will we lose interest in certain cultural genres—traditional news reporting, literary novels, nonfiction books—in favor of others—news briefs, pulp fiction, video games—that either require less of our minds or deliver more immediate rewards?

It's hard to know for sure: When it comes to information and communication, the last few decades have probably been the most rapid period of transformation in history. Access to technology may be creating new divisions of haves and have-nots in the form of the social, economic, and cultural gap between those with effective access to information technology and those without such access, known as the **digital divide**. This is the divide between those who are connected and those who are not; between those with high-speed access and those in the slow lane; between those with the education and media literacy to navigate around the more innovative and independent sites and those who mainly visit the big commercial sites (Klinenberg 2007); between "digital natives" born into the age of the Internet and older "digital immigrants" who have to try to keep up with the changes (Palfrey and Gasser 2008). As computers and the Internet become more important to everyday life around the world, understanding the causes and effects of the digital divide (Norris 2001) will be one of the most important tasks for sociologists of culture and communication.

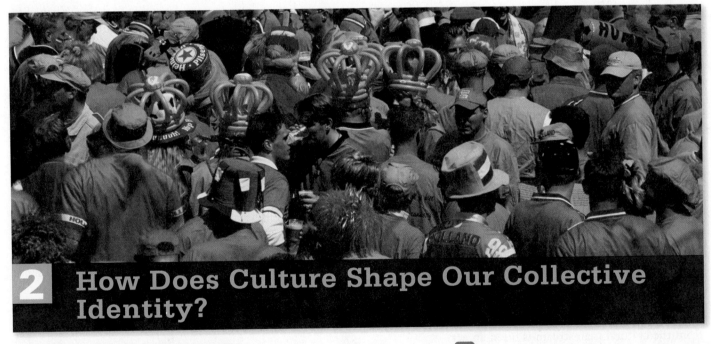

2 How Does Culture Shape Our Collective Identity?

CULTURE AND GROUP IDENTITY

Watch the **Big Question Video** in **MySocLab**

We all think of ourselves as belonging to numerous different groups. Some of these groups are relatively easy to define—for example, nationality or religion—but others are less clear. Are football fans a group? What about university students? If so, how can you tell? More fundamentally, what makes up group identity, and how do sociologists study it? It turns out that culture is central to group identity—both in defining a group and in maintaining it. Some scholars suggest that we should only use the word *culture* to refer to differences and similarities that form the basis for groups coming together or clashing with each other (Appadurai 1996:13).

In the absence of clear ways to define where one group ends and another begins, we need to take our cues from shared behaviors. One way of thinking about identity in cultural terms is through the concept of **group style**, or the set of norms and practices that distinguishes one group from another (Eliasoph and Lichterman 2003). Different groups have different **norms**—shared assumptions about correct behavior—and because most people belong to many groups (for example, your school, your national identity, and your gender); we learn to adopt the right style for the right occasion. Adopting the right style is not always a simple matter, though—think of how difficult it would be for you to fit in if you were transported to a different time or place. Group style is thus a way for people to communicate belonging or not belonging. According to this account of identity formation, culture is a practice of communication.

Mainstream Culture, Subcultures, and Countercultures

Some groups deliberately set themselves off from **mainstream culture**—the most widely shared systems of meaning and cultural tool kits in a society. In the United States, well-known examples include hippies in the 1960s and on-line gamers in the 2000s. Historically, these groups were often considered to be deviant. But contemporary sociologists refer to such groups as **subcultures**, or relatively small groups of people whose affiliation is based on shared beliefs, preferences, and practices that exist under the mainstream (literally *sub-cultures*) and distinguish them from the mainstream. Other examples include rock climbers, hunters, ballroom dancers, and chess players. The American sociologist Claude Fischer (1975) claimed that subcultures are most likely to emerge in cities, where—unlike in small towns and traditional villages—the large, concentrated population allows many such groups to flourish. Some subcultures may have a clearly articulated sense of common purpose or definition, while others may be only loosely connected by mutual interests.

While subcultures tend to exist in harmony with mainstream culture—there's nothing socially threatening about rock climbers—cultural-studies scholars in the United Kingdom argued that some subcultures express differences in political and economic power and that setting yourself apart from the cultural mainstream is often an act of "resistance through rituals" (Hall and Jefferson 1975). This type of subculture is usually called a **counterculture**—a group whose ideas, attitudes, and behaviors are in direct conflict with mainstream culture and who actively contest the dominant cultural practices in the societies of which they are a part.

In the 1960s, hippies were a counterculture, as are contemporary militias and the recent Tea Party and Occupy Wall Street movements. Sociologists consider culture an arena of struggle within which different mainstream cultures, subcultures, and countercultures are unequally ranked and often stand in opposition to another, each fighting for supremacy in determining what counts as culture and seeking to reap the rewards that come from it (Clarke et al. 1975:11).

Read the **Document** *The Code of the Streets* in **MySocLab**.

United States: Hegemony, Culture Wars, or Multiculturalism?

Subcultures and countercultures only make sense when there is a dominant mainstream culture that they can challenge. But is there a single mainstream culture in the United States in the twenty-first century?

The early-twentieth-century Italian revolutionary Antonio Gramsci argued that the dominant classes in a society maintain their rule by encouraging certain moral and cultural understandings that are favorable to them. When elites gain legitimacy and power from widely shared yet taken-for-granted beliefs about what is right or wrong, proper or improper, valuable or not, this is called **hegemony**. For example, it's common sense these days that people should work in order to earn enough money to survive and that people who choose not to work should only be entitled to the bare minimum of financial support, but such common sense ultimately serves the interests of wealthy business owners who need to find hard workers for their businesses. Gramsci argued that movements seeking to radically transform a society needed not just to win political power but to overthrow cultural hegemony—to fight common sense with good sense. Culture, in other words, is not just entertainment; it's a war.

These days, such **culture wars** in the United States usually refer to arguments over the proper role of family and

What distinguishes a subculture from the mainstream?

Countercultures such as punks use their appearance and behaviors to deliberately set themselves off from mainstream culture. What are other examples of contemporary "resistance through rituals"?

religious values in certain questions of state policy: abortion rights, immigration rights, and gay rights are three of the most important. The sociologist James Davison Hunter argued in the early 1990s that people tended to line up on the same sides on many of these issues—positions he labeled "progressive" and "orthodox"—and that being progressive or orthodox didn't necessarily correspond to social class or political affiliation. The main battle lines of American electoral politics, he concluded, were shifting from economic questions to moral questions (Hunter 1991). The journalist Thomas Frank made a compatible argument about the defection of white working-class voters from the Democratic Party. On the basis of an increasing turn away from economic issues and toward moral issues, these voters have come to identify with the Republicans and to see the Democrats as a party of the elite, even though Republican economic policies are clearly the more elite-driven of the two parties (Frank 2004).

At the same time, the idea of culture wars suggests that there are two dominant cultures squaring off against each other: a liberal culture and a conservative culture. This is at odds with another important way to describe the contemporary group-identity landscape of the United States: multiculturalism. **Multiculturalism** refers to beliefs or policies promoting the equal accommodation of different ethnic or cultural groups within a society. Immigrant societies such as the United States have to reckon with a considerable number of different cultural backgrounds and systems of meaning, which make a simple liberal-versus-conservative understanding of culture an insufficient one.

Historically, the standard metaphor used to describe the model of cultural accommodation in the United States is the *melting pot*. Immigrants come from all sorts of diverse cultural backgrounds but are gradually assimilated into American society until they become, at some point, genuinely American, at a minimum by learning to speak English. The melting pot ideal is now generally recognized by sociologists as problematic because it privileges a specific (white, English-speaking, middle- and upper-class) notion of what it means to be American—a notion that is hard to take seriously when 40 percent of Americans are nonwhite and 30 percent do not speak English in their home (see Figure 5.2). The melting pot is thus an example of **ethnocentrism**: an inability to understand or accept cultural practices different from one's own. Perhaps reflecting these realities, the melting pot idea has declined somewhat in mainstream discourse since the twentieth century, although it still thrives in right-wing political discourse,

How is the concept of culture wars at odds with the multicultural landscape of the United States?

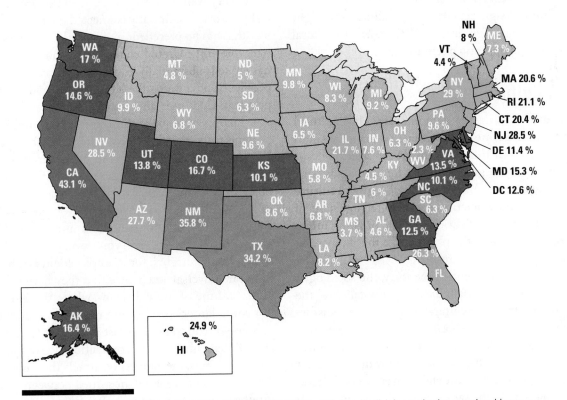

FIGURE 5.2 THE MULTILINGUAL UNITED STATES Although English is our dominant national language, America has always had a history of multilingualism, and with every new wave of immigration the linguistic diversity of the United States continues to grow. As the map shows, the percentage of Americans who do not speak English at home varies widely, from only 2.3 percent in West Virginia to 43.1 percent in California.

Source: U.S. Census Bureau (2012).

Immigrants come to the United States from all sorts of national, ethnic, cultural, and linguistic backgrounds. Why is it important for sociologists studying immigration to practice cultural relativism?

particularly with respect to immigration and English-language-use policy.

The problem with ethnocentrism is that it leads us to make incorrect assumptions about others on the basis of our own experience. If Clifford Geertz had observed the Balinese cockfight from an ethnocentric point of view, he simply would have concluded that many Balinese made risky and irresponsible bets. Or imagine if you went to a Chinese restaurant and concluded that the owners must not have heard about forks and knives because they brought you chopsticks. Although we have all been raised in specific cultural contexts that will influence our thinking in unacknowledged ways—and so we can never escape ethnocentrism entirely—these kinds of assumptions make it difficult to understand other cultures with any kind of depth. We will misinterpret shared meanings or fail to grasp what is important in a given situation. For this reason sociologists do their best to practice **cultural relativism**—evaluating cultural meanings and practices in their own social contexts. For example, Geertz didn't try to discover the cultural significance of the Balinese cockfight in general but rather its significance *for the Balinese*. Cultural relativism is thus the opposite of ethnocentrism.

☐ Global Culture

The existence of subcultures demonstrates that cultural practices can help define group identity for very small groups. But what about the other end of the scale? Does it make sense to talk about group identity for a group as large as the entire human race? What would such a **global culture** that incorporates cultural practices common to large parts of the world look like? Globalization and the ongoing interconnection of people across the planet make this an increasingly plausible idea, if not yet a reality.

Writing in the early twentieth century, the sociologist Max Weber attempted to explain the rise of capitalism as the consequence of a large-scale cultural and religious transformation. He observed that Calvinism (a variant of Protestantism) preached that an individual's salvation or damnation was predestined by God, and thus people couldn't directly affect their chances to go to heaven through prayer or good deeds, as Catholics believed. At the same time, Calvinists were anxious to look for signs of whether God had chosen them for salvation, and they came to believe that practicing hard work and thrift was such a sign. Weber argued that this **Protestant ethic**, when applied to an emerging money economy such as eighteenth-century America, encouraged savings and investment instead of luxury and thus had the unexpected consequence of launching the capitalist cycle of investment, production, and reinvestment. When capitalism subsequently spread around the world, in other words, it was not just an economic system that spread but a cultural one as well (Weber [1905] 2002).

In Weber's time, the cultural values associated with the Protestant ethic had only spread as far as Western Europe and North America for the good reason that culture did not travel very well, and only under certain circumstances. But today's world is culturally connected on a planetary scale in a way that has no precedent in history. What's more, the dominant role of the United States in the global cultural landscape has eroded substantially. It has been the case for decades that people in India watch the latest Hollywood movies, but now people in California are watching Bollywood movies, too.

Thanks to globalization, certain cultural systems have become truly global. Some of these are obvious: Microsoft Windows, for instance, is used by hundreds of millions of people worldwide and provides the basis for a common technological vocabulary that transcends language. Other aspects of global culture are more abstract: Concepts such as citizenship, economic development, and human rights are widely assumed to apply to everyone everywhere (Meyer et al. 1997). Human rights, for example, could not have achieved the near-universal acceptance that they have except within a global culture of individualism, where the individual—and not some larger social grouping such as the family or the nation—is held to be the most important (Elliot 2007).

Global cultural interconnection doesn't mean that we all watch the same movies or attach the same meaning to symbols. Instead, the relationships between place and culture have become more complex. Some cultural events and products are now widespread and *homogenous* like never before: McDonald's has restaurants in over 120 countries. But other aspects of culture have become more diverse and *heterogeneous:* A number of indigenous languages that were dying out have seen revivals in recent decades in part in reaction to globalization (Van Der Bly 2007). Therefore, we should think about global culture not as a single thing but as a set of *flows:* some ideas, people, and commodities circulate smoothly, and others do not (Appadurai 1996).

National Cultures

Even in the era of globalization, though, the most important group identity in the modern world is surely the nation. The entire world is divided into nation-states, and most people are a citizen or subject of a single one of them. So it is not surprising that **national culture**, the set of shared cultural practices and beliefs within a given nation-state, is an important principle for sociology. Are there differences between cultural norms, assumptions, and identities between different nations? If so, what are they, what produces and reproduces them, and what effects do they have? These are the questions that sociologists try to answer about national cultures.

What produces and reproduces global and national cultures, and what effects do they have?

Today it seems obvious that the world should be divided into nations and that people should think of themselves in these terms: I'm American and you're Canadian, she's British and he's Chinese. But it wasn't always so. The rise of **nationalism**—the fact that people think of themselves as inherently members of a nation—was a large-scale cultural transformation, perhaps even a sign of a new global culture. Nations are *imagined communities:* Their members share an assumption of commonality with each other, even though they come from diverse class and ethnic backgrounds, and most will never meet (Anderson 1991). In a country like the United Kingdom, with a strong national government and a common language, this is a plausible enough assumption. But what about Indonesia, composed of 13,000 islands and home to over 700 languages? With the notable exception of some separatist regions at the periphery, Indonesians generally also imagine themselves to be a single national community. And importantly, they view their community as limited, as one among many. A national community is not like a religious community, whose practitioners may hope to convert the entire world to their faith. Indonesians don't want to make all Italians Indonesians.

National communities came about with the origination of *print capitalism*—the mass production of books and then newspapers written in local languages for simultaneous mass consumption by an increasingly literate public (Anderson 1991). When French people read French newspapers and German people read German newspapers, they not only learn what's happening in their respective countries; they

also confirm their membership in two different shared national cultures. Even today, when newspaper readership is on the decline, other forms of shared media consumption follow the same pattern. A study of the geography of Twitter, for example, found that people's networks are generally national and unilingual—although in theory your experience of Twitter could be a truly global one, in practice it is likely to reinforce your sense of belonging to a certain national imagined community (Takhteyev, Gruzd, and Wellman 2012).

In contemporary life, cultural sociologists generally take nations for granted the same way we all do, and many of them study the differences between national cultures: What makes national cultures different from one another, and what are the implications of the differences? Americans are generally thought to be more individualistic than people in other countries, for example, but they are far less likely to live alone than are residents of apparently less individualistic nations, such as Sweden, Norway, Finland, and Denmark (Klinenberg 2012). Why might this be? It can't be because of genetics or different types of human nature: There isn't anything fundamentally different about people in different countries. It turns out that a combination of different factors—including economic prosperity, the rising status of women, the communications revolution, mass urbanization, and the longevity revolution—all influence whether people want to and are able to live alone, and these factors vary widely across national contexts. Explore the Infographic on page 124 to learn more about the new culture of living alone.

Indeed, many important social, political, economic, and cultural institutions are organized along national lines, and these have systematic effects on the way people live their lives and the kinds of attitudes and worldviews they develop. (The effects are not always uniform; social security policies vary substantially between countries, for example, and heavily impact the elderly while having a smaller impact on others.) These different worldviews can in turn have a big impact on other features of national life. In Japan, CEOs are paid on average 16 times more than workers; in the United States, it is 319 times more. Researchers have struggled to explain this enormous and persistent difference between the two countries on the basis of economic considerations alone, suggesting that there are likely cultural factors at work.

One important area of research is early childhood, because it is when we are children that many of our cultural assumptions are formed. One study of preschools in Japan, China, and the United States revealed the very different roles that preschools play in forming cultural identities in

The Culture of Living Alone

Percentage of households that are people living alone

Seattle 42%
WA
Portland 34%
OR
ID
MT
ND
MN
WI
MI
Minneapolis 43%
SD
Detroit 38%
Chicago 35%
Cleveland 40%
New York 31%
(Manhattan 46%)
VT
ME
NH
MA
NY
CT
RI
PA
NJ
MO
DE
Washington 48%
CA
San Francisco 40%
NV
UT
WY
CO
NE
IA
IL
IN
OH
KY
VA
Las Vegas 28%
Denver 40%
KS
St. Louis 45%
MO
Knoxville 51%
TN
NC
SC
AZ
Santa Fe 41%
OK
AR
Atlanta 45%
Santa Monica 48%
San Diego 30%
Phoenix 28%
NM
Los Angeles 30%
MS
AL
GA
Fort Worth 28%
Dallas 35%
TX
LA
AK
Houston 32%
New Orleans 36%
FL
Tampa 37%
HI
Miami 36%
Miami Beach 49%

Labels show one-person household percentages for cities.

38%
35
32
29
26
23
20

Map is shaded by county.

In 1950 the number of people living alone in the U.S. was about 4 million. Today that number has skyrocketed to 33 million, or 28 percent of American households. What does this trend say about America? For a long time, ours has been a culture organized around the classic idea of the nuclear family and a belief in living and doing things together. But does the choice to live alone mean that Americans are disconnected from each other and no longer care about community life? The truth is that people living alone are not isolated, but actually very well connected. In fact, as compared with married people, people who live alone are more likely to spend time friends and neighbors and they're even more likely to volunteer with civic organizations. And most of all they are more likely to live in cities, where high population densities, and the concentration of restaurants, coffee shops and social groups, provides this new group of people with the capacity to live alone but not *be* alone.

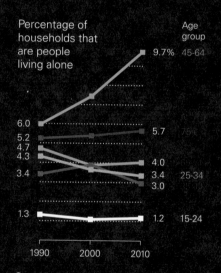

Percentage of households that are people living alone

Age group

9.7% 45-64
6.0
5.2
4.7
4.3
3.4
5.7 75+
4.0
3.4 25-34
3.0
1.3
1.2 15-24

1990 2000 2010

Sources: Based on data from Susan Weber and Andrew Beveridge, Queens College, CUNY; U.S. Census Bureau.

⊙→ Explore the Data on the Culture of Living Alone in MySocLab and then ...

▪ Think About It

In 1950, living alone was most prevalent in rural areas around the Northwest. Today, it is concentrated in big cities. Why this shift in the location of going solo? And how have people who live alone changed the culture of cities?

▪ Inspire Your Sociological Imagination

Women are more likely than men to live alone, but men are more likely to be socially isolated. Why is this? And what are some of the challenges related to the rise of living alone and social isolation - for individuals, families, cities, and nations?

these three countries (Tobin, Wu, and Davidson 1989). By recording classroom activities and then discussing the videos with teachers and parents, the researchers found that U.S. preschools put heavy emphasis on creativity and respect for the children as individuals. In China the emphasis was on instilling order and discipline in the children, an understandable objective in the context of China's single-child families where "little emperors" are often seen as spoiled by their parents and grandparents. In Japan, meanwhile, educators left children to their own devices to a much greater degree than in the other two cases, forcing them to learn to get along respectfully with others.

These might seem like stereotypes, but that's exactly the point. If there are durable differences in cultural norms between different countries, we would expect to find evidence of them in institutions such as preschool. As the authors of this study indicate, preschool both *reflects* national culture—because teachers and parents are influenced by certain ideas and try to pass them along—and helps *reproduce* it—because children inherit these same ideas.

Preschools follow very different educational approaches in different countries. Why is preschool an important place to study national cultural differences?

3 How Do Our Cultural Practices Relate to Class and Status?

CLASS, STATUS, AND CULTURE

 👁 Watch the **Big Question Video** in **MySocLab**

How do you know whether someone is wealthy or powerful? You can't see their bank account or know who is in their phone address book. The chances are that you know because of cultural signs: the way someone dresses, how they speak, the sports they play, the music they like, the kinds of things they like to do, in short, **taste**—their cultural preferences.

Although we normally think about social class in mainly economic terms, taste—and culture more broadly—plays a crucial role in setting and maintaining class distinctions. In one famous study, the French sociologist Pierre Bourdieu even argued that taste is fundamentally the distaste for the taste of others. In culture wars, as in all others, the stakes can be high.

Cultural Capital

Contrary to popular assumption that it is the land of opportunity, the United States is an intensely class-bound society, second in the developed world only to the United Kingdom. Someone who is born into the working class is very likely to stay working class for her entire life, and the same is true for someone born into the upper class. One way of understanding why that is the case is to think about the kinds of resources people can bring to bear in their lives. One kind of resource is money and other economic assets; another is social connections and networks of friends and acquaintances. Bourdieu referred to these as *economic capital* and *social capital*, respectively. He also suggested that there is a third type of resource important for determining class position: In addition to the money you have and the people you know, your success in life is also influenced by your **cultural capital**. This is your education, your attitudes, and your preferences, which collectively confer upon you a higher or lower status in the eyes of others. (Bourdieu 1984).

Cultural capital is serious business. In the summer of 2011, the character The Situation from *Jersey Shore*—a very popular but low-status reality TV show—prominently wore clothing from Abercrombie and Fitch. The company, worried about having its higher-status brand tarnished by association with *Jersey Shore* (and also probably looking for some easy publicity) offered to pay The Situation to *stop* wearing its clothing—the very opposite of a standard marketing arrangement!

We use our cultural capital all the time in interactions with others and often don't even realize we are doing so. Bourdieu did not consider public or over-the-top displays of status symbols to be an important form of cultural capital; instead, he emphasized the various ways that people display taste in everyday life. Discussing why you enjoyed the Spanish director Pedro Almodóvar's latest film, for example, signals to others that you have good taste in movies. Taste also implies distaste; if the person you are talking to doesn't know who Almodóvar is, you are likely to make negative judgments about

What is cultural capital, and in what ways have American elites become cultural omnivores?

his own tastes and status. Even if you don't *consciously* judge other people on their tastes, the chances are that tastes will influence the kinds of people you want to spend time with or avoid. Tastes, therefore, help maintain status boundaries between different groups (Holt 1998).

Cultural capital requires scarcity: Cultural experiences that everyone can share cannot serve as the basis for status distinctions. Before the Swedish home-products company IKEA began to sell its inexpensive furniture, the aesthetic it applied (minimalist Scandinavian modernism) was considered a sign of high status. But because the middle class can afford IKEA furniture and shops there extensively, this aesthetic is no longer an embodiment of significant cultural capital. The issue is not money but difficulty: In order to provide a basis for signaling distinction, high-status cultural consumption must not be easy to participate in, and if it becomes easy it will stop being high status.

Does this notion of cultural capital apply to contemporary life in the United States? The United States has a more pervasive mass culture than many other countries, and recent research has suggested that American elites are becoming less snobbish and increasingly behaving as **cultural omnivores**, or cultural elites who demonstrate their high status through a broad range of cultural consumption, including low-status culture. American elites today are more likely than average to consume not only high culture but popular culture as well. It is a sign of distinction to have wide-ranging tastes (Peterson and Kern 1996). At the same time, we shouldn't overstate the inclusive nature of elite tastes. While, for instance, cultural elites show a fondness for country music (a low-status genre more associated with

Cultural capital is only valuable if it is rare or hard to obtain. Now that the middle class can easily buy modernist furniture at Ikea, that kind of furniture is no longer an important status symbol.

the working class), the type of country music elites generally enjoy is not the commercial country of Garth Brooks or Tim McGraw but rather more alternative country acts such as Wilco or Blue Mountain (Holt 1997).

Symbolic Boundaries

The kinds of distinctions that people make between themselves and others on the basis of taste are just one kind of **symbolic boundary**. Two other important symbolic boundaries are *socioeconomic status*—the amount of money you make and the kind of job you have—and *morality*—the moral considerations that guide the way you live (or appear to live) your life. Sometimes these three types of symbolic boundaries overlap in people's thinking about status and class, and sometimes they don't.

For instance, in debates about the scope and generosity of public assistance in the United States, politicians and commentators often draw the distinction between the "deserving poor" and the "undeserving poor." The former are thought to be hardworking people who nevertheless have struggled to get ahead, while the latter are lazy "welfare queens" or drug addicts. Leaving aside the fact that evidence of this distinction is slim, it is nevertheless a case where moral boundaries are being drawn independently of socioeconomic ones. A similar moral distinction is often drawn between hardworking business leaders and corporate fat cats. Some sociologists have argued that moral boundaries in the United States are more important for indicating status than they are in other countries and that cultural boundaries are less important (Lamont 1992).

When we use discuss symbolic boundaries, we often use terms such as "out of place" or "knowing your place." In many cases, this is just a metaphor—there isn't literally a geographical place you are out of. But sometimes there is: Symbolic boundaries often take geographical form. A person dressed a certain way or with a certain skin color can appear perfectly normal in one neighborhood and strange (or threatening) in another. The symbolic boundaries associated with cultural practices have spatial boundaries as well. Graffiti artists in 1970s New York City developed a highly structured artistic community with informal but well-maintained norms of conduct and apprenticeships for beginners. But they made their art in public places in violation both of the law and of middle-class norms of public space use (significantly, most graffiti artists were people of color and were not middle class). In other words, their artwork was both symbolically and spatially beyond set boundaries.

There were two main responses to the graffiti movement: One was an attempt—in particular by local politicians and media—to portray graffiti as deviant and criminal; the other was an enthusiastic embrace of graffiti by trendy art galleries in some New York neighborhoods. Even though they disagreed about its merits, graffiti's admirers and detractors both agreed about it being out of place and were eager to move it off the streets (an inappropriate place for art) and into the galleries (an appropriate place for art). Sometimes "out of place" is both a metaphor and literally true (Cresswell 1996).

How Culture Reproduces Class

An important topic for sociologists concerned with power and inequality is the process that causes class boundaries and distinctions to be maintained over time, known as **class reproduction**. There are lots of reasons why some people are rich and others poor, but how do those boundaries get maintained in the short term and the long term? Bourdieu's theory of taste attempts to explain short-term class reproduction. In countless everyday interactions, we remind ourselves and others about our relative statuses and thus ensure that our status differences stay prominent. But what explains class and status reproduction over the long term? Why are middle-class children likely to grow up into middle-class adults and working-class children likely to grow up into working-class adults?

How do symbolic boundaries relate to culture?

One obvious answer is money: Wealthier families will have an easier time affording private schools, SAT preparation courses, college tuition, and personal tutors, for example, and they will also likely leave sizeable inheritances to their children. But money only explains part of the story: Sociologists have shown that people make meaningful choices about how to live that are limited but not solely determined by their economic circumstances. The question of how and why we make the choices we do is what culture explains.

The ethnographer Paul Willis (1977) followed a set of boys from working-class homes in a British industrial town in the 1970s. They frequently behaved badly in school, were rebellious, and didn't seem to care much about their futures. A standard opinion at the time was that such cases were simply people failing to make the right choices to get ahead in life. But Willis found it was quite the opposite: The boys' apparently unproductive behavior in school was in fact them adapting to their class circumstances. The same attitudes that got them in trouble with their teachers turned out to serve them very well in factory work a few years later, where standing up to authority and not working hard on command help workers gain collective leverage against their bosses. The boys were learning how to be working-class men.

A more recent study compared middle-class and working-class families in the United States to see how different class positions affect parents' approaches to childrearing and what the implications of the differences are for children's futures. During the study, it became clear that there were two quite different approaches. Middle-class parents followed an approach of *concerted cultivation*, actively fostering their child's talents and intervening on their behalf, thereby instilling a sense of entitlement. Working-class parents, by contrast, followed an approach of *accomplishment of natural growth*, caring for their children but leaving them to fend for themselves socially, thereby instilling a sense of constraint (Lareau 2003). The middle-class children's sense of

What explains class and status reproduction over the long term?

entitlement will make it more likely that they push to succeed socioeconomically when they are older, while the reverse is true of the working-class children's sense of constraint, making it more likely that as they get older the children will stay in the class they were born into.

The implication of both of these studies is that class is reproduced not only through the money you have but through the culture you practice.

4 Who Produces Culture, and Why?

THE CONDITIONS OF CULTURAL PRODUCTION

⊙ Watch the **Big Question Video** in **MySocLab**

In 1845, Karl Marx and Friedrich Engels argued that the people who have the most wealth and power in a society generally also have the greatest ability to produce and distribute their own ideas and culture (Marx and Engels [1845] 1972). In nineteenth-century Europe, these people were capitalists, such as factory owners and bankers, who valued their rights to private property and their freedom to run their businesses as they saw fit. By using their influence with newspaper owners and intellectuals, they were able to make liberty and freedom the dominant ideas of the age.

Marx and Engels's argument allows us to see cultural production as a historical phenomenon. Ideas and fashions don't just change randomly over time; they respond to other changes in a society's political and economic circumstances. At the same time, in the nineteenth century it was much more difficult to spread ideas than it is today. Printing

presses were expensive, and much of the population was illiterate. Today, with the Internet and social media, is it still the case that powerful people and classes have control over the production of culture? Sociologists of culture need to pay careful attention to the *conditions of cultural production:* Who controls the production of ideas in society, and to what ends?

☐ The Public Sphere

A basic premise of public life in a democracy such as the United States is that everyone is allowed to participate. In theory, everyone over 18 can vote, can run for public office, and can try to convince other people of their point of view. In practice, public participation is massively unequal—for example, former felons are stripped of their right to vote in many states, and it is very hard to attract an audience for your ideas or your art if you don't have a fair amount of money—but as an ideal, this vision of equal participation in public life is a powerful one.

The German sociologist Jurgen Habermas calls this ideal the **public sphere**, and it is the most influential sociological account of how ideas are produced and exchanged in modern society (Habermas 1962). According to Habermas, the highest form of public life in capitalist society is private citizens assembled in a public body to confer about matters of general interest. In this ideal public sphere, citizens set aside their own interests, as well as their wealth and status, and meet as equals to collectively debate and generate ideas about how to govern collectively.

How does the concept of the public sphere explain how culture is produced in society?

In eighteenth-century Europe, when the public sphere began to emerge, it was centered in a range of institutions such as newspapers, pubs, social clubs, and coffee shops—in short, any location where people could gather and discuss the news of the day. The public sphere stood apart from the state and offered citizens a way to criticize and influence the government, which was a novel idea in an age of absolute monarchies. In modern welfare states such as the United States, the public sphere is where different social groups organize to become political actors and compete for influence. Activists such as the Tea Party or Occupy Wall Street movements, and lobby groups such as the National Rifle Association or the AARP, are examples of the kinds of groups that are prominent in today's public sphere. An important way they compete is by trying to shape public opinion through the production of ideas, for example in newspapers, on television, and with advertising.

Some sociologists have criticized Habermas's theory of the public sphere for ignoring the power differences that inevitably prevent all citizens from participating equally in public life. For example, the Tea Party movement has received many millions of dollars in funding from a small number of wealthy conservatives, while Occupy Wall Street has raised much smaller amounts of money, generally from small donations. As a result, the Tea Party has been able to spend more money on advertising and promotion, on bankrolling their preferred political candidates, and on other activities that give them influence in the public sphere. In general, sociologists argue that the same things that give some people power over others in private life—such as race, gender, class, and education—will give some people more influence in the public sphere, regardless of Habermas's ideal of equal participation (Fraser 1992). Furthermore, they argue that there has never been one overarching public sphere, as Habermas suggested. Instead, subordinated social groups—or subcultures—have frequently constituted their own **counterpublics**, alternative public spheres through which they produce and circulate their own values, beliefs, and ideas. Factory and union culture in the first half of the twentieth century, the network of black churches that formed the backbone of the civil rights movement, and the bars and clubs where the gay liberation movement began are all examples of American counterpublics over the years.

Fragmented publics do not necessarily need to be subordinate, either: The concept can apply to any subculture. One researcher describes the users of social networking sites such as Facebook as constituting a **networked public**, or online public sphere. Networked publics attract participation from teenagers in particular because of things they offer that face-to-face public settings cannot. Social networking allows for persistence (you can browse through your friends' profiles and message histories years after initial friend requests and conversations), searchability (you can seek out other people with similar interests and connect with existing friends regardless of geographical proximity), replicability (it is hard to distinguish the "original" from the "copy" when copy-and-paste is ubiquitous), and invisible audiences (much of our activity on social networks is potentially being observed by people we don't know, and perhaps at totally different times), and these features make networked publics distinct public spheres (Boyd 2008). Regardless of whether there is one public sphere or many, the concept encourages us to think about how ideas and culture are produced and how people participate in that production.

The Culture Industry versus Cultural Democracy

Who controls popular culture today, and who benefits from it? Is it the corporations that produce it at a profit, or the public who consumes it, shares it, and enjoys it? If record labels, movie studios, and advertising agencies heavily push the latest songs and movies on us, when we enjoy them are we dupes or are we exercising cultural free will? Sociologists have been largely split on these questions between two perspectives: one that sees popular culture as an industry, and one that sees popular culture as a democratic arena—a cultural public sphere.

Writing after the Second World War, the German sociologist and philosopher Theodor Adorno argued that the popular culture that dominates the public sphere encourages a passive, conservative public. He was referring to popular music, movies, and other types of mass culture, all of which he labeled the **culture industry** (Horkheimer and Adorno [1947] 2002). His chief complaint was that popular culture encourages audiences to passively consume what they are watching, reading, or listening to rather than participating or engaging creatively with the work. The kind of culture that the culture industry produces is standardized, commoditized, and does not challenge the status quo; at the end of the day, it is advertising rather than art.

Other sociologists have argued that Adorno's critique of popular culture (along with others like it) was too pessimistic. They instead believe that popular culture provides an arena through which we all debate the meaning of the good life and the conditions for attaining it—an explicitly cultural version of Habermas's public sphere. One response, for example, to Adorno's claim that most people passively receive the culture that is offered to them is that popular culture is user driven. Cultural producers want to attract an audience, so they tailor their art to reflect popular preferences (Gans 1999). Movie studios wouldn't keep releasing the same kind of movies if people didn't want to watch them, and when people vote with their time and money by choosing not to watch a certain kind of movie, studios will probably stop making that kind of movie. According to this perspective, popular culture is an element of *cultural democracy*. In the cultural marketplace, lots of different tastes—including those of subcultures that elites disapprove of—are accommodated. Different cultural styles exist "because they satisfy the needs and wishes of some people, even if they dissatisfy those of other people" (Gans 1999:91).

The debate between the culture industry and cultural democracy perspectives on cultural production generally concerns the kinds of art and media produced by large corporations. The culture industry perspective argues that people passively accept what they are given by corporate media, and the cultural democracy perspective argues that corporate media gives people what they legitimately want. But there is another possibility, which is that people don't just passively accept corporate culture but actually intentionally disrupt and subvert it in reaction to the common view that corporations have too much influence in social life. Naomi Klein calls this *culture jamming* (Klein 2000). Most of us can't avoid constant exposure to corporate media on television and the Internet, but also on signs and billboards in public spaces. Culture jamming relies on this constant exposure in order to mock it, perhaps by directly modifying billboards with graffiti. Culture jammers reject the idea that marketing has to be passively accepted as a one-way information flow.

Culture jamming takes corporate imagery everyone is familiar with and subverts it to show anti-corporate or countercultural messages. Is this form of cultural protest effective?

Is popular culture an industry or a cultural democracy?

☐ The Medium Is the Message

Debates over whether popular culture is democratic, conservative, or something else often focus not only on the content of popular culture but just as often on its form. If the same content is broadcast on cable TV and on Twitter, will it communicate the same thing? The answer from communications theory is that it won't. As Marshall McLuhan famously declared, the medium is the message (McLuhan 1964). By this, McLuhan meant that different media encourage different ways of communicating, of organizing power, and of centralizing or decentralizing social activity.

Compare listening to a news bulletin on the radio with reading the same news on a website. There are some obvious differences: For example, when you hear the news on the radio, you hear only what the announcer says, while on a website you have the opportunity to follow hyperlinks and look up unfamiliar things on Wikipedia. In this respect, the web offers a richer experience than the radio. But there are some other differences that may not be as obvious. On the radio you can't follow hyperlinks, but you also have a harder time skimming the material the way you can on a website. Radio dominates one of your senses—hearing—and prompts you to devote most of your attention to receiving and processing the information you are hearing. A website, by contrast, provides you with a more ambiguous sensory experience. There might be sound and video on the webpage, but there might be just text. You might be listening to music in the background, or you might have an instant messaging window open simultaneously. Reading news on a website requires more of your direct engagement than listening to the radio does. Different forms of communication can thus provide very different experiences even when communicating the exact same content.

For this reason, sociologists say that media are biased (Innis 1951). Bias here doesn't refer to political bias—the way, for example, that many people believe Fox News has a right-wing slant—but rather to the different types of engagement that different forms of communication encourage. Some scholars further argue that different media actually change our notions of truth and our values (Postman 1985). As a result, sociologists of culture and the media need to pay careful attention to changing patterns of media consumption and engagement. If we read fewer books and more webpages, the implications may be much broader than just how we get our news and entertainment.

Cultural production in the United States is increasingly occurring online. But an arguably greater transition was from the age of typography to the *age of television* (Postman 1985). From the sixteenth century until midway through the twentieth century, public discourse in the West was based in writing, a medium biased towards careful and considered thought. Personal communication largely occurred via letters, which took a long time to write and be delivered, encouraging people to thoughtfully consider what they wanted to say. Similarly, large-scale communication occurred through books and pamphlets, which also encouraged thoughtfulness. According to some communications scholars, meanwhile, the age of television has been an age of irrelevance, impotence, and incoherence in public discourse. How much of what we see on the news has any actual relevance for our lives in the sense that it will cause us to make different decisions? Endless reporting of distant natural disasters, for example, is irrelevant to our daily lives, and this helps promote a loop of impotence because we become used to passively receiving information without expecting to be able to act on it in any meaningful way. What's more, the information we receive through television tends to arrive in a series of short, disconnected sound bites, which make it difficult for us to put them in any coherent context. Ultimately, the bias of television as a medium is toward stimulation and entertainment, possibly at the expense of understanding.

Do we still live in the age of television? Things have changed since the 1980s, when these trends were first identified. Ronald Reagan was president, the Internet only existed in

Does communication change with the form or medium?

a few laboratories, and no one had cell phones. Our media consumption habits have changed as well. On the one hand, Americans watch more television than ever before—American households had the TV turned on 8.5 hours per day on average in 2011, compared to only 6.5 hours per day in 1980 (Nielsen 2011:16). And, in fact, 40 percent of American households have the TV turned on during all waking hours—regardless of if anyone is watching or not (Gitlin 2007:18). On the other hand, we spend a lot of time on the Internet, where media consumption isn't necessarily as passive as it is with television. Have things gotten better or worse? Is this still the age of television?

Evidence suggests that many of the trends from the age of television have actually intensified. Long-form fiction reading has substantially declined, for example; the percentage of American adults who have read a novel, play, or the like in the last year shrunk from 57 to 47 percent between 1982 and 2002 (Gitlin 2007:213). And although we watch more television than ever before, we spend far less of that time watching the news: In 1980, 23 percent of Americans watched the evening news on average each night, compared to only 7.5 percent in 2010 (see Figure 5.3; Pew Research Center 2012). At the same time, it is possible that the entertainment we watch on television is of higher quality than it used to be, with the increasing popularity of high-brow TV shows on channels such as HBO and the increasing sophistication of more mainstream fare on the large networks

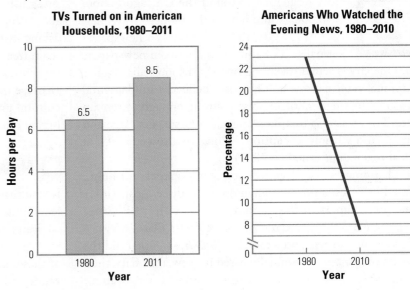

FIGURE 5.3 IS THIS STILL THE AGE OF TELEVISION? Although Americans watch more television than ever before—in fact, 40 percent of American households have the TV turned on during all waking hours—there have been dramatic changes in what role television plays in our lives.

Source: Nielsen (2011).

(Johnson 2005). But arguably the most important trend is an increase in cultural multitasking—when you watch TV, how often are you also checking Facebook, browsing the Internet, or instant messaging with a friend? The contemporary media environment is a "torrent": a nonstop flow of information that we rarely if ever disengage from. The torrent doesn't so much command our active attention as it forms a sensory background for our lives (Gitlin 2007). As we all live our lives in an increasingly online and interconnected fashion, just how cultural production continues to change in the years ahead will be a crucial question for both sociologists and the public at large.

5   What Is the Relationship between Media and Democracy?

MEDIA AND DEMOCRACY: A CHANGING LANDSCAPE

Watch the Big Question Video in **MySocLab**

Before he helped to found the Chicago School of sociology and launch the modern social science of the city, Robert Park was a newspaper journalist. The connection between newspapers and the city is actually a strong one. As the journalist Walter Lippmann once argued, "There is, I believe, a fundamental reason why the American press is strong enough to remain free. That reason is that the American newspapers, large and small, and without exception, belong to a town, a city, at most to a region" (Blethen 2002).

Lippmann's observation about newspapers all being based in cities is not true anymore. The three most widely read newspapers in the United States are the *Wall Street Journal, USA Today,* and the *New York Times. USA Today* is a national newspaper, and while the *Wall Street Journal* and the *New York Times* are nominally based in New York City, their readership is largely national or even global. What about the other half of Lippmann's argument? Is the American press still "strong enough to remain free"? With newspaper readership in free fall, does this even matter? Should we be asking instead about whether blogs are strong enough to remain free? What is the relationship between media and democracy, and how has it changed since Robert Park's time? Because the media are arguably the most important form of cultural production in our society, these are important and urgent questions for cultural sociologists.

☐ Newspaper Citizens

In the first half of the twentieth century, Park and his colleagues at the University of Chicago treated the city as a laboratory to study social relations. One of the most important groups of people they studied was immigrants. Many of these had only recently left their home countries and still wanted to keep track of goings-on at home. In the days before television, radio, and the Internet, newspapers provided the only practical means of doing so. Park observed that foreign-language newspapers were an important institution in Chicago, and reading, which was generally an elite practice in the countries where immigrants had previously lived, became not only common but a necessity in the U.S. city (Park 1923:274).

Foreign-language newspapers didn't just provide a link to home countries. They also addressed the experience of the new groups to which immigrants—whether German Americans, Russian Americans, or Chinese Americans—belonged. Immigrants were changed through the process of immigration, and the newspapers provided a new set of common themes, stories, characters, and even a vocabulary for making sense of the new world. The new American metropolises of the early twentieth century were enormous, chaotic, and sometimes mysterious. Police departments and courts, department stores and restaurants, hotels and boarding houses, train stations, stock exchanges, concert halls and saloons: No one could possibly experience it all, but newspapers would delve into these worlds, allowing readers to sample tastes of the city life they might not experience firsthand. News was aimed at the common reader, with stories of love and romance targeted to women, and sports and politics targeted to men.

Some newspaper publishers, such as William Randolph Hearst, saw the news as a form of entertainment. Others, such as Joseph Pulitzer, saw the news as information. But they commonly saw newspapers as vehicles of social integration. Benedict Anderson emphasized the role of newspapers in creating national imagined communities, but Hearst and Pulitzer's papers also created urban imagined communities. According to the historian Richard Hofstadter, newspapers created "a mental world" for migrants moving from the countryside to the city. For these migrants, the urban environment could be both cruel and fascinating, both mysterious and enticing, and newspapers were one of the main guides they used to interpret it. Newspapers thus helped close the social distance between readers and emphasize their common circumstances (Hofstadter 1960:188). The notorious showman and scam artist P. T. Barnum put it more directly: "He who is without a newspaper is cut off from his species" (Barnum [1880] 1990).

City newspapers helped to make people citizens, but citizens of what? What community did newspapers help make people feel a part of? In a small village, people could keep up with the goings-on of their neighbors directly through word of mouth, but in large cities, Park argued, newspapers helped perform this role by reporting on events of local importance (Park 1923:277–78). According to Park, and most media scholars who have followed, if we are to have a politics built on public opinion and informed debate, the newspaper must tell us about ourselves, informing us who we are by letting our experiences and ideas surface on its pages.

☐ Making the News

If the news is vital to democracy, then it matters a great deal how the news operates. **Journalism** is above all a form of communication: It is the production and dissemination of information of general public interest. But sociologists of the media are in broad agreement that the news does a lot more than just pass along facts to the public. By deciding what to cover and how to cover it, journalists don't simply report on the news, they actually help to create and change it (Schudson 2003:11).

How do journalists make the news?

How does the news have this kind of power, and is it a good thing? There are plenty of arguments about the power of the media. Common left-wing critiques suggest that the mass media support corporate power, militarism, and the interests of the wealthiest. Common right-wing critiques suggest that the media make culture liberal and spread feminism, environmentalism, and the acceptance of homosexuality. Political insiders on all sides believe the media exerts agenda-setting power that can change the course of political events and determine careers.

The problem is that it is difficult to prove that the media actually have this influence. One famous incident of apparent media influence was during the Vietnam War. Up until 1968, TV news coverage was favorable to the war, sanitizing violence and especially U.S. casualties. That changed in 1968, most famously with CBS news anchor Walter Cronkite's February editorial calling for negotiations with the Viet Cong, and the popular narrative is that media criticism of the war prompted a turning point in public opinion. But when the coverage became more critical, polls found a temporary increase in support for the war as people rallied to support the president and the campaign.

Because the media are so visible and audible, they are presumed to be an important force in society. But if the public doesn't passively receive whatever the media tell it, how do the media have their influence? According to media scholar Michael Schudson, the media act as a cultural system: They set the context for making events in the world intelligible. They do this by helping construct a community and a public conversation. Regardless of your opinions on a given issue, when you hear about it in the news you are more likely to treat it as an event of importance. This is why public relations experts say, "There's no such thing as bad press." The news amplifies issues and makes them publicly legitimate.

☐ Media Bias: Domination or Framing?

Are the media biased? There is no doubt that certain topics get very little coverage in the news. Abortion is hotly debated, as are tax breaks for businesses. But the desirability of capitalism is very rarely mentioned. There are different explanations for why this is the case.

Edward Herman and Noam Chomsky have developed a "propaganda model" of the media: The role of the media, they argue, is to inform, entertain, and ingrain citizens with national values and to suppress dangerous oppositional perspectives. In the case of state-run media in nondemocratic countries, this propaganda role is obvious, but Herman and Chomsky claim that the private-sector media in countries such as the United States operate in the same way. They give five reasons why this is the case: first, the concentration of media ownership in a small number of wealthy hands; second, the fact that advertising is the primary source of revenue for the media; third, the media reliance on government officials, corporate leaders, and public relations as sources for reporting; fourth, the power of governments and big business to discipline and threaten media that is too critical; and finally, the ubiquity of anticommunist sentiment to be aroused (Herman and Chomsky made their arguments in the context of the Cold War, and Chomsky has subsequently suggested that the war on terror is the contemporary equivalent).

The result of these five factors, according to Herman and Chomsky, is that the media will give sustained attention to stories that are useful to powerful institutions and very little attention to stories that are not. For example, there were similar periods of state violence in Cambodia and Indonesia during the 1970s, but the media largely ignored the episode in Indonesia (a U.S. ally) while relentlessly covering that in Cambodia (a U.S. enemy). Their argument can be seen as a modern version of Marx and Engels's belief that the ruling ideas of an age are the ideas of the ruling class. Herman and Chomsky give provide a model to explain how, in the contemporary United States, ideas useful to ruling elites are promoted and other ideas are silenced (Herman and Chomsky 1988).

Herman and Chomsky's propaganda model is an example of a media domination argument: They hold that the media tell (or try to tell) the public what to believe, and the message they communicate is a biased one. Today, sociologists of the media more commonly argue that the news is slanted because of media **framing**. Reporters cover a diversity of topics, but they tend to do so through certain existing storylines and narratives. Schudson gives the example of the coverage of race in local news. Local news consistently shows a higher percentage of blacks as perpetrators of crime and as recipients of public assistance than is in fact the case. Is this bias? Are reporters trying to push a certain ideological line? Schudson argues that they generally are not, but that their coverage fits and helps confirm the frame of African Americans as prone to criminality and poverty. "Media frames, largely unspoken and unacknowledged, organize the world both for journalists who report it and, in some important degree, for us who rely on their reports" (Gitlin 1980:7).

The explanation for how framing operates has as much to do with institutional factors as personal ones. On the one hand, journalists themselves tend to be economically conservative, upper middle class, and socially liberal. Minorities and the poor are underrepresented in the newsroom. This means that journalists tend to cover stories in ways that make sense to the white upper middle class, for example by assuming the virtue of individualism and political moderation. On the other hand, there are institutional factors that impact how the news gets made. The media are generally for-profit enterprises, and they want to tell exciting stories to sell newspapers or attract viewers. This means that the news tends to focus on visible events, action and conflict, and personal drama. For the same reason, the media tend to focus on bad news; as the saying goes, "if it bleeds it leads."

Why do certain topics get very little news coverage?

☐ Corporate Media Concentration

One of the premises of the free press in a democracy is that citizens will be exposed to a variety of perspectives and sources of information in order to participate meaningfully in public life. But just six corporations own most of the media in the country. How much choice do U.S. media consumers actually have? Three trends in the U.S. media landscape suggest that the relationship between media and democracy is only likely to grow more troubled (McChesney 1999; Klinenberg 2007).

The first is consolidation: Fewer and fewer corporations own more and more of the media outlets in a given market. Consolidation limits consumer choice—in an extreme case, the corporation Clear Channel once owned all the commercial radio stations in the city of Minot, North Dakota. This is a monopoly and is still comparatively rare, but oligopolies (markets controlled by a handful of firms) are now the norm in the media. Consolidation also makes it difficult for new entrants to break into the market, increasing the likelihood that the media market will stay dominated by the same players.

A second trend is conglomeration, which describes a firm controlling multiple types of media functions. For example, the Walt Disney Company, one of the big six U.S. media corporations, owns ABC, ESPN, hundreds of radio stations, and various print media operations. When Disney has a new movie to release, it can rely on its subsidiaries to promote the movie on its stations and television programs and to ensure that the coverage is positive. This is called *synergy,* and Disney is the master of synergy.

How much choice do U.S. media consumers actually have?

The final trend is hypercommercialism. It has long been standard for movies to feature some sort of product placement—advertising where shots or mentions of a product are integrated into the movie itself as opposed to a separate ad. But product placement has soared to new heights in recent years and shows no sign of abating. The 2010 romantic comedy Valentine's Day, for instance, featured product placements for 60 different products—one every 125 seconds! This is an example of hypercommercialism, and it is a defining feature of today's corporate media—blurred lines between advertising and editorial content in newspapers; the ubiquity of outdoor advertising; the spread of media companies into retail businesses, such as the ESPN Store; and sponsored programming, such as the corporate naming of nearly all professional sports venues.

According to communications scholar Robert McChesney, these three trends have put enormous commercial pressure on journalism. Within the bounds of profitability and corporate acceptability, the media produces a wide range of content; outside of these bounds, nothing.

☐ Media, Democracy, and the Internet

Writing one hundred years ago, the journalist Walter Lippmann was skeptical of the media's ability to provide the public with the information necessary for a democracy. He argued that "news and truth are not the same thing." Democracy requires truth, but the news can only describe and discuss events from day to day. Lippmann believed that democracy required a collective intelligence, which could only be had with extensive social organization, and that here the press could only play a small part, although a necessary one (Lippmann 1922:358).

The notion that the press is vital to democracy is an old one. Thomas Jefferson, for instance, famously said that "Were it left to me to decide whether we should have a government without

newspapers, or newspapers without a government, I should not hesitate a moment to prefer the latter." Many First Amendment scholars believe that the media are necessary to provide a forum for debate (to help constitute the public sphere, in other words), give a voice to public opinion, serve as citizens' eyes and ears in politics, and serve as a public watchdog over government and business (Graber 2003).

But the relationship between the media and democracy looks different in the age of corporate media consolidation and the Internet. Corporate consolidation inevitably means that media are less responsive to the local communities that they serve, and the quality of democratic politics and cultural life suffers as a result (Klinenberg 2007:26). Less local staffing, less local news gathering, and less interaction with the local community means less ability to play the democratic role Park and Lippmann thought was necessary.

At the same time, people are fighting back, and they're increasingly doing so online. Citizen journalism has exploded in the last decade, in large part because barriers to entry are so low. In the mid-1990s, a group called Radio Mutiny set up an unsanctioned pirate radio station in West Philadelphia as a challenge to corporate media, but doing so took nine months of hard work to build the transmitter (Klinenberg 2007). Setting up a blog, by contrast, takes only a minute or so. The Internet has lowered the bar for entering into the public sphere, allowing the people formerly known as the audience to assert their own voices, if not nearly as forcefully as the conglomerates such as Clear Channel, Disney, and even Google.

The most spectacular incidence of Internet activism and democracy of recent years is the 2011 Arab Spring uprising in the Middle East, and particularly the mass Tahrir Square demonstrations in Egypt that overthrew the

Increasingly, corporate marketers believe the best advertising is the kind you don't even realize is an ad. Do product placement and other forms of hypercommercialism threaten the integrity of the media?

Massive protests swept through the Middle East in 2011, reaching their peak with millions of people gathering in Tahrir Square in Cairo, Egypt to overthrow the Mubarak Regime. Many have argued that social media played an important role in allowing these protests to be organized and spread. What other ways might social media be changing the way democracy is practiced around the world?

Mubarak regime. Across the region, people protested against their governments, most visibly by gathering in large numbers in public squares. Within a few months, four national governments were forced from power, and a number more only narrowly avoided that fate. Here social networks, and in particular Twitter, were often held to be crucial to activists' organizing efforts, by allowing people to coordinate their protests and get up-to-the-minute information on what was happening elsewhere. At the same time, governments in Egypt and other parts of the Middle East also used social media in their attempts to repress the civilian uprising.

Despite the ongoing development of grassroots and citizen-led media activism, it would be a mistake to view the Internet as the remedy for the troubles of the contemporary media landscape. Although it empowers people to easily post and share content with each other, setting up a blog is of course no guarantee that anyone will read it. There is evidence that readership online follows roughly the same pattern as readership offline—a large majority of people get their news from a tiny number of sites, while a large majority of sites get virtually no traffic at all (Hindman 2008). Moreover, the Internet has not necessarily made it any easier to monitor the activities of the powerful—a key traditional role of journalism. And corporations are increasingly finding ways to subvert the apparently democratic nature of social media by hiring people to post and monitor content. Finally, the actual efficacy of online activism, for example in the Arab Spring, has yet to be proven. There is no doubt that activists are using Twitter as a key tool for communication and mobilization, but we don't yet know if this actually makes a difference to the outcomes. It is more realistic to say that the Internet has created both new opportunities and new dangers for the free media and for democracy.

CONCLUSION CULTURE ONLINE AND OFFLINE

It is the nature of culture that it changes dramatically over time and across locations. The collective meaning and shared rituals of the Balinese cockfight from 50 years ago would probably be scarcely recognizable to contemporary Indonesians. And no doubt the culture of early twenty-first-century America will seem equally strange to Americans in 50 or 100 years. What would be shocking is if culture stayed the same.

But even compared to a baseline of ongoing cultural change, it is fair to say that a dramatic cultural transformation has been occurring in recent decades in the United States and throughout the world with the rise of the Internet and global cultural flows. Many of the most pressing questions for cultural sociologists in coming years, therefore, will likely be concerned with the cultural implications of the Internet and other new forms of interconnectivity.

We shouldn't make the mistake, though, of assuming that the increasing prominence of the Internet in society means that all of our important cultural questions will be online ones. The persistence of offline forms of social life—street life, public performances, print media, poorer communities that do not have easy access to the necessary technology, and more—in an online world will be an increasingly urgent focus of research and public policy. Will the digital divide get wider or narrower in years to come, and what will be the implications for cultural production, communications, and democracy?

In what ways has the Internet created new opportunities and new dangers for the free media and for democracy?

Watch the Video in MySocLab
Applying Your Sociological Imagination

Study and **Review** in **MySocLab**   **Watch** the **Video** Inspiring Your Sociological Imagination in **MySocLab**

 1

What Is Culture? *(p. 114)*

 Watch the **Big Question Video** in **MySocLab** to review the key concepts for this section.

This section explored how sociologists talk about culture and the systems of collective meaning we make as a group.

THE MANY MEANINGS OF CULTURE (p. 114)

Culture as a System: The Balinese Cockfight (p. 115)

• **What are some collective symbols of contemporary U.S. culture?**

Explore A Sociological Perspective: What is the meaning of this? in **MySocLab**

Culture as a Practice: Habitus and Tool Kit (p. 117)

• **How is culture actually practiced?**

Culture and Communication (p. 117)

• **In what ways is culture a form of communication?**

KEY TERMS

culture *(p. 114)*
symbol *(p. 115)*
ethnography *(p. 115)*
value *(p. 115)*
habitus *(p. 117)*
tool kit *(p. 117)*
language *(p. 117)*
cultural universal *(p. 118)*
mass communication *(p. 118)*
digital divide *(p. 119)*

2

How Does Culture Shape Our Collective Identity? *(p. 119)*

 Watch the **Big Question Video** in **MySocLab** to review the key concepts for this section.

This section explored how cultural practices both reflect and define group identities, whether the group is a small subculture, a nation, or a global community.

CULTURE AND GROUP IDENTITY (p. 119)

Mainstream Culture, Subcultures, and Countercultures (p. 120)

• **What distinguishes a subculture from the mainstream?**

Read the **Document** *The Code of the Streets* by Elijah Anderson in **MySocLab**. This reading examines the subculture of the inner city poor and how their norms and values contradict those of the dominant society.

United States: Hegemony, Cultures Wars, or Multiculturalism? (p. 120)

• **How is the concept of culture wars at odds with the multicultural landscape of the United States?**

KEY TERMS

group style *(p. 119)*
norm *(p. 120)*
mainstream culture *(p. 120)*
subculture *(p. 120)*
counterculture *(p. 120)*
hegemony *(p. 120)*
culture war *(p. 120)*
multiculturalism *(p. 121)*
ethnocentrism *(p. 121)*
cultural relativism *(p. 122)*
global culture *(p. 122)*
Protestant ethic *(p. 122)*
national culture *(p. 123)*
nationalism *(p. 123)*

Global Culture (p. 122)

National Cultures (p. 123)

- **What produces and reproduces global and national cultures, and what effects do they have?**

Explore the **Data** on The Culture of Living Alone in **MySocLab**

3 How Do Our Cultural Practices Relate to Class and Status? *(p. 125)*

Watch the **Big Question Video** in **MySocLab** to review the key concepts for this section.

In this section, we discussed how people's cultural habits help define and reproduce the boundaries between high status and low status, upper class and lower class.

CLASS, STATUS, AND CULTURE (p. 125)

Cultural Capital (p. 126)

- **What is cultural capital, and in what ways have American elites become cultural omnivores?**

Symbolic Boundaries (p. 127)

- **How do symbolic boundaries relate to culture?**

How Culture Reproduces Class (p. 127)

- **What explains class and status reproduction over the long term?**

4 Who Produces Culture, and Why? *(p. 128)*

Watch the **Big Question Video** in **MySocLab** to review the key concepts for this section.

The cultural field is the place for creativity and meaning making. But it is also a battlefield. In this section, we explored who controls the media and popular culture, and what messages they communicate.

THE CONDITIONS OF CULTURAL PRODUCTION (p. 128)

The Public Sphere (p. 128)

- **How does the concept of the public sphere explain how culture is produced in society?**

The Culture Industry versus Cultural Democracy (p. 129)

- **Is popular culture an industry or a cultural democracy?**

The Medium Is the Message (p. 130)

- **Does communication change with the form or medium?**

5 What Is the Relationship between Media and Democracy? *(p. 132)*

👁 **Watch** the **Big Question Video** in **MySocLab** to review the key concepts for this section.

The media are arguably the most important form of cultural production in our society. This section examined the media's relationship to democracy and the new ways in which it is changing how democracy works.

MEDIA AND DEMOCRACY: A CHANGING LANDSCAPE (p. 132)

Newspaper Citizens (p. 132)

Making the News (p. 133)

- **How do journalists make the news?**

Media Bias: Domination or Framing? (p. 134)

- **Why do certain topics get very little news coverage?**

Corporate Media Concentration (p. 134)

- **How much choice do U.S. media consumers actually have?**

Media, Democracy, and the Internet (p. 135)

- **In what ways has the Internet created new opportunities and new dangers for the free media and for democracy?**

👁 **Watch** the **Video** Applying Your Sociological Imagination in **MySocLab** to see these concepts at work in the real world

6

POWER and POLITICS

Listen to the **Chapter Audio** in **MySocLab**

by STEVEN LUKES
and JEFF MANZA

T he decade of the 1960s is famous today as a period of protest and turmoil all around the world. In the United States, protests against the Vietnam War were reaching their peak and other kinds of social movements were also sprouting up, especially on college campuses. One particularly dramatic set of protests took place at Columbia University in New York City in April 1968. Student rebels, demanding a variety of changes in the governance of the tradition-bound Ivy League campus, had taken over the office of University President Grayson Kirk. After occupying the office for several days, police officers stormed President Kirk's office and forced the students out. Here is how one observer described the scene:

> One and a half hours after the president's suite had been cleared of student demonstrators, Grayson Kirk stood in the center of his private office looking at the blankets, cigarette butts and orange peels that covered his rug. Turning to A.M. Rosenthal of the New York Times and several other reporters who had come into the office with him he murmured, "My God how could human beings do a thing like this?" It was the only time, Truman [Kirk's dean] recalled later, that he had ever seen the President break down. Kirk's windows were crisscrossed with tape and on one hung a large sign reading "Join Us." His lampshades were torn, his carpet was spotted, his furniture was displaced and scratched. But the most evident and disturbing aspect of the scene was not the minor damage inflicted by the students. The everything-in-its-place

MY SOCIOLOGICAL IMAGINATION
Steven Lukes

My first book was about the life and ideas of Emile Durkheim, one of the founders of the sociological tradition, whose classic works raise large questions about how to understand what "social" means and why the explanations typical of economics and psychology, at the level of individuals and their interactions, will always be inadequate. They also, however, leave other questions unaddressed: They largely neglect power relations, class, and other social conflicts within societies. My subsequent work has addressed both sets of questions, with books on individualism, on power, and on Marxism. I started to think sociologically about morals when still an undergraduate student: Where our moral judgments come from if not from our social context, and why they should apply beyond it, are questions I continue to pursue. And reading Durkheim's great book on religion led me to ask to what extent our religious, scientific, and even logical thought is socially shaped.

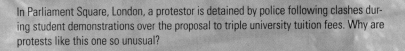

In Parliament Square, London, a protestor is detained by police following clashes during student demonstrations over the proposal to triple university tuition fees. Why are protests like this one so unusual?

Watch the Video in **MySocLab**
Inspiring Your Sociological Imagination

décor to which Kirk had grown accustomed was now in disarray—disarray that was the result of the transformation of an office into the living quarters of 150 students during the past six days (Goffman 1971:288)

Commenting on this report, the famous sociologist Erving Goffman wrote:

The sociological question, of course, is not how could it be that human beings would do a thing like this, but rather how is it that human beings do this sort of thing so rarely. How come persons in authority have been so overwhelmingly successful in conning those beneath them into keeping the hell out of their offices? (Goffman 1971:288, cited in Lemert 1997:133–34).

Once we think about it, Goffman's observation is remarkably astute. Instead of thinking of protests against power and injustice as unusual disruptions of the status quo, in many ways the critical question for the sociologist studying power and politics is simply this: Why is it that, in most times and places, people accept injustice and learn to live with it? Why don't the vastly more numerous poor and middle classes do more to seize the wealth of the rich?

> ## We are often not fully aware of the impact that power has on us, and sometimes we are not aware of its operation at all.

In this chapter, we will explore these questions by examining power and its political underpinnings. Power is a complex idea. We are often not fully aware of the impact that power has on us, and sometimes we are not aware of its operation at all. Sometimes we can be mistaken about the causes of what afflicts us, and we may see power at work when it is not, attributing our misfortunes to conspiracies of one sort or another. One huge task for the sociologist studying power is to bring to light what is involved when power is at work. What are its typical *mechanisms*, or modes of operation? When we go along—as we often do—with policies and relationships that work against our interests, why do we do that? Is power at work in securing our compliance, and, if so, how is our compliance secured? And where are we to *locate* power: Where does power lie? Who is the *they* that have power? Are we looking for individuals, or groups, or impersonal institutions? Are the answers to such questions sometimes hidden from, even inaccessible to, people caught up in power relationships? As we will see, power is most effective when it is least observable to participants and observers alike. And if that is so, then the task facing the sociologist of power is all the more daunting.

Student rebels assist each other in climbing up into the offices of Columbia University President Grayson Kirk at the campus in New York City, April 24, 1968.

THE BIG QUESTIONS

👁 **Watch** the **Big Question Videos** in **MySocLab**

In this chapter, we explore three central questions.

What are the distinct forms of power? In this section we explore the three dimensions of power, using a sociological lens to examine not only the most visible ways in which power is expressed but also its more subtle forms.

How does the state distribute power in a society? Here we examine the institutions of power, which sociologists refer to as the state. We explore how and why the states matter in the distribution of power, and why states tend to promote the interests of the powerful.

Who has power in the United States today? Our discussion of the dimensions of power and political institutions leads us to an examination of the American political system. How is the United States different than other similar countries in the way power is distributed in national politics?

1   What Are the Distinct Forms of Power?

THE THREE DIMENSIONS OF POWER

👁 **Watch** the **Big Question Video** in **MySocLab**

Power in the most general sense simply means the capacity to bring about some outcome; in other words, either to effect changes or to prevent them from occurring. In social and political contexts the effects of power will be those that are significant to people's lives. When these effects of power negatively affect people's interests, we can speak of power being held or exercised *over* them. In such cases, the sociologist's quest is to try reveal what this involves. There are also other ways of identifying social and political power: for instance, as *collective* power to achieve shared goals (as when people cooperate to promote a cause or pursue a campaign) or as *positive* power, where power serves others' interests (as, ideally, parents, teachers, philanthropists, and social workers are supposed to do).

Who has power in the one-dimensional view?

In this chapter we will first focus on what is involved in having and exercising power over others and then turn to an analysis of how power over others can be extended to the capacity to achieve goals through the political system.

It is useful to think of power as containing three distinct "dimensions." The first of these dimensions—the one-dimensional view—involves situations where we can see power at work when one party prevails in a conflict. A second dimension of power, however, becomes visible once we consider the ways in which those with power prevent or deflect challenges to their authority from arising in the first place; this is referred to as the two-dimensional view of power. Finally, the three-dimensional view reveals the ways in which those with power convince those without power

that the current arrangement is good enough. We begin with the one-dimension view.

☐ The One-Dimensional View of Power

The most straightforward situation where we can see power at work is one where there is a conflict between two or more individuals or groups and one of them prevails. Let's call the more powerful individual or group "A" and the less powerful individual or group "B." In any decision-making body, such as a legislature, when a vote is taken on an issue over which A and B take opposing sides, if A wins the vote, we can say A has exercised power over B.

There are countless examples of power at work in this observable form, involving conflict over an issue or issues for which the participants have interests that are in contention. The conflict can be interpersonal—between lovers or within families—or it can occur within or between organizations. It can even exist between countries. A bully in the schoolyard, a mugger in the street, a landlord versus a tenant, a struggle between employers and unions over wages, a group of people rising against a dictatorship, a country locked in civil war or at war with other countries—all of these involve power in a directly visible form. Sometimes, the balance of power can shift and the usually powerless agent can gain and sometimes exercise power. In some cases, the power of the powerful is illegitimate (such as the bully or the mugger), sometimes legitimate (the landlord's rent

In a display of one-dimensional power, anti-government protesters demonstrate in the streets of Syria in 2011 demanding the ousting of President Bashar al-Assad.

might be legal and fair), and sometimes (as in war within or between countries) what is right and wrong itself may be what is at issue (imagine how history would have been written differently if Nazi Germany had won World War II).

Power is often exercised just by following the "rules of the game." For example, when companies compete for market share in selling some good or service, it is the economic game; when a group of legislators wins a vote, it is the political game. But in other cases, those who win do so not by following the rules of the game but rather by manipulating them in some way. Using threats or bribes to get what you want or cheating are examples of how someone or some group can gain power by breaking the rules. For example, by using coercion or threats or by offering special incentives or outright bribes, a person or group can achieve power by breaking the rules of the game.

Exercising power by breaking the rules of the game is, however, an uncertain undertaking. For example, when threats of violence escalate into the actual use of force, it means that the mere threat itself has failed. The use of force often signifies weakness. For example, when governments headed by dictators face social rebellions, as we saw in some of the Arab Spring protests in the Middle East in 2011, they often use military force to try to stop the protests. This may stop or slow down the protests, but in many cases these government will eventually fall if protests continue even in the face of force. Too much force is rarely sustainable over the long haul. In this sense, the use of force is failed power: If the more powerful A must use force against the less powerful B, A has not succeeded in getting B to comply but only to temporarily give in.

Who has power on the first dimension? Scholars and writers sometimes speak of a ruling class or a **power elite** (as C. Wright Mills called it in a famous book in 1956). The idea is that a small group of power holders is consistently able to get what it wants. The political scientist Robert Dahl (1958, 1961) famously put such claims to the test in the late 1950s, suggesting that they would be confirmed if there are "cases involving key political decisions in which the preferences of the hypothetical ruling elite run counter to those of any other likely group that might be suggested" and "in such cases, the preferences of the elite regularly prevail" (Dahl 1958, p. 466). The key political decisions, Dahl suggested, must be over important issues that "involve actual disagreement in preferences among two or more groups" (Dahl

1958, p. 467). Dahl used this approach in a study the city politics of New Haven in the 1950s. He concluded that the evidence showed that different groups prevailed over different key issues and thus that the ruling elite hypothesis was refuted. He concluded, instead, that power in New Haven was distributed *pluralistically* and that perhaps this was so throughout the United States as whole.

The **pluralism** thesis advanced by Dahl would become one of the most widely influential and debated theories in the study of American politics. Supporters of pluralism argue that as long as competing groups (or interest groups) have sufficient power to participate, the final outcome of any policy or political controversy will reflect the preferences of the majority of the citizens. Critics of pluralism maintain that it provides too narrow a view of the nature of power because it is applicable only where there is obvious, observable conflict. Whether or not Dahl's famous pluralist account was right for New Haven in the mid-1950s, it is clear that his work and that of his followers were focused on just one dimension of power: that which is fought over and distributed through visible, open conflict. Yet as we will now see, there are also more subtle ways that power operates, and in those other domains it is much harder to argue that power is evenly distributed.

☐ The Two-Dimensional View of Power

One problem with treating power as a one-dimensional process focused only on outcomes is that it ignores the question of why some important issues never come up for discussion or debate in decision-making arenas. We can define a second dimension of power in which a power holder (A) prevents a subordinate group or individual (B) from raising issues that would challenge A's power.

Power in this second dimension consists of the ability of some actors to prevent others from ever getting alternative

President Barack Obama attempts to set the agenda by focusing on topics he believes are most important, such as health care.

ideas proposed or considered in the first place. This process, like one-dimensional power, is present at all levels of social life, from interpersonal relationships to international relations. It is the power to decide what gets decided and consists of **agenda setting**—the act of consciously or unconsciously averting the challenge of potential issues—issues that threaten the interests of the dominant or powerful. The ability to control or set the agenda is a critical resource of power whether we are talking about intimate relationships between couples or families or tracing power all the way up to Congress or the United Nations. When power is exercised through agenda control, the *grievances* of excluded or marginal groups can be denied a hearing. There are a variety of different ways agenda control can be achieved, the most common being the literal manipulation of agendas through the control of procedures, thereby affecting what gets discussed and decided.

This second dimension of power requires us to stretch our understanding of what counts as important issues: they are not *just* those that are the subject of open conflict but *also* those that are prevented from becoming the subject of political challenge. Small children might prefer that more of the family budget be spent on candy than vegetables or that more (or less) time be spent with relatives, but parents typically do not let small children have much say over what kinds of foods the family buys or how many visits with relatives the family takes. The same kind of dynamic arises in politics. Researchers have puzzled over why some topics are the focus of intense discussion and debate while other equally or even more important topics are ignored. For example, why do some issues become social problems while other equally pressing issues do not?

Among the most important examples of this, from a sociological perspective, is the relative lack of attention to issues surrounding the persistence of poverty, racism, and rising inequality versus the enormous amount of attention given to the health and well-being of big business, banks and Wall Street, and corporate profits. For example, every newspaper in America has a section devoted to business, covering the comings and goings of business executives and the profitability (or lack thereof) of various local and national companies, and every day the ups and downs of the stock market are widely covered. But there is no comparable devoted coverage of the daily grind of poverty, or the insecurity faced by millions of American families, or the trials and tribulations of the groups that try to represent the interests of the poor.

These are hardly random examples. The study of agenda setting has paid special attention to the mass media (such as television, newspapers, and in recent years talk radio and influential Internet news sites). When the media gives a large amount of attention to a particular issue, it becomes much more likely that it will receive attention by politicians and policymakers. The fact that coverage of big business is so pronounced is perhaps unsurprising once we observe that most important media outlets are owned by corporate entities or conglomerates themselves. The search for profit in the news media also skews what we read about in other ways. Much of the focus of the media today is driven by editors' perceptions of what sells—that is, what citizens are most interested in reading about. For example, there is an old saying in the media industries, "if it bleeds, it leads": sensational stories about murders and other violent crimes (and usually the more gory the better)

Why is agenda setting in politics important?

have always generated a lot of attention. Celebrities and celebrity gossip also generate intense fascination. The celebrity in trouble with the law, or celebrity couples falling in and out of love or marriage, can be sure to provoke especially intense coverage, with only the names changing from year to year. By contrast, the media usually pays much less attention to challenges to the status quo and seldom provides opportunities for these challenges to reach other, like-minded people.

There is another important source of agenda control that arises in many situations. Subordinate individuals or

News stories about celebrities, like Lindsay Lohan's probation case, always generate intense fascination from the public. Are these types of news reports more important than reports on wars or poverty?

groups may desire some kind of change but believe achieving that change is not possible, so they choose not to even try. Because they don't even attempt to bring about change, the powerful individual or group is not threatened. Inactivity itself may be the reason why challenges to power don't appear. There are many reasons why achieving change (or challenging power holders) may appear daunting: A power holder may possess such superior resources or such adamant opposition to change as to make change seem impossible, or institutions (such as the government or other large organizations) may channel protests in harmless directions or provide other obstacles. Sometimes a power holder avoids challenges because they never get raised in the first place.

The Three-Dimensional View of Power

The first and second dimensions of power, however important they are, do not exhaust the possibilities. Seeing power three-dimensionally involves understanding the various ways in which its workings can be hidden from the view of those subject to it and even from those who possess power. Let us look more closely how this might happen, beginning with how power can sometimes be invisible.

First, consider the assumption that power always involves behavior—that is, some kind of action, whether conscious or unconscious. But we have already noted that one can have power without exercising it. Indeed the very meaning of power suggests this: Power signifies an ability or capacity, the existence of which can, of course, be proven by observing its action. But if power over others consists of the ability to affect others' interests in a negative way, then this does not necessarily result from positive actions by the powerful. It can also result from the *anticipation* by those others of what they believe the powerful would do if they were not to comply with their interests. So, for example, censorship involves active intervention, but it can be rendered unnecessary if journalists, writers, and others engage in self-censorship.

Second, people sometimes defer to, or are even attracted towards those with power. The power of wealth, privilege, and **status**—the prestige accorded to individuals and to important social or economic roles—is often at work without the powerful having to lift a finger to exercise it or even being conscious of its impact or its reach. Status hierarchies and class distinctions are regularly sustained in this way. Many of us behave differently in the presence of the powerful or famous than with other people. When your boss visits the office or when a celebrity walks into a restaurant, we may make extra efforts to try to ensure their happiness. In this way, the powerful do not even need to assert their authority to secure respect or obedience on the part of others.

Another way in which the third dimension becomes visible is when we question the view that whenever conflict is absent, people are content. So if the existence of power can be proven by observing its exercise, such a proof will involve observing that (power holder) A prevails over (weaker party) B where there is an obvious conflict between them, or observing how A suppresses or thwarts B's challenge by keeping the conflict between them hidden. But just because the presence of conflict enables one to prove the existence of power, it does not follow that conflict is necessary to power. This ignores the crucial point that the most effective—and potentially the most sneaky—use of power is to prevent such conflict from arising in the first place by persuading B that whatever A wants is in B's best interests. Power holders attempt to do this by shaping the perceptions and beliefs of the powerless. Where the powerful are in the business of preserving and protecting the status quo, the effects of such power are to encourage people to accept their role in the existing order of things—because

When is power least visible?

they cannot imagine any alternative, because they see it as natural and unchangeable, or because they see it as divinely ordained and beneficial. All of these reasons have been said to play powerful roles in why ordinary people accept the rule of kings or dictators. But to assume that the absence of a grievance is the same thing as genuine consensus rules out the possibility of manipulation in how people think.

The powerful may also be in the business of preventing change by exploiting their power in an attempt to shape perceptions and get people to accept as true all kinds of mythical and simplistic versions of reality. Those in power may do this by playing not only on their followers' fears, prejudices, and limited information but also on the many ways in which people are susceptible to biased and faulty reasoning. In general, the power to frame issues can help to shape people's beliefs. Where power is held or exercised over them, it can be the power to mislead, convincing people to support leaders or favor policies that work directly against their interests. In the most extreme form, such as propaganda issued by a dictator's government, the attempt at persuasion is open and direct. Sometimes efforts at persuasion come with both the threat of a punishment and an offer of a reward. Bosses may try to persuade their workers to be more accepting of unpleasant assignments by offering them a modest pay raise or some other benefit.

The three-dimensional view enables us to see that power over others is not always simply a matter of being able to prevail over them when conflicts of interest occur, or even to set the agenda of what such conflicts are about. It will also consist of being able to secure the dependence, allegiance, or compliance of others. That compliance may occur without the powerful needing to act, and it can exist without conflict when the powerful shape the preferences of others in ways that work against their interests. The third dimension of power, in other words, reveals itself when the powerless embrace the interests of the powerful as their own. Consider the famous slogan uttered by Charles Wilson, then president of General Motors (GM), during congressional testimony in 1953, when he declared "what is good for General Motors is good for America." All Americans benefit, in other words, from policies that make GM more profitable. What Wilson had in mind when he made this statement was that when GM is profitable, it will hire more workers and generate more business for the subcontractors who supply GM with parts used in the manufacture of automobiles. But GM—or any large corporation—does not exist only to provide jobs for Americans; it also tries to maximize its profits and payouts to its shareholders. In order to maximize profits, GM has an interest in trying to keep the wages it pays its workers as low as possible, to have minimal regulations applied to its products, to try to pay as little in corporate taxes as it can, to not have to spend large sums to reduce the pollution it causes, and so forth. None of these things are likely to be in the general interests of all Americans or even of all GM workers not in the top management. The existence of a third dimension of power urges that we pay attention to the ways in many or even most Americans may not think of all of the ways that things can be "good for General Motors" without necessarily being good for them.

Thus far, we have suggested that a sociological understanding of power compels us to examine not only the most visible ways in which power is expressed but also its more subtle forms. Power may be revealed in open conflict, but it may also reflect the ability of a power holder to keep challenges from arising in the first place or even the capacity of a power holder to convince subordinate groups that it is in their interests to support the existing arrangement (see Table 6.1). Is power everywhere? Explore *A Sociological Perspective* on page 149 to see Michael Foucault's view. Next we examine how and where power becomes obvious, in the political institutions of what political sociologists and political scientists call the *state*.

TABLE 6.1 THE THREE DIMENSIONS OF POWER

	First Dimension	**Second Dimension**	**Third Dimension**
Power of A over B	A has superior resources and wins open conflicts.	A constructs or benefits from barriers that prevent B from challenging A's position or even raising a challenge in the first place.	A influences B to support or think the way A does, even when it is not in B's interests to do so.
Powerlessness of B versus A	B has few resources to win open conflicts.	B fails to get its challenge to A to be taken seriously, or B is so frustrated by lack of power that B fails to issue challenge to A.	B comes to believe in A's ideas even when it is not in B's interests to do so.

Source: Based on Gaventa (1980).

A SOCIOLOGICAL PERSPECTIVE

Is power everywhere?

French philosopher and historian Michel Foucault (1926-1984) held radical ideas on power that have been hugely influential across the social sciences. He famously suggested that we live in a "disciplinary society" and argued we are all subjected to a disciplining power that we can't see but that is all around us. Many contemporary examples are consistent with Foucault's theory of power. Surveillance does indeed appear everywhere. Computers now record many of our daily activities, including things we purchase and websites we browse. Businesses purchase databases of information that provide a remarkable level of detail about us to better target ads. There has been a dramatic increase in government surveillance of individual activity since the terrorist attacks of 9/11. Supercomputers housed at the National Security Agency track every e-mail we send, looking for clues of connections to foreign terrorist networks (Brooks and Manza 2012, chapter 1).

Our everyday activities are also monitored more than ever before, with the development of technologies like closed-circuit TV cameras and webcams linked to live feeds. Foucault's theory of power was not limited to surveillance; he was also interested in how our minds and bodies are disciplined and shaped by the powerful forces that are everywhere around us, such as how institutions like schools, prisons, mental institutions, sports teams, and others train (or retrain) individuals to conform in certain ways (including not just their minds but also their bodies). But what is all this surveillance and disciplining ultimately used for? Foucault's focus was never on individuals and groups who dominate and are dominated; he always saw power as operating through individuals rather than against them. His ideas have inspired many interesting studies but more contemporary students of power have replaced Foucault's radical view with one of power as a force standing above us.

What are the different forms of power and who deploys that power in your world?

Who has control of your information and what power does that information afford them?

⊙▸ **Explore** A Sociological Perspective in **MySocLab** and then . . .

■ Think About It

Thinking about the subtle forms of power in our everyday lives opens up many new ways of thinking about the world around us, and our place in it. What are some of the techniques of surveillance that you have encountered in the last 24 hours? What do you think happens to the data that has been collected about you?

■ Inspire Your Sociological Imagination

Some people believe that Americans have given up too many civil liberties in the fight against terrorism since 9/11, and that the government is going way too far in terms of reading emails and monitoring telephone, bank and credit card records. Others feel that these steps are necessary to prevent further acts of terrorism. What do you think? Is it possible to use sociological evidence to help us decide this controversy?

2 How Does the State Distribute Power in a Society?

THE INSTITUTIONS OF POWER

👁 Watch the **Big Question Video** in **MySocLab**

Power in all of its forms can be expressed in any setting in a multitude of ways, but it is most consequential when it is expressed through the major political institutions of any society. The complete array of these institutions is known as the **state**. Governments make laws, spend large sums of money on a huge number of areas, tax individuals and companies, and prepare for (and sometimes go to) war. Large government **bureaucracies**, which define policies and procedures and issue and administer regulations that are to be adhered to by others. Courts and legal institutions interpret and enforce laws and government policies (and sometimes find those policies unconstitutional). Taken as a whole, these decisions are supposed to make our lives better, but they also have a huge impact on the overall distribution of power in any society. For these reasons, the study of power quite naturally turns to an examination of the institutions of the state.

☐ What Is the "State"?

Sociologists use the term *the state* to refer to all of the formal political institutions of any society. In the United States these include the three branches of government (the executive, legislative, and judicial branches) as well as all of the bureaucracies that support the work of each branch. Other government institutions at lower levels of administration—such as local governments or intermediate regional governments (like the "state" government in California or Texas, or regional governments such as provinces in Canada)—can also be considered part of the state, but in this chapter we will focus on national political institutions.

It is important to note that a state is not simply just an elected government, like the Obama administration or even the Obama administration and the Congress together (although elected officials are certainly key parts of the state when they hold office). The state also includes the legal system (and the courts that enforce the law), including the Constitution, as well as those permanent bureaucracies that remain in place regardless of who is the head of the current government. In the United States, for example, a new president only appoints a few thousand new administrators and staff upon taking office, but the entire federal government employs over 3 million people. Most of these employees remain in office no matter who the president is. When the president leaves office and a new Congress and President are elected, those permanent bureaucracies tend to continue doing what they were before the change in elected government. This is one reason why bringing about change in national politics—irrespective of which major party is in office—is so difficult to achieve.

We have already noted that the policies and programs that states make alter the balance of power among individuals, groups, and within society as a whole. Adam Smith (1723–1790), a great theorist of the emerging social order of capitalism, famously described it as an economic system governed by an "invisible hand" of the free market, in which successful entrepreneurs and efficient producers would be rewarded and those with bad ideas or products competed out of business. This imagery, although not at all representative of Smith's more complex views, has proved a remarkably powerful one over the nearly 250 years since Smith's famous work *The Wealth of Nations* was first published in 1776. But that image is misleading in one critical respect, which Smith himself in fact noted. In order for markets to function properly, the state has to provide a wide range of legal guarantees and rules, and have the capacity to enforce those rules when they are violated. For example, market exchanges rely on contracts. A contract exists when one person agrees to provide a certain good at a certain price and the other person agrees to pay that price. As long as both parties do what they promise, the terms of the contract are fulfilled. But what happens when one party fails to do what it promises, if the person who promised to pay a certain price decides at the last minute not to pay up? It is state institutions—sometimes the courts, sometimes government agencies—that normally provide the necessary assurance that if one party fails to live up to its contractual commitments, it will be penalized (this is not true, of course, for illegal organizations like the Mafia, which have their own methods of enforcing rule violations). For most individuals and business organizations, the critical backing provided by the state makes contractual exchange possible.

The role of the state in enforcing contracts has grown over time to include a wide range of other supports to help make a market economy work. One of the most important thing states do is *regulate* the economy in ways that try to provide a level playing field for all participants; through regulation the state tries to prevent economic actors from harming innocent third parties. Some examples of such regulatory policies include:

- Laws and policies that prevent large corporations from taking advantage of their size to cut special deals with suppliers or using their size to drive competitors out of business and create uncompetitive monopolies (for example, in the 1990s when the Microsoft corporation provided low-priced operating software for new computers but then made it difficult for consumers to run non-Microsoft programs).
- Laws preventing stock market traders from using insider knowledge to unfairly profit (for example, if employees at a company knows of a new product that will increase the value of the firm's stock, they are not entitled to use that knowledge to buy up the company's stock in advance of the new product's release and later sell at a profit).

- Laws and regulations that prevent firms from making false advertising claims about their products (for example, not allowing a food manufacturer to call a nonorganic food products organic).
- Laws and regulations that require companies to meet minimal standards in terms of safety for workers and consumers (for example, laws barring a children's clothing manufacturer from making clothes that might catch on fire).
- Laws and regulations that make companies or individuals compensate innocent third parties when their actions cause harm (for example, if a company's factory creates pollution that impacts the health of families living near the factory).

These examples identify some of the many ways that modern states act to try to solve some of the problems and limitations of a market economy. In each of these cases, one can argue that these policies are in the general interests of the broad public—by making sure that there is competition between firms and protecting consumers and innocent third parties. These policies also give individuals who want to start a business a reasonable expectation that if the goods or services they provide are of high enough quality, they will be able to compete against existing businesses on fair terms.

How do states regulate the economy?

Regulators are not always popular with businesses. Here, Elizabeth Warren, former head of the Consumer Financial Protection Bureau, makes opening remarks during a mortgage disclosure forum.

Most of these policies sound straightforward. And they are, to some large extent, in the general interests of all of us (including most legal businesses, which do not want to be undermined by competitors who cheat in one way or another). But the *details* of any of these policies have enormous consequences for the distribution of power. Businesses typically resist attempts to pass regulations that might lower profit margins but that protect citizens. A famous historical example from the 1960s was the way in which GM resisted efforts to require its cars to be safer until a consumer advocate named Ralph Nader was able to show that one GM car, the Corvair, was so unsafe in crashes that it was causing the unnecessary deaths of some of its owners. A more recent example can be seen in the aftermath of the banking and financial crisis in 2008. The collapse, or near collapse, of many American and international banks required a mammoth government bailout and triggered a long period of economic hardship and insecurity for years to come. Following the crisis, many government leaders called for limits on financial speculation to reduce the likelihood of another financial calamity. These restrictions would make it harder for banks and investment firms to make extremely high profits but would make it less likely that they would declare bankruptcy (and thereby threaten other banks and the economy as a whole). But the financial sector as a whole has resisted many of these proposed changes, in many cases successfully. Many observers of the banking industry note that the big banks are bigger than ever, and the risk of another financial collapse remains nearly as great as before the crisis (Johnson and Kwak 2010; Krippner 2011; Madrick 2011).

Why States Matter in the Distribution of Power

The policies and programs adopted and maintained by the state are hugely important in many different ways. Policies can, for example, be designed to ensure that poor families receive a greater share of the economic pie than they would if the market was left completely untouched, or, by contrast, policies can be designed to ensure that the rich are allowed to maintain or even increase their share of wealth. These policies, known as tax and transfer policies, are especially important for the distribution of income and wealth. All governments must tax their citizens to pay for government services, but whether the rich will pay a higher share than the poor varies widely across countries. All governments provide some benefits for some categories of people who might otherwise be destitute, but again, countries vary widely in how much of these benefits they provide.

Taken as a whole, *who gets what* is at least partly a function of government policy. There are many specific examples of how states impact who gets what in any society. Here are a few:

- States set or alter the rules of the game within which individuals and groups contest each other for power—policies can favor big business, small business, farmers, or workers and unions, but not all at the same time.
- States allocate a huge amount of resources through various kinds of spending programs, collectively known as the **welfare state**. These programs include old-age pensions (primarily known as Social Security in the United States), health insurance for many people who would not be able to acquire it on their own, unemployment insurance, welfare for poor families, and many other such programs.
- States decide who bears the burdens of public spending programs, primarily through tax policies.
- States have the power to decide such life-and-death matters as whether a country goes to war or whether the death penalty is legal. Other life-defining public policies include whether or not food and health care shall be provided to those who cannot afford to pay for it themselves.

In each of these policy areas, states make choices that impact the distribution of power across the entire society. In many important ways, states provide the institutional backdrop for market economies to function and directly or indirectly ensure that investments can be made profitably. Sometimes states will directly intervene on behalf of the powerful, especially in periods of political conflict and stress. But states are not simply tools of the ruling classes of a society. States also make some policy decisions, as we will see, that can empower the poor and help the disadvantaged obtain a greater share of the benefits of economic growth.

The legislatures, courts, and bureaucracies that make up the state are places where all three forms of power can be found, although they are most visible in terms of direct, overt conflict over state policy (the first dimension of power) or in terms of what issues are made the subject of public discussion and debate (the second dimension of power). The role of the state in persuading less powerful individuals and groups that their interests are served by policies that protect and promote the interests of the powerful (the third dimension) is a subtle but important aspect of the overall operation of the state: to convince people that the existing world in which they live is just and fair.

How do states impact who gets what in a society?

Promoting the Interests of the Powerful

In this section, we will examine some general reasons why states more often than not adopt policies in the interests of the powerful. This pattern is found throughout the world.

The civil rights movement pushing for the integration of schools in the 1960s helped change the context of political power.

Why is this so? Or more specifically, how and why do states tend to adjust their policies to support the goals of powerful business interests?

Social scientists who have studied this question have proposed two broad sets of answers. The first view is what we might call the *business confidence* theory of the state (Block 1987). It holds that whatever the preferences of government officials (for example, whether a liberal Democrat or a conservative Republican is president), the state as a whole has a powerful incentive to make sure that big business interests have the confidence and security they need to want to make investments that will create jobs and produce economic growth. When entrepreneurs and business executives think that business conditions are not favorable, their incentives to make those investments decline. Because the overall health of the economy is so important, states are driven to adopt policies that will convince business leaders that the economy will remain healthy in the near future. In the era of economic globalization, maintaining a healthy business environment at home is important for discouraging companies from moving abroad, or alternatively, for encouraging foreign companies to invest in your country. A newly elected government has to take these issues into consideration.

The second argument for why states tend to promote the interests of the powerful focuses on the relative political power of different groups (Domhoff 2006; Hacker and Pierson 2010). Large corporations and rich individuals simply have more resources to influence political life than do other groups representing working-class and middle-class people. For example, corporations will try to influence elections and election outcomes by donating large amounts of money to candidates they favor. Corporate executives and rich individuals are also far more likely to have access to politicians than are poor people. They tend to travel in some of the same circles and clubs and their donations will open doors when something of importance is being debated and discussed. The upshot of this disproportionate influence is that policies will often tend to favor the interests and

Why do states tend to promote the interests of the powerful?

preferences of the powerful and well organized. As we will see in the next section, there is plenty of evidence in support of this argument.

Taken together, these two theories tend to suggest that policy will always favor the powerful. But exceptions do occur; sometimes the powerless get what they want instead (Piven and Cloward 1997). In the 1930s, a wide range of new government programs were adopted that included the Social Security system (eventually creating pensions for all Americans over 65), unemployment insurance, mammoth job creation programs, increased regulation of business, and increased taxes on the rich. These New Deal programs adopted under Franklin D. Roosevelt were bitterly resisted by most wealthy Americans and many business interests. Similarly, in the 1960s, the federal government created both Medicare (health insurance for everyone over 65) and Medicaid (health insurance for the poor), adopted civil rights legislation that gave women and minorities new rights and opportunities to compete on a more equal footing with white men, and significant increases in welfare spending programs. These examples suggest that it is hardly the case that the powerful always win. In particular, when the poor are well organized into social movements, they can sometimes exert influence over the direction of policy. If there is one thing that both the 1930s and 1960s had in common, it is that in both eras large social movements of poor people (mostly unions and the unemployed in the 1930s, and the civil rights movement in the 1960s) changed the context of political power. But large social movements of the poor are relatively rare. How is power distributed in more normal circumstances? We turn to an examination of that question in the next section of the chapter.

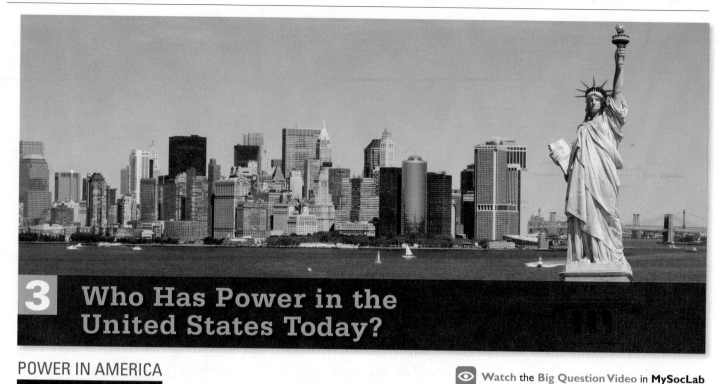

3 Who Has Power in the United States Today?

POWER IN AMERICA

👁 Watch the Big Question Video in MySocLab

A sociological analysis of power provides a different way of understanding American politics than what reading the newspaper or watching television news reports normally provides. Ordinarily, we think or hear only about the first dimension of power: who wins elections (or who is ahead in the polls leading up to an election); the outcomes of debates over the passage of particularly important laws or government programs by Congress and the president; or conflicts over American foreign and military policy. Most of what we read about national politics—in Congress, the presidency, and the Supreme Court—involves such openly contested conflicts over public policy decisions. These are important aspects of any **democracy**, a political system in which all citizens have equal rights to participate in political life. But when we inspect more closely, we also find the other dimensions of power shaping political outcomes.

Who Wins? Policy and Politics in the First Dimension

The first dimension of power in American politics concerns the question of who wins (or more specifically, who can achieve their goals) when there is open conflict. In many cases, at least in recent years, these conflicts have sometimes put most or all Republicans on one side and most Democrats on the other side of the conflict. Other issues are more complicated and do not always cleanly break along party lines. When the issues under discussion become especially heated—for example, in the fall of 2008 when President George W. Bush and the Congress decided to bail out the country's leading banks in the hopes of preventing a financial calamity—the debates that follow can hold everyone's attention. Most of the time, however, the issues being discussed and debated in Washington, DC, are obscure to most Americans. On most issues, only professional policy analysts and congressional insiders fully understand all of the details of policy proposals and fully understand what it is at stake. Many important decisions are made largely outside of the public's view.

When it comes to the national politics of the first dimension, our sociological perspective on power and politics urges that we take a step back from a narrow focus on these day-to-day conflicts to ask: what are the broad patterns buried in these outcomes? We do not have enough space in this chapter to consider most political outcomes, but we can focus on one set of policies that are among the most important: policies that impact the distribution of wealth and inequality. More specifically, we consider (1) *tax policies*, especially some of the political changes in the ways taxes are paid that have enabled the superwealthy to take home a much greater share of the economic pie than they do in all other rich, democratic countries most like the United States; and (2) *antipoverty programs*, or more specifically why it is that the policies of the American government do the least, of any of the rich countries most similar to us, to reduce poverty and help families live in a minimally acceptable way.

In 2009, protesters marched in a demonstration outside the offices of American International Group (AIG). AIG received over $180 billion in federal bailout money and used $165 million of that to pay out employee bonuses that year, outraging the public.

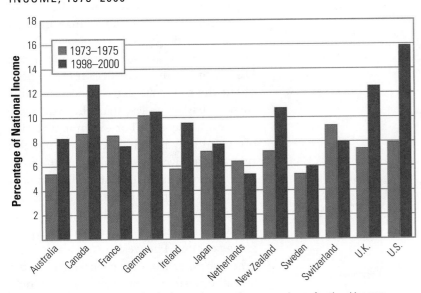

Taxation and Economic Inequality The United States has an extraordinarily high concentration of income and wealth at the very top, with the top 1 percent of households receiving nearly 24 percent of all income in 2007 (declining slightly to 21 percent in 2008); the top 10 percent received about half of all income, while the remaining 90 percent of all families received only about 50 percent of all income. One factor that is unique about the fact that the rich are *so* rich today is that it is not true elsewhere. Figure 6.1 shows that compared with some of the countries that are most like the United States, the share of total income received by the top 1 percent is far lower, and in some of these countries it has not grown significantly in recent years at all. In other countries, especially in the Anglo-American world (i.e., Britain, Australia, Canada, and the United States), the rich have gotten richer, but only in the United States do they command such a large share of all income.

One of the implications of Figure 6.1 is that democratic countries can be prosperous *and* organize their economies so that the rich do not gobble so much of

FIGURE 6.1 TOP 1 PERCENT OF FAMILIES SHARE OF NATIONAL INCOME, 1973–2000

Percentage of National Income

Legend:
- 1973–1975
- 1998–2000

Countries (x-axis): Australia, Canada, France, Germany, Ireland, Japan, Netherlands, New Zealand, Sweden, Switzerland, U.K., U.S.

Notes: The first bar for each nation is the top 1 percent's average share of national income (excluding capital gains) in 1973–1975 (except for Ireland, for which data are unavailable until 1976; the first bar for Ireland averages the years 1976–1979). The second bar for each nation is the top 1 percent's average share in 1998–2000 [except, for reasons of data availability, France and Germany (1996-1998), the Netherlands (1997–1999), and Switzerland (1994–1996)].

Source: Leigh (2007). (The figure uses Leigh's data on the top 1 percent excluding capital gains, adjusted for consistency across nations.)

the benefits of economic growth. And in fact, if we look at the historical data we will find that this was once the case in the United States. Figure 6.2 shows that for the period from the 1930s through the 1970s, the rich were much less rich than today, leaving more for everyone else. For example, between 1968 and 1978, the top 1 percent of earners only received about 8 percent of income, whereas in 2007 they received a whopping 24 percent.

Why is it better to be really rich in America now than, say, 40 years ago? Or why is it better to be a rich person in the United States as opposed to, say, France? The short answer is because of important policy changes that have altered the way incomes and wealth are distributed and consumed. The political organizations of the upper class have successfully convinced Congress and various presidents to make it easier for them to retain most of their income and wealth and to pass on nearly all of it to their children or favorite charity (Winters 2011). The most obvious way is through the tax system, that is, how much taxes citizens in different income brackets are required to pay. The tax rate on earnings above a certain amount of income becomes a crucial factor in whether or not the rich will have more than everyone else or a *lot* more than everyone else. The United States, as in all rich countries, has long had a **progressive income tax system** in which the rich are expected to pay a greater share of their income than are the middle class. The logic is that those who have higher incomes can better afford to contribute a somewhat higher share of their income to pay for government programs that benefit everyone. This logic is common to all democratic societies, and public opinion polls show that Americans support requiring the rich to pay higher tax rates than everyone else.

But in spite of this commitment to a progressive system of taxation, tax burdens on high earners have declined dramatically in the past 30 years. Figure 6.3 tells the remarkable story of the history of tax rates on high incomes in the United States. At the end of World War II (when especially high taxes were adopted to help pay for the war effort), the highest earners were paying over 90 percent of their earnings above the top threshold (in 1944, that was $200,000). In the early 1960s, the top rate was reduced to around 70 percent of earnings above the highest bracket (in 1964, that amount was $400,000), lower but still about twice as

FIGURE 6.2 INCOME SHARE OF TOP 1 PERCENT, TOP 5 PERCENT, AND TOP 10 PERCENT OF AMERICAN FAMILIES, 1913–2008

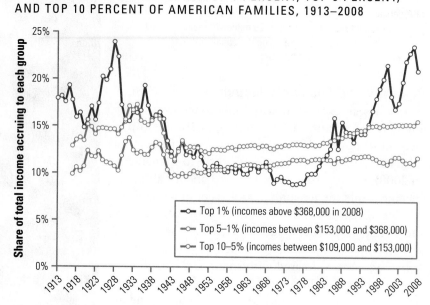

Source: Saez (2012).

What do tax policies tell us about how power is distributed in the U.S.?

high as it has been since the mid-1980s. In the early 1980s, in two dramatic waves of tax cuts on high earnings during the presidency of Ronald Reagan, the rich saw their tax rates fall below 30 percent, bumped up a bit in the early 1990s under presidents George H. W. Bush and Bill Clinton, settling at 35 percent today. The tax rate on high earners is also significantly lower than in other rich democratic countries.

Other changes to the tax code in the United States in recent decades have benefited the super-rich and typically enable them to pay much less than the official tax rate would suggest. For example, the rich often not only have high earnings but also typically receive considerable income from their investments. Much of this investment income is treated differently than other kinds of income and may be taxed at a rate as low as 15 percent (the so-called capital gains tax rate). The wealthy can also shelter other earnings from taxation, reducing the overall tax rate paid by rich families. Commonly known as *loopholes*, these tax breaks are useless for the vast majority of American families but extremely valuable for the very rich. For example, the very wealthiest Americans often make liberal use of off-shore tax

FIGURE 6.3 TAX RATE ON HIGHEST-EARNING AMERICANS

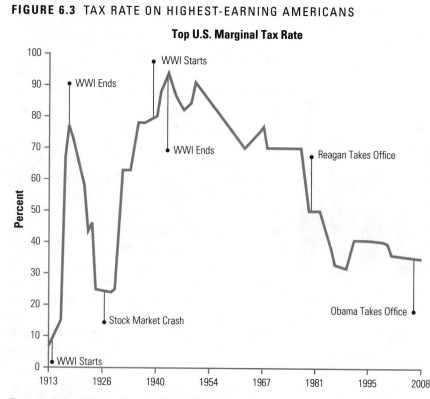

Figure based on 2011 data from the Citizens for Tax Justice.

Billionaire Warren Buffet believes the richest people in the country should be taxed at a higher rate than others, but many disagree with this. What do you think?

shows that the actual average taxes paid by corporations are far lower than the official tax rate would suggest. Not only has the overall rate of corporate taxes fallen, many industries have enjoyed special tax deals that allow them to pay even lower rates. For example, the oil industry has regularly received special tax breaks and loopholes, ostensibly to encourage these companies to drill for more oil, even as oil prices have soared and oil company profits reach record highs.

Even the lower rates of corporate taxes paid today (as shown in Figure 6.4) do not tell the whole story. In fact, yet more loopholes enable some corporations to reduce their taxable income down to nothing. The all-time champion of avoiding corporate taxes appears to be General Electric (GE), known for its household appliances like refrigerators and light bulbs and more recently for green-power products as well its finance arm, GE Capital. In the 1980s, GE had so successfully avoided paying taxes that then-president Ronald Reagan (who was earlier in his life a paid spokesperson for GE) ordered his staff to try to close some of the

shelters, by creating investment schemes in little countries like the Cayman Islands that have no income tax, as a way of avoiding or radically reducing taxes they would otherwise pay to the American government. Wealthy individuals and families can afford to employ lawyers and tax accountants skilled in the manipulation of these rules to seek every possible vehicle to reduce their tax rate, something that ordinary Americans would not be able to do (Winters 2011).

Recently, the billionaire investor Warren Buffet has highlighted just how tax loopholes and reduced rates on certain kinds of income can benefit the wealthiest Americans (Buffet 2011). He noted that he paid federal income taxes at a lower rate—about 18 percent on his 2010 income—than did his secretary and other lower-level employees at his firm, Berkshire Hathaway. The very wealthy 2012 Republican Presidential nominee Mitt Romney similarly revealed, when he released his tax returns, that he was paying less than 15 percent of his income in federal taxes.

Just as wealthy individuals and families have benefited from many changes in the tax laws over the past, so too have corporations. Private companies now pay much less in taxes than they used to. Figure 6.4 shows the dramatic changes in corporate tax revenue as a percentage of the entire economy since the 1960s. The figure's top panel shows the decline in corporate income tax as a percentage of total federal tax revenue, while the bottom panel

FIGURE 6.4 TWO VIEWS OF CORPORATE TAX RATES SINCE WORLD WAR II

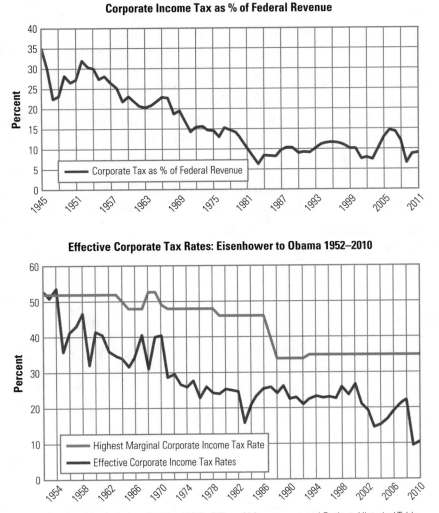

Source: The President's Budget for Fiscal 2012; Office of Management and Budget, Historical Table 2.1; and Bureau of Economic Analysis, National Income and Products Accounts Table 1.12.

loopholes GE was using to avoid taxes. But the company is a powerhouse in Washington, DC, and it has persisted. More recently, the *New York Times* reported that in 2010 GE managed to pay *no* corporate income taxes at all, despite making $14 billion in profits across the world. In fact, the *New York Times* reported, GE was so successful in eliminating its taxes that the federal government actually owed GE $3.2 billion! (This money is provided in the form of tax credits that can be used to pay off future tax obligations, not that it appears likely that GE is going to incur any.) GE's tax lawyers and accountants, many of whom formerly worked for congressional tax committees or the Internal Revenue Service, aggressively use a variety of tax shelters to write down profits, and the company further lobbies Congress each year for special tax breaks often buried in legislation and unnoticed by the media or the public. GE's successful avoidance of all taxes may be extreme, but any corporation can reduce its tax bill by using similar strategies as well (Kocieniewski 2011).

Reduced tax burdens allow corporations to retain more of their earnings, and in recent years they have lavished pay and other perks (including generous stock options) on their top managers. We know most about the compensation of the chief executive officers (CEOs) of companies, as firms are required to report the annual incomes of their CEOs. This requirement produces very clear information about the trends over time. As shown in Figure 6.5, whereas the average Fortune 500 CEO made about 35 times the average full-time salary at the same firm in the 1970s, today it is around 243 times more! Another way to look at it is to look at the differences in pay between the CEOs of America's largest companies. From the 1930s through the 1970s, CEO compensation averaged (in 2010 dollars, adjusted for inflation) about $1 million per year. That was a lot of money, but compensation began to shoot up in the 1980s and by 2005 had reached $9.2 million (a 900 percent increase) and was

only slightly lower at $8.5 million after the recession of 2007 and 2008 (Mischel et al. 2009).

Looking at the big picture, we would argue that in the fight over how the benefits of economic growth are distributed, dramatic changes in individual and corporate tax rates indicate that in recent decades rich individuals and families, as well as large corporations and their top executives, are winning. The struggle over who should pay what taxes will continue, and it is possible that in the future tax rates on the highest earners will once again increase.

Antipoverty Policy: Why Are So Many Americans Poor?

Another distinctive feature of **public policy** (policies adopted or implemented by the government) in the United States that bear on the patterns of inequality has been the inability of America to reduce the levels of poverty to the same degree as other rich countries around the world. Every government in the modern age has established programs to try to make sure that poor families have access to some basic necessities of life, like food and shelter. Taken as a whole, these programs and policies are known as the welfare state, and they are designed to help address a number of important **social problems**, a term used to describe a wide range of issues that are thought to have harmful consequences (such as poverty, crime, drug abuse, homelessness, inequality, racism, sexism, and discrimination). For example, capitalist economies have never produced enough decent-paying jobs for everyone who needs one, inevitably leaving some families in poverty. Antipoverty programs operate as a kind of insurance program for misfortune. Adults (and their children) may fall into poverty for any number of different reasons: because they are unable to work because of a physical or mental disability, because of an extended illness or accident, because the economy is in recession and unemployment is high, or because of just plain bad luck.

Because we can't know in advance who among us will end up homeless and destitute, we all contribute a little to provide protection for those who do end up in that state. Antipoverty programs also attempt to give poor children the same opportunity as middle-class children to succeed in life (or at least seek to improve their chances). The logic is that poor children who are poor through no fault of their own should not be held back as a consequence.

Although every country has welfare-state programs designed to reduce poverty, some do a lot better than others. We now know that in rich countries it *is* possible to dramatically reduce the number of children and families living in poverty, if government programs make a commitment to doing so. How do we know this? A number of scholars have studied the problem, using very carefully developed data about household income and living standards

FIGURE 6.5 RATIO OF AVERAGE ANNUAL CEO COMPENSATION TO AVERAGE WORKER COMPENSATION, 1965–2010

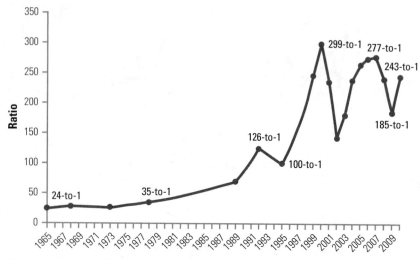

Source: Adapted from Mishel and Bivens (2011).

FIGURE 6.6 PERCENTAGE OF POOR CHILDREN PRE AND POST-GOVERNMENT ACTIONS

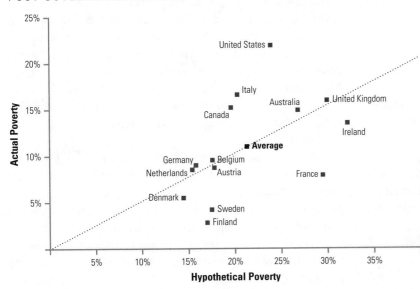

Figure based on data from Smeeding et al. (2009).

United States to reduce poverty; notice that in the United States, both percentages are only modestly different from one another, whereas in other countries a significant difference exists. Consider for example the United Kingdom. If people only lived on what they earn, there would be a significantly higher rate of poverty as they would have no government programs to try to lift families with children out of poverty. Instead, the United Kingdom dramatically reduces its poverty (by over 50 percent) through its antipoverty programs.

The ineffectiveness of the American welfare state in reducing poverty has many consequences. Of special note is the impact on children. When children grow up in poverty in any country, the likelihood is that many will have problems as adults. Of course some children will grow up in poverty and achieve great success as adults, but the odds are stacked against them. When one-fifth or more of children are growing up in poverty (and over one-third of minority children), the importance of the issue for all of American society is magnified. These poor children will grow up to become the adults of the future.

But what does this mean as an indicator of who has power in the United States? The limited welfare state highlights some of the unique features of the American political system that systematically disadvantage the poor and the middle class politically. Social welfare programs tend to be most generous in countries that are characterized by strong unions, in countries with a socialist or social democratic party that has regularly won elections, and in countries with a political system dominated by a strong central government (as opposed to a more decentralized type of government where power is divided between the national government and regional and local governments). The American welfare state benefits from none of these conditions. The stranglehold of a two-party system, consisting of the Republican and Democratic parties, has meant that there is no "left" political party that consistently promotes policies that would reduce poverty and inequality.

to be able to compare across countries. One commonly used measure is to count as poor all families who have less than half the income of the median family of the same size (that is, the same-sized family at the 50th percentile of all families). This way of measuring poverty has the advantage of taking into account *relative* standards of living in different countries. A poor person in a rich country like the United States will have a higher income than a poor person in Chad, one of the poorest countries in the world, but basic living standards are higher in the U.S. as well.

Using such a definition of family poverty and comparing the United States to other rich countries, we can now look at the data. And here we see that, in fact, the United States does very badly in comparison to the rich democracies most like us (Smeeding et al. 2009). Figure 6.6 displays the raw facts: Rates of poverty in the United States are higher than in any of the comparison group of similar nations, although interestingly this is most clear *after* government programs are taken into account. Using comparable data about family income across countries, the researchers are able to estimate what the (hypothetical) poverty rate in each country would be if there was no government policy to try to correct it (the x-axis); the y-axis estimates the *actual* poverty rate once government intervention is taken into account (such as programs that provide welfare benefits to poor families). The chart is based on truly comparable data from each country and all sources of income, an important point that makes it a unique way of understanding where the United States stands. Two results are of special importance. First, a number of countries have high hypothetical poverty rates based just on market incomes before government action is taken into account. In some cases, this is as large as in the United States. Second, no country does as little as the

So who wins on the first dimension of power? In other words, who is able to exert their will in order to prevail in national politics? We cannot possibly examine all of the policy outcomes that take place. In any given year, there are literally hundreds of important issues that come up for discussion and debate and are decided in Congress, by the President and his administration, or by the Supreme Court. But our more limited survey of important areas of policy concerning inequality and the welfare state suggest that certain patterns tend to recur over and over again, throughout the ups and downs of American history. Compared to the nations most similar to the United States in terms of wealth, economic development, and longstanding democratic government, we have to conclude that powerful actors appear to prevail more often, and receive far more rewards when they do, than in other countries. In short, it is better to be rich in the United States than in any other similar country, and it it is worse to be poor than in any similar country.

But all of this does not mean that there are *never* opportunities for the less powerful to win in the first dimension of power. There are political issues where the outcomes are more mixed or where entrenched power holders have indeed lost ground. In particular, in recent decades, issues involving social and cultural equality—such as rights for minorities, women, and gays and lesbians—have often produced outcomes that have given members of historically disadvantaged groups important opportunities and protections. America was once a country that denied equal rights and opportunities to members of various different groups. And this was the reality not that long ago: It was not until 1965, for example, that African Americans had full legal rights to vote in all Southern states, and only in 1972 was full educational equality between the genders guaranteed. Today America is as supportive of equal rights and equal opportunity for minority groups as most other countries.

Who Sets the Agenda? Politics in the Second Dimension

We have now seen some important examples of how the American political system produces outcomes that reward the powerful. Why aren't other approaches, ideas, and policies taken more seriously? Why is the range of acceptable political debate in the United States so relatively narrow compared with other similar countries? The second dimension of power calls our attention to ways in which powerful actors sometimes maintain their power (or the status quo) by preventing issues from coming up in the first place. To understand how agenda setting occurs and is more limited in America than in other places, we now examine some of the reasons why certain kinds of issues never get discussed in the first place. As we will see, several features of America's political institutions and economic system combine to help keep that from happening. In particular, we want to highlight two key points: (1) the two-party political system, and (2) the highly unusual amount of money donated to candidates for political office in American politics.

A Two-Party Political System America is very unusual in having just two major parties who contend for office— the Democratic and Republican parties. Most democratic countries around the world have at least three, and sometimes four or more, parties who win seats in the national legislature. In these countries, a much wider range of options and opinions are presented to voters at every election, and a wider range of opinions and parties are represented in national legislatures. For example, in most countries there is a party that is more liberal, or to use the European term, "social democratic," than the Democratic Party in the United States. Most countries also have a political party that occupies the political center, standing between the left-wing and right-wing parties. Many countries also have a Green party that wins seats in the legislature.

Why are there only two parties in America? The electoral system established by the Constitution—a "first-past-the-post" electoral system, in which the candidate (and party) winning the most votes in a single district wins the seat—makes it virtually impossible for third parties to gain traction. By contrast, systems of **proportional representation (PR)** found in most other countries allow minority parties to gain representation based on the share of the vote they win. In PR systems, voters select a party, not a candidate. The proportion of votes received by each party translates into seats in the national parliament. In many cases, a party receiving as little as 5 percent of the vote will receive seats in the legislature and gain a foothold in the political system. In the United States, by contrast, only the candidate winning the most votes in a congressional district or state wins a seat in the House or Senate, respectively. As a result, a new political party seeking to build support cannot do so gradually (as under PR systems) by electing a few representatives and building a reputation with voters. Regional third-party efforts—most notably the Populists of the late nineteenth century in parts of

Why are there only two political parties in America, and why does it matter?

the American South, and the Midwestern Progressives in the twentieth century—have occasionally been viable for a period of time, winning some seats in Congress. But these efforts are relatively easily turned aside by the major parties and their voters co-opted into one or the other of the major parties. The two-party system had become firmly established by 1840, and there has been only one successful example of a third party entering the political system and displacing one of the dominant parties since then—the Republican Party breakthrough in the intense conflicts of the pre–Civil War era in the 1850s and 1860 (when Abraham Lincoln won the presidency on a Republican ticket). In all other cases, third parties have failed.

The range of viable political parties in other democratic countries has important consequences for how agendas are set and what kinds of political issues are discussed in the media and in their national legislatures. Imagine how different Congress might be today if a libertarian, a socialist, a conservative, and a green party all won seats in the national legislature alongside the Democratic and Republican Parties. In such a case—which would be similar to what happens in many European countries—there are simply more political positions under discussion. It is also likely that no one party would have a majority of seats, and winners would have to form a coalition of parties in order to govern (thus encouraging a wider range of discussion and compromise than a two-party system requires). A multiparty system also changes the nature of electoral campaigns, where citizens have a wider menu of options to consider (and a wider range of opinions being expressed). The daily coverage of political life in the media (such as on political talk shows on television) is also very different. When there are only two significant political parties, by contrast, the effort to be balanced is much easier: You only need to hear from two different parties, two different points of view. A more complex political environment prevents the kind of "he said/she said" of today's political discourse in America.

Money and American Politics   American politics are also exceptional in the amount of money that is available, or must be raised, by candidates for political office. Not surprisingly, most of the money given to support candidates running for office comes from wealthy individuals and large corporations and business groups. In recent decades, incentives for political candidates to seek funding have increased dramatically. Political strategists and campaign managers have reached a consensus that high-spending media campaigns are the most efficient way to reach voters and that serious candidates for office need to raise funds. Table 6.2 shows that since 1978

TABLE 6.2 TRENDS IN NATIONAL ELECTION CAMPAIGN FINANCE, 1978–2006 (IN MILLIONS OF DOLLARS, INFLATION ADJUSTED)

Election Year	Total Business Contributions	Total Labor Contributions	Total Ideological Contributions	Total Individual Contributions
1978	66.5	31.8	8.3	NA
1980	93.4	35.3	13.1	NA
1982	106.7	43.2	22.9	NA
1984	122.4	48.4	28.3	NA
1986	111.4	54.2	34.0	NA
1988	152.3	58.0	32.9	NA
1990	139.4	52.7	22.4	NA
1992	263.1	62.4	26.7	459.8
1994	262.7	63.6	30.4	353.6
1996	407.7	71.8	33.5	536.5
1998	357.3	65.5	37.8	407.2
2000	669.7	104.7	54.0	817.6
2002	615.5	96.1	68.6	719.3
2004	769.4	101.6	77.1	1,014.2
2006	631.7	88.9	67.1	703.0
Δ 1978–2006 (Midterm Elections)	950%	280%	810%	
Δ 1980–2004 (Presidential)	823%	288%	589%	
Δ 1992–2004 (Individual)				154%

Note: All estimates shown in 2006 dollars. "Total" includes hard and soft (unregulated) contributions from 1992 through 2002 to all candidates for national office (U.S. House, Senate, and presidency). After 2002, totals include hard and estimated 527 (ideological advocacy) contributions. Note that 1992, 1994, 2000, and 2004 are presidential years and thus reflect higher overall contributions than in midterm congressional elections without a presidential ballot.

Source: 1978–1984: Corrado (1987); 1986–2000: Federal Election Commission reports (http://www.fec.gov) and Center for Responsive Politics (http://www.opensecrets.org).

Money and Politics

The role of money in American elections highlights how social inequalities shape the political process. Contributions made by individuals during federal elections are an increasingly important way for Americans to get involved in supporting their candidates of choice. But these contributions also reflect deep socioeconomic fault lines.

The **majority of campaign contributions** from individuals originate from a handful of large and disproportionately wealthy metropolitan areas.

The **50 metro areas with the most individual contributions** of more than $200

Seattle
Portland
Minneapolis-St. Paul
New York
$224 million
Boston
Chicago
$113 million
Detroit
Cleveland
Pittsburgh
New York
Sacramento
Columbus
Philadelphia
San Francisco
Indianapolis
Cincinnati
Baltimore
Denver
Kansas City
Louisville
Washington
$217 million
Los Angeles
$124 million
Las Vegas
St. Louis
Nashville
Raleigh-Durham
San Diego
Phoenix
Albuquerque
Atlanta
Fort Worth · Dallas
Austin
San Antonio
Houston
New Orleans
Orlando
Tampa
West Palm Beach
Miami

Total contributions, in millions

$10 $20 $100 $200

A fraction of Americans contributed money in the 2008 election, and an even tinier portion contributed over $200.

In **2008**, the percentage of adults who ...

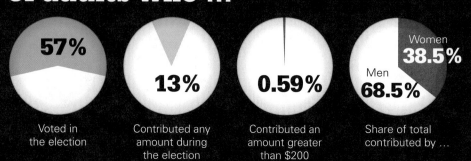

57%
Voted in the election

13%
Contributed any amount during the election

0.59%
Contributed an amount greater than $200

Women **38.5%**
Men **68.5%**
Share of total contributed by ...

⊙→ Explore the Data on Money and Politics in **MySocLab** and then ...

■ **Think About It**

In what ways is the fact that campaign contributions from individuals come from a few wealthy metropolitan areas an example of power in the second dimension?

■ **Inspire Your Sociological Imagination**

What is a possible explanation for the fact that male donors out-contribute female donors by more than 2 to 1?

Sources: Based on data from the Center for Responsive Politics; U.S. Election Project; American National

there has been a nearly tenfold increase in real dollars contributed by business interests to candidates for American national elections, as well as steady and seemingly relentless growth in contributions from affluent individuals. By comparison, contributions from labor unions have stayed relatively constant and now total merely a fraction of what corporations are spending.

Changes on the supply side have also influenced these trends: The vast increase in wealth at the top has expanded the resources for the rich to invest in the political system. And rising household affluence creates a similar dynamic. Giving among the wealthy for all purposes—civic, charitable, and religious as well as political—has increased in this era of rising inequality. While much of this giving may have benign political consequences, no such simple conclusions would be appropriate when it comes to political money. Explore the Infographic *Money and Politics* on page 162 for more information on this topic.

Where does this extraordinary flow of political money come from? Contributions come from either individual donors or **political action committees (PACs)** organized by a wide range of individual businesses and business associations, unions, professional associations, and ideological groups such as the National Rifle Association or Emily's List (a group that works to elect prochoice Democratic women). PAC contributions can be reasonably divided into three broad categories: business-related, labor, and ideological PACs (with the latter running the gamut from far left to far right). In addition to money given by PACs, individuals account for a large proportion of total donations. And the vast majority of the largest of these contributions continue to be made by wealthy individuals or families. If we combine the rising amounts being given by wealthy individuals with the growing disparities between business and labor PACs, it is clear that, from the standpoint of who gives, the signals imparted to elected officials overwhelmingly favor the wealthy.

Of perhaps equal concern in recent years is the impact of political money in funding agenda-setting organizations. The remarkable growth in the resources flowing into think tanks and foundations has been an especially significant factor, especially those funded by business organizations and

Read the Document *Is Congress Really for Sale?* in **MySocLab**

conservative foundations. Beginning in the 1970s, these organizations began providing resources on an unprecedented scale in support of what are known as policy-formation organizations, like the American Enterprise Institute, the Brookings Institute, the Heritage Foundation, the Cato Institute, and others. The growing capacities of these policy organizations to intervene in political debates, get their representatives on the media, and provide policy advice to presidents and Congress is by now well established. These organizations play a significant role in setting the policy agenda. To the extent that the policy organizations with the greatest resources are disproportionately promoting a conservative policy agenda—as numerous studies have found—they contribute to a larger environment in which many egalitarian policy ideas are simply not on the agenda for discussion (Hacker and Pierson 2010).

One would be hard pressed to imagine that contributors give large amounts and get nothing in return, although the consequences of large and increasing amounts of money are far more subtle then is commonly understood. Politicians rarely "sell" their votes, and having more money than your political opponent does not automatically guarantee victory. What three decades of research on political money has established, however, is that to be a serious candidate for elected office, especially Congress, one has to be able to raise money from either corporations or rich individuals, or both. This weeds out possible candidates who do not appeal to donors, and not surprisingly, this tends to limit who can run for office. And finally, while large donors are not guaranteed any particular outcome, they do get access to elected officials that ordinary citizens do not typically have. Access can translate into small, but often significant, benefits like tax breaks hidden in legislation and rarely subjected to public scrutiny (Clawson et al. 1998; Manza et al. 2004).

Republican Presidential candidate Mitt Romney expects to spend over $500 million for his 2012 campaign for President, and Democratic incumbent Barack Obama will spend a similar amount. How is it possible for candidates to raise so much money?

The Third Dimension: Do Americans Believe in Policies Benefiting the Powerful?

Recall former GM President Charles Wilson's maxim, quoted earlier in the chapter, that "what is good for General Motors is good for America." Allowing GM or any large corporation to fully maximize its profits may require a range of public policies that would clearly *not* be good for the rest of America on some important dimension(s) of well-being. Policies that allow the very rich to earn and keep most of their exceptionally high and growing incomes while poor and working- and middle-class families see few of the benefits of economic growth of the past 30 years hardly constitutes policies that are in the interests of everyone. Some would add that the failure to tax the rich and large corporations more extensively means doing less to lift children and families above the poverty line, having schools and universities that are not as good as they might be, having fewer police officers and fire fighters, and not repairing or maintaining streets and bridges and public parks as much as we might. The very richest Americans need not worry about these things—they can send their children to top private schools, and can afford to live in gated communities that provide a high level of security far from the sources of pollution, and crime. But what about everyone else? Why do they not always insist that they have access to the same quality schools and health care as the rich?

These are the tensions raised by the third dimension of power. The question is properly posed as whether, and to what extent, Americans may have come to actively embrace policies that allow public policy to favor the richest Americans? As we have noted, this is the most challenging part of studying power, and one that necessarily becomes controversial in that we encounter the problem of knowing what, exactly, is in any one individual's or group's best interests. That is, how do we really know that "what is good for General Motors" is not, in fact, good for most Americans? Once again, the challenge of studying power on the third dimension may involve knowing things that are impossible to know (like what someone might think if they had full knowledge and information about the impact of government policies).

But we do believe that several decades of social science research on what the public thinks about government and public policies give us one way of beginning to answer the question. Scholars who conduct opinion **surveys**—or polls—of a **representative sample** (a small group of people selected at random) of Americans have in fact made a lot of headway in developing sophisticated research tools for

studying how people reason about their underlying beliefs or preferences. The term used to characterize the results of opinion surveys is **public opinion**. These methods are not perfect for examining the third dimension of power, but they do provide at least a first look at the issue, a way of thinking about the empirical problem of consciousness.

Let's consider these questions in relation to Americans' attitudes about inequality and public policies designed to reduce inequality and poverty. What do we know from decades of research on public opinion in these areas? The single most important and well-established finding about what Americans believe when it comes to public policies involving the unequal distribution of income, the welfare state, and national security policy is the following—and contradictory—set of beliefs:

- Most Americans believe that the political system favors the preferences of the powerful, that the rich should pay more taxes than the poor, that government should spend more on specific social programs in the abstract and do more to help those who cannot provide for themselves through their job. Americans are, in principle, egalitarians (they would prefer more equality than we have today).
- But most Americans have also come to accept the view that government overall is too big, that in the abstract the market is better at solving social problems than the government, and that taxes are too high. Americans favor individual initiative and free markets and oppose "big government." They are, in other words, not willing (in spite of their desire to have more equality) to support expanding government programs that have been shown to reduce poverty and inequality in other countries.

Americans hold what can only be characterized as contradictory views about these questions. Perhaps that is not so surprising; as individuals, most of us hold somewhat contradictory beliefs about many things. We may want a large helping of ice cream while knowing that it is not healthy to have one. So too when it comes to poverty and inequality: We may want more equality but not the higher taxes on the rich that might be required to achieve it. Our individual opinions are often confused because we don't think about these questions all the time, and so when we are asked we may give inconsistent answers. But when you look at the average responses of all Americans, it is now clear, as two political scientists recently have put it, that Americans are "conservative egalitarians" (Page and Jacobs 2009). In other words, Americans do not consistently connect their beliefs about equality into support for government programs that

What contradictory views do Americans hold on policies involving the unequal distribution of income?

FIGURE 6.7 AMERICANS ARE LESS SUPPORTIVE OF HELPING THE POOR AND THE OLD

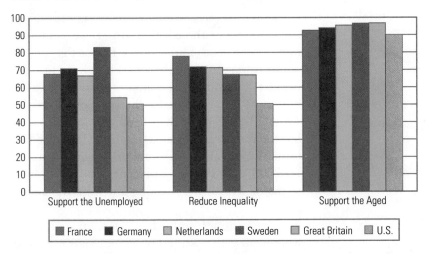

Note: Survey respondents were asked whether it should be the government's responsibility to guarantee a decent standard of living for the unemployed, reduce income difference between the rich and poor, and guarantee a decent standard of living for the old.

Source: Author's tabulations from 2006 International Social Survey Program.

have, but they are often not willing to have the government—the one institution fully capable of having an impact—do the job. A good example of this can be seen in the debate over whether or not the federal government should adopt a national health insurance plan that would cover all Americans. The government of every rich country around the world takes steps to ensure that all citizens have health coverage. The sole exception is the United States, where approximately 50 million people (almost one in six Americans) is uninsured or has very limited health insurance. Consistent with what we have been arguing here, increasing proportions of Americans in recent years have supported increased government spending on health care for all citizens (see the top line in Figure 6.9). Support for increased spending has reached 70 percent in recent years.

Yet, as the bottom line in Figure 6.9 shows, only around 50 percent of Americans support a government-run national health insurance program, and until a slight blip upward in 2006 through 2008 the proportion was under 50 percent. In other words, there is about a 20 percent gap between the proportion of Americans supporting better health care in the abstract and the proportion wanting a government-run program. The latter figure, which has been fairly steady for nearly 50 years, shows that opponents of national health insurance can easily remind citizens of how much they dislike government when national health insurance is proposed. Over the past century, there have been repeated efforts to pass a national health insurance measure. Until 2010, when the Obama administration narrowly succeeded in getting a measure through Congress that would cover almost all Americans, all of these previous attempts failed (Quadagno 2006). And it remains uncertain what the ultimate fate of the Obama administration's health care reforms will be (Starr 2011).

might actively alter the balance of power in favor of the powerless.

One concrete example is that Americans are significantly less supportive of social spending programs than are citizens in comparable countries. Drawing on data from an international survey that fielded identical questions in many countries, Figure 6.7 shows how Americans are *much* less supportive of helping the unemployed, reducing income inequality, and to a lesser extent helping senior citizens. Citizens in comparable countries (France, Germany, the Netherlands, Sweden, and Great Britain) all exhibit much higher levels of support for each proposition.

In addition to their generally lower level of support for social programs than citizens in other countries, even when Americans do prefer more effort be devoted to reducing poverty or inequality, Americans are always less convinced that government-based programs are the best way to go. Deep hostility to big government is one of the hallmarks of American public opinion in the last three decades. When asked how much confidence they have in their government, less than 20 percent of Americans in recent polls have indicated they have confidence in government doing the right thing all or even most of the time, whereas the percentage reporting little or no confidence has shot up during this same period (see Figure 6.8). People's confidence in government has declined dramatically over the past 35 years.

The upshot of all of these views is that Americans have adopted an approach to the appropriate role of government that is very limited. Americans want more equality than they

FIGURE 6.8 PERCENTAGE OF RESPONDENTS WITH "HARDLY ANY" CONFIDENCE IN CONGRESS AND THE EXECUTIVE BRANCH, 1972–2010

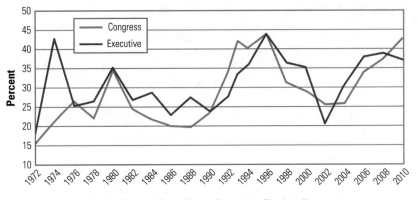

Source: Author's analysis of General Social Survey Cumulative File, http://www.norc.gss.org.

FIGURE 6.9 TRENDS IN SUPPORT FOR INCREASED SPENDING AND GREATER GOVERNMENT INVOLVEMENT IN HEALTH CARE, 1974–2006

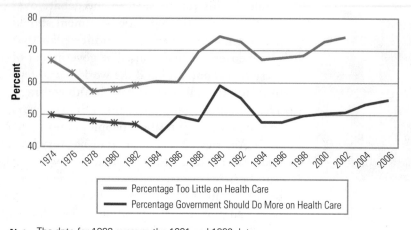

Note: The data for 1992 average the 1991 and 1993 data.

Source: Author's analysis of General Social Survey.

Hostility toward big government is important because, as we have noted earlier in this section, history suggests that the only way a country can have more equality and less poverty is by expanding the role of the state in society. Charitable organizations, while often well-meaning and able to help, are never large enough to lift significant numbers of people out of poverty. Free markets are good for many things, but without significant regulation and appropriate types of taxation, free markets will produce high levels of economic inequality (and the process of loosening regulations on banks in the past 30 years reminds us of how important regulation

can be). It is only the government that has the resources and ability to produce more equality and less poverty.

Finally, let us consider a third example: public attitudes about the elimination of the estate tax (also known as the inheritance tax, or the "death" tax as opponents labeled it). The estate tax is a tax that is paid when someone dies and leaves money to someone other than a spouse. By the 1990s, the estate tax had been eliminated on all but the very largest estates (so people leaving a few thousand dollars to their children paid no taxes). By 2003, only the top 2 percent of households in terms of wealth were paying any inheritance tax at all.

Even though only the very richest families were paying the estate tax, a campaign to repeal it culminated in 2003 with the elimination of last remaining inheritance taxes. A study of this campaign by two political scientists asked the excellent question: "Why would the public broadly support the repealing of a tax paid by only 2 percent of America's wealthiest taxpayers?" Yet polling data consistently showed that a significant majority of Americans favored the elimination of all estate taxes, no matter how the question was posed (see Table 6.3 for one example). Even more remarkably, a 1935 poll conducted by *Fortune* magazine found that even in the middle of the Great Depression, majorities of Americans favored setting no limits on how much someone could inherit (Graetz and Shapiro 2005; see also Bartels 2008, chap. 7).

TABLE 6.3 SUPPORT FOR REPEALING THE ESTATE TAX "There has been a lot of talk recently about doing away with the tax on large inheritances, the so-called ['estate tax'/'death tax']. Do you FAVOR or OPPOSE doing away with the [estate tax/death tax]?"

	Favor Repeal	Oppose Repeal	N
Total sample	67.6%	27.2%	1,346
Among those who ...			
have family incomes of less than $50,000	62.9%	29.9%	620 (46%)
want more spending on most government programs	66.3%	28.3%	1,232 (92%)
say income gap has increased *and* that is a bad thing	64.9%	31.9%	596 (40%)
say government policy contributes to differences in income	64.6%	30.1%	813 (63%)
say rich people pay less than they should in federal income taxes	65.2%	31.4%	674 (30%)
All of the above	63.4%	32.8%	134 (10%)

Source: Bartels (2008).

Because almost everyone except the very rich were paying little or no inheritance taxes at the time it was repealed, the successful elimination of the all such taxes has to be considered one of the major puzzles of recent American politics. Why would Americans support policies that so clearly were not going to impact them? Several answers have been advanced to account for public support for repeal of the estate tax. One is what we might call wishful thinking, or optimism bias: American may simply be unrealistically optimistic about their chances of someday becoming wealthy. Table 6.3 appears to confirm this. Over 60 percent of families with annual incomes below $50,000 favored repeal of the tax, as did respondents to the survey who say they want more spending on government programs or that they think income inequality is too high. A second factor is simple ignorance of the facts of the estate tax, although there is conflicting evidence as to whether people with better information were more likely to oppose the tax. At any rate, by the time the matter came up for vote in Congress, in spite of the fact that repeal amounted to a naked handover of funds to the children of the very wealthiest of Americans, the combination of broad public support and a vigorous campaign for repeal pushed the measure over the top. America is now the only rich, democratic country in the world that imposes no inheritance taxes at all.

Our conclusion is that on the third dimension of power, ordinary Americans do not, for the most part, believe *all* of the things that the powerful might desire them to, but in many cases they have come to believe in conservative principles about how bad big government is that have allowed inequality to grow unchecked in recent decades. This rejection of a greater government role in American society is consequential because the only realistic way—based on everything social scientists and policymakers have learned in the last 100 years—that inequality can be reduced is through increased taxes and more social spending by the federal government. But when politicians and political activists propose to do something that would reduce inequality or provide more social benefits for the poor, defenders of privilege have been able to mobilize a powerful, principled opposition among a majority of Americans.

CONCLUSION THOUGHTS AND QUESTIONS FOR FURTHER INVESTIGATION

The sociological study of power and politics, as we have proposed it in this chapter, analyzes the various ways in which power is exerted and maintained, proceeding from what is clearly observable to what is normally hidden. It is not simply concerned with votes, elections, and public policy but *also* with the underlying sources of political outcomes. In other words, just as a good police detective needs to dig beneath the surface to explore the hidden factors that might be behind a murder, so too must political sociologists examine power by going beyond the *outcomes* of political life to understand how power operates. We have argued that three dimensions of power are central, but ordinarily the media focus solely on the most visible dimension (where there is open conflict). Once we learn to think about power and politics on all three dimensions, we have learned a different way of thinking about political life. It is, in short, an application of the sociological imagination to the study of power.

Because power and power relations are such a pervasive aspect of social life, the study of power has to be considered a central task for all of sociology (and for all citizens). We know from opinion polls and surveys that the vast majority of Americans are unhappy with their government and system of democracy. Armed with the approach we have outlined here, many questions, challenges, but also opportunities open up for all of us—students, citizens, workers, parents, retirees—to think about what might be done to make democracy in the United States and elsewhere work better. We have mostly focused on national politics in the United States, but power can often be studied and, where appropriate, more easily challenged at lower levels of societies. In our towns and cities, workplaces and other organizations, or even in our own families, power can be analyzed in terms of three dimensions and how they reinforce one another. And analysis is always the precursor to effective change.

Watch the **Video** in **MySocLab**
Applying Your Sociological Imagination

Study and **Review** in MySocLab   **Watch** the **Video** Inspiring Your Sociological Imagination in MySocLab

1 What Are the Distinct Forms of Power?
(p. 144)

Watch the **Big Question Video** in **MySocLab** to review the key concepts for this section.

In this section, we examined the three dimensions of power, using a sociological lens to examine not only the most visible ways in which power is expressed, but also its more subtle forms.

THE THREE DIMENSIONS OF POWER (p. 144)

The One-Dimensional View of Power (p. 144)

- **Who has power in the one-dimensional view?**

The Two-Dimensional View of Power (p. 145)

- **Why is agenda setting in politics important?**

The Three-Dimensional View of Power (p. 147)

- **When is power least visible?**

Explore A Sociological Perspective: Is power everywhere? in MySocLab

KEY TERMS

power *(p. 144)*
power elite *(p. 145)*
pluralism *(p. 145)*
agenda setting *(p. 146)*
status *(p. 147)*

2 How Does the State Distribute Power in a Society? *(p. 150)*

Watch the **Big Question Video** in **MySocLab** to review the key concepts for this section.

In this section, we examined what the institutions of power (the state) actually do. We also explored why states matter in the distribution of power and why states tend to promote the interests of the powerful.

THE INSTITUTIONS OF POWER (p. 150)

What Is the "State"? (p. 150)

- **How do states regulate the economy?**

Why States Matter in the Distribution of Power (p. 152)

- **How do states impact who gets what in a society?**

Promoting the Interests of the Powerful (p. 152)

- **Why do states tend to promote the interests of the powerful?**

KEY TERMS

state *(p. 150)*
bureaucracy *(p. 150)*
welfare state *(p. 152)*

3 Who Has Power in the United States Today? (p. 154)

👁 **Watch** the **Big Question Video** in **MySocLab** to review the key concepts for this section.

Finally, our discussion of the dimensions of power and political institutions led us to an examination of the American political system. This section discussed how the U.S. is different form other similar countries in the way power is distributed in national policies.

POWER IN AMERICA (p. 154)

Who Wins? Policy and Politics in the First Dimension (p. 154)

- **What do tax policies tell us about how power is distributed in the U.S.?**

Who Sets the Agenda? Politics in the Second Dimension (p. 160)

- **Why are there only two political parties in America, and why does it matter?**

⊙➜ **Explore** the **Data** on Money and Politics in **MySocLab**

📖 **Read** the **Document** *Is Congress Really for Sale?* by Paul Burstein in **MySocLab**. This reading examines what influence interest groups, individual campaign contributions, public opinion, and others have on policy makers in the U.S.

The Third Dimension: Do Americans Believe in Policies Benefitting the Powerful? (p. 164)

- **What contradictory views do Americans hold on policies involving the unequal distribution of income?**

👁 **Watch** the **Video** Applying Your Sociological Imagination in **MySocLab** to see these concepts at work in the real world

KEY TERMS

democracy *(p. 154)*

progressive income tax system *(p. 156)*

public policy *(p. 158)*

social problem *(p. 158)*

proportional representation (PR) *(p. 160)*

political action committee (PAC) *(p. 162)*

survey *(p. 164)*

representative sample *(p. 164)*

public opinion *(p. 164)*

7

MARKETS, ORGANIZATIONS, and WORK

((• Listen to the **Chapter Audio** in **MySocLab**

by RICHARD ARUM
and JEFF MANZA with
ABBY LARSON, MICHAEL
McCARTHY and
CHRISTINE BAKER-SMITH

W hen we think about companies in the United States, names like Walmart, Google, Apple, or Chevron come to mind. But of the nearly 6 million companies with employees, just over 5 million are small businesses owned and operated by someone who employs less than 20 people. Entrepreneurship is a topic that fascinates many of us, not simply because small businesses are an important part of the economy, and most of us know a family member or friend who works for themselves, but also because entrepreneurship and self-employment are aligned with many young Americans' hopes and dreams: to tell an employer to take this job and shove it, to be one's own boss, to build something from scratch.

But what exactly does self-employment look like for young, college-educated adults today? One of the chapter's authors asked a national group of college students about their entrepreneurial aspirations during their senior year of college in 2009 and then followed up with them after they graduated. During their senior year, 5 percent of students reported that they planned to own their own businesses within two years of completing college, while 36 percent of respondents reported that they aspired to be entrepreneurs at some point in their lives.

When we asked Sarah, a female business major who recently graduated from a large public university in a small city, what job she hoped to have in five years, she described her entrepreneurial ambitions without hesitation: "I expect to successfully be running my own company." She had in fact already started a small entertainment company that offered the services of "art development

MY SOCIOLOGICAL IMAGINATION
Richard Arum

I grew up as a white, privileged, Jewish kid in the suburbs of New York, but in a manner a little different than the norm. While my friends were surrounded with adult role models who were in professional fields such as law and medicine, I grew up connected to a broader set of individuals, including cultural icons and civil rights heroes such as Muhammad Ali. This early personal exposure shaped who I was and the choices I would end up making as an adult. In the years following, I received a teaching certificate from Harvard University and subsequently worked as a teacher in a segregated public high school in Oakland, California. In that institutional setting, in order to make sense of the dysfunction of the school as an organization as well as the impact that the school was having on the lives of the students, I increasingly was drawn to asking sociological questions of the world. In order to move beyond simply asking these questions, I enrolled at the University of California– Berkeley with the objective of developing sociological tools and skills to better understand the problems around schooling in America. Developing a sociological imagination for me was an attempt to develop a set of analytical competencies to participate actively in policy discussions that could substantively improve the outcomes of youth.

Founded by business partners Shelly Hwang and Young Lee, Pinkberry is one example of an entrepreneurship that has made it big. Since its opening in 2005, Pinkberry, which sells upscale frozen desserts, has grown from one store in West Hollywood, California to a franchise including over 100 stores nationwide.

Watch the **Video** in **MySocLab**
Inspiring Your Sociological Imagination

(and) independent branding in music production." Like many entrepreneurs, she was collaborating with her romantic partner in the business. In addition, Sarah reported that she used some of what she had learned in college toward this endeavor, from her accounting, marketing, finance, and communication courses. If Sarah's emerging company is to be successful, however, she has to understand not just the local market but how to run her firm as an organization as well as how to manage employees.

Stable organizations and individual careers inside these organizations that were so common in the middle of the twentieth century are now undergoing rapid change.

Although in the year or two after graduation only 2 percent of graduates in our study actually ended up fully immersed in self-employment, it turns out that the students' estimate of being self-employed at one point in their lives is not far from what we would expect from national data. About 20 percent of men and women have been self-employed by the time they are in their early thirties, and more than 30 percent have been self-employed by the time they are in their early fifties. However, while many people do start their own business or work from themselves at some point, most do not last in this status for long. Most start-up businesses typically fail within the first few years.

Our research also explored how the character of self-employment has changed dramatically in recent decades. While self-employment had been in decline in most developed economies throughout the twentieth century, and many social scientists believed that it was likely to disappear in the face of markets increasingly dominated by large companies, self-employment surprised many social scientists by reemerging and beginning to grow in the last quarter of the twentieth century. When we looked close, we found an additional surprise. Traditional self-employment—an activity dominated by small shopkeepers, restaurateurs, and craftsmen—is indeed declining. But new forms of self-employment emerged to replace it. In particular, two types of self-employment are growing: professional freelancers (including artists, designers, and writers, who value independence and flexible job hours) and low-income, marginal, informal forms of self-employment, such as in-home childcare or day labor. Although professional and unskilled forms of self-employment are increasing for both men and women in most settings, countries still differ on the extent to which traditional forms of self-employment are prevalent (see Figure 7.1)

Why is this occurring? The forms of self-employment that are growing are related to a larger restructuring of the American economy, in which companies are increasingly outsourcing work to self-employed people, both professionals and people with relatively few skills. Stable organizations and individual careers inside those organizations that were so common in the middle of the twentieth century are now undergoing rapid change. In this chapter, we explore how and why these changes in economic life have occurred, introducing sociological ideas about markets, organizations, and work.

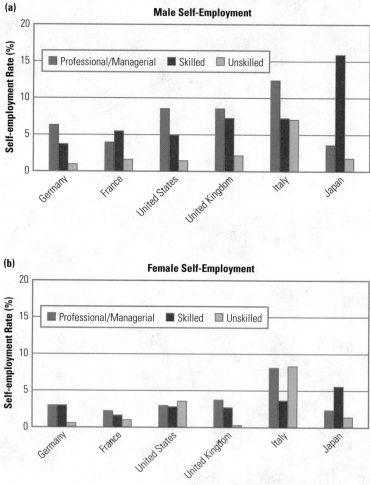

FIGURE 7.1 SELF-EMPLOYMENT IN SELECT COUNTRIES

Source: Figure based on data from Arum and Müeller (2004).

THE BIG QUESTIONS

👁 **Watch** the **Big Question Videos** in **MySocLab**

1 **How do social factors impact markets?** We live in what is sometimes called the "age of the market," and sociologists are increasingly aware that markets are part of the social structure of society. In this section, we explore how a sociological understanding of markets differs from an economic understanding.

Why are organizations important for social and economic life? To gain a deeper understanding of how modern economies work—and ultimately how social forces influence the economy as a whole—sociologists place considerable importance on analyzing the organizations that exist within markets.

2

3 **What is the relationship between organizations and their environment?** The ecological framework of organizational sociology challenges whether organizations actually adapt to their environments or whether the organizations that survive do so because they were uniquely suited to the environment from the start. In this section we explore this relationship between organizations and their environment.

How are jobs structured? The kinds of jobs we have are important to us as individuals for our sense of self. But the overall distribution of jobs across an entire society significantly defines the economic system and what type of society it is. In this section, we explore how work is organized in modern workplaces in the United States.

4

5 **What makes a good job?** A good job for one person may not be such a good job for someone else. In this section we examine what constitutes a good job in America and how American workers fare relative to their peers in similar

1　How Do Social Factors Impact Markets?

THE CREATION AND FUNCTIONING OF MARKETS

👁 **Watch** the **Big Question** Video in **MySocLab**

e live in what is sometimes called the "age of the market." **Markets**—places where buyers, sellers, and producers engage in exchange of commodities and services—are the foundation of economic life. The power of economic markets has not always, however, been so clear. For much of the twentieth century, following the Russian Revolution in 1917 and the establishment of communist governments first in the Soviet Union and later in Eastern Europe, North Korea, and Cuba, alternatives to market capitalism as a way of organizing a country's economy existed. While these governments professed an ideological commitment to communism—that is, a society organized without private property and based on the principle that individuals should be able to consume societal resources based on their needs, not their ability—in practice, the government and/or communist party owned and controlled the means of production. In the socialist economies of Eastern Europe, the government employed what was known as **central planning**, in which the government decided what kinds of goods and services would be produced and how much they would cost. For a time, centrally planned economies appeared to be doing reasonably well; in the 1960s and 1970s, there were debates among economists and other observers about whether **capitalism** (an economic system based on private property and market exchange) or **socialism** (an economic system where the government owns property and controls production) was superior. But a long period of stagnation and decline began in the 1970s, which, coupled with the lack of democracy in these societies, led to their downfall in the late 1980s (and in the Soviet Union, in 1991).

Today, the socialist alternative has, in relative terms largely been diminished as a viable alternative to market

capitalism. All over the world, including all of the most developed countries, the vast majority of goods and services are provided through economic markets (with government-run services the primary alternative). It is fair to say that almost every arena of social life today has a market attached to it. You can buy all of the necessities of life for a price, even life itself. For example, babies and new organs can be purchased for a price, although usually only in illegal markets. You can also pay to have your dead body frozen until some future time when (it is hoped) you can be brought back to life.

Entrepreneurs—people who invest in and start businesses—are constantly inventing new markets to sell goods and services to potential buyers. For example, human travel options have been relentlessly expanded to include such exotic options as traveling to the South Pole, climbing Mount Everest, and perhaps even traveling in space. In recent years, a whole range of new services for pets has been introduced, including doggie day cares (places where you can drop your pet off to be watched and entertained by a human staff while you are at work), dog-walking services (a dog-walking professional comes to your house or apartment and walks your dog a couple of times a day), animal psychologists (who offer to help your pet with their emotional life), elaborate dog grooming services (to make dogs look their best) and other such services.

These and other examples show that markets and market ideas are increasingly penetrating areas of social life that were once considered outside of the market domain. Even the most intimate spaces of individuals' lives now have markets available. Families that can afford to will frequently hire others to take care of their children, prepare their meals (at home or at restaurants), clean their houses and take care of

Social forces support market exchanges even in alternative countercultural settings, like the Burning Man festival held once a year in the Nevada desert.

their yards, and provide them with security from thieves. The sociologist Arlie Hochschild (2012) recently analyzed even more dramatic examples of the outsourcing of our lives, finding that specialists now exist to provide services such as helping them find lovers, "nameologists" to help them name their children, even "wantologists" to help them figure out what it is they want out of life. One way to see how pervasive markets are in everyday life is to count the number of markets that you encounter on a daily basis. Do you rent an apartment or own a house? What did you eat for breakfast? Did you listen to music or news online? Use an Internet service to check your e-mail? Send a text message? What did you wear? How did you get to class or work? All of these involve markets.

Even important functions of government that were previously handled by government employees are increasingly being subcontracted to private entrepreneurs. This even includes warmaking (for example, private military contractors hired by the U.S. government have increasingly joined American soldiers on the ground in recent wars), but also a wide variety of other government services and activities. Local governments in particular have often sought to cut costs by using private firms to handle what was formerly done by government employees. Sandy Springs, Georgia—a city of 94,000 people—has even subcontracted almost all traditional government functions to private companies, including its local court system, where a judge who is paid $100 an hour presides. The city employs just seven full-time workers (Segal 2012).

Given its pervasiveness, there is an increasing awareness among sociologists that markets are part of the social structure that provides the architecture of modern societies. So ubiquitous are markets in our society as a means by which to organize social behavior that we do not often give them much thought: They are a taken-for-granted part of how we live our lives. It is exactly for this reason, then, that we need to examine them with the tools of the sociological imagination.

☐ Defining Markets

What a market is may seem intuitive—one of those "you know it when you see it" kind of things. The stock market is, most certainly, a market, and one we all hear a lot about. Movies that feature the frenetic shouts of traders on Wall

How do sociologists define markets differently than economists?

Street as they hustle to buy and sell companies for profit represent one image of financial markets, and the daily (or even hourly) news reports on the ups and downs of the stock market suggest that the stock market must be important. People buy and sell shares in companies based on their assessment of whether the value of a company will go up or down in the future. But there are also a lot of ambiguous cases. What about a free online dating site? Is that also a market? Certainly there are "buyers" (people who respond to ads) and "sellers" (those who put up profiles seeking dates). But no money changes hands. What about services that facilitate housing exchange for vacations? Consider the annual cultural festival Burning Man, held in the Nevada desert. Once you have purchased your ticket and have traveled to the festival, there are both formal and informal rules against the exchange of currency, and goods and services are exchanged through a barter economy only. Do markets operate there?

These examples highlight the complexity of defining what we mean by the market, and indeed the way sociologists define markets has been evolving since sociology first emerged as a discipline. In classical economics, a market implies an exchange of goods and services between buyers and sellers. In this definition, exchanges can happen in the blink of an eye (when we hand over money or click a computer screen), and the price of the good or service being exchanged is determined by the demand for whatever is being sold. Both sides of the transaction (buyer and seller) are assumed to have knowledge about the good or service they are buying or selling, and both participants are thought to be making decisions that they think will improve their individual (or their family's, or company's) well-being. Economists call this perspective on markets the **rational choice perspective**, and it is a powerful one because it relies on a simple set of assumptions about what motivates individuals and organizations as they enter into market exchanges.

Missing from this definition, however, are many of the concerns and considerations about social forces that sociologists think are important. Many of the earliest social theorists such as Karl Marx and Max Weber closely studied economics, and they sought in their writings to make sense of markets in new ways. Sociologists would ask of the economist's definition of the market questions such as what is necessary for these exchanges to occur? For example, *how* do buyers and sellers find each other? How do people know that they won't be cheated? What role does power play in the market?

The sociological definition views markets not as random, one-shot exchanges between a buyer and seller but rather as *repeated* interactions that people—buyers, sellers, and producers—carry out according to formal and informal rules. For a market to exist, there must be shared understandings about what kinds of commodities will be traded, who can trade, and how the trades take place. And for this to happen, important societal institutions—such as governments and laws—as well norms of appropriate behavior come into play. Indeed, without all of these other forces, market exchanges would often be impossible or very limited.

Three Key Social Factors in Markets: Networks, Power, and Culture

The sociological study of markets has focused on a combination of three critical social factors that influence how markets work: (1) social networks, (2) power, and (3) culture. In this section, we briefly describe each.

Social Networks Today, the term *social network* is widely associated with concepts such as Facebook and Twitter among myriad others—technological platforms that connect individuals and facilitate the exchange of information and, increasingly, goods and services. When sociologists talk about **social networks**, however, they are also interested in a slightly different aspect of social relationships: the ties between people, either through family/kinship relationships or through relationships involving friends, colleagues, classmates, or even friends of friends. Whereas classical economic theories of markets view them as ruthlessly impersonal, and set aside who people are and whether or not they know each other, sociologists argue that connectivity between people is an important part of how market exchange happens.

In his bestselling book *The Tipping Point*, Malcolm Gladwell (2000) gives a telling example of why social networks matter in retelling the story of Paul Revere. On the night of April 18, 1775, two prominent men set out on horseback to warn Boston area residents that the British army was on its way and the Revolutionary War was underway. William Dawes rode to the south, where he knew very few people.

How do networks, power, and culture impact markets?

Little came of his heroic effort, and he is largely forgotten. Revere, on the other hand, rode to the north where he was well known. Revere was able to alert his friends and associates, and they alerted others, and in short order a small army was created to fight the British forces. Revere took advantage of his social networks in a way that Dawes could not, and as a result he is remembered as a hero and Dawes is largely forgotten.

People who study markets through the lens of networks tend to argue in a similar fashion that economic activities, including market activities, are often built on kinship and friendship, and trust and goodwill, between people who know each other. Markets need these social ties in order to maintain levels of trust necessary to carry out economic exchange. These ideas were famously theorized by the sociologist Karl Polanyi ([1944] 1957), who argued that economic action is *embedded* in social interactions—that is to say, economic exchange takes place within the context of socialized life. People often buy and sell from people they already know. It's easy to think of examples of how knowing someone can influence preferences and market participation; the fact that shoe companies pay professional basketball players enormous sums just to wear their shoes (in the hopes of influencing potential buyers) is a good example. Sociologists who have studied banks and loans have found that while large corporations may be able to court a number of banks to secure loans, the fact of having done business before often influences preferences (Uzzi 1999). While one might anticipate that a business that discovered lower interest rates from another bank would immediately switch banks, many businesses will prefer to stay with the bank that they know and to ask that bank for lower rates. Developing a relationship with a bank over time can have advantages on both sides. For example, having a history of trust built up may provide a certain level of wiggle room for the business when it comes time to negotiate the terms of the loan, as the bank has certain information about the trustworthiness of the business to repay the loan.

In other research, social networks have proven important for the ways they exchange information related to the market. One famous example of how connections matter for economic outcomes can be found in a line of work established by Mark Granovetter in the 1970s showing that someone's chances of getting a job are highly influenced by who they know (Granovetter 1973). Studying how people found jobs in the Boston area in the early 1970s, Granovetter interestingly found that it wasn't someone's first-degree connections (the people that one knows personally) but rather second-degree connections—friends of friends—who were most helpful for securing new jobs. Later research has found mixed results for this specific argument. But the general point that Granovetter was making—that hiring does not simply involve an employer choosing from among the best available applicants but rather that referrals and recommendations from friends and acquaintances play a vitally important role as well—remains central to how we understand the hiring process. Sociologists sometimes tell their students that one of the most valuable things they can get out of college is a network of educated friends who may later in life provide information and opportunities of which they wouldn't otherwise be aware!

Social networks also matter a great deal for how individual careers develop, either inside a single company or in moving from one job to another. Managers inside companies may promote the "best" people on staff, but how do they decide who that is? In part, they often think the people they consider friends or enjoy being around are well qualified for promotion. Or they talk with other managers looking for talent—and those other managers may suggest their friends as particularly talented. Moving from one job to another is also often facilitated by who you meet in your current job. As people move to new companies and become involved in hiring, they often look to people they knew at the previous firm. Networks create opportunities in these kinds of ways.

Power In the classical economic view of markets, the identity of market actors should not matter in predicting how markets function. It is on this basis that some economists have argued that markets are the great equalizer. Gary Becker, a Nobel Prize–winning economist who studied human behavior through the lens of the market, famously argued that in the market everyone is the same, "rich or poor, men or women, adults or children, brilliant or stupid persons, patients or therapists, businessmen or politicians, teachers or students" (Becker 1976). But when sociologists observe how markets actually work, they tend to find not equality but inequality, and an important set of benefits that accrue to those who are already powerful. It is by now thoroughly established, on the basis of decades of research, that employers do not treat all potential applicants simply on the basis of merit but rather also look closely at demographic characteristics such as the age, gender, race, and ethnicity of a job applicant. Being a white male at an appropriate age for the job does not guarantee you will be hired, but it certainly helps.

Markets are affected by relative power and status in a wide variety of other ways. One way is the importance of power relationships between firms operating within the same market. The idea behind this perspective is that if you look closely, in most market exchanges, one party has relatively more power than the other, and this relative advantage in power shapes how the interaction between the parties unfolds. An easy example to visualize is the kind of market exchange envisioned in the book and film series *The Godfather*. Here, market outcomes are determined by coercion and brute force. One has the choice to either do business with the mob and its leader, the Don—to buy from their suppliers, to hire workers from the unions it controls, or to pay for its "protection"—or to face the consequences.

While the way that power influences this particular kind of market exchange is extreme, we can also see how different

The actor Marlon Brando in his famous role as the head of a mafia crime family in the first two Godfather movies (1972 and 1974). How does organized crime attempt to solve the classical problems of organizations? How does their approach differ from other (non-criminal) organizations?

articulations of power play a role in other kinds of markets. It is well known that larger firms can often get better deals on the same product than smaller firms—something Walmart has employed to great benefit in driving small businesses across America out of operation by undercutting their prices (Lichtenstein 2009). Another important set of examples can be seen in the auditing industry. Auditing firms do what is called due diligence, providing what is understood to be a disinterested review of a company's financial books. In recent years, a number of corporate accounting scandals have been in the news, which has made it clear that large, powerful firms can often manipulate the allegedly independent auditing firms. Auditing firms often face problems of conflict of interest and resource dependency. Auditors are paid by the very companies whose books they are required to validate. One can see how power enters the picture as companies are able to play auditing firms against one another and have the potential to exercise power in attaining the kinds of auditing sign-offs they desire.

Culture Finally, there remains the question of how people know the rules by which markets run. Without common understandings about who can participate in markets and how market interactions are to take place, the coordination of exchange would be very difficult. Sociologists have used this idea to make sense of how formal and informal rules help construct and coordinate markets. When we think of market rules and regulations, it's easy to think of formal rules. In the trading of stocks and bonds, for example, a famous rule prohibits what is called insider trading. What this means is that if you are a member of a company and you have information about the company's strategy or know, for example, that the firm is going to be sold or acquired, you are not legally permitted to trade your company's stock using that information. This is to help create an equal playing field among market participants who would not have this kind of insider information. Many such rules are set by governments—which set the rules of the game, and as Polanyi argued, are essential for creating and sustaining markets. Many of the rules that govern market behavior, however, are not formal or even explicit rules but rather are informal and taken for granted. Sometimes imagining these kinds of rules is difficult, exactly because they are so built in to the way that we live our lives. It's often only when taken-for-granted-rules are broken that we notice how powerful they are.

But informal rules also are significant. We have to know how to participate in any market we enter. An example we are all familiar with is in the dating market, where unspoken rules have to be mastered; they include things like how and when to express interest in someone else, as well as the appropriate levels of enthusiasm, for example. Knowing whether and how you can bargain for the best deal with someone else in a market situation (say an employer or a seller of services) is an important type of normally hidden, but often crucial, cultural knowledge.

Sometimes the unwritten rules of a market can be changed by participants to create new opportunities. In a famous study of the rise of the life insurance industry, sociologist Viviana Zelizer (2012) found that only after the cultural norms about the appropriateness of putting a monetary value on a life changed did the life insurance industry take off. For this to happen, people in the insurance industry had to justify and legitimize the idea that a human life has some kind of economic (as well as social) value to friends and family. Only after this value was established was a market for life insurance viable; the industry had, in essence, not only to convince people to buy life insurance, but to convince them that if someone dies the heirs could be compensated with money for their loss. We take this for granted today, but in order for that market to emerge an important cultural shift in the very meaning and value of a human life had to occur.

2 Why Are Organizations Important for Social and Economic Life?

ORGANIZATIONS IN THE MODERN WORLD

👁 Watch the **Big Question** Video in **MySocLab**

When we say that we live in the age of markets, we have to add one important caveat: These markets are not typically just made up of a bunch of individuals selling goods to other individuals. Rather, contemporary markets contain within them a variety of organizations that determine and shape the boundaries of that market. In almost everything we do, we encounter an organization: From birth in a hospital to the day care centers, schools, churches, and businesses we participate in, to the government itself—an endless array of organizations impact our daily lives. Virtually every market has a set of key organizations that operate within it in both

Eradication of an illness can force charitable organizations to redefine their missions.

competitive and noncompetitive ways. To gain a deeper understanding of how markets and modern economies work—and ultimately how social forces influence the economy as a whole—sociologists have placed considerable importance on analyzing how organizations work.

What exactly makes up an organization? An **organization** can be defined as a group engaged in a specific activity that has an identifiable purpose or goal and that has an enduring form of association. Given this admittedly broad definition, it is no surprise that there are many different types of organizations. Organizations can be huge (e.g., the U.S. Army) or as small as two or three people. But in spite of such vast differences, research on organizations finds that they typically have many things in common. In this section we discuss several of these features.

Organizational Persistence

One nearly universal finding about organizations, and one that provides an important clue to understanding how they work, is that once established, organizations tend to persist. This holds true even in the face of important challenges to their existence. A famous case in point is an organization known as the March of Dimes, a charitable organization established in 1938 by President Franklin Roosevelt and others to fight polio, a medical condition that could cripple an individual (Roosevelt himself was a victim of polio). The organization asked citizens to donate a dime to help the fight against polio. In 1955, a new vaccine (known as the Salk vaccine) was approved for use, and it proved so successful that it essentially eliminated polio. The organization had achieved its goals. So did it go out of business? No. After a long internal discussion, the organization's leaders decided to look for new medical conditions to fight by raising money from the public, ultimately changing the mission to fighting birth defects and other childhood diseases in 1958. It has since expanded into an all-purpose health research organization (Rose 2003).

Why do organizations like the March of Dimes persist even when their original purpose is moot? One reason is that the people who are involved in them have a strong interest in their survival. People who work for an organization for a living, for example, want the organization to survive so they keep their jobs. Organizations also have a name and a reputation that is known to others. That name brand is (usually) valuable, and rather than going completely out of existence an organization may survive by being absorbed into (or bought by) another organization.

But most importantly, organizations (especially as they grow) tend to develop **bureaucracies**, where rules are written down and defined roles of members of the organization are made clear. Once a bureaucratic form of an organization emerges, an organization is on the road to establishing a long-term presence. In a bureaucratized organization, people can join and leave the organization, but the organization itself persists because it has established operating principles and procedures that do not rely on any one individual to maintain them. In these cases, the organization has now become more than the sum of all the individuals within it.

From Start-Up to Bureaucratic Firm: The Case of Apple

The famous case of Apple Computer provides a good example of how bureaucracies develop as organizations grow (even in the computer industry, which prides itself on avoiding bureaucracy!). In the now classic narrative of how Apple became a world leader, Steve Jobs and Steve Wozniak, brilliant college drop-outs with entrepreneurial vision and technical curiosity and know-how, began designing the first Apple personal computers in a garage in Los Altos, California, in the mid-1970s. In 1977, the company released the Apple II computer, one of the first commercially successful personal computers. With the buzz created by the Apple II and the revenue it generated, Apple was able to hire a number of outstanding young engineers and computer scientists and expand the range of the products it could offer. Apple's next breakthrough came in 1984, when the company introduced the first Macintosh

Why do organizations persist?

computer to glowing reviews but initially disappointing sales. As its sales increased, Apple began to transform itself into a multinational corporation with a board of directors and professional managers hired to market and run the growing organization. Around the same time as the Macintosh was released, Apple's board forced Jobs out of the company (Wozniak had left earlier). Apple continued to market and sell the Macintosh and other products without its founders for over a decade. The once small company had now morphed into a bureaucratic organization (albeit one where a high level of personal freedom for its employees was tolerated, setting a new model that other high-tech firms like Google have emulated). Eventually, having faced several product setbacks in the late 1980s and early 1990s and solid but unspectacular sales of the Macintosh, the company brought Jobs back as CEO. Under Jobs, Apple developed breakthrough products that would revolutionize the computer world: the iPod, the iPhone, and the iPad.

Although the story of Apple Computer is frequently presented as a story about the triumphant return of Jobs, the visionary individual who combined a fascination with both technology and design with a willingness to explore new products, Apple is also a fairly typical story of an organization that evolved (successfully, in this case) over time from a small organization created by a couple of individuals to a larger, bureaucratic organization. Apple's survival during its ups and downs in the 1980s and 1990s, before the introduction of its breakthrough products in the late 1990s and 2000s, depended in large part on the creation of an organizational structure that had the resources and stability to cushion the ups and downs of its computer business. Perhaps if Jobs had not returned to Apple, it would have remained a much smaller company, or even gone out of business. But either way, its evolution makes it a dramatically different type of organization today than when Jobs and Wozniak founded it.

☐ The Downside of Bureaucracy

While the process of bureaucratization of an organization can provide strength and stability, it can also create complex new problems for how decisions get made. We have a number of shorthand expressions for these problems: bureaucracies, as we all know, are famous for "red tape," for being "inefficient," and for being "bloated" and ineffective. Calling someone a "bureaucrat" can often be an insult. Let's probe these issues a bit further.

Max Weber's Theory of Bureaucracy In order to ensure stability and predictably, organizations rely strongly on rules and regulations. The German sociologist Max Weber, observing the German civil-service sector in the early twentieth century, provided the most influential description and analysis of bureaucratic organizations in these terms (Weber [1922] 1978). The move of any organization toward a bureaucratic form, Weber thought, was a necessary response to the complexities of modern large-scale markets and big governments. An organization that embraced bureaucratic means was attempting to find ways to allocate resources and make decisions more efficiently than it otherwise would. The hallmark of a bureaucracy, according to Weber, was the existence of formal procedures and rules, which are supposed to ensure both consistency (the same problem or task is addressed the same way each time) and accountability (individuals in the bureaucracy are accountable to those above them). Bureaucracy, Weber thought, was an inevitable feature of the modern world. Yet Weber also saw many negative aspects of bureaucracies. While undertaken with efficiency as the end goal, bureaucratic organizations also create stifling routines and boring jobs, and make it difficult for organizations to respond to changes in the environment in which they operate.

Weber's theory of bureaucracy emphasizes three central features. First, bureaucracies establish positions of authority that are hierarchically organized—that is, the higher up you go in a bureaucracy, the more authority is vested in that position. Bureaucracies are hierarchically organized so that there is a chain of command, and everyone working in the bureaucracy is responsible to the office above him or her (the president or CEO of an organization is typically responsible to an outside board of some kind). Second, written rules define the scope and responsibility of each position within a bureaucratic organization. Third, while organizations may have volunteers, they are only properly considered bureaucratic when the decision-making officers of the organization are full-time, salaried positions. These officials—known less charitably as "bureaucrats"—were said by Weber to treat their jobs as a calling and to have a stake in the overall functioning of the organization.

Weber's classical theory captured many of the key features of the bureaucratic organizations that were rising in the late nineteenth and early twentieth centuries. But there were also things he missed. In particular, Weber focused on the formal aspects of bureaucratic organizations, but he did not analyze the informal aspects of how bureaucracies actually work. Later critics and researchers who have studied many organizations in both the for-profit and nonprofit sectors have noted just how often the formal aspects of a bureaucracy do not function as they claim. Rules are routinely broken or ignored and often can only proscribe what someone does in an actual job in a vague way. Bosses are only sometimes able to effectively supervise their subordinates. Bureaucratic officials are also self-interested in ways that Weber's model did not anticipate. For example, bureaucrats often seek to increase the amount of resources available to their unit whether or not that is the wisest use of the organization's resources. Having a bigger budget under your control provides many benefits, even if the money might have been better spent somewhere else in the organization.

Why are decisions difficult in bureaucratic organizations?

The Garbage-Can Model

In the real world, bureaucracies are often messy places where rules and regulations are difficult to define and implement. Both people and organizations have to make decisions, and the problems they face are not that different. Individuals, for example, might come to an important decision (let's say what college to attend) based on the information to which they have access, but they also are influenced by the success of previous decisions, their long-term goals, their estimation of their likely success, and other factors. But individuals can only make a *rational* decision when they have enough information to analyze all possible options and implications. It is easy for any of us to go wrong when we don't know what we are doing or are not sure what we are trying to achieve. In most cases, we don't know everything and have to guess.

The same thing is true in organizations, but because there are many people involved, and often multiple options and multiple possible goals, the problem of accurately deciding on a rational course of action is especially difficult. The ideal conditions for making precise decisions seldom occur in bureaucratic organizations. Organizational decision making seldom follows a clear path but rather has been described by organizational theorists as often similar to tossing a set of questions and answers into a garbage can and then seeing what matches come out. The **garbage-can model** of decision making is a useful metaphor. Think about an organization such as a legislature, like the U.S. Congress. When a legislator proposes a bill, she must gather enough support to bring it to a committee that is in charge of the topic. To do so, she may add various pieces to the bill to win the support of committee members. Once this step is complete, the legislator must present the bill to the general assembly and get its support for passage. Finally, even when the bill has successfully passed both these legislating bodies, it must obtain the signature of the executive in order to become law. In each of these steps the bill may be modified to meet the needs of a particular member. For example, in the committee there may be a member who has an interest in this bill accomplishing an additional task. The member may "hold the bill hostage" until this additional language has been added. The same thing may happen in the general assembly as well, with even more legislators. And finally, the executive may also make demands for changes and modifications to the bill before granting executive passage. Thus the bill, though it has progressed through a process of decision making, is no longer completely rational in terms of logically connecting back to an original intent. The bill has instead emerged from a sort of "garbage can" of all the wants and needs of those involved in the process.

While legislatures have particular features of decision making that encourage garbage-can approaches, large corporations often operate in a similar fashion. When General Motors or any large car manufacturer decides to introduce a new car (or make significant changes to an existing model), many different departments are involved: Engineers are consulted on how to maximize the new car's fuel efficiency and design the motor, design experts conceptualize the "look" of the new car, and operations managers figure out how it can be built at a cost that will enable the company to earn a profit. On paper this all sounds simple; each division does its job. At each step of the way, however, the different divisions fight over every detail, and often unsatisfactory compromises have to be reached. Fuel efficiency may not be compatible with the design team's choices; a powerful engine may reduce fuel efficiency; the requirements to manufacture the car at a reasonable cost may hinder both engineers and designers. And because the company cannot know for sure what tastes people will have two or three years later when the car will be introduced, there is often a lot of guess work involved. The end result is often much less than either the engineers or designers envisioned in the first place.

Loose Coupling

What if a unit of an organization truly wanted to keep its decisions from falling into the garbage-can model? How could it accomplish this? One way is to disentangle itself from the rules and regulations of the larger institutions within which it operates. It can try to do this through what is known as **loose coupling**, the attempt to decentralize decision making to allow for multiple approaches to emerge. Loose coupling is evident in many different organizational environments. Consider the diverse way in which schools in America are organized. While schools operate within districts, states, and a federal system, there are multiple layers and linkages between local schools and federal

Designing a circuit board for an electric car might be easier than convincing individuals to adopt these new technologies.

mandates and regulations. Periodically, efforts to establish national guidelines and goals are asserted, such as the No Child Left Behind (NCLB) Act of 2001. NCLB mandated many changes within schools to create a standards-based assessment system; while some have happened, others have not. How is it possible that local schools have not complied with all parts of this federal law?

Schools, while legally connected to each level of the system, are many levels removed from the federal government. The space between these different levels allows local schools to operate with a significant degree of autonomy. While, for example, NCLB may mandate that every school engage in hiring qualified teachers, the federal government cannot directly supervise every school in the country, making its task of punishing noncompliers difficult. It thus relies on each of the levels of the system to help it regulate compliance with its laws. This can be like the child's game of telephone, where each level's focus on the original intent of the policy grows less and less clear. Each level also has its own concerns and agendas, leaving its interest in enforcing federal guidelines at the top uncertain. At the local level, the school may comply in some ways with those mandates most likely to be enforced, but not others, based on its own organizational interests and goals that are separate and apart from the federal agenda. In this way the education system in America is loosely coupled.

Loose coupling can be a negative thing, but it also provides institutions with the flexibility to maneuver with regard to more local environmental concerns and changes. For example, a few years ago the New York City Department of Education mandated that schools adopt a zero-tolerance policy for student possession of cell phones on campus. The district policies required that all student cell phones be confiscated and held until parents were notified and came to school to pick up what had been defined as contraband. Administrators and teachers in many schools, however, understood that while the intention of the policy was perhaps laudable, attempts at implementation would at best be laughable. Virtually all of today's students have cell phones with the full support of their parents, who use these devices to keep in touch with them. Confiscating phones of the entire student body and summoning a mob of irate parents would not be effective practice. Clearly, loose coupling can be a barrier to some institutional goals, yet for some organizations or in some situations it can improve adaptation and survival.

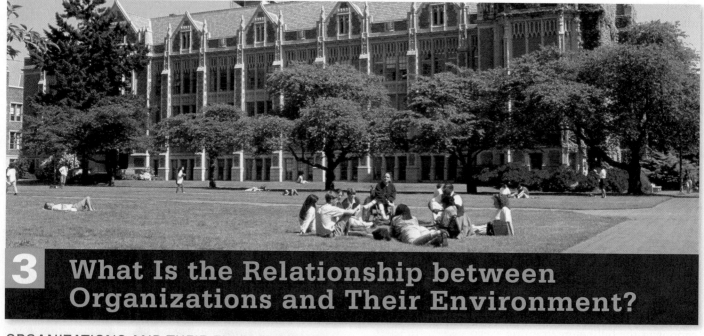

3 What Is the Relationship between Organizations and Their Environment?

ORGANIZATIONS AND THEIR ENVIRONMENTS

👁 Watch the **Big Question** Video in **MySocLab**

T he sociological imagination, as we have discussed throughout this book, urges us to look at the social contexts in which individuals and groups interact with one another. The same idea can be applied to organizations. Like individuals, organizations operate in the context of a larger environment, consisting of other firms, government policies, international competition, and many other forces. Just as individuals are impacted by the environments they live in, so too are organizations. In this section of the chapter, we consider some classical ideas about organizations and their environments.

In nature every animal, plant, or other organism lives within a particular environment. Evolutionary theory tells us that this environment influences not only the life and death of the organism but also the ways in which the organism grows and changes across generations. Like organisms, organizations depend on their environment to provide resources necessary for survival. Where an animal might depend on its environment to provide food and water, an organization depends on its environment for economic, social, and political resources. Without these resources the organization will perish. This ecological metaphor is a useful one for understanding how organizations work.

Organizational Structure

An ecological framework of organizational structure raises the question of whether successful organizations continually adapt to the environments they operate in or whether the organizations that survive do so because they were uniquely suited to the environment from the start. Either way, however, organizations must have features that are suitable for their environment if they are to stay alive and prosper. This might mean that an organization has developed an impermeable shell that protects it from environmental demands, or it might mean that the organization has maintained such a fluid structure that it can easily mobilize to adapt to changing environments. Scholars in this field suggest that organizations that survive are generally those that have created a structure that is a good match to an initial environment and then have made themselves difficult to change (Hannan and Freeman 1989). This strong resistance to change is referred to as **structural inertia**. The better the initial match, the stronger the inertia and thus the greater the staying power of the organization. This inertia, however, could be terminal when the environment dramatically changes and the absence of adaptation leads to organizational mortality.

It is not hard to see why structural inertia sets in. An organization that is successful early in its history has little reason to change; as the expression goes, "don't fix it if it isn't broken."

But structural inertia may also prevent the organization from surviving at some point. How would this happen? Though it is necessary, once it is set in place it is nearly impossible to change. Think of the *Titanic*. What made it so great was its size and thus its inertia, yet this is also what caused it to be unable to avoid hitting the iceberg. Organizations are like the *Titanic* as they become successful, and the very things that allowed them to be successful may actually make them eventually fail.

Organizations not only face threats from the environment and their own inertia, they also must survive in an arena with competition. The competition may be different for each organization, but all organizations must compete for resources within their environment. Organizations that survive have often successfully identified and fulfilled a **niche** (a distinct segment of a market or social process) for which the organization's services or products are in demand. Though there is still competition from other similar organizations, an organization that is effective at servicing a niche usually survives.

This competition is easiest to imagine among for-profit institutions—think of any new, successful product innovation as representing a niche, or a firm successfully offering a new kind of service—but we can even see it in the comparison between for- and non-profit institutions of higher education. All of the organizations in higher education (such as New York University, the University of California–Berkeley, Miami Dade Community College, or the for-profit University of Phoenix) attempt to create for themselves a market niche. By identifying a particular market of students that the institution can serve, a school limits the amount of competition it must face to survive in its environment. Take, for example, the difference between a state university and an elite private university. While the state university has institutional competition in the form of similar schools like other state universities, its identification as a public institution allows it to limit the demands placed on it and its competition for survival. For the most part, this university does not need to compete with private colleges for the same students. Students interested in or able to afford attending private colleges are likely to be somewhat different than their peers who chose among only state schools during their college application process. They may have different goals, different resources, and other features. A state school, for example, may have a much more specified array of majors than a private college—a state school might have majors in veterinary medicine, business, and the like, while a private university may focus more on general subjects like economics and biology. Different types of students are drawn to each of these types of schools. Similarly, while the state university does not need to compete as heavily with private colleges for its applicants once it has its own niche, it also reduces the actions demanded of it by limiting the types of people it serves. By clearly identifying itself as one that serves students who are interested in particular majors, the state school has provided itself with the freedom to put resources into these specific majors. These resources then give the institution a stronger ability to compete for organizational survival against those that are outside its niche but still in the larger institutional environment, like private colleges.

To better understand what these resources might be, let's consider the example of nonprofit organizations in the United States, such as private charities, churches, or research and advocacy groups. Every organization needs money to pay its staff, for office space, and for such things as sending as

How can an organization's structure help or hurt its chances for survival?

Pressures for disability accommodations can take multiple forms.

advertising. Where does the money come from? Nonprofit organizations do not earn money in the way that for-profit entities (like a grocery store) might, and thus rely largely on donations. To be successful and survive, however, a nonprofit must pay careful attention to its environment. One source of funding could be individuals who might donate to a cause because they have been impacted by it or simply because they care about it. These people make up part of the organization's environment. Similarly, legislators and other individuals with access to large amounts of money might take up the cause, providing significant economic resources to the organization. But in either case, entrepreneurial effort is required to identify and persuade potential donors to support a nonprofit organization in the face of many competing and seemingly worthy organizations also asking for funds.

The existence of a market for donations, however, also demonstrates a different aspect of the organizational environment: the social dimension. These same big donors may also speak out publicly for the cause, thus increasing the reach of the organization. By increasing its reach, the organization may be able to gather more small donors, thus increasing resource availability. Additionally, by increasing the renown of the organization and its status among those with high social status, the organization gains *legitimacy*. Even more clearly, if a legislator were not just to provide substantial financial support but also to pass a bill or law or make a big speech about the cause, this legislator has then given the organization another form of legitimacy or recognition. This legitimacy may ensure that the organization has the power to operate in areas where it had not in the past, may provide a legal pathway for the actions which the organization advocates, or even restrict the actions of its adversaries. In this case legitimacy becomes a resource to the organization.

☐ Organizational Similarity

The 1990 American with Disabilities Act (ADA) was a landmark legislation that declared that those citizens with disabilities should have the same access to physical spaces such as buildings and bathrooms as their non-disabled peers. ADA includes a set of rules for the physical buildings in which organizations operate. These rules and regulations mandate that certain facilities in every commercial and public-service building be accessible to all individuals, including those who are challenged with a mobility disability. Organizations then have to modify their physical structures to comply with these rules. Modification of a building by adding additional wheelchair ramps, elevators, handicap accessible bathrooms, and the like, however, is very expensive and time consuming, and the likelihood of being caught for failing to comply is low. So why do organizations comply?

There are three different reasons an organization might comply with these demands. These reasons are related to a sociological concept called **organizational isomorphism**, whereby organizations in the same field tend to change over time to become increasingly similar to each other over time (DiMaggio and Powell 1983). Isomorphism is a complicated concept, but an important and valuable one to grasp. The phenomenon of isomorphism has been found repeatedly in research across a wide range of organizations and industries, and it constitutes one of the classic insights of organizational sociology.

Theories of isomorphism arise from the simple fact that organizations in the same field (or market, or industry) tend to become more similar over time. Why might that be the case? The most straightforward way this occurs is when organizations are pressured to comply with certain legal regulations or requirements (such as the ADA's requirements that all buildings must provide wheelchair access). When applied to all organizations in the field, what is known as **coercive isomorphism** occurs. In this case, organizations all do the same thing because they have been compelled to take such actions. If they did not, they would face consequences that might include being sued by a customer or being fined by a government agency.

But compulsion is hardly the only way isomorphism occurs. There are two other reasons organizations might adopt similar behaviors or policies to one another. Imagine that an organization, in response to the ADA, must make a significant investment in these physical building changes. While these expenses may be considerable, the damage that could be done to the organization's legitimacy by not doing this might be even greater. Imagine if protestors began picketing in front of the building because of the building's refusal to provide access to disabled persons. By contrast, if an organization moves quickly to promote equal access it may be able to advertise itself as especially fair, sensitive, and responsive (implying that its competitors are not). Responding to these kinds of incentives is a kind of **normative isomorphism**: The organization is responding to pressures that are exerted on its legitimacy. Here *normative* indicates the general feelings or expectations of the people that the organization serves (for example, employees and customers or clients). Failing to attend to those expectations and needs of its supporters, the organization would fail to address the

normative environment in which it lives and thus would potentially lose its legitimacy within that environment.

Now let us assume the organization feels pressure both legally and from those whom it serves to create structures that allow disabled attendees entrance to the building. How does it know which type of infrastructure would be appropriate to build? Facing this uncertainty, it might look around its environment; the organization can then engage in **mimetic isomorphism**. Mimetic isomorphism is the process of literally imitating parts of other organizations visible in one's environment. By making itself look like all the others, the organization does not attract negative attention that might call its legitimacy into question.

It is easy to see how isomorphism can be integral for organizations responding to changes in their environment, but is it also useful for organizations even when there isn't a fundamental change in the environment? Organizations that are able to mimic their peers give themselves protection against threats to their survival that come in the form of legal, normative, and structural pressures in everyday life within the environment. Doing more or less what the other guy is doing in the face of these pressures is almost invariably the safest approach to take.

4 How Are Jobs Structured?

THE DIVISION OF LABOR IN MODERN SOCIETIES

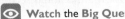 Watch the **Big Question** Video in **MySocLab**

One of the most important things that markets and organizations do is provide jobs and economic opportunities for individuals. Most people below retirement age work in a job that provides either a wage paid by an employer or income from self-employment. Most people work a lot, Americans in particular.

In 1970, hours worked per person were similar in Western Europe and the United States. Today, however, an American worker employed full time works an average of 46 weeks per year, while a French worker works 40.5 weeks and a Swedish worker just 35.4 weeks (see Figure 7.2). The average full-time worker in America works about 150 hours more than the

FIGURE 7.2 AVERAGE HOURS WORKED IN A CALENDAR YEAR

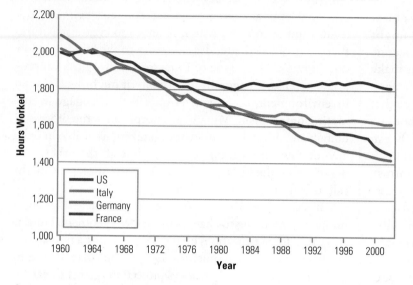

Source: Alesina, Glaeser, and Sacerdote (2005).

average number of hours worked per year by full-time workers in other similar countries, an extra month of work time. If the typical American worker sleeps about eight hours a night and takes two weeks of vacation a year, he or she is spending 30 percent of his or her waking hours at work.

Just as the kind of job we have is important to us as individuals for our sense of self, the overall (or aggregate) distribution of jobs across an entire society significantly defines the economic system and what type of society it is. All societies have a **division of labor**, in which some people do some things and other people do other things. If you were dropped down in a strange place with the assignment of figuring out your surroundings, one of the first things you might want to know about this strange place is what kinds of jobs people have, or what the division of labor in that society looks like. Hunting-and-gathering societies, or agrarian societies of past and present, are defined by the basic fact that the overwhelming majority of individuals are engaged in those activities. They have a relatively simple division of labor. By contrast, rich contemporary societies like the United States are defined by a complicated division of labor in which there are hundreds of different kinds of jobs in a bewildering array of organizational settings.

Increasing Specialization in the Division of Labor

How is work organized in modern workplaces? How has it changed over time? The specialization of tasks within and between organizations, and among workers toiling within

organizations, provides a useful starting point for thinking about the organization of work in entire societies.

From the mid-nineteenth century onward, accelerating in the twentieth century, there has been an explosion in the types of jobs people could work in, a process that continues right up to the present (especially if we recall the recent appearance of the "wantologist" identified by Arlie Hochschild [2012]). The **Industrial Revolution**—the rise of large-scale production of goods and products for mass markets—centered on the emergence of the factory as an increasingly central place where economic activity occurred. The first factories used relatively simple technology, and much of the work had to be done by skilled craftsworkers who were capable of producing a finished product more or less by themselves. As technology advanced, as well as more sophisticated forms of management and supervision, however, jobs were subdivided into different specialties. In the late nineteenth and early twentieth centuries in America and Europe, factories increasingly became dominated by assembly-line production, in which each worker would perform one or a small number of tasks.

Alongside the increasing specialization inside factories was rapid growth of both new and old professional and managerial occupations. The increasing wealth that the industrial revolution created both required and supported the creation of a large set of occupations that provided services and support to the manufacturing sector. Colleges and universities, once primarily reserved for the very wealthy or for religious instruction, underwent a mammoth expansion from the late nineteenth century onward. Occupations like physician, lawyer, accountant, business manager, professor and teacher, and many others expanded very rapidly, and became linked to educational credentials that provided a ticket to entry into the field.

The continuing growth of specialization in the kinds of jobs people have has continued right up to the present. Today the Census Bureau has a detailed job classification system that identifies over 12,000 different job titles that people can have. Reviewing the list, we find such fine-grained distinctions as that between an abrasive grader (which refers not to a professor who issues low grades to her students, but rather someone who "operates pebble mill to grind emerge, rouge, and other abrasives and separate them according to fineness") but also an abrasive grinder (someone who "tends the machines that grind specified radii on abrasives"). It is not hard to quickly reach the conclusion that there is a seemingly endless variety of jobs in a modern economy.

How is work organized in modern workplaces?

Monitoring work increases productivity, although it can also produce resistance, as researchers learned during the Hawthorne studies, conducted during the 1920s and 1930s.

☐ The Labor Process

The vast number of jobs might seem to imply that only specialists can perform their jobs. But most jobs are performed inside organizations and are controlled in a variety of different ways by the supervisors and managers who stand above individual workers in any organization. The **labor process** is the term that sociologists have developed to describe how most jobs are organized and controlled by managers from above, as well as the relationship between workers and management. The study of the labor process attempts to open up the workplace by examining how workers actually do their jobs, how managers try to control and direct them, and how the relationships between the two unfold. It represents another way in which the sociology of the economy moves into areas that classical economics paid relatively little attention to.

What forces have shaped the labor process? The most famous early line of research had its origins in attempts to understand why some workplaces were more productive than others. In the famous **Hawthorne studies** in the 1920s and 1930s conducted by Harvard industrial sociologist Elton Mayo and his associates, for example, a variety of experiments were conducted with different teams of workers to see what factors might induce workers to produce more output in the same amount of time (among other things, the researchers found that cooperation between the workers was especially important).

Since the 1960s and 1970s, however, questions about how to make work more efficient has tended to fall to engineers and business management scholars. The sociology of work today has come to focus on a very different set of questions about the organization of the labor process. An important shift was marked by the appearance of a book entitled *Labor and Monopoly Capital* by Harry Braverman (1974). This widely discussed book argued that in order to maximize profits, capitalist firms and their managers are continually driven to reduce their employees' ability to control what they do on the job. Braverman pointed to the rise of **scientific management**, a late-nineteenth-century movement

What forces have shaped the labor process?

sparked by the writings of Frederick W. Taylor, an early industrial engineer, as central to modern management strategies. Scientific management is premised on the idea that managers need to figure out how to understand and control what the workers under them are doing. Instead of allowing workers to decide how something should be done, or done differently, effective management requires controlling all of those decisions and keeping workers focused on precise tasks. The pinnacle of scientific management is the well-developed **assembly line** system of production, in which every task a worker must perform is completely scripted for her or him. Henry Ford, the founder of the Ford automobile company in Detroit, was the first to fully implement such a design early in the twentieth century, and it was much copied thereafter. 📖 **Read** the **Document** *Hanging Tongues: A Social Encounter with the Assembly Line* in **MySocLab**.

The workplace Braverman described was one in which workers were continually facing a process of **deskilling**, in which management constantly seeks to ensure that workers are not able to have the upper hand because of their more detailed knowledge of what needs to be done. Take for instance the craft of shoemaking. Prior to the development of capitalism, Braverman argued, a shoe was typically made in its entirety by a craftsman known as a cordwainer (i.e., a shoemaker). A single person would make the pair from start to finish. In order to mass produce shoes in an efficient way, shoe companies and their managers had to study and break down each step in the process, and assign each to a different person on a factory assembly line (today usually in a place like Vietnam or China). These modern factory workers probably do not know how to make the shoe in its entirety (including how to make the raw materials as well as how to assemble the entire shoe). Their individual tasks at work are heavily routinized and fairly easy to learn. The workers in such a factory are easily replaceable and have a weak position to resist what management wants as a result.

Braverman's thesis generated an enormous amount of debate about the extent and depth of deskilling in modern workplaces. Some sociologists argued that industrialization has had a more complex pattern, in some cases deskilling jobs while in other cases creating *new* types of jobs that require more skills. And modern technology has in many cases increased the amount of skill required in particular jobs (for example, requiring knowledge about computers which direct robots). If we look at the overall pattern of job growth over time, it does seem clear that there has been a long-term shift towards jobs that require *more* skill and *more* education, not less, one reason why the income differences between college graduates and those without college degrees has been growing in recent years (Goldin and Katz 2010). Two sociologists who tested this proposition came to exactly this conclusion. Grouping all job titles into 10 categories ranging from the least skilled to the most skilled and asking where job growth is occurring across these categories (Wright and Dwyer 2000), they found that in the 1960s, the pattern of fastest growth was for the most skilled job categories (8–10), and the lowest growth was at the bottom (see Figure 7.3). The 1960s were a time of solid economic growth in the United States. What about the 1990s, another period of solid (even spectacular) economic growth? Here, the authors find a more mixed pattern, in which the fastest-growing occupations are those at the top (10), but the second-fastest-growing title is at the very bottom (1), followed by the medium- to higher-skilled categories (6–9). On balance, though, there is little evidence that workers are being pushed into the least skilled (or most deskilled) jobs.

Other research that has examined either specific occupations or workplaces paints a much more nuanced picture of the relationship between the skills of workers and

FIGURE 7.3 1960 AND 1990 GROWTH OF HIGH AND LOW QUALITY JOBS Employment growth today is in both high and low quality types of jobs.

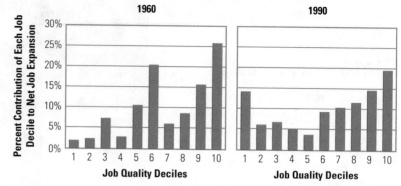

Notes: Jobs grouped into 10 categories based on analysis of relative quality; 1 = lowest; 10 = highest.

Source: Wright and Dwyer (2000).

management's attempts to squeeze as much out of their workers as possible (Vallas, Finlay, and Wharton 2009). For example, many kinds of skills that workers develop in their jobs are not easily measured but important. An assistant who can anticipate what the boss needs ahead of time, a restaurant cook who has learned how to substitute one ingredient for another when supplies run short without ruining the dish, or a teacher who can sense when a student is not understanding some key point all possess important skills that require the ability to respond to problems that even the most elaborate program of scientific management cannot anticipate or control. While many jobs may not require or enable an individual worker to become a true craftsman, this does not mean that there are not still important skills and knowledge being applied.

Ongoing changes in the organization of work and the labor process are reflected in the new workplaces of the twenty-first century (explore *A Sociological Perspective* on page 189 to see how workplaces have changed). As we noted earlier in the discussion of organizations, increasingly, the large assembly-line factory in which an individual worker performs a single task (or set of tasks) is being replaced by workplaces where cooperation among workers is encouraged and jobs are more interchangeable and interconnected. This change is still ongoing, but it represents one of the most important shifts in the nature of work since the advent of the modern assembly line in the age of Ford.

A SOCIOLOGICAL PERSPECTIVE

How have work organizations changed?

In the last few decades, the world of work has not only changed the kind of work people do – it has also altered the physical and organizational environments in which work is performed. Gone are the days of the "traditional" workplace in both factories and offices. Office work was once marked by a sea of cubicles, with rows and rows of desks disconnected from each other by privacy walls and doors. Known for its orderliness, such workplaces often stressed employee conformity and sameness. The same is true of the classic assembly-line workplaces of large factories. They were organized with an emphasis on standardization and surveillance, often with little room for interaction among employees while they worked. In place of these spaces of employment is a new model of workplace organization that emphasizes cooperation and teamwork on the part of individual workers.

More than ever before, for U.S. workers the world of work is in a store in the retail sector. In fact, the largest employer in the U.S. is Walmart (with over 1.5 million employees). For those in professional jobs – especially in computing, business, law, medicine, and administration – increasing attention has been devoted to designing "alternative" workplaces that stress cooperation and interaction. At the forefront of this are the work campuses created by many high-tech companies like Google and Yahoo. They give new meaning to the term "world of work" as their workplaces become worlds of their own: brightly colored, pet-friendly complexes of spaces traversed by employees on bikes and replete with cafes, child-care centers, massage rooms, socializing areas, and gift shops. These attractive workspaces are not, however, typical of most of the kinds of work done at places like Walmart.

What are the benefits for owners who enforce rigid structure and oversight for factory workers, and what are the effects of that structure on workers, morale and productivity?

Are there other factors that contribute to creativity, cooperation, and productivity in the workplace beyond the structure of a particular work environment?

The "campus" style workplaces of many technology companies seems attractive. Why can't more companies be organized this way? What changes might be required to make this happen?

Explore A Sociological Perspective in **MySocLab** and then ...

Think About It

What were the advantages and disadvantages of the work organizations of 50 or 100 years ago when compared to today? Is it better to be a young person entering the world of work without a college degree today than 50 years ago? Why or why not?

Inspire Your Sociological Imagination

Think of a job you have had, or a workplace you know about. What would be required to make that workplace more like the campus-style workplace of high-tech firms (as pictured above, or described in the chapter)? Would workers continue to be productive with dramatically reduced supervision and more control over how they do their jobs?

5 **What Makes a Good Job?**

GOOD JOBS, BAD JOBS, NO JOBS: WORK IN AMERICA

👁 Watch the **Big Question Video** in **MySocLab**

The question of what makes for a good job may seem deceptively simple. Yet we have no clear consensus about how to identify the "best," or "good," jobs in the United States or elsewhere. Holding differences in pay constant, is it better to be a secretary or a truck driver, an insurance claims processer or a cable television installer? And further complicating things is the fact that what is a good job for one person may not be so great for someone else. That said, there are some features of jobs that make them more or less attractive, and in almost all cases having a job is vastly superior to not having a job. In this section we consider some of these issues, as well as compare work in America with work in other similar countries.

How do levels of autonomy and trust relate to job satisfaction?

☐ Work Satisfaction

Although any job can be boring, repetitive, difficult, stressful, or in some cases physically or mentally dangerous, there are also potentially positive aspects of work in almost any organizational setting. Work is a place where you can meet new friends you might not otherwise have met, learn new skills you might not otherwise have, learn more about yourself and what you are good at (or not good at), develop contacts that can help you move up (or move on), or find a lover. Work may sometimes be boring, but the idea that leisure time is always fun and interesting may also be a bit of an exaggeration. Too much leisure time can be boring too. People who are unemployed not only miss a paycheck, but they also

report missing the structure in their daily lives that having a job provides.

For scholars who have devoted significant attention to the question of what makes a job satisfying, there are several aspects of jobs that appear to stand out as especially important features of what makes them "good." Perhaps the most obvious aspect is how well they pay (people almost universally tend to rate jobs as better when they pay more). But beyond the rate of pay, several things stand out: the amount of **autonomy** in a job (that is, how much a particular job allows a worker to control his or her activities); its status; the amount of trust it entails (i.e., how much trust from an employer a job grants the person in the job); the level of skill and the importance of credentials in the job; and the amount of security the job provides (that is, how likely a worker is to be able to stay employed in the job).

The level of autonomy and discretion (or trust) in a job is important because satisfaction in the work performed is invariably lower when every action is tightly controlled or monitored. Having the trust of one's employer (handling secrets, not being monitored or supervised closely by anyone) is invariably associated with greater responsibilities and higher pay. By contrast, in very low-trust workplaces, cameras may monitor workers' every move and the ability to choose when to take a break (or even go to the bathroom!) may be monitored and controlled by someone else. Those in low-trust office environments typically have their access to the Internet severely limited or blocked completely (and if they do have the freedom to use the Internet freely, the websites they log

Workplace authority and productivity are enhanced by trust in organizational leadership.

into may be monitored by their employer). In high-trust occupations, such as in professional occupations (those requiring advanced degrees and certification to practice), or in management positions, people work without much or even any direct supervision. They may be trusted with important responsibilities and company secrets. They are generally able to control the pace of their work efforts: they can go online and read the newspaper or the sports page or plan their evening activities when they choose. For an increasing number of workers, flexibility in when they work is common. Even when individuals in these occupations work long hours—some of the occupations that have people working the longest hours are the most thoroughly professionalized and have the most ostensible autonomy and discretion—these workers often have the freedom to pick and choose how they structure their days and where they fit the extra work hours.

The amount of skill required in a job and the possession of supervisory authority round out the main components of what differentiates jobs from one another. Having authority in the workplace—for example, having one or more subordinates to supervise—is frequently, though not always, associated with making a job more attractive. Supervising others means higher pay and, in many situations, the ability to concentrate on more desirable or challenging work tasks while assigning more routine or less desirable tasks to someone else. The skill required to perform a job is an important part of what provides security and ultimately more pay. Some jobs can be learned in a matter of hours or days. Operating a cash register or making a hamburger at a fast-food restaurant are skills that can be mastered easily and quickly by anyone. As a consequence, an employee in such a job is easily replaceable. By contrast, jobs that require long apprenticeships or educational credentials—such as learning how to be plumber or becoming a lawyer—are far more difficult to achieve, providing a stronger foundation for job security and claims for increased pay. Within job titles, there can, of course, be a vast disparity in pay (compare a partner at a Wall Street law firm versus a lawyer who works by herself taking cases when she can get them). But all in all, the possession of a professional credential like a law degree and experience practicing law affords a higher income, greater status and better working conditions.

Finally, it is hard to be secure in a job when one does not know whether or if one's job will still be there six months or a year from now. Relatively few jobs provide exceptionally high security; these tend to be government jobs, teaching jobs (college professors may even possess tenure, the granting of which provides a guarantee against being fired for almost any reason), and many experienced and in-demand professionals or other people can count on being able to work and earn under virtually any circumstance. The vast majority of jobs, however, provide considerably less security. Small businesses frequently fail, and medium and large firms can also go out of business or lay off large numbers of workers when business declines. There is evidence that in recent years job insecurity has risen; Americans are more likely to have an uneven flow of income from year to year than 30 or 50 years ago (Hacker 2006). Explore the Infographic on page 192 to learn how we measure labor market activity in America.

Comparing Work in America with Similar Countries

How do American workers fare relative to their peers in similar countries? We noted earlier that American workers on average work longer hours and take fewer paid vacations than do workers in other countries. Why might that be the case? And how does the overall mix of jobs in the United States compare to other countries?

Capitalist market economies like the United States can organize work in a variety of different ways, but two factors are especially important: the role of unions and how much (and what kind) of government laws or regulations exist that protect workers in their jobs. Some countries tend to have stronger government regulations and make it easier for employees to create organizations called **unions** (which represent workers as a group in their negotiations with employers), while others let the free market decide more of how work is organized. If we put America on a spectrum comparing it

How does work in America compare to work elsewhere?

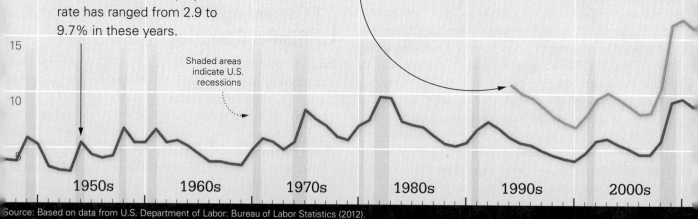

65 percent

60

55

50

45

40

35

30

25

20

15

10

― Unemployment

Since 1947, the federal government has measured unemployment each month by asking a large sample of Americans (in the Current Population Survey) whether in the past week they were working, out of work but looking for a job, or out of work and not looking for a job. **The unemployment rate is officially defined as the percentage of respondents who were out of work and looking for work.** Using this definition, the unemployment rate has ranged from 2.9 to 9.7% in these years.

― Underemployment

But what about people who want a job but are not actively looking for work because they have grown too frustrated to look, or people who work part-time but want a full-time job? Since 1994, the government has asked further questions to get a fuller measurement of total unemployment. This figure, compared to the first figure, shows a much higher level of unemployment, at times reaching almost 17 percent.

Ratio of employed to employable population

Another way to think about employment and unemployment is to look at the ratio of employed people to the entire population in prime working years (defined as ages 25-54). Since 1947, the percentage of Americans with a job rose steadily, falling during periods of recession (highlighted by the gray bars). But the recent recession has shown a rapid and unprecedented fall, and no real recovery, since 2008.

Shaded areas indicate U.S. recessions

1950s   1960s   1970s   1980s   1990s   2000s

Source: Based on data from U.S. Department of Labor: Bureau of Labor Statistics (2012).

Explore the Data on Measuring Labor Market Activity in **MySocLab** and then . . .

Think About It

Americans are increasingly supporting themselves by cobbling together two or more part-time jobs. How might the rewards of holding multiple jobs be different than holding one full-time job? Should we consider these multiple job holders underemployed if they are working an average of 40 or more hours per week?

Inspire Your Sociological Imagination

While the overall percentage of individuals employed is greater now than in the 1950s, this is largely because more women are in the labor force today. The percentage of men who are neither employed nor looking for work is higher today than in earlier decades. How have societal norms changed that make it increasingly acceptable for men not to be in the labor market?

to other advanced economies, it would be on the far end with fewer government regulations of employment and a relatively weaker labor movement to negotiate with employers over the conditions of work (see Figure 7.4).

What are the consequences of these two factors? Unions do many things such as providing workers with the power to negotiate more effectively with their employers, but they also help monitor and protect working conditions. Unions in America have been going through a precipitous decline in recent years. Measured as a proportion of the workforce that is organized into unions, unionization rates reached their peak in the 1950s when nearly 35 percent of the workforce was organized into unions. By 2010, just a little more than 10 percent of the workforce was protected by a union.

With the decline of unions, many large American companies have been free to develop a strategy of trying to compete in a competitive global marketplace through the development of company policies known as **lean production**. The main aim of lean production, from the perspective of management, is to continually identify and constantly reduce the costs of production. Some of this has involved the introduction of new technologies; some of it has involved reducing waste in the production process. Neither of these kinds of developments are necessarily bad (or good) for workers. But another side of lean production has been more consistently harmful to workers: the elimination of job perks and forms of security that workers once took for granted. Most commonly, this means doing away with many of the perks of a job that once were provided (including in recent years health and pension benefits), but in extreme cases it may even include things like regular breaks, a set work schedule, and job security. Employers often find that they can shave costs by eliminating the traditional nine-to-five job that was customary in the twentieth century, replacing full-time workers with part-timers who may accept lower wages and no (or few) benefits. Part-time work is often beneficial to employers because it cuts costs in terms of wages and fringe benefits, as the workers often do not qualify for benefits such as health care and pensions. The shift toward part-time work and temporary work can be seen in Figure 7.5. In 2000, almost one in five employees in the United States worked part time. And since 1970, most of the growth in part-time work has occurred among employees who would prefer to work full time (Kalleberg 2000). While the aims of employers to cut costs accounts for much of this increase in part-time work, so does the expansion of industries that tend to rely more on part-time work. Since the 1970s, the service, retail, and finance industries have taken up a larger share of the workforce, while manufacturing has declined.

Second, there has been a significant increase in outsourcing over the past 30 years, which is continuing right up to the present. **Outsourcing** occurs when firms turn over

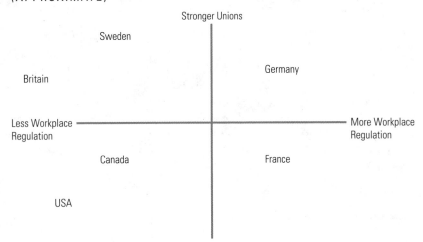

FIGURE 7.4 CROSS-NATIONAL COMPARISON OF WORKPLACE REGULATION AND UNION STRENGTH (APPROXIMATE)

the execution of tasks such as payroll, administration, janitorial services, and food services to third parties. One common type of outsourcing occurs when a company or an organization (including state, local, and federal governments) concludes that it can save money by firing some of its current workers and hiring a private contractor to perform the same job (while paying its workers lower wages and benefits than the larger organization was providing).

The last important point to note is that American workers are heavily dependent on their employers for nonwage needs. Consider healthcare and retirement. While both have dimensions that are public, relative to other advanced capitalist countries American workers are much more reliant on their jobs for health and retirement benefits. In 2005, expenditures on occupational social programs accounted for 10.1 percent of gross domestic product, far above the Organization for Economic Cooperation and Development (OECD) average of 2.9 percent. What drives this difference is that many Americans secure health care and retirement benefits through their work. One result is that some Americans do not have any healthcare at all. In 2008, over 47 million U.S. citizens had none, and even more are underinsured. Between 2007 and 2008, 86.7 million Americans were uninsured at some point. A system that relies on employer-provided healthcare has many pitfalls, especially because employers are not forced to provide healthcare to their employees.

Retirement benefits are a similar story. Almost half of the retirement income received by individual workers when they retire comes from private savings accounts and employer pension plans of one kind or another, far above the average of other rich countries (which is closer to 20 percent). In the more typical case, public pensions (like the Social Security system in the United States) provide a much higher amount of the income a worker received while working. For many decades after World War II, workers were able to count on pension plans offered by their employers that were based on the amount of time they

FIGURE 7.5 INCREASING INVOLUNTARY PART-TIME EMPLOYMENT IN THE UNITED STATES

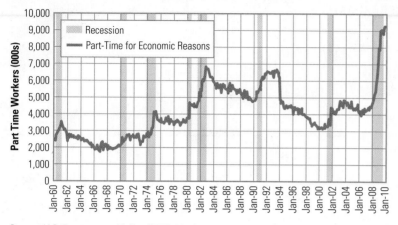

Source: U.S. Department of Labor. (2008; 2012).

had worked for the company. Since the 1980s, particularly as unions have declined, employers are increasingly abandoning those plans in favor of less generous retirement programs like 401(k) savings plans. Unlike the older plans, the employer is not obligated to provide a base amount of retirement income. Instead, in these plans the employer contributes to a fund for the employee, but it is up to the worker to contribute to the fund as well. For high-income workers, contributing to a retirement account is relatively easy, but for workers whose earnings are low this is often difficult or impossible.

All of this amounts to a work context where, relatively speaking, employees in America have less power than workers in other countries. The most significant alternative to the American system of work is what is sometimes called the **social democratic model**, typically associated with countries in Northern Europe. Social democratic countries spend far more on social programs to help the poor and the unemployed than in the United States, and they also provide health insurance and retirement benefits that are not so closely linked to someone's job. Social democratic countries also typically provide much more protection for workers in their jobs; it is harder to fire someone, workers have more protections against mistreatment from their employers, and they have more paid vacation time and paid leave when they have a child than American workers (Pontusson 2005).

The strong regulation of most jobs in Europe has proved, however, to be something of a double-edged sword. Employers may be more reluctant to hire workers when they know they cannot fire them very easily and when they have to pay higher taxes for their workers' pension and health benefits than in the United States. This has also encouraged companies in Europe to hire workers on a temporary basis without full social benefits, creating a new division between full-time employees who enjoy world-class benefits and vacations and a growing temporary and contingent workforce that does not. Whether these trends will deepen is now one of the most pressing questions facing European politicians and policymakers (Castles 2004).

CONCLUSION MARKETS, ORGANIZATIONS, AND WORK IN THE TWENTY-FIRST CENTURY

Using a sociological imagination to examine the interrelationships between markets, organizations, and work, we have noted throughout this chapter many ways in which rapid change now appears to be underway in the rich, developed countries like the United States. We began by noting how market forces appear to be penetrating many arenas of social life that were once handled by individuals, families, churches, or other social organizations. Markets are also growing into arenas that governments once held monopolies on.

Work and organizations are not immune to these pressures and are changing as well. Although the vast majority of organizations still seek to maintain compliance from the top down to the bottom, there are emerging counterexamples of a growing number of organizations. These organizations have viewed what we have called loose coupling—the weakening of the relationship between executives at the top and the rest of the firm—as a strength, not a weakness. At the center of this alternative type of organization is the idea that bureaucracies tend to stifle creativity and that it is better to create organizations where members share tasks and responsibilities, and all participate in management to some extent. Further, work teams operating independently of one another may come up with innovations more rapidly than the classical bureaucratic firm. Some of the most common examples can be found in the high-tech sector. At firms like Google, Facebook, and many start-up companies, instead of a chain of command there are often a bunch of different work teams, typically with about three to seven members, who work together on various projects. No one member of the team is irreplaceable, and the team takes advantage of its collective intelligence. The team has to report to higher management, and at some point if nothing is accomplished the team is broken up and members are reassigned to other, more productive units.

This does not mean that all of the insights of organizational theory that we have discussed in this chapter are going out the window. Quite the contrary: The pressures to emulate one another—what sociologists call isomorphism—appear to be driving some of the ongoing changes in work and organizational forms we have observed. For example, when one company or organization figures out how to cut its costs or implement a new style of workplace organization, other firms study that change and may implement it. Change is happening, but not in a random way. Whether these changes, alongside the growing penetration of markets into new arenas of society, will make life better or worse remains to be seen.

Watch the Video in MySocLab
Applying Your Sociological Imagination

Study and **Review** in MySocLab   **Watch** the **Video** Inspiring Your Sociological Imagination in MySocLab

---

 1

How Do Social Factors Impact Markets?
(p. 174)

 Watch the **Big Question Video** in MySocLab to review the key concepts for this section.

We live in what is sometimes called the "age of the market," and sociologists are increasingly aware that markets are part of the social structure of society. In this section, we explored how a sociological understanding of markets differs from an economic understanding.

THE CREATION AND FUNCTIONING OF MARKETS (p. 174)

Defining Markets (p. 175)

- **How do sociologists define markets differently than economists?**

Three Key Social Factors in Markets: Networks, Power, and Culture (p. 176)

- **How do networks, power, and culture impact markets?**

KEY TERMS

market *(p. 174)*

captialism *(p. 174)*

socialism *(p. 174)*

central planning *(p. 174)*

entrepreneur *(p. 174)*

rational choice perspective *(p. 175)*

social network *(p. 176)*

 2

Why Are Organizations Important for Social and Economic Life? *(p. 178)*

 Watch the **Big Question Video** in MySocLab to review the key concepts for this section.

To gain a deeper understanding of how modern economies work—and ultimately how social forces influence the economy as a whole—sociologists place considerable importance on analyzing the organizations that exist within markets, a topic explored in this section.

ORGANIZATIONS IN THE MODERN WORLD (p. 178)

Organizational Persistence (p. 178)

- **Why do organizations persist?**

From Start-Up to Bureaucratic Firm: The Case of Apple (p. 179)

The Downside of Bureaucracy (p. 180)

- **Why are decisions difficult in bureaucratic organizations?**

KEY TERMS

organizations *(p. 179)*

bureaucracy *(p. 179)*

garbage-can model *(p. 181)*

loose coupling *(p. 181)*

3 What is the Relationship between Organizations and Their Environment? *(p. 182)*

Watch the **Big Question Video** in **MySocLab** to review the key concepts for this section.

In this section we explored the relationship between organizations and their environment. Do organizations actually adapt to their environments, or do the organizations that survive do so because they were uniquely suited to the environment from the start?

ORGANIZATIONS AND THEIR ENVIRONMENTS (p. 182)

Organizational Structure (p. 183)

- **How can an organization's structure help or hurt its chances for survival?**

Organizational Similarity (p. 184)

- **Why would an organization change to be more similar to others in its field?**

4 How Are Jobs Structured? *(p. 185)*

Watch the **Big Question Video** in **MySocLab** to review the key concepts for this section.

In modern societies jobs are specialized and have distinct labor processes associated with them. In this section we examined various theories about job specialization and the management of the labor process.

THE DIVISION OF LABOR IN MODERN SOCIETIES (p. 185)

Increasing Specialization in the Division of Labor (p. 186)

- **How is work organized in modern workplaces?**

The Labor Process (p. 187)

- **What forces have shaped the labor process?**

Explore A Sociological Perspective: How have work organizations changed? in **MySocLab**

Read the **Document** *Hanging Tongues: A Social Encounter with the Assembly Line* by William E. Thompson in **MySocLab.** This reading chronicles the author's experiences working in a Midwest beef processing plant. Using participant observation, he explains how workers interact, cope, and maintain a sense of self-worth while doing one of society's "dirty" jobs.

5 What Makes a Good Job? *(p. 190)*

Watch the **Big Question Video** in **MySocLab** to review the key concepts for this section.

A good job for one person may not be such a good job for someone else. In this section we examined what constitutes a good job in America and how American workers fare relative to their peers in similar countries.

GOOD JOBS, BAD JOBS, NO JOBS: WORK IN AMERICA (p. 190)

Work Satisfaction (p. 190)

- **How do levels of autonomy and trust relate to job satisfaction?**

Explore the **Data** on Measuring Labor Market Activity in **MySocLab**

Comparing Work in America with Similar Countries (p. 191)

- **How does work in America compare to work elsewhere?**

Watch the **Video** Applying Your Sociological Imagination in **MySocLab** to see these concepts at work in the real world

KEY TERMS

autonomy *(p. 190)*

union *(p. 191)*

lean production *(p. 193)*

outsourcing *(p. 193)*

social democratic model *(p. 194)*

8
CITIES and COMMUNITIES

(((Listen to the **Chapter Audio** in **MySocLab**

by PATRICK SHARKEY
with MAX BESBRIS

A few years ago, the *New York Times* published a map showing the location of every incident of homicide occurring in New York City from 2003 to 2009 (see Figure 8.1). Even during a time when violent crime was dropping rapidly, the number of blue dots covering the five boroughs of New York City provides a sense of how common this most extreme form of violence is. While violence is often thought of as a social problem related to poverty, policing, and the criminal justice system, in cities like New York the sheer volume of deaths due to homicide makes it an urgent public health problem.

At the same time, there are several features of homicide that make it unlike virtually every other major public health burden. The first is that homicide targets young people. Whereas cancer and heart disease are the leading causes of death among older adults, in New York and many other cities across the country, homicide is the leading cause of death among older adolescents and young adults—often by a wide margin.

Yet homicide is not spread evenly across the population of young people. Take a moment to view the map in Figure 8.1 of homicides from one year to the next, and you will notice how similar the spatial pattern of violence looks over time. In many neighborhoods of New York City, one of the most densely packed urban areas in the world, there are almost no homicides. But in some neighborhoods of Brooklyn, the Harlem section of Manhattan, and the South Bronx, there is a consistent concentration of extreme violence. The neighborhoods where violence is concentrated are also some of the poorest, most racially segregated neighborhoods in the city, a pattern that is present in most urban areas across the country.

An additional unique feature of homicide, one that I study in my research and that distinguishes it from most other diseases and

MY SOCIOLOGICAL IMAGINATION
Patrick Sharkey

My research focuses on the way that places—meaning the environments surrounding individuals, from the residential block to the town or city in which they live—affect the life chances of individuals and groups in the United States. Much of my work looks at multiple generations of American families and analyzes the degree of inequality in families' neighborhood environments over long periods of time and the consequences of living in persistently poor or disadvantaged neighborhood environments over multiple generations. A more recent strand of my research focuses more closely on the specific ways that living in a poor neighborhood may affect the day-to-day lives of children, with particular attention paid to the way that violence and other stressors in children's environments "get into the minds" of children to affect their behavior, their health, and their academic performance.

A group of young people examine the victim of drug related violence in one of Rio de Janeiro's notorious *favelas*, or slums. Cities are often thought of as sites of violence and disillusionment and we will see why throughout this chapter.

Watch the **Video** in **MySocLab**
Inspiring Your Sociological Imagination

causes of death, is that the effects of homicides are not limited to the victims of lethal violence. In a recent study, I found that children who are given a standard assessment of reading and vocabulary skills perform substantially worse if they are assessed in the days following a local homicide that occurs in their neighborhood (Sharkey 2010). In other words, local violence does not just affect those who are there to witness it but "gets into the minds" of youth throughout the community.

How is it that a homicide a few blocks away might affect the performance of a child who did not know the victim, and did not witness the event, on a basic test of reading and language skills? We are still figuring out the precise answer to this question, but extensive research demonstrates that stress arising from community violence can cause anxiety, disrupt sleep, and reduce children's ability to concentrate and focus (Osofsky 1999). If the shock of a single homicide affects children's behavior and performance so drastically, what is it like to live in one of the neighborhoods in which those blue dots on the map, each representing a homicide, are so tightly clustered together?

The study of homicide sheds light on the way that different aspects of communities, such as the presence or absence of violence, can alter the experiences and opportunities of individual residents, often reinforcing patterns of inequality in society as a whole. But it is not just homicide that is concentrated in space, prevalent in some neighborhoods and absent in others. There are many social phenomena that are clustered together in space, and much of our social world is organized by geography. Where you live plays a central role in influencing where you go to school, with whom you interact, and what types of institutions surround you. The fact that public schools are typically organized and partially funded by residential districts means that the quality of a child's educational opportunities depends, in large part, on that child's address. Research tells us that residents of poor and segregated neighborhoods have less political influence than residents of neighborhoods with more racial and economic diversity (Cohen and Dawson 1993). A great deal of evidence indicates that the geographic locations of jobs and

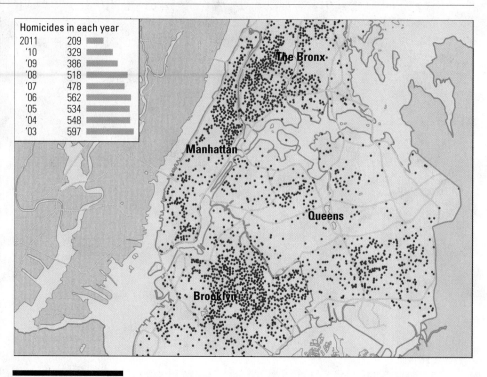

Homicides in each year	
2011	209
'10	329
'09	386
'08	518
'07	478
'06	562
'05	534
'04	548
'03	597

FIGURE 8.1 MURDER IN NEW YORK CITY This figure shows the spatial distribution of murders in New York City. Why are some parts of the city murder-free?

industry have important influences on the likelihood that individuals will be able to find and maintain steady employment (Holzer 1991). In a similar way, the quality of public attractions like parks and recreation centers, the effectiveness of institutions such as the police, and the degree of exposure to toxic soil and clean air all depend directly on where we live.

For all of these reasons, the environments that surround us have important implications for our lives and our life chances. But to understand why violence is so concentrated, why school quality varies so dramatically, or why toxins are so prevalent in some communities, we have to take a step back and attempt to understand how cities and communities in the United States and elsewhere are formed and change over time.

In this chapter, we will examine not only how the world became urban but what it means to *live* in an urban world. We will consider the new opportunities and some of the major social problems—like concentrated poverty and segregation—that can result from urbanization. As the chapter closes, we widen our view to look at the way in which cities are connected across the world through immigration, communication, and transnational business. By moving from local communities to worldwide connections, we are able to learn a tremendous amount about the structure of our society.

> **There are many social phenomena that are clustered together in space, and much of our social world is organized by geography.**

THE BIG QUESTIONS

👁 **Watch** the **Big Question Videos** in **MySocLab**

Sociologists have struggled for more than a century to understand how cities and communities form and how they affect social life, and our discussion of these issues is guided by exploring the following five big questions:

What draws people to cities? Most of the human population now lives in urban areas. This basic fact is important because it raises a number of intriguing questions about how to define what a city is and how city life has affected different aspects of our individual lives. These questions will be explored throughout the chapter. As we will learn, a sociological understanding of cities is more complex than the "official" definitions provided by government agencies.

How do neighborhoods form and change? The development of cities and communities is not natural but rather is driven by political and economic forces. Individuals and groups with different, sometimes competing interests struggle to build communities in very different ways. Patterns of change over time can be seen as the product of these struggles. The types of communities that have emerged over time are dramatically diverse.

Does living in cities influence who we are, who our friends are, and how we live? Cities are distinguished not only by their size, density, or other measurable characteristics but by how they affect the way we interact, work, and live together.

Why are so many social problems found in cities? Cities have increasingly become the sites of the world's most extreme wealth and poverty. Urban areas have always been great engines of wealth creation, but a growing proportion of the world's poverty is now moving from undeveloped, rural areas into densely populated urban slums.

How will cities change in an increasingly connected world? Cities link the world together. To fully comprehend the forces that shape our world, we must expand our view well beyond individual city streets and communities, and even beyond the boundaries of individual nations.

1 What Draws People to Cities?

HOW THE WORLD BECAME URBAN

👁 Watch the **Big Question Video** in **MySocLab**

For the first time in human history, more than half of the world's population lives in urban areas (United Nations 2010). This statement, which is based on estimates from the United Nations, raises a basic yet important question: Just what does it mean to be *urban*? As it turns out, this is a difficult question to answer. In the United States, the Census Bureau classifies **urban areas** as areas with a population density of at least 1,000 people per square mile, plus all surrounding areas that have an overall density of at least 500 people per square mile (U.S. Census Bureau 2009). Everything else—meaning all areas that are less dense and that are not adjacent to an urbanized region—is classified as *rural*. Whereas the official definition in the United States is based on density, the United Nations does not have a standard definition, instead relying on each nation to define urban areas on its own. What it means to be urban is clearly not a settled issue.

Regardless of how imprecise the UN estimates are, they reveal an unmistakable trend: Our world is becoming increasingly urbanized. Sociologists have long been interested in the process of **urbanization**, meaning the growth in the proportion of the population living in cities and urban areas. Unlike the definition used by the Census Bureau, however, a sociological perspective on cities does not end with quantitative descriptions of places nor with figures on the geographic concentration of people, the movement of people across places, or the size of cities and towns. In addition to describing how cities and communities form and change, a sociological perspective focuses on how these and other dimensions of places affect the way that people interact with

each other, how they form friendship ties and communities, where and how they work and produce goods, and how they generate culture and subcultures.

We will consider many different ideas about what a city is and what it does in this chapter. Before we get there, however, let us first consider a more basic question: How did our world come to be dominated by cities?

☐ Urbanization and the Growth of Cities

The last few centuries of human history have been marked by the movement of the population from the country to the city. Sociologist and demographer Kingsley Davis (1965) argued that, in the modern world, the process of urbanization follows an "S curve" whose shape is driven by the timing of industrialization. According to this model, which is illustrated in Figure 8.2, before the emergence of widespread industry, the pace of urbanization is slow and gradual—this is the long tail at the bottom of the S. With the onset of industrialization, cities grow rapidly as large segments of the population move from rural areas to urban areas, drawn by plentiful jobs in the city and technological advances that reduce demand for labor in rural areas—this is the steep, upward slope of the S. After cities reach their carrying capacity, demand for labor subsides, the cost of urban space rises, and cities may become overcrowded. As a result, migration into the city slows and the pace of urbanization levels off; this is the flat top of the S.

The cities that have emerged from this process of urbanization are very different from those that were present before the age of industry. Cities first arose over 5,000 years ago, but they were small, poorly connected enclaves that lost population just as easily as they gained it. Often surrounded by a wall for defense and occupying somewhere between a few thousand and more than one hundred thousand residents, these city-states usually functioned as trading centers and the capitals of empires. They were centers of culture and commerce, but they were not built for growth—for instance, while the overall population of Europe increased from the eleventh century to the nineteenth century, the proportion of the population that was urban remained roughly the same. This meant that life for the vast majority of the population occurred in rural, sparsely populated, agricultural settings where interactions between strangers were rare and day-to-day life focused on producing immediate sustenance.

Industrialization changed all that. Britain, which was the first nation to industrialize, experienced rapid urbanization from 1800 to 1900, with continental Europe and the United States (and eventually much of the rest of the world) not far behind. The main cause of population growth in cities was not higher birth rates compared to rural areas but rather migration: the movement of people from the country to the city. England's cities grew as its population was drawn away from rural areas, where agriculture was becoming more and more mechanized. The population moved toward its cities, where factories were sprouting up, requiring less land than farms and more manual labor to make them run.

One of the best examples of the urbanization process can be found in the **Great Migration** of African Americans from the rural South to the industrial cities of the Northeast and Midwest United States. In 1900, there were only a few hundred thousand African Americans who were born in the South and had migrated out in their lifetimes; by 1980, there were over 4 million (Tolnay 2003). In the city of Detroit alone, the population of African Americans grew from just over 4,000 in 1900 to about 24,000 in 1920, over 350,000 in 1950, and over 750,000 by 1970 (Farley, Danziger, and Holzer 2000). The individuals and families that migrated out of the South were driven by declining agricultural opportunities, which were amplified by the severity of racial discrimination and racial inequality. They were pulled northward, and later westward, by the intense demand for workers in the new factories of Northeastern, Midwestern, and Western cities. But they were also pulled by the emergence of African American cultural institutions in Northern cities and by the hope that racism would be less severe outside of the South (Lemann 1991).

The sheer magnitude of this shift in population altered the demographic, economic, and cultural landscapes of cities throughout the Northeast, Midwest, and West. On the one hand, African Americans did have new opportunities for economic mobility outside of the South, and black culture flourished in cities throughout the Northeast and Midwest.

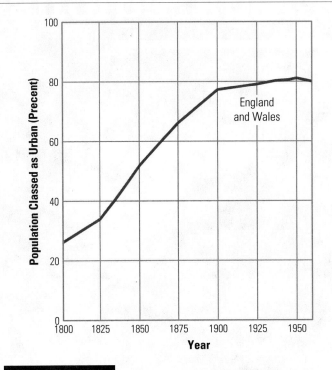

FIGURE 8.2 ENGLAND AND WALES AREA POPULATION
The "S curve" of population growth during industrialization, 1800–1960, in England and Wales.

Source: Davis (1965).

On the other hand, the growth of the black population in Northern cities was met with informal and formal efforts designed to maintain the "color line" in urban neighborhoods and schools. Racial segregation became a severe problem in cities throughout the country and has continued to be a problem ever since. We will examine the emergence of social problems associated with the ghettos that arose in many such cities later in the chapter.

Urban, Suburban, and Rural Patterns of Settlement

As the world's population continues to urbanize, the boundaries separating cities from towns, and from other cities, have become less clear. Several new urban forms have appeared in the United States and elsewhere, including a crop of **conurbs**, which are defined as continuous urban regions extending across city and suburban political boundaries. Examples in the United States include places like Dallas/Fort Worth or Seattle/Tacoma, where the airports are often named after the two cities. **Megacities**, cities with populations of over 10 million people, like Mexico City and Lagos, Nigeria, are another recent phenomenon that has emerged throughout the world, with several in China alone. These new urban forms are often embedded in a larger **megaregion**, where

What major forces have led to urbanization?

Megaregions

Boston-Washington Corridor
54 million

Chigago-Pittsburgh
46 million

London-Leeds-Chester
50 million

Amsterdam-Brussels-Antwerp
50 million

Delhi-Lahore
121 million

Greater Tokyo
55 million

Hong Kong-Shenzen
121 million

Osaka-Nagoya
36 million

Rio de Janeiro-Sao Paulo
43 million

Many of the world's largest cities are growing at incredible rates and merging to form vast megaregions. Megaregions are characterized by large populations and significant economic activity. These vastly populated areas are defined by the individual cities they encompass and the relationships that form between them.

POPULATIONS OF MEGAREGIONS AROUND THE WORLD

Sources: Based on data from Florida, Gulden, and Mellander (2007); UN-HABITAT (2010).

40 megaregions

in the world each boast
economies of
$100 billion

or more . . .

Less than
20%
of the world's population resides in megaregions.

Megaregions produce
2/3s
of the earth's economic output.

9 out of 10 innovations come from megaregions.

◉ Explore the Data on Megaregions in **MySocLab** and then . . .

■ Think About It
Megaregions are hubs for innovation and they attract talent from around the world. However, many living in these areas face poverty and other serious problems. What factors do you think might contribute to inequalities in megaregions?

■ Inspire Your Sociological Imagination
9 out of 10 innovations originate in megaregions. Think about which products and systems you utilize that may have originated in a megaregion. Do you think those products could have been produced outside of the megaregions? What challenges to innovation exist outside megaregions?

Once a largely rural area, the San Fernando Valley was quickly suburbanized in the 1930s. What other suburbs in the United States may have followed a similar trajectory?

two or more large cities in geographical proximity are linked together through infrastructure and through economic activity (Gottman 1966). Megaregions include areas like the Northeast corridor of the United States. This region, stretching from Boston, through New York City, Philadelphia, and Baltimore, to Washington, D.C., is continuous, contains almost 50 million inhabitants, and produces over $2.5 trillion of economic output annually (Short 2007). It is estimated that over 20 percent of the human population is concentrated in 40 megaregions across the world, with the largest in rapidly developing countries like India and China (Florida 2008). Explore the Infographic on page 204 to learn more about megaregions.

The new scale of urban areas creates challenges that will not necessarily be solved at the neighborhood or city levels. Issues like water treatment, transportation, and the provision of housing and social services now transcend the official borders of cities, requiring coordination among localities that are often in competition with each other for residents and businesses. Addressing these border-transcending concerns is especially important in the United States, where local governments have a great deal of decision-making power (Downs 1994).

It is not just densely populated urban areas that have seen major changes over the last 100 years. Traditional **suburbs**, areas within metropolitan regions but outside the political boundaries of central cities, have also seen a great transformation. Before the twentieth century, suburbs were not densely populated and specialized in trade rather than agriculture (Baldassare 1992). With increases in commuter railways and steadily rising car ownership, so-called "bedroom communities," where workers lived but did not work, began to form around major urban areas in the late nineteenth century. As urban areas grew, these suburbs were often formally incorporated into the city, with new suburban communities created further out.

An example of the processes of change in suburban areas can be found in Southern California's San Fernando

What urban and suburban forms emerged during the twentieth century?

Valley, located directly north of the Los Angeles Basin. In the early 1900s, the Valley was a mostly rural mass of land where wealthier Los Angelenos built country homes on the border with the city. As development increased, the city of Los Angeles, pushed by a number of prominent businessmen, annexed more and more of the Valley. By the late 1930s, most of the Valley had been incorporated into the city.

As the century continued, the pace of suburbanization quickened, fostered by government subsidies for car and home ownership and highway construction. In the Northeast, Midwest, and later in the West, suburbanization was also driven by **white flight**, which refers to the movement of white families out of central cities and into the suburbs, a pattern typically driven by changing demographics of cities experiencing an influx of African Americans or other racial and ethnic minorities. The San Fernando Valley again provides a prototypical example of this process, as the Valley became a destination suburb for whites who left Los Angeles as blacks and Latinos moved into the city's South and East sides.

The term *white flight* brings to mind issues surrounding racial conflict and tension within America's cities. What is frequently overlooked are the ways the federal government facilitated, and in fact subsidized, the exodus of whites from central cities. Since the 1930s, the government has played a central role in supporting home ownership by guaranteeing or providing mortgages directly (Massey and Denton 1993). Instead of using its role in the home mortgage industry to promote homeownership for all groups,

Edge cities like Tysons Corner, Virginia, are often located at the junction of major freeways just outside major cities.

the federal government adopted a set of standards to rank the riskiness of potential loans. Homes in racially homogeneous white neighborhoods were ranked highest, while homes in primarily black or racially mixed neighborhoods were ranked lowest and were typically ineligible for investment. The practice of **redlining** emerged from the system used to determine areas ineligible for loans—predominantly black or racially mixed communities were literally outlined in red on maps to signify that they had received the lowest rankings and were thus ineligible for loans. This practice spread throughout the banking industry; even after World War II, the Federal Housing Administration discouraged loans to racial minorities and prohibited loans that would lead to racially or economically integrated neighborhoods. Home ownership, especially in the suburbs, was largely restricted to whites.

Over time, America's suburbs have become more diverse as African Americans have increasingly moved into the suburbs and more recent immigration streams have increased the number of Asians and Latinos as well. In the San Fernando Valley, for instance, whites are no longer the majority of the population. However, racial and class segregation remains high in most American suburbs, and suburban poverty continues to grow (Holliday and Dwyer 2009). As the number of Americans living in the suburbs has grown, the boundaries of suburbs have stretched further and further away from central cities, a process known as **suburban sprawl**. With growing concern about damage to the environment, increasing traffic congestion, and growing commutes, new forms of settlement have arisen as alternatives to, or new versions of, the traditional suburb.

One example is the **edge city**, which has emerged as a new urban form on the periphery of large urban centers (Garreau 1991). Edge cities are self-contained worlds typically located at the junctions of major freeways and featuring business and social and cultural spaces condensed into a small geographical area. Edge cities like Valencia, California (about 30 miles north of downtown Los Angeles), or Tysons Corner, Virginia (about 20 miles west of Washington, D.C.), have developed as suburban counterparts to the traditional downtown areas of large central cities. Instead of individuals commuting from the suburbs to central business districts to do their shopping, seek entertainment, or go to work, edge

cities concentrate all of these activities in places that were often undeveloped just a few decades prior. What is unique about edge cities is the fact that they contain many of the traditional attractions of downtown areas, but not very many people actually live within them. Commuters arrive to work in the office parks and to shop in the malls, but at the end of the day they depart and head elsewhere.

Because edge cities generally are not well served by public transportation, mobility into and out of the edge city requires a car. This dependency on cars has meant that the emergence of edge cities is a phenomenon unique to the United States—until recently, that is. The growth of automobile ownership in developing nations like China, India, and countries in the Middle East has led to a steep increase in the number of edge cities in other parts of the world.

As cities and the suburbs around them have changed, so too have the nation's rural areas. Residents of America's rural areas are no longer isolated from urban life, as even traditionally rural states like Nebraska are increasingly urban. More than half of Nebraska's population is clustered in 3, out of 93, counties. Unsurprisingly, these three counties contain the state's three largest cities (Sulzbergur 2011). Large agriculture companies farm huge swaths of land in places as diverse as Iowa's cornfields and California's central valley, and their need for low-wage labor has attracted an increasingly diverse population to nonmetropolitan areas around the country. Over the past several decades, Latinos and Asians have been the fastest growing ethnic groups in rural America, posing a new set of questions for sociologists to consider: How does ethnic diversity change the cultural landscape of rural areas? How does cultural assimilation in rural areas differ from assimilation in cities? For researchers who have studied ethnic diversity and immigration in mainly urban settings, these questions will become increasingly important as new immigrant groups spread out beyond the cities that have traditionally been the ports of entry to the United States.

2 How Do Neighborhoods Form and Change?

NEIGHBORHOODS AND URBAN CHANGE

👁 Watch the **Big Question** Video in **MySocLab**

Up to this point we have focused on the forces that lead to urbanization and the emergence of new types of suburban and urban forms. We now turn to a different set of questions about the internal dynamics of cities: Why do cities come to look the way they do? How do neighborhoods form within cities, and how are a city's residents, resources, and institutions distributed across space? How and why do communities change over time?

Urban Ecology: The Chicago School

These were some of the central questions confronted by a group of sociologists associated with the University of Chicago in the early part of the twentieth century, known collectively as the "Chicago School" of urban sociology. Using the city of Chicago as a laboratory, the ideas of the Chicago School on urbanism, urban forms, and urban change have been extremely influential to the discipline, even though some of these ideas have been challenged or dismissed outright in the years since they were written.

One of the central ideas in early Chicago School writings is that the form of cities can be understood as the result of a process in which different segments of the population sort themselves into the areas of the city in which they thrive—a perspective referred to as **urban ecology**. This perspective, laid out most clearly in the work of Robert Park and Ernest Burgess, borrowed from biology the idea that organisms adjust to their surroundings and find the best fit within their environment. The urban ecology approach was used to explain the formation of different types of areas based on their role or

What is urban ecology?

function within the city, as well as the sorting of individuals and groups into the areas that provided the best "fit." For example, immigrants may cluster in certain areas within the city because they can interact with other people and with institutions that share their culture and history. Over time, assimilation occurs as individual members of the group begin to interact with more and more individuals from other ethnic groups and begin to integrate with the wider culture and the wider economy, identifying less with the culture of their homeland. Boston's North End neighborhood provides a good example of this process, as it experienced an influx of Italian immigrants who came to work in the city's ports in the mid- to late-1800s. Over time, these immigrants and their descendants moved into other businesses and into other parts of the city, becoming more integrated into the wider social and economic life of Boston.

This example shows how the social and economic integration of different groups within the city relates directly to the form and spatial layout of the city's neighborhoods. Hanging to this day in the seminar room of the University of Chicago's Sociology Department is a hand-drawn figure mapping out Burgess's "concentric zone" model of urban community structure (see Figure 8.3). Burgess saw cities as a series of rings spreading out from the center of the city, which he identified as the central business district (CBD), or "The Loop" in Burgess's map of Chicago. The CBD was seen as the eye of the metropolis, where the majority of business, high-end shopping, and high culture (museums and symphonies) were located. This was no accident, according to Burgess. Retailers pay the most for land that provides access to the greatest number of customers, while manufacturing—located in the zone that surrounds the CBD—does not rely on heavy pedestrian foot traffic and only requires accessibility to commuting workers. Surrounding the "factory zone" was a "zone of transition," which featured low-quality housing for newly arrived immigrants and the poor. As individuals assimilated or moved upward into the working and middle classes, Burgess's model suggests that they moved *outward* into residential areas with higher-quality housing and into "commuter zones" for the wealthy, who were willing to pay more for space and separation from urban life (Park and Burgess [1925] 1967).

Burgess's model has been criticized as far too rigid, failing to account for variation in the spatial structure of cities outside of the Northeast and Midwest—not to mention cities outside of the United States. With the growth of elaborate highway systems and communication technology, the model has become less relevant over time. Even as a description of Chicago in the first half of the 1900s, however, the idea of integration and assimilation as "natural" processes that lead to the sorting of groups into different sections of the city has been shown to be incomplete. For instance, research on Chicago's African American community in the early part of the twentieth century suggests that the boundaries surrounding this section of the city would more appropriately be described as solid barriers instead of permeable "zones of transition." While other ethnic groups may become socially and spatially integrated over time, the informal and formal policies used to restrict African Americans to one particular area of the city meant that the black community remained separate from the city's larger economic, social, educational, and political life— occupying a "city within a city" (Drake and Cayton 1945).

The Political Economy of Cities and Communities

A more general critique of the urban ecology perspective is that it fails to consider the role of political and economic forces that affect the development of cities. More recent research calls our attention to the active ways that local government officials and private investors drive politics in pursuit of one outcome: growth. From this perspective, the city can be understood as a **growth machine**, where investors and governments work to increase the size of the city's population and the level of economic activity occurring within it (Logan and Molotch 1987). The growth of cities and regions provides retailers with more business, newspaper editors with wider readerships, and university campuses with larger applicant pools. Growth also provides local governments with a larger tax base and greater ability to request funding from state and federal governments.

In the pursuit of growth, local governments regulate the use and distribution of land within the city through the establishment of taxation rates, through policing and the protection of private property, through the city's responses to the demands of different groups of citizens or their representatives, and through the regulation of utilities and transportation. In all

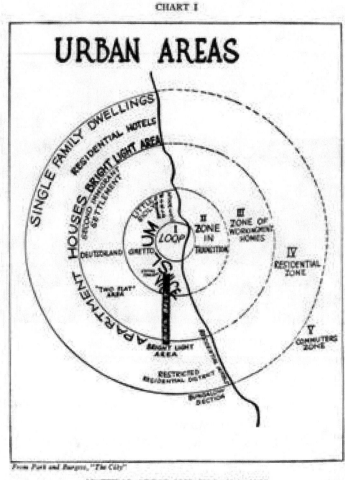

CHART I

URBAN AREAS

From Park and Burgess, "The City"

NATURAL AREAS AND URBAN ZONES

FIGURE 8.3 BURGESS'S CONCENTRIC ZONES MAP OF CHICAGO   The "concentric zone" model of neighborhood organization within cities has been highly influential and debated ever since it was originated in the 1920s. Do cities simply self-arrange so types of houses and neighborhoods meet the needs of its residents?

of these arenas, policy decisions often are influenced by a tight group of urban elites, including local developers and builders along with the leaders of key institutions, such as local media outlets and universities. These groups of influential members of the community seek investment and promote the development of cultural attractions such as museums, professional sports teams, universities, and even public parades that are designed to foster civic pride and attract residents.

From this perspective, urban change can be thought of not as a natural process of ecological change but as the direct result of political and economic interests working to promote growth. Thinking of cities as the product of intensive and strategic investment then changes the way we understand everything about cities, even the way certain buildings and neighborhoods look. Research on the transformation of New York City's SoHo neighborhood from a manufacturing district to a wealthy, fashionable residential and retail community provides a good example (Zukin 1982). In SoHo, redevelopment groups composed of representatives from the business community and the city government pushed forward changes in zoning and land

In the 1920s, the Strip District of Pittsburgh was an economic center of factories and warehouses. It has since been transformed into a lively neighborhood community of lofts, restaurants, and shops.

use that transformed who could live in the neighborhood and what businesses could operate in the neighborhood, recreating the physical space and the types of individuals within it. The physical transformation of the neighborhood was part of a broader effort to create a new neighborhood identity, a rebranding of SoHo as a destination for artists and a center for culture and shopping—as opposed to a working-class section of the city dominated by factories.

Issues like racial and ethnic segregation also come to be seen in very different terms when the city is viewed as a growth machine. The sorting of different groups into neighborhoods across the city is viewed by some as the product of a concerted effort on the part of political and economic elites to protect investment and promote growth. Los Angeles offers a good illustration of this process. With its dizzying array of ethnic enclaves, its sprawling geography and car culture, its history of oppressive policing, and its obsession with image, Los Angeles has come to be seen as the quintessential example of an American city where change is driven by a powerful set of economic elites.

For example, the research of Mike Davis documents the way that "growth coalitions" sought to keep poor African American and Latino populations from spreading into spaces deemed historically important by allocating tax subsidies to favored developers and by excluding groups representing the city's poor communities from taking part in decision making on urban planning (Davis 1990). Davis labeled the Los Angeles metropolis a "fortress of exclusion" that featured strategic investment in favored neighborhoods and a set of policing and land-use policies designed to keep the poor and racial and ethnic minorities out of these areas. Specifically, Davis documents the city's removal of homeless shelters and mental health facilities from neighborhoods where wealthy property owners wanted to develop new real estate investments. Not coincidentally, these property owners had previously donated large sums of money to city and county politicians who made decisions about the placement of social service facilities. His analysis reveals how the city even commissioned new park benches and bus stops in investment-ready areas designed to be physically uncomfortable in an effort to prevent homeless individuals from loitering. This vision of the different zones within Los Angeles, some designed and policed to exclude some groups, does not resemble Burgess's vision of Chicago—instead of transition zones, Davis describes "no-go" zones where the poor were

How do political and economic interests work together to promote growth and affect urban change?

relegated and contrasts them to the glittering redeveloped commercial zones and gated housing communities of the wealthy. The irony is that planning is so concentrated, the beautiful commercial neighborhoods and the destitute poor areas are sometimes right next to each other, as is the case with Los Angeles's downtown and its infamous Skid Row. The former contains skyscrapers, architectural landmarks, symphonies, stadiums, and museums, while the latter is lined with shantytowns and garbage.

This research moves away from the vision of neighborhoods as natural areas to one where urban communities are seen as the product of a contentious process in which different groups, bringing different resources and differential influence to the political discussion, are pitted against each other.

Davis labeled the Los Angeles metropolis a "fortress of exclusion" with a set of policing and land-use policies designed to keep the poor and racial and ethnic minorities out of favored neighborhoods.

3 Does Living in Cities Influence Who We Are, Who Our Friends Are, and How We Live?

LIVING IN AN URBAN WORLD

Watch the **Big Question** Video in **MySocLab**

I n his book *Going Solo*, Eric Klinenberg (2012) documents remarkable growth in the number of Americans living by themselves—with the highest rates in places like Washington, D.C., Denver, and Minneapolis. In the Manhattan borough of New York City, about half of all households are occupied by a single individual. Living alone can mean very different things to different people, but Klinenberg's research suggests that the growth in the number of Americans on their own is not necessarily a negative trend. Many of the individuals with whom he spoke expressed great satisfaction with their living situation and remained closely linked with friends and family.

Other research takes a less optimistic view on individual and community life in modern society, expressing concern with growing levels of **social isolation** in society, meaning a lack of interpersonal connections and a decline in civic life. For example, research conducted in the 1990s showed that Americans have been spending less time with family, less time in groups like bowling clubs, and less time engaged in civic organizations since the mid-1960s (Putnam 2000).

What do these trends tell us about life within cities? As we will see, sociologists have worried for a long time about how urban life affects the ties that individuals form to family, to neighbors, and to their communities. More broadly, urban sociology has long been concerned with the question of what it means to live in an increasingly urban world, a challenging question that forces one to link large-scale, macro forces to micro, day-to-day experiences and interactions between individuals. As was true for the study of urban change, one of the most influential arguments about the effects of urban life was put forth by a sociologist in the Chicago School.

Urbanism as a Way of Life

Louis Wirth, writing in 1938 in Chicago, defined a city as "a large, dense, and permanent settlement of heterogeneous individuals" (Wirth 1938). Size, density, and heterogeneity —these sound like fairly straightforward characteristics of a place that are easy to measure. However, these quantifiable characteristics were only a beginning point for Wirth. He went on to argue that these are the essential characteristics of cities because of the way that large, densely populated, and residentially stable places alter the lives of individuals and the nature of social interactions within them. Drawing on his observations of city life in Chicago, Wirth argued that city dwellers interact in largely anonymous, superficial, and transitory ways in their day-to-day exchanges with one another. He attributed this to the unique "specialization" of urban residents into different types of occupations and careers, the "differentiation" of urban individuals by social class, and the "segregation" of urban spaces by race, all of which do not exist to the same degree in smaller, more intimate communities. According to Wirth, diversity in cities does not necessarily lead to interaction among different groups living in close proximity, who coexist with only "the faintest communication, the greatest indifference, the broadest tolerance, occasionally bitter strife, but always the sharpest contrast" (Wirth 1938:20).

Wirth's thoughts on city life relate closely to the theories of German sociologist Georg Simmel, whose ideas laid the foundation for studying the effects of urbanism on individuals (Simmel [1902] 1972). Noting the large-scale migration to cities that had occurred all over Europe

Claude Fischer's theory of subcultures helps us understand why certain neighborhoods take on a particular identity—take, for example, Haight-Ashbury in San Francisco, which became a center for the hippie movement in the 1960s.

during the nineteenth century, Simmel argued that the shift in the environment surrounding such a substantial portion of the population must have consequences on the ways individuals act and interact. Simmel studied turn-of-the-century Berlin and came away with mixed feelings toward city life. He argued that the constant barrage of stimuli found in urban settings and the impersonal character of economic interactions lead individuals to live life with an indifferent, blasé attitude that provides a shield against the chaos of the city. However, Simmel also saw the city as liberating individuals from the social controls found in small, tight-knit communities. The exposure to many different kinds of people, which is only afforded by the size and density of an urban area, opens the individual up to a seemingly infinite number of new ways of life. From Simmel's perspective, the anonymity of the city allows individuals the freedom to express themselves in new ways and to escape the tendency toward conformity in small towns. It is in the city, then, that individuals find both freedom and isolation.

These early views of urbanism settled on the idea that something about the city itself produces a different psychological outlook for individuals, leading to new experiences but also to feelings of alienation. Subsequent scholars have rethought these claims and reached different conclusions. Sociologist Herbert Gans, who studied community life in a diverse array of urban and suburban settings, found isolation and alienation in these communities but also found strong interpersonal ties between neighbors and active community life. Based on his observations, Gans called into question Wirth's assertion that urbanism in particular, as opposed to the larger factors of economic and political structures of modern life, had any consequential effects on the way people live (Gans 1968). Gans agreed that there are differences between the type of life in nonurban and urban areas but argued that these differences are due to factors like age, race, occupation, and the income of individuals and

not to urbanism. According to Gans, we should not think about an "urban way of life," or, for that matter, a "suburban way of life," but instead we should focus on demographic and economic differences between groups in different places, as opposed to ecological factors like size, density, and heterogeneity.

Other urban scholars have argued that there are, in fact, differences in lifestyle that are fostered by cities that cannot be accounted for simply by demographics—but the consequences of city life are complex. Cities encourage unconventional behavior, according to the urban sociologist Claude Fischer, as the sheer size and density of urban spaces lead individuals to sort into subcultures with similar interests or occupations. As a result, cities have higher rates of artistic innovation, higher rates of crime, and more "extreme" lifestyles (Fischer 1975). Institutional structures that support these subcultures (venues that host punk rock bands, bars that cater to professional clientele, etc.) rise up in response to the demands of growing subcultural groups. Fischer's theory of subcultures helps us understand why certain neighborhoods take on a particular identity; for example, why youth from the suburbs move into neighborhoods like Haight-Ashbury in San Francisco, which became a center for the hippie movement in the 1960s, or Colonia Roma in Mexico City, which recently has become a destination for young artists and urban hipsters who work in design-related industries. In both cases, these neighborhoods catered to a unique subpopulation of the city and developed a new character that reflected the lifestyles of their residents.

How has urbanization affected our lives and communities?

Other scholars have also highlighted the positive aspects of urban environments and the ways that cities foster community. One of the most influential of these figures who wrote in defense of the urban way of life was Jane Jacobs, who argued that vibrant neighborhoods that encourage the use of public spaces can foster social connections, interaction, and public safety (Jacobs 1961). Jacobs fought her most well-known battle to protect her own neighborhood, New York's Greenwich Village, from redevelopment. She contended that the neighborhood's dense, tree-lined streets, which combined businesses and residences, promoted social interaction by giving ownership of public space to all different types of community members. Jacobs thought that cities could indeed be cold and isolating, as Wirth saw them, but they did not have to be. She argued that the physical layout of neighborhoods has a lot to do with the quality of life within them. Mixed-use neighborhoods, like the Greenwich Village of the 1950s, provided Jacobs with an example of how active street life and pedestrian traffic lead to more "eyes on the street," which, as she saw it, increases neighborliness and creates a safe community. The legacy of Jacobs' vision of urban life can be seen in the ideas of a school of urban design known as "New Urbanism." The planners, architects, and urban designers that are collectively known as the New Urbanists call for a return to mixed-use, walkable urban communities as a response to growing suburban sprawl (Duany, Plater-Zyberk, and Speck 2001). As suburbs have moved further and further away from central cities, the influence of the New Urbanists has grown and the communities they envision have come to be seen by many as a more sustainable model for urban design.

How have times and technology changed how people in communities interact with each other?

☐ Communities and Networks

As is clear by this point in the chapter, one of the fundamental concerns of urban sociologists is the question of how urbanization affects **community**, often thought of as the degree to which individuals connect with, support, and interact with each other. How to define the boundaries of an individual's community is another question. Most of the classic sociological thinking on urban communities has implicitly conceived of an individual's community as comprising family members and neighbors, along with nearby friends. But times, and technologies, have changed. Think about your own community, the people with whom you interact on a regular basis. Is your entire community located in the immediate space surrounding you? Our guess is that for most readers, no matter whether you live in the smallest of towns or the biggest of cities, the answer is no.

In the late 1970s, sociologist Barry Wellman picked up on this problem with classic conceptions of community

that focused entirely on the space surrounding an individual. Wellman and other researchers pushed the field toward a view of community that focused on the **social ties** of individuals within cities, or the various types of connections that individuals make with other people, no matter the setting.

Wellman argued that thinking strictly about geography and the layout of neighborhoods limited urban sociology's focus, making it unable to fully capture how community works in modern life (Wellman 1979). From this perspective, when sociologists saw a lack of community cohesion, it was because they failed to see the wider networks in which individuals are enmeshed. For example, we might have strong friendships with people through school or work, even though these friends do not live in the same neighborhood. And when scholars pushed back against the idea that community life had declined, they too were limited by their focus on neighborhoods and neighborly ties. Wellman claimed that community was neither "lost" nor "saved" but instead was "liberated." What he meant was that individuals in cities do not lack strong intimate ties, nor are the ties that they have solely derived from family or neighbor relationships within close proximity. Instead, city dwellers draw on different networks that are spread over large geographies. In cities, people rely on different sets of friends, family, colleagues, neighbors, and associates for different reasons.

These ideas form the basis of research on **social networks**, the study of the ties that link people and groups together. Early research in the field helped to clarify the role that technology plays in shaping the way we construct our social networks and our communities. With the growth of communication technology and the rise of the Internet, community can no longer be thought of as something contained within a geographic area. The range of activities in which we participate provides opportunities for friendships and the formation of social ties in the home setting, at work, in religious communities, and of course online.

As of mid-2012, there were over 900 million active Facebook users, creating the capacity for individuals to maintain a constant connection with a limitless group of "friends." We are just beginning to understand how these online social networks are changing personal and social life. Just as early urban scholars worried about how cities would erode social life, early scholars of online social networks suggested that online activity serves as a poor substitute for a lonely crowd that is less interested in face-to-face, or voice-to-voice, interaction. As access to online networks has expanded, this negative view has subsided. Research suggests that online networks may expand and enhance our offline networks by strengthening social ties that provide support and creating new ties that provide access to new information and potentially useful contacts (Ellison, Steinfield, and Lampe 2007).

In these ways, online networks may not be weakening social life but rather enhancing **social capital**, which refers to the resources available to individuals through their relationships and networks (Coleman 1988). What sociologists have learned is that social capital does not emerge solely from close personal relationships with good friends and loved ones. In fact, the most useful ties are often those that connect people to new networks of individuals whom they do not already know and to new ideas and resources held by individuals within these networks.

This idea is captured in a classic study of job-referral networks conducted by the sociologist Mark Granovetter

What impact has technology had on community life?

and famously titled "The Strength of Weak Ties" (Granovetter 1974). Granovetter found that the professionals he interviewed *did not* hear about their job through contacts that they saw or interacted with frequently. Instead, they got word of potential employment options from contacts whom they saw only occasionally or rarely. Whereas an individual's closest friends may all know each other and have similar sets of information sources, these weak ties were most useful because they had access to unique information and unique contacts, opening up new opportunities for the job seeker.

With the expansion of weak ties on social and professional networking sites, we may be nearing a golden age of networks, where everyone is connected. Considering this new reality, one wonders whether concerns about the erosion of community are outdated or whether the traditional focus of urban sociology on local neighborhoods has become less relevant.

A great deal of urban sociology suggests otherwise. Despite the fact that individual networks may not be limited by physical proximity, there is strong evidence that communication and interaction within the local, physical neighborhood remains essential to community life. Research demonstrates that when residents of a neighborhood have a high level of cohesion and trust, they are more able to organize as a community and enforce common norms of behavior in public spaces. As a result, communities with high levels of cohesion and trust have lower levels of crime and violence, even if the community is very poor (Sampson, Raudenbush, and Earls 1997). Explore *A Sociological Perspective* on page 214 to learn more about how redesigning an urban neighborhood can enhance a community.

The breakdown of this type of community cohesion can lead to disastrous consequences. Perhaps the best example comes from a study of a deadly heat wave that occurred in Chicago in 1995 (Klinenberg 2002). In research designed to explain why so many people died in the series of days when Chicago's temperature rose above 100 degrees and stayed there, the most vulnerable population was found to be the elderly who were living in neighborhoods where violence had become a constant threat, where the active bustle of street life had slowed to a trickle, and where residents felt forced to retreat into their homes, isolated from their neighbors and from public life.

This type of disaster serves as a reminder that the life of the city does not always resemble the somewhat romantic vision of a "street ballet," as Jane Jacobs described the urban scenes outside her window in New York's Greenwich Village. The city is home to some of society's most pressing social problems, including crime, violence, and severe poverty.

SOCIOLOGICAL PERSPECTIVE

urban neighborhoods be redesigned to enhance community?

w York University professors Richard Sennett and Eric nberg are involved in a project with colleagues at the don School of Economics to reexamine problems of n design and planning with an eye towards designing dings and neighborhoods to be more livable, open, and munity oriented for residents. Recently, Sennett and enberg asked their sociology students to redesign a ic housing building on Manhattan's Lower East Side in York. The team's work was specific to one area in New but their ideas and solutions can be applied to urban gn problems around the country.

The student team's goals were to create areas for residents and neighbors to come together away from busy intersections and traffic; to make the area more pedestrian friendly; to provide open spaces without visual or symbolic barriers; and to create opportunity for small businesses to bring the community together. In order to accomplish these goals, the team made recommendations to open up garden areas by removing high walls around the park areas and repurposing nearby impersonal spaces, like a gas station, into green space and areas for residents to gather and spend time together.

Areas like Cleveland's Lakeview Terrace public housing complex are among the many urban areas where a neighborhood redesign could impact the feel of the community for its residents. What political, economic, and social factors might work against such a redesign?

Without a formal neighborhood redesign, what could residents of public housing neighborhoods do themselves to create a better sense of community?

Through grants and nonprofit funding, some communities like this one in Detroit, are clearing unused land to create community gardens to produce food for its low-income residents. How can the creation of a community garden affect how residents and neighbors interact with one another?

What other ways might local residents, businesses, and governments increase the health and safety of our neighborhoods?

Explore A Sociological Perspective in **MySocLab** and then ...

Think About It
does our physical environment affect how we live and become
mmunity? To what extent does the environment condition how

■ Inspire Your Sociological Imagination
Is there a part of your neighborhood or city that could benefit from
change? Choose a location and think of three ways you could

4 Why Are So Many Social Problems Found in Cities?

SOCIAL PROBLEMS AND THE CITY

👁 Watch the **Big Question Video** in **MySocLab**

In *The Condition of the Working Class in England in 1844*, Friedrich Engels takes the reader into the rows of dilapidated cottages lining the side streets of Manchester, England, and documents the squalor in which the majority of working-class residents lived (Engels [1845] 1972:430–31):

> *Right and left a multitude of covered passages lead from the main street into numerous courts, and he who turns in thither gets into a filth and disgusting grime, the equal of which is not to be found—especially in the courts which lead down to the Irk [river], and which contain unqualifiedly the most horrible dwellings which I have yet beheld.*

Engels is one of many urban scholars who have described, through visual imagery or statistical portraits, the array of social problems that often come bundled together in the poorest urban slums, tenements, or high-rise housing projects. These scholarly accounts have led to various public policies, social reform efforts, and social movements designed to confront the unequal conditions that lead to urban poverty. Engels, who worked closely with Karl Marx as a leader in the communist movement, used his description of urban squalor as a launching point for a critique of the capitalist system in England after the Industrial Revolution. Similarly, in the United States, Jane Addams combined her analysis of inequality in American society with activism around social issues as well as direct intervention, creating the first "settlement house" in Chicago (Addams 1910). The Hull House, founded in 1889, was designed to promote social integration by providing services and supports to neighborhood residents from various ethnic and immigrant backgrounds.

Responses to the conditions of the urban poor are not always so empathetic, however. The problems associated with urban poverty are often explained as the result of cultural deficiencies of the urban poor (Banfield 1970), not as linked to any broader structure of inequality. Public policy targeting the urban poor often reflects this scornful view and can be seen in much of the rhetoric surrounding debates on welfare policy and criminal justice. Consequently, many of the policies directed at poor urban areas have sought to alter or remove the poor rather than provide aid.

Perhaps the most notorious example can be found in the form of the 1949 Housing Act, which provided federal funding to help local governments acquire sections of cities with slum housing in an effort to redevelop these "blighted" (or deteriorated) areas. This policy, which came to be known as **urban renewal**, resulted in the destruction of entire swaths

Industrialization caused problems of overcrowding and a lack of housing. As a consequence, the poor were forced to crowd together in tenements or even rent coffins as depicted here.

of poor and working-class neighborhoods in cities across the country and the replacement of these communities with carefully planned areas featuring new commercial space, transportation infrastructure, and high-rise apartments. Although urban renewal was framed as a reform effort designed to improve housing for the poor and improve blighted neighborhoods, scholars have shown that developers and the business community reaped most of the benefits of the policy. The residents of such communities were frequently an afterthought, as documented in a famous study of Boston's West End neighborhood, a working-class Italian American community that was torn down and redeveloped in the 1950s (Gans 1962). Over the years, many scholars studying communities that are identified as "blighted" and targeted for redevelopment have found socially cohesive communities in the midst of poverty, places where residents reject the "slum" label attached to their communities by outsiders.

Beyond redevelopment, urban renewal was used in many cities to consolidate growing populations of African Americans and to reinforce racial segregation in urban neighborhoods. In Chicago, urban renewal resulted in a series of high-rise public housing projects that were constructed to house the city's growing black population. The new projects helped alleviate the serious shortage of housing for African Americans, who lived in overcrowded, low-quality housing in the city's "black belt." But the location of the projects within the black sections of the city also served to reinforce segregation in the city as a whole. These communities were then isolated from the largely white sections of the city surrounding them through the construction of the Dan Ryan Expressway, which was built alongside some of the largest projects in the city, providing a buffer between the city's white and black neighborhoods.

This example brings to light the way that race is intertwined with many of the major debates and controversies surrounding cities and urban poverty. Nowhere is this connection more apparent than in the issue of the **urban ghetto**, a term used to refer to sections of cities that are characterized by severe racial or ethnic segregation and deep poverty.

Read the Document *Death of a Neighborhood* in MySocLab.

Concentrated Poverty and the Urban Ghetto

In 1945, St. Clair Drake and Horace Cayton published a comprehensive study of "Bronzeville," the name given to the African American section of Chicago's South Side. The authors described a vibrant community where black cultural and social life thrived despite high poverty, overcrowded and dilapidated housing, and unrelenting discrimination. They documented lively scenes from parks where "Bronzeville's teeming thousands swarm, lounging on the grass, frolicking in the Black Belt's one large swimming pool, fishing and rowing in the lagoon, and playing softball, tennis, or baseball" (Drake and Cayton 1945:603). While noting that

Today's Bronzeville looks a lot different than it did in 1945. Despite the rampant poverty, however, there are continued attempts to create community, often through religious institutions.

certain sections and streets of Bronzeville were known as "lower-class" areas, the authors pointed out that the poor were not confined to any single section of Bronzeville but were "scattered from one end of the community to the other" (Drake and Cayton 1945:602). And while "gambling dens" and "call-houses" were more prevalent within the lower-class sections of the city's black belt, churches were also widespread. Indeed, they describe "the evening hours of Bronzeville's lower-class areas" as "noisy with the cacophony of both hymns and blues" (Drake and Cayton 1945:611)

This classic study of community life in Bronzeville was published before the civil rights movement had begun to flourish, before a wave of riots had swept through America's cities in the 1960s, and before the economic downturn of the 1970s. If we move forward in time 40 or so years after Drake and Cayton wrote, to the end of the 1980s, sociologists studying the same streets and parks in Chicago provide a very different portrait of city life on the South Side. A more recent study of the same streets describes vacant streets that resemble war zones stripped of all commercial activity, desolate and depopulated, where violence and drug abuse are prevalent and unemployment is rampant: "The windows and doors of apartments and houses are commonly barricaded behind heavy metal gates and burglar bars. Public facilities and spaces are not spared ... most parks are 'no-go' areas, especially after nightfall" (Wacquant 2009:55).

This imagery captures the emergence of a new form of urban poverty that became prevalent in the period following the civil rights era of the 1960s and that has become associated with a wide range of uniquely urban social problems. The new urban poverty can be characterized by several distinguishing features, including a growing concentration of the urban poor within a smaller number of extremely high-poverty neighborhoods, the persistence of severe racial segregation despite fair housing laws, and the growth in concentrated joblessness and related social problems. Although the social problems present in urban America were sensationalized by inflammatory political rhetoric and television shows like *COPS*, the change in the character of poor urban neighborhoods is nonetheless visible in statistics on concentrated poverty (see Figure 8.4) and violent crime.

So how did we get from the poor yet vibrant "Black Metropolis" of the 1940s to the desolate, violent black ghetto of the 1980s? In his book *The Truly Disadvantaged* (Wilson 1987), William Julius Wilson put forth one of the most influential sociological arguments of the past 50 years to help explain this change. Wilson's theory begins by documenting how manufacturing jobs began to disappear from cities in the Northeast and Midwest, leaving minority populations without the stable, working-class jobs that had drawn them northward in the Great Migration. With the decline in manufacturing jobs in central cities, joblessness skyrocketed and there were fewer "marriageable" black men who could support a family and play the role of breadwinner—the rate of single-parent-headed families rose sharply, as did the rate of welfare receipt. In addition to the transformation of urban labor markets, Wilson demonstrated how civil rights legislation allowed middle-class African Americans to expand the boundaries of

What changes have led to neighborhoods with concentrated poverty in the United States?

urban ghettos or to leave them altogether. Whereas the earlier research on Bronzeville described a community in which different segments of the black community lived, worked, and played in close proximity, the movement of middle-class blacks out of the traditional black ghetto had the unanticipated consequence of removing the "middle-class buffer" from black neighborhoods. When the middle class left, the community institutions they left behind, including the church and the schools, deteriorated rapidly.

The result of these and other more subtle changes was a **concentration of poverty** in the urban ghetto that was associated with high levels of violence, homelessness, joblessness, and welfare receipt. If the ghetto of the 1940s was a place where all classes of African American families were forced to live, the ghetto of the 1980s was a place where the most impoverished communities of racial and ethnic minority groups had been abandoned.

Despite the changes that have occurred in poor urban communities over time, the research of urban ethnographers—scholars who study people and places by immersing themselves in a community—typically captures a more complex reality of life in the nation's most disadvantaged

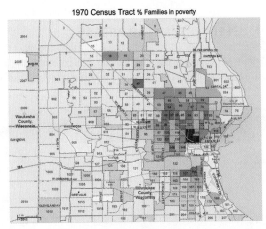

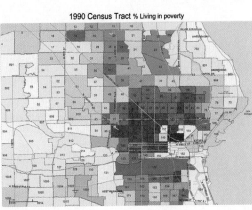

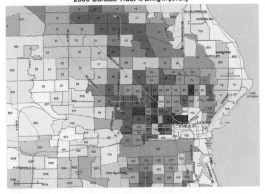

Legend:

Suppressed by Census
n/a (<100 base cases)
< 1%
1% to 5%
5% to 10%
10% to 15%
15% to 20%
20% to 25%
25% to 30%
30% to 40%
40% to 50%
50% to 75%
75% to 100%

☐ State Capital
○ City Pop. 30K to 50K
• City Pop. 50K to 100K
● City Pop. 100K to 250K
⊗ City Pop. 250K to 500K
◉ City Pop. Over 500K
○ Place Pop Less than 30K
— State
— County
☐ Census Tract - thick outline
⊡ Census Tract - thin outline
  Airport/Airfield
  Park/Forest
  Cemetery
☐ Military
  Prison

© 2012 Social Explorer

FIGURE 8.4 NEIGHBORHOOD POVERTY IN MILWAUKEE These maps of Milwaukee show that particular neighborhoods went into steep economic decline after the 1970s. While there was some relief in the decade between 1990 and 2000, the latest data show how concentrated neighborhood poverty is a long-term problem that spans decades. ⊕ **Explore** in **MySocLab** to see more neighborhood maps showing the poverty rates in Milwaukee.

communities. On the one hand, sociological research on the urban ghetto has provided vivid portraits of the ways in which the threat of violence comes to structure daily life in the poorest, most racially segregated sections of urban America, forcing youth to make constant strategic decisions about where and with whom to spend their time and how to negotiate potentially dangerous interactions (Anderson 1999). On the other hand, scholars studying the most intensely violent neighborhoods find individuals and families that rely on dense networks of support for childcare, friendship, emotional support, and financial assistance in times of crisis (Stack 1974; Venkatesh and Celimli 2004). Even in the most distressed neighborhoods across the country, a strong sense of community can flourish.

Segregation and Urban Diversity

Whereas figures on concentrated poverty reveal the degree to which the poor are clustered into a small number of neighborhoods, figures on racial and ethnic **segregation** describe the degree to which individuals from different racial and ethnic groups live within the same communities. When thinking about current levels of segregation, it helps to turn back to one of the key pieces of civil rights legislation passed in the late 1960s, the 1968 Fair Housing Act. The legislation made discrimination in the public and private housing markets illegal and carried with it the hope that America's neighborhoods would no longer be divided by race. Yet decades later, racial segregation has declined only slightly in most of America's major cities, as is visible from Table 8.1.

Although these figures focus on the segregation of African Americans from whites, this portrait of urban America is incomplete without considering the diversity of ethnic neighborhoods across the country. The United States has seen an explosion of immigration since the passage of the Hart-Cellar Act in 1965, which overrode the previous national origins quota system and rapidly changed the flow of immigrants coming to the United States. Whereas in the early part of the century most immigrants came from Europe, a majority of immigrants now arrive from Latin America, the Caribbean, Africa, Asia, and the Middle East (Waters, Ueda, and Marrow 2007).

The impact of immigration on urban life is complex. There is some evidence that immigrants have played an important role in revitalizing some of the most distressed urban neighborhoods around the country, bringing new life to neighborhoods that had lost population and business activity for decades. Some have suggested that immigration has helped to facilitate the racial and ethnic integration

TABLE 8.1 PERCENTAGE OF BLACK ISOLATION IN SELECT U.S. METRO AREAS

This table shows changing percentages in the rates of black residential isolation, which refers to the percentage minority in the neighborhood where the average minority resident lives. In 2010, the average black person in Detroit lived in a neighborhood that was 80.9 percent black. In many northern, formerly industrial areas, isolation remains quite high. Other metropolitan areas like Houston and Los Angeles have seen a drop in black isolation, mostly due to an influx of immigrants into traditionally black neighborhoods.

Area Name	1980 Isolation	1990 Isolation	2000 Isolation	2010 Isolation
Detroit–Livonia–Dearborn, MI	81.5	85.2	85.7	80.9
Chicago–Joliet–Naperville, IL	83.8	78.3	73.7	66.8
Milwaukee–Waukesha–West Allis, WI	69.4	69.1	67.2	65.5
Cleveland–Elyria–Mentor, OH	77.6	76.7	70.9	64.7
Philadelphia, PA	74.5	73.4	67.8	62.9
New Orleans–Metairie–Kenner, LA	69.4	68.8	70.3	62.9
Baltimore–Towson, MD	72.5	69.4	65.8	62.4
St. Louis, MO–IL	73.1	68.4	64.3	62.0
Washington–Arlington–Alexandria, DC–VA–MD–WV	70.7	66.1	63.6	59.2
Atlanta–Sandy Springs–Marietta, GA	71.8	63.2	61.2	58.1
Miami–Miami Beach–Kendall, FL	65.1	61.1	60.7	56.6
New York–White Plains–Wayne, NY–NJ	62.1	60.7	58.7	53.9
Boston–Quincy, MA	59.6	52.3	45.8	40.7
Houston–Sugar Land–Baytown, TX	63.3	51.8	45.0	37.2
Los Angeles–Long Beach–Glendale, CA	60.2	42.1	34.3	29.1

Source: Logan and Stults (2001).

of once-segregated neighborhoods. For instance, recent research has identified an emerging set of **global neighborhoods** around the country, which can be defined as neighborhoods that contain members of several different racial and ethnic groups (Logan and Zhang 2010). Los Angeles's East Hollywood, which contains a substantial number of immigrants from Latin America, Armenia, and Southeast Asia, is one such neighborhood. The emergence of these new global neighborhoods raises important questions about the future of the nation's cities, as new evidence suggests that growth in the ethnic diversity of urban neighborhoods may chip away at the traditional boundaries separating whites and blacks, leading to the hopeful idea that an increasingly diverse urban landscape may lead to the decline of racial segregation.

How diverse are America's cities?

At the same time, the neighborhoods of immigrants have not been immune to changes that have taken place in urban neighborhoods over the past several decades. For instance, the number of Latino Americans living in high-poverty *barrios* (the Hispanic equivalent of the black ghetto) rose alongside the growth in the concentration of poverty among African Americans in the 1970s and 1980s (Jargowsky 1997). The new urban poverty has generated new challenges for immigrant families as the traditional pattern of upward mobility with each passing generation is no longer the dominant model of assimilation. Instead, immigrants' trajectories are better characterized by a pattern of **segmented assimilation**, in which immigrants follow one of several possible pathways of assimilation (Portes and Zhou 1993). One path is the traditional trajectory of upward mobility and cultural assimilation into the mainstream. But another, increasingly prominent path involves downward economic mobility and assimilation into the urban poor. A third path for immigrants is to integrate into the economic mainstream while sustaining ties to the culture in the origin community by remaining within residential enclaves. This is true of Chinese Americans in San Francisco, who make up a close to a fifth of the city's population and are a large part of the city's civic life. As the proportion of nonwhite Americans continues to grow, this latter path may become increasingly common over time.

While we have focused on concentrated poverty and related urban problems in an American context, scholars of urban poverty have begun to focus more attention on how the ghettos of America compare to the favelas in Brazil, the townships in South Africa, and the banlieues of France—all of which are areas around the world with severe, concentrated poverty (see Table 8.2). Further, in the developing world, there is growing evidence that some of the most extreme poverty is shifting from rural areas to urban areas (Montgomery, Stren, and Cohen 2003), creating new challenges for cities. Concentrated poverty is a global problem, and it is becoming increasingly clear that the problems of cities should be thought of in global terms.

TABLE 8.2 URBANIZATION OF POVERTY IN THE DEVELOPING WORLD
While the percentage of the world's population living in urban areas increases at a steady rate (now over 50 percent), urban areas' share of the world's poor is growing at double the pace.

1993	Urban Share of the Poor (%)	Urban Share of Population (%)
Latin America and Caribbean	47.7	72.3
Middle East and North Africa	15.3	52.8
Sub-Saharan Africa	24.3	29.8
South Asia	21.9	25.7
India	22.5	26.2
World Total (Excluding China)	24.2	41.6
2002	**Urban Share of the Poor (%)**	**Urban Share of Population (%)**
Latin America and Caribbean	59.0	76.2
Middle East and North Africa	19.9	55.8
Sub-Saharan Africa	30.2	35.2
South Asia	24.1	27.8
India	25.2	28.1
World Total (Excluding China)	28.2	43.4

Note: Urban and rural poverty measures using a poverty line of $1.08 per day (in 1993 PPP)

Source: Ravallion, Chen, and Sangraula (2007).

5   How Will Cities Change in an Increasingly Connected World?

CITIES AND THE CONNECTED WORLD

Watch the **Big Question** Video in **MySocLab**

There are many ways to demonstrate the degree to which the world has become connected. One powerful way is to see it.

A few years ago New York's Museum of Modern Art hosted a unique exhibit called New York Talk Exchange. You can get a good taste of the exhibit from Figures 8.5 and 8.6, as well as the webpage devoted to the project: http://senseable.mit.edu/nyte/. The exhibit featured visual representations of the real-time connections between New York City and the rest of the world being made through Internet traffic and telephone conversations. Put together by designers at Massachusetts Institute of Technology's Media Lab, the arcs of light shining into and out of New York provide a beautiful reminder of how closely connected the world has become. The image in Figure 8.5 shows the *location* of these arcs, which shone brightest in the major cities of Western Europe but also extended to Jamaica, Ghana, China, and elsewhere around the globe. The connectedness of New York City to the rest of the world, whether it be by commerce, family, information, or anything else, is on full display.

York City's five boroughs, originated in Santo Domingo and Santiago, the two largest cities in the Dominican Republic (Sassen 2008). About 10 percent of international calls out of Brooklyn are made to Kingston, Jamaica, and 17 percent are made to the combination of Kingston, Santo Domingo, and Haiti. For the most part, these are not business transactions being made over the phone but rather phone conversations

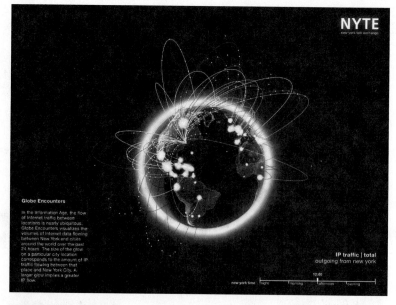

FIGURE 8.5 THE NEW YORK TALK EXCHANGE: GLOBAL ENCOUNTERS   What are the different possible reasons for heavy Internet (IP) traffic? Are the reasons the same across cities? Think about what kinds of information are flowing between New York City and London, England, versus Santo Domingo, Puerto Rico, both of which seem to have large glows.

Immigration and the Urban Landscape

Data from the New York Talk Exchange exhibit (see Figure 8.6) show that about 20 percent of transnational phone calls coming into the Bronx, one of New

linking residents of the Bronx and Brooklyn with their families and friends in their home nations. The shining lights in small cities throughout the world provide visual evidence of a new reality: Humans cross national boundaries to live and work in greater numbers than ever before.

The United Nations estimates that in 2010 roughly 214 million people lived in a nation different from the one in which they were born (DeParle 2010). In the United States, the liberalization of immigration policy has led to rapid growth in immigration that has accelerated over time. About 43 million immigrants are now estimated to live in the United States alone, an increase of almost 20 million from just two decades ago. Connections to their origin countries go beyond verbal communication. Estimates suggest that $300 billion of financial assistance in the form of **remittances**, or money sent from migrant workers to family and friends at home, flows from the United States each year. In some countries like Jamaica, El Salvador, and Lebanon, up to 20 percent of the national income comes from workers who send money back from abroad (DeParle 2007).

The growing presence of immigrants has had an enormous impact on America's cities. Although there is some evidence that immigrants are beginning to locate directly in suburban areas, America's major cities continue to be the primary points of entry for the majority of immigrants from abroad (Tavernise and Gebeloff 2010). For instance, immigrants make up more than a quarter of the population in the nation's 17 largest cities, compared to just 7 percent of the population outside of these cities (Card 2007). Whereas Chicago School models of immigrant assimilation assumed that immigrant groups would move out of zones of transition and integrate into mainstream society over time, the emergence of ethnic enclaves—large, stable sections of cities where the local labor market, residential market, and culture are dominated by a specific ethnic group—was not anticipated by early urban theorists. Figure 8.7 shows how immigration has affected the racial and ethnic composition of Miami, the primary destination for Cuban Americans.

☐ Globalization and the City

Just as people move and communicate across the world, technology allows products and services to flow rapidly across national boundaries—and the nodes of activity are located in the world's global cities. A **global city** is an urban center where the headquarters of transnational firms that create and

In what ways are the world's cities linked together?

control the international flow of information and commerce are located (Sassen 2007). Global cities have a concentration of people and infrastructure that allows for the coordination of the international economy. They are the hubs of international finance and technology in a world where business activity crosses national boundaries easily, where products are marketed across the world, and where capital moves fluidly. In early work on the emergence of global cities, attention was focused on New York, London, and Tokyo (Sassen 1991), but scholars have now identified a range of global or "globalizing" cities that coordinate regional business activity that spans the boundaries of nations, including cities as diverse as Sao Paulo, Brazil; Jakarta, Indonesia; and Moscow, Russia (Castells 2000).

The emergence of global cities has implications that extend beyond international finance and technology. These cities, and the cross-national activity that runs through them, have wide-ranging impacts on the social and economic structure of urban areas and on the lives of the residents within them. The spatial layout of cities, the policies implemented by local governments, and the economic structure of cities are all affected by the globalization of urban areas (Marcuse and van Kempen 2002). In this sense, there is an increasingly strong connection between the *local* conditions of urban populations and the *global* networks of firms.

Beginning in the 1980s, scholars began to put forth arguments about how the process of globalization alters

FIGURE 8.6 THE NEW YORK TALK EXCHANGE: THE WORLD INSIDE NEW YORK The image shows how New York City connects with other parts of the world, and it reflects the racial and ethnic separations within the city itself. Flushing, a neighborhood in the borough of Queens, is clearly very diverse, but is this kind of diversity constant throughout the city?

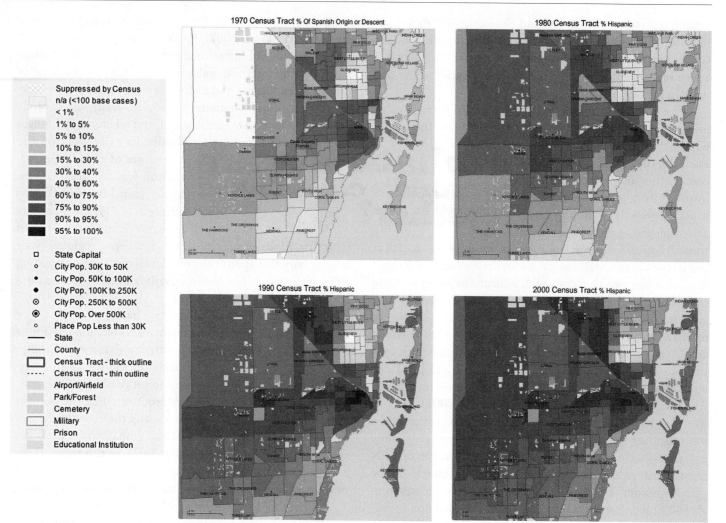

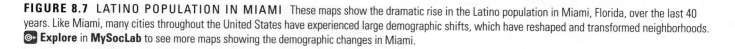

FIGURE 8.7 LATINO POPULATION IN MIAMI These maps show the dramatic rise in the Latino population in Miami, Florida, over the last 40 years. Like Miami, many cities throughout the United States have experienced large demographic shifts, which have reshaped and transformed neighborhoods. ◉ **Explore** in **MySocLab** to see more maps showing the demographic changes in Miami.

the basic economic structure of urban areas, leading to new relationships among city governments, corporations, and residents as well as new forms of class struggle. As America's urban economies transformed in the 1970s, the manufacturing jobs that once formed the base of urban labor markets began to decline rapidly and were replaced by service-sector jobs, including everything from relatively low-wage work in retail stores to high-salary work in banking, that have come to dominate many urban economies in the postindustrial information age. International cities like New York and London reshaped their urban landscapes to provide the infrastructure and the amenities required to attract and retain the international firms that would make them centers of global business (Zukin 1992).

How have immigration and globalization changed cities and urban neighborhoods?

Some scholars of globalization argue that this shift has led to a severe polarization of urban labor markets. For instance, sociologists argue that the globalization of economic activity is leading to an increasingly sharp divide between the global elite, who control international commerce, and the global service class, who cater to the elite. For the new international firms and businesspeople, the global city "consists of airports, top-level business districts, top-of-the-line hotels and restaurants, a sort of urban glamour zone" (Sassen 1996:635). The Palermo Soho neighborhood in Buenos Aires, which contains high-end fashion boutiques and trendy new restaurants, is one such glamour zone. The neighborhood is a hot spot for young upper-class locals and tourists, who hop the bars and cafés late into the

This cafe in Palermo Soho, a fashionable neighborhood in Buenos Aires, represents the types of establishments prevalent in "urban glamour zones," where the global elite can shop and eat, often isolated from the poorer and even middle class residents of the city.

night. Focusing on the other end of the class spectrum, sociologists studying the political economy of urban areas have documented how these changes play out in the relationships between city governments and different groups of city residents. As cities attempt to lure in the corporations and businesspeople necessary to transform into a world city, some argue that urban governments have shifted attention away from local residents—public spaces are left untended, the homeless are removed from public areas, and walled enclaves rise up to protect the city's areas of centralized global activity (Davis 1990).

The research of scholars analyzing class struggles within global cities reminds us of a basic question: Whose city is it? There is a built-in tension in the dual quest to make cities competitive in regional and global markets, and to make cities livable for all groups of residents. As several of the scholars whose work we have reviewed make clear, this tension becomes greater in the age of globalization. It is one of the central tensions that will determine the future of the nation's, and the world's, urban areas.

CONCLUSION   **OUR URBAN FUTURE**

As far back as 1968, urban scholars have predicted that improvements in air travel and telephone communication would make location in an urban area less critical, leading to declines in urbanization in a "post-city" age (Webber 1968). In subsequent years many theorists echoed these predictions, arguing that the growth of information technology would lead to a demographic shift back to rural areas.

Here we are a few decades later, and communication and information technology have improved beyond anyone's expectations—yet urbanization continues, and cities are more important than ever to the world economy. All signs point to a decidedly urban future.

What this future will look like is much less clear. We have described the various forms that cities are beginning to take, from the proliferation of edge cities at the junction of major highways in the United States to growing megaregions in Asia and elsewhere. The new cities are increasingly global, driven by

growth in information technology and services as opposed to industry. The forces that determine which cities are able to grow in this new environment are also changing. Urbanist Richard Florida suggests that the cities that will grow in the new urban environment are those that can offer not only the traditional services that cities provide, like housing and high-quality schools, but also the cultural amenities and the feel of an open, diverse, and tolerant urban environment that can attract the group of professionals he labels the *creative class* (Florida 2003). The creative class includes artists, engineers, professors, designers, and architects, who collectively produce creative culture within a city. Focusing on culture and lifestyle, Florida argues that cities need to compete for creative people before they can compete for business. Florida's arguments are sometimes criticized for failing to take into account larger forces like political power and the economic structure of cities, but his outlook has been extremely influential among city planners and managers (Peck 2005).

The idea that people and ideas are the drivers of urban innovation and growth is echoed in economist Edward Glaeser's optimistic book *The Triumph of the City* (Glaeser 2011). Glaeser views cities as the centralized locations where ideas and knowledge are able to diffuse across a population, creating an emergent set of innovations that combine specialized perspectives and talents in a way that is only possible in an urban setting. From this perspective, cities will be the key to solving the world's most pressing human problems.

The focus on the role of cities as centers of innovation, creativity, and economic growth should not distract us from the role of cities as the sites of the world's most extreme inequality. As cities globalize and complete the shift toward an information- and technology-based economy, many urbanists see a widening gap between those who benefit from the shifts and those who do not. Some envision a world where technology and the flow of information are increasingly central to economic production,

Today, cities are often focused on attracting dynamic technology companies and their economically powerful employees. This workspace at a tech company in Tel Aviv offers the kind of amenities educated employees are coming to expect from their employers as it tries to be at the epicenter of the next Silicon Valley.

allowing multinational institutions to dictate policy that extends across states, with national and local governments declining in importance (Castells 2000).

These are long-term, global visions of our urban future. Glancing out of our offices and onto the streets of New York City, we can't help but consider the more immediate future of cities and neighborhoods. At this point in time, in many cities across the United States, the future is remarkably uncertain. Many cities around the country experienced a revival in the 1990s, as some of the most severe urban problems of the 1980s, like crime and violence, declined rapidly in the latter half of the decade. Over the nation as a whole, violent crime dropped by about 40 percent over the 1990s, with substantial improvements in cities as diverse as San Diego, Dallas, Chicago, Indianapolis, and New York (Zimring 2007). Over the same period in which crime was dropping, rates of home ownership in cities throughout the country rose, joblessness dropped, and property values soared.

Now, just a few years later, these positive developments in America's cities seem like distant memories. The combination of a housing crisis and a major economic recession has eroded the gains in employment and the growth in home ownership that emerged in the 1990s. In a section of Queens where more than two-thirds of mortgages are in the category of high-risk, subprime loans, a resident described the hollow feeling of a neighborhood emptying out: "Every two or three houses it's empty . . . . It's not a good feeling. You see the weeds growing tall and the junk mail piling up" (Fernandez 2008).

As the foreclosure crisis spreads throughout communities in New York and elsewhere, research tells us that the risk of a rise in crime also grows (Immergluck and Smith 2006). In combination with the widespread joblessness that has characterized this most recent economic recession, these developments threaten to reverse the revitalization of urban neighborhoods across the United States.

These changes lead to a cautious view of our urban future, one that focuses on the role of cities as the sites of the world's growing inequality. The more optimistic view is found in the work of urbanists like Glaeser, who calls cities "our species' greatest invention." Elements of both perspectives are certainly true. What is undeniable, however, is that as the world continues to urbanize, our species' future will increasingly be determined by our cities' future.

Watch the Video in **MySocLab**
Applying Your Sociological Imagination

Study and **Review** in **MySocLab**　　　◉ **Watch** the **Video** Inspiring Your Sociological Imagination in **MySocLab**

1

What Draws People to Cities? *(p. 202)*

◉ **Watch** the **Big Question Video** in **MySocLab** to review the key concepts for this section.

Most of the human population now lives in urban areas. This basic fact is important because it raises a number of intriguing questions. This section explored how to define what a city is and how city life has affected different aspects of our individual lives. We learned a sociological understanding of cities is more complex than the "official" definitions provided by government agencies.

HOW THE WORLD BECAME URBAN (p. 202)

Urbanization and the Growth of Cities (p. 202)

- **What major forces have led to urbanization?**

Urban, Suburban, and Rural Patterns of Settlement (p. 203)

- **What urban and suburban forms emerged during the twentieth century?**

◉➜ **Explore** the **Data** on Megaregions in **MySocLab**

2

How Do Neighborhoods Form and Change? *(p. 207)*

◉ **Watch** the **Big Question Video** in **MySocLab** to review the key concepts for this section.

The development of cities and communities is not natural but rather is driven by political and economic forces. This section explored the types of communities that have emerged over time due to individuals and groups with different, sometimes competing, political and economic interests.

NEIGHBORHOODS AND URBAN CHANGE (p. 207)

Urban Ecology: The Chicago School (p. 207)

- **What is urban ecology?**

The Political Economy of Cities and Communities (p. 208)

- **How do political and economic interests work together to promote growth and affect urban change?**

3 Does Living in Cities Influence Who We Are, Who Our Friends Are, and How We Live? *(p. 210)*

 Watch the **Big Question Video** in **MySocLab** to review the key concepts for this section.

This section explored how cities are distinguished not only by their size, density, or other measurable characteristics but by how they affect the way we interact, work, and live together.

LIVING IN AN URBAN WORLD (p. 210)

Urbanism as a Way of Life (p. 210)

● **How has urbanization affected our lives and communities?**

Communities and Networks (p. 212)

● **What impact has technology had on community life?**

Explore A Sociological Perspective: Can urban neighborhoods be redesigned to enhance community? in **MySocLab**.

4 Why Are So Many Social Problems Found in Cities? *(p. 215)*

 Watch the **Big Question Video** in **MySocLab** to review the key concepts for this section.

In this section, we discussed how cities have increasingly become the sites of the world's most extreme wealth and poverty. Urban areas have always been great engines of wealth creation, but a growing proportion of the world's poverty is now moving from undeveloped, rural areas into densely populated urban slums.

SOCIAL PROBLEMS AND THE CITY (p. 215)

Concentrated Poverty and the Urban Ghetto (p. 216)

● **What changes have led to neighborhoods with concentrated poverty in the United States?**

Read the **Document** *Death of a Neighborhood* by Rob Gurwitt in **MySocLab.** This reading examines how an urban renewal program in the 1950s essentially destroyed an inner-city neighborhood in Connecticut and what city planners can learn from the mistakes that were made.

Segregation and Urban Diversity (p. 218)

● **How diverse are America's cities?**

5 How Will Cities Change in an Increasingly Connected World? *(p. 220)*

 Watch the **Big Question Video** in **MySocLab** to review the key concepts for this section.

KEY TERMS

remittances *(p. 221)*
global city *(p. 221)*

In this section, we discussed how cities are the nodes that link the world together. To fully comprehend the forces that shape our world, we must expand our view well beyond individual city streets and communities, and even beyond the boundaries of individual nations.

CITIES AND THE CONNECTED WORLD (p. 220)

Immigration and the Urban Landscape (p. 220)

- **In what ways are the world's cities linked together?**

Globalization and the City (p. 221)

- **How have immigration and globalization changed cities and urban neighborhoods?**

 Watch the **Video** Applying Your Sociological Imagination in **MySocLab** to see these concepts at work in the real world

9

SOCIAL STRATIFICATION, INEQUALITY, AND POVERTY

(((**Listen** to the **Chapter Audio** in **MySocLab**

by FLORENCIA TORCHE,
RICHARD ARUM, and JEFF MANZA

 ow does growing up poor impact children? We would like to think that all children have an equal chance to succeed in life. How true is this? This is a question that social scientists have been especially interested in examining in recent years. Despite the levels of wealth and economic productivity that capitalist societies such as the United States have achieved, many families continue to live in poverty, in many cases even lacking the resources to meet their everyday needs. And evidence is accumulating that children are especially harmed by poverty, sometimes in subtle and hidden ways. One of these hidden possibilities is that the stress of a mother's poverty may be toxic to her child even *before* birth. Until recently, researchers believed that the fetus was fully isolated from its environment by the placenta, which would shield it from any damaging exposures. We now know that this is not the case, as researchers have confirmed that alcohol, tobacco, and drugs affect the fetus. But what about the stresses causes by poverty? Is it possible that the stress faced by mothers living in poverty can affect the fetus just like smoking or drug use? If so, it would suggest that the impact of poverty is even worse than we had previously thought.

The ideal research design to study the impact of stress during pregnancy would involve assembling a group of pregnant women and giving stress to half of them selected at random (treatment group) while not giving stress to the other half (control group). Of course, for ethical reasons, this sort of experiment is not possible. But in 2005, an earthquake in Chile provided one of us with an alternative strategy to assess the impact

---

MY SOCIOLOGICAL IMAGINATION
Florencia Torche

I grew up in Chile observing social inequality from a very early age. My research focuses on the way in which inequality is reproduced across generations, that is how advantages and disadvantages are transmitted from parents to children. In particular, I am interested in education and analyze the extent to which education both contributes to the transmission of inequality across generations and promotes opportunity. Much of my work uses an international comparative perspective in an attempt to understand how variation across nations—in terms of levels of economic development, the educational system, and the welfare state—affects patterns of inequality. My most recent research examines the extent to which social background has profound effects on early life—starting as early as in the prenatal period—including how these early patterns have consequences for an individual's health, developmental and socioeconomic outcomes later in life.

Poverty affects children even before they are born, in visible ways such as lack of food and healthcare, and in less visible ways such as maternal stress.

Watch the Video in **MySocLab**
Inspiring Your Sociological Imagination

of stress. Because the earthquake came unannounced, and because it affected some Chilean cities but left others untouched, it created a kind of natural experiment similar to what might have happened if we had assigned some pregnant mothers to have added stress and other not. In other words, those women who happened to live in the earthquake were, like poor mothers everywhere, exposed to extra stress during their pregnancy, while others who happened to live in areas far away from the earthquake served as the control group for the study. By comparing these two groups of pregnant women, Florencia Torche was able to measure the effect of stress separate from other factors usually associated with it.

The findings were striking. Babies exposed to the earthquake in the first trimester of gestation were far more likely

Is it possible that the cause of stress faced by mothers living in poverty can affect the fetus just like smoking or drug use?

to be born preterm and low weight, two conditions that have been shown to have very serious consequences. Babies born preterm require much more medical attention and are at a higher risk of dying in the first year of life and of experiencing health, developmental, and cognitive problems if they survive. And this is only an extreme impact; other, less obvious negative consequences of being exposed to stress can be found among a much larger group of babies in the study.

Why did the earthquake affect the chances of being born preterm? The most likely explanation is that the acute stress elicited by the earthquake has an effect on the placenta. Basically, stress sends a message to the fetus that says, "the outside world is not too safe, so you should get out as soon as possible," which sets a biological clock for early delivery. Because premature birth predicts developmental problems later on, this study strongly suggests that being exposed to a stressful environment due to poverty even before birth may have a negative effect on a child's outcomes. Given strong evidence that poor mothers have more stressful pregnancies, this leads to a very troubling conclusion: Even before they are born, poor children are much more likely to be exposed to stress that impacts their development in their mother's womb, and that stress is very damaging and will have life-long impacts. This is, as we will see, just one of the many ways in which poverty has negative consequences for individuals and society as a whole.

As we will see, a central value in modern societies is "equality of opportunity," which means that everyone, regardless of the resources of the families they are born into, has a fair chance at succeeding in life. But the fact that poverty handicaps children literally from conception and results in cumulative disadvantages as children grow up deeply questions the goal of equality of opportunity. This is just one example of how inequality is recreated across generations. In this chapter, we will examine why inequality exists, how it is maintained over time, and what are the consequences of inequality for society.

The effect of poverty adds up during children's lives, producing cumulative disadvantages that are increasingly hard to overcome.

THE BIG QUESTIONS

👁 **Watch** the **Big Question Videos** in **MySocLab**

1 **What is inequality?** At the heart of the study of social stratification is the concept of inequality. We know that some people simply have more than others. But why? Has the enormous gap between rich and poor always existed? How have societies and thinkers justified inequality? What is the sociological concept of class? We examine all of this in the first section of the chapter.

Why is America so unequal? Inequality in the United States today is about as high as it has ever been since we started measuring it in the early twentieth century, and poverty rates have remained persistently high. How does the United States compare with other developed countries most similar to it? And does the United States have more people living in poverty than other countries? Why is America so unequal?

3 **Do we all have an equal opportunity to succeed in life?** Social mobility, which refers to the movement of individuals from their family's social position to their social position in adulthood, is one of the most important topics in the study of social stratification. Inequality of opportunity arises whenever some individuals or groups have privileged access to better jobs and/or schools by virtue of the family they were born into. In this section we examine how social mobility is measured, why countries differ in opportunity, how the United States compares to other countries, and the relationship between education and mobility.

How much poverty exists in the United States and around the world? Poverty is a complicated concept. Beyond a minimum of resources to ensure subsistence, it is difficult to define what our "basic" needs are. In this section we examine two ways of viewing poverty and examine how much poverty there is in the United States and in other countries around the world. We will also look closely at the problem of childhood poverty.

1 What Is Inequality?

INEQUALITY: AN INTRODUCTION

👁 **Watch** the **Big Question Video** in **MySocLab**

The sociological subfield of **social stratification** examines inequalities among individuals and groups. It is the systematic study of inequality. In this chapter, we will explore a wide range of different questions and puzzles about why there is so much poverty and inequality in the United States today. In order to do that, we will need to make comparisons to the past as well as to many other countries around the world, including those most similar to the United States. We begin by introducing the concept of inequality, which is at the heart of the study of social stratification.

Has the enormous gap between rich and poor always existed?

☐ The History of Inequality

Some people have more than others. **Inequality**—the unequal distribution of valued goods and opportunities—is a feature of virtually all known human societies. But throughout history, the form and level of inequality have varied widely. Primitive hunting and gathering societies, for example, typically shared their limited food supplies and resources among all members of the tribe more or less fairly, although decision-making powers were exercised by tribal chiefs, and privileges were given to the medicine man (known as the

shaman). In these primitive communities, mere survival was often in question, and there was little, if any, surplus left over after basic necessities were met. Without significant opportunities for some individuals to gain at the expense of others, there was relatively little possibility for large inequalities to emerge.

Slavery was one of the first ways that systematic inequalities began to appear. Slaves are individuals without any rights of citizenship who can be compelled to work for others. The system of slavery allows for the creation of wealth for the slave owners that the slaves do not share in. This was true in the slave societies of the ancient world, notably in Athens and Rome, but also elsewhere throughout human history wherever slavery was practiced.

While slavery produces an extreme form of inequality, the dominant system of inequality throughout the world prior to the advent of capitalism was what is known as **feudalism**, a social order in which those who own land (landlords) are entitled to receive the products of the laborers, or **serfs**, who are legally obligated to work for the landowner. The largely agrarian settlements and societies of the Middle Ages (ca. 500 CE–1500 CE) were places where a handful of families of landlords were able to accumulate sometimes considerable fortunes. However, the vast majority

FIGURE 9.1 COMPARATIVE LEVELS OF PER-PERSON INCOME PER CAPITA

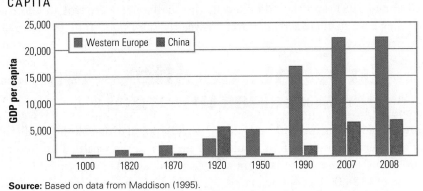

Source: Based on data from Maddison (1995).

of human beings lived, for generations, at the verge of starvation and died very young (the life expectancy at birth in Medieval England was about 30 years; today it is 80 years). The traders and merchants of early urban settlements in the Middle Ages were also sometimes able to become rich, and urban areas (including the city-states that began to appear towards the end of the Middle Ages) began to show that somewhat more diversity of income and wealth was possible. The tiny stratum of economic elites in these societies generally lived entirely apart from the rest of the population, sometimes in grand castles, and there were no significant "middle" classes like those of capitalist societies today.

The world of inequality is much more complicated today. The industrial revolution allowed for rapid and sustained economic growth; societies as a whole got richer, and within them vastly greater inequalities also would emerge. The changes were dramatic. Between 1500 CE and 1820 CE, average incomes around the world grew from $545 to $675, a very modest change. But in areas where the industrial revolution was taking off, the change was more dramatic; average incomes in Western Europe reached

$1,269 in 1820 and would soar to over $5,000 in 1950, over $17,000 by 1990, and $22,000 by 2007 (this is average income per person, adjusted for inflation) (Maddison 1995). The United States was similar to Western Europe until around the time of the Civil War, after which it began to become richer faster, going from a per capita income of approximately $2,400 per person in 1870 to $5,500 in 1920, nearly $9,000 in 1950, $23,000 in 1990, and approximately $31,000 per person by 2008 (see Figure 9.1). To gain some further perspective, we can compare Western Europe with China; through 1300 CE, the two regions had similar levels of income (with China leading for much the period before), but they then begin to diverse substantially as the take-off period for Western Europe begins.

The pace of change, and improved living standards, has accelerated in recent years. As Figure 9.1 shows, in 130 years, average incomes in Western Europe increased four times, but in just the 40 years between 1950 and 1990 they increased almost 3.5 times as much (and average incomes have continued to rise since then). A similar pattern can be observed in the United States (see Figure 9.2, again using

FIGURE 9.2 UNITED STATES AND CHINA, PER-PERSON INCOME PER CAPITA

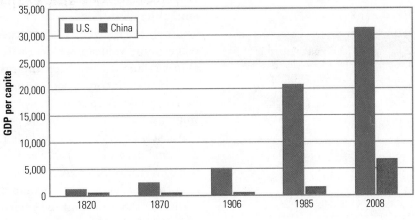

Source: Based on data from Maddison (1995).

China as a comparison), where incomes changed slowly from 1820 to 1870 but doubled between 1870 and 1906, doubled again between 1906 and 1951, and then doubled again by 1985. Since 1985, they have further increased over 50 percent, to over $31,000 per person.

These figures are impressive, but they highlight just how unequal America has become. The average income per person (for both children an adults) is currently around $31,000. This implies that the average family of four would have an income of $124,000. But we know that is high; a family of four with an income of $124,000 would be placed in the top 10 percent of all families, not around the middle. The reason for the disparity is that when we think of averages, we are often thinking about medians instead. The **median** is the midpoint of all families, where half of all such families are above and half are below. The median family income is around $60,088 (in 2009), an amount vastly below the average. How can this be? Why is the gap between the two statistics so large? The short answer is because the gap between the very richest individuals and families and everyone else has grown enormously in recent years (although it has always been large). Much of the income being generated is concentrated at the top. Indeed, almost all of the gains of economic growth since the early 1970s have gone to a very small group at the very top (see Table 9.1).

Those individuals and families who enjoy extraordinary wealth are truly unprecedented in human history. *Forbes* magazine does an annual survey of the richest people in the world. Topping *Forbes'* analysis of the richest individuals in the world in 2012 was the Mexican telephone mogul Carlos Slim Helu, who was estimated to have a net worth of $69 billion. The next two richest people—Americans Bill Gates and Warren Buffett—possessed approximately $61 and $44 billion in wealth, even *after* donating many billions to

In what specific ways are societies unequal?

a charitable foundation they jointly control (Forbes 2012). All across the globe, the rich have gotten richer, and today they collectively control an enormous share of the world's wealth. It's a good time to be super-rich. One recent study estimates that the top 1 percent of the world's population controls about 32 percent of the entire world's wealth. But it's not so good to be poor; the bottom 30 percent of the world's population—some 2 billion people—have less than 1 percent of the wealth and live on less than $2 a day (Davies et al. 2007).

☐ The Who and What of Inequality

In *what* specific ways are societies unequal? And *who* exactly are we comparing to whom? Let's start with the "what" question: Social scientists have focused most of their attention on a few especially important and unevenly distributed things. Inequalities of income and wealth are central, and the most widely discussed, but they are also fundamentally different concepts, and it is important to understand the difference. **Income** refers to the receipt of money or goods over a particular accounting period (such as hourly, weekly, monthly, or yearly). There are multiple possible sources of income: earned income from a regular job, income received from investments or ownership of income-generating properties or businesses, income transfers from the government (such as Social Security), income received from family or friends (including inheritances), and illegal or "underground" earnings (such as from crime or informal and untaxed work or business activity). Most people, before retirement age, receive most or all of their income from their job, but some have multiple sources of income.

Wealth, by which we mean the net value of the assets owned by individuals or family, is another important indicator of long-term household resources. The most commonly owned wealth asset is real estate. Approximately 70 percent of Americans own the primary residence in which they live. Because homes tend to appreciate (or increase in value) over time—at least until the last few years, when home values have declined sharply—home ownership has historically been the primary way that families with modest incomes can accumulate wealth (by buying a house and living in it for many years while it appreciates in value). A smaller subset of the population owns **net financial assets (NFA)**. These include the total value of savings, investments, and other convertible assets (less outstanding debts). Wealth differences between individuals and groups are often far larger than income differences. For example, while the top 1 percent of American households received approximately 23 percent of income in 2007 (as we will

TABLE 9.1 U.S. FAMILY INCOME, 2010

Quintile	U.S. Estimate
Top 5%	Above $181,314
Fifth Quintile	Above $99,891
Fourth Quintile	$62,151-99,891
Third Quintile	$39,212-62,150
Second Quintile	$20,700-39,211
Lowest Quintile	$0-20,699

Source: U.S. Census Bureau (2010).

see later), they commanded about 35 percent of all wealth (see Figure 9.3).

Income and wealth are critical measures of inequality, and these are the measures that are most commonly studied. But they are not the only relevant ones. Actual **consumption**—what individuals and families households are actually able to buy and consume—provides a different perspective on their well-being than income alone. Interestingly, for poor and middle-class families, consumption often *exceeds* reported income. For poor families, this is usually because other family members or friends provide money or goods or because some income is unreported (Edin and Lein 1997). Even very poor families are often able to acquire goods like telephones, televisions, and even cars—items that at some point in the past were available only to the rich. Figure 9.4 (page 236) shows evidence of how consumption of key goods has increased dramatically over time. Nevertheless, the gap between the poor and the middle class in terms of consumption remains very large. Poor households are much more likely to go without medical care or adequate food, maintain the quality of their

housing, have adequate transportation (keeping in mind that in most parts of America car ownership is an essential part of "getting around"), and so forth.

Consumption trends for average middle-class families are also often at odds with their incomes, but for a different reason. Since the 1980s, middle-class families were able to consume more than they earned by taking out loans, typically secured by their homes. These loans could be used to purchase any number of different things, including paying for college tuition for children, a new car, or to refurbish a kitchen or bathroom. Whatever the money was used for, the basic point was that many middle-class families were spending more than their incomes allowed. The downside was that the average debt load for middle-class families soared between 1975 and 2008 before leveling off, averaging about $48,800 per household in 2010 (see Figure 9.5 on page 236).

Finally, inequality of **well-being** captures a number of different dimensions of life that are essential to our everyday lives but that are distributed unequally. Among the most important aspects of well-being are health, exposure

FIGURE 9.3 WEALTH INEQUALITY

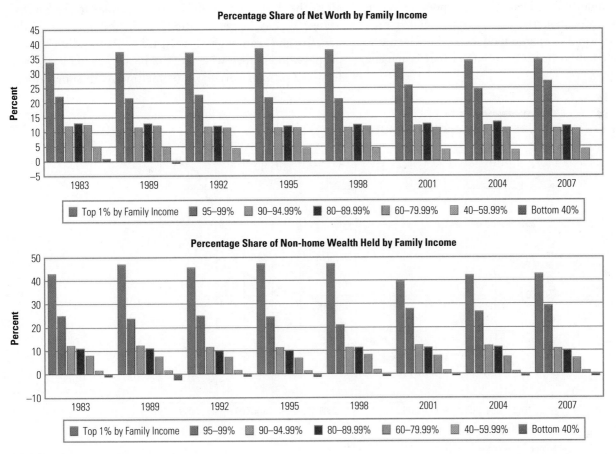

Source: Wolff (2010).

FIGURE 9.4 RISING CONSUMPTION IN THE UNITED STATES

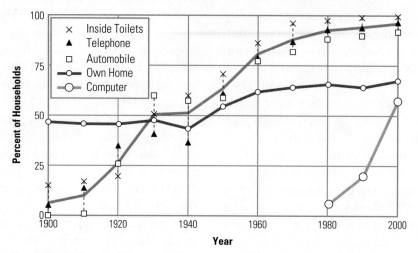

Note: The blue line shows the average of toilet, telephone, and automobile; the data points for the individual items are connected to the line.

Source: Fischer and Hout (2006).

to crime and violence, exposure to environmental risks like air or water pollution, and even one's general level of happiness. Inequalities of income and wealth are often related to well-being; for example, the rich and the middle class can purchase better quality healthcare than the poor as well as other things that provide better health (gym memberships, better quality and more organic food, etc.). They can also afford to live in neighborhoods or suburbs where crime and pollution is low.

☐ Class and Inequality

The system of inequality today does not, of course, consist only of the rich and everyone else. In most countries, and all of the developed countries most similar to the United States, there is a large **middle class** that enjoys some of the benefits and trappings of wealth. In this middle class are people working for a wide range of businesses in mostly professional or managerial jobs (sometimes with supervisorial

FIGURE 9.5 RISING HOUSEHOLD DEBT

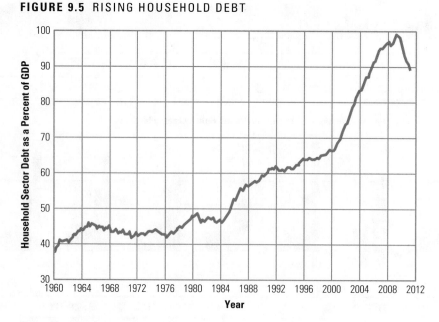

Source: Economagic.com

responsibilities), or small business owners running successful businesses. Those who have manual jobs, such as skilled factory workers, can also earn incomes that put them in the middle class. Middle-class people and their families (middle-class lifestyles often involve two working adults combining their incomes) enjoy enough income to allow them to buy homes, cars, computers, large televisions, and have savings and retirement accounts.

But how exactly do sociologists conceptualize what is meant by "the middle class"? For sociologists, class has long been a central concept in the study of inequality. Sociologists use the term **class** in general to identify groups of people in similar social and economic positions, who have similar opportunities in life, and who would benefit (or be hurt) by the same kinds of government policies. Classes are groups, not individuals (although individuals make up classes). Using the concept of class to understand some

What is the sociological concept of class?

of the broad patterns of inequality in American society can be useful beyond what we can learn by studying individuals and families.

What makes up a class? There is disagreement about how to define classes, and sociologists disagree about how many different classes there are. But most agree that classes are made up of people sharing a similar economic situation who have (1) conflicting economic interests with other classes (for example, workers want more pay while business owners want more profits); (2) share similar **life chances** (that is, members of the same class are likely to have similar incomes and opportunities as they get older); (3) have similar attitudes and behaviors; and (4) have the potential, at least, to engage in collective action (such as when workers organize a union).

Class analysis is, then, the study of how, when, and where classes exist along these four dimensions. Classes are most visible when there are sharp differences between them on some key political controversy, and people get together to protest on the basis of economic grievances. This is perhaps most obvious in a situation where revolutionary change is in the air and large numbers of people demand a more equal distribution of economic goods and opportunities. But revolutions and other types of collective action by entire classes are relatively rare. What about everyday life?

Karl Marx introduced the concept of class in his many economic and political writings in the nineteenth century (most famously in *The Communist Manifesto*, coauthored with Friedrich Engels) (Marx and Engels [1848] 1983). Marx's concept of class was that any society has a single, critical division between two classes (one dominant, one subordinate) as a result of the economic system. In capitalist

societies, this meant that the important class distinction was between business owners (or what Marx and Engels called the **bourgeoisie**) and workers who do jobs for pay (a group they referred to as the **proletariat**). Other classes could exist, but they were of minor importance. But since Marx wrote, it has long been clear that only a much broader notion of class can provide a meaningful description of contemporary capitalist societies. Various middle-class groupings—such as business managers, professionals, and those who are self-employed—are not usefully lumped together with factory workers or the baristas at Starbucks. Any sophisticated theory of class in American (or any other modern) society will need to attend to the groups in the middle.

But to ask the question "what is middle about the middle classes?" (Wright 1986) is to raise a whole host of problems for developing a theory of class. There have been three broad solutions to this problem. The first solution is to distinguish classes based on income. Those with high incomes belong in one class, those with incomes near the median are in the middle class, and those with low incomes are in the lower classes. Simple, right? But the problem with using income to define classes is that there are no clear-cut boundaries between classes (does having an annual income of $79,000 place a person in the middle class while an income of $80,000 places another person in the upper class?). Further, sociologists have argued that more important than the amount of income is the *source* of income. How people earn gives us a better way of predicting how people will behave, who their friends are, and what kinds of opinions they may hold. For example, a part-time college instructor may have the same *current* income as the unionized janitor who cleans up at the end of the day. But, having earned advanced degrees and possessing a different skill-set than the janitor, the instructor has the potential to earn far more income over her life than the janitor, even if she is currently not earning more. The sociological concept of class attempts to capture these varying life chances in dividing society into class locations.

A second approach to class that some analysts employ is to move in the opposite direction from a simple income measure and utilize a much broader definition of class based on components such as education, income, and current occupation. Using this approach, researchers can construct a score for an individual's **socioeconomic status (SES)**. The basic premise of the SES approach is that by combining a number of different attributes of any individual, we can properly place him or her in relation to others, and assign him or her a class. While different weights can be assigned to each, one basic decision rule is that someone scoring high on all three dimensions (income, education, occupation) is "high SES," someone scoring low on all three is "low SES," and everyone else is "middle SES."

SES is useful for many purposes and does more than income measures to distinguish among people for research purposes. But a key aspect of class theory is that members of the same class should have some context for acting together to try to improve their lives in some way. People in the same SES location are not ever likely to act together on that basis. A third approach to class, and the one favored by most sociologists, is to focus solely on each person's occupation in adulthood. Following Marx, this approach views the place of each individual in the economic system as crucial. And unlike income or SES, there are many examples of occupational groups having similar political views and acting together to push for higher wages or to change government policies (e.g., in unions or professional associations like the American Bar Association or the American Medical Association). Most of the occupation-based approaches divide different occupations into a small group of distinct classes. The most popular of these schemes is that of sociologists Robert Erikson and John Goldthorpe (Erikson and Goldthorpe 1992), who have identified five core classes displayed (in a slightly simplified way) in Table 9.2. The Erikson–Goldthorpe scheme makes distinctions between those individuals who own their own businesses (or are self-employed) and those who work for someone else. Among those who are employed, distinctions are made between those who have jobs that either entail supervising others or require employer trust and those that do not; between those involving manual work or not; and, among manual workers, those that require special skills and training.

☐ Justifying Inequality

If inequality, as we have noted, is universal in human societies, it is not surprising that many thinkers, scholars, and politicians have concluded that income or wealth inequality is both inevitable and even *necessary* for societies as a whole to function. Exploring these ideas helps us to understand both the nature of inequality and some of the controversies it generates.

Justifications of inequality have taken many forms over the centuries, including those based on tradition, such as the idea that the level of inequality reflects God's will or, more simply, that privilege based on inheritance is a natural process in which people are born into their station in life. While such ideas persist in some parts of the world today, in most places two basic justifications of inequality stand out as particularly important. The first idea is that inequality ensures that those with "talent" are given proper encouragement to develop their talents and pursue excellence for the benefit of all. The second is that inequality leads to greater economic efficiency by encouraging people to take risks and invest in businesses in the hopes of receiving higher returns than if they just worked for someone else.

These two justifications of inequality have been defended in a variety of ways. One way is by using the example of an imaginary world in which all incomes and rewards are identical (as we've noted, no such society can be found in the modern world, but that has not stopped proponents of inequality to use the image to defend inequality). The fear is that in such a world, where the doctor, the janitor, and the fast-food worker all receive the same income, it would be difficult to attract the most qualified people to become doctors (or fill other important positions). How could we motivate them to undergo the lengthy training period that is required to become a doctor if they could immediately start making the same amount of money as a janitor? Defenders of inequality often point to historical examples of communist societies in the twentieth century, most notably the Soviet Union and other countries in Eastern Europe, to argue that attempts to legislate more equality can have disastrous consequences for motivating people to do their best possible work.

How is inequality justified?

TABLE 9.2 THE ERIKSON–GOLDTHORPE CLASS SCHEME

Salariat/Service Class: Professionals, managers, and administrators; higher-grade technicians; supervisors of nonmanual workers

Routine Nonmanual Workers: Nonsupervisorial employees in administration and commerce positions; sales workers; secretaries, clerks, and other rank-and-file white-collar workers

Petty-Bourgeoisie: Business owners (other than farm); self-employed workers and consultants; artisans, etc.

Farm Owners: Farmers and ranchers (landowners)

Skilled Workers and Supervisors: Skilled manual workers; supervisors of manual workers (foremen); lower-grade technicians/repairmen

Nonskilled Workers: Semi- and unskilled manual workers

Farm Laborers: Farm and ranch employees

Source: Erikson and Goldthorpe (1992)

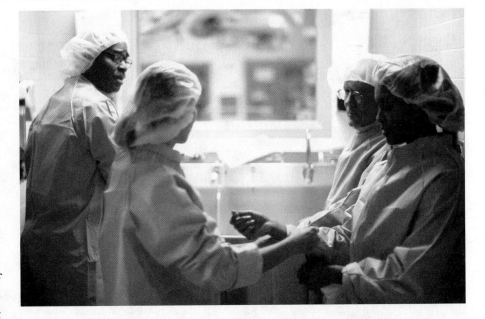

One justification for inequality is that wide differences in pay are needed to recruit talented people into important jobs, such as specialized surgeons, and to motivate lengthy training. But how large should these differences be to achieve motivation?

The talent justification for inequality holds that talent is unevenly distributed because all individuals are born with different biological traits. Genetic differences between people produce differences that societies should recognize and take advantage of. The idea is that some of us are simply born with abilities that the rest of us do not have. Societies provide unequal rewards in order to ensure that those born with special gifts will be motivated to develop those talents. For example, it might be argued that there is only one golfer in the world with the gifts of Tiger Woods, and hence it is appropriate that Woods should be compensated for having developed special talents. Similarly, it can be argued that a great lawyer or surgeon has gifts that vastly exceed those of the average lawyer or surgeon, so he or she should be rewarded accordingly. However, recent research by cognitive psychologists suggests that this is not so simple. Talent is largely something that can be acquired (through careful training), not something individuals are simply born with (Ericsson et al. 2006). Having the opportunity to develop a talent is often a privilege that comes with having enough resources to afford great teachers, mentors, coaches, trainers, and the ability to travel to conferences or events to meet others developing similar talents.

The efficiency justification, by contrast, argues that inequality enables everyone to live better because the possibility of disproportionate rewards motivates individuals to take risks and create things of value. For example, why would anyone make a potentially risky investment in a new business opportunity unless there was some potential to profit from it? The rich are even sometimes referred to as "job creators," an idea based on the notion that investing in businesses is what creates jobs. Of course not all rich people are wealthy because they have invested in a business (many have inherited wealth, while others become wealthy even while employed by someone else). But to the extent that investment is driven by a desire to make money, society as a whole would suffer from a lack of investment if business owners were not allowed to earn more.

The view that rewarding talent and making society more efficient by encouraging people to invest in new businesses provides a firm foundation for inequality. These arguments have proved quite powerful in the political realm when questions of poverty and inequality occasionally arise. But these justifications nevertheless raise as many questions as they answer. First of all, to say that inequality in general is beneficial begs the question of *how much* inequality is beneficial. "Efficiency" appears achievable across many different level of social inequality, with some very **egalitarian** countries — where disparities between the poor and the rich are small — achieving growth rates and standards of living comparable to those of the United States (which, as we will see in the next section, is a very inegalitarian country). In other words, the comparative evidence suggests that you do not need to have as much inequality as we do today in the United States to get the benefits of motivating people to work hard and maximizing their potential that much lower levels of inequality can provide. Further, very high levels of inequality have significant costs as well as benefits. While modest inequalities can be desirable in many ways, high levels of inequality give the appearance of injustice and may eventually give rise to sharp conflicts between groups. Further, those who are on top in highly unequal societies have incentives to prevent redistribution and to maintain the status quo, and promoting ideas about rewarding talent or promoting efficiency may serve merely to justify a world they benefit from. The very rich in unequal societies, for example, are likely to dominate the political system, even if it is otherwise democratic.

We will explore in more detail the ways in which excessive inequality can be harmful to societies later in this chapter. First, however, we need to gather some basic facts about the nature of contemporary inequality.

2 Why Is America So Unequal?

UNEQUAL AMERICA IN COMPARATIVE PERSPECTIVE

👁 **Watch** the **Big Question Video** in **MySocLab**

T oday, inequality in the United States is about as high as it has ever been, at least since good data about incomes became available in the early twentieth century. Inequality is also, as we shall see, higher than in any other rich, democratic country (although there are less developed countries that have more inequality). And in spite of its enormous wealth, the United States has more people living in poverty than most other similar countries. These two facts are both of considerable importance, requiring us to think hard about how and why America is so unequal.

Trends in Income Inequality in the United States and around the World

When did inequality start increasing? Is this a new trend, or has inequality been growing for a long time as the United States has experienced urbanization and industrialization? Researchers have been able to examine tax returns as a source of information about income in order to measure income inequality since 1917, soon after the Federal Income tax was established permanently by the 16th Amendment. Because in the United States everyone has to file a tax return, even if they don't pay taxes, it is possible to track the incomes of all U.S. families over a long historical time period.

What does this analysis show? One way that researchers have used to measure long-term

trends in inequality is the share of total national income that goes to different groups in the country. In a perfectly equal society, the income share of the wealthiest one-tenth of families, for example, will be exactly 10 percent of the national income. The higher the income share of the wealthiest 10 percent, the more inequality there is. Figure 9.6—drawn from the pioneering work of economists Emmanuel Saez and Thomas Piketty (Saez and Piketty 2010)—gives us a picture of inequality since 1917.

FIGURE 9.6 SHARE OF INCOME IN THE TOP 10 PERCENT OF FAMILIES AND THE TOP 1 PERCENT OF FAMILIES IN THE UNITED STATES, 1917–2010

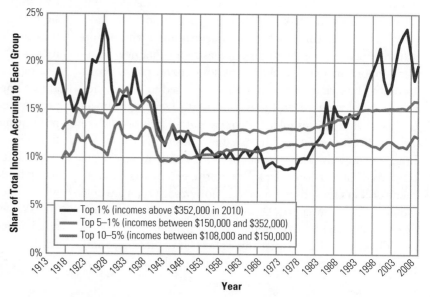

- Top 1% (incomes above $352,000 in 2010)
- Top 5–1% (incomes between $150,000 and $352,000)
- Top 10–5% (incomes between $108,000 and $150,000)

Source: Saez (2012).

A SOCIOLOGICAL PERSPECTIVE

Why is inequality in the United States today so high?

Inequality was very high during the 1920s, a period in which the stock market and the banking industry were extremely profitable. The wealthiest 10 percent received almost half of the total national income, including families that accumulated large amounts of industrial and financial wealth. Inequality dropped sharply after the 1930s, impacted by the Wall Street crash of 1929 which destroyed big financial fortunes and induced the Great Depression. World War II (1939–1945) pushed economic growth during and after the war.

With the infusion of well-paid jobs in new industries and expanded consumption possibilities for U.S. families, middle class families prospered. In the 1960s, the U.S. government launched the "Great Society," a policy aimed at reducing poverty and racial inequality, which hit record lows in the 1960s-early 1970s, but began to rise again in the late 1970s. Since then, like in the 1920s, the financial industries grew rapidly and allowed some people to become very wealthy. By 2010, the share of total income going to the wealthiest one-tenth of families reached the 1920s levels – these families received again about 45 percent of the total national income.

Under what circumstances have ordinary people–like the demonstrators in the 1930s shown here–been willing to challenge high levels of economic inequality?

The Occupy Wall Street movement that began in the fall of 2011 raised serious questions about the huge salaries being received by Wall Street bankers while ordinary Americans had no increase in household income in 12 years. Do you think this movement or another like it will grow in the future?

Is the nature of inequality cyclical or are there ways individuals, communities, and governments can better maintain more equitable levels of inequality over time?

⊙→ **Explore** A Sociological Perspective in **MySocLab** and then …

Think About It

Which types of policies would result in less inequality in a society? Beyond the most obvious "taxing those who have more and giving to those who have less," what other initiatives may reduce inequality?

Inspire Your Sociological Imagination

In which ways do people notice that the level of inequality is changing around them? Does inequality have an effect on the way neighborhoods, cities, schools, and politics work?

241

As we can see, the income share of the wealthiest 10 percent has always been more than 10 percent. *How much more* has changed consider-able over time. The post-war period from the 1940s to the 1970s marks a historical low in the level of inequality in the United States. In the 1960s, only about one-third of the total income in the country went to the wealthiest one-tenth of families. We can also see that there has been much change in inequality since 1917. Explore *A Sociological Perspective* on page 241 to see how inequality has changed in the last century.

How different is the level of income inequality in the United States compared to other countries around the world? As the Infographic on page 243 suggests, the United States is very unequal compared to other rich countries. We have twice as much inequality as Sweden and about one-third more than most other European countries. This is instructive in that these are the countries that have similar levels of economic development to us, as well as similar educational systems and democratic political institutions. The United States is the most unequal country of the developed world, and that difference is substantial. Indeed, to find countries with *more* inequality, we would have to include in the comparison group a couple of countries in Latin America and Africa that have extremely high levels of inequality (South Africa and Nambia are the most inegalitarian countries in the world).

The most egalitarian countries in the world are Scandinavian countries—Sweden, Norway, Finland, and Denmark. These nations have a type of political system in which the government plays a strong role in ensuring a minimum standard of living for citizens, through policies such as promoting full employment, providing universal access to healthcare, and redistributing resources from those who have higher incomes to those who have lower incomes via taxes and transfers. These policies have tended to reduce poverty and inequality, although there are still very rich people in countries like Sweden (which has three of the world's richest 100 billionaires, quite a high number for a tiny country) (Esping-Andersen 1990).

☐ Why Did Inequality Increase?

Which factors explain the increase in economic inequality over the last decades, not only in the United States but in other countries as well? On the one hand, the fact that inequality has also risen in most advanced industrial countries suggests that at least some of these factors are shared across the industrialized world. On the other hand, the fact that inequality is higher and has risen faster in the United States than

How does income inequality in the U.S. compare to other countries around the world?

in other countries suggests that something different is going on in the United States. Researchers are hard at work trying to address this question, and the accounts they have offered are still preliminary because the trends are so recent. We do know, however, that several factors have played a role.

The Changing Relationship between Technological Expansion and Education　From the 1970s onwards, the United States has experienced major technological advancements, including the universalization of personal computers in the workplace and the expansion of computer networks and telecommunication technologies. There was a time not so long ago when nobody used computers and when face-to-face meetings or typed letters instead of e-mail and smartphones were the norm for communication.

Technology matters for inequality because it complements some jobs while it replaces others, making them obsolete. For example, changes in computer networking have replaced bank tellers (an occupation that requires middle-level skills) with ATMs and online access to your bank. At the same time, these improvements in computer technology have increased the need for a new type of bank worker, a sales-oriented financial analyst who usually has an MBA or at least a BA. In general, technology complements jobs that require higher levels of education—a college degree or more—while it replaces jobs with middle and lower levels of education. This has happened with many jobs. As a result, having a college degree or more pays off more than before—increasing the so-called college premium—whereas people with less than a college degree see their earnings decline or have increasing trouble finding a job.

Why has economic inequality in the U.S. increased since the 1960s?

Social scientists call this **skill-biased technological change (SBTC),** which simply means that technological advancements are creating jobs that require high skill, which usually means a college degree or more. SBTC is causing growing inequality. But why now? After all, major technological advancements are not a new phenomenon in U.S. history. For example, the expansion of electricity in the late nineteenth century may have been even more revolutionary than the introduction of the personal computer and the Internet. The reason is that technological innovations are only part of the story accounting for growing inequality. The other part is the extent to which education expands to meet the needs of technological development. If the number of college graduates increases at the same pace as technology, so that the educational system meets the needs of the economy, then college graduates will not receive a premium simply because there will be more of them.

Income Inequality

eveloped by the Italian statistician and sociologist, Corrado Gini, the Gini Index
s the most commonly used measure of overall income inequality. The Index
s from 0 to 1, where 0 indicates complete equality (all families have the same
e) and 1 indicates complete inequality (one family gets all the income, and all
families gets nothing). The larger the Gini is, the more inequality there is.
e inequality in America has grown since the 1960s, mainly because "the rich
creasingly richer," not because "the poor are getting poorer."

Based on data from U.S. Census Bureau (2012); C.I.A. World Factbook (2012).

**data from 2000-2012, compared to sub-Saharan Africa and Latin America,
Gini values of 0.5 are common, the United States is somewhat more
but compared to other rich countries, especially in Europe, the U.S. is
nequal.**

Gini Index
United States

0.44
0.36

1970 1980 1990 2000 2

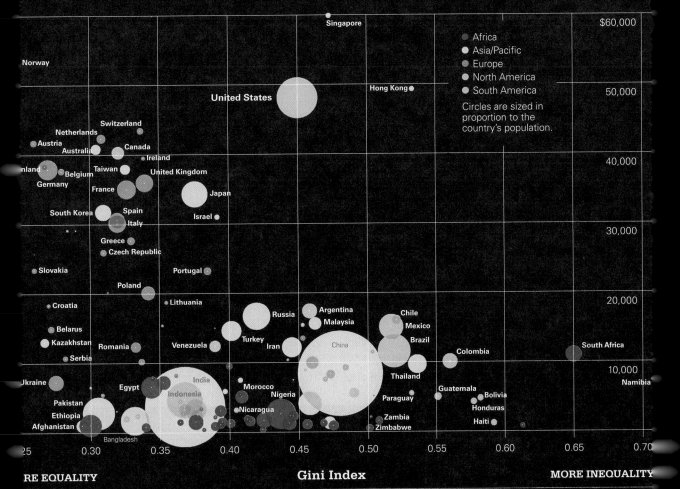

Circles are sized in proportion to the country's population.

- Africa
- Asia/Pacific
- Europe
- North America
- South America

RE EQUALITY

Gini Index

MORE INEQUALITY

0.30 0.35 0.40 0.45 0.50 0.55 0.60 0.65 0.70

Explore the Data on Income Inequality in **MySocLab** and then …

ink About It

e the main factors explaining the growing
ween high-income families and everyone

Inspire Your Sociological Imagination

Why do you think poorer countries are more unequal than richer ones? Does a
country's poverty cause inequality, or does inequality cause poverty?

What has happened in the United States in the last few decades is that higher education has not expanded at the pace required by technological change. As a result, people who have a college degree have become scarcer relative to the needs of the economy, and because of their relative scarcity they have been receiving higher salaries. As two economic historians have put it, a dynamic economy is characterized by a "race between education and technology" (Goldin and Katz 2010). If technology advances too fast, then educational expansion does not match the expansion of technology in the workplace and the college premium increases. This, some researchers argue, is what has happened in the United States since the 1980s. (Many recent college graduates, since the recession that began in 2007, may puzzle over this claim, as unemployment has grown and it is harder even for college graduates to find good jobs. But we are describing a much longer trend and one that is likely to continue once the American economy starts growing again.)

SBTC explanations are powerful because they are consistent with the timing of the trend in inequality—in particular with the greater gains of those at the top of the income distribution. But SBTC cannot be the whole story. First of all, inequality began to increase in the late 1970s, before massive implementation of computers in the workplace, which only happened in the late 1980s. Also, technological expansion has been comparable in Europe and the United States, but inequality has increased more in the United States. Further, the earnings of professionals in many fields most closely related to technological innovation—such as engineers and computer system analysts—are not the ones that have grown the most. So we need to consider other explanations as well, in particular: deindustrialization, government policies, and the decline of labor unions.

Deindustrialization and Restructuring Developed countries like the United States have also undergone a steady decline in industrial or manufacturing jobs, while there has been a parallel increase in service jobs such as those related to healthcare, finance, and retail. In 1950, almost 40 percent of jobs were in industry and manufacturing. Today, only 20 percent are. While "service" is a big category, for many workers this process of deindustrialization meant substituting bad jobs for good ones—jobs that pay less, offer fewer benefits such as healthcare and pensions, and are more likely to be part time. For example, some jobs that have been growing recent years—like food preparation workers, security guards, childcare workers, customer service representatives, healthcare aides, and cashiers—are all low-wage, low-benefit jobs that an increasing numbers of people hold. Meanwhile, factory jobs that typically pay higher wages than these jobs have been declining in recent decades.

Why have manufacturing jobs disappeared so rapidly in the United States and other countries? The heart of the answer is not that there is less manufacturing being done in the world but rather that it is increasingly being done elsewhere, in places where workers will accept lower wages and companies can, as a result, make higher profits. At the center of this important change is **globalization**, which involves the growing permeability of national borders and the increase in flows of goods, services, and even people across national borders. One of the most important aspects of globalization is the increasing *trade* between countries, which results in cheaper imported goods from these countries and often allows companies to relocate manufacturing jobs in other countries. Because developing countries can often produce products at lower cost than in richer countries, trade can depress the wages of low-skill domestic workers who produce these goods.

Globalization has also led, in short, to what is known as **outsourcing**—the contracting of parts of the production process to another party, often abroad, such as when the customer service representative who helps you with your credit card bill issue does so from India. Outsourcing is extremely common in manufacturing, where different components can be made in different places with only final assembly taking place in the United States. As *New York Times* columnist Thomas Friedman (2012) indicates, the world is now so thoroughly integrated that products are imagined, designed, built, and marketed through global supply chains, wherever their cheap productive and organizational talent is available. Products are not "Made in America," even if final assembly takes place here. Rather, they are "made in the world." Take Apple Computer as an example. A few years after Apple began building the first Macintosh computer in 1983, the late Steve Jobs bragged that it was "a machine that is made in

Foxconn is a large Taiwanese multinational company with large plants in China where Apple products are manufactured. Foxconn workers make an average of $1.5-2.20/hour, a fraction of what a similar worker would make in the U.S. but much more than an average Chinese worker, who makes about 35-65 cents per hour. Foxconn has been criticized for poor working conditions of its workers. Whose responsibility is it to protect workers' health and rights – Apple, the Chinese government, or consumers?

FIGURE 9.7 AVERAGE HOURLY WAGE AND PRODUCTIVITY, 1947–2009

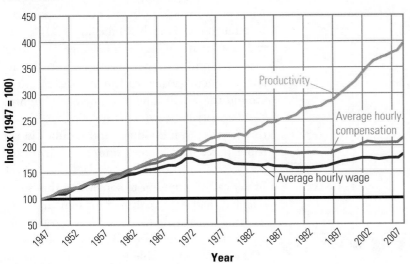

Source: Economic Policy Institute (2009).

The cumulative impact of economic restructuring can be seen most clearly in the flattening out of wages for workers in the middle and lower half of the American economy. Figure 9.7 provides the grim details. Average wages have stagnated since the 1970s, even though the average worker is far more productive in 2010 than the same worker would have been in 1970 (**productivity** is a measure of the output per worker per hour).

Government Policies   So far we have focused on economic changes in driving the overall pattern of income inequality, but the pattern is also very much the result of government policies. The most important of these policies is taxation, while for the very poor the failure to raise the minimum wage has been especially consequential.

Taxes have a big impact on the overall level of inequality in a society because of their impact on high earners, and because taxes are used to pay for government programs that support the poor, the elderly, the disabled, and other disadvantaged individuals and families. A **progressive tax system** is one in which tax rates are higher on richer people than poorer people, with the idea being that it is fairer to ask those who can afford to pay more to do so. Most tax systems around the world, including in the United States, are progressive. When the tax rates on high earners are high, it will constrain their incomes (why try to earn more if you going to give most of it back in the form of taxes?). Of course, it is never that simple; because the tax code contains a large number of deductions and exemptions, the actual rate paid by high earners (who typically employ a small army of tax lawyers and consultants to reduce their tax burdens) will be lower than the official rate. Still, the rates paid by the highest earning Americans have fallen dramatically over time, from over 90 percent to 36 percent today (see Figure 9.8). This decline, along with other important changes to tax rates, such as reduced taxes on certain kinds of income, has meant in practice that the actual rates paid by high earners are much less. 2012 Republican presidential candidate Mitt Romney, who has an estimated net worth of $250 million, paid just 13.9 percent of his income in federal taxes in 2010 on more than $21 million in income.

Another important trend in government policy has been the failure of federal government to raise the **minimum wage** to keep up with inflation. While the minimum wage had grown steadily between the 1940s and the late 1960s, it was frozen in the 1980s (see Figure 9.9). Freezing it meant that it lost much of its value in real terms because it was not adjusted for inflation. Prices kept rising, but the minimum wage did not. So after adjusting for inflation, the real (inflation-adjusted) value of the minimum wage dropped from about $9 an hour in 1978 to less than $6 an hour in 1990 and has remained constant thereafter (having been raised enough to keep pace with inflation but not to make up for past losses).

America." Today, all of the 70 million iPhones, 30 million iPads, and 59 million other hardware products Apple sold in 2011 were manufactured overseas. Many of these popular products are made by an enormous Chinese manufacturing company called Foxconn, in a complex of factories located in Shenzhen, China, that employs over 300,000 workers. At these plants, Apple products are made by workers who labor long hours for low pay under demanding and sometimes risky conditions. Many of these popular products are made by an enormous multinational manufacturing company called Foxconn, with large factories in China that employ hundreds of thousands of workers to assemble and clean iPhones and iPads. At these plants, Apple products are made by workers who labor long hours for low pay under demanding and sometimes risky conditions. According to a recent *New York Times* report, an explosion killed two workers and hurt a dozen in a Foxconn plant in Chengdu, China. In Wintek, another Apple manufacturing partner in China, hundreds of workers were injured after being ordered to use toxic chemicals to clean the iPhone screens, highlighting a record of poor safety procedures at these factories that has long been documented (Duhigg and Barboza 2012).

Deindustrialization is a critical piece of the larger pattern of **economic restructuring**, which refers to changes in the way the economy, firms, and employment relations are organized that have taken place since the 1970s. The post–World War II decades of the 1950s and 1960s were characterized by an organizational type in which many employees, once hired, were offered long-term job stability and protected from economic volatility. The deep economic recession of the early 1970s shook this system. Based on a desire to cut costs and increase profits, firms increasingly sought to squeeze their workers and make terms of employment more flexible. For example, it became much easier for employers to dismiss employers, to reduce benefits, and to avoid having to bargain with unions.

FIGURE 9.8 TOP MARGINAL TAX RATES, 1960–2011*

*Top Marginal Tax Rates refers to the rate that applies to the wealthiest taxpayers.

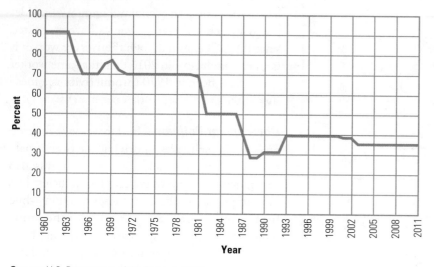

Source: U.S. Department of the Treasury (2011).

The 1 Percent

Most people would rather be rich than poor. But how much is too much? In the fall of 2011, a social movement calling itself Occupy Wall Street exploded on the scene, first in New York City and later across America and in other countries around the world. The movement highlighted the disparity between what it called the "1 percent"—that is, individuals and families in the top 1 percent of income and/or wealth—and everyone else (the "99 percent"). Occupy Wall Street called attention to something that social scientists had been analyzing for some time: the growing disparity between the very top and everyone else (Neckerman and Torche 2007). One of the most remarkable trends in inequality in America, especially over the past 25 years, has been the pulling away of the top 1 percent. And, as more detailed research shows, it is really the top half of the top 1 percent—those individuals and families in the top 0.5 percent—who have done best. In fact, the higher up you go, the better things look.

Table 9.3 displays this picture starkly for the year 2007 (again, drawing from the important work of the economists Saez and Piketty). In this year, the top 400 taxpayers (either individuals or married couples filing jointly) received 1.6 percent of all income received that year. The average income of this rarefied group was a whopping $344,800,000. The next highest group identified in the table is the top one-hundredth of the top 1 percent. This only slightly less rarefied group had an average income of $26,548,000. 14,588 taxpayers fell into that category, including a few well-known

The stereotypical portrait of the minimum-wage earner is a teenager working for purchase money. In fact, as many as 70 percent of minimum-wage earners are adults, many of whom are minorities and women (Morris and Western 1999). Even if the minimum wage affects only a small proportion of the working population (about 5 to 6 percent of all workers currently make the minimum wage), it does matter for inequality because it affects the well-being of families at the bottom of the income distribution *and* because many workers are paid just over the minimum wage (so when it does not go up, those workers are not likely to see any increases either).

Who is the "1 percent"?

Union Decline Labor unions are collective organizations that represent workers in their dealings with employers. As with the decline in the minimum wage, the decline of unions is thought to contribute to inequality because unions tend to raise average wages and reduce the amount of profits that employers are able to keep for themselves. The proportion of employed workers belonging to unions reached a peak in the 1950s in the United States; at that time, about one-third of all workers belonged to a union. Unionization has dropped dramatically since then, particularly during the 1980s. As of 2010, only 12 percent of all workers belonged to a union, and the majority of union workers are employed in government jobs where wages are less unequal. Today, only about 7 percent of private-sector employees are in unions, a figure that continues to decline each year. This decline leaves America with the weakest unions of all the rich countries and reduces the collective power of workers to push for a greater share of profits.

FIGURE 9.9 THE DECLINING VALUE OF MINIMUM WAGE, 1960–2009

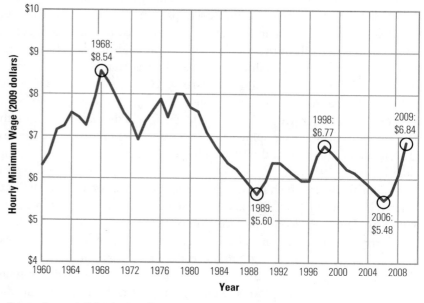

Source: Economic Policy Institute (2009).

TABLE 9.3 MATERIAL POWER IN THE UNITED STATES, BASED ON 2007 INCOMES

THE MATERIAL POWER INDEX EXPRESSES THE INCOME OF TOP TAXPAYERS AS A MULTIPLE OF THE AVERAGE INCOME OF THE BOTTOM 90 PERCENT OF TAXPAYERS.

Threshold of Taxpayers	Number of Taxpayers	Average Income	% of All Income	% Income Cumulative	Material Power Index
Top 400	400	$344,800,000	1.6	1.6	10,327
Top 1/100th of 1%	14,588	$26,548,000	4.5	6.1	819
Top 1/10th of 1%	134,888	$4,024,583	6.2	12.3	124
Top half of 1%	593,500	$1,021,643	7.0	19.3	32
Top 1%	749,375	$486,395	4.2	23.5	15
Top 5%	5,995,000	$220,105	15.1	38.6	7
Top 10%	7,493,750	$128,560	11.1	49.7	4
Bottom 90%	134,887,500	$32,421	50.3	100.0	1

Note: Based on IRS tabulations of individual income tax returns for 2007, CPS-estimated number of potential tax units and National Income Accounts total income figures. Income includes realized capital gains. Each income level is exclusive of the category above it. Average income of the top 400 taxpayers is from the Internal Revenue Service (2009). The total number of taxpayers filing returns in 2007 is 149,875,300, and the total reported gross personal income is $8,701 billion.

Source: Winters (2011).

celebrities, singers, actors, and athletes. By the time we've calculated the incomes of the top 15,000 people, we've already consumed over 6 percent of all income received in 2007! This is in a country with a population of about 313 million people. By contrast, the bottom 90 percent of all taxpayers had an average income of $32,421 and received just slightly over 50 percent of all income. In other words, the top 1 percent of all earners received 23.5 percent of all income, the bottom 90 percent a little over twice as much (50.3 percent).

We can get a different view of the trends when we look over time. When we do so, we find a very stark fact: Virtually all of the economic gains of the past three decades have gone to the top 1 percent of the population (and among the top 1 percent, the top half has done much better than the bottom half). We can see this most clearly when we look at over-time changes in household incomes at different levels of American society (see Figure 9.10). Broken out in this way, we see that households incomes have been nearly flat for all categories except the top 5 percent, with the partial exception of the period in the late 1990s, while the top 1 percent and especially the top 0.5 percent have pulled away from everyone else.

In view of these trends, it is entirely appropriate to pay careful attention to the top layers of American society. In the vast writings on the American upper class, two distinct "wings" have been the subject of much lore: the recently rich, sometimes called the new rich, and an older, more established social upper class, which has longer and deeper upper-class pedigrees. The new rich are often portrayed in literature and films as somewhat uncouth and excessively reliant on the use of money to buy their way into the best schools and clubs rather than taking the time to master the social graces that go along with upper-class status. The "old money" social upper class, by contrast, is said by the newcomers to be snotty,

pampered, lazy, and resting on their laurels (or even worse, the laurels earned by previous generations of rich families).

We have relatively little systematic social science research on whether and to what extent these images reflect any real or important conflict. One of the great paradoxes of the social science of inequality is that we know *much more* about the lives of the very poor than the very rich. While the rich live behind gated enclaves that are hard for researchers to penetrate, the poor have been put under the social science microscope over and over again in the past 100 years. It's remarkably easier to get research grants to study poor children and their families than anything pertaining to studying rich people. Our knowledge of the rich rests on a much thinner research foundation.

FIGURE 9.10 CHANGES IN HOUSEHOLD INCOMES IN THE UNITED STATES OVER TIME

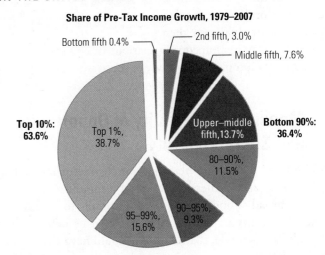

Share of Pre-Tax Income Growth, 1979–2007

Bottom fifth 0.4%
2nd fifth, 3.0%
Middle fifth, 7.6%
Top 10%: 63.6%
Top 1%, 38.7%
Upper–middle fifth, 13.7%
Bottom 90%: 36.4%
80–90%, 11.5%
95–99%, 15.6%
90–95%, 9.3%

Source: Economic Policy Institute (2010).

3 Do We All Have an Equal Opportunity to Succeed in Life?

INEQUALITY, EDUCATION, AND SOCIAL MOBILITY

👁 Watch the Big Question Video in MySocLab

So far we have discussed inequality as a snapshot of where individuals and whole societies are at a particular point in time. But this is only part of the story. One important type of inequality is inequality of opportunity—which refers to the ways in which inequality shapes the opportunities for children and young adults to maximize their potential. Equality of opportunity would exist in a world where all children have similar chances to succeed in life, regardless of whether they were born in wealthy or poor families. If everyone, regardless of their **social background**—their family, the community they live and grow up in—has similar chances of success in life as an adult, we could say that opportunities are truly equally distributed. If, in contrast, an individual's chances to do well in life depend on the advantages or disadvantages of birth and early childhood, then we say opportunity is unequally distributed. This is one of the most important topics in the study of social stratification.

Measuring Inequality of Opportunity and Social Mobility

While most Americans accept some degree of inequality in outcomes as an inherent feature of a capitalist economy, there is broad support in the United States today for the ideal of equality of opportunity. Most of us believe very strongly, for example, that children should have the opportunity to flourish even if they are born into families with limited resources. This idea is part of what is known as the American Dream, and it is one of the most cherished aspects of life in United States. Politicians and social theorists have also sometimes called for equality of opportunity on the grounds that it benefits society; they argue that if poor children have no chance to succeed in life, their talent will be wasted, and this is inefficient for the society as a whole.

But do we have something approximating equality of opportunity? Measuring opportunity in any society is not a simple research question. Whereas we can measure other kinds of inequalities—income, wealth, consumption, even well-being—in relatively straightforward ways (even if the details are complicated!), there is no one obvious way of determining how much opportunity individuals really have. The solution that social scientists have settled on is that of examining what is known as **social mobility**, the pattern of intergenerational inheritance in a society. Social mobility is a measure of the extent to which parents and their children have similar or different social and economic positions in adulthood. A high-mobility society is one where there is relatively little connection between parents' and children's place in life. A high-mobility society approximates the ideal of equality of opportunity; in such a society, where a child ends up in life is determined largely through her or his own achievements. By contrast, when there is a relatively close connection between parents and their children's positions when children reach adulthood, social mobility is low. An immobile society can at the extreme become a **caste society**,

How is inequality of opportunity measured?

one in which the advantages or disadvantages of birth determine fully your social position (such as was traditionally the case in India, where being born into a lower caste gave one few chances in life).

In a perfectly mobile society, parents' resources would be completely irrelevant for children's outcomes; that is, everyone would have the same chances of succeeding in life regardless of their family background. In a perfectly immobile society, however, chances of success would be entirely determined by parental resources. Children of poor parents would grow up to be poor, while children of rich parents would grow up to be rich. The question about mobility is thus a question about "who gets what?" Specifically, we ask the question: To what extent do family resources (that is, who your parents are) determine how well you will do in life?

Accounts of individual social mobility often focus on individual effort and ability. Stories about mobility usually highlight exceptional individuals who overcame massive difficulties and experience upward mobility—the "rags to riches" story—and less frequently, individuals who decline in spite of the many opportunities they had and experience downward mobility. Countless movies and novels have portrayed either of these situations. These anecdotal cases often highlight the extent to which individual upward and downward mobility can be linked to specific individual attributes: hard work overcoming disadvantage, drug abuse offsetting privilege, and so forth. Sociologists have shown, however, that mobility is not simply an attribute of individuals. If it were, there wouldn't be much variation across different societies. But when we look at differences in mobility rates across countries, we find that there are, indeed, societies that provide more opportunity to their citizens for upward mobility, regardless of their family backgrounds, than others. In every society there are exceptional people who defy norms and expectations, but there are also general patterns that can be identified.

Oprah Winfrey is an example of a "rags to riches" upward mobility story. Born into poverty in rural Mississippi to a teenage single mother, and raised in an inner city neighborhood in Milwaukee, she overcame severe adversity to become a billionaire and philanthropist. How exceptional is Winfrey's story? What would it take for biographies like Winfrey's to be more prevalent in the U.S.?

How do chances for mobility in the United States compare to other countries?

Social Mobility in Comparative Perspective

One way in which social scientists measure mobility in different societies is by identifying the strength of the **correlation**—that is, the relationship between two variables that change together—between parents' income (or any other measure of socioeconomic standing) and children's income. A correlation of zero means that there is no literally no connection whatsoever between parents' income and children's income. That is, parents' income does not make any difference on how small or larger their children's income will be. This identifies a situation of perfect mobility. A correlation of one, in turn, means that parents' income fully determines children's income, which identifies a situation of perfect **immobility**. Specifically, it means that if your parents have an income that is, say, 50 percent higher than the average income, you too as an adult will have an income 50 percent higher than the average. In real existing societies, the intergenerational correlation is always somewhere between zero and one.

Figure 9.11 displays the correlation of earnings in the United States and other advanced industrial countries for which we have comparable data. As the figure shows, the chances of mobility substantially vary across countries. Countries such as Italy, France, and the United States have relatively high intergenerational correlation, that is, lower mobility on this measure. On the other extreme, Nordic countries such as Denmark, Norway, and Finland have weaker correlations between parents' and children's income, indicating higher chances of mobility. For example, the intergenerational correlation in Norway is .16. That means that, on average, you pass 16 percent of your economic advantage to your kids. If I earn $100,000 more than the mean income, then, on average, my kids will earn $16,000 more than mean. By contrast, the intergenerational correlation of .41 in the United States means that if your earnings are $100,000 higher than the mean, then your kids will, on average, make $41,000 more than the mean.

The Norway/U.S. comparison reflects a very substantial difference in the mobility systems of these two countries.

FIGURE 9.11 INTERGENERATIONAL CORRELATION OF EARNINGS IN THE UNITED STATES AND OTHER ADVANCED INDUSTRIAL COUNTRIES

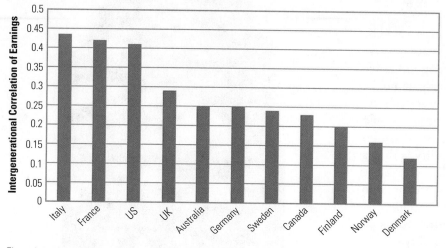

Figure based on data on data from Blanden (2009).

within **labor markets**, but perhaps most importantly on the policies that governments adopt. Families matter because parents play a large role in shaping how much education and other social and intellectual assets children acquire, and it is education and other assets that will determine children's incomes. Labor markets—the way workers are hired and promoted—matter because it is in the labor market that education pays off in economic terms. Government policies matter because government regulates both labor markets and educational systems. Governments decide whether and to what extent disadvantaged children should get compensatory assistance (such as the Head Start Program, which provides education and health services to low-income children and their families), which may help them overcome disadvantages associated with their family background. Governments also decide how equal schools are in rich and poor areas and how much support students receive for going to college.

These three factors—families, labor markets, and government policies—are highly correlated with the level of inequality in conditions children face when they are growing up. High inequality of opportunity usually means that advantaged families can invest much more than disadvantaged families in their children's education and that the quality of schools that wealthy children attend will be much better than schools serving poor children. High inequality is also closely related to a high payoff of a having a college degree (in fact, as we discussed, there is a growing college premium in the United States). And high inequality is related to the role of the government. If the government has a weak system of policies to compensate for the disadvantage that poor children face, these children will have much less opportunity to succeed as adults (thus reinforcing inequality).

Norwegian children may get a modest boost (or penalty) from their parents' achievements. But the overwhelming majority of their adult earnings will be dependent on their own achievements. American children, by contrast, receive about two and half times more advantage (or disadvantage) from their parents than Norwegian children. Who your parents are matters much more, on average, in the United States than in Norway. The gap is smaller with other countries, but this kind of evidence must raise serious doubts about the proposition that America is truly the land of opportunity, at least by comparison with countries most like us. However, unlike the case of income inequality, there are other rich countries with similar rates of social mobility to the United States, notably in Southern Europe.

Measuring the social mobility through the earnings correlation between parents and their adult children in the developing world is more challenging because high-quality data are scarce. But we do have some high-quality research on a number of countries in Latin America. Based on the best available estimates, the intergenerational correlation is much higher in countries such as Brazil, Chile, or Peru than in advanced industrial countries, reaching values between .5 and .6. This means that, on average, parents pass along more than half of their economic advantage (or disadvantage) to their children.

Factors Influencing Mobility

What specific factors in a society affect how much mobility there is? This too is not an easy question, as there are a large number of different factors that influence social mobility. For example, the amount of mobility will depend on how families work, on how individuals are slotted into jobs

What factors affect how much mobility there is in a society?

Social scientists have shown that the overall level of inequality of conditions in a country is indeed typically related to the level of intergenerational mobility (or equality of opportunity) in that country. Specifically, higher inequality overall is associated with lower mobility. Figure 9.12 plots the level of inequality when children were growing up in each country in the x-axis against the intergenerational earnings correlation in the y-axis (i.e., the vertical axis). As we can see, countries with higher levels of inequality display stronger intergenerational correlations between parents' income and children's earnings. In contrast, mobility is much higher in low-inequality country mobility.

Figure 9.12 suggests a clear relationship between inequality and mobility. We cannot, however, jump to the conclusion that high inequality *causes* low mobility. The reason is that there may be other factors that produce both inequality of conditions and low intergenerational mobility. The figure, however, does suggest that a society's overall level of inequality plays an important role and helps to explain the differences in mobility between countries.

Education and Social Mobility

Sociologists have emphasized the primary role of education in understanding social inequality and how individuals move in and out of poverty from one generation to the next. In all complex societies, privileged, high-status positions by definition are scarce—that is, after all, what makes them privileged. The very existence of high-status positions in a society is possible only when there are also lower statuses, less privileged ones. What sociologists have discovered is that in modern societies, these privileged positions in general are rarely directly inherited by children of the upper class, but rather they are allocated through education systems. Upper-class parents are (almost always) unable to directly transfer privileged occupational positions to their children; a doctor or lawyer cannot simply pass on the family business to her child unless the child can get into and through medical school or law school. Instead, these parents invest for decades in their children's education in the hopes that similar occupational opportunities will be conferred indirectly.

To understand this important insight into how education and social inequality are linked, it is worth reviewing how sociologists have emphasized different aspects of this relationship over the past century. Education has a dual character with respect to attaining privileged, high-status positions. On the one hand, education systems can function to challenge other traditional forms of allocating privileged positions in society. In traditional societies, for example, occupations are often simply passed on from parent to child. If a father was an agricultural laborer, his sons would also likely be agricultural laborers. The establishment and spread of public education broke down these traditional forms of occupational inheritance and substituted a new way of deciding who will get what. Educational systems do this through what are known as principles of **meritocracy**, a system where rewards and positions are distributed by ability, not social background or personal connections.

Education systems, however, can also be used to maintain and preserve privileged access to scarce

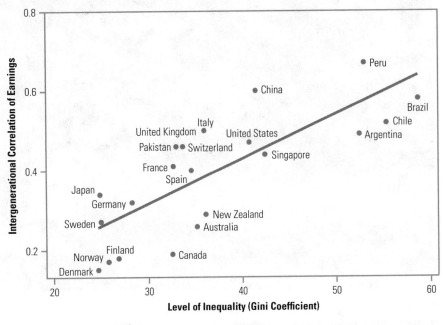

FIGURE 9.12 RELATIONSHIP BETWEEN INCOME INEQUALITY AND MOBILITY IN SELECTED COUNTRIES, AROUND YEAR 2000

Source: Corak (2012).

positions if families with more resources are able to invest in more or better education for their children, for example by moving to a better neighborhood, or paying for private school or private tutoring. Furthermore, educational systems produce credentials, groups can use these credentials to separate those with privilege from those without. In modern societies, high-status positions increasingly require educational credentials. It no longer matters how good you are at a particular thing—for example, teaching or healing people—without the proper educational certificate, you are typically denied access to privileged jobs such as being a doctor or university professor.

Sociologists recognize that schools play a fundamental role in society, not simply by training individuals for employment but, more importantly, by working to select those who will be granted access to more desirable occupations. To the extent that schools facilitate the movement of talented individuals from lower social origins to privileged occupations, sociologists consider the society "open" rather than "closed." When individuals from disadvantaged socioeconomic backgrounds attain privileged occupational positions with associated higher social rewards (such as status, prestige, and income), social mobility has occurred. Sociologists have repeatedly demonstrated that schools play a critical role in either blocking or facilitating social mobility. Read the **Document** *Class Conflict: Tuition Hikes Leave College Students in Debt and Torn between Paid Work and Course Work* in **MySocLab**.

What is the relationship between education and social inequality?

4 How Much Poverty Exists in the United States and around the World?

LIFE AT THE BOTTOM: THE PROBLEM OF POVERTY

👁 Watch the Big Question Video in **MySocLab**

Poverty is a complicated concept. In the simplest of terms, it is a condition that involves the inability to afford basic needs such as food, clothing, shelter, and healthcare. But beyond a minimum of resources to ensure subsistence, it is difficult to define what basic needs are. Adam Smith, the founding father of economics, wrote in his classic 1776 book *The Wealth of Nations* that

"A linen shirt is, strictly speaking, not a necessary of life . . . . The Greeks and Romans lived, I suppose, very comfortably though they had no linen. But in the present times, through the greater part of Europe, a creditable day-labourer will be ashamed to appear in public without a linen shirt, the want of which would be supposed to denote that disgraceful degree of poverty which, it is presumed, nobody can well fall into without extreme bad conduct" (Smith [1776] 1976:466).

It may be the case that having a cell phone today is as necessary as having a linen shirt in the late eighteenth century, when Smith was writing. What about a car? A computer? It is entirely possible to argue that, given that the importance of transportation (particularly where mass transit options are limited) and access to information and communication that are crucial for finding a job or going to school, having access to such items are indeed basic needs.

The way in which the government measures poverty in the United States is by setting an income threshold—the minimum income necessary to afford basic necessities. This threshold is called the **poverty line**. The official poverty line was defined for the first time in the early 1960s as part of a major government effort to reduce the amount of poverty in the United States (what came to be known as the War on

Poverty), and once established it has simply been updated each year to take inflation into account. The poverty line varies by family size. For example in 2010, the poverty line for a family of four was $22,314. So families of four with incomes less than $22,314 were considered poor. The poverty line for a person living alone was $11,139. So if someone living alone earns less than $11,139, he or she will be considered poor. Using the official definition of poverty, in 2010, about 15 percent of Americans lived in poverty (more than 45 million people, out of a total population of approximately 313 million).

The official measure of poverty the U.S. government employs has not been changed since the 1960s, except for adjusting for inflation. Many criticisms have been raised of this measure (for example, the measurement accounts for some kinds of income that poor people may receive, like food stamps, but it also does not take into account taxes they pay or adjust for differences in cost of living across states). These criticisms are important but, as researchers have shown, the trends in poverty that we will describe later do not change if adjustments for these things are made.

The most important problem with the official measure of poverty, however, is that it does not take into account changing standards of living—from Adam Smith's linen shirt to today's cell phones and computers. So many European governments use a measure of **relative poverty**, which attempts to capture changes in living standards. The most common definition of relative poverty is defined as those families with incomes below 50 percent of the median income (the median is the midpoint of the income distribution in the country, with half of the population above and half below). The median income serves as a benchmark of what is common or typical in a society, so being 50 percent below the median means being significantly disadvantaged in comparison with other members of society. The idea of relative poverty is that someone who makes less than half the median income is excluded from the shared benefits of society. A relative measure of poverty is in fact a measure of inequality because wider economic disparities will result in a larger proportion of families living far below the median income. The official definition of poverty used by the American government is a measure of **absolute poverty,** one that attempts to define the minimum amount of income necessary to meet basic needs, but one that does not adjust for changes in living standards. Using a relative measure of poverty, millions more would be considered poor in the United States. However it is measured, though, poverty is unquestionably a major problem in the United States.

FIGURE 9.13 POVERTY TRENDS IN THE UNITED STATES, 1959–2010

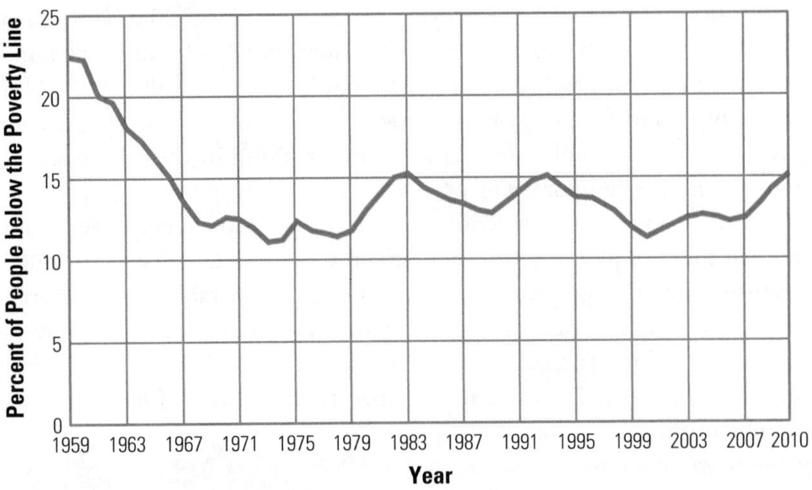

Source: U.S. Census Bureau (2011).

Poverty in the United States: Who Are the Poor?

Figure 9.13 plots the proportion of people living in poverty in the United States since 1959 based on the definition given by the U.S. Bureau of the Census. As we can see, the proportion of poor people declined sharply over the 1960s due to sharp economic growth and the Great Society programs (see *A Sociological Perspective* on p. 241), but there has been less improvement since then. In 2010, the last year for which we have data, the proportion of people in poverty reached 15.1 percent. This is partly due to the economic recession that started late in 2007 and the slow recovery that has followed since 2009. This is not an unusual trend—throughout the period considered, poverty is very much affected by the "business cycle"—changes in economic performance. Poverty increased after the recessions of the early 1970s, early 1990s, and early 2000s, when the economy worsened and unemployment increased. But the economic context is not the entire story. As we will see, the government can play an important role in shielding people from economic vulnerability. Before moving to that, let's examine who the poor are.

Even though people living in poverty are diverse, there are a number of factors that increase the likelihood that someone will be poor. Among these, the most important are education, employment status, minority status, age, and family structure. Education matters because, as we have discussed, schooling is an important determinant of the skills that people can sell in the market in exchange for a wage. Having less than a high school diploma puts anyone at higher risk of poverty. Employment status and type of job are basically the outcome of education and other skills and other assets. Having and maintaining a job that pays wages higher than the poverty line will keep anyone out of poverty. But there have never

been enough jobs for all who want and need one, and even full-time jobs at the minimum wage are not enough to lift a family out of poverty. So those who either do not have jobs or have very low pay will be poor. Minority status also matters in the United States. African Americans, Hispanics, and Native Americans are much more likely to live in poverty than whites. However, it is important to mention that the largest numbers of poor people are white. For example, in 2005 there were 16.2 million whites, 9.1 million African Americans, and 9.2 million Hispanics living in poverty. Finally, family structure also matters. Families in which there is a single parent—usually a female—are much more likely to be poor. This phenomenon has been called "feminization of poverty," and it highlights the difficulties of complementing the roles of primary caregiver and provider on a single income.

One widespread belief about the poor is that most do not have jobs. This is not true. In fact, most of the people living in poverty engage in the labor market at least some of the time. About two-thirds of families living below the poverty line have at least one working family member. The proportion of poor adults engaged in the labor market is higher among families with children. In 2001, for example, there were 19.4 million families with children that lived in poverty. Of these 14.3 million, or 73 percent, had at least one part-time worker. And 7.4 million of these families—more than half—had a full-time worker.

These statistics highlight that many poor people in the United States are engaged in the labor market. They are known as the **working poor,** people who cannot make enough income to be free from poverty even if, as many do, they work full time. How can this be? Many jobs simply do not pay enough to lift people working in them above the poverty line. For example, according to the Bureau of Labor Statistics, a food preparation

Which factors increase the likelihood of poverty?

worker earns $8.71 an hour, and a home care aid makes $9.75 an hour. If these workers worked 40 hours a week for 48 weeks a year, they would make, respectively, $16,723 and $18,720 a year, which is well below the poverty line for a family of four (which in 2010 was $22,314). But this is not all. For the working poor, poverty is not just about low income. Low-paying jobs are often unstable, and many people working in these jobs work on a temporary or part-time basis. Such jobs are not secure enough to build economic security, save money, and rely on them to plan for the future. Even those families that are usually above the poverty line may be very vulnerable to economic and family circumstances. A recession, a divorce or spousal abandonment, or a severe illness can change the picture for families living close to the poverty line in ways for which middle-class families have more of a cushion. Most poor families have very little in the way of savings to fall back upon in the event of any crisis. They live, in short, at the edge of insecurity.

How does the level of poverty in the United States compare to similar countries?

☐ Poverty in International Comparative Perspective

Is the level of poverty in the United States comparable to other advanced industrial countries? The United States has experienced similar economic trends in terms of deindustrialization and economic restructuring, which suggests levels of poverty similar to other wealthy countries. On the other hand, America's policies towards poverty reduction are quite different than the policies of other countries in Western Europe, Canada, or Australia. The United States spends less to directly alleviate poverty through "welfare" programs than any other wealthy country, although the United States does spend a lot on education and health care relative to other countries (Garfinkel, Rainwater, and Smeeding 2010).

Comparing poverty levels across countries is no easy task. It requires a common measure of income, a common poverty line, and a way to make currency similar across nations. One important comparative study has undertaken this task to compare 11 advanced industrial countries (Smeeding 2006). In order to compare poverty, the author uses both an absolute poverty line, such as the one used in the United States, and a relative poverty line, such as the one used in Western Europe. Taking everything into account, the answer is that poverty is higher in the United States than in other advanced industrial country. Figure 9.14 shows the comparison across 11 countries in 2000. The pink squares indicate how many people are poor before any government programs are taken into account, using a relative poverty measure defined as all individuals and families with incomes 50 percent of the median income or below. In this measure, which does not take into account any government programs to help the poor, just the incomes received from employment and other sources, the United States ranks right in the middle of the countries. But this changes once we calculate a more realistic approach to poverty that includes all income (from government as well other sources) that is really available to families (blue squares). This broader measure shows that the United States's poverty rate is higher than that in any of the countries considered. The reason is that the United States does much less to redistribute income from the wealthy to the poor than other countries. As shown in the gray circles, in every country the government reduces poverty, but the reduction is much less in the United States. The United States reduces poverty created by market incomes by 26 percent, compared to an average of 61 percent across advanced industrial countries.

In case this result might reflect the use of a relative measure, we can also compare absolute poverty rates in different countries. Here again, the United States has a significantly higher poverty rate. The bar graph on the right uses the official poverty line in the United States for every country. Using an absolute standard that captures a comparable income threshold across countries, poverty is higher in the United States than in other advanced industrial countries. These data suggest, then, that one important reason for the excess poverty in the United States is that policy is doing far less to reduce poverty than most other countries.

☐ Poverty and Children

A particularly important concern that social scientists and government officials have about poverty is how it impacts children. Why is childhood poverty a powerful predictor of poverty in adulthood? Childhood poverty creates a vicious cycle that reproduces disadvantage across generations. This is an especially important problem in the United States. While 13.7 percent of adults were poor in 2010, as many of 22 percent of children younger than 18 lived in poverty. The reason why children are more likely to live in poverty is that poor households tend to have more children than wealthy households and that poor children are more likely to live with a single parent than nonpoor children.

Poor children have more than their share of problems. We noted in the chapter introduction that they usually weigh less at birth and are more likely to die in their first year of life than nonpoor children. When they start school, they score lower in standardized tests. Poor children are also absent from school more often and exhibit more behavior problems than affluent children. Poor teenagers are more likely to drop out of high school, have a baby when they are young, and get in trouble with the law. Young adults who were poor as children complete fewer years of schooling, work fewer hours, and earn lower wages than young adults raised in better-off families. As a result, children raised in poverty are more likely to end up poor and in need of public assistance when they become adults (Mayer 1997).

FIGURE 9.14 RELATIVE AND ABSOLUTE POVERTY RATES IN 11 ADVANCED INDUSTRIAL COUNTRIES

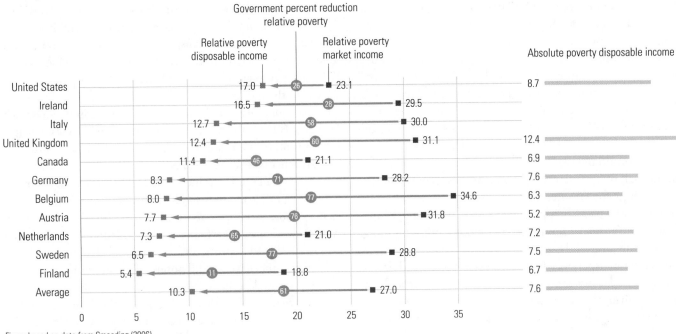

Figure based on data from Smeeding (2006).

Homelessness

One of the most extreme forms of poverty is **homelessness**, literally the lack of permanent shelter to live in. Homelessness is a significant social problem in many parts of the world, including the United States. Individuals and families can become homeless for any number of specific reasons, including wars and violent conflicts that can in some cases create millions of refugees. But under more normal circumstances, the one nearly universal condition is that of extreme poverty (although other problems such as mental illness or personal disasters are significant). Most people who become homeless will not remain so indefinitely, but even brief periods of homelessness can be devastating. Life on the streets and even in homeless shelters can be dangerous, and not having a regular address makes many aspects of daily life difficult.

The problem of homelessness in America grew considerably in the 1980s, when the closing down of mental hospitals, decline of social programs for the poor, destruction of low-cost housing in urban areas, and rise in unemployment among high-risk groups combined to increase the number of people without regular residences (Jencks 1995). While a variety of government programs aimed at reducing homelessness have stabilized and reduced the size of the homeless population since the early 1990s, the problem has hardly been eliminated. The most rigorous estimate of the homeless population in the United States is the annual survey conducted by the Department of Housing and Urban Development (HUD) using innovative methods of locating the homeless. HUD has estimated that on a single night in

Why is poverty bad for children? In some cases the reason is obvious. Lack of basic nutrients, shelter, immunization, and access to healthcare is detrimental to children's development. When extra money prevents hunger, homelessness, or when it buys medical care and other necessities, it can make a huge difference in the lives of children. But in the United States, unfortunately, most poor families struggle to meet these basic material needs and often do not receive enough help from the government to give their children all of the basic necessities of life.

But the detrimental consequences of poverty are not limited to cases of extreme deprivation. As researchers in the social and biological sciences have shown, living in poverty is an important source of stress, and stress is extremely bad for children (as we also noted in the introduction). Poverty is not just about the ability to afford things. Poverty is also usually associated with exposure to environmental toxins, neighborhood violence and insecurity, anxiety about making ends meet, difficulties in accessing institutional services such as healthcare or schools, and many other stressors. Poverty and its attendant stressors can shape the neurobiology of the developing child in powerful ways, which may compromise cognitive development and concentration, thus affecting school attainment. This is a direct effect of poverty on the child. Poverty is stressful for parents too, and it may affect the investments of time and resources that parents make in children, as well as parents' interactions with children. This is an indirect effect of poverty on children—stress takes a toll on parents, which in turn will affect children's learning and development.

How does growing up in poverty harm children?

January 2010, there were about 650,000 homeless people. Of this total, about 400,000 lived in shelters, and the remainder were unsheltered (U.S. HUD 2010). HUD also estimated that about 1.6 million people were homeless at some point during the previous 12 months. But these estimates do not consider the millions of people who are living doubled up, temporarily or indefinitely, with family or friends. Attempts to estimate this more inclusive population produce much higher estimates of the total homeless population; one study estimated that 14 percent of all Americans have at some point in their lives been homeless (Link et al. 1994).

Although homelessness is most common among single men, the lack of a regular dwelling creates especially significant hardships for families with children and is yet another example of how poverty impacts the innocent young. Using a broader definition of homelessness that includes doubling up with family or friends, it has been estimated that some 1.5 million children experience homelessness in the United States at some point during the year, a number that is particularly disturbing given the strong evidence of high levels of stress and dislocation it causes for children (Bussuk et al. 2011).

CONCLUSION SHOULD WE BE CONCERNED ABOUT EXCESSIVE INEQUALITY?

To what extent does inequality matter? The simplest answer to this question is the most straightforward: higher levels of inequality mean that the poor have fewer resources to acquire needed goods and services than they would in more egalitarian countries; at the same time, the lives of middle-class families have stopped improving as they did for the much of the twentieth century. This is a vitally important fact in its own right. The further down the income distribution you look, the more difficult it becomes for families to meet basic needs. The fact that the rich are absorbing a larger share of the total income being produced in the United States and many other countries makes it difficult for families to address those needs or to envision a brighter future for themselves or their children.

But beyond the consequences of rising inequality for household well-being and shared prosperity, what else can be said? We've discussed in this chapter how economic inequalities are related to child development and education, but what are some other consequences? A few issues are worth paying attention to. One is political. Every adult citizen has one and only one vote, but there are other ways to influence political outcomes. Perhaps the most important of these is by donating money to candidates for political office. And rising wealth at the top makes it easier for affluent individuals to "invest" in the political system, and the interests and concerns of the rich are not necessarily those of the rest of the country. In fact, the American political system has, in recent years, undergone

a remarkable infusion of money into the political system. The money is coming both from corporations but increasingly from very wealthy individuals. To run for political office, certainly at the national level (like Congress) but increasingly in state and sometimes local elections, requires candidates to raise great amounts of money from large corporations and rich individuals. This raises suspicion that the rich are exerting too much influence over the political system. While researchers are divided on that question, there can be no doubt that the more money rich individuals have, the more they donate to their favorite candidates for office (Domhoff 2010; Hacker and Pierson 2010).

Another issue to consider is the fact that societies with high levels of overall economic inequality have appeared, in a number of studies, to have poor overall societal health, while societies that are more equal seem to have better health. The main reason researchers have suggested to explain this finding is that rich people will be in a position to purchase much *more* healthcare than they otherwise would, potentially squeezing out poorer people who are less likely to have coverage (Wilkinson 2006).

Another more subtle consequence is the desire to keep up with the rich when it comes to consumption. Walk into any department store in America and you will see an array of desirable, high-priced items. To the extent that people look up to those who have more than they do, they will never feel completely satisfied with the possessions they do own, and they want more. Most Americans want bigger houses, faster cars, fancier jewelry, and so forth. This has become a problem because many American families are taking on ever-higher levels of debt to try to attain such goods. As a world leader in levels of household debt, many social scientists have noted the precariousness of this situation for the American national economy (Sullivan et al. 2001). In periods when credit becomes tighter and the economy slows, consumer spending driven by credit will shrink significantly. "Luxury fever" also impacts subjective well-being—we are never fully satisfied with what we have (Frank 1999). Even though the United States has a higher average income than virtually all other countries in the world, international surveys show that Americans are not as satisfied as we would expect. High levels of income inequality are the most likely culprit (Oishi and Diener 2011).

Inequality is always going to be with us, but the *amount* of inequality that a society allows is not set in stone. As we have seen throughout this chapter, governments *can* choose to adopt policies that can reduce the amount of income and wealth controlled at the very top, and they *can* choose to adopt policies that will reduce the number of people living in poverty. Many very successful and rich countries have made those choices. But the United States has not. America has high levels of poverty and inequality, and government policies of recent decades have done little to ensure that the benefits of economic growth are shared more equitably among the entire population.

Watch the Video in MySocLab
Applying Your Sociological Imagination

What Is Inequality? *(p. 232)*

◉ **Watch** the **Big Question Video** in **MySocLab** to review the key concepts for this section.

At the heart of the study of social stratification is the concept of inequality. In this section, we explored the history of inequality and the ways societies and thinkers have typically justified inequality. We also discussed the sociological concept of class.

INEQUALITY: AN INTRODUCTION (p. 232)

The History of Inequality (p. 232)

- **Has the enormous gap between rich and poor always existed?**

The Who and What of Inequality (p. 234)

- **In what specific ways are societies unequal?**

Class and Inequality (p. 236)

- **What is the sociological concept of class?**

Justifying Inequality (p. 238)

- **How is inequality justified?**

KEY TERMS

social stratification *(p. 232)*

inequality *(p. 232)*

slavery *(p. 232)*

feudalism *(p. 232)*

serf *(p. 232)*

median *(p. 234)*

income *(p. 234)*

wealth *(p. 234)*

net financial assets (NFA) *(p. 234)*

consumption *(p. 235)*

well-being *(p. 235)*

middle class *(p. 236)*

class *(p. 237)*

life chances *(p. 237)*

class analysis *(p. 237)*

bourgeoisie *(p. 237)*

proletariat *(p. 237)*

socioeconomic status (SES) *(p. 237)*

egalitarian *(p. 239)*

Why Is America So Unequal? *(p. 240)*

◉ **Watch** the **Big Question Video** in **MySocLab** to review the key concepts for this section.

Inequality in the United States today is about as high as it has ever been since we started measuring, and poverty rates have remained persistently high. In this section, we compared the United States with other similar developed countries and asked why America is so unequal.

UNEQUAL AMERICA IN COMPARATIVE PERSPECTIVE (p. 240)

KEY TERMS

skill-biased technical change (SBTC) *(p. 242)*

globalization *(p. 244)*

outsourcing *(p. 244)*

economic restructuring *(p. 245)*

productivity *(p. 245)*

progressive tax system *(p. 245)*

minimum wage *(p. 245)*

3

Do We All Have an Equal Opportunity to Succeed in Life? *(p. 248)*

 Watch the **Big Question Video** in **MySocLab** to review the key concepts for this section.

Social mobility is one of the most important topics in the study of social stratification. In this section we examined how social mobility is measured, why countries differ in opportunity, how the United States compares to other countries, and the relationship between education and mobility.

Read the **Document** *Class Conflict: Tuition Hikes Leave College Students in Debt and Torn between Paid Work and Course Work* by Ellen Mutari and Melaku Lakew in **MySocLab**. This reading examines the costs and benefits of higher education and argues that we all benefit when everyone has equal access.

KEY TERMS

4 How Much Poverty Exists in the United States and around the World? *(p. 252)*

👁 **Watch** the **Big Question Video** in **MySocLab** to review the key concepts for this section.

Poverty is a complicated concept. Beyond a minimum of resources to ensure subsistence, it is difficult to define what our "basic" needs are. In this section we examined two ways of viewing poverty and just how much poverty there is in the United States and in other countries around the world. We also looked closely at the problem of childhood poverty.

LIFE AT THE BOTTOM: THE PROBLEM OF POVERTY (p. 252)

Poverty in the United States: Who Are the Poor? (p. 253)

• **Which factors increase the likelihood of poverty?**

Poverty in International Comparative Perspective (p. 254)

• **How does the level of poverty in the U.S. compare to similar countries?**

Poverty and Children (p. 254)

• **How does growing up in poverty harm children?**

Homelessness (p. 255)

👁 **Watch** the **Video** Applying Your Sociological Imagination in **MySocLab** to see these concepts at work in the real world

10

RACE and ETHNICITY

((• Listen to the Chapter Audio in MySocLab

by ANN MORNING, with NANDI DILL,
RACHEL GARVER, and JOHN HALUSHKA

What exactly is race? Does biology play a role in it? What about culture? Is it something that people invented, or has it always been part of the human experience? The study of race and ethnicity has long been central to American sociology and has also featured prominently in other fields, like anthropology, psychology, and biology. Yet in spite of this longstanding scholarly attention, we have yet to come up with widely agreed-upon definitions of *race* and *ethnicity*.

About 10 years ago, I traveled around the northeastern United States to interview anthropology and biology professors about how they understood the concept of race. What I found surprised me because it ran counter to what many of my graduate school professors had told me—that social and natural scientists today all agree that race is a human invention without any basis in biological characteristics. When I actually spoke with anthropologists and biologists, though, it immediately became clear that their views on race varied a great deal and hardly reflected the consensus that my graduate school advisors presumed.

One of the discoveries that intrigued me the most was the way they used *me*—or more specifically, my physical appearance—to back up their views. In several instances, the professor I was interviewing would say something about *my* race in order to support his or her definition of the term in general. What struck me most, though, was that even with the same "data" at

Today, experts in the social and the natural sciences debate whether the distribution of human biological characteristics around the world—like dark skin, light hair, or particular genetic traits—can be mapped onto the three or four racial categories that European scientists invented in the 1700s.

Watch the **Video** in **MySocLab**
Inspiring Your Sociological Imagination

hand—namely, me and my physical features—these academics came up with wildly different interpretations of race.

In one of my very first interviews, a cultural anthropologist at a large urban public university asked me how I identified myself in racial terms. It's a question I'm used to because with my African, European, Asian, and American Indian ancestry, people are often curious about my background. The anthropologist's reaction was to use me as evidence that race does not really have any biological underpinning. "You're a perfect walking example of why [race] doesn't work," he concluded. "I just wonder, looking at you," he went on, "how anybody could maintain that there are these hard and fast races...."

A few weeks later, a biology professor at a state university explained to me how race might come up in a lecture on genetics. Skin color, he suggested, "could be used as an example of quantitative genetics ... the general thought is that by and large, although there are some environmental influences, there are four sets of genes which determine skin color." Peering over his glasses at me, he mused, "I take a look at you, and you might have—don't be offended—you have, if there are four ... that means there are eight genes, and I would say you have three or four black genes and four or five white genes ... Just on skin color." In contrast to the cultural anthropologist who felt that my appearance disproved the existence of races, this biologist thought I was a textbook example of how race is rooted in DNA.

Finally, one rainy afternoon a physical anthropologist at an Ivy League university gave me a tour of his large laboratory, pointing out various human skeletons and the traits he argued reflected their racial heritage. Soon our talk turned to the uncertainty involved in determining race from skeletal remains. "Environments have changed enormously," the anthropologist explained. "There's been more intermixing." Then he turned to me and said, "I mean, if you give me your skull and so forth, and I look at your nasal aperture, I'm not going to have a clue that you have any black ancestry." But then he corrected himself: "Now I might, given your teeth, because they're large."

As these anecdotes suggest, contemporary scientists' ideas about race—and what it has to do with biology, society, or anything else—span a wide spectrum. The cultural anthropologist thought it was impossible to identify clear-cut races (and thus that they do not exist); the biologist thought that race could easily be traced back to an individual's genetic profile; and the physical anthropologist allowed that identifying a person's race is not always easy but that ultimately our bodies display telltale signs of our racial heritage. For me, these encounters sum up a fundamental characteristic of today's scientific perspectives on human difference: thoughtful and highly trained specialists, working with the same data, have yet to reach a consensus on the basic question of what race is.

> **Thoughtful and highly trained specialists, working with the same data, have yet to reach a consensus on the basic question of what race is.**

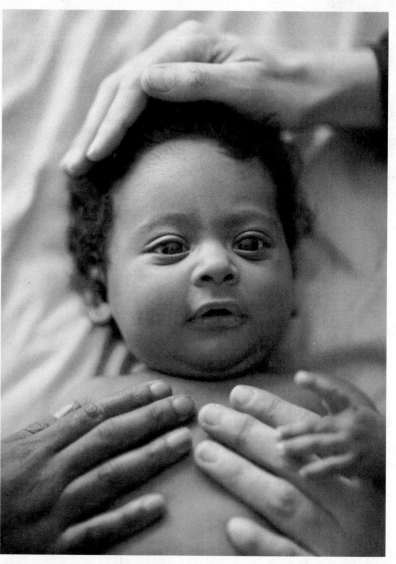

What exactly is race? Sociologists make clear distinctions between race and ethnicity and use the two terms to describe different kinds of categories and identities.

THE BIG QUESTIONS

👁 **Watch** the **Big Question Videos** in **MySocLab**

1 **What is the difference between race and ethnicity?** More often than not, the words *race* and *ethnicity* get used interchangeably, as if they mean the same thing. And indeed they have more than a passing resemblance. But sociologists make clear distinctions between race and ethnicity and use the two terms to describe different kinds of categories and identities.

Is race real? If there's one thing academics agree on, it is that race is real. Where they part ways is on the question of whether race is anchored in deep-seated physical differences between individuals or whether it is an invention that is not determined by human biology but which nonetheless is "real" because it has an unmistakable impact on daily life. **2**

3 **What is racist and what isn't?** In classroom discussions of race and ethnicity, students often preface their comments with phrases like, "I don't know if I should say this, but …" or "I'm not sure what the right term for this group is, but …" Concern about the "political correctness" of our ideas, speech, and behavior is a prominent feature of both public and private conversations on race today. Sociologists have thought a lot about prejudice and discrimination, providing ample food for thought on racism in the contemporary United States.

Do race and ethnicity matter anymore? In the wake of President Obama's historic election, many people have wondered whether it is fair to say that the United States has entered a "postracial" era. Sociological research suggests that while it may not be too soon to talk about a "postethnic" era, race is still closely linked to socioeconomic inequality. **4**

5 **How are race and ethnicity changing in the twenty-first century?** At the start of the twenty-first century, the face of America is very different from what it was 200 years ago. Immigrants come from a wider range of countries than ever before; people are more likely to marry partners from a different racial background; and changing attitudes have led more and more people to identify themselves as multiracial. These and other demographic changes will certainly have an impact on the nation's racial and ethnic makeup, on its patterns of socioeconomic inequality, and on its inhabitants' attitudes and beliefs about race and ethnicity.

1 What Is the Difference between Race and Ethnicity?

UNDERSTANDING RACE AND ETHNICITY

👁 Watch the Big Question Video in **MySocLab**

The introduction to this chapter described disagreement among social and natural scientists about the best way to define race. When we focus only on sociologists, however, we find that they share fairly precise understandings of both race and ethnicity.

The sociological distinction between the two terms runs counter to everyday practice, where *race* and *ethnicity* are often used as synonyms for each other. People from all walks of life—journalists, teachers, doctors, advertisers, and politicians—routinely use the two terms interchangeably. Even dictionaries lump together the two words. As part of its definition for race, the *Oxford English Dictionary* (2011) describes it as "[a] group of several tribes or peoples, regarded as forming a distinct ethnic set," or alternatively as "any of the major groupings of mankind, having in common distinct physical features or having a similar ethnic background." Similarly, one of its definitions for the adjective *ethnic* is "pertaining to race."

Why do we tend to treat race and ethnicity as the same thing? Sometimes the term *ethnicity* is seen as a polite replacement for *race*—a way to avoid using a term that is associated with racism, racial inequality, and racial discrimination. Another, less well-known factor may have to do with the federal government's designation of Hispanics (also referred to as "Latinos") as an "ethnic group," when Americans in general increasingly seem to view them as simply another racial group, akin to blacks, whites, and Asians.

But the confusion between race and ethnicity is also due simply to the fact that, at their core, the two concepts share a great deal in common. Both are systems for classifying human beings into groups based on shared ancestry. The crucial distinction between them lies in the different kinds of characteristics that are used to assign people to ethnic or to racial groups.

Sociological Definitions of Race and Ethnicity

Max Weber (1864–1920), one of sociology's founding figures, was also one of the first sociologists to define ethnicity and race. Weber described ethnic groups as "those human groups that entertain a subjective belief in their common descent," spelling out that "it does not matter whether or not an objective blood relationship exists" (Weber 1978). The most striking aspect of Weber's definition is that the key ingredient for ethnic membership is *belief* in shared descent. The subjective dimension of ethnicity would go on to become a central fixture of later sociologists' thinking.

Weber did not portray race as equally subjective, however. Instead, like most scholars of his era, he felt that races stemmed from "common inherited and inheritable traits that actually derive from common descent." This is an essentialist view of race (called **essentialism**); that is, it presumes that an individual's

How do contemporary sociologists define race and ethnicity?

Barack Obama, pictured here as a young man with his maternal grandparents, is often considered to be the United States' first black president. Given his multiracial family tree, however, there is no logical or scientific reason to classify Obama as "black" rather than "white."

racial identity depends on fundamental and innate characteristics that are deep-seated, inherited, and unchangeable. These traits are thought to be part of a person's "essence," their very being. Whereas Weber observed that many different characteristics or experiences could serve to indicate who belonged to which ethnic group—including physical resemblance, historical memories, and common cultural practices—he believed that it is physical makeup alone that determines an individual's race. In a nutshell, ethnicity is based on people's cultural practices, and race on their biological traits.

While contemporary sociologists share Weber's view of ethnicity, most reject his definition of race. Instead, sociologists today believe that racial identification is as subjective a process as ethnic classification. The major difference between race and ethnicity lies in the basis on which group boundaries are drawn. In other words, we look for different clues or signs when we think about a person's ethnicity as compared to their race.

Why then do contemporary sociologists reject Weber's description of race as based solely on inherited physical traits? The difference in viewpoints is subtle but meaningful. In a sense, today's sociologists have taken to heart Weber's message about the subjectivity of group definitions and have come to believe that even our perceptions of biological similarity are subjective. So our racial classifications are based not on some objective measure of physical resemblances (as Weber claimed) but rather on our beliefs and socially influenced perceptions of which kinds of people are biologically similar and which are different.

A useful illustration comes from the United States's **one-drop rule**, a custom that became enshrined in many state laws around the turn of the nineteenth century. According to this longstanding method of identifying a person's race, someone with one black grandparent and three white grandparents is a black person because their "drop of black blood" means they somehow have more in common with blacks than with whites. This is the same reasoning that leads us to label President Obama as black even though his mother was white. Clearly, there is no natural biological rule that makes him more black than white. Instead, there are social rules—cultural customs—that determine how we classify people by race and even how we "see" race.

Now we have all the ingredients we need to lay out definitions of race and ethnicity. In this chapter, we define **ethnicity** as a system for classifying people who are believed to share common descent, based on perceived cultural similarities. We define **race** as a system for classifying people who are believed to share common descent, based on perceived innate physical similarities. Framing the two concepts in this way makes clear how much they have in common, but it also highlights the fundamental difference between them.

Key Distinctions between Race and Ethnicity

Contemporary sociologists have written extensively on the similarities and differences between the concepts of race and ethnicity (Cornell and Hartmann 2004; Cornell and Hartmann 2007).

Which Matters More: Race or Ethnicity? One of the first things that researchers point out is that in any given place, the notions of race and ethnicity may not be equally important for people (Cornell and Hartmann 2007). In the United States, race has historically mattered much more than ethnicity. For most of the nation's history, being white was a necessary requirement in order to enjoy the full benefits of citizenship. Not only did whiteness protect one from enslavement in the antebellum period (1789–1860), but even after the Civil War, it opened access to the voting booth, to better jobs, to schools and hospitals, and to more affluent neighborhoods. Until 1952, only white immigrants could become U.S. citizens, and it was not until 1967 that nonwhites were allowed to marry whites throughout the nation. Although ethnic groups such as Irish, Italian, and Jewish Americans have faced considerable discrimination, their exclusion was not written into U.S. law to the same extent as race-based barriers. Not surprisingly then, racial differentials in key socioeconomic outcomes—like income, wealth, and educational attainment—are much wider today than

Which matters more, race or ethnicity?

Recognized ethnic groups are often, but not always, descendants of immigrants. These Hopi people constitute a distinct ethnic group in the United States, even though their ancestors were indigenous to the area, not recent arrivals.

comparable gaps between ethnic groups. In other words, being white rather than black makes a bigger difference than being Swedish rather than Polish, or Jamaican rather than Haitian—and that has been true throughout the nation's history.

Distinguishing Racial and Ethnic Labels So far we have talked about race and ethnicity in the abstract, without specifying just which groups are ethnic and which are racial. Any list or taxonomy, however, depends entirely on time and place. In my research on censuses conducted around the world (Morning 2008), I discovered that the official racial and ethnic categories used by different countries to classify their populations vary widely. In Guatemala, ethnic groups on the census include "Garifuna" and "Ladino" people; in Bulgaria, the main categories are "Bulgarian," "Turkish," and "Gypsies." The New Zealand census classifies people as "New Zealand European," "Maori," "Samoan," "Tongan," "Chinese," and "Indian" (among others), while Sri Lanka recognizes ethnic groups like "Sinhalese," "Sri Lanka Tamil," "Indian Tamil," "Sri Lanka Moor," "Burgher," "Malay," "Sri Lanka Chetty," and "Bharatha."

Despite such immense local variation, there is a rule of thumb we can use to distinguish racial labels from ethnic ones. Race is anchored in color terms—like "black" and "white"—that denote vast, continental groupings that include millions if not billions of people. "Black" might refer to people from sub-Saharan Africa or the Caribbean, "white" to natives of Europe. Even if they are not frequently used today, color terms like "red," "yellow," and "brown" refer to similarly large-scale groups: indigenous (or native) Americans, Asians, and Hispanics.

In contrast, ethnic groups tend to be much smaller in size and associated with local, national, or regional geography rather than with continents. It is not surprising then that different countries recognize startlingly different sets of ethnicities; they are concerned with groups that differentiate themselves within national borders. Sometimes these ethnic groups are considered native to the area, like Hopi or Navajo people in the United States; other times they are recognized to be descended from immigrants, like Korean Americans, German Americans, and Cuban Americans. Often though the historical distinction between native and migrant is murky. When the United States annexed large swaths of Mexican territory in the nineteenth century, many people went overnight from being residents of Mexico to becoming residents of the United States. Were these Mexican Americans then an immigrant or a native ethnic group?

Power Relations: Race as a Tool of Domination The concept of race gained much of its power and reach from Europeans' imperial encounters with Africans, Asians, indigenous Americans, and others beginning in the fifteenth century. Prior to that, Western medieval societies were divided by religion (i.e., Christians versus non-Christians), and going back even further, the ancient Greeks distinguished between themselves and "barbaric" peoples. But a color-coded hierarchy of race as we understand it today did not yet exist in the Western imagination. Instead, it was not until European explorers, armies, clergy, and settlers sought to dominate peoples across the globe that the race idea formed. Europeans came to believe that the differences they observed in appearance and behavior between themselves and others could be explained by intrinsic, racial characteristics. Equally importantly, they were persuaded that races fell along a hierarchy in which they occupied the top rung, so European domination and colonization of others was only natural. Beliefs about racial difference then grew out of a context of conquest, exploitation, and enslavement and were further cultivated to justify power inequalities.

With this colonial era as a backdrop, many scholars have argued that race—as opposed to ethnicity—has several features that reflect its historical use as a tool of domination. One has already been mentioned: races tend to be conceived as forming a hierarchy, with superior races on top and inferior ones on the bottom. Ethnic groups, in contrast, are not generally viewed this way. The distinction between Jamaican American and Trinidadian American, for example, is not widely associated with superior versus inferior value judgments. (Members of these groups, however, may be quick to point out their own ethnicity's relative merits.)

Another key difference is that racial categories tend to be imposed on individuals or groups by others, while ethnic labels

How did race come to be used as a tool of domination?

are more likely to be chosen for themselves by the individuals or groups concerned. This contrast can be described as external versus internal classification. Racial terms like "black," "American Indian," "Asian," and even "white" have historically originated with European-dominated states that enacted policies toward these groups that treated them as homogeneous masses, even if the individuals so categorized did not identify at all with those labels. The "Hispanic" category is an excellent case in point. Although the U.S. government considers Hispanics to be an ethnic and not a racial group, they have effectively been "racialized" into being considered by many to be a race comparable to whites, blacks, and so forth. Yet the very notion of a Hispanic race—or even a Hispanic ethnicity—is a very recent one, stemming from the federal government's attempts in the 1970s to develop a set of official racial classifications (Graham 2002). Before then it was not obvious that people from Central America like Mexicans and Guatemalans had much to do with people from the Caribbean like Cubans and Dominicans, let alone with people from South America like Peruvians and Argentines. So although they did not choose or invent the label for themselves, people with origins in any of these places now find themselves in a society in which, regardless of how they prefer to identify themselves, they are labeled by the government, other institutions, and other people as Hispanic.

Due in part to the United States's long history of classifying its inhabitants by race, individuals usually cannot choose their race (although they can fill out whatever they like on forms). A person who is considered by others to be black will probably not be taken seriously if she insists that she is white or prefers to think of herself as white. In contrast, ethnic terms are free from regulation by the U.S. government—that is, there is no official list of ethnic groups—and individuals have much more leeway in choosing the ethnic identity they prefer for themselves. Americans who ancestors arrived from many different European countries can choose which ethnic group(s) they identify with (Waters 1990). For example, a person with German, Irish, and French ancestry might prefer to describe himself simply as "Irish American" without facing others' insistence that he identify as German, French, or something else. Moreover, his reason for doing so—for example, because he inherited an Irish last name, or spent time in Ireland, or grew up in an Irish American neighborhood—would probably not be questioned.

 Is Race Real?

THE SOCIAL CONSTRUCTION OF RACE

 Watch the **Big Question Video** in **MySocLab**

Sociologists often describe race as a **social construct**, or a social phenomenon that was invented by human beings and is shaped by the social forces present in the time and place of its creation. The idea of *invention* often leads people to assume that something that is socially constructed is not real. But since when are inventions not real? Thomas Edison invented the light bulb, but it is real. Steve Jobs invented the iPad, and it's real. The Beatles invented the real song "I Want to Hold Your Hand." Similarly, the belief that human beings come in four or five colors or flavors called "races" is invented—and it's real. Or to put it differently, races are real—but they are not biological. They are real social groupings that have real effects on people's lives, much like religious groups. No one would say religion is not "real"; it has exercised an enormous influence on human affairs since time immemorial. People have lived and died for their religious beliefs and identities. But we don't usually think of religious groups as being determined by individuals' biological characteristics. Instead, we understand that a complex array of social processes go into making a person a member of a particular religious group. The same is true of race.

Race and Society

The definition of race as socially constructed means several things. First is the idea that race is a classification system that is invented, created by human beings, and therefore man-made rather than natural. Second is the perspective that it is *socially* created—not the work of a single individual but rather the product of masses of people who form a society. In that sense, race is a lot like language: no single person invented English, or Spanish, or Korean, but languages are real social phenomena that millions of unnamed people have shaped. Third, the social foundation of race implies that as societies change, so do their ideas about race. Many sociologists, historians, and anthropologists investigate just how societal factors—such as economic conditions and organization, shifts in cultural values, or political upheavals—influence beliefs about race.

One puzzle that has fascinated researchers is how Americans' ideas about who is white have changed over time. Many people whom we consider to be white today would not have been classified as such a century ago. Americans of Irish, Italian, Jewish, and other European ancestries were routinely excluded from the white category. Consider for example the nineteenth-century Ohio newspaper that complained of Germans "driving 'white people' out of the labor market" (Jacobson 1998: 47). Or a century earlier, Benjamin Franklin's complaint that "[t]he number of purely white people in the world is proportionally very small," for

> *…the Spaniards, Italians, French, Russians, and Swedes are generally of what we call a swarthy complexion; as are the Germans also, the Saxons only excepted, who, with the English, make the principal body of white people on the face of the earth. (quoted in Jacobson 1998: 40)*

In Franklin's view, only the English and some Germans could be counted as white, unlike Swedes, Italians, and Russians. The historian Matthew Frye Jacobson, who uncovered these long-ago examples of racial categorization, argues that the massive wave of European immigration to land in the United States over the period of roughly 1880 to 1920 had a major impact on who was considered white. If whiteness had seemed self-evident at the founding of the Republic, when the European-origin population was largely of English

descent (though with Irish, Scottish, Dutch, and French members as well), its boundaries were much less clear when immigrants began arriving from places like Poland, Italy, Greece, Hungary, and Russia in the late nineteenth century. As a result, politicians, scientists, and everyday people started to view the newcomers as members of separate races, distinct from—and inferior to—"true" whites, who were of northwestern European origin.

So why do we consider Polish Americans and Greek Americans today to be white? Or, in the memorable phrase of one anthropologist, "How did Jews become white folks?" (Sacks 1994). Paradoxically, it is because prejudice against these "nonwhite" Europeans became so great that Congress passed a law—the 1924 Immigration Act—that sharply limited the numbers of people who were allowed to emigrate to the United States from Southern and Eastern Europe. The sharp downturn in European immigration that followed meant that over the following generations, fewer and fewer Americans of European descent were immigrants who spoke foreign languages and practiced unfamiliar customs, while more and more were native-born, English-speaking U.S. citizens who embraced American cultural forms, from music and dress to sports and food. In other words, southern and eastern Europeans underwent cultural **assimilation**, a process by which immigrants come to be incorporated into their new society by taking on the cultural tastes and practices of the new society. For example, the first-generation Pole had a second-generation Polish American son, who might simply have a third-generation American daughter. And part of the process of becoming American for these immigrant groups was being quietly folded into the white population. At the end of this section, we'll explore whether other groups may become white in the future.

Changing American definitions of who counts as white lend support to the **constructivist** view of race—that is, the argument that racial categories are social creations, not biological facts. If race were simply a matter of our physical makeup, the boundaries of the white category would not have shifted so dramatically over the last 200 years; people's bodily characteristics have not changed over that time. What changed instead were Americans' beliefs about who belonged to what race, so they went about constructing and reconstructing race categories.

Race and Biology

The hardest thing for most people to accept about the constructivist perspective on race is that it seems to contradict what they see with their very own eyes. How can anybody claim that race is not a biological fact, when we can easily "see" race? Every day we come across people whom we can

How have Americans' ideas about who is white changed over time?

Racial categories are not simply straightforward reflections of human physical diversity; they have everything to do with the beliefs that are prevalent in the societies that use them. In the U.S., people from countries like India are considered to be part of the same 'Asian' race as people from countries like China, despite their surface physical differences. But in Canada, they are classified as members of separate races.

immediately identify in racial terms, for example as white or Asian.

The simple answer is this: We can easily spot surface physical differences between people. But the ways in which we then assign people to racial groups is purely a matter of socialization—that is, of having been trained (consciously or not) to pick out particular bodily characteristics and then associate them with particular groups.

Consider a very simple example. Pretend you are in a laboratory with a researcher who puts three colored blocks in front of you—red, yellow, and blue—and asks you to divide them into two groups. You might decide that red and yellow go together, while blue remains its own category, or perhaps you might choose to group red and blue together, leaving yellow on its own. There is no obvious similarity here, no clear-cut grouping of which two colors go together. But if every time you make a choice, the researcher corrects you by putting the yellow and blue blocks together and leaving the red apart, you will learn very quickly that the colors yellow and blue fit together. From that point forward, you will easily be able to classify yellow and blue—but not red—as part of the same group, even when you're asked to sort toy cars or beach balls instead of blocks. Matching items to groups based on color will become an automatic reaction you don't even have to think about; after a while, it will seem natural that yellow and blue go together, but not red.

Race works the same way. We grow up learning to look for certain pieces of information about a person's body (notably their skin color, hair color, hair texture, and eye color and shape) while disregarding other things, like height, weight, ear shape, and hand size, to come up with an idea of which race they belong to. And today at least, we're usually right: The race we think the person belongs to is in fact the race with which he or she identifies. But that does not mean that our racial classification of others, and their racial identification of themselves, are based on some innate racial characteristics they possess and that we simply observe. Instead, it's more like a situation in which, instead of blocks, we have yellow-colored, blue-colored, and red-colored people, and we've all been trained to think of the yellow and blue people as being in a different racial category than the red ones. In other words, both the observers and the observed share exactly the same mental rules of who belongs to what race. But that does not mean there is anything natural or necessary

Is race determined by biology?

about blues and yellows being matched together, or about reds being held apart.

Human beings vary in their surface (and other) biological traits as we move around the world. And we are very good at spotting physical differences between the members of our species. We can generally see physical differences between Norwegians and Italians, Italians and Nigerians, Nigerians and Ethiopians, Ethiopians and Indians, and Indians and Koreans. We can even see physical differences between siblings! But we don't generally consider those differences to indicate that a brother and sister are members of different races. Similarly, we may or may not consider the physical differences we notice between different groups around the world to reflect racial differences. For example, we can see surface differences between Norwegians and Nigerians and Koreans, and indeed we usually consider them to be members of different races. In these examples, racial difference maps onto observable physical difference. But in other cases, like the comparisons of Norwegians to Italians, or Nigerians to Ethiopians, or Indians to Koreans, we see physical differences between them but classify them as members of the same racial group. Despite their distinctive surface characteristics, in the United States today Norwegians and Italians are considered to be racially white, Nigerians and Ethiopians black, and Indians and Koreans, Asian. It is not biology that dictates that Indians and Koreans are members of the same race while Ethiopians are not, but rather socially created and widespread rules for grouping people.

In the last few decades, some scientists have started to argue that even if surface physical features are not a reliable indicator of race, genetic characteristics—that is, patterns in our DNA—reveal the existence of human racial groups. This assumption underpins criminal forensic experts' analysis of DNA evidence (extracted from crime-scene specimens like blood or saliva) to try to guess the perpetrator's race. It is also behind the new pastime of genetic genealogy, where companies analyze their clients' DNA to estimate the racial

In Brazil, race labels are meant to give more specific details about people's appearance in terms of facial traits, skin color, eye color, hair color and hair texture. This focus on physical appearance means that a person's race depends on how they look as much as if not more so than on their ancestry. As a result, even full siblings can be considered to be of different in races in Brazil. Would you say that the members of this family in Brasilia all belong to the same race?

makeup of their family tree. But just as in the case of sorting blue and red blocks, racial analysis of DNA starts with man-made rules for assigning individuals to racial groups. Before looking at a customer's—or a suspect's—DNA sample, scientists have to decide which characteristics of the DNA will be indicative of which kind of racial ancestry. And to do that, they have to come up with a list of which race(s) they believe are out there, and then sample individuals from those assumed races to find out what kinds of genetic characteristics they typically have. In the United States, genetic genealogy firms generally try to identify European, African, or East Asian ancestry. In the United Kingdom, where much of this forensic technology was developed, the categories of interest are "Caucasians, Afro-Caribbeans, and Asians from the Indian subcontinent" (Evett et al. 1996: 398). In both cases, scientists divide humankind into racial categories that are familiar given their society's histories. But the technology could be used with any kind of geography-based grouping—even a simple division of human beings into "red" and "blue" races. Once two or more categories have been created, and individuals selected to provide representative DNA for each of those categories, then it is simply a matter of working through a statistical algorithm for assessing how similar the particular customer's (or suspect's) gene variants are to those typically found within the "red" or "blue" sample. Crucially, the genetic genealogy companies' estimates can never be disproved or properly assessed: If you are informed that your ancestry is 30 percent African, 40 percent Asian, and 30 percent European, what independent and reliable data can you use to verify this statement?

For many people, the constructivist view of race is hard to truly grasp because it flies in the face of what we think we see and know. Its basic premise is that even though we may *think* race is grounded in human biology, it isn't really—it just claims to be.

☐ Race and Place

The sociological view that race is socially constructed is grounded in a comparative (or cross-national) perspective. Depending on location, the race concept has emerged in different forms, at different times, or perhaps not at all. (By

Why is race understood differently around the world?

"race concept" or "race thinking," I mean people's beliefs about race including their notions of what it is, which groups are races, and who belongs to which race.) Because Western scholars have focused less on societies outside Europe and North America, the study of race thinking elsewhere is still in its infancy. But the research that has been done in this area offers some fascinating insights on important questions about race around the globe.

One question that researchers ask is how we can explain the noticeable variations in the way people around the world think about race. One study of West Africa found that local racial groupings like black, white, and red had little to do with individuals' surface physical appearance but instead were based on whether individuals were believed to have noble ancestry (which in this context meant Arab heritage) (Hall 2011). Similarly, Brazilians do not link physical appearance to racial group the same way Americans do; in Brazil, dozens of racial labels exist to classify people based on very specific combinations of skin color, hair color, hair texture, facial features, and so forth. As a result, full siblings can be of different races in Brazil, a situation that is unthinkable by American standards. Finally, scholars have noted that while contemporary Americans attribute racial differences to genes, people elsewhere (and at different times) have thought of racial difference as residing in the blood, or the mind, or the soul (Nelkin and Lindee 1995). What causes the race concept to take on such different forms?

To date, researchers have concentrated on two types of explanation for such variations in race thinking. The first is that as the Western race concept spread across the globe in the wake of imperial conquest, it blended with local traditional beliefs and prejudices to create many new versions of race (Dikötter 2008). For example, South Koreans' ideas of race today likely reflect a mixture of ideas brought by U.S. military personnel stationed there since the mid-twentieth century, historical Korean and Japanese color preferences, Confucian beliefs about groups' proper places, and longstanding images of Korea as being a nation based on shared blood (Kim 2008).

The second approach for explaining local variants of race tends to focus on demographic, economic, and political factors. Why, for example, have Americans traditionally classified people with white and black ancestry as black, while Australians thought that mixture between whites and Aboriginal peoples would result in white, and not native, descendants? A key difference lies in the economic roles that European settlers expected African Americans and Aboriginal Australians to play. Because black slaves in the United States were a source of free labor, it was in white Americans' best interest to increase their numbers, and the one-drop rule of treating mixed-race people as black was one way to add to the black population. In contrast, for white Australians Aboriginal people represented a source of free land, but to successfully occupy that land, they had to empty it of Aborigines. For the European settler community in Australia then, it was preferable to erase the Aboriginal population by absorbing it into the white one—or by removing it and concentrating it on undesirable lands (Wolfe 2001).

But why then did Brazilians develop a belief in the potential "whitening" of the descendants of black slaves rather than do the same thing as Americans and treat everyone with black ancestry as black in order to increase the slave population? Here demography (the characteristics of human populations) seems to have played a decisive role. Portuguese colonists made up a much smaller share of the Brazilian population than English settlers did in North America, and so they worried about being outnumbered by the people they enslaved. One solution to their problem was to fuel divisions within the African-descent population that would lessen the likelihood of slave rebellions, and color was a key tool for doing so. In other words, the Brazilian system for using many different race labels to describe people, rather than lumping them into a single "black" category as in the United States, was originally a way to create and emphasize distinctions between people whose solidarity might otherwise jeopardize Portugal's colonial venture in South America. Again, there is nothing natural or inevitable about the way human beings have created racial categories; the conventions and classifications we come up with are reflections of the social, economic, and political worlds we live in.

3 What Is Racist and What Isn't?

CONTEMPORARY RACISM

👁 **Watch** the **Big Question Video** in **MySocLab**

Americans use the word *racist* to describe an astonishingly long list of things. In addition to labeling people as racist, we also talk about ideas, speeches, sermons, movies, songs, books, policies, laws, and political parties as being racist. Whether something or someone is racist is often the subject of heated debate. Is the April 2010 Arizona law making unauthorized immigration a crime racist? Are sports mascots and team names representing American Indians racist? These controversies stem in part from the lack of an explicit, widely shared notion of what racism is.

☐ What Is Racism?

For sociologists, the term **racism** includes two phenomena: *prejudice* and *discrimination*. **Prejudices** are negative beliefs or attitudes held about entire groups. They are broadly applied and are based on subjective and often inaccurate information. Prejudices involve prejudgments of individuals based on **stereotypes**, which are simplified generalizations about a group. These blanket images are hard to change because, as psychologists have shown, we tend to look for and remember information that seems to confirm our stereotypes while ignoring or dismissing information that does not support them. Explore *A Sociological Perspective* on page 273 to see how we often confuse race with ethnicity by drawing heavily on stereotypes when we dress up in costumes on Halloween.

Discrimination differs from prejudice in that it involves actions rather than beliefs. It includes any behavior that harms individuals or puts them at a disadvantage on the basis of their group membership. Discrimination maintains and reinforces social hierarchy by keeping subordinate groups from advancing. This can vary in degrees of severity. The mildest form of racial discrimination is the use of negative words or phrases in reference to a particular group. While names or phrases may be hurtful or even work toward perpetuating stereotypes, they do not impact people's life chances. A more extreme type of discrimination involves placing limits on people's opportunities based on their racial group. This involves preventing specific racial groups from equally accessing schools, employment, housing, and other institutions that are part of membership and participation in society. At its most extreme, discrimination can be carried out as acts of violence against an individual or members of a racial group. In the era following the Civil War, lynching was an act of racial discrimination used to intimidate, punish, and terrorize primarily blacks in the South. Many other societies, such as South Africa, Rwanda, and Bosnia, have also experienced violent forms of racially and ethnically charged discrimination, including **genocide**, which is the deliberate and systematic killing of a category of people.

Acts of racial or ethnic discrimination can be classified as individual or as institutional and structural. **Individual discrimination** is an intentional action carried out by an individual or small group that is meant to harm members of a certain group. An employer refusing to hire blacks, a landlord who does not rent apartments to Mexican Americans, or a group of teenagers who paint swastikas on a Jewish synagogue are all examples of individual-level discrimination. In these cases, individuals or small groups take purposeful actions to negatively affect members of specific racial or ethnic groups.

People are not the only actors who may discriminate, however. Sociologists maintain that institutions can also be discriminatory. **Institutional (or structural) discrimination** occurs when the actions or policies of organizations or social institutions exclude, disadvantage, or harm members of particular groups. Jim Crow—a system of laws and social norms that governed interactions between blacks and whites in the American South in the early twentieth century—represented an institutionalized system of discrimination. Schools, housing, transportation, and public facilities all formally engaged in discriminatory practices by keeping blacks and whites separate and in grossly unequal facilities. South Africa's system of apartheid is another example of this institutional form of discrimination where whites were able to secure their social position by excluding nonwhites from the majority of institutions.

An important difference between individual and institutional discrimination is that while individuals who discriminate do so intentionally, institutions' discriminatory policies may or may not arise from the intention to put certain groups at a disadvantage. An example of intentional institutional discrimination would be the United States' 1790 naturalization law, which explicitly stipulated that only white immigrants could become citizens. An example of unintentional discrimination could be the federal sentencing guidelines that penalize individuals in possession of crack cocaine more heavily than those possessing powder cocaine. Although the guidelines do not explicitly refer to race—and so do not appear to be intentionally discriminatory—the fact that powder cocaine is used disproportionately by whites and crack by blacks means that African Americans are more likely than whites to face the heavier penalties dictated by the sentencing guidelines. As this example suggests, however, it is not easy to determine whether institutional discrimination is intentional or not. Even though the guidelines do not overtly base criminal sentences on race, they may well have been adopted because they were likely to have a disproportionately harsh impact on African American offenders. Either way, sociologists consider institutions to be discriminatory if the ultimate impact of their actions is to exacerbate inequality, regardless of whether or not that was the intention.

What is the difference between prejudice and discrimination?

📖 **Read** the **Document** *Names, Logos, Mascots, and Flags: The Contradictory Uses of Sport Symbols* in **MySocLab**.

☐ Why Does Racism Occur?

Some of the earliest research on prejudice and discrimination was conducted by psychologists, who saw racism as an expression of particular personality disorders. Yet psychological approaches to prejudice have been criticized for overlooking the context that gives shape to the beliefs and behaviors that underlie racism. They also treat racism as if it

A SOCIOLOGICAL PERSPECTI

Who are you going to be for Hallow

loween costumes sometimes reinforce popular no-
s about race and ethnicity that a sociological perspec-
challenges, such as the belief that race is something
an readily see. Using recognizable symbols, they sug-
that racial and ethnic groups can be differentiated by
al cues. What results are exaggerated misrepresenta-
s drawn heavily from stereotypes that may be humor-
to some and offensive to others.

These types of costumes also confuse race and
nicity. For example, retail stores often label costum
"Asian" or "Arabian" which are both broad geograp
egories typical of racial groupings. However, the in
features of the costumes, such as attire and headpi
represent cultural markers often associated with sn
more narrowly-defined ethnic groups. Presented th
race and ethnicity are shown to be interchangeable

How could wearing this costume impact
a child's perception and understanding
of Native American culture?

Cute or harmful? Do even
innocent representations
of cultural stereotypes
reinforce prejudice?

Explore A Sociological Perspective in **MySocLab** and then ...

Think About It

would you create a Halloween costume to represent the racial
ethnic group(s) to which you identify? Is it possible to make this
ume without the use of stereotypes? Would it be recognizable

Inspire Your Sociological Imaginatio

What characteristics do racial and ethnic costumes tend
common, regardless of the specific groups they are mea
tray? And how do gender stereotypes influence the desig

were an abnormal condition, when in fact, historically, large numbers of Americans have held prejudices and acted in a discriminatory fashion. Accordingly, sociologists have developed normative theories, which pay attention to the role of social rules and guides to behavior that vary across social contexts. Normative theories of prejudice consider the type of situations where norms are in place that could encourage or give rise to prejudicial beliefs or discriminatory acts. Through socialization, people learn the norms that operate in an environment or society at large. Research has shown that even very young children absorb racial prejudices and act upon them—for example, when choosing play partners (Van Ausdale and Feagin 2001). In short, people learn to think and act in a racist fashion—they are socialized into racism.

How can people be socialized into racism?

The challenge remains, however, to explain why racism comes to permeate a given society in the first place. Sociologists have responded by highlighting the connection between racism and power. Whether we think of the origins of racial thinking in contexts of imperialism and slavery, or more contemporary manifestations like the official racial segregation of schools until the 1950s, it is evident that racist exclusions and handicaps both reflect and perpetuate imbalances in the amount of power that different groups hold. Race-based hierarchies do not occur by chance but rather are the product of human efforts to acquire and preserve social privileges. In other words, we can ascribe racism to groups' sustained efforts, conscious and unconscious, to shore up their own status in society.

Does Racism Still Exist in the United States?

Researchers have used a wide variety of methods to gauge racial prejudice and discrimination in the post–civil rights era.

Prejudice Surveys today show relatively low public support in the United States for Jim Crow–era measures like racial segregation in public facilities or transportation. For example, in 1942, 68 percent of whites polled in a national survey were in favor of separate schools for black and white students, but in 1995, only 5 percent supported such an arrangement. Similarly, in 1958, 96 percent of whites surveyed opposed racial intermarriage, but by 1997, that figure had dropped to a third (33 percent). And while only 37 percent of whites in 1958 said they would be willing to vote for

Does racial prejudice and discrimination still exist in the U.S. today?

a black presidential candidate, in 1997, 95 percent said they would (Schuman et al. 1997).

Such surveys are not a sure-fire indicator of public prejudices, however. The optimistic interpretation of survey findings is that whites have become less prejudiced toward blacks over time. The pessimistic interpretation is that whites have simply become less likely to admit to racial prejudice, but their true sentiments have not changed much over time.

Accordingly, some scholars have turned to analyses of everyday talk for a better measure of how Americans truly think about race. Through long, in-depth interviews, they have found ample evidence that whites in particular often try to avoid openly discussing race and that they frequently use "color-blind" rhetoric that downplays the possibility of racism still playing a role in American life (Bonilla-Silva 2002; Frankenberg 1993). These studies pay attention to the strategies individuals use to resolve the tensions and complexities within present-day racial beliefs, like the conflict between prejudice and the idea that our nation is an egalitarian one.

Evidence that racial prejudice persists has also been taken from mass media portrayals of racial groups. These portrayals are often based on stereotypes in which minority groups are presented in roles that are defined by negative or demeaning characteristics. Studies of newspapers, television programming, and movies as well as the Internet use a research method called content analysis that looks for patterns in presence and meaning in order to study how racial groups appear in the media. Research has found that since the 1970s and 1980s, media representation of racial groups has become more diverse and positive, with minority groups taking on more prominent roles.

Discrimination Racial discrimination is not easy to measure in an era in which such behavior is widely frowned upon and, in some instances, legally prohibited. In many social settings it has become a form of deviance, a phenomenon that sociologists often try to study using indirect, unobtrusive, or anonymous measures. Surveys and interviews on the other hand pose the same problems for discrimination research as they do for the investigation of prejudice. For example, employers are not likely to admit to interviewers that they practice racial discrimination—and they may not even be aware of it. To adequately explore discrimination, social scientists often try to observe behavior through two principal strategies: experiments and ethnographies.

Deryl Dedmon, 19, was sentenced to two concurrent life sentences for murdering a black man, 47-year-old James Craig Anderson, by running him over with his pickup truck in June 2011. What do you think this case says about the existence of racism in the contemporary United States?

One experimental study of discrimination garnered so much public attention that presidential candidate Howard Dean cited it during his 2004 campaign. Sociologist Devah Pager (2003) tested the influence of a criminal record on the resumes of black and white job applicants. With the help of two black and two white college students pretending to apply for entry-level jobs at 350 different companies, Pager demonstrated that the negative effects of a criminal record are 40 percent greater for black job applicants than white job applicants. Considering the disproportionate number of black men who have been incarcerated, this bias disadvantages a large segment of the black applicant pool. The study was also remarkable for showing that white applicants *with a criminal record* were more likely to be considered for a job than black applicants without one. Pager (2007:91) concluded, "Being black in America today is just about the same as having a felony conviction in terms of one's chances of finding a job."

Another widely noted experiment involved creating fictitious résumés of both high and low quality, and then randomly assigning some résumés either a stereotypically white name (like "Emily" or "Greg") or a stereotypically black one (like "Lakisha" or "Jamal"). The researchers sent out these fake résumés in response to over 1,300 sales, administrative support, clerical, and customer service job listings found in the *Boston Globe* or *Chicago Tribune* Sunday newspapers. Their results showed that when controlling for applicant quality and neighborhood, résumés with "white names" received 50 percent more follow-up phone calls than résumés with "black names." Moreover, an increase in the quality of the applicant did not reduce this difference. In fact, the study showed that the disadvantage of a "black name" increased as the quality of the résumé increased (Bertrand and Mullainathan 2004). Like the Pager study, this experiment makes a strong case that racial discrimination plays a significant role in employment in the United States today.

A different approach to investigating racial discrimination is to observe it ethnographically. Deirdre Royster's

(2003) study of 25 black and 25 white working-class men with comparable levels of intelligence, education, and dispositions toward work debunked the idea that the job market is a meritocratic and fair arena where the most qualified candidates are the first to be hired. In contrast, Royster found that employment was determined by social networks that led to personal referrals and recommendations among the white blue-collar community. Not only were black blue-collar workers disadvantaged by the absence of connections to owners, managers, or supervisors that were integral for white workers in finding employment, but the white blue-collar community erroneously perceived blacks as having an advantage through affirmative action policies and practices. This myth of "reverse racism" meant that white workers were often unwilling to make recommendations or referrals for black workers. Although the advent of affirmative action policies has been used to claim reverse discrimination, sociological research maintains that discrimination against racial minorities, specifically black applicants, remains a significant explanation for racial stratification in employment.

4 Do Race and Ethnicity Matter Anymore?

THE IMPACT OF RACE AND ETHNICITY TODAY

Watch the **Big Question Video** in **MySocLab**

The empirical evidence of ongoing prejudice and discrimination that social scientists have documented contradicts an image that many have of the United States. The passage of the Civil Rights Act of 1964 and the Voting Rights Act of 1965 – both of which legally prohibited discrimination – is often thought of as the culmination of the civil rights movement, marking the end of the long and arduous struggle to secure civil and political rights of African Americans and other minority groups. Many Americans point to the passage of these laws as the moment when race became insignificant in the United States. No longer were racial minorities legally prohibited from pursuing their academic, political, or economic aspirations. How could skin color be a barrier to success any longer?

How do sociologists explain racial gaps in socioeconomic status?

Sociologists have taken this question seriously. In addition to developing experimental, survey, and ethnographic measures of contemporary racism, they have conducted sophisticated statistical analyses that compare the socioeconomic status of different racial groups. According to almost any measure they have explored, a clear racial hierarchy emerges, with whites (and sometimes Asians) on top, and Hispanics, blacks, and American Indians on the bottom.

Racial Disparities in Socioeconomic Status

To begin to answer the question of whether race and ethnicity matter in the contemporary United States, we need a statistical snapshot of how different groups live today. What the numbers reveal is that ethnicity no longer seems to have much of an impact on key life outcomes like who individuals marry, what kind of job they have, or where they live. In contrast, however, race continues to make a big difference on all these dimensions and more.

Income and Wealth Nonwhite families have experienced substantial gains in household income since World War II. Despite these gains, sociologists and economists have documented persistent gaps in family income between white and nonwhite households for the last 40 years (see Figure 10.1). Although the income gap between white and minority families narrowed following the civil rights movement, this narrowing leveled off in the 1970s and has not changed much since. For example, the average black household in 2010 had a median income of $32,068. This is just 60 percent of the median white household of $54,620, an income disparity that has not changed significantly since the 1970s (U.S. Census Bureau 2011; Brown et al. 2003; Marger 2003; see Table 10.1). When we compare Hispanic families to white families during the same period, we see that the income gap between these groups has actually increased. In 1972 the median family income of nonwhite Hispanic households was 74 percent of white households, a ratio that has shrunk to 69 percent in 2010 (U.S. Census Bureau 2011).

In addition to income gaps, black and Latino families are more likely than white families to fall below the poverty line.

In 2009 a quarter of all black and Latino families were living in poverty, compared to just 10 percent of white families (see Table 10.1). The disproportionate number of black and Latino families that fall below the poverty line largely accounts for the different income patterns between white and minority families. However this general trend should not obscure the fact that there is a stable base of middle- and working-class minority families that earn incomes comparable to white families. In fact, if we compare college-educated blacks to college-educated whites, the racial gap in income is substantially diminished, although it does not entirely disappear (Marger 2003:279; Conley 1999).

Although there remains a substantial income gap among whites, blacks, and Latinos, it is important to note that whites are not at the top of the income hierarchy in the United States. As Table 10.1 illustrates, Asian Americans have the highest median household income among racial and ethnic groups in the United States. However, we should be cautious with our interpretation of these data. Because these data are not separated by country of origin or specific Asian ethnicity, they may cover up the fact that Asian families tend to fall at both ends of the income spectrum. For example, some Asian groups, such as Vietnamese and Cambodian Americans, are at the bottom of the income hierarchy, while other Asian groups, such as Chinese, Filipino, and Japanese Americans, are at the top of the income hierarchy (Marger 2003:367). These household income figures may also be misleading because they do not take into account the number of people in a household whose income contributes to the total. In other words, Asians' higher median household income may simply be the result of their households containing more working members than do white households.

In addition to the racial gap in household income, sociologists have also identified a racial gap in household wealth. Wealth refers to "the accumulated sum of assets (house, cars, savings and checking accounts, stocks and mutual funds, retirement accounts, etc.) minus the sum of debt (mortgages, auto loans, credit card debt, etc.)" (Kochlar, Fry, and Taylor 2011:4). While black Americans have made gains in income, education, and occupation since the civil rights movement, the black-white wealth gap endures and is central to current patterns of racial inequality (Conley 1999). The accumulation of wealth depends heavily on intergenerational transfers between parents and children (e.g., gifts, informal loans, and inheritances). Because black families have experienced multiple generations of exclusion from home ownership and other forms of asset accumulation, they have been unable to build up a base of assets to pass on from generation to generation (Massey and Denton 1993; Oliver and Shapiro 1997; Brown et al. 2003). Black families that are able to purchase a home are more likely than any other racial group to live in a segregated neighborhood, which diminishes property value and home equity, and they are more likely to receive unfavorable terms on their home mortgage than comparable whites (Brown et al. 2003:14). As a result the net worth of black families persistently lags behind the net worth of white families. Explore the Infographic *Race and Inequality* on page 278 to learn more about the changing demographic patterns and persistent trends in socioeconomic inequality in the United States.

FIGURE 10.1 REAL MEDIAN HOUSEHOLD INCOME BY RACE AND HISPANIC ORIGIN: 1967–2010

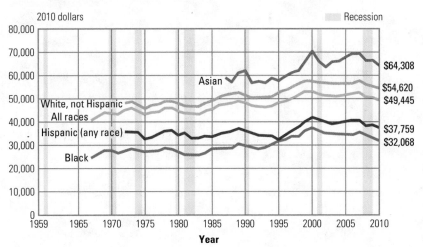

Source: U.S Census Bureau (2011).

TABLE 10.1 INCOME, POVERTY, AND UNEMPLOYMENT

Race/Ethnicity	Median Household Income in 2010	Percent of White Income	Percent of Families in Poverty in 2009	Unemployment Rate in 2012
White	$54,620	100%	9.9%	7.4%
Black	$32,068	59%	27.4%	13.6%
Hispanic	$37,759	69%	26.6%	10.5%
Asian	$64,308	118%	12.1%	6.7%

Source: U.S. Census Bureau (2011); U.S Bureau of Labor Statistics (2012).

Race and Inequality

O ver the past 100 years the United States has experienced dramatic shifts in its racial composition. **In 1910, 89 percent of the U.S. population consisted of non-Hispanic whites, and the Census Bureau predicts that figure will drop to just 46 percent by the year 2050, making the U.S. a "majority-minority" nation for the first time in its history.** Despite these changing demographic trends, patterns of socioeconomic inequality remain a persistent feature of race relations in the United States. The most striking indicator of inequality is the racial gap in wealth. The recent economic recession took a far greater toll on the wealth of minority families, exacerbating these already existing inequalities.

Becoming a Majority-Minority Nation

Percentage of population that is white (non-Hispanic)

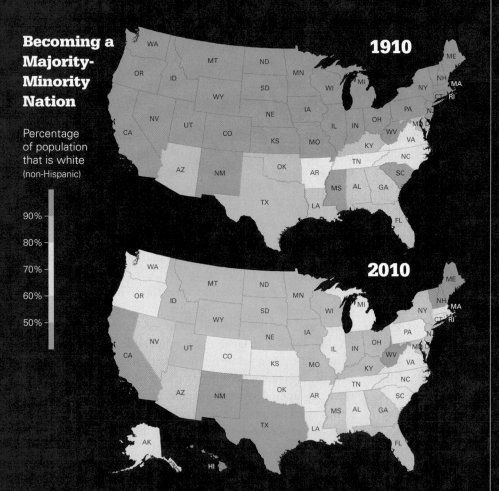

90%
80%
70%
60%
50%

1910

2010

Sources: Based on data from U.S. Census Bureau (2012); Pew Research Center (2011).

◎→ **Explore** the **Data** on Race and Inequality in MySocLab and then...

▪ **Think About It**
How might trends in fertility, mortality, and/or migration contribute to the decrease in the share of the white population, and to the relative increase in the Hispanic and Asian populations?

▪ **Inspire Your Sociological Imagination**
What might be some of the effects of America becoming a majority-minority nation?

The Wealth Gap

Despite changing demographic trends, the racial gap in wealth remains a persistent feature of socioeconomic inequality in the United States, reflecting generations of discrimination and disadvantage faced by minority families. The racial wealth gap is the largest it has been in the past 25 years, reflecting the uneven impact of the Great Recession.

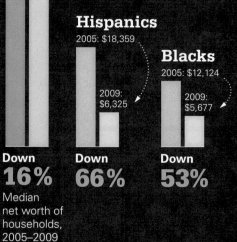

Whites
2005: $134,992
2009: $113,149

Hispanics
2005: $18,359
2009: $6,325

Blacks
2005: $12,124
2009: $5,677

Down 16%
Down 66%
Down 53%

Median net worth of households, 2005–2009

Employment and Unemployment Since the passage of the Civil Rights Act of 1964, which legally ended discrimination in the labor market, African Americans have been able to move into middle- and upper-middle-class occupations from which they had previously been excluded (Landry and Marsh 2011). Many of these middle-class occupations are concentrated in the government sector, such as primary and secondary education, social work, and public administration. This is largely because antidiscrimination laws were more easily enforced in public bureaucracies than in the private sector (Brown et al. 2003). A smaller proportion of African Americans were also able to move into upper-middle-class occupations such as law, medicine, and executive and managerial positions. Despite these gains, blacks remain underrepresented in professional and managerial positions and overrepresented in the lower-wage service sector (Conley 1999:11). Moreover, sociologists have noted that upper-middle-class blacks still only earn about 85 percent of the income of whites in similar professions (Landry and Marsh 2011:385).

Despite the upward mobility of middle-class blacks since the civil rights movement, African Americans continue to lag behind whites in a key dimension of inequality: unemployment. In 2012 the unemployment rate for blacks was 13.6 percent, nearly twice the rate for whites (7.4 percent) (U.S. Bureau of Labor Statistics 2012; see Table 10.1). The black-white unemployment gap has been a durable feature of racial inequality since the 1960s. In fact, the unemployment rate for blacks has been consistently double that of whites in the 50 years since the civil rights movement (Conley 1999).

Education African Americans have experienced substantial gains in educational attainment over the last three decades. Between 1980 and 2010 blacks' rates of high school completion have risen by nearly two-thirds and rates of college completion have more than doubled, while rates of high school drop-out have shrunk by nearly half (see Figure 10.2a). Hispanics have experienced similar patterns of educational attainment since 1980. Between 1980 and 2010, rates of high school completion have risen by over 40 percent for Latinos while rates of college completion have doubled, and rates of high school drop-out in 2010 are half of what they were in 1980. However, many of the educational gains made by blacks and Hispanics during this period were paralleled by gains among whites. Thus, although blacks and Latinos have made a great deal of progress over the last three decades, gaps in educational attainment between whites, blacks, and Hispanics remain. At the same time, rates of educational attainment among Asians have remained high and stable since the 1980s. Asian Americans have the highest rates of educational attainment in the country. Rates of college completion

The unemployment rate for African Americans has been consistently double that of whites in the 50 years since the civil rights movement.

What patterns of educational attainment have minority groups experienced over the last 30 years?

among Asians are nearly triple those of blacks and quadruple those of Hispanics (see Figure 10.2b). Sociologists point out that the high levels of educational attainment among Asians are largely tied to the fact that Asian immigrants tend to come from middle- and upper-middle-class families, in contrast to the poor and working-class backgrounds of many Latino immigrant groups (Steinberg [1989] 2001).

Residential Segregation Despite the fact that the Civil Rights Act of 1968 outlawed discrimination in housing markets, African Americans continue to be the most residentially segregated group in the United States (Massey and Denton 1993; Sharkey 2008). In addition to being spatially isolated, black families are also more likely to live in low-income neighborhoods over successive generations than

FIGURE 10.2 GAINS IN EDUCATIONAL ATTAINMENT

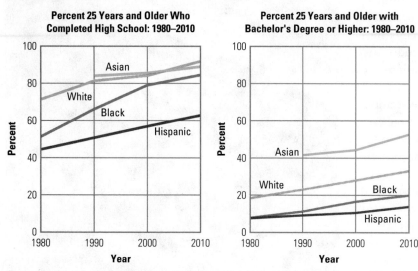

Percent 25 Years and Older Who Completed High School: 1980–2010

Percent 25 Years and Older with Bachelor's Degree or Higher: 1980–2010

Source: National Center for Educational Statistics (2011a); National Center for Educational Statistics (2011b).

any other racial group. Over half of all black families live in the poorest neighborhoods in the United States and have done so over multiple generations since the 1970s (Sharkey 2008:933). Black children who grew up in poor neighborhoods in the 1970s were more likely than any other group of children to remain in those poor neighborhoods as adults.

Sociologists have documented how growing up in poor, isolated neighborhoods—or **ghettos**—severely truncates the life chances of black families. Residents of ghetto neighborhoods are more likely to attend low-quality schools and be exposed to crime and violence, and are less likely to have access to economic opportunities and employment networks (Sharkey 2008). Sociologists have also shown that residents of segregated inner-city neighborhoods have less political influence than residents of more racially diverse suburban neighborhoods (Massey and Denton 1993).

Criminal Justice Supervision On any given day in America, over 2 million adults are serving time behind bars, accounting for a quarter of all prison and jail inmates worldwide (Liptak 2008). However, incarceration is not evenly distributed in the population. African American men account for 40 percent of the prison population—while accounting for only 12 percent of the general population (Pager 2007:3). In 2010 black men were seven times more likely to be incarcerated than white men and about twice as likely as Hispanic men (U.S. Bureau of Justice Statistics 2011; see Figure 10.3).

The incarcerated population is heavily concentrated among young African American men without a college degree. Among black men who finish high school, but do not attend college, nearly one in three will serve time in prison.

For those who drop out of high school, 60 percent will be incarcerated at some point in their lives (Western 2006). Sociologist Bruce Western calls this cohort of young, disadvantaged men the "mass imprisonment generation." For this generation of young black men, incarceration has become a common life event, more likely than college attendance or military service. Sociologists estimate that a third of adult black men have a felony conviction on their record. When misdemeanor convictions and arrests are taken into account, about half of all black men have a criminal record (Pager 2007:157).

Health and Healthcare Coverage Racial inequality is not just reflected in socioeconomic indicators like income, wealth, and education; racial and ethnic groups also show disparities in a variety of indicators related to health. For example, coronary heart disease is the leading cause of death in the United States, but African Americans are much more likely to die from this condition than any other racial group (Centers for Disease Control and Prevention 2011; see Table 10.2). African Americans also have the highest rate of infant mortality in the United States, a rate that is more than double that of whites, Asians, and Hispanics. One of the most striking disparities in mortality is in the area of homicide. For example, in 2007 the homicide rate for black males was over 10 times the rate for white and Asian males and about 4 times the rate for Latinos and Native Americans. Moreover, blacks have by far the highest rates of HIV infection among any racial or ethnic group in the United States.

Why do disparities in health exist among racial groups?

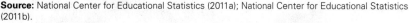

FIGURE 10.3 INCARCERATION RATES PER 100,000 IN 2010

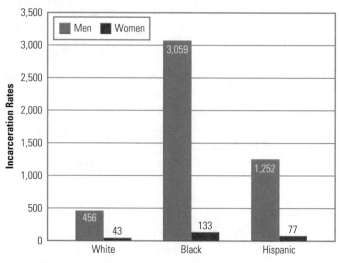

Source: Bureau of Justice Statistics (2011).

TABLE 10.2 VARIOUS HEALTH-RELATED INDICATORS

Race	Rates of HIV Infection of Persons over 13 Years of Age per 100,000 in 2008	Rates of Infant Mortality per 100,000 in 2006	Rates of Homicide per 100,000 in 2007	Death Rates for Coronary Heart Disease in 2008
White	8.2	5.58	2.7	134.2
Black	73.7	13.35	23.1	161.6
Hispanic	25.0	5.41	7.6	106.4
Asian	7.2	4.55	2.4	77.1

Source: Center for Disease Control and Prevention (2011).

The rate of HIV infection among African Americans is about 10 times the rate for whites and Asians and about 3 times the rate for Hispanics (see Table 10.2).

Many of these disparities in health are related to differences in healthcare coverage. According to the U.S. Census Bureau (2011), about 30 percent of Hispanics and 20 percent of African Americans lack a regular source of healthcare, compared to less than 12 percent of whites. As a result, African Americans and Latinos are far more likely than whites to rely on hospitals and clinics for their usual source of health care (U.S. Department of Health and Human Services 2000).

Political Participation and Representation Since the passage of the Civil Rights Act of 1964 and the Voting Rights Act of 1965, African Americans have experienced significant gains in political participation and representation. For example, between 1964 and 1972 over 2 million blacks were registered to vote in southern states, and since the 1970s close to 9,000 African Americans have been elected to political office (Marger 2003:287–288). In recent decades, black elected officials have become increasingly prominent in national politics. For example, during the 1990s and early 2000s African Americans such as Colin Powell and Condoleezza Rice occupied prominent positions in the Clinton and Bush administrations. In 2011 there were 44 black members of Congress, not to mention the fact that the president of the United States at the time of this writing, Barack Obama, is African American. However, despite the increasing visibility of African Americans in national politics, most black political officials remain predominantly at the state and local levels (Marger 2003).

Despite the gains in political participation that resulted from the civil rights movement, African Americans still face obstacles in exercising their voting rights. For example, a disproportionate number of African Americans are denied their voting rights because of felon disenfranchisement laws. *Felon disenfranchisement* refers to the loss of voting rights following a felony conviction. As noted earlier, African Americans make up a disproportionate segment of the population under criminal justice supervision. As a result, one in seven African Americans is denied the right to vote because of felon disenfranchisement laws. In some states, especially in the South, this number is as high as one in four (Manza and Uggen 2008). The disenfranchisement of such a large segment of the African American population has been shown to have significant consequences for electoral outcomes. Two scholars have estimated that if ex-felons had been allowed to vote in Florida in 2000, Al Gore would have carried the state by at least 30,000 votes and thus would have won the presidential election that year (Manza and Uggen 2008).

How have the high incarceration rates among African American men impacted their political participation?

How Do We Explain Racial Stratification?

Along almost any dimension of social and economic status, there are clearly significant gaps between different racial groups in the United States today. But how can we account for these inequalities?

Biology A century ago, American scholars would have embraced essentialist explanations that attributed nonwhites' poorer health outcomes to their natural physical inferiority, or that tied group differences in income levels to their inborn intellectual capacity. Sociologists today dismiss such biological explanations for racial disparities for several reasons. For one thing, they do not consider races to be biologically determined groupings but rather socially invented ones. For another, biologists claim that a trait like intelligence—if it were rooted in a person's genes—would probably not be distributed across the human species following the same pattern that supposedly racial traits like skin color are. And finally, attempts to measure and distinguish racial capacities or tendencies for things like intelligence, criminality, or other behavioral traits have been so obviously biased by researchers' stereotypes of nonwhites that they have provided very little in the way of a credible empirical basis on which to build essentialist theories of racial socioeconomic disparities.

How do sociologists account for racial inequalities?

Cultural Explanations Another longstanding approach to explaining racial socioeconomic inequality has been the cultural model. In the past, this meant attributing distinct and unchanging beliefs, norms, and values to separate racial groups and hypothesizing that these fixed cultures drove their members to certain behaviors that were advantageous or disadvantageous in the labor market, in school, or elsewhere in social life. Today, however, a more dynamic and complex notion of culture prevails, one where culture includes flexible worldviews and behaviors that people develop in response to their social context. In other words, this outlook connects culture and social structure as a way to explain racial stratification. In sociologist Elliot Liebow's ([1967] 2003) classic ethnography in Washington, D.C., it was found that black street-corner men's behaviors were not due to any intrinsic characteristics or to fixed cultural preferences but rather to the concrete obstacles these men faced in finding steady and adequate employment. Liebow argued black street-corner men's frequent decisions to turn down work did not reflect the cultural lack of a work ethic but rather a rational calculation concerning the marginal gains and physical stress brought by day labor. Therefore, he concludes that social policy aimed at eliminating racial inequality should not seek to reform individuals or modify cultural norms regarding traits such as persistence and patience but rather expand the structural opportunities open to them. In other words, culture may contribute to racial stratification not because it involves an unchanging set of values that group members are destined to hold but because it is largely a response to the structural obstacles certain races face in pursuing the American dream of upward mobility.

Structural Context Many sociologists explain racial stratification by pointing to opportunities and constraints that result from the structural environment—that is, from political arrangements, economic organization, and legal institutions. For example, the ebbs and flows of the U.S. economy create or restrict employment opportunities in ways that may affect racial groups differently. Early twentieth-century European immigrants were welcomed by a rapidly expanding U.S. economy. In contrast, immigrants since 1970, who are primarily from Asia and Latin America, have faced a tighter U.S. economy with higher unemployment and relatively fewer entry-level and low-skill jobs that can lead to long and stable careers. Consider too the many different ways in which racial groups have "arrived" in the United States: Native Americans were at first forcibly excluded, then segregated in reservations; Africans were brought against their will to perform slave labor; and Mexican Americans and other Latino groups were originally incorporated through U.S. territorial conquest. And although voluntary immigration has historically fed the growth of both the Asian and European American populations, it is worth noting that the former faced an array of immigration, residential, and administrative restrictions that the latter did not. In summary, the economic, political, legal, and social roles these groups were assigned at the start of their American experience have had long-lasting effects on their socioeconomic status. The particular social, economic and political climate a group encounters when it arrives in the United States influences its initial status and potential path.

Historical Discrimination Racial inequalities created by formal and informal discrimination in the past continue to shape the stratification we see today. For example, historical legal and informal prohibitions against residential integration isolated racial minorities into underresourced neighborhoods, denying them access to quality public education, sufficient employment opportunities, and community infrastructure such hospitals or libraries that were taken for granted in white neighborhoods. Across the United States, there also existed thousands of "sundown towns," which prohibited the settlement—or even the presence overnight—of blacks, Asians, or Jews by force of law or physical threat (Loewen 2005). When blacks were able to move into certain areas, it often spurred "white flight," or the exodus of white residents. The historical residential segregation of African Americans and others has not only meant a loss of opportunities in the past that put their descendants at a disadvantage. The children and grandchildren of those who lived in underresourced neighborhoods in the past tend to live in the same places today, and they continue to suffer the same consequences in terms of education, health, and employment (Sharkey 2008).

Contemporary Discrimination We have already seen that many researchers, across different disciplines and using a wide array of techniques, have come to the conclusion that racial discrimination is alive and well in the United States. It may take the form of employment discrimination, where workers are treated differently by race when hiring, promotion, or firing decisions take place; it may show up on the housing market, when a person's race influences which neighborhoods or homes brokers and real estate agents will show them. Discrimination can be subtle or it can be blatant, and it can be intentional or unintentional. Whenever it materializes, however, it contributes to the racial

The mortgage lending crisis that emerged in 2007 hit black and Hispanic families disproportionately hard. African-American and Latino borrowers are estimated to have been nearly twice as likely as whites to lose their homes to foreclosure, like this house in Detroit.

inequality that has been a feature of U.S. society from its very beginnings.

What to Do about Racial Stratification?

Racial stratification has been an enduring characteristic of the U.S. because for most of its history, white political elites expected and actively promoted such hierarchy. Moreover, the majority of the population felt it was natural and even desirable for whites to occupy the top economic, political, and social rungs. For at least the first 150 years of the nation's existence, white supremacy was effectively the law of the land, ensuring through both formal policies and informal practices that whites had unrivalled access to the best jobs, housing arrangements, education, and public facilities, among other things.

The idea that such racial stratification is unfair and undesirable has only recently been accepted by large numbers of Americans. The civil rights movement, largely a phenomenon of the 1950s through the 1970s, was at the heart of this sea change. Thanks to its strategy of large-scale, peaceful protest and of key court battles, in which Americans of all races participated, U.S. laws were rewritten or introduced to prohibit the favoritism toward whites that earlier laws had protected.

Civil rights–era laws—like the Civil Rights Act of 1964 or the 1965 Voting Rights Act—largely embraced a principle of color-blindness, forbidding the use or consideration of race in varied contexts like employment. However, a tool developed later in the fight against racial inequality is grounded instead in a color-conscious approach: the policy of **affirmative action**.

Affirmative action is a practice that involves considering individuals' race when making decisions that are likely to have an impact on existing patterns of racial inequality. The examples that have drawn most attention in the United States are those of college admissions and of employment. Should college admissions offices or employers take into account the race of the individuals who apply to their organizations in order to ensure that their student bodies or work forces are similar in racial makeup to the surrounding population?

Affirmative action is hotly debated, in part because it involves opinions on a whole series of issues that people don't often stop to tease apart. First, a person's view of affirmative action will depend on whether she believes racial inequality exists in the United States today. Second, even if she does think so, she may believe its causes cannot be addressed by social policy. If racial inequality simply reflects the biological and behavioral capacities of each race, there may be little public policy can do about it. If instead she believes that racial inequalities can be lessened by social policy, she may not think race-based affirmative action is a good instrument for doing so. Perhaps class-based affirmative action would be better. And finally, even if she thinks race-based affirmative action is the way to go, she may be unsure of how exactly to implement it. Should all institutions be required to implement it? (Currently very few are obligated by law to do so.) Should it take into account the races that people identify themselves with or the races that other people ascribe to them? And should it call for "hard" affirmative action—for example, numerical quotas or points—or "soft" affirmative action, like race-targeted college advertising or scholarships? In summary, affirmative action is a complex policy whose subtleties are often lost in raucous public debate.

After more than 150 years of racial privilege for whites, however, Americans are torn about whether we can eliminate racial stratification simply through formal, or legal, color-blindness. As President Lyndon B. Johnson famously put it in 1965: "You do not take a man who for years has been hobbled by chains, liberate him, bring him to the starting line of a race, saying, 'you are free to compete with all the others,' and still justly believe you have been completely fair."

5 How Are Race and Ethnicity Changing in the Twenty-First Century?

RACE AND ETHNICITY IN THE FUTURE

👁 Watch the **Big Question** Video in **MySocLab**

"Interracial," "multiracial," "postracial"—is the United States on its way to becoming some, all, or none of these? One thing is clear: The face of America has changed a great deal since the nation's founding over 200 years ago. At that time, the former colony contained for the most part people from only three parts of the world: Northern Europe (especially England, Ireland, and the Netherlands); West Africa; and indigenous North America. The first U.S. census, in 1790, did not classify any races other than those covering these origins; official categories for Asians were almost a century away, and for Hispanics, closer to two. Yet by 2010, the most common ethnic ancestries among Americans were no longer limited to longstanding English or African American communities. Instead, the descendants of later European arrivals like Germans, Italians, and Poles are now among the most numerous in the nation, and "Mexican" ranks sixth on the list of the most common ancestries Americans report (Brittingham and de la Cruz 2004). An even bigger shift is apparent in the percentages of the U.S. population that the census classifies as white and black. In 1790, over 80 percent of the population was recorded as white, with the remainder labeled black (American Indians were usually not enumerated on the census at that time). By the 2010 census, however, whites' share of the total population had dropped to 64 percent, and blacks' from 19 to 12 percent. The Hispanic or Latino population is now slightly larger than the black one, at 12.5 percent, and Asians, Native Hawaiians, and other Pacific Islanders have grown to nearly 5 percent of the U.S. population. American Indians and Alaska Natives, neither of whom were carefully enumerated in the eighteenth century, together make up 0.7 percent. A final measure of change can be seen in the more than 9 million individuals (almost 3 percent of the total population) who were identified on the 2010 census with two or more races (Humes, Jones and Ramirez 2011). They exercised a right to identify with more than one race that had been available on the census only since 2000.

Changes in demographic makeup, however, are only part of the story of how race and ethnicity are changing in our lifetimes. In this concluding section, we will explore not only the factors behind transformations in the nation's population composition but also investigate how racial and ethnic stratification, identities, classifications, and conceptions are rapidly changing. In all these areas, we will take a look backward in time to see what trends have brought us to the present and to consider the predictions that social scientists make about the future.

☐ A Changing Population

In November 1993, *TIME* magazine put on its cover a beautiful young woman who smiled at readers over the title, "The New Face of America." Her tawny skin, light brown eyes, and chestnut hair gave no clue to her ethnic origins. And no wonder: The image was not a picture of a real person, but rather a morphed composition assembled from photographs of dozens of individuals from a wide array of ancestries. According to *TIME*, the morphed face was "15% Anglo-Saxon, 17.5% Middle Eastern, 17.5% African, 7.5% Asian, 35% Southern European and 7.5% Hispanic." Its purpose was to illustrate "How Immigrants Are Shaping the World's First Multicultural Society."

Although the United States is far from being the first multicultural society, the exaggeration tells us something about the story that Americans tell themselves about how the country has changed over the last two centuries. As the *TIME* magazine headlines suggest, it is a narrative about a nation whose growing tolerance leads to greater immigration and interracial mixture over time.

What this account overlooks is that the United States has always been a multiracial—not to mention multicultural—society. From its earliest beginnings as a collection of English colonies, racial intermixture was common. As far back as the 1630s and 1640s, colonial records attest to interracial sexual unions and mixed-race offspring (Williamson 1980). As the enslavement of Africans continued over the next two centuries, interracial mixing—notably through the coercion of black female slaves by white male slaveowners—was so widespread that by 1915, the U.S. Census Bureau estimated that three-quarters of the black population had some nonblack ancestry (U.S. Census Bureau 1918). Similarly, Latino people are largely of mixed European, Native American, and African descent. Yet we do not usually include Hispanics and African Americans in our picture of multiracial America because their mixed ancestry is old, dating back to the eras of slavery and colonial conquest. Instead, we prefer to think of multiraciality as something new, linked to the contemporary era in which individuals have had new freedom to enter voluntarily into interracial relationships. The artificiality of this picture of multiracial America is sharply conveyed by the writer Danzy Senna's comment on the *TIME* magazine photomorphed image: "Of course, anyone could see that women just like the computer face they had created did exist in Puerto Rico, Latin America, and Spanish Harlem" (quoted in Streeter 2003: 305).

If neither interracial unions nor multiracial people are new in the United States, what *has* changed is our attitudes toward them. In 1967, the Supreme Court struck down all state laws banning interracial marriage. In 1997, the federal government revised its official racial classifications to permit individuals to identify with more than one race. Both decisions signaled a sea change in Americans' willingness to recognize and even accept new ways of thinking about race. These policy shifts are mirrored in both public attitudes and behaviors. In 1958, 96 percent of whites surveyed disapproved of intermarriage, but nearly 40 years later, in 1997, that share had dropped to 33 percent (Schuman et al. 1997). Correspondingly, in the last 30 years, the percentage of newlyweds married to someone of a different race or ethnicity has more than doubled: Less than 7 percent of the individuals

Professional golfer Tiger Woods is of Asian, African, European, and American Indian descent. He is just one of a long list of 21st-century celebrities—like Jessica Alba, Paula Abdul, or Keanu Reeves—whose multiracial or multiethnic ancestry is widely known and accepted.

How have attitudes toward interracial unions and multiracial people changed in the United States?

who married in 1980 had a spouse of another race or ethnicity, but in 2010, more than 15 percent did. More than a third of U.S. adults now say they have an immediate family member or close relative who is married to someone of a different race (Wang 2012). National statistics also show an increase in the mixed-race population. From 2000, when the U.S. census first counted multiracial people, to 2010, the number of people identified with more than one race rose from fewer than 7 million to more than 9 million, or nearly 3 percent of the total population (Humes, Jones and Ramirez 2011).

These statistics have several limitations. Figures on interracial marriages do not include people who live together or have other intimate relationships. Census counts of mixed-race people exclude large numbers of people who

TABLE 10.3 THREE WAVES OF IMMIGRATION

Approximate Time Period	Immigration Wave	Origin Countries
1820–1870	The Frontier Expansion	• Brought over 7 million immigrants, largely Irish, German, and Scandinavian, who were drawn to homesteading and farming opportunities. • Immigration from Asia also began in this era, although efforts would soon be made to stem it, starting with the 1882 Chinese Exclusion Act designed to bar Chinese migrants from entry.
1880–1925	Ellis Island	• Brought southern and eastern Europeans in large numbers for the first time, channeling them to cities and industrial work.
1965–present	Immigration and Nationality Act	• After a long hiatus, immigration picked up in mid-twentieth century. • Immigration and Nationality Act of 1965 was designed to even out old immigration barriers that sought to exclude immigrants not from Northern Europe. • Today's immigrants are more diverse than ever, with most coming from Asia, Latin America, and the Caribbean.

Note: This table refers to the countries from which immigrants arrive in the U.S. In contrast, the discussion of "immigration eras" in Chapter 12 refers to the immigration laws that were in place at different points in U.S. history.

have multiracial ancestry—like most African Americans and Latinos—but who are not aware of or choose not to report their mixed background. These and other shortcomings make it difficult to compare the numbers of interracial unions and multiracial people today to those in the past. However, the statistics that are available do point to an upward trend underway for both.

Immigration is the other major demographic trend to reshape the racial and ethnic makeup of the United States. Here there is no question that the twenty-first century is very different from the nineteenth century. The United States has undergone three major waves of immigration since its founding, and each has left its mark on the nation's demographic composition, as indicated in Table 10.3 (Kritz and Gurak 2004). According to the Population Reference Bureau, 20 percent of the world's migrants live in the United States (Martin and Midgley 2010). And in sharp contrast to the European predominance in the two previous immigration waves, today's immigrants are overwhelmingly from Asia, Latin America, and the Caribbean. Of the foreign-born individuals who entered the United States in 2008 or later, 40 percent came from Asia and 35 percent from Latin America and the Caribbean. The top six sending countries of immigrants to the United States are Mexico, China, India, the Philippines, Vietnam, and El Salvador (Walters and Trevelyan 2011).

As remarkable as these changes are, demographic changes in the twenty-first century may be just as striking. The U.S. Census Bureau has forecast that before midcentury, the non-Hispanic white population of the United

How has the U.S. census adapted to the evolving shifts in how Americans identify themselves?

States will shrink to less than half of the total. Current Bureau projections for 2050 put the white share of the U.S. population at 46 percent, Hispanics at 30 percent, blacks at 12 percent, Asians at 8 percent, American Indians and Alaska Natives at 1 percent, and multiracial people at 3 percent. These estimates are of course based on many assumptions—about fertility, mortality, and migration—that may not hold true. These projections presume the continuation of trends that have been underway for decades now: the decrease in the white population and stability in the black and American Indian ones, compared to dynamic growth among both Hispanic and Asian Americans. However, another factor may play a role in ways that are difficult to anticipate now: namely, the choices that people will make about how to identify themselves in racial and ethnic terms and the options they are given for doing so.

☐ Changing Classification and Identity

The twentieth century saw several major shifts in how Americans identified themselves—and were identified by others—in terms of race and ethnicity. And in fact, census racial and ethnic categories have changed almost every 10 years in the United States (Lee 1993). The only group that has consistently been named on the census is white; everything else was added later, anywhere from the eighteenth to the twentieth century (see Table 10.4). Will the next 100 years usher in another round of momentous change in the ways Americans classify by race and ethnicity?

TABLE 10.4 RACE CATEGORIES ON U.S. CENSUS IN 1810, 1910, AND 2010

1810: Free White Males; Free White Females; All Other Free Persons, Except Indians Not Taxed; Slaves

1910: White; Black; Mulatto; Chinese; Japanese; Indian; Other

2010: White; Black, African Am., or Negro; American Indian or Alaska Native; Asian Indian; Chinese; Filipino; Japanese; Korean; Vietnamese; Native Hawaiian; Guamanian or Chamorro; Samoan; Other Asian; Other Pacific Islander; Some other race

Sources: U.S. Census Bureau (1918); Lee (1993); Nobles (2000).

The growing demographic diversity of the United States suggests that it will become more and more common for Americans to share workplaces, schools, families, and social settings with people of different races.

Perhaps the most significant change in recent years has been the federal government's shift in 1997 to allow people to identify themselves with more than one race when filling out the census or other official documents. Although government policies are not a direct reflection of how everyday people think about racial and ethnic categories, the emergence of grassroots organizations for mixed-race people in recent decades suggests that Americans have grown increasingly accepting of the idea that a person might belong to more than one race (DaCosta 2007; Williams 2006).

A change that has yet to take place but that seems likely in the future is the inclusion of "Hispanic/Latino" as a race on government forms. At present the U.S. government considers Hispanics to constitute an ethnic group and so does not include it on the census race question. In the wider society, however, the terms *Hispanic* and *Latino* tend to be used as if they were akin to races: journalists, politicians, academics, and everyday people use phrases like "blacks, whites, and Latinos," suggesting that Hispanics are seen as a racial group like "whites" and "blacks." Moreover, the current lack of a "Hispanic or Latino" category on the census creates problems for people who would rather identify themselves using those terms instead of being forced to choose among options like "white," "black," and "American Indian or Alaska Native." As a result, large numbers of Hispanic people select "Some other race."

☐ Changing Stratification

Immigration inflows that are more diverse than ever, rising rates of interracial marriage, and new openness to multiracial identities—what impact will these demographic and social changes have on racial inequality in the United States? Some observers believe they all point the way to a more racially inclusive and egalitarian society. Consider for example these newspaper headlines: "A New Generation Is Leading the Way: What Young People of Mixed Race Can Tell Us about the Future of Our Children" (Jackson Nakazawa 2003) or "The New Face of America: Blended Races Making a True Melting Pot" (Puente and Kasindorf 1999). The basic idea is that demographic trends reveal a new openness to bridging historical racial divides, and therefore that race is growing less significant as a factor in social, political, and economic life.

A closer look, however, suggests that while race may be becoming less important for some groups, it remains a powerful barrier for others. The question, as sociologists Jennifer Lee and Frank Bean (2004: 221) put it, is "whether racial boundaries are fading for all groups or whether America's newcomers are simply crossing over the color line rather than helping to eradicate it." It is important to note, for example, that although the rate of interracial marriage overall has grown considerably in recent years, Asian and Hispanic newlyweds are more likely than blacks to have spouses of a different race (Wang 2012). In addition, individuals of mixed-race ancestry are more likely to identify themselves (or be identified) as multiracial if they have Asian ancestry but to be assigned to a single race—black—if they have African ancestry (Gullickson and Morning 2011). And as we have seen, race is still associated with pronounced differences in socioeconomic status, with blacks, Hispanics, and American Indians generally worse off than whites and Asians. These kinds of findings have led some scholars to conclude that the color line is hardly disappearing from American life; it is simply shifting from one that separated whites from nonwhites to one that distinguishes blacks from nonblacks. In other words, we may have a new "beige majority" (Lind 1995) where whites, most Asians, light-skinned Latinos, and mixed-race people can all lead lives relatively free of racial discrimination, while darker Hispanics, some Asians, Native Americans, and blacks remain stigmatized by color (Gans 1999).

Other sociologists take a more optimistic view. Over the next 20 years, the post–World War II "baby boom" generation, born between 1946 and 1966, will gradually retire from the work force. They will be replaced by a younger cohort that has a much smaller percentage of whites, thus placing larger shares of nonwhites in the relatively good jobs that the baby boomers held. In his recent analysis of the U.S. labor market, Richard Alba (2009) foresees a smooth transfer of opportunities for a comfortable middle-class life from whites to nonwhites without competitive conflict. Older whites will simply leave good jobs vacant, and a mix of younger people, white and nonwhite, will move into them. Alba stresses that this is not a foregone conclusion; for example, he calls on the nation to invest more wisely in blacks' and Hispanics' education to better prepare the future work force. His vision, however, reminds us that race and ethnicity—both as ideas and as structuring

What impact will demographic and social changes have on racial inequality in the United States?

social forces—have never been static, and that even as short a time span as a quarter-century may bring about striking changes.

CONCLUSION DEVELOPING A SOCIOLOGICAL IMAGINATION ON RACE AND ETHNICITY

In trying to uncover the cultural and structural forces that shape our lives, even when we are not aware of them, sociologists often come up with answers that are not intuitive, because they go against the grain of common sense. The study of race is a good example. It is an everyday term for Americans, and one that we usually think is a straightforward descriptor of people's physical characteristics. What sociology tells us, though, is that there are no such simple, obvious groupings of human beings based on bodily traits, and that labels like "black" and "white" tell us more about the way societies choose to classify people than it does about the individuals who get assigned to those categories. In this area as in so many others, developing a sociological imagination means looking beyond widespread beliefs that are too often taken for granted.

👁 **Watch** the **Video** in **MySocLab**
Applying Your Sociological Imagination

What Is the Difference between Race and Ethnicity? *(p. 264)*

👁 **Watch** the **Big Question Video** in **MySocLab** to review the key concepts for this section.

KEY TERMS

essentialism *(p. 264)*
one-drop rule *(p. 265)*
ethnicity *(p. 265)*
race *(p. 265)*

More often than not, the words race and ethnicity get used interchangeably, as if they mean the same thing. In this section, we discussed how sociologists make clear distinctions between race and ethnicity and how they use the terms to describe different kinds of categories and identities.

UNDERSTANDING RACE AND ETHNICITY (p. 264)

Sociological Definitions of Race and Ethnicity (p. 264)

- **How do contemporary sociologists define race and ethnicity?**

Key Distinctions between Race and Ethnicity (p. 265)

- **Which matters more, race or ethnicity?**
- **How did race come to be used as a tool of domination?**

Is Race Real? *(p. 267)*

👁 **Watch** the **Big Question Video** in **MySocLab** to review the key concepts for this section.

KEY TERMS

social construct *(p. 267)*
assimilation *(p. 268)*
constructivist *(p. 268)*

If there's one thing academics agree on, it is that race is real. But is race anchored in deep-seated physical differences between individuals or is it an invention that is not determined by human biology but is real because it has an unmistakable impact on daily life?

THE SOCIAL CONSTRUCTION OF RACE (p. 267)

Race and Society (p. 268)

- **How have Americans' ideas about who is white changed over time?**

Race and Biology (p. 268)

- **Is race determined by biology?**

Race and Place (p. 270)

- **Why is race understood differently around the world?**

3 What Is Racist and What Isn't? *(p. 271)*

 Watch the **Big Question Video** in **MySocLab** to review the key concepts for this section.

Concern about the "political correctness" of our ideas, speech, and behavior is a prominent feature of both public and private conversations on race today. Sociologists have thought a lot about prejudice and discrimination, providing ample food for thought on racism in the contemporary United States.

CONTEMPORARY RACISM (p. 271)

What Is Racism (p. 272)

- **What is the difference between prejudice and discrimination?**

Explore A Sociological Perspective: Who are you going to be for Halloween? in **MySocLab**

Read the **Document** *Names, Logos, Mascots, and Flags: The Contradictory Uses of Sport Symbols* by Stanley D. Eitzen in **MySocLab.** This reading demonstrates the importance of language and symbols in society.

Why Does Racism Occur? (p. 272)

- **How can people be socialized into racism?**

Does Racism Still Exist in the United States? (p. 274)

- **Does racial prejudice and discrimination still exist in the U.S. today?**

4 Do Race and Ethnicity Matter Anymore? *(p. 276)*

 **Watch** the **Big Question Video** in **MySocLab** to review the key concepts for this section.

Many people today wonder whether it is fair to say that the United States has entered a "postracial" era. This section discussed how sociologists suggest that race is still closely linked to socioeconomic inequality today.

THE IMPACT OF RACE AND ETHNICTY TODAY (p. 276)

Racial Disparities in Socioeconomic Status (p. 276)

- **How do sociologists explain racial gaps in socioeconomic status?**

Explore the **Data** on Race and Inequality in **MySocLab**

- **What patterns of educational attainment have minority groups experienced over the last 30 years?**
- **Why do disparities in health exist among racial groups?**
- **How have the high incarceration rates among African American men impacted their political participation?**

How Do We Explain Racial Stratification? (p. 281)

- **How do sociologists account for racial inequalities?**

What to Do about Racial Stratification? (p. 283)

5

How Are Race and Ethnicity Changing in the Twenty-First Century? *(p. 284)*

Watch the **Big Question Video** in **MySocLab** to review the key concepts for this section.

The face of America today is very different from what it was 200 years ago. In this section, we explored the demographic changes in the U.S. that have impacted its racial and ethnic makeup, patterns of socioeconomic inequality, and attitudes and beliefs about race and ethnicity.

RACE AND ETHNICITY IN THE FUTURE (p. 284)

A Changing Population (p. 284)

- **How have attitudes toward interracial unions and multiracial people changed in the United States?**
- **How has the U.S. census adapted to the evolving shifts in how Americans identify themselves?**

Changing Classification and Identity (p. 286)

Changing Stratification (p. 287)

- **What impact will demographic and social changes have on racial inequality in the United States?**

Watch the **Video** Applying Your Sociological Imagination in **MySocLab** to see these concepts at work in the real world

11

GENDER and SEXUALITY

(((Listen to the Chapter Audio in MySocLab

by PAULA ENGLAND

In 2011, *Forbes* magazine reported that 12 women held CEO positions at Fortune 500 companies. Women have headed companies like Yahoo, PepsiCo, Xerox, and Avon, achievements few dreamed possible just decades earlier. These women, and many of today's women leaders in other fields, exude confidence and assertiveness. Naturally, we would assume these qualities would extend from a woman's professional life to her personal life, but do they?

Can a woman be a strong leader, communicator, and innovator at work and also feel like asking a man on a date is inappropriate because of her gender?

A few years ago I was conducting research on sex and relationships among college students. During one of my interviews I met Janine, a graduate student studying for her master's in business administration (MBA). As we spoke about dating, relationships, and sex, she expressed her preference for traditional dating rather than "hooking up." Janine took great pride in waiting for men to ask her on dates. Her reasoning for never asking men on dates was that she believed men wouldn't see her as "relationship material" if she did. What a paradox, I thought—a woman who feels absolutely entitled and confident about scaling upper management, which was off-limits to women a few decades ago, but who wouldn't even consider asking a man on a date. Clearly some things have changed and others have stayed the same!

In this chapter we will consider patterns and change in both gender and sexuality. The term **gender**, as used by sociologists, refers to the way in which social forces structure how being male or female affects what is expected of you, how you are treated, what opportunities you have, and the results for individual men and women. We will also examine sexuality and how sociologists study it because the topics of gender and sexuality are related in several ways. We will discuss cultural ideas about how women and men are supposed to act—at work, in social gatherings, as well as in romantic and sexual relationships. We will also explore how affirming or rejecting of same-sex romantic relationships our society and some of its subgroups are.

MY SOCIOLOGICAL IMAGINATION
Paula England

My mother didn't have enough money to go to college, and never considered a career after she married at age 19 and became a stay-at-home mom to four children. Later, when I was grown, she claimed she was lucky to be able to stay at home with her kids. But she also talked about feeling underappreciated by my dad. Gender inequalities often made her feel "less than." Dad had the education, not her, and she often felt that principals, doctors, and community leaders didn't respect "just a housewife," even though she saw importance in what she was doing.

I became fascinated by sociology, seeing it as a way to understand social causes of human suffering. I wondered how much my mother's suffering would have been lessened had the gender regime been different. My early research focused on why some occupations are filled mostly with men and others mostly with women, why women earn less than men, and why mothers earn less than women without children. These topics interested me because I wanted to understand the social forces that hold women back. Later, I began to study the increasing trend toward young couples having unplanned pregnancies followed by births outside of marriage. Currently, I'm conducting a study of relationships and sex among college students, trying to understand how the sexual revolution intersects with the gender revolution.

Ideas about gender are often closely linked to cultural expectations. How do cultural ideas influence how women and men believe they are supposed to act at work, in social gatherings, or in the types of relationships they have?

Watch the Video in **MySocLab**
Inspiring Your Sociological Imagination

THE BIG QUESTIONS

◉ **Watch** the **Big Question Videos** in **MySocLab**

From the early writings of the founding sociologists over a century ago until about 1970, not many sociologists studied gender or sexuality. These topics were seen as more in the realm of nature than society. But since about 1970, sociologists have used their methods and approaches to study these topics. In this chapter, we will examine how sociologists answer the following big questions about gender and sexuality:

1 **Where do the differences between men and women come from?** In this section we will explore the differences between men and women, and examine where these differences come from, with a focus on what sociologists have shown.

How have the lives of women and men changed in the last 50 years? Women's lives have changed so much in the last 50 years that we often call the changes a gender revolution. Here we explore some of these changes as well as how they have affected men's lives.

2

3 **How are our sex lives shaped by biology and society?** There is no question that sexual attractions and behavior are affected by biology, but, as we will see in this section, they are also strongly affected by social construction.

How has sexual behavior changed in the last 50 years? Sexual behavior of young unmarried adults has changed substantially over the last several decades, but what about the extent to which sexual and relational behavior is affected by gender norms and inequalities? In this section we will explore sexual behavior as well as gender differences in the sexual realm.

4

Where Do the Differences between Men and Women Come From?

GENDER DIFFERENCES

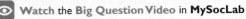 **Watch** the **Big Question Video** in **MySocLab**

All around us we see differences between the way men and women (or boys and girls) dress, the activities they engage in, and what they say they want. More boys than girls play sports, more girls than boys play with dolls, many college majors and occupations contain either mostly men or mostly women, and more women than men are stay-at-home parents.

But sometimes we exaggerate the size of these differences. Take, for example, the common belief that males score higher than females on standardized math tests. One way to quantify this is by computing the difference between the average (also called the mean) male and female score. In 2011 data on the mathematics part of the SAT Reasoning Test that many students take to apply to college, men's average score, on a scale from 200 to 800, was 531, and women's was 500, with a difference of 31. (The SAT is very similar to the ACT; many of you may have taken one or the other.) Another way sociologists examine the gender difference is to plot the whole distribution of scores for each sex, showing the percentages for men and women at each score. Figure 11.1 shows both the male and female means and the whole male and female distributions for the 2011 Math SAT test. Each of the two curves has a large bulge in the middle, which tells you that more people score in the middle of the distribution than at either extreme. You can see

that the male mean (at the center of the male distribution) is a bit higher than the female mean. But you can also see how much the two distributions overlap, and that the mean difference looks rather small compared to the amount of overlap. Thus, even on a characteristic where one sex has a higher average, there will be many members of the sex with the higher average who are below the average of the sex with the lower average. It is important to keep this in mind so as not to exaggerate gender differences.

FIGURE 11.1 MALE AND FEMALE DISTRIBUTIONS AND MEANS ON THE SAT TEST

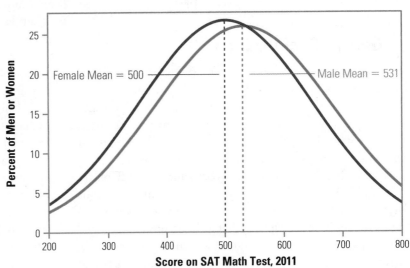

Numbers computed and distributions drawn by Paula England from data reported by The College Board (2011). Calculations assumed a smoothed normal distribution, except truncated at 200 and 800, the top and bottom possible score of the test.

But when men and women really do differ, what shapes these differences? Many people believe that sex differences in behavior and preferences are "natural," caused by biological differences such as differences in hormones, anatomy, or brain structure. There is some truth to this. One example of a biological influence is the evidence that testosterone, a hormone present in both men and women but generally in much greater amounts in men, encourages some kinds of aggressive or dominance-seeking behavior. This suggests that the higher levels of aggressive behavior that we see in men, on average, are caused in part by the fact that men have higher testosterone than women. Yet causation is not just one-way, from hormone to behavior; changes in the social environment can also change testosterone levels. For example, one study showed that men's testosterone levels increase before a competitive athletic event, and those of the winners stay elevated afterwards, while the testosterone levels of the losers drop afterward (Mazur and Booth 1998). Another biologically based difference is that only women can breastfeed infants. But men participate much more in infant care in some societies than others, showing that society also has an effect.

Sociologists focus on social causes of phenomena, and, while biology clearly has a role in differences between men and women, research in sociology has shown that social arrangements have powerful effects on differences between men and women. The entire system of social processes that create and sustain gender differences and gender inequality is often referred to as the **social construction of gender**. Societies have a broad gender system that consists of interactions in small groups in which what is expected of a person and rewarded depends upon his or her sex, and institutions like schools, churches, corporations, or governments that set policies or rules that affect males and females differently (Risman 2004). To the extent that men have more power than women in politics, the economy, and the family, the gender system is called **patriarchy**.

Gender Socialization

One way that gender is socially constructed is through socialization. Socialization is the means by which members of a society are inculcated into, or taught, its norms and practices. Some of what gets taught is conventions about gender—what boys should do differently than girls, or women differently than men. Parents are important agents of socialization. Most parents dress boys and girls differently, decorate their rooms differently, have different aspirations for them, and give them different toys. Parents' socialization practices have changed in that girls are now encouraged to take part in a broader range of activities. For example, many parents now encourage their girls to play sports and give them what used to be thought of as boys' toys, such as Legos and racing cars. But not many parents have started

Fathers of the Aka tribe in West Africa spend more time in close contact with their infant children than in any other society, indicating that society can play a role in influencing sex differences.

to give their boys dolls. Studies show that fathers—more than mothers—are particularly discouraging of boys doing anything that they see as feminine, like playing with dolls or ballet dancing (Maccoby, Emmons, and Jacklin 1974). Peer groups are also agents of socialization. Male peer groups often ostracize boys who are not seen as stereotypically masculine enough and ridicule boys believed to be gay (whether they are or not) (Pascoe 2007).

Another important agent of socialization is the mass media—popular music, movies, television shows, Internet sites, and advertisements. Most of us see and hear hundreds of media messages every day. In movies and television, women portrayed in romantic roles are almost always young and thin and look like models. In contrast, men can be cast in a romantic role even if they are older and heavy. Ads typically show women rather than men doing housework. Men are seen in powerful roles in the economy, politics, and athletics. Some of this simply reflects the current social reality, but men and women are portrayed in a narrower range of roles in the media than they take in real life (Holtzman 2000). Socialization does not only affect children but continues through adulthood as those around us continue to affect us, we continue to see and hear media images, and we are affected by major institutions such as religion and government.

Sex versus Gender

A person's **sex** is a biological matter. Humans group into two sexes, where males and females differ in anatomy, chromosomes, and average levels of certain hormones. But men and women overlap on many of the defining characteristics, and some people, called intersex individuals, are born with some defining anatomical characteristics of each sex. As introduced previously, a person's gender is a result of how society shapes differences and inequalities between men and women. One interesting group of people challenges many of our assumptions about sex and gender and how they go together. **Transgendered** individuals are those who were assigned one sex category at birth, based on the usual anatomical criteria, but feel strongly they belong in the other sex category. Some undergo surgery to correct this perceived incorrect assignment. Transgendered people are often subjected to extreme ridicule and even violence because of the actions of people who are intolerant of those who challenge the notion that one's sex is something fundamental and unchanging. Sometimes the term *transgender* is used to refer to a broader group of people who change or challenge sex or gender categories—perhaps dressing conventionally male while being in a female body (or vice versa) or rejecting the need to look male or female in dress and style altogether (McKenna and Kessler 2006). This challenges people's belief that sex and gender are binaries—having only two categories.

How do we distinguish the concepts of sex and gender?

Gender Differences Vary by Setting and Time

There are two main reasons why we know that many of the typical differences we observe between men and women are, at least in part, socially constructed. First, these gender differences vary between different social settings—that is, between different cultures and even between different situations within one society. Second, gender arrangements have changed over time. If biology were driving all the differences between men and women, we would not expect things to vary by the social setting or change over time.

One example of gender changing between different social settings is that men and women conform more closely to norms of masculinity or femininity when they are aware of being watched. One research team discovered this in a study in which they asked college students to play a video game in which they first defended and then attacked by dropping bombs. The number of bombs a student dropped in the video game was taken as a measure of aggressive behavior. The researchers were interested in whether there were gender differences in aggression because most people think of men as more aggressive than women, and some past studies have found this sex difference (Hyde 1984; Hyde 2005). But how much of that difference is just a matter of people doing what others expect of them rather than enduring differences in preferences? To find out, the researchers randomly assigned half of the students who had agreed to be in their study into each of two groups. As long as a truly random process is used, this guarantees that the two groups should be equivalent on just about anything before the treatment. In this **random-assignment experiment,** participants in one group were led to believe that their actions during the

How do social expectations affect the interactions between men and women when they know they are being watched by others?

video game would be monitored by the researcher. The other group received a different treatment; they were given the impression that no one would be monitoring their games. Among this second group, men did not drop any more bombs than women. In the first group, the group that believed they were being watched, men dropped significantly more bombs than women (Lightdale and Prentice 1994).

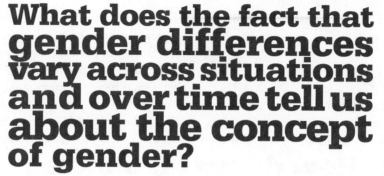

What does the fact that gender differences vary across situations and over time tell us about the concept of gender?

told there is no gender difference (Correll 2004). Another experiment randomly assigned two groups in the same way and then asked each group to take a math test. In the group told that men perform better, the male students scored higher, on average, than the females; but in the group told that there is no gender difference in the population, the men and women scored the same (Spencer, Steele, and Quinn 1999). In these studies, we see that what people hear from others about whether their sex is better at something affects their confidence and even their actual performance—and this is true even if the generalization they are told is untrue. Thus, stereotypes that are untrue or exaggerated will tend to produce the very difference they claim is true, even if the difference didn't exist before.

The researchers concluded that gender-stereotypical behavior is more likely to happen when people believe that they are being watched. Of course, people are being watched by others in a good deal of their life—in school, at home with family, at work, at social gatherings, or out on the street. This suggests that some of how women and men act results from trying to live up to what they think others expect from someone of their sex. Apparently this social pressure, even with no rewards or punishments, has an effect. Although this study only focused on aggression, you can imagine all sorts of other gender differences that social expectations might affect.

☐ The Impact of Stereotypes

Some social expectations are based on **stereotypes,** beliefs about a group that are often untrue or exaggerated as a description of the group. These beliefs are then applied to individual members of the group for whom they may not be true at all. Educators worry about the stereotype that girls and women perform worse in math because math is so crucial for many technical majors and careers. Men do better on the math SAT test, on average, as we saw in Figure 11.1. But a recent review of many studies showed that most other standardized math tests show only small gender differences, with the average differences virtually disappearing on most tests but the SAT since the 1990s (Hyde et al. 2008). The lower average scored by girls on some standardized tests is odd because, when they take math classes in high school or college, they average higher grades than boys (Dee 2007).

Researchers have wondered if exposure to the idea that men perform better at math helps to produce the very reality it claims to merely describe. To find out, one researcher randomly assigned male and female college students to two groups—one in which they were told that men perform better on tests, on average, and one in which they were told that there is no average gender difference on such tests. Then male and female participants were asked to assess their own skills on a scale. In the group that had been told that men perform better, women assessed themselves lower on the scale than men did, but this difference was smaller in the group

Social context can also determine how "macho" men act. A team of sociologists showed this in a recent experiment in which male and female college student participants were randomly assigned to two groups. First, the students were given a gender identity survey. Then they were given feedback on whether their answers to the survey showed them to be more feminine or masculine. But, in fact, what they were told about their scores on the survey was made up. Men randomly assigned to one group were told they scored somewhat feminine; those randomly assigned to the other group were told they scored quite masculine. What was interesting was the effect on men who were told that they were somewhat feminine. When the participants were given a second survey, these men expressed more support for war, more negative attitudes toward gays, more interest in SUVs, and persisted a longer time at a strength test (Willer et al. 2011). Interestingly, women's attitudes on the second survey showed no change as a result of whether they were told they were more masculine or feminine. The authors concluded that men desire to appear masculine, and if they have reason to think others doubt their masculinity, they redouble their efforts to engage in behavior culturally coded as masculine. Women seem to be less worried about how feminine they appear, reflecting less social pressure on them to act feminine.

These studies do not necessarily prove that biological influences have no impact on gender differences. But, because the studies show that gender differences fluctuate depending on the social situation, we can be sure that some of the differences we observe come from social forces. In addition, the fact that gender inequality has changed over time is further evidence that gender is at least partly socially determined and that biology does not completely dictate destiny. Next, we will examine these changes.

2 How Have the Lives of Women and Men Changed in the Last 50 Years?

THE GENDER REVOLUTION

👁 Watch the **Big Question** Video in **MySocLab**

Women's lives have changed so much in the last 50 years that we often call the changes a gender revolution. Most of the changes consist of ways in which girls and women have taken on activities and roles previously limited mostly to men. More girls than ever are playing on sports teams, more girls hold offices in student government than previously, more women than men now get college degrees, women's employment has increased, some women have moved into traditionally male professions, women hold some elected offices in state legislatures and Congress, and some women retain their birth-given last name when they marry. In this section we look more closely at a few of these changes in women's lives as well as how these changes have affected men's lives since the 1970s.

What are some of the reasons that women's employment increased dramatically between 1960 and 1990?

Rising Women's Employment and Education

Of all the changes in the lives of women over the last several decades, the biggest is the increase of women in the paid workforce. Even married women with small children now hold jobs outside the home at high rates. Figure 11.2 shows the percentage of men and women in the United States who were employed from 1962 forward, among adults 25 to 54 years old. (People are counted as employed if they held a paying job anytime in the last year.) Men's employment declined slightly. Women's employment, which had been rising slowly most of the century, rose dramatically between 1962 and 1990 and then plateaued, with little increase since then. Yet it leveled off at a fairly high level, with over 70 percent of women employed. While women's employment is still lower than men's (whose rates are about 90 percent), the two sexes have converged substantially.

The two main reasons that women's employment increased were economic. First, as wages increased during the 1960s and 1970s, so did the incentive for women—or couples—to decide in favor of a woman working for pay (Bergmann 1986). In addition, the economy changed to include a higher share of jobs in service work (jobs like secretary, receptionist, nurse, and store clerk), which had always employed many women. As the demand for service workers rose, more opportunities became available for women (Oppenheimer 1970). One result of this growth of women's employment is that many families that include a husband and wife are now dual-earner families.

Since 1973, men's wages have not increased (if adjusted for changes in the cost of living). In fact, the earnings of men who have no more than a high school education—who often work in factories, as drivers, or in construction—have decreased, which has encouraged employment of their wives. But men in managerial and professional jobs (like lawyer

FIGURE 11.2 PERCENT OF MEN AND WOMEN EMPLOYED, 1962–2010

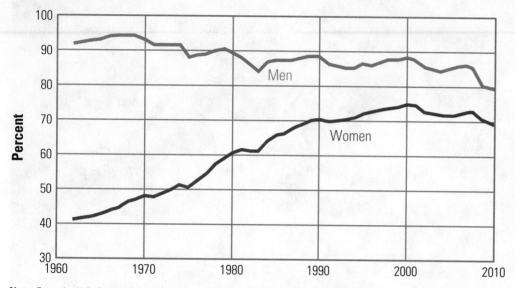

Note: From the U.S. Current Population Surveys (CPS), applies to men and women (age 25 to 54) who are considered employed if they ever held a job during the year.

Source: Figure based on data from calculations from Current Population Survey (2010).

lower grades than girls for decades, so these facts alone cannot explain the dramatic shift. Researchers are still trying to figure out why the gender gap favoring college degrees for men has reversed to one favoring college degrees for women. They suspect that one reason is that, even when girls were performing better in high school, parents prioritized paying for sons to attend college in the era when most women became full-time homemakers. Today both young men and women plan to work for pay during much of their future lives, so now girls doing as well as their brothers are just as likely to go to college, and if they are doing better, they are more likely to complete college.

and engineer) have seen their pay increase more than the cost of living, yet the typically well-educated wives of these men have increased their employment dramatically as well (Juhn and Murphy 1997). Laws against sex discrimination made it more possible for well-educated women to achieve high-level careers. The **feminist movement** encouraged these laws and their enforcement and gave some women a sense of entitlement to have a career as well as a family.

Which sex obtains more college degrees has changed dramatically. If we go back to 1950, women received only 24 percent of the bachelor's degrees granted (Digest of Education Statistics 2001:table 247). As Figure 11.3 shows, women steadily increased their share of degrees over time, passing men in number of degrees in 1986. By 2007, 57 percent of bachelor's degrees went to women. Similar trends are occurring in many countries around the world. Among African Americans, women are an even higher percent of graduates (McDaniel et al. 2011). The fact that more women than men obtain a college degree reflects the facts that girls, on average, study a bit harder and get higher grades in elementary and high school, that they like school better, that fewer of them have discipline problems in school, and that fewer are involved in crime (Steffensmeier and Allan 1996; DiPrete and Buchmann forthcoming). But, on average, boys have been more involved in crime and have received slightly

Change in Women's Jobs and in the Pay Gap

In the past, many women worked in traditionally female occupations such as maid, secretary, nurse, or teacher. But since about 1970 an increased number of women have entered traditionally male fields, becoming managers, lawyers, doctors, engineers, or professors, and more women have enlisted in the military. Sociologists measure **occupational sex segregation** with an index that ranges from 1 for complete segregation (all occupations are either 100 percent male or 100 percent female) to 0 for complete integration (each occupation has the same percentage of females as the

FIGURE 11.3 PERCENT OF U.S. BACHELOR'S DEGREES GOING TO WOMEN, 1970–2009

Figure based on Paula England's calculations from *Digest of Education Statistics* (2008).

In the last 40 years, occupational sex segregation has declined significantly. One example of this is that more women have entered into engineering, still a largely male-dominated field.

paid workforce as a whole). Using this measure, occupational sex segregation declined substantially in the 1970s and 1980s but has declined more slowly since then (England 2011).

Women with college and graduate degrees have entered traditionally male occupations much more frequently than women graduating only from high school. In the United States, as well as most countries, the male jobs not requiring a college degree—such as carpenter, welder, electrician, or truck driver—have seen only small numbers of women join their ranks. Interestingly, college women are more likely to choose traditionally male majors (like natural science and engineering) in less affluent, developing nations than in the United States (Charles and Bradley 2009).

Despite some integration, jobs remain quite sex segregated. This is partly because socialization still encourages young men and women to aspire to different jobs. Another factor is hiring discrimination. Although it has been illegal to refuse to hire people for a job because of their race or sex since the Civil Rights Act was passed in 1964, the law has not entirely ended discrimination.

Women's earnings have also increased. Figure 11.4 shows the median women's earnings as a percent of the median men's earnings for each year. (The median for either sex is the level where half the people of that sex are below it and half are above.) The figures include only those who worked full time the whole year. Women earned about 60 to 65 percent of what men earned from the 1950s to the 1980s. After 1980, this began to equalize so that by about 2000, women earned 76 percent of what men did. Since 2000 there hasn't been much more progress toward equality.

Why do women still earn less than men?

Why do women still earn less than men? One explanation is that employers pay people more when they have more years of experience, and women are more likely than men to have dropped out for a time to take care of children. A second reason is that women are concentrated in lower-paying occupations. Some of this is because women choose occupations—for example those helping people—that pay less than other jobs requiring the same amount of education. This may reflect different socialization by gender. Another part of the concentration of women in lower-paying jobs is that, as mentioned earlier, some employers discriminate against women when hiring in higher-paying jobs, leaving the women no choice but to seek lower-paying jobs (Reskin and Roos 1990).

One form of discrimination that explains part of the pay gap is that some employers pay women less than men in the same job. This has been strictly illegal since the passage of the Equal Pay Act in 1963, unless the difference is based on seniority, performance, or some factor other than sex itself. But it sometimes happens.

Another factor in the pay gap is that employers often set lower pay rates in jobs filled mostly by women than in different jobs requiring the same amount of education but filled mostly by men (England 1992; Levanon, England, and Allison 2009). For example, secretaries (mostly women) in some organizations earn less than assembly workers on the factory line or janitors (mostly men) even though the secretaries need as much education and as much (though different kinds of) skill. Why do employers fail to pay mostly female jobs as much as comparably demanding yet different male jobs? Research that I

FIGURE 11.4 MEDIAN WOMEN'S ANNUAL EARNINGS AS A PERCENT OF MEN'S

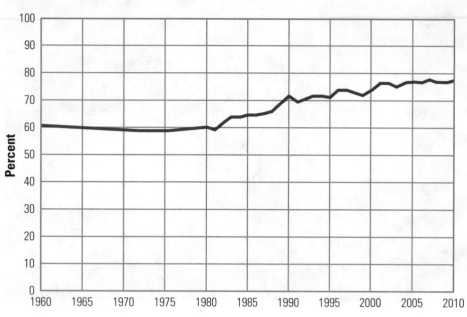

Note: Figures apply to full-time, year-round workers only.

Source: Institute for Women's Policy Research (2011).

conducted earlier in my career convinced me that employers often do this out of a biased perception that whatever is done by women must be easier and not as important for the company. Often the bias is unconscious, but many researchers see it as a form of discrimination. While this is not recognized as illegal discrimination in U.S. federal law (England 1992), it is in some other nations. If you won't hire someone into a particular job because she is female, or you pay a woman less than a man in the same job when her seniority and performance are the same as his, these actions are violations of U.S. law. But our laws do not cover setting lower pay levels in whole jobs because they are filled largely with women, even though there is evidence that employers do this.

Some employers discriminate against women simply because they are mothers, although in most cases this is illegal. One study investigated this type of discrimination by sending fake resumes to real job ads. Two identical resumes were developed that showed the same credentials and experience except that, in the section of the resume where many people list their hobbies or community activities, one resume said the woman was an officer in the Parent Teacher Association (revealing that she is a mother), while the other resume said the woman was an officer in some other community club. Just this difference resulted in a significant difference in how many calls for interviews were received. Interestingly, the same manipulation to fake men's resumes showed no fatherhood penalty (Correll, Stephen, and Paik 2007).

Some of these factors in the gender pay gap are also factors in why the pay gap is smaller than before. Women's

employment has become more continuous, with more women staying employed when they have small children, so the average woman's years of job experience are now closer to those of the average man. Because salaries tend to increase with more years of experience, this convergence between men's and women's years of experience has reduced the pay gap. As more women than ever have chosen traditionally male, high-paying fields, such as law, medicine, and management, this has increased women's pay relative to men's. Also, enforcement of antidiscrimination law has reduced employer discrimination. All these factors have contributed to the reduction of the gender pay gap. But progress toward gender equality in employment, occupations, and pay has slowed down since the 1990s. Figure 11.4 shows this slowdown for pay equality. Interestingly, it was around the same time that attitudes about gender, which had become more egalitarian among both men and women in the 1970s and 1980s, moved in a more conservative direction (Cotter, Hermsen, and Vanneman 2011).

The Impact on Men

It isn't only women's lives that have been changing. Men's and boys' lives have changed too. Since the 1970s, married men began spending substantially more time with their children and doing a bit more housework. In this way their roles expanded to take on some traditionally female activities, parallel to the way more women moved into traditionally male activities. But what is striking is how asymmetric these changes were. Men moved much less into what had been women's arenas than vice versa. In fact, probably the larger change for boys and men was not taking on formerly female activities, but how all the movement of girls and women onto what had been their turf impacted them. Another important change comes not from the gender system but from changes in the economy since the 1970s that made the "American Dream" of a good-paying job more unattainable for those men not in the top portion of the earnings distribution. Let's look at how these changes affected men's lives.

We saw that women's employment increased dramatically, especially from the 1960s to about 1990. As this happened, men's attitudes, like women's, became more accepting of female employment (Cotter et al. 2011). But men didn't move in large numbers into being full-time homemakers; we saw in Figure 11.2 that 90 percent of men are still employed.

Employed fathers spend more time caring for their children than they did 50 years ago, but so do employed mothers, and women's hours of paid work have increased much more than men's hours in household work. Why do men's roles seem to be more resistant to change than women's?

Indeed, norms of masculinity seem relatively unchanged in insisting that married men are supposed to have a job—so much so that when men aren't employed, couples more often divorce (Sayer et al. 2011). Even if norms had shifted to make men's employment more optional, it would have been impractical for most couples, as the wives entering employment typically didn't make as much money as their husbands, so families would have taken a reduction in pay if men quit their jobs. Many advocates of work-family balance and gender equality have hoped that more couples could have each partner employed half the time while they share child rearing and household work relatively equally. But that is very difficult to do without financial sacrifice in the U.S. economy. In all countries in the European Union, the law requires that employers pay part-time workers the same amount per hour as full-time workers in the same job. In the American economy, part-time jobs typically pay substantially less per hour than the same job done a full 40 (or more) hours per week. Thus, few couples could move from one full-time earner to each partner working part-time without a loss in pay. For all these reasons, the biggest change for men as a result of women's increased employment was not that more men started staying home or working part time but that many of them got used to being part of a two-earner

Why haven't the changes in men's roles been as dramatic as the changes in women's roles?

couple. The obvious benefit of this for men is that they share in the increased earnings that result. But it also means that women are more able to support themselves and more apt to leave unhappy marriages (Sayer et al. 2011).

With more women working for pay, women also don't have as much time for housework, so we might expect that women would look to men to do more housework than before. Men's housework has increased, but only a small amount. Between 1965 and 2000, on average, married mothers decreased their housework by 15 hours per week, mainly because more of them took jobs, but married fathers increased their housework by only 5 hours per week (Bianchi, Robinson, and Milkie 2006). Employed fathers increased the time they spent caring for children substantially, but so did mothers (Bianchi et al. 2006). This is an example of how women have entered traditionally male spheres (in this case employment) more than men have taken on traditionally female activities.

As more women chose traditionally male fields of study in college, and careers previously filled mostly by men, very few men decided in favor of traditionally female majors, like elementary education, and only a trickle of men moved into occupations filled mostly with women. Thus, the desegregation of occupations and fields of study was a largely one-way street with women moving into traditionally male fields while few men entered traditionally female fields (England 2010). Men didn't enter female-dominated occupations in large numbers for two reasons. One is that these occupations, as we saw earlier, often pay less than male-dominated occupations—even when you compare jobs requiring the same amount of education. Second, the social stigma of doing anything that makes a male seem feminine is much greater than any parallel stigma of females engaging in male-identified activities. It has long been a feature of our culture that males are ridiculed for doing anything seen as feminine. Thus, men risk both lowering their income and being stigmatized if they undertake activities and jobs thought of as feminine. Some still do so because of a real sense of calling in a caring profession or because some unusual life circumstance brought them into a nontraditional role. While they may earn less than if they chose a more male-dominated field, just as women do, research shows that men are not treated worse than women within the female jobs but, if anything, tend to be welcomed and rise to the top of these fields (Budig 2002).

Looking at the lives of kids, there is one important way that the gender revolution has extended to boys. The social scene in today's high schools and colleges often features friendship groups containing both sexes. So, compared to decades past, more boys and young men have the experience of a female friend or even a female best friend.

In sum, the large changes in gender roles of the last 50 years have moved men into what had been female realms much less than they have moved women into previously male-dominated activities. It has been less appealing for men to enter traditionally female activities such as child care, homemaking, and female occupations because they often pay less than traditionally male occupations, if at all, and such moves are much more stigmatized than women taking on male roles. Of course, the changes in girls' and women's lives have created changes for boys and men. Boys have had to get used to girls competing with them more openly in school, and men find women competing for the same types of jobs they have. Men have gotten used to employed wives, and most now accept women's employment.

At the same time that all this has happened, since about 1973, earnings have become much more unequal among men. Earnings for men at the top have increased enormously, while those of men at the very bottom have decreased, and those of men in the middle class have stagnated (Eckstein and Nagypal 2004; Gordon and Dew-Becker 2007; Autor, Katz, and Kearney 2008). (These figures are after adjusting for changes in the cost of living.) As global competition has increased, few employers provide secure employment for life. Whole industries have moved largely overseas, taking away many good-paying, skilled manual jobs in factories. Thus, for most men, it is increasingly difficult to count on being able to hold a job steadily, to earn more than their fathers, and to earn more as they get older—all features of the American Dream. Yet there is still a strong norm that suggests men are responsible to be breadwinners in families, even as acceptance has grown for women also sharing this role. Men are still judged—in a way that women are not—by their earnings, even as changes in the U.S. economy have made it more difficult for many men to do as well as before and as they face increasing competition from women who have equal education.

Angelina Jolie's young daughter Shiloh is rarely seen dressed in feminine clothes. How has the gender revolution played a role in allowing this to be acceptable in today's society?

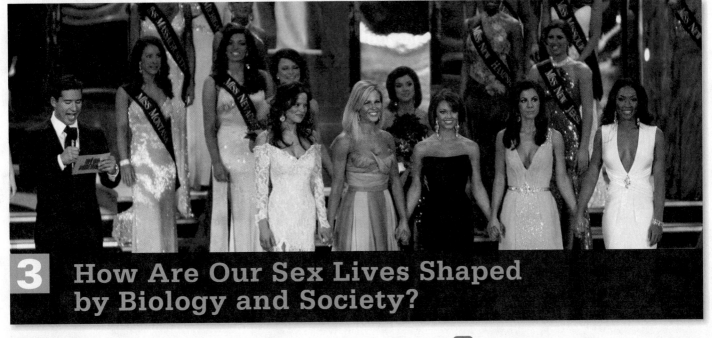

3 How Are Our Sex Lives Shaped by Biology and Society?

SEXUALITY

👁 **Watch the Big Question Video in MySocLab**

We've already examined many aspects of men's and women's lives, but we've so far ignored one key area: sexuality. You might not expect a discussion of sex in a sociology textbook because we often think of sex as an entirely natural, biological matter, not socially constructed at all. It seems all biological because nonhuman animals as well as humans have sex, and the age at which we are interested in sex is affected by hormones. There is no question that sexual attractions and behavior are affected by biology, but, as we'll consider in this section, they are also strongly affected by social construction (Gagnon and Simon 1973).

Societies put many restrictions on sex. In some societies, homosexual behavior is illegal, punishable by prison time (Ottosson 2010), while, by contrast, the right to same-sex marriage is protected by law in some nations and a few U.S. states. Premarital sex and childbearing have been stigmatized in some historical periods, and still are today in some nations, but they are extremely common in other societies. Even the style of dancing in the U.S. has become increasingly sexualized over past decades, as you can see from *A Sociological Perspective* on page 306.

Social norms regulate fine details about what appearances are seen as sexually appealing or disgusting. In China prior to 1950, upper-class girls' feet were bound, a painful process that stunted their growth; men found tiny feet sexually alluring (Mackie 1996). Today's notion that ultrathin women are the most beautiful would mystify people in many cultures, where such women would be seen as unhealthy and not sexy at all!

☐ Sexual Orientation

The term **sexual orientation** refers to whether individuals are attracted to members of the other sex, the same sex, or both. Today we use the terms *heterosexual, homosexual* (homosexual men are often referred to as gay[1] and women as lesbians), or *bisexual*. But not everyone fits neatly into one of

In the "Long Neck" tribe in Northern Thailand, women are seen as more beautiful if they have long necks, and some take drastic measures to achieve this beauty. What drastic measures do American women take to alter their bodies?

_____
[1]Sometimes the term *gay* is used to describe either men or women who have sex with members of their own sex.

A SOCIOLOGICAL PERSPECTIVE

What do dancing rituals say about our attitudes on sex and gender?

Dancing has recurring relevance throughout the life course, especially to mark maturation and romantic development. Some middle school dances have often led to struggles between students experimenting with sexual behavior through dancing and schools trying to control the degree of intimacy acceptable. Dancing also reveals a lot about gender norms. In the old system, men asked women to dance, and men led women during dancing, deciding the movements and the style. This system is still followed today in ballroom, tango, and many other dancing styles. Dance indirectly reveals norms of pleasure entitlement.

The sexualized motions of "freak dancing" seem designed to provide sexual stimulation to men more than to women. At some of today's college parties, men still initiate, but by coming up behind the woman and starting to dance with her, sometimes touching her. Women kissing other women has become a popular activity on the dance floor. Sometimes this is a way for young women to explore whether they might be bisexual or lesbian. Other times it is to get male attention. Gay men and lesbians sometimes dance in ways similar to the scripts of heterosexuals. Other times they innovate their own scripts.

How has the power between men and women changed as dancing styles have become less formal over time?

What causes us to mimic the dance rituals of our peers rather than create our own individual rituals?

Have contemporary dance rituals blurred the line between dancing and intimacy?

◉▸ **Explore** A Sociological Perspective in **MySocLab** and then . . .

Think About It

What does the norm that men should ask women to dance or initiate contact tell us about a society?

Inspire Your Sociological Imagination

If the rules of society changed so that your sex didn't affect any aspect of what was expected of you, how would it change dancing

these three categories. One researcher writing decades ago suggested that there was a continuum from homosexual to heterosexual and that people could be various places along this scale (Sell 1997; Kinsey et al. [1948] 1998; Kinsey et al. [1953] 1998). A recent study followed women who, at the beginning of the study, identified as something other than heterosexual. The study found that about two-thirds of these women shifted the sexual orientation they identified with over 10 years. They moved in all directions between identifying with the labels *lesbian, bisexual,* and *heterosexual,* and even preferring no label. Also, the study showed that behavior (which sex one has sex with), attraction (which sex one is attracted to), and identity (whether one refers to oneself as lesbian, bisexual, or heterosexual) are not always consistent (Diamond 2008).

An interesting question is where our sexual orientation comes from. As with other aspects of sex, there is evidence that both biology and society have their effects. Evidence that genetics affect sexual orientation comes from research on twins and other siblings. Starting from samples of gay men or lesbians, some of whom were twins, researchers asked them about the sexual orientation of their siblings. They compared how often same-sex siblings of homosexual individuals were also homosexual when they were identical twins, fraternal twins, and adoptive siblings. Siblings differ in their degree of genetic relatedness—with identical twins having identical genes, fraternal twins being as related as nontwin siblings, and adoptive siblings being the least genetically similar. The researchers found that a higher percentage of the identical twins of gay men were also gay, compared to a lower percentage of the fraternal twins of gay brothers and an even lower percentage of the adoptive brothers of gay men. A similar pattern was found for women (Bailey and Pillard 1991; Bailey et al. 1993; Bailey et al. 2000). On the one hand, the study proves that genes don't entirely determine sexual orientation because, even among identical twins, when one is homosexual, most of the time the other is not. Because identical twins are genetically identical, if they don't have the same sexual orientation, something else from their social experiences must explain their differences (Stein 2001). On the other hand, the study shows that there is some influence of genes on sexual orientation as the finding is that siblings who are more genetically related are more similar in sexual orientation than siblings who are less genetically related.

☐ Sexual Behavior

How do biology and society affect other aspects of our sexual behavior? A big debate in this area is whether men like casual sex more than women, and, if so, if this is because of

some biological difference or is a result of social influences (Schmitt 2003). Evolutionary theories say that this is a gender difference that we would expect to have evolved millennia ago. According to these theories, in any population, variation in genes occurs at random. Some of the randomly occurring new genes lead to things that enhance survival, others hurt survival, and still others are neutral. Over many thousands of years, the genes that enhance survival will be more represented in the population because the people (or other animals) with these genes are more likely to survive long enough to reproduce, and their descendants will carry those genes. If there are sex-specific genes, then genes that helped women to produce offspring that survive will be carried in women today, while genes that helped men produce offspring that survive will be carried in men today. Because a woman carries a fetus for nine months, her number of surviving children will not be enhanced much by frequent sex with multiple partners. But this is different for males, who could potentially impregnate many women in the nine-month period it takes a woman to gestate

What evidence do researchers point to that supports a biological influence on sexual orientation?

Nightclubs and college parties often feature women showing more skin than men. Why is this?

one child. Thus, any combination of genes that encouraged frequent, casual sex would increase men's number of offspring, and the representation of this combination of genes in the future gene pool. But it probably would not increase women's. According to one evolutionary theory, this is why evolution led to more preference for casual sex among men (Buss 1994).

Even if evolution is one factor in why men seek casual sex more than women, sociologists point to a social factor that is part of the explanation as well. Our culture features a **double standard of sexuality** (Crawford and Popp 2003; England, Schafer, and Fogarty 2008; Kreager and Staff 2009). This is the tendency to judge women more harshly than men for having casual sex. One piece of evidence that a double standard is in play is that we have many more pejorative terms to refer to women who we think have sex too casually—terms like *slut* or *whore*—than we have for men doing the same thing. Many men engage in the same behavior, but we are less likely to call them similar names. There are some terms like this to refer to men (such as *man whore* or *player*), but they seem less consistently negative. Indeed, within male peer culture, being a player is often a positive source of status. Recognizing the double standard, sociologists point out that women are more motivated than men to avoid casual sex because it does greater damage to their reputations. It is not entirely a matter of a biologically dictated lack of interest.

One way that we know biology has some relevance to sex is that among youth of the same age, those who are experiencing puberty and have the associated increases in certain hormones are more likely to have sexual fantasies and engage in sexual behavior. But the same study that shows this also shows that social factors are relevant as well. For example, youths brought up in religious households that discourage early sex are less likely to engage in such behavior (Udry 1988). Further evidence of social influences on sex is the fact that the prevalence of sex before marriage has changed quite drastically in most modern societies, as we'll discuss later.

☐ Sexual Minorities

The term **sexual minority** refers to anyone who is not heterosexual, or who is transgendered, having changed their sex or gender from what was assigned to them at birth. To understand what it means to be a member of a sexual minority, consider the situation of a hypothetical young 17-year-old named Tom, who has just recently begun to identify himself as gay. If Tom is typical of the young American gay men interviewed in one study, he was first aware of attractions to other males at age 8, first knew the meaning of the term *homosexual* at age 10, first applied the term *homosexual* to his

own attractions at age 13, and first had sexual contact with another male at 14, yet he didn't think of himself as gay until age 17, won't tell any of his friends he is gay until age 18, and won't tell his family till age 19 (Savin-Williams 1998). Why the secrecy and the delay in squaring one's identity with one's urges? The answer lies in the messages about sexual orientation that one gets from social experiences growing up. This is called **heteronormativity**, a situation where the culture and institutions send the message that everyone is heterosexual, or at least that this is the only normal way to be.

To see what heteronormativity is like, consider all the experiences our hypothetical young man is likely to have had growing up. Tom listens to rock music, and most of the songs are about sex or romance between men and women. The plots of most television shows or movies feature romances or sexual escapades between men and women. In his high school, bias against gays abounds (Pascoe 2007). His male friends frequently insult each other with the term no one wants to be called, "fag," and another common put-down is, "That's so gay!" Tom was never on the receiving end of these insults, and he doesn't want to be, either; that's one reason he doesn't want to tell people at his high school that he is gay. At his family's church, nothing is said pro or con about homosexuality, but a friend of his who belongs to a more conservative church says that, at his church, the preacher talks about the evils of being gay from the pulpit. The only weddings Tom has heard about are between a man and a woman, and he has never met a married couple consisting of two men. He has heard that gay marriage is legal in a few U.S. states but knows it is not in most; he's not sure why, but he doesn't want to ask. He certainly can't imagine gaining popularity, and figures he might invite ridicule, if he asks a boy to his senior prom. It is little wonder that he gets the impression that his same-sex attractions are something to hide. His experience is typical of young people growing up gay, lesbian, or bisexual in America. You can see from Tom's example some of the difficulties of growing up as a member of a sexual minority in a heteronormative environment.

But some members of sexual minorities experience even worse things. Those who show affection for someone of the same sex are often ridiculed by youth peer groups, regardless of whether they appear masculine or feminine. Some employers refuse to hire those they think are gay or fire people upon discovering it. Such discrimination, even if completely open, does not violate any federal law; discrimination in employment based on race, religion, sex, or national origin is illegal, but discrimination based on sexual orientation is not prohibited by U.S. federal law. In renting or selling housing, it is illegal to discriminate based on race according to federal law, but there is no protection if someone won't rent

What challenges do lesbian, gay, bisexual, transgendered, and questioning individuals encounter?

A lesbian couple kisses outside a court in Buenos Aires, Argentina to protest a judge's decision against same-sex marriage.

to gay people. Surveys indicate that nearly half of sexual minority members report that they experienced some kind of discrimination in housing or employment based on sexual orientation, about 40 percent have been threatened with violence, and about 80 percent have been verbally harassed because of their sexual orientation. Terms used for any of these kinds of bias directed at a person because of their sexual orientation are **heterosexism** or **homophobia;** these terms are often used interchangeably. Probably as a result of these various forms of ridicule and harassment they face, gay and lesbian youth are 2 to 3 times as likely to commit suicide as heterosexual youth (O'Brien 2001). If one dresses or looks in a way that social norms see as more appropriate for the other sex, one may be stigmatized and sometimes even visited with violence in school or on the street, whether or not one is actually gay or lesbian.

Despite this grim picture of what a young person growing up as a member of a sexual minority has to face, the scene has changed substantially over the last few decades, due in part to a social movement for gay rights (Armstrong 2002) and to a change in public opinion to more tolerance of sexual diversity. The gay rights movement has sought to make gay, lesbian, bisexual, and transgendered people appear as individual human beings rather than as negative stereotypes, to support legislation against various sorts of discrimination based on sexual orientation, and to get rid of legislation that explicitly forbids sexuality or marriage between those of the same sex.

The gay rights movement got its start in the 1960s in New York City and San Francisco. It was dominated by white men. In response to feeling that their concerns were marginalized in the movement, a group called Queer Nation was formed in 1990 (Armstrong 2002). This group highlighted the concerns of nonheterosexual persons of color, lesbians, bisexuals, transgendered persons, and those who didn't like pigeonholing people into any of these categories and preferred the umbrella term *queer*. Since then you can notice that on many college campuses, sexual minorities use the word *queer* in a positive way despite its pejorative connotation in the general population.

Many things have changed in a way more friendly to the lives of sexual minorities. Some states and municipalities have laws against discrimination in employment and housing on the basis of sexual orientation, although there are no such federal laws. The U.S. military dropped its ban on service by gay and lesbian soldiers in 2011. Most colleges and

Robert Su and Ramon Escamilla are married in City Hall in San Francisco in June of 2008. What do you think is the future of same-sex marriage in America?

universities have LGBTQ (Lesbian, Gay, Bisexual, Transgender, and Questioning) centers providing services and a place to socialize. Many cities have such centers as well. Some high schools have Gay/Straight Alliance groups. There are newspapers and magazines directed at the LGBTQ community. There are neighborhoods with high concentrations of sexual minorities in some large cities.

Yet these changes have brought about a strong backlash. Groups who hold more traditional views oppose public acceptance of gay lifestyles that fundamentally challenge their ideas of gender and family. Some opposition stems from religious teachings from some churches that homosexuality is wrong. Other churches and temples interpret their religion to be tolerant of same-sex love and sex. These conflicting views have coalesced in recent political controversies over gay marriage. In 1993, a state court in Hawaii said that the state law limiting marriage to unions of one man and one woman was unconstitutional unless the state could show some compelling reason for it. In response to the possibility that the law would be struck down by the court, political mobilization led to passage of an amendment to the Hawaii's state constitution stating that the legislature could limit marriage to male-female couples. Opponents of gay marriage, afraid that other states would get rid of their restrictions of marriage to male-female couples, lobbied Congress to pass a law stating that states prohibiting gay marriage would not have to recognize the gay marriages allowed in other states. (Prior to this most states had recognized marriages contracted in other states, so that, for example, a couple married in California who moved to Oregon would be considered married in Oregon as well.) In 1996, Congress adopted the federal Defense of Marriage Act (DOMA). It said that for purposes of any federal benefits that hinge on marriage, marriage refers only to the legal union of one man with one woman. Under this law, for example, partners in a lesbian or gay male marriage do not have the same right to pass property from one to the other upon death without paying any federal estate tax, a right enshrined in federal law for married couples. After DOMA was passed, this right was limited to male-female couples even in states where same-sex marriage is legal. DOMA also said that states that have not legalized same-sex marriage are under no obligation to treat as married those same-sex married couples who married in a state where same-sex marriage is legal and moved into a state in which it is not legal.

A few U.S. states have legalized same-sex marriage; the first was Massachusetts. However, many more states have passed state versions of something like DOMA.[2] Other states have provided an option of domestic partnerships for same-sex couples that have some of the benefits of marriage. The Netherlands became the first country to allow same-sex marriage in 2001, and since then Belgium, Canada, Spain, South Africa, Norway, Sweden, Portugal, Iceland, and Argentina have followed suit. Consider the Infographic on same-sex marriage on page 311 to see how this trend has taken shape in the U.S.

---

[2]See http://www.care2.com/causes/what-states-allow-gay-marriage.html for up-to-date information on states allowing and prohibiting same-sex marriage.

Same-Sex Marriage

I n 2008, same-sex marriage was legal in California from **JUNE 16** until **NOV 4**, when voters passed Proposition 8, prohibiting it. A federal appeals court ruled Proposition 8 unconstitutional in 2012, but while this ruling is being appealed new same-sex marriages are not allowed.

Status of same-sex marriage by state

■ **8** states (along with the District of Columbia) allow same-sex marriage*

■ **30** states have constitutional amendments that define marriage as consisting of a man and a woman

■ **11** states have passed laws that ban recognition of same-sex marriage

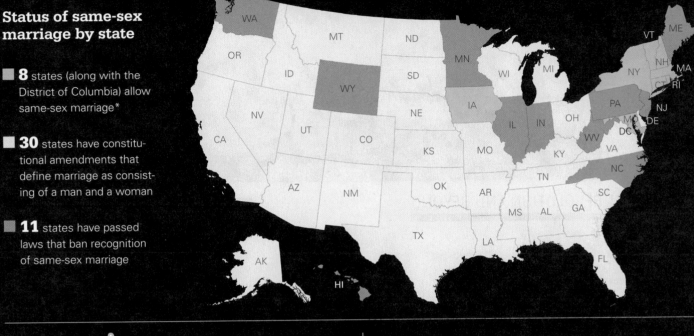

in **1996** **27%** of Americans supported legalization of same-sex marriage
65% opposed legalization

in **2009** **37%** supported
54% opposed

in **2011** **53%** supported
45% opposed

*States may have changed their status since this was written. See http://www.care2.com/causes/what-states-allow-gay-marriage.html for current information.

◉➜ **Explore** the **Data** on Same-Sex Marriage in MySocLab and then . . .

■ **Think About It**
Attitudes toward same-sex marriage are changing. Since 2004, 6 states have passed laws making same-sex marriage legal, and surveys show that public approval is on the rise. What do you think has led to this shift in public opinion?

■ **Inspire Your Sociological Imagination**
Changing attitudes about who is allowed to marry isn't the only shift we've seen in the past 50 years. What other once gender-specific roles have now become accepted roles for either sex? What do you think this shift in public opinion means for our country?

In 2011:

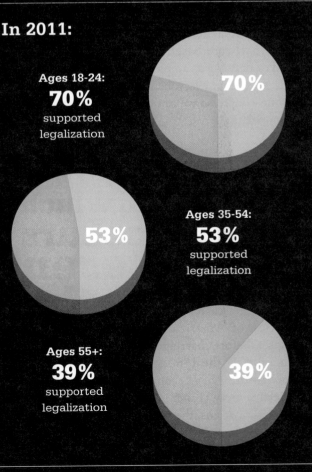

Ages 18-24:
70%
supported legalization

70%

Ages 35-54:
53%
supported legalization

53%

Ages 55+:
39%
supported legalization

39%

Sources: Based on date from Gelman et al. (2010);l The Pew Research Center (2011); Gallup (2011).

4 | How Has Sexual Behavior Changed in the Last 50 Years?

THE SEXUAL REVOLUTION AND BEYOND

Watch the **Big Question** Video in **MySocLab**

Over the last 50 years sexual behavior of young unmarried adults has changed substantially. There has been some, but much less, change in the practices of married couples. To look at changes in sexual behavior, it is best to rely on data from surveys that were based on **probability samples**. This method of drawing a sample to survey from the U.S. population ensures that everyone has an equal probability of being in the sample, so we can be sure that it is representative of the population.

☐ Premarital Sex

Surveys using probability samples have asked Americans about the age at which they first had intercourse as well as the age they first married, if they have. These surveys paint a picture of a substantial increase in the proportion of Americans having sex before marriage. Among people coming into adulthood after the 1960s, 90 percent or more have had premarital sex; it has become accepted in most groups in American society (Finer 2007). Evangelical and fundamentalist Christians, the most conservative of Protestants in their teachings on this subject, often have strong beliefs against premarital sex, and some even take virginity pledges. Yet studies show youth from these conservative

How have relationships in which premarital sex occurs changed in recent decades in the U.S.?

religious denominations do not actually start sex later and are not more likely to wait until marriage for sex than youth from other religious groups. Instead, more religious youth, from almost any denomination or faith tradition, tend to start sex later (Regnerus 2007).

Although many American high school students have sex, most American parents disapprove. One study compared attitudes of American and Dutch middle-class parents by interviewing parents of 16-year-olds in both nations. The researcher asked parents how they would feel about their son or daughter having a girlfriend or boyfriend sleep overnight in the family's home. Almost all Dutch parents said this was okay. They thought sex should be in a relationship with a nice person and saw sex as a natural and appropriate progression of a relationship. They preferred to have their teen child have sex at home in a safe, comfortable place. They wanted to talk to their child about using protection from sexually transmitted infections (STIs) and pregnancy. In answer to the same question, almost all the American parents said they were vehemently against their child having sex. They expressed concern that kids who have sex are driven by "raging hormones," not making considered decisions. They saw teen sex as the outcome of a "battle of the sexes" rather than envisioning a caring relationship among the teens. Even if

FIGURE 11.5 HOW FAR COLLEGE STUDENTS WENT SEXUALLY ON THEIR MOST RECENT HOOKUP

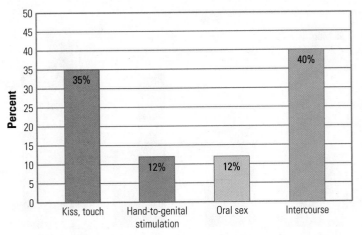

Note: Categories farther to the right may also include behaviors to the left, but not vice versa.

Source: Paula England's calculations from Online College Social Life Survey, 2010 version.

they knew that sex was common and their own child might be doing it, most didn't want to approve of it in their own home (Schalet 2011).

As the proportion of people having premarital sex was increasing between cohorts coming of age in the 1960s and 1980s, the median age that people first had sex outside marriage decreased from 20 to 17. But more recently, since the late 1980s, the trend has reversed. That is, the proportion of teens having sex by a given age has decreased. For example, in 1988, 51 percent of teens 15 to 19 had intercourse at least once, but among those aged 15 to 19 in 2008, only 43 percent had intercourse (Martinez, Copen, and Abma 2011).

While premarital sex has become almost universal, what has changed over time is in what context it typically occurs, with the acceptable contexts getting more casual. In the 1950s and 1960s, those who had premarital sex often did so only with the person they later married. In the 1970s, sex became common in relationships, and increasingly young couples in relationships are involved in **cohabitation**, the term that sociologists and demographers use to describe the act of living together as an unmarried couple. These relationships may be serious enough that couples are considering marriage, or they may involve couples who are not engaged but just dating, and who cohabit for practical reasons, such as

to save money by sharing rent. It is only in recent decades that sexual activity has become common in casual liaisons where there is no expectation that either party expects a relationship to ensue. Such a liaison is today often referred to in youth culture as a **hookup.**

On college campuses today, when students say they hooked up, this can mean anything from just making out to having intercourse. In an online survey I conducted with students at over 20 colleges and universities, one of the questions asked students whether they had ever hooked up in college with someone with whom they were not in a relationship. For those who said yes, they were asked to report on what happened sexually in their most recent hookup. Figure 11.5 shows what percentage was in each category, where hookups were classified by how far students went sexually (so, for example, if you made out and had intercourse, you were classified as having intercourse).

Figure 11.5 shows that 40 percent of hookups involve intercourse. These are often cases where the couple had hooked up together before. Thirty-five percent of hookups involved no more than kissing and nongenital touching. Most hookups were with someone the student already knew at least moderately well. Qualitative interviews I did with students showed that, while many hookups led nowhere, some relationships started with hookups, sometimes with one or more dates between hooking up and defining the relationship as exclusive (England et al. 2008).

Gender Inequality in Sex and Relationships

The availability of the birth control pill in the 1960s made it more possible to have sex as a young adult, go to college, and delay marriage until after college without fear of pregnancy

In your experience, do you think that hookups often lead to relationships?

before marriage. This helped women to prepare for careers by going to college. Thus, the availability of the pill and the advent of more premarital sex went along with increased gender equality in education and the labor market (Bailey 2006).

Yet while women's career aspirations are now much more equal to men's than previously, gender differences in what is expected in the romantic and sexual realm has changed surprisingly little, even at the same time that norms of whether premarital sex was acceptable were changing. In my college online survey mentioned earlier, when asked who asked whom out on their most recent date, students reported that the man did the asking in about 90 percent of cases. When asked who initiated sexual activity on a hookup, more reported that men did than women.

Interestingly, hookups lead to orgasm much less often for women than men. Figure 11.6 shows the percent of male versus female college students who reported having an orgasm depending on whether the event they were reporting on was a first-time hookup with this partner, the second or third hookup with this partner, the fourth or more hookup with this partner, or the most recent time in a relationship of at least six months when they did something sexual beyond just kissing. The figure shows that both men and women are much more likely to orgasm with a partner when they've hooked up several times before. This is partly because they go farther sexually. Talking to women, my research team and I learned that it is also because partners learn more about how to please each other with experience. Both men and women have an even higher chance of orgasm in relationships. This is again partly because they go farther sexually and have more practice with each other. Interviews with men and women students revealed that it is also because of the affection in relationships that makes partners care more about each other's pleasure.

The gender gap in orgasm is much larger in early hookups than in later hookups with the same partner, and the gender gap in orgasm is smallest in relationships (see Figure 11.6). Women have orgasms only one-third as frequently as men during first hookups. This gender gap in orgasm is much bigger than the gender gap in pay! Using in-depth interviews, a team of researchers I was part of found that men report really caring about the pleasure of their girlfriends but being much more selfish in hookups. In contrast, women seemed to feel an obligation to try to give pleasure to their male partners whether they were in casual hookups or relationships. Interpreting this finding, we argued that the sexual double standard may explain this. That is, perhaps

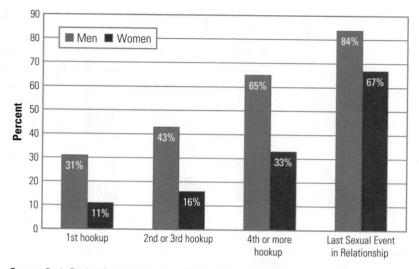

FIGURE 11.6 PERCENT OF COLLEGE MEN AND WOMEN REPORTING ORGASM IN VARIOUS CONTEXTS

Source: Paula England's calculations from Online College Social Life Survey, 2010 version.

men and women are more ambivalent about whether women deserve sexual pleasure in a hookup than they are about men's entitlement to pleasure in a casual context (Armstrong, England, and Fogarty 2012).

Overall, while sex before marriage has become more acceptable, the extent to which sexual and relational behavior follows gendered expectations has changed very little. While of course there are exceptions, the expectation that men ask women on dates, initiate sexual activity, propose marriage, and are less severely judged for casual sex still remains.

Read the **Document** *The Balance of Power in Dating* in **MySocLab**.

Births Outside of Marriage

Since the 1960s, as the average age at marriage has increased and premarital sex has become more common (Ellwood and Jencks 2004), births outside of marriage have become more common. An increase has been seen in all education, income, and racial groups. But young women and men from lower-income families, who often don't have the academic record or money to complete college, are much more likely to have children before marriage. The highest rates occur among the most disadvantaged African Americans. The premarital sexual behavior of those at lower income levels isn't so different from that among those attending college and earning higher income. The key difference is that those at lower education and income levels are less consistent in using birth control; researchers are not yet sure why this is (England, McClintock, and Shafer 2011). One factor in the

How much change has occurred in the ways sexual and romantic behavior are scripted by gender?

increase in nonmarital births is that, as premarital sex has become more common, the stigma of your pregnancy publicly revealing that you've had sex before marriage is much less than previously. Researchers suggest that because of this, couples do not as often marry in response to a pregnancy as previously (Akerlof, Yellen, and Katz 1996).

☐ Generational Differences

During the 1990s, a national survey on sex used a probability sample to ask Americans of all adult ages detailed questions about their sexual behavior and their attitudes about sex. One way the researchers assessed trends was to compare the answers of different generations. When they compared the responses of those above and below 45 years of age, they found, consistent with the studies reviewed earlier, that the younger generation were more likely to have had sex before marriage and to have cohabited before marriage. In the earlier generation (people over 45 in the 1992 survey), the most common response to the question of how many sexual partners the respondents had in their lifetime was one partner, whereas in the younger generation (under 45 in 1992) the most common response was two to four partners (Michael et al. 1994). The main explanations of the increase in the typical number of partners are earlier first intercourse, later first marriage, and more individuals divorcing and remarrying in the more recent generation. Comparing the generations, the researchers also found that oral sex was more commonly practiced—and seen as more appealing—by the younger generation. One of the most important findings of the study was that the image we often get from the media of America as a sex-crazed country is highly misleading. While it is true that younger cohorts often have a number of partners before—or after the end of—a marriage, the vast majority of married people are faithful to one partner. Of married respondents in the survey, 94 percent said they only had one partner in the last year, and when asked how often they have sex, the most common response was "a few times a month." Despite the popular idea that "swinging singles" have sex more than married people, in fact, married or cohabiting people were much more likely to report frequent sex in the last year. This is simply because having a regular partner that you live with makes sex much more accessible.

CONCLUSION   THE PUZZLE OF GENDER INEQUALITY

As we've seen, gender and sexuality are linked. When people are committed to the idea that men and women are naturally and appropriately different, a bias against same-sex relationships often results because such relationships challenge the idea that roles need to be assigned based on one's sex. Gender and sexuality are also linked because our cultural beliefs about how we are supposed to act—at work, in social gatherings, or anywhere—affect how we act when we have sex as well. Gender norms also create the sexual double standard under which peers judge women more harshly than men for casual sex.

Neither gender nor sexual practices are static. That is how we know that they are, at least in part, socially constructed, although they are undoubtedly affected by biology as well.

Many sociologists used to believe that the changes in the system of gender and sexuality were unidirectional and continuous. For a few decades it looked like things were getting ever more permissive regarding sexuality and ever more equal between men and women. A person's sex came to dictate less about how the person was treated or expected to act. Many gender inequalities in job opportunities, pay, and leadership declined. Tolerance for sexual minorities increased. Premarital sex lost much of its stigma.

But recent research has made clear that change in these matters does not go in only the direction of more permissiveness in sexual matters and more and more equality between men and women. Some changes have plateaued or even reversed. We've seen that many forms of gender-equalizing change—declining segregation of occupations, reduction of the sex gap in pay, and egalitarian attitudes—moved most dramatically in the 1970s and 1980s, with slow-downs or reversals since 1990. In the sexual arena, intercourse among teens became more common, but then the trend reversed more recently.

We've also seen that some things change much more than others. Women's roles changed more than men's. Gender change is discussed as "women's progress" because women changed their roles much more than men. More women entered employment, went farther in school, and entered previously male-dominated fields of study and occupations. Movements in the opposite direction—of men becoming homemakers or entering female-dominated fields of study and occupation—have happened much less. In part this is because activities women have traditionally done pay less and receive less respect, and as long as that is true, men will have an incentive to avoid these roles, and women will have an incentive to abandon them.

Another instance of some things changing much more than others is that women's dramatic movements into employment and traditionally male careers were not matched by large changes in how gendered sexual behavior is. The sexual script that sees men as the initiators of dates, sex, and proposals of marriage has not changed dramatically. And a sexual double standard still exists such that women are judged more harshly for casual sex.

One of the remaining puzzles for sociologists studying change in gender and sexuality is to understand which things change, why equalizing changes sometimes reverse, and why some things are so resistant to change.

👁 **Watch the Video in MySocLab**
Applying Your Sociological Imagination

Study and **Review** in MySocLab    **Watch** the **Video** Inspiring Your Sociological Imagination in **MySocLab**

 1

Where Do the Differences between Men and Women Come From? *(p. 295)*

 **Watch** the **Big Question Video** in **MySocLab** to review the key concepts for this section.

Are differences between men and women all natural, or are they shaped by society as well as biology? This section explored the differences between men and women and examined where these differences come from.

GENDER DIFFERENCES (p. 295)

Gender Socialization (p. 296)

Sex versus Gender (p. 297)

- **How do we distinguish the concepts of sex and gender?**

Gender Differences Vary by Setting and Time (p. 297)

- **What does the fact that gender differences vary across situations and over time tell us about the concept of gender?**

The Impact of Stereotypes (p. 298)

KEY TERMS

gender *(p. 292)*

social construction of gender *(p. 296)*

patriarchy *(p. 296)*

sex *(p. 297)*

transgendered *(p. 297)*

random-assignment experiment *(p. 297)*

stereotype *(p. 298)*

2

How Have the Lives of Women and Men Changed in the Last 50 Years? *(p. 299)*

 **Watch** the **Big Question Video** in **MySocLab** to review the key concepts for this section.

Women's lives have changed so much in the last 50 years that we often call the changes a gender revolution. This section explored some of these changes and how they have affected men's lives.

THE GENDER REVOLUTION (p. 299)

Rising Women's Employment and Education (p. 299)

- **What are some of the reasons that women's employment increased dramatically between 1960 and 1990?**

Change in Women's Jobs and in the Pay Gap (p. 299)

- **Why do women still earn less than men?**

The Impact on Men (p. 302)

- **Why haven't the changes in men's roles been as dramatic as the changes in women's roles?**

KEY TERMS

feminist movement *(p. 300)*

occupational sex segregation *(p. 300)*

How Are Our Sex Lives Shaped by Biology and Society? *(p. 305)*

Watch the **Big Question Video** in **MySocLab** to review the key concepts for this section.

There is no question that sexual attractions and behavior are affected by biology, but as we discussed in this section, they are also strongly affected by social construction.

SEXUALITY (p. 305)

Sexual Orientation (p. 305)

* **What evidence do researchers point to that supports a biological influence on sexual orientation?**

Explore A Sociological Perspective: What do dancing rituals say about our attitudes on sex and gender? in **MySocLab**

Sexual Behavior (p. 307)

Sexual Minorities (p. 308)

* **What challenges do lesbian, gay, bisexual, transgendered, and questioning individuals encounter?**

Explore the **Data** on Same-Sex Marriage in **MySocLab**

How Has Sexual Behavior Changed in the Last 50 Years? *(p. 312)*

Watch the **Big Question Video** in **MySocLab** to review the key concepts for this section.

Sexual behavior of young married adults has changed substantially over the last several decades, but what about the extent to which sexual and relational behavior is affected by gender norms and inequalities? This section explored sexual behavior and gender differences in the sexual realm.

THE SEXUAL REVOLUTION AND BEYOND (P. 312)

Premarital Sex (p. 312)

* **How have relationships in which premarital sex occurs changed in recent decades in the U.S.?**

Gender Inequality in Sex and Relationships (p. 313)

* **How much change has occurred in the ways sexual and romantic behavior are scripted by gender?**

Read the **Document** *The Balance of Power in Dating* by Letitia Ann Peplau and Susan Miller Campbell in **MySocLab**. This reading examines what constitutes power in a relationship, and what factors can tip the balance of power away from equality.

Watch the **Video** Applying Your Sociological Imagination in **MySocLab** to see these concepts at work in the real world

12

IMMIGRATION

((Listen to the Chapter Audio in MySocLab

GUILLERMINA JASSO
with LESLIE-ANN BOLDEN,
CARSE RAMOS, and
HAREL SHAPIRA

Marie Jana Korbelová was born in Prague in 1937. Her father, a Czech diplomat, had served as press attaché to what was then Yugoslavia. In 1939, Czechoslovakia was occupied by Nazi Germany, and the family fled to London to escape political persecution. At the end of World War II, her father was briefly welcomed back and served in the new Czechoslovakian government, appointed as ambassador to Yugoslavia. When the Communist Party seized control of the Czechoslovakian government, however, Marie's father was once again forced to resign his position and flee, this time from communism. The family came to the United States in 1948 and was granted political asylum. They ultimately settled in a Denver suburb, and Marie became a U.S. citizen in 1957.

In high school, Marie was a bright, active, and politically engaged student, founding her school's first international relations club. She subsequently attended Wellesley College, where she majored in political science and was an active member of the College Democrats of America. On breaks, Marie interned at *The Denver Post*. Shortly after her graduation in 1959, Marie—who now went by Madeline—married a journalist named Joseph Albright, and the couple moved east, ultimately settling in Long Island. After giving birth to three daughters, Madeline Albright earned a PhD in public law and government from Columbia University. She then relocated her family to Washington, DC, taking a faculty position at Georgetown University and advising Democratic Party leaders on foreign policy questions in her area of expertise. When president Bill Clinton came into office in 1992, he appointed her as ambassador to the

---

MY SOCIOLOGICAL IMAGINATION
Guillermina Jasso

I was born half a mile from the border with Mexico in the old Mercy Hospital that faced Jarvis Plaza in Laredo, Texas. But I did not know that my parents were "immigrants." In the Texas textbooks, "immigrants" were Southern and Eastern Europeans who lived in crowded tenements and had bad habits. Every year Martin High School, the only public high school, graduated a class of securely anti-immigrant students, the vast majority of whose parents or grandparents had come from Mexico. No one had told these Shakespeare-quoting, Bach-playing, Rodgers and Hammerstein-whistling, Lerner and Loewe-dancing boys and girls that we, too, threatened the American way of life.

I grew up passionate to understand the way the world works. In time I got a PhD, and began studying fairness, theoretically with probability distributions, empirically with vignettes. One day in 1977 I got a call from the Commissioner of the Immigration and Naturalization Service. Would I join his staff and advise him on the social science underlying immigration issues? "But I don't know anything about immigration," I said. "You know more than you think you know," he said quietly, "and you can learn the rest."

And that is how I started studying immigration. And how I learned that my parents were immigrants and that I was born in the fabled second generation.

Immigration—for migrants, the countries they leave, and the countries they enter—
is one of the most pressing sociological topics of this era.

Watch the **Video** in **MySocLab**
Inspiring Your Sociological Imagination

United Nations, and in 1997, Madeline Albright became the first woman in U.S. history to serve as secretary of state.

Albright's immigrant story is one of great personal and professional accomplishment. It is, in every sense, a feel-good story. But there are many other immigrant stories, and not all have such exceptional endings. Many immigrants earn low wages and struggle to survive in their new country. They lack many of the same rights, protections, and opportunities as American citizens. They often face prejudice and hardship in their new lives. Immigrants have even died in detention facilities because their health problems were ignored and not treated, an extreme example of how the decision to move to another country is often far from simple.

Many immigrant stories fall somewhere between triumph and tragedies, reflecting a complex portrait of the struggle to survive. Take for instance the case of Miguel Mendoza and his family, whom one of the authors met in the course of research on immigrants in the United States. Miguel came to the United States with very little money or education, but had big dreams of providing a better life for his children than the one he could in the Dominican Republic. Miguel worked hard, and with his wife saved enough to open a corner convenience store, known as a bodega, in an immigrant neighborhood in New York City. The Mendoza family lived above the bodega to save money, and they worked hard, often as much as 15 hours a day, and eventually were able to open three additional bodegas and buy their own home.

Miguel Mendoza and his wife worked very long hours—first to acquire the bodegas, and after to keep them profitable.

Immigration is an important part of the fabric of social life and one that is becoming increasingly important in the twenty-first century.

They were not at home as often as they would have liked, and their children often spent time with friends in the neighborhood, some of whom were involved in criminal activity, selling drugs and guns. In an effort to steer his sons on the path to success as he saw it, Miguel decided that they should work in the bodegas with him, but his older son used the bodega to also sell drugs and guns for his friends, got arrested and was sent to prison. Miguel almost lost his life's work in his efforts to keep his son out of prison, and also to prove that he did not know of his son's illegal activities out of his bodega. In an effort to not repeat the mistakes made with their oldest son, the parents were very strict with their second son and their daughter, with mixed results. Their daughter rebelled when they tried to limit her activities, left home at 17 to move in with her boyfriend, did not attend college, and became pregnant at 18. Only the second son managed to fulfill their parents' hopes, going off to college in the Midwest, graduating and eventually settling on the west coast.

The stories of the Mendozas and Korbelovás represent just two of the millions of stories of immigrants in America. Immigration is particularly important for the history of American society. We all (or nearly all) have an immigration story. The sole exceptions the descendants of the native peoples of the continental United States and of Hawaii and Alaska, but even these "native" peoples are themselves descendants of migrants from several thousand years ago. Yet in spite of the nearly universal nature of the immigrant experience, social and political controversy over rising immigration in recent years has increased, in the United States and in many other countries as well.

THE BIG QUESTIONS

👁 **Watch** the **Big Question Videos** in **MySocLab**

1 What is immigration, and how has it changed over time? What kinds of things do sociologists study when they study immigration, and why is the study of immigration important for understanding the world we live in? In this section we examine the basic concepts and ideas in the study of immigration and then examine some of these in the context of the United States and its immigrant history.

Why do people move? People move for many reasons, but the most fundamental of these is the desire to make a better life for themselves and their children. Sociologists are interested in the characteristics of both those who move and those who stay, as well as the countries they come from and the countries in which they settle. Distinguishing between these different categories of people and places provides important insights into the dynamics of the migration process.

How do immigrants fare in their new environments? Sociologists are especially interested in what happens to migrants after moving as they encounter a new society and its social, economic, and political systems. In this section we explore a host of interesting questions raised by the process of assimilation—during which immigrants adapt to the new society they are living in.

What are the consequences of immigration? Immigration is controversial in the United States and around the world because it has wide-reaching effects on the origin country, on the destination country, and on individuals and families in both countries, including natives, immigrants, and the children of immigrants. In this section we examine the benefits and potential costs of immigration.

1 What Is Immigration, and How Has It Changed Over Time?

IMMIGRATION: A SOCIOLOGICAL PERSPECTIVE

👁 Watch the **Big Question Video** in **MySocLab**

People move for many reasons. They grow up in one town, may go somewhere else for college, and may move to yet another place to work. Some people are forced to leave their homes because of war, economic hardship, or natural disasters. Others move because their parents move. But whatever the underlying reasons and whatever the distance traveled, whether from one city to another or from one country to another, the movement of people is a fundamental feature of our world. Indeed, from the earliest human migrations out of Africa, there have always been substantial numbers of people living away from the place where they were born. And this continues to be true today. In 2010, about 216 million people lived outside the country where they were born (World Bank 2011a). Who are these people? Why do they move? And where do they go? In this chapter we explore these questions, using sociological perspectives and imagination to understand immigration and its impacts.

Migration is the process by which individuals move from one place to another. The idea that migration is a *process* provides the foundation for a sociological approach to immigration as a whole. To think of migration as a process is to think of it not simply as a single event but rather as a long unfolding that takes place over time—starting with the initial idea, continuing with the planning stage, then the actual migration, followed by short-term and long-term impacts and consequences. Although migration is one process, sociologists sometimes distinguish between **emigration**, the act of leaving one place, and **immigration**, the act of arriving

and settling in another. In order to understand migration we need to consider this long unfolding process and, importantly, the conditions and characteristics not only of the individual migrants but also of the places which they leave and to which they go.

Taking account of the larger social context, including the economic and political situation a potential migrant faces, forms the second key to the sociological approach to immigration. It involves considering how the decision to emigrate and the consequences of immigrating are the result not only of individual motivations and personalities but also of those bundles of forces known as **social structures**, including laws, policies, and customs across the social life, both economic and political, noticing gender, race, religion, language, and family dynamics. Certainly, when it comes to migration, individual motivations are important, and a basic factor in migration is that people are seeking to make better lives for themselves. But, of course, sociologists assume that everyone wants a better life, and thus we ask: Why does moving from one place to another make it more possible for some people to secure better lives? Why do some people who live in one place tend to migrate more than people from other places? And finally, why do people from certain places tend to migrate to specific places?

Connected to the focus on process and the examination of both emigration and immigration, sociologists distinguish between **receiving countries** (sometimes called host or destination countries), which refers to those countries to which migrants go, and **sending countries**, which are the countries

TABLE 12.1 WORLD MIGRATION: MAJOR SENDING AND RECEIVING COUNTRIES, 2010

Country	Millions of Persons
A. Top 15 Sending Countries	
Mexico	11.9
India	11.4
Russian Federation	11.1
China	8.3
Ukraine	6.6
Bangladesh	5.4
Pakistan	4.7
United Kingdom	4.7
Philippines	4.3
Turkey	4.3
Egypt	3.7
Kazakhstan	3.7
Germany	3.5
Italy	3.5
Poland	3.1
B. Top 15 Receiving Countries	
United States	42.8
Russian Federation	12.3
Germany	10.8
Saudi Arabia	7.3
Canada	7.2
United Kingdom	7.0
Spain	6.9
France	6.7
Australia	5.5
India	5.4
Ukraine	5.3
Italy	4.5
Pakistan	4.2
United Arab Emirates	3.3
Kazakhstan	3.1

Source: World Bank (2011a).

from which migrants originate. As you can see in Table 12.1, some countries have high numbers of emigrants (meaning they are sending countries) while other countries have high numbers of immigrants (meaning they are receiving countries), and some have significant numbers of both.

The United States the destination of some 40 million migrants, is the top receiving country, and Mexico, the origin of almost 12 million migrants, is the top sending

country. Saudi Arabia, Canada, Spain, Australia, and the United Arab Emirates also stand out as major receiving countries, while China, Bangladesh, the Philippines, Turkey, and Egypt are also primarily sending countries. Some countries have both immigration and emigration streams. These include Russia (with 12.3 million immigrants and 11.1 million emigrants—due no doubt to population shifts since the fall of the Soviet Union), Germany, India, the United Kingdom, Ukraine, Pakistan, Kazakhstan, Italy, and France (which, with 1.7 million emigrants, does not make the top 15 sending countries). Later in the chapter we examine in greater detail why it is that some countries are sending or receiving countries or both, but for now, the important thing to keep in mind is that migration in the world is not random but rather highly *patterned;* that is, it has an order and particular shape, with some people and places having a greater likelihood than others to be involved in migration.

As individuals and families seek to move from one place to another, their comings and goings are not always happy. Indeed, throughout history, many societies have sought to limit or regulate both immigration and emigration. Regulations on emigration range from absolute prohibition on people leaving (as in the communist countries of Eastern Europe during the years of the Cold War, roughly 1948–1989) to restrictions on certain groups of people (such as Jews in Germany during the period of Nazi rule between 1933 and 1945) to enforced departure or exile (as in the case of Dante, condemned in 1302 to perpetual exile from his native Florence). The Berlin Wall—built in 1961 as a barrier between West Berlin and both East Berlin and the surrounding East German territory—is a prominent symbol of the efforts of governments to keep people from leaving. More recently, many countries have been concerned about **brain drain**, the departure of well-educated and skilled citizens to other countries where they can use their skills more productively and make more money. Countries have adopted a variety of strategies to discourage their most skilled younger people from leaving. Many such initiatives are aimed at improving economic growth in the hope that more job opportunity will improve retention rates. Countries also sometimes focus on members of the country's **diaspora** (people settled far from their homeland), hoping to entice them to return to the origin country.

Similarly, throughout history, groups and societies have also sought to regulate immigration. As with emigration, such regulations range from absolute prohibition (preventing anyone from entering a country) to enforced importation (as in the great slave migrations of the eighteenth and nineteenth centuries). In between these extremes lie the elaborate regulations common today throughout the world, which reject some immigrants outright and admit others under a variety of provisions for temporary or permanent stays. For both temporary and permanent residence, there is an intricate system by which foreign-born persons become

Building the Berlin Wall, 1961. The Communist Government in East Germany sought to reduce the movement of citizens out of the country by building a wall and stationing armed guards with orders to shoot to kill anyone attempting to leave the country.

eligible for a **visa**—the authorizing entry document. The decision about who is entitled to a visa becomes a critical part of immigration policy.

These regulations, at both exit and entry, represent a major element in understanding migration not only as an individual decision but also as subject to government policies and social and economic forces. On the one hand, when analyzing immigration sociologically we need to think about the social, economic, and political situation of both the sending and receiving country, but we also need to think about the **emigration and immigration policies**, the set of rules and regulations established by each country with regards to the movement of people across borders. Although a person may wish to leave a country, leaving may be prohibited or the choice about where to go may be highly constrained. In the next section we highlight these issues by considering the history of immigration policy in the United States.

The Basic Structure of Immigration Policy in the United States

Persons born in other countries and their descendants have a substantial presence in the United States. That this has been true for all of America's history is why the country is often called a "nation of immigrants." And more people would like to move to the United States than current law permits. From these two central facts flow the complicated system of visas—which allow individuals to live legally in a country on a temporary or permanent basis—and the broad diversity in the rights and duties provided to foreign-born residents.

Under current U.S. law, foreign-born persons living in the United States include **legal permanent residents (LPRs),** also called *legal immigrants*, who are authorized to live and work in the country permanently but are not citizens; **foreign-born citizens** of the United States, including naturalized citizens (LPRs who have taken the additional steps necessary to become U.S. citizens) and derivative citizens (chiefly children who acquire citizenship when their parents naturalize or who are adopted by citizen parents); **legal temporary residents** (also called *nonimmigrants*), who

are in the U.S. under a variety of legal, temporary statuses; and **unauthorized migrants** (often referred to as *illegal immigrants*) who are in the country without a proper visa. All these groups face some limitations on employment. Some temporary visas prohibit employment, and others have varying degrees of employment restriction. Even persons in the most privileged group—foreign-born citizens of the United States—cannot become president or vice-president of the United States. Thus, visa status in many ways defines the circumstances of a foreign-born person. And importantly, a foreign-born person's behavior and choices often cannot be interpreted without understanding his or her visa situation.

The process through which temporary entry into the United States can be obtained is complex and varied. U.S. law defines a nonimmigrant as an alien (foreign-born person who is not a citizen or national of the United States) who seeks temporary entry to the United States for a specific purpose. Currently there are 23 classes of nonimmigrant visas, denominated by a variety of letters and numbers, including visas for tourists, students, and specialty workers. Some of the nonimmigrant visas are valid for, or associated with, relatively short stays. Others are associated with long—sometimes very long—stays. For example, an F-1 student can remain until the course of study is completed; similarly, foreign media correspondents and employees of international organizations may live and work in the United States for "temporary periods" that may reach or exceed twenty years.

Temporary humanitarian status is provided to refugees, asylees, and parolees. **Refugee status** is a form of protection that may be granted to people who have been persecuted or fear they will be persecuted on account of race, religion,

What privileges does U.S. citizenship confer?

nationality, political opinions, or membership in a particular social group. Refugees are generally outside their home country; a referral for refugee status can be sought only from outside the United States. **Asylum status** is available for persons who meet the definition of refugee but are already in the United States or seeking admission at a port of entry. In order to be eligible for refugee or asylum status, a person must meet the appropriate legal standard for proving that she has a "well-founded fear" of persecution should she be returned to her home country; that the persecution was perpetrated by the government (or a group that the government is unwilling or unable to control); and that the persecution was, as noted, on account of her race, religion, nationality, political opinions, or membership in a social group.

The classes of admission to legal permanent residence (LPR) are of two main types: those that are numerically unlimited and numerically limited. Numerically unlimited LPR is granted to the spouses, minor children (under age 21), and parents of adult U.S. citizens. Numerically limited LPR is granted to three main categories of immigrants: family immigrants (comprised of adult children and siblings of U.S. citizens and the spouses and unmarried children of LPRs and arranged into four family preference categories); employment immigrants (via five employment preference categories, for jobs where not enough American workers can be located); and diversity immigrants (winners of the lottery visas designated for persons from countries underrepresented in recent immigration). The person who qualifies for a particular visa is called the **principal**. The three numerically unlimited categories for spouses, minor children, and parents of adult U.S. citizens are for principals only. Most of the other categories provide LPR visas not only for the principal but also for the spouse and minor children of the principal.

Overall, the United States admits about 1 million persons a year to LPR status (see Table 12.2). The number of numerically limited LPR visas granted annually is about 226,000 to family immigrants, 140,000 to employment immigrants, and 50,000 to diversity immigrants. The majority of new LPRs have numerically unlimited visas (U.S. Department of Homeland Security 2002–2011).

The largest share of new legal immigrants consists of persons born in Mexico—16 percent over the 2001–2010 decade. The second largest group consists of persons born in China—at 6.31 percent, less than half the Mexico contingent. In third through fifth place are India (6.31 percent), Philippines (5.59 percent), and Dominican Republic (3.13 percent). The ranking remains the same for 2011. Over half of new LPRs are already living in the United States. In the 10-year period from 1996 to 2005, the proportion who gained LPR status in the United States was 55.8 percent; it increased to 59.2 percent in the 2006 through 2010 period. An important and interesting feature of legal permanent immigration is that women are the majority of new

Mikhail Baryshnikov, the brilliant Russian dancer, choreographer, and actor, migrated from Russia to the United States in the mid-1970s, and became a U.S. citizen in 1986.

immigrants—almost 55 percent. This is due to the strong family focus of visa allocation, with wives and mothers of U.S. citizens accounting for large fractions of the spouse and parent visas.

The process of applying for an immigrant visa is arduous and time consuming. Persons waiting for numerically limited visas may have to wait many years (U.S. Department of State n.d.). The current upper extreme is over 23 years for persons from the Philippines approved for visas as the siblings of U.S. citizens; at the other extreme, visas for world-class "priority workers" in the employment first preference category (persons of extraordinary ability in the sciences, arts, education, business, or athletics; outstanding professors or researchers; and multinational managers or executives) are available immediately. There is a long queue for numerically limited visas (U.S. Department of State 2011). Over 4.5 million persons are already approved and waiting for the approximately 366,000 numerically limited visas available each year. This means that currently over 12 years' worth of visas are already claimed.

TABLE 12.2   RECENT ANNUAL FLOWS OF NEW LEGAL PERMANENT
RESIDENTS TO THE UNITED STATES

Fiscal Year(s)	All Immigrants`	Excluding Immigration Reform and Control Act (IRCA)
A. Average Annual Flow		
1991–1995	1,046,063	781,848
1996–2000	773,021	771,307
2001–2005	980,478	980,344
2006–2010	1,119,850	1,119,735
B. Annual Flow		
2006	1,266,264	1,266,047
2007	1,052,415	1,052,322
2008	1,107,126	1,107,010
2009	1,130,818	1,130,735
2010	1,042,625	1,042,563
2011	1,062,040	1,061,989

Notes: Flows of new LPRs represent all persons granted LPR status during the period. In most years, over half of all new LPRs are already living in the United States. Through fiscal year 2000 the figures in the "Excluding IRCA" column refer to the total, non-IRCA-legalization number of new LPRs. This number was reported as "total non-legalization" in Table 4 of the Immigration and Naturalization Service and Department of Homeland Security yearbooks through the 2004 yearbook. The yearbooks for 2005 through 2011 do not report the non-IRCA-legalization total, but it is possible to obtain it by subtracting the IRCA legalization total from the grand total in Table 7. During the period 1991 to 2011, IRCA legalizations declined from a high of over 1 million in 1991 to less than 1,000 in every year since 1998, with a low of 8 in 1999 and totals of 188, 217, 93, 116, 83, 62, and 51 in fiscal years 2005 through 2011, respectively.

Source: Based on data from U.S. Department of Homeland Security (2002–2011).

The Legal Permanent Resident Visa System

An important insight in recent immigration research is that immigrant behavior cannot be understood without understanding immigrants' legal status in the United States—how they came, whether they have the coveted **green card** (the paper evidence of LPR status) and, if so, how they got it. For example, any assessment of the work and jobs of immigrants requires information about their authorization to work; understanding home ownership among immigrants requires understanding the risk of deportation they face; and understanding the children of immigrants and their behavior and choices in schools requires understanding whether they have a claim to U.S. citizenship. Sociologists now appreciate that a move from illegal to legal status represents a highly consequential form of upward social mobility (Bean and Stevens 2003; Jasso, Massey, Rosenzweig, and Smith 2008). Those immigrants who gain legal permanent resident status have the opportunity to build a future without fear of deportation. In time, they become eligible for the same civic and social programs as American citizens. For these reasons, obtaining permanent residence is of critical importance for individual immigrants and their families.

Most individuals seeking LPR status require a sponsor who files the initial petition that establishes the prospective immigrant's eligibility and starts the visa process. In the case of family immigrants, the sponsor is the relative who is already a citizen or LPR of the United States; for employment immigrants, the sponsor is the employing individual or firm. (The requirement for a sponsor may be waived in certain cases, such as for the widow(er) and child of a deceased U.S. citizen or for the spouse and child of an abusive citizen or LPR under the Violence against Women Act.)

Becoming a U.S. Citizen

How does an immigrant become a U.S. citizen? In general, there are two paths to citizenship for foreign-born persons. The first is naturalization, and the second is deriving citizenship from one's parent(s). **Naturalization** is the process by which a person who is 18 years of age or older acquires citizenship. Eligibility for naturalization requires a period of time as an LPR, physical presence in the United States, knowledge of English, knowledge of the history and government of the United States, "good moral character," and attachment to the U.S. Constitution.

When a parent becomes a U.S. citizen, children who are LPR, unmarried, under 18, and in the parent's legal and physical custody automatically become citizens; they "derive" citizenship from their parent. There are, of course, many intricate rules for special cases, such as adopted children and legitimated children. Children born in the United States

A SOCIOLOGICAL PERSPECTIVE

What makes a border a barrier?

These days, the nearly 2,000 mile long border between the United States and Mexico is fortified with walls, watch towers, check points, and Border Patrol agents. For most of America's history, people were free to move between the United States and Mexico. It was not until the middle of the nineteenth century, after the Mexican-American War, that the border between the United States and Mexico began to take physical shape. A group of people were hired by the governments of both countries to walk across the 2,000 miles of mostly open desert and demarcate a physical border using only 52 small stone monuments, often with hundreds of miles separating each one.

How is it that 52 stones set across 2,000 miles of land were thought of as an appropriate border between the U.S. and Mexico by both countries at one time?

Why do Americans think differently (or do they?) about the U.S. border to Canada than they do about the U.S. border to Mexico?

There was no formal enforcement of the border until 1924 when the U.S. Border Patrol was established. In the 1990s, after The North American Free Trade Agreement (NAFTA) was signed, restrictions on the movement of people between the U.S. and Mexico were increased while restrictions on the movement of goods between the counties decreased. In 1994, legislation funded the building of walls and military infrastructure on the border. Following the terrorist attacks of 9/11, enforcement of the border intensified as it began to be seen as a national security issue and part of the War on Terror. By 2010, the once open border had been transformed into a closed militarized one.

What changed the United States government's view and policies on immigration from the influx of 16 million European immigrants from the late 1800s-early 1950s to today? What economic, social, or political events impacted those changes?

@ **Explore** A Sociological Perspective in **MySocLab** and then ...

■ Think About It

In 1986, the Border Patrol had a budget of $151 million; by 2002 it was $1.6 billion. During this same time the number of Border Patrol agents more than doubled. What do you think would happen if we got rid of Border Patrol agents and went back to having no fence between the U.S. and Mexico? As you think about it, consider this: during the same time period that the Border Patrol doubled in size (1986-2002), the number of people crossing the border illegally also doubled in size.

■ Inspire Your Sociological Imagination

The U.S. / Mexico border represents a formidable and very physical border to cross. But in our everyday lives we are continuously crossing borders, moving from one social space into another, from a space where we belong to one where maybe we do not belong as much. What borders do you have to contend with in your everyday life? Do you cross them all? Are there consequences to crossing or not crossing them?

become citizens at birth, even if their parents were not citizens at the time they were born. The major current exception to this pertains to children of certain diplomats, who are regarded as "not subject to the jurisdiction" of the United States and therefore not covered by the Fourteenth Amendment to the Constitution. Explore *A Sociological Perspective* on page 327 to learn more about how immigration across borders have changed over time.

How do immigrants become U.S. citizens?

☐ A Brief History of U.S. Immigration

For much of its history, the United States has welcomed foreigners—although sometimes reluctantly, and in some periods relatively few in number. The federal government began collecting statistics on immigration in 1820, and historical data are now published every year in the official reports (the *Yearbook of Immigration Statistics* and its predecessors). These data alone suggest quite a bit about the history of immigration. Figure 12.1 displays the trends in immigration into the United States, distinguishing between volume with and without inclusion of the persons admitted to lawful permanent residence via amnesty provisions of the Immigration Reform and Control Act (IRCA) of 1986. The plot features vertical lines to separate four distinct immigration eras, which we discuss in turn in the rest of this section. (In contrast, Table 10.3 in Chapter 10 displays three "waves" of immigration, reflecting immigrants' different countries of origin in different time periods.)

The First Immigration Era (1789–1874): Prerestriction The **first immigration era** can be characterized as a period when immigration was largely unrestricted. At the first census in

1790, almost 4 million persons were enumerated, of whom about 700,000 were slaves from Africa and the remainder free whites and indentured servants, mostly of English, Dutch, and German origin. However, while immigration was largely unrestricted, naturalization was not. The Naturalization Act of 1790 limited naturalization to "free white persons," a class excluding nonwhites, indentured servants, and married women. Thus, there were two kinds of immigrants during the first immigration era—those eligible to naturalize and those not. The latter included millions of slaves brought by force into the United States.

It is striking to note that the right to vote, one of the key markers of citizenship in a democratic society, was not as linked to naturalization during the first immigration era as it is today. Back then, a majority of states allowed immigrants to vote in federal, state, and local elections without requiring them to become citizens, sometimes advertising this right for immigrants as a way of attracting them to live in the state. It was not until 1926 that the last state (Arkansas) abolished noncitizen voting (Keyssar 2000). American democracy in the nineteenth century embraced immigrant voters in a variety of different ways. The major political parties would compete to attract the loyalties of members of different ethnic communities, holding enormous parades and festivals during election season.

The Second Immigration Era (1875–1920): Qualitative Restrictions If the first immigration era was marked by openness and lack of restrictions, the year 1875 marks the start of the **second immigration era** and the beginnings of explicit immigration policy. During this period, there were no numerical limitations on immigration, only a growing set of exclusion criteria based on personal characteristics or behavior. Prostitutes and convicts were the first to be barred as undesirable immigrants (1875). Next, the Chinese Exclusion Act of May 6, 1882, suspended the immigration of Chinese laborers. Within three months, the Immigration Act of August 3, 1882, established the first financial test, declaring inadmissible anyone likely to become a public charge and imposing a head tax of 50 cents per passenger. The list of inadmissibles would continue to grow—persons with certain contagious diseases, further classes of convicts, polygamists (1891), anarchists and persons advocating overthrow of the government of the United States (1903), and on and on. The high-water mark of restrictions placed on immigration during the second immigration era came in 1917 with passage of legislation that imposed a literacy test on adult immigrants (albeit with waivers for the illiterate wives of literate immigrants) and barred persons from the Asia-Pacific region.

The new focus on personal characteristics was felt in immigration statistics. In 1899 the

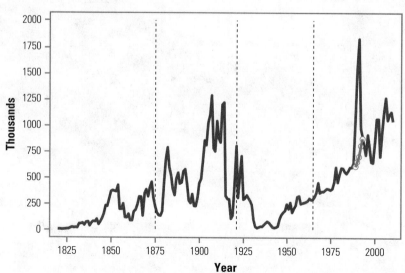

FIGURE 12.1 IMMIGRATION TO THE UNITED STATES: 1820–2010

Note: The main solid red line represents the annual number of new legal immigrants. The short blue plot with circles represents the annual flow excluding IRCA legalizations. The vertical blue lines separate the four immigration eras.

Source: Based on data from U.S. Department of Homeland Security (2010).

Bureau of Immigration began collecting data on "race or people." According to the Dillingham Commission Report (U.S. Immigration Commission 1911), "This departure was necessitated by the fact that among immigrants from southern and eastern European countries, as well as from Canada and other sources of immigration, the country of birth does not afford a satisfactory clue to the actual racial or ethnical status of such immigrants" (Vol. 3, p. 44).

However, restrictions based on personal characteristics proved insufficient to quell growing discontent with an otherwise open immigration policy. Anti-immigrant tensions grew in many parts of the United States as the number of immigrants living in large cities mushroomed rapidly. Immigrants were increasingly competing with natives for jobs and economic opportunities, as well as beginning to stake claims to political power in places where they were especially numerous (such as Boston and New York). A growing anti-immigrant backlash developed, exemplified by extreme stereotypic images of immigrants in newspapers, popular cartoons, films, and literature. Occasionally, violent conflicts between immigrants and natives broke out. Politicians in both parties began to feel pressure from their constituents to close the door to new immigration.

The Third Immigration Era (1921–1964): Worldwide Qualitative Restrictions plus Quantitative Restrictions on Eastern Hemisphere

These pressures eventually led to a **third immigration era**, inaugurated with the passage of the Emergency Quota Act in 1921. This act limited the number of immigrants from any Eastern Hemisphere nationality to 3 percent of the number of residents of that nationality living in the United States in 1910, for a total of 357,000. A more dramatic Immigration Act of May 26, 1924, also known as the National Origins Act, provided for a transition quota system to be followed by a permanent system with a much smaller total quota of 154,000 and, more restrictively, reflecting the national origins of the white population in 1920. This legislation was primarily designed to restrict the numbers of immigrants from Southern and Eastern Europe, following the influx of large numbers of Jews, Italians, and Slavs in the early 1900s. Immigration from Northern and Western Europe, though subject to the overall ceiling, enjoyed more generous quotas (for example, 66,000 for Britain and 26,000 for Germany out of the 154,000 total). Additionally, the 1924 act barred from immigration persons ineligible to naturalize.

The new restrictions of the third immigration era triggered new institutions and new laws. First, since immigration from the Western Hemisphere remained unrestricted, people from the Eastern Hemisphere might want to enter the United States illegally by crossing the borders from Canada and Mexico. Thus, two days after passage of the National Origins Act, the government established the U.S. Border Patrol with the mission to deter illegal entries. The Border Patrol's first two stations were in El Paso, Texas, and Detroit, Michigan.

Second, however, there would now certainly be illegal entrants, the Border Patrol notwithstanding, and some of them might be deserving. Thus, the Registry Act of 1929 provided for the legalization of persons, not otherwise ineligible, who had entered before July 1, 1924. Since then, the qualifying date for inception of illegal residence has changed several times; it currently stands at January 1, 1972. Third, the John Jay Treaty (1794–1795) had guaranteed safe passage to American Indians across the border with Canada; now there was concern for honoring that commitment. Thus, the act of April 2, 1928, provided that the Immigration Act of 1924 was not to be construed as limiting the right of American Indians born in Canada to cross the border. As part of guaranteeing free passage, American Indians born in Canada may become LPRs.

During the long period of racial bars to naturalization (and immigration), a major concern had been how to define "white"—a concern that prompted such colorful highlights as a 1909 query whether "Jesus of Nazareth himself" would be denied naturalization (Smith 2002). More broadly, the theme of "becoming white" recurs vividly in immigration history, involving, for example, Irish, Italians, Jews, and others (Ignatiev 1995; Jacobson 1999).

There would be more, and dire, consequences of the 1924 act. Under the national origins quota system, the United States routinely denied entry to hundreds of thousands of refugees and asylum seekers, primarily Jewish, fleeing Nazi persecution before and during World War II. This famously included those aboard the S.S. *St. Louis*, the transatlantic liner that in 1939 reached both Cuba and the United States only to be forced to return to occupied territories in Europe (where some of its passengers would later be tragically sent to concentration camps). But the days of racial bars to naturalization were numbered. World War II had largely ended unemployment in the United States and created millions of new jobs. Even with retirees, housewives, and students entering the labor force, there were still labor shortages, especially in agriculture and railroad maintenance, in the years after the war. To meet the new demand, the United States and Mexico entered into a series of agreements, starting in 1942, which came to be known as the **Bracero Program**, under which Mexican workers came to the United States. The postwar boom created even more jobs, and the Bracero Program continued until the late 1960s. At its peak in the mid to late 1950s, the Bracero Program brought 400,000 to 500,000 Mexican laborers into the United States each year on temporary, nonimmigrant visas (Calavita 1992).

What are the four eras of immigration in U.S. history?

The contentious nature of immigration policy, however, would continue to arouse discontent and debate. In this period, pressure would come not from those in favor of keeping the doors closed but from those who favored a more open immigration policy. The case of agriculture and the Bracero Program suggests, in part, that some employers were interested in maintaining a supply of low-wage labor. Civil libertarians and liberals also did not like the quota system, but for different reasons (noting, for example, the unfairness in the distribution of opportunities to enter the country and the denial of many basic rights to those admitted on a temporary basis).

The Fourth Immigration Era (1965–present): Both Qualitative and Quantitative Restrictions on Both Hemispheres

After a long period of contentious debate, major immigration reform would finally come in the form of the Immigration Act of 1965, which ushered in the **fourth immigration era** with its numerical restrictions on both Eastern and Western Hemispheres—which continues to the present. The 1965 act eliminated the national origins quotas and established a two-tiered immigration system—a numerically unlimited tier for the immediate relatives of U.S. citizens and a numerically limited tier of visas for everyone else. Initially, numerically limited visas were allocated differently in the two hemispheres, continuing earlier practice—first-come, first-served in the Western Hemisphere (now with a ceiling), while in the Eastern Hemisphere based on preference categories giving priority to nonimmediate relatives and employment-based immigrants. In 1976 the preference category system was extended to the Western Hemisphere.

The preference category system for allocating numerically limited visas was restructured by the Immigration Act of 1990, effective in 1992. The new system, still in effect today, provides separate ceilings and preference categories for family-based and employment-based visas. As noted earlier, the number of visas available annually in the family preference categories is at least 226,000 but may be larger (though never larger than 480,000) depending on the previous year's volume of numerically unrestricted immigration; in the employment-based categories, the annual number of visas available is at least 140,000 but may be larger if there are unused family preference visas. Additionally, U.S. immigration law provides for immigration on humanitarian and diversity grounds. On humanitarian grounds, persons admitted to the United States with refugee visas or granted asylum status may adjust to LPR after residing in the United States for one year. On diversity grounds, the United States grants 50,000 visas annually to nationals of countries from which the number of immigrants was less than 50,000 in the preceding five years. Eligibility requirements include a high school degree or equivalent, or two years of work experience (within the preceding five years) in an occupation requiring two years of training or experience; selection is by lottery.

The history of the lottery visas has an interesting link to race. In the 1970s, as it was becoming clear that the family reunification provisions of the 1965 Immigration Act engendered increased flows of relatives of previous immigrants, a new concern arose in policymaking circles. For persons in countries without a foothold in the immigration stream, there would be little possibility of immigrating to the United States. For example, documents of the U.S. Select Commission on Immigration and Refugee Policy, whose final report

The Bracero Program in the 1940s and 1950s brought large numbers of low-wage agriculture workers from Mexico on short-term contracts that did not permit them to become permanent U.S. residents.

was issued in 1981, convey a sense of urgency about opening a new channel for "independent" immigration, and at least part of the concern involved the small numbers of black immigrants from Africa. A number of procedures for selecting immigrants in the envisioned open immigration channel were discussed, including a point system (Jasso 1988). Eventually, the United States established the Diversity Visa Program, making available new visas for blacks and others from Africa. Note that there was no scarcity of black immigrants from the Caribbean; the dearth was of black immigrants from Africa.

Immigration policies have undergone important further changes since the terrorist attacks of September 11, 2001. Shortly after these attacks, the federal government passed a number of measures to make it more difficult for people around the world, but especially from countries with large Muslim populations, to travel to the United States or to obtain visas for shorter or longer-term residence, including for such things as studying at an American university. Enhanced monitoring of foreigners who do gain entry from these countries has also increased significantly in recent years. These measures have raised important questions about how open America intends to be in the future. Explore the Infographic on page 331 to see where immigrants settle in America.

Coming to America

28% Asia

2% Northern America

California has the highest percentage of foreign born residents at 27%

<1% Oceania

12% Europe

4% Africa

Width of arrows represent the percentage of foreign-born residents from each region of the world.

Squares show the distribution of immigrants by state. Each square represents 100,000 foreign-born residents.

29% Mexico

8% Other Central America

7% South America

9% Caribbean

Where do immigrants to America come from, and where do they settle? As this map shows, while foreign-born immigrants reside in every part of the United States, over half live in four states—California, New York, Texas, and Florida—and over one-fourth live in California. In terms of percent foreign-born within each state's population, California ranks first with 27.2 percent, followed by New York, New Jersey, Florida, Nevada, Hawaii, and Texas—all with more than 15 percent foreign-born.

In 2010, there were about 40 million foreign-born people living in the United States. As the map shows, more than half were born in Latin America and the Caribbean, and over a quarter were born in Asia. The top country of birth was Mexico (at 29.3 percent), followed by China (including Hong Kong), India, the Philippines, and Vietnam.

Source: Based on data from U.S. Census Bureau (2012).

⊙➔ Explore the Data on Coming to America in **MySocLab** and then ...

■ Think About It
According to 2008 estimates of legal temporary residents, the top origin country is India (21.9 percent). What might account for the different origin-country pattern for this subset?

■ Inspire Your Sociological Imagination
Why do you think immigrants are consistently drawn to states like California, Florida, and New York?

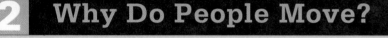

2 Why Do People Move?

SELF-SELECTION, PUSH AND PULL FACTORS, AND MIGRATION DYNAMICS

Watch the **Big Question Video** in **MySocLab**

People consider moving for many reasons. Perhaps most fundamentally, moving may provide a better life for themselves and their children. The central way that sociologists approach the question of why people move, however, is to examine the potential gains migrants make between their expected well-being in the origin country versus the life they envisioned for themselves or their families in the destination country. The outcome of this comparison depends jointly on the potential migrant's own characteristics and on the characteristics of both the origin country—including its push factors—and the destination country—including its pull factors. **Push factors** in the home country are those that drive people to leave; while **pull factors** in the receiving country are those that attract people to go there. Some of the important push factors include economic hardship or political strife in the home country. Simultaneously, pull factors include the economic and political characteristics of the receiving countries. For some people, there will be a benefit from migration, and for others not. To illustrate, a key comparison is between expected wage in the origin country versus the expected wage in the destination country (adjusted for purchasing power); countries differ in how they reward skills and occupations, and thus some individuals will benefit economically from a move and others not, and among those who benefit, some will benefit more than others.

What factors influence the desire to move?

Further, countries are connected to one another in many different ways. For example, people from Mexico are more likely to go to the United States than to Europe not only because there are higher wages in the United States but also because the two countries share a 1,969-mile land border and a long history, with their peoples and economies connected to each other in very strong ways. Mexico and the United States are strong trade partners; the United States is Mexico's largest trading partner, buying more than 80 percent of Mexican exports in 2010, and Mexico is the third largest buyer of U.S. exports. The United States has many companies based in Mexico and a high degree of investment there. Thus, people in each country have many business or professional colleagues, friends, and family members in the other country.

☐ The Desire to Move and Migrant Energy

Although migration is a universal phenomenon, most people will not move to another country. The *desire to move* and the **migrant energy** it unleashes—varies in strength. Some people may want very much to move, others may want a little to move, and others may not want to move at all. Persons with a high desire to move (or, equivalently, with large amounts of migrant energy) are said to be highly positively **self-selected** for migration.

To understand what factors impact the desire to move, sociologists link it to other personal characteristics, such as earnings or health. We ask, for example, is the desire to move stronger among the rich or the poor? Among the healthy or the unhealthy? The answers to these questions help illuminate the reasons why some people make the decision to move while others do not. If in an origin country the desire to move is strongest among the highly skilled, we say that selection on skill is positive; and if the desire to move is strongest among the unskilled, we say that selection on skill is negative. Similarly, if the desire to move is strongest among the healthiest, we say that selection on health is positive; and if the desire to move is strongest among the unhealthiest, we say that selection on health is negative. The type of selection helps illuminate the characteristics and dynamics of different migration flows.

Sociologists and other social scientists sometimes isolate one force or one dimension and explore its dynamics in the migration process. Freedom from want is a good example. Many theories of the migration process begin with the assumption that people move to maximize their well-being, and, more specifically, often assume that well-being varies with the difference between the wage in the origin country and the wage in potential destination countries, after the costs of migration. In other words, migrants consider whether their economic circumstances would be better in a new country if they could move there. Thus, the higher the cost of migration, the greater the required improvement in the wage.

Whatever the migration dynamic may be, once set in motion, it often acquires a life of its own. This can happen in several ways. First, there is habit. For example, if a young man's father and grandfather both went abroad every year to work in the harvest, it becomes an expectation, perhaps even a norm, that the young man will do the same. Second, the costs diminish with each generation because crucial information can be passed from parent to child. These and other mechanisms may intensify as networks of migrants form and enlarge (Massey et al. 1993).

Movers and Stayers

From this landscape of the search to make life better, we can isolate and examine the processes set in motion. Consider again the fact that not everyone with a high desire to move will actually move, and some with low desire to move will in fact move. Why? There are two sets of reasons. First, recall our earlier discussion of government policies on exit and entry. Some individuals may be barred from leaving the origin country or entering the destination country. Others may be forced to leave the origin country

What is the distinction between a mover and a stayer?

Shown here, an immigrant woman works in a bakery in Florida. One of the great puzzles of immigration research is why some people choose to move to a foreign land, while other similar people do not.

or to enter the destination country. Second, family dynamics intervene, forcing some persons to move or making it impossible for others to move, however great their desire to move (Mincer 1978).

Social scientists have found it useful to distinguish between **movers** (those who migrate to the destination country) and **stayers** (those who stay in the origin country). Linking movers and stayers to the desire to move yields what economist Jacob Mincer called *tied movers* and *tied stayers*. Thus, the set of movers is diverse in that it includes both movers-at-heart (with high desire to move) and tied movers (with low desire to move). Similarly, the set of stayers is diverse in that it includes both stayers-at-heart (with low desire to move) and tied stayers (with high desire to move).

A recent survey of immigrants admitted to U.S. LPR status in 2003—the U.S. New Immigrant Survey, of which the author of this chapter is one of the directors—obtained information on how many years each new LPR had wanted to become a legal permanent resident. Approximately half—50.9 percent—provided a specific number of years. The rest said either that they had always wanted LPR—28.8 percent—or never wanted LPR (18 percent). The set of movers thus included both persons with very high desire to move (the ones who said "always"), persons with an intermediate desire to move (the ones who provided a specific number of years), and persons with very low desire to move (those who said "never")—that is, a mix of movers-at-heart and tied movers. There are, this suggests, a wide range of different motivations to move to the United States.

3 How Do Immigrants Fare in Their New Environments?

THE ASSIMILATION PROCESS

👁 Watch the **Big Question** Video in **MySocLab**

Sociologists are especially interested in what happens to a migrant after moving, as he or she encounters a new society and its social, economic, and political systems. The process of **assimilation**—whereby immigrants adapt to the new society—raises a host of interesting questions. To what extent do individuals embrace and adopt the language and cultural values and norms of their new countries? What is pace of their adaptation? Are certain groups more likely than others to form isolated enclaves, or conversely, are certain immigrants especially good at learning to "fit in"? How deeply and successfully do immigrants become Americans, Canadians, or Australians? And how fast is this process?

Questions about assimilation are important because they help assess how migration contributes to developing the migrant's own potential. Such questions also help assess how the migrant contributes to the destination country and its social, economic, and political development. Migration arouses fears that many immigrants will not adapt to their new country's dominant ways of living, and by failing to assimilate they will (if their numbers are large enough) threaten the social fabric. This idea goes all the way back to the founding of the American Republic. For example, George Washington (1794), in a letter to his vice president, John Adams, worried that if immigrants settle with people from their own country, they would not assimilate, and "… the settling of them in a body … may be much questioned; for, by so doing, they retain the language, habits, and principles (good or bad) which they bring with them. Whereas by an intermixture with our people, they, or their descendants, get assimilated to our customs, measures, and laws: in a word, soon become one people."

☐ Measures of Assimilation

Research suggests that assimilation is multifaceted. Most immigrants quickly adopt certain features of their new country while retaining some of the values and norms of their place of origin. Of course, which aspects are adopted, and the speed with which they are adopted, may vary greatly across individual immigrants and immigrant streams. Thus, many new questions arise for researchers to study.

Social scientists use a variety of indicators to gauge how well immigrants have assimilated. Some of the indicators are obvious and include remaining in the country (that is, not returning to their original country), learning English, and becoming a U.S. citizen.

Other indicators of assimilation cover a wide range of domains and behaviors involving whether and how immigrants become more like natives. These include socioeconomic status, geographic distribution, family size and household structure, intermarriage, and behaviors such as smoking. **Socioeconomic status** (SES) describes an individual's schooling, labor force participation, occupation, income, and homeownership. By measuring the SES of immigrants, sociologists are able to gauge the extent to which immigrants and natives are on an equal footing in the social hierarchy. If immigrants arrive poorer than natives, then the closer the SES of immigrants is to the native population, the greater the degree of assimilation. English fluency and SES are considered important indicators of the potential for social and economic incorporation (Alba and Nee 2003; Jasso and Rosenzweig 2006; Portes and Rumbaut 2006)

Spatial concentration refers to the geographic distribution of a population. Sociologists are interested in the extent to which immigrants live in isolation from the native-born population or, by contrast, together with the native-born population. The greater the degree to which immigrants live apart from the native-born population and only near each other, the lower the degree of assimilation. In general, sociologists have found that both higher SES and longer duration in the receiving country lead to lower spatial concentration.

Another measure of assimilation is **intermarriage**, which refers to both marriages between immigrants and natives and to marriages across racial or ethnic lines. Both types of intermarriage share the common feature that they reveal very close relationships between people from different groups and often involve breaking away from some traditional marriage patterns, thus reducing the likelihood of passing on the culture of the home country to the next generation.

Finally, social scientists examine what may be called little measures of assimilation. They pertain to adopting the local currency, the local way of reckoning temperature, and the local way of measuring length and weight. In the United States, this involves adopting the dollar as the monetary currency, the Fahrenheit scale for temperature, and the British system for length and weight. In addition, immigrants usually begin to share in what are taken to be important local customs and activities. In the United States, such local customs can range

from celebrating national holidays such as Thanksgiving to playing national sports like baseball, to cooking and eating national foods like hamburgers and hotdogs.

Read the **Document** *Mexican Americans and Immigrant Incorporation* in **MySocLab**.

Recent Research on Immigrant Assimilation

Three fundamental ideas are important in studying immigrant assimilation in the contemporary United States. First, it is critical to define the population whose assimilation is studied, as assimilation may not be a meaningful concept for some sets of foreign-born residents, such as those who are here temporarily and have no desire to remain in the United States. Second, most immigrants are self-selected and thus motivated to assimilate. Third, given the heavy focus on family reunification within the visa allocation system, many new LPRs have spouses, parents, or children who were born U.S. citizens or who have already become citizens. Thus, they have a built-in guide to things American, a caseworker and advocate, under the same roof or nearby. And, importantly, many of them already satisfy the intermarriage criterion of assimilation.

While it is useful to assess measures of assimilation in all foreign-born residents—as they may signal anticipatory assimilation or wishful assimilation—it is among LPRs that assimilation assumes critical importance. Unless they leave, LPRs are in the United States for the long haul, and their children will be Americans. Thus, assessing the progress and integration of LPRs provides a window into the future of the social, economic, and political institutions of the United States.

Table 12.3 reports basic characteristics of the cohort of immigrants granted LPR in 2003, studied in the New Immigrant Survey. This group, which is representative of all new adult LPRs in 2003 and which comes from 168 countries, is exactly the kind of group in which it is important to assess assimilation. However, these individuals have only recently been granted LPR and thus are at the start of the immigrant career, so to speak. Full assessment of their assimilation will come later as the cohort is reinterviewed every few years. Nonetheless, because the survey collected information about their years before coming to the United States and because more than half are adjustees and have already been living in the United States, it may be possible to shed light on the assimilation process.

As noted earlier, recent research has shown that the immigrant visa type provides powerful information about how

> # What measures help us gauge how well an immigrant has assimilated?

TABLE 12.3 BASIC CHARACTERISTICS OF NEW LEGAL IMMIGRANTS AGED 18+

Immigrant Class of Admission	Percent Female	Age		Schooling		English Fluency		Percent Adjustees	
		Men	Women	Men	Women	Men	Women	Men	Women
Spouse of Natural Born (NB) U.S. citizen (16.2%)	59.6	31.6	32.1	13.0	13.8	60.8	60.5	84.2	81.1
Spouse of Foreign Born (FB) U.S. citizen (17.9%)	66.0	34.2	33.1	12.3	12.5	43.4	38.0	79.3	65.2
Parent of U.S. citizen (11.9%)	66.2	65.5	62.7	8.75	6.93	20.8	19.7	25.3	33.6
Minor child of U.S. citizen (3.38%)	41.9	20.2	20.2	11.5	11.9	50.5	46.9	46.1	41.4
Adult single child of U.S. citizen (3.28%)	54.3	31.6	34.8	12.3	12.3	48.9	38.3	31.8	33.6
Adult married child of U.S. citizen (1.72%)	57.7	40.6	39.9	13.2	12.4	48.7	45.5	20.4	16.8
Spouse of adult child of U.S. citizen (1.51%)	48.1	42.4	37.4	12.9	11.2	35.7	25.5	8.92	12.9
Sibling of U.S. citizen (3.94%)	51.4	48.5	48.2	11.8	11.1	35.1	22.7	8.97	12.9
Spouse of sibling (2.49%)	52.8	50.3	46.2	13.0	10.8	37.6	19.6	3.98	3.98
Spouse of Legal Permanent Resident (LPR) (2.44%)	83.5	43.2	40.2	8.65	7.76	16.3	10.6	47.7	63.9
Child of LPR (2.81%)	49.2	34.3	35.0	11.0	11.1	27.7	17.2	23.5	19.5
Employment Principal (6.02%)	32.8	37.3	36.8	15.7	15.2	78.6	80.7	78.9	55.4
Employment Spouse (3.63%)	77.1	40.4	35.3	14.7	15.2	70.1	76.4	56.5	76.4
Diversity Principal (5.53%)	41.1	32.3	32.8	14.5	14.5	52.5	45.4	8.45	11.5
Diversity Spouse (2.58%)	48.7	37.7	34.5	14.6	13.1	39.1	38.8	5.17	3.55
Refugee/Asylee/Parolee Principal (5.35%)	42.8	40.7	38.3	12.8	11.8	39.9	35.1	100	100
Refugee/Asylee/Parolee Spouse (1.22%)	74.8	45.3	43.0	13.3	10.9	36.5	30.1	100	100
Legalization (7.98%)	49.8	38.7	37.9	9.03	8.43	17.0	9.06	100	100
Other (0.05%)	–	–	–	–	–	–	–	–	–
All Immigrants	56.5	38.7	39.1	12.3	11.6	44.7	38.4	57.9	57.0

Note: Based on data from the New Immigrant Survey (2003), Adult Sample. Sample size is 8,573. Estimates based on weighted data. The measure of English fluency requires that the interview was conducted entirely in English.

the green card was obtained, networks to which immigrants have access, and, in general, their life chances. For each of the major visa types, the table presents the proportion in the cohort, the percent female, and, separately by gender, average age and schooling and percent adjustee and fluent in English. Consistent with the well-known fact noted earlier, over half of the cohort is female, and the proportion female is even higher in the most numerous visa categories, those for spouses and parents of U.S. citizens.

The results in Table 12.3 pertain to measures of assimilation, which may be thought of as outcomes. How about access to help in the assimilation process? One way to address

What do sociologists take into consideration when researching immigrant assimilation?

this question is to examine the new immigrants' connections to U.S. citizens. Accordingly, in addition to the 16 percent of the new LPRs married to native-born U.S. citizens, 18 percent are married to a naturalized citizen, 12 percent are the parents of adult U.S. citizens, 10 percent are the children or children-in-law of U.S. citizens, and 6 percent are the siblings or siblings-in-law of U.S. citizens—for a total of 62 percent related by blood or marriage to a U.S. citizen. Moreover, LPRs sponsored by employers may not have close kin who are U.S. citizens (though some do), but they certainly have employers and colleagues at their workplace who are U.S. citizens or knowledgeable about the United States.

Thus 72 percent of the new LPRs have ready access to natives or naturalized citizens who can be helpful sources of information about adapting to the United States.

The chief exceptions to this pattern of ready access to help with assimilation are diversity immigrants, humanitarian immigrants (refugees, asylees, parolees), and legalization immigrants. Of these, refugees may have ties to a sponsoring church or nongovernmental organization. The others may be more on their own, so to speak. However, at least one subset of diversity immigrants—blacks born in Africa—are highly accomplished, with some of the highest average schooling and rates of English fluency (Jasso 2011). The official immigration statistics have not collected information on race since 1961, and thus before the New Immigrant Survey it was not possible to ascertain the presence of blacks among immigrants (including those born in Africa). The New Immigrant Survey not only confirms their presence but shows their very high attainment.

As you can see, data from the New Immigrant Survey are making it possible to study questions of assimilation more systematically and in a population clearly relevant to discussions of assimilation. Consider, for example, the proposition that new LPRs may have begun their Americanization long before they moved to the United States. We saw earlier that 28.8 percent of the immigrants surveyed in 2003 had "always" wanted to become a legal permanent resident of the United States, and that another 50.9 percent had wanted it for a varying number of years before they got their green card. These two groups are ripe for study of their assimilation. But what about the 18 percent of the 2003 cohort who never wanted to move to the United States? Some in fact did not stay. Some obtained LPR in the United States as insurance in case economic or political upheavals threatened their country. Others obtained LPR because they travel frequently to the United States and thought it would be simpler than getting a tourist visa every time they want to visit. Of course, some among the 18 percent will actually fall in love with the United States, starting the assimilation process somewhat later than others in their cohort.

A Closer Look at Language and Spatial Concentration: Ethnic Enclaves

Humans communicate in words, and it is natural that immigrants would gravitate toward those with whom they can communicate. If they know English, they can communicate with anyone and go anywhere; if they only know their native language, they have a restricted set of communication partners and limited options for finding a job, a place to live, and places to shop, eat, and go to the movies. Thus, new immigrants with limited English fluency may choose to live near kin or conationals—who, besides being able to communicate with them, can impart useful information about the destination locale and can indeed join with them in a form of mutual protection society.

Geographic areas that attract large numbers of persons of any single kind have come to be called **ethnic enclaves**. As numbers of residents, as well as shops and restaurants featuring goods and foods of the country of origin, grow, these enclaves acquire distinctive names and images. They include Little Havana in Miami, Little Italy in New York and Baltimore, Koreatown in Los Angeles, Spanish-language *barrios* and *colonias* all across America, and the Chinatowns of San Francisco, New York, and Los Angeles.

Our discussion is framed in terms of decisions that immigrants make about where to live and work. But the very idea of an enclave has roots in historical periods when people were forced to live with their similars (on some dimension). Examples include settlements outside the city walls (such as Irishtowns for expelled Vikings and Irish after the Norman invasion of Ireland in the twelfth century), distinctive quarters of a city (such as the biblical and medieval Jewish quarters), and Jewish ghettoes in Europe and black ghettoes in the United States.

What are the benefits and challenges of ethnic enclaves?

Here, immigrants to America are studying English. Language acquisition is a key part of the assimilation process for migrants in a new land.

It is important to distinguish between geographic places and the people who pass through them. For example, Little Italy in New York City (not far from the offices of the authors of this chapter) is a well-defined geographic area with its own coordinates. Originally, it was place where large numbers of Italian immigrants settled. But over-time, it lost its distinctive ethnic character. Today, it has the flavor of a theme park—a place with Italian restaurants and shops selling Italian-themed goods for tourists and visitors—but it is otherwise a diverse place with many different kinds of people living there.

From the standpoint of the assimilation process, the key questions raised by this discussion include: Which immigrants are more likely to live or work in an enclave? For given skills, what is the wage penalty associated with working in an enclave? For given language skills, how is the speed of learning English affected by living or working in an enclave? Also, does a special form of English that is different from standard English develop in enclaves?

Research on these questions is ongoing. For now, the available research suggests the following: Higher economic rewards are associated with knowledge of English overall, but the cost of not knowing English is smaller in areas with greater concentration of persons speaking the same non-English language. Foreign-born individuals who expect to spend less time in the United States (either because they do not intend to stay or because they are elderly) are more likely to live in locations with high concentrations of people speaking the same language and less likely to invest in learning English, whereas those who expect to stay permanently are more likely to move out of the enclave.

4 What Are the Consequences of Immigration?

THE IMPACTS OF IMMIGRATION

Watch the **Big Question** Video in **MySocLab**

I mmigration is controversial in both the United States and around the world because it has wide-reaching effects on the sending country, on the receiving country, and on individuals and families in both countries, including natives, immigrants, and the children of immigrants. Social scientists and government officials have spent a great deal of time trying to estimate both the benefits and costs for the United States. Sociologists are also particularly interested in the impact of immigration pay on families and children, as we explore in this section.

☐ Immigration Dilemmas for Families

The process of obtaining LPR status discussed earlier is more straightforward for individuals than for families and is easier, overall, the greater the financial resources of the prospective immigrant (and sponsor). To appreciate the complexity of the process for families and the effect of financial resources, consider two families from the Dominican Republic.

In the first family, the wife is a physician and the husband is a software engineer with a baccalaureate degree who was sponsored by a U.S. firm for an employment visa. They have two children, a five-year-old and a six-month-old infant. Both the wife and the two children were included on the husband's visa application as accompanying family members. After all the requisite documents were collected (including national identity cards, police records, military service records, etc.) and the family was interviewed, they obtained visas. For this family, the process was smooth. They arrived in 2008 and settled in an affluent suburb in New Jersey. Eventually they had a third child. The total duration of the visa process was about three years.

Contrast this story with that of a second family. In this family, the husband is a welder and the wife a bank teller. They had hoped that his occupation would qualify him for a visa in the subcategory for skilled workers. However, no opportunity ever materialized. They became eligible, however, when the wife's brother, a naturalized U.S. citizen, offered to sponsor her. To prepare for their visas, they collected all the same documents that the first family had collected, including birth certificates for their three children—ages 17 (girl), 13 (boy), and 6 (girl). Additionally, however, because the visa is in a family-sponsored category rather than an employment-based category, they needed an affidavit of support signed by the sponsor. After much figuring and calculating and searching for a joint sponsor, they concluded that the financial requirements for the whole family could not be met. Reluctantly, and sadly, they decided to leave their three children with the children's grandparents in the Dominican Republic. The couple arrived in New York City in 2008 and moved into the predominantly immigrant neighborhood of Washington Heights. For them, the visa process lasted 12 years—9 years longer than for the first family we described (because the visa queue is so much longer in the family-based categories than in the employment-based categories).

Because of the amount of time that had passed, the children in this second family could no longer be brought as accompanying children; they would have to be sponsored. There would be a wait for visas to become available. So the couple set out to work as hard as possible in order to accumulate the financial resources to sponsor their children and qualify financially for the affidavit of support. The children's priority date was February 15, 2010, and visas became available in July 2012. Unfortunately, the eldest daughter married, losing her eligibility, and, further, the couple was unable to find the resources to sponsor both of the two younger children. The family thus faced the wrenching decision of which child to bring to the United States—the middle child or the youngest?

The couple decided to bring the middle son, who shows great promise as a student. This child attends school and works part time in the neighborhood grocery store to supplement the family's income in order to satisfy the financial requirements for bringing the youngest child. There is a pervasive grief in the family because there is no visa category available for the eldest daughter—no pathway for the married child of an LPR. Only if one of the parents naturalizes would it become possible to sponsor her as the married child of a U.S. citizen. The couple does not even become eligible to naturalize until 2013, and they are worried that they will not yet have the requisite English language skills.

There is a note of joy, however. While in the United States, the couple had a fourth child. This is a golden child, a U.S. citizen by birth. The family is blended—and divided. Around this time, the grandparents in the Dominican Republic experienced some health problems, and the couple started to think they should bring their third child, now 10 years old. But how? They cannot yet sponsor her immigration because they cannot meet the financial requirements. The family continues to hope that somehow they will find the resources or that the rules will change or that they will find a new joint sponsor.

There is a further lingering regret. If the family could have immigrated when it first applied, all the children would be completely fluent in English and speak it without an accent. But the long waits for numerically limited family visas and the financial requirements made that impossible. With every passing day, the dream fades.

Notice how different the two scenarios are, and notice the part played by money. The second family's story could have been as short as the first's had they commanded the resources to satisfy the financial requirements for bringing all three of their children as accompanying children when the adults obtained LPR—when it was straightforward to bring them, the children were all still young and unmarried, and there was no further wait for a numerically limited visa.

The irony is that family reunification is the cornerstone of U.S. immigration law, and yet the many complexities in the law, the many moving parts, often serve to divide families. The further irony is that the United States long celebrated its welcoming of the poor but now makes it all but impossible for poor people to come here legally.

☐ Children of Migration

What about the children of families that migrate? The distinct sets of children affected by international migration are (1) foreign-born children living with their foreign-born parents in the United States; (2) native-born children living with their foreign-born parents in the United States; (3) foreign-born children living in the origin country, including (a) those left behind by parents who are in the United States and (b) those living with their foreign-born parents but who already have a link to the United States (such as being in the queue for a numerically limited visa); and (4) native-born children living in the parental origin country, including (a) those sent by parents who are in the United States to be raised in the origin country and (b) those living with their foreign-born parents who have no intention of returning to the United States. Each of these sets of children has been studied and discussed by sociologists and other social scientists.

What happens to the children of immigrants?

Much attention has been paid to children living in the destination country that were born to foreign-born parents—the **second generation**. These are the golden children, U.S. citizens from birth, raised in the United States, eligible to become president of the United States, heirs to both the parental migrant energy and all the opportunities of the new country. A large research literature indicates that these quintessential second-generation children do better than their parents.

And indeed, classically, they have outperformed their parents and outperformed their third- and higher-generation counterparts. Many of the great scientific and artistic advances in the United States have been made by these second-generation children. Why has this so often been the case?

To understand the second-generation effect, it is important to understand the conditions under which it can be expected. When immigrants come from countries where they were unable to develop their potential, so that they have lower schooling and fewer skills than they would have obtained under more favorable circumstances, it is completely natural that their children, inheriting similar potential but placed in a situation where they can develop that potential, will outperform the parents. Moreover, the children inherit at least a portion of their parents' migrant energy, and thus will outperform third- and higher-generation children of similar potential.

The great migration at the turn of the twentieth century brought to the United States immigrants who for reasons of poverty or religion or gender were severely underschooled— brilliant men who had left school in the third grade to fend off starvation, brilliant women who were illiterate. It is no surprise that their offspring would become great scientists, musicians, and writers.

But much has changed in the 110 or 120 years since the great migration. In particular, the United States increasingly favors the immigration of the highly skilled. So what would one expect today? First, the children of highly educated parents will not outperform their parents. How can they? If their parents have PhDs, what can they do to outschool their parents? Moreover, they have attenuated migrant energy; no matter how much of it they inherit, it cannot match the migrant energy of the actual migrants. Second, however, they are likely to outperform third- and higher-generation

counterparts of the same potential because they do inherit some of their parents' migrant energy.

A recent study of the 8-to-12-year-old children of immigrants in the New Immigrant Survey compared English fluency between children born in the United States and children brought before the age of four (Jasso 2011). The children born in the United States had a significantly higher probability of being fluent in English than those who immigrated at a young age.

Another question concerns the effects on children of growing up in unauthorized status or with parents who are unauthorized. For many families, this is an indefinite condition, with some or all family members unauthorized and no remedy in sight. Research on children ages 8 through 12 found that the probability of being fluent in English was higher among children whose parents had illegal experience than among children whose parents had never been unauthorized (Jasso 2011). Why would having parents with unauthorized status have a positive effect on children's fluency

Robert K. Merton (1910-2003), one of the most distinguished sociologists in the twentieth-century, was a second generation immigrant. Merton's Yiddish-speaking Jewish parents moved to the U.S. from Russia in 1904, settling in Philadelphia where Merton was born and raised.

in English? One possible reason is that children who have seen the hardships of illegality are equipping themselves for their new life. Another is that they may have gained English fluency by translating for their parents (Valdés 2003).

Children left behind in the origin country or sent there after birth in the U.S. by parents who remain in the United States also merit special study. But why would a child be left behind? There are several reasons. First, as mentioned above, some visa categories do not provide visas for the children of new LPRs; examples include visas for the parent of a U.S. citizen and for the unmarried child under 21 of a U.S. citizen. Second, new LPRs who can bring their minor children as accompanying children may not have the financial resources necessary for bringing all of them. Third, by the time a numerically limited visa becomes available, the children may have lost eligibility for visas as accompanying family members, either because they married or because they aged out. The story of the second family above exemplified some of these reasons for leaving children behind.

How does the new LPR who has children abroad decide whether to sponsor the child for immigration or instead send financial support for him or her abroad? Recent research indicates that parents are more likely to sponsor children who are more educated and live in low-wage countries, whereas they are more likely to send money to children who are less educated and live in low-wage countries (Jasso and Rosenzweig 2012). Thus, parents appear to maximize their children's income and redress inequality between them.

Additional questions that merit further study concern the effects of household structure and of the larger social environment on children of immigrants. These reflect views that children may suffer greatly if one or more family members is unauthorized—either via mechanisms of compassion or because the family's coping strategies may significantly curtail opportunities for the nonunauthorized child. Other questions pertain to the possibly beneficial effects of native step-siblings and half-siblings. Finally, discriminatory tendencies in the larger social environment may negatively affect the child's development, either directly or by limiting parents' ability to invest in their children and nurture their cognitive and noncognitive skills. Of course, there will always be children who rise above all adversity, and indeed, use it as a force for good. But their numbers may not be large.

Social and Economic Benefits and Costs

Migration potentially produces benefits and costs not only for the migrants and their native sponsors but also for the larger society and economy. Research on the 1996 cohort

What are the social and economic benefits and risks of immigration into the United States?

of new legal immigrants shows that soon after admission to LPR, the average gain in earnings from the last job abroad to the first job in the United States (with foreign earnings adjusting for cost of living by converting them into dollar amounts based on estimates of the country-specific purchasing power of the currencies) was $10,306 for men (a 68 percent increase) and $6,146 for women (a 62 percent increase). At the same time, however, 28 percent of the new male immigrants and 27 percent of the new female immigrants were earning less at their job in the United States than in their last job abroad (Jasso, Massey, Rosenzweig, and Smith 2000).

For the United States as a whole, questions about the impacts of immigration are pervasive. Many Americans express concern about the effects of immigration on population size, population growth, the environment, competition in the workplace, the jobs and earnings of natives, public health, public safety, the national treasury, and state and local budgets. Such concerns are not always easy to address, in part because the effects of immigration are spread out across a vast economy and a vast society but may be disproportionately felt in certain locales.

Periodically, there are large-scale efforts to study in a rigorous way the impacts of immigration on the United States. These include several major government commissions and panels, such as the Dillingham Commission (1907–1911), the U.S. Select Commission on Immigration and Refugee Policy (1979–1981), the U.S. Commission on Immigration Reform (1990–1997), and the National Academy of Sciences–National Research Council's Panel on Demographic and Economic Impacts of Immigration (1995–1997). These commissions consult with a wide variety of experts in an effort to reach some general conclusions, and they provide substantial evidence for assessing the impact of immigration.

A more recent effort to assess the impacts of immigration on the United States was carried out by President George W. Bush's Council of Economic Advisers, which issued a "White Paper" on June 20, 2007. The report, like previous reports such as that of the National Research Council (Smith and Edmonston 1997), noted the difficulties in disentangling the effect of immigration from the effects of other economic forces and in projecting costs and benefits into the future, while also noting the progress that social scientists have made in addressing this question.

The report presented three key findings:

1. On average, U.S. citizens benefit from immigration. Immigrants tend to complement (not substitute for) natives, raising natives' productivity and income.
2. Careful studies of the long-run effects of immigration on government budgets conclude that it is likely to have

a modest positive influence (on average, immigrants pay more in taxes than they receive in government benefits).

3. Skilled immigrants are likely to be especially beneficial to natives. In addition to contributions to innovation, they have a significant positive fiscal impact.

The report concluded that immigration not only helps fuel the country's economic growth but also has a positive effect on the income of native-born workers.

In summarizing the research that led to its key findings and final conclusion, the report notes a number of striking facts. For example, an astonishing 40 percent of PhD scientists working in the United States were born abroad. As the technical requirements of an increasingly high-tech economy increase, the United States is not producing enough mathematicians and scientists to fill the jobs being created by the new economy. However, America is fortunate that many highly skilled scientists, mathematicians, computer programmers, and engineers from other countries want to live and work in the United States. The presence of these workers helps keep American companies competitive in global markets and generates other jobs here.

☐ Remittances

When migrants leave their hometown and country of origin, they take their skills and abilities to another place. They also often leave behind relatives and friends—sometimes close family members like spouses and children. Whether the trip is temporary or permanent, migrants often provide monetary gifts, bequests, loans, or other financial help to those left behind. Indeed, often the very purpose of the migration is to obtain financial resources to support the family in the origin country. These transfers are known as **migrant remittances**, and they constitute an extremely important source of income for individuals, families, and households around the world and especially in developing countries (Maimbo and Ratha 2005; Rapoport and Docquier 2006; World Bank 2011a).

The World Bank (2011a) estimates that worldwide remittance flows exceeded about US$440 billion in 2010. The United States was the top source, with $48.3 billion in recorded remittances. About $325 billion went to developing countries. As the World Bank (2011b) notes, "remittances sent home by migrants to developing countries are three times the size of official development assistance and represent a lifeline for the poor."

Remittances sent back home represent only one of two directions of monetary and nonmonetary flows. Money and goods are also sent from the origin country to assist migrants in the destination country, for example, to pay college tuition, buy a home, start a business, or make a film. Accordingly, the broader term **transfers** is used to denote flows

in both directions. To illustrate, migrants in the United States send remittances to other countries—estimated by the World Bank (2011a) at $48.3 billion in 2010. At the same time, international students and others living in the United States—temporarily or permanently—often receive allowances and other financial assistance from their family abroad. An extreme case of such financial help involves the most expensive apartment ever sold in New York City (at the time of the sale), purchased in March 2012 for $88 million for a student from Russia [Barrionuevo 2012]).

Sociologists and other social scientists study migrant remittances, attempting to understand three main things: (1) the amounts of transfers in both directions; (2) the determinants of sending or receiving transfers; and (3) the consequences of remittances for individuals, households, and countries. With respect to the magnitude of remittance flows, researchers almost universally

Does immigration benefit the United States?

Immigrant workers, even many of those earning low wages, such as this migrant worker in Oregon, will often send money back home to help family and friends.

believe that the true size, including unrecorded flows through both formal and informal channels, is larger than the recorded flows (World Bank 2011a). Recorded statistics, incomplete though they may be, provide a window into remittance flows. Table 12.4 reports the top 15 remittance-sending and remittance-receiving countries. As shown, besides the United States, other countries in the top five remittance-sending countries are Saudi Arabia, Switzerland, Russia, and Germany. The top five remittance-receiving countries are India, China, Mexico, the Philippines, and France. India and China have large populations, and, not surprisingly, remittances received exceed $50 billion each, more than twice the remittances received by the much smaller Mexico and Philippines.

The second focus among researchers pertains to the characteristics of migrants and their link to sending transfers, especially remittances, and the amount of remittances. Ideas about altruism and about familial contracts and insurance permeate the research literature. Two key findings have been established. First, temporary migrants are more likely to send remittances. Second, sending remittances seems to be unresponsive to external shocks such as economic recessions. Finally, the patterns of results suggest that sending remittances may be usefully interpreted as part of a familial contract.

Data from the New Immigrant Survey provide the first information on the remittance behavior of a cohort of legal immigrants in the United States. The data indicate that, during the 12 months preceding the interview, about 20.3 percent of the 2003 cohort sent money to relatives and friends and 12.4 percent received money (Jasso 2012). These averages hide a lot of variation in transfer behavior across visa classes. Persons who obtained their green card as the parent or minor child of a U.S. citizen had among the lowest rates of remittances (7.41 percent and 3.79 percent, respectively) and among the highest rates of receipts (16.6 percent and 24 percent, respectively). At the other end of the spectrum, the highest rates of remittances were among employment-based and legalization immigrants (31.3 percent and 40.2 percent, respectively), with correspondingly low rates of receipts (5.15 percent and 1.41 percent).

What about effects of remittances? There is little doubt that remittances improve the daily lives of recipients. Remittances can be used to pay utility bills, send children to school, improve housing, obtain medical care, or purchase vehicles. Other questions pertain to the effect of remittances on a country's development, its economic growth, and economic inequality. Rapoport and Docquier (2006) conclude that the overall effect of remittances on origin countries' long-run economic performance is positive. Especially for poor countries, remittances sent back provide a valuable infusion of resources that enhance living standards.

Remittances would, however, be even more valuable if the costs of sending funds were reduced. The amount sent is never the amount received; high bank fees greatly reduce

TABLE 12.4 MIGRANT REMITTANCES: MAJOR SENDING AND RECEIVING COUNTRIES, 2010

Country	Billions of U.S. Dollars
A. Top 15 Sending Countries	
United States	48.3
Saudi Arabia	26.0
Switzerland	19.6
Russian Federation	18.6
Germany	15.9
Italy	13.0
Spain	12.6
Luxembourg	10.6
Kuwait	9.9
Netherlands	8.1
Malaysia	6.8
Lebanon	5.7
Oman	5.3
France	5.2
China	4.4
B. Top 15 Receiving Countries	
India	55.0
China	51.0
Mexico	22.6
Philippines	21.3
France	15.9
Germany	11.6
Bangladesh	11.1
Belgium	10.4
Spain	10.2
Nigeria	10.0
Pakistan	9.4
Poland	9.1
Lebanon	8.2
Egypt	7.7
United Kingdom	7.4

Source: World Bank (2011a).

the value of remittances. These fees are estimated to average 13 percent and go as high as 20 percent (Maimbo and Ratha 2005) or in extreme cases to 25 percent (Rapoport and Docquier 2006). Obviously, both the sender and the recipient—and the receiving country—would be better off with less expensive mechanisms for sending funds.

CONCLUSION IMMIGRATION AND THE FUTURE

International migration raises a host of interesting questions for social scientists and government policymakers, and for both families and countries. The initial scientific questions about immigration—such as who migrates, how do they fare in the destination country, and what are the impacts of immigration—quickly lead to further questions. Does the ease of learning and using the destination country's language depend on certain affinities between the two languages, such as whether they are gendered or distinguish between the formal and the familiar "you" (e.g., French *tu* versus *vous*)? How do cities develop and evolve to incorporate migrants and migration streams? In the future, migration questions and the larger questions of social science will merge, shaping and deepening our understanding of both.

In a very real sense, immigration serves as a superb laboratory for all the social sciences, revealing how humans develop, maintain, and discard identities; how family and household structures change; how societies develop, maintain, and discard hierarchies; how groups allocate scarce benefits; how groups decide whom to include and whom to exclude; and how economic inequality and inequality between subgroups grow and diminish. As the world becomes increasingly connected and globalized, the study of immigration is becoming central for sociology. Recent work argues that migration and social stratification are so intertwined that soon it will be impossible to study one without the other. The same might be said about all the topical domains of sociology and many of the chapters in this book—on family, religion, cities, and political behavior.

What is striking about the history of immigration into the United States is how deeply controversial it has been. For a country that was built by immigrants, that has historically prided itself on welcoming new immigrants, and that has benefited so immensely from the special skills, talents, and hard work of waves of immigrants, it is remarkable how anti-immigrant sentiment has frequently roiled beneath the surface. Today, immigration is once again increasingly controversial, with many politicians calling for new limits on who may live in the United States.

What will the future bring? The biggest challenge is to revise immigration law, making it simpler, more coherent, and more intelligent. But that is daunting because no one knows how to approach the question of giving and taking away visa entitlements. It has become fashionable for politicians and others in public life to say they are eager to undertake comprehensive immigration reform but that first the problem of illegal migration must be addressed. This may not be entirely sensible. Illegal migration is a direct consequence of the rules for legal migration. Put simply, persons ineligible for legal visas will, under different circumstances, become illegal migrants. As long as people are excluded or limited, there will be illegal migration. To their great credit, the legislators of the 1920s understood this, and that is why, as we saw, not long after passage of the 1924 National Origins Act, Congress passed a law providing a mechanism for illegals to legalize (the Registry Act of 1929). It will take enormous ingenuity to take this tolerance into account when deciding how to allocate visas. At first blush, it might seem impossible, given that prospective migrants with the lowest tolerance for illegality—who could be excluded from eligibility without seriously increasing illegal migration—may be the ones deemed most desirable.

More deeply, the United States is perennially at a crossroads, caught between two visions of America, one an open society that welcomes many foreigners, the other a relatively closed country that only lets in a few. Throughout American history, there is unease with newcomers, especially if they do not resemble natives. Yet the children of the newcomers, and certainly their grandchildren, morph into natives, and it is universally proclaimed that the latest wave of newcomers is different from the current descendants of earlier waves of newcomers. The correct comparison would be between each wave of newcomers as it was perceived by contemporaneous natives. Is it time for a new fifth era? Or will the future be a new version of the fourth era's restrictions? Will the image of the second and third generations trump the reality of the first generation? Will the future diamonds be visible in the rough stones?

As better data become available and knowledge about international migration and its impacts on sending and receiving countries grows, more and more of the classical questions sketched in this chapter will begin to be answered. And new questions will emerge. Immigration is a vast frontier, and its study a great adventure that illuminates not only immigration but also everything in its reach—language acquisition and use, identity construction, urban development, inequality. This duality echoes the classic idea in American history: Immigrants thought they were building new lives, but what they were building was a new nation.

1 What Is Immigration, and How Has It Changed Over Time? *(p. 322)*

👁 **Watch** the **Big Question Video** in **MySocLab** to review the key concepts for this section.

What kinds of things do sociologists study when they study immigration? And why is the study of immigration important for understanding the world we live in? In this section we defined the basic concepts and ideas in the study of immigration, and then examined some of these in the context of the United States and its immigrant history.

IMMIGRATION: A SOCIOLOGICAL PERSPECTIVE (p. 322)

The Basic Structure of Immigration Policy in the United States (p. 324)

● **What privileges does U.S. citizenship confer?**

The Legal Permanent Resident Visa System (p. 326)

Becoming a U.S. Citizen (p. 326)

● **How do immigrants become U.S. citizens?**

⊙→ **Explore** A Sociological Perspective: What makes a barrier a border? in **MySocLab**

A Brief History of U.S. Immigration (p. 328)

● **What are the four eras of immigration in U.S. history?**

⊙→ **Explore** the **Data** on Coming to America in **MySocLab**

KEY TERMS

migration *(p. 322)*

emigration *(p. 322)*

immigration *(p. 322)*

social structure *(p. 322)*

receiving country *(p. 322)*

sending country *(p. 322)*

brain drain *(p. 323)*

diaspora *(p. 323)*

visa *(p. 324)*

emigration and immigration policy *(p. 324)*

legal permanent resident (LPR) *(p. 324)*

foreign-born citizen *(p. 324)*

legal temporary resident *(p. 324)*

unauthorized migrant *(p. 324)*

refugee status *(p. 324)*

asylum status *(p. 325)*

principal *(p. 325)*

green card *(p. 326)*

naturalization *(p. 326)*

first immigration era *(p. 328)*

second immigration era *(p. 328)*

third immigration era *(p. 329)*

Bracero Program *(p. 329)*

fourth immigration era *(p. 330)*

2 Why Do People Move? (p. 332)

👁 **Watch** the **Big Question Video** in **MySocLab** to review the key concepts for this section.

People move for many reasons, but the most fundamental of these is the desire to make a better life for themselves and their children. Sociologists are interested in the characteristics of both movers and stayers as well as the countries they come from and the countries in which they settle. Distinguishing between these different categories of people and places provides important insights into the dynamics of the migration process.

SELF-SELECTION, PUSH AND PULL FACTORS, AND MIGRATION DYNAMICS (p. 332)

The Desire to Move and Migrant Energy (p. 332)

● **What factors influence the desire to move?**

Movers and Stayers (p. 333)

● **What is the distinction between a mover and a stayer?**

KEY TERMS

push factors (p. 332)

pull factors (p. 332)

migrant energy (p. 332)

self-selected (p. 332)

movers (p. 333)

stayers (p. 333)

3 How Do Immigrants Fare in Their New Environments? (p. 334)

👁 **Watch** the **Big Question Video** in **MySocLab** to review the key concepts for this section.

Sociologists are especially interested in what happens to migrants after moving as they encounter a new society and its social, economic, and political systems. In this section we explored a host of interesting questions raised by the process of assimilation—during which immigrants adapt to the new society they are living in.

THE ASSIMILATION PROCESS (p. 334)

Measures of Assimilation (p. 334)

● **What measures help us gauge how well an immigrant has assimilated?**

Recent Research on Immigrant Assimilation (p. 335)

● **What do sociologists take into consideration when researching immigrant assimilation?**

A Closer Look at Language and Spatial Concentration: Ethnic Enclaves (p. 337)

● **What are the benefits and challenges of ethnic enclaves?**

KEY TERMS

assimilation (p. 334)

socioeconomic status (SES) (p. 335)

spatial concentration (p. 335)

intermarriage (p. 335)

ethnic enclave (p. 337)

 Read the **Document** *Mexican Americans and Immigrant Incorporation* by Edward E. Telles in **MySocLab**. This reading examines how Mexican American immigrants and their children assimilate or become incorporated into mainstream society.

What Are the Consequences of Immigration? *(p. 338)*

Watch the **Big Question Video** in **MySocLab** to review the key concepts for this section.

Immigration is controversial in the United States and around the world because it has wide-reaching effects on the origin country, on the destination country, and on individuals and families in both countries, including natives, immigrants, and the children of immigrants. In this section we examined the benefits and potential costs of immigration.

Watch the **Video** Applying Your Sociological Imagination in **MySocLab** to see these concepts at work in the real world

13

FAMILIES and FAMILY LIFE

 **Listen** to the **Chapter Audio** in **MySocLab**

by KATHLEEN GERSON
with STACY TORRES

 hat's a typical family." We've all heard this phrase before, but is there a typical family? And how can we really know what life is like in someone else's home? Often our perceptions as outside observers are quite different from the perceptions of those who are family members. Consider the story of 24-year-old Josh, who grew up in Oceanside Terrace, a small working-class suburban community on Long Island not far from the hustle and bustle of New York City. In a survey, Josh had reported growing up with his biological parents and two brothers in a household where his mother stayed home during his preschool years. From the outside, Josh's childhood home seemed to be what Americans tend to think of as a typical, traditional family, but his family experience was much more complex than it appeared. Josh was back for a brief visit to celebrate his parents' anniversary before moving to a new job on the West Coast when I sat down with him one morning to talk about his family life.

Josh grew up with his biological parents and two brothers in the kind of household Americans like to call "traditional" (for an overview of this period, see Coontz 1992). His father was a carpenter, and his mother stayed home during his preschool years, but Josh recounts a sequence of events that left him feeling as if he lived in three different families. The first, anchored by a breadwinning father and a home-centered mother, did indeed take a traditional form. Yet this outward appearance mattered less to him than his parents' constant fighting over money, housework, and the drug habit his father developed in the army. "All I remember is just being real upset, not being able to look at the benefits if it would remain like that, having all the fighting and that element in the house," Josh tells me.

MY SOCIOLOGICAL IMAGINATION
Kathleen Gerson

My sociological imagination began when I realized I was part of—yet stood apart from—the world around me. Born in the deep South, I grew up in a community where traditional homes and worldviews were the norm. Yet my own family was headed by a single mother strongly committed to social justice. As I developed a sense of being both an insider and an outsider, I learned to see the world from several vantage points at once. A move to San Francisco during adolescence deepened my questioning of what others took for granted. By the time I reached college, these experiences had attuned me to the power of social contexts. Sociology offered a place to address the big issues facing contemporary societies. With that aim in mind, my research focuses on gender, work, and family life, with an eye to understanding the new work and family pathways emerging in the United States and other postindustrial societies. Although I rely on a range of methods, I specialize in qualitative interviewing. My goal is to uncover how personal biographies intersect with social institutions to bring about social change. I have written books and articles that offer innovative frameworks for explaining the revolution in gender, work, and family patterns, and my current research focuses on the new worlds of work and care, where occupational paths and personal relationships are increasingly uncertain.

A "one size fits all" model cannot describe the many shapes that today's families take nor the quality of the interactions among their members.

Watch the Video in **MySocLab**
Inspiring Your Sociological Imagination

As Josh reached school age, his home life took a major turn. His mother found a job as an administrator in a local business and, feeling more secure about her ability to support the family, asked her husband to move out and "either get straight or don't come back." Even though his father's departure was painful and unusual in this neighborhood where two-parent homes were the norm, Josh also felt relief. His parents' separation provided space for his mother to renew her self-esteem through her work outside the home. Josh missed his father, but he also came to accept this new situation as the better of two less-than-perfect alternatives.

A "one size fits all" model cannot describe the many shapes that today's families take, nor can it capture the quality of interactions among their members.

Yet Josh's family changed again a year later when Josh's father "got clean" and returned home. Even more remarkable, when his parents reunited, they hardly seemed the same couple. Time away had given his father a new appreciation for the family and a deepened desire for greater involvement in his children's lives. Josh's mother displayed major changes as well, for taking a job had given her pride in knowing she could stand on her own. As his father became more attentive and his mother more self-confident, the family's spirits and fortunes lifted. In Josh's words, "that changed the whole family dynamic. We got extremely close."

In the years that followed, Josh watched his parents build a new partnership quite different from the conflict-ridden one he experienced in his earliest years. He developed a new and closer relationship with his father, whom he came to see as one of his best friends. He also valued his mother's strengthening ties to work, which not only nourished her sense of self but also provided enough additional income for him to attend college.

Josh's story exemplifies several important but often hidden truths about family life in contemporary societies. First, families are not "types" but are rather a set of dynamic processes and unfolding pathways that develop in unexpected ways over time. Despite the apparent stability and continuity his family may have shown on a survey checklist, a closer look revealed a domestic life that actually changed in fundamental ways. Second, families can look very different depending on one's point of view. Survey and census questions may reveal a snapshot of how a family looks at one or even several points in time, but an in-depth interview that charts the ups and downs of family life is more likely to reveal how family life is an unfolding pathway where crucial events often trigger unexpected transitions and unforeseen outcomes. Third, families come in all shapes and sizes, and it is misleading to assume that one type is better than another. A "one size fits all" model cannot describe the many shapes that today's families take, nor can it capture the quality of interactions among their members.

Finally, and perhaps most crucially, Josh's story reveals how the tumultuous changes of the last several decades require us to think in new ways about family life in the United States and other advanced, postindustrial societies. In a rapidly changing world, his parents were neither able nor willing to maintain a static set of arrangements for organizing their marriage or providing emotional and financial support to their children. As they developed new responses to a host of unexpected events, Josh's family changed dramatically. Its shift from a breadwinner-homemaker to a single-parent to a dual-earner home exemplifies both the growing diversity of family forms and the increasingly fluid nature of family life. These changes offer today's young adults options their parents barely imagined and their grandparents could not envision. Yet they also pose new challenges for creating and sustaining intimate relationships, for bearing and rearing children, and for integrating earning a living with caring for others. In the context of twenty-first century America, some families may thrive and others may not, but all of today's families face uncharted territory.

Families are films, not snapshots, and family life is an unfolding, unpredictable process. Actress Sandra Bullock adopted her son, Louis, just months before making the decision to divorce her husband.

THE BIG QUESTIONS

👁 **Watch** the **Big Question Videos** in **MySocLab**

To make sense of family life, both in the American context and beyond, this chapter will consider a variety of questions.

1 **What is a family?** To begin at the beginning, we first need to examine the meaning of the term *family*. What is a family, and what are the various ways to define it? Answering this question leads to the next one.

2 **Why has family life become the topic of such heated debate?** To understand the contemporary debate over "family values," we need to map out the competing views about the current state of the American family as well as how we got here and what we need to do in response.

3 **What challenges do we face as we develop relationships and balance family and work?** Some pressing issues that affect American families today include the decline of permanent marriage and the new contours of adult commitment, as well as the blurring of gender divisions and the rise of work-family conflict.

4 **What is it like to grow up in a twenty-first century family?** The experiences of children growing up in twenty-first century families and transitioning to adulthood are very different than they once were. How have these changes affected children and young adults?

5 **What causes inequality among families?** The causes of family inequality are complex and difficult to isolate, especially because the economy is changing and gender, race, and ethnic diversity intersect with class differences.

6 **What social policies around the world best support changing families?** Finally, we will place this overview of American family life today in a comparative perspective. By examining how other countries have experienced and tackled many of the same challenges, we will be in a better position to create the supports that American families will need to thrive in the

1   What Is a Family?

THE MANY WAYS WE DEFINE *FAMILY*

Watch the Big Question Video in **MySocLab**

The family is a core institution in all societies. It provides the first and most immediate context for our physical, emotional, and social development. As we age, family issues confront us with many of life's most crucial choices—whether and whom to marry, how to shape our sexual activity, whether to bear children and how many to bear, and how to raise the children we choose to have. Families influence us in ways so deep that it is difficult to exaggerate their importance. Yet their power to shape our destiny depends on their links to other institutions. Families are shaped by the societies they inhabit, but they also have the power to transform those societies.

Most of us think we know what a family is, even if we cannot always offer a precise definition. As the saying goes, we think we know a family when we see one. Yet "the family" can have many meanings. In this section we will explore how we define family, starting with a global and historical perspective.

What are some family forms that can be found throughout human history and across diverse societies and households?

earning an income, a wife who focuses on childrearing and housekeeping, and their biological children. Yet this term is inaccurate and misleading. From a global and long-term historical perspective, it is clear that the independent homemaker-breadwinner household is a relatively rare, modern, and short-lived arrangement. Many other family forms can be found throughout human history and across diverse societies and cultures. Patterns such as arranged marriages, **polygamy** (when a person, typically a man, has multiple marital partners, typically wives), and multigenerational households, for example, were common prior to the rise of modernity in the West, and they continue to hold sway in many non-Western cultures. Some societies, especially those ruled by monarchies, have allowed marriages between cousins and even siblings among the ruling elite in order to keep the transfer of inherited power within an enclosed family system. And some cultures, deemed **patrilocal**, require a wife to live with her husband's parents and obey their authority.

The homemaker-breadwinner household that Americans often label *traditional* actually rose to prominence in the mid-twentieth century, largely as a consequence of post-World War II prosperity and the growth of the suburbs. While a majority of American households took this form for much of the 1950s, many did not. Working-class and minority communities, in particular, were more likely to find

☐ A Global and Historical Perspective

Though families are a universal social institution, their forms vary greatly across diverse social settings. Americans tend to think that the traditional family consists of an independent household anchored by a husband who concentrates on

the middle-class ideal of the traditional family either out of reach or unappealing. Equally important, many husbands and wives who lived in these "traditional" households found them unnecessarily stifling. When renowned feminist Betty Friedan spoke of middle-class women's confinement to domesticity as "the problem that has no name" (Friedan [2001] 1963: 57) and sociologist William Whyte (1956) referred to the conformity expected of the "organization man," they both identified a growing sense of unease about the reigning 1950s family structure.

Since that time, American families have changed in vast and unexpected ways, reminding us that the history of family life is a history of change. We have seen the rise of a diverse array of family forms, including dual-earner, single-parent, same-sex, and single-adult homes, which now vie with breadwinner-homemaker households for social and cultural support. Because these changes leave no one untouched, family life has become the site of both private struggles and public contention. If the 1950s produced a misleading belief in "the ideal family," the twenty-first century leaves us facing instead a series of puzzles and paradoxes. Is the family declining, or is it here to stay? Do families shape people, or do people shape families? Is there one best family form, or is it better to have a variety of family forms and practices? When it comes to these (and many other) questions, there are no simple answers. Instead, we need a sociological lens that allows us to see family life from a variety of perspectives, just as a prism allows us to see light in all of its hues.

☐ Kinship System or Household?

For demographers, *families* refer to groups of people who live together in households and share legal ties. Anthropologists, in contrast, see families as **kinship systems**—the social links and boundaries, defined by biology and social custom, that establish who is related to whom. In modern settings, and especially in the contemporary United States, it is common to stress the emotional bonds that connect people who care deeply about each other, whether or not they are linked by concrete bonds of law or biology. Many people today thus refer to their close friends—and even their pets—as "family" (Powell et al. 2010).

None of these definitions is either right or wrong, nor is one inherently better than another. The value of any definition depends instead on its usefulness in explaining the social world, and that can change with the social puzzle that needs solving. Sociologists thus conceive of the family as a social institution with multiple dimensions—"the familistic package," as sociologist William J. Goode once described it (Goode 1982). This package of social relationships can consist of a network of **kin**, a group of people who share a residence, or even the cultural meanings and perceptions that ordinary people use to decide which groupings they consider family and which they do not.

Since the peaking of the homemaker-breadwinner household in the mid-twentieth century, we have seen the rise of a diverse array of family forms, including single-parent homes.

Sociologists also distinguish between the families we inherit and the families we create (Streuning 2010). Our "family of orientation" consists of the people linked to us by birth—our parents, siblings, and extended kin. Our "family of procreation," in contrast, consists of the relatives we gain over the course of our lives through marriage and childbearing—our spouses, partners, and children. Yet in postindustrial societies, these terms seem overly simple and out of date. Now that openly acknowledged same-sex relationships are on the rise and many people sustain committed partnerships that do not involve legally sanctioned marriage or childbearing, the term *procreation* cannot encompass the wide range of chosen families that are emerging in the contemporary United States and elsewhere.

Our definitions also shape the questions we can pose about family life. If we define families as systems of kinship, our focus turns to questions about how kinship links and boundaries are mapped in any given society: Who counts as a member of the **nuclear family**—that is, the socially recognized parents and their dependent children—and who counts as extended kin? In premodern societies, for example, kinship lines include a number of people who extend far beyond the nuclear unit to encompass a whole clan, and in some tribal societies, the biological parents are not necessarily recognized as the social parents. For example, the work of the pioneering anthropologist Bronislaw Malinwoski found that among a tribe known as the Trobriand Islanders, a child's uncle—that is, his or her mother's brother—performed many of the social functions that modern Western societies associate with fatherhood, such as providing material support and enforcing discipline, while a child's biological father acted in a similar way toward his sister's children (Malinowski 1913).

Who do you consider to be your family? Many people today refer to their close friends (and even their pets) as "family."

Modern societies, in contrast, draw boundaries that limit kin to a much smaller number of people, rarely extending beyond cousins and second cousins (Levi-Strauss 1964). Because modern societies are large and complex, they have fewer concerns about intermarriage within kinship groups than do simple societies. Yet this complexity also requires more attention to creating legal standards for who is and is not a family member as well as for establishing the lines of responsibility and obligation among family members. The rise of divorce, remarriage, and out-of-wedlock childbearing has complicated these concerns. Equally important, the rise of reproductive technologies means that a rising number of children have both social parents and biological parents, including a sperm donor, an egg donor, or a surrogate mother. As the boundaries and definitions of parenthood blur and grow rapidly, kinship systems become more difficult to chart.

If we view families as households, our attention turns to residence patterns: Who lives together in households, and how are these households distributed geographically? The U.S. Census Bureau, for example, focuses on household units. In collecting and analyzing census data, the bureau defines *family* as a set of people living together who are connected by biological or legal ties and distinguishes these family households from nonfamily households, which consist of two or more individuals living together who are not linked by biological or legal ties—such as a group of college roommates or young singles sharing an apartment. By using this definition, moreover, the Census Bureau explicitly includes married couples (with and without children) and single parents living with their children in the category of family while excluding childless couples who are not married but living together, whether straight or gay.

Yet many people disagree with such a strict definition, preferring instead to use more subjective measures. A recent national survey found that Americans offered a variety of criteria for deciding when a household is a family (Pew 2010). Being married and having children are cited most often, with 99 percent agreeing that a married couple with children makes a family. Yet that figure drops to 88 percent for a married couple without children, to 86 percent for

singles with children, to 80 percent for an unmarried heterosexual couple with children, and to 63 percent for a same-sex couple with children. Less than half believe that same-sex couples without children (45 percent) and unmarried heterosexual couples (43 percent) are a family. These definitions are also linked to differences in ethnic and class cultures. Minority subcultures and residents of poor neighborhoods are more likely to create wide networks of caretaking and financial support that resemble the kinds of bonds we associate with kinship. We can even think of these relationships as "fictive kin"—that is, people whom we rely on, provide support for, and feel close to as if they were family members (Hill Collins 1991; Stack 1974).

How do kinship systems and residence patterns contribute to different definitions of family?

Read the Document *Beyond the Nuclear Family: The Increasing Importance of Multigenerational Bonds* in **MySocLab**

Personal and Cultural Ideals of Family Membership

To understand the varying ways that individuals define the family and decide whom they consider a member of their own family, it is necessary to investigate the ways that families embody a set of personal and cultural ideals. This perspective turns our attention to the perceptions, beliefs, norms, and values that inform multiple, and often conflicting, views of family life: What constitutes membership in our own and others' families, and how should family members treat each other? Many of the most heated controversies taking place in the United States today—from the legitimacy of gay marriage to parental rights for surrogate parents to abortion rights to employment among mothers—reflect a growing political and social divide between those who believe it is essential to maintain a relatively narrow definition of the family and those who believe it is necessary to conceive of families in much broader and more flexible ways.

Because family life has multiple aspects, sociologists strive to understand the family from a variety of vantage points. Most important, families embody a wide array of interrelated institutions that link the most intimate aspects of human experience to each other and to the wider world of public pursuits. These organized arrangements and patterned behaviors include processes of mate selection and sexual behavior; patterns of marriage, divorce, and adult commitment; patterns of fertility and childbearing; domestic activities such as housework and childrearing; the division of household labor; patterns of caregiving and breadwinning; patterns of authority relations among partners, spouses, and children; processes of social placement that link families to the class structure; and the structuring of individual development over the life course.

What does it mean to describe family life as multidimensional?

As we examine the many ways that family life unfolds—as an institution and a set of lived experiences—we first need to understand how and why family life in contemporary American society has become the topic of such heated debate (Risman 2010).

2 Why Has Family Life Become the Topic of Such Heated Debate?

CONTEMPORARY AMERICAN FAMILIES:
A CONTROVERSIAL TOPIC

Watch the Big Question Video in **MySocLab**

Given the many ways that we can define *family*, it is no surprise that the study of family life lends itself to controversy. Yet during various points in American history, the topic did not provoke nearly as much heated debate. In the mid-twentieth century, few people objected to defining the family—or at least the ideal family—as a household with a breadwinner husband, a homemaker wife, and their dependent children. Why, then, is family life so controversial today? The most obvious reason is that, unlike the post-World War II era, one family type no longer dominates others. In 1950, with the baby boom underway, almost 80 percent of U.S. households consisted of a married couple, and three-quarters of the wives in these couples did not hold a paid job. Yet recent decades have witnessed a rapid erosion of this once predominant form, which now accounts for less than 15 percent of American households. Instead, a mosaic of living arrangements—including dual-earning married couples, couples in **cohabitation** (nonmarried couples living together, both straight and gay), single-parent homes, and single adults living alone or with others—coexist side by side. Figure 13.1 shows how the composition of households has changed over the past 40 years.

The rise of diverse family forms has not only transformed the residential landscape; it has also undermined an earlier consensus about what makes a group of people into a family. Although dual-earner and single-parent homes have always existed alongside the homemaker-breadwinner home, they were a numerical minority. In the United States today, however, there is no numerical majority. The once-labeled "traditional family" must now compete with other types of relationships for social resources and cultural legitimacy. In the wake of such a vast social shift, it is perhaps inevitable that a thorny political debate would ensue. On one side are those who argue that the erosion of the traditional couple, with an earner-husband and caretaker-wife, endangers society; on the other are those who argue that supporting many different family forms is necessary for social justice and personal well-being. These differing perspectives suggest different causes and reach different conclusions about the consequences of family change (Giele 1996).

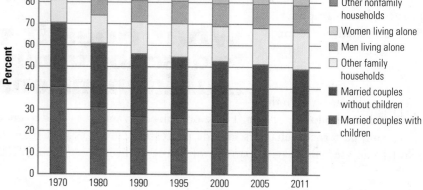

FIGURE 13.1 CHANGES IN COMPOSITION OF U.S. HOUSEHOLDS, 1970–2011

Legend:
- Other nonfamily households
- Women living alone
- Men living alone
- Other family households
- Married couples without children
- Married couples with children

Source: U.S. Census Bureau (2011).

The Family Values Perspective

Some critics argue that a weakening of **family values**—the orientations people have toward family responsibilities—has created rising selfishness and unfettered individualism, which has in turn fueled the growth of nontraditional living arrangements. Proponents of this *family decline* perspective see lower marriage rates, along with rising rates of cohabitation, divorce, and premarital sex, as a decline in adult commitment. They worry that the increasing number of single mothers and out-of-wedlock pregnancies endangers children. Even in two-parent families, they are concerned about the growth in employed mothers, the blurring of gender distinctions, and the weakening of fathers' position as head of household. And they see the acceptance of same-sex partnerships as a devaluation of heterosexual marriage. Taken together, they fear that all of these changes undermine the family bonds needed to raise healthy children and create a stable society. To halt this supposed family decline, social policies should thus aim to reinvigorate "traditional marriage" and make it harder to choose other options. (Prominent proponents of the family decline perspective include Blankenhorn 1995; Blankenhorn

What concerns do proponents of **the family decline** perspective have regarding the nature of families today?

2009; Popenoe 1988; Popenoe, Elshtain, and Blankenhorn 1996; and Whitehead 1997. For rebuttals to the family decline perspective, see Bengston, Biblarz, and Roberts 2002; Moore et al. 2002; Skolnick 2006; and Stacey 1996).

By focusing on the central role of eroding moral values, however, the family-decline perspective ignores the many uplifting values that diverse family forms embody, such as a stress on equality and freedom to choose in intimate matters. In important ways, the cultural-decline argument thus offers an evaluation of new family forms rather than an explanation of why they have emerged.

The Economic Restructuring Perspective

In contrast, a second perspective focuses on the social-structural factors, rather than the cultural norms, that have prompted family change. This *economic restructuring* approach does not dispute the trends that signal family change, but its supporters argue that basic social and economic forces, not a decline in family values, has inevitably eroded the foundations of the breadwinner-homemaker family and required new family arrangements. Changes in men's job opportunities, such as the decline of both unionized blue-collar work and secure white-collar career paths, have left fewer men with the ability to earn enough money to support a family on their own. In a parallel development, the growth of service work has expanded the pool of jobs for women, while expanded educational opportunities have encouraged and allowed them to pursue professional careers once reserved for men. These deep-seated changes in the

Expanded educational opportunities have allowed and encouraged women to pursue professional careers once reserved for men.

The Gender Restructuring Perspective

The focus on economic causes is important, but it tends to ignore the role of cultural forces and especially the growing desire among many women—and men—to live in families that do not resemble the heterosexual, gender-divided household that predominated in the mid-twentieth century. A third perspective on family change, which focuses on *gender restructuring*, adds another wrinkle to the economic restructuring approach that stresses institutional forces.

Focusing on the interdependence of paid and domestic work, the gender restructuring perspective highlights the growing mismatch between the structure of jobs (and careers) and the caretaking needs of families. While the family revolution has sent mothers into the labor force and created single-parent and dual-earner households, complementary changes have not occurred in the structure of jobs or care giving. To the contrary, employees who wish to move ahead are expected to place their job before family pursuits, yet parents, especially mothers, are expected to shower their children with attention. (see Epstein et al. 1999; Hays 1996; Moen and Roehling 2005; Williams 2000; Williams 2010). The expansion of new options is thus on a collision course with resistant institutions. Families may have changed, but the structure of the workplace and the organization of childrearing continue to presume a breadwinner-homemaker model that is no longer practical or desirable for most families.

These growing conflicts leave parents stressed, overburdened, and contending with time squeezes every bit as severe as their financial squeezes. They also create dilemmas about how to resolve a host of competing needs and values. How do adults balance the desire for personal independence with the value of lifelong commitment? How do parents trade off between the need to earn money and the need to care for their children? How do children experience growing up in diverse and changing families where new opportunities coexist with new uncertainties? How are these opportunities and uncertainties distributed across families in different class and ethnic subcultures? And is it possible to develop social policies that reconcile the growing divide between those who wish to restore the once dominant homemaker-breadwinner household and those who support more diverse and **egalitarian relationships** (where caretaking and breadwinning tasks are shared more or less equally by both partners)?

Focusing on the contradictions and dislocations of family change allows us to examine the ways that contemporary family life involves a mix of new opportunities and new insecurities. This perspective acknowledges the irreversible nature of change, but it does not assume that long-term

occupational structure have allowed women to pursue more independent lives, but they have also made it more difficult for families to survive on only one income.

From an economic restructuring perspective, blurring gender boundaries, the rise of dual-earner families, and a new emphasis on individual choice and self-reliance are inescapable consequences of a new economic order. These changes have produced a mix of new opportunities and new insecurities. The financial stability that middle-class families once enjoyed is waning, replaced by a growing divide between the top tier of well-compensated, securely employed professionals and everyone else. If families are more vulnerable today, it is not because they have rejected good family values but rather because they cannot rely on a stable, predictable economic and social system to provide for their needs. In this context, social policies that try to restore the traditional family are doomed to fail. Instead, such policies should focus on broadening the safety net so that all types of families can thrive in an uncertain postindustrial economy.

By recognizing the institutional constraints over which most families have little control, the economic restructuring perspective does not assume nontraditional choices reflect poor values. Instead, family shifts stem from growing constraints on the practicality of traditional options, along with expanding desires to take advantage of new opportunities. Because these shifts are irreversible, it is shortsighted and even harmful to try to turn back the clock or to blame people for their values.

How do proponents of the economic restructuring approach explain changing family arrangements?

outcomes are already determined. Instead, it draws our attention to the dilemmas and paradoxes created by inconsistent and contradictory social arrangements (Lorber 1994; Risman 1998). To make sense of modern families, we need to understand the interplay between inescapable social forces, such as the rise of a postindustrial economy with uncertain job paths, and the efforts of individuals, families,

What role do cultural and economic forces play in the gender restructuring perspective on family life?

and societies to craft innovative resolutions to the dilemmas created by incomplete change. These dilemmas take many forms, from tensions in forging adult commitments and sharing earning and caretaking tasks, to new challenges in growing up and making the transition to adulthood, to new class and ethnic inequalities. We examine each of these dilemmas in the sections that follow.

3 What Challenges Do We Face as We Develop Relationships and Balance Family and Work?

THE NEW CONTOURS OF ADULTHOOD COMMITMENT

Watch the Big Question Video in **MySocLab**

I n 2006, the Census Bureau reported that for the first time in U.S. history, less than half of American households contained a married couple and only 20 percent of households contained married couples with children (U.S. Census Bureau 2006). Compared to 1960, when the average age of marriage hovered around 20 for women and 23 for men, people are more likely to live together before getting married, to postpone a first marriage until their late 20s or early 30s, and to divorce or separate if the marriage proves unfulfilling (see Figure 13.2; Pew 2010).

Despite these trends, rumors of the death of marriage are greatly exaggerated. The overwhelming majority of Americans, around 90 percent, eventually marry, and most of those who divorce choose to remarry (Casper and Bianchi

2002; Cherlin 2009). Time and again, studies report that Americans consider having a good marriage as one of their most important goals (Kefalas et al. 2011). Indeed, the fight for same-sex marriage rights serves as a powerful indicator of its continuing importance. Marriage to one person for life may no longer be required, but marriage remains highly valued. Explore the Infographic on how mate preferences have changed over the years on page 360.

☐ Love and Marriage

American culture has always embodied a tension between creating lifelong commitments and retaining a measure of personal autonomy about whether and how to build intimate

FIGURE 13.2 CHANGES IN MARITAL AND LIVING PATTERNS, 1960–2008

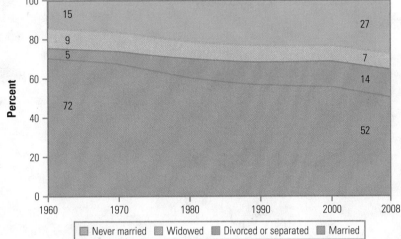

Note: Ages 18 and older. Numbers may not total to 100 percent due to rounding.

Source: Pew Research Center (2010).

expected (and allowed) to pursue goals outside the home (Cancian 1987; see also Parsons and Bales 1954). Although these gender differences were defined as complementary, they inevitably created tensions between the ideal of individualism, which grants everyone the right to pursue autonomous goals, and the notion that women should maintain the intimate bonds of marriage and childrearing through selfless commitment to caring for others.

Today's postindustrial economy, which gathered steam in the later decades of the twentieth century, has changed the social context in which family members must balance the tension between commitment and self-development. The gender revolution, illustrated most vividly by the rise of women's employment, has created a form of economic individualism in which almost everyone, including women no less than men, expects to support him- or herself. The reproductive revolution, demonstrated by the expansion of contraceptive options, has given people more control over their reproductive choices. The sexual revolution has undermined the sexual double standard, destigmatized premarital sex, and allowed gay and other previously hidden relationships to move out of the closet. The divorce revolution has made it easier to leave a marriage without being found at fault. And the life course revolution has lengthened the lifespan, providing more time to make, unmake, and remake intimate bonds (Luker 2007; Rosenfeld

relationships (Swidler 1980). These contradictory values go back as far as the nation's founding, when both individualism and community became central to national identity (Bellah et al. 1985). Yet this tension has found different expressions as social conditions have changed. Prior to industrialization, parents exercised great control over their children's mate choices, but this control subsided when the rise of industrialization in the nineteenth century demanded a socially and geographically mobile labor force. This new economic system fostered a new family unit, the "conjugal family" consisting of a relatively autonomous married couple able to seek its fortune outside the parental household (Goode 1963). The conjugal unit not only fit well with the industrial system; it also elevated the importance of emotional considerations, such as love and companionship, over parental approval as the appropriate criteria for choosing a mate.

The industrial system also produced the physical, economic, and mental separation of the home and the workplace. As many forms of work, and especially the manufacture of goods, moved outside the home to become paid jobs, the family became the site for unpaid tasks, such as childrearing and housework. This new division between the domestic and public spheres, intertwined in earlier periods, engendered a strict division—even polarization—of feminine and masculine roles. In a process that one sociologist has called "the feminization of love," women became responsible for emotional and caretaking duties, while men were

How has marriage become deinstitutionalized in today's postindustrial economy?

Americans today can cohabit prior to (or instead of) marriage, and recent estimates suggest that close to 45 percent of Americans are likely to cohabit at some point in their lives.

What Women and Men Want

What do women and men want in a mate? According to sociologist Christine B. Whelan, they generally want the same thing: mutual attraction and love. Whelan's research shows that both women's and men's rankings of desirable qualities in potential partners have changed drastically between 1939 and 2008. Of particular interest is the fact that a desire for education and intelligence in a partner has risen for both men and women.

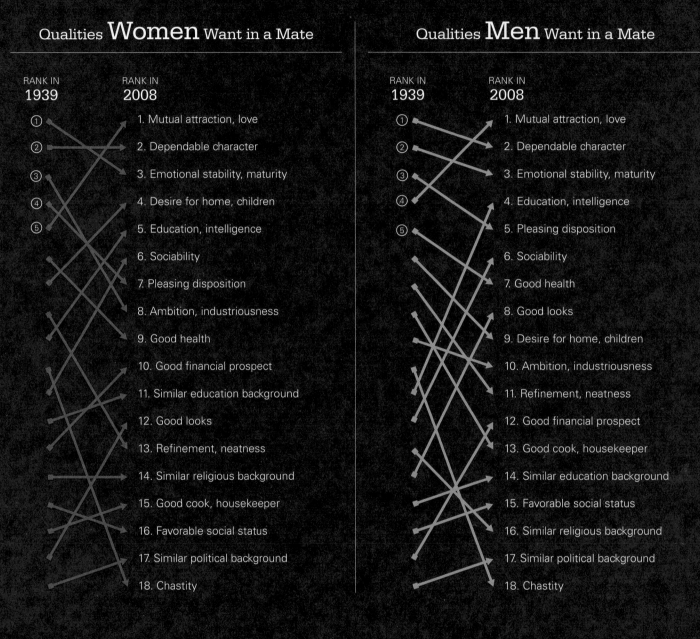

Qualities Women Want in a Mate

RANK IN 1939	RANK IN 2008
1	1. Mutual attraction, love
2	2. Dependable character
3	3. Emotional stability, maturity
4	4. Desire for home, children
5	5. Education, intelligence
	6. Sociability
	7. Pleasing disposition
	8. Ambition, industriousness
	9. Good health
	10. Good financial prospect
	11. Similar education background
	12. Good looks
	13. Refinement, neatness
	14. Similar religious background
	15. Good cook, housekeeper
	16. Favorable social status
	17. Similar political background
	18. Chastity

Qualities Men Want in a Mate

RANK IN 1939	RANK IN 2008
1	1. Mutual attraction, love
2	2. Dependable character
3	3. Emotional stability, maturity
4	4. Education, intelligence
5	5. Pleasing disposition
	6. Sociability
	7. Good health
	8. Good looks
	9. Desire for home, children
	10. Ambition, industriousness
	11. Refinement, neatness
	12. Good financial prospect
	13. Good cook, housekeeper
	14. Similar education background
	15. Favorable social status
	16. Similar religious background
	17. Similar political background
	18. Chastity

Source: Based on data from Boxer, Noonan, and Whelen (forthcoming).

Explore the Data on What Women and Men Want in **MySocLab** and then ...

Think About It

What do these changes in what men seek in a mate tell us about how larger social and economic changes influence personal relationships? How do you think women's mate preferences have changed?

Inspire Your Sociological Imagination

What traits do you look for in a partner, and in what ways do you think they are different than the ones your parents or grandparents sought in a partner? Why do you think your preferences are different in this way?

2009; Skolnick 2006; Weitzman 1985). All of these changes have combined to deinstitutionalize marriage by creating a wide array of alternatives to traditional marriage, including cohabitation, **serial relationships** (when people enter and exit a series of intimate partnerships), gay partnerships, and permanent singlehood (Cherlin 1992; Smock 2000; Smock and Manning 2010). Recent estimates suggest, for example, that close to 45 percent of Americans are likely to cohabit at some point in their lives. Americans today can cohabit prior to (or instead of) marriage, engage in sexual activity and bear children without marrying, and leave a marriage if it seems unworkable.

The shift from a system in which getting married was a prerequisite for forming a family to one in which it is one option among many has transformed the meaning of marriage itself. Marriage is now a highly valued, but nevertheless voluntary, bond that adults may decide whether or not to make or, indeed, unmake. As they ponder this decision, contemporary adults are more likely to stress the importance of love, respect, and mutual interests than to seek relationships built around a notion of different but complementary gender roles. One recent survey found that most married adults believe that love (95 percent) and companionship (82 percent) are very important reasons to get married, compared to only 31 percent who cite financial stability, and most singles agreed. In another, 62 percent said that sharing household chores is very important for a successful marriage, while 53 percent cited an adequate income (Pew 2007a; Pew 2010). These ways of measuring a successful marriage place more stress on sharing and less on distinct spheres linked to gender. In fact, the concept of static roles can no longer adequately describe the blurring gender distinctions between women's and men's activities in the home or outside of it. These new ideals for marriage also mean that people apply new—and higher—standards when choosing a mate and deciding how to define a worthwhile relationship. Yet the stress on emotional rather than financial bonds also makes marital ties more fluid and voluntary. Now that marriage is both optional and reversible, love has conquered marriage (Coontz 2005).

Mothers, Fathers, and Work-Family Conflict

Once considered separate spheres, the relationship between the home and the workplace evokes a very different metaphor today. As women, especially mothers, have joined the paid labor force and new technologies have blurred the lines between home and work, the image of family life as a distinctly private realm—a "haven in a heartless world"—has given way to the image of families in conflict with the wider world, especially with the world of work (Shorter 1975). Mothers and fathers are now more likely to share breadwinning, but they also face daunting challenges about how to integrate their paid jobs with their families' caregiving needs (Blair-Loy 2003; Hochschild 1997; Jacobs and Gerson 2004; see also Folbre 2008). In fact, although we generally use the term *work* to refer to paid jobs, unpaid work in the home is also a form of work. **Care work**, whether it is paid or unpaid, is as essential to a household's survival as is bringing in an income. Even though we often pay others outside the household to perform care work, we tend to ignore its economic value, especially when it is performed by a family member without a wage or salary attached.

Despite the media portrayal of an "opt-out revolution," to use a term coined by journalist Lisa Belkin (2003) to portray women who leave the workplace to care for children, young women now pursue careers in unprecedented numbers (Damaske 2011; Stone 2007). According to one study, employment among college-educated women in professional and managerial occupations has increased across generations, with less than 8 percent of professional women out of the labor force for a year or more during their prime childbearing years (Boushey 2008). Even though women's labor force participation rates have stopped rising, this stall has occurred at a very high level (well over 70 percent), especially compared to several decades ago, when the rate hovered around 30 percent. Today, women's participation in the paid labor force stands at almost 73 percent, down from a peak of almost 75 percent in 2000 (compared to men, whose participation rate has dropped from a peak of 96 percent in 1953 to about 86 percent) (Percheski 2008).

While mothers with children under the age of one show a small decline in their work force participation compared to a peak in the late 1990s, mothers whose children are older than one year show no similar drop. In fact, the difference in employment rates between mothers and childless women has declined. Most mothers now hold a paid job outside the home, even when their children are very young. Almost 55 percent of married mothers with children under the age of one year are employed, and that figure rises to more than 60 percent for married mothers with children under six years and 75 percent for those with children between 6 and 18 years (Cohany and Sok 2007; Cotter, England, and Hermsen 2010). Table 13.1 provides more details.

It is clear that the image of women opting out is highly misleading. It also ignores the constraints, such as a lack of widely available childcare and employer reluctance to tailor jobs to caretaking needs, which prompt some women to pull back temporarily and make it difficult for others to return to the labor force. Women's march into the workplace may have reached a plateau, but there is no widespread exit of women (at any educational level or marital status) from the world of paid work. Moreover, despite the persisting perception that women leave work for family reasons and men because they lose their jobs, the ups and downs of women's employment, like that of men's, reflect the opening and closing of work opportunities as the economy shifts. Indeed, the recent recession

TABLE 13.1   CHANGES IN WOMEN'S LABOR FORCE PARTICIPATION, 1950–2010

Women's Labor Force Participation Rates by Marital Status, Children in the Household, Age, and Percent of Full-Time Workers, 1950–2010

	1950	1960	1970	1980	1990	2000	2010
Single	40.6%	41.8%	45.6%	52.5%	66.7%	68.9%	63.3%
Married, husband present	21.6	30.5	40.8	49.4	58.4	61.1	61.0
No children in household	30.3	34.7	42.2	46.7	52.3	54.8	54.3
Children under 6 in household	11.9	18.6	30.3	43.2	58.2	65.3	63.6
Children 6–17 in household	28.3	39.0	49.2	59.1	74.7	79.0	77.5
Aged 20–24	46.0	46.1	57.7	67.7	71.3	73.1	68.3
25–34	34.0	36.0	45.0	65.4	73.5	76.1	74.7
35–44	39.1	43.4	51.1	65.5	76.4	77.2	75.2
45–54	37.9	49.8	54.4	59.6	71.2	76.8	75.7
55–64	27.0	37.2	43.0	41.7	45.2	51.9	60.2
Percent of women workers who work year-round full-time	–	36.9	40.7	43.7	57.5	59.9	58.6

Sources: Gerson (1985); United States Census Bureau (2012); Bureau of Labor Statistics (2010). For presence of children, 2010 data are from 2008.

has been dubbed a "man-cession" because men (who are more likely to work in declining sectors, such as blue-collar work) lost jobs at a higher rate than did women. Whether women's earnings contribute to a dual-earner partnership or provide the sole support for a household, they are integral both to the economy and to the financial well-being of their families. Indeed, according to one study of contemporary women's work paths, employed women now see their decision to work at paid jobs as "for the family" (Damaske 2011).

Despite women's movement out of the home, the organization of work remains largely based on the principle that each employee can count on someone else to take care of a family's domestic needs. Indeed, the pressure to put in longer hours at the workplace has intensified, with over a quarter of men and more than 10 percent of women workers putting in more than 50 hours a week and 60 percent of married couples working a combined total of at least 82 hours (Jacobs and Gerson 2004). While part-time jobs are available, they often require working inconvenient schedules and provide neither sufficient income nor sufficient opportunities for advancement (Presser 2003). Indeed, many of those holding part-time jobs actually work at more than one. The best jobs remain reserved for those who work full time and overtime for an uninterrupted span of decades.

In what ways does the clash between family needs and work pressures affect family life?

The clash between family needs and workplace pressures spills over into family life in a variety of ways. It has produced an unequal **second shift**, a phrase coined by sociologist Arlie Hochschild, where employed mothers are more likely than fathers to add the lion's share of domestic duties to their already crowded work schedules (Hochschild 1989; Hochschild 1997). This inequality produces marital tensions, or what Hochschild calls "a scare economy of gratitude" in which everyone feels unappreciated and shortchanged. Faced with these tensions, couples may develop strategies that help them cope, but these strategies do not—and cannot—change the underlying conditions from which the tensions stem. Hochschild thus recounts the efforts of Nancy and Evan Holt, who decide to split tasks by their location in the house—with Evan responsible for outside duties, such as taking care of the dog and cleaning the garage, while Nancy remains responsible for everything else. While the Holts hope this arrangement will ease tensions in the household, it instead allows the couple to create a family myth of equality that actually contributes to strains. Paradoxically, the growth of employment among mothers (in both dual-earner and single-parent families) has occurred alongside increased pressure for parents, especially mothers, to give their children more time and attention. This norm of

Fathers' parental involvement still lags behind mothers', but men are doing more domestic work than their fathers and grandfathers.

intensive motherhood conflicts with the countervailing norm that everyone should work hard and contribute financially, leaving women to face a "damned if you do and damned if you don't" set of options (Hays 1996). If a mother takes a job, she faces accusations of neglecting her children, but if she does not, she must defend her position as a stay-at-home mom, a social status whose symbolic value and social support have declined sharply. Research in this area reports that employed and nonemployed mothers both expressed unease about not meeting their mothering obligations or living up to the standards expected of mothers (see Hays 1996).

The blurred boundary between home and work produces time crunches and cultural contradictions, but it also creates new opportunities and possibilities. Women and men are both more likely to say they want to integrate earning and caring in their own lives and to establish a more flexible, egalitarian relationship with a lifelong partner. Fathers' parental involvement still lags behind mothers', but men are doing more domestic work than their fathers and grandfathers (Coltrane 2004; Deutsch 1999; Sullivan and Coltrane 2008). The gender gap in parenting is shrinking, and couples with more equal sharing express higher levels of satisfaction and are less likely to break up (Cooke 2006). More surprising, despite the image of the stressed, neglectful parent, parents today actually spend more time with their children than their counterparts did several decades ago. Mothers and fathers may both hold paid jobs, but they are also focusing more on their children when they are not at work (Bianchi 2000; Bianchi, Robinson, and Milkie 2006).

Work-family conflicts nevertheless remain difficult to manage, largely because the organization of jobs and childcare has not changed to accommodate shifts in gender relationships and the family economy. Individual workers, especially among professionals and other well-paid occupations, face growing pressures to put in long days at the office, while less educated workers increasingly take jobs

with nonstandard schedules and little long-term security. In addition, the *combined* working time of whole families has risen dramatically (see Figure 13.3), with dual-earning and single parents feeling most caught between the demands of work and the needs of domestic life (Gornick and Meyers 2003; Williams 2010). These types of households have always been stretched thin, but many more Americans live in them today. The future of family well-being will thus depend on restructuring jobs and childcare to help workers resolve the time squeezes created by widespread, deeply anchored, and irreversible social changes to the nature of the economy and the structure of families (Esping-Anderson 2009; Hochschild 1989).

FIGURE 13.3 CHANGES IN COUPLES' COMBINED WORKING TIME, 1970 AND 2000 (MARRIED COUPLES AGES 18–64)

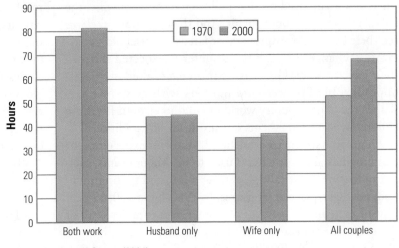

Source: Jacobs and Gerson (2004).

Watch the **Big Question Video** in **MySocLab**

4 What Is It Like to Grow Up in a Twenty-First Century Family?

GROWING UP IN TODAY'S FAMILIES

The rise of family diversity has also transformed the experience of childhood as well as the transition to adulthood. A growing percentage of children now grow up in a home with either two employed parents or a single parent or a same-sex-couple (Galinsky et al. 2009; Johnson et al. 2005; U.S. Census Bureau 2006; U.S. Census Bureau 2007). Children are also more likely to live in homes that change shape over time. While children have always faced predictable turning points as they move from infancy to adulthood, more children today experience unpredictable family changes as well. Compared to their parents or grandparents, they are more likely to see married parents break up or single parents remarry. They are more likely to watch a stay-at-home mother join the work force or an employed mother pull back from work when the balancing act gets too difficult. And they are more likely to see their financial fortunes rise or fall as a household's composition changes or parents encounter unexpected shifts in their job situations. Growing up in an era of fluid marriages, unpredictable finances, and mothers with new work ties shapes the contemporary world of childhood, even for those children whose own parents remain steadfastly traditional.

The transition to adulthood, like the experience of childhood, is also not what it used to be. Major events, such as graduating from school, getting a job, and getting married, now take place at later ages. In 1960, by age 30, 65 percent of men and 77 percent of women had completed all of the major life transitions that form the historic benchmarks of adulthood, including leaving home, finishing school, becoming financially independent, getting married, and having a child. By 2000, however, only 46 percent of women and 31 percent of men by age 30 had completed these transitions (Furstenberg et al. 2004); Newman (2009) also reports that these trends are not confined to the United States, as many European countries are also witnessing even greater increases in the number of 20-somethings still living with their parents. Let's explore how these changes have affected children and young adults.

☐ The Changing Face of Childhood

Among all children in 2000, only 21 percent lived in a two-parent household with an employed father and a nonemployed mother, while 59 percent lived with an employed mother, including 41 percent who lived with two employed parents, 3 percent with an employed mother and nonworking father, and 15 percent with an employed single mother (Johnson et al. 2005). Table 13.2 displays these results. It shows that the remaining children lived with either a single mother who did not have a paid job (5 percent), a married couple where neither were employed (4 percent), a father-only household (6 percent), or with neither parent (5 percent). The proportion of children born to unmarried mothers is at an all-time high of almost 37 percent, although about half of these nonmarital births are to cohabiting couples (U.S. Census Bureau 2006; U.S. Census Bureau 2007).

How have these changes affected children? Fortunately, worries about the harmful effects of having an employed mother or even experiencing a parental breakup are overstated. Decades of research have found that, on the whole,

TABLE 13.2 PROFILE OF PARENTS LIVING WITH CHILDREN UNDER 18

| | All parents | Married | Unmarried | Among unmarried parents | | |
				Divorced/ Separated	Living with a partner	Never married
	%	%	%	%	%	%
Men	45	50	23	22	42	14
Women	55	50	77	78	58	86
18-29	19	15	32	14	40	52
30-49	73	76	61	76	56	46
50-64	8	9	6	10	4	2
65+	<1	<1	<1	<1	<1	<1
Whites	65	68	52	63	59	36
Blacks	11	7	24	16	13	41
Hispanics	17	16	19	16	24	19

Note: Hispanics are of any race. Whites and blacks include only non-Hispanics.

Source: Pew Research Center (2010).

children do not suffer when their mothers work outside the home. Instead, a mother's satisfaction with her situation, the quality of care her child receives, and the involvement of a father and other caretakers are more important than whether or not a mother holds a paid job (Galinsky 1999; Harvey 1999; Hoffman, Wladis, and Youngblade 1999; Waldfogel 2006). The children of employed mothers do just as well in their cognitive development and, among children in low-income families, they do better (Burchinal and Clarke-Stewart 2007). Those who see a mother's employment as harmful generally point to thin research results showing small, temporary, and nonsignificant negative effects of being in day care for a small number of children (Crouter and McHale 2005). Indeed, despite the difficulties of balancing work and family, employed mothers and two-income homes are, in the words of Rosalind Barnett and Caryl Rivers, "happier, healthier, and better off" (see Barnett and Rivers 1996; 2004).

In the case of one- versus two-parent homes, children living with both biological parents do fare better on average, but this difference declines substantially after taking account of a family's financial resources and the degree of parental conflict prior to and after a breakup. Most of the negative consequences of divorce can be traced to the high conflict and emotional estrangement preceding a breakup, along with the hostility and loss of economic support that often follows in its aftermath (Cherlin et al. 1991; Furstenberg and

What does research indicate about the effects of divorce on children?

Cherlin 1991; Hetherington and Kelly 2002; McLanahan and Sandefur 1994). The effects of divorce on children vary greatly, with one researcher concluding that "while certain divorces harm children, others benefit them" (Li 2007). Children in high-conflict families whose parents divorce fare better, for example, than children raised in high-conflict families whose parents do not divorce (Amato and Booth 1997; Rutter 2010). While some analysts argue that all divorces are harmful in the long run, with a "sleeper effect" emerging many years later (Marquardt 2005; Wallerstein et al. 2000), others point to the large variation in divorce's consequences. One study found that over one-third of grown children felt their parents' marriage was more stressful than the divorce, which came as a relief when it reduced the long-term daily conflict between parents (Ahrons 2006). All in all, the effects of parental breakups—both negative and positive—vary with and depend on the circumstances that surround the divorce before and after it takes place.

Most research demonstrates that the diversity within family types, however defined, is as large as the differences between them. Some researchers show, for example, that family composition does not predict children's well-being (Acock and Demo 1994), while others make the same case for different forms of parental employment (Parcel and Menaghan 1994). In my own research, I found that almost four out of five young adults who had work-committed mothers believed this was the best option, while half of those whose mothers did not have sustained work lives wished they had. Similarly, a slight majority of those who lived in a single-parent home wished their biological parents had stayed together, but almost half believed it was better for their parents to separate than to continue to live in a conflict-ridden or silently unhappy home. In addition, a majority of children from intact homes thought this was best, but two out of five felt their parents might have been better off splitting up (Gerson 2011).

Children can thrive in a variety of domestic circumstances, but family process is more important than family form. What matters is how well parents and other caretakers meet the challenges of providing economic and emotional support rather than the specific forms in which these challenges are met. Children care about how their families unfold, not what they look like at any one point in time. Family life is dynamic, as families are not a stable set of relationships frozen in time but rather involve situations that can change daily, monthly, and yearly as children grow. All families experience change, and even the happiest ones must adapt to these changes if they are to remain so. Family pathways can move in different directions as some homes become more supportive and others less so.

What explains why some family pathways remain stable or improve, while others stay mired in difficulty or take a downward course? My study of "the children of the gender revolution," who grew up during the recent period of family change, finds that flexibility in earning and caregiving provides a key to understanding how and why some families are able to provide for children's well-being while others are not (Gerson 2011). Flexible family strategies can take different forms. In two-parent homes, children fared well when couples shared breadwinning and caretaking fairly equally or when they took turns and traded places as mothers pursued committed careers or fathers encountered roadblocks at the workplace. Chris, for example, tells how his family life improved dramatically when his mother's promotion at a hospital, where she worked as an intensive care nurse, allowed his father to quit a dissatisfying job as a printer and retrain for work as a machine technician, which he found much more satisfying.

In single-parent, divorced, and remarried households, children fared better when mothers were able to find jobs that kept the family afloat and fathers remained closely involved in their children's day-to-day care. Letitia thus recounts how her home life changed for the better when her father became the primary caretaker, providing emotional support that her inattentive and often absent mother could not. In the wake of her parents' separation and her father's remarriage, she also gained a more nurturing stepmother (in her words, "my real mother") whose commitment to work also contributed to the family's financial stability.

Despite the differences in family circumstances, all of these responses involved breaking through rigidly drawn gender boundaries between women as caretakers and men as breadwinners. In a world where parents may not stay together, where men may not be able or willing to support wives, and where women may need and want to pursue sustained work ties, most families will encounter unexpected challenges, whether they take the form of financial crises or uncertainties in parental relationships. When families are able to respond by rejecting narrow roles in favor of more expansive and flexible family practices, they are better positioned to create more financially stable and emotionally supportive homes for children. Flexible approaches to breadwinning and caretaking help families adapt, while inflexible ones leave them ill prepared to cope with the economic and marital challenges that confront twenty-first century families.

☐ Becoming an Adult

The markers used to decide who is—and who is not—an adult are very different today than they were several decades ago, with people much more likely to stress economic achievements over family commitments. In 2002, 90 percent of Americans considered completing one's education and achieving financial independence to be quite or extremely important to being considered an adult, followed by working full time (84 percent), supporting a family (82 percent), and becoming financially independent (81 percent; see Figure 13.4). In contrast, less than one third of Americans considered such family events as getting married and having a child (33 percent and 29 percent respectively) as requirements for adulthood (General Social Survey 2002; Furstenberg et al. 2005).

The extended time it takes to complete the transition to adulthood has produced a new life stage that some call "delayed adulthood" and others see as "the age of independence" (Rosenfield 2009). Like most social changes, this expanding period of early adulthood—after adolescence but before making lifelong commitments—can contain benefits and drawbacks. Sociologist Christian Smith (2011), for example, argues that young adults now get "lost in transition" without a moral compass to guide them, while Michael

FIGURE 13.4 PERCENT WHO SAY AN EVENT IS QUITE IMPORTANT OR EXTREMELY IMPORTANT TO BECOMING AN ADULT

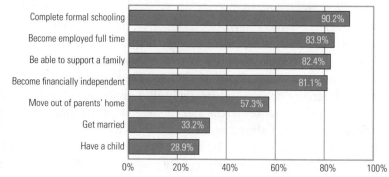

Source: Figure created based on data from GSS (2002); Furstenberg et al. (2004).

Kimmel (2008) points to the emergence of a place he calls "guyland," where young men engage in potentially self-destructive pursuits such as excessive drinking and partying. Others, however, see notable benefits in the emergence of a period when young adults are freed from childhood (and parental) controls and have an opportunity to develop a more independent self. The research of sociologist Michael Rosenberg (2009) has found that the rise of new kinds of relationships, including interracial and same-sex couples, reflects new opportunities for young adults to forge a life that is less constrained by the prejudices of earlier eras and more in tune with the realities of contemporary life.

Whatever the viewpoint, young adults now have more time to pursue independent goals before making major lifelong commitments and to develop ways of living that diverge from their parents' paths. This new period has also fueled a gender revolution in young women's and men's aspirations and plans. National surveys and my own in-depth interviews find that a majority of young people hope ultimately to create a lasting relationship, but not one that is based on separate spheres for mothers and fathers. Instead, most women and men want to create a flexible, generally equal partnership where they share paid work and family caretaking while also reserving considerable room for personal independence (Pew 2007b). In my interviews with young adults aged 18 to 32, I found that four-fifths of the women want an egalitarian relationship, and so do two-thirds of the men (Gerson 2011). In addition, three-fourths of those reared in dual-earner homes report wanting to share breadwinning and caretaking fairly equally with a partner, and so do more than two-thirds of those from traditional homes and close to nine-tenths of those with single parents.

Yet young women and men also fear their goals will be hard to achieve and may prove out of reach. Worried about finding the right partner and integrating family with work, they are pursuing fallback strategies in young adulthood. Young women and men both emphasize the importance of work as a central source of personal identity and financial well-being, but this outlook leads them to pursue different strategies. Women are more likely to see paid work as essential to their own and their family's survival and to prefer self-reliance over economic dependence within a traditional marriage (see Figure 13.5). Men, in contrast, are more likely to worry about the costs of equal sharing and to prefer a neo-traditional arrangement that allows them to put work first and rely on a partner for the lion's share of caregiving.

Images of young people avoiding adulthood and "failing to launch" cannot capture the complex experiences of today's young women and men. New generations do not wish to create a brave new world of disconnected individuals. In the long run, they hope to balance autonomy with a satisfying, committed relationship. However, they also believe they need to take time to create a financial base, discover their own strengths and needs, prepare for an uncertain economy that demands more education and higher levels of training, and find a partner whose family vision meshes with their own.

What are the benefits and drawbacks of the expanding period of early adulthood experienced by U.S. young adults?

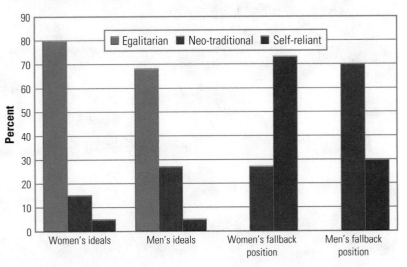

FIGURE 13.5 IDEALS AND FALLBACK POSITIONS OF YOUNG WOMEN AND MEN

Source: Gerson (2011).

The extended time it takes to complete the transition to adulthood has produced a new life stage, where young adults can pursue independent goals, such as work and leisure pursuits, before making lifelong commitments.

5 **What Causes Inequality among Families?**

FAMILIES AND SOCIAL INEQUALITY

👁 **Watch** the **Big Question Video** in **MySocLab**

F amilies of all classes and ethnicities are changing, but different groups are changing to different degrees and in different ways. Single-parent families, for example, are more likely to be found among African American households, where 65 percent of children live with either one parent or neither parent, compared to 34 percent of non-Hispanic white children, 24 percent of Hispanic children, and 17 percent of Asian children (Blow 2008). And while the overwhelming majority of Americans eventually marry, marriage rates have declined most steeply for the less educated and for members of racial minorities, where men's school and work opportunities are especially squeezed (Porter and O'Donnell 2006). Because economic inequality is linked to family differences, with a disproportionate number of poor and economically disadvantaged families found among single-parent families, it follows that ethnic minorities are also more likely to be overrepresented in lower income levels (see Figure 13.6).

The causes of family inequality are complex and difficult to isolate. Does inequality reflect different family values,

FIGURE 13.6 SHARE OF NEVER MARRIED, BY RACE, ETHNICITY, AND EDUCATION

(A)

(B)

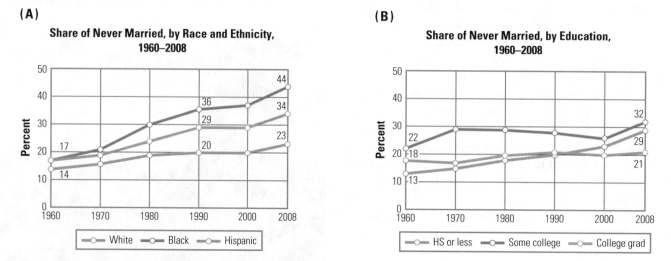

Note: Ages 18 and older. Hispanics are of any race. Whites and blacks include only non-Hispanics.

Source: Pew Research Center (2010).

Many middle class parents engage in a form of intensive parenting that some call "concerted cultivation," involving a high degree of scheduled activities.

or does it stem from unequal access to economic and social resources? Sociologist Annette Lareau (2003) proposes a circular link between class cultures, especially childrearing practices, and the transmission of inequality from one generation to the next. She argues that middle-class parents engage in a form of intensive parenting called "concerted cultivation," which involves a high degree of scheduled activities, a stress on the acquisition of language skills, and a sense of entitlement when interacting with social institutions such as schools. In contrast, working-class families engage in "natural growth," which involves unstructured play and leisure activities, a more informal approach in conversations, and more deference to authority figures such as teachers and doctors. While all families strive to provide their children with love and nurturance, she argues that different childrearing styles leave middle-class children better equipped to succeed in high-pressure, well-compensated jobs and occupations, thus continuing the cycle of inequality.

Yet diverse class and ethnic subcultures also share many values and practices. Sharon Hays (1996; 2003) finds that standards of intensive mothering, which bear a strong resemblance to Lareau's notion of concerted cultivation, exist in all classes. Studies of poor and middle-class single mothers find many similarities in their reasons for choosing motherhood over marriage as well as their strategies for raising children (Edin and Kefalas 2005; Hertz 2006). Poor single mothers are more likely to begin childbearing in late adolescence or early adulthood, while middle-class single mothers are more likely to postpone until their late 30s and early 40s as biological deadlines near, but both groups offer similar reasons for having a child while not being married. In separate studies of unmarried mothers in poor neighborhoods and middle-class single mothers by choice, both sets of researchers found that all these women valued motherhood highly and were not willing to forgo the experience simply because the right partner could not be found (Edin and Kefalas 2005; Hertz 2006). Though they possessed vast differences in financial resources, both groups relied on a support network of friends and relatives, including some men, to help rear their children.

People who grow up in the same class or ethnic subculture also vary greatly, and many move up and down the class ladder over the course of their lives. Some children are able to move to a higher class position than that of their parents, while others are not. Mobility across the generations has declined in recent years, but most children born into the bottom quintile of the income distribution are likely to move higher to some degree. One researcher reports that among children born into bottom fifth of the income distribution, 42 percent will stay there, but 24 percent will move to the fourth quintile, 15 percent will move to up to third quintile, 12 percent will move up to second quintile, and 7 percent will make it to top quintile. Among children born into the top quintile, 40 percent will remain there, but 54 percent will fall (Furstenberg 2007). Even siblings who grow up in the same family may follow different paths. Another researcher reports that the income differences among adult siblings are greater than the average income differences between families (Conley 2004). Because children who grow up in the same households are likely to diverge as adults, it is difficult to attribute their trajectories to a shared class or family culture.

In addition, the uncertainty of the twenty-first century economy makes it increasingly difficult to draw clear class boundaries. While there are many ways to define class, the most typical definition focuses on occupation. People are generally classified as middle class or upper middle class when at least one family member is employed in a professional, managerial, or similar occupation, while they are deemed working class if the adult earners are employed in blue-collar, pink-collar, or other service or wage work not requiring a college education. The poor encompass those families that fall at or below the official poverty level, although the official level often underestimates the number of people whom many would agree live in poverty. More important, many working-class and middle-class American families now find themselves facing financial uncertainty, knowing that the loss of a job or a family member would trigger a downward slide. These families live on a "fault line," precariously balanced between maintaining a class position and dropping below it (Newman and Tan 2007; Rubin 1994; Warren and Tyagi 2003).

Complicating matters even more, race and ethnic diversity intersects with class and gender inequality. Sociologist Patricia Hill Collins (1991) points out that class, race, and gender combine in ways that make it difficult to separate their distinct effects. Not only are African Americans and Latinos more likely than whites and Asians to be concentrated at lower income levels, but so are women of all races

How do race, ethnicity, and gender intersect with class to create inequality among families?

and ethnicities. None of these categories can be considered alone. On the other side of the class divide, an emerging black middle class signals growing diversity among African Americans, just as the rise of women professionals has created similar diversity among women.

In the long run, a range of factors—including supports and obstacles provided by neighborhoods, schools, and jobs in addition to the family environment—structure children's experiences and shape their life chances. All in all, family differences, such as poor people's tendency to marry less often than other income groups, stem more from differences in resources and opportunities than from differences in values.

6 What Social Policies around the World Best Support Changing Families?

THE UNITED STATES
IN COMPARATIVE PERSPECTIVE

⊙ Watch the **Big Question** Video in **MySocLab**

Alleviating the difficulties created by inconsistent change depends on accepting the irreversibility of family change and creating a range of institutional supports for this new reality. Individual families cannot make these adjustments on their own. Only collective social policies can create the supports that twenty-first century families need to thrive or even survive.

☐ Social Policy around the World

The United States lags far behind many other postindustrial societies in adopting social policies that support new family forms. France, for example, allows any two people to form a civil union that bestows all the legal rights and responsibilities of a married couple. France, along with all the Scandinavian countries, also offers universal childcare, and Scandinavian countries guarantee paid parental leave for everyone (Gornick and Myers 2009). In Sweden, Iceland, and Norway, these leave policies not only support employed mothers; they also encourage fathers' parental involvement by specifying that a father cannot transfer his leave time but must "use it or lose it." Most Europeans can also build their families without regard to such considerations as healthcare and educational access, which are available to everyone whether or not they are married or employed full time.

In thinking about how the United States approaches family change, it is helpful to compare it with other nations at a similar level of economic development. From Europe to the Far East, all the postindustrial nations have experienced similar social shifts, including a rise in women's labor force participation, the postponement of marriage and childbearing, and the proliferation of diverse family forms. Yet the policy responses to these shared demographic trends are quite distinct.

Some countries, especially in Scandinavia, have developed policies based on the principle of providing universal family supports regardless of who you are. This egalitarian approach covers a range of specific policies, including paid parental leaves, universal day care, and antidiscrimination workplace policies along with universal health care and free education. Taken together, this approach aims to reduce both gender and class inequality while providing for children's well-being regardless of the kind of family they live in.

In contrast, other countries, such as Italy, have adopted an approach that encourages maternal care but does not support women's employment or more egalitarian family forms. This familistic approach offers mothers with children, even if they are single, economic incentives for bearing children and staying home to rear them. It does not, however, stress day care, antidiscrimination at work, or others measures that would facilitate employment among mothers, encourage fathers to share in caretaking, or generally acknowledge the rise of new family and gender arrangements. Ironically, in Italy, Japan, and other countries that have resisted the incorporation of women in the public sphere, many women have responded by resisting marriage and motherhood, creating a shortage of births not seen in societies with more egalitarian policies. Explore *A Sociological Perspective* on page 372 for a closer look at social policies around the world.

FIGURE 13.7 PARENTAL LEAVE FOR TWO-PARENT FAMILIES IN 21 COUNTRIES

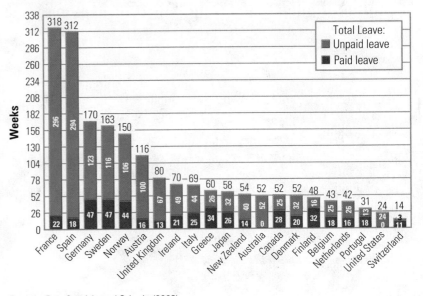

Source: Ray, Gornick, and Schmitt (2009).

How do government policies towards families differ around the world?

☐ Social Policy in the United States

Where does the United States fit in this picture? Unlike either egalitarian or familistic approaches, U.S. social policies stress the principle of individual opportunity. This individualistic approach stresses policies aimed at providing a chance to succeed—or fail—in the labor market but not at creating programs of family support for everyone. Unlike familistic approaches, there is less concern for recreating the traditional family through maternal support; but unlike egalitarian approaches, there is less concern with equality of outcomes or facilitating the inclusion of mothers into the labor force or the inclusion of fathers in caring for dependents (see Figure 13.7). In practice, this means that American social policy has focused more on whether and how to prevent discrimination and far less on creating universal family support programs. Indeed, we continue to debate the advantages and disadvantages of the family revolution rather than accepting its irreversibility and restructuring other institutions to better fit the new realities.

☐ Where Do We Go from Here?

What, then, would a more effective, inclusive policy approach look like? In an era of massive family change, we need to think more broadly about what equal opportunity really means. Individuals live in families, and we cannot separate

A SOCIOLOGICAL PERSPECTIVE
Is childcare the same around the world?

United States: Parents often struggle to find affordable, high-quality childcare for the most part without help from the government. Low-income families, in some cases, can find subsidized childcare if they meet certain criteria but higher income families are not eligible for such services. Census figures show that 48 percent of children four years and younger with working mothers were cared for by relatives and the number of stay home mothers (5 million) has declined since 2008.

Japan: A chronic childcare shortage makes finding daycare slots a competitive process. Worried that women would choose either a career or motherhood, Japan, in 2008, announced a 10-year goal of providing working parents with daycare for children ages 1-5.

If the Unites States offered the same level of parental leave for fathers as offered in Sweden, how could the father-child relationship change?

Sweden: Policies like the "use it or lose it" paid parental leave encourage greater involvement of fathers because leave days cannot be transferred. Parents may take up to 480 total parental leave days when a child is born or adopted, and the government subsidizes childcare for its citizens.

France: The state provides free preschool for children from two years of age. A system of "child minders" helps to supplement its daycare centers. A child minder receives training, undergoes regular inspections, and can care for up to five children at a time.

Can you think of some possible benefits for governments to provide subsidized childcare for all of its citizens?

How would affordable and available access to childcare affect mothers' contributions to the workplace?

⊙→ **Explore** A Sociological Perspective in **MySocLab** and then . . .

■ Think About It
The U.S. lags far behind many other postindustrial societies in adopting social policies that support new family forms. What enables other countries to adopt different, more supportive approaches to accommodating families with children, including paid parental leave and universal daycare?

■ Inspire Your Sociological Imagination
What are the long-term implications of these different approaches for both the economic development of each country and for the well-being of families and individuals?

Workplace antidiscrimination policies need to cover "family responsibilities" discrimination, which will help protect all of those who shoulder responsibilities for caring for others. Here, workers in Belgium are demonstrating in support of giving fathers two weeks fully paid paternity leave.

the fate of individuals from the well-being of their families. We thus need family policies that reaffirm classic American values, such as equal opportunity, tolerance of diversity, and individual responsibility, but do so in the context of collective support for the diverse needs of the new family arrangements that are essential pieces of modern social life.

More concretely, this means a host of specific policies in diverse arenas: family support policies, workplace policies, and legislation to protect the vulnerable of all ages, family statuses, and sexual orientations. Legislative efforts need to encompass equal opportunities for all kinds of families and interpersonal relationships, including single parents, same-sex couples, dual-earner families, and single adults. At the workplace, antidiscrimination policies need to be expanded to include what Joan Williams (2007) calls "family responsibilities" discrimination, so that those who shoulder responsibilities for caring for others will not face huge penalties for devoting time to this essential but undervalued task. Family-support

What would a more effective, inclusive policy approach to family support in the United States look like?

policies should thus aim to reduce poverty and inequality along with creating a wider institutional framework for dependent care, including the care of children, the elderly, and anyone in need of it. Community childcare supports, in particular, will help employed parents and nurture the next generation. Jobs that offer flexible avenues for working and career building will not only help families integrate paid work and care work but also help employers attract and retain committed workers.

Antidiscrimination policies that protect the rights of all parents with caregiver responsibilities will not only even the playing field for employed mothers but also create fairer workplaces for men (of all sexual orientations and class positions) who wish to be involved as caretakers. No one policy can address all the challenges that twenty-first century families face, but taken as a whole, these approaches will go a long way toward helping families develop their own strategies for meeting the challenges that await them in the decades to come.

CONCLUSION THE FUTURE OF FAMILIES

Despite the rapid pace of change, most Americans remain quite upbeat about the future of the family. According to a recent Pew survey, 67 percent say they are optimistic about the future of marriage and the family. Yet Americans are also concerned about some family trends, such as the rise in divorce and unwed childbearing, and politically divided over others, such as gay marriage, abortion, and the growth of paid childcare (Pew 2010). Another Pew survey thus found that 71 percent believe the growth of unwed motherhood is a big problem (Pew 2007b).

The focus of attention may shift from employed mothers to abortion rights to single motherhood to gay marriage, but underlying political cleavages remain between those who support diversity in family life and those who would like to restore the breadwinner-homemaker family that predominated a half century ago.

The uneven and inconsistent character of family change means not only that people will live in different types of families but also that they will have different outlooks on family life. Those who are pioneering new family forms have good reasons to favor social policies, such as supports for employed parents and same-sex couples, that will help ease their dilemmas. But those who favor traditional family arrangements are more likely to view such policies as unwarranted support for options they consider unpalatable and even unacceptable. These differences play an important role in national elections, where a sizable "marriage gap" has emerged alongside the highly publicized gender gap. Married couples, and especially those who depend only on a man's income, are more likely to vote for conservative candidates, while single women and men are more likely to vote for candidates who identify themselves as liberals (Edlund and Pande 2002).

To complicate matters, those who oppose family change are not immune to it. Regions of the country with the highest rates of unwed motherhood and divorce are more likely to lean toward conservative views on family life that stress the role of cultural decline in creating new challenges. In contrast, regions with the lowest rates are more likely to take a liberal approach that is less concerned with individual values and more focused on economic restructuring (Cahn and Carbone 2010). It appears that those most susceptible to the uncertainties of family change are also the most unsettled by it.

These ambivalent and conflicting views make it difficult to assess the prospects for the future. Family diversity is here to stay, but so is the debate over family diversity. There is, however, another approach that takes seriously the feminist view that gender restructuring is not only at the heart of family change but also represents a set of values worth enacting. Because family change is inevitable and offers new possibilities for equality, this view argues that the challenge is to accept the growing need for more egalitarian arrangements and restructure society to make that possible (Ferree 1990).

There are some signs that the family values debate may be cooling. New generations, who watched their parents and other adults invent a mosaic of new living arrangements, now take for granted options that earlier generations barely imagined. Jason's story is instructive. Although he grew up in a white, working-class suburb where traditional views predominated, he watched his parents struggle with unexpected crises and experienced changes that broadened his views on family life. Like his peers throughout the United States, the experience of growing up in a changing family prompted a rejection of older certainties and a more tolerant perspective on his own family options and the choices of others. These more tolerant outlooks among those who came of age amid the family and gender revolution may result in a decline in the resonance of politically divisive cultural wedge issues (DiMaggio et al. 1996; Jayson 2007; Teixeira 2009). Even among young adults who identify as highly traditional and very religious, a growing number say they "are tired of the culture wars [and] want to broaden the traditional evangelical agenda" (Banerjee 2008).

Facing their own conflicts about marriage, sexuality, work, and parenthood, young adults are increasingly weary of a divisive political rhetoric that blames families for conditions beyond their control. Most say they prefer a politics that avoids finger-pointing in favor of a more tolerant vision that stresses similar needs rather than putting social groups in conflict. These aspirations point toward the possibility of a more inclusive politics that focuses on the common needs of diverse families and replaces an image of moral decline with a concern about realigning our social institutions to better fit the new circumstances of twenty-first-century families.

Yet without social supports for more versatile ways of constructing families, new generations have good reason to remain skeptical about their chances of achieving these ideals. In the absence of institutional supports, American families face uncharted territory. The rise of alternatives to permanent marriage means that sexual partnerships are necessarily more optional and fluid. And economic shifts, such as the rise of service-sector jobs and the decline of blue-collar ones, make women's participation in the world of paid work inevitable. These intertwined and reinforcing changes create a host of new options, but they are also on a collision course with other social institutions that remain based on a mid-twentieth century model of static family forms. If families are films, not snapshots, then we need public discussions and social policies that see family life as an unfolding, unpredictable process in which anyone, at any time, may need some kind of help. In the context of this irreversible but unfinished family revolution, people need social supports for the diverse and changing families that exist today.

Watch the Video in MySocLab
Applying Your Sociological Imagination

1 What Is a Family? *(p. 352)*

👁 **Watch** the **Big Question Video** in **MySocLab** to review the key concepts for this section.

To begin this chapter, we first needed to examine the meaning of the term family. What is a family, and what are the various ways to define it?

THE MANY WAYS WE DEFINE *FAMILY* (p. 352)

A Global and Historical Perspective (p. 352)

- **What are some family forms that can be found throughout human history and across diverse societies and households?**

Kinship System or Household? (p. 353)

- **How do kinship systems and residence patterns contribute to different definitions of family?**

📖 **Read** the **Document** *Beyond the Nuclear Family: The Increasing Importance of Multigenerational Bonds* by Vern Bengston in **MySocLab**. This reading examines the changes in multigenerational bonds that have emerged as family forms have changed.

Personal and Cultural Ideals of Family Membership (p. 354)

- **What does it mean to describe family life as multidimensional?**

KEY TERMS

polygamy *(p. 352)*
patrilocal *(p. 352)*
kinship system *(p. 353)*
kin *(p. 353)*
nuclear family *(p. 353)*

2 Why Has Family Life Become the Topic of Such Heated Debate? *(p. 355)*

👁 **Watch** the **Big Question Video** in **MySocLab** to review the key concepts for this section.

To understand the contemporary debate over "family values," this section mapped out the competing views about the current state of the American family, how we got here, and what we need to do in response.

CONTEMPORARY AMERICAN FAMILIES: A CONTROVERSIAL TOPIC (p. 355)

The Family Values Perspective (p. 356)

- **What concerns do proponents of the family decline perspective have regarding the nature of families today?**

The Economic Restructuring Perspective (p. 356)

- **How do proponents of the economic restructuring approach explain changing family arrangements?**

The Gender Restructuring Perspective (p. 357)

- **What role do cultural and economic forces play in the gender restructuring perspective on family life?**

KEY TERMS

cohabitation *(p. 355)*
family values *(p. 356)*
egalitarian relationship *(p. 357)*

What Challenges Do We Face as We Develop Relationships and Balance Family and Work? *(p. 358)*

 Watch the **Big Question Video** in **MySocLab** to review the key concepts for this section.

This section examined the decline of permanent marriage and the new contours of adult commitment, as well as the blurring of gender divisions and the rise of work-family conflict.

THE NEW CONTOURS OF ADULTHOOD COMMITMENT (p. 358)

Love and Marriage (p. 358)

- **How has marriage become deinstitutionalized in today's postindustrial economy?**

Explore the **Data** on What Women and Men Want in **MySocLab**

Mothers, Fathers, and Work-Family Conflict (p. 361)

- **In what ways does the clash between family needs and work pressures affect family life?**

What Is It Like to Grow Up in a Twenty-First Century Family? *(p. 364)*

 Watch the **Big Question Video** in **MySocLab** to review the key concepts for this section.

In this section, we discussed how the experiences of children transitioning into adulthood are very different from how they once were and what this means for today's children and young adults.

GROWING UP IN TODAY'S FAMILIES (p. 364)

The Changing Face of Childhood (p. 364)

- **What does research indicate about the effects of divorce on children?**

Becoming an Adult (p. 366)

- **What are the benefits and drawbacks of the expanding period of early adulthood experienced by U.S. young adults?**

5 What Causes Inequality among Families?

(p. 368)

Watch the **Big Question Video** in **MySocLab** to review the key concepts for this section.

The causes of family inequality are complex and difficult to isolate, especially because the economy is changing and gender, race, and ethnic diversity intersect with class differences.

FAMILIES AND SOCIAL INEQUALITY (p. 368)

- **How do race, ethnicity, and gender intersect with class to create inequality in families?**

6 What Social Policies around the World Best Support Changing Families? *(p. 370)*

Watch the **Big Question Video** in **MySocLab** to review the key concepts for this section.

Finally, we placed American family life today in a comparative perspective. This section examined how other countries have approached social policies for families and how we can learn from their tactics.

THE UNITED STATES IN COMPARATIVE PERSPECTIVE (p. 370)

Social Policy around the World (p. 370)

- **How do government policies towards families differ around the world?**

Explore A Sociological Perspective: Is childcare the same around the world? in **MySocLab**

Social Policy in the United States (p. 371)

Where Do We Go from Here? (p. 371)

- **What would a more effective, inclusive policy approach to family support in the United States look like?**

Watch the **Video** Applying Your Sociological Imagination in **MySocLab** to see these concepts at work in the real world

14

SOCIOLOGY of RELIGION

((· **Listen** to the **Chapter Audio** in **MySocLab**

by GERALD MARWELL
with ADAM MURPHREE

I always begin teaching the sociology of religion by asking each student to describe his or her religious upbringing and present beliefs. Forty years ago, most of my students would have identified with a conventional religious tradition—Catholic, Baptist, Jewish, and so forth. Today, the most common responses are very different: "I believe in God, but don't go to church"; "If following a particular religion makes someone happy, I'm not going to look down on them"; "When you get down to it, I think all religions are really about the Golden Rule—treat others the way you want to be treated."

My NYU students are hardly typical of American youth. Fortunately, however, sociologist Christian Smith and his associates (Smith et al. 2009) actually interviewed a nationally representative sample of young people ages 18 to 23. Although they find many conventionally religious people in this age group, as well as a substantial number of atheists (who do not believe in any god) or agnostics (who do not believe that god's existence or nonexistence is knowable), Smith's results are similar to what I have observed among my students.

Smith calls the most common religious pattern among today's youth "moralistic therapeutic deism (MTD)," which he describes in terms of five "key beliefs" (154):

1. A god exists who created and ordered the world and watches over human life
2. God wants people to be good to each other, as taught in the Bible and by most religions.
3. The central goal of life is to be happy and to feel good about oneself.

MY SOCIOLOGICAL IMAGINATION
Gerald Marwell

My mother said I was always an "oppositional" child. I grew up in a religious home and went to parochial school, but I never understood what these old stories had to do with me or my world. And I was angry that my friends were out playing ball while I was stuck listening to old men telling me to sit still. I went to MIT to become an engineer, but I discovered interests in economics and psychology instead. I disagreed with the oversimplified psychology that underlies economics and hoped that sociology, the most general of the social sciences, might let me pursue both of my interests. And I fell in love: with all of sociology, and all of social science. Where else can you spend your life thinking about the human condition and get paid for it? Most of my work has been on offering alternatives to economic theories of "collective action," or cooperation, particularly in social movements. Religion is not so different from social movements, in that it requires commitment and faith. So, in my late 60s I finally took up the question that has puzzled me my entire life—why are so many people religious? Why is religion so important in the world?

It is important to almost all religious communities that their young become believers and practitioners. They incorporate children into aspects of their religion as early as they can. Here, very young Native Americans participate in tribal religious practices as part of this learning process.

Watch the **Video** in **MySocLab**
Inspiring Your Sociological Imagination

4. God does not need to be particularly involved in one's life except when God is needed to solve a problem.

5. Good people go to heaven when they die.

Smith argues that MTD is moralistic because young people believe the basic job of religion is to help us be good people—to have good morals. They also tend to think that most people are intrinsically good and that all religions help people to stay good, mostly because all religions teach some version of the golden rule.

MTD is also therapeutic because most young people believe that religion in moderation is generally, if not always, good for people. It helps people be happier and healthier. It gets them through crises. It gives them groups to belong to and share with. It makes for closer families with shared memories and feelings.

Religious people, and the real religions they practice are more complex and internally contradictory than we tend to think.

However, MTD is a very general religion. Perhaps reflecting America's historical idealization of religious tolerance, all religions are seen as essentially true at their core—the belief in God regardless of the form he or she takes (deism). At the same time, most elaborated religious **doctrine**—the official beliefs and rules of particular religions—is perceived as being unrealistic and boring. Established religions are seen as often unreasonable in their repressive rules, unscientific beliefs, and overbearing organizations. Many young people are suspicious of organized religion. They attend church rarely, if at all, except to be with their families.

Religious people, and the real religions they practice are more complex and internally contradictory than we tend to think. For sociologists of religion, this means that we get to study the wonder of the human condition and complex cultures and the consistencies and oddities of human behavior, all at the same time.

Perhaps because their whole lives are encompassed by their families, children are more likely to be religious than any other age group. Here we see orthodox Jewish and Muslim adolescents engaged in important rituals of their faiths.

THE BIG QUESTIONS

👁 **Watch** the **Big Question Videos** in **MySocLab**

1 **What is religion, and how is it organized?** Sociologists have no single agreed-upon definition of religion. Nevertheless, they understand that the actual religious behavior of people in every religion is enormously variable and fluid. In this section we examine the incredible number of religions throughout the world and throughout history, as well as the idea that religion is a social institution and that organized religion has important social functions.

How do people choose their religions? With all the religions in the world, how do people pick a religion for themselves? Here we look at the patterns of religious choice, including the impact of race, ethnicity, and social class. **2**

3 **Why are women and older people more religious than men and the young?** In this section we discuss differences in religiosity by gender and age.

Why do people kill each other in the name of religion? In this section we ask why there has been so much religious conflict over history and in the present, and discuss the difficulty of distinguishing religious conflict from ethnic or class conflict. **4**

5 **What is the future of religion?** We save for last what has historically been the most important question for sociologists of religion: Is secularization or increased religiosity the future of religion?

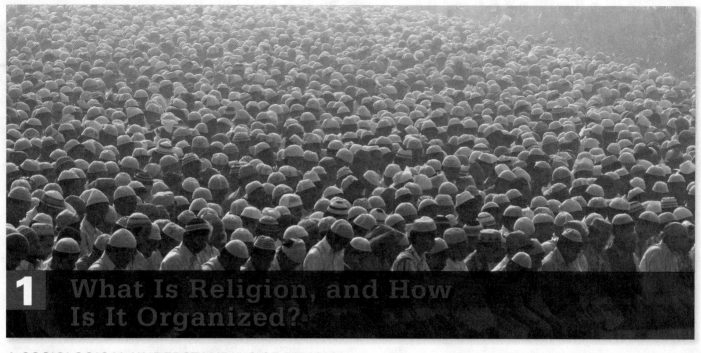

1　What Is Religion, and How Is It Organized?

A SOCIOLOGICAL UNDERSTANDING OF RELIGION

◉ Watch the **Big Question Video** in **MySocLab**

The study of religion and society occupies a unique place in the history of sociology. The first intellectual to call himself a sociologist, Auguste Comte, thought that sociology would lead to a modern "religion of humanity," with scholars such as himself fulfilling the functions of priests. More importantly, religion was central to the work of two of the most-read sociologists in history, Max Weber and Emile Durkheim. Weber wrote what is probably the most frequently read book in sociology, *The Protestant Ethic and the Spirit of Capitalism* (Weber [1904] 1958), in which he argued that the ascetic form of Protestantism that flourished in nineteenth-century America was critical in the development of full-blown capitalism.

Perhaps the second most-read sociological book is Durkheim's *Suicide* (Durkheim 1898), which begins with a puzzle rooted in religion: Why do areas populated mainly by Protestants have much higher suicide rates than areas populated mostly by Catholics? Later in his career Durkheim wrote perhaps the most profound and influential sociological treatise on religion ever written, *The Elementary Forms of Religious Life* (Durkheim 1912), in which he examined the religion of Australian aborigines and proposed that the idea of god basically represented the community or society.

In this chapter we therefore walk in the footsteps of giants and attend to issues foundational to a sociological understanding of society.

What are different ways that sociologists define religion?

☐ Defining Religion

Many sociologists are (and were) deeply religious people of one faith or another; many are not (Gross and Simmons 2009). Privately, religious sociologists may hope that their work supports the argument for religion, even for their own religion. However, no sociologist with a reasonable reputation would argue professionally and publically that hers was the one true faith, while all others were wrong. Sociologists understand their field as part of the scientific approach to human affairs, and they know that science cannot answer a question that is so certainly a matter of faith.

Furthermore, sociologists do not even agree as to what they mean when they describe "religion." There are many, many different and conflicting definitions in the literature. To get a feeling for these differences, I have found it instructive to focus on two distinctive approaches: one that emphasizes sacredness, and a contrasting definition that emphasizes the supernatural. In *The Elementary Forms of Religious Life* (Durkheim 1912), Durkheim defines religion as the way that societies deal with things that are **sacred**—those things that are worthy of awe and special treatment and are not just mundane or everyday parts of life: sacred objects like the Torah, sacred behaviors such as the communion ritual, sacred places like Mecca, sacred times like Easter day, and sacred people such as monks or the Dalai Lama. In other words, religion creates

There may be no God in Buddhism, but these Thai Buddhists seem to be praying to something during a religious festival.

symbolic boundaries between certain people, objects, times, places, and other things and events in the world. And the object that is most sacred, on which everyone depends, and for which god is a symbol, is the community of which they are a member. Sociologist Jay Demerath (2006) calls this Durkheim's idea of "we-ligion."

Compare Durkheim's definition with one used by the contemporary theorists Rodney Stark and Roger Finke: "Religion is concerned with the supernatural; everything else is secondary.... [It] consists of very general explanations of existence, including the terms of exchange with a god or gods" (Stark and Finke 2000:89–91). In this view, religion is a set of ideas describing the relations between the natural and the **supernatural**, including how earthly beings can obtain goods from other-worldly entities, be they healthy crops or eternal salvation.

Many interesting questions are raised by the differences between these two definitions. If supernatural beings are required for religion, where does that leave Buddhism, the "religion" of about 360 million people? Buddhist doctrine is formally atheistic—no god or gods are part of the belief system. On the other hand, many practicing Buddhists act as if they believe in spirits, and many of them pray to statues of the Buddha for assistance. Furthermore, because most Buddhists believe in the transmigration of souls (i.e., reincarnation), do "souls" qualify as supernatural beings?

Alternatively, defining religion as the way people deal with the sacred means that religion has plenty of room for Buddhism and also a number of phenomena not conventionally thought of as religion. For example, a good case can be made for including the revolutionary communism of early-twentieth-century Europe, or of late-twentieth-century Mao Zedong, as a religion.

We usually call political worldviews such as communism ideologies. Interestingly, however, religion also fits the common definition of **ideology**—a set of ideas that constitutes one's goals, expectations, and actions. If sacredness turns ideology into religion, consider the fact that communism has its sacred texts—"The Communist Manifesto," Mao's Little Red Book; its sacred prophets—Lenin, Marx; and even its mystical beliefs—such as the historical necessity of the triumph of the working class. Thus, many sociologists do consider communism the equivalent of a religion. Perhaps an even better case can be made for Nazism. For most Germans of his time in power, Adolph Hitler became a god, or at least a sacred being. Hitler's book Mein Kampf was a sacred text; racial purity and Aryan superiority were sacred ideas. Conquest was pursued with religious fervor.

More importantly, a "sacredness" definition of religion has led sociologists to recognize a common, even necessary form of religion they call **civil religion**. Consider the way Americans feel about their Constitution—for most, it is a sacred text; or about the flag—a sacred symbol; or about July 4—a day of ritual and worship at the shrine of sacred America. Consider the frequently repeated claim that "Ground Zero," where the World Trade Center once stood, is "sacred ground." According to what religion is it sacred? Not Protestantism nor Hinduism, nor any recognized religion. From a Durkheimian perspective, the civil religion that makes these things sacred is the same as all religions—it is the worship of the community and society, from which all good things eventually flow and on which we are completely dependent. In that sense, all religions are "civil" religions.

The Fluidity and Variability of Religion
Regardless of which definition they use, sociologists take a rather fluid approach to understanding religion. Religion is not defined by one set of doctrines or another. Instead, it is defined by the behaviors, beliefs, and commitments of the people of a group or society. Yes, doctrine matters, because religious doctrine is also the product of people's behaviors (writings, arguments), beliefs, and commitments, but doctrine is only part of what defines a working religion.

In the real world the rigidities of doctrine are often neglected by the faithful. For example, in Catholic doctrine it is clearly wrong to use contraception, yet 98 percent of

In Morocco, some Muslim women are veiled, some are not. It does not prevent affection between this mother and daughter.

sexually active Catholic women in the United States have done just that (Guttmacher Institute 2011), most without a moral qualm. What, then, is the correct description of the Catholic religion? As another example, most Islamic scholars agree that the Koran only asks women to dress "modestly" and does not require them to be veiled in public. Yet women in Saudi Arabia must be fully veiled or risk arrest. The Wahabbi sect that controls religious matters in Saudi Arabia insists that wearing the veil is an essential part of being a good Muslim. In other words, it is part of their Islam. In Morocco, some women who think of themselves as pious do not wear a veil, while others do. And these women, with different opinions, can be seen everywhere walking and talking together in friendship.

Even more fluid are the religious traditions and practices of most East Asian societies (Demerath 2003). In Japan, Korea, China, much of Indonesia, and elsewhere, people seem to feel free to combine elements from different religions, almost using religion as a toolbox with applications to a variety of problems and life issues. For example, in Korea, Confucian prayers for one's ancestors may be combined with Christian prayers for God's help or grace. The Japanese often celebrate births according to Shinto (Japanese folk religion) traditions, marry in Christian rituals, bury their dead with Buddhist ceremonies—and call themselves nonreligious.

The Incredible Variety of Religions

Instead of asking what the one true faith might be, sociologists from Weber and Durkheim onward have tried to understand the empirical reality before their eyes: the hundreds or thousands of different contemporary and historical religions to be found around the world, and the complex overlaps, syntheses, conflicts, and differences among these faiths. What made and makes religion so fascinating is that it is everywhere, in societies remarkably different from one another, and that it is so clearly produced socially and thus requires a sociological explanation.

To help grasp the incredible variety of religions that exist, we provide Table 14.1 and the accompanying Infographic on pages 385–387. Both the table and Infographic include only religions that are active and involve relatively large numbers of people today. They do not include religions that are from

the past or that are estimated to have fewer than 1 million adherents today. Note that the inclusion of Scientology is problematic, in that although the movement claims more than 2 million adherents, outside estimates are as low as 70,000.

Even as a picture of contemporary religion Table 14.1 is very approximate and incomplete. A complete and nuanced listing would take at least a book. For example, to save space we have compressed Roman Catholics, Eastern Orthodox, Baptists, and other religions into a single category: "Christianity." The adherents of those sects might strongly disagree with their lost uniqueness. At the same time, we give separate space to Jehovah's Witnesses and Mormons, whose adherents consider themselves Christians but also have crucial additional beliefs and doctrines that make them very different from the rest of Christendom.

Table 14.1 also combines Sunni, Shiite, and Sufi Muslims. In fact, all of the major religions had early periods in which geographically separated areas practiced somewhat different versions. Only later were these forged into a relatively consistent pattern through force or compromise. Later still, perhaps, these experienced schisms that produced newer and divergent versions of what was for a while considered a single religion.

The Infographic is devoted to showing where in the world the five (or six) religions with by far the most adherents dominate: Christianity, with approximately 2.2 billion adherents, is the largest; Buddhism, with 360 million, is the smallest. The sixth "religion" is **irreligion** (the absence of religion)—which dominates numerically in many countries generally considered Christian, and also in many Far Eastern countries like China and Japan. The next largest religion in Table 14.1 is Sikkhism, with approximately 23 million adherents, far less than the "big five/six."

"Chinese Syncretism" is perhaps the most complicated of the major religious traditions. The Chinese have long exhibited a highly **syncretic** approach to religion, that is, one that combines elements of different religions, making their beliefs and practices difficult to classify. At one point, Chinese religious scholars articulated "the Unity of the Three Religions," which taught that Buddhism, Taoism, and Confucianism were all ultimately equivalent and complemented each other. Thus, people could mix the three traditions. The Chinese emperor typically employed Buddhist, Taoist, and Confucian religious figures in his court simultaneously. Similarly, today many Chinese turn to a diverse set of sources, including folk religion and practices we might consider "superstition," to attempt to manipulate "luck" and secure favorable circumstances. Thus, even as the Communist Party has attempted to repress or regulate it, religion remains for many Chinese something one does rather than something one is.

The 19 smaller religions of over one million adherents each are divided into five groups, the largest of which contains religions that are related to Christianity. Most, like the Mormons, have prophets or sacred books in addition to those of conventional Christianity. Note that there are no "Islam-related" religions listed. The Druze would qualify, but this sect has fewer than 1 million adherents. Islam is the newest and perhaps "tightest" of the big five religions, and perhaps has been more able to fight the development of new, cult-like offshoots.

The world did not begin with five, or even one, "big religions." The big religions became so widespread relatively recently as history goes, mostly by sending missionaries backed by advanced scientific knowledge, or by conquest.

Although there are 25 religions listed in Table 14.1, this number pales against the number of religions that

TABLE 14.1 MAJOR RELIGIONS OF THE WORLD

	Est. Adherents	Established	Where Originated
The Big Five/Six			
1. Christianity Includes: Catholic, Orthodox, Protestant	2,200 million	30 CE	Israel
2. Islam Sunni, Shi'a	1,300 million	622 CE	Saudi Arabia
3. Hinduism	900 million	Prehistory	India
4. Chinese Syncretism	400 million	Prehistory	China
5. Buddhism Theravada, Mahayana, Vajrayana	360 million	520 BCE	India
6. Nonreligion Atheism, agnosticism	1,100 million		
Christianity-Related			
7. Judaism Orthodox, Conservative, Reform. Religion of the Hebrews, the "Chosen People." The root religion of Christian and Muslim monotheism. This-world and ethical oriented.	14 million	1300 BCE	Israel
8. Mormonism Consider themselves Christians. Believe Book of Mormon, not accepted by other Christian groups, is divinely inspired. Emphasizes self-discipline and family devotion.	12 million	1830 CR	USA
9. Spiritualism Focus on understanding and communicating with disembodied entities using methods such as séances, automatic writing, and other techniques. Believe all people have immortal spirits.	11 million	1850 CE	USA, UK, France
10. Seventh Day Adventists Affirm Protestant beliefs. Adhere to the teachings of Ellen White, considered a prophet. Emphasize healthy living. Follow strict dietary codes and observe a day of rest on Saturday.	10 million	1863 CE	USA
11. Jehovah's Witness Affirm Christian God but believe the Trinity is unbiblical. Believe 144,000 chosen will go to heaven, while others live forever on a new earth. Emphasize evangelism and healthy living.	7 million	1879 CR	USA
12. Unification (Moonies) Believe founder Sun Myung Moon is the second coming of Christ. Emphasizes forming harmonious families to bring about the Kingdom of God on Earth.	1–3 million	1954 CE	South Korea

(TABLE 14.1 *Continued*)

	Est. Adherents	Established	Where Originated
13. Aladura Mix Anglican and African rituals, focusing on healing and this-worldly salvation. Prominent role played by prophets who are believed to have extraordinary healing powers.	1 million	1918 CE	Nigeria
14. Rastafari Believe god (Jah) became incarnate in Haile Selassie. Emphasize worldly salvation, freedom from oppression, and return to Africa. Practice dietary restrictions and ritual marijuana use.	1 million	1920 CE	Jamaica

Hinduism-Related

	Est. Adherents	Established	Where Originated
15. Sikkhism Believe salvation consists of escaping the cycle of reincarnation and uniting with god. Emphasize moderate living and distinctive dress, including the turban, that symbolizes devotion.	23 million	1500 CE	India
16. Jainism Believe that the soul is eternal, uncreated, and can attain divinity. Practice complete nonviolence, including towards animals, and asceticism. Meditate through chanting mantras.	4 million	550 BCE	India

Far Eastern (Chinese, Buddhist) Religion–Related

	Est. Adherents	Established	Where Originated
17. Taoism Believe in living according to the Tao, the principle behind everything that exists, to achieve inner peace and longevity. Yin and yang. Cultivate detachment from worldly concerns.	20 million	550 BCE	China
18. Falun Gong Focus on regulating the body's vital energy through stretching and meditation exercises. Believe adherents can gain superhuman powers through these practices	10 million	1992 CE	China
19. Confucianism Emphasize ethical practices. Cultivate virtues such as loyalty, honesty, and concern for others. Focus on maintaining social harmony. Not concerned with supernatural forces or beings.	5 million	500 BCE	China
20. Shinto (Japanese folk) Believe in spiritual entities called kami. Practice rituals focused on securing blessings and avoiding evil through calling on the kami. Kami are believed to reside in shrines.	2–4 million	<300 BCE	Japan

Composites of Major Religions

	Est. Adherents	Established	Where Originated
21. Baha'i Believe god has successively revealed himself through the prophets of major religious traditions. Practice daily prayer and hold monthly communal feasts.	5–7 million	1863 CE	Iran
22. Cao Dai Emphasize the underlying similarity of all religions. Venerate a diverse array of saints including political, religious, and artistic figures. Salvation is escaping the cycle of reincarnation.	4–6 million	1926 CE	Vietnam

New Religious Movements

	Est. Adherents	Established	Where Originated
23. New Age Diverse and personalized, practices using tools and techniques such as crystals, tarot cards, astrology, and yoga. Tend to see the divine as an impersonal force. Believe in reincarnation.	5 million	1900s CE	USA and Europe
24. Wicca Generally believe in coequal god and goddess as well as lesser deities. Worship and rituals occur in covens or individually. Core principle is "Do what you will as long as no one is harmed."	1–3 million	1930s CE	UK
25. Scientology Participate in special counseling sessions ("auditing") to purify mind and spirit and to unlock inner potential. Church materials and auditing sessions provided in exchange for donations.	70,000–2 million	1954 CE	USA

Sources: ReligionFacts.com, "Big Religion Chart (http://religionfacts.com/big_religion_chart.htm)," was the major source for information in this table.

A Global View of Religion

The world has not always been dominated by a handful of big religions. Hundreds or even thousands of local animistic or pagan religions preceded the relatively recent spread of the "big five." This spread came mostly through the efforts of missionaries backed by advanced scientific knowledge, or through conquest. This map shows where the five active religions with 300 million adherents or more are the majority today. Of special interest is the separation of the blue Christian countries into dark blue [■] (where more than half the population claims to be religious) and light blue [□] (where more than half claims to be non-religious). Also consider the fact that most Chinese practice a syncretic, or blended, religion [■] that might combine elements of many kinds of religion, along with non-religion.

United States
Mormonism
Seventh Day Adventists
Jehova's Witness
Scientology
New Age
Wicca

Great Britain
Spiritualism

Israel
Judaism is the majority religion.

China
Taoism
Falun Gong
Confucianism

South Korea
Unification (Moonies)
Cao Dai

Jamaica
Rastafari

Japan
Shinto

Colors indicate the predominant religion in each country.

The primary locations of each of the other 19 religions with more than one million adherents are shown in italic.

Nigeria
Aladura

India
Sikkhism
Jainism
Baha'i

Islam   Christianity   Non-religious/Christian   Buddhism   Hinduism   Chinese Syncretism

Six countries are shown as split Islam/Christianity: Bosnia and Herzegovina, Cote d'Ivoire, Kazakhstan, Nigeria, Tanzania and Eritrea.

Source: Based on data from C.I.A. World Factbook (2012); ReligionFacts.com; European Commission's Eurobarometer (2005).

Explore the **Data** on A Global View of Religion in **MySocLab** and then . . .

Think About It
Why are so many Christian countries experiencing the rapid rise of non-religion at this time?

Inspire Your Sociological Imagination
The Islamic population of the world is growing. But is it likely to become the dominant religion in other countries? Why or why not?

ethnographers, archeologists, and historians have identified as present prior to the consolidation of the major religions, not to mention the probably thousands of religions that existed prehistorically and for which we have never found a trace. To give some perspective, note that in 1800 the two small islands of Papua New Guinea held almost 800 separate tribes, each with its own language and probably its own version of religion.

To talk about these religions, let us briefly consider the concepts of animism and paganism. Neither of these were or are specific religions, but they are useful ways to designate whole classes of early religions, and we do not have the space to describe the many useful distinctions among types of early religions that have been discussed by anthropologists and other scholars.

By animism, I mean to broadly refer to religions that ascribe human characteristics to animals, plants, and inanimate objects such as rocks and mountains; and/or see "spirits" as present and active in the world; and/or believe in some underlying force that animates everything from the weather to human activity. These kinds

What is the function of the religious social institution?

of religious thinking, which often lead to ritual practices to appease the spirits or harness the forces, seems to be common in tribal cultures all over the world, although in wildly varying forms. Although it no longer dominates the world, animism has not died out. What are generally called "folk" religions such as those in China or Shinto in Japan, have large elements of animism, and various major religions such as Islam are combined with folk animistic elements in places like Indonesia, as is Christianity with animism in parts of South America. And who is to say that the Star Wars blessing—"may the Force be with you"—isn't a prediction that animism will rise again in the future?

Paganism is a term coined by early Christians to refer to the other, nonmonotheistic religions of their times, with Roman, Greek, and Babylonian paganism being their major referents. I use the term to refer to religions that generally envision a set of gods and attendants who rule the world (polytheism) and can be appealed to through ritual, prayer, and sacrifice. Pagan religions often created representations of these gods in concrete forms, or idols, which were central to their rituals. Paganism generally reflected the more centralized ideas of the empires and large societies that integrated and conquered tribal societies. It survives today in consciously "neopagan" religions such as Wicca, and perhaps most prominently in the large and varied collection of Hindu gods and avatars. Radical Protestants frequently disparaged Catholicism as "pagan" because of its "excessive" reverence (idolatry) for Mary, its many saints, and its omnipresent statues and religious images.

☐ Religion as a Social Institution

So diverse, complex, and dynamic are the religions of the world that one might argue that religion differs with every individual. Mr. Y's Catholicism, which stresses the sense of belonging and the beauty of the liturgy, might be different from his wife's, which stresses the importance of obedience to God's laws and the sacredness of the family. Neither Mr. nor Mrs. Y knows or cares about the intricate **theology**—discussions of the interpretation of religious matters—that mesmerizes their priest, and so on.

In fact, the authors of an influential contemporary analysis of religion, Habits of the Heart (Bellah et al. 1985), were particularly taken with the example of a woman named Sheila, who called her religion "Sheilaism." She described Sheilaism as taking the bits and pieces from various religions that she thought were useful or convincing and combining them into her own personal religion.

Such privatization of religion is probably an important contemporary trend. But it is not the central sociological reality about religion. Instead, religions are first and foremost what sociologists call **social institutions**—structured and enduring practices of human life built around well-established rules or norms, or centered in important organizations (like the government, courts, churches, schools, or military)—in other words, the way things are done.

From a Durkheimian perspective, the primary social function of the religious social institution is the promotion of social order. Most actual religious institutions specialize in teaching and demanding that people follow societal norms—especially those thought of as the commandments of god or the gods or, as in Buddhism and Confucianism, the lessons of revered teachers or prophets. Religion is full of "oughts" (what is right) and "ought-nots" (what isn't), and of threats of punishment or failure in this world or the next if one does not follow these rules. In other words, religion is one of society's central mechanisms for social control over the behavior of people. It is no accident that in many older societies it was the shamans, rabbis, imams, and priests who were also the judges in the legal system.

In most historical places, there tended to be one very dominant religion, often closely aligned with political power. Because religions tend to see themselves as the truth, they have long had a tendency to fight to dominate the community or society in which they are embedded. In small, early communities there was little deviation from a single set of animistic or pagan beliefs. This was the assumptive world that everyone shared, and one lived with it much as we believe in atoms or evolution.

In the Holy Roman Empire there were minority religions, sometimes persecuted, sometimes not. Gradually, however, after a millennium, everyone was expected to be Catholic. But what came together later fell apart. After the sixteenth-century

Protestant Reformation, the Anglican Church became the state church of England, the Lutheran Church became the state church in Sweden, and so on throughout those states of Europe where Protestantism had won definitive victories (not, for example, in France and Germany, where Catholics and Protestants were still both entrenched). This is why America's early legal commitment to religious **pluralism**—accepting many different religions, or all religions, as legitimate—and to the separation of church and state was so important and so unique.

Denominations   Separation of church and state allowed many flowers to bloom in the religious garden. In the United States, Roman Catholicism is just one **denomination** among many. A denomination is an organized religious group with at least a few different doctrines that distinguish it from other such groups that are also adherents of the "same" religion. Denominations usually are combinations of a few to many specific congregations. After decades of immigration, Roman Catholicism became the largest Christian denomination in the United States, but it still only represents a minority of religious Americans. Most Americans were and are Protestants. But there are many denominations among Protestants: the Baptists are the largest, but there are many Presbyterians, Congregationalists, and so forth. It is estimated that there are more than 200 different denominations in the United States, and many of these have been divided into competing branches.

Denominations are where we find much of the "organization" in what we call "organized religion." Denominations train and ordain priests, ministers, rabbis, and imams. They may assist churches in financial trouble. They frequently, if not always, determine the "correct" doctrine. They provide model liturgies to be followed and lessons to be taught in the church sanctuary and religious education programs.

It is within as well as between denominations that the "big" religious wars are fought. For example, several Episcopalian congregations recently left that denomination because it made an openly homosexual priest a bishop. When the Catholic Church decided to move from the Latin mass to one in the regional language of each area, so that parishioners could understand what was being said, many congregations threatened to defect—although few did. The Mormons suffered internal wars over polygamy (where a man may have more than one wife at the same time), which the church historically approved but had to disapprove if it wanted to be accepted under American law. Later, the Mormons fought over and eventually changed their original position forbidding black people from holding leadership positions. We may expect more internal conflicts in many denominations as they deal with the changing societies in which they function and the changing views of their members.

What role do denominations and congregations play in organizing religious activity?

Congregations   According to Mark Chaves (2004) and others, however, denominations are not the key organizational aspect of American religion (with the possible exception of the Catholic Church). Instead, the most important level of organization is the local **congregation**—the specific church or temple or mosque that people actually attend.

Because congregations are founded and disbanded with great frequency, and because there are many institutions that may or may not be congregations, it is difficult to get exact figures for the number of congregations in America. Nevertheless, it is estimated that there are about 335,000 religious congregations in the United States (Chaves 2011). Of these, about 300,000 are Protestant and kindred churches, and 22,000 are Catholic and Orthodox churches. Non-Christian religious congregations are estimated at about 12,000.

More than half of all congregations are regularly attended by less than 100 individuals. In other words, there are many small churches in America, often with part-time or unpaid ministers or no minister at all.

The rituals of different Christian denominations can provide radical contrasts. In some Pentacostal denominations, the handling of "serpents" evokes feelings of immediacy and of inviting the protection and the spirit of the lord. In Eastern Orthodox denominations, traditional priestly attire and rituals evoke a sense of continuity with the past and reverence for God's everlasting presence.

On the other hand, more than half of all church attendance is actually in the largest churches (top 10 percent in size). Some of these churches, those with 2,000 or more members, are called megachurches. In any given week, the largest of these—Joel Osteen's Lakewood Church in Houston, which sits 16,000—may have 45,000 people attend its three services. Interestingly, several of these large churches, including Lakewood, are nondenominational, which is the fastest-growing segment of the church world. These churches do not feel that they need some denomination telling them what to do, telling them how to pray, or taking a share of their collections.

The enormous supply of churches must mean that there is a tremendous demand for church among Americans. In fact, large numbers of Americans do go to church regularly, although not as many as they think. In surveys, 40 to 45 percent of Americans—about 118 million people—report that they went to church the past week. However, it appears that Americans overstate their attendance. Research that counted people in the pews in one county found that only about 20 percent actually attended in a specific week—half of the 40 percent who claimed they had attended in a telephone survey. It seems that people who think of themselves as regular churchgoers don't want to "mislead" the survey by admitting they didn't go last week. And half of them didn't (Chaves, Hadaway, and Marler 1993).

Sixty million is still a lot of people in church on any given week. Organized religion will not go away soon, at least in the United States. And not only religious people like to go to church. Some who are not really believers in the doctrines of the church, or even in god, still attend. As Durkheim argued so long ago, many people go to church for the shared experience—the celebration of community, family, and common identity. As the many Jews in New York who go to Christmas services and love the music know, and the many Christians who attend Jewish Passover seders know, people often love ritual—if not all ritual, at least the rituals they learn as part of their communities. Ritual is something all the church members know and can do together, in part as a sign of their togetherness. *Collective effervescence* is what Durkheim called it, and the church has always been important for providing that experience (explore *A Sociological Perspective* on page 391 for more on this topic).

Serving the Needs of the Community

Furthermore, besides the government, which operates fairly impersonally and often ineffectively, there is no other institution in the United States that provides as directly and personally for community needs. Community here does not mean some residential community. In an urban world, every city, and almost every suburb, is home to several congregations. The community of primary interest to each congregation is the community of coworshippers, not the city or suburb (Chaves 2004).

In most churches, membership qualifies you for help with all kinds of problems and for a variety of other services. The large congregations, attended by more than half of all churchgoers, are much more than religious institutions. They often provide alternatives to public schools, counseling for troubled parishioners, sports and social programs for teenagers, financial counseling, help with elderly parents, nursing homes, and even graveyards. Even small churches will help members in trouble, with visits to the sick and personal support when needed.[1]

Many churches and denominations do extend their charity beyond their membership. For example, Lutheran Social Services is one of the most important providers of welfare in the country. Of course, much of its budget comes from the government, and it is not allowed to use "Lutheranness" as a reason for receiving charity. Its religious background stems from the mission that the Lutheran Church felt that it had a responsibility to perform. However, Chaves (2004) warns that despite their charitable rhetoric, charity is actually a minor and sporadic activity of most congregations.

Modern technology allows a mega-church minister to preach in a hall that seats 9,600 worshipers, and also reach additional members in other venues and at home.

---

[1] For a sense of how deep the support from churches might be, look at the website of the third largest, and probably first, Protestant megachurch, Willow Creek, especially the bottom of its home page: http://www.willowcreek.org/home1.aspx.

A SOCIOLOGICAL PERSPECTIVE

What is religion's function?

What role does religion play in your life? Does it provide a sense of community? Do you find comfort in its rituals? Even though he believed that religious traditions were withering away in the face of science and modernization, Emile Durkheim thought that religion served a crucial social function for people and society, which included: (1) bringing the community together to participate in ritual, that is, scripted collective activity that employs certain cherished symbols; (2) generating a collective effervescence by successful ritual, in which the individual is overcome by the feeling of being one with the community; and (3) producing long-lasting solidarity, or a feeling of belonging together, that will sustain the community until the ritual is repeated.

How might the experience of attending a concert serve a similar social function for the people in this photo as would attending a religious service?

Many would argue that the individuals in these two photos are worshipping different gods. But what makes their social experiences similar?

⊙→ Explore A Sociological Perspective in **MySocLab** and then …

■ Think About It

How is the communal feeling of commitment to an 'alma mater' different from the communal feeling of commitment to a church or denomination?

■ Inspire Your Sociological Imagination

Next time you participate in some kind of ritual – formal or informal, religious or secular – consider Durkheim's idea. What went into making the ritual happen and making it relatively successful or unsuccessful? And what does it produce?

PATTERNS OF RELIGIOUS CHOICE

👁 Watch the **Big Question Video** in **MySocLab**

With all the religions in the world, how do people pick one religion as their own? Of course, this is a trick question. Most people don't sit down, consider a list of religions, and then choose to be one or the other. Most people are born into a religion—the religion of their parents. And throughout history most parents belong to the religion that has long been institutionalized in their society or community or perhaps just family. Thus, if you manage to hear about religions other than the one you are born into, you might decide to change, but the odds, and social pressure, are decidedly against that. Besides, most children love and respect their parents and are very likely to want to maintain their relationships by being like their parents in their views of the world.

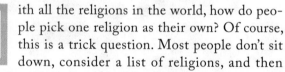

In today's world most, if not all, people are aware that there are other religions than their own. They are also very aware that some form of irreligion (the absence of religion) is an alternative embraced by at least some people, somewhere. So, yes, many people change religions, or at least denominations. However, even in the United States, the most religiously pluralistic of all countries, it is estimated that only one-fifth of all people formally change their religions or denominations during their lifetimes (Newport 2006). On the other hand, given the fluidity of real religions, individuals may change their personal religious feelings or ideas or practices but remain within the same denomination over time.

☐ Birds of a Feather

We do know that there are definite patterns regarding the social backgrounds of people who end up in different religions, denominations, and congregations. In the United States, Sunday remains the most segregated day of the week, and church the most segregated place in the country—and not just by race. It is also segregated by class and lifestyle and various forms of preferences. Adults attend churches voluntarily, so birds of a feather are permitted to flock together, and they do so even more than they do in other institutions (which are also segregated, although not as fully).

Perhaps the most important ingredients of American church segregation, besides religion itself, are area of residence and social status. But it might be best to start with a story that is particularly telling for understanding the complex role that churches play for people in the United States, and to some extent everywhere—the rise (and fall) of the ethnic church, particularly the immigrant church.

The Ethnic Church   The United States is often described as "a nation of immigrants," a fact that profoundly affects the landscape of American religious organizations. As Germans, Swedes, Chinese, and other ethnic groups emigrated to America, they did not fit very well into the established churches, even churches of their own denominations. German and Swedish

Lutherans needed German- and Swedish-speaking versions of Lutheranism, where they could pray in the language they knew and mix comfortably with people from their own background. Thus, immigrants established thriving ethnic churches of their own.

An instructive illustration is the Korean American church—a set of Protestant churches that conduct services in Korean or serve a primarily Korean American membership (see Chang 2006 for a history). Although some came to the United States earlier, particularly after the Korean War, most Korean immigrants arrived after the 1965 change in American immigration law, which repealed the previous massive discrimination against non-Europeans. There are therefore many first- and second-generation Korean Americans in the United States.

In Korea, about 25 percent of the population describes themselves as Protestant. In the United States, however, 75 percent of Korean Americans are Protestants. To some extent this difference might reflect a special American attraction for Korean Protestants as compared with Buddhists. More interesting, however, is the fact that almost 40 percent of Korean Protestants in the United States were previously not religious, or of another religion! That is a lot of "converts," and is the first clue for understanding the role and attraction of the ethnic church.

For Korean immigrants, the Korean church is much more than a religious institution. It is the center of their community; a place they can speak Korean, eat Korean food, and share community and community values with others from a common culture. The church provides a kind of safe haven where immigrants and their children can negotiate the treacherous path from culture to culture. Were it really about religion, many or most Koreans could have attended established Protestant churches. They did not. The enormous number of Korean American converts to Christianity probably does not reflect some strong response to Christian doctrine. Instead, non-Christian Koreans clearly wanted, even needed, to associate themselves with the principal institutional center of their community, the various Protestant churches. Durkheim would have it no other way.

The centrality of non-English speaking churches for immigrant communities is not new in the United States. Polish-speaking Catholic congregations in Chicago served the same function. Italian immigrants struggled to have an Italian Catholic service and community in a New York diocese whose priests were mostly Irish, but they eventually succeeded.

In Savannah, GA, young Americans in a Korean-American Methodist church learn Korean, keeping their connection to the ethnic community.

Today, many Catholic churches have special services for Spanish-speaking parishioners or services in Vietnamese on the West Coast, featuring Hispanic and Vietnamese priests, respectively.

The Black Church   Undoubtedly, the most important segregated church in the United States is the historically black church. About 60 percent of all African Americans (more than 80 percent of African American church members) belong to traditionally black denominations, and additional African Americans belong to denominations that are integrated but attend almost completely segregated congregations (Greeley and Hout 2006).

Most black churches were established by free blacks—both in the North before the Civil War and most importantly after the Civil War. Black churches are generally religiously conservative, but because they represent a severely exploited and repressed minority, they also have emphasized a kind of **liberation theology**, a theology that emphasizes Christ's focus on helping the poor and downtrodden. For black churches this is particularly reflected in the biblical story of the Exodus—the escape of the Jews from slavery in Egypt. "Let my people go" is a favorite theme of sermons and prayers.

Until fairly recently (and perhaps even now), African Americans were not welcome in most white churches in either the North or South, certainly not as equals Even if they had been accepted, a good sociologist should have predicted that a predominately black church would come to be the focus of the black community, much like the churches of immigrants. The community needed a collective center dominated by its needs and concerns, and the church provided it. On top of everything else, after being freed from slavery blacks became immigrants inside America. They left the South for the North in a great migration. In the South, they left the plantations for towns and cities. Even though they spoke English, they faced most of the needs of immigrants, and more.

The importance of the black church became very clear during the civil rights struggle of the 1950s, 1960s, and

1970s. The movement leaders were mostly ministers from black churches, especially in the South. The Rev. Martin Luther King Jr. was the son of the pastor of the largest and most affluent black church in Atlanta. This gave King the backing he needed so that he could dedicate himself to the movement. No other institution in the South could provide financial support, space for meetings, and community-supported professionals like the ministers who were not so dependent for their livelihood on the white power structure. The churches also provided sanctuary for activists—although that sanctuary was sometimes bombed or attacked. The church was also the source of the gospel songs and the liberation message that buoyed the spirits of the activists. Almost all observers agree that without the black church the civil rights movement would have been in danger of collapse.

White Conservative Christians: A Speculative Note

Pushing the immigrant analogy even further, one might speculate that the relative success of conservative churches in America during the past three or four decades has similar sociological characteristics. The conservative Protestant church was strongly rooted in the Bible Belt of the American South and in the rural North. Since World War II, people have been moving off of the farms and out of the small towns that were the homes for these communities. Sons and daughters have moved into cities and suburbs and become more economically successful in the affluence of the times. They were, in a sense, immigrants into the urban, industrialized world of modern America. And the church was their community center and source of continuity in this somewhat alien culture.

The Fall of Ethnic Churches

The Korean American church is thriving, with the American melting pot seeming to have little effect. But history is long.

Consider America's largest immigrant group—the Germans. Some came to America in colonial times, but the largest wave arrived in the first half of the nineteenth century and settled mostly in the upper Midwest. They were a varied group—they thought of themselves as Prussians and Bavarians (Germany was not unified until 1871), and they were Catholic and Lutheran and Amish and Mennonite. But for all of them there were immigrant churches where German was spoken and where German culture was central to daily life. In Milwaukee and Chicago there were German counterparts to the Polish Catholic Church. The Germans practically dominated American Lutheranism.

Where is it all now? Besides a few Amish or Mennonite settlements, most of the edifice of the German church is gone, and so are the Swedish-, Polish-, and Italian-speaking churches. The process might take four or more generations. It probably requires a significant decline in immigration, so

that those uncomfortable in the host American culture are not replenished. But it would be disingenuous to think that such churches will last forever.

Residential Segregation

This section began by suggesting that the most important factor distributing people into congregations is place of residence. Different kinds of people tend to live in different places. Just look at the campus churches at your college or university. They are full of students who live on or near campus. This constitutes a group of people very much alike on all kinds of characteristics, including, to begin with, age and level of education.

Few congregations serve broad areas of a city or county. With a few exceptions, congregations tend to reside in neighborhoods and be seen as neighborhood institutions. A congregation in the suburbs south of Chicago rarely attracts members from a northern suburb or from the city's core. Neighborhoods tend be collections of people who are economically or ethnically similar.

Throughout history, immigrants, and hence ethnic groups, have tended to move into areas where people they know already reside, particularly relatives and friends from home towns. They get help and a sense of comfort. The already beaten path is the way to helpful information and to safety. It is also the way to relevant churches. Returning to our Korean American illustration, consider the fact that 44 percent of the people living in Palisades Park, New Jersey, are of Korean ancestry (U.S. Census Bureau 2010). This is no accident.

For a long time the suburbs contained mostly white, middle-class immigrants from the city. Their congregations were of a certain type. And so were inner-city congregations. Congregations in the Bible Belt have socially different members from congregations in San Francisco or Seattle. The influence of place on congregational selection is enormous, if not completely dominant.

Social Class and Religious Preferences

Probably the most famous sociological statement about religion—"religion is the opiate of the people"—was penned by Karl Marx (1844), who wrote relatively little more about religion. Nonetheless, Marx linked religion to inequality and human suffering in a way that was convincing for many observers. As he saw it, religion was an illusion and a distraction that both dulled the pain of economically exploited people and offered a false substitute for the politics of class struggle necessary for their liberation.

If Marx is right, religion, like drugs, should appeal most to the poorest members of society—and perhaps to the rich and powerful who exploit the poor and who profit the most from their piety. The real picture, however, is much more complicated.

Norris and Inglehart (2004) present a nuanced, contemporary version of Marx's thesis that is based upon their research around the world. They conclude that growing up in societies that provide less personal security (physical, financial) is more likely to lead people to find security through religion and prayer than is growing up in societies that provide of a sense of security to more people (18). Those individuals who live in poverty are generally the most insecure of all. A sick child can mean the inability to go to work and a spiral into the loss of housing and other necessities. Notice, however, that Norris and Inglehart do not simply equate "security" with current or personal poverty. People who grow up insecure but manage to prosper may still feel very insecure. Most importantly, people who do relatively well in societies that are insecure still are influenced by the collective attitudes towards religion and therefore share the religiosity of their mostly insecure compatriots.

The poor, then, are more likely to be religious and to rely on religious institutions. In some cases their dependence on these institutions is such that they call on their religious leaders to help them deal with the real world, even in rebellious ways. As one sociologist argues, "[religion] can serve as an apology and legitimation of an unjust status quo, on the one hand, yet also as a source of resistance and protest" (Neptad 1995:107). Two of the most-cited examples of this are the aforementioned historically black churches (and many supportive white churches, especially in the North) in the civil rights movement, and the role of many local Catholic churches in the revolutions by the poor in Latin America. The latter is often discussed under the rubric of liberation theology.

Caste and Religious Switching in India
Perhaps the most striking relationship between stratification and religious choice, however, is the way that the caste system traditional in Hinduism has affected the birth and growth of various religions on the Indian subcontinent. Among Hindus, the caste system provides a relatively rigid and religiously sustained ordering of people into a social hierarchy. In Hindu doctrine, people are born into different castes, which have different functions in the society. The system has sometimes been called Brahmanism because the Brahmin (or priestly) caste is at the top of this pyramid. At the bottom are the enormous number of untouchables or dalits (which

is technically not a caste—a religious complexity not worth going into here), with other castes ranged in between. One cannot escape the social standing of one's caste in this lifetime. Where one is born is supposed to be ordained by one's behavior in one's previous life. Good behavior mostly consists of submitting to the status and conditions into which you were born.

Weber called this system one of the most logically consistent theodicies ever invented. A **theodicy** is an explanation of why bad things happen to good people. To oversimplify, in Hinduism bad things happen to you because of what you did in a previous life, not because of what you do in this life. Being good now gets you a better situation in your next life. It is a potent means of social control—probably much better than the Christian notion that God "has his reasons" for doing bad things to good people.

Not everyone is willing to accept the strictures of caste. This is one of the reasons for the popularity of so many different religions in India. Although he accepted reincarnation, the Buddha (an Indian) was strongly opposed to caste, saying that "Birth does not make one a priest or an outcaste. Behavior makes one either a priest or an outcaste." Sikhism was partly founded in rejection of caste. Although Baha'i was developed in Persia, the largest Baha'i community in the world—2.2 million—is in India. There are an estimated 2.4 million Christians in India. All of these religions were and are particularly attractive to members of lower castes and the "untouchables" who sought to escape their karmic fate. For example, two-thirds of Indian Christians come from the "untouchables" (scheduled groups) or lower castes.

Particularly interesting is the attractiveness of Islam to the same constituencies. Islam came to India as the religion of Mughal conquerors, so there were other reasons for conversion if one was ambitious. But Islam became a major way out of the caste system for many Indians and continued as an

Traditional Hindu weddings in India are often full of vibrant colors and energy.

alternative for a very long time. Ironically, some scholars describe a "caste" system among Indian Muslims which divides the upper-caste Ashraf, supposedly descended from the invading Arab and Persian rulers, from the lower-caste Ajlaf, who were Indian converts. Status advantages are not easy to erase.

Denominations and Social Class in the United States

Because they come from such different backgrounds—educationally, geographically, and in other important characteristics—different denominations in the United States contain surprisingly different kinds of people. Figure 14.1, based on a recent survey, shows, for example, that Jews, Hindus, and Episcopalians in America are about three times as likely to be college graduates as Pentecostals, Jehovah's Witnesses, and Baptists. Fewer than one in five Baptists earns more than $75,000 per year, while more than half of Episcopalians make that much (Leonhardt 2011).

In some ways Figure 14.1 underrepresents the background differences among denominations. Methodist college graduates are much more likely than Baptist college graduates to be the children of college graduates. The children of first-generation collegians may be more comfortable in an urban, middle-class society than their parents and

may find the appeal of conservative Christianity fading. Or perhaps it will be their grandchildren? On the other hand, they may remain most comfortable in the church in which they were raised. That church itself, however, might subtly or markedly compromise its points of difference with mainline Protestantism as its members become more like their neighbors in their lifestyles and experiences. For conservative Christians this is a time of change, as the grandchildren of the Bible Belt accommodate to the urban world of modern America.

☐ Conversion

So who converts to what, and why? Leaving aside moves to irreligion (discussed in a later section) we know that in the United States, at least, people convert from one denomination or religion to another for a variety of reasons.

Most religions seek to recruit, or proselytize, more members—as each should, if it is the true religion and cares for everyone's spiritual well-being (or for their eternal souls). There are a few exceptions. Hindus do not generally proselytize (although there are some aggressive gurus). Jews actually make it difficult

Who converts to what denomination or religion, and why?

FIGURE 14.1 INCOME AND EDUCATION OF VARIOUS U.S. RELIGIOUS DENOMINATIONS

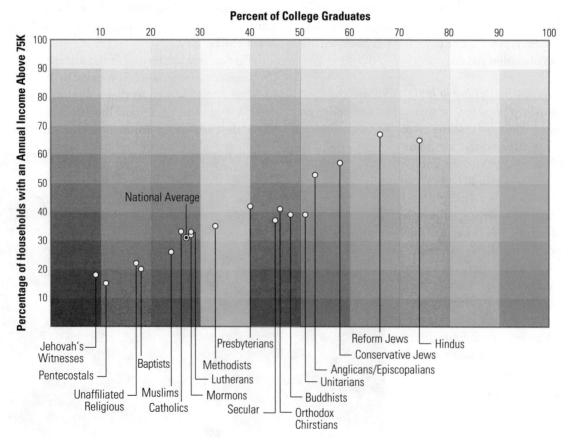

Source: Pew Research Center(2006).

Wiccans usually worship in the woods, close to nature. For New York City Wiccans, that is a tall order. Shown here, a coven meets in Washington Square Park near New York University.

for people to convert, primarily because Judaism is only partly a religion. More powerfully, it is an ethnic group. In Israel, the determinant of whether one is Jewish or not is mostly whether or not one had a Jewish mother. An individual does not have to be a practicing Jew, just have had a Jewish mother herself. The notion that the Jews are the "chosen people" may be the key idea in Judaism, and it obviously leads to all kinds of exclusionary assumptions.

In turn, the idea that being Jewish is both an ethnicity and a religion has led sociologists and others to the notion of cultural Judaism, defined as claiming one's Jewishness but not accepting the doctrines of the religion. Such Jews should probably be called "ethnic Jews" because they are unwilling to give up their identification with the group despite agnostic or atheistic beliefs. Conversions among denominations within Judaism are probably as frequent as they are among Christians. For example, the children of Orthodox Jews born in the United States seem to have less than a 50 percent chance of remaining Orthodox as adults, with 29 percent becoming Conservative, 17 percent becoming Reform, and 12 percent becoming secular Jews (Amont 2005)

Read the **Document** *Are American Jews Vanishing Again?* in MySocLab.

Among Christians, most conversions are between denominations. Conversions between Catholics and Protestants—or either and Mormons—are considered much more of a leap. We know something about these conversions. For a long time, intermarriage was the dominant reason for people changing denominations (and for Jewish–Christian conversions as well). The strong notion that families should go to church together was important here. So was a simple attempt to make life less complicated or to decide "what to raise the children." There is some recent evidence that people have become more comfortable retaining their religious commitments within dual-faith or dual-denominational marriages. Perhaps this stems from older ages at marriage or from such marriages just being more common and acceptable.

Who is drawn to emerging new religions?

New Religious Movements

One segment of organized religion that depends on converts is **new religious movements**, an umbrella term for new religions and offshoots of "foreign" religions that have a foothold in the United States. Examples may be found in Table 14.1 and include such religions as Wicca, Scientology, the Moonies (the Unification Church), various Buddhist or Hindu sects, and so forth. Some would include as new religious movements the Mormons, Jehovah's Witnesses, and other relatively new versions of religious doctrine.

Who is drawn to these new religions? Rodney Stark has studied the Moonies, the Mormons, and other such churches and concludes that "… people must have a degree of privilege to have the sophistication needed to understand new religions and to recognize a need for them. This is not to say that the most privileged will be most prone to embrace new religious movements, but only that converts will be from the more, rather than the less, privileged classes (Stark 1996:39)." He points out that Christianity was once just such a movement—a Jewish "Jesus cult"—and its converts tended to suffer from "relative deprivation"—that is, resentment among the somewhat privileged that they actually deserved even more privilege and respect. On the other hand, Stark argues, sect movements that seek to purify existing traditions, that is, to make them more like the "old-time," "true," "essential," "authentic," version of the religion, appeal to the lower classes. Stark also asserts irreligious people are the most likely to join new religious movements and concludes that this reflects a deep desire for some spiritual connection among those who do not accept traditional faiths.

3 Why Are Women and Older People More Religious than Men and the Young?

RELIGIOSITY BY GENDER AND AGE

👁 Watch **the Big Question Video in MySocLab**

Women are particularly likely to convert to new religious movements. Some of these, like Wicca, a neopagan cult with female goddesses, are explicitly aimed at women. But most new religions seem attractive to women. In Stark's research on early Christianity, women were more likely to convert. It was also probably true of the beginnings of Islam. In more modern and radical cults, consider the following data: 73 people were killed in the showdown between the U.S. government and the Branch Davidian cult in Waco, Texas, and 45 of them (62 percent) were female; in the mass suicide at Jonestown by the members of the People's Temple cult, 66 percent were women.

Why do women take up new religions? Perhaps because they are treated so badly by the old religions. Unsurprisingly, most religious traditions support, or even mandate, traditional gender roles. They bar women from most positions of authority, restrict their dress, and sometimes blame them for the evils in the world (Eve in the major monotheistic traditions, Pandora in Greek mythology, Izanami in the Shinto creation story). Until very recently, almost all priests, ministers, rabbis, imams, monks, gurus, shamans, and other such higher functionaries of the religious establishments were male. All of Jesus's disciples were male. Women often had to sit in separate sections of the church or synagogue or mosque. They could not lead prayers, and because most were illiterate they were not even able to read the prayers.

Why are women more religious than men?

New religions tend to be better for women. As a striking example, consider the beginnings of Islam. Most Westerners seem to think of Islam as backwards in its treatment of women. In fact, Mohammad prescribed a liberating revolution for women in the context of his time. In the Arab world before Islam, women were chattel, the property of their fathers and then of their husbands and then of anyone their husbands gave them to. They had no rights. Mohammad gave them rights of protection, divorce, and property, among other advances. Similarly, early Christianity gave women the right to not be killed having unsafe abortions they didn't want, not to be treated as chattel, or not to be left to die from exposure because their father wanted a son, among others. All of these were common practices in the Roman paganism of the time.

☐ Women as Generally More Religious

Despite these and other advances for women, "new religions" today still develop in an environment in which women are disadvantaged, in general, and second-class citizens within most of the established religions of the world, in particular. One would think such treatment would lead women to reject traditional religion to a greater extent than men. Yet most research finds just the opposite. One literature review argues strongly that despite their poor treatment, "[t]he greater religiosity of women must be one of the oldest and clearest findings in the psychology of religion" (Beit-Hallahmi and Argyle 1997:142).

But wait a minute. One of the great things about science is that we keep reevaluating what we think we know. This is what D. Paul Sullins did in 2006, and his reanalysis of the available data challenged the received wisdom, concluding: (1) Women were more likely to describe themselves as pious or religious across almost all societies studied, but men were more likely or equally likely to be active "organizational participants" (i.e., go to church regularly, etc.) in about 25 percent of countries. (2) Most importantly for our purposes, there was little difference in piety between male and female Jews (particularly Orthodox Jews) or male and female Muslims, and males were much more likely to participate in religious activities than women in countries dominated by those faiths (Sullins 2006). Since Sullins published his analysis, more extensive data from Saudi Arabia, Egypt, Jordan, and Iran have confirmed his findings for Muslim countries (Moaddel 2007).

Why might the relationship between gender and religiosity be different among Jews and Muslims than among Christians? Consider the gender differences in the way that faith is or was lived in traditionally Muslim countries, or among Jews in some earlier, more traditional period. All male orthodox Jews were expected to spend much of their time studying the Torah and the Talmud—in other words, in religious study. In contrast, women and girls were not allowed to participate in such activities. Women were much less likely to go to temple than men, and most did not even know how to participate in the prayers that were the major part of the service. Women performed a variety of small rituals at home, but their intellectual and perhaps emotional engagements with religion were comparatively limited.

The status of Muslim women is similar. Young Muslim boys are trained to memorize the Koran; girls are not (although some may choose to do so). The number of women who pray at the mosque is generally a fraction of the number of men. Those who do attend are shunted off to the rear or side. One of the five pillars of Muslim practice is the Hajj, or ritual visit to Mecca, which religious Muslims try to perform at least once in their lifetime. Yet males always outnumber females at the Hajj by very large margins. In general, then, Muslim men might attend services more often in some countries, while more or equal numbers of Muslim women consider themselves religious. The proposition that women are always more religious than men is really quite questionable.

Questions about Muslim and Jewish gender differences do not invalidate the consistent finding of greater female religiosity in most Christian settings. Beit-Hallami and Argyle (1997) offer a number of possible explanations. As psychologists, they give great weight to the idea that men and women have different personality distributions, with men being more aggressive and hence more likely to challenge the religion of their parents. Like most Western social scientists, they do not include the idea that women prefer their "different but equal" roles in traditional religious life. The evidence from women's choices after being allowed to vote, to hold jobs, and so forth just seems too contradictory for many social scientists to accept this position.

My own preferred reason for greater female religiosity among Christians is more sociological. I begin by noting that in practice Christianity may be more egalitarian than Orthodox Judaism or Islam. Although all priests are male, most traditional Catholic men and women occupy similar positions towards their faith in that the priest does most of the work and the thinking for them. The men do not have to know any more than the women. They need to be obedient. In radical Protestantism, on the other hand, every person, male and female, should have a personal relationship with God and read the Bible. Again, the ministers and theologians might be men, but their importance is downgraded before the individual parishioner's role in his or her religious life.

In virtually all societies (with the possible exception of contemporary Scandinavia), being religious is conventional. At the same time, in almost all societies we know of, including most seemingly modern societies, control over women, particularly their sexuality, is more important than control over men—so the training of women for compliance and conventionality is a central concern of almost all cultures. Furthermore, women in traditional societies are kept at home much more than men. For conventional Christian women, the church is a safe and acceptable place to be in public and with other adults. They do not go to bars, or sports clubs, or places of work. For all women, often denied education or economic opportunity, being pious is one of the few means by which they can be just as good as, or better than, other people. Men can gain respect by earning money, by being good at sports, by doing well in scholarship, or by seducing women. Religion and motherhood are the key bases of self-validation available to most traditional women, including those in the developed world.

Why are older people more religious?

☐ Do We Become More Religious as We Age?

One of the more interesting, if less important, reasons women are more religious than men in most places is that on average women are older. In most developed countries women outlive men by about five years. And, as many of us know from our own experience, older people are more religious than younger people.

FIGURE 14.2 ATTENDANCE AT RELIGIOUS SERVICES, BY GENERATION

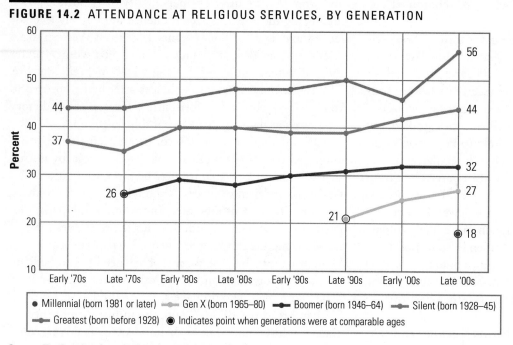

Source: The Pew Forum on Religion and Public Life (2010).

For a long time, the age difference in religiosity was thought to derive from the confrontation with death becoming increasingly acute as we age. Alternatively, mature wisdom and perspective were seen to replace the rebelliousness of youth.

Today, however, most sociologists agree that the most important reason older people tend to be more religious is not aging but what is called "cohort" differences: Older people were brought up in more religious times than younger people. Your grandparents were always more religious than you (most of you, that is). This can be clearly seen in Figure 14.2.

As Figure 14.2 shows, the "generations" (usually called "cohorts" by sociologists) born earlier are always more likely to say they go to church than the generations born later, and each generation starts at a lower level of attendance in their early 20s than the previous generation (or cohort).

The data in Figure 14.2, however, does not track the religiosity of individuals over their lifetime, which is a much more difficult job. To do so, we would have had to start the research more than 50 years ago. We have only a few such long-term studies that measured religiosity, and they are for selected, not-very-representative samples. Nevertheless, these can give us some idea of individual change. One such study follows a group of Oakland, California, students who were interviewed while in high school in the late 1920s and then interviewed several additional times, most recently in the 1990s when they were well into their 70s (Dillon and Wink 2007). Figure 14.3 shows their religious trajectories, by gender, where the measure of "religiousness" is a complex combination of practices and beliefs. Note that, as expected, women in the sample were always substantially more religious than men.

The respondents were most religious when they were teenagers. The women remained at the same level in their late

30s, declined in religiosity into their 60s, and increased in their late 70s. Men simply declined rather markedly into their 60s, with some recovery in their late 70s. For both men and women, therefore, there is some evidence the ages between 60 and 80 might contain some increase in religiosity. Or it might indicate that more religious people live a bit longer.

Unfortunately, data were not collected during this sample's college-age years. We know from other work that this stage of life, which is when most people in the United States leave home, is the stage when they are most likely to reassess their religious commitments and decline in religious participation, whether they went to college or not. For example, Smith (2009:244–46) followed a representative sample from ages 13–17 to ages 20–22. He found that between 33 and 40 percent of these young people declined in religiosity, some sharply, while only 3 to 7 percent increased (the rest were "stable").

To represent what I think the religious life histories of the Oakland sample would look like if we had data for their 20s, I have added lines to Figure 14.3 that

FIGURE 14.3 MEAN CHANGE IN RELIGIOUSNESS OVER TIME BY GENDER

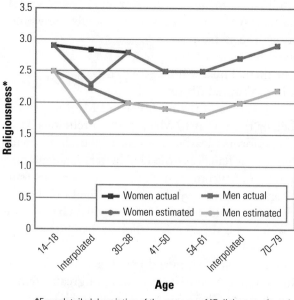

*For a detailed description of the measure of "Religiousness" used in this figure see Dillon and Wink (2007, p. 82)

Source: Dillon and Wink (2007).

estimate these data points (marked as "interpolated" in the figure). I propose that the "real" low point in religiosity would have been during their 20s. The resulting trendlines fit with the following narrative of religiosity over the life course, at least in the United States: (1) Because parents, schools, and churches invest heavily in the religiosity of children, and most children accept these lessons, children's religiosity is high, if somewhat incoherent. (2) With relative independence from their parents during the post-high-school years, many of these young people lose interest in religion, or in their inherited religion, or begin to be influenced by other, less religious views. (3) After people have children themselves, they tend to move to communities where churches are more important and to think that they should teach their children about religion. This is particularly important for women, who most often bear the responsibility for childrearing. Thus, there is a tendency to return to church during this life stage, which for the Oakland sample was probably ages 28 to 40. (4) After their children leave the home, some of the middle-aged return to their earlier, less religious practices and views. (5) In the oldest part of the life course, people leave their jobs and lose friends and spouses. For many, the church and the support of religion might become more important, whether they fear death or not.

4 Why Do People Kill Each Other in the Name of Religion?

RELIGIOUS CONFLICT

👁 Watch the **Big Question** Video in **MySocLab**

To this point we have mostly focused on figuring out what people get out of religion. Unfortunately, however, there is also a much darker side to the relationship between religion and society. In this day and age we have all confronted the paradox of people killing each other in the name of religion. Muslims killing Americans in New York, killing Jews in Palestine, killing other Muslims who won't toe their religious line in Pakistan; Jews killing Muslims in Lebanon; Catholics killing Protestants in Northern Ireland, and vice versa; Buddhists and Hindus killing each other in Sri Lanka; Muslims and Christians killing each other in Nigeria; periodic eruptions between Hindus and Muslims in India; Sunni Iraq fighting a vicious war against Shi'a Iran—all this and more in only the past half-dozen decades.

History is replete with religious war. After all, people who know that their religion is right have every reason to spread that religion and to defend it by force against heathens or heretics. Particularly in the first century after Mohammad's death, Islam was primarily spread by the sword. In the twelfth and thirteenth centuries, Christians launched the Crusades against Muslims. In the sixteenth century, Protestants and Catholics fought the Thirty Years' War over control of various parts of Europe. In the nineteenth and twentieth centuries Jews were slain in pogroms by Russian Orthodox Cossacks. In the first two decades of the twentieth century,

Muslim Turks and Kurds probably killed from 1 to 1.5 million Christian Armenians. Even civil religion might be said to have its violence: During the Civil War, Northern soldiers sang "The Battle Hymn of the Republic" as they marched off to do their sacred duty to save the Union.

If MTD subscribers (and most people) are right in thinking that religion fosters morality, we seem to have some weighty negative evidence. But then, appearances can be deceiving. It is often hard to tell when a religious war is a war about religion. Consider, for example, the Catholic-Protestant war in Northern Ireland. In a very telling sentence (supposedly a quotation from a nameless participant), Demerath (2003) describes the war as "Protestant atheists vs. Catholic atheists." He points out that with one or two prominent but really marginal exceptions, virtually all religious figures in Northern (and Southern) Ireland were against the killings and confrontations. Furthermore, one could easily argue that major class and ethnic conflicts were the real sources of the war. Northern Ireland was ruled by the well-off descendents of British colonialists. Thus, ethnicity and class, as well as religion, separated the sides. In Sri Lanka, the Buddhists are overwhelmingly ethnic Sinhalese, and the minority Hindus (18 percent of the population) are ethnic Tamils. They speak different languages, and the Tamils have long considered themselves discriminated against economically and politically. For most Tamils, the war is about the need for secession so that they can have their own country. Neither group seems to think the other should change their religion. Perhaps this too is an ethnic and economic war rather than a religious one.

We could look at many "religious" wars and find ethnic or tribal conflict more central to the problem. Serbs killing Muslims in Bosnia called it "ethnic cleansing," not "religious cleansing." Muslims and Jews lived together fairly peacefully in British-controlled Palestine until the 1920s, when Zionists, who believed that Jews needed their own homeland so that they could defend themselves from lethal anti-Semitism around the world, particularly in Germany and other parts of Europe, began immigrating in great numbers. Threatened by the flood of Jews, Palestinian Arabs rioted and demanded the British halt the migration (Sela 1994). Note that most of the founders of Israel were more or less irreligious, as are most Israelis today. As mentioned earlier, these secular people define Jewishness in ethnic rather than religious terms. One has the right to become an Israeli citizen if one's mother is Jewish, not if one believes in the sacredness of the Torah and that Jews are God's chosen people: ethnicity, not religion. Jews are not fighting Muslims because they believe theirs is the one true faith.

All this is not to say that there are no wars or internal mass killings that are not at least somewhat religious in basis. Even the United States has seen the killing of doctors who perform abortions by fundamentalist vigilantes who claim to be acting on religious grounds. Earlier, Mormons were violently driven out of upstate New York and later Nauvoo, Illinois, because of their different religious ideas. Since the fall of the military dictatorship, some Egyptian Muslims have been attacking the churches of Christian Copts, who are about 10 percent of the population, calling Christians "blasphemers" for disagreeing with Islam.

Perhaps the most compelling incident of what seems to be religious violence is part of the long-term conflict between Hindus and Muslims in India. The partition of India into India and Pakistan (which at first included what would become Bangladesh) took place in 1947, shortly after Britain decided to end its colonial control over the subcontinent. The partition was hasty and unplanned. More than 7 million Muslims moved to Pakistan, and an approximately equal number of Hindus, Sikhs, and others moved from the territory that became Pakistan to what remained of India. From being approximately 25 percent

Why is it difficult to distinguish religious conflict from ethnic or class conflict?

Hindu militants storm the disputed mosque at Ayodhya preparing to demolish it and clear the site for a Hindu temple.

Muslim before partition, the new India contained less than 13 percent. The new Pakistan had hardly any Hindus at all. It is estimated that between half a million and a million people died in the process as Hindus and Muslims fought over land or just over resentments in both communities.

After partition communal conflict between Hindus and Muslims was common in India, although almost always local. Anything that might go wrong could begin a cycle of hostility. Muslims had conquered most of India in the sixteenth century and ruled until the eighteenth century, a fact not lost on the majority Hindus. To this day, some of them continue to write vicious screeds on the horrors of Muslim occupation, particularly in the blogosphere. For many Hindus the partition meant that India was now specifically a Hindu country, perhaps with more reason than the idea that America is a Christian country. This idea sparked the growth of a political philosophy of "Hindutva," which asserts that India should be for Hindus, and eventually led to the election of an avowedly Hindutva party to a majority in the parliament.

In the early 1990s, Hindutva politicians and a number of Hindu "holy men" focused on a mosque in Ayodhya that they claimed had been built on top of an important Hindu temple (what cynics have called one of the mythical birthplaces of the mythical god Rama). They demanded that the mosque be razed and the Hindu temple rebuilt. The government was opposed, envisioning the turmoil that would ensue and the hundreds of other sites that might become controversial. In December 1992, an estimated 200,000 Hindus descended on the mosque and, despite some opposition from a small number of police, razed the mosque themselves (led by Hindu "skinheads," of all things). All over India communal violence broke out, with more than 2,000 people being killed.

Was this really a religious conflict? It at least warns us that conflicts between religious groups can have elements of everything—class resentments, ethnic drives for control of land or governments, long memories of past or imagined injuries, and religious intolerance or fear. Religion is a potent marker of "us versus them." It speaks for the "rightness" of our cause. For many people in this world, security comes only from being a member of a powerful group. That group's fate is our fate—and that includes nationalism as well as ethnicity or religion. Religion provides institutional support for our side because it has professional people to do the organizing. It works well in times of conflict.

5 What Is the Future of Religion?

SECULARIZATION VERSUS INCREASED RELIGIOSITY

 Watch the **Big Question Video** in **MySocLab**

If you have read this far, you might think we have surely hit all the high points in the sociology of religion. But this is emphatically not the case. I have actually saved for last what has historically been the most important question for sociologists of religion—is **secularization** or increased religiosity the future of religion? For most of the twentieth century, social scientists generally argued that with modernization and the development of science, the relevance of religion to the life of society would progressively decline. In this view, the world is becoming "demystified." We are abandoning superstition and becoming more and more secular. This has usually been referred to as the secularization hypothesis and was an important sociological theory even at the turn of the twentieth century

More recently, however, Stark and his colleagues (for example, Stark and Finke 2000), have challenged this more-or-less accepted idea. They have presented data and arguments about the growth and strength of religion in highly developed countries like the United States, and claim that there is a deep-seated human need for religious commitment and practice that overrides modernization. Others have disagreed with Stark and his collaborators, and the battle has been drawn.

As with many terms in the sociological arsenal, secularization has been used in somewhat different ways by different theorists. At its simplest level, secularization has been taken to mean that people abandon religion as unscientific or irrelevant to modern existence. Books are written about "The Death of God" and the rise of irreligion in modernized societies.

But most sociologists have actually meant something more subtle by secularization. As Weber argued, sociologists do not necessarily expect people to abandon all belief in God or in their church or in religious ideas. Instead, their argument focuses on the authority religion has over the lives of people: Do people actually limit or suit their behavior according to the dictates of religion? Those who argue for secularization see this authority shrinking in the modern world as life becomes more complex and modern institutions that have little to do with religion claim more and more authority over parts of people's lives.

For example, in a society dominated by agriculture, religion appears central to everything—from appeasing the weather gods to prayers for fertility or for god's support in war. In contrast, businesspeople in modern industrial societies do not pray for their production line to work. Even in religious America today people have to work on supposed religious days of rest so that the assembly line is not shut down. Hospitals and doctors, not priests and shamans, are experts on health. Education is delivered by professionalized schools, mostly state rather than religious. Most people have hardly any idea of the relationship between weather and food and only pray to have enough money to feed their teenage children. We can easily add many examples to this list.

It is hard to argue with the authority version of secularization in highly developed societies. Everywhere in Europe and America, the authority of churches over the way society is run has diminished over time. Stores are open on Sundays. People don't go to church. Catholic women use birth control. Most Jews are not kosher. Evangelical Christians have high divorce rates and get abortions.

How do sociologists define secularization?

□ European Irreligion

Even if one asks simply whether people are religious or not, one can easily make the case that the nonimmigrant people of Europe have become very secular indeed. On any given Sunday only about 10 percent of Europeans go to church. Fewer than half of the people of Scandinavia, Holland, Germany, France, Britain, or Belgium, or of many countries that were previously part of communist Europe, say they believe in god (European Commission 2005:8).

Surveys tend to show that although Europeans are not opposed to religion in other people, they want the religious to keep it private. They do not want religion in their politics. Europeans actually tend to be put off by very religious people, so they are probably more suspicious of what they see as the excessive religiosity of Muslim immigrants than they are of the fact they are Muslims. When asked, most Europeans say that religion is not very important in their own lives.

How can this be? Don't Western Europeans "need" traditional religion for moral order or for some vision of life after death? Somehow they manage without. For example, Europeans have less than 25 percent of the homicide rate in the United States—for irreligious Norway it is close to 15 percent (Geneva Declaration Secretariat 2008). The poor in Europe are given a relatively generous safety net and need neither starve nor die without medical care. If "do unto others" is the essence of Christian morality, Europeans do not seem particularly immoral.

□ American Exceptionalism

Among the developed countries of the world (Australia, Canada, Japan, and Israel look a lot like Europe regarding religion), it is the United States that is considered the exception that needs to be explained. Modern as any Western European country, the United States retains a level of conventional religiosity far above almost all of the other developed countries of the world. As noted above, at least twice as many Americans as Europeans say they attend church regularly. About 80 percent of Americans say they believe in god. Two-thirds of Americans say they would not vote for an irreligious person to be president (of course, the United States has had many relatively irreligious presidents—Jefferson, Lincoln, and Franklin Roosevelt, among others.) And religious issues like abortion, homosexuality, public support for religious education, and prayer in schools are often central issues in American politics.

The Rise of Conservative Protestantism These issues have become so important primarily because of the rise in power and numbers of evangelical, conservative, or fundamentalist Protestants, particularly during the 1970s and 1980s. These conservatives consistently describe themselves as highly

Conservative Protestants and Catholics have turned abortion and homosexuality into defining political battlegrounds. Not everyone wants to fight those battles.

religious, consistently report higher church attendance, and otherwise are considered more religious than adherents of "mainline" Protestant denominations.

Greeley and Hout (2006) show that about 75 percent of the growth of conservative Protestantism was due to their relatively high fertility, which was particularly striking in contrast to the sharply declining fertility of mainline Protestants during the same period. A second major factor in conservative growth was an increase in the ability of conservative Christians to retain their young people. At one time, evangelicals who prospered would often change to the more socially and financially prestigious mainline churches. With increasing affluence, that became less necessary, as more successful evangelicals made for more acceptable communities for the upwardly mobile.

According to Putnam and Campbell (2010) a third factor also fueled the post-1960s rise of conservative Protestantism—a profound reaction to the revolutionary social changes of the time. Because conservative white Protestants are centered in the South, reaction against the civil rights revolution was certainly a factor. However, Putnam and Campbell argue that the key revolution had to do with changing gender roles and "sexual liberation." Repelled by these changes, many more conservative Americans sought to defend a more stable commitment to "traditional family values"—especially for their children—and turned to those churches that they saw as sharing this conservative vision.

As part of this reaction the prominence of conservative Protestantism was further boosted by the entrance of evangelical ministers into politics, with organizations such as the Moral Majority, culminating in the election of the conservative evangelical George W. Bush. In all, it appeared, and to many still appears, that evangelicals were the future face of religion in America. In the next section we can see that this might not be the case.

Why Is America So Religious? Many reasons have been advanced for American religious exceptionalism. For example, Stark and his colleagues have argued that in most countries there has been only one established religion, while in the United States many different religions compete—a much better marketing situation. If we could buy only one cereal, those of us who do not like it might stop eating cereal. Of course, the advertising budgets for cereal are enormous, which no doubt supports the American addiction to these morning grains. At the same time, if one looks at religion as a commodity, one also realizes that expenditures on promoting religion are much, much higher. Consider all the TV shows and ads on TV, in newspapers, and now on

How does religiosity compare in Europe and America?

the Internet. At 2 AM one night I found at least seven different programs promoting religion. Even more tellingly, we pay more than 300,000 clergymen to give sermons that are mostly about convincing parishioners that they should be faithful.

An alternative argument is that religion thrives in America because the nation is so ethnically, geographically, and religiously diverse. Each group clings to its religion as a means of preserving its community and culture. Another possibility is that the absence of a highly developed welfare state makes churches crucial in America. In European countries the state does more to provide medical, social, and educational services. In the United States, public schools are underfunded and often useless; many people cannot get health insurance; the police are often ethnically alien to minorities and the poor; most jobs are not unionized and unions cannot help most people with difficulties at work; and so forth. In the absence of strong and available alternative institutions, Americans turn to their churches for hope, help, and sustenance.

☐ The Decline of Religion in America

It is likely that no single reason uniquely accounts for America's exceptionalism but that several or all factors work together to make the United States different. However, it is not clear how long that difference will be sustained. There are signs that religiosity in America may be moving in the European direction, particularly if we ignore the effects of massive immigration.

Currently, surveys indicate that the fastest growing religion in the United States is "no religious preference." From 2.7 percent in 1960, and 8 percent a decade ago, the number of people so identifying themselves has grown to about 16 percent today, and because young people are much more likely to think of themselves as not religious, the number is likely to increase.

If not for immigration, the Catholic Church would be seen as hemorrhaging believers. Twenty years ago Catholics made up about 22 percent of the American people. Today the percentage is about the same despite the fact that about 80 percent of the enormous numbers of recent immigrants to America have been Catholic. Moreover, the Catholic Church is having great difficulty finding men to take up religious vocations and become priests (to be sure, however, they could end the problem for at least 50 years if they simply allowed women to become priests or allowed priests to marry).

We can also expect the relative number of conservative Protestants to decline over the coming decades. As conservative Protestants have become more urban and educated, differences between their birth rates and those of other Americans have declined. Evangelical intellectuals are already complaining that they are losing their young to more secular orientations. Figure 14.4 (based on Putnam and Campbell 2010:125) is a dramatic summary of trends among youth aged 18 to 29, comparing those who declare themselves to be evangelicals with those who say that they have no religious preference ("nones"). The contrasting projections are stark and argue for continued secularization in America.

The major argument (see especially Hout and Fischer 2002) for the key inflection point in both curves—1990—is that the rise of conservative Christian political assertiveness that characterized the previous decades repelled many Americans, who prefer a separation of the church from politics. Young people who had previously identified in a marginal way with a specific religion did not lose all of their faith—most still believe in God and pray. However, they no longer want to be associated with the right-wing politics that now characterizes religious denominations, so they become "nones."

The Rise of Religion in the Rest of the World

As Norris and Inglehart conclude, a good case can be made for the secularization hypothesis in the developed modern world, even the United States. And yet, as Norris and Inglehart also say quite clearly, if we look at the contemporary world as a whole, we can make just the opposite argument—the world seems to be getting more, not less, religious. A higher percentage of people are probably more religious

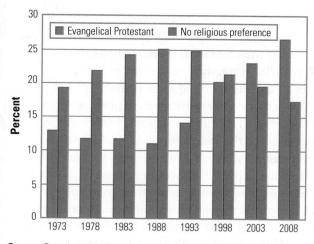

FIGURE 14.4 EVANGELICALS AND "NONES" AMONG AMERICAN YOUTH (AGES 18–29), 1973–2008

Source: Based on data from Putnam and Campbell (2010).

now than they were two or three decades ago, and in many countries, like Russia, Iran, and elsewhere in the Middle East, religious authority seems to have increased rather than withered.

I would add a caution. The measures we have of religiosity around the world are not very deep and may mask processes of secularization that are occurring in countries that are "developing." The pictures on our TV screens tend to present the sensational, not the long-term gradual processes suggested by those who promote the secularization hypothesis.

However, on the assumption that Norris and Inglehart are right, what is the major reason for the increase in religious persons around the world? Although the causes might be complex, surely one of the most important is simple demography. Everywhere in the world, as in the United States, religious people have more children than irreligious people. The difference is even greater between societies. Religious societies have much higher birth rates than irreligious ones. In part, this simply reflects the levels of development of those societies. Before modernization all societies were mostly religious, and all societies had high birth rates and high death rates. People simply did not know how to stop having babies or how to stop death. Eventually, sanitation, medicine, and other factors brought the death rate down in industrializing and modernizing societies, leading those societies to have high birth rates but low(er) death rates, so that their populations "exploded." In the contemporary world a less-developed society does not have to invent sanitation or medicine. These ideas and materials can be brought in from outside, so the drop in death rates can happen quickly.

As the more developed countries learned how to control deaths, their birth rates also came down. People found that children could be expensive and confining in an industrial and urban world. Some of these societies (e.g., Japan, Russia, Spain) now actually have declining populations. Meanwhile, less developed countries today may have reduced death rates, but they still have high birth rates (although they are coming down) and are still religious. Thus, the number of religious persons in the world increases with these exploding populations.

Even if we return to the idea of secularization as authority, the world has seen surging religious militancy in much of the Muslim world, with relevant consequences for politics in those countries. Women are either deciding to wear veils or being forced to wear veils. Iran, once run by a secular shah and a socialist prime minister, is now controlled by its religious establishment. In Egypt, the Muslim Brotherhood has reentered the political arena and will share power in the next government, and so on.

Reasons for this reemergence have complex roots but are partly a matter of the reassertion of cultural pride in a segment of the world that had been colonized and dominated by Western political, economic, and, most importantly for religion, cultural imperialism. Under these circumstances, many people found that only religion provided an alternative symbol of difference and nationalism and a legitimate basis for organization, so that it could serve as a rallying mechanism for the assertion of independence and power.

The Resurgence of Conventional Religion in Russia and China

The second most important story in the recent growth of conventional religion concerns two of the largest societies in the world, Russia and China. The stories are quite different, but they are important nevertheless.

In Russia, the revival of Russian Orthodoxy after the fall of the antireligious communist state has been remarkable. We do not really know how many Russians gave up Orthodoxy under the communists. Surely, many remained conventionally religious, perhaps practicing privately or in restricted circumstances.

The new noncommunist but authoritarian government in Russia has allied itself with the Orthodox Church. The government seeks to use religion to exercise some control over the vast country it is trying to manage—to provide some agreement on norms and way of life. The Church has become the most trusted institution in Russia. From so-called secular communism to relatively religious in practically the blink of an eye, Russia can be used as compelling evidence of the rise of religion in the contemporary world.

So can China, but in a completely different way. In China, the communist regime has not disappeared. It has, however, changed many of its policies, including its approach to conventional religion. Persecution of religious organizations has been relaxed, and religion is now allowed to

go about its business so long as it is not controlled by "outside" forces and acts within the boundaries set by the government. It is not completely free, but not squashed, either.

The major beneficiary of this new situation appears to be Protestant Christianity, particularly in its Pentecostal variants. Small "house" churches have appeared in many areas of China, and there are now estimated to be as many as 100 million Chinese adherents. This is perhaps less than 10 percent of the enormous 1.3 billion person Chinese population but equal to almost half of all the Christians in the United States—and quickly growing.

Pentecostalism, which is generally inward-looking and hence not as likely to compete for political power, seems relatively well-suited for a situation in which the government is determined to keep power to itself. It is also probable that Confucianism, Taoism, and other traditional Chinese religions have been growing during this period.

Religion and the Promise of Prosperity

And then there is the rise of the prosperity gospel all over the world. Listen to Joel Osteen, who leads the largest megachurch in America: "It's going to happen ... Suddenly, your situation will change for the better ... [God] will bring your dreams to pass" (Osteen 2004:196–98). All because you believe in Christ and extol him. "God wants you to have a house," he says. Three of the 12 largest megachurches in America are led by ministers who preach prosperity theology.

For many of the newly urbanized people of the world who see the wealth of Christian America and are finally in position to dream of success for themselves, the prosperity gospel, born in America, and convincingly American, seems to be the answer. Christianity with a prosperity theology has been most explosive in Africa. In its 2006 survey of African religion, the Pew Foundation asked participants if God would "grant material prosperity to all believers who have enough faith." About 90 percent of Kenyan, South African, and Nigerian Pentecostals said yes. Ninety percent also agreed that religious faith was "very important to economic success" (Pew Research Center 2011).

For sociologists of religion the success of prosperity Christianity is deeply ironic. Weber's Protestant Ethic argued that ascetic Protestantism had set the stage for Americans to develop habits of thrift, hard work, and wealth accumulation that are the hallmarks of successful capitalism. Those religious Calvinists believed in the doctrine of grace, in which neither prayer nor good "works" could bring salvation. But they sought signs that they were among those elected by God for his own reasons—and prosperity and hard work were the signs they understood as suggesting they would achieve salvation.

What is the prosperity gospel?

Prosperity theology stands Weber's analysis on its head. Instead of prosperity being a signpost towards salvation, prosperity becomes the goal of being religious. Prayer and good works, instead of being useless in gaining salvation, are now the price of being prosperous. Grace comes to the people who donate to the church of the prosperity preacher—it is not something with which you are born.

How much more modern is prosperity theology than a theology focused on salvation! Most of us no longer die at 35 but at twice that age or more. Salvation will and can wait. A nest egg will be necessary to sustain us in comfort.

CONCLUSION A PROPOSITION ABOUT DEATH AND RELIGIOSITY

An old and revered saying in science is that "the more you learn the more questions you have." I hope that you have learned by reading this chapter. I have learned a lot by writing it. And true to the saying, I am left with a lot of questions and ideas. I hope you are as well.

I therefore want to end this chapter with a question, something to look into in the future. I will phrase the question as a proposition. It may be true, or sort of true, or not true at all. I have seen no research on the point.

My proposition derives directly from the last paragraph in the discussion of the prosperity gospel in the last section. After thinking about it, I suspect that one of the reasons highly devel oped countries experience declines in religiosity is that over the long term those countries have experienced soaring life expectancies.

At the time of Christ, average life expectancy in the Roman Empire was less than 30 years. By 1870 life expectancy in England, the richest country in the world, was still only 40 years. Three of ten babies born died by the age of one. Death was everywhere. Everyone had seen many people die. A 30-year-old had seen her mother and one or more children die, a 10-year-old her grandmother and a brother, and maybe her father. Death was even more present everywhere else in the world. No wonder people were preoccupied with death and the afterlife.

Today, life expectancy in England is about 80, in the United States 78, in Japan 82. Most young people have known no one who has died, or perhaps their aged grandparents, or a soldier in some war. But death is not an everyday event unless one lives in a retirement community. Young people don't live there. Furthermore, I suspect that many old people are not as repulsed by death as their ancestors. With long lives behind them, their peers dying, and illnesses sapping their activity, death does not seem so cruel and forbidding. People over 70 have America's highest suicide rate. Death has come gradually, in little steps. As the current cliché has it, death is a natural part of life—especially when one is 85.

So perhaps the focus of religion on the afterlife, or next life, or on helping people to deal with death, is not as important as it used to be. And if religion is therefore less useful, it may also be less compelling. Or is it? Perhaps you would like to do some research. If you and they can bear to talk about death, talk to your grandparents. Figure out some way of getting information on this question that would be useful. Be a sociologist of religion!

Watch the Video in MySocLab
Applying Your Sociological Imagination

Study and **Review** in **MySocLab**   **Watch** the **Video** Inspiring Your Sociological Imagination in **MySocLab**

1 What Is Religion, and How Is It Organized? *(p. 382)*

 Watch the **Big Question Video** in **MySocLab** to review the key concepts for this section.

Sociologists have no single agreed-upon definition of religion. Nevertheless, they understand that the actual religious behavior of people in every religion is enormously variable and fluid. This section examined the incredible number of religions throughout the world and throughout history, the concept of religion as a social institution, and the social function of organized religion.

A SOCIOLOGICAL UNDERSTANDING OF RELIGION (p. 382)

Defining Religion (p. 382)

- **What are different ways that sociologists define religion?**

Religion as a Social Institution (p. 388)

- **What is the function of the religious social institution?**

Explore the **Data** on A Global View of Religion in **MySocLab**

- **What role do denominations and congregations play in organizing religious activity?**

Explore A Sociological Perspective: What is religion's function? in **MySocLab**

KEY TERMS

doctrine *(p. 380)*
sacred *(p. 382)*
supernatural *(p. 383)*
ideology *(p. 383)*
civil religion *(p. 383)*
irreligion *(p. 384)*
syncretic *(p. 384)*
theology *(p. 388)*
social institution *(p. 388)*
pluralism *(p. 389)*
denomination *(p. 389)*
congregation *(p. 389)*

2 How Do People Choose Their Religions? *(p. 392)*

 Watch the **Big Question Video** in **MySocLab** to review the key concepts for this section.

With all the religions in the world, how do people choose a religion for themselves? This section explored the patterns of religious choice, including the impact of race, ethnicity, and social class on religious preferences.

PATTERNS OF RELGIOUS CHOICE (p. 392)

Birds of a Feather (p. 392)

- **What leads to segregation in American churches?**

Social Class and Religious Preferences (p. 394)

Conversion (p. 396)

- **Who converts to what denomination or religion, and why?**

KEY TERMS

liberation theology *(p. 393)*
theodicy *(p. 395)*
new religious movement *(p. 397)*

Read the **Document** *Are American Jews Vanishing Again?* by Calvin Goldscheider in **MySocLab.** This reading argues the Jewish population is thriving and American Jews are a model for other ethnic communities in how to assimilate while retaining a sense of ethnic culture.

New Religious Movements (p. 397)

- **Who is drawn to emerging new religions?**

---

3 Why Are Women and Older People More Religious than Men and the Young? *(p. 398)*

👁 **Watch** the **Big Question Video** in **MySocLab** to review the key concepts for this section.

In this section we discussed differences in religiosity by age and gender.

RELIGIOSITY BY GENDER AND AGE (p. 398)

Women as Generally More Religious (p. 398)

- **Why are women more religious than men?**

Do We Become More Religious as We Age? (p. 399)

- **Why are older people more religious?**

---

4 Why Do People Kill Each Other in the Name of Religion? *(p. 401)*

👁 **Watch** the **Big Question Video** in **MySocLab** to review the key concepts for this section.

This section examined why there has been so much religious conflict over history and in the present, as well as the difficulty of distinguishing religious conflict from ethnic or class conflict.

RELIGIOUS CONFLICT (p. 401)

- **Why is it difficult to distinguish religious conflict from ethnic or class conflict?**

What Is the Future of Religion?

(p. 403)

 Watch the **Big Question Video** in **MySocLab** to review the key concepts for this section.

We saved for last what has historically been the most important question for sociologists of religion. In this section, we explored the future of religion.

SECULARLIZATION VERSUS INCREASED RELIGIOSITY (p. 403)

- **How do sociologists define secularization?**

European Irreligion (p. 404)

American Exceptionalism (p. 404)

- **How does religiosity compare in Europe and America?**

The Decline of Religion in America (p. 405)

The Rise of Religion in the Rest of the World (p. 406)

The Resurgence of Conventional Religion in Russia and China (p. 407)

Religion and the Promise of Prosperity (p. 407)

- **What is the prosperity gospel?**

 Watch the **Video** Applying Your Sociological Imagination in **MySocLab** to see these concepts at work in the real world.

15

EDUCATION

((• Listen to the **Chapter Audio** in **MySocLab**

by CAROLINE H. PERSELL

J ake steps out of his dorm onto a vast campus with a computer center, multiple theaters, many seminar rooms, dining halls, art studios, tennis courts, a hockey rink, and much more. Mary enters her school through a security check and faces packed halls, large classrooms, and peeling paint. The first day of school differs dramatically for the 1 percent of young people attending elite private boarding schools like Jake's and the millions like Mary who attend crowded, decaying inner-city schools. The differences extend far beyond the physical facilities, however, and raise provocative questions about relative educational opportunities.

Classes at elite boarding schools are often taught as seminars with no more than 15 students. Teachers know their students well and can provide extra help if needed. Students write a great deal and are carefully taught how to write well—how to make an argument and support it with evidence. Virtually everyone participates in extracurricular activities such as student government and yearbook. In contrast, in the typical public high school, less than 10 percent of students are involved in such activities.

Young people who attend elite boarding schools also benefit from college advisors who actively promote their virtues to the top colleges and universities. When we asked college advisors at such institutions to describe their jobs, one told us, "I put the applicants' folders in the trunk of my car and drive around to [the Ivy League] colleges and talk to the admissions officers about our applicants. I try to make the case for a particular student if I think the college is making a mistake." Having such advisors at one's disposal clearly makes a difference: Graduates of elite boarding schools are disproportionately represented at the most elite private colleges and universities despite the fact that most do not do as well academically as public school graduates once in college.

MY SOCIOLOGICAL IMAGINATION
Caroline H. Persell

While I was in graduate school at Columbia University, James Coleman and others published a major study showing that schools made little difference in the achievement of students because the variations within individual schools was almost as great as the variations between schools. This rocked the scholarly world and got me thinking about whether it captured all the colors in the educational spectrum. In my visits to many inner-city schools, I had seen students and teachers with lots of energy, ambition, and intelligence working hard to do the best they could in the underresourced conditions they were in. At the same time, I knew that other types of schools, like private boarding schools, were not included in the Coleman study, and wondered how education differed for students at such schools. A question of enduring interest to sociologists is how social and economic advantages are transferred from one generation to the next in a society that purports to frown on inherited privilege. Peter Cookson and I addressed this question by studying elite boarding schools in the United States and England and found out that they perpetuate intergenerational inequality not just with money but through a range of school practices.

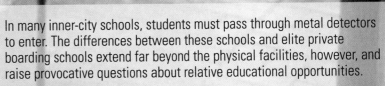

In many inner-city schools, students must pass through metal detectors to enter. The differences between these schools and elite private boarding schools extend far beyond the physical facilities, however, and raise provocative questions about relative educational opportunities.

Watch the **Video** in **MySocLab**
Inspiring Your Sociological Imagination

413

Mary's teachers see about four times as many students in a given day than Jake's do (160 vs. 40) and have much less time to work individually with students who need help or to help them improve their writing. Mary's larger classes (25–28 students) make seminars around an oval table impossible. College advisors are responsible for anywhere from 300 to 600 students each year and find it hard to give personalized advice to each one. They also lack the resources to visit college campuses and get to know college admissions officers personally. These and other differences between schools to be explored in this chapter suggest some of the ways schools help develop the potential of some children more than others.

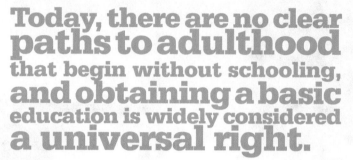

Today, there are no clear paths to adulthood that begin without schooling, and obtaining a basic education is widely considered a universal right.

Most of us take it for granted that success in life requires many years of formal schooling. But the extent of education, its formal and informal purposes, and its relation to other institutions have changed dramatically over time. For most of human history, there was no formal education system separate from the family and community. Early schools taught literacy and basic arithmetic so adults could read sacred scriptures such as the Bible, Torah, or Koran; write letters; and do simple counts and tabulations. But even in Europe and North America, a classical liberal education was available only to a small, male elite. Like many of the United States' founding fathers, Thomas Jefferson thought that in a democracy all citizens needed to be literate to understand the major issues of their times. Yet in Jefferson's era, 7 of 10 Americans worked as farmers or farm laborers. As late as 1870, no more than 2 percent of 17-year-olds in America were high school graduates.

In the United States as elsewhere, the number of schools multiplied with the rise of industrialization, the growth of cities, the desire of working people for advancement, and emerging occupations that placed a premium on education. Children could no longer learn the skills and knowledge needed for adult life simply by observing their parents or neighbors, spurring reformers such as Horace Mann to call for the formation of "common schools" that would be funded by taxes and attended by all. In most industrialized countries, a new system of universal mass education gradually took hold. The United States, however, led the way in these changes.

Today, while there are no clear paths to adult success that do not include formal schooling, the U.S. is no longer leading the world in educational attainment. By 2008, large numbers of countries including Japan, the United Kingdom and Germany had higher rates of high school graduation than the United States (see Figure 15.1). In addition, other countries (such as South Korea) had begun to graduate a larger share of young adults from college than the United States did. While educational participation in recent decades expanded dramatically abroad, in the United States improvements in educational attainment over the past three decades were considerably more modest.

FIGURE 15.1 UPPER SECONDARY (HIGH SCHOOL) GRADUATION RATES, 2009

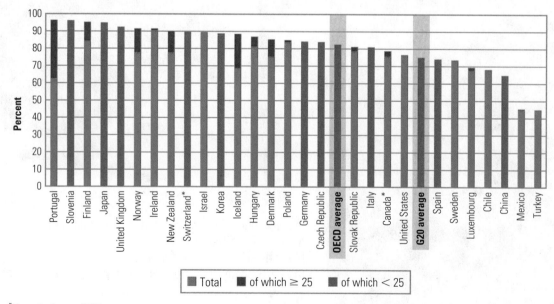

*Year of reference 2008.
Countries are ranked in descending order of the upper secondary graduation rates in 2009.

Source: OECD (2011).

THE BIG QUESTIONS

👁 **Watch** the **Big Question Videos** in **MySocLab**

To understand why and how the institution of education has become so important in our lives, we need to consider the following five big questions:

1 **What are the major functions of schooling?** We will examine the various purposes of schooling in this section, from socialization to preparation for work as well as for citizenship and community life.

How is education related to important life outcomes? Education is strongly related to many important life outcomes, including work and economic opportunities, health and life expectancy, and marital success and happiness. **2**

3 **Is education equally available to all?** Is education the great equalizer in U.S. society, or does it reproduce existing inequalities? Here we examine the sociological research that investigates whether educational access, experiences, and outcomes are similar for persons of different social classes, races, and genders.

How do educational systems differ? How can there be such wide variations in the quality and types of schooling, particularly by social class and race? To address this question, we examine differences in educational systems around the world and the various ways that U.S. schools are organized. **4**

5 **How do digital technologies affect education?** We examine how digital systems of monitoring and control may transform teaching and learning, the impact that substituting digital media for live contact between teachers and learners may have, and the effect that the spread of technology may have on

1 What are the Major Functions of Schooling?

THE PURPOSES OF EDUCATION

👁 **Watch the Big Question Video in MySocLab**

When we think about education, its more formal purposes usually come to mind—such as learning skills and knowledge. And these are obviously useful both for individuals and for society. But education also serves other major purposes, such as incorporating new members into society, sorting people into various occupations, and increasing the economic development of a society. Education also serves some other, less formal functions (which tend to be discussed more by sociologists than educators) that may surprise you—including providing a marriage market for older students, teaching religion, and preventing crime by keeping youths off of the streets. Let's examine a few of the major functions of schooling.

What are the goals of education?

☐ Socialization

One major function of schooling is socializing young people into the habits, attitudes, and practices of contributing members of a community, religion, or nation. Thinking about your own schooling, what habits, attitudes, or practices do you think your schools encouraged? Not surprisingly, a big debate in education concerns the content of that socialization. Is education largely about learning attitudes, moral values, and behaviors and producing happy, well-adjusted young people? Or is education about intellectual skills and content? Most people agree schools should be about both social and cognitive learning but differ over their relative importance.

Others differ on whether education should be intellectual and broad in its orientation (as in a liberal arts curriculum) or more narrowly focused on specific occupations.

Starting in kindergarten, we are taught how to behave in school, including how to line up, be quiet on demand, be neat, fit in with a social system, follow rules, respect authority, obey, compete, and achieve success within the boundaries of the system (Gracey 2012). This is part of what sociologists call the **hidden curriculum** of schools, referring to often unstated standards of behavior or teachers' expectations. For example, most teachers want students to raise their hands and wait to be called on before speaking. More middle-class children may learn this at home or at preschool than do poor children. Thus the school practice may be more familiar to some than to others. Other children are taught at home to show respect for adults by being very quiet around them, so they may never speak up in class. Teachers may think they are not paying attention or learning when they sit silently. The way children conform to the hidden curriculum of a school may affect how their teachers assess them and interact with them. The hidden curriculum of schools also includes the gender roles they encourage or enforce, loyal citizenship, and obedience to authority.

☐ Future Preparation

As schools have expanded, they are increasingly used to sort and select young people for future opportunities, a second major purpose of education. If you want to be a police officer, for example, but have only a high school diploma, your options are limited because more cities are requiring police officers to have at least some college education. Using education to screen employment applicants is variously called credentialism or the allocation or sorting function of education. **Credentialism** refers to the requirement of certain specific degrees or certificates before you can be considered for a particular job. Employers may assume that applicants with more formal schooling have more knowledge and skills, including a variety of "soft skills"—knowing how to dress, act, and present oneself at work, being able to work well with other people—that may enhance a person's job performance. Students attending schools with more frequent and intense contact with adults—think again of the elite boarding schools described at the beginning of the chapter—may learn more soft skills than public school students who have less informal contact with adults. Given the dramatic increase in educational participation, it is harder to be considered for employment without various credentials—whether a high school diploma, college degree, or graduate or professional degree.

The case of the late Steve Jobs, founder of the Apple Corporation, illustrates many of these issues. Jobs attended Reed College in Oregon for less than a year before he dropped out. He felt he was wasting his parents' meager savings because he was not doing well taking required courses that held little interest for him. However, there was much he wanted to learn, so he asked professors if he could audit the courses that interested him, and they agreed. He was a

Why might formal schooling and credentials be less important for entrepreneurs, such as the late Steve Jobs?

FIGURE 15.2 HOURS STUDIED BY CONTEMPORARY STUDENTS IN MORE OR LESS SELECTIVE COLLEGES

Study Hours by College Selectivity

(Bar graph. Y-axis: Weekly Study Hours, ranging 0 to 16. X-axis: College Selectivity. Legend: Highly Selective ≈ 15.3, Selective ≈ 11.5, Less Selective ≈ 10.5.)

Source: Arum and Roksa (2010).

voracious learner without formal credentials. He also lacked many of the soft skills. In his first job at Atari, his body odor was so offensive that people refused to work near him, a problem his boss solved by putting him on the night shift by himself. Lacking degrees and soft skills, Jobs would have been hard pressed to get a full-time job in any major organization. The one route open to him was starting his own corporation, where the knowledge, skills, and talents he had could be used productively.

Sometimes it is difficult to see the distinction between credentials and knowledge. Some students may feel that what matters is simply the degree, not what they learned along the way. However, in many fields—architecture, social work, computer programming—simply having an educational credential does not ensure that you have the knowledge, problem-solving skills, creativity, and interpersonal qualities needed to perform well.

As more students attend college in the United States and around the world, some sociologists have investigated whether they are studying or learning as much as students in the past. Research on contemporary college and university students in the United States shows they study less than half as much as students in the 1950s, although students at highly selective colleges today still do study more than their peers in less selective institutions (see Figure 15.2; Arum and Roksa 2010). They also are not making large gains in critical thinking, complex reasoning, or the ability to communicate in writing as they move through college. Is this because they are working so much outside of school? Not according to the researchers, who found that today's students spend much more of their time socializing in person and online than they do studying or working. Are these students developing their soft skills and building social networks that will be helpful in the future? Can they get along in the world with social skills alone, or will their failure to enhance their cognitive skills have lifelong consequences? More research is needed to address these questions.

☐ Economic Functions

Business leaders have become increasingly interested in education because they depend on schools and colleges to prepare much of the work force. But is education really an engine for the economic development of a society? Teaching citizens to read and do simple arithmetic clearly fosters economic growth. In developing countries with limited resources, the evidence suggests that the most effective approach to economic development is to provide elementary education to everyone. Having achieved primary education for all, many Asian countries—including China, India, Singapore, Taiwan, and South Korea—are now focusing heavily on math, science, and engineering in secondary and higher education, with the goal of further developing their economies.

Throughout the twentieth century, the United States led other nations in educational achievement, providing more formal schooling to its citizens than other countries. According to some researchers, this high level of human capital played a key role in spurring economic growth in the United States during this time (Goldin and Katz 2008). Today, the United States no longer leads the world in either the amount of education received or in educational achievement (which we will discuss later in this chapter). Part of this may be the high cost of higher education in the United States compared to other countries.

At the end of World War II, federal policymakers in Washington, DC, turned to education to solve a different economic problem, the concern that millions of returning war veterans would flood the labor market. Partly for this reason, Congress passed the G.I. Bill in 1944, which allowed honorably discharged veterans to enroll in any accredited higher-educational program they were accepted into while receiving a small living allowance and having the tuition paid by the government. Some 7.8 million former soldiers took advantage of the G.I. Bill to participate in an education or training program. In this way, the national government used education to regulate the flow of workers into the labor market and avoid high unemployment (100 Milestone Documents).

Is education a key to the economic development of a society?

2 How Is Education Related to Important Life Outcomes?

EDUCATION AND LIFE OUTCOMES

Watch the **Big Question** Video in **MySocLab**

In a modern society, educational attainment has profound effects on our life outcomes. For example, consider identical twins Maria and Ana who followed different life and educational pathways. Maria became pregnant at 16 and dropped out of high school. Ana graduated from high school and went on to college. At age 40, Maria is not married and is struggling to get full-time work as a sales clerk or cashier in a store. Her three children each have babies. Ana is married to an accountant, has two teenage children, and is working full time in a hospital as a medical technician. Their lives reflect larger trends showing that the number of years of education individuals obtain is related to many important consequences in their lives, including intellectual development, occupations, earnings, working conditions, and health. Let's look more closely at these important life outcomes and consider the role education plays in them.

Economic Outcomes

As Ana and Maria found, people with more education are more likely to work full time and less likely to be unemployed than people with less education, at all ages. As they enter the labor force, more educated citizens are also more likely to find jobs in higher-status occupations than those with less education. This is not surprising because occupational status and working conditions are highly related to the skills and education demanded in the most competitive professions and fields. You could not become a surgeon or a lawyer, for example, without an advanced degree and highly specialized training.

As Figure 15.3 shows, those of us with more education also earn more, on average, than those with less schooling, even when family background and academic ability are statistically controlled (Pallas 2000). Furthermore, the pay gap between high school and college graduates has been rising since the late 1970s (Goldin and Katz 2008; Murnane, Willett, and Levy 1995). Scholars attribute this expanding pay gap to several factors. First, although unions push for higher wages and benefits for working people, the number of private-sector workers in these labor unions is shrinking. Second, U.S. manufacturing jobs are shifting overseas where workers are willing to work for lower wages. Finally, there is a growing concentration of financial assets in large global corporations where managers tend to get paid more when they control more assets.

Why do people with more education reap larger socioeconomic rewards? Sociologists offer two competing explanations. **Socialization theory** sees education as transmitting knowledge, skills, and values that persist in adulthood and that employers believe increase productivity. It draws on *human capital theory* in economics by suggesting that individuals with more schooling are paid more because they are more productive. When you obtain more education, you are "investing" in yourself; hence the term *human capital*.

In contrast, **allocation theory** sees education as channeling people into positions or institutions that offer different opportunities for continuing to think, learn, and earn. According to this theory, education signals to employers that you have the desired abilities and attitudes, regardless of whether you acquired these traits in your formal schooling (Spence 1974). Think of it this way: Socialization sees education as changing you so you are different in key ways that influence how much you earn. Allocation doesn't change you but rather moves you into different routes—whether a high-speed interstate highway or a two-lane winding country road, or somewhere in between—which lead to different earnings.

> # Why do people with more education reap larger socioeconomic rewards?

FIGURE 15.3 MEDIAN ANNUAL EARNINGS OF FULL-TIME WORKERS BY EDUCATIONAL ATTAINMENT AND GENDER

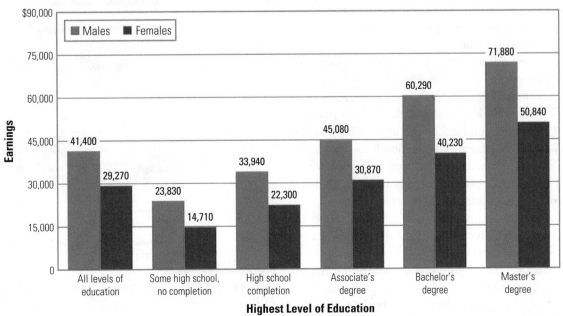

Source: U.S. Census Bureau (2009).

Another aspect of allocation theory is the idea of **social closure**, which argues that education serves a credentialing function that limits entry into some professions and thus raises the rewards of people in them. Today more and more occupations require people who want to break into them to jump through a lot of hoops. At one time, to work in finance, you needed to be able to read, write, and do arithmetic. You could start as a "runner" on Wall Street, carrying orders or messages around to different people or firms. Now, you need at least a college degree, plus increasingly a masters of business administration (MBA) from one of the top universities in the country, and you may need to take a test to become licensed as a financial advisor. One study of 488 occupations found that such closure practices affect earnings in many occupations including those in business and finance, health, education, social services, criminal justice, and others (Weeden 2002). Closure practices include licensing, educational credentialing, certification, association representation, and unionization. These practices operate independently of the human capital you have.

Both socialization and allocation theories recognize that occupational positions are related to education and subsequent life-course outcomes (Pallas 2000). What occupational differences matter? Schooling clearly influences the types of tasks you do at work, the amount of control you have over your work, and how much you supervise the work of others. Some (e.g., Bowles and Gintis 1976; Ross and Van Willigen 1997) argue that employers use educational credentials to bolster the authority of managers in the workplace, while others assume that education provides the knowledge and skills needed for direction, supervision, and planning. Whatever the reasons, the result is that more educated workers do less manual and routine work, and more mental work. They are also more likely to supervise the work of others and have more control over the nature and pace of their jobs. Moreover, larger national and international firms with more assets are more likely to require higher levels of education and pay higher salaries.

Do people from different social-class backgrounds obtain the same economic payoff from similar levels of education? Considerable research on this question suggests that economic outcomes vary by the social class of our parents (see Figure 15.4). For members of the upper class, social background is strongly related to education level (Cookson and Persell 1985; Espenshade and Radford 2009). Children from wealthy families are extremely likely to graduate from college and increasingly likely to obtain graduate or professional degrees. Their occupations and income depend to some degree upon their education but are also influenced by their social connections and wealth.

For members of the middle class, educational background explains more of the variation in occupation and income than do social origins, especially for individuals who are white and male. This is because many middle-class jobs

are related to educational credentials and to the contacts that people make in college. Individuals from lower-class or poor backgrounds are likely to obtain less education and to take longer getting it than members of other classes. Yet even when they do obtain more education, they are less likely than their middle- and upper-class peers to enter high-status and high-income occupations. Why is this so? One explanation is that people from lower-class backgrounds may have less direct knowledge of such occupations due to the fact that higher-status jobs are less likely to be advertised and more likely to be obtained as a result of informal referrals (Granovetter 1974). However, more educated persons from lower-class backgrounds are still more likely to be employed and earn more than people of similar social origins with less education.

Civic and Political Participation

In general, more educated individuals have wider and bigger social networks than their less educated peers, which helps increase their chances of job referrals. Those of us with more education are also more likely to participate in social, voluntary, civic, arts, and political events and activities than

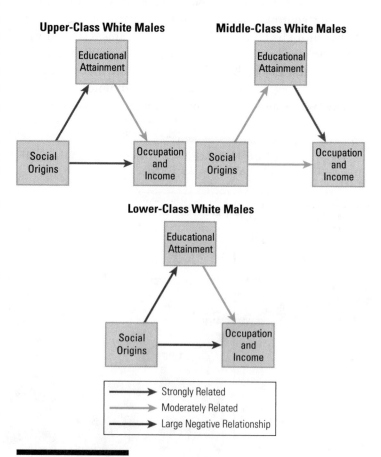

FIGURE 15.4: RELATIONSHIP OF CLASS BACKGROUND, EDUCATION, AND OCCUPATION

Source: Persell (1990).

How does formal education promote certain forms of political values and civic participation, while discouraging others?

those with less education, a finding consistent across cultures. Because more educated people have a wider array of social ties and involvement, it is not surprising that they report feeling higher levels of social support—that is, feeling that there are others on whom they "can rely for advice and encouragement" (Pallas 2000; Ross and Mirowsky 1989). They are also somewhat more likely to talk to others when they have a problem (Ross and Mirowsky 1989).

Do people with more education participate more and have more social ties because they have higher status occupations and incomes or simply because they have more education? Even when they have comparable occupations and incomes, people with more education still participate at higher levels (Pallas 2000). Such evidence is more consistent with the socialization view of education than the allocation view.

☐ Health and Life Expectancy

People with more education are also more likely to demonstrate healthy behavioral habits and to report being in better physical condition. They are less likely to smoke, for example, and, among those who do smoke, are more likely to quit. Given these differences, it is not surprising that people with more education tend to live longer. This is true for men and women, blacks and whites. For men, the difference in life expectancy is about five years, while for women it is about three years.

Why is education so positively related to health and life expectancy? A major reason is the association between education and working conditions. Consistent with allocation theory, people with less education are more likely to be channeled into physical labor, sometimes in difficult, toxic, or dangerous conditions. I remember talking with a maintenance man who was working on a broken sewer line. He said, "When I'm out here shoveling shit in the rain, I know I shoulda went to college." Such workers are also likely to have less autonomy on the job and more likely to take orders from others, which tends to be more stressful (Marmot 2004; Whitehead, Townsend, and Davidson 1992; Wilkinson 1996). Having insurance is also positively related to better health (Finkelstein et al. 2011). At the time of this writing, however, not all employers provided insurance, and a quarter of the U.S. population had no coverage.

Consistent with socialization theory, there is also some evidence that more highly educated people have better access to health information, can understand it better, can better comprehend probabilities, and are in a better position to obtain the help they need (Pallas 2000). They may also be more likely to observe good health habits such as taking medicines on a prescribed schedule, using seat belts in their vehicles, and avoiding unhealthy behaviors.

☐ Family Life

Education is also related to how likely you are to marry, your marital happiness, the type of person you select as a spouse, the age when you have children, and your likelihood of divorce. In the United States today, more-educated people are more likely to marry than less-educated people. Among women aged 25 to 34, 59 percent of college graduates are married, compared with 51 percent of non–college graduates (Martin 2006). Among those aged 35 to 44, 75 percent of college graduates compared to 62 percent of non–college graduates are married, and for those 65 or older the gap is 50 percent of college graduates married compared to 41 percent of nongraduates. There is also a happiness gap in marriage, which is a change from the past. The percent of those without a college education

Why is education positively related to health and life expectancy?

who rate their marriage as "very happy" has dropped in recent years, while it has risen or held steady among the better educated (Zernike 2007).

We are also increasingly likely to marry individuals with educational levels similar to our own—a practice sociologists call **educational homogamy**. The odds of a high school graduate marrying someone with a college degree declined by 43 percent between 1940 and the 1970s. In the first decade of the twenty-first century, the percentage of couples who have similar educations reached its highest point in 40 years. If both parents have similar educational levels in a family, there are implications for the educational and financial resources available to children in the family. Further, this practice of educational homogamy is related to lower rates of divorce.

How is education related to marital happiness?

A big change in recent decades is that educated Americans are marrying at an older age, having fewer children, and having them somewhat later. Women in particular are waiting longer to marry as they get more education. People who marry somewhat older are less likely to get divorced than people who marry younger. This might explain the "divorce divide" that has opened up between those with and without college degrees (Martin 2006), with divorce being more common among those without degrees.

People who marry older and have more education have met a greater variety of people, they know more about what is important to them, and they may be less likely to see marriage as their only alternative in life. These factors, plus the possibility of more financial security, affect marital happiness and divorce rates.

3 Is Education Equally Available to All?

EDUCATIONAL INEQUALITY

⊙ **Watch the Big Question Video** in **MySocLab**

Given the importance of education in our lives, many sociologists focus on whether education is equally available to all. Is education the great equalizer in U.S. society, or does it reproduce existing social inequalities? Sociologists have done considerable research to investigate whether educational access, experiences, and outcomes are similar for persons of different social classes, races, and genders.

☐ Social Class Differences

Consider three babies born at the same time but to parents of different social-class backgrounds. The first baby is born into a wealthy, well-educated business or professional family. The second is born into a middle-class family in which both parents attended college and have middle-level managerial or social service jobs. The third is born into a poor family in which neither parent finished high school or has a steady job. Will these children receive the same education? Although the United States is based on the promise of equal opportunity for all, in reality the educational experiences of these three children are likely to be quite different.

Inequality in the United States   Education in the United States is not a single, uniform system that is available to every child in the same way. Children of different social classes are likely to attend different types of schools, to receive different kinds of instruction, to study different curricula, and to leave school at different rates and times. As a result, when children end their schooling, they differ more than when they entered, and these differences may be used by other social institutions such as employers to select or reject them. When this happens, social reproduction rather than equal opportunity is occurring.

High economic inequality in the United States affects how much education people receive. In states with more income inequality—with bigger gaps between high- and low-income families—young people who grow up in wealthier families obtain more education and children in poorer families obtain less education. In states with smaller gaps between high- and low-income families, family income is not as strongly related to the amount of education children obtain (Mayer 2001). The reason seems to be that in states with greater income inequality, individuals with more education earn much more than people with less education, so wealthier families may work even harder to ensure their children get more education (Mayer 2001).

But the United States also has a historical belief in equal opportunity for all regardless of their social origins. The paradox of growing inequality and the belief in opportunity for all creates a special problem for the United States, which some scholars term the "management of ambition" (Brint and Karabel 1989:7). Many more people aspire to high-paying careers than can actually enter them, partly because pay gaps are so large. One result has been the growth of educational credentialism, which means that more and more education is required for all jobs, especially professional and managerial occupations (Collins 1977). As the required amount of education lengthens, the hurdles may be more difficult to overcome for youth from low-income backgrounds. Exactly how does social class affect student achievement and persistence?

The social class of families and individuals has been consistently related to educational success throughout history (Coleman et al. 1966; Gamoran 2001; Mare 1981;

Persell 1977). Although there are a number of exceptions, students from higher-social-class backgrounds tend to get better grades and to stay in school longer than do students from lower-class backgrounds. In the last 50 years, family income has become more important than race in explaining the educational achievement gap. Indeed, income now is associated with more than twice the black-white achievement gap, which was double the income achievement gap 50 years ago (Reardon 2011). Family income is becoming more important for children's school achievement and is now nearly as important as parental education. Why?

Social-class backgrounds affect where we go to school and what happens to us once there. As a result, lower-class students tend to encounter less-prepared teachers, are often exposed to less-valued curricula, are taught less, and are expected to do less work in the classroom and outside. Hence, they learn less and are less well-prepared for the next level of education. This happens because social class is related to the neighborhoods where people live, neighborhoods are related to the funding available to schools, and funding is related to school quality. School experiences are related to educational expenditures, which vary widely by state (see Figure 15.5), and even within districts some schools may spend more per pupil than others. Schools and districts that spend more can hire more educated and experienced teachers. They can provide resources that foster education like good libraries, laboratories, field trips, and current textbooks. They can also offer more extracurricular activities such as athletics, drama, and music. Research suggests that for some students such activities make the difference between schools being tolerable or intolerable.

Although students have many reasons for dropping out of school or for failing to continue, their experiences in school may contribute to their desire to continue or to quit. One large national study found that 24 percent of public high school students dropped out, compared to 12 percent of Catholic and 13 percent of other private school students (Coleman, Hoffer, and Kilgore 1982). More students are involved in extracurricular activities in Catholic and private schools than in public schools. In addition, social and economic background is a more important cause of lost talent among U.S. youth in the late high school and post–high school years than gender or race (Hanson 1994). Poor students may feel they need to begin working as soon as possible.

Similarly, college attendance depends on a number of factors, including access to the necessary financial resources. Social class affects college attendance in other ways besides

How does social class affect student achievement?

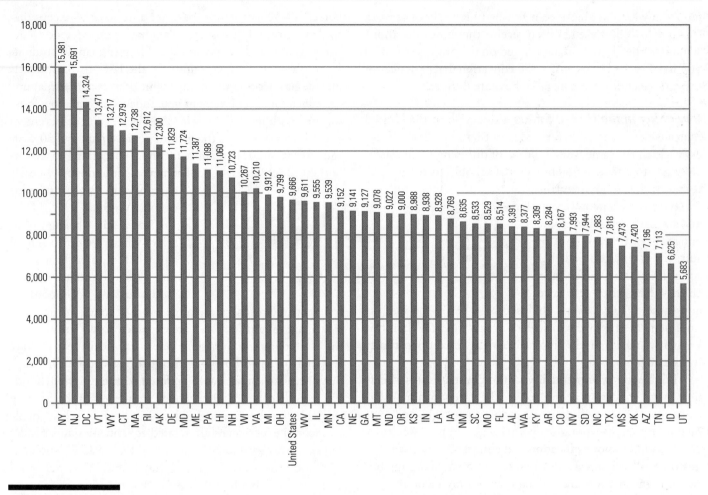

FIGURE 15.5 ELEMENTARY AND SECONDARY PER-PUPIL SPENDING BY STATE, 2006–2007

Source: U.S. Census Bureau (2007).

financial ones. Class is related to the types of schools students attend, which in turn are related to college attendance. Graduates of private high schools are more likely than graduates of public high schools to attend four-year (rather than two-year) colleges (Falsey and Heyns 1984), attend highly selective colleges (Persell, Catsambis, and Cookson 1992), and earn higher incomes in adult life (Lewis and Wanner 1979). Even within the same school, higher-class students are more likely to be in higher tracks, and students in higher tracks (like Advanced Placement [AP] classes or the International Baccalaurate) are more likely to attend college than students in lower tracks (such as honors or college tracks) (Alexander et al. 1978; Alexander and McDill 1976; Jaffe and Adams 1970; Rosenbaum 1976; Rosenbaum 1980). This doesn't mean that low-income students never complete high school or college, but it does mean that higher-income students are more likely to do so even when they have the same academic abilities. 📖 Read the Document *Savage Inequalities* **MySocLab**.

The United States in Comparative Perspective The

United States has greater social-class inequality than other industrial or postindustrial societies around the world, with Germany, Japan, Italy, France, Switzerland, England, Sweden, and the Netherlands all having considerably less social-class inequality than the United States. And the degree of inequality in a country is related to achievement on international educational achievement tests. The countries with the least socioeconomic inequality—Sweden and the Netherlands—are also the countries where a family's social-class background is less related to their children's school achievement and attainment (Blossfeld and Shavit 1993). Sweden and the Netherlands also have fewer people living in poverty.

At the national level, countries with higher levels of social-class inequality tend to do worse on international tests of educational achievement than countries with lower inequality. In the United States, while the most privileged do well on standardized assessments, those from disadvantaged backgrounds do poorly, and overall U.S. results are mediocre, according to three international studies of 97 countries and jurisdictions around the world (Condron 2010). The United States ranked 17th in reading, which was above average; 23rd in science, which was barely above average;

Education Around the World

How much do countries spend on education? In 2008, the average amount of money spent by countries who are part of the Organization for Economic Co-operation and Development (OECD) was 5.9% of their Gross Domestic Product, making education one of the largest expenditures — along with military and healthcare — of these countries' resources.

It is not only governments who spend money on education. The fees that college students are asked to pay differ dramatically across and within countries. While in some countries like Iceland and Mexico public colleges are free, in other countries, like Korea and the United States, even public colleges require large tuition fees.

Around the world — except for Korea and Mexico — the more education you have, the more likely you are to have a job. Moreover, in some countries, like Czech Republic or Spain, if you don't have a college education you will have a very hard time getting a job. Similarly, in the United States, college graduates are three times more likely to be employed than those who did not graduate from high school.

Expenditure on education as a percentage of GDP, 2008

Country	%
Iceland	7.9%
Korea	7.6
Israel	7.3
Norway	7.3
United States	**7.2**
Denmark	7.1
Sweden	6.3
Argentina	6.1
France	6.0
Mexico	5.8
Switzerland	5.7
OECD Average	**5.9**
United Kingdom	5.7
Netherlands	5.6
Ireland	5.6
Brazil	5.3
Austria	5.4
Spain	5.1
Japan	4.9
Italy	4.8
Germany	4.8
Russian Fed.	4.7
Czech Republic	4.5
China	3.3

Cost of higher education, average tuition fees, 2008-2009

- Public instituions
- Independent private institutions

Country	Public	Private
Australia	$ 4,140	$ 8,933
France	750	4,734
Iceland	0	10,542
Italy	1,281	4,713
Mexico	0	5,365
Korea	5,315	9,586
Switzerland	879	7,262
United States	**6,312**	**22,852**

Unemployment rates of 25-64 year olds by educational attainment, 2009

- High school education or less
- College degree or higher

Country	HS or less	College+
Australia	7%	3%
Canada	13	5
Czech Republic	22	2
Estonia	24	6
France	12	5
Germany	17	3
Hungary	21	4
Israel	11	5
Korea	3	3
Mexico	4	4
Spain	22	9
United Kingdom	10	4
United States	**16**	**5**
OECD Average	**12**	**4**

Source: Based on data from OECD (2011)

Explore the Data on Education Around the World in MySocLab and then ...

Think About It

What factors do you think might be related to the size of educational expenditures as a percentage of gross domestic product (GDP) in a country?

Inspire Your Sociological Imagination

What consequences might result from the fact that both public and private higher education costs much more in the U.S. than in other countries?

and 32nd in math, which was below average, in the 2009 Program for International Student Assessment tests of 15-year-old students (OECD 2010). It is not clear that the samples of students selected in all the countries are comparable, however. Shanghai, China, which consistently scored first in all three areas, is populated by many students who migrate from other provinces to study in what are considered better schools. One reason for the poor showing by the United States seems to be greater school resource inequality, as we see later in the chapter. Teacher quality also varies in schools around the world and affects student learning (Montt 2011). Another reason may be variations in how diligent students are, with young people in some parts of the world studying more. This is illustrated in the film *Two Million Minutes*, which compares six outstanding high school students in the United States, China, and India, showing how much more time U.S. students spend working at jobs and socializing compared to the Indian and Chinese students, who spend many more hours per week (and more weeks per year) on their studies. Explore the Infographic on page 425 to learn more about what other countries invest in education and how education is related to unemployment.

Racial and Ethnic Gaps

Beyond class differences, considerable research analyzes racial and ethnic gaps in educational achievement. Despite individual exceptions, African American, Latino/a, and Native American students tend to fare worse, on average, than those who are white or Asian American, and the disparity has persisted over the last 30 years. Gaps occur in standardized test scores, grade point averages, rates of placement in gifted or special education programs, dropout rates, and college attendance and graduation rates (Hallinan 2001; Nettles and Perna 1997; Persell and Hendrie 2005).

The historical legacy of slavery, racial discrimination, and segregation has created severe social and economic inequalities for racial minorities that affect their education. Sociologists have discovered that black and white children of the same age and birth weight, whose parents have the same education, occupation, and income, whose mothers were the same age when they had their first child, who have the same number of children's books in their homes, and who were equally likely to receive support from the U.S. government's Special Supplemental Nutrition Program for Women, Infants, and Children (WIC), obtained statistically similar scores on their reading and number tests (Fryer and Levitt 2004a; Fryer and Levitt 2004b; Yeung and Pfeiffer 2009).

The unfortunate reality is that black and white children are *not* equally likely to share these measures of life chances. And the achievement gap between even those similarly matched white and black children reappears by the third grade. How can we explain this? Racial differences in educational achievement can be explained by historical and current systems of racial inequality, including neighborhoods, families, schools, and peers which become important for older children. Racial differences in achievement are due to social inequalities rather than to genetic differences. This is shown in research that takes into account grandparental resources, neighborhood characteristics, and peers as well as information on parents, students, and schools (Yeung, Persell, and Reilly 2010). Grandparents classified as white have more education, more wealth, and live in neighborhoods with less poverty than black grandparents. When their children become parents, they also differ in their educational attainment, income, occupation, wealth, and neighborhoods. White children in the third generation are much more likely than black children to live in neighborhoods with little poverty, attend schools with many more children of average or high **socioeconomic status (SES)**—which is a broad definition of a person's class based on components such as education, income, and current occupation—and have more friends who stay out of trouble. When grandparental resources and neighborhoods are considered together with parental resources, neighborhoods, parenting practices, school SES, and peers, these factors together reduce the racial gap to insignificance (Yeung et al. 2010).

Gender Differences

Are there gender as well as class and racial differences in educational attainment or achievement? If so, how do we explain them? Throughout the world, boys and girls obtain similar amounts of education in relatively affluent and industrialized nations. In poorer nations, especially those with large portions of the population working in rural agriculture and countries with large Muslim populations, girls are considerably less likely than boys to obtain even an elementary school education (Persell, James, Kang, and Snyder 1999). When examining gender differences in academic performance, the results vary depending on the age of the students being compared and whether grades or test scores are examined (Buchmann, DiPrete, and McDaniel 2008).

Why are there racial differences in educational achievement?

Young women graduate from college at higher rates than young men in the United States, Canada, Australia, New Zealand, and most countries in Europe.

With respect to test scores, gender gaps in the United States have remained relatively stable for 30 years (Hedges and Nowell 1998). Boys often have higher test scores in math and girls in reading, but there is considerable cross-national variation in the direction and size of the gaps (Baker and Jones 1993). Few gender gaps are found in the early grades, but the disparities grow as children advance through the system (Buchmann et al. 2008). On the SAT reasoning test, the male sample of test-takers is more selective because fewer males than females take the test, so we cannot readily compare them.

With respect to grades, girls do consistently better than boys, although this was not always the case. It used to be that girls' grades dropped in the later years of high school and college. Girls also have better soft skills, and they are now equally likely to take demanding math classes (Mulkay et al. 2005) and more likely to take AP classes in the United States.

With respect to educational attainment, girls are more likely to graduate from high school and attend college in the United States than boys, especially among students of color. In 1960, 65 percent of all BAs were awarded to men; by 1982, men and women earned an equal number of degrees; and in 2008 and 2009, females earned 57 percent of bachelor's degrees (National Center for Education Statistics 2010:Table 297). Women also have higher college completion rates in most countries in Europe, Canada, Australia, and New Zealand. Among 30 developed countries, a male advantage in college completion

What educational differences exist between males and females?

exists only in Switzerland, Turkey, Japan, and Korea. There are further gender differences in the rate of delayed enrollment in college (with males having higher rates). Women and men in the United States are about equally likely to earn MAs, PhDs, and law, medical, and dental degrees. While women do obtain more education, they are more likely than men to attend two-year, public, and nonselective colleges (Buchmann et al. 2008).

Parents with more education and other resources have children who are more likely to be highly educated, according to considerable research in sociology and economics. Are these family resources equally allocated by gender? Girls and boys are typically exposed to the same environment. Nevertheless, for children born before 1960, girls reached educational equality with boys only in the minority of families with two college-educated parents. The gender gap in college graduation rates was the largest in families where parents had a high school education or less. But for children born after the mid-1960s, one study (Buchman and DiPrete 2006) found, "a female advantage emerged first among families with absent or less-educated fathers. It remains largest among these families, but has gradually extended to all family types" (Buchmann et al. 2008:327).

It is possible that girls' higher aspirations to attend college may partially explain their superior performance in high school and their higher rates of college graduation. The fact that girls spend more time on homework and are less likely to have disciplinary problems may also help them perform better (Buchmann et al. 2008). But the stronger performance of girls might also reflect their desire to narrow the gender pay gap through education. Men with some high school education earn 62 percent more than their female counterparts, while men with master's degrees earn 41 percent more than women with similar educations (refer to Figure 15.3). Perhaps as young women realize they are likely to spend a good part of their adult lives working, they decide to put more effort into schooling in an effort to obtain better jobs.

Once they go to college, do men and women study the same subjects and pursue similar degrees? In recent decades, more women have chosen to major in traditionally male-dominated fields (computer science, natural sciences, and business, for example), but relatively few men have decided to major in nursing, early childhood education, or other traditionally female-dominated fields (Jacobs 1995; England and Li 2006) (see Figure 15.6). The gender gap in education favors girls compared to boys with respect to achievement and attainment but favors males compared to females with respect to attending selective colleges and choosing majors leading to higher paying careers.

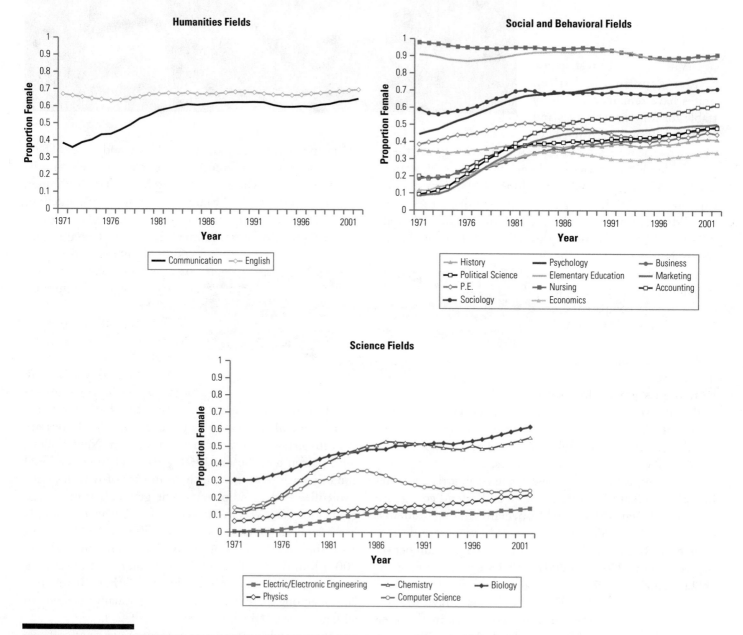

FIGURE 15.6: PROPORTION OF BACHELOR'S DEGREE RECIPIENTS WHO WERE WOMEN, 1971–2002

Based on England and Li (2006:666).

4 How Do Educational Systems Differ?

EDUCATIONAL SYSTEMS AROUND THE WORLD

Watch the **Big Question Video** in **MySocLab**

Your experience as a student in the United States is quite different from the experience of a student in France or China. Children growing up in different countries encounter educational systems that differ in three important ways. First, they vary in access, with different proportions of children of various ages, genders, and races attending school. Second, schools vary in how they are controlled and financed. In some countries, the nation funds and controls schools, setting the curriculum and standards for teachers, student achievement, and other issues. France is often cited as an example of a country where the education commissioner knows what is being taught in any school on any particular day and hour. In other countries, educational institutions are controlled and funded by provinces or local governmental authorities, meaning that all pupils may not receive the same level of government funding or be exposed to the same curriculum. A third issue concerns the relative size of public and private education and whether public money is used to pay for private education. National differences on these three dimensions contribute greatly to variations in educational systems and their outcomes across time and place.

☐ Access

In some countries, K–12 education is free and access to education is provided by governments. But other countries use markets to distribute access by charging school fees

Is schooling equally available to all children around the world?

(e.g., South Africa for secondary school) that limit access for the poor. Some countries require children to attend school and enforce this requirement, while others forbid certain children (for example, girls in Afghanistan) to attend for cultural reasons. In the United States and other affluent countries, free public schooling is available to all and children are required to attend school, usually until they are 15 or older, unless they are homeschooled, privately tutored, or otherwise educated. However, in some less wealthy countries, governments have chosen to spend some of their education money on developing universities instead of providing universal primary education. Some countries may charge school fees, or have schools but no books or laboratories, and not all teachers may be trained. Consequently, around the world, access to education varies widely, with sometimes large differences by gender, class, and race. Explore *A Sociological Perspective* on page 430 to learn more about home-schooling.

Large differences exist with respect to higher education around the world. In many countries, postsecondary college or university education is free to students. In the United States, students and their families pay tuition and fees even in state universities. Almost three-quarters of U.S. students attend public nonprofit colleges and universities, and about 1 in 10 attends each of the following: private independent nonprofit colleges or universities, private religious institutions, or private for-profit institutions. Costs of higher education have soared in recent years, especially at state institutions; financial aid has been allocated less on

A SOCIOLOGICAL PERSPECTIVE

Why is home-schooling on the rise?

Although the majority of people around the world are educated at public or private schools outside the home, there are a significant number who stay at home for their education. In the United States about 1.5 million children are home-schooled, an increase from 1.7 percent in 1999 to 2.9 percent in 2007. Of that population, some home-schooled children attend up to 25 hours per week in traditional schools. White students from higher income and two-parent families constitute the majority of home-school situations.

In 2003, the National Home Education Research Institute conducted a survey of 7,300 U.S. adults who had been home-schooled. Their findings generally suggest that home-schooled people outperform those who attended schools on standardized tests, are more involved in their communities, and are more likely to vote. This is not surprising given the social class background of the parents responsible for home-schooling.

The National Center for Education Statistics reports that parents' most common reason for home-schooling is a desire to provide religious or moral instruction. What are some other reasons a parent would choose to home-school his or her child?

Can you think of changes in public or private schools in recent years that would have impacted the rise in the number of home-schooled children?

⊙→ Explore A Sociological Perspective in **MySocLab** and then . . .

■ Think About It

Decisions to home school children are typically justified in terms of children's well being. Why might a commitment to home-schooling also increasingly be attractive (or desirable) for contemporary parents who wanted to stay at home, rather than participate in the labor force?

■ Inspire Your Sociological Imagination

Some experts argue that home-schooling gives students a one-sided view of the world, as parents may only present their own points of view in teaching. Can you think of other drawbacks?

Some students have access to traditional printed resources, some don't, while still others have access to digital media in their schools. Are such differences truly consequential?

the basis of need and more on the basis of merit; and students have been borrowing increasing amounts of money to finance their educations. All of these trends make access to higher education in the United States less rather than more available to lower-income students.

Control and Financing of Schools

While most affluent countries have national public elementary and secondary education systems with uniform curricula, testing, and financing, some do not. The United States is a notable exception to the pattern of a national system. The U.S. Constitution states that powers not delegated to the federal government are reserved by the states, and courts have interpreted education to be one such function. As a consequence, states have their own departments of education, which may set curriculum and standards for public schools. There are also locally elected school boards that approve school budgets and help shape educational policy.

In the United States, 44 percent of school funding comes from local sources (primarily real estate taxes), 48 percent comes from state tax monies, and 8 percent comes from the federal government if a school district is qualified to receive one or more forms of federal aid. One of the consequences of state and local control and funding is vastly unequal expenditures on K–12 education in the United States, unlike many other countries. Data are available at the state level (refer to Figure 15.5), but *within* most states there are also very large variations in per-pupil expenditures. Even within particular school districts, there are variations in how much money different schools receive (Condron and Roscigno 2003).

Like the United States, South Africa also funds schools locally, with similarly unequal results. Systemic differences in the funding of schools are related to other issues such as teacher quality, curriculum, and student achievement, and to unequal educational opportunities by social class and race. In many European countries, universities as well as elementary and secondary schools are paid for by the federal government, although often a smaller proportion of the population attends them than in the United States.

Public versus Private Education

Countries vary widely with respect to whether they have private schools, who attends these schools, and whether public funding pays for them. Private schools include all institutions managed by an entity other than a state or public authority. At the secondary level, about 28 percent of students in the developing world are in the private sector, as are 14 percent of students in the developed world (World Bank 2012). Many countries (such as the United States) do not provide direct public support for private education, although they may provide indirect support, such as tax exemption for property. Other countries, such as the Netherlands, support all forms of education with public tax monies, including religious and private schools. Almost 70 percent of schools in the Netherlands are administered by private school boards, and about 60 percent of all students there and in Belgium attend private schools.

However, in most of Western and Eastern Europe, Canada, and Israel, the vast majority of primary and secondary school students attend public schools (Torche 2005). In the United States, about 11 percent of students attend private schools (OECD 2001), although the numbers vary widely by state. In New York, for example, about 25 percent of students attend such schools, compared to about 1 percent in Wyoming (Coleman et

Are schools funded the same way in different societies?

How widespread is public education?

al. 1982). Some research shows that states with more private schools spend more on public education than states with fewer private schools, suggesting that competition for students may influence the level of support for education (Arum 1996). While some researchers have found that student achievement is higher in private schools than public schools (e.g., Coleman and Hoffer 1987), others stress that variability within the public and private sectors is far greater than the variation in achievement between the sectors (Haertel et al. 1987). The elite boarding schools discussed at the beginning of the chapter represent 10 percent or less of private schools in the United States and only 1 percent of all U.S. high schools. Achievement differences between public and private school students are not that great when family background of the students is taken into account. They do differ in whether and where students go to college, however.

Access, control, and financing highlight some of the ways educational systems can vary at the national level. Within countries, there are differences in the way schools are organized, and U.S. schools have several additional features that differ from schools in many other countries.

☐ Organizational Practices

Two of the major differences in educational practices between the United States and other developed countries are testing and tracking.

Testing While teachers have always given students tests and other assessments, the United States has seen an increasing emphasis in the last several decades on large-scale "high-stakes" achievement tests. The stakes are high because a single test may determine whether students move to the next grade or even if they can graduate from high school. Such tests may also be used to hold educators, schools, and school districts accountable. Yet other nations with strong educational systems and high student achievement are not testing students every year and are not judging teachers by their students' test scores (Tucker 2011).

According to proponents of achievement testing, the purpose of using such tests is to set higher standards for student learning and raise student achievement. However, when some students do poorly on a test, schools and teachers can respond in several different ways. They can work harder with the students obtaining low scores, providing them with more personal attention, tutoring, and additional learning experiences in an effort to improve their achievement test scores. Such responses usually require additional resources, which many schools lack, especially ones that are already underfunded. Another possible response is that schools try to shed students with lower scores by encouraging them to drop out or transfer. This is clearly an unintended consequence of

high-stakes testing and one that hurts the most educationally needy and vulnerable students. Many teachers, while not opposed to high standards, say that the existence of mandatory testing leads to "teaching in ways that contradicted their own ideas of sound educational practice" (Winter 2003:B9).

One study analyzed an urban elementary school's response to the Texas Accountability System and the Student Success Initiative requiring third-grade students to pass a reading test to be promoted to the fourth grade (Booher-Jennings 2005). The researchers in this study found that teachers devoted more resources to helping those students who were on the brink of passing the Texas Assessment of Knowledge and Skills test, while at the same time they reduced the size of the group whose scores counted by referring more students to special education. Why would teachers participate in such a system? This research found that the institutional environment defined a good teacher as one with high pass rates. Teachers became competitors rather than partners with their colleagues, which weakened the faculty's ability to work together toward common goals. "The singular focus on increasing aggregate test scores rendered the school-wide discussion of the 'best interests of children' obsolete" (Booher-Jennings 2005:260).

This study raises important questions about how the Congressional No Child Left Behind (NCLB) Act of 2001 is implemented. The intended goals of NCLB are to reduce the achievement gap between low-income or minority children and higher-income or white children by holding educators accountable. Some of the key provisions of this federal law are state-level annual tests of third to eighth graders in reading and math, plus at least one test for students in grades 10 through 12. States and districts are required to report school-level data on students' test scores for various subgroups: African American, Latino/a, Native American, Asian American, white non-Hispanic, special education, limited English proficiency, and low-income students. NCLB rewards or punishes school districts, schools, and teachers for the tested achievement of their students but does not prescribe consequences for students (Dworkin 2005).

Under this system, schools with too many low scores are labeled "failures" regardless of the reason for the low scores. But when their success is measured differently, for example by how much their students are learning, about three-quarters of the schools are succeeding (Downey, von Hippel, and Hughes 2008). Schools' actual impact on learning was measured by observing how much more students learned during the school year than during summer vacation. Students in 75 percent of the schools were learning at a reasonable rate and much faster during the school year than in summer vacation.

High-stakes testing provides the wrong incentives for teachers and students. Teachers seek to survive by teaching

How has high-stakes testing affected the quality of education in the United States?

How might tracking affect learning and opportunities for students?

to the test or "gaming the system" rather than seeking to help all children learn more. Students are poorly prepared for life, which does not consist of choosing the most correct answer out of four or five offered. They need to learn how to think, solve difficult problems in new ways, and plan and execute complex projects. The heavy reliance in the United States on test-based incentives for teachers has not improved student achievement (National Research Council 2011). The heavy stress on teacher accountability diverts the focus from poverty, unemployment, and inequality, which are the underlying reasons for many children struggling in school. Testing is also a major basis for assigning students to different ability or curriculum groups, a practice called *tracking*.

Tracking Schools don't talk about **tracking**, but sociologists use the term to describe how schools assign students to distinct groups based on ability or curriculum. Early assignments in elementary school are often based on reading levels, and the curriculum is said to be the same for all students. However, even a shared curriculum may be taught differently to different groups. And, over time, different ability groups are likely to be assigned to different courses of study.

How does tracking affect learning and educational opportunities?

Tracking in the United States today is widespread, particularly in large, diverse school systems and in schools serving primarily lower-class students (Lucas and Berends 2002). It is less prevalent, and less rigid when it occurs, in upper-middle-class suburban and private schools and in parochial schools (Vanfossen, Jones, and Spade 1987). In recent years, tracking has become more subtle. High school courses now tend to be classified as regular, college prep, honors, and AP, or something similar. Low-income students and parents, in particular, may be unaware of what the distinctions mean and not realize that decisions made in seventh or eighth grade affect what courses are possible in high school. Even if their school has AP courses, students may be unaware that grades received in AP or honors courses may be given greater weight when their grade-point averages are computed, and thus may differentially affect their chances for college admission or scholarships. They also may not realize the importance of taking certain courses, such as calculus, for doing well on college entrance examinations. Many inner-city or low-income schools do not offer even a single AP course, while many affluent suburban schools offer a dozen or more. Differences in the courses students take,

especially in such areas as mathematics, science, and foreign language, go a long way toward explaining differences in achievement test scores (Darling-Hammond 2001).

How exactly does tracking affect learning and opportunities? Research suggests that tracking creates instructional, social, and institutional differences in students' learning experiences. Numerous researchers have observed **instructional differences** between tracks, with higher-ranked groups being taught more words in reading, for example (Gamoran 1984; Gamoran 1986). Teachers of high-track students set aside more time for student learning and devote more class time to learning activities (Oakes 1985). Others found variations in the content, pacing, and quantity of instruction in different tracks (Dreeben and Barr 1988). Also, high-track teachers use more interesting teaching methods and materials (Hallinan 1987). In secondary schools, college-track students consistently receive better teachers, class materials, laboratory facilities, field trips, and visitors than their lower-track counterparts. Finally, teachers hold higher expectations and the other students support learning more in the higher-ability groups. As a result, the achievement of students in the higher groups tends to develop more than it does in the lower groups (Hallinan 1987).

Socially, tracks create settings that shape students' self-esteem and expectations about academic performance. Being assigned to particular tracks immediately ranks students in a status hierarchy, formally stating that some students are better than others (Rosenbaum 1976). Higher-track students receive more empathy, praise, and use of their ideas, as well as less direction and criticism, than do lower-track students (Freiberg 1970). Teachers spend more time in low-track classes on discipline, and students in those classes perceive their teachers as more punitive than do students in high-track classes (Oakes 1985). Students at the top are taught critical thinking, creativity, and independence, while students at the bottom are denied access to these educationally and socially important experiences (Oakes 1985). The social-class background of students is also related to the prevalence of tracking in the schools, to the nature of the available tracks, and to the ways track assignments are made. Tracking clearly segregates children by social class and ethnicity (Tyson et al. 2005; Tyson et al. 2011).

Institutionally, tracking creates groups of students who are understood by teachers and parents as having certain qualities and capacities above and beyond the actual skills they possess. Ability groups limit teachers' perceptions of what grades are appropriate for students in different tracks (Reuman 1989). Both parents and teachers rated children in higher reading groups as more competent and likely to do better in the future than children in low reading groups, even when children's initial performance levels and parents' prior beliefs about their children's abilities were comparable (Pallas et al. 1994).

Tracking persists because many teachers feel unprepared to effectively manage classrooms with a range of student abilities (Darling-Hammond 2001:474). In the 1980s, tracking came under considerable attack, and a movement toward detracking gained support (Braddock and McParland 1990; Oakes 1985; Oakes 1992; Wheelock 1992). But even when teachers strongly support and have succeeded in ending

tracking in some communities, they have encountered serious resistance and opposition from higher-class parents. Detracking is often perceived as a threat by privileged parents who feel tracking gives their children educational benefits. They often mount strong political resistance to removing tracking systems. For example, being in an honors course confers advantages in the competition for college admissions. Detracking was able to occur when politically savvy teachers were able to involve powerful parents in meaningful ways in the process of implementing it (Oakes et al. 1997).

Some aspects of school organization are related to social class and race. Prosperous and white children are twice as likely as poor or minority children to attend private schools, for example, and much more likely to attend schools with fewer low-income or minority children. Schools serving mostly low-income students tend to be organized and to operate differently than those serving more-affluent students, with more testing and tracking than in schools serving higher-income students. Both organizational practices and educational resources are patterned along the social fault lines in society, with the result that all babies are not raised in the same educational nurseries. One difference is the type of educational technology students experience in their lives.

5 How Do Digital Technologies Affect Education?

EDUCATION AND TECHNOLOGY

Watch the **Big Question** Video in **MySocLab**

Most college students today have never lived in a world without digital technologies—handheld devices, smartphones, video games, personal computers, and the Internet. We have already seen that students today typically spend more time socializing, whether in person or online, than students in

the past, and less time studying, but they may be learning other things this way. How do these technologies affect education?

Advances in web technology have great relevance for education. Web 1.0 remained largely one-directional, a place for us to search for and read information. Web 2.0 includes such easy Internet publishing tools as software for blogging, wikis, Real Simple Syndication (RSS), video posting sites like YouTube, photo sites like Flickr and Instagram, online video games, and distributed file-sharing projects like BitTorrent. Web-based networks like Facebook and Twitter allow people to participate, interact, form groups, tag, evaluate, organize, and remix material.

Suppose you've decided to go see a movie and grab a bite to eat afterward. You're in the mood for a comedy and some incredibly spicy Mexican food. Some Internet experts believe the next generation of the Web—Web 3.0—will make tasks like your search for movies, food, and other information faster and easier. Instead of the multiple searches you would need to do on the current Web 2.0 Internet, you might type a sentence or two in your Web 3.0 browser and let it do the rest. In this case, you could type "I want to see a funny movie and then eat at a good Mexican restaurant. What are my options?" The Web 3.0 browser will analyze your statement, search the Internet for possible answers, and then organize the results for you so you can make a decision (adapted from Strickland 2012). Web 3.0 is expected to add intelligence by being able to understand the meanings of words in context, analyze data you have given it, learn about your preferences, and even predict your "needs and behavior to provide richer and more meaningful and useful interactions" (Baraniuk 2008:242). Apple's new intelligent personal assistant, Siri, is an early step into Web 3.0, but so far such innovative technologies have not been used in education.

In the early years of the Internet, there was a cartoon of a dog sitting at a computer and the caption said, "On the internet, no one knows you are a dog." However, on Web 3.0, "everybody knows what kind of dog you are, your favorite leash color, the last time you had fleas, and the date you were neutered" (Clifford 2009). Teachers trying to teach the dog new tricks are beginning to take advantage of the Internet, given the wealth of information and potential applications available.

☐ Uses of Technology in Education

Some schools are beginning to use Web 3.0 data systems for monitoring student learning in real time. As students complete an assignment electronically, their work is assessed by a computer (or perhaps even a teacher for some kinds of work). The results can be accessed any time by teachers, administrators, parents, and students to see how students are progressing. If such a system is coupled with diagnostic assessments identifying areas of understanding that are giving particular students trouble and offering them help, this could significantly enhance learning. However, if the system only identifies which students are having problems, it won't do much to improve education.

How do schools use digital technologies to enhance learning?

Do students using new forms of digital technologies learn more in school?

On a smaller scale, some teachers are experimenting with new forms of pen technology. Digital pens not only write but also have a small recording device in them that can record sounds. If a student is being asked to do something—say, solve a math problem—while the teacher is explaining the process, the recording in the pen can indicate exactly where the student got confused and what the teacher was saying at the time. This has the potential to help teachers pinpoint exactly where students need help, and maybe even improve their teaching.

In higher education, digital technologies are being used in multiple ways, including videos (for example, through YouTube or TED); podcasts; social networks (like Piazza) for homework; blogs for discussing problems; the posting of syllabi, readings, class notes, and supplemental materials online; and exclusively online courses. Digital technologies have the potential to make learning far more interactive, assuming that creative programs are developed to help students understand key concepts, theories, methods, and processes in a subject. Many digital materials in education are not particularly interactive, however. Online courses offered by many colleges, universities, and for-profit institutions may be little more than videotaped lectures, podcasts, or slide shows. Perhaps they will become more interactive over time. But developing such materials takes a lot of work, and the reward structure of both higher education and K–12 education offers few incentives to teachers for developing such materials. Highly selective colleges and universities appear to be relying less on total online instruction than less selective universities. It will be interesting to see which institutions give college credit for work done

How might digital technologies magnify inequalities in education and society?

completely online and which do not, and what their reasons will be. Research shows that fewer students complete online classes compared to face-to-face courses. One large study of 51,000 community-college students found that those enrolled in online courses failed and dropped out more often than those whose coursework was classroom based (Brown 2011).

Another issue is how technology may change the role of teachers. Will digital technologies eliminate instructors, as happened to the foreign language teachers in one New Jersey high school after administrators decided it would be cheaper to buy a digital system to do the job? To our knowledge, there is no systematic research showing students learn better from such digital systems than from teachers. Or will instructors play different roles, such as helping students work out individualized programs that involve a variety of learning methods and styles? As educational systems face increasing cost pressures, more will likely look for ways to use technology to save money, but this may not necessarily be better for students.

Online teaching and learning is already flourishing and will continue to thrive by providing supplemental resources for students taking courses for credit, and for adult or continuing learning. If you are taking an advanced math course and are struggling to solve quadratic equations, for example, you can go to YouTube and find literally thousands of short videos explaining how to solve such equations. You can see which ones were accessed most or read reviews to see which ones other people found most helpful. For continuing

Does digital media connect students with others or work to isolate them more?

education, there are thousands of online videos demonstrating skills such as tiling a bathroom or tying knots. But these examples also reveal something important about what may be learned most effectively online: namely, specific tasks. What may be harder to teach online are critical thinking skills. How, for example, do we learn what *kinds* of problems require the use of quadratic equations? How can we learn to assess the quality of the data used in the equation? It may be harder to use technology to show when and why one approach may be superior to another. It is also unlikely that exclusively online educational experiences can impart some of the informal skills that in-person education does, to say nothing of the inspiration that learning from a creative, devoted teacher can spark.

Implications of Digital Technologies in Education

Antonio and Emily have no smartphones or computers in their home, and the school they attend has 50 computers for 5,000 students. Compare their situation with that of Courtney and Stanton, who attend an affluent suburban high school where classrooms are equipped with "smartboards" and computers are available for every student. Courtney and Stanton also have their own smartphones, numerous computers in their homes, and parents who are adept at using them. The comparison illustrates one of the most important implications of using technology for education, namely the potential for a growing **digital divide**—the social, economic, and cultural gap between those with effective access to information technology and those without such access. Sociologists have studied how access to the Internet varies by social background. Even when people do have access, the quality of that access varies by class, race, and gender (Hargittai 2010). If education depends increasingly on home access and use of the Internet, students with multiple devices and users in their social networks will find it easier to complete school assignments successfully. Those without such access will depend on libraries or school labs (often with limited hours and help) to do their work. The growing use of digital technologies outside of school will likely magnify existing inequalities in education and society unless serious efforts are made to counteract such tendencies.

A second major implication of digital technologies is that schools will find it increasingly difficult to control the ideas and information students find. Of course, this trend is not entirely new. It began with the invention of the printing press and the growth of mass media and libraries. Where the Internet differs is that material on it may be totally unscreened by anyone beyond its producer. As anyone who has surfed the web knows, a great deal of information of widely varying quality is readily available online. The result is that teachers, schools, and parents won't necessarily know the quality of the information and ideas to which young people are exposed.

A third implication of digital technologies is the formidable demand they make for students' time and attention. We now live in the information equivalent of a giant buffet filled with tempting delicacies to eat. What will we stuff into our heads? How do we learn to regulate our time? Some schools use Internet blocking programs to restrict access to social networks, online games, and pornography in school. Some ban the use of Wikipedia (the collectively written digital encyclopedia) for research, while others allow it to be used as a starting point but require that other sources also be consulted. Many schools are becoming increasingly aware of the importance of teaching students how to critically assess the information they find online. As these various responses suggest, technology will require educators to be adaptive and creative and may raise as many new challenges as it solves.

CONCLUSION THE FUTURE OF EDUCATION IN A GLOBAL ECONOMY

We care about education because it shapes so many important aspects of our adult lives, from intellectual development to career prospects, income level to physical health, civic and political engagement to marriage patterns. In this chapter, we explored some of the major functions of education as well as how it relates to all of these important life outcomes. We also examined inequalities in education and how educational systems in the United States differ from others around the world, as well how digital technologies are affecting education.

Looking forward, sociologists may fruitfully study the effects of globalization on education. What are the implications for education of fewer manufacturing jobs in the United States? What are the consequences of turning publicly controlled educational systems into privately controlled, for-profit operations? Will the content and ways of learning change, and if so, how? A few sociologists, like Meyer (1977), have studied educational curricula around the world, and some have studied how students learn. More work might be done studying educational goals, including examining who is involved in the process of setting goals and what they favor.

A number of thinkers are pondering what people need to learn to function well in the twenty-first century, and they identify some common competencies. Sociologists could productively study the social contexts and processes that help or hinder the development of these capabilities. First are *critical-thinking and problem-solving skills.* Looking at the social context surrounding an activity or market, a defining characteristic of sociology, is part of critical thinking. Critical thinking involves analyzing how parts of a whole interact to create various outcomes in complex systems; analyzing and evaluating evidence from many different sources, including its timeliness, credibility, and usefulness; assessing arguments, claims and beliefs, and alternative points of view; integrating and connecting information and arguments; drawing inferences and conclusions from information; and reflecting on what has been learned and what more needs to be learned. The rise of the Internet with huge quantities of instantly available information of widely varying quality makes these skills particularly important today.

Second are *communication and collaboration skills* across networks, including global ones involving diverse cultures. This includes being able to lead and influence others by reasoning and persuasion rather than by trying to command obedience. Clear communication involves being able to articulate thoughts and ideas effectively orally or in writing; to listen effectively to discern meaning, knowledge, values, attitudes, and intentions; and to understand how to communicate to inform, instruct, motivate, and persuade. It might also include being multilingual. Communication is not just about grammar, punctuation, or spelling but the ability to think clearly and write with focus, energy, and passion (a real voice). It also entails using multiple media and technologies, being able to judge their effectiveness and weigh their impact. Effective collaboration involves working well and respectfully with diverse teams; being flexible, helpful, and willing to compromise to accomplish common goals; and sharing responsibility and credit for collaborative work.

Third is *agility and adaptability* because the world and the economy are changing so quickly. People need to expect and be able to deal with disruptions, whether from outside events like 9/11 or dramatic weather patterns or from inside innovations, changes, and reorganizations. They may need to adapt to varied roles, responsibilities, schedules, and contexts and be able to work in ambiguous situations with changing priorities. They need to be able to accept feedback on their work; deal positively with criticism, setbacks, and praise; and understand, negotiate, and balance diverse views to reach solutions.

Fourth is *learning how to take initiative* and be entrepreneurs, whether in the corporate world, communities, or education. Individuals need to learn to set clear goals, balance short-term and long-term goals, use their time effectively, work independently, and be self-directed learners to explore and expand their learning.

Fifth, is *curiosity, imagination, and creativity.* Many problems require solutions that have not yet been proposed. People need not only to wonder why things are the way they are and how they got that way but be able to imagine how they might be substantially improved or even done in a completely new way. Creativity and innovation involve using a wide range of idea creation techniques (such as brainstorming); developing both incremental and radical ideas; and elaborating, refining, analyzing, and evaluating ideas. They include experimenting and adapting from what is learned.

If these are widely agreed-upon goals of education, it is difficult to see how frequent multiple-choice tests might help develop these qualities in students. Investigators might also consider the role played by education over the life course. Some subjects, for example, arts, music, and literature, may become even more important for individuals after they finish their formal working years, even if they aren't used in their occupations.

Watch the Video in MySocLab
Applying Your Sociological Imagination

✔ **Study** and **Review** in MySocLab   👁 **Watch** the **Video** Inspiring Your Sociological Imagination in **MySocLab**

1   What Are the Major Functions of Schooling? *(p. 416)*

👁 **Watch** the **Big Question Video** in **MySocLab** to review the key concepts for this section.

In this section, we examined the various purposes of schooling in this section, from socialization to preparation for work as well as for citizenship and community life.

THE PURPOSES OF EDUCATION (p. 416)

Socialization (p. 416)

- **What are the goals of education?**

Future Preparation (p. 416)

Economic Functions (p. 418)

- **Is education a key to the economic development of a society?**

2   How Is Education Related to Important Life Outcomes? *(p. 418)*

👁 **Watch** the **Big Question Video** in **MySocLab** to review the key concepts for this section.

Education is strongly related to many important life outcomes, including work and economic opportunities, health and life expectancy, and marital success and happiness.

EDUCATION AND LIFE OUTCOMES (p. 418)

Economic Outcomes (p. 419)

- **Why do people with more education reap larger socioeconomic rewards?**

Civic and Political Participation (p. 420)

Health and Life Expectancy (p. 421)

- **Why is education positively related to health and life expectancy?**

Family Life (p. 421)

- **How is education related to marital happiness?**

3 Is Education Equally Available to All?

(p. 422)

> Watch the **Big Question Video** in **MySocLab** to review the key concepts for this section.

4 How Do Educational Systems Differ?

(p. 429)

> Watch the **Big Question Video** in **MySocLab** to review the key concepts for this section.

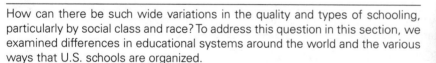

👁 **Watch** the **Big Question Video** in **MySocLab** to review the key concepts for this section.

In this section, we examined how digital systems of monitoring and control may transform teaching and learning, the impact that substituting digital media for live contact between teachers and learners may have, and the effect that the spread of technology may have on inequality in education.

👁 **Watch** the **Video** Applying Your Sociological Imagination in **MySocLab** to see these concepts at work in the real world

16
CRIME, DEVIANCE, and SOCIAL CONTROL

((· Listen to the Chapter Audio in MySocLab

by TROY DUSTER
and JEFF MANZA

Why do some kinds of behavior violate societal rules while other similar behaviors do not? How is it that *deviant* behavior is defined as such, and violations punished? We don't ordinarily observe the process by which deviance is defined until we notice what happens when someone tries to challenge those rules. During the early 1990s, when both authors were at the University of California at Berkeley (as a sociology professor and PhD student in sociology, respectively), the campus and surrounding community became embroiled in a controversy that that brought these issues sharply into focus. In the fall of 1992, a tall, thin, angular 20-year-old Berkeley undergraduate named Andrew Martinez began coming to his classes wearing only his key chain. Known as the "naked guy," Martinez quickly achieved local and later national and international fame. At that time, neither the campus nor the city of Berkeley had any rules or regulations requiring that someone wear clothes (Zengerle 2006). Long known for its progressive political traditions, Berkeley citizens and elected officials grappled with the novel question of whether Martinez should have the right not to wear clothes.

For several weeks, Martinez continued to walk the streets of the city and campus and attend his classes completely in the nude. Naked guy "sightings" became events. One student at the time described later how thrilled she and her friends were when the naked guy came (clothed—it was winter) to a party they organized (Richards 2006). Defending his actions in a local newspaper and elsewhere, Martinez articulately suggested that in his view clothing was oppressive. He claimed that "[w]hen I walk around nude, I am acting how I think it is reasonable to act, not how middle-class values tell me I should act. I am refusing to hide my dissent in normalcy even though it is very easy to do so." He even helped to organize, with a local nude theater troupe known as the X-Plicit Players, a "nude-in," which succeeded in getting two dozen sympathizers to participate.

While many people simply ignored him, some students and residents complained to campus administrators and the local

MY SOCIOLOGICAL IMAGINATION
Troy Duster

The first 16 years of my life were spent in a low-income, racially segregated neighborhood on Chicago's near South Side. It was a period in the United States in which racial segregation was taken for granted at barber shops, bowling alleys, swimming pools, and many public accommodations—even in the urban North. Frank Wong, the son of a Chinese restaurant owner in the area, was the only student in my high school who was not African American. Then, at age 17, I crossed town to attend Northwestern University, where I was one of only seven African Americans on a campus of over 7,000 whites. Anthropologists call it "culture shock" when the deep assumptions about what is normal are disrupted by new circumstances, whether by travel to a foreign country or by being thrust into an unfamiliar social world where previously held assumptions have little or no relevance. For me, sociology provided a handle on my situation, a way to understand why and how people explain away their privilege as if it were an individual accomplishment. I watched with the astonishment of the outsider how people from wealthy families concluded unreflectively that the way the world was ordered was natural and right. Of course, many poor people also see the way the world is organized as normal, so that was no surprise. But it was the attempt to explain the "why" that caught my attention, intrigued and stoked my intellectual curiosity, and brought me into sociology.

Cyclists ride naked through London for the World Naked Bike Ride, an international event where people meet and ride through the streets together in efforts to promote green transportation. Is this deviant behavior?

Watch the Video in **MySocLab**
Inspiring Your Sociological Imagination

police. Soon thereafter, campus officials decided enough was enough, and he was suspended from the campus. Martinez continued to appear naked in public, even attending a City Council meeting unclothed to plead his case. But it was to no avail; the council passed a measure banning public nudity, and shortly thereafter began arresting Martinez whenever he appeared naked in public. Eventually, Martinez disappeared from public life, and the public controversy he had created quickly disappeared from the news.

> **Once we ask ourselves why wearing clothing is an obligation, we open up a whole series of questions that go right to the heart of how society exerts its force over individuals, and with what consequences.**

The story of the naked guy may seem like an "only in Berkeley" story, a strange and easily forgotten episode. Yet it actually raises a number of profound questions. For starters, why *do* we have to wear clothes? Who decided that clothes are a necessary part of our everyday appearance? To be sure, it ordinarily doesn't usually matter *what* you wear, as long as you wear something (although controversy has erupted in recent years in many school districts and communities over the preference of some young men to wear jeans very low on their hips, allowing their underwear to show). Further, why do governments, in this case the Berkeley city government, assume the authority, in the name of the public, to arrest and punish someone simply because he or she refuses to wear clothes? It's not likely to become a leading civil rights cause anytime soon, but once we ask ourselves why wearing clothing (or clothing that does not show our undergarments) is an obligation, we open up a whole series of questions that go right to the heart of how society exerts its force over individuals, and with what consequences. That is the subject of this chapter.

The Naked Guy of Berkeley, Andrew Martinez, attending a class at the University of California-Berkeley in 1992.

THE BIG QUESTIONS

👁 **Watch** the **Big Question Videos** in **MySocLab**

What is deviance? In order to understand deviance, we first need to ask the question, "What is normal?" We explore the origins of deviant behavior by examining the role of groups and group boundaries in the creation of social norms. We also explore the distinction between statistical and social deviance.

How is morality defined and regulated? Societies have long tried to dictate and control individuals' behavior and morality. We explore two moral crusades, against alcohol and morphine use in the United States, to highlight how the process of defining normal behavior is achieved and how certain kinds of behavior come to be labeled deviant or even criminal. We then look at some contemporary moral crusades and consider the future of moral regulation.

Who defines deviance? Insights into deviant behavior come from studying the social and economic positions, cultural practices, and attendant political power of dominant groups. In this section we explore the relationship between deviance and power.

How is social control maintained? Finally, we examine how and where social control—the ways societies regulate and sanction behavior in such a way that it encourages conformity and discourages deviance from the norms—comes to be formalized in the institutions of the criminal justice system. We then examine how the criminal justice system in America has grown massively in recent decades, turning increasingly to formal punishment as a means of sanctioning deviance.

1 What Is Deviance?

DEVIANCE AND THE GROUP

👁 **Watch** the **Big Question Video** in **MySocLab**

Before we can consider what is deviant, we need first to ask the question: "What is normal?" Who decides what is normal and, therefore, what is deviant? To do so, we begin with the most fundamental of the building blocks of normality and deviance: the group.

☐ Establishing Group Boundaries

From small ones like families and sports team to larger ones like neighborhoods, organizations, and even entire nations, individuals belong to groups. Sociologists define a **social group** as a collection of people who interact with one another and who have a shared sense of belonging. Most humans across the globe are born into families that impose fundamental rules such as when and how to eat food and whom to obey. In *Civilization and Its Discontents*, Sigmund Freud pointed out that all cultures impose upon their young some very strict rules about the most basic of needs (for example, at an early age, the child is told to stop "playing with your food!"), which sets up the first great conflict between individual and society. Freud saw this as one of the first lessons of dominance and social control—and thus among the first lessons about the futility of rebellion. Anyone who has reared a child understands Freud's

How do groups distinguish themselves?

idea as a metaphor for what happens throughout life, that the child ultimately gives up and gives over to the behavioral rules. And here we come to the first axiom in the study of deviance and control: namely, that this early struggle is first and foremost about the *parents'* notion of normality and only secondarily about the child. Deviance and control always constitute a paired relationship, and even in this earliest of all subsequent pairings, it is the more powerful group (the parents) who determine what is normal and thus what is deviant.

Groups outside the family exert similar pressures to conform throughout an individual's life. How do groups achieve this power? One way is through *positive affirmations*—or claims—that groups use to establish boundaries. There are an infinite variety of markings, behaviors, and attributes that are possible, from cutting three lines across the forehead to pledging fraternity or sorority X versus Y; from wearing certain kinds of clothing and body piercings; and using a specific language and code of behavior. Such positive affirmations signal who is in the group and who is out. But merely being a compliant member in good standing of a group is not the whole story; the *negative affirmations* of group membership—what we aren't allowed to do if we are to retain membership—constitute the other side of group influence. Both are important.

The Positive Affirmations of Group Membership   All groups set markers at their boundaries. Beginning with our earliest group—our family—we quickly learn who is and who is not in the group. While groups are often defined through objective criteria such as having a shared language or the same job, the identity of the group is more importantly tied to the way group members define themselves and are defined by others. In school those who study too hard are referred to as "nerds" and the ones who play sports are called "jocks." These are not innocent labels but include value judgments. It is the symbolic ideas and values about who the group members are, what sociologists call **symbolic boundaries**, that really give a group its identity (Lamont and Molnar 2002).

One way to think about symbolic boundaries is in terms of how different spaces are defined. When you enter a church, for example, you are not simply crossing a physical boundary between the church doors and the outside world but also a symbolic boundary between a religious space and a secular one. The very meaning of the space is different, as is how we are supposed to behave in it. Immigration—the process of moving from one country to another—provides another good example of how physical and symbolic boundaries work to define groups. Countries often mark boundaries between themselves by establishing physical borders, perhaps most dramatically on the U.S.-Mexico border. Such borders signal to us that we are moving from a territory belonging to one group to territory belonging to another.

However, boundaries are used to differentiate not only physical space but also symbolic space. Just because immigrants cross from Mexico into the United States does not mean they have "become" American. On the contrary, as the conflict over immigration in the United States shows, people use a whole range of symbolic boundaries to differentiate those who are considered American from those who are not. These symbolic boundaries involve setting up differences between our ideas of "us" and "them," including ideas about who Mexicans are and why they may be considered "different" than Americans.

Group boundaries are a key aspect of understanding deviance because of the role groups play in defining and setting limits of acceptable behavior. We have powerful incentives to do as the group says we must. Being part of a group means behaving within the boundaries of the community, and breaking those boundaries involves reprimands or even the risk of being removed from the group altogether. Behaviors defined as deviant involve crossing boundaries, in terms of both group members who transgress the boundaries of the group as well as nonmembers who try to break those boundaries.

Groups police their boundaries so as to prevent "outsiders" from entering. Symbolic and physical boundaries are set up with the explicit purpose of keeping outsiders out, and the crossing of such boundaries is considered an act of deviance. Consider again the example of immigration: "illegal immigration" is defined as the unauthorized crossing of a boundary. In this way deviance takes place both when someone moves "outside" the boundaries he or she is expected to live in and when he or she enters another group's space.

The Negative Affirmations of Group Membership   Just as all groups have rules of what members *must do*, they also all have explicit designations of what members *must not do*. This second set of excluded behaviors, or prohibitions, is the key ingredient of deviant behavior: It is behavior that violates

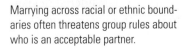
Marrying across racial or ethnic boundaries often threatens group rules about who is an acceptable partner.

the group consensus of what *we must not do*. Any couple that has dated or married across sharply defined group boundaries (blacks and whites, Chinese and Koreans, same-sex couples, Hindus and Muslims, etc.) has likely experienced expressions of disapproval from other group members. The major religions contain many explicit rules believers must follow. For instance, the Christian commandments forbid murder, adultery, and theft. The Koran forbids these three and adds alcohol consumption. Such prohibitions empower authorities to punish those who deviate, with the punishment of ostracism for violators serving as the ultimate way groups maintain boundaries.

Explicit rules banning certain kinds of behaviors are often written down. The oldest known written set of laws in human history to be placed before the public is the Hammurabi code. It originated in the ancient city of Babylon, around 1780 BCE. Most known for the famous retributive justice penalty of "an eye for an eye," the Hammurabi code also included a specific set of punishments that aimed to best fit specific deviant acts. Since the time of the Hammurabi code, as groups and societies began to prescribe punishments for specific acts, they have revealed in the process much about what they truly value. For example, during the early and middle parts of the nineteenth century, governing bodies in the western region of the United States sometimes imposed the death penalty for horse thieves, while a conviction for murder could be punishable by just a few years in prison. This speaks loudly to what was most valued by those with the power to decide punishment at that time.

Sentences and punishments, when they appear whimsical or irrational, raise questions about the legitimacy of the group or society making the rules. Indeed, in the late eighteenth and early nineteenth centuries, as the first prisons and criminal justice systems began to appear in Western societies, their credibility was often undermined by the arbitrary manner in which punishments for crimes were determined and given out. Some thieves were hung for stealing cloth worth very little, while rapists and murderers often served only a few months in prison. Moreover, for the same crime, one person could get 20 years' imprisonment while another served a few weeks. Leading nineteenth-century philosophers argued that it was imperative to find a way to "make the punishment better fit the crime." Numerous social theorists, essayists, historians, and moral philosophers observed, lamented, analyzed, and commented upon how the chaotically uneven punishments were undermining the legitimacy of the government's use of its punitive powers. The first major reform of the penal

codes was inspired by this situation, and codification finally occurred in the mid-nineteenth century and swept through most Western societies.

The most important influence on the reform movement was a book published in 1764 by an Italian social theorist, Cesare Beccaria. Simply titled *On Crimes and Punishments*, in it Beccaria set forth a theory of how and why justice should be meted out to the perpetrator. His main concern was that the citizenry have a sense that the criminal justice system was fair. A key element was the open, transparent, and public nature of laws, and the corresponding transparency of the punishment attached to criminal activity. This left room for the possible fluidity of the severity of punishment (attached to a specific crime) if there was a public outcry about the unfairness, an issue that remains heavily debated today in extreme cases such as the man sentenced to a 50-year-to-life sentence for stealing a few DVDs for his children at Christmas (one was reported to be *Snow White*); as this was his "third strike" under California's three-strike criminal justice law (in which anyone receiving a third felony conviction would be sent to prison for a life sentence) (Cannon 2005).

☐ Statistical versus Social Deviance

As we think further about the nature of deviance, it is important to make a distinction between how frequent or rare some behaviors are on the one hand, and whether or not those behaviors violate written or unwritten rules. Rare behaviors are "deviant" in the sense that they are uncommon but are not necessarily deviant in the sociological sense. Consider the following example. In a class of 60 students, a small group of students may choose to wear a baseball cap, a scarf, or a beret during class. In this case, wearing head coverings could be defined as **statistically deviant**—that is, most students do not wear head coverings during class—but it would not be defined as **socially deviant**, that is, behavior that violates societal rules (schools in America generally allow students to wear head coverings). Wearing hats in class, even if only a few students wear them, is considered socially acceptable, not deviant. To be sure, if one or two of those students chose to take off their clothes and get naked, it would be socially deviant—as the case of Andrew Martinez suggests.

The distinction between statistical deviance and social deviance is important because what is considered deviant (or even criminal) has little to do with how common it is. We might think that being socially deviant means doing

How does statistical deviance differ from social deviance?

something most people don't do, and likewise that acting "normal" means doing what most people do. But that is simply not always the case. Take smoking marijuana or committing adultery. Most Americans have smoked marijuana at some point in their lives, a criminal act in most states. Yet most people who have smoked marijuana would not think of themselves as criminals (even those who regularly use the drug). Similarly, adultery is statistically very common in the United States, with some estimates suggesting that more than 20 percent of married persons have committed adultery at some point in their lives. While adultery is no longer a criminal act in the United States, in spite of the fact that so many husbands and wives cheat on each other, it is still considered deviant. It violates a social norm about marriage and crossing boundaries of what is considered acceptable behavior for a married partner.

When thinking about social deviance, then, it is important to distinguish between deviant behavior and deviant persons. Just because someone engages in some form of behavior that others in the group or society would label as deviant does not mean that the person will be so characterized. Indeed, in the normal course of life, each of us will transgress some rule, and when large numbers of people start disregarding the same rule, the typical response is to **normalize** the deviant behavior—that is, to recast the behavior into a frame that rescues the person as "normal" even as the behavior is deemed "deviant."

Social Norms: The Unstated Rules of Everyday Life

Contemporary societies like the United States have vast legal systems and criminal codes that specify what is criminal or illegal activity in far greater detail than our forebears could have envisioned. When the explicit, written rules are violated, we have names for the so-called deviants—ranging from *murderer* to *thief*, from *arsonist* to *rapist*. Later in the chapter, we will discuss these formal rules and the ways they are administered through the criminal justice system. Yet a vital aspect of social control that is at least equally important is the enforcement of the unstated, unwritten, and nonarticulated rules—what sociologists call norms. In every society, even those with elaborate written rules and criminal codes, there are inevitably an enormous number of *unwritten* rules of behavior that individuals have to master in order to avoid appearing deviant. The French sociologist Emile Durkheim,

What is a social norm?

writing over a century ago about such matters, called this "the unstated terms of the social contract" (Durkheim [1890] 1997). Durkheim was referring to the fact that rules of behavior do not need to be written down in order to require conformity.

For example, when you enter an auditorium and there is only one person seated, "everyone knows" that unless that person is a friend the seats on either side of him or her are off limits. If there is an alternative, the norm is that you are not supposed to sit right next to a stranger. **Norms** are basic rules of society that help us know what is and what is not appropriate to do in any given situation. At a very basic level, these unstated rules tell us a lot about the nature and character of our society. One of those norms is the "norm of engagement." Nowhere is it written down, but North Americans have a near universal understanding that they must always be engaged with some object or person (Goffman 1963). If you doubt that this is true, try the following experiment: In the presence of those who know you (family, friends, or people at work), sit for several minutes and do nothing. Have no object in your hand (no book or magazine, smartphone, iPad, or other object) and have no music or television playing to provide a possible object of your attention. Just sit there. Within a few minutes, you will experience what happens when the norm of engagement is violated: Those around you will start to become uncomfortable and wonder what is wrong with you. Should you persist long enough in this comatose state, at some point your family or friends will start to worry that perhaps some kind of mental disturbance is occurring.

It is not easy to trace where such unwritten rules of behavior come from. In contrast to written rules and laws, which have a history that can be traced through **archival research** using historical records, legal case law, and other sources, the origins of norms are more obscure and often impossible to uncover. Yet we can be sure that they have their roots in societal process where the desires and preferences of powerful groups get extended throughout an entire society. The norm of engagement that sociologist Erving Goffman discusses likely has its roots in fears of idleness ("an idle mind is the devil's workshop") and is perhaps also linked to the idea that we should always use our time productively in some fashion. The norm of personal space may have its roots in larger ideas about personal privacy. But whatever the precise origin of these norms, we can be sure that they grew out of a social process of defining what is normal in light of other ideas about proper behavior.

2 How Is Morality Defined and Regulated?

THE PROBLEM OF MORAL REGULATION

Watch the **Big Question Video** in **MySocLab**

A t the center of the societal struggle over what is and what is not deviant is a provocative question: What is morality and appropriately moral behavior? At all times and places, societies struggle with questions of **moral behavior**—that is, which types of behaviors will be considered good and right (or *moral*) versus those which are bad and wrong (or *immoral*). Some common examples in contemporary America would include whether or not drug use or homosexuality are compatible, or not, with our understanding of morality. What is considered immoral behavior is constantly at issue because in any society different groups will inevitably have different views and understandings. When societies attempt to outlaw certain kinds of previously common and widespread behavior across society, it is invariably a highly controversial process. How does moral and immoral behavior come to be defined, and how does the definition of moral behavior change over time? How and why does society attempt to control and police the behavior of individuals, and with what consequences?

What is the distinction between interested and disinterested punishment?

Interested versus Disinterested Punishment

A useful place to start is to note a distinction between what has been called *interested punishment* versus *disinterested punishment* (Ranulf 1938). This distinction refers to two different

kinds of deviants and two different kinds of reasons for punishment: those that arise out of a desire to protect wealth and private property, and those that attempt to direct and control the behavior of individuals. First, because there is an existing distribution of wealth and power in any society, the most privileged groups and classes have a strong and direct interest in maintaining their wealth and their political domination. To be sure, we all have an interest in having our private property protected, but for holders of great wealth the stakes are much higher. Laws against theft and fraud, originating in the desire of the powerful to protect their wealth and privilege, eventually would filter down into ordinary criminal-law rules against theft of all kinds. Transgressors, insurgents, and rebels who threatened wealth-holders could expect firm punishment, and it was a short step from there to generalizing these types of punishment to protect everyone's property.

On the other hand, there are countless numbers of laws that have been placed on the books that have nothing to do with the distribution of wealth. These laws relate to behaviors such as tobacco use, alcohol and drug consumption, gambling, and prostitution—and can even include such behavior as the way one dresses, engages in demonstrative behavior in public places, or has same-sex liaisons. Because these rules, and their transgressors, have little to do with wealth redistribution, these kinds of rules and laws have been described as disinterested punishment. This kind of punishment is designed not to protect property but rather to control the morals and social behavior of people. Initially, these laws were explicitly written and targeted at the poor and the working classes, and were in many cases created by upper-class groups seeking to control and shape the lower classes. But in order for proposals for specific kinds of moral regulation to prevail, they would have to find broad popular support as well.

The two kinds of punishments are not entirely independent. Throughout American history, right up to the present, the effort to control morality among certain lower-status groups—minorities, the poor, immigrants, and others—has been closely connected to the interests of the powerful in maintaining social order (Beisel 1997). Moral reformers have always hoped that encouraging good behavior on the part of the poor will make them better workers, more committed citizens, and less likely to revolt against those with more wealth and power.

The Temperance Movement as Moral Crusade

To understand how moral and immoral behavior gets defined and then redefined over time, it is useful to study some historical examples and see how they evolved over time. One important one in American history is the case of the campaign against alcohol. Once upon a time, at the beginning of the nation and for its first two centuries, Americans drank so much alcohol that we could appropriately be called the "Alcoholic Republic" (Rorabaugh 1979). In the early eighteenth century, Americans drank five gallons of alcohol per capita every year. By 1830, per capita consumption had gone up even further, to seven gallons. That is the equivalent of nearly two bottles of 80-proof hard liquor per adult person per week—even factoring in abstainers (Okrent 2010:8). (To get a comparative sense, at the end of the twentieth century, we were down to two gallons per capita.)

So how did the United States go from being a nation soaked in alcohol to being the only industrialized country to enact a constitutional amendment banning the consumption of alcohol, during the period known as **Prohibition** (1920–1933)? The roots of this shift can be

traced to the nineteenth century, during which Americans witnessed a dramatic pendulum swing in attitudes toward alcohol. In the 1850s, while it was common for an adult male to down several swigs of hard liquor every single day, it was typically done in the home, not in taverns, saloons, public bars, or in the streets. As more and more people moved from rural farms to cities, with industrialization and the massive influx of European immigrants in the last half of the century, all that would change.

The new immigrants were often concentrated in the poorest sections of cities in the industrializing North. The older generation of Americans—mainly from northern and western Europe—felt threatened by what they perceived as a change in "American values" and traditions. More specifically, the movement for the prohibition of alcohol was a crusade to reestablish the traditional values that the upper middle classes experienced as slipping away (Gusfield 1963). It was, in short, the late-nineteenth-century version of "let's take the country back!"

Still, it is remarkable that we could go from a nation in which a pint of liquor a day was normal to a period of constitutionally mandated prohibition. How did this happen—and more importantly, why? The story begins in a small town in Ohio in 1873, when a small group of middle-class white women entered a saloon, sunk to their knees, and prayed for the souls of the owners that they might stop serving alcohol. While this is often cited as the launch of what is known as the Temperance Movement ("temperance" in this period meant moderation, not abstinence), historians note that there had been strong and insistent calls for moderation of alcohol consumption for much of the previous three decades. No single factor explains the success of the movement to rid the nation of alcohol, but there is a consensus that the new

Protest against alcohol Prohibition, 1931. The remarkable shift from a country with high alcohol consumption to one with a complete ban on all alcohol is one of the most extraordinary efforts to legislate morality across an entire society. Was it doomed to fail?

immigrants—"the infidel foreign population," as one historian has described them (Okrent 2010:26)—became the increasingly public face of alcohol excess. Eighty percent of licensed saloons were owned by first-generation Americans, and they "set at once to selling liquor ... to Italians, Greeks, Lithuanians, Poles—all the rough and hairy tribes ..." as one of the muckrakers of the Progressive Era put it (quoted in Okrent 2010:26).

What does the history of alcohol and opium use tell us about what is normal and deviant?

The small group of women who prayed at the Ohio saloons in December 1873 would be the initial spark that would eventually become the Women's Christian Temperance Union (WCTU). Within three months of that first pray-in, the spark ignited the closing of taverns in over 75 communities. In the next few decades, this small group would have remarkable successes in getting school boards across the nation to insert new instructional materials denouncing alcohol as an evil and then getting legislation passed at both local and state levels outlawing the sale of alcohol. Jurisdictions soon came to be known as either "dry" (no alcohol sales permitted) or "wet." A good part of the movement's effectiveness came from the fact that the most determined advocates and leaders were primarily, if not exclusively, the wives of the most successful upper-middle-class professionals; their husbands were bankers, doctors, lawyers, or very successful businessmen. During the peak of its power in the first decade of the twentieth century, the membership in the WCTU was overwhelmingly drawn from the ranks of the most privileged groups in American society. In 1919, Prohibition advocates succeeded in getting a constitutional amendment passed that made alcohol consumption illegal anywhere in the United States.

Yet, less than two decades later, the pendulum would swing back with ferocity. Millions of Americans refused to stop drinking, creating a campaign of mass civil disobedience that undermined the legitimacy of the new constitutional amendment. In the face of continued widespread drinking, attempts to enforce the ban on liquor would prove exceptionally difficult. The symbolic act that would break the back of Prohibition occurred when then New York governor

Franklin Delano Roosevelt, shortly before he would become president, raised a glass of liquor at a public event, signaling yet another shift in the constitution of the moral center when it came to alcohol. Prohibition would soon thereafter be repealed, and the consumption of alcohol today is permitted with relatively few restrictions (e.g., laws against driving or operating machinery while under the influence of alcohol are among the few major restrictions).

☐ The Campaign against Opium

While the alcohol crusade was one major example of a moral crusade that successfully, if only temporarily, made everyday behavior into deviant behavior, a very different morality play of normality and deviance was being played out in the matter of another mind-altering substance, opium, and its two derivates, morphine and heroin.

Opium has been around for thousands of years, but morphine was not discovered and developed until the first decade of the nineteenth century. It took 50 years before it would become the most effective painkiller in medical history—in large measure owing to the discovery of the hypodermic needle in 1856. This would occur just in time for the Civil War.

The toll of human suffering during the Civil War was monstrous, not just in terms of the huge proportion of the U.S. population that was killed but also those who suffered maiming injuries and debilitating health consequences that would last their full lifetime. In this context, morphine would be introduced, fast becoming the drug of choice for dealing with pain of any and all kinds. When the war ended,

An Opium Den in New York's Chinatown, circa 1910.

ex-soldiers often returned home with strong habits. While injections of morphine were legion for many sources of pain, a new pathway into the blood would come from ingesting the drug in the form of a soothing syrup. For just a few pennies, one could purchase such a product at the local pharmacy. Prescriptions were not part of the U.S. regulatory system until 1914 across the nation. So anyone, of any age, could purchase bottles of this syrup, with a content of as high as 10 to 14 percent morphine. There was no Food and Drug Administration until the dawn of the twentieth century. Thus, there were no requirements to label ingredients, much less disclose proportionality of contents.

Here we come to the most fascinating feature of "the tale of two drugs" (alcohol vs. morphine). Between the end of the Civil War and 1904, records from pharmacies indicate that the heaviest usage of morphine was by middle-class, middle-aged, white females (Terry and Pellens 1970). This was the same four-decade period in which alcohol producers and distributors were being demonized and alcohol consumers were being characterized harshly by those seeking to demonize alcohol. Yet during this very same period, morphine use was characterized primarily as a medical problem. Rather than getting labeled as social deviants, morphine consumers were the objects of sympathy, more pitied than despised. Morphine producers and distributors were not vilified; they were mainly ignored and did not register as a problem of any moral character, certainly not of a transgression of the moral order.

All that would soon change. Up until the first decade of the twentieth century, anyone could walk into a pharmacy and purchase morphine or heroin (or any drug) for a few pennies without a prescription. New York State was the first to break with this practice, with the passage of the Boyle Act of 1904. The New York State legislation (and the federal law modeled upon it a decade later, known as the Harrison Act in 1914) was originally intended to give medical doctors control over the distribution of drugs by requiring prescriptions for the first time. However, when it came to the opiates, these laws would have the opposite effect. Physicians were suddenly confronted with scores of "patients" waiting for their prescriptions while regular patients were crowded out of waiting rooms. The response was to simply prescribe *en masse*—signing many prescriptions and having an assistant distribute them to those who waited in long lines (Duster 1970). The federal government strenuously objected to this practice and took several physicians to court to stop it. In 1916, the Supreme Court sided with the government position, ruling in *Webb v. U.S.* that prescriptions must be individually prescribed based upon an individualized medical assessment. This ruling suddenly criminalized the practice of *en masse* prescriptions, sent several newly created law-violators to prison, and scared the medical profession away from the treatment of opiate users.

Within a few years, a black market in the production and distribution of the opiates was created, and opiate addicts were suddenly portrayed as morally reprehensible, not simply the victims of physiological dependency. Thus, in the short space of two decades, the morphine and heroin addicts had been transformed in the public eye—no longer as middle-class, middle-aged, white, female victims of a health and medical problem but as working-class, male, youthful criminals, and increasingly "of color."

It is one of the least appreciated ironies of American history that just when the pressure to end Prohibition peaked in the early 1930s, laws would emerge to demonize what had previously been *normal* opiate use: those soothing syrups with a high morphine content consumed primarily by middle-class, middle-aged white women. These two juxtaposed stories offer a good example of the structural forces that shape who gets to be normal and who gets labeled as deviant. What lessons can we learn from these two drugs whose inverted histories in late-nineteenth- and early-twentieth-century America overlapped? The important element to note in this story is that the pharmacology of the drugs did not change. Rather, it was the pattern of consumption that changed, and *that* changed everything about what was determined to be deviant behavior and who could be categorized as engaging in immoral, deviant behavior.

By the late 1930s, alcohol had shifted from being the metaphorical "demon rum" (the evil inherent in the mind-altering substance) to being a substance that some could gracefully handle (the casual social drinker) and some could not (the problem drinker). In sharp contrast, morphine, heroin, and opium had shifted from being a medical analgesic that victimized unwittingly our best citizens (in the late nineteenth century) to a drug that drove the unfit to willful, licentious thrill-seeking. Again, nothing about the pharmaceutical product had changed—but those perceived as the primary consumers had been dramatically transformed into morally reprehensible deviants in just three decades. As we shall see in the next section, the seemingly arbitrary answer to the question of what constitutes normality and deviance is not so arbitrary at all. It is mainly about the location of power and the capacity to use the levers of state power to exercise control.

Contemporary Moral Crusades

The attempt to regulate morality remains very much a part of contemporary American society. One important example, which has many parallels to the campaigns against alcohol and morphine, can be seen in the **war on drugs**. Launched by President Ronald Reagan in 1985 and widely embraced by government officials across the country, the government significantly increased surveillance of and criminal penalties for the sale, possession, and consumption of nonprescription drugs. Today, jails and prisons are filled with millions

Popular comedian and talk show host Ellen DeGeneres with her wife, Portia de Rossi. Homosexuality was long considered deviant. Why is that no longer the case?

of drug offenders in the name of social order (we will provide more details later in the chapter). The reasons for the vast increase in the criminalization of drugs since the 1980s are complicated, but certain facts are indisputable: Far more African Americans are being arrested and convicted than actual patterns of drug use would suggest, and similarly far more poor people than white, middle-class people (not to mention affluent people) are being arrested and convicted than actual patterns of drug use would suggest (Tonry 1995). The white college student experimenting with illegal drugs, or the suburban couple or business executive who enjoy occasionally getting high, are drastically less likely to face criminal charges than are poor people or minorities. The criminalization of drugs has become a way of policing poor neighborhoods and communities, and the costs to everyone—the individuals being arrested and convicted over minor drug offenses, their families and communities, and society at large through the extraordinary expense of keeping drug offenders in prison—are very high (Hagan 2010).

Another important moral crusade in recent decades in America, but one that has seemingly failed, has been the effort to ban or limit homosexuality and punish gays and lesbians on the basis of their sexual orientation. For centuries homosexuality was largely practiced "in the closet," although to be sure gays and lesbians were subject to arrest and harassment by police wherever they were discovered. Gay bars were continually being subjected to police raids, but the practice of homosexuality remained sufficiently under the radar of public consciousness that few explicit campaigns against homosexuality needed to be launched. All that would change in 1969 when patrons of a gay bar in New York's Greenwich Village—the Stonewall Inn—fought back when police raided the bar one night in August. After three days of riots and growing protests in support of the Stonewall patrons, the movement for gay liberation and freedom was born. From that moment forward, gays have demanded and increasingly obtained full rights of citizenship, and laws against homosexuality have declined or disappeared.

What does the failure of the crusade against same-sex relationships say about the future of moral crusades?

But this did not happen without a terrific fight, one that continues to this day. Opponents of homosexuality sought—with varying degrees of success—to follow in the footsteps of earlier moral crusades to reassert the illegality of homosexuality or to restrict the rights of gays and lesbians at every opportunity. Many states and local governments across America passed laws restricting the employment rights of gay individuals, for example to prevent then from teaching in public schools or working at childcare centers or other public institutions. The military enforced an affirmative ban against homosexual soldiers (only recently repealed by President Barack Obama). The AIDS epidemic was initially cast as a "gay disease," even though many heterosexuals were also diagnosed as HIV-positive.

The moral crusade against homosexuality was vigorously pursued by anti-gay activists, but ultimately did not succeed in either making same-sex unions either illegal or successfully ostracizing gays. Increasing numbers of gays and lesbians in public life began to acknowledge their sexual orientation, with Massachusetts congressmen Gerry

Stubbs and Barney Frank openly acknowledging they were gay in the early 1980s. Slowly, it became possible for gays to affirm their sexual orientation without fear of punishment or sanction by employers, family members, or friends. The individual ritual of "coming out of the closet," as gays and lesbians across the country openly acknowledged their sexuality, would become so common that today virtually all Americans have at least one gay family member or friend. In 2003, the Supreme Court acknowledged (in *Lawrence v. Texas*, 539 U.S. 558) the shift in public attitudes and societal trends by overturning a 1985 ruling that had allowed the states to keep antigay laws on the books. Today, the struggle over homosexuality has shifted to a bitter campaign over the rights of gays and lesbians to marry (which has been established in a few states and other countries around the world but remains unavailable in most states). But the effort to criminalize same-sex relationships has failed.

The apparent failure of the crusade against same-sex relationships portends an uncertain future for such crusades (and the effort to legislate morality). Growing numbers of younger and middle-aged Americans, irrespective of their political or religious views, favor lifestyle freedom over laws and regulations telling people what they can and cannot do (e.g., Baker 2005). Increasingly, the line seems to be drawn at the point of behavior that threatens to harm others; drinking is fine, but driving a car while drunk is now subject to major criminal penalties that have dramatically increased in recent years. The growing campaign to legalize marijuana—with many states legalizing the use of medical marijuana and campaigns for outright legalization gaining ground in some parts of the country—exemplifies the changing dynamics of moral regulation. It is increasingly difficult for opponents of marijuana to persuade citizens that it makes sense to allow alcohol consumption (which can be far more problematic in many ways for both individuals and society) while still outlawing marijuana. Nevertheless, the historical account we have provided in this section certainly suggests that attempts to regulate the behavior of the poor, immigrants, and other disadvantaged groups are not likely to completely disappear.

3 Who Defines Deviance?

DEVIANCE, CRIME, AND POWER

Watch the **Big Question Video** in **MySocLab**

What is the connection between economic and political power and the definition of deviant behavior? Recall that our first experience with the idea of normality and its boundaries (deviance) is from the small social group into which we are born, almost universally the kinship unit. But if the small and relatively homogeneous group is our first encounter with who gets to define normality, as we grow up and encounter other groups, stronger and more compelling forces determine *which* group's view of normality will prevail. As we have seen in the last section, foremost among these forces is that power, whether hidden or direct, plays a role. In the historical example of how alcohol and the opiates traded places as the symbols of normal and deviant behavior, the advocates with greater access to political power began to surface. It was only when powerful groups sought to criminalize alcohol and opiates that those campaigns succeeded. In this section we turn our attention to other important struggles over defining deviance in which the role of economic and political power in shaping punishment becomes explicit.

☐ Labeling Deviance and Crime

Much of the discussion in the chapter so far has pointed to one important conclusion: What is considered deviant, or criminal, is somewhat arbitrary. In the 1960s, some sociologists began exploring contexts where deviant, criminal, or abnormal behavior were defined by individuals in positions of authority, and they found plenty of evidence of such arbitrariness. This research included riding around in police cars and seeing what police officers actually do, which includes overlooking a lot of things that could be considered violations of the law (Bittner 1967; Cicourel 1967); studying public defenders' offices and noting how often cases were disposed of through having lawyers on both sides work together to get guilty pleas from certain suspects (but not others) (Sudnow 1965), studying intake decisions at mental institutions (Goffman 1959), and many others. This body of research, which has been repeatedly confirmed in later studies, tells us that when we look at what actually happens in the field, as opposed to what is supposed to happen according to written rules, there is a great deal of arbitrary decision making going on.

One of the more interesting of the new theories that emerged in this period challenged the idea that there are real and objective differences in behavior that is normal versus what is deviant. Most sociologists today argue that the *process* by which a behavior comes to be defined as deviant is critical to understanding what causes it. In other words, instead of focusing on the behavior of individuals, they argue we need to look at how the behavior came to be defined as deviant. Deviant behavior is "caused" by the process through which a behavior comes to be defined, or as they say, labeled, as deviant.

These ideas are associated with what came to be known as the **labeling theory** of deviance, the idea that many kinds of behaviors are deviant solely because they are labeled as such. One of the leading proponents of the labeling theory of deviance, the sociologist Howard Becker, argued that deviance, rather than an objective thing, is a social construction that evolves over time (Becker 1963). An act that may be considered normal at one point in time comes to be defined as deviant at another point in time. In this way, a

basic premise of labeling theory is that social control does not simply respond to deviance; it actually constitutes deviance. And so to understand deviance we need to focus on how social control actively makes certain behaviors deviant. It involves thinking about deviance not as a momentary act, such as the moment at which someone robs someone else, or smokes marijuana, but rather as a process which involves looking at how a behavior *becomes* deviant. Understanding this process involves two things. First, it requires looking at why and how certain behaviors and people get labeled as deviant. Second, it requires looking at the impacts of these labels on the behaviors of the people who are labeled. Once labeled deviant (or a troublemaker or a criminal), an individual may come to act in that way. If a criminal record makes it more difficult to get a job, as many studies have documented, turning back to crime to support oneself or one's family may be the only logical way to survive. Further, once labeled a troublemaker or deviant, an individual's actions are more closely scrutinized by the authorities, including teachers, police officers, employers, etc. In this way, the odds that the deviant will be caught in further acts of deviance go up.

☐ From Deviance in the Streets to Deviance in the Suites: White-Collar Crime

One of the most important developments in the study of deviance and crime, and one that extended the idea of labeling theory into arenas where power is particularly important, was the introduction of the concept of white collar crime. First introduced by the famous criminologist Edwin Sutherland in 1949, the term **white-collar crime** refers to unethical business practices committed by people in the course of their work lives. Historically, white-collar crimes were handled almost solely in civil courts. This was, in Sutherland's view, often perverse: Some kinds of white-collar crime can have as much or more of a negative impact and cause injury to more people in a society than ordinary street crimes (such as burglary, robbery, vandalism, shoplifting, or assault). For example, when a corporation or business owner knowingly markets an unsafe product, far more people may suffer significantly greater harms than any thief or bank robber can cause. Sutherland concluded that when business activity damages innocent people's property or physical well-being, it is completely arbitrary to absolve the wrongdoer of criminal responsibility (Sutherland 1949).

White-collar crime can take many forms, from those that are closer to street crimes (e.g., stealing money from your employer or using the Internet to defraud others) all the

How does labeling theory explain deviance?

way up to those involving powerful businesses and corporate leaders who make decisions or seek profits in ways that cause injury or harm to innocent people. Perhaps not surprisingly, there has been much more agreement that lower-level white-collar crimes, such as embezzlement or fraud, are properly situated in criminal (as well as civil) courts; the treatment of higher-level white-collar crime, which is often more consequential, has remained more controversial.

The Enron Scandal   We can get a better handle on the notion of white-collar crime, and the difficulties in applying punishments, by considering a couple of recent examples. Both of these cases involve a complex mixture of greed, political influence, and corruption. The first involves a giant energy corporation known as Enron. Prior to its bankruptcy in late 2001, Enron appeared to be one of the most successful corporations in the world. In 1996, Enron reported profits of $13.3 billion. Just three years later, in 1999, the company's reported profits had tripled to $40.1 billion. And the very next year, in 2000, profits were reported to have soared to the $100 billion mark, making it number seven among the Fortune 500 list of companies, leap-frogging over well-known companies IBM, Walmart, AT&T, and Philip Morris. For an astounding six years in a row, *Fortune Magazine* named Enron as the "most innovative company" in America. In the fall of 2001, however, it would be revealed that these were fictitious profits based on enormous accounting fraud and price manipulation.

Before Enron's operations were revealed to be fraudulent, the company benefitted from its close relationship with many elected officials, including President George W. Bush (who famously and playfully nicknamed Enron CEO Kenneth Lay "Kenny boy"). Enron executives provided enormous amounts of money to support the election campaigns of favored politicians, and as a result frequently received special treatment from government agencies. One example of the many ways in which Enron was able to take advantage of its growing political power and influence comes from the sale of electricity in California, where it won exclusive contracts to provide much of the state's energy. During the period from April 1998 to April 2000, Californians were paying on average $30 per megawatt for electricity. In June of 2000, several power plants were suddenly closed for maintenance by Enron, and prices sharply increased to $120 per megawatt—an extraordinary increase of 400 percent in just two months. Then things became worse when Enron arranged for the appearance of "congestion" (scheduling power deliveries that it never intended) so that it could charge special "congestion fees" of $750 per megawatt (Fox 2003:208). Pacific Gas and Electric, California's largest utility company, was caught in the middle and would file for bankruptcy, having run up a deficit of nearly $9 billion as a direct consequence of Enron's manipulation of the state's energy grid during this period.

Perhaps the most infamous moment in the entire Enron case involved tapes that later came to light that capture an Enron trader's derisive, scornful laugh at the plight of a California grandmother whose energy bill had just quadrupled because of his participation in an unscrupulous manipulation of the power grid. "All that money that you stole from those poor grandmothers in California? Grandma Millie. Now she wants her … money back for all the power you've just charged … !" The Enron trader replies, "F … Granny!" and then has a loud, sustained laugh with his buddies that should curdle the blood of any decent soul.

Enron's illegal manipulation of energy prices in California would prove to be just the tip of the iceberg of its unscrupulous practices. The company was also using a mammoth accounting fraud to create profits where none existed. The "Enron scandal," as it came to be known, involved creating false profits by reporting phony income from fictitious off-shore companies created by Enron's financial officers. When the first journalists and government officials began raising questions about the company's accounting practices, senior Enron executives began selling their shares in the company while repeatedly promising shareholders that all was right with the company, and even urging others (including Enron's own employees) to buy the company's stock. In November 2001, within days after the scandal was revealed, the value of the stock would fall from its peak of $90 (in 2000) to just a few pennies. The full details of the scandal are complex, but the bottom line is that when the company filed for bankruptcy, all of the company's shareholders, its 20,000 employees (many of whom received stock bonuses that executives knew would eventually be worthless), and communities around the world where Enron was operating suffered as the company collapsed. The entire huge accounting firm of Arthur Anderson, where several of the accountants who had helped Enron with their fraud were employed, had its reputation destroyed and was forced to fold, costing thousands more people their jobs. In contrast to most cases of white-collar crime, the fraud in the Enron case was so extreme and blatant that three senior executives would serve time in prison, though Lay himself died before he could begin his prison sentence. Still, given the depths of the fraud at Enron, it is a remarkable commentary on the shortcomings of white collar justice that only three people were sent to prison.

The U.S. Banking and Financial Crisis   A second, even more dramatic example of the complexities of regulating white-collar crime can be seen in the banking and

What does the 2008 U.S. financial crisis tell us about power and deviant behavior?

financial crisis that hit the United States, Europe, and ultimately the global economic system in 2008. To understand this case more fully, and how and why many banks and other financial corporations were able to take actions that generated billions of dollars in profits while causing millions of homeowners to lose their homes, we need to briefly investigate the historical background. After the banking collapse during the Great Depression of the 1930s, new laws and regulations were put in place to prevent another collapse of the banking system. Banks were limited in the kinds of risky investments they could make. While many in the banking world objected to these constraints, for decades they served to reduce the risk of financial crisis. But beginning in the 1980s, as memories of the Great Depression faded, powerful banking interests persuaded Congress to begin loosening the rules and allowing them to take on more risk in the search for higher profits. For example, in 1982 Congress voted to deregulate the savings and loan (S&L) industry. Risky investments by S&Ls ensued almost immediately, and within a decade some had gotten rich while scores of these institutions failed. As a direct consequence, taxpayers were slapped with a bill of $124 billion. But that was only the beginning.

In the 1990s, the growing movement to tear down banking and financial regulations had reached a fever pitch. Congress and President Bill Clinton, at the urging of the financial industry, undid many of the remaining restrictions on the banks. In this increasing "anything goes" environment, financial companies aggressively pursued new avenues of profit. One of these, which would ultimately trigger the development of the financial crisis, was the mass marketing of new home-mortgage products, known as *subprime loans,* to consumers who had little hope of repaying them. Playing on the desire of most Americans to own their own home, the subprime loans typically had a low initial "teaser" rate, but the fine

print revealed that they would eventually jump to a much higher rate. Many of the people taking out these loans did not understand the risk they were accepting, and laws that once might have protected them had been eliminated in the name of deregulation.

The story is more complicated than we can fully convey here, as the levels of fraud throughout the home-mortgage industry were breathtakingly pervasive and complicated. One key point was that the banks and loan companies making the subprime loans discovered that they were able to make handsome profits reselling the loans to other investors, who then assumed all of the risk. So they soon began giving out loans to virtually anyone they could find who would sign the paperwork. The secondary institutions (other banks, insurance companies, and investment firms) who bought up the subprime loans were continually assured they were safe. At this level, far removed from the original loan, the new loanholders could not understand, nor were fully informed, about the risks they were accepting.

The crisis began to unfold in 2007, when the American economy went into recession, unemployment started to rise, and home prices began to decline at the same time that many subprime loans were being reset to their higher rate. Large numbers of subprime borrowers began defaulting on their loans. As a result, the repackaged loans went into default, and in short order the entire financial sector would face a severe crisis that would ultimately require the federal government to provide many billions of dollars to keep the big banks from going out of business. The phrase "too big to fail" came to be applied to large banks that had taken on

Countrywide Financial Corporation CEO Angelo Mozilo testifying before Congress about his firm's promotion of subprime mortgages. Despite widespread fraud in the marketing and sale (and resale) of these loans, resulting in billions of dollars in losses, not a single executive in the mortgage industry has spent a day in prison for their role in this calamity.

these risky loans; although all other businesses in America go bankrupt when they make poor decisions, in this case the risks to all of American society if large banks were allowed to fail was too great to let happen. The federal government's "bailout" of the banks would keep them in business, but the full cost of the financial crisis of 2007 and 2008 is still being felt today. Unemployment rates shot up after the crisis began, and the American economy has performed very poorly by historical standards since then.

By effectively lobbying Congress to overturn regulations of financial institutions and energy production, powerful corporate actors enabled the redefinition of what would constitute normality, deviance, and criminality. By their own admission in Congressional testimony, many bank and financial executives acknowledged routinely practicing deception in withholding vital information from their own clients in relation to mortgage and subprime loans (and in the sale of financial products related to those loans). Goldman Sachs, the most famous financial firm in the world, paid $50 million in fines and faced many embarrassing revelations about its executives' behavior and treatment of their clients during the crisis. In late 2011, the CBS television news journal *60 Minutes* aired a two-part segment in which two whistle-blowers testified as to just how routine and systematic fraudulent mortgage-loan practices had indeed become "normal" (December 4, 2011). These midlevel managers had explicitly warned senior management, only to be ignored, then offered monetary settlements to remain silent, then fired for not cooperating with the firms' cover-up.

The actions of Enron in the 1990s and early 2000s, and later those of many in the financial sector in the 2000s, were fraudulent and in violation of federal and state law, but the criminal justice system had great difficulties deciding whether and how to punish them. To be sure, a handful of top Enron officials did receive modest prison sentences, but so far virtually no one in the mortgage industry has served prison time. One of the most aggressive offenders in the subprime scandal was Angelo Mozilo, president and CEO of Countrywide Financial, one of the companies that led the way in issuing and profiting from subprime loans. Despite making about $500 million while at Countrywide, Mozilo not only did not go to prison, he ended up settling the case against him by paying a fine of $47.5 million. Contrast this with the rough treatment of low-level drug offenders we mentioned in the previous section. Such examples typify the frequently light treatment of white-collar crime, and they raise two critical points. First, what kinds of deviant behavior get punished, and how strong the punishment, is linked in part to who the perpetrator is. Second, we are reminded

again that what counts as a punishable crime is in large part shaped by the overall distribution of power.

At the peak of the media coverage on predatory bank loans, the first author of this chapter was confronted by a provocative question from his nephew: "So which is worse, to rob an old lady of her purse, or to rob her of her pension?" This rhetorical question captures an old idiom about the differences between "blue-collar crime," or street crime, and white-collar and corporate crime. It is hard, if not impossible, to make the case that robbing an old lady of her purse is a worse offense, but it is certainly vastly more likely to be punished by the criminal justice system.

State Deviance, Terrorism, and War Crimes

If powerful corporations can engage in deviant behavior without much risk of criminal penalty, so too can governments. In the case of what we might call **state deviance**— that is, policy and actions carried out by government officials in their official capacities—criminal courts and international law rarely issue sanctions even against actions that lead to the deaths of innocent people. Just as the criminal justice system has trouble punishing corporations and corporate executives, so too are government officials often able to avoid any criminal sanction even when their actions cause significant harm or death to others. It reminds us, once again, that power matters.

We will explore these issues in more detail in this section in the context of the so-called **war on terror**—the effort of the American government since the attacks on the World Trade Center in New York and the Pentagon on September 11, 2001, to find, capture, or kill those individuals and groups suspected of plotting terrorist actions. In the name of fighting terrorism, the United States government and leading government officials have assumed the right to violate international law and widely accepted views about human rights in the modern world. Yet no government official has been formally punished for any of these activities.

What Is Terrorism?   In recent years, few topics have received more attention than **terrorism**—the use of violence to achieve some political objective. No one defends terrorism. Anyone who uses force to kill innocent people violates the universal rule against murder. But who the real terrorists are is not always so clear.

Let's start with a historical example before turning to the current war on terror. Great Britain maintained a global empire from the eighteenth century until after

When does violence committed during wartime become criminal?

World War II. It did not end in 1781 with its defeat at the hands of American revolutionaries, although the American revolutionaries did strike the first successful blow against it. In many places, not just America, other people subject to British rule objected to their lack of control over their own land, and they often struggled against long odds and a much better-equipped British army to win their freedom. In all such instances, those fighting British rule were labeled as terrorists. For example, in the 1950s in Kenya, members of a group fighting for independence from British rule, known as the Mau Mau, were called terrorists by the British, even though the British massacred more than 20 times as many civilians as the Mau Mau killed British. When British soldiers fired on crowds of unarmed protestors, as happened several times in Kenya and many other times throughout the history of the British Empire, it was never labeled terrorism by the British press or by the British government, but rather defended as necessary to protect the British Empire. As long as the British ruled, its opponents were always terrorists, and the British army was not (even when it killed innocent people).

What is terrorism? To appreciate how the modern understanding of terrorism developed, it is important to first explore the concept of a "theater of war." 500 years ago European armies were composed of men who designated the battlefield as the sole appropriate arena of conflict. Much like contemporary prize-fighters who are limited to the ring, boxing gloves, and rounds set off by agreed-upon parameters, these battlefields delimited the legitimate landscape for the war. While there were skirmishes that leaked off the battlefield, the arena of conflict was established by this limited notion of an agreed-upon terrain.

In the theatre of war, generals deploy troops, have their men dig trenches, and take hills to capture the high ground. But what of situations in which one army so outnumbers another, or is so much better equipped, that there is no real contest? Do generals really want to go into battle when their numbers are one-tenth that of their enemy? No, at least not on a straightforward battlefield encounter, where their inferior numbers inevitably lead to doom. Instead, strategy enters the formula, and tactics evolve. Methods such as cutting armies off at passes and starving them by destroying supply lines began to enter the theater of war as *legitimate* strategies. That is, before opponents ever got to some place called the field of battle, it was legitimate to intercept and harass them, to use decoys, and even send false signals, among other tactics. "All is fair in love and war" goes the saying.

We can see that it is only a matter of degree to shift away from grand strategy on or around the battlefield, to the cunning of ambush (before the "battle"), to the next major development, **guerilla warfare**, where a fighting force hides from its enemy and carries out targeted raids designed to wear down its numerically superior opponent. So long as European nations were doing battle with each other, there was the notion of a theater or arena of battle, more or less agreed upon as to the terms of action and ultimate settlement. However, in the colonial period, European powers had to do battle with people who were to face them with inferior arms and employing different rules of the game. Their inferior arms meant that Europeans could slaughter thousands of natives at will. That slaughter was never called terrorism. Yet one may ask, what greater terror is there than to be enslaved upon one's own land by a people who have contempt for your culture and your way of living?

More important to this line of argument, however, is that the colonized would later employ tactics that would shift the very meaning of war. Now, rather than regular soldiers conducting a battle in designated uniforms, increasingly *the people* themselves might be the enemy. In some

Hero or war criminal? Ernesto "Che" Guevara (center) leads a guerilla army campaign in Latin America. Guevara would later be killed without trial by the Bolivian government, assisted by the CIA.

ways, the Americans started it during the Revolutionary War. The British Redcoats, marching in formation, were fair game for the locals. The locals were usually not in uniform. They could devise clever ways of attacking an initially superior enemy. Later, other colonized peoples around the world would further blur this distinction. Women could and did carry muskets and fire them. Children could be used as runners. In guerilla war, any actor in the occupied territory could be a soldier in disguise.

Seen from this angle, the emergence of terrorism in the contemporary world is a progression from the battlefield to the strategic ploys of generals to avoid the battlefield, to guerilla warfare, and finally to terrorism. If we are to understand terrorism, we must try to penetrate the social and political situation of the perpetrators of terrorist acts. On the surface, the most powerful nations clearly dominate the weaker nations, and the United States has by far the strongest military in the world. In the theater of war, a weak nation would no more do battle with a strong nation than a welterweight would get into the boxing ring with a heavyweight. But outside the ring, the welterweight, even the lightweight, is equal to the heavyweight, by using different rules of engagement. And, indeed, outside the theater of war, the guerilla warrior begins to equalize matters by finding ways to make the fight fairer.

State Terror: The Case of Torture and Drone Strikes

While Americans have heard a great deal about the attacks on 9/11 and the continuing threat of a terrorist attack from Al Qaeda since then, we far less frequently discuss aspects of the war on terror where the United States government has sanctioned and employed tactics such as the kidnapping and torture of suspected terrorists, using drone strikes

to attack housing complexes occupied by suspected terrorists as well as children and adults not involved in any terrorist activity, and assuming the right to kill without trial people accused of membership in terrorist organizations (Brooks and Manza 2013: chap. 1). Why is it terrorism when Al Qaeda kills Americans but not terrorism when the U.S. government engages in actions such as these? To answer that question, it is useful to first examine why the U.S. government turned to the use of torture, the kidnapping of suspects, and in some cases their execution. In the aftermath of the attacks of 9/11, a single powerful metaphor dominated much of the thinking of government officials (and one that exerted considerable influence within the media and broader public as well). The metaphor was that of a "ticking time bomb," the idea that additional terrorist plots and attacks were imminent, and in order to foil them immediate and unconditional action was necessary. Officials in the White House crafted legal memos that claimed to justify the use of a variety of tactics that were not in accord with current international or American constitutional law (and that would later be denounced by virtually all legal scholars who examined them). Using these memos as a cover for their actions, for several years the government rounded up many people suspected of being involved in terrorist activity and took them to hidden locations where they could be subjected to "enhanced interrogation" techniques, otherwise known as torture, in the hopes of gathering intelligence. We know now—as a result of many important journalistic revelations—that many of the interrogation techniques used by agents of the Central Intelligence Agency (CIA) and special military units defied the international human rights protections codified in the **Geneva Conventions**, a series of international

The bombing of the World Trade Center, September 11, 2001 (left) and bodies of innocent people killed by an American drone strike in Afghanistan, which residents say claimed 150 lives (right). Why is one of these attacks considered terrorism and the other not?

A SOCIOLOGICAL PERSPECTIVE

Who is responsible for the deplorable acts at Abu Ghraib?

In April 2004, shocking photos taken in the Abu Ghraib prison were released by the media. Not only did the photos provide clear evidence of prisoner torture, but they exhibited that the prisoners were being abused in quite ritualized, and often sadistic, ways by U.S. soldiers. Indeed, the techniques used to humiliate prisoners crossed particular moral and cultural boundaries – as soldiers deployed animals, nudity, sex, and religion to debase inmates. Was this the act of a few wayward, deviant soldiers, as many military officials insisted, or are there other societal factors to consider?

Why were only a handful of low-level officers at Abu Ghraib punished?

How might the institutional deviance of a military culture have supported these seemingly individual acts of deviance?

Why is torture considered deviant and illegal under international law?

Why do you think that people were particularly unnerved by the images of female soldiers engaged in torture while smiling for the camera?

Explore A Sociological Perspective in **MySocLab** and then ...

Think About It

Some defenders of torture argue that it is a good way to get terrorists to provide information in a timely fashion. Others argue that the information provided under such conditions is rarely truthful but merely provided to stop the torture. Under what conditions, if any, is it okay for governments to order soldiers to torture prisoners?

Inspire Your Sociological Imagination

One of the possible defenses of the soldiers at Abu Ghraib is that they were part of an organization that was trying to get information from these prisoners. Is it ever possible for the organization, as opposed to individuals, to be responsible for whatever legal violations occur?

agreements about the fair treatment of prisoners of war. (For some of the most important of these accounts, see Hersh 2005; Mayer 2008; Lichtblau 2008). We also know, from these same sources, that many of the people subjected to torture had little or no connection to any terrorist or terrorist activity.

The techniques of torture used in these investigations, especially in the period from 2002 to 2005, are important to learn about. They included sleep and sensory deprivation, isolation, and repeated beatings as well as humiliation, forcible administration of drugs, and (most famously and brutally) "waterboarding," a technique that simulates the sensation of drowning. Evidence of these top-secret interrogations was uncovered and revealed over an extended period of time, and the full story of the administration's use of torture cannot yet been written. But the first unambiguous evidence of torture came with the release of photographs of inmate abuse at the Abu Ghraib prison in April 2004, reported by *New Yorker* reporter Seymour Hersh and broadcast in a special *60 Minutes* report (explore *A Sociological Perspective* on page 462). An official military review of treatment of inmates at Abu Ghraib rebuked the prison's commanding officers. Interviews with prison officials and military investigators, as well as evidence shown in the photos that were released (and more graphically in photos not released for public viewing), documented gross mistreatment of inmates. This included evidence that inmates had been raped and sodomized, physically and deliberately injured, urinated upon, and subjected to attacks by guard dogs. At least one inmate was killed, and many others suffered serious injuries.

The initial response of the U.S. military to the abuses at Abu Ghraib was to place blame on specific (and mostly lower-level) military personnel and their immediate supervisors, implying these were random, unauthorized occurrences (Hersh 2005). Whatever the particulars of the "chain of command" at Abu Ghraib, later evidence suggested that the systematic use of torture was relatively widespread and sanctioned by officials at the very top of the U.S. government. Abu Ghraib was only one of a number of sites where torture was employed. Some of these were "black sites," foreign prisons operated by the CIA or the American military in which individuals accused of terrorist activities could be interrogated outside the reach of any legal authority. Secret prisons were located in countries such as Poland, Romania, and Lithuania, and other facilities have been identified in Africa and the Middle East. The existence of black sites was initially denied by the government, but in September 2006, President George W. Bush publicly acknowledged their existence. In addition to the use of black sites, suspects have sometimes been turned over to foreign governments known for their use of torture and other aggressive techniquesof interrogation and punishment (Mayer 2008).

In spite of the worldwide condemnation of the American government's use of torture from 2002 to 2005, only a handful of low-level officers at the Abu Ghraib prison have been punished. Why is this the case? As the strongest military power in the world, the United States does not have to play by the same rules as everyone else; it can, and does, refuse to participate in international legal proceedings that have been brought against high government officials involved in planning and sanctioning the use of torture.

After 2005, President Bush ended the use of torture in investigations, and President Obama made that a binding legal requirement on the U.S. military by issuing an executive order banning the use of torture in 2009. But other policies in the war on terror that have continued or even increased in recent years have raised similar questions about state deviance and war crimes. For example, the American military has widely used unmanned drone planes in Afghanistan, Pakistan, and Yemen to attempt to kill suspected terrorists. These strikes—which involve sending U.S. planes into countries where the governments have repeatedly demanded they not fly—have also killed hundreds of innocent civilians (Mayer 2009; Bergen and Tiedemann 2010). In June 2012, in response to a particularly horrific incident in which 18 innocent people were killed, the American government agreed to reduce its use of drone strikes in Afghanistan except in cases of self-defense (Associated Press 2012). But the drone strikes continue elsewhere (in Pakistan and Yeman, for example) and the larger issue of culpability of the powerful remains. Imagine if the Canadian or Mexican government repeatedly sent airplanes into the United States to kill people it said were involved in terrorism, and lots of innocent Americans, including children, were being killed in those bombings. Would Americans not view that as mass murder and demand that the people responsible for the attacks be held criminally liable?

☐ Power and Deviance: A Final Note

It should now be clear that the central insights from the sociological study of deviance do not come from attempts to explain the personal characteristics, attributes, or pathologies of pirates or terrorists, of alcohol runners or drug cartel operatives, of predatory loan sharks peddling subprime loans or of CIA agents torturing suspected terrorists. Rather, insights into such deviant behavior come from studying the social and economic positions of those who define and label deviance and crime, and how they can shape those definitions to suit their own purposes. The answer to the question of how and why some kinds of behaviors are punished while other, seemingly similar ones are not comes from the explicit values articulated by those in power.

4 How Is Social Control Maintained?

THE INSTITUTIONS OF SOCIAL CONTROL

Watch the **Big Question Video** in **MySocLab**

As we have seen so far, society imposes rules about normal and deviant behavior, most definitively by establishing criminal laws and criminal codes, which deliver the final word about what is deviant behavior when the prison door slams shut. When some kinds of deviance become crimes, they pass into the realm of the *institutions of social control*—such as the police, criminal courts, and prisons and jails—that are all around us.

In this section we examine how and where **social control**—the various ways societies regulate and sanction behavior to encourage conformity to and discourage deviance from the norms—comes to be formalized in institutions. At the center of this process is, of course, the criminal justice system. But before we get there, however, we must first turn to some basic features of the system of societal sanctions that lie behind the formal institutions of social control.

Sanctions and Rewards as Forms of Social Control

A key dimension of social control occurs through **sanctions**, or punishments that groups and societies establish to enforce norms. Sanctions include punishments of various kinds—at the extreme, imprisonment. But sanctions are not the only way social control is promoted. We often follow rules and norms not just because we are worried about punishment but also because we may seek rewards that good behavior provides. Positive rewards might include things like praise, awards, and salary raises. Doing what the boss wants, no matter how irrational

it may be, can be a good way of moving up in the company (whereas challenging the boss can put an employee at risk).

Sociologists also distinguish between formal and informal sanctions and rewards. **Formal sanctions** are those used to enforce the norms that are written into law, and are usually carried out by a group of people who have been given the specific task and power to do so, including the police or school principals. Examples of such sanctions are fines or arrests (and possible prison sentences), while formal rewards might be getting good grades or promotions. On the other hand, **informal sanctions** might include such things as insults or giving someone a dirty look, while informal rewards include things like giving people compliments.

To make this more complex, it is important to note that although most of the time social deviance will elicit a negative response, there are actually some occasions in which acting in a deviant way, especially against the authorities, may elicit a positive response, while conformity, or simply following the rules and norms, elicits a negative response. Think of the classic example of Robin Hood. Robin Hood was a thief, and robbery is generally agreed upon as a deviant act. However, Robin Hood's act of stealing from the very rich and giving the money to the destitute poor is often viewed as heroic. Or consider the case of Mahatma Gandhi or Martin Luther King Jr. Violating laws against public protests, Gandhi and King are heroic figures today for refusing to bend to the will of an oppressive authority. The model of civil disobedience they popularized is now universally acknowledged as right and proper in certain situations.

Similarly, there are also occasions in which conforming to the norms will be met not with a positive response but a negative one. Consider for example people who do whatever it takes just to please others and get their approval. In school, these conformists may be ridiculed by other students as the teacher's pet, while at the same time they may be rewarded by their teacher (or not, if their conformity is too obvious and becomes grating for the teacher). In the extreme case, simply following the orders of Adolf Hitler and the Nazi government during World War II is not regarded as an appropriate defense for murdering people in concentration camps. In these situations, it is not so simple as to say that following rules and norms entails approval while not following social norms means disapproval. Knowing how to strike the right balance reflects a full understanding of the written and unwritten rules.

The ambiguities in the line between deviance and conformity have created pressures to expand formal sanctions. Historically, as societies have grown and become more complex, there has been a shift from emphasis on informal means of social control towards more formal means. In the contemporary world, the dominant form of social control is through the criminal justice system, and its central institution of discipline, the prison.

☐ The Criminal Justice System

Modern societies have developed elaborate institutions of criminal justice for sanctioning certain kinds of deviant behavior. The **criminal justice system** includes criminal law (in the United States, both the federal government and each state have their own criminal codes, although in many other countries a single national criminal code exists), the police forces that identify and apprehend offenders, lawyers, the court system that evaluates evidence of guilt and assigns sentences where a conviction is obtained, and the jails and prisons where offenders may be sentenced to serve time (as well as probation and parole offices that supervise convicted offenders not in prison). **Jails** generally hold people who are accused before a trial, or people convicted of misdemeanors, crimes that have a maximum sentence of less than one year of **incarceration**, or imprisonment. **Prisons**, by contrast, are where convicted felons serving a sentence of one or more years are held once they have been convicted of a serious crime.

Societies punish offenders of criminal law for four basic reasons (Manza and Uggen 2006:chap. 4): (1) to exact *retribution* for the victims of criminal acts; (2) to *deter* offenders, and others, from committing crimes in the future; (3) to *incapacitate* or otherwise prevent offenders from committing

further crimes; and (4) to *rehabilitate* or reform offenders. **Retribution** is a form of simple vengeance, founded on the notion that those who have committed crimes should suffer for the harm they have caused others. Modern proponents of retribution argue that the punishment should fit the crime already committed rather than future crimes that the criminal or others might commit. In contrast to retribution, which is designed to redress crimes already committed, **deterrence** endeavors to prevent future crimes by creating a disincentive to violate the law by threatening punishment.

Not all convicted offenders are sentenced to jail or prison; in fact, many will receive **probation**, a form of punishment where an offender is allowed to live in her or his community as long as no further offenses are committed for the length of the sentence. The goals of retribution and deterrence do not require imprisonment. However, the other two purposes of punishment relate specifically to the use of imprisonment. Putting someone in a jail or prison can serve one of two purposes: It removes them from society (so that they commit no further offenses, at least for some period of time), but it can also provide a context for **rehabilitation**, which involves the attempt to help offenders stop committing further crimes through therapy, education, and job training (the latter arising from the view that if former offenders are able to find decent jobs after leaving prison, they are more likely to desist from further criminal activity).

Analysts may differ on which purpose of punishment is most important, and indeed the various purposes are not incompatible with one another. A long prison sentence could both deter others from engaging in the same behavior *and* remove the offender from her or his community. Such a sentence can both deter someone from committing further crimes and also provide a context for rehabilitation to occur. Whatever the exact understanding of the general purposes of punishment, it has long been the case that imprisoning someone is something extraordinary, generally reserved for the extreme violations of the law. Yet, as we explore in the next section, in recent years in the United States this is no longer the case.

How does the criminal justice system exert social control?

☐ Mass Incarceration in America Today

The American criminal justice system in recent years has undergone a remarkable change. The incarcerated population in the United States has grown 700 percent over the past 40 years—in other words, there are seven times more people in prison today than in 1972, adjusted for overall population size (i.e. it takes into account that the entire population of America has grown in this period). For the first

FIGURE 16.1 STATE AND FEDERAL PRISON POPULATION, 1925–2010

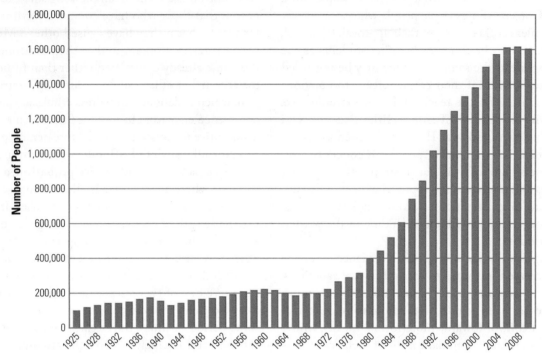

Source: Bureau of Justice Statistics (2011).

three-quarters of the twentieth century, except for a notable uptick during the depression years of the late 1930s, the incarceration rate (that is, the number of prisoners per capita) remained relatively constant. People who committed serious crimes would be sent to prison, but most offenders would receive other penalties. Beginning in the early 1970s, however, the number of people housed in prisons began to grow steadily every year and would continue to do so for the next 30 years before finally leveling off around 2005 (see Figure 16.1). More people were being sentenced to prison, sentences became longer, and judges and parole boards had greatly reduced discretion to late people off for good behavior. New categories of deviance—mostly having to do with drugs—became increasingly criminalized, with sellers and simple users much more like to be sentenced to prison than before.

The growth of the prison population in the United States over the past 40 years is unprecedented around the world. The United States incarcerates vastly more people per capita than almost any other country in the world today (see Figure 16.2). Many scholars have come to describe this level of punishment as **mass incarceration**, a situation where vastly greater numbers of people are held in prisons than in earlier periods of history or in comparison to similar countries (Garland 2001). The countries closest to us in

Why is the incarceration rate in the United States so high?

having high incarceration rates are countries like Russia, Cuba, and South Africa, not the West European countries, Canada, Australia, or Japan, which are otherwise much more similar to the United States. The United States sends 6 to 8 times as many people in prison as those countries, and more than 10 times as many people as Japan!

What was behind this enormous increase in the prison population? An obvious answer would be that rates of crime rose in that same period so that more people were going to prison because more people were committing crimes. This answer would, however, be incorrect. In fact, between the 1970s and the early 1990s, crime rates were essentially unchanged, and even more remarkably, since the early 1990s crime rates have *fallen*, in some cases quite dramatically (see the Infographic on page 468). Yet in spite of a declining crime rate, more and more Americans have been issued felony convictions, and many have ended up in prison.

Another possible answer for the increase in crime would be that even if they aren't increasing, crime rates in America are much higher than they are in other countries, so it makes sense that there should be so many more people in prison than in other countries. This too turns out not to be true. Many Americans are surprised to learn that overall crime rates in the United States are not particularly high by comparison with other countries. We know this from

FIGURE 16.2 GLOBAL PRISON POPULATIONS The exceptionally high number of inmates in the United States can be seen on this map.

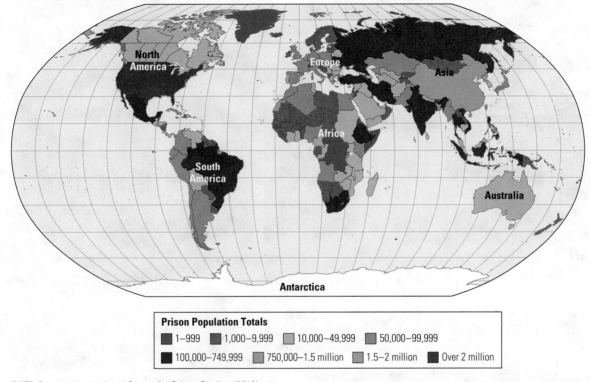

Prison Population Totals

■ 1–999   ■ 1,000–9,999   ■ 10,000–49,999   ■ 50,000–99,999

■ 100,000–749,999   ■ 750,000–1.5 million   ■ 1.5–2 million   ■ Over 2 million

DATA Source: International Centre for Prison Studies (2012).

high-quality data from international "victimization surveys," in which citizens in many countries are asked identical questions about whether they have been the victims of a long list of crimes, ranging from petty theft to sexual assault to aggravated assault (the only kind of crime that respondents aren't asked about is murder—because the victim obviously wouldn't be around to answer the survey!—but murder is one of the types of crime that is always well recorded, and international records are comparable). Victimization surveys are considerably more reliable than official government statistics because governments and police departments vary widely in how they record crimes.

According to the victimization surveys, the United States has crime rates that are close to the average of similar nations, with the exception of a relatively high rate of murder—a rare crime in any society. The current murder rate in the United States—about 5.5 per 100,000 population—is 2 to 3 times the comparable rate in some European countries, and this a worrisome difference. Violent crimes cause more fear than any other type of crime. But the odds of any of us being murdered are still exceptionally small in the United States. The majority of murders are committed by family or friends, not strangers. When a murder does occur, it will usually be reported in the media, and this regular reporting (and often frequent follow-ups) tends to exaggerate how

common murder really is. But when it comes to all kinds of crimes, the United States is not very different than most other similar countries, ranking somewhere in the middle (with more crime than some countries and less than others). Many scholars have suggested that the very high number and relatively widespread availability of guns has much to do with the higher incidence of murder in the United States.

In light of this evidence, it is clear that the rise of mass incarceration in the United States is a puzzle. When we look at the relationship between all crimes and prisoners per capita, the United States is completely different than all similar countries in terms of how many people we are sending to prison. There is nothing in this astounding development that is "natural": All other societies most like the United States with similar crime rates put far fewer people in prison. There is no rulebook for how many people have to be given felony convictions for their behavior and no close connection to actual levels of criminal activity.

So why has criminalization of deviant behavior in America increased so dramatically in recent years? This is a question that many social scientists are now debating, and there are several competing theories about it. Three major factors behind the rise of mass incarceration have proved especially important. First, the latest moral crusade against

Incarceration Rates in the U.S.

The United States prides (and sings about) itself as being "the land of the free." But with the highest rate of incarceration in the world, it may also have become the land of the unfree for many. With the exception of slavery, there is no other time in U.S. history when so many people have been confined against their will. What's more, the largest increase in incarceration rates occurred in the last 30 years, since the 1980s.

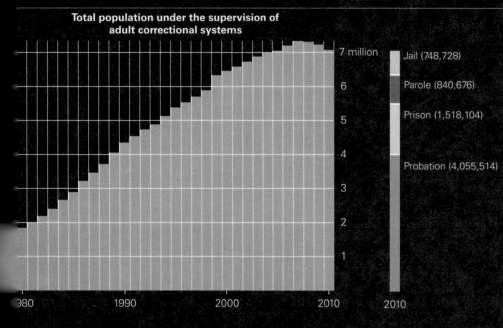

Total population under the supervision of adult correctional systems

- 7 million
- 6
- 5
- 4
- 3
- 2
- 1

1980 — 1990 — 2000 — 2010

- Jail (748,728)
- Parole (840,676)
- Prison (1,518,104)
- Probation (4,055,514)

2010

The Rise of Mass Punishment in the United States

Is the United States alone in these trends? Yes and no. Many other countries have also experienced increasing incarceration rates in the last few decades, most notably England, Australia, Brazil, and South Africa. Yet their increases do not come close to those of the U.S. Instead, it turns out that countries with incarceration rates most similar to the U.S. are vastly different in political, economic, and cultural terms—such as Russia, with its long legacy of totalitarian rule and state socialism and Rwanda, with its recent history of mass genocide.

More People Sent to Prison Even Though the Crime Rate Fell

We usually think about trends in crime as a big part of what predicts how many people will be in prison. Yet since the early 1990s, America has seen a significant and dramatic decline in crime rates, while at the same time the incarceration rate (the percentage of people in prison) has continued to increase. This simple fact raises troubling questions about the criminal justice system.

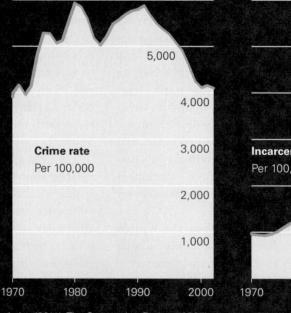

Crime rate
Per 100,000

- 5,000
- 4,000
- 3,000
- 2,000
- 1,000

1970 — 1980 — 1990 — 2000

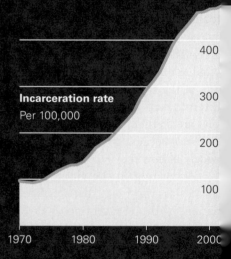

Incarceration rate
Per 100,000

- 400
- 300
- 200
- 100

1970 — 1980 — 1990 — 2000

Sources: Based on data from Bureau of Justice Statistics (2011); The Sentencing Project (2005).

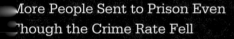

Explore the **Data** on Incarceration Rates in the U.S. in **MySocLab** and then . . .

Think About It

Sending large numbers of people to prison often impacts the family, friends and even the community of the convicted offender. Do you know anyone who has been sent to prison? How was their family impacted by

Inspire Your Sociological Imagination

What are some alternatives to sending people to prison? What are the advantages and disadvantages of alternative sanctions that might be tried? What kinds of sociological evidence might

Over 25 years after President Ronald Reagan signed legislation designed to punish drug offenders more harshly, drug use remains similar to what it was, but America's prisons and jails are now filled with drug offenders. Who "won" the war on drugs?

certain kinds of individual behavior, this time targeted against drugs (particularly certain kinds of drugs that are disproportionately consumed by poor people and minorities) has had a major impact. The "just say no" campaign, launched by President Ronald Reagan in 1985, spread quickly around America and encouraged police and criminal justice officials to arrest and convict those accused of the possession or sale of drugs. State governments, as well as the federal government, passed mandatory minimum sentences for drug offenders, which had the effect of dramatically increasing the proportion of people in prison for drug-related offenses (see Figure 16.3). For example, in 1988, shortly after the beginning of Reagan's war, 17 percent of all people convicted of felonies were drug offenders. Just 14 years later, that figure had nearly doubled to 32 percent.

A second key factor in the steady increase in incarceration rates involves politics (Hagan 2010). Beginning in the 1960s, many politicians began to have success running for office as proponents of "tough on crime" laws. Perhaps the first major politician to make fighting crime an overtly political issue was Republican presidential candidate Barry Goldwater, in 1964. Although Goldwater would lose that election badly, other politicians followed in his footsteps in promising to reduce crime. Richard Nixon won the presidency in 1968 promising a "law and order" government, declaring war on "the criminal elements which increasingly

threaten our cities, homes, and our lives" (quoted in Hagan 2010:150). Around the country, politicians promoted longer sentences and more punishment. Liberal judges—that is, judges thought to be too lenient on criminals—were increasingly targeted for removal from the bench (many states and local jurisdictions elect judges, making this possible). Public support for harsher policies was reflected in opinion polls and surveys.

Why did Americans want more and more people in prison? The period from the late 1960s onward saw the convergence of three important trends that would fundamentally transform the criminal justice policy environment: (1) a conservative backlash to the social movements and cultural trends of the 1960s; (2) an economic downturn in the 1970s that precipitated a search for reasons, and scapegoats, for social problems after 1973; and (3) urban riots in the 1960s in many cities left lasting images that made urban crime the focus of intensive media scrutiny. The most careful research suggests that Republican politicians, where they controlled state governments, moved first and fastest on crime, with the Democrats following suit later (Western 2006:chap. 3; Manza and Uggen 2006:chap. 4). Coming out of the bloody political battles of the 1960s, Republican politicians found political opportunity in platforms calling for tough penalties, but many Democratic politicians increasingly came to accept the new tough-on-crime policy environment.

The role of **racism**—stereotypes based on perceived characteristics rooted in skin color—has long been particularly important in relation to crime (and criminal justice policies). Racial stereotyping about criminality has been pervasive throughout American history. In the early twentieth century, Theodore Roosevelt, expressing widely held views of the time, called for "relentless and unceasing warfare against lawbreaking black men" on the grounds that "laziness and shiftlessness ... and above all, vice and

FIGURE 16.3 FELONY CONVICTIONS IN STATE COURTS, 1988 AND 2002

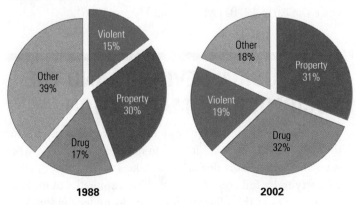

1988   **2002**

Source: *Felony Sentences in State Courts* series (Washington, D.C.: U.S. Government Printing Office, 1989, 2004).

criminality of every kind, are evils more potent for harm to the black race than all acts of oppression of white men put together" (quoted in Klinkner and Smith 1997:337). **Lynching**—the violent killing of an individual, usually by a self-appointed group, without trial and in a public place—was frequently justified by black criminality. The first woman to hold a Senate seat, Rebecca Latimer Felton of Georgia, told her supporters in 1897 that "[Rapes of white women] will grow and increase with every election where white men equalized themselves at the polls with an inferior race and controlled their votes by bribery and whiskey. . . . If it takes a lynching to protect woman's dearest possession from drunken, ravening human beasts, then I say lynch a thousand a week if it becomes necessary" (quoted in Williamson 1984:128; for other examples, see Mendelberg 2001: chap. 2).

More recently, perceptions about who is committing crimes continue to be biased against racial minorities. Research on the media coverage of crime shows that African American are significantly overrepresented in portrayals of criminal offenders (Entman and Rojecki 2001). Research on the adoption of especially punitive crime policies shows they have been found in states with significantly higher African American populations (Manza and Uggen 2006:chap. 2; Garland 2010). For example, the evidence suggests that whites are at least as likely to use illegal drugs as blacks, but blacks are *three times more likely* to be sent to prison for a drug-related offense (Western 2006:46–47). A number of analysts have reached the conclusion that the rising prison population reflects a "new Jim Crow," as Alexander (2010) has put it; African Americans men are being rounded up and sent to prison in such high numbers that prison is increasingly the dominant institution in the lives of many young black men. 📖 Read the **Document** *The Rich Get Richer and the Poor Get Prison* in **MySocLab.**

☐ Consequences of Mass Incarceration

When individuals go to prison, they suffer a set of penalties that go beyond their time in prison, and the impacts are not just to individuals but also to families, communities, and societies as a whole. For sociologists, the study of mass incarceration must take into account not just why people commit crimes, and why societies choose to punish those actions, but also the larger consequences for everyone else and society as a whole. In this final section on the criminal justice system, we consider a few of these additional consequences of mass punishment.

Having a criminal record has many consequences for the individual offender. Careful research suggests that it means

What are some consequences of mass incarceration?

that you will have a harder time finding a good job, you will make less money over your lifetime, and you will likely have more difficulty maintaining a stable family life. As a felon, you automatically become ineligible for a whole series of government programs (like public housing, many educational loan programs, and various social programs designed to help those in poverty) that otherwise might have helped you in your life. You may lose custody of your children. You will lose the right to vote in all but two states while you are in prison, and in most states you won't be able to vote until you have also finished serving any parole time after your release (and in some states you will lose the right to vote for life). Social science research has, in recent years, been very careful in investigating whether these negative outcomes are specifically the result of criminal convictions or something else. They do this by using a variety of experimental designs that compare convicted felons to otherwise similar people in the general population (Western 2006; Pager 2007; Wakefield and Uggen 2010).

But, as we noted, the impact of mass incarceration is not limited to the growing numbers of individuals receiving a felony conviction or being sent to prison. Families are often torn apart by prison sentences. Parents are separated from children, couples are divided, and a body of research has shown that children are deeply impacted by having a parent in prison. Their grades are likely to be lower, and they have lower self-esteem and more stress than their peers (e.g., Hagan and Foster 2009). The cost of building and maintaining a large prison system is becoming staggeringly expensive, crowding out other important purposes for which those funds could be used. As state government budgets become increasingly tighter, American democracy is increasingly being impacted by mass incarceration; the second author of this chapter has estimated that 5.3 million American citizens lost the right to vote in the 2004 presidential election, and a number of recent election outcomes, including the 2000 presidential election in which George W. Bush narrowly defeated Al Gore, would have been different but for the fact that so many more people have lost the right to vote since the early 1970s (Manza and Uggen 2006).

CONCLUSION **DEVIANCE AND THE SOCIOLOGICAL IMAGINATION**

The sociological study of deviance raises powerful questions for the sociological imagination, and in many ways studying what is normal and what is deviant is to take a microscope to all of a society in its full complexity. We have explored a number of these puzzles in this chapter. For example, understanding how

New York City police officers employing "stop and frisk" tactics against young minority men, a practice that has become very controversial because of severe bias in who is being stopped.

and why certain kinds of actions come to be labeled and punished for being socially deviant in one context while other similar or worse actions in another do not is an enduring issue in all human societies. There are no obvious answers, but as we explore more deeply we do find one important pattern that recurs no matter what the particular form of deviance: Those individuals and groups with power have a special capacity to define or impose particular definitions of deviance and to turn that definition into written laws and forms of punishment (or avoid having those same laws applied to them). Defining deviance downward—when the powerful define ordinary behavior of the weak as deviant—is a common pattern that the study of deviance reveals.

A particularly dramatic example of this conclusion can be seen in the war that created the United States of America. Imagined what would have happened if Britain had won the War of Independence. There is little doubt that George Washington, John Adams, Thomas Jefferson, and scores of others that history today has anointed heroes of the American Revolution would have been hung as traitors (Paul 2009). In fact, in 1779, at a particularly bleak moment in the war, Jefferson abandoned his Virginia home and "headed for the hills" just to escape such a likely fate (Gordon-Reed 2008:136). And had the British prevailed, those colonists who sided with the British would have been anointed heroes. Of course, because the American revolutionaries did win the war, Washington, Adams, and Jefferson are our heroes; those who sided with the British were branded traitors, and some were put to death.

As we finish writing this chapter, this lesson can be seen in a terrific current controversy in New York City over the police department's use of "stop and frisk" tactics, whereby police officers are free to detain anyone they think might be carrying a weapon or posing a threat to the police officer. Almost 700,000 people were frisked in 2011, and well over 80 percent of those were either African American or Latino. Although young black and Latino males between the ages of 14 and 24 make up just 4.7 percent of New York's population, they received 42 percent of all stops. While the stops are supposed to be to look for weapons, in the vast majority of cases where an arrest is made what is found is not a gun but rather a small amount of marijuana or other drugs (New York Civil Liberties Union 2011). Over 50,000 people were arrested for simple marijuana possession in New York in 2010 and 2011, in most cases resulting from a stop-and-frisk event. Because so many of the people being stopped are young minority men, it is hardly surprising to learn that most of the people being arrested for marijuana use, and thereby put into the criminal justice system, are young black men.

When a group is intensively policed in the way that young minority men have been in New York City, their deviance—even if it is minor—will be uncovered. This does not mean, of course, that it is a fair process. In fact, as we have already noted, the best data we have suggest that whites use as many or more drugs than nonwhites, yet whites in New York are just a tiny percentage of those being convicted for drug possession. Societies often pay far more attention to the possibility of deviance from below than above. It would indeed be interesting—even if it is inconceivable that it would be undertaken—to see what would happen if stop-and-frisk tactics were routinely applied to residents of wealthy suburbs!

One of the challenges of the sociological imagination is the need to look beneath the surface of social life to uncover the normally hidden forms of inequality and injustice in the world around us. In no arena of social life is this more apparent than in the case of deviance and criminal justice. Once we begin to scrutinize what is "normal" and what is "deviant," a new way of looking at the world presents itself.

Watch the **Video** in **MySocLab**
Applying Your Sociological Imagination

What Is Deviance? *(p. 446)*

Watch the **Big Question Video** in **MySocLab** to review the key concepts for this section.

In order to understand deviance, we first need to ask the question, "What is normal?" This section explored the origins of deviant behavior by examining the role of groups and group boundaries in the creation of social norms. We also examined the distinction between statistical and social deviance.

DEVIANCE AND THE GROUP (p. 446)

Establishing Group Boundaries (p. 446)

- **How do groups distinguish themselves?**

Statistical Versus Social Deviance (p. 448)

- **How does statistical deviance differ from social deviance?**

Social Norms: The Unstated Rules of Everyday (p. 449)

- **What is a social norm?**

KEY TERMS

social group *(p. 446)*

symbolic boundary *(p. 447)*

statistically deviant *(p. 448)*

socially deviant *(p. 448)*

normalize *(p. 449)*

norm *(p. 449)*

archival research *(p. 449)*

How is Morality Defined and Regulated? *(p. 450)*

Watch the **Big Question Video** in **MySocLab** to review the key concepts for this section.

Societies have long tried to dictate and control individuals' behavior and morality. In this section, we explored two moral crusades in the United States to highlight how the process of defining normal behavior is achieved and how certain kinds of behavior come to be labeled deviant or even criminal. We then examined some contemporary moral crusades and considered the future of moral regulation.

THE PROBLEM OF MORAL REGULATION (p. 450)

Interested Versus Disinterested Punishment (p. 450)

- **What is the distinction between interested and disinterested punishment?**

The Temperance Movement as Moral Crusade (p. 451)

The Campaign Against Opium (p. 452)

- **What does the history of alcohol and opium use tell us about what is normal and deviant?**

Contemporary Moral Crusades (p. 453)

- **What does the failure of the crusade against same-sex relationships say about the future of moral crusades?**

KEY TERMS

moral behavior *(p. 450)*

Prohibition *(p. 451)*

war on drugs *(p. 453)*

Who Defines Deviance? *(p. 455)*

 Watch the **Big Question Video** in **MySocLab** to review the key concepts for this section.

Insights into deviant behavior come from studying the social and economic positions, cultural practices, and attendant political power of dominant groups. In this section we explored the relationship between deviance and power.

DEVIANCE, CRIME, AND POWER (p. 455)

Labeling Deviance and Crime (p. 456)

- **How does labeling theory explain deviance?**

From Deviance in the Streets to Deviance in the Suites: White-Collar Crime (p. 456)

- **What does the 2008 U.S. financial crisis tell us about power and deviant behavior?**

State Deviance, Terrorism, and War Crimes (p. 459)

- **When does violence committed during wartime become criminal?**

Explore A Sociological Perspective: Who is responsible for the deplorable acts at Abu Ghraib? in **MySocLab**

Power and Deviance: A Final Note (p. 463)

How Is Social Control Maintained? *(p. 464)*

 Watch the **Big Question Video** in **MySocLab** to review the key concepts for this section.

This section examined how and where social control comes to be formalized in the institutions of the criminal justice system. We also explored how the criminal justice system in America has grown massively in recent decades, turning increasingly to formal punishment as a means of sanctioning deviance.

THE INSTITUTIONS OF SOCIAL CONTROL (p. 464)

Sanctions and Rewards as Forms of Social Control (p. 464)

The Criminal Justice System (p. 465)

- **How does the criminal justice system exert social control?**

Mass Incarceration in America Today (p. 465)

- **Why is the incarceration rate in the United States so high?**

Explore the **Data** on Incarceration Rates in the U.S. in **MySocLab**

Read the **Document** *The Rich Get Richer and the Poor Get Prison* by Jeffrey Reiman in **MySocLab.** In this excerpt, Reiman provides compelling evidence that demonstrates the inequities in the criminal justice system.

Consequences of Mass Incarceration (p. 470)

- **What are some consequences of mass incarceration?**

Watch the **Video** Applying Your Sociological Imagination in **MySocLab** to see these concepts at work in the real world

17

SOCIAL MOVEMENTS and REVOLUTIONS

by JEFF GOODWIN

On September 17, 2011, several hundred people marched to Wall Street in lower Manhattan with the goal of occupying public space in front of or near the Stock Exchange. The ultimate goals of the protesters were unclear, but they were clearly opposed to the tremendous economic and political power of banks, financial institutions, and corporations generally. They claimed to speak for the 99 percent of the population who have no control over these institutions. Wall Street was blocked by police, but the protesters occupied a small park—known as Zuccotti Park—not far away. Many of the protesters began to sleep overnight in the park, which became a site for political discussions and for organizing marches and other protests. Thus began the so-called Occupy Wall Street movement.

The protesters were evicted by police from Zuccotti Park just two months after they occupied it. In the meantime, however, the movement organized several demonstrations in New York City with thousands of participants, including a demonstration in Times Square on October 15 in which perhaps 50,000 people participated. The mass media began to focus on the movement, and politicians began speaking about inequality and the economic problems of the "99 percent." Protesters unexpectedly began to occupy public parks and other public spaces in dozens of cities and towns across the United States—in Washington, Boston, Chicago, New Orleans, Portland (Oregon), Oakland, and beyond. Police eventually evicted protesters from virtually all the parks they had occupied, but these evictions did not end the movement, even if they made it less visible. Activists continued to meet and organize a range of protest activities against banks and corporations.

Occupy Wall Street raises a number of questions that have preoccupied sociologists interested in social movements and revolutions. Why did this movement develop when it did? Who participated in it? Why did the protesters use certain tactics and not others? What changes has the movement brought about? What might cause it to decline or disappear? Is this a revolutionary movement? Is a revolution possible or likely in a country like the United States? Or are other countries, with different problems and political institutions, more likely to have revolutions in the future?

MY SOCIOLOGICAL IMAGINATION
Jeff Goodwin

I grew up at a time when the U.S. government was trying hard to destroy domestic social movements, especially the black power and the anti–Vietnam War movement, as well as revolutions overseas, particularly in Cuba, Vietnam, and Chile. I remember vividly the killing of students at Kent State University who were protesting the invasion of Cambodia, something that was pretty scary for a young kid. I was also scared and anxious when my older brother was drafted into the military, but fortunately he was not sent to Vietnam. All this made me interested in why people protest and rebel, sometimes violently, and why governments sometimes use violence against their opponents. I came to understand how the sociological imagination which C. Wright Mills described—the capacity, that is, to see how seemingly personal grievances are in fact linked to social structures and shared with others—is a prerequisite of political protest. While I was studying rebels in college and graduate school at Harvard, I also joined the ranks of movements that were trying to stop the U.S. government from supporting brutal armies in Central America and the racist government in South Africa. I have been studying social movements (and occasionally participating in them) as well as revolutions ever since.

The Occupy Wall Street movement grew in size and spread very rapidly across the United States in the fall of 2011.

 Watch the **Video** in **MySocLab**
Inspiring Your Sociological Imagination

THE BIG QUESTIONS

👁 **Watch** the **Big Question Videos** in **MySocLab**

Scholars and activists themselves have asked four key sets of questions about social movements and revolutions. This chapter examines how sociologists have answered these questions.

What are social movements? Social movements play a crucial role in contemporary societies. Through them we can learn about the world around us. We start the chapter by defining social movements and exploring what we can learn by studying them.

Why do movements emerge, and who joins them? The most frequently asked question about social movements is why they emerge when they do. In this section we examine how movements take shape and look at who joins or supports social movements.

What do movements accomplish? Why do movements use certain tactics and not others? Why do movements decline or disappear? In this section we look at what movements do and what changes and outcomes movements bring about, including unintended consequences.

What are revolutions, and why do they occur? Finally, we look at why some social movements are revolutionary and what causes revolutionary situations to occur. When and why have revolutionary movements been able to take state power? We conclude the chapter by examining how democracy shapes social conflict and the prospects for revolution.

1 **What Are Social Movements?**

STUDYING SOCIAL MOVEMENTS

Watch the Big Question Video in **MySocLab**

hroughout history, people have complained about the things they disliked. Sometimes they do more than complain; they band together with others to try to change things. In modern societies, more than ever before, people have organized themselves to pursue a dizzying array of goals, and they have used a wide variety of tactics to attain those goals. There are the strikes, pickets, and rallies of the labor movement, aimed at unionization and better wages but also (sometimes) at political goals. The women's movement has tried to change family life and gender relations through persuasion and lawmaking. Animal rights activists have broken into labs and "liberated" experimental animals. And there have been many conservative and right-wing movements as well, from Americans opposed to immigrants in the 1840s (and today) to those who have bombed abortion clinics in recent years.

Some of these movements have looked for opportunities to claim new rights while others have responded to threats or violence. Some have sought political and economic emancipation and gains, while others have fought against lifestyle choices they disliked or feared. Some have created formal organizations, others have relied upon informal networks, and still others have used more spontaneous actions such as **riots**, which are unplanned collective protests, loosely organized at best, involving attacks on property and (sometimes) persons. Movements have regularly had to choose between violent and nonviolent activities, illegal and legal ones, disruption and persuasion, radical and moderate demands, reform and revolution.

Social movements are conscious, concerted, and sustained efforts by ordinary people to change (or preserve) some aspect of their society by using extrainstitutional means. *Extrainstitutional means* are collective actions undertaken outside existing institutions, like courts and legislatures, although movements may also work through such institutions at least part of the time. Movements are more conscious and organized than fashions or **fads** (behavior that spreads, often rapidly, among a specific population and is repeated enthusiastically for some period of time before disappearing, often rapidly). They last longer than a single protest or riot. There is more to them than formal organizations, although such organizations usually play a part. They are composed mainly of ordinary people as opposed to wealthy elites, politicians, or army officers. They need not be explicitly political, but many are. Movements protest against something, either explicitly as in antiwar movements or implicitly as in the back-to-the-land movement that is disgusted with modern urban and suburban life.

Why do we care about social movements? Examining protesters and their points of view is certainly a good way to comprehend human diversity. For example, why do some people think animals have rights, or others that the United Nations is part of a sinister conspiracy? But aside from studying social movements to understand a diverse array of viewpoints, movements are also windows onto a number of aspects of social life. These include politics, human action, social change, and the moral basis of society.

Politics, Human Action, and Social Change

Social movements are a main source of political conflict and change. They often articulate *new* political issues and ideas. As people become attuned to some social problem they want solved, they often form some kind of movement to push for a solution. Political parties and their leaders rarely ask the most interesting questions or raise new issues; bureaucracy sets in, and politicians spend their time in routines. It is typically movements outside a society's political institutions that force insiders to recognize new fears and desires among specific social groups. During the Obama administration, for example, politicians were generally not discussing growing inequality in the United States or the power of corporations; it took the Occupy Wall Street movement to initiate a public discussion about these issues.

Scholars of social movements ask why and how people do the things they do, especially why they do things *together*; this is also the question that drives sociology in general, especially sociological theory. Social movements raise the famous question asked by philosopher Thomas Hobbes regarding social order: Why do people cooperate with each other when they might get as many or more benefits by acting selfishly or alone? The study of social movements makes the question more manageable: If we can see why and how people voluntarily cooperate in social movements, we can understand why and how they cooperate in general. Political action sheds light on action in other spheres of life. It gets at the heart of human motivation. For example, do people act to maximize their material interests like wealth and power? Do they act out rituals that express their beliefs about the world or simply reaffirm their place in that world? What is the balance in movements between symbolic action—which is intended to spread a message—and instrumental (i.e., goal-oriented) action—which is intended to bring about some specific change? What is the balance between selfish and altruistic behavior?

Social movements are also a central source of social and political change. In the United States, movements are at least partly responsible for most of the progressive laws of the past century, including women's right to vote, the right to organize unions, and civil rights for African Americans and other minorities, including homosexuals. Of course, there are other sources of social change, including corporations, which are out to make a profit: they invent new technologies that change our ways of working and interacting. Corporations are always inventing new ways of extracting profits from workers and inventing new products to market. These changes typically disrupt people's ways of life: A new machine may throw people out of work or make them work harder. Toxic wastes may be disposed of near a school. People react to these changes, and resist them, by forming social movements.

But while corporations are the main source of technical change, they are rarely a source of change in values or in social arrangements. Why? In modern societies with tightly knit political and economic systems, the big bureaucracies demand economic and political control and stability. So they try to routinize social life in order to prevent the unexpected. They resist changes in property relations, for example, which are one of the key components of capitalism.

So innovation in values and political beliefs often arises from the discussions and efforts of social movements. Why don't societies just endlessly reproduce themselves intact? It is often social movements that develop new ways of seeing society and new ways of directing it. They are a central part of what has been called "civil society" or the "public sphere," in which groups and individuals debate their own futures (Cohen and Arato 1992).

What can movements teach us about social life?

Moral Sensibilities

Social movements are similar to art: They are efforts to express sensibilities that have not yet been well articulated, that journalists or novelists have not yet written about, and that lawmakers have not yet addressed. We all have moral sensibilities—including unspoken intuitions as well as articulated principles and rules—that guide our actions or at least make

These students from Oberlin College are protesting hydraulic fracking in Ohio. Why are students so often involved in social movements?

us uneasy when they are violated. Social movements are good ways to understand these moral sensibilities. For example, movements have challenged ideas about who deserves legal rights, including the right to vote. Radical abolitionists like Frederick Douglass fought to end slavery and give rights to African Americans; women's movements have fought for the right to vote and for reproductive rights (including access to contraceptives and abortions); antiabortion activists argue that human fetuses have rights; and many people now believe that certain animals have at least some rights, like the right not to be used in scientific experiments. It's safe to say that many fewer people (and other species) would have rights today were it not for social movements, which have dramatically changed the moral sensibilities of societies over the past two centuries.

Social movements play a number of crucial roles in contemporary societies. We learn about the world around us through them. They encourage us to figure out how we feel about government policies and social trends and new technologies. In some cases they even inspire the invention of new technologies or new ways of using old technologies. Most of all, they are one means by which we work out our moral visions, transforming vague intuitions into principles and political demands.

☐ Understanding Social Movements Today

Sociologists and other scholars have emphasized different aspects of social movements at different historical moments. They once largely feared movements, seeing them as dangerous mobs. Later scholars were much more sympathetic, emphasizing that movements are quite rational, carefully weighing the costs and benefits of their actions. Others stressed the political nature of movements. The **political process perspective** emphasizes that movements are primarily concerned with politics, not individual psychological states, and are a normal response, under certain circumstances, to routine political processes. Movements emerge and may be successful if those political processes create opportunities for certain kinds of collective protest. Still other scholars emphasize the cultural side of movements, exploring the work that goes into creating powerful symbols, convincing people that they have grievances that can be remedied, and building a sense of solidarity or connectedness among certain people.

What aspects of movements are contemporary sociologists interested in?

Recently sociologists have begun to recognize and study even more aspects of social movements. For example, many movements have a global reach, tying together protest groups and networks across many countries and even forming international organizations. The environmental movement and the protest against the World Trade Organization and the unregulated globalization of trade are examples. Yet most of our models still assume a national movement interacting with a single national state.

Our understanding of social movements has grown as movements themselves have changed. Like everyone else, scholars of social movements are influenced by what they see happening around them. Much protest of the nineteenth century took the form of riots, so it was natural to focus on the nature of crowds and "mobs." Scholars who examined the labor movement and the American civil rights movement recognized that claims of new rights necessarily involve the state, so it was natural for them to focus on the political dimensions of protest. Social scientists who came of age in the 1960s and after were often favorably disposed toward the social movements around them and so portrayed protesters as reasonable people. Many of the movements of the 1960s and after were not about rights for oppressed groups but about lifestyles and cultural meanings, so it was inevitable that scholars sooner or later would turn to this dimension of protest.

Likewise in recent years, several important social movements have become more global in scope. The so-called alter-globalization movement against the power of multinational corporations and international lending agencies is one example. Many movements are also interested in changing our emotional capacities, especially movements influenced by the women's movement, which argued that women were disadvantaged by the ways in which different emotions were thought appropriate for men and for women. Research on social movements will undoubtedly continue to evolve as social movements themselves evolve.

These protesters in Seattle are opposed to the politics of the World Trade Organization. Why has unregulated global trade led opponents to forge ties across the borders?

2 Why Do Movements Emerge, and Who Joins Them?

MOVEMENT ORIGINS AND RECRUITMENT

Watch the **Big Question Video** in **MySocLab**

The most frequently asked question about social movements is why they emerge when and where they do. Where we think a movement comes from colors the way we view its other aspects, too: its goals, participants, tactics, and outcomes.

How Movements Take Shape

In general, theories of movement origins focus either on the characteristics of participants or on conditions in the broader environment which potential participants face. It is also possible to link these two perspectives.

Scholars have discovered a wide range of factors that explain why a movement emerges when and where it does: political factors such as divisions among authorities or lessened repression from the police and army; economic conditions such as increased income, especially among those sympathetic to a movement's cause, or alternatively an economic crisis that throws many people out of work; organizational conditions such as social-network ties or formal organizations among aggrieved populations (such as churches, schools, and athletic leagues); demographic conditions such as the increased population density and human connectedness that comes with industrialization (if you live a mile from your nearest neighbor, it is hard to organize collectively); and cultural factors such as moral intuitions or sensibilities that support the movement's

cause. And of course potential protesters must understand factors such as these as real opportunities for collective protest before they can take advantage of them.

Resource Mobilization and Political Process Approaches

In the 1960s and 1970s, a group of researchers noticed that social movements usually consist of formal organizations (McCarthy and Zald 1977). Known as the **resource mobilization approach**, this theoretical perspective emphasizes the importance of resources, like labor and money, for generating and sustaining social movements. The more resources a movement is able to employ or mobilize, the more successful it is likely to be. This school argues that there are always enough discontented people in society to fill a protest movement, but what varies over time—and so explains the emergence of movements—is the resources available to nourish it. These researchers accordingly focused on how movement leaders raise funds, sometimes by appealing to wealthy people, sometimes through direct-mail fundraising from thousands of regular citizens. As a society grows wealthier, moreover, citizens have more money to contribute to **social movement organizations (SMOs)**—the formal organizations that support and sometimes initiate movements—and so there are more movements than ever before. With this point of view, the focus shifted decisively away from the kinds of individuals who might join a movement and toward the organization and resources necessary to sustain a movement. Today, scholars

What factors explain why movements emerge when and where they do?

still consider resources an important part of any explanation of movement emergence.

The theoretical paradigm that has concentrated most on movement emergence is the political process approach mentioned earlier (e.g., McAdam 1982). According to this perspective, economic and political shifts occur, usually independently of protesters' own efforts, that open up a space or opportunities for the movement. Because this approach views movements as primarily political, making demands of the state and asking for changes in laws and policies, it regards changes in the government or state as the most important opportunity a movement needs. Most often, this consists of a slackening in the repression that organizers are otherwise assumed to face, perhaps because political authorities are divided (the movement may have found some allies within the government) or because powerful political and economic actors have divergent interests. There may be a general crisis in the government, perhaps as a result of fighting (or losing) a foreign war, which distracts leaders and may bankrupt the government. In many versions of this perspective, the same factors are seen as explaining both the rise of the movement and its relative success.

Resources, organization, and a sense of new opportunities all undoubtedly encouraged the civil rights movement that grew rapidly beginning in 1955. By then, the migration of African Americans out of the rural South provided them with more resources and denser social ties; churches and organizations through which money could be channeled to civil rights work; and a new, more optimistic cultural outlook. These factors encouraged more extensive political mobilization, especially through the National Association for the Advancement of Colored People (NAACP), which in turn won inspiring legal victories, especially *Brown v. Board of Education* in 1954, which held that racially segregated schools violated the Constitution.

is recruited, the very existence of social ties among potential recruits is seen as a prerequisite for the emergence of a movement. If most political process theorists emphasize conditions in the external environment (especially the government) that allow a movement to emerge, network theorists look at the conditions within the community or population of those who might be recruited. Those people with dense ties, or who belong to certain formal organizations, find it easier to reach, persuade, and mobilize other people and thereby build a movement.

Scholars who have studied the 1969 Stonewall rebellion in New York City and the subsequent development of a militant gay and lesbian movement emphasize the critical importance of social networks. The Stonewell rebellion involved violent confrontations between police and gay men and lesbians over the course of several days following the arrest of gay patrons at a bar called the Stonewall Inn in Greenwich Village. This rebellion, apparently a spontaneous eruption of gay militancy, in fact marked the public emergence of a long-repressed, covert urban subculture. The gay movement was also able to draw upon preexisting networks of activists in the radical movements then current among American youth. The "gay liberation" movement recruited from the ranks of both the anti–Vietnam War movement and the women's movement. It also borrowed its confrontational tactics from these movements. Many lesbians and gay men had already been radicalized and educated in the arts of protest by the feminist and antiwar movements.

The theoretical approaches discussed thus far redefined somewhat the central question of movement emergence. Scholars began to see movements as closely linked to one another because leaders and participants shifted from one to the other or shared social networks, or because the same political conditions encouraged many movements to form

Social Networks Alongside resource mobilization and political process approaches, a number of sociologists have emphasized the **social networks** through which people are mobilized into social movements. Social networks are the webs of ties or connections that link individuals (and organizations) to one another, thereby facilitating communication and other exchanges. Although networks have been used primarily to explain *who*

This march in New York City occurred on the first anniversary of the Stonewall rebellion, then known as "Gay Liberation Day."

at the same time. So researchers began to ask what caused entire waves or "cycles" of social movements to emerge rather than asking about the origins of single movements. One cannot fully understand any one of the movements of the 1960s cycle of protest, for example—including the civil rights movement, the women's movement, the farm workers' movement, and the anti–Vietnam War movement—without knowing something about the other movements in this cycle.

Cultural Approaches In recent years, some sociologists who take a cultural approach have linked social movements to broad historical developments, especially the shift from an industrial or manufacturing society to a postindustrial or knowledge society in which fewer people process physical goods and more deal with symbols and other forms of knowledge. Social movements are seen as efforts to control the direction of social change largely by controlling a society's symbols and self-understandings.

In cultural approaches, the goals and intentions of protesters are taken very seriously. For instance, the origin of the animal protection movement has been linked to broad changes in sensibilities over the last 200 years that have allowed citizens of the industrial world to recognize the suffering of nonhuman species—and to worry about it. Such concerns would simply not have been possible in a society

In the *Sex in the City* movie, an animal rights activist tosses fake blood on Kim Cattrall's character for wearing a coat made of animal fur. Why have some people become so concerned with the suffering of animals in recent decades?

where most people worked on farms and used animals both as living tools (horses, dogs, dairy cows) and as raw materials (food, leather, etc.). The point is to observe or ask protesters themselves about their perceptions, desires, and fantasies without having a theory that predicts in advance what protesters think and feel. Perceptions are crucial in this view.

From this perspective, the work of sociologist Charles Kurzman (1996) helped change the way scholars think about shifts in political opportunities for protest. Political process theorists had insisted that these were objective changes, independent of protesters' perceptions, but Kurzman's research shows that the perceptions may matter as much as the underlying reality. Kurzman's research on the Iranian Revolution (1978–1979), in which the monarch (or shah) was overthrown by a popular uprising, indicates that there were no objective political changes on the eve of the revolution that suddenly weakened the monarchy or created new opportunities for protest. Indeed, despite considerable police repression and expressions of U.S. support for the monarchy, protest against the shah continued to grow and people gradually came to believe they could topple the regime. A movement can sometimes succeed, apparently, if it thinks it can. In other words, cultural perceptions can play as important a role as changes in the state or society. Political process theorists had apparently not tested their model in cases where perceptions and objective realities diverged: Protesters may fail to see (or seize) opportunities, and they may imagine opportunities for protest when none seems to exist. The slackening of police repression, divisions among wealthy elites and politicians, and so on (the "opportunities" of political process theorists) may only have an effect if they are perceived as such. And people may sometimes rebel (and sometimes win), as in Iran, even when the political environment does not at first seem promising.

Cultural sociologists have reached different conclusions than resource mobilization and political process theorists in part because they have examined different kinds of social movements. Most political process theorists, for example, have focused on movements of groups who have been systematically excluded from political power and legal rights, in other words groups that are demanding the full rights of citizenship. Cultural approaches have been more likely to examine movements of those who already have the formal rights of citizens—who can vote, pressure legislators, and run for office—but who nonetheless feel they must step outside normal political institutions to have a greater impact. Resource mobilization theorists also assume that people know what they want and simply need the resources and organization to pursue it; cultural sociologists recognize that in many cases people only gradually figure out what they want, often because movement organizers persuade them of it (e.g., that animals can suffer like humans, that marijuana should be legal, that the U.S. government is the tool of Satan).

Cultural sociologists have reasserted the importance of perceptions, ideas, emotions, and grievances, all of which resource mobilization and political process theorists once thought did not matter very much or could simply be taken for granted. But these are examined today in the context of broader social and political changes, not in isolation from them. It is not as though people first develop goals and then decide to go out and form movements to pursue them; there is an interaction among ideas, mobilization, and the broader environment. Some people get pulled into movements by friends or family and are only slowly converted to the movement's cause; their political beliefs are a consequence, not a cause, of joining the movement. Research suggests, for example, that over 40 percent of committed antiabortion activists had ambiguous views about abortion or even considered themselves "pro-choice" when they initially joined the movement; it was only after they spent some time in the movement, interacting with long-term activists, that they came to emphatically oppose abortions (Munson 2008).

Recruitment: Joining or Supporting Movements

Once activists form groups or networks and begin to think of themselves as a movement (or at least a potential movement), their next step is usually to try to expand their ranks by recruiting others to their cause. Like accounts of movement origins, sociological theories of recruitment have evolved over time from an emphasis on individual traits to one on availability, and finally toward a synthesis of these dimensions.

How do movements recruit supporters?

Individual Traits among Protesters

Scholars once tended to see protesters as swept up in crowds, acting in abnormal and sometimes irrational ways because of frustration with their individual circumstances. In some theories marginal and alienated members of society were seen as most likely to join social movements; in others it was those who were insecure or dogmatic. Such claims were usually demeaning to protesters, who were thought to be compensating for some sort of personal inadequacy or psychological problem, but subsequent empirical research did not generally support the image of protesters as more angry or alienated than others.

The economist Mancur Olson (1965) suggested that protesters are perfectly rational, arguing that they do not join groups if they think they can gain the benefits that these groups pursue without taking the time to participate. In other words, people may become "free riders" on the efforts of others, letting others protest while benefitting from their successes. You don't have to join the environmental movement to enjoy the clean air that it wins for all of us—so why join it? Another reason to free ride is that your own participation in or contribution to a collective effort won't make a noticeable difference once the group consists of more than a few dozen people. What can a group of 101 people accomplish that a group of 100 can't? So to attract participants, Olson argues, movements must provide "selective incentives" that are enjoyed only by those who participate, such as interesting political discussions, the possibility of making new friends, insurance for trade union members, and the like. Olson challenged scholars to show how organizers manage to overcome the free rider problem.

Olson helped inspire the resource mobilization paradigm, which shifted attention from what kinds of *people* protest to what kinds of objective *conditions* facilitate protest. Attitudes and grievances were dismissed as insufficient to cause protest, for many people had the right attitudes and interests but did not participate. As part of this new agenda, **biographical availability** was seen as necessary for participation: People with few family or work obligations—especially young people without children—were particularly available to devote time to movement activities (McAdam 1988).

Recruitment via Social Networks

Researchers have found that the best predictor of who will join a movement, in addition to biographical availability, is whether an individual knows someone already in that movement. In many movements, a majority of participants are recruited this way. Social networks are thus usually a precondition for the emergence of a movement as well as the explanation for who was subsequently recruited to it. Physically scattered or socially isolated people are the least likely to join a movement. In the extreme case of "bloc recruitment," organizers bring a whole social network or organization virtually intact into a movement. This suggests that—contrary to Olson's view—people do not make decisions to join movements (or not) as isolated, self-regarding individuals but in concert with others in their networks.

Different kinds of social networks can be used for recruitment. They may not be political in origin or intent. Black churches and colleges were crucial to the Southern civil rights movement in the 1950s, fundamentalist churches helped defeat the Equal Rights Amendment in the 1980s, and mosques facilitated the Iranian Revolution. Networks developed for earlier political activities can also aid recruitment into a movement that develops later—one reason why a history of previous activism makes someone more likely to be recruited. The clustering of movements in waves or cycles makes this mutual support especially important, as one movement feeds into the next. Because of these networks, prior activism and organizational memberships help predict who will be recruited (and who will not be).

Social media like Facebook and Twitter can also be used to recruit people to political protests, as was seen during the so-called Arab Spring of 2011 as well as in the Occupy Wall Street movement later that year. These media allow multitudes of people who have never met before and who have no other connections to communicate with one another. They make it possible to organize huge protests in a much shorter span of time and over greater distances than was previously possible. They allow activists to direct people to assemble at specific places and at specific times before the authorities have time to react. This can be especially important where authoritarian regimes are likely to break up protests violently. On the other hand, government authorities may also monitor social media—or attempt to shut them down altogether—in their attempts to control protest. So social media can be used to organize as well as disrupt movements.

Without denying the importance of personal contacts and communication networks, recent studies have also examined the cultural messages transmitted across these networks. For example, "suddenly imposed grievances" that are produced by dramatic and unexpected events may be important for recruitment. The partial nuclear meltdown in 1979 at the Three Mile Island power plant in Dauphin County, Pennsylvania, which led to the evacuation of nearly 200,000 people, alerted the public to the risks of nuclear energy, giving a big boost to the antinuclear movement (Walsh 1981). Recruitment is also more likely when people feel that they have a chance of success. This sense of optimism and efficacy has been called "cognitive liberation" (McAdam 1982). People may have lots of grievances as well as ties to individuals in a movement seeking to redress those grievances, but they are unlikely to join that movement if don't think it can succeed.

Scholars view direct personal contacts as important because they allow organizers and potential participants to achieve a common definition of a social problem and a common prescription for solving it. In successful recruitment, organizers offer ways of seeing a social problem that resonate with the views and experiences of potential recruits. The Occupy Wall Street movement, for example, spread very rapidly across the country in 2011 because its message about the power of banks and corporations and the plight of the "99 percent" resonated with people during a time of economic crisis and home foreclosures. Networks are important *because* of the cultural meanings they transmit. Networks and meanings are not rival explanations;

they work together. Explore the Infographic on page 485 to learn more about who makes up the Occupy Wall Street movement.

How Framing and Cultural Attitudes Shape Recruitment

Scholars of movements have also emphasized the framing work involved in recruiting people to movements. **Framing** generally refers to the specific ways that ideas and beliefs are presented to other people. Scholars of movements focus on how activists try to frame or present their ideas so that they make sense to or resonate with the beliefs of potential recruits and supporters. Scholars have distinguished three successive types of framing that are necessary for successful recruitment: *diagnostic,* in which a movement convinces potential converts that a problem needs to be addressed; *prognostic,* in which it convinces them of appropriate strategies, tactics, and targets; and *motivational,* in which it exhorts them to get involved in these activities (Snow and Benford 1988). Frames are more likely to be accepted if they fit well with the existing beliefs of potential recruits, if they involve empirically credible claims, if they are compatible with the life experiences of the audiences, and if they fit with the stories or narratives the audiences tell about their lives. Frames, in short, must resonate with the salient beliefs of potential recruits. When the frames of activists and potential recruits fit together in this way, scholars speak of "frame alignment."

Collective identity is another concept used to get at the mental worlds of people which helps explain recruitment to movements. A **collective identity** is one's belief that one belongs to a certain group (or groups) with distinctive characteristics and interests (for example, women, the working class, feminists). In order to devote time and effort to protest, people must usually feel part of a larger group they think they can help. Not all identities come easily to people; they may have to be consciously created, which is one of the things that some movements do. The gay and lesbian movement, for example, still devotes a lot of its energy to making it possible for gays and lesbians to feel comfortable with themselves and to identify themselves publicly as gay or lesbian (i.e., to "come out of the closet"). Obviously, people who for whatever reason find it difficult to identify themselves publicly with a certain group are unlikely to become politically active on its behalf.

Another cultural approach emphasizes how attitudes and worldviews matter. Political scientist Ronald Inglehart (1977) has argued that new "postmaterial" values and beliefs have emerged in the advanced industrial nations since the 1960s. Through most of human history, in his view, people have been forced to worry about basic material needs such as food, shelter, and security, but since World War II the advanced industrial world has been largely spared traditional privations. Those born after World War II—at least the college-educated and affluent middle class—were "freed" to

Occupy Wall Stree[t]

Constructing a profile of the typical participant in the Occupy Wall Street movement, as for any movement, can be quite difficult. Participants in movements are like the layers of an onion. At the core are the devoted, full-time (or nearly full-time) leaders and activists who do most of the strategic thinking and planning for the movement. Then there are the part-time activists who do a lot of the difficult but necessary work involved in recruiting participants and organizing meetings and protests. Then there are movement's "foot soldiers," the people who show up at meetings and protests—and who must show up if the movement is to come to the attention of the public, the media, and the authorities. And then there are people who express support for the movement in public opinion polls and may contribute money to it.

Sources: Based on data from Fast Company (2011); Panagopoulos and Costas (2011); Pew Research Center (2011).

◉ **Explore the Data** on Occupy Wall Street in **MySocLab** and then . . .

▮ **Think About It**
How might the views of OWS activists about the President and Congress lead them to use "extra-institutional" political tactics?

▮ **Inspire Your Sociological Imagination**
What do you think is behind the reasoning that younger people tend to support the OWS movement while older people tend to oppose it?

What do supporters of the O.W.S. Movement look like?

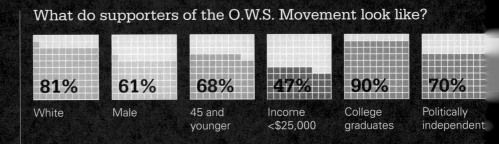

81% White	**61%** Male	**68%** 45 and younger	**47%** Income <$25,000	**90%** College graduates	**70%** Politically independent

Political views of those active in the movement in N.Y.C.

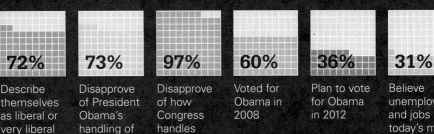

72% Describe themselves as liberal or very liberal	**73%** Disapprove of President Obama's handling of his job	**97%** Disapprove of how Congress handles its job	**60%** Voted for Obama in 2008	**36%** Plan to vote for Obama in 2012	**31%** Believe unemployme[nt] and jobs are today's mos[t] important problems

What does the public think of the Occupy movement?

Percentage in each group that supports or opposes the movement.
Figures may not add to 100 because of rounding.

		Supports	Opposes	Neither/ don't know
	Overall	44	35	22
Politics	Republican	21	59	20
	Independent	46	34	21
	Democrat	60	21	19
Age	18-29	49	27	24
	30-49	45	32	23
	50-64	45	38	17
	65+	33	47	20
Education	College graduate	48	40	12
	Some college	50	33	17
	High school or less	39	33	28
Family income	$150,000+	36	55	10
	$100,000-$150,000	46	43	11
	$75,000-$100,000	49	37	14
	$30,000-$75,000	48	34	18
	<$30,000	43	30	27

pursue "higher" goals such as control over their lives, environmental protection, and satisfying work rather than worrying primarily about their paychecks. The spread of mass communication and higher education contributed to the same trends. The result has been less emphasis on economic redistribution, class-based political organizations, or the pursuit of political power—again, at least where the affluent middle class is concerned. Instead we have seen movements critical of large bureaucracies, meaningless work, complex technologies, and many different forms of oppression. One can certainly better understand who is likely to support the environmental movement or the animal-rights movement by using the concept of postmaterial politics. These movements have a primarily middle-class social base, even though they are not pursuing the narrow economic interests of this class. So the growth of a postindustrial sector of the economy can help explain not only changes in political concerns over time but also different sympathies across parts of the population at any given time.

It turns out that another contemporary movement has a primarily well-educated and middle-class social base: the followers of the late Osama bin Laden (Kurzman 2002). While many Westerners assume that the Islamic world is mired in religious superstition and rejects modern rationality, bin Laden's followers are much better educated than their peers and use the latest technologies and media. They are not motivated by narrow class or economic interests but by their opposition to the policies of the U.S. government in the Middle East, even as they use religious language and look nostalgically backward to a golden age of Islam. Attitudes and worldviews matter for recruitment, but they are not always what we assume them to be.

Recruitment, however, involves more than ideas about how the world works. Its moral and emotional dimensions are equally important. In fact, all the key factors that explain recruitment depend heavily on their emotional impact on people. Social networks, for example, are often grounded in the emotional bonds among their members: We pay attention to people in our networks, and what they say, because we are fond of them or trust them. The term **moral shock**

is also meant to incorporate some of the moral and emotional dimensions of recruitment to movements. A moral shock is an unexpected event that surprises, distresses, and outrages people, often to the point of motivating them to join a movement to eliminate the source of their outrage. Moral shocks may be so strong that they lead people without social ties to activists to seek out or even form a group to redress their grievances (Jasper 1997). An example of a moral shock is the impact of the *Roe v. Wade* Supreme Court decision of 1973, which legalized abortions under certain circumstances, on many religious Americans, especially Catholic women. For these women, it was as if the Supreme Court had legalized the murder of certain kinds of children. Although they had not been politically active previously and knew no political activists, these women formed the core of the early antiabortion movement (Luker 1984).

Recent scholarship on movements pays more attention to what goes on inside people's heads (and hearts) than previously. Protest is no longer seen as a compensation for some psychological problem but part of an effort to impose meaning and morality on the world, to forge and express a collective identity, to create or reinforce emotional bonds with others, and to define and pursue collective interests. These are things that all humans desire and seek. There is today considerable consensus that positions in networks and cultural orientations (cognitive, moral, and emotional) are equally important in recruitment. But there are also cases in which cultural messages can be used to recruit people in the absence of social networks, relying on moral shocks instead of personal ties. For virtually all social movements, only a small fraction of potential recruits actually join, and it takes all the factors we have considered to understand who does and does not sign up.

While many Westerners assume that the Islamic world is caught up in religious superstition and rejects modern rationality, it is known that the followers of the late Osama bin Laden are actually much better educated than their peers and use the latest technologies and media.

MOVEMENT TACTICS AND OUTCOMES

👁 **Watch** the **Big Question Video** in **MySocLab**

I f you are in a social movement, the most pressing question you face is: *What is to be done?* How do you choose tactics that will help your cause? How do you recruit more people, attract the news media, put pressure on the rich and powerful, or favorably impress decisionmakers? Tactical decisions are the real "stuff" of social movements. Fortunately, a few sociologists have looked at how these decisions are made, how and when protesters innovate in their tactics, and what the tradeoffs are between different kinds of tactics. Practitioners as well as academics have also addressed these issues.

The Strategies and Tactics of Movements

The tactical choices of activists are usually made in the heat of conflict and so can be hard to explain in a rigorous fashion. These choices depend in part on the instincts of movement leaders, who themselves may not always be able to explain why they made one choice rather than another. Decisions are sometimes made quickly, and it may be difficult to reconstruct the process later—when being interviewed by a sociologist, for instance.

Tactical choices are usually made during the course of interactions with other decisionmakers: with one's opponents, of course, but also with the police, the media,

Why do movements use certain tactics and not others?

legislators, potential allies, and many others. To take just one example, before most rallies or marches today, leaders negotiate with the police over where they will go, what they will do, how many will be arrested (if any), and so on. Leaders must also make tactical choices with regard to their own followers as well as opponents: how to placate disaffected factions, how to keep members coming back to future events, how to increase or simply maintain the membership. As a result, any given action is probably designed for several different audiences at the same time. But an action that satisfies one may not please another.

With regard to their opponents, protesters hope to change their behavior through persuasion, intimidation, or imposing costs (financial or otherwise) upon them. Raising the costs of "business as usual" is generally necessary when movements confront powerful elites (especially the wealthy) who have not been elected. They can simply ignore protesters or try to repress them if they become threatening. Strikes and boycotts, however, hurt the wealthy economically and may lead them to make concessions to protesters so that their factories and farms can continue to make profits.

Movements also seek to undermine their opponents' credibility with the public, media, and government officials. With regard to such officials, protesters hope to change laws, policies, regulatory practices, and administrative rules and to avoid repression. From the courts, protesters typically strive to have unfavorable laws struck down or at least interpreted

FIGURE 17.1 WHICH SMOs HAVE RECEIVED THE MOST MEDIA ATTENTION DURING THE TWENTIETH CENTURY?

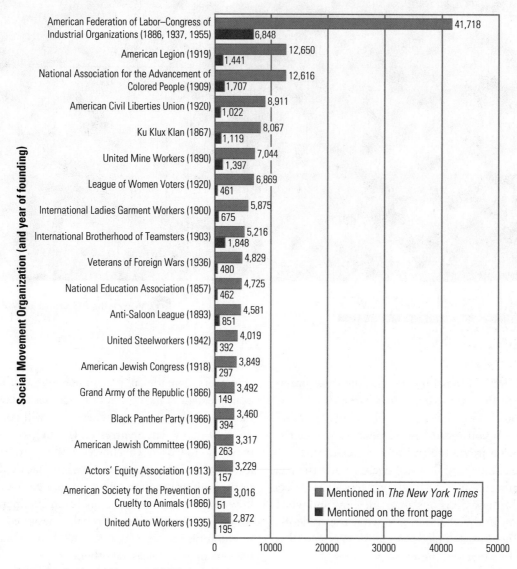

Source: Based on data from Amenta et al. (2008).

in a new way. With both courts and police, they hope for tolerance of their protests. Social movements seek to use the news media to spread their message and sometimes to undermine their opponents (see Figure 17.1). Protesters may also approach professional groups, such as engineers, to change their standards. They may seek allies in other protest groups. And from the public at large, they may hope for new recruits, sympathy, contributions, or at least changes in awareness. Finally, they even have goals for their own members: personal transformations and continued fervor for the cause. In other words, movements have a lot of goals to balance in their tactics, and striking the right balance is sometimes extremely difficult.

Movement leaders, moreover, are only familiar with a limited number of tactics. The sociologist Charles Tilly (1986) developed the concept of a "repertoire of contention"

to describe the range of tactics available to protesters in any given society in a particular period. Most social movements in that society draw on the same repertoire because it is largely fixed and unchanging, at least in the short run. There are many possible tactics that movement leaders are not familiar with or do not have the knowledge to utilize, including (hypothetically) tactics that might be extremely beneficial to the movement. Tilly was interested in explaining how repertoires of contention changed over long stretches of time, while other scholars have been concerned with explaining why particular leaders choose certain tactics and not others from the existing repertoire: Why a march rather than a letter-writing campaign? Why wait a week before responding to your opponents' actions rather than acting immediately? Why choose one cultural frame rather than another for a speech or website?

Shown here, the sit-in protest in support of affirmative action has taken over the steps of the Michigan state capitol building. Why are some protest tactics used repeatedly over the years?

Saul Alinsky, one of the greatest community organizers of the twentieth century, wrote a great deal about tactics in the course of trying to improve the living conditions of poor neighborhoods, particularly in Chicago (Alinsky 1971). Alinsky developed tactical principles that are not unlike those of army generals: Try to take your opponents by surprise, and try to make them think you are more powerful than you are. Try to use tactics your own followers enjoy and are familiar with. The idea of keeping the pressure on one's opponents is important because you never know where and when your opponent will be vulnerable or will make a blunder. The greater the pressure, the greater the chance you will trip them up. Alinsky also recognized that it is usually necessary to portray your enemy as an utter villain, a real flesh-and-blood person who can be blamed, not an abstract principle. Thus, protest movements during the Arab Spring of 2011 demonized dictators like Hosni Mubarak in Egypt. Protesters called for the replacement of the authoritarian regime in Egypt with democracy, but they usually called simply for the overthrow of Mubarak, who symbolized all that was wrong in the country. Such demonization can lead to strong emotions and polarization. Alinsky's rules are quite general, but they can be helpful reminders to social movement leaders.

In describing civil-rights sit-ins, sociologist Aldon Morris (1984) exemplifies the resource mobilization approach to tactics. He is not so much concerned with the origins of the sit-in tactic or the strategic thinking behind its use. Rather, he is concerned with revealing the indigenous organizations and social networks through which the sit-ins rapidly spread, arguing against a view of the sit-ins as spontaneous eruptions. Morris also touches on another important issue: the emergence of "movement centers" with resources, social ties (especially preachers and NAACP activists), and regular meetings (usually at churches). Other theorists have called these "free spaces," places relatively free from surveillance where oppositional ideas and tactics can develop and spread.

Other scholars have looked at the use of violent strategies by social movements and have tried to dispel some of the myths surrounding these. They point out that guerrilla warfare and terrorism are rational political responses to state violence and conflicts over territory, not the handiwork of psychopaths or religious fanatics, as the media often suggest.

Scholars as well as journalists are often hesitant to emphasize the rationality or achievements of political violence, in part because of their moral discomfort with it. In the case of the antiapartheid movement in South Africa, this has led some scholars to avoid discussing violence altogether and to portray the movement, misleadingly, as an entirely nonviolent civil-rights struggle like that in the United States. But political violence, like war, is routine politics by other means. That said, recent research indicates that nonviolent movements may be twice as likely to succeed as violent movements, even against very repressive regimes (Chenoweth and Stephan 2011). This is because ordinary people usually find it much easier to participate in nonviolent movements, so they tend to be much larger than violent movements, and because government officials and soldiers are more likely to defect to nonviolent movements.

Although social movements are defined, in part, by their use of extrainstitutional tactics (that is, outside existing political institutions) to pursue their political goals, protest can

We often think of protests as occurring "in the streets," but they can occur within institutions as well. Here gay rights advocates call for the repeal of the "don't ask, don't tell" policy during a Senate hearing.

also take place *within* institutions. For example, gays and lesbians in the U.S. military have fought with allies outside the military to overturn the so-called "don't ask, don't tell" policy that prohibited them from serving as openly gay or lesbian. Thus, free spaces *outside* regular institutions are not always enough for movements to flourish; sometimes they can also thrive *within* dominant institutions.

The choice of strategies and tactics is certainly an area in which additional research is needed. One limitation of existing research has been that most scholars have thought about the movement as their unit of analysis: how each grows, operates, and affects the world around it. But tactical choices are made in close interaction with other actors in the same "field of conflict," including opponents and allies, actual and potential. These interactions are like a game of chess: Each player's tactical moves are shaped as much by the moves of the other players as by one's preferred or ideal course of action. So movements often end up doing things they would rather not do but feel they must—such as killing civilians. But this is not surprising. In an ideal world, after all, people would not need to make hard choices about political tactics; they would already have the things their movements are fighting for.

Why do movements decline or disappear?

The Decline and Disappearance of Movements

Not surprisingly, scholars have had much more to say about why social movements arise than why they decline or disappear altogether. Nonetheless, several hypotheses about movement decline have attained some prominence.

Read the **Document** *The Rise and Fall of Aryan Nations* in **MySocLab**

Changing Political Environments   Most explanations for movement decline focus on the surrounding political environment, which may constrain as well as facilitate movements. Of course, the very success of a movement in changing laws or government policies may undermine the motivations that many people had for participating in that movement. Movement organizations may also be legally

recognized by the government, leading to their institutionalization and declining reliance upon disruptive protest. Government concessions of this type, even if they do not redress all the grievances and concerns of movement participants, may nevertheless be sufficient to satisfy or placate many people, who will then drift away from the movement or from protest tactics. Social movements, in short, may become victims of their own limited successes. The U.S. labor movement is a prime example of this dynamic. After militant and sometimes deadly strikes in the 1930s led to the legal recognition of trade unions and the right to collective bargaining, unions gradually turned away from strikes and the aggressive recruitment of new members. As a result, the proportion of workers who belong to unions has been declining since the 1950s. Explore *A Sociological Perspective* on page 491 to learn more about the U.S. labor movement.

Internal Dynamics and Evolution   Movements may also decline as a result of their own internal dynamics and evolution. The women's movement, for example, has gradually lost its radical vision and militancy (Epstein 2001). This was a result in part of intense ideological conflicts among radical feminists within the movement, who had provided much of the movement's activist core and ideological inspiration. Gradually, and partly because of its own success in opening up new professional careers for women, the women's movement as a whole took on a middle-class outlook. It became more concerned with the career opportunities and material success of individual women than with the group solidarity of women or addressing the concerns of poor and working-class women. A number of women's organizations have now been successfully institutionalized, including the National

A SOCIOLOGICAL PERSPECTIVE

Will the labor movement revive?

Why do movements decline or disappear? Sometimes they become victims of their own limited success, as was the case with the American labor movement. After decades of internal divisions and repression by private armies and government officials, an industrial labor movement emerged in the United States in the 1930s. New tactics like sit-down strikes (in which striking workers occupied their factories), as well as divisions among employers, allowed workers to win significant concessions, including the right to unionize and bargain collectively.

These concessions encouraged union officials to focus less on mass mobilization and more on reaching deals with employers. When profits were threatened beginning in the late 1960s, however, business groups became more aggressively anti-union. Since the 1970s, workers' rights and protections have been steadily undermined and many industries have been de-unionized. After a long decline, many workers and activists hope Occupy Wall Street's direct-action tactics will reinvigorate the American labor movement.

Sit-down strikes like this one at a GM factory in 1936 resulted in expanded rights for workers. How did a changing political environment impact this movement?

How might an alliance with the Occupy movement help to revive the American labor movement?

Encouraged by the loss of unions' capacity to mobilize, business leaders pushed to erode collective bargaining rights, an effort that continues to this day. Shown here, air-traffic controllers march during a 1981 strike. After 12,000 controllers went on strike, President Reagan fired all the workers who did not return to work. What other factors were responsible for the decline of the labor movement?

◉▸ **Explore** A Sociological Perspective in **MySocLab** and then …

■ Think About It

What factors contributed to the union victories of the 1930s? Is it likely that conditions like those of the 1930s will happen again?

■ Inspire Your Sociological Imagination

Think of the people you know in the full-time workforce. How many are members of unions? Are those who are in unions satisfied with their union? Why or why not? How many of those who are not in a union wish they were? Why?

Organization for Women (NOW), but they have not been able, and most have not been concerned, to bring about gender equality within the larger society.

The sociologist Joshua Gamson (1995) emphasizes yet another way in which a movement's internal dynamics may lead to break up and decline. As we have seen, movements typically require—or themselves attempt to create—clear and stable collective identities. How can we make claims and demands upon others, after all, if we do not know who "we" and "they" are? Many recent movements have been centrally concerned with establishing, recasting, or defending collective identities, including previously stigmatized identities. But collective identities, sociologists argue, are not "natural" or given once and for all; they are culturally constructed and continually reconstructed. Some identities, moreover, may obscure or devalue other identities that people have. As a result, people have often attempted to blur or reconfigure certain identities. Hence, Gamson's question: Must movements organized around a particular identity self-destruct?

Gamson shows how the gay and lesbian movement has been shaken in recent years by "queer" theorists and activists who have challenged fixed sexual identities like "gay," "lesbian," and "straight." Queer activists have also challenged the assimilationist goals of mainstream (and generally older) gay and lesbian activists, some of whom object to the very use of a stigmatized label like "queer." To some extent, Gamson points out, queer activism developed out of the growing organization of bisexual and transgendered people, whose very existence challenges the notion of fixed sexual and gender identities.

Ultimately, the gay and lesbian movement, and indeed all movements, face a dilemma: To be politically effective they may feel a need to emphasize exclusive and secure collective identities, but this may paper over and effectively ignore important differences among movement participants—differences based on race and class, for example, which may later erupt in a way that weakens the movement. How movements handle this dilemma in order to avoid self-destruction—how they weigh and balance competing and potentially disruptive identity claims—is an important question for future research.

Repression   Movements may also decline because the political opportunities and the free space that have helped give rise to them begin to contract or disappear. Divisions among the wealthy and powerful may be resolved or (perhaps because of such unity) authorities may decide to harshly repress or crack down on a movement. Both of these factors are usually invoked to explain the violent demise of the democracy movement in China in 1989. A number of scholars have also pointed to repression as a key factor in the decline of the U.S. labor movement since the 1950s. More specifically, union decline is largely explained by aggressive employer opposition to unions, which has been facilitated by laws and policies that favor employers over workers. One does not see the same type of employer resistance to unions in much of Europe (or Canada), mainly because laws discourage it. As a result, unions have held their own in these countries or even become stronger. American unions have also been hurt by factory closings in recent years; many businesses have transferred their operations to parts of the country (mainly the South) or to other countries where unions are weak and wages relatively low.

A primary reason for the existence of a legal framework in the United States that encourages business opposition to unions is the long-standing *political* weakness of the American labor movement. Unlike all other developed capitalist countries, the United States has never had a strong labor or leftist political party (although some scholars have suggested that the Democratic Party briefly functioned like one during the 1930s and 1940s). Scholars refer to the historical weakness of labor and socialist parties in the United States as "American exceptionalism." The precise reasons for this exceptionalism continue to be debated, with factors such as the two-party system, racial and ethnic antagonisms among workers, and the American creed of individualism receiving considerable emphasis.

Many scholars point out that while repression usually works, it does sometimes fail. Police violence sometimes demobilizes protesters and crushes insurgents, but it sometimes backfires, spurring even more people to take to the streets or to take up arms. What explains this? Research on Central America during the 1970s and 1980s (Brockett 1993) suggests that ruthless repression was most effective when authorities used it before movements had become strong—before a cycle of protest had begun. However, after such a cycle of protest was underway—when people were already active and organized—repression tended to backfire. Organized activists redoubled their efforts, went underground, and often turned to violence, joined by others seeking protection, justice, and sometimes revenge.

U.S. counterinsurgency efforts in Iraq failed because they were based on a misunderstanding of insurgent social movements (Roxborough 2007). U.S. officials assumed that popular attitudes towards insurgents and the government are based on short-term cost-benefit calculations, failing to see how insurgencies are deeply rooted in class, ethnic, or religious conflicts. Accordingly, attempts by the United States to win over the "hearts and minds" of the Iraqi population by providing material benefits proved insufficient. Insurgent movements are less interested in popularity or legitimacy per se than in monopolizing political control at the grassroots; such movements constitute an alternative government. Effective counterinsurgency, then, requires establishing local political control, a project that requires a great deal of time and manpower—something that outside powers may be unwilling to commit.

One of the unintended consequences of the bombing of a federal building in Oklahoma City in 1995 (shown here during a memorial service two weeks after the bombing, which killed 168 people) was a decline in the activities of right-wing militia groups.

☐ Outcomes

Social movements have a number of effects on their societies, some of them intended and others quite unintended. A few movements attain many or most of their goals, while others at least manage to gain recognition or longevity in the form of protest organizations, but many if not most are suppressed or ignored. While sociologists used to talk about the success or failure of movements, today they are more likely to talk about movement *outcomes* in recognition of the unintended consequences of movements. Some movements affect the broader culture and public attitudes, perhaps paving the way for future movements. Others leave behind social networks, tactical innovations, and organizational forms that later movements can adopt and use. At the extreme, some movements may simply arouse such a backlash against them that they lose ground. For example, the mobilization of far-right militia groups against the U.S. government which led to the Oklahoma City bombing in 1995 inspired closer surveillance and repression of these groups than had previously existed—not to mention extremely negative media coverage. Their number and activities declined sharply after the bombing.

Measuring a Movement's Success and Achievements
When thinking about what movements can achieve, it is useful to distinguish between *acceptance* (or recognition) and the winning of *new advantages* (Gamson 1990). Acceptance occurs when a movement or SMO comes to be regarded as a legitimate representative of a group by its opponents. Acceptance is generally crucial for the stability and longevity of a protest group, especially when its main opponent is the state. New advantages are the benefits a movement or SMO achieves for its constituency, such as old-age pensions, voting rights, clean air, or healthcare. These are the things that most ordinary participants—as well as free riders—are looking to attain from movements.

Acceptance and new advantages don't necessarily go together; a movement can attain one but not the other (or neither). The sociologist William Gamson has described four general types of movement outcomes based on whether a movement is fully accepted or not and whether it wins many new advantages or none (see Table 17.1). Movements that win a "full response" (i.e., full acceptance and many new advantages) are the most successful; the least successful movements are those that "collapse" by failing to win acceptance or any new advantages. There are also two outcomes that fall somewhere between success and failure. A movement is "preempted" when it wins new advantages but fails to win acceptance; and a movement is "coopted" when it is accepted by its opponents but fails to win any new advantages for its constituents. Of the 53 groups Gamson studied, 20 received a full response and 22 collapsed, while 5 were subject to cooptation and 6 to preemption (Gamson 1990:37).

Explaining movement outcomes is complicated by the fact that success in the short and the long term may not coincide. In some cases, these even conflict with each other, as when a movement's initial successes inspire strong countermobilization on the part of those under attack. The pro-choice movement, for example, was quite successful in liberalizing abortion laws in a number of states and then seemed to win a huge victory with the *Roe v. Wade* Supreme Court decision in 1973. But this decision, as we have seen, which legalized certain types of abortion, sparked a formidable countermobilization by the antiabortion movement. This countermobilization has succeeded in making it more difficult to attain an abortion in many parts of the United States, especially if one is a minor. On the other hand, movement efforts that are unsuccessful in the short run may

How can we measure a movement's success or achievements?

TABLE 17.1 FOUR TYPES OF MOVEMENT OUTCOMES

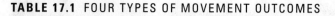

		Acceptance	
		Full	**None**
New Advantages	**Many**	**1. Full Response** Examples: American Federation of Labor American Federation of Teachers	**2. Preemption** Examples: American Free Trade Tobacco Night Riders
	None	**3. Cooptation** Examples: Bull Moose (Progressive) Party American Association of University Professors	**4. Collapse** Examples: International Workingmen's Association National Student League

Source: Gamson (1990:29 and Appendix A).

turn out to have big effects in the long run, as in the case of martyrs who inspire outrage and additional mobilization.

Cultural Consequences   Overall, researchers have shown that only a few large and enduring movements have had profound effects on their societies. The labor movement won the 40-hour work week and the right to collective bargaining with employers. The civil rights movement eliminated laws enforcing racial segregation and won voting rights for African Americans, and the women's movement won laws against sex discrimination and forever changed the way people think about gender differences. A large number of movements have met with considerable repression. Others have attained some acceptance for their own organizations without obtaining tangible benefits for those they represent (i.e., they have been coopted). Still others have pushed the government to establish a new agency or regulator in response to their demands, only to discover later that this agency was ineffectual or taken over by the movement's opponents. Scholars of social movements would like to believe that the movements they study affect the course of history, but they have often had to assert this without much good evidence.

The cultural and personal consequences of activism—many of them unintended—have received considerable attention from sociologists in recent years. The activist identity is itself an important effect of social movements, just one of many cultural effects of movements. These cultural effects are perhaps the hardest movement impacts to study, yet they may be some of the most profound and longest-lasting outcomes. Many movements help articulate new ways of thinking and feeling about the world. Thus, animal

protectionists developed widespread sympathy for nonhuman species into an explicit ideology of outrage at the harm done to animals. Other movements raise issues for public debate, forcing informed citizens to think about a topic and decide how they feel about it. The pro-choice and pro-life movements are prime examples. Today, citizens are virtually expected to have an opinion on the abortion issue. A majority may reject a movement's perspective, but it can still cause them to think more deeply about their own values and attitudes. Even those who disagree with antiabortionists still have to decide *why* they disagree. Still other social movements inspire scientific research or technological change, as the environmental movement has.

There may be even broader cultural effects of social movements. On the one hand, they give people a moral voice, helping them to articulate values and intuitions and think through issues that they do not have time to think about in their daily lives. (Should women be able to have abortions? Should lesbians and gay men be able to marry and adopt children? Should the government provide a job to everyone who wants one?) This is extremely satisfying for most movement participants as well as the general public (see Table 17.2). On the other hand, social movements can also generate extremely technical, scientific, and practical knowledge. They engage people in politics in an exciting way—rare enough in modern society. Unfortunately, some movements may go too far, when instead of trying to be artists they try to be engineers, telling others what is good for them rather than trying to persuade them. This has often happened when movements have taken state power and tried to impose their views on others, which brings us to the topic of revolutions.

TABLE 17.2 WHAT DO AMERICANS THINK OF SOCIAL MOVEMENTS AND THEIR GOALS?

The Labor Movement:

30 percent want it to have more influence.

42 percent want it to have less influence.

The Civil Rights Movement:

52 percent of blacks think that new laws are needed to reduce discrimination.

15 of whites think such laws are needed.

The Women's Movement:

69 percent of women think it has improved their lives.

27 percent of women disagree.

The Gay and Lesbian Movement:

50 percent support same-sex marriage.

45 percent oppose it.

The Pro-Choice and Pro-Life Movements:

41 percent consider themselves pro-choice.

50 percent consider themselves pro-life.

The Environmental Movement:

62 percent think it has done more good than harm.

36 percent think it has done more harm than good.

The Occupy Wall Street Movement:

44 percent support it.

35 percent oppose it.

The Tea Party Movement:

20 percent agree with it.

27 percent disagree with it.

Sources: Based on data from Jones (2011); Newport (2011); Alfano (2009); Silver (2012); Saad (2012); Pew Research Center (2011a; 2011b).

4   What Are Revolutions, and Why Do They Occur?

UNDERSTANDING REVOLUTIONS

👁 Watch the Big Question Video in **MySocLab**

In everyday conversation, *revolution* has come to mean virtually any fundamental change. Transformations of ways of thinking, technologies, and even fashions and consumer goods are often described as revolutionary. Sociologists, however, generally define **revolution** as a type of profound political or social change. Social movements, by contrast, are a type of sustained collective action that sometimes help bring about revolutions, but they sometimes produce only small changes or none at all.

☐ Defining "Revolution"

Sociologists generally define *revolution* in one of two ways. Some define revolutions as any change of government or political regime brought about, at least in part, by social movements or popular protest. Others define revolutions (or "social revolutions") more narrowly as entailing not only a change of regime but also fundamental changes in a society's economic institutions and class structure (e.g., the French, Russian, and Chinese revolutions). (Although some government officials may support revolutions, revolutions differs from *coups d'etat*, which involve the overthrow of a government by political authorities, often led by military officers, with little if any popular support or active participation by ordinary people.) "Social" revolutions thus differ from those revolutions (sometimes called "political revolutions") that bring about new political regimes, but little if any change in economic or class structures (e.g., the English and American revolutions). Of course, what begins as a political revolution may end up being a social revolution. For example, the political revolution in Russia in February 1917, which overthrow the king or czar, helped pave the way for the social revolution of October 1917, in which the radical Bolshevik Party (later renamed the Communist Party) seized power and oversaw a dramatic transformation of Russian society, including the dispossession of landlords and factory owners.

For some analysts, including Marxists, revolutions necessarily involve a substantial redistribution of property or the creation of a new type of economy or "mode of production." Yet other analysts argue that revolutions may radically alter everyday life for millions of people without bringing about much economic change—through dramatic political and cultural changes, for example. However defined, most scholars agree that social revolutions have been relatively rare, if momentous, occurrences. By most counts, fewer than two dozen major social revolutions have taken place during the past two centuries (see Table 17.3).

The revolutions that occurred in the Middle East and North Africa during the so-called Arab Spring of 2011 were political as opposed to social revolutions. They overthrew dictators and brought about changes in political regimes, but they did not substantially change economic institutions, the distribution of property, or class structures. The revolution in Egypt might even be described as a half-revolution. It overthrew the dictator Hosni Mubarak and destroyed Mubarak's powerful political party, but some elements of the old political regime—above all, the armed forces and the judiciary—survived the revolution intact and continue to wield tremendous power. Egypt's rich elite (which includes many military officers) has also held onto its wealth and economic power.

These nonviolent protesters in Tahrir Square in Cairo, Egypt, are shouting slogans against the dictator Hosni Mubarak.

Revolutions, Violence, and Other Forms of Conflict

Many sociologists view violence as an essential characteristic of revolutions, and many, if not most, revolutions have in fact involved considerable violence among the parties contending for state power. Foreign states, moreover, have often intervened militarily in revolutionary situations or attacked newly installed revolutionary governments. Some revolutionary regimes, furthermore, have employed considerable

TABLE 17.3 MAJOR SOCIAL REVOLUTIONS

Country	Year
France	1789
Mexico	1910
Russia	1917
Yugoslavia	1945
Vietnam	1945
China	1949
Bolivia	1952
Cuba	1959
Algeria	1962
Ethiopia	1974
Angola	1975
Mozambique	1975
Cambodia	1975
Laos	1975
Iran	1979
Nicaragua	1979
Eastern Europe	1989

Note: The listed dates are conventional markers that refer to the year in which revolutionaries initially overthrew extant political authorities. Revolutions, however, are best conceptualized not as events but as processes that typically span many years.

violence in order to reorganize society along new lines, and some have even perpetrated genocide or mass murders or have attacked neighboring countries. Still, the extent of violence in revolutions is quite variable, and some have occurred with comparatively little bloodshed. Some sociologists, furthermore, have detected a trend in recent decades toward nonviolent revolutions (for example, Iran in 1979, Eastern Europe in 1989, and Tunisia and Egypt in 2011). For these reasons, violence is best viewed as a potential and variable component of revolution, not as one of its defining characteristics.

Whether one employs the broader or narrower definition of revolution, the concept clearly stands apart analytically from such kindred forms of political conflict as wars (interstate or civil), popular rebellions, riots, and *coups d'etat*. Historically, however, these latter forms of conflict have often been closely connected with revolutions or revolutionary situations. Interstate wars sometimes help to cause revolutions by weakening armies—thereby creating political opportunities, as political process theorists would say—as well as by inflaming popular grievances, including perceived threats to one's nation; in turn, revolutions often result in interstate wars, usually because foreign powers seek to destroy those revolutionary movements or regimes they perceive as threats. France, Russia, Vietnam, Cuba, Iran—all were invaded shortly after revolutionaries took power. The revolutionary situations created by radical social movements, furthermore, often take on the form of civil wars, and radical movements bring about actual revolutions if they successfully seize state power.

Similarly, social movements that initially seek reforms within the existing political system—the kind of movements this chapter has focused on thus far—become **revolutionary movements** if they ultimately attempt to overthrow the government, which often happens when the political order breaks down or when the government persistently refuses to implement the reforms desired by such movements.

Spontaneous riots, furthermore, may help to precipitate revolutions, and riots have occurred frequently as a result of the breakdown of political authority that characterizes revolutionary situations. Finally, *coups d'etat* may become "revolutions from above" if their leaders mobilize masses of people and implement radical political or socioeconomic changes. In sum, while revolutions, and especially social revolutions, are a distinctive and comparatively rare form of political conflict, they are often connected, whether as cause or consequence, with other and more frequently recurring types of conflict, including social movements.

Revolutionary Situations

Many movements and rebellions have arisen over the past two centuries with the explicit aim of deposing oppressive political authorities and, often, remaking the social order from top to bottom. When such movements obtain substantial popular support, one may speak of the existence of a **revolutionary situation**: a situation in which two or more political institutions or movements claim to be the rightful or legitimate rulers of a certain territory or population.

There have been hundreds of revolutionary situations around the globe during the past two centuries. Most movements that try to bring about revolutions, however, do not succeed in overthrowing the government. If the government's armed forces remain strong and cohesive, revolutionaries are typically defeated or confined to peripheral regions within the national territory. Most revolutionary situations, in other words, do not result in actual political, let alone social, revolutions. A revolution typically requires the prior weakening or collapse of the government's "infrastructural power"—its capacity, that is, to enforce its will upon the society that it claims to govern. While revolutionary movements sometimes muster the power to incapacitate governments (by winning over military officers, soldiers, and government officials, for example), such movements just as frequently overthrow governments that have already been fatally weakened by interstate wars, economic and fiscal crises, or divisions and conflicts among the rich and powerful. The French Revolution, for example, occurred in part because the monarchy was in a state of fiscal collapse, and the Bolsheviks were able to seize power in Russia partly because the Russian army had been decimated in what was then known as the Great War (i.e., World War I).

Characteristics of Revolutionary Situations

Revolutionary situations can be understood as moments when regimes come into sharp conflict with radical social movements that are demanding power; such situations arise when the regime can no longer manage or accommodate the competing interests and demands of the groups they are meant to govern. A revolutionary situation opens up the possibility of deep political and social change should the radicals emerge victorious.

The famous Russian revolutionary Vladimir Ilyich Lenin famously stated that revolutionary situations display "three major symptoms": (1) a crisis or split among the upper classes; (2) unusual suffering among the lower classes; and (3) "a considerable increase in the ... independent historical action" of the lower classes (Lenin 1915:213). Since Lenin's time, scholars of revolutions have developed these basic insights. Perhaps the most crucial "symptom" Lenin lists—acute suffering among the masses—typically involves a sharp decline in the material conditions of the population. Accordingly, some scholars of revolution understand revolutions as a product of relative deprivation—a feeling that one does not have what one deserves. More likely, what Lenin had in mind are disruptions of everyday life that unsettle people's routines and thereby instigate their defiance of economic and political authorities. In this sense, revolutionary situations require the weakening or breakdown of "the regulatory controls inherent in the structures of institutional life" (Piven and Cloward 1977:11). Economic crises, wars, and even natural disasters typically cause these dislocations. The consequences are felt in the immediate lives of ordinary people, who endure the loss of work or lowered wages, who are sent into bloody and often unpopular wars, or who suffer the breakdown or even collapse of institutions upon which their survival depends—work, markets, transportation, policing, schools, and so forth.

For governments, furthermore, such shocks disrupt the existing balance of political forces. In order to preserve regime stability, political elites may feel compelled to seek new allies, incorporating new sectors of the population—who consequently find themselves with enhanced influence—and perhaps discarding old allies. On the other hand, some authorities may respond to profound social dislocations by attempting to exclude from political influence formerly incorporated groups or by significantly elevating the costs of their incorporation. These dislocations may also place increasing strain on politically excluded groups. As disturbances redefine the inclusiveness of the political regime and activate ordinary people in new ways, political alignments are redrawn and the balance of power shifts. Acute shocks typically release ordinary folk from passivity, activating their grievances through new organizational structures and institutional avenues. In sum, one precondition for revolutionary situations consists of massive disruptions that break down routinized systems of social control. Subsequently, explosions of political protest may place regimes under great duress.

During the Arab Spring, people very rapidly poured into the streets, demanding the removal of repressive dictators.

What makes some social movements revolutionary?

Tunisians gather around a statue depicting the vegetable cart of Mohamed Bouazizi, who set himself on fire in December 2010 in an act of protest that triggered the so-called Arab Spring.

But most of these dictators—in Tunisia, Egypt, Libya, Yemen, and Syria—had been in power for decades. What was new was the economic crisis gripping the region. People were upset with rising food and fuel prices, and young people in particular could not find the kind of work for which they had been educated—or any work at all. It is telling that the Arab Spring began with protests in Tunisia in December 2010 which were a response to the self-immolation of an educated young man, Mohamed Bouazizi, who was trying to survive by selling vegetables from a cart. But Bouazizi did not have a proper permit for his cart, and he burned himself in protest (he later died in hospital) after a municipal official and her aids confiscated his cart and publicly humiliated him.

Fracturing the Foundations of a Regime

Profound social dislocations like mass unemployment may be necessary for the emergence of revolutionary situations, but they are clearly insufficient. Lenin identifies another indispensable condition for revolutionary situations: The shock must create a crisis or division among the upper classes, which in turn fractures the foundations of the government. Such divisions and the resulting political destabilization provide an opening that may itself magnify pressures from below and that newly mobilized people can exploit. Such a crisis typically occurs when the usual consensus over arrangements for settling the competing claims of the upper classes collapses, often as a result of wars or state-led efforts at economic modernization that generate growing fiscal pressures on elites. As agreement over how the costs of fiscal and institutional reform should be distributed disintegrates, the institutional coherence of the regime comes under enormous strain. The state's capacity to control and enforce its will upon the population within the territory it claims to govern may begin to contract and even collapse.

Upper-class disunity and state breakdown may follow two general scenarios. In the first, a crisis, such as a fiscal emergency provoked by international war, may generate instability as elites resist the burdens imposed by state officials. The ensuing crisis in the regime, involving the disintegration of state power and legitimacy, then serves to facilitate and exacerbate rebellion by ordinary people who are mobilizing through existing networks and organizations. This is the story of the French, Russian, and Chinese revolutions (Skocpol 1979). In the second scenario, the shock unleashes mounting and threatening pressure from below from a social movement or movements. No longer bound by the institutions of social control, this movement generates a crisis among the upper classes, who are pulled into opposing directions by the developing movement itself. One upper-class faction might prefer to repress the growing pressures from below, extracting more resources to cover fiscal gaps, clamping down on democratic rights, and generally resorting to coercion; another faction, by contrast, might prefer to enact reforms, resigning itself to accommodating popular demands in order to preserve its rule. In this scenario, were it not for the additional stress from social movements, the upper classes might converge on a unified and stabilizing response, preventing regime collapse. This is the story of the Cuban, Iranian, and Nicaraguan revolutions and of the Arab Spring. In either scenario, the cohesion of the police and armed forces is crucial for preventing the fall of the regime. If the costs of war, repression, or reform divide or weaken the military and undermine its ability to act in a unified and decisive manner against popular movements, then revolution becomes likely or even inevitable.

In short, the second condition listed by Lenin (and emphasized by political process theorists) involves elite division and institutional collapse, which either results from or results in a popular movement from below. In either event, the upper classes find it impossible to coexist in harmony under the existing regime. The revolutionary crisis intensifies as the actions of disaffected upper-class groups impair the efficacy of state institutions.

What causes revolutionary situations?

Revolutionary Movements and the Seizure of State Power

These two conditions, when combined, would seem to be sufficient to produce a revolutionary situation. If ordinary people are thrust into collective action because of the erosion of the regulatory capacity of key institutions, and upper-class divisions lead to a collapse in the state's infrastructural power, a powerful insurrection would seem likely. However, Lenin raises a third condition. The final ingredient that he has in mind is the *capacity* of a social movement to take advantage of the institutional shock and state collapse in order to place radical transformation on the national agenda. Simply stated, an existing regime is likely to weather a weakening of state institutions and pressures from below if the lower classes prove incapable of organizing into a radical social movement that can effectively topple it.

Consider the case of Morocco during the Arab Spring. Morocco is one of the poorest countries in North Africa and the Middle East—poorer than Tunisia and Egypt—and the vast majority of its people are struggling economically. But while there were some protests calling for political reforms in Morocco following the revolutions in Tunisia and Egypt, they were comparatively small and intermittent. As a result, Morocco's King Mohammed VI was easily able to hold onto power after enacting a few modest reforms.

Requirements for Organizing a Revolutionary Movement

For a strong revolutionary movement to take shape, two requirements must be met. First, ordinary folk must possess considerable collective leverage over the rich and powerful. This condition is met when ordinary people play important roles in crucial institutions—roles that are necessary or highly valued, which gives their threats of withdrawing their contributions to such institutions disruptive force. Important industries, for example, depend upon the labor of ordinary workers in order to function; when workers withdraw that labor during a strike, these industries shut down, and their owners cannot make profits. Thus, when the lower classes enjoy structural power rooted in their essential institutional roles, their capacity for generating costly disruptions is enhanced (Schwartz 1976). In the context of shock and crisis, elite vulnerability to such disruptions grows. The central point is that the institutional roles of the lower classes must translate into a capacity to undertake collective actions that challenge the power of the upper classes.

Most accounts of the Egyptian uprising in 2011 focus on the occupation of Tahrir Square in central Cairo by thousands of people. But the dictatorship of Hosni Mubarak may have been more shaken by the strikes and work stoppages that occurred during the occupation, culminating in a general strike in the days before Mubarak's resignation (Schwartz 2011). (A general strike occurs when workers in an entire city or country refuse to work, as opposed to workers in a single industry or factory.) The strikes hurt many businesses across the country—the tourist industry was already reeling from the loss of business caused by the political unrest—which may have convinced military officers (many of whom are also businessmen) that Mubarak had become a threat to their own interests. The military refused to disperse the protesters in Tahrir Square, urged Mubarak to resign, and took power for themselves.

A second requirement for what Lenin called "independent historical action" by the masses is the political and ideological resources necessary to convert increased political activity and leverage into decisive collective action. This means ideas, organization, and tactics as well as the ability of activists to obtain, process, produce, and deploy information among followers. Clearly, ideas and ideology play an important role in the origins and outcomes of revolutions. However, they do not operate as autonomous forces that drive the contenders in a revolutionary situation. After all, radical ideologies have existed and appealed to many people in most if not all modern societies. They have seldom, however, given rise to strong revolutionary movements, much less to revolutions.

Culture, broadly understood, matters in revolutionary situations when particular ideologies are able to shift the balance of forces, weakening authorities and upper classes. When social dislocations and state crises offer openings for radical social movements, the tactical decisions and framing work of activists can be decisive. When the strategies and ideologies promoted by radical activists resonate with ordinary people—that is, when "frame alignment" occurs—and when they are not only consistent with but also promote increased popular mobilization, thereby maximizing its disruptive impact, they can be the final necessary ingredient that provides such mobilization with the capacity to overthrow a regime. In fact, Lenin ended his famous statement on revolutionary situations with an important qualification: "Not every revolutionary situation," he explained, "gives rise to a revolution; revolution arises only out of a situation in which the above-mentioned objective changes are accompanied by a subjective change, namely, the ability of the revolutionary class to take revolutionary mass action strong enough to break (or dislocate) the old government, which never, not even in a period of crisis, 'falls', if it is not toppled over" (Lenin 1915:213). Revolutions, in other words, are only possible when there are strong social movements that can topple governments in deep crisis.

Political Environments that Encourage Revolutionary Movements

Revolutionary situations are much more likely to arise in authoritarian and repressive political contexts than in democratic and liberal ones. In fact, no popular revolutionary movement has ever overthrown

Vladimir Lenin (1870–1924), shown here in October 1917, was not only the most famous leader of the Russian Revolution but also studied and wrote about revolutions more generally. What did he consider the main causes of revolution?

a long-consolidated democratic regime. The great social revolutions of the twentieth century, for example, toppled kings and dictators (as in Russia, China, Cuba, Iran, and Nicaragua), extremely repressive colonial regimes (as in Vietnam and Algeria), and the Soviet-imposed single-party regimes of Eastern Europe. But none overthrew a regime that even remotely resembled a democracy. In fact, revolutionary movements tend to prosper when governments sponsor or defend—with violence when necessary—economic and social arrangements that are widely regarded as unjust. In certain societies, economic and social arrangements may be widely viewed as unjust (i.e., as not simply unfortunate or inevitable), yet unless state officials are seen to sponsor or protect those arrangements—through legal codes, taxation, conscription, and, ultimately, force—revolutionary movements aimed at overthrowing the state are unlikely to become strong. People may blame their social "superiors" or employers for their plight, for example, or even whole classes of such elites, yet the government itself may not be challenged unless there exists a widely shared perception that it will stand behind and defend those elites at all costs.

Indiscriminate, but not overwhelming, violence by weak states against social movements and oppositional politicians and activists unintentionally helps revolutionaries. For reasons of simple self-defense, people who are targeted by the state may join clandestine groups or even arm themselves. People whose families or friends have been victimized by the state may also join or support revolutionary movements in order to seek revenge against the perpetrators. Social movements and political parties have generally turned to disruptive strategies, including armed struggle, only after their previous efforts to secure change through legal means were violently repressed. Under repressive conditions, ordinary people often view mass disruption, including armed struggle, as a legitimate and reasonable means of political contestation.

Authoritarian and repressive states, in sum, unintentionally facilitate the development of revolutionary social movements by generating or reinforcing popular grievances, contributing to widespread feelings of moral outrage, focusing those feelings on the government (or dictator), foreclosing possibilities for peaceful reform, enhancing the plausibility and legitimacy of revolutionary ideologies, and (often) compelling people to employ disruptive and even violent strategies in order to defend themselves and to pursue effectively their collective interests and ideals.

The connection between repressive authoritarianism and revolution is clearly illustrated by the Arab Spring of 2011. The six countries that experienced broad popular uprisings—Tunisia, Egypt, Libya, Bahrain, Yemen, and Syria—are dissimilar in many ways. These countries have different levels of economic development and urbanization; some are ethnically divided, others more homogenous; some have been very close allies of Western powers, others not. But what they all had in common were longstanding dictators (or a monarch, in the case of Bahrain) who would not tolerate threats to their continued rule. Their violence and intransigence forced their political opponents to give up their dreams of incremental reforms and take to the streets. Only disruptive mass movements, most concluded, could bring an end to the reign of these autocrats. And of course they were right. Mass protests in Tunisia and Egypt convinced the armed forces in those countries to abandon their support for dictators. In Libya, Yemen, and Syria, mass protest led to divisions in and defections from the armed forces, resulting in much bloodier conflicts. Only the king in Bahrain has managed to retain the solid support of his military forces—supplemented by troops from neighboring Saudi Arabia—in the face of a broad popular uprising.

How does democracy shape social conflict?

Democracy and Social Conflict   By contrast with authoritarian regimes, more liberal and democratic governments tend to pacify and institutionalize, but hardly do away with, class and other forms of social conflict. Elections have been aptly described as a "democratic translation of the class struggle." Democracy channels a variety of social conflicts—including, but not limited to, class conflicts—into party competition for votes and the lobbying of representatives by interest groups. The temptation to rebel against the government, which is rarely seized without trepidation under any circumstances, is generally quelled under democratic regimes by the knowledge that new elections are but a few years off, and with them the chance to cast out unpopular rulers. In addition, democracies have generally provided a context in which social movements can win concessions from economic and political elites, although this often requires a good deal of disruption. But movements that aim at overthrowing elected governments rarely win much popular support unless such governments (or the armies that they command) effectively push people into rebellion by indiscriminately repressing protesters. By and large, however, the ballot box has been the coffin of revolutionaries. This explains why there have been so few large-scale attempts to overthrow long-established democracies in Western Europe and North America.

This does not mean that political radicalism and militancy go unrewarded in democratic societies. Democracy, to repeat, by no means eliminates social conflict; in fact, in many ways democracy encourages a flowering of social conflict by providing the political space within which those groups outside ruling circles can make claims on political authorities and economic elites. Not just political parties, then, but a whole range of social movements, trade unions, interest groups, and professional associations can become the organizational vehicles of political life in democratic polities. These institutions of civil society, however, are generally just that—civil. Their repertoires of contention include electoral campaigns, lobbying, strikes, boycotts, demonstrations, and civil disobedience—forms of collective action that may be quite disruptive and undertaken for quite radical ends but that are not aimed at bringing down the government.

Democracy, then, dramatically reduces the likelihood of revolutionary change, but not because it brings about social justice. Formal democracy is fully compatible with widespread poverty, inequality, and popular grievances of all sorts. This is why movements for social justice so often arise in democratic contexts. But, again, these movements almost always view the state as an instrument to be pressured and influenced, not as something to be seized or smashed. Revolutionary movements, for their part, develop not simply because people are angry or aggrieved but because the government under which they live provides no other mechanisms for social change, violently repressing those who peacefully seek incremental reforms. This said, the spread of democracy will not necessarily render revolution *passé* as a form of political struggle. Radical leaders and parties have sometimes been able to amass a broad following in democratic contexts and to win elections (for example, Salvador Allende in Chile in 1970, and Hugo Chavez in Venezuela in 1998, 2000, and 2006). Perhaps during the twenty-first century we will see some democratically elected governments attempt to revolutionize economic and political institutions. As yet, however, the democratic route to revolution has never been successfully traveled.

TABLE 17.4 WHAT DO AMERICANS THINK ABOUT THE RICH AND ABOUT CLASS CONFLICT?

77 percent think there's too much power in the hands of a few rich people and large corporations.
19 percent disagree.
76 percent think there is a wider gap between the rich and middle class compared to 10 years ago.
16 percent think the gap is narrower.
46 percent think rich people are wealthy because they know the right people or were born into wealthy families.
43 percent think rich people are wealthy because of their own hard work, ambition, or education.
66 percent think there are strong or very strong conflicts between rich and poor.
30 percent think there are no or not very strong conflicts between rich and poor.
71 percent of people between 18 and 34 think there are strong or very strong conflicts between rich and poor.
55 percent of people over 65 there are strong or very strong conflicts between rich and poor.

Sources: Based on data from Pew Research Center (2011); Teixeira (2012); Morin (2012).

CONCLUSION THE FUTURE OF MOVEMENTS AND REVOLUTIONS

We began this chapter by looking at the Occupy Wall Street movement. Like other social movements, the Occupy movement did not emerge spontaneously but grew out of the planned actions of preexisting networks of activists. The movement's tactics were not spontaneous either. Activists in the Occupy movement, like activists before them, chose tactics with which they were already familiar. The tactic of occupying public spaces was inspired by the occupation of Tahrir Square during the revolution in Egypt earlier in the year. And the movement spread rapidly across the country, like movements before it, because it framed its ideas about inequality and the power of banks and corporations in a way that appealed to a great many people during a time of economic crisis. There were also networks of activists in cities and towns across the country, most of whom had been active in previous movements, who could spread the movement's ideas and organize occupations of their own. None of this would surprise sociologists who have studied past movements.

What about the future of the Occupy movement? Police repression—expelling the occupiers from public spaces—has undoubtedly weakened the movement by reducing its visibility. But many people remain active in the movement's "working groups" and other informal networks. By the time you read this, the movement may have declined or disappeared, grown even larger, or transformed itself into a movement (or set of movements) with a different name and focus. Much will depend on whether the movement is able to discover or innovate upon tactics that will energize and unite its followers, including fresh recruits, and win concessions from the rich and powerful. If the movement continues to talk about the power of the wealthy "1 percent" but is unable to do anything about it, participants will likely tire of the movement and move on (see Table 17.4). Because the United States is a liberal democracy, we can predict with some certainty that there is very little chance that the Occupy movement will become a revolutionary movement. The movement will also find it very difficult—should it try—to convince a great many people that the U.S. government should be overthrown, violently or nonviolently, although it may convince many people (and probably already has) that the government has been corrupted by money. This could lay the foundation for another anti-corporate movement (or movements) in the future.

We will undoubtedly see many more social movements and revolutions in the years ahead. As long as ordinary people feel that the rich and powerful are oppressing them (or at least ignoring their needs and interests), and as long as people can safely connect with one another and find ways to pressure (or overthrow) the rich and powerful, movements and revolutions will remain part of the human condition.

Watch the **Video** in **MySocLab**
Applying Your Sociological Imagination

What Are Social Movements? *(p. 477)*

👁 **Watch** the **Big Question Video** in MySocLab to review the key concepts for this section.

We began this chapter by defining social movements and exploring what we can learn by studying them.

STUDYING SOCIAL MOVEMENTS (p. 477)

Politics, Human Action, and Social Change (p. 478)

- **What can movements teach us about social life?**

Moral Sensibilities (p. 478)

Understanding Social Movements Today (p. 478)

- **What aspects of movements are contemporary sociologists interested in?**

KEY TERMS

riot *(p. 477)*

social movement *(p. 477)*

fad *(p. 477)*

political process perspective *(p. 479)*

Why Do Movements Emerge, and Who Joins Them? *(p. 480)*

👁 **Watch** the **Big Question Video** in MySocLab to review the key concepts for this section.

The most frequently asked question about social movements is why they emerge when they do. In this section we examined how movements take shape and looked at who joins or supports social movements.

MOVEMENT ORIGINS AND RECRUITMENT (p. 480)

How Movements Take Shape (p. 480)

- **What factors explain why movements emerge when and where they do?**

Recruitment: Joining or Supporting Movements (p. 483)

- **How do movements recruit supporters?**

⊙ **Explore** the **Data** on The Occupy Wall Street Movement in MySocLab

KEY TERMS

resource mobilization approach *(p. 480)*

social movement organization *(SMO)* *(p. 480)*

social network *(p. 481)*

biographical availability *(p. 483)*

framing *(p. 484)*

collective identity *(p. 484)*

moral shock *(p. 486)*

3 What Do Movements Accomplish? *(p. 487)*

Watch the **Big Question Video** in **MySocLab** to review the key concepts for this section.

Why do movements use certain tactics and not others? Why do movements decline or disappear? In this section we examined what movements do and what changes and outcomes movements bring about, including unintended consequences.

MOVEMENT TACTICS AND OUTCOMES (p. 487)

The Strategies and Tactics of Movements (p. 487)

● **Why do movements use certain tactics and not others?**

The Decline and Disappearance of Movements (p. 490)

● **Why do movements decline or disappear?**

Explore A Sociological Perspective: Will the labor movement revive? in **MySocLab**

Read the **Document** *The Rise and Fall of Aryan Nations* in **MySocLab.** In this reading, Robert Balch uses participant observation and interviews to study Aryan Nations, an Idaho-based white separatist movement that disintegrated in 2000.

Outcomes (p. 493)

● **How can we measure a movement's success or achievements?**

4 What Are Revolutions, and Why Do They Occur? *(p. 496)*

Watch the **Big Question Video** in **MySocLab** to review the key concepts for this section.

This section explored why some social movements are revolutionary and what causes revolutionary situations to occur. When and why have revolutionary movements been able to take state power? We concluded the chapter by examining how democracy shapes social conflict and the prospects for revolution.

UNDERSTANDING REVOLUTIONS (p. 496)

Defining "Revolution" (p. 496)

● **What makes some social movements revolutionary?**

Revolutions, Violence, and Other Forms of Conflict (p. 497)

Revolutionary Situations (p. 498)

● **What causes revolutionary situations?**

Revolutionary Movements and the Seizure of State Power (p. 500)

● **How does democracy shape social conflict?**

Watch the **Video** Applying Your Sociological Imagination in **MySocLab** to see these concepts at work in the real world

KEY TERMS

revolution *(p. 496)*

revolutionary movement *(p. 497)*

revolutionary situation *(p. 498)*

18
ENVIRONMENTAL SOCIOLOGY

((• **Listen** to the **Chapter Audio** in **MySocLab**

by COLIN JEROLMACK

In the remote and rugged region of northwestern Alaska, on a small island separated from the coast by five miles of choppy Arctic waters, lies the village of Shishmaref. While its nearly 600 indigenous Inupiat inhabitants enjoy some of the conveniences of modern living such as television and snowmobiles, they maintain a traditional lifestyle in which they obtain the necessities of life through hunting, fishing, and barter. For centuries, the Inupiat of Shishmaref and the mainland have developed and relied upon a vast stock of knowledge about animal migration patterns, ocean currents, and seasonal variations in ice thickness in order to persevere in such an unforgiving climate. However, in recent years their environment has changed in rapid and threatening ways. Since 1979, more than 20 percent of the polar ice cap has melted as a result of rising global temperatures, and scientists project that summer Arctic sea ice could disappear entirely by 2030. The Inupiat fear that their livelihoods, their villages, and their culture will vanish along with the glaciers.

These days, the sea surrounding Shishmaref freezes later and thaws earlier than ever before. With the decrease in sea ice, which forms a protective barrier around the island, Shishmaref has become vulnerable to storm surges. Large waves eat away 10 miles of the coast every year and literally pull houses out to sea. Lacking the resources to fortify the island perimeter, villagers recently voted to abandon their homes and relocate to the mainland. Many residents worry about the loss of their community and way of life, and

MY SOCIOLOGICAL IMAGINATION
Colin Jerolmack

As a beginning graduate student interested in city life, I spent a lot of time wandering around the streets of New York's Greenwich Village. I was particularly drawn to neighborhood parks that were undergoing renovations because the process of deciding how to redesign the parks afforded a window into how community members used, imagined, and complained about their public spaces. I was surprised to learn that many civic associations and park users complained about pigeons, whose feces made park benches unusable and posed a potential disease threat. However, in observing public behavior I saw that pigeon feeding was a popular activity among park visitors. I realized that urban wildlife impacted how people interpreted and experienced their public spaces, for better and for worse. Over time, I became fascinated by the ways that the natural environment shapes city life, and I came to see that people's responses to urban wildlife revealed how they draw boundaries between environment and society. Because of the humble pigeon, I developed a passion for environmental sociology without even leaving the metropolis.

The coast of northwestern Alaska is crumbling into the sea as global warming melts the frozen earth that glues the landscape together. Shown here, a home destroyed by beach erosion tips over in the Alaskan village of Shishmaref.

Watch the Video in **MySocLab**
Inspiring Your Sociological Imagination

the state government worries about who will pay the estimated $200 million cost of building a new village and moving all the residents.

In 2009, I traveled to northwestern Alaska to study the consequences of climate change for indigenous people. My guide was Caleb Pungowiyi, a resident of the town of Kotzebue and a senior advisor to Oceana, a nonprofit ocean conservation organization. Caleb did not need to look at the annual reports on sea ice retreat to determine that exceptional global warming is occurring—he could look to his backyard. Hunting expeditions, and travel in general, have been curtailed because snowmobiles are falling through ice that once was rock solid. Hotter, drier summers are leading to a rash of brush fires. Permafrost—the eternally frozen earth under the tundra that holds the landscape together— is melting, leading to coastal erosion, landslides, and sinkholes that are destabilizing towns and swallowing up houses. As animals such as caribou and bearded seals adjust their migration and mating habits in response to warming temperatures, hunting becomes a less reliable means of securing food.

Given the high cost of groceries that must be flown in from Anchorage and the lack of steady jobs, indigenous Alaskans are caught in a double bind: their traditional lifestyle may soon cease to be viable, but there are few feasible alternatives. The future of this region likely holds many more scenarios like Shishmaref—impoverished and politically marginalized

communities forced to abandon their ancestral homes and many of their customs in the face of global warming.

Though the evidence for climate change may not be obvious in places like New York City, in the extreme conditions of the Arctic the signs of global warming are clearly recognizable. While scientists compile records to demonstrate that the changes occurring in Alaska and elsewhere are unprecedented, the Inupiat already know this to be true because of the unprecedented challenges they face on a daily basis as they struggle to secure their existence.

The plight of indigenous Alaskans introduces us to the core concern of **environmental sociology**: understanding the ways that society simultaneously shapes and is shaped by the physical environment (Catton and Dunlap 1980). While their traditional lifestyle and culture were forged as adaptations to their natural world, the contemporary environmental crisis that threatens to overwhelm the Inupiat has social origins. There is now a virtual consensus in mainstream environmental science that much of the global warming we are witnessing is the result of burning fossil fuels. Environmental problems, then, have both societal causes and social consequences. There is another sense in which the predicament of the Inupiat is emblematic: indigenous groups, minorities, and the poor have historically suffered the most from environmental degradation. The costs of environmental problems are unevenly distributed, reflecting and reproducing social inequality.

Environmental problems have both societal causes and social consequences.

Can you think of other ways that warmer temperatures will affect the environment?

THE BIG QUESTIONS

👁 **Watch** the **Big Question Videos** in **MySocLab**

The Alaskan case touches on a number of important questions that the field of environmental sociology seeks to address.

1 **How does social life relate to the natural environment?** Environmental sociologists study the *interaction* between environmental facts and social facts and emphasize their interdependency (Freudenberg and Gramling 1989). Every society consumes and transforms the natural environment to satisfy its needs and desires, yet every society must also adapt to its physical surroundings and confront natural limits. And, while there is an objective natural world "out there," how we interpret and interact with it are always influenced by cultural, political, and economic processes.

How has human activity harmed the environment? The most pressing environmental problems of our time—such as deforestation, water pollution, and global warming—are the result of human activities. Finding solutions to these problems will require collective social action, and making those solutions equitable may prove to be the biggest challenge of all.

2

3 **How do environmental factors impact inequality?** Consider the devastating natural disaster Hurricane Katrina, which overwhelmed New Orleans' man-made levees in 2005, killing 2,000 people and displacing over 1 million more. As the storm menaced the Gulf Coast, wealthier residents were able to evacuate because they had automobiles and the finances to pay for hotel rooms. The poorest residents—many of whom were black—did not have the means to get out and became stranded in their homes as the water rose. As a result, they were disproportionately represented in the storm's death toll. When sociologists examine environmental catastrophes like Katrina, they ask: how does the structure of society shape the effects of these natural events?

How can we create more sustainable societies? As the global population expands and environmental degradation worsens, it seems that there are simply not enough natural resources for every human being on the face of the earth to use as much oil and electricity, and dispose of as much waste, as citizens of wealthy nations. How can members of rich countries be convinced to adopt more sustainable lifestyles? And how can we balance the dire need to enact international environmental regulations with the aspiration of developing countries to follow in the

4

1   How Does Social Life Relate to the Natural Environment?

UNDERSTANDING ENVIRONMENT-SOCIETY RELATIONS

Watch the **Big Question** Video in **MySocLab**

Many social transformations have accompanied the transition of societies from traditional to modern forms: capitalism supplanted feudalism; people migrated from small villages to large cities; the division of labor intensified; close-knit communities gave way to mass societies characterized by impersonal and contractual ties; and so on. Yet as societies went through these dramatic social changes, their relationship to the physical environment was also rapidly transformed. In fact, many social theorists have concluded that the transition of societies from traditional to modern forms was, to a large degree, driven by the development of technology that enabled the greater exploitation of natural resources. Environmental sociologists see the relationship between environment and society as dynamic and interdependent, and they seek to understand how this relationship varies over time and across social contexts.

☐ Traditional Societies

The term *primitive,* though sometimes considered to have a negative meaning, can be usefully employed to think about how traditional societies have typically interacted with their environment. *Primitive* evokes the image of a preindustrial society in which people live close to the land, build simple homes out of natural materials, rely on their feet for transportation, hunt and gather, make only superficial changes to the environment, and consider nature to be sacred.

The field of anthropology was born over a century ago out of the study of preindustrial societies. As Western powers colonized far-flung regions of Africa and Latin America, they encountered people who lived much like the imaginary "primitive" society described above. Anthropologists lived among these strangers in order to understand their cultures and lifestyles. Here were people, it seemed, virtually untouched by the forces of modernization. And here were societies characterized by a lack of control over, and a dependence on, nature. These environment-society relations structured their cultural and religious systems.

The anthropologist Bronislaw Malinowski (1948) spent the years surrounding the First World War observing native culture in the Trobriand Islands of the Western Pacific. He noticed that the islanders performed elaborate ceremonial rites before they set out on fishing expeditions in the ocean but that such rituals were entirely absent from their fishing trips in the lagoon. The reason for this difference was simple. Fish were plentiful in the lagoon, and the waters were calm. Thus, islanders could predict that fishing would be safe and produce a high yield. The yields from ocean fishing were far less predictable, and such trips could be treacherous. Facing a situation that was out of their control, they resorted to magic to try to bring a sense of order and predictability to the natural world. This finding explained many of the systems of magic that anthropologists found in traditional cultures, and it helped explain the relative absence of these systems in modern societies, which tame nature through the application of science.

In Papua New Guinea, indigenous societies were traditionally organized into clans that each adopted a particular animal as the sacred symbol—or totem—of the group. We can find traces of totemism in "modern" societies as well, such as when sports teams use an animal as their mascot and group name.

Social scientists noted another common feature of traditional societies—they often attributed spiritual significance to nature. Emile Durkheim, one of the founders of sociology, produced one of the most well-known explanations of "primitive" religion based on his study of Aboriginal tribes in Australia. He noted that these tribes were organized into clans based on spiritual rather than blood kinship, with each clan adopting a particular plant or animal—called a totem—as the symbol of the clan. Clans considered their totem plants or animals to be sacred, and so killing and consuming them was generally taboo. Clans inscribed ceremonial objects with the emblem of their totem, which made these objects sacred as well. This belief system, called **totemism**, was common among many indigenous groups—including American Indians.

Durkheim realized that it was only once plants or animals became a symbol of the clan that they were elevated to the status of sacred. He took this as evidence that the Aborigines did not actually consider nature to be divine. Rather, the totem was sacred because it stood for the clan. Durkheim did not think that the Aborigines were as different from modern societies as they first appeared. Every society has its sacred objects and rituals that help bring together its members as a community. Americans, for instance, salute the flag and play the national anthem before sporting events. "Primitive" people chose animals and plants as their sacred objects, Durkheim believed, simply because their lifestyles were intimately connected to nature (Durkheim 1915).

☐ Modern Societies

As natural forces came to be more understandable and predictable through the accumulation of scientific knowledge, the environment became a safer, more useful, and more urban place. Humans ceased to be the playthings of nature, applying technology to exert greater control over their surroundings. The first step in this process was the agricultural revolution. Through animal and plant domestication and the invention of the plow, tangled forests gave way to manicured fields. Irrigation channels reduced humans' dependency on

rainfall. Permanent settlements sprang up, trade intensified, and roads were developed.

The next great technological leap was the Industrial Revolution, ushered in by the invention of the steam engine. While the Industrial Revolution gave rise to modern capitalism, it was—as Karl Marx and Friedrich Engels (1932) observed—founded on the "subjection of nature's forces to man." Entire forests were destroyed for their lumber, mountains were leveled to expose coal seams, holes were punched deep into the earth's surface to extract oil, rivers were dammed and rerouted, fields were smothered in cement, and smokestacks blackened daylight skies. We used technology to alter our environment in seemingly miraculous ways: Projects such as the diversion of the Colorado River westward through almost 300 miles of tunnels, dams, and aqueducts made possible the transformation of a bone-dry desert into the expansive metropolis of Los Angeles; and the city of Chicago even succeeded in permanently reversing the directional flow of its river so that sewage and industrial toxins were carried away from the city. The Industrial Revolution hastened urbanization. Cities became the centers of industry, and the advent of trains and highways allowed people to fill in the countryside with sprawling suburbs.

Marx and Engels argued that that "the whole internal structure" of a society, including the "nature of individuals," was dependent on the extent to which its members could harness technology to transform natural resources into social goods (Marx and Engels [1932] 1977:161). The lack of productive technology of early hunter-gatherer societies, they believed, kept the social structure of these groups very simple. There was little division of labor—perhaps just one chief who had authority over everyone else—because almost

How do modern societies differ from traditional ones in their relationships to the physical environment?

Modern science and the Industrial Revolution drained the natural world of magic and reduced nature to a commodity. But how do we determine the value of clean air or a pristine landscape?

all of the members of a tribe had to busy themselves with looking for food sources. Because everybody performed the same tasks, there was little individuality. Once humans began to transform vast stretches of forests into fields through agriculture, a more complex social structure could develop. A division of labor emerged because it only took a fraction of a society's members to produce enough food for everyone. Other members could be enlisted to produce tools or serve as warriors. An elite class also began to take shape as those who owned the agricultural food surpluses—and the land—could translate these resources into economic power.

As societies moved from agriculture to the production of goods, made possible on a grand scale by the technological advances of the Industrial Revolution, their social structure became even more stratified. A sophisticated division of labor emerged as peasants migrated to cities to work for a wage and factory owners maximized efficiency by dividing up the job of a single skilled craftsman into discrete tasks that could be carried out by a team of relatively unskilled workers.

Marx and Engels's thesis leaves us with a puzzle: Why did some societies develop more quickly than others? Why, for example, did the Industrial Revolution take place in Western Europe and not Southern Africa? Jared Diamond, a professor of geography, argues that global inequalities emerged in prehistoric times and are rooted in differences in people's environments—namely, geographic differences in the availability of naturally occurring food sources (Diamond 1997).

Diamond provides a compelling illustration of his thesis. A thousand years ago, the favorable climate of present-day New Zealand enabled a group of Polynesian settlers known as the Maori to develop a thriving agricultural society. At one point, a group of Maori moved to the Chatham Islands. For hundreds of years, this society—which became known as the Moriori—remained isolated from the Maori on the mainland. But because the Chatham Islands did not support the tropical crops that the Moriori brought with them, they reverted back to the hunting-and-gathering lifestyle of their preagricultural ancestors. Because natural resources were so scarce, the Moriori remained a small society with little division of labor. Meanwhile, the Maori continued to improve their agricultural technology so that they could support

many people. Population density and resource abundance spawned a division of labor: a stratum (or segment of society) of craft- and tool-making specialists, a group of political leaders, and a warrior class. Over time, the Maori invaded and conquered other societies and acquired new technologies from them, such as guns. Everything came around full circle in 1835, when the Maori arrived in the Chatham Islands with axes, guns, and other weapons. Finding a tiny, peaceable society with simple technology and a rudimentary political system, the Maori slaughtered and enslaved the Moriori with ease.

Though cut from the same cloth, in the intervening centuries the Maori and Moriori developed in different directions based on adaptations to their environment. Diamond contends that the societies around the globe that developed the fastest were those graced with an abundance of plants and animals that could be readily domesticated. Many parts of Europe and Asia (particularly western Asia in the region known as the Fertile Crescent) naturally possessed many of the large mammals that could be domesticated—horses, pigs, cows, and sheep—as well as many of the cereals and grains that would become the backbone of agriculture, such as wheat. As these societies flourished and modernized, they settled new places, conquered the locals, and brought their technology, animals, and crops with them. This is the modern history of the Americas, whose relatively resource-deprived and preindustrial indigenous societies met their demise at the hands of technologically advanced invaders from Europe.

We've come a long way from the world of rain dances and enchanted forests. As Max Weber famously observed, the cold, hard rationality of science and economics drained the natural world of magic and mysticism. Modern societies primarily view the environment as a source of natural resources. And their success at taming and exploiting it encourages cultural attitudes of humans as separate from, and superior to, the natural world—a belief called **anthropocentrism** (literally, "man in the middle").

☐ The Environment-Society Dialogue

Marx, Engels, and Diamond are sometimes labeled **determinists** because their theories imply that a society's environment, or the technology that it has developed to exploit its environment, determines everything else—from its social structure to individuals' thoughts. But it is perhaps more appropriate to say that they view material conditions as the most fruitful *starting point* for understanding the development of society. Marx and Engels's conception of social change is in fact rooted in the assumption that there is a reciprocal relationship between environmental and social conditions. The transition from an agricultural to a capitalistic mode of production, for example, was realized through social revolutions that reorganized society around commodity production.

Though many scholars reject the argument that the environment is the most important determinant of social structure, the notion that the environment guides and constrains social life has become an important part of sociological thought. For example, in the early 1900s an influential group of sociologists at the University of Chicago turned to **ecology**—the branch of science that studies the relationship between organisms and their environment—to explain the physical and social organization of modern cities. They examined how natural landscape features like rivers served as both resources and barriers that dictated where industries were placed and how city streets were laid out. Further, these Chicago sociologists saw the city as the "natural habitat of civilized man," in which various sections of the city were akin to ecological niches (Park and Burgess 1925:2). Human behavior, it was believed, could be largely understood as social adaptations to a particular urban area: Ethnic and neighborhood conflict was rooted in competition for scarce resources, such as jobs, and deviance was largely a product of living in derelict slums—not individual pathology. Urban sociologists continue to explore the ways that the built environment shapes behavior and social outcomes, such as important recent studies on the effect that one's neighborhood has on his or her chances for upward mobility.

Beliefs, values, and ideas also play an important role in guiding environment-society relations. For instance, there is evidence that the Europeans who settled the Americas committed wanton environmental destruction, slaughtering wildlife and burning forests in excess of their material needs, because they viewed the untamed wilderness as alien and literally God-forsaken. They aimed to reproduce the "civilized" pastoral landscapes of their beloved European countryside (Taylor 1998). Historian William Cronon points out that the rapid development of Chicago, which transformed from prairieland to a teeming metropolis in only a few decades, cannot be explained by environmental factors alone. Despite the fact that other emerging cities such as St. Louis arguably boasted more natural advantages and were situated closer to existing markets and settlements, "boosters" successfully sold the promise of a great city to speculators on the East Coast who bought up prairie lots that they had never seen. These investments, in turn, actually brought the dream of the Midwestern metropolis to life (Cronon 1992).

How does the environment shape behavior and social outcomes?

Why do different people interpret the environment differently? The value that a person places on the Amazon rainforest, for example, depends on his or her position in society: The multinational lumber company sees a profitable commodity to be harvested, environmentalists see a priceless natural sanctuary to be left untouched, and the few remaining indigenous communities see a home that enables their physical and spiritual well-being. The profit-seekers' orientation encourages them to cut down the forest, while

Environmentalists rejoiced at the reintroduction of the endangered grey wolf to Yellowstone Park, but many local farmers viewed the event as a threat to their community and lifestyle. What are other examples of how social contexts shape the way that people interpret nature?

the preservationists' orientation encourages them to protect it against any human incursion. Where do these differing orientations come from? The answer, many sociologists argue, can be found by studying the social contexts in which environment-society interactions are embedded. Research shows, for example, that people's socioeconomic status and political orientation strongly condition whether or not they believe scientific claims about climate change or whether they consider human-induced ecological disruptions to be a problem at all (Taylor and Buttel 1992).

To get a handle on how social contexts shape people's interactions with the environment, sociologist Rik Scarce documented the conflict that erupted over the reintroduction of the grey wolf into Yellowstone Park. In sociological terms, he was interested in the **social construction** of the environment—the process by which the natural world was interpreted and made meaningful to people who lived in the vicinity of the park. In an era that celebrates the restoration of ecosystems to their original state, the return of once-endangered grey wolves was a feel-good story to many people. But Scarce found that local farmers had a different view. One concern was economic: Wolves would eat their livestock. But their animosity toward the wolves ran deeper. For years, farmers felt that their community was slowly being undermined by the growing presence of wealthy neighbors who valued the area only for its wilderness and did not involve themselves in local life. This feeling led farmers to interpret the reintroduction of grey wolves as a misguided effort by "outsiders" to impose their will on the local community (Scarce 2005). People's attitudes toward ecological restoration in Yellowstone were patterned by their social position in society, revealing how our relationships with nature reflect who we are and what we value (Greider and Garkovich 1994). We interact with the environment, then, not just in a material sense—but also in a profoundly social sense (Bell 1994).

2 How Has Human Activity Harmed the Environment?

CONTEMPORARY ENVIRONMENTAL PROBLEMS

Watch the Big Question Video in **MySocLab**

If our relationships with nature reflect who we are, then it may be time to take a long, hard look in the mirror. In pursuit of material comfort and profit, individuals and corporations have irreparably damaged the oceans and surface of the Earth and destabilized its natural equilibrium. The end of the last ice age over 10,000 years ago ushered in an era of natural global warming known as the Holocene. But in just 200 years we have sped up the process of global warming so much, and altered the Earth's topography and chemistry so dramatically, that we seem to have pushed the Earth into a new geologic era. Fittingly, geologists propose to call this era Anthropocene (Zalasiewicz et al. 2010). Given the social and economic origins of so many contemporary environmental problems, it is appropriate that sociologists are increasingly turning their attention to an area of study that was once thought to be the exclusive domain of the natural sciences.

Global Warming

In 1958, the chemist Charles David Keeling began monitoring the levels of carbon dioxide (CO_2) in the atmosphere. The results were startling. Each year evidenced a greater concentration of CO_2 than the last, and the escalation corresponded with global increases in the burning of **fossil fuels**, which are energy sources such as coal, oil, and natural gas that are made of fossils that decomposed over millions of years under high pressure. Though the concentration of atmospheric CO_2 held steady for thousands of years, over the last 50 years it has increased by 20 percent. CO_2 emissions can linger in the atmosphere for a century and produce what is called the **greenhouse effect** by allowing the sun's heat to pass through to the Earth's surface while stopping it from spreading back into space. As a result, the Earth's average temperature continues to rise. This is called **global warming**. To be sure, experts debate the precise degree to which CO_2 emissions contribute to global warming, but there is now wide agreement in the mainstream scientific community that human activity is the primary culprit.

Climatologist Michael Mann and his colleagues have demonstrated that global temperatures were more or less constant over the past one thousand years and that the spike in global temperatures over the past half-century maps onto the spike in atmospheric CO_2 (see Figure 18.1). The Intergovernmental Panel on Climate Change estimates that Earth's global surface temperature increased about 1.5°F over the twentieth century, and it estimates an increase of 7.2°F this century. While some skeptics point to the occasional April snowstorm or an unusually harsh winter as evidence that global warming is not happening, such an argument confuses short-term weather events with long-term climate trends. The long-term warming trend is unmistakable, and it is unequal to anything human history has witnessed.

While a growing number of automobiles, planes, and factories are producing ever-greater carbon emissions, deforestation is crippling the Earth's natural ability to absorb CO_2. Sea ice in the Arctic is melting so quickly that it may only be a few decades until the Arctic Sea is devoid of ice in the summer; and the thickness of wintertime sea ice may thin from 12 feet to less than 3 feet (Kolbert 2007). Because the ocean absorbs more heat than does ice (which deflects light), sea ice retreat hastens the warming of the ocean, which in turn speeds up the melting of the ice floating on its surface. As a result of melting mountaintop glaciers, and because water expands as it warms, the sea level is rising. The small island nation of the Maldives, whose highest point is only 6 feet above sea level, is already contending with the effects of sea level rise. The ocean is advancing over the rims of its islands and may eventually cover them entirely. The nation's president held an underwater cabinet meeting to draw attention to its plight, and he even considered purchasing land in other countries in case the entire nation is forced to abandon its homeland.

The sea level is predicted to rise anywhere from several inches to several feet this century, depending on the extent to which nations act to limit carbon emissions. Assuming a "business-as-usual" scenario, meaning that companies and industries are allowed to continue environmentally harmful production practices in the pursuit of profit maximization, millions of people could be displaced, and some coastal cities like New Orleans might need to be abandoned, while many others would have to build massive levees. Global warming also means that millions of farmable acres around the world may become arid and useless. While this would

FIGURE 18.1 RISING RATES OF ATMOSPHERIC CO₂ AND GLOBAL TEMPERATURES

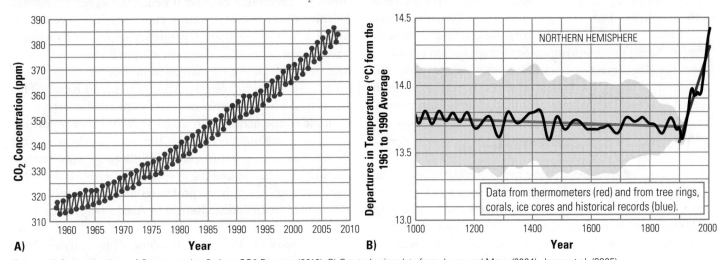

Source: A) Scripps Institute of Oceanography: Scripps CO2 Program (2012); B) Created using data from Jones and Mann (2004); Jones et al. (2005).

The Maldives, a small island nation, may soon be completely underwater as melting glaciers and warming ocean temperatures make the sea level rise. Some climatologists predict tens of millions of global "environmental refugees" in the coming decades as more coastline is swallowed by the sea.

directly threaten critical food sources, it would also alter the earth's ecosystems so dramatically that many plant and animal species would be unable to adapt. While polar bears have become the poster child for animal endangerment due to global warming, scientists predict that as many as 20 to 50 percent of all animal species may become extinct over the next 100 years because of rising temperatures (Kolbert 2007). Of course, some species would thrive in warmer weather—we can expect mosquitoes to expand their habitat, introducing malaria to new locales.

The notion of global warming does not fully capture the complexity of how carbon emissions impact the earth's climate. Global warming upsets the balance of ecosystems to such a degree that they become destabilized. Some regions of the planet may even become temporarily cooler because of the disruption of oceanic and atmospheric circulation. And climatologists predict that extreme weather events, from heat waves to droughts to floods, will likely occur with greater frequency. We may see so-called "hundred-year storms" like Hurricane Katrina happening several times in a single generation as tropical storms are able to gather greater force from the additional heat and evaporation given off by warming oceans. Because of the variety of environmental changes that warming temperatures are producing, a growing number of scientists prefer to use the term **climate change** instead of *global warming*. Whatever name one chooses, the changes that corporations and consumers are producing in our environment through carbon emissions pose the single greatest hazard to both our ecosystems and humanity. Putting the brakes on global warming has been called the most important task of this century—and beyond.

☐ Natural Resource Depletion

It is likely that no one will soon forget the explosion of the Deepwater Horizon drilling rig off the coast of Louisiana on April 20, 2010, which killed 11 workers and spewed over 50,000 barrels of petroleum *per day* into the Gulf of Mexico for three months. Technology seemed unable to stem the flow, as rust-colored crude oil burst through the underwater

How have human behaviors led to climate change?

containment cap and crept toward the shorelines despite the use of chemical dispersants and controlled burns on the ocean's surface. The petroleum created an 80-square-mile "kill zone" in the ocean where virtually all sea life was destroyed. Black tar washed up on the coast, injuring wildlife and scaring off vacationers. Gulf Coast fishermen were out of work for months.

The United States is the world's leading consumer of oil, burning through almost 19 million barrels every day—half of which must be imported (India, whose population is about four times larger than that of the United States, consumes 3 million barrels per day). Of that amount, 72 percent is used to power its automobile-centered transportation system (Energy Information Administration 2009). No one knows how long the world's supply of "black gold" will last, though many experts predict a timeframe of several generations, not centuries. Despite this forecast, wealthy countries have been slow to move away from their dependency on oil. In fact, most have sought to increase domestic oil production and invest in new techniques of oil extraction in order to reduce their reliance on imports from the Middle East and Russia. The Deepwater Horizon explosion is only the most conspicuous example of the many environmental disruptions occurring worldwide as almost no stone is left unturned in the quest for more oil and corporate profit. Drilling rigs move further and further offshore and dig deeper and deeper. And industry is setting its sights on protected natural areas like the Arctic National Wildlife Refuge in Alaska because of their potential caches of oil.

Ever since the Industrial Revolution, humanity's energy requirements have escalated exponentially. And the most

The explosion of the Deepwater Horizon drilling rig symbolizes the environmental and human costs of our dependency on increasingly scarce natural resources like oil. Why has the United States been slow to adopt renewable energy sources such as solar and wind power?

valuable sources of energy, like petroleum, come from deep underground or within mountains. As highlighted in Table 18.1, oil, coal, and natural gas—which are nonrenewable resources, meaning that there is a limited supply that cannot be replaced—currently provide about 85 percent of the energy consumed around the world (Energy Information Administration 2010a).

The Industrial Revolution was built on coal, which released plumes of black smoke into the sky as it fired everything from steam engines to the furnaces that melted iron. Today, coal combustion still generates a third of the electricity consumed by Americans and is the world's greatest source of electricity (Department of Energy 2011). Like drilling for oil, obtaining coal can be disruptive and unsafe. Massive tunnels are burrowed into the ground or the tops of mountains are sheared off with the aid of dynamite. Thousands of miners around the world are killed each year by underground explosions or corridor collapses. Cleaning and processing coal produces large amounts of toxic sludge, which is often stored behind makeshift dams next to where the coal is extracted. In one infamous incident in West Virginia, 132 million gallons of sludge breached a dam and poured down the mountainside, leveling a town and killing 125 residents (Erikson 1976). Though coal combustion is a leading

What natural resources are being depleted and why?

source of air pollution and global warming, it is attractive because coal reserves are widely dispersed around the globe. This means that many countries do not need to rely on imports because they can extract it domestically.

Perhaps the most environmentally harmful form of resource depletion is deforestation. Tropical rainforests provide a natural habitat for two-thirds all species on the planet, including many plants that are used in medicine, and play a crucial role in capturing CO_2 and converting it into oxygen. Though forests are often cut down to produce paper and lumber, most deforestation is a result of farming. As the global demand for beef continues to grow, firms and individual ranchers are eager to burn down stands of trees and replace them with pastures where cattle can graze

TABLE 18.1 GLOBAL ENERGY SOURCES (QUADRILLION BTU)

Total World	2005	2010	2015	2020	2025	2030	2035
Liquids (gasoline, diesel, and kerosene)	170.8	173.2	187.2	195.8	207	216.6	225.2
Natural Gas	105	116.7	127.3	138	149.4	162.3	174.7
Coal	122.3	149.4	157.3	164.6	179.7	194.7	209.1
Nuclear	27.5	27.6	33.2	38.9	43.7	47.4	51.2
Other (including renewables like solar and wind)	45.4	55.2	68.5	82.2	91.7	100.6	109.5
Total	**471.1**	**522**	**573.5**	**619.5**	**671.5**	**721.5**	**769.8**

Sources: History: U.S. Energy Information Administration (EIA), International Energy Statistics database (as of March 2011); and International Energy Agency, *Balances of OECD and Non-OECD Statistics* (2010). Projections: EIA, *Annual Energy Outlook 2011;* AEO2011 National Energy Modeling System, and World Energy Projection System Plus (2011).

FIGURE 18.2 TOTAL CATTLE HERD SIZE AND DEFORESTATION IN AMAZON

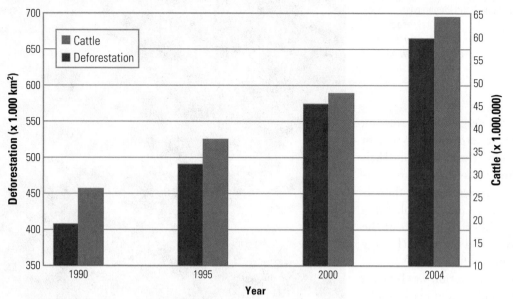

Source: Figure based on data from Greenpeace (2009).

(see Figure 18.2). A Greenpeace report attributes 80 percent of deforestation in the Brazilian Amazon to cattle ranching, and the United Nations estimates that, through the slashing and burning of CO_2-absorbing trees, meat production contributes more to global warming than either car tailpipes or industrial smokestacks (Greenpeace 2009). Deforested areas also suffer greatly from soil erosion, sometimes degenerating into desert-like landscapes. Ecologists estimate that deforestation is causing the extinction of as many as 50,000 plant and animal species every year (137 species per day), and they predict that the rainforests, which once covered 14 percent of the earth's land surface, may be entirely gone by the end of this century unless major restrictions are put in place and enforced (Kolbert 2007).

Animal and plant species also face extinction because we consume them faster than they can reproduce. A dramatic example is the collapse of the cod fishing industry. Cod were once so numerous off the eastern coast of Canada that explorers reported catching them with baskets. Over the course of the twentieth century, massive mechanized trawlers replaced small fishing boats. The sea filled up with gigantic nets that scraped the bottom of the ocean floor. Profits soared as trawlers worked around the clock, processing and freezing the fish below deck. At their peak in 1968, trawlers hauled in 800,000 tons of cod in a year. But by the early 1990s, cod were so overfished that their entire population was estimated to be just 1 percent of what it had been 30 years before. A complete ban on cod fishing was implemented in 1992, leading to the loss of over 40,000 jobs. To this day, however, the cod population has not rebounded. Though the fishing industry now places restrictive quotas on the amount of a given species that can be caught, the number of marine species that are threatened by "factory fishing" steadily increases (*E Magazine* 2001).

One of the most precious natural resources, and maybe the one most taken for granted in developed countries, is water. Though global access to clean water has increased dramatically over the past several decades, many worry that supply will not keep pace with demand. Around the world, the amount of water held in *aquifers*—naturally occurring underground wells—is declining. The Ogallala aquifer, which is tucked beneath parts of eight states in the American Midwest and which supplies almost a third of the groundwater used for irrigation in the United States, is currently only regenerating 10 percent of the amount of water that is taken out each year. The typical American uses 70 gallons of tap water each day and pays pennies. But anticipated future water shortages may very well make water the most valuable natural resource of the next century.

Expanding populations and global development are also leading to conflict between cities, states, and nations as they vie to secure the rights to access, divert, and dam bodies of water to secure their own livelihood. The longest river in the world, the Nile, is a case in point. The Nile has nurtured Egypt for thousands of years. In order to prevent annual flooding and create a reliable water reservoir, Egypt constructed an enormous dam across the Nile in the 1960s. It is estimated that the Aswan Dam increased Egypt's irrigated land area by one-third, and the dam also became an important source of hydroelectricity. However, upstream countries such as Uganda and Tanzania complain that colonial-era agreements prevent them from building their own dams. The 10 upstream nations demand a new treaty that grants them greater rights to the Nile's precious water. As a downstream nation, Egypt worries that such a treaty would mean that the river flow is greatly diminished by the time it reaches the Aswan Dam, and conservationists fret over whether the Nile can support such massive development without being reduced to a trickle.

Natural resource depletion is not a unique problem of the modern era. Historians point to Easter Island as evidence. It appears that the small island off the coast of Chile was the site of a thriving society between the 1200s and the 1600s. However, extensive deforestation led to soil erosion and the extinction of many species of edible plants and animals. By the 1800s, the civilization collapsed amid famine and warfare over scarce resources. In today's global economy, societies need not be self-sufficient because they can import goods. But we should not overlook the lesson of Easter Island. Diamond writes that the rate and scale of global resource depletion and population expansion is slowly nudging our entire planet toward collapse (Diamond 1995). This outcome can be avoided, but doing so will likely require an unusual way of thinking: making decisions about resource consumption that are based not primarily on what is profitable or convenient for us but on what will benefit future generations.

Why is there an excess of solid and chemical waste in wealthy countries like the U.S.?

☐ Solid and Chemical Waste

While natural resource depletion can be thought of as an input crisis, the world faces an output crisis that is just as serious. Though the production of some amount of waste is unavoidable, wealthy countries like the United States create such an excess of garbage that they have been labeled "throw away societies." Much of this is about convenience: Disposable razors, diapers, and cups mean that we do not have to sharpen blades, clean messy cloth diapers, or walk around with our own beverage containers. But all those plastic bags, Styrofoam peanuts, and wrappers add up.

Given that elaborate packaging helps producers sell commodities and that most consumers pay a flat fee for garbage removal regardless of how much they throw out, both buyers and sellers have little incentive to be more conscientious about waste. In addition, many products—from pens to toasters to cars—are designed nowadays to provide a limited amount of use before they need to be replaced. This allows producers to make more money. Consumers generally accept it because these less durable products are cheaper, and it is easier to buy a new one than to get the old one fixed. But those old pens, toasters, and cars have to go somewhere.

Despite the mantra of "reduce, reuse, recycle," the amount of trash that each American produces in a day has nearly doubled between 1960 and 2011 (from about 2.5 pounds to almost 5 pounds; for more details on these trends, see the Infographic on page 520). This equals 250 million tons of solid waste per year. To this annual figure must be added the nearly *8 billion* tons of industrial waste generated by American businesses and the untold amounts of hazardous waste—from paint can lids to spent nuclear fuel—that require special collection and storage methods (Environmental Protection Agency 2011). Less than a third of plastic and glass bottles produced in the United States actually get recycled, and recycling still requires massive energy inputs (Environmental Protection Agency 2011).

Most of our waste is simply dumped into massive holes and covered over. Though it may be out of sight and out of mind, much of our trash (like that old TV) will linger in landfills for centuries. The problem is that these landfills keep filling up, and nobody wants a trash heap in their backyard. New York City ran out of landfill space in the early 2000s and currently pays hundreds of millions of dollars per year to ship its trash to cash-strapped regions of Pennsylvania and Virginia, where poorer residents now *do* live with trash heaps in their backyard.

Landfills are also toxic stews, where battery fluid mingles with mercury, and household cleaners and other industrial hazards slowly leach into the surrounding earth and groundwater. In 1953, the Hooker Chemical Company covered over a giant chemical dump known as Love Canal and sold it to the city of Niagara Falls, New York, for a dollar. Convinced that the hazardous waste was safely

The United States has been called a "throw away society" because the Average American disposes of almost 5 pounds of trash every day. How much garbage do you produce daily?

What Our Garbage Says About Us

Why are Americans producing so much more trash today than they did 50 years ago? The kinds of jobs we have, products we make, and things we buy have changed dramatically over this period, directly impacting the type and quantity of trash we generate. Contemporary America has been called a "throwaway society" because of consumers' preference for the convenience of disposable plates, cups, diapers, and other household products.

Changes in the amount and kind of waste produced also reflect technological innovations. Plastic—which today comprises over ten percent of consumer waste—was not yet produced on a mass scale in the 1960s. Conversely, the percentage of consumer waste derived from paper has actually decreased in this period as Americans increasingly prefer to read digital versions of newspapers, magazines, and books rather than hard copies.

Source: Based on data from U.S. Environmental Protection Agency (2011).

 Explore the **Data** on **What Our Garbage Says About Us** in **MySocLab** and then …

■ **Think About It**

Many items that we throw away could in fact be diverted from trashcans. Which types of waste do you think can be reused or composted?

■ **Inspire Your Sociological Imagination**

Even though we recycle more than we used to, we still generate more waste. What is a possible explanation for this, and how might we reverse the trend?

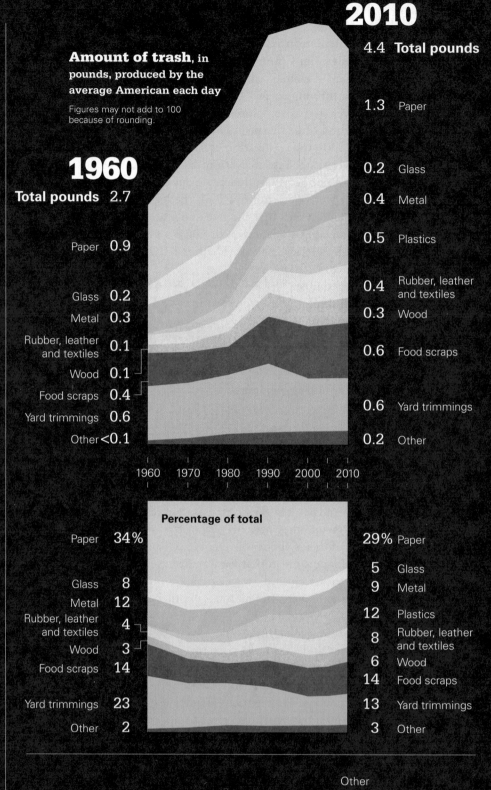

2010

Amount of trash, in pounds, produced by the average American each day

Figures may not add to 100 because of rounding.

1960

Total pounds 2.7

Paper	0.9	4.4	**Total pounds**
		1.3	Paper
Glass	0.2	0.2	Glass
Metal	0.3	0.4	Metal
		0.5	Plastics
Rubber, leather and textiles	0.1	0.4	Rubber, leather and textiles
Wood	0.1	0.3	Wood
Food scraps	0.4	0.6	Food scraps
Yard trimmings	0.6	0.6	Yard trimmings
Other	<0.1	0.2	Other

1960 1970 1980 1990 2000 2010

Percentage of total

Paper	34%	29%	Paper
Glass	8	5	Glass
Metal	12	9	Metal
		12	Plastics
Rubber, leather and textiles	4	8	Rubber, leather and textiles
Wood	3	6	Wood
Food scraps	14	14	Food scraps
Yard trimmings	23	13	Yard trimmings
Other	2	3	Other

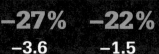

Key categories of paper products that contributed to the reduction of paper waste in the United States from 1994 to 2010	Newspapers	Office paper	Other commercial printing	Bags and sacks
	−27%	**−22%**	**−63%**	**−54%**
	−3.6 million tons	−1.5 million tons	−4.3 million tons	−1.2 million tons

sealed below ground, the city built a school on the site and oversaw the construction of about 100 nearby homes. It took 25 years for residents to realize there was a problem. After a period of heavy rain in 1978, rusted metal drums filled with carcinogenic waste broke through the surface of people's backyards; puddles of oozing toxins choked trees and plants to death; and children playing outside returned home with chemical burns. The number of area miscarriages, birth defects, and cancer cases skyrocketed. While the Love Canal tragedy led to more stringent federal regulations of toxic waste disposal, there are still thousands of sites in the United States where toxic waste has been improperly disposed (Szasz and Meuser 1997).

Convenience has its consequences. But the full cost of all of the industrial waste and throwaway products and packaging that sustain modern lifestyles and corporate profits is not reflected in their sticker price. Though efficient waste management systems seem to make rubbish disappear, the environment pays the penalty. As Love Canal indicates, the cost may also be borne by people's bodies. This is especially true in poor countries, where erratic trash collection and the lack of proper facilities for the disposal of toxins means that waste may spread disease as it festers in the streets.

Tailpipe emissions from automobiles harm the atmosphere—and our lungs. What alternative forms of transportation do you think might be available for commuters in cities like Los Angeles?

Air and Water Pollution

The freeways of Los Angeles were designed to whisk commuters across the sprawling city at speeds of 55 miles per hour. These days, however, the average rush hour speed on Los Angeles freeways may be 5 or 10 miles per hour, and "rush hour" now means a time window as wide as 5:00 to 10:00 A.M. and 3:00 to 7:00 P.M. The average Los Angeles resident spends almost four days a year sitting in traffic. Yet even as those millions of cars sit idle on congested freeways, they continue to pollute the air. Los Angeles is legendary for its **smog**, a smoky haze produced when tailpipe emissions that linger in the atmosphere chemically react with the sunlight. Los Angeles continues to endure "smog alerts," where schools are closed and residents are warned to stay inside because of poor air quality. Smog can burn the lungs and irritate the eyes and nose, and it has been known to aggravate asthma, bronchitis, and other respiratory illnesses.

Why are air and water pollution more of a threat in developing countries?

Toxic air pollution is as much a product of smokestacks as tailpipes. In one year, a single coal-based electrical plant pumps tens of thousands of tons of noxious gases into the atmosphere. These include nitrogen oxide and sulfur dioxide, which react with water molecules in the air to create acid that returns to earth when it rains. So-called **acid rain** has been shown to kill plant life and marine animals. Industrial pollutants have also severely depleted the atmosphere's ozone layer, which shields the Earth's surface from the sun's ultraviolet radiation. UV rays are harmful to a number of plant and animal species and have been linked to cancer and cataracts in humans. The toxins most responsible for ozone depletion are chlorofluorocarbons (CFCs), which until recently were commonly found in aerosol sprays and liquid coolants.

No one can avoid inhaling microscopic pollutants produced from the combustion of fossil fuels. Their effects can mimic those of cigarette smoke, and it is estimated that 50,000 Americans die each year from cardiopulmonary diseases linked to breathing in toxic particles (Dollemore 2008). In October 2010, it was estimated that almost 600 residents of Hong Kong had died since the beginning of the year because of air pollution. Over the same nine-month period, experts also attributed a staggering 4.63 million doctor visits and 45,000 hospitalizations to poor air quality caused by coal-burning plants and automobiles (Bryskine 2010). Though city air quality is improving somewhat in developed societies as a result of cleaner technologies, it is worsening in developing countries that must rely on cheaper, dirtier methods to produce energy. Mexico City's smog is so thick that the nearby mountains are often shrouded in brown haze. Clean air and healthy lungs are luxuries it can't afford.

Clean, potable water is another luxury that many people in developing countries cannot afford. Over half the world's rural population still lacks access to clean water, leading desperate people to rely on polluted sources—including sewage—to supply their cooking, bathing, and drinking needs. Exposure to contaminated water causes tens of thousands of deaths each year worldwide from preventable diseases such as dysentery and cholera—diseases that Americans never have to worry about.

The United States, however, is hardly immune from concerns about water quality. Aside from acid rain, contamination of rivers, streams, and aquifers from agriculture and industry is common. Cow manure, which is often filled with infectious agents such as *E. coli*, regularly enters waterways as runoff after a rainstorm. Agricultural runoff, which can also include chemical agents from synthetic fertilizers, is the single biggest source of water pollution in the United States. Despite this fact, farm waste for the most part is not regulated under federal laws. When it comes to industry, a *New York Times* investigation found thousands of instances where companies openly flouted the Clean Water Act but were never punished. In one case, the drinking water in a West

Virginia town was contaminated with lead, manganese, and nickel because coal companies purposely injected over 2 billion gallons of toxic sludge into the ground over a period of five years. Residents who continued using the stained yellow drinking water suffered from severe rashes, rotting teeth, miscarriages, and kidney and bladder diseases. The problem of chemical wastes being discharged into drinking water goes beyond the coal industry, encompassing natural gas extraction ("fracking"), dry cleaners, gas stations, and sewage treatment plants (Duhigg 2009).

Pollution is cheap. Consumers want inexpensive goods and sources of energy, and producers operate in a cutthroat environment where they must keep down costs to be competitive. Unless firm, enforceable limits are placed on the amount of air and water pollutants that businesses can generate, or unless businesses are given financial incentives for adopting "greener" (or more environmentally friendly) practices, we should expect pollution to worsen. It is unlikely that most producers and consumers will voluntarily discontinue "business as usual" and pay the higher cost of sustainability.

3   How Do Environmental Factors Impact Inequality?

THE ENVIRONMENTAL MOVEMENT AND SOCIAL INEQUALITY

 Watch the Big Question Video in **MySocLab**

I n response to the unfolding ecological crisis, a powerful social movement has emerged over the last half-century that challenges "business as usual." The movement has made notable gains in remedying some of the damage wrought by society on the environment. But socially produced environmental problems

have also led to new social problems. And not everyone suffers equally: The wealthiest people tend to reap most of the benefits and suffer few of the costs of environmental problems. One of the most vital contributions that sociologists have made to the study of environmental problems is an understanding of how they are linked to social inequality.

☐ The Environmental Movement

As early as the 1800s, there were those who sensed something tragic about the destruction of natural landscapes in the face of urbanization. None may be more famous than the philosopher Henry David Thoreau. His 1854 book *Walden* documented a two-year experiment in which he built and lived in a cottage on the wooded outskirts of Boston. Living simply and close to the land, he wrote, rejuvenated the spirit and reawakened the senses. A rallying cry against overcivilization and the social ills of the city, *Walden* framed the discourse for future generations of **preservationists** (Brulle 1996)—those who believe that the environment has intrinsic value and should be maintained in as pristine a state as possible. The leading figure of early efforts to preserve the countryside and wilderness was John Muir, who successfully petitioned U.S. president Theodore Roosevelt—an avid outdoorsman—to set aside the Yosemite area as a protected national park in 1906. Among Muir's many other lasting legacies was founding the Sierra Club, which to this day is the most influential environmental protection group in the United States. Firmly a believer in preserving nature in pristine form, Muir rejected the utilitarian view of **conservationists**—who argue that the point of environmental protection ought to be to responsibly manage natural resources so that they are available for commercial use by future generations.

It took until the second half of the twentieth century for environmental problems to begin to be seen as dire threats to humanity. There may have been no greater wakeup call than Rachel Carson's 1962 book *Silent Spring*. The book's title referred to an imagined future where songbirds could no longer be heard because they had all been killed by pesticides like DDT. Carson blamed the government for allowing the use of toxins without knowing the long-term consequences, and she compared pesticides to nuclear fallout. "Can anyone believe," Carson pleaded, "it is possible to lay down such a barrage of poisons on the surface of the earth without making it unfit for all life?" (Carson 1962:8).

Silent Spring directly led to the ban on the use of DDT in the United States. But, perhaps more fundamentally, the book led Americans to question their faith in better living through chemistry. Carson argued that science had been hijacked by the titans of industry, who were driven by short-term profit, and that there was little reason to assume that chemical producers cared about public safety. She also challenged society's anthropocentrism, contending that humans are only one component of a fragile ecosystem that, if further degraded, could undermine the foundations of mankind's existence. Grassroots movements began to spring up across the country, advocating for stronger government regulation of the chemical industry.

Before the decade of the 1960s ended, and amid the emergence of the civil rights movement, several catastrophes brought the environmental movement to a head. In 1969

Over a century ago, the preservationist John Muir gave U.S. president Theodore Roosevelt a tour of Yosemite in order to convince him to protect the area's natural beauty. What pristine environments are most threatened today by development?

alone, a massive oil spill off the coast of California killed thousands of marine animals and blackened the shoreline of Santa Barbara while Cleveland's Cuyahoga River actually caught on fire because the surface of its brown, oozing, toxic water was covered in oil. These events sparked tremendous public outrage, resulting in the first Earth Day the following year and in a string of significant political victories for the environmental movement. Most notably, the Nixon administration—which was generally on the side of "big business" and thus viewed environmentalism as a threat to productivity and profit—bowed to this unprecedented groundswell of popular protest by creating the Environmental Protection Agency (EPA) and signing the Clean Water Act into law. Meanwhile, best-selling books like Paul Ehrlich's *The Population Bomb* (1968) sounded alarm bells about the potential collapse of societies as an exploding global population pressed up against the limits of finite natural resources. Though new technologies demonstrated that humans could extend natural limits (for example, genetically altering plants to increase crop yields), more and more people recognized that technology was not a cure-all as the scope of environmental risks kept increasing.

Despite growing public concern about our planet's health, efforts to enact environmentally friendly policies are routinely thwarted by political alliances between private businesses and conservative lawmakers—many of whom voice skepticism about scientific claims regarding environmental problems or contend that "going green" will harm the economy (Dunlap and McCright 2011). President George W. Bush,

The Cuyahoga River Fire was one of the key moments that inspired the environmental movement of the late 1960s and 1970s. Can you think of any contemporary environmental problems that have resulted in popular political protest?

for instance, memorably refused to sign the Kyoto Protocol, an international pledge to cut carbon emissions, because he said that it was not clear that global warming was caused by people and that the pact would result in a loss of productivity and jobs. More recently, companies engaged in fracking, a process by which natural gas is extracted from shale rock by the injection of millions of gallons of toxic chemicals into the ground, have been able to avoid submitting to more stringent environmental regulations and having to disclose the contents of what they pump into the earth (which they argue is a trade secret) by maintaining close ties with business-friendly governors of the states where they drill.

Environmental Justice

In the summer of 1978, a trucking company illegally dumped 31,000 gallons of used transformer oil along hundreds of miles of roads in Warren County, North Carolina. The location was no accident: This was the poorest county in the state, and 65 percent of its residents were black. Adding insult to injury, the state decided to place a hazardous waste landfill in the area that would store the used oil but also serve as a repository for toxins from other counties. Rather than accept their fate, locals fought back. As a group, they lobbied against the proposal, filed a civil lawsuit, and were arrested for staging protests. The language and strategies they employed helped shape an emerging social movement (Szasz and Meuser 1997).

While the environmental movement of the 1960s and 1970s advocated for the preservation of natural areas and for increased federal regulations to protect air and water, many minorities and people in poverty felt that the movement did not address the problems that affected them. Their concerns were grounded in the disproportionate number of hazardous waste facilities that were placed in their communities and in the higher rates of asthma and other environment-induced illnesses that they had to endure. A 1987 report issued by the United Church of Christ found, based on a comparison of zip codes across the United States, that race was the most significant predictor of living close to a hazardous waste facility (e.g., garbage incinerator, sewage treatment plant). As shown in Figure 18.3, the higher the concentration of minorities in a particular zip code, the greater the number of hazardous waste facilities it contained (Commission for Racial Justice 1987). The report's findings echoed the pioneering research of sociologist Robert Bullard, who showed that 21 of Houston's 25 garbage dumps and incinerators were located in black neighborhoods even though blacks only comprised 25 percent of the city's population (Bullard 1983).

Poor people of color bear the burden of such a disproportionate share of environmental hazards, and their communities are so routinely targeted as sites for hazardous waste facilities that some sociologists label the phenomenon **environmental racism** (Bullard 1990). Though environmental racism suggests conscious discrimination against minorities, it is often the case that polluting industries choose the path of least resistance, placing facilities where land is cheaper and where residents are not politically organized (Brulle and Pellow 2006). Such decisions seem to often be based on economics rather than race, but the enduring association between poverty and nonwhites in the United States means that the areas where environmental hazards are clustered usually have the highest concentration of minorities. In the past, discriminatory housing practices forced minorities to live in undesirable neighborhoods with greater levels of pollution; today, those with low incomes simply cannot afford to move to cleaner, healthier places.

New York University's Institute for Environmental Medicine has been looking at the link between air pollution and health in the South Bronx. Home to many poor and working-class people of color, the South Bronx also hosts over a dozen waste-transfer stations, a sewage-treatment plant, and miles of congested expressways. It has one of the highest hospitalization rates for asthma among children in New York. By placing air-monitoring devices in students' backpacks, the NYU researchers found that children in the South Bronx were exposed to unhealthy levels of air pollution from car exhaust on a regular basis. They also saw that the students exhibited symptoms of asthma, such as wheezing, during the times

What is environmental racism and how can it be remedied?

FIGURE 18.3 PERCENT PEOPLE OF COLOR LIVING NEAR HAZARDOUS WASTE FACILITIES

Within 1 km.

Between 1 km. and 3 km.

Legend:
- People of Color
- African American
- Hispanic or Latino
- Asian/Pac. Islander
- Native American
- Other

Between 3 km. and 5 km.

Beyond 5 km.

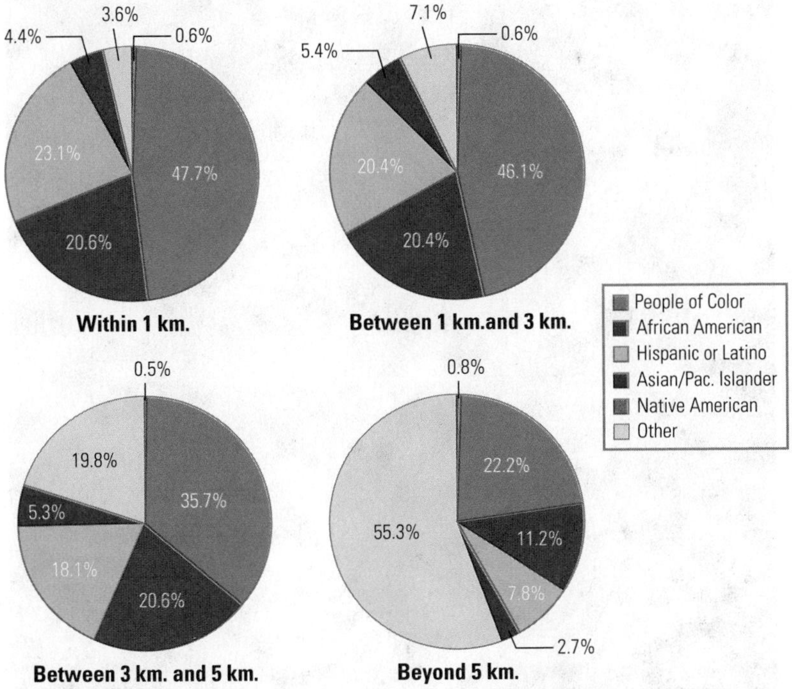

Source: Based on data from the Commission for Racial Justice (2007).

when the amount of air pollution was highest (Fernandez 2006). This and other studies show that people in the poorest neighborhoods, most of whom are nonwhite, often do not breathe the same air or drink the same water as their wealthier counterparts (Szasz and Meuser 1997).

To address what they perceive as environmental racism or classism, poor and minority communities have organized grassroots political campaigns and sued polluters in court. The goal is **environmental justice**, conceived of as the achievement of equal protection from environmental hazards for all people, regardless of race, class, or geography. Environmental justice also entails giving community members a voice in shaping decisions that affect their environment and their health.

Sociologists Robert Brulle and David Pellow identify two major strands of the environmental justice movement that emerged in the 1980s. The antitoxics movement was based primarily in white working-class communities and drew its inspiration from the local response to the Love Canal catastrophe. Fueled by concern for her children and her neighbors, a homemaker named Lois Gibbs turned her neighborhood homeowner's association into a citizen action group. She also helped forge a national coalition of community organizations facing similar environmental threats. These groups shared information, organized protests, filed class-action lawsuits against polluters, and helped make the nation aware of the extent to which factories and industry were poisoning the communities around them.

Around the same time, people of color (e.g., blacks, American Indians, and Hispanics) who were inspired by the Warren County landfill protests began forming a movement that tackled similar issues, such as the location of hazardous waste facilities and illegal dumping. What made their movement unique was its framing and strategies. People of color explicitly defined local environmental problems as a violation of their civil rights, and many of them adopted the civil disobedience tactics of the 1960s, such as staging massive protests and occupying the offices of politicians and polluting companies (Brulle and Pellow 2006).

Environmental justice groups have achieved some notable gains, such as shutting down dangerous incinerators and landfills and convincing the EPA to create an Office of Environmental Justice (Brulle and Pellow 2006). In one landmark case, Navajo Indians in New Mexico—who were unwittingly exposed to harmful levels of radiation for decades by mining companies that extracted uranium on behalf of the U.S. military—helped propel the passage of a law in 1990 that requires the government to compensate people who have suffered from nuclear bomb testing and uranium mining. Increasingly, environmental justice movements are cropping up in developing countries, where they challenge the business-as-usual tradeoff of pollution for profit and attempt to hold wealthy countries accountable for local environmental problems caused by global warming.

📖 **Read** the **Document** *Dumping in Dixie: Race, Class, and the Politics of Place* in **MySocLab**

The Social Dimension of Natural Disasters

In July of 1995, the residents of Chicago baked in one the city's most severe heat waves. In just one week, over 500 people died as a direct result of the heat. Medical workers were so overwhelmed that they had to store the corpses in refrigerated meat-packing trucks until they could perform autopsies. Were these deaths the unavoidable consequence of natural events? While the mayor, and for the most part the media, framed them

Why are some people more vulnerable to a natural disaster than others?

this way, NYU sociologist Eric Klinenberg argued that the massive loss of life was in fact a "structurally determined catastrophe" that could mostly have been prevented. The heat wave did not take lives at random. Rather, Klinenberg discovered that vulnerability was concentrated in "the low-income, elderly, African-American, and more violent

Many of the people left behind after Hurricane Katrina forced the evacuation of New Orleans were poor and black. How does the sociological concept of "environmental inequality" challenge typical understandings of natural disasters?

regions of the metropolis" (Klinenberg 1999:250). Poor neighborhoods were underserved by municipal agencies that could have reached out to social isolates and people without air conditioners, and their local hospitals were overwhelmed and understaffed. Klinenberg also argued that the city had allowed poor neighborhoods to become so deteriorated and dangerous that residents feared leaving their homes even as the temperatures rose to dangerous levels. As a result, they quietly and anonymously perished.

While sociologists do not deny the destructive power of natural disasters such as floods, earthquakes, and heat waves, they analyze the ways in which the outcomes of such events—such as who lives and who dies, who evacuates and who remains—are patterned by social forces. In the wake of Hurricane Katrina, most of the desperate faces of those stranded on their roofs or packed into the temporary shelter of New Orleans' Convention Center were poor and black. Despite these arresting scenes, politicians and media pundits hotly debated whether or not poor people of color disproportionately suffered from the storm. Sociologists played a key role in offering evidence of social disparities and revealing government neglect of the vulnerable.

NYU sociologist Patrick Sharkey found that blacks, along with the elderly, were much more likely to die as a result of Hurricane Katrina than would be expected given their presence in the population; and he showed that deaths were concentrated in New Orleans' black communities (Sharkey 2007). A panel of social scientists convened by the Social Science Research Council (SSRC) showed that many of the people who stayed behind lacked the necessary means to evacuate, most notably a car and money for a hotel. The SSRC panel also documented the major role that governmental disorganization and miscommunication played in hindering assistance to vulnerable residents. The Federal Emergency Management Agency (FEMA), for instance, failed to coordinate evacuation plans with local officials and neglected to give the go-ahead to the U.S. military to begin airdrops of food and water rations (Social Science Research Council 2006).

Socially patterned differences in vulnerability are even more pronounced on a global scale, as revealed by the earthquake that rocked poverty-stricken Haiti in 2010. Lacking the money to erect reinforced buildings, Haitians had little choice but to inhabit structures that crumbled under the force of the 7.0-magnitude quake, killing over 100,000 people and leaving over 1 million more homeless. The substandard quality of the nation's infrastructure, from roads to hospitals, also contributed to the high number of casualties.

Global Environmental Inequality

In 1984, over 40 tons of highly toxic gas escaped from a pesticide plant in Bhopal, India, and killed nearly 10,000 people who lived in a nearby slum. In the subsequent 20 years, as many as 20,000 premature deaths resulted from lingering bodily effects of exposure. The factory belonged to the Union Carbide Company, an American chemical producer that was lured to India by its lower environmental standards and lax rule enforcement. Though Union Carbide denied responsibility, the facility was operating with "safety equipment and procedures far below the standards found in its sister plant" in West Virginia (Broughton 2005:2).

In the global economy, production and consumption are usually disconnected. If we look at the labels on our clothing or the packaging of our electronics, we will likely see that they were made in China or another country where companies can pay workers cheaper wages than in the United States—and where companies can pollute more. In this way, wealthy countries benefit from cheap industrial and consumer goods while developing countries bear the environmental and health risks.

More and more sociologists are reconnecting the points of production and consumption and documenting the environmental suffering that the developing world endures to prop up Western lifestyles. In one study, ethnographers studied an impoverished shantytown in Argentina surrounded by an immense petrochemical compound (Auyero and Swistun 2009). The village's 5,000 residents suffered from convulsions, rashes, psychological problems, bloody noses, and constant headaches—all of which are linked to ingesting lead and other toxic industrial chemicals. The source of much of the pollution was Shell Oil, an American company that used the facility to carry out the dirty process of refining crude oil so that it is ready for global consumption and industrial use.

Despite overwhelming evidence, the researchers found that residents remained unsure about the causes of their illnesses and rarely mobilized against Shell. This was because Shell, as a powerful and wealthy company, was able to manipulate how residents perceived and responded to contamination. Many of the locals worked for Shell, and Shell also ran a town health clinic and performed its own environmental tests. Because residents could not afford independent doctors or consultants, their main source of information

about illness and exposure came from biased Shell representatives, and locals faced losing their jobs if they protested. Their enduring suffering is one of the hidden social costs of the world's refined oil (Auyero and Swistun 2009).

The greatest environmental problem that the world faces today—global warming—may also be the greatest source of environmental inequality. While rich nations have, by far, contributed the most to global warming, poor countries disproportionately suffer from its effects. For those who must make a living off the land, small changes can have huge impacts on their ability to subsist. A report issued by Columbia University researchers concluded that climate change is already forcing as many as 50 million people, almost all of them living in the least developed countries, to migrate to new areas in order to secure a livelihood. Given the dismal forecast of continued deforestation, melting glaciers, rising sea level, and an increase in the frequency and intensity of extreme weather events, we can expect hundreds of millions of worldwide "environmental refugees" by the year 2050 (Cooperative for Assistance and Relief Everywhere 2008).

4 How Can We Create More Sustainable Societies?

CONSUMPTION, PRODUCTION, AND SUSTAINABILITY

👁 Watch the **Big Question Video** in **MySocLab**

Many experts believe that the global population is growing so rapidly that in several generations the Earth may no longer be able to support everyone. The problem is not merely numbers, for if we were all hunter-gatherers we would consume far less resources and produce much less waste. According to biologist

Paul Ehrlich, the impact that a given group of people has on the environment is a function of the size of its population multiplied by its degree of affluence and its level of technology. For example, wealthy, developed countries tend to use an exponentially greater amount of natural resources *per person* than poor, less developed countries. Americans comprise only 5 percent of the world's population but consume about 25 percent of the world's energy. A single American consumes as much energy as dozens of people in developing countries.

Where does all this energy go? The last time I went to a concert, I looked out and saw the glow of thousands of cellular phones and the flashes of countless digital cameras—devices that did not exist just several decades ago. As the concert let out, many folks listened to their iPods on their way to the parking lot, where they got into their cars. Many likely turned on any number of appliances when they got home: microwaves, televisions, laptops, and so on. Understandably, most people in poor countries would like to enjoy the material comforts that wealthy nations take for granted. But something has to give. Even though new technologies enable us to stretch Earth's natural limits, ecologists believe that we will eventually hit the wall.

Innovations in food production are predicted to lag behind population increases, rising levels of air and water pollution are damaging our habitat's ability to sustain us, and the Earth's finite resources are being exhausted. Despite the fact that current consumption and pollution patterns are already unsustainable, the world's energy demand in 2030 is predicted to be 40 percent greater than it was in 2007. Over three-quarters of that increase will likely come from dirty, nonrenewable fossil fuels (UNDP 2010). As depicted in Figure 18.4, scientists predict that global carbon emissions will increase by more than 30 percent between 2007 and 2035. Ecologists argue that, to avoid impending environmental and social crises, societies must work toward a model of **sustainability**, which refers to development and consumption that satisfies a society's current needs without imperiling the ability of future generations to do the same.

☐ The Tragedy of the Commons

A key principle of economics is that competition among commodity producers trying to capture a greater share of the market leads to lower prices for consumers. Many economists point to this as evidence that a free market self-regulates and produces optimal collective outcomes. But in the influential article "The Tragedy of the Commons," ecologist Garrett Hardin (1968) contended that the opposite is often true: Each individual acting in his or her own self-interest will, in the long run, bring ruin to everyone.

Imagine a shared pasture (the "commons"), Hardin wrote, where herders graze cows.

Because they earn a living from their cows, all herders have an interest in maximizing the number of cows they have grazing in the pasture. The herder who adds a cow to the pasture reaps all the benefits from that cow, but the negative impacts on the pasture created by overgrazing are distributed across all herders. Because, in the short term, he gains more than he loses, each herder concludes that he should keep adding cows to the pasture—until finally the pasture is entirely overgrazed. The freedom of each herder to pursue his interests produces collective devastation.

Hardin's analogy of the commons highlights the tension between short-term and long-term rewards, and between individual and collective interest. Economists rightly point out that businesses will adopt more sustainable practices if and when there is a market for them. But ecologists, pointing to societies that collapsed in the past such as Easter Island, argue that preventing future environmental calamity requires making sacrifices today. As discussed earlier, the cod-fishing industry went bust because each trawler sought to maximize its own haul of fish without regard for future generations. And global warming threatens us all because it is in the short-term economic interest of people, firms, and nations to continue business-as-usual practices rather than pay the cost of going green. The lesson is that we cannot expect the majority of people to regulate themselves as long as the negative consequences of their actions (1) will not be apparent until far in the future or (2) fall on other people.

What warnings do the "tragedy of the commons" and the "treadmill of production" concepts offer when thinking about sustainability?

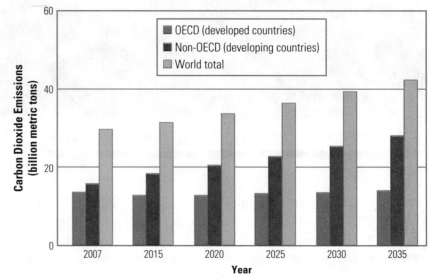

FIGURE 18.4 WORLD ENERGY-RELATED CARBON DIOXIDE EMISSIONS, 2007–2035

Source: Energy Information Administration (2010).

In order to promote environmentally friendly behavior, Hardin argued, we would need to restrict the amount of a particular resource that a single entity can use (e.g., permits or quotas), enact economic sanctions that punish polluters (e.g., taxes or fines), and create economic incentives that reward sustainable practices (e.g., tax breaks). The idea, in other words, is to replace self-regulation with political regulation. Our entire planet is our "commons." If we continue to eschew regulation and foul our own nest, future generations may find it uninhabitable.

The Treadmill of Production

A number of sociologists agree with Hardin but go even further, arguing that uncontrolled destruction of the environment is an essential feature of the contemporary economic system. Allan Schnaiberg forcefully advanced this perspective through his concept of the "treadmill of production." While one of the principles of ecology is balance and a tendency toward equilibrium, such as when a forest fire clears out the underbrush so that new trees can grow, the pursuit of profit tends toward disequilibrium. The basis of capitalism is continued economic expansion—measured in profits, market shares, gross domestic product, and so on. Producers, laborers, and governments all share an interest in growing the economy by increasing production and consumption. Doing so, of course, entails the consumption of more energy and the production of more pollution. Thus, economic expansion increases wealth, but at the expense of the environment. Schnaiberg argued that the treadmill of production helps ensure business's profits by externalizing the environmental costs of their activities to the poor and the powerless, meaning that economic growth also increases environmental inequality (Schnaiberg 1980).

Economic growth is driven by competition. While competition among producers leads to technological innovation and lower prices, it can also discourage sustainable business practices. Why should one producer voluntarily pay the higher cost of adopting cleaner technology if she does not have to? This would decrease her profits, and if she raised prices to reflect her higher cost of doing business, consumers would go elsewhere.

There is an important place, then, for regulation. However, businesses faced with costly environmental laws may simply move their facilities to regions that have fewer restrictions. Similarly, countries or states sometimes loosen environmental regulations in order to lure businesses away from other regions. These two dynamics set in motion a "race to the bottom," whereby companies and governments conspire to remove or avoid environmental protections that harm profit. The toxic effects of the race to the bottom are evident from the Bhopal gas leak in India to the smog-choked skies of Beijing.

The implication of the treadmill-of-production idea is that achieving environmental sustainability will likely require a major restructuring of the economy away from a materials-intensive growth model. And the lesson of the race-to-the-bottom phenomenon is that political remedies will have to be harmonized across regions so that polluters do not pick up and move somewhere else when new regulations are put in place. These are tall orders, but some important steps have already been taken in this direction.

Toward Sustainability

While technological innovation will most likely play a central role in helping societies reduce their impact on the environment, it is no silver bullet. Reining in pollution on the scale and timetable needed to head off an ecological crisis will also require that governments take a more active role in regulating pollution and steering the economy away from the treadmill of production. Last but not least, sustainability requires civic engagement. While the notion of the throwaway society points to the unsustainability of contemporary lifestyles, it implies that everyday citizens can vote for sustainability with their wallets by changing their patterns of consumption. Explore *A Sociological Perspective* on page 530 to learn more about sustainable agriculture.

What implications do technology, politics, and individual lifestyles have for sustainability?

The Role of Technology Technology will have a major role to play in making societies more sustainable. Recall that 85 percent of the world's energy comes from fossil fuels. Because fossil fuels are nonrenewable, and because their combustion is the leading source of global warming, transitioning to **renewable energy** sources that are capable of being replaced by natural ecological cycles, such as wind, sunlight, and water, would have major environmental benefits. This is already happening. Solar panels and wind turbines have started to take their place alongside hydroelectric dams as viable and important sources of "green energy." Between 2007 and 2008, renewable energy consumption in the United States grew a record 10 percent. Despite this promising sign, as of 2008 over 90 percent of the energy consumed by Americans was still derived from nonrenewable resources (Energy Information Administration 2010b). We can expect, however, that the decades ahead will see an enormous increase in renewable energy production. The federal government has begun actively promoting renewable energy as both good for the environment and good for the economy. Factories have sprung up across the United States to meet the growing demand for wind turbines and solar panels, providing local jobs in an era of outsourcing.

A SOCIOLOGICAL PERSPECTIVE
Can environmental damage be reversed?

Agriculture is responsible for 15-30 percent of global greenhouse gas emissions. Yet agriculture is also one of the areas where the most can be done to reverse environmental damage and to enhance people's standard of living. One example of sustainable and equitable agriculture is the fair trade and organic foods movement, where communities producing goods like chocolate or coffee band together to increase their wages and improve their working conditions, while growing food in ways that promote the health of the surrounding ecosystem.

The Movimento sem Terra (MST) of Brazil was formed by peasants who were evicted from their leased farms by corporations. By protesting and occupying private land, the MST has become a global symbol of peasant farmers' efforts to produce food in a way that sustains both their land and their communities. In the United States, there has been an explosion of urban farming and community gardens. Such lifestyle choices reduce the carbon emissions associated with long-distance transportation and factory farming, and they enable people to take back control of their food supply.

What similarities or differences are there between the Brazilian farmers' efforts to produce sustainable food and take care of their land and U.S. farmers producing food within government subsidizing programs?

What impact does a public or personal produce garden have on the local environment and community health?

How can local supermarkets take advantage of locally grown food and what long-term impact can this partnership have on the environment?

How does the fair trade movement protect farmers and lands throughout the world?

Explore A Sociological Perspective in **MySocLab** and then ...

■ Think About It
More and more people are demanding locally grown and organic produce. In what ways are such food choices more sustainable and healthy than fast food?

■ Inspire Your Sociological Imagination
As people become increasingly concerned about the contents and origins of what they eat, many are questioning the safety of genetically modified produce and consuming fewer processed foods. What changes in the environment and society do you think are responsible for this consumer movement? Can you think of examples of popular foods that have come under scrutiny because they are now considered unhealthy or unsustainable? Why do you think it might be harder for poor people to have access to healthy food?

The mass production of plug-in electric vehicles means fewer cars on the road producing tailpipe emissions. But where the electricity comes from that powers these cars matters: If it is derived from burning fossil fuels like coal, then the decrease in tailpipe emissions might be canceled out by increased smokestack emissions.

Because nuclear power does not produce greenhouse gases, it has increasingly been touted as a sustainable source of energy. Indeed, the United States, France, and Japan have included nuclear power as a key ingredient of their green energy portfolios for the coming decades. However, in addition to the fact that spent fuel rods must be securely stored for 10,000 years before they cease to be a public health risk, high-profile accidents leave people questioning whether nuclear power is environmentally friendly. On March 11, 2011, an earthquake off the coast of Japan unleashed a tsunami that flooded the Fukushima Daini Nuclear Plant and knocked out its power. As the nuclear fuel overheated, explosions tore through the reactors. Radioactive plumes forced evacuations throughout the region and contaminated crops and groundwater. Though a very rare event, the Fukushima disaster fueled enough anxiety about nuclear energy that the German government promptly abandoned the chancellor's pronuclear policies and agreed to shut down all of its nuclear power plants—which provide almost a quarter of Germany's energy—by 2022.

As more people around the world pursue middle-class lifestyles, the demand for automobiles escalates. Unless we develop cars that do not rely on oil, any gains made in reducing carbon emissions through wind, solar, or nuclear power will be cancelled out by tailpipe emissions. The development of hybrid vehicles has been an important step in reducing carbon emissions, and their popularity shows that there is a market for "green" cars. Hybrids are powered by gasoline combustion, like traditional vehicles, yet they also draw energy from batteries. By using less gas, hybrids can produce significantly lower carbon emissions. However, hybrids still pollute. A number of manufacturers aim to create alternative fuel vehicles that do not emit any carbon.

One promising path to this objective is the electric vehicle (EV), which draws all of its energy from batteries. Rather than filling up at a gas station, the driver plugs the EV into an electrical outlet. EVs have actually been around for decades and are beginning to be mass produced. But several technological obstacles must still be overcome before they become attractive to consumers: The batteries are heavy, bulky, and expensive and require several hours to recharge, and EVs can travel less than half the distance of gas-powered vehicles before they need to refuel. Given the strides made over the past decade, however, there is reason to believe that EVs will soon be competitive with gas-powered vehicles. For EVs to truly be green, though, the electricity that powers them must come from clean and renewable resources rather than coal or oil.

The Role of Politics Politics has played an important part in promoting the development of green technology; but many environmentalists are pushing governments to assume a larger role in moving societies toward sustainability. While the American government offers tax rebates to businesses that adopt green technology, environmentalists seek federal legislation that would place a legal limit on carbon emissions. In the absence of federal regulations, some regions, states, and cities have taken it upon themselves to create climate action plans. States in the northeastern United States and Canada, for instance, have set a target to reduce the region's total carbon emissions to 10 percent below 1990 levels by the year 2020. And New York City aims to reduce its citywide carbon emissions to 30 percent below 2005 levels by 2030. One way to reduce regional carbon emissions is to limit suburban sprawl. Because cities cluster people and the businesses that serve them within a self-contained area where many errands can be done on foot, bike, train, or bus, urban living is a surprisingly green lifestyle. The state of Oregon has long recognized this—since the 1970s, it has enforced land-use laws that concentrate residential and commercial growth in urban areas.

One method for achieving carbon reduction goals is through a **cap-and-trade program**. The idea is that governments set a limit on the total amount of carbon emissions that are allowable (the cap) and then sell permits to businesses that entitle them to a designated amount of emissions. If firms need to emit more than their permit allows, they must purchase pollution credits from firms that are emitting less than their permit entitles them to (the trade). Such a system ensures a reduction in the total amount of carbon emitted into the atmosphere, rewards firms that move toward clean technology, and makes dirty firms pay for their pollution. The European Union was an early adopter of a trading program for greenhouse gases.

To prevent a race to the bottom, in which firms move their operations to regions that have not implemented limits on greenhouse gas emissions, nations would need to work out an international agreement in which all countries sign

Walking and bicycling are two of the most environmentally friendly—and healthy—ways to get around. What could your city or town do to make these transportation options more attractive?

on to reduce the global carbon footprint. Though achieving such a task is daunting, there is historical precedent. In 1987, countries from around the world gathered in Montreal to tackle the threat of ozone depletion. Acknowledging that the primary source of the so-called ozone hole over Antarctica came from aerosol sprays and liquid coolants containing CFCs, 196 countries eventually signed on to an agreement to phase out the production of these pollutants by 2000. Under guidance from the United Nations, wealthy nations set aside a special fund to help developing countries meet the phase-out requirements. Dubbed the Montreal Protocol, the CFC phase-out agreement is usually considered the most successful international environmental treaty of all time (see Figure 18.5).

Though curbing carbon emissions is more complicated, the Montreal Protocol is a useful framework. Important efforts have been made, most notably the 1997 Kyoto Protocol. Industrialized nations committed to reducing greenhouse gas emissions by an average of 5 percent below 1990 levels by 2012, set aside a fund to aid developing countries in adapting green technologies, and laid the foundation for an international cap and trade agreement. However, Kyoto highlighted the tension between environmental and business interests. The United States, at the time the world's largest polluter, refused to ratify the agreement because it would hamper economic growth. Meanwhile, environmentalists argued that the 5 percent carbon emissions goal was far too meager to prevent dangerous levels of global warming. Newly industrialized countries such as China and India were largely exempt from emissions reductions on the controversial but reasonable grounds that wealthy nations had been allowed to develop without pollution restrictions.

With the Kyoto Protocol set to expire, countries gathered again in Copenhagen in 2009 to try to hammer out the next treaty. Though the United States and China—the world's largest polluters—seemed open to committing to a reduction in carbon emissions, in the end no legally binding international agreement was produced. Developing countries remained unconvinced that their ability to modernize would not be overly constrained by the agreement, and countries disagreed over the extent to which wealthy nations ought to adopt stricter emissions targets to reflect the disproportionate role they played over the twentieth century in contributing to global warming. These conflicts make it apparent that the obstacles to solving environmental problems can be more political than technological, and finding equitable solutions is often challenging.

The Role of Lifestyle Changes While economics and politics are key arenas where changes are necessary in order to move toward sustainability, environmentalists stress that small changes to one's lifestyle can also have a major impact. California alone uses 19 billion disposable plastic bags every year—600 bags every second (Californians Against Waste 2011). These bags are made from the nonrenewable resource petroleum, and their production releases toxins into the air. Essentially nonbiodegradable, after one use plastic bags usually wind up in a landfill or become litter that fouls the land and waterways and chokes unsuspecting animals. To avoid this waste, many people are turning to reusable bags made out of durable materials like canvas. Similarly, consumers concerned about the waste produced by billions of paper cups and Styrofoam containers are switching to

FIGURE 18.5 LEVELS OF CFC PRODUCTION BEFORE AND AFTER THE MONTREAL PROTOCOL (1987)

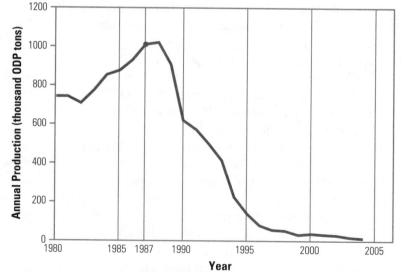

Source: European FlouroCarbons Technical Committee (2012).

travel mugs and reusable food containers. Public campaigns against bottled water highlight the large amount of waste—1.5 million tons annually—that this convenience produces and the strain it places on precious resources (in most parts of the developed world, tap water is perfectly safe to drink) (Baskind 2010).

Businesses respond when consumers demand green alternatives. Because of consumer anxiety about the toxic chemicals that wind up in the ground and water as a result of conventional farming practices, organic produce is now widely available in supermarkets. And in many parts of the country, consumers can tell their electric company that they would like part or all of their energy to come from renewable resources. Given the added cost, not everyone can afford to make these choices, but more and more consumers are deciding that the benefits are worth it.

A lifestyle choice that has major implications for sustainability is transportation. While there is always room for improvement, cities like New York and Portland have taken great strides to make walking, biking, and public transportation more attractive by adding bike and bus lanes and extending service hours and regional service. But old habits die hard. As I look out my office window in Manhattan, a sea of cars (especially yellow cabs!) chokes the six-lane road. Large SUVs containing a single occupant idle for minutes at a time, and tailpipe exhaust fills the air above them. Meanwhile, a few cyclists zip by, regularly beating cars to the same destination, but the nearby bike lanes remain underutilized. Many of those automobile commuters will fight traffic for over an hour to get to their homes in Long Island or New Jersey, even though a commuter train does the same journey in less time.

Certainly, many Americans seem to have no choice but to drive most of the time—particularly if they live outside of urban areas. Green transportation advocates recognize this reality. Rather than expecting people to ditch their cars, they urge people to be more selective about when and how they use them. Can they carpool? Is the train a viable option? Considering one's alternatives for a particular trip, rather than simply making one's car the default choice, could go a long way in reducing greenhouse gas emissions.

Depending on where you live and how much money you have, certain sustainable practices may not be an option for you. But everyone can take steps to learn more about the wider ecological impacts of their lifestyle and then decide what environmentally friendly changes are possible or attractive to them. One easy way to do this is to calculate your carbon footprint. A number of websites will estimate the amount of carbon emissions that you or your household are responsible for each year based on information you provide about transportation choices, electricity usage, and so on. After computing your carbon footprint and comparing it to the national and global average, the websites offer tips on how you can take steps to reduce your environmental impact (check out http://www.nature.org/initiatives/climatechange/calculator).

CONCLUSION LINKING ENVIRONMENTAL AND SOCIAL FACTS

Environmental sociology opens up new vistas for social analysis. Studying the ways in which environment and society are enmeshed fosters dialogue between the natural and the social sciences. Environmental sociology encourages us to recognize that the "natural" is always linked to the social. Because the ways that we interact with our environment—whether we seek to protect or destroy it—are based on our interpretations of it, solving environmental problems will require acknowledging, and reconciling, disparate environmental worldviews.

Environmental sociologists make it clear that solving environmental problems will require significant social change, not just new technology. But is the pursuit of profit incompatible with sustainable development? Certainly, history has shown that capitalism leads to environmental degradation. However, the last several decades have witnessed the emergence of green technologies and innovative environmental policies such as cap-and-trade programs for carbon emissions. While there is still a long way to go, societies are nonetheless making strides toward sustainability without sacrificing their gross domestic product. This has led a number of scholars to argue that economic growth *can* be adapted to sustainable goals. As society's preference for environmentally friendly products and industries escalates, so goes the argument, firms will compete for market shares by producing green commodities and technologies. Can we leave it to the economy to produce sustainability? Would this alleviate environmental inequality or exacerbate it?

Sociologists agree that there is a correlation between socioeconomic status and environmental risk. But what, exactly, is the nature of this relationship? While some studies clearly show that poor people of color are more likely to live near toxic waste facilities, this reveals a correlation but not causation. We are left wondering: Did companies discriminate by locating the facility there, or is it simply the case that both the residents and the firm settled in an area because it was affordable? Also, given that the majority of those in poverty are nonwhite, sociologists are often unable to determine whether it is race or class that plays the most important role in determining environmental risk.

How do we define and measure environmental risk? Even if we find that a poor neighborhood has higher rates of asthma than the surrounding areas, for instance, how can we actually demonstrate that the increased rate is because of nearby smokestacks and not other factors such as diet or exercise? At this point we do not have enough data, or the right instruments, to precisely map the connections among geography, socioeconomic status, and risk. Gaining the ability to do so is crucial because environmental justice will only be achieved if we can reveal the mechanisms of injustice.

Watch the Video in **MySocLab**
Applying Your Sociological Imagination

1   How Does Social Life Relate to the Natural Environment? *(p. 510)*

 Watch the **Big Question Video** in **MySocLab** to review the key concepts for this section.

In this section, we explored how every society consumes and transforms the natural environment to satisfy its needs and desires while also adapting to its physical surroundings and confronting natural limits.

UNDERSTANDING ENVIRONMENT-SOCIETY RELATIONS (p. 510)

Traditional Societies (p. 510)

Modern Societies (p. 511)

- **How do modern societies differ from traditional ones in their relationships to the physical environment?**

The Environment-Society Dialogue (p. 513)

- **How does the environment shape behavior and social outcomes?**

KEY TERMS

environmental sociology *(p. 508)*

totemism *(p. 511)*

anthropocentrism *(p. 513)*

determinist *(p. 513)*

ecology *(p. 513)*

social construction *(of the environment) (p. 514)*

2   How Has Human Activity Harmed the Environment? *(p. 514)*

 Watch the **Big Question Video** in **MySocLab** to review the key concepts for this section.

The most pressing environmental problems of our time—such as deforestation, water pollution, and global warming—are the result of human activities. This section described contemporary environmental problems and discussed how they are caused by industrial production and consumption.

CONTEMPORARY ENVIRONMENTAL PROBLEMS (p. 514)

Global Warming (p. 515)

- How have human behaviors led to climate change?

Natural Resource Depletion (p. 516)

- What natural resources are being depleted and why?

Solid and Chemical Waste (p. 519)

- Why is there an excess of solid and chemical waste in wealthy countries like the United States?

 Explore the **Data** on What Our Garbage Says About Us in **MySocLab**

Air and Water Pollution (p. 521)

- Why are air and water pollution more of a threat in developing countries?

KEY TERMS

fossil fuel *(p. 515)*

greenhouse effect *(p. 515)*

global warming *(p. 515)*

climate change *(p. 516)*

smog *(p. 521)*

acid rain *(p. 521)*

3

How Do Environmental Factors Impact Inequality? (p. 522)

👁 **Watch** the **Big Question Video** in **MySocLab** to review the key concepts for this section.

This section explored how sociologists examine environmental catastrophes, such as Hurricane Katrina, and how the structure of society shapes the effects of these natural events.

THE ENVIRONMENTAL MOVEMENT AND SOCIAL INEQUALITY (p. 522)

The Environmental Movement (p. 523)

Environmental Justice (p. 524)

● **What is environmental racism, and how can it be remedied?**

📖 **Read** the **Document** *Dumping in Dixie: Race, Class, and the Politics of Place* by Robert Bullard in **MySocLab.** This reading demonstrates the concept of environmental racism.

The Social Dimension of Natural Disasters (p. 525)

● **Why are some people more vulnerable to a natural disaster than others?**

Global Environmental Inequality (p. 526)

4

How Can We Create More Sustainable Societies? (p. 527)

👁 **Watch** the **Big Question Video** in **MySocLab** to review the key concepts for this section.

In this section, we discussed the social, political and economic obstacles to adopting sustainable lifestyles in developed and developing countries, and we explored the ways in which we might be able to overcome these obstacles.

CONSUMPTION, PRODUCTION, AND SUSTAINABILITY (p. 527)

The Tragedy of the Commons (p. 528)

The Treadmill of Production (p. 529)

● **What warnings do the "tragedy of the commons" and the "treadmill of production" concepts offer when thinking about sustainability?**

Toward Sustainability (p. 529)

● **What implications do technology, politics, and individual life-styles have for sustainability?**

⊙➔ **Explore** A Sociological Perspective: Can environmental damage be reversed? in **MySocLab**

👁 **Watch** the **Video** Applying Your Sociological Imagination in **MySocLab** to see these concepts at work in the real world

19

POPULATION, AGING, and HEALTH

(((Listen to the Chapter Audio in MySocLab

by LAWRENCE L. WU
and JENNIFER L. JENNINGS

 ow do social scientists think about population, aging, and health? We decided to answer this from the perspective of one us (Wu), in a setting that is probably familiar to most of you—a holiday gathering. My parents divorced when I was a teenager, and I am a gay man, so holiday gatherings for the Wu family are usually at my sister's—she is married and has two kids. Like most grandparents, my mother enjoys spending time with my niece and nephew, so she flies from Los Angeles for the holidays to stay at my sister's. Holiday gatherings mean holiday meals, and around the holiday dinner table (two tables, actually) usually sit, on my side of the family, my sister, my brother-in-law, my niece, my nephew, me, and my mother; and on my brother-in-law's side of the family are his mother (but not his father, who passed away recently); his sister, her husband, and their two kids; and one of his two brothers, his wife, and their three kids. We do what many families do at holiday gatherings: We eat too much, drink too much, exchange presents, talk, and watch the kids play.

And talking, at least in my family, means recounting family history, a topic that invariably comes up during the holidays. Here's a quick sketch of my family's history. Both my parents were born in China, in Shanghai, in 1930. They came to the United States in 1949, attended college, met each other in 1956, and married in 1957. I was born a year later, and my sister was born about two years after me. (This means that both of us were born at the tail end of the baby boom, something we discuss in greater detail below.) At least as interesting, demographically speaking, is my parents' generation. My mother's parents had a total of four children, all of whom were born in China: my two uncles (one of whom died of AIDS in the late 1980s), my mother, and one daughter who died a few months after she was born. My father's parents had seven

MY SOCIOLOGICAL IMAGINATION

Lawrence L. Wu

I was born in New York City but mostly grew up in Los Angeles, in the northwest corner of the San Fernando Valley in a city called Chatsworth. As a sociologist, my areas of specialization are in social demography, particularly in the social demography of the family, meaning that I have written on fertility (and especially nonmarital fertility), cohabitation, marriage, and divorce. Many social demographers use big data sets in their research, and I am no different, so I'm more than a bit of a numbers geek (something that you'll see, for better or worse, in this chapter). As you'll also learn, what fascinates me the most as a social scientist is the fact that so much of our social world has changed so very quickly and what this means, in turn, for each of us as individuals living in an ever-changing world. This also means that as a numbers geek, one of my other areas of specialization is in statistical methods for studying change, both change historically and change as people's lives unfold from birth through adolescence and into adulthood.

Why are sociologists so fascinated with studying population change, aging societies, and health?

children, all of whom were also born in China: my father, one uncle, and five aunts.

This pattern of large families in past generations and much smaller families in current generations turns out to be central to understanding a key demographic debate of the past few decades. For example, in the 1960s and 1970s, when I was growing up, it was taken for granted that *the* most pressing population issue was rapid population growth. *The Population Bomb*, published in 1968 by American biologist and educator Paul Ehrlich, summarized this view, noting that the world's population was growing much too rapidly and that there would soon be very dire consequences (Ehrlich 1968). Ehrlich's argument was not new; in fact, 180 years earlier, English scholar Thomas Malthus (1798) also argued that rapid increases in population would lead to widespread misery.

Today, many **demographers** (social scientists who study population issues) agree that there is not one but two pressing problems related to population growth. One is, as before, the problems facing nations and regions in the world in which population growth continues to be very rapid and

> **The pattern of large families in past generations and much smaller families in current generations turns out to be central to understanding a key demographic debate of the past few decades.**

in which it would be highly desirable for population growth to be curbed. The second, seemingly paradoxically, concerns nations and regions of the world in which populations are aging rapidly and may even experience decline, sometimes at a very rapid pace. For those nations facing rapid population aging and potential decline, it would be highly desirable for these trends to be curbed.

There is a larger demographic story that helps to resolve this apparent paradox in which the problem in some cases is too rapid population growth and other cases the possibility of too rapid population decline in the future. And as we will see, these very different patterns of population growth also have profound implications for aging and population health. Aging societies face dramatically different challenges than younger ones. In aging countries the challenges of improving population health have shifted from reducing infectious diseases (like tuberculosis) to managing chronic diseases like heart disease and diabetes for a growing fraction of the population. In this chapter, we discuss why this is so.

THE BIG QUESTIONS

👁 Watch the Big Question Videos in **MySocLab**

How do populations change over time? The world had 1.75 billion people in 1910, 3.5 billion in 1967, and 7 billion in 2012, thus taking 57 and then 45 years for the world's population to double in size. When will the world's population next double in size? In this section we also look at how mortality and fertility have changed for different nations and what these changes might imply for the demographic futures of these nations.

What happens in aging societies? Some countries have many very young people but very few old people, while others have many old people currently and will have even more old people in the future. What do these differences mean for health conditions in countries like these? In this section, we ask about the demographic implications when populations begin to age. We then focus on how sociologists measure health in an aging population.

How do social contexts affect health? We often think of health behaviors as individual choices. In this section, we explore how social contexts affect our health behaviors and how events that happen throughout our lives affect our health as adults. The relationships we have with others also play an important role in determining whether we engage in positive health behaviors.

Who gets sick and why? Low socioeconomic status is a strong predictor of poor health. If you are highly educated, you are more likely to live a longer and healthier life than people who are not. This has been true throughout history and across many different countries. We explore why these patterns persist and the major explanations that sociologists have advanced to explain them.

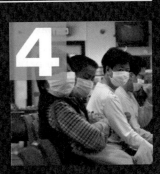

1 How Do Populations Change over Time?

POPULATION DYNAMICS

👁 Watch **the Big Question Video in MySocLab**

The Population Bomb, written by Paul Ehrlich and published in 1968, summarized a pervasive mid-twentieth-century concern—that the world's population was growing much too quickly and that this ticking time bomb would soon have catastrophic effects (Ehrlich 1968). Table 19.1 suggests why Malthus, Ehrlich, and so many others were alarmed. The table gives a condensed history of population growth in which we've organized the numbers to answer the question: How long has it taken for the world's population to double in size? We reached a landmark around 2012, when the world's population hit 7 billion, so we've made the table end there. In any case, the table tells what seems (but only seems) to be a simple story.

We start our story in Table 19.1 in 480 BCE, when the world's population is estimated to have been about 110 million. It wasn't until 800 CE that the world's population reached 220 million, thus taking 1,280 years to double. In 1330, or 530 years later, the world's population doubled again, and it doubled again between 1330 and 1810. (The world's population fluctuated dramatically during this latter period because of the Black Plague and the repeated epidemic outbreaks that followed.)

The really crucial part of the story starts in 1810, when the world's population began growing very rapidly. The number of human beings alive doubled in the 100 years between 1810 and 1910, doubling again during the next 57 years, and again in the next 45 years, at which point we get to the 7 billion people alive today.

So the story that Table 19.1 tells is simple but dramatic: It once took 1,280 years for the world's population to double, but the most recent doubling took only 45 years. Wouldn't these numbers imply that Ehrlich was right? To answer this, let's pose the same question, but instead of looking backward historically, let's ask it looking forward into the future. This means asking: How many years will it take for the world's population to double again, from 7 to 14 billion? And will the next doubling be in about 30, 40, 50, or 60 years?

TABLE 19.1 DOUBLING OF THE WORLD'S POPULATION THROUGH HISTORY

Date	Population (in millions)	Years to Double Population Size
480 BCE	110	
800 CE	220	1,280
1330 CE	440	530
1810 CE	875	480
1910 CE	1,750	100
1967 CE	3,500	57
2012 CE	7,000	45

Sources: Based on data from U.S. Census Bureau (2012).

Perhaps surprisingly, the answer is "none of the above" (Lam 2011). That is, what nearly all demographers who study this question would say is that, unlike what Ehrlich believed and unlike past history, the world's population is unlikely to double again to 14 billion, certainly not in the foreseeable future. Thus, most demographers would view Ehrlich's claim as either simply wrong or, at the very least, as a much too simplistic portrait of what is a more complicated situation.

To understand this, we need to step back a bit. To demographers, the assertion that the world's population will continue to explode in size is a claim about **population dynamics**, that is, how the size of the world's population has changed, and will be changing, over time. And for demographers, population dynamics involve issues that reach beyond the simple numbers in Table 19.1. In particular, understanding population dynamics requires a detailed understanding of demography's "big three": **fertility**, **mortality**, and **migration**, that is, the set of processes underlying births, deaths, and the movement into and out of a given population. Part of this is obvious in that how a region's or nation's population changes over time is determined by these three factors. Thus, to know how many people will be in the United States in 2020, we need to know the size of the U.S. population in 2010, plus births between 2010 and 2020, minus deaths during this same period, plus the numbers who move into the United States, minus the numbers who move out of the United States.

So far, all this is just arithmetic, a type of accounting exercise; what could be simpler? Well, the less simple part is at the heart of population dynamics—how it is that populations change over time. And if population size is determined by fertility, mortality, and migration, then it necessarily follows that understanding population change requires both describing change in fertility, mortality, and migration as well as understanding what might be causing these changes. It is these aspects of population dynamics—how fertility, mortality, and migration have changed or will change—that make these population issues both much more interesting and much more challenging to social scientists. And this is why the story in Table 19.1 tells only a part of the story and why most demographers believe, unlike Ehrlich, that 7 billion people will not double anytime in the foreseeable future.

The First Demographic Transition

So if Table 19.1 tells only an incomplete story, what is the larger, more complete story? The answer is something that demographers call the **first demographic transition** (see, e.g., Notestein 1953; Davis 1963; Coale 1973; Hirschman 1994; Bulatao and Casterline 2001), that is, the transition by a region or country from a pretransition period of high fertility and high mortality to a posttransition period of low fertility and low mortality. The way we will be telling the story is to concentrate on a set of **stylized facts**, that is, a series of facts or empirical regularities that we know with great certainty. These stylized facts allow us to describe the characteristic features of the first demographic transition.

As a stylized fact, the first demographic transition is a story about historical change, and the important part to remember is that it is a story about change in two things, fertility and mortality. The story is in one sense quite simple, but what is less simple is the story's implications, which are less obvious and thus more interesting. This story has two moving parts, mortality and fertility, and three historical periods: pretransition, midtransition, and posttransition.

Here's how this story goes. For nearly all of human history (and thus before the first demographic transition), both mortality and fertility were very high. Fertility tended to be a bit higher than mortality, but only very slightly, and this meant that the world's population grew, but only very slowly. Fast-forwarding to today and looking at a country like the United States, we get to a situation of both low mortality and low fertility. So the story is one of high fertility and high mortality pretransition, and of low fertility and low mortality posttransition.

The next piece of the puzzle, and a really interesting part, is what happens in the middle of the first demographic transition. And this part of the story is that mortality first declines, followed by a decline in fertility. So putting all of these pieces together, the story of the first demographic transition involves (1) an initial pretransition period characterized by high fertility and high mortality, then (2) a transitional period in which mortality first declines followed by a decline in fertility, and then (3) a posttransition period in which both fertility and mortality are low.

Now let's focus on the transitional period in the middle, where mortality begins to decline but fertility remains high. Think about this. Slow population growth for nearly all of human history was the result of births and deaths more or less cancelling. Now we enter a period in which mortality declines, meaning fewer deaths, but fertility remains high, meaning as many births as previously. The simple arithmetic of many births but fewer deaths equals rapid population growth. This means that in this middle period, we see something very different and something very new. This is the world that Thomas Malthus and Paul Ehrlich observed and wrote about and which seemed to them to imply a population time bomb. But their story didn't take into account the other crucial part of the first demographic transition, which is that fertility does not remain high; it eventually declines,

How do fertility and mortality change during the first demographic transition?

Sudan is currently experiencing a period of rapid population growth, growing from 9 million people in 1950 to 44 million in 2010.

but only after mortality has begun its decline. And this is another crucial part of the story: In the middle of the first demographic transition, population growth can be very rapid when mortality falls but fertility remains high.

The final part of the story, which is perhaps the most interesting and most consequential, is that once fertility decline has begun (or in some versions of the story, once it passes a certain threshold), it does not reverse; thus, without exception, demographers have observed that high fertility pretransition eventually declines to much lower levels posttransition. So without exception, at least to date, we have never seen nations and regions that have gone through the first demographic transition return to pretransition levels of high fertility. Fertility levels, posttransition, have been observed to fluctuate, sometimes falling a bit, sometimes rising a bit, but we have never seen posttransition fertility levels return to the high levels of fertility that characterize things pretransition. And these are the stylized facts characterizing the first demographic transition.

How do fertility and mortality differ around the world?

Changes in Fertility and Mortality around the World

We can now better understand why Malthus and Ehrlich were so alarmed, but also why 7 billion in 2012 will be very unlikely to become 14 billion in the foreseeable future. In the 1950s and 1960s, a large number of countries had experienced recent and quite marked declines in mortality. But because these mortality declines were recent, they were not yet accompanied by a decline in fertility. As a result, the world's population soared in the middle of the twentieth century, increasing at an extremely rapid rate. In this sense, it is not surprising that many people like Ehrlich were so alarmed about the extremely rapid growth of the world's population. But what was less obvious was that fertility decline would also take place. And fertility decline is indeed a remarkable stylized fact—something that has been extremely well documented by demographers, namely that just

about everywhere, fertility decline has either taken place, is well underway, or is in its initial stages.

Fertility decline is thus the key to why the 7 billion humans alive in 2012 will almost certainly not imply 14 billion humans in the foreseeable future. Although fertility remains high in many poor nations and regions of the world, fertility decline has begun in virtually all of these nations. This, then, is also the more complete story behind the numbers in Table 19.1. For most of human history, fertility and mortality were high but mostly cancelled, so that population growth was slow. This implies a long time for the world's population to double in size. Then at some point, mortality begins to decline, but fertility remains high, resulting in very rapid increases in population. At a last stage, mortality decline is accompanied by fertility decline, and we saw a hint of this in Table 19.1 in the slowing of the doubling time for the world's population.

We can tell the same story not only for the world as a whole but also for specific nations. In the next few sections, we will look at this from 1950 to 2010 for one poor country, Sudan, and two rich countries, the United States and Japan. And to foreshadow things, the important actor in this story is once again changes in fertility.

Fertility and Mortality Change in Sudan Let's begin by looking at Figure 19.1 and working through what it tells us about Sudan's population, starting with some basics. The top graph for Sudan tells a story of very rapid population growth, from 9 million in 1950 to 44 million in 2010. Thus in terms of the doubling times we looked at in Table 19.1, the story for Sudan would be that its population doubled in size between 1950 and 1980 (30 years) and doubled again between 1980 and 2005 (25 years).

FIGURE 19.1 CHANGE IN FERTILITY AND MORTALITY IN SUDAN, THE UNITED STATES, AND JAPAN, 1950–2010

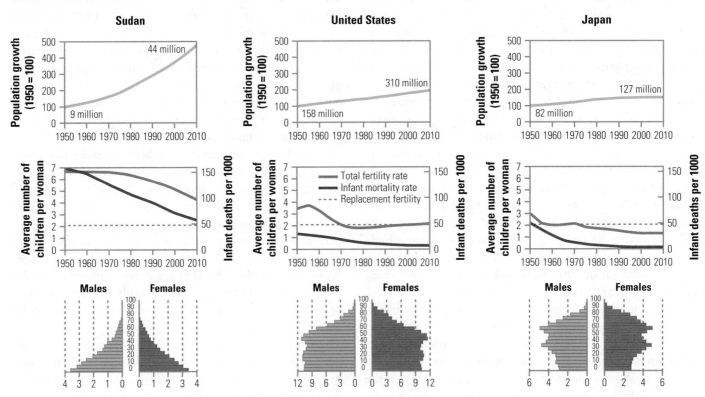

Source: Based on data from United Nations, Department of Economic and Social Affairs (2011); U.S. Bureau of the Census (2012).

The middle graph tells the story of the first demographic transition for Sudan—why its population has been growing so rapidly—which is that Sudan is very much in the middle of its first demographic transition. This graph plots mortality (red curve, scale on the left-hand axis) and fertility (blue curve, scale on the right-hand axis), and shows how they have changed in Sudan between 1950 and 2010. And the patterns we see follow exactly the storyline for what happens during a nation's first demographic transition, which is that we first see high fertility and high mortality, then mortality decline, followed at some later point by fertility decline. Thus for Sudan in 1950, both mortality and fertility were high. Our measure of fertility, the **total fertility rate**, was just under 7 for Sudan in 1950. (The total fertility rate is defined by both a level, 7 in this case, and a calendar year, 1950, and what it means is that were fertility in Sudan to remain at 1950 levels, the average woman would have about 7 children over her lifetime.) But mortality in Sudan was undergoing a steady but quite rapid decline during this period; by contrast, fertility did not begin declining until 1980 or so—and note that Sudanese fertility remains high even at present, at an average of roughly 4 children per woman in 2010. So we get the standard first demographic transition arithmetic: rapid decreases in mortality, but much later and slower decreases in fertility, which in turn imply very rapid population growth. And this is exactly what we see in Sudan: 9 million people in 1950, 44 million in 2010.

Fertility and Mortality Change in the United States What is the story for the United States? A first thing to notice is that the United States has far more people than Sudan, with 158 million people in the U.S. in 1950 and 310 million in 2010. But as the top graph for the United States in Figure 19.1 shows, population growth has been far slower in the United States than in Sudan. The middle graph for the United States shows part of the reason why. U.S. mortality has been fairly steady throughout this period, but the same was not true of fertility, which hit a peak of 3.7 children per woman in 1955 at the height of the baby boom but then declined, fluctuating between 1.9 and 2.1 children per woman between 1970 and 2010.

So the story of the first demographic transition is repeated in the United States as well, but at the end of the story, with low mortality but moderately high fertility in 1950 and low levels of mortality and low fertility in 2010.[1] Thus, we see in Figure 19.1 the start of the first demographic transition in Sudan and the end of it in the United States.

---

[1]The more correct story for the United States is that it began its first demographic transition around the early 1800s and had largely completed it by the 1930s. The U.S. baby boom, which we discuss in more detail below, led to a temporary increase in fertility, but at levels far below pretransition levels of U.S. fertility.

That we see the start and end of the first demographic transition in Sudan and the United States has very real consequences, which we can see when comparing the bottom graphs for these two nations. These graphs give what demographers call **age pyramids**, in which we have plotted the age distribution for these countries in 2010, with the numbers at the youngest ages at the bottom of the graph and the numbers at the oldest ages at the top, and with males and females on the left- and right-hand sides, respectively. The age pyramid for Sudan is just that, a sharp pyramid, in which the largest numbers in the population are the very young and the fewest are the very old. This reflects the fact that Sudan is a poor nation, with poverty influencing how mortality strikes at those of different ages. And this age and mortality story goes like the following: Although mortality has declined in Sudan, infant mortality is still quite high, and the same is true for child mortality. This, coupled with high fertility, means that many babies are born but many also die; of those babies that survive to early childhood, some also die; and so forth. And the result is an age structure for Sudan in which there are many who are very young but few who are very old, reflecting the fact that life expectancy in Sudan is far shorter than in wealthier nations.

What about changes in mortality and fertility in the United States? As Figure 19.1 shows, the 2010 age pyramid for the United States is completely different from the age pyramid in Sudan. What we see in the United States are roughly the same numbers of those who are very young and those who are much older, with the age structure beginning to resemble a pyramid only after age 60. And this again reflects how mortality strikes at those of different ages, but with dramatically different results for a wealthy nation like the United States. And thus the age pyramid for the United States does not look like a pyramid until far older ages—nearly all babies born in the United States survive to early childhood, nearly all children survive to adolescence, nearly all adolescents survive to early adulthood, and so forth, with mortality only influencing the U.S. age distribution in notable ways after age 60.

The other very important fact is that U.S. fertility has for several decades been at what demographers call **replacement fertility**. The idea is simple in that if, on average, each person in a generation had two children, this would imply a more or less unchanging size in the population—each father and mother would, on average, produce two offspring, thus replacing themselves by this number of offspring. (Demographers usually put replacement fertility at 2.1 children per woman to deal with the relatively small numbers of those who die before reaching the typical ages of childbearing.)

Fertility and Mortality Change in Japan

Figure 19.1 also provides data for Japan, another rich nation. The top graph

for Japan shows that the population in Japan has grown from 82 million in 1950 to 127 million in 2010. So Japan experienced population growth between 1950 and 2010, as was true for Sudan and the United States, but Japan's population growth has been far slower than either of these countries. As we see in the middle graph, Japan has completed its first demographic transition, with low levels of both fertility and mortality. What is particularly important to note is that Japan has had below-replacement levels of fertility for several decades, in sharp contrast to the United States, where fertility levels have been around replacement levels for several decades. The consequences of these differences—replacement levels of fertility spanning several decades in the United States but below-replacement levels of fertility spanning several decades in Japan—are very apparent when comparing the age pyramids for the United States and Japan, particularly their shapes at younger ages. As we noted earlier, the U.S. age pyramid doesn't resemble a pyramid until older ages, with roughly the same numbers of people in each five-year age group until age 60 to 64. Japan's age pyramid is very different, with sharply declining numbers at younger ages. The fact that we see sharply declining numbers in Japan's age pyramid at younger ages lines up almost with trends in Japanese fertility shown in the middle graph for Japan—since the 1970s, Japan has had below-replacement levels of fertility, with a total fertility rate in Japan of 1.3 in 2010.

So stepping back a bit, we have seen that fertility in Sudan is substantially above replacement, fertility in the United States is at replacement, and fertility in Japan is below replacement. And these facts, together with mortality, are clearly reflected in the age pyramids for these three countries. But if Japan is at below-replacement fertility, why is it that we see increases in Japan's population between 1950 and 2010? We could ask the same question for the United States, given that U.S. fertility has been at roughly replacement levels for several decades. There are two answers to this question—immigration and population momentum—which we discuss in the next section.

Immigration and Population Momentum

We already know the answer to why population size in Sudan has been increasing rapidly—it is in the middle of its first demographic transition, and so is still experiencing very rapid population growth. But the United States and Japan are both posttransition, so why is population increasing in these countries?

Let's begin with immigration, because at one level it just involves the usual demographic arithmetic and so is easy. The United States has historically been a nation of immigrants, meaning of course that virtually all of those in the United States today are not Native Americans but instead

Since the 1970s, Japan has experienced below-replacement levels of fertility. What are the consequences of this?

arrived, or are descendants of those who arrived, in the United States at various points in history, from those descended from the people who arrived on the Mayflower to those who are very recent immigrants. (Recall that, as we mentioned at the very beginning of this chapter, Wu's parents were born in China but moved to the United States.) In 2010, there were an estimated 21.2 million legal immigrants and 10.8 illegal immigrants (Hoefer, Rytina, and Baker 2010) out of the 310.4 million people living in the United States. By contrast, Japan's immigration history is very different in that Japan's immigrant population has always been extremely small. So part of the answer for why the population of the United States is larger in 2010 than in 1950 lies in the continuing flow of immigrants, both legal and illegal, to the United States. (The more complete answer for how migration affects change in a nation's population involves the numbers of in- and out-migrants, but in the case of the United States, in-migration vastly outnumbers out-migration.)

The other reason why the populations of Japan and the United States have continued to grow over the last 60 years is **population momentum**. This refers to the tendency of a population that has been changing in size to continue to change in size even if factors such as fertility and mortality have shifted to levels that would, in the long run, imply no change in population size. Population momentum is thus very similar to the momentum of a physical object. Take, for example, a jet airplane that has been climbing rapidly. If the pilot were to ease off on the jet thrusters, the plane would continue climbing, at least for a while. So growth in the population of the United States or Japan is not unlike a jet that has been climbing, with the jet continuing to climb for a while even if the pilot eases up on the thrusters. This also means there is a level of fuel supplied to the jet thrusters that makes the plane eventually fly at a constant altitude—neither climbing nor descending. Anything less than this level means that the jet will eventually begin to descend,

and anything above this level means that the jet will continue climbing.

The jet plane analogy for Japan is that the pilot is supplying less fuel than what is required to keep the plane at a constant altitude. Population momentum means that Japan's population did in fact continue to grow between 1950 and 2010. But as this analogy also suggests, Japan grew more rapidly during the first 30 years and less so in the last 30 years of this 60 year period—Japan's population was 82 million in 1950, 116 million in 1980, but only 127 million in 2010.

We began this chapter by noting that people like Malthus and Ehrlich thought that there was a ticking time bomb in the extremely rapid growth in the world's population. And while you should now know that what they worried about reflected a too simple view of population change, it nevertheless would be highly desirable for the extremely rapid population growth in countries like Sudan to be curbed. But we also noted that demographers now worry about a second and completely different problem—that of population aging, in which some regions and countries of the world are facing rapid increases in the numbers of older people. And you now know a lot about (and have the sociological and demographic tools to think about) these two very different sorts of population change.

👁 **Watch** the **Big Question Video** in **MySocLab**

2 What Happens in Aging Societies?

THE IMPLICATIONS OF AN AGING POPULATION

I n this section, we will discuss the demographic implications when populations begin to age. We will first explore what the first demographic transition implies for the health conditions of populations. We will then turn to the aging of the baby boom generation in the United States and Japan and compare how quickly aging might occur in these two countries.

☐ The Epidemiological Transition

As we saw in the first section, the first demographic transition carries with it a shift from age pyramids like that in Sudan to those that we see in the United States and Japan. How might the first demographic transition influence health when we think about overall health in a nation's population? The answer is something that social scientists now call the *epidemiological transition* (Omran 1971). **Epidemiology** is the study of health-related events in populations, their characteristics, their causes, and their consequences. The **epidemiological transition** refers to the transition of a population from health conditions primarily involving infectious disease (often extremely deadly to infants, children, and young adults in poor and developing countries) to health conditions primarily involving chronic disease (often shaping the health conditions of individuals,

How does the epidemiological transition explain differences in health conditions affecting those in poorer and richer countries?

and especially the elderly, in rich countries like the United States and Japan). And the story behind the epidemiological transition is that the first demographic transition has very important implications for the sorts of diseases and health conditions affecting countries like Sudan and countries like the United States and Japan.

Infectious diseases are diseases due to bacteria, viruses, parasites, and other infectious agents. The common cold, the flu, and HIV are examples of viral infections, while bacterial infections involve bacteria—for example, the time you got sick when you ate something that wasn't cooked properly. Infectious diseases do not usually kill people in countries like the United States and Japan, but they are an extremely common cause of death, especially for infants and young children, in poor and developing countries like Sudan.

However, we have seen a steady decline in mortality even in very poor countries like Sudan. And at least part of the reason that mortality has declined is that many poor countries have been able to tackle at least some sources of infectious disease, for example, by cleaning up and protecting water supplies and by immunizing and providing better healthcare and nutrition to infants, children, and mothers. But as should be obvious, advances in our scientific understanding of infectious disease do not in any way guarantee that mortality will decline—instead, declining mortality often requires very serious social action and social policies on the part of poor and developing countries.

The epidemiological transition also involves a transition to chronic disease. **Chronic diseases** (or, more generally, **chronic health conditions**) are diseases and health conditions that are persistent; examples include serious heart and respiratory problems, diabetes, high blood pressure, obesity, cancer, Parkinson's disease, Alzheimer's disease, and HIV/AIDS. Many of these chronic health conditions are not the result of an infectious disease but instead involve risk factors that you and I can influence, at least in part, by things like eating right, exercising, avoiding tanning booths or too much sun, and being careful about sexually transmitted diseases.[2] This is why one of the first reasearchers who wrote about the epidemiological transition characterized it as a long-term shift in mortality and disease patterns in which infectious disease is "gradually displaced by degenerative and *man-made* disease" (Omran 1971, emphasis added).

The other notable fact about chronic health conditions is not only that they tend to strike at older ages but that they typically do not kill when they first strike, and when they do kill, they often do slowly. This is the chronic aspect of these health conditions—if you suffer from a chronic health condition, you may die of it eventually, but in countries like the United States and Japan, you most often will not die from it right away. And for many of these chronic conditions (obesity, high blood pressure, heart or lung disease, some but not all cancers, HIV/AIDS), you can live for a quite long time and lead something resembling a normal life even when having a chronic condition means that you do not have perfect health.

☐ Aging of the Baby Boomers

The **baby boom** refers to the period following World War II from 1946 to 1964, during which the United States experienced a notable, extended, but ultimately temporary spike in fertility. Those born between 1946 and 1964 are referred to as the *baby boom birth cohorts* (or the *baby boomers*). (A **birth cohort** refers to persons born during the same period of time.)

We can see the U.S. baby boom in the middle graph of Figure 19.1, which shows that the U.S. total fertility rate stood at 3.4 in 1950, rose to a peak of 3.7 in 1955, and fell in later years. The baby boom can also be seen very clearly in

FIGURE 19.2 AGE PYRAMIDS FOR THE UNITED STATES AND JAPAN, 1950–2010

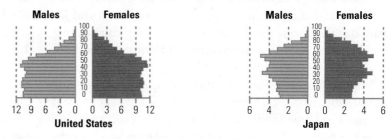

Source: Based on data from the U.S. Census Bureau (2012).

the age pyramid for the United States (see Figure 19.2). The peak of 3.7 in 1955 for the total fertility rate corresponds with the broad peak in the U.S. age pyramid covering those who were 50 to 54 in 2010 (the youngest of the baby boomers) to those aged 60 to 64 in 2010 (the oldest of the baby boomers). Note also that there is another broad peak in the U.S. age pyramid, one covering ages 15 to 19, 20 to 24, and 25 to 29 in 2010 and thus corresponding to those born in the years 1981 through 1985, 1986 through 1990, and 1991 through 1995. Many in these birth cohorts are the children of the baby boomers; thus we see a *reflection* of the baby boom in the children of the baby boomers.

Something very similar shows up in Japan's age pyramid. Japan also experienced a baby boom and, as in the United States, this shows up in the sharp peak at ages 60 to 64 in Japan's age pyramid, with this peak corresponding to those in Japan who were born between 1946 and 1950. These Japanese baby boomers then proceeded to have their children in their 20s and 30s, in the 1970s and 1980s, and we see this reflection once again as the second peak at younger ages in Japan's age pyramid. (The peak for the children of Japan's baby boomers is sharper than in the United States because Japanese baby boomers had their children, on average, in a narrower band of ages than the U.S. baby boomers.)

If we then fast forward to 2010 and beyond, most of the baby boomers in the United States and Japan are still alive and can be expected to live for at least another 15 to 25 years. We will return to exactly how long people might be expected to live in the next section, but what this means is what some have called the *graying* of societies like the United States and Japan. You can see this in Figure 19.2—the baby boom bulge in the age pyramids, coupled with how long the baby boomers are likely to live, means that there will be many more elderly in the future in the United States and Japan than there are now. (The oldest of the U.S. baby boomers—those born in 1946—turned 65 in 2011 and so were the first of the baby boomers to reach the typical ages at retirement.) 📖 **Read** the **Document** *A Gradual Goodbye: If People Are Living Longer, They Will Have to Work Longer Too* in **MySocLab**.

---

[2]One health condition that is now both chronic and infectious is HIV/AIDS. HIV/AIDS caused many deaths in the United States in the 1980s and 1990s but can now be treated, if diagnosed promptly, in ways that make it much more of a chronic condition.

Aging and Population Dynamics

We now know that countries like Sudan are growing much more rapidly than countries like the United States and Japan. But this also raises the possibility that population aging will be more rapid in some countries than others. And both phenomena—the pace of population growth and the pace of population aging—are fundamentally questions involving population dynamics. Figure 19.2 tells us a lot about what we need to know (and thus can reasonably expect looking into the future) about the pace of population aging in the United States and Japan. And the answer is that we can reasonably expect that population aging will be far more rapid in Japan than in the United States.

The reason for this is easy to see, and it lies in the shapes of the U.S. and Japanese age pyramids. Population aging refers to the relative numbers of young and old people in a population, and the age pyramids give us very detailed information about this for the United States and Japan for one particular calendar year—in the case of Figure 19.2, the calendar year 2010. Now predicting what the future will look like is speculative; it requires guesses about mortality (that is, how future mortality will strike those of different ages) plus guesses about fertility (that is, how future fertility will fill in the numbers at the bottom of future age pyramids). Looking again at Figure 19.2, you may have already guessed the answer, which is that Japan will, in all likelihood, be aging much more quickly than the United States. And the fundamental reason for this is fertility—the fact that fertility in Japan has been at subreplacement levels for many decades.

Should these trends continue into the future, Japan's population can be expected to decline once mortality begins thinning the ranks of Japan's baby boom generation. How quickly might Japan's population decline? Any answer to this question again has to be speculative, but we can nevertheless give fairly precise answers under the speculative "what if" scenario of "what if a nation's fertility remains at a particular subreplacement level for a long time?" Table 19.2 gives these numbers by asking how long it would take for population to halve in size—that is, decrease by a factor of two—if fertility remains at a particular subreplacement level for a very long time.

What Table 19.2 shows is that if fertility in a population were to remain just a bit below replacement, population decline would be very gradual, but that population decline can be very rapid at other subreplacement levels of fertility. Thus, were a hypothetical nation to have an average of 1.9 children per woman rather than the replacement level of 2.1 children per woman and were this to continue for a long time, this hypothetical nation's population would indeed decline, but quite slowly, taking roughly 280 years to halve in size. However, were a hypothetical nation to have an average of 1.4 children per woman and were this to continue for a long time, this hypothetical nation's population would take only 54 years to halve in size—an extremely rapid pace of population decline. And because Japan's fertility has been between 1.2 and 1.4 for several decades, there is the distinct possibility that Japan will experience very rapid population decline. And what has been both surprising and fascinating to demographers is that many countries besides Japan have equally low levels of subreplacement fertility. (The list includes Austria, Cuba, the Czech Republic, Germany, Greece, Hong Kong, Italy, Poland, Russia, Singapore, South Korea, Spain, and Taiwan.) Thus countries like these not only face the prospect of rapid population aging but also the possibility of rapid population decline at some point in the future should fertility remain at very low subreplacement levels.

Health in an Aging Population

What does it mean to be healthy? As defined by the World Health Organization (2011), health is "a state of complete physical, mental, and social well-being and not merely the absence of disease or infirmity." What makes health different than many social goods is that it is difficult to carry out life without it. If you are unhealthy, it is difficult to get more education, to perform well at work, or to maintain meaningful relationships.

Life expectancy is one of the most common measures uses to describe the health of a population. It is defined as the average number of years a population at some age can expect to live. As we discuss earlier in this chapter, life expectancy has increased substantially in the last century in developed countries. Americans' life expectancy at birth,

Will some countries age more quickly than others?

TABLE 19.2 YEARS UNTIL A NATION'S POPULATION WILL DECLINE BY A FACTOR OF 2 OVER THE LONG RUN WERE THERE TO BE A CONSTANT LEVEL OF SUB-REPLACEMENT FERTILITY

Mean number of children per women	2.0	1.9	1.8	1.7	1.6	1.5	1.4	1.3	1.2	1.1	1.0
Years until population halving	901	279	161	112	84	66	54	45	38	33	29

Source: Based on calculations using a formula from Kohler, Billari, and Ortega (2002).

for example, was 78.1 years in 2009 (World Bank 2011). Americans' life expectancy has increased by 8.3 years since 1960, but it nonetheless lags behind other countries around the world. The Japanese, by contrast, can expect to live 82.9 years.

Life expectancy tells us how long we might expect to live, but knowing when we might die does not tell us everything we might want to know about health. Because of this, social scientists also track **healthy life expectancy**, the average number of healthy years one can expect to live if current patterns of death and illness remain the same. The U.S. government is currently tracking three measures of healthy life expectancy: expected years of life in good health, expected years of life free from limitation of activity, and expected years of life free from selected chronic diseases (USDHHS 2008).

How do sociologists measure health?

Another measure of health status is the number of **physically and mentally unhealthy days** that Americans rated their physical or mental health as not good. In 2008, adults 18 to 24 reported 2.1 physically unhealthy days, while those 75 and older reported 6. Poor mental health, however, is more common among young adults. Those 18 to 24 years old reported 4 mentally unhealthy days over the last month, whereas those 75 and older reported 2 days (USDHHS 2008).

Chronic disease prevalence also provides a different portrait of Americans' health status. In 2008, almost 1 out of every 2 American adults 18 and older reported that they had a chronic disease (USDHHS 2008). As we discuss later, Americans have a substantially higher burden of some chronic diseases, like heart disease and diabetes, than other similar countries around the world, even when we compare people of the same age.

Together, these measures of health tell us how sick our population is and provide a framework for understanding the impact of an aging population on society as a whole. Researchers continue to debate whether increases in life expectancy will translate into increases in the number of years that we live free of disease or will simply prolong the amount of time that we spend sick at the end of our lives.

Health Care in Aging Societies
Because of declines of fertility and increases in life expectancy in developed countries, many countries are now facing significant problems financing the retirement and healthcare costs for the elderly. By 2030, 1 in 8 people in the world will be 65 or older (NIA 2007). By 2050, it is projected that 1 in 5 Americans will be over the age of 65 (Pew Research Center 2009). In aging societies, the number of younger working people for each person 65 and older has been shrinking so that there are fewer people who will be able to share the cost of healthcare for the elderly.

Since 1965, the United States has provided healthcare for citizens 65 and older through a program called **Medicare**. Until recently, Medicare only covered hospital care and outpatient services and included no prescription drug benefits. Many important dimensions of health, such as dental services, are not included in Medicare, and Medicare does not cover the entire cost of a recipient's medical bills. In 2006, Medicare beneficiaries' median out-of-pocket spending on healthcare was $3,103 a year (Nonnemaker and Sinclair 2011). Ten percent of beneficiaries spent $8,300 a year. For many of the elderly, costs this high can mean having to choose between food and medicine or having to skip medicine frequently.

For many reasons—in particular, medical advances and technology—healthcare has also become more expensive for everyone over time. For example, between 1986 and 1994, we paid an average of $12,000 per heart attack patient to extend their life for a year. Between 1999 and 2002, we paid $300,000 to extend life for an additional year (Chandra 2012). Because of three factors—the rising cost of healthcare, the aging of American society, and the decline in the number of younger people to help share the cost—9 percent of the United States' gross domestic product (GDP) will be spent on healthcare by 2035 (Congressional Budget Office 2011).

As American life expectancy has increased, we face new problems, such as caring for larger numbers of the elderly and managing chronic disease.

Chronic diseases like cancer and heart disease now kill a higher fraction of Americans, creating the need for different end-of-life care options than we have had in the past.

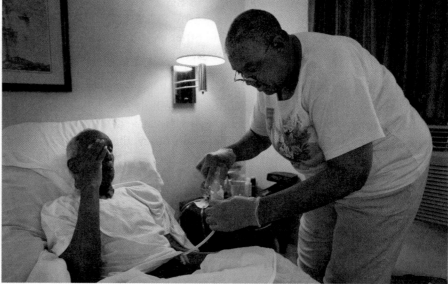

But as difficult as these problems are for the United States, we might very reasonably expect these problems to be even more daunting in Japan. That is, even though both the United States and Japan are graying societies, what we saw in Table 19.2 raises the possibility that Japan's population will not only grow older but will also grow smaller, with fewer new workers replacing those that retire.

Death and Dying around the World

We often think of death as the most individual event in our lives. We often hear people lament that they will "die alone," and people have a wide variety of personal preferences about the kind of death they hope to have. But these preferences are a function not just of individual idiosyncratic tastes but of the cultures, religions, and nations in which we are embedded.

The rise of chronic disease as the cause of death, rather than an acute event like a heart attack, creates new challenges for caring for people at the end of their lives. Chronic diseases generally unfold slowly, so those suffering from them can expect to experience a series of health emergencies that ultimately culminate in their death. This change may have important implications for how we choose to manage death; for example, by not only trying to prevent death but by reducing the pain and stress that can accompany the end of life, a period that now extends for much longer than ever before.

The United States tends to operate around a heroic model of medicine, where we expect doctors to "do everything they can" to prolong lives. A relatively small number of Americans have defined the conditions under which they prefer to die in a legal document, called an **advance directive**. For example, an advance directive might specify that someone does not want to be placed on a ventilator if that is necessary to sustain his or her life. Others might suggest that they only want **palliative care**, which is defined by the World Health Organization as "an approach that improves the quality of life of patients and their families facing the problem associated with life threatening illness, through the

prevention and relief of suffering by means of early identification and impeccable assessment and treatment of pain and other problems, physical, psychosocial and spiritual." One of the best-known types of palliative care is **hospice care**, which focuses on eliminating suffering—physical and mental—for terminally ill patients. Hospices in the United States have traditionally provided care for terminal cancer patients but have expanded rapidly with the aging of the population. Hospice organizations now estimate that up to 42 percent of deaths in the United States involve some kind of hospice care (National Hospice and Palliative Care Organization 2011).

How has the rise of chronic disease in developed countries created challenges in caring for the elderly?

According to data that bring together measures about the quality, cost, and availability of end-of-life care from around the world (Economist Intelligence Unit 2010), there is substantial variation between countries in end-of-life care. Developed countries like the United Kingdom and Australia are consistently rated to provide the best quality of care, while India, Uganda, Brazil, and China are rated as the worst.

We have seen that aging societies, and the individuals who live in them, are in many respects the victim of their own success. The multiple social challenges that they face — chronic disease, financial burdens, and issues around an extended period of end-of-life care — exist precisely because of increases in life expectancy over the last century. Aging societies also provide a clear example of a larger sociological principle: Our social institutions adapt to the changing social contexts and conditions that they face. In the next section, we will further consider how social contexts affect not only social institutions, but individual and population health.

Watch the Big Question Video in MySocLab

3 How Do Social Contexts Affect Health?

A SOCIOLOGICAL VIEW OF HEALTH

When you walk into the doctor's office, health feels like an individual problem. You have a few worrisome symptoms—a cough and some difficulty breathing. Your doctor asks you about how you've been eating, whether you smoke, whether you've been exercising, and what you know about your family history. You admit that you've been skipping the gym. And it's true that you have been more stressed than usual at work. You walk away with orders to stop smoking and to fill a prescription to calm your cough.

Doctors are interested in the immediate causes of illness that can be remedied with medical treatments. They focus on why you got this illness at this time. The cause of your poor health could lie deep in your past—for example, you lived in a polluted city as a child—but in their offices, they attempt to address the immediate symptoms rather than to consider their social causes.

Sociologists take a decidedly different approach to the study of health. First, they focus on the social causes of disease within a population rather than on the immediate causes of an individual's illness. Sociologists want to know why people in some countries are much more likely to die early than those in others, or why poor populations consistently die earlier than more affluent ones. Most approaches to health research focus on individual genetic risk factors or individual behavioral risks. Instead, sociologists are interested in how interactions between individuals and the societies in which they live affect health.

Second, sociologists consider how social contexts shape individual health behaviors. When confronted with an overweight person, sociologists look beyond the individual's self-control to explain that outcome. Sociologists focus on how social contexts may lead individuals to eat more, and exercise less, than is healthy. They also consider how social interactions and norms affect people's willingness to stop engaging in behaviors that are bad for their health.

Finally, doctors generally focus on how our current day-to-day lives affect illness because those are the contexts they can influence. In contrast, sociologists think about how the contexts we inhabit throughout our lives affect our health. For example, babies who weigh too little when they were born are more likely to have a range of health problems as they age. Because poor early health conditions may be as important as your later health behaviors, sociologists consider how events occurring now and in the past affect your health.

The Population as Patient

In the 1980s, an English epidemiologist named Geoffrey Rose had an important insight about the way most health systems work. Rose realized that individuals are part of societies with particular rates of disease. For example, Americans are more likely to be overweight than people in Japan not only because of individual factors. The rate of disease in any society is a product of social forces. Doctors ask, "Why is this person overweight?" Rose wanted us to ask, "Why is the American population as a whole heavier than the Japanese population?"

The sociological approach to improving health differs from the medical approach. Doctors focus on treating high-risk groups—for example, those most likely to have hypertension. Getting fewer people to become sick in the first place, however, might require a different strategy.

How could that be possible? Most risk factors, like blood pressure, have no clear cutoff above which high blood pressure leads to a stroke or a heart attack. Your risk increases as your blood pressure increases. The medical field necessarily establishes arbitrary cutoff points on a continuum that determine when you should receive treatment for high blood pressure (hypertension). We give people drugs for hypertension over a certain cutoff and keep an eye on patients right below that cutoff.

The trouble is that high-risk groups make up a small fraction of the overall population. But as the example of hypertension makes clear, health risks operate on a continuum; they are not an "either/or" phenomenon. Most of the cases of stroke don't come from people at high risk of hypertension but from those who had elevated blood pressure. For that reason, Rose believed that we could save more lives by decreasing everyone's blood pressure a little bit than by reducing the blood pressure of the most high-risk cases. This is often referred to as the *population model for prevention*, and it focuses on "shifting the distribution of risk" (Rose 1985).

Shifting the distribution of risks means changing whole societies. A number of recent public health initiatives have attempted to do that. For example, in New York City, chain restaurants are now required to list the number of calories in each item. The goal of this policy is to encourage New Yorkers to choose healthier options and to create pressure for businesses to offer them. As a result, the average New Yorker would eat fewer calories, pushing fewer over the line that doctors consider "obese." By changing features of the social environment and treating the population as the patient, this initiative puts the population model of prevention into action. It remains an open question, of course, whether this approach will improve population health. Explore the Infographic on page 553 to learn more about long-term effects of obesity in the United States.

Obesity has increased substantially in recent decades, a pattern that many have attributed to changes in the American diet.

How does the sociological approach to health differ from the medical approach?

☐ The Effects of Social Contexts on Individual Behavior

How might other social forces beyond the country in which you live affect your health? Suicide provides an interesting example. On its face, suicide is the most individual of acts. In the late nineteenth century, sociologist Emile Durkheim sought to understand how suicide rates differed across social groups and how social change affected rates of suicide. In his book *Suicide* (Durkheim [1897] 2006), he showed that suicide rates are affected by the amount of social integration and social regulation in people's lives.

One of Durkheim's most paradoxical results was that social integration and regulation could be either helpful or harmful. In communities where *either* social integration or regulation is extremely low or high, more people are likely to commit suicide. Strongly integrated groups benefited from the sense of inclusion that strong social ties foster. But Durkheim also showed that too much integration is also associated with higher rates of suicide, as group needs take precedence over individuals' need to survive. On the other hand, social ties not only integrate individuals but regulate their behavior. Without these ties, Durkheim argued that individuals' desires could exceed their ability to fulfill them and thus lead to higher suicide rates.

Sociologists recognize that the contexts that people inhabit and the relationships they have with others play an important role in shaping the choices that they make. They ask what features of social contexts enable or constrain particular behaviors. Sociologists examine how norms around behavior may affect individuals' choices. For example, norms about binge drinking appear to vary across age groups.

Obesity in the U.S.

In the past 50 years, obesity rates in the United States have increased almost universally, affecting people of all races, ages, levels of education, and genders. The United States has the highest obesity rate of any country in the world (U.S. Department of Health and Human Services, 2010). High obesity rates have serious implications on everything from individual health and life expectancy to national healthcare costs.

Percentage of adults who are obese

20% 25% 30% 35% 40% 50%

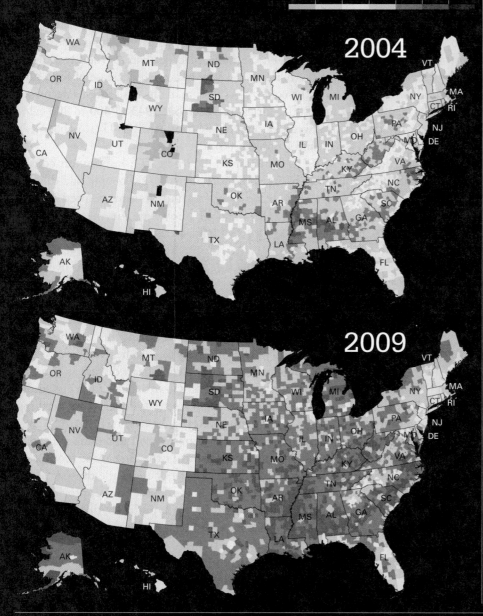

2004

2009

Studies predict that by 2020, close to half (45%) of the U.S. adult population will be obese if present trends continue (Stewart, Cutler, and Rosen 2009).

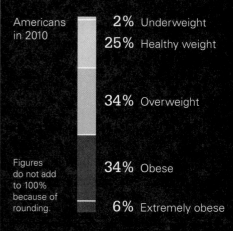

Americans in 2010

2% Underweight
25% Healthy weight
34% Overweight
34% Obese
6% Extremely obese

Figures do not add to 100% because of rounding.

Compared to people of healthy weight, people who are overweight or obese are at higher risk of:

- Coronary heart disease
- High blood pressure
- Type 2 diabetes
- Stroke
- Endometrial cancer
- Breast cancer
- Colon cancer
- Respiratory problems
- High cholesterol
- Liver disease
- Gallbladder disease
- Osteoarthritis
- Abnormal menses
- Infertility

Because obesity can lead to so many health problems, it has a significant economic effect on our healthcare system. It is estimated that these costs totaled around $117 billion ($61 billion direct and $56 billion indirect) in the year 2000 alone (U.S. Department of Health and Human Services 2001).

Sources: Based on data from Centers for Disease Control and Prevention (2012).

Explore the Data on Obesity in the U.S. in **MySocLab** and then ...

Think About It

Why is the American population as a whole heavier than the population of any other country in the world? What social forces might be responsible?

Inspire Your Sociological Imagination

What are the pros and cons of public health initiatives aimed at fighting obesity, such as a tax on sodas or requiring that calories be listed on menus?

Twenty-six percent of 18- to 24-year-olds report binge drinking (defined as more than four drinks for women and more than five drinks for men on one or more occasions in the last 30 days). For those 65 and older, that number drops to only 4 percent (CDC 2011).

How might social contexts contribute to age differences in binge drinking? Social contexts shape what counts as "normal" behavior and what behaviors are socially sanctioned or accepted. If all of the students in your dorm binge drink on the weekends, it's more likely that you will, too. Social contexts also provide opportunities for engaging in binge-drinking behaviors. If you can walk down your hallway to a party where binge drinking is happening, it's easier to engage in the behavior than if you have to actively seek out opportunities to do so. Some social contexts like colleges may create stress that leads people to engage in health-risking behaviors to alleviate stress. Binge drinking, which may alleviate stress in the short term but cause negative health outcomes in the long term, is just one example of a coping behavior that is influenced by social context.

The relationships we have with others also impact the choices we make. Our social relationships affect our health in three major ways: through social influence, person-to-person contact, and access to resources (Smith and Christakis 2008).

Obesity provides one of the best examples of the process of social influence. While obesity is often thought of as a result of choices that we privately make, most eating is social. Imagine that the person across the table from you decides to order the all-you-can-eat buffet. Because it is more convenient for your meal if you both order from the buffet, you probably follow your friend. If your friend goes back for a second and third helping, you might be less shy about doing the same. Sociologists have in fact produced empirical evidence that suggests that people who are obese are more likely to have friends who are obese (Christakis and Fowler 2007). While it is complicated to determine the direction of causality, as we choose our own friends and it is often said that "birds of a feather flock together," this is nonetheless suggestive that social norms are at work.

Person-to-person contact is also important for the spread of infectious diseases. For those of you who watch movies, you already have many examples at your fingertips about how person-to-person contact in the presence of a highly contagious disease can lead to pandemic flu or disease. In this way, the people with whom we ride the bus and the people in the next cubicle over have important impacts on our health.

A final way through which social relationships affect our health is through access to resources. Think about the last time you had to find a doctor. You probably asked your friends and family if they knew of a good doctor for your condition. Social relationships also affect your access to information. If other college students are talking about getting the new human papillomavirus (HPV) vaccine, you may learn important information about the benefits of the vaccine through your conversations.

The Accumulation of Health Risks across the Life Course

An unusual natural experiment during World War II provided some of the most compelling evidence we have about the accumulation of health risks across the life course. In the winter of 1944, Germans placed a ban on food transports in the Netherlands, leading to a rapid decrease of food supplies in the country. As a result, daily adult rations decreased from 1,800 calories in December 1943 to 400 to 800 calories between December 1944 and April 1945 (Roseboom, de Rooij, and Painter 2006).

The Dutch famine had catastrophic human consequences; by its end, more than 18,000 people had died. It had an unintended effect, however—it gave social scientists the opportunity to understand how events that happen early in our lives may affect our long-term health outcomes.

Sociologists studying the Dutch famine made a fascinating observation: People born during the height of the Dutch famine were more likely to have heart disease. When we think about the causes of having heart disease as an adult, we generally think about how our behavior during adulthood affects that outcome. This study suggested something different: What happens to you *in utero* has enduring consequences. The timing of exposure to the famine mattered, however—those exposed during the first three months of gestation were more likely to be obese, while those exposed later were less likely to be obese. These studies provide support for the **fetal programming hypothesis**; that is, the idea that things that happen to you during critical periods of development can change the way that the tissues and structures of your body function.

The example of the Dutch famine illustrates another unique feature of the sociological approach to health. When sociologists consider the effects social contexts you have inhabited throughout your life have on your health, they call this a **life-course perspective**. Of particular interest are the long-term impacts of adverse childhood conditions, which can have negative effects on health long after they are no longer experienced. Increasingly sociologists are thinking about health in a life-course framework. For example, rather than only examining the effects of being obese as an adult, they focus on the

> # How do our social worlds and relationships help determine the health choices we make?

cumulative effects of obesity as a child, as a teenager, and as a young adult on your adult health outcomes. There are three types of life-course models that sociologists study.

The first life-course model is a **sensitive-period model** (or **latency model**). In this model, very early life exposures can affect adult outcomes but may remain latent for years. Trying to improve health in adulthood does not work if the damage is done once. The idea is that things that happen to you even before you were born—that is, while you were in your mother's womb (such as the Dutch famine)—can have long-term implications for your adult health outcomes, but their effects do not show up for a long time.

The second life-course model is the **cumulative-exposure model**. Smoking may provide the best example of this model. If you are a smoker, you accumulate exposure to carcinogens over a long period of time. Each cigarette adds up, and by the time you are older, you are more likely to have emphysema and lung cancer if you have exposed yourself to these carcinogens over a longer period of time.

The final model is the **social-trajectory model**. According to this approach, your early life experiences determine where you end up in the social pecking order, which in turn influence your health. For example, if you are sick as a child, you may do more poorly in school. As a result, you are less likely to go to college and thus less likely to get a higher paying job. Because you work in an industry that does not provide health insurance, your health is further negatively affected. Differences in life conditions throughout the life course may contribute to differences in health across countries, as we will see in the next section.

Where you are born plays a large role in determining the condition of which you are likely to die. In America, leading causes of death are heart disease and cancer.

Differences in Health across Countries and Local Contexts

Imagine you were to enter a lottery. Unlike the lotteries most of us are familiar with, where hard cash is the prize, this lottery would determine the country in which you would be born. By the luck of the draw, you could be born in the United States, where less than 1 percent of babies die in their first year of life. Or you could be born in Afghanistan or Angola, where more than 1 in 10 babies do not survive their first birthday (WHO 2011).

If you do make it past your childhood, what you are likely to ultimately die of varies substantially across countries. In the United States, you are most likely to die of heart disease or cancer. In Afghanistan and Angola, you are most likely to lose your life to diarrhea, the flu, or pneumonia.

We rarely stop to think about how much our lives are influenced by where we happened to be born or by the socioeconomic backgrounds of our parents—choices over which

How do sociologists use life-course perspectives to examine health issues?

we have no control. But, as we have learned in this section, social contexts have important impacts on the health of people who inhabit them. Who you are and where you live play a substantial role in determining how long you will live and how healthy you will be while you are alive.

What's curious is that there are large differences between the United States and other similar highly developed countries, such as England. In 2005, researchers compared the prevalence of heart disease, diabetes, and cancer in the United States and England and paid special attention to disparities by socioeconomic status (SES; Banks et al. 2006). The United States spends more than twice as much as England on medical care (about $5,270 versus $2,160 per person), and we often hear that the United States has "the best medical system in the world." You would think that this would amount to better health outcomes. Explore *A Sociological Perspective* on page 556 to learn more about the quality of healthcare around the world.

There are many factors that determine quality of healthcare. At an elementary level, physician density—the ratio of medical doctors to people in a given population—greatly affects how many patients can visit the doctor and how much time doctors can devote to each individual patient. Physician density varies greatly across the globe and provides some insight to the way medical care differs from country to country. According to the World Health Organization, there must be a minimum of 2.3 health workers—meaning medical doctors, nurses, and midwives—per 1,000 people in order to sufficiently meet the healthcare needs of a population (World Health Organization 2008).

In the United States there are approximately 2.7 physicians per 1,000 people (2004), slightly lower than that of other Western nations. In many developing countries, particularly in Africa, a lack of medical professionals is a major obstacle to adequate healthcare. In Sierra Leone, for example, there are only 0.016 physicians per 1,000 people (2008) – even fewer in Ghana, indicating that healthcare needs of people in these countries are far from being met. On the other hand, Cuba has one of the highest physician-to-population ratios at about 6.4 physicians per 1,000 people (2007), indicating that the wealth of a nation it is not the sole determinant of the healthcare resources available to its people (TCIA World Factbook).

Women wait in a Tillaberi hospital for their children to be seen by medical staff. Facing food shortages and drought, a cholera outbreak threatens the people of several villages. Would a cholera outbreak in the U.S. pose the same or less of a deadly threat to our cities?

How do countries like Cuba and Venezuela make the healthcare needs of their people a top priority (per capita) over Western countries when they don't have the same financial resources to draw from?

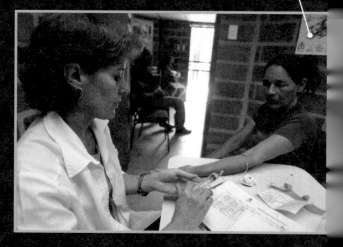

Emergency rooms and clinics in the U.S. are often crowded and overflowing with people needing medical attention. What are some of the social and economic issues related to this reality that go beyond the immediate healthcare issue of the individual?

⊙► **Explore** A Sociological Perspective in **MySocLab** and then . . .

■ **Think About It**

Why do Americans have worse health outcomes, even though we

■ **Inspire Your Sociological Imagination**

How would the healthcare you receive be different if you were borr

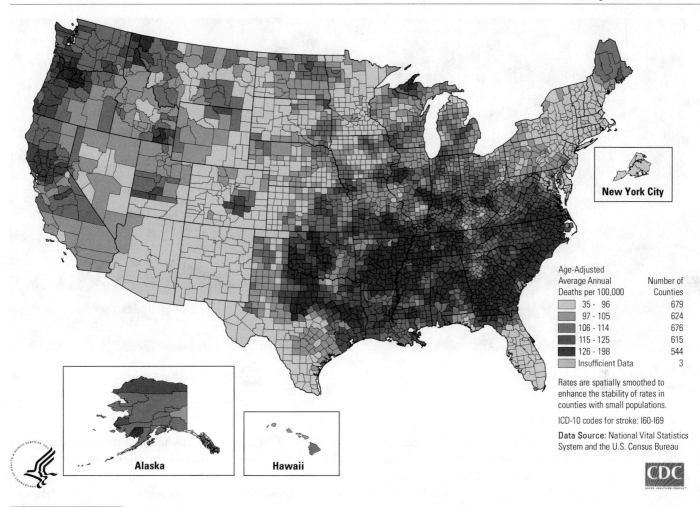

FIGURE 19.3 STROKE DEATH RATES, 2000–2006

Source: CDC (2012).

These researchers found, when comparing only white Americans and white English people, that the United States had substantially higher rates of chronic disease. You might think this is because people in the United States are more likely to diagnosed. To address this problem, the researchers compared people in the two countries only based on biological markers of these conditions. Still, they found that people in the United States were substantially less healthy.

Finally, the researchers found that people of higher SES are more healthy in both countries. However, people of higher SES in the United States were about as healthy as people of lower SES in the United Kingdom. While the researchers could not determine the cause of these differences, proposed explanations include higher levels of inequality in the United States, longer and more stressful working hours, and the absence of universal health insurance.

Researchers have also determined that there are important differences in health across different geographic regions of the United States. In 1962, the Centers for Disease Control came across a puzzling finding. People in North and South Carolina, as well as Georgia, had substantially higher rates of stroke than other parts of the country (Casper et al. 2003). Over time, as the map in Figure 19.3 shows, the region now referred to as the "Stroke Belt" came to encompass Alabama, Arkansas, Georgia, Indiana, Kentucky, Louisiana, Mississippi, North Carolina, South Carolina, Tennessee, and Virginia. While the explanation for this pattern is poorly understood, scholars have hypothesized that factors like current and prenatal diet, water sanitation, pervasive untreated hypertension, and poor-quality healthcare may all play a role.

In this section, you have discovered that social contexts matter. Next we will consider how your individual factors, including SES, race, and gender, interact with the social contexts in which you live to influence your health outcomes.

How does where you live impact your health?

4 | Who Gets Sick and Why?

MEASURING HEALTH

◉ Watch the **Big Question Video** in **MySocLab**

A s we discuss in this chapter, social scientists use a range of measures to track the health status of populations, including life expectancy and chronic disease prevalence. Because health has many different facets, each of these measures provides a snapshot of a different piece of the health puzzle. Yet no matter how the numbers are cut, Americans live shorter, less healthy lives than we would expect based on the wealth of the country.

☐ Health and Socioeconomic Status

What are the strongest predictors of one's health? You might guess that it's whether you have health insurance. Or perhaps it's whether or not you smoke, what you eat, or how often you exercise. In fact, an extraordinarily strong predictor of one's health is your SES (Adler and Ostrove 1999). SES has a number of dimensions, including education, income, and occupation. If you are highly educated, you are more likely to live a longer and healthier life than those who are not. The same is true of income and occupation. When researchers talk about **health disparities**, they mean differences in health status linked to social, economic, or environmental conditions. These conditions include SES, race and ethnicity, gender, and geographic location.

The association between one's social status and health is one of the most consistent findings in social science. It holds across every time period of history and place that has been studied, whether the leading causes of death are infectious diseases like tuberculosis or chronic diseases like heart disease

(Marmot 2004). Social status matters beyond being poor. There is a clear **socioeconomic gradient in health**, a term that means that those with lowest status are less healthy than those in the middle, who are less healthy than those at the top.

The idea of SES as a **fundamental social cause of health** attempts to explain the persistence of the association of health and SES across time and place (Link and Phelan 1995). Over time, the risk factors for poor health have changed considerably. In earlier times, they included poor sanitation and housing, which hastened the spread of infectious diseases. But as these factors explaining the relationship between SES and health became less prevalent, other risks emerged. Health information, such as the relationship between smoking and health, became more commonplace. Technologies such as intensive care for premature infants diffused. Why is it the case that higher SES people continue to enjoy better health even as the world changes?

Fundamental cause theory holds that higher SES individuals have access to knowledge, money, power, and social connections that are deployed throughout the life course to avoid disease and death. These resources can be deployed in a range of situations. As a result, this theory predicts that no matter what the causes of bad health, socioeconomic gradients will emerge.

In present times, SES is important because it gives people the ability to make use of knowledge about how to improve one's health, for example, to heed advisories to stop smoking. It also includes the use of resources to gain access to better institutional resources, such as safer neighborhoods.

How does socioeconomic status affect health?

Central to this theory is the idea of flexible resources that are deployed strategically throughout the life course.

The theory of fundamental causes blends the multiple dimensions of SES. However, SES is a multifaceted concept that encompasses access to material resources, access to information, relative status, and control over one's work. These measures of SES have different relationships to health, and the mechanisms that link education to health may not be the same as those that link occupation and health. Another concern is that the causal relationship between SES and health may differ across these measures. It could be the case that poorer health is a cause of lower occupational status. Finally, different dimensions of SES may matter differently throughout the life course. Financial resources may be particularly important at some times, but education may be more important in others. Next, we review the evidence linking each of these components of SES to health.

Education   It is clear that those with more education live longer, healthier lives, but does having more years of education *cause* better health? Because individuals play a strong role in choosing the amount of education they get, it could be that healthier people choose to—or are able to—attend school for longer.

Researchers have used a number of creative natural experiments to establish causality. Some of the best-known studies rely on changes in compulsory education laws. Compulsory education laws determine at which age students can stop going to school. Early in the twentieth century, states varied widely in the number of years of education they required. Over time, states began to increase the number of years students were required to attend. When these laws changed, students were required to get more years of education than their peers who were slightly ahead of them in school. But there is no reason to believe that these laws changed because health was improving, so they provide an ideal setting to determine whether getting more education *improves* health. These studies find that students who attended school for more years had higher survival rates as adults, which suggests that education does in fact have a direct effect on health (Lleras-Muney 2005).

Income explains some of the association between education and health, but not all of it. Health behaviors clearly play an important role. Those with more education use illegal drugs, alcohol, and tobacco less. Even for people with the same income, people with more education use preventative healthcare more, and they do a better job of managing existing conditions—for example, remembering to take their medications. By some estimates, the better health behaviors of the more educated can explain 40 percent of their health advantage (Cutler, Lleras-Muney, and Vogl 2008).

Scholars continue to debate why more education leads to better health behaviors. First, it may be that education improves one's ability to understand health information, which leads to better behavior. Second, education may improve one's ability to self-govern, which may equip those

How does education impact our health? Some believe having a better education can improve our ability to self-govern, which may equip us with the ability to change our health behaviors when necessary.

with more education to change their health behaviors when necessary. Finally, a central component of fundamental cause theory holds that SES allows individuals to take advantage of new advances in medical technology.

Income and Wealth   Those with higher incomes also have better health even after we control for their educational attainment. Determining the causal relationship between education and health is more complicated than in the case of education. Because education largely happens early in the life course, getting educated generally happens well before the onset of poor health. (To be sure, poor health in early childhood affects how much education children get.) In contrast, health can affect one's income because it affects participation in the labor force. People who are sick may work fewer hours or retire earlier, both of which reduce their income. Poor health also reduces one's wealth. When people become sick, they may have to rely on their savings when they can't work, or spend some these savings on health. As a result, researchers continue to debate the direction of causality.

Where income and wealth clearly matter, however, is in affecting children's health. Parents with more income can purchase more nutritious food, safer environments, and better medical care for their children. The effects of family income on child health, moreover, appear to increase over time (Case, Lubotsky, and Paxson 2002). That is, the difference of the health of poorer and more affluent children is greater later in childhood. Chronic conditions, such as asthma, become more common as children age. Families with more resources can use them to control these health conditions and minimize their effects.

Researchers continue to debate whether the effects of income of health are larger for those with less money. For the poor, an extra dollar at the bottom may matter more than for those above a basic standard of living. Alternatively, it could be the case that every dollar helps to increase health. The answer to this question is important because it provides insight into the mechanisms linking income and health. If the effects are largest for the poorest, hardship—for example, not having enough or nutritious food—may explain the link between income and health. If the relationship is more linear, that would suggest that lower relative social standing leads to worse health.

Occupation   The most influential study of the effects of working conditions on health comes from a fascinating set of studies of British civil servants called the Whitehall studies (Marmot 2004). All participants in this study were part of a white-collar profession; the lowest ranked civil servants died sooner than those in the middle, who died sooner than those at the top. The researchers hypothesized that the mechanism linking rank and health was control of one's environment. The workers at the bottom had less control over their working conditions and in particular were more likely to get heart disease.

This study and others pointed to the idea that those with higher status experience less psychosocial stress. The right amount of stress helps the human body perform better. The body's stress-response system mobilizes you to respond to a threat in your environment. Your heart beats faster, and your blood pressure and blood sugar rise. When you no longer face a threat, your body's systems return to their normal state.

This stress response is part of everyone's life, and it is healthy so long as it is not constant. When your body responds this way too often—what some researchers call "toxic stress"—it can no longer regulate itself effectively. As a result, people facing persistent stress are more likely to develop cardiovascular disease in particular and a range of other illnesses.

☐ Health and Race/Ethnicity

On almost every health measure, African Americans have worse health outcomes than non-Hispanic white Americans. They live almost 5 fewer years than white Americans do—a difference of 78.2 versus 73.2 years (Arias 2011). Babies born to black women are more than two times more likely to die before age 1 than those born to white women

(CDC 2011). African Americans also have higher rates of chronic conditions; for example, they are twice as likely to have high blood pressure (CDC 2011).

What explains these differences? Four main arguments have been made. The first is a genetic explanation, an argument that can traced to the pre–Civil War debate about slavery. Science played an important role in those debates, as medical evidence was called on to determine whether blacks were biologically inferior to whites and only capable of being slaves (Krieger 1987). The "scientific" basis for these claims has been disproven, and current research in genetics continues to show that the study of human diversity is not well captured by socially constructed racial groups.

The second argument is that racial differences really represent class differences. If this was true, there would be no residual racial differences in health once we control for SES. The current literature suggests that black disadvantages in health remain even after these controls are introduced, suggesting that we need to identify causes beyond SES.

The third argument is a psychosocial stress explanation. Exposure to discrimination in everyday life may increase stress. When the body mobilizes its responses to stress too often, it loses its ability to regulate itself, which leaves the body at increased risk for disease. Stress may also lead to the adoption of coping behaviors, such as eating or drinking, that have negative effects on health.

The fourth argument relates to the quality of treatment that African Americans receive in healthcare settings. Because cardiovascular disease is a leading cause of death, a substantial fraction of this literature has focused on its treatment. It is well documented that black patients who come to the hospital with a heart attack are less likely to get certain treatments, such as bypass surgery. These racial disparities can't be explained by differences in health insurance or health status (Institute of Medicine 2002). Racial disparities in care are not limited to invasive surgical procedures, as persistent racial disparities exist in the provision of basic therapies such as aspirin (Barnato et al. 2005).

Two main explanations have been proposed to explain these findings. One set of scholars has assumed a persistent pattern of racial disadvantage, mostly based on work contrasting black and white outcomes, that systematically channels nonwhite patients to lower-quality hospitals and doctors. The alternate account draws on the fact that black patients are treated in a small number of hospitals—for example, 85 percent of all black heart attack patients are treated in only 1,000 hospitals (Chandra 2009)—while only 40 percent of all white heart attack patients are treated in those hospitals. These scholars argue that geography is a strong determinant of racial disparities in healthcare,

How do sociologists explain health disparities between races?

How do sociologists explain gender differences in health?

FIGURE 19.4 NUMBER OF SUICIDES BY RACE

Source: Based on data from Centers of Disease Control and Prevention (2011).

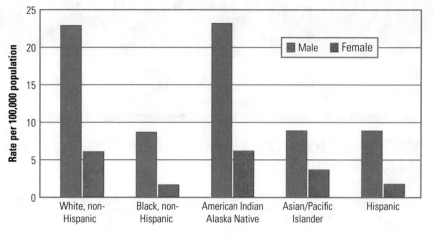

as mortality disparities are largely driven by between-hospital, rather than within-hospital, differences in quality (Skinner et al. 2005).

It is important to note two key facts about the relationship between race/ethnicity and health. First, it is not the case that nonwhite Americans have better health on every outcome. One of the clearest examples of this is suicide (see Figure 19.4). Non-Hispanic whites have substantially higher suicide rates, at 14 per 100,000 for whites, 10 for blacks, and 8 for Asians and Hispanics (CDC 2011).

Second, there is not a universal nonwhite health disadvantage. The story is also different for Hispanic Americans, who have survival rates that are equal to or sometimes better than those of non-Hispanic whites (Elo et al. 2004). Many explanations have been explained for this finding, and researchers continue to debate its causes. One explanation for this "Hispanic paradox" is the idea that people who migrate are healthier to begin with. Another points to the better health behaviors of Hispanics; for example, Hispanics are substantially less likely to smoke than African Americans or non-Hispanic whites (American Lung Association 2012). Whatever its causes, there is substantial variation in racial and ethnic disparities across groups and across diseases.

☐ Health and Gender

Gender differences in health present a challenge to the idea that more resources equal better health. Although women tend to have fewer resources, they live approximately five years longer than men. (National Center for Health Statistics 2011). The gap between men's and women's mortality in America has been declining since the 1970s, when women had an almost eight-year lead in life expectancy (Read and Gorman 2010).

When we look at disease rather than death, these patterns are different. Men tend to engage in more risky behaviors, which make them more likely to die through accidents and homicides when they are younger. Men with chronic diseases tend to have more life-threatening ones such as heart disease and cancer. Women, on the other hand, suffer from more chronic conditions like arthritis, anxiety, and depression; these largely do not lead to premature death but do reduce women's quality of life.

Two main approaches have been used to examine gender differences in health. The first is the biological approach, which holds that women's health advantages derive from differences that protect women in pregnancy such as more flexible circulatory systems and more robust immune systems. These factors may explain women's increased life expectancy but do not explain why they have higher rates of chronic disease.

Other explanations for gender differences point to a range of social factors that differentially affect health by gender. Notions of masculinity that are tied to risk-taking behaviors, such as drunk driving, make men more at risk for accidental deaths. The masculine idea of "being tough" also results in men receiving less preventative healthcare than women and delaying seeking medical care in more urgent situations (Springer and Mouzon 2011).

CONCLUSION WHY ARE WE SO INTERESTED IN POPULATION CHANGE, AGING, AND HEALTH?

We began this chapter by noting that in the 1960s and 1970s, it was taken for granted that *the* most pressing population issue was very rapid population growth and that this ticking time bomb would spell disaster for the world. But you now know the reasons behind what might otherwise seem like a paradox—why it is that most who study these issues now point to not one but rather two problems of population change, too rapid population growth in some countries versus rapid population aging (and the possibility of very rapid population decline) in others. And you also now know that although your health might seem like something only involving you, your genes, and your doctor, your health is in fact profoundly shaped by larger social contexts and forces. These are the reasons that sociologists have been so fascinated by population change, aging, and health.

Another reason why we are so fascinated with population change, aging, and health is that these are aspects of the social world that have been changing very rapidly. The very earliest sociologists—Marx, Weber, and Durkheim—all were fascinated by how the modern world was different from what the world was like in earlier times. Sociologists today continue to study change—change affecting societies, but also change affecting the lives of individuals, how it is that the lives of others have unfolded over time, and what your life might look like in the future.

👁 **Watch the Video** in **MySocLab**
Applying Your Sociological Imagination

1 How Do Populations Change over Time? (p. 540)

 Watch the **Big Question Video** in **MySocLab** to review the key concepts for this section.

The world's population has doubled in size twice since 1910—first taking 57 and then 45 years. When will the world's population next double in size? This section also examined how mortality and fertility have changed for different nations and what these changes might imply for the demographic futures of these nations.

POPULATION DYNAMICS (p. 540)

The First Demographic Transition (p. 541)

- **How do fertility and mortality change during the first demographic transition?**

Changes in Mortality and Fertility around the World (p. 542)

- **How do fertility and mortality differ around the world?**

KEY TERMS

demographer *(p. 541)*

population dynamics *(p. 541)*

fertility *(p. 541)*

mortality *(p. 541)*

migration *(p. 541)*

first demographic transition *(p. 541)*

stylized fact *(p. 541)*

total fertility rate *(p. 543)*

age pyramid *(p. 544)*

replacement fertility *(p. 544)*

population momentum *(p. 545)*

2 What Happens in Aging Societies? (p. 546)

 Watch the **Big Question Video** in **MySocLab** to review the key concepts for this section.

Some countries have many very young people but very few old people, while other countries' populations have many old people currently and will have even more old people in the future. What do these differences mean for health conditions in countries like these? In this section, we asked about the demographic implications when populations begin to age. We then focused on how sociologists measure health in an aging population.

THE IMPLICATIONS OF AN AGING POPULATION (p. 546)

The Epidemiological Transition (p. 546)

- **How does the epidemiological transition explain differences in health conditions affecting those in poorer and richer countries?**

Aging of the Baby Boomers (p. 547)

 Read the **Document** *A Gradual Goodbye: If People Are Living Longer, They Will Have to Work Longer Too* in **MySocLab**. In this excerpt, *The Economist* magazine examines the issue of retirement. As the average life expectancy increases in wealthy societies, retirement from work at age 65 can mean many years of economic inactivity.

Aging and Population Dynamics (p. 548)

- **Will some countries age more quickly than others?**

Health in an Aging Population (p. 548)

- **How do sociologists measure health?**

Death and Dying around the World (p. 550)

- **How has the rise of chronic disease in developed countries created challenges in caring for the elderly?**

KEY TERMS

population aging *(p. 546)*

epidemiological transition *(p. 546)*

epidemiology *(p. 546)*

infectious disease *(p. 546)*

chronic disease (chronic health condition) *(p. 547)*

baby boom *(p. 547)*

birth cohort *(p. 547)*

life expectancy *(p. 548)*

healthy life expectancy *(p. 549)*

physically and mentally unhealthy days *(p. 549)*

chronic disease prevalence *(p. 549)*

Medicare *(p. 549)*

advance directive *(p. 550)*

palliative care *(p. 550)*

hospice care *(p. 550)*

How Do Social Contexts Affect Health? *(p. 551)*

👁 **Watch** the **Big Question Video** in **MySocLab** to review the key concepts for this section.

We often think of health behaviors as individual choices. In this section, we explored how social contexts affect our health behaviors and how events that happen throughout our lives affect our health as adults. The relationships we have with others also play an important role in determining whether we engage in positive health behaviors.

A SOCIOLOGICAL VIEW OF HEALTH (p. 551)

The Population as Patient (p. 551)
- **How does the sociological approach to health differ from the medical approach?**

◉ **Explore** the **Data** on Obesity in the United States in **MySocLab**

The Effects of Social Contexts on Individual Behavior (p. 552)
- **How do our social worlds and relationships help determine the health choices we make?**

The Accumulation of Health Risks across the Life Course (p. 554)
- **How do sociologists use life-course perspectives to examine health issues?**

Differences in Health across Countries and Local Contexts (p. 555)
- **How does where you live impact your health?**

◉ **Explore** A Sociological Perspective: What is the quality of healthcare around the world? in **MySocLab**

Who Gets Sick and Why? *(p. 558)*

👁 **Watch** the **Big Question Video** in **MySocLab** to review the key concepts for this section.

Low socioeconomic status is a strong predictor of poor health. If you are highly educated, you are more likely to live a longer and healthier life than people who are not. This has been true throughout history and across many different countries. This section examined why these patterns persist and the major explanations that sociologists have advanced to explain them.

MEASURING HEALTH (p. 558)

Health and Socioeconomic Status (p. 558)
- **How does socioeconomic status affect health?**

Health and Race/Ethnicity (p. 560)
- **How do sociologists explain health disparities between races?**

Health and Gender (p. 561)
- **How do sociologists explain gender differences in health?**

👁 **Watch** the **Video** Applying Your Sociological Imagination in **MySocLab** to see these concepts at work in the real world

20
GLOBALIZATION

(((**Listen** to the **Chapter Audio** in **MySocLab**

by VIVEK CHIBBER

We have all had this experience at some point: We pull up in our car at a fast-food restaurant, place an order at the speaker, and then drive on to the window to pick up our food. The person at the window greets us with a smile; she asks us if we would like to add anything to our order and then hands us our bag of food. Usually, we peer into the bag to make sure she got everything we asked for—"Did you remember to add extra ketchup?" She assures that she did, we smile back, and then drive away.

Sounds simple, right? Not any longer. Here is what is happening in many of your local fast-food drive-throughs. You drive up and place your order—but the person listening to you and taking the order is not the one who greets you as you drive up to the window. Your order goes to a worker wearing a headset and sitting in front of a computer hundreds of miles away. That worker then types your order into the computer and it appears on the screen of the cashier whom you meet at the drive-through window. What used to be a simple exchange between you and an attendant a few feet away has turned into a three-part transaction between people hundreds of miles from one another but completed in the same amount of time. It is as if distance just doesn't matter anymore.

We have all heard that globalization is breaking apart production processes. Products that used to be made under one roof are now produced in separate sites thousands of miles apart, and assembled by workers in many different locations before they reach us. Could that happen with services too? It used to be taken for granted that while the manufacture of goods can be broken up and dispersed across distant locations, a service has to be provided on site. It would never occur to most of us that something as personal as taking an order at a restaurant could also be outsourced, just like the manufacture of a car.

Just how far has globalization gone? What is driving it, and what are its limits? These are the questions that we tackle in this chapter.

MY SOCIOLOGICAL IMAGINATION
Vivek Chibber

I came to sociology largely by accident. When I graduated from college, I knew I wanted to go to graduate school to study the political economy of capitalism — how it works, where it come from, and why people put up with it. But issues like these were rapidly receding from the research agenda of most disciplines. I had no particular interest in sociology. But as it happened, there was a good group of people at the University of Wisconsin sociology department who focused on just this subject. So I decided to do my PhD there, mainly because I thought I would get what I wanted — and become a sociologist in the process. My research interests are still largely the same, though with a focus on the developing world.

How far-reaching is globalization? What is driving it and what are its limits? These are questions we will explore in this chapter.

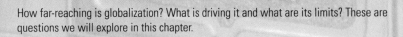

Watch the **Video** in **MySocLab**
Inspiring Your Sociological Imagination

THE BIG QUESTIONS

👁 Watch the Big Question Videos in **MySocLab**

In this chapter we examine the basic facts about the process of globalization—what it is, when it started, what its driving forces are, and what its effects have been. Of course, we are examining a process that is still very much underway and that is constantly evolving.

1 **What are the origins of globalization?** It is hard to come across any discussion of economic policy without a reference to the idea of globalization. What does it mean, and how can sociology make sense of it? In this section we examine globalization and its origins.

How far-reaching is globalization? To evaluate how far-reaching the process of globalization has been, we examine two issues. First, we need to know to what extent countries are participating in international trade and investment. Second, do countries integrate equally with different parts of the world?

2

3 **What drives globalization?** In this section we explore how recent phenomena such as outsourcing, global value chains, and regional trade agreements have become important components of globalization. We also examine China's explosive economic growth and the human costs that sometimes accompany globalization.

What are the benefits and drawbacks of globalization? Has globalization lived up to its promise? Here we assess whether globalization has been good for economic growth.

4

1 What Are the Origins of Globalization?

GLOBALIZATION AND ITS ORIGINS

👁 Watch the **Big Question Video** in **MySocLab**

Globalization is not a carefully defined scientific concept. It has become part of sociological research, but it was adopted by social scientists because it was already in common currency in the media and popular discourse by the 1980s. Like any popular concept, it is often used in different ways by different people, and this ambiguity has even been imported into some social science discussions. But one thing most of its usages have in common is that they refer to the process through which national economies are becoming linked with one another. For this chapter, we define **globalization** as the integration of economic activities across national borders.

To get a sense of what this means, imagine a world in which every country is a self-contained economic unit. Everything that is consumed by its population is made within the country, whether it is clothing, food, electronics, home construction, or other goods; and everything that is produced gets consumed within the national borders. There is no trade, and there is also no immigration. This would be a perfectly *deglobalized* world. By deglobalized, we mean a world in which every country consume only what it produces for itself—there is no trade. But now suppose that over time, some countries began to interact with one another economically. Perhaps they began to trade some of their products, with some selling their agricultural products to their neighbors and others selling electronic goods. This would begin a process of trade in which countries would begin to **export**—that is, sell their goods to other countries—and **import**—that is, buy goods produced in other countries. Or entrepreneurs in one country could keep selling to their own home markets,

but they could decide to move their production to another country, perhaps for cheap labor. This would begin a process of **foreign investment**, in which it is not goods that leave a country but investments. Or it could also turn out that some people decide that there are better jobs to be had in a neighboring country and begin a process of **emigration**, the process of traveling from their home to another economy. All of these decisions would be part of a process of globalization, of moving from a condition of economic isolation to one in which economies are linked to each other in various ways.

As the example above showed, economic integration can be carried out in a number of ways. Perhaps the most common is through international trade. This is a process in which people in one country sell products or services to customers in another country. But integration can also be carried out through the movement of **factors of production**—capital and labor (land is also a factor, but land can't travel across borders!). Firms in one country can invest in another one, either by moving their facilities to another country or by buying up existing plants and equipment in the target country. Finally, people can also move between countries, bringing about a flow of labor that adds to the pool of workers in one country while reducing it in another. All of these activities are dimensions of globalization.

☐ The Beginnings of Globalization

When did globalization begin? Has the world always been globalized, or is it a recent phenomenon—and if so, how recent? The answer to that question depends on which of the different dimensions of globalization we are interested in. Depending on our focus, the answer is different. For example, if we equate globalization with the spread of international trade, we get a very different answer than if we equate it with one country investing in another.

International trade has existed for centuries, even millennia. It is possible to trace it back to the most ancient societies, stretching back thousands of years. So, not surprisingly, those sociologists who equate globalization with trade have announced that the world began to globalize as far back as 5,000 years ago. If we accept this definition, there is nothing special about the last few centuries; all that has changed over the past 5,000 years is the *degree* of economic integration. But most social scientists reject this definition and also the idea that globalization has proceeded more or less evenly over millennia. Clearly, something has changed in the recent past. To most people who study the subject, the 1870s marked a turning point in global economic integration. This shows up in a large number of indicators—the degree of trade, the flows of investment, and most of all, the convergence of international prices. Price convergence is simply when the price of a good sold in different places tends toward the same level, for instance, when a car in Mexico City sells at the same price as it would in Atlanta. It seems safe to say that there appears to have been a dramatic uptick in globalization in the past couple of centuries, especially since the 1850s.

Why did globalization not start earlier? Two important changes had to occur before globalization could really take off. One was change in infrastructure—especially in transportation and communication. The second was a transformation in society's economic systems.

What are the two key changes responsible for globalization taking off?

In transportation, two changes around the middle of the nineteenth century were truly revolutionary. First, the expansion of railways across the giant land masses of Europe, Asia, and Latin America were critical to allowing goods produced in the interior of the country to be brought out to the coasts and made available for import. Before the advent of the railway, economic production and consumption had to be largely local, or confined to a small geographical area. The long journey from one region to another meant that perishable goods had to be consumed locally or they would rot in transit. Between 1820 and 1914 in the United States alone, more than 250,000 miles of railroad lines were laid down (Hurd 1975). But the United States was not alone. In Western Europe, Russia, India, and Australia, railway construction boomed, connecting inland markets that had so far been isolated through hundreds of thousands of miles of new lines.

The second great advance was in the advent of the steamship. Railways could transport goods across national borders only within the same land mass. For intercontinental trade to take off, there also had to be a revolution in oceanic travel. Steamships were available for transport in the early nineteenth century, but they were too expensive for anything but occasional use. Until the 1850s, they were mostly utilized for transporting high-cost luxury items, primarily on inland rivers. A series of technological advances made steamships more efficient and lowered their costs around the middle of the century. By the 1870s, they were becoming the major source of transoceanic transportation (O'Rourke and Williamson 2000:33–35).

While the railroad and steamship were important in lowering transportation costs, the invention of the telegraph

Infrastructural Transformation The most obvious reason that globalization did not take off earlier is that the means to bring it about were still somewhat primitive. The integration of national economies requires considerable advances in communication and transportation. On this score, the really revolutionary changes in the modern era occurred after the 1850s.

A mid-nineteenth century steam engine transporting goods across the United States. The American railway lines created a national market for many consumer goods, and also played a crucial role in making them available for export to Europe.

brought about a revolution in communication. It is hard to imagine today, but the telegraph probably had a greater impact on economic activity than either the telephone or the computer in the twentieth century.

Social Structural Transformation   While the great leaps in technology and transportation were critical for globalization to take off, their effectiveness would have been limited had it not been for another transformation. This was a change in the way that people related to markets. The fact is that up until the mid-nineteenth century, markets played a relatively minor role in the lives of most people in the world. The vast majority of humanity lived in the countryside as **peasants,** or agricultural producers who predominately produced goods for their own consumption rather than to sell on the market. It was only as this class of peasants was integrated into market production that the pace of globalization could pick up speed.

Globalization is a process through which the sale of goods and services spreads across national borders, expanding across the world. But for this to happen, there has to be an expansion of the market for those goods and services—people have to want to *buy* them. But even in the nineteenth century, most people in the world mostly consumed what they produced for themselves on their farms and in their locality. This meant that they only went to markets periodically for those things they couldn't produce at home. And this, in turn, meant that the *demand* for goods and services in the market always remained limited. The only group that was a reliable source of demand for consumption goods was people living in cities because they didn't have their own land like peasants did. But cities in the nineteenth century only accounted for a small proportion of the global population. Most of humanity was still located in the countryside, and this part of the population was geared toward self-subsistence, or living off the land. The economic system in most areas was still **precapitalist** in that the place for market-produced goods was still very limited.

This is why globalization remained limited well into the nineteenth century. As long as most of the world economy was still precapitalist, consisting of peasants who toiled on their own plots of land, producing for themselves much of what they consumed, the market for goods and services remained very small. For globalization to take off, the scope of markets would have to expand, so people would want to buy the goods coming from distant parts of the world. The demand for market-produced goods would have to increase. For this to happen, peasants had to be induced or forced to become dependent on the market for their survival. This could happen in two ways. Either wealthy landlords or farmers could offer to buy up their land, or they could be pushed off the land by various means—sometimes they lost the land because they fell into debt, or they had to sell bits of it off to pay taxes. Either way, peasants would find themselves suddenly without their traditional means of survival—the ability

to work their own plots with their own labor. Once this happened, they had little choice but to work for a wage—either in the city in factories or small shops, or in some other kind of employment. Or they could stay in the countryside. Perhaps they could find work as rural wage laborers, or maybe they could lease out some land and farm it for a rent.

This process, through which peasants gradually lost access to land and the ability to produce their own necessities without having to buy them, is known as the rise of a **capitalist economy**. Capitalist economic systems are distinguished by the fact that almost everyone has to buy on the market whatever they consume. Onetime peasants now had to purchase the wheat or rice that they once grew on their own plots. They had to buy clothes that they spun in their own homesteads. In other words, they became market dependent. The fact that so many people had to turn to the market for goods meant that demand for goods expanded enormously in the second half of the nineteenth century. This growing demand provided the real basis for the uptick in globalization.

The growing demand for goods was one of the reasons that states expended so much energy on expanding transportation infrastructure. As people in distant rural areas turned to the market for purchase of goods, the state felt considerable pressure to improve material infrastructure so goods produced in one part of the country could be delivered to other parts where they were in demand. In fact, much of the transportation was used not just for internal consumption but for export markets. For example, starting in the 1880s, the United States became a major source of wheat for Western Europe. This export of wheat from Midwestern America across the Atlantic was a major component of nineteenth-century globalization. It is an example of how the change in social structure combined with improvements in material infrastructure and technology to create the first real explosion in globalization.

The Course of Globalization: From the Nineteenth Century to Today

Globalization had become a very powerful force by the early 1900s. So can we assume that, once the necessary preconditions were in place, it proceeded smoothly through the course of the twentieth century? For many analysts, there is a sense that globalization is something like a tidal wave, an unstoppable process against which governments are more or less helpless. We have seen that it took some very profound changes for it to take off—there was certainly nothing automatic about globalization before 1850. But once these changes had in fact taken place, once capitalism spread across Europe and much of the world, did the integration of economies become unstoppable? In fact, it did not. As Figure 20.1 shows, after 1913, the world actually underwent a process of **deglobalization** for more than 50 years. By de-globalization, we mean a process in which international economic integration decreases over time.

Figure 20.1 shows a commonly used measure of global economic integration, which is trade as a proportion of **gross domestic product (GDP)**, or the value of all goods and services sold on the market within a defined period. The intuition behind this measure is that globalization cannot get very far unless countries are trading with one another. The extent to which a country is involved in trade is therefore a good rough indicator of how deeply connected it is to other economies. For many advanced economies, trade as a proportion of total economic activity actually went down between 1914 and the 1970s. This means that their economies become less integrated with the rest of the world in these years in spite of the fact that they had become more capitalist and despite the dramatic improvements in transportation and communication. These economies became more globalized from 1850 to 1914 and then deglobalized between 1914 and 1970.

The process of deglobalization began with World War I. The years of military conflict caused enormous disruption in normal patterns of trade and investment, which derailed the process of economic integration that had begun in preceding decades. Once the war ended, governments tried to put trade and investment back on track. But then, just a little more than 10 years later in 1929, the global economy was hit by what has come to be known as the Great Depression. The Depression also caused enormous disruption to international trade and investment because as economies all over the world collapsed, exporters found that the markets for their goods disappeared almost overnight. This was another powerful shock to the whole process of globalization.

The war and the Great Depression certainly derailed the economic integration that had begun after 1850. But shocks are temporary phenomena. Economies recover and trade and investment resumes its normal course. There had

Has globalization expanded steadily since the nineteenth century?

to be something more to the story in these decades if globalization didn't manage to reach the levels of 1914 until the very end of the century. Might there have been something else that created obstacles to reglobalization? In fact, there was—the power of the state. State action, a set of policies that enabled governments to assert greater control over their national economies, played a major role during this period of deglobalization.

The most important factor that worked against the resumption of a globalized world was that, after the Great Depression, governments all over the world passed measures to insulate their economies from excessive vulnerability to global economic shocks and to gain more control over the flow of economic activity. After the wrenching experience of two world wars and the Great Depression, governments resolved to achieve greater control over the own national economies. They wanted to have greater influence over the goods that entered and exited their countries as well as the flow of capital into and out of national production. Toward this end, they implemented a number of measures designed to put brakes on the free flow of goods and services. Two instruments crucial for this were tariffs and capital controls.

A **tariff** is a tax that is imposed on imports or exports. It adds to the price of the traded good, thereby making it more expensive. It raises revenue for the government, but it also makes the good less attractive to customers because it is now more expensive than its rivals. This has the predictable effect of reducing the flow of this good into the market. Everything else being equal, it is a trade-depressing measure. **Capital controls** are restrictions imposed by the government on the movement of investment out of, or into, the country. An example would be a case where a shoe manufacturer wanted to sell his factory and open up a new one in another country. In order to transfer his funds to a bank in that country, he would first have to get permission from his own government. In this way, his government would exert some control over the movement of funds out of its borders. These capital controls are designed to give government greater sway over the flow of investment, allowing it to increase or decrease the quantity of investment as a response to changing economic conditions. The government can make it harder for investors to "take their money and run" out of the country; it can also make it harder for investors to enter the country if the state feels that some investors are hurting national interests. Together, tariffs and capital controls act as brakes on the free flow of capital and goods. The decades between 1930 and 1970 were marked by a very wide use of both of these measures as well as a host of other instruments designed to allow states more control over economies. This was what turned the temporary shock of 1929 into a more enduring era of deglobalization.

FIGURE 20.1 RATIO OF MERCHANDISE TRADE TO GDP, CURRENT PRICES (IMPORTS AND EXPORTS COMBINED)

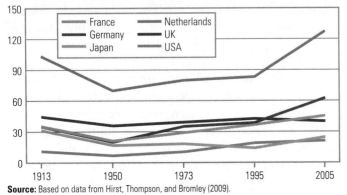

Source: Based on data from Hirst, Thompson, and Bromley (2009).

The fact that it was state policies that triggered a process of deglobalization helps us understand why *re*globalization ensued in the 1970s after a decades-long hiatus. Starting in the 1970s, and then increasingly from the 1980s onward, states moved to remove many of the controls and restrictions they had placed on trade and capital flows. This was part of the turn to more market-based policies that governments across the world have enacted since the 1970s. As states changed course and began to allow more mobility to goods and money, the process of economic integration resumed its course, much as it had in the early twentieth century. It is this second phase of globalization that we have lived through for the past quarter-century and that seems so often to be a force out of our control.

What conclusions can we draw from this past century? The big lesson is that there is nothing natural or inevitable about globalization. Even though trade and migration have been around for thousands of years, all economies remained localized and quite limited in their degree of international integration until quite recently. It took some very dramatic changes in underlying conditions for globalization to expand beyond its centuries-old limits. Just as importantly, even after capitalism spread across much of the world, globalization still did not become an unstoppable force. After the first 50 years of increasing integration of production across national borders, the world experienced 50 years of deglobalization. This was made possible by state action. It wasn't until states turned to a more market-oriented strategy that globalization resumed its course. This tells us that the ebb and flow of globalization since 1900 has been governed mainly by political factors and that globalization has depended upon a suitable political environment. States may very well have the power to begin a new era of deglobalization if citizens demand it (Gindin and Panitch 2012).

Another way of putting this is that globalization has always been politically driven—the main forces controlling the degree and the pace of globalization have been governments and their policies, not technology. This is an important point to keep in mind because it is common to hear in the media and in political debates that we cannot stand in the way of globalization. This makes it seem as though it is an inexorable force. But we have seen in this section that it is not. It is made possible by political decisions taken by governments, and it has been scaled back, also as a result of governmental decisions.

2 How Far-Reaching Is Globalization?

GLOBALIZATION'S REACH

👁 Watch the Big Question Video in **MySocLab**

We now know something about the origins of globalization. The next question is, just how far-reaching has this process been? There are two issues that we have to examine. First, how far-reaching has been the resumption of international trade and investment? We need to know to what extent countries are participating in international trade and investment. Second, do countries integrate equally with different parts of the world? Sometimes we get the impression that in today's world every corner of the world is more or less equally connected to the others. But is this true? Or is it the case that countries tend to group together with their neighbors in what is called *regionalization*?

The Degree of Globalization

So far we have focused on the fact that globalization receded in the middle parts of the twentieth century before it resumed course in the 1970s. But Figure 20.1 (on page 570) also showed us another important fact—that even in the first decade of the twenty-first century the degree of globalization was not much more than it had been in the early twentieth century. In fact, some countries—like Japan and England—have still not caught up with their levels of globalization 100 years ago. Japan traded 31 percent of its domestic production in 1914, compared to only 24.7 percent in 2005, and England slid from just under 45 percent in 1914 to 40 percent in 2005.

So even while trade and export dependence has increased in the past 30 years, it is not entirely new. How could this be so? How could trade dependence have been as great then as it is now for so many countries? One reason is that in 1914, the countries with the more advanced economies were also colonial powers. England and France were both very deeply integrated with their colonial empires. This opened up markets for their goods. Firms selling in the colonies of their home country had real advantages over their rivals from other countries because they had better knowledge of the conditions and often had better access to sales and marketing networks. This created a powerful drive for colonial exporters to expand into the markets in the lands their governments ruled. This kind of trade integration was not usually very beneficial to entrepreneurs in the colonized countries. But it did create a very globalized world, even if its benefits were weighted toward the rich West.

Now let's see if trends in international investment show a greater level of integration than simple trade. When firms from one country make investments in another, it is known as **foreign direct investment (FDI)**. So as international investment increases in size and scope, it shows up in international statistics as an increase in the flow of FDI. For international production to become more integrated, the share of FDI should be increasing over time. This means that more of what is produced across the world comes from international investment as opposed to investment by local firms. If we look at the data, the result is not what we might expect. In 2010, the gross fixed capital investment in the world economy was almost $14 trillion. Of this, total FDI, calculated as the sum of inward and outward-oriented FDI, amounted to $2.57 trillion. This means that foreign investment never accounted for more than one-fifth of total global investment (UNCTAD 2011:24, table 1.5). Flows of FDI tend to be quite volatile, rising and falling from year to year. But since the 1990s, the range has remained around

10 to 20 percent (Sutcliffe and Glyn 2010:87–88). Another way of putting this is that more than 80 percent of global investment today is carried out within national borders, usually more. This tells us that factories and firms are not as footloose as some of the popular images might have us believe. Almost all investors stay within their own national border.

The Importance of Regions

Now let us turn to the second question, which is whether, even if globalization is increasing, it is bringing together the parts of the world into a seamless whole. Or does economic integration cluster around small regions?

A good place to start is to see how far goods actually travel. In a nonglobalized world, goods tend to stay in small geographical zones. They do not travel very far because their consumption is carried out close to the regions where they were produced. If globalization was a process in which countries transmitted goods to all corners of the world, we would expect to find that as it takes hold the distance traveled by goods also increases. However, for most countries, with the United States as a major exception due to its trade relations with China, there has not been a very significant change in the average distance for imports and exports in this period. However, there is variation in trend in the 1965–2000 period. During this time, 77 countries experienced a decline in the distance of their exports and imports and 39 countries had an increase in their trading distance (Carrere and Schiff 2004).

This regional bias for trade is further confirmed by the increase in the regional share in total trade over the last few decades. The *trade intensity index,* which is the ratio of intraregional trade share relative to the region's share in global trade, is used to obtain a measure of regional bias. All regions demonstrate this bias, with Latin America (except for Mexico) showing the strongest regional bias (UNCTAD 2007). In other words, we can see that the share of intraregional trade is increasing for a number of blocs, such as the European Union. Explore the Infographic on page 574 for a closer look at regional trade.

Another good indicator of the importance of regionalization over globalization is the role of the **transnational corporation (TNC)**. A TNC is a corporation that sells products in more than one country. Most trade and foreign investment is actually carried out by TNCs, not by small firms. In 2006, there were 77,000 TNCs in the global economy, employing 62 million workers and with assets of over $4.5 trillion. Examining the trading activities of these giant corporations is a good window into the dynamics of

How extensive is international trade and investment?

globalization. Two facts stand out about TNCs. First, most of them locate their branches and affiliates in other countries. So 65 percent of TNC affiliates are located abroad. This tells us that they are in fact organizing their trading activities across national borders, as one would expect in a process of globalization. But how far do they actually go?

This is where the second interesting fact comes in. It turns out that most of the trading and investment activity of TNCs is in neighboring or nearby countries, not in far-flung regions. The world's largest firms are concentrated in the triad of the European Union, North America, and Japan. In a very careful analysis of 380 of the Fortune 500 companies in 2001, economist Alan Rugman has shown that, on average, sales in their home region were 71.9 percent of the total sales. As little as 2.4 percent of the 380 companies could be classified as global, that is, they generated their revenue across the three largest regions of North America, Europe, and Asia and the Pacific and had headquarters in all of these regions. An example of such a firm would be IBM, which is an American company with 43.5 percent of its sales in its home region. The rest of its sales come from Asia (20 percent) and Europe, the Middle East, and Africa (28 percent). Only 6.6 percent of the 380 companies were biregional, that is, had at least 20 percent of their sales from at least two regions but less than 50 percent in their home region. For example, BP, which is a British company, had 36.3 percent of its revenues from the European market and 48.3 percent from the American market. Three percent were host-region oriented, that is, more than 50 percent of their sales came from a single region that was not their own. DaimlerChrysler was the largest in this group. This Europe-based company had 60 percent of its sales in North America. However, an overwhelming majority were home-market oriented. That is, 320 out of the 380 had a majority of their sales in their home region. For example, Walmart, which is the number-one firm on the Fortune 500, had 94 percent of its sales in North America. On average, the sales in the home regions of such firms are 80 percent. Moreover, very few of these firms have a significant presence outside of these three regions, such as in Latin America or the Indian subcontinent. Of the 500 largest TNCs, only 9 are truly global, that is, derive at least 20 percent of their business from each of the following regions: Asia, North America, and Europe. For the vast majority of the TNCs, over 80 percent of their sales are done within the geographical region in which they are located. So here, too, regionalization dominates over globalization (Rugman 2005).

We see the same pattern with labor flows. The stock of international migrants has increased from 65 million in 1965 to 165 million in 2000 at an average rate of 1.3 percent

IBM is one of the oldest and largest transnational corporations in the world.

Why does economic integration cluster around regions?

per year between 1990 and 2000. However, a closer look at migration statistics reveals that the top migration corridors are between neighboring countries. As of 2010, the top migration corridor was United States–Mexico, followed by cross-border flows between Ukraine and Russia. Other prominent corridors are India–Bangladesh, India–United Arab Emirates, and Turkey–Germany (World Bank 2011; World Bank 2009; UN Wall Chart 2009).

Hence, what appears to be happening is not a flattening out of the world as a whole. Globalization is not creating a seamless web of links between all corners of the world but rather is promoting the growth of *regional blocs*—economic ties that are most densely woven between neighboring countries and that get much thinner between countries located farther away. The three main blocs are around North America, Europe, and East Asia. The economies of these

Globalization or Regionalization?

The flow of trade, investment, and population across national borders has swelled, but the origins and destinations of these flows are not usually on opposite ends of the globe. Instead, they are likely to be relatively near each other. In this way, what is often called globalization is in large part actually an increase in regional trade, investment, and migration.

Since the bulk of world trade is carried out by large transnational corporations (TNCs), their trading activity provides a good window into the dynamics of globalization. It is remarkable the extent to which the sales of the largest corporations, even those that have the largest portion of their sales outside of their home countries, are concentrated in their home regions. Corporations headquartered in the United States are most likely to sell products in North America, those of Europe within the European Union within Europe, and those of Japan within the Asia-Pacific region.

Source: Based on data from Rugman (1995).

![Explore icon] **Explore the Data** on Globalization or Regionalization in **MySocLab** and then ...

■ **Think About It**

Why is it that cross-border trade so often stays close to home?

■ **Inspire Your Sociological Imagination**

Could you make a case that the geography of *sales* might underestimate globalization?

ARROWS REPRESENT PERCENTAGE OF SALES BY REGION

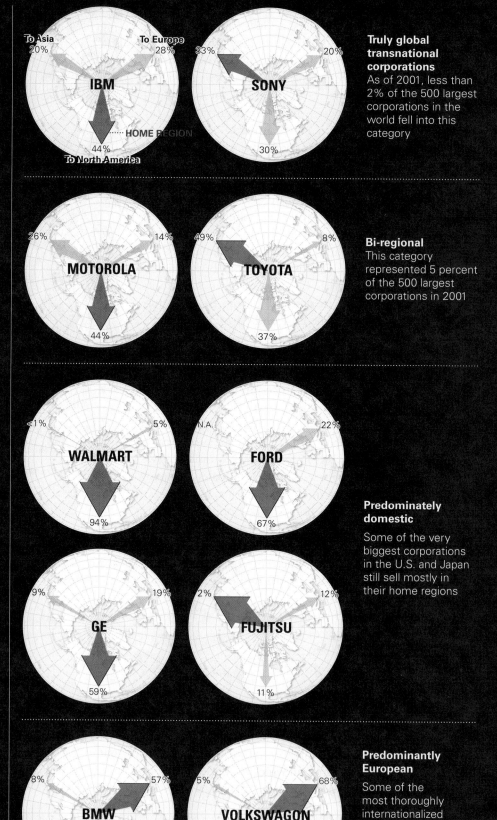

To Asia 20% | To Europe 28% | IBM | HOME REGION | 44% To North America

33% | 20% | SONY | 30%

Truly global transnational corporations
As of 2001, less than 2% of the 500 largest corporations in the world fell into this category

26% | 14% | MOTOROLA | 44%

49% | 8% | TOYOTA | 37%

Bi-regional
This category represented 5 percent of the 500 largest corporations in 2001

<1% | 5% | WALMART | 94%

N.A. | 22% | FORD | 67%

Predominately domestic
Some of the very biggest corporations in the U.S. and Japan still sell mostly in their home regions

9% | 19% | GE | 59%

2% | 12% | FUJITSU | 11%

8% | 57% | BMW | 30%

5% | 68% | VOLKSWAGON | 20%

Predominantly European
Some of the most thoroughly internationalized companies in Europe still sell mostly to other European countries

regions are getting more tightly integrated around production and finance. How this is happening is the subject of our next section.

Taken together, the information on trade and investment has some important implications. It means that even with all the deepening of economic integration over the past quarter century, global production and exchange still primarily revolves around the national economy. Furthermore, the degree of integration is not even very new. Even though globalization is a singularly modern phenomenon, as we saw earlier in this chapter, the trends of the last 20 years or so are not unprecedented. The world has been through a comparable degree of globalization before and even managed to reverse it through state action. So even

while the world is more integrated than it was 40 years ago, the degree is still rather limited, and it is certainly not unprecedented. Furthermore, what is being integrated is not the world as a whole but smaller regions within that world. Three such regions really stand out: one around North America, the other in Europe and North Africa, and the third in East Asia and now spreading into South Asia as well. Economic activity tends to flow within these regions, and less so between them.

 Read the **Document** *Arnold Schwarzenegger, Ally McBeal and Arranged Marriages: Globalization on the Ground in India* in **MySocLab**.

3 What Drives Globalization?

GLOBALIZATION'S DRIVING FORCES

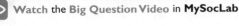 **Watch** the **Big Question** Video in **MySocLab**

We now know some of the basic facts about globalization—what it means, when it started, and how far it has gone. We have encountered some surprising findings. The world has not moved in a steady path from less globalized to more globalized. And in fact, what seems to be emerging is a world comprised of economic regions, not a seamless web of economic integration. What are some of the key forces driving globalization?

☐ Outsourcing and Global Value Chains

Most people know that a common phenomenon in recent years has been the practice of **outsourcing**, when producers take activities that they once did in-house and farm them out to other firms in remote locations. Outsourcing is part of a larger process that is called the creation of **global value chains**, which are sets of linked operations that organize the production of any particular product. This is an important concept to understand because much of what we know as globalization has been driven by the creation of global value chains.

Take the production of an automobile. This involves a long set of activities, starting with the manufacture of steel and rubber, their transportation to an auto plant, the manufacture of mechanical parts, their assembly into a car frame, painting, installation of upholstery, and so forth. All these activities are linked together in a chain of operations. In the era of deglobalization, it was common for many of these processes to be carried out in-house, under one roof. This means that the value chain was compact and geographically contained. But in recent years, as transportation and communication costs have declined and as a means of locating cheaper labor, companies have turned to breaking apart various components of the value chain in their operations and moving the various operations to remote locations. Activities that were once carried out under one roof now take place hundreds of miles away. But they don't typically move across the world. Instead, they tend to move to neighboring regions.

Consider the process of producing clothing. The production of clothing involves three primary steps: the spinning of thread, the weaving of fabric, and the final assembly of the clothing. These three steps have important differences. Spinning, especially of synthetic fibers, is immensely capital intensive, which means it involves high-technology machinery usually operating on a very large scale. The weaving of fibers into cloth is somewhat less capital intensive and involves a lower level of technical sophistication. The final assembly of clothing is very different: It involves a lot of manual labor, with relatively little use of automated machinery. In addition, it can be split up into many small-scale factories (Dicken 2011:308). Together, these three steps make up the value chain of clothing production.

What has happened is that these three steps, especially the final

What role do global value chains play in globalization?

assembly step, now typically take place in different places. A lot of the spinning and weaving that goes into garments is still done in the United States, but since the 1980s, the more labor-intensive part of the value chain has moved to Mexico and the Caribbean. Garment producers set up assembly operations in these low-wage countries in areas that are set up as *export processing zones*. These are locations where the governments give foreign manufacturers special privileges and tax breaks in return for setting up operations there. The TNCs get low-cost operations, and the host country gets more jobs for its labor force. The garment producer sets up operation, and brings in cloth woven in the United States. This is then further processed and assembled in the export processing zone and reexported into the United States. A chain of operations that was once located within the same plant has now been dispersed across nations. But its dispersal hasn't sent those operations all the way across the globe. Typically, it has been spread out over neighboring countries, or countries that are near each other.

What has this meant for the countries that are participating in regional integration? We can ask this question from a bottom-up perspective or a top-down one. From the bottom-up perspective, we look at what the implications have been for labor—for the people actually doing the work in the export processing zones or the TNCs. From the top-down angle we look at what it has meant for overall economic growth—has it sped up development and industrialization? Has it meant faster growth for the global South (the poorer developed countries in the world)? There is no better place to look than China as a hothouse for what globalization has meant on the ground.

Workers at a clothing factory in Guadalajara, Mexico making garments for Walmart. It is very common for firms to hire mostly women, because employers believe that they are a more manageable labor force than men. Not surprisingly, sexual harassment complaints from workers in these factories are very high.

☐ China's Export Zones: A Case Study

China's explosive economic growth of the past few decades has been a striking example of a country attempting to take advantage of the changing geography of global production. China has become a center of manufacturing as part of fragmented global supply chains. A truly immense quantity of goods sold in the United States is labeled "made in China"—over $399 billion worth in 2011 (Department of Commerce 2012). Yet China has established itself in a very particular position in the global value chain. Instead of designing products or producing the more sophisticated components like computer processors, Chinese factories most often *assemble* components produced elsewhere into final products, which are then reexported to consumer markets like the United States. For instance, in 2006, 80 percent of the value of exported consumer electronics simply represented the value of the imported components, not any work actually done in China.[1] The final assembly step that is performed in China is often one of the simplest in the production process. Instead of advanced technology or highly skilled labor, it requires above all a large, willing, and *low-cost* labor force. This is what China offers to the multinational corporations that build factories or hire contractors there.

The supposed promise of this kind of manufacturing is that by hooking into the global economy, it will stimulate the growth of other, more advanced industries. Indeed, China's exports have played a central role in its astonishing economic success of the past three decades and have meant real benefits for ordinary workers in China. Wage levels and working conditions are not worse in factories producing for exports than in other jobs in China.[2] Young people in rural China migrate in massive numbers to the coastal regions where export manufacturing has blossomed because it offers them an opportunity to improve their families' livelihoods that is simply not available in agriculture.

Nonetheless, the benefits of economic growth do not change

the fact that the life of a worker in China's export assembly factories is grueling. In fact, this is no small part of the appeal for the multinational corporations that locate manufacturing in China. Consider this story, told by a former Apple executive to a reporter for *The New York Times*. A few weeks before the iPhone was to be released, Apple redesigned the screen but was intent on keeping to the original deadline. So, on the very day the redesigned screens began to arrive around midnight at the assembly factory in China, a foreman went over to the workers sleeping in the company's dormitory and roused them from their sleep. They were each given a biscuit and a cup of tea. They were then told to go to their workstations, at which point they began a 12-hour shift assembling the iPhones. The result? Within four days, the plant was producing 10,000 units a day.

In the executive's words, "The speed and flexibility is breathtaking. There's no American plant that can match that" (Duhigg and Bradsher 2012). This speed and flexibility comes from the fact that Chinese workers have to work far longer and harder than employees in any American factory. On paper, workers in China—as in the

---

[1] For electronics, a full 80 percent of value-added is produced outside of China (Koopman, Wang, and Wei 2009).

[2] For instance, in the 10 large electronics assembly firms in southern China investigated by China Labor Watch in 2010 and 2011 (employing around 250,000 workers in total), the typical production-line employee made well above the local government's minimum wage, usually about 1.5 to 2 times China Labor Watch's own estimate of the minimum cost of living (China Labor Watch 2011:126–33).

Women working in an electronics plant in Guangdong, China. These plants have become notorious for their long hours and very weak protections for their employees.

What are the benefits and costs of China's export zones?

United States—have a 40-hour week, but in reality workers have no choice but to put in extensive overtime, even if it is sometimes labeled "voluntary"—after all, workers could "choose" to lose their jobs instead of "voluntarily" working overtime. The actual working day is 10 to 14 hours long, often with only a 10-minute break. During peak seasons of heavy output, employees in some factories work seven days a week. Including overtime, workers typically earn between $350 and $450 a month, compared to minimal living expenses of $200 to $300 a month. Because employees are often migrants, it is common for them to live in company dormitories, where they are bunked 6 to10 people per room (China Labor Watch 2011). In all, working at one of these factories is almost more than a job: It encompasses the entirety of the workers' lives.

In addition, Chinese workers lack the kinds of institutional protections long taken for granted in advanced economies like the United States. Chinese factories usually do have unions, but they do nothing to represent workers' interests to their employers. In interviews conducted by a human rights group, China Labor Watch, employees who went to the so-called worker care centers at every factory said they were offered only "psychological consolation" instead of real help solving problems in their jobs; in many firms, workers were unaware there was a formal union organization at all. Employers also seek to skirt what protections do exist. For instance, they try to keep their workers in the dark about provisions for compensation for work-related injuries guaranteed by labor law or their contracts. Other companies utilize external "labor dispatch agencies" that free the company of any contractual relationship with—and thus legal responsibility for—their workers at all. Lacking these basic protections and mechanisms for addressing grievances, it should be no surprise that working conditions are often unsafe: There are many reports of workers being exposed to dangerous chemicals and of being injured or killed in workplace accidents (China Labor Watch 2011; Duhigg and Barboza 2012).

The Chinese example shows that while the spread of global value chains has indeed provided some benefits to labor in host countries, this has come with a cost. Firms often go to these areas not just for the cheaper labor there but also because they have fewer protections and less recourse against employers' demands for greater flexibility and responsiveness from their employees. But there are potential costs on the other side as well, to the workers of the country from which the firms are exiting. In a careful study carried out for the U.S. Trade Deficit Review Commission, Cornell University economist Kate Bronfenbrenner found that employers in the United States used the threat of exit as a means of gaining advantage over employees, especially in union-organizing drives. Two facts stand out about this tactic. First, the threats were effective more often than not. The study found that when employers warned of the likelihood of plant shutdowns and flight to other locations, more than two-thirds of organizing drives failed. The second interesting fact is that managers actually followed through with plant closings in less than 3 percent of the cases where they issued the threats. In other words, in most of the cases, managers were using workers' fears about globalization against them. Even though the chance of capital flight was very low, workers believed that the threat was real (Bronfenbrenner et al. 2000).

How representative are these studies? It is not easy to say because teasing out the actual effects of globalization on wages and working conditions is no simple task. Workers' pay, their conditions of work, and their hours are affected by many factors, of which globalization is just one. Isolating globalization's effect is hard to do because none of the changes occur in an experimental setting. What we can say is that the increase in global capital flows and trade has not brought clear-cut benefits to labor. What the effects are, whether they are positive or negative, depends on how globalization interacts with other factors—such as the level and quality of democracy, trade union strength, and economic growth.

Shown here, workers outside a Goodyear Tire plant are protesting management's threats to move production to Indonesia unless the union accepts their demands. This is an example of how employers often use the threat of exit to extract concessions from unionized employees.

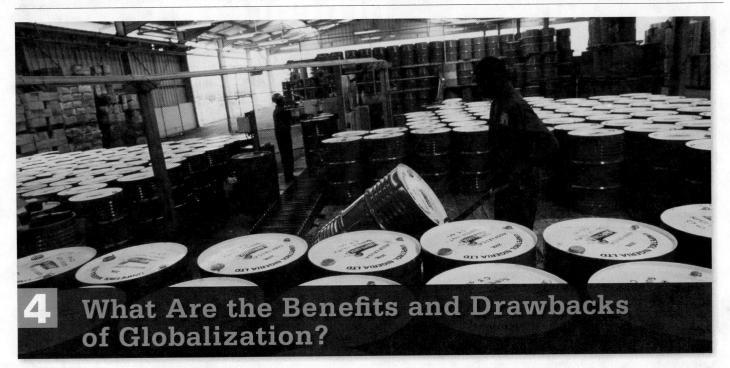

4 # What Are the Benefits and Drawbacks of Globalization?

THE EFFECTS OF GLOBALIZATION

👁 Watch the **Big Question Video** in **MySocLab**

Take a minute to review *A Sociological Perspective* on page 580. As you can see, the process of globalization is also occurring in the cultural domain. We often associate globalization with material goods. Food is one such item, and there is no more iconic restaurant in American culture than McDonald's. But it is also taking place in the entertainment industry. In both spheres, it has been a two-way street. The main promise of globalization has been that, by freeing up opportunities for trade and investment, it should give a boost to economic growth. Globalization is, in this sense, part of the turn to more market-based economic policies that have been promoted by governments all over the world since the 1980s. You might wonder what models of development were in place before the 1980s, when trade and investment flows really took off again. In this section we will first take a brief look at the kinds of economic policies that were practiced by developing countries in the years of deglobalization—the 1930s to 1980—in order to better appreciate what changed in recent years. We will then take a look at the empirical record of these past years and compare it to the record of the earlier decades to get a sense of how the two compare. This will allow us to draw some conclusions about the relative merits of globalization as a model of economic development.

Is globalization good for economic growth?

▯ Economic Policies in Developing Countries: 1930s to 1980s

From the 1930s to the 1980s, most countries in the developing world oversaw very ambitious periods of rapid industrialization. These were years in which these nations—in Latin America, Asia, the Middle East, and Africa—tried to change their economies from agriculture to industry. To do this, they relied a great deal on the involvement of the state—to regulate markets, provide protection to firms, control prices, and protect local industry from global competition. This model has come to be known as state-led development, but its more technical designation is **import-substituting industrialization (ISI)**. In economic literature, ISI has become associated with the kind of development policies poor countries used in the middle of the twentieth century. But in fact it has been used by every country that has tried to industrialize since the eighteenth century. It was used by England to ward off competition from Dutch entrepreneurs, then by the United States in the early 1800s to catch up with England, then by European countries in the middle of the nineteenth century, and then by the developing countries during the twentieth century (Chang 2002).

At the heart of ISI was a commitment to nurture national industry in the face of international competition.

A SOCIOLOGICAL PERSPECTIVE

Are there cultural aspects of globalization ?

One of the most visible ways in which culture is being globalized is through the entertainment industry. The United States exports not just manufactured goods, but also movies and television shows to almost every continent in the world. But Hollywood is not the only globalizer when it comes to entertainment. The movie industry in Mumbai, India – known as Bollywood – is also a major exporter of movies, mainly to the Middle East and Africa, but also to the West.

Another very visible aspect of cultural globalization is the spread of certain cuisines – like American fast food restaurants or Starbucks coffee shops. But here too, the flux has been in both directions. While it is possible to observe American fast food in Beijing, it is also common to find Chinese cuisine in American cities, big and small. In England, Indian cuisine is now so much a part of national culture that it is jokingly referred to as England's "official cuisine."

The influence of Asian film on Hollywood is not new. Can you think of examples where an Asian influence is obvious?

Is the impact of cultural globalization always positive? What are some possible drawbacks?

International artists are also subject to globalizing influences. Where classic movies and television cast American actors to portray international characters, today's market allows actors from around the world to work in their chosen fields in many countries. How has this shift influenced our perception of other cultures?

⊙ **Explore** A Sociological Perspective in **MySocLab** and then . . .

■ Think About It

Movies are just one example of cultural products that have been exported through globalization. Can you think of others?

■ Inspire Your Sociological Imagination

One way to appreciate the influence of globalization is by thinking of products in our life that are not globalized. Most of what we eat is grown or produced in places thousands of miles away. Can you

When countries try to industrialize, their entrepreneurs face some considerable disadvantages. Usually, they have to produce for markets in which goods are already being sold by more experienced firms from richer countries. Take the case of textiles, where a new firm might try to enter a developing country. If a new manufacturer decides to set up a textile factory, she has to face the fact that the shirts she produces will compete against shirts being sold by other firms, usually from richer countries, but certainly by firms with more experience and more money than she has. How can she break into the market? To help her in this venture, her government might implement measures to make things easier. It could impose tariffs on shirts imported from other countries to raise their price; it could provide her with cheap credit to lower costs; it could also help her acquire the latest technology. All these measures are part of a strategy to give her some help against imported goods that she has to compete against. If successful, she will be able to push the imported shirts out of the market and become the dominant seller in the local market—she will have substituted her own goods for the imports. This is why the strategy is called import substitution.

For ISI to work, it takes extensive state intervention in markets, as we just described. During the decades stretching from the Great Depression to the 1980s, this meant that states were enabling their national firms to succeed in local markets and push out foreign producers. So, for example, as Brazilian textile producers grew in their own experience and power, they pushed American textile producers out of the market. This is why ISI and deglobalization in some products went together. When globalization took off in the 1980s, it was part of a larger shift toward more market-friendly policies associated with neoliberalism. In the developing world, neoliberalism came in the form of a policy package known as the **Washington Consensus**. This was a term coined by economist John Williamson, and it describes the main components of a policy package that replaced ISI in the developing world during the 1980s.

The policies that were implemented under the Washington Consensus were broadly oriented to opening up the domestic economy to international finance and capital, to lowering trade barriers and liberalizing the domestic economy. This is also why they are associated with recent globalization—because they aimed to open up emerging economies to goods and capital from the advanced world and also to encourage more exports from the former to the latter. Hence, just as the middle decades of the twentieth century were a time in which state controls and deglobalization went together, so at the end of the century, liberalization and globalization went together. This is important to keep in mind when we try to assess the impact of globalization on economic growth. It is not very easy to separate the effects of economic integration from the effects of deregulation, less state intervention in the economy, and

the fewer controls over financial flows. The two dimensions of economic policy acted together, and separating the effects of one from the other is not always possible. The North American Free Trade Agreement of 1994 is a good example of how integration and deregulation go together.

☐ NAFTA: A Case Study

The North American Free Trade Agreement (NAFTA) has been one of the most widely studied instances of globalization in recent years, and it has also attracted its share of scholarly debate (Feller 2008). In the debates that preceded its ratification, supporters of NAFTA, including then president Clinton, argued that it would result in rising incomes for everyone and lead to the creation of tens of thousands of jobs in the United States (Hufbauer and Schott 1993; Clinton 1993). Opponents decried the lack of effective labor and environmental protections in the treaty and worried that it would exert a downward pressure on wages and living standards, as companies would be able to move their operations in order to take advantage of lower wage and production costs abroad without losing access to domestic markets (Franklin 1993).

Assessing NAFTA's consequences nearly two decades after it came into force on January 1, 1994 is tricky because it is hard to disentangle the effects of the free trade agreement from other factors that shape social and economic outcomes. Notably in Mexico, NAFTA's implementation was quickly followed by a massive financial crisis in 1994 and 1995 (also known as the "Mexican peso crisis"), which may or may not have been linked to the agreement. Everyone agrees that NAFTA produced a significant increase in cross-border

What are the consequences of NAFTA?

One consequence of economic globalization since the 1980s has been an increase in the frequency of financial crises. In most of these instances, the result has been a cut-back in social programs and an increase in unemployment. Here we see protestors in Mexico City hurling rocks at government offices in the wake of the peso crisis of 1994.

trade and financial flows, and its defenders, including many business groups, think tanks, and politicians, claim that this contributed to economic growth (Abramowitz 2008; Office of the United State Trade Representative 2008). Critics of NAFTA, however, insist its positive benefits have been largely limited to already economically advantaged groups, and they blame it for contributing to elevated levels of income inequality and stagnating wages and living standards for workers and other non-elite groups (Public Citizen 2008). Economist Robert Scott, for instance, has found that the subsequent explosion in the United States' trade deficit with Mexico engendered a net loss of over 680,000 jobs north of the border, with more than 60 percent of such "job displacement" occurring in the manufacturing sector (Scott 2011). Declining industrial employment had particularly harmful consequences for the job prospects of unskilled workers and weakened labor's bargaining position with employers; thus, NAFTA fed escalating pay and income disparities as well as a growing gap between median wage levels and productivity growth (Bernstein and Mishel 2007).

Meanwhile, the substantial rise in FDI into Mexico resulted in only minimal employment gains while intensifying various forms of inequality (Audley et al 2003). In part, that is because many of the newly created jobs by NAFTA were in the informal sector or did not provide standard benefits (such as paid vacations or social security). Nearly all of the growth in manufacturing employment was due to greater work opportunities in the low-wage and highly exploitative *maquiladoras*, which are mostly foreign-owned export assembly plants that comprise a significant, and rapidly growing, segment of Mexico's industrial sector. Furthermore, expanded employment in manufacturing was largely outweighed by losses suffered in Mexico's agricultural producers as a result of the influx of cheaper, sometimes heavily subsidized U.S. farm imports (Henriques and Patel 2004). The result was a massive migration out of the Mexican countryside (Bacon 2012). Improved access to Mexican markets benefited large U.S. agricultural producers but did not prevent the elimination of hundreds of thousands of smaller family farms during the NAFTA era. These sorts of considerations have led some one-time supporters of NAFTA to conclude that it failed to provide the boost to living standards they expected while exacerbating a wide array of socioeconomic problems (DeLong 2006).

☐ Has Globalization Lived Up to Its Promise?

One of the most direct ways to assess whether globalization has fulfilled its promise is by looking at growth rates. And here the evidence seems pretty clear. Figure 20.2 compares the rate of growth in GDP during the ISI era—that is, 1950 to 1980—with growth rates in the decades of rapid globalization. Two facts stand out. The first is that economic growth was better during the ISI era throughout the developing world. We see that in all four of regions covered—East Asia, Latin America, Africa, and the Middle East—growth slowed down after the end of ISI. Second, we see that some regions did better than others. East Asia managed to sustain decent growth, even though it was lower than in the earlier years. But Latin America and the Middle East witnessed a more dramatic slowdown. This tells us that even though globalization did not deliver as promised, the disappointment with its results was greater in some regions than in others. In fact, the slowdown in growth inside the developing world was part of a global decrease in growth rates after 1980. The advanced countries witnessed a deceleration of their own. This is a bracing discovery. We have seen in other chapters that inequality within countries has increased over the past 30 years, in some cases dramatically. When we combine that with the finding that growth rates have also slowed down, it tells us that economic conditions for the poor and very poor have become much worse. It means that income growth has been very meager in national economies, and on top of that, what little income growth there has been has flowed mainly into the bank accounts of the very rich. This is true in the developed and in the underdeveloped world.

In sum, the impact of globalization on the economic performance of low-income countries has been mixed at best. To begin with, globalization has failed to reduce the gap between wealthy and poor countries. In fact, global inequality has been accentuated as Northern industrialized countries are now further ahead than they were in the postwar years, before open markets and transnational production took hold. Besides growing world inequality, globalization has not only reinforced polarization between wealthy countries and less developed countries, it has also generated sharp disparities within the global South.

What is the impact of globalization on the economic performance of low-income countries?

Workers in a maquiladora plant in Tehuacan, Mexico. Notice the crowded and dusty conditions.

FIGURE 20.2 REGIONAL ECONOMIC GROWTH RATES, 1950–2008

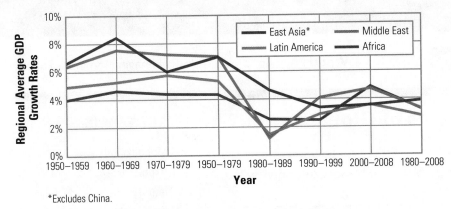

*Excludes China.

Source: Based on data from Maddison Statistics on World Population, GDP and Per Capita GDP, 1-2008 AD

Whereas the few East Asian industrializers were able to sustain robust pre-1980 growth rates—and even fewer countries, namely China and India, were able to take off in the era of open world markets—most low to middle-income countries which benefited notably during the decades of state-led development and regulated markets saw their growth, productivity, and investment stagnate with the turn to globalization.

CONCLUSION GLOBALIZATION IN RETROSPECT AND PROSPECT

There are three big ideas that you should take from this chapter. The first is that globalization is and always has been a politically driven phenomenon. In other words, it is not the result of unavoidable economic forces sweeping away all that comes before them. We have seen that it took very specific political and social conditions to bring it about. The first of these was the spread of capitalism as a specific economic system. Capitalism makes everyone within the economy market dependent—everyone has to fully participate in buying and selling in order to survive. Until this happened, there were very tight limits on how far globalization could proceed. And for the change to come about, it took massive efforts by states. The turn to capitalism was not automatic. It was brought about by long and arduous policy directives from governments, either enticing peasants to give up their plots of land or coercing them into it. Even after the turn to capitalism, massive investments in transportation and communication technology were still needed for globalization to take off. These also required a governmental action because infrastructure investments did not promise immediate profits for private investors. Railroads, for example, were either built within the public sector or needed large subsidies to attract private investors. When globalization took off in the 1870s, it seemed like it was driven by purely economic forces, but behind it was the heavy and ever-present hand of the state.

The importance of the state is also evident in the way economic integration ebbed and flowed in the twentieth century. It is important to remember that the onset of globalization has not been in the form of a steady growth from 1870 to now. In the early twentieth century, it probably seemed like market integration was an unstoppable force which all governments and all economies were powerless to stop. Yet by 1950 it already seemed like a thing of the past. The world during the years after World War II was one in which there was still plenty of trade and international investment, but it was subordinated to production and exchange within national borders. The reglobalization that has occurred since the 1980s has again been driven by state policies—such as the lowering of tariffs, the opening up of capital markets, and the deregulation of markets. Taken together, all these points show that globalization has been the product of social and political initiatives. And this means—crucially—that there is nothing natural about it. It can be modified, and even significantly changed, by state policy.

The second point is that even while globalization is a reality, we should not exaggerate its extent. We are often told by the media and political leaders that we are in an era of unprecedented economic integration. The *New York Times* columnist Thomas Friedman famously announced in his best-selling book that, with globalization, the world had become flat—meaning that every part of the world was becoming woven into the same seamless fabric (Friedman 2005). But as we have seen, there are two caveats to this observation. First, in historical terms, the extent of real economic integration today is probably no more than it was in 1912. So it is not accurate to say that we are in a new world. Rather, we are now catching up to a world from a century ago. Second, whatever integration exists is more closely structured around regions than it is around the globe. This means that things like distance, culture, history—all the things that sociologists study—still matter a great deal in economic dynamics.

Third, we have seen that globalization is not a panacea. In fact, on most counts, the years of increased economic integration have witnessed worse economic outcomes than earlier years. This does not mean that we should push for a new era of deglobalization, as there are also benefits that come with economic integration. And as we pointed out earlier, it is not easy to disentangle the effects of globalization itself from the effects of neoliberalism and the deregulation of markets more specifically. It could very well be that globalization accompanied by a more active state, more redistribution, and more regulation of market outcomes could yield better results than would a new era of deglobalization. But while some kind of globalizing economy might be desirable, we can probably conclude that the kind we have *actually had* has not lived up to expectations. But how do we modify it if it is an unstoppable force? The point is that it is not. Now that we know that globalization has always been governed by political forces, that it has relied on state support and state indulgence, we can also have some confidence that if we are unhappy with its results, there is something that an activated citizenry can do about it.

1 What Are the Origins of Globalization?
(p. 567)

 Watch the **Big Question Video** in **MySocLab** to review the key concepts for this section.

What does globalization mean, and how can sociology make sense of it? In this section we examined globalization and its origins.

GLOBALIZATION AND ITS ORIGINS (p. 567)

The Beginnings of Globalization (p. 567)

- **What are the two key changes responsible for globalization taking off?**

The Course of Globalization: From the Nineteenth Century to Today (p. 569)

- **Has globalization expanded steadily since the nineteenth century?**

KEY TERMS

globalization *(p. 567)*

export *(p. 567)*

import *(p. 567)*

foreign investment *(p. 567)*

emigration *(p. 567)*

factors of production *(p. 567)*

peasant *(p. 569)*

precapitalist *(p. 569)*

capitalist economy *(p. 569)*

deglobalization *(p. 569)*

gross domestic product (GDP) *(p. 570)*

tariff *(p. 570)*

capital controls *(p. 570)*

2 How Far-Reaching Is Globalization? *(p. 571)*

 Watch the **Big Question Video** in **MySocLab** to review the key concepts for this section.

To evaluate how far-reaching the process of globalization has been, we examined two issues in this section: First, to what extent are countries participating in international trade and investment? Second, do countries integrate equally with different parts of the world?

GLOBALIZATION'S REACH (p. 571)

The Degree of Globalization (p. 572)

- **How extensive is international trade and investment?**

The Importance of Regions (p. 572)

- **Why does economic integration cluster around regions?**

 Explore the **Data** on Globalization or Regionalization? in **MySocLab**

 Read the **Document** *Arnold Schwarzenegger, Ally McBeal and Arranged Marriages: Globalization on the Ground in India* by Steve Derné in **MySocLab.** This reading examines the impact of globalization on the lives of affluent and middle-class Indian society.

KEY TERMS

foreign direct investment (FDI) *(p. 572)*

transnational corporation (TNC) *(p. 572)*

3 What Drives Globalization? *(p. 575)*

 Watch the **Big Question Video** in **MySocLab** to review the key concepts for this section.

4 What Are the Benefits and Drawbacks of Globalization? *(p. 579)*

 Watch the **Big Question Video** in **MySocLab** to review the key concepts for this section.

GLOSSARY

absolute poverty A measure of the minimum requirements needed for people to have basic standards of food, clothing, health, and shelter. Any individual or family falling below this fixed amount is defined as living in poverty. The official U.S. government definition of poverty is an absolute measure based on an estimate of minimum living standards first established in the 1960s and adjusted for inflation thereafter.

access The ability or right to approach, enter, exit, communicate with, or make use of research sites and materials.

acid rain Rain containing acid that is formed when the gaseous air pollutants nitrogen oxide and sulfur dioxide react with water molecules in the atmosphere.

advance directive Written instructions (such as a living will) that a person prepares in the event that he or she is no longer able to make decisions at the end of life.

affirmative action Government policies regarding employment and education that seek to increase the representation of minorities and women in fields from which they have historically been excluded. Affirmative action is undertaken in an effort to counter the historical effects of discrimination and exclusion.

age pyramid A diagram that plots the age distribution of a population, with the numbers at the youngest ages at the bottom of the graph and the numbers at the oldest ages at the top, and with males and females on the left- and right-hand sides, respectively.

agency The capacity of individuals (or groups) to make free choices and exert their own will.

agenda setting The ability to decide which of the many possible topics for discussion, debate, and possible action that exist in the world will actually be considered. Agenda setting can take place in any institutional setting where decisionmaking occurs.

allocation theory A theory regarding the impacts of education that focuses on how education channels people into positions or institutions that offer different opportunities for continuing to think, learn, and earn.

anthropocentrism The belief that humans are separate from and superior to the natural world.

apartheid A system of racial segregation in South Africa, which was explicitly adopted in 1948 and ended in the early 1990s. All citizens were classified into racial groups, and residential areas were explicitly segregated on the basis of these categories, as were education, medical care, and public facilities.

archival research Research involving the use of printed records from the past, including documents, publications, and government and organizational records. These records are usually stored in special collections maintained by libraries, government agencies, or other organizations.

assembly line A type of factor in which each worker performs one or a handful of small, discrete tasks, with a conveyer belt moving pieces to each workstation. A finished product results from the input of many workers across an entire factory.

assimilation The process by which immigrants come to be incorporated into their new society by taking on the cultural tastes and practices of the new society.

asylum status A form of protection available to immigrants seeking admission to another country because of political violence or repression in their home country. Typically, applicants seeking asylum status must demonstrate that their life would be in danger if they were forced to return to their home country.

autonomy In work, the power to decide what and how one performs one's daily tasks, free of close supervision.

baby boom The post–World War II period in the United States from approximately 1946 through 1964. During this period, fertility was high. The birth cohorts born during the baby boom years produced a generation of Americans that was the largest in U.S. history.

biographical availability An individual's freedom to participate in a movement or protest due to a (relative) lack of constraining obligations created by work, school, family, or community.

birth cohort A group of individuals in a population born within a given time period. Thus the 1995–1999 birth cohort refers to those born between 1995 and 1999.

bourgeoisie The group in a capitalist economy who own businesses and employ people to work for them. This term is used in the Marxist tradition to refer to the most powerful class in a capitalist society.

Bracero Program A set of agreements between the United States and Mexico from 1942 to 1964 to import temporary workers from Mexico.

brain drain The departure of a significant number of the most educated and skilled citizens, who go to live and work in other countries.

bureaucracy A type of organization that has rules and responsibilities for each position (or job) spelled out, in which selection into those positions occurs on the basis of merit (not typically by election or inheritance). Many bureaucracies are also responsible for setting out policies and procedures that are to be adhered to by others.

cap-and-trade program A system in which a limit is placed on the total amount of carbon emissions that are allowable (the cap) and in which businesses buy and sell permits that entitle them to a designated amount of emissions (the trade).

capital controls Government policies that limit the movement of capital (i.e., funds available for investment) into or out of a country.

capitalism An economic system organized around private property and market exchange. In a capitalist economy, goods that are produced for consumption are distributed via exchange on the market.

capitalist economy An economic system in which goods and services are exchanged through markets, in which prices are established by what buyers are willing to pay, and in which property is privately owned. Under capitalism, markets extend to the hiring of workers at wages determined by negotiations between individuals (or unions) and employers. The role of government in regulating a capitalist economy varies widely, producing different types of capitalist economies around the world today.

care work All types of caring for other people, typically in one's own family, including childcare, elder care, or taking care of a disabled or sick adult.

caste society A society in which a person's social position is determined by the family he or she is born into.

causal inference A statement about cause and effect that claims that a change in one variable is the cause of a change in another variable.

causality When change in one variable is a direct cause of change in another variable. For example, long-term smoking is established as a cause of increased risk of lung cancer.

central planning An economy in which governments plan the amount of goods to be produced and their price for consumers. Central planning was commonly practiced in communist countries in the twentieth century, such as the Soviet Union, China, and countries in Eastern Europe.

chronic disease (or chronic health condition) A health condition that is long lasting, including heart disease, cancer, arthritis, diabetes, asthma, and chronic obstructive pulmonary disease.

chronic disease prevalence The total number of cases of a particular disease in a population, or the proportion of disease cases compared to the population as a whole.

civil inattention The act of ignoring other people to an appropriate degree even while noticing that other people are present.

civil religion The sacred beliefs, practices, and symbols associated with a particular nation-state or community, which may or may not contain elements of a traditional organized religion.

class The sociological concept that refers to a group of people who share a similar social and economic position in society.

class analysis The study of society focused on class or changes in the system of class inequality. Emphasis is placed on examining how, when, and where people's actions and beliefs are influenced by their economic position.

class reproduction The processes that cause class boundaries and distinctions to be maintained over time.

climate change The variety of changes in weather patterns that warming temperatures are producing.

code of ethics A set of guidelines that outlines what is considered moral and acceptable behavior in some context (such as within an organization or profession).

coercive isomorphism Similarities between organizations that arise out of legal or other requirements. Organizations become similar because they have no choice.

cohabitation The act of an unmarried straight or gay couple living together.

collective identity One's belief that one belongs to a certain group (or groups) with distinctive characteristics and interests (for example, women, the working class, or socialists). Not all such identities come easily to people; they may have to be consciously created, which is one of the things that some movements do.

community A group of individuals who interact with and often support each other on the basis of a shared aspect of personal identity. Communities of people often live in close proximity, but the term can apply to communities linked in other ways.

comparative-historical perspective A method of research that examines differences across countries or in different historical periods to try to understand what factors cause some specific change to occur.

concentration of poverty When a geographically bounded area experiences extremely high rates of economic disadvantage leading to higher rates of social problems.

congregation A specific religious body that meets regularly.

conservationist One who argues that the point of environmental protection ought to be to responsibly manage natural resources so that they are available for commercial use by future generations.

constructivist One who holds the view that social categories such as race or gender are social creations, not biological facts.

consumption The act of purchasing and using goods and services.

conurb A geographically continuous urban area that stretches across city political boundaries.

correlation The existence of a relationship between two variables. A correlation exists when a change in one variable is related to a change in another variable. It does not necessarily imply, however, that the change in one variable is the *cause* of the change in the other. Correlation can be contrasted with **causality**.

counterculture A group whose ideas, attitudes, and behaviors are in direct conflict with mainstream culture.

counterpublic Alternative public organizations created by disadvantaged social groups.

credentialism A requirement that one must obtain certain specific degrees or certificates before he or she can be considered for a particular job.

criminal justice system The entire body of laws and institutions that regulate and punish criminal activity. This includes written laws, courts, and other organizations where guilt or innocence is determined, as well as the places (such as jails and prisons, but also probation and parole offices) where those who have been convicted of a criminal offense are supervised.

critical mass Describes the size of a group or social network large enough to sustain some kind of important activity. A social movement, for example, attains critical mass when it is large enough to engage in sustained protest.

cross-national comparison Research that focuses on explaining the differences between countries, such as understanding why some outcome is observed in one country and not another.

cross-sectional research Research based on data that is collected at one point in time.

cultural capital The type and level of education and cultural knowledge possessed by an individual. Having a high level of cultural capital signifies one's high status in the eyes of others.

cultural omnivore A cultural elite that demonstrates high status through a broad range of cultural consumption and knowledge, including low-status culture.

cultural relativism The idea that cultural meanings and practices must be evaluated in their own social contexts.

cultural universal A cultural trait common to all humans and societies.

culture Systems of belief and knowledge shared by members of a group or society that shape individual and group behavior and attitudes. A society's culture includes its language, customs, symbols, rituals, and other forms of meaning that are widely shared.

culture industry The production for profit of popular music, movies, books, television, social media, and other types of mass-culture products by capitalist enterprises.

culture wars Disagreements about the proper role of family and religious values in society.

cumulative-exposure model A model highlighting a gradual process of worsening health with continued exposure to toxins.

curriculum The structure of coursework and content of a sequence of courses making up a program of study in a school or school system.

data analysis The scientific process by which researchers interpret the data they have collected.

data coding The organization of data based on key concepts and categories.

data display A visual projection of patterns in data, for example, as tables or figures.

deglobalization Periods of history when economic trade and investment between countries declines.

democracy A concept with multiple meanings, all of which concern the ability of ordinary people to exert direct control over their leaders. As form of governance in the modern world, democracy can be said to exist where leaders are chosen in free elections where anyone can run and the news media are freely allowed to discuss the issues and candidates. Broader conceptions of democracy incorporate a more direct role for citizen participation where everyone has the right to participate and equal resources to do so.

demographer One who studies population issues, particularly in relation to fertility, mortality, and migration, and how these processes vary among individuals in a population.

demographic data Information on the size, structure, or distribution of the population, and how these change over time.

demography The study of population size, particularly in relation to fertility rates (the ratio of live births in a population), mortality (the ratio of deaths and the life expectancy of individuals), and migration across borders.

denomination An organized branch of a larger religious tradition.

dependent variable A variable that fluctuates in relation to other ("independent") variables. In research, the dependent variable is the object of explanation, or what the researcher is trying to explain.

deskilling The process of breaking down the tasks involved in the production of goods or services into parts that can be done by someone without specialized training.

determinist One who believes that a society's environment, or the technology it has developed to exploit its environment, determines everything else—from its social structure to individuals' thoughts.

deterrence Policies or laws that are designed to discourage an individual or group from engaging in some kind of behavior.

deviant An individual whose actions or attitudes fall outside the generally accepted norms of a given group or society. What is "deviant" behavior is subject to change, depending on which group(s) have the power to define what is "normal."

diaspora A group of people dispersed from their original homeland and settled in other areas for long periods of time who nonetheless retain cultural practices, memories, and ties to that space.

digital divide The social, economic, and cultural gap between those with effective access to information technology and those without such access.

discrimination Any behavior, practice, or policy that harms, excludes, or disadvantages individuals on the basis of their group membership. Discrimination is often used by dominant groups to control opportunities and reduce the challenges from subordinate groups.

disinterested behavior A type of behavior by an individual that is not based on economic or political interests or motives.

division of labor The specialization of individuals in any organization or group, or in society as a whole, particularly in relation to work. There is thus a division of labor in all of society (with different people working in different occupations), a division of labor in individual organizations (where different people perform different tasks) and a division of labor in individual families and communities.

doctrine The official beliefs and rules of a particular religion or social and political group. Most commonly used to refer to more rigid belief systems.

double standard of sexuality Judging women more harshly than men for having sex outside of marriage or outside of relationships.

ecology The branch of science that studies the relationship between organisms and their environment.

economic restructuring Changes in the way the economy, firms, and employment relations are organized.

edge city A concentrated area of business, shopping, and entertainment just outside of the historical urban centers of commerce. Edge cities differ from classic suburbs in having a considerable amount of land devoted to economic activities, not just residences.

educational homogamy The practice of people marrying individuals with educational levels similar to their own.

egalitarian A society, organization, or group characterized by having little or very low levels of inequality.

egalitarian relationship A relationship where all members of the relationship share more or less equally in performing required tasks. In the case of intimate relationships, this includes sharing household chores, including child or elder care.

emigration The act of leaving one's country of birth to move to a new country.

emigration and immigration policies Government policies regulating the right of people to move into or out of a country.

empirical generalizability The application of conclusions from findings about one group or setting to the larger population. An empirical research result is generalizable when the same result can be found in another context.

entrepreneur One who invests money in a business.

environmental justice The achievement of equal protection from environmental hazards for all people, regardless of race, class, or geography; environmental justice also means giving community members a voice in shaping decisions that affect their environment and their health.

environmental racism A concept that describes how poor people of color disproportionately bear the burden of environmental hazards.

environmental sociology The study of how society simultaneously shapes and is shaped by the physical environment.

epidemiological transition The transition of a population from health conditions primarily involving infectious disease to health conditions primarily involving chronic disease.

epidemiology The study of health-related events in populations, their characteristics, their causes, and their consequences.

epistemology The study of what we think we can know about the world.

equilibrium price In economic theory, the price of a product when the demand for the product is exactly the same as the supply of the product.

essentialism The view that members of a group share a fundamental, inherited, innate, and fixed quality or characteristic. This outlook presumes that races are natural groupings whose boundaries are determined by deep-seated and unchangeable traits that are found within each individual.

ethnic enclave A place where people of a particular ethnicity live in high concentration.

ethnicity A system for classifying people who are believed to share common descent, based on perceived cultural similarities.

ethnocentrism The inability to understand, accept, or reference patterns of behavior or belief different from one's own.

ethnographer A sociologist who enters the everyday lives of those he or she studies in hopes of understanding how they navigate and give meaning to their worlds.

ethnography A qualitative research method for studying the way of life of a group of people by close observation of them over a relatively long period of time.

ethnomethodology A line of sociological inquiry (introduced by Harold Garfinkel) that studies the ways (tools and methods) members of a particular group construct social order and make sense of their everyday lives.

experiment A method of research in which one group gets a treatment of one kind or another, while a control group that is otherwise similar does not get the treatment. Experimental research designs are easiest to conduct in a laboratory, but increasingly sociologists are developing experiments in the real world.

export Goods or services that are sold outside the country in which they are produced.

extended case method A method of conducting ethnography that emphasizes the contribution of research to social theory. An ethnographer using the extended case method starts from a theoretical problem or puzzle.

factors of production The inputs—such as land, labor, capital, and technology—that go into the production of any good or service.

fad Any kind of behavior that spreads (often rapidly) among a specific population and is repeated enthusiastically for some period of time before disappearing (often rapidly).

family values A term generally associated with views and ideas about the family that highlight the virtues of heterosexual marriage and childrearing in a traditional nuclear family with defined gender roles. Family values can also be applied to other kinds of nontraditional unions.

feminist movement A social movement whose members advocate equality between men and women in rights and opportunities.

fertility The process by which members of a population produce live births.

fetal programming hypothesis The idea that things that happen to a person during critical periods of development can change the way that the tissues and structures of his or her body and brain function.

feudalism A social order in which those who own land (landlords) are entitled to receive the products of the laborers (serfs) who are legally obligated to work for the landowner.

fieldwork The collection of data about a group through firsthand observation of the group. It usually involves traveling to a setting in which the group lives or works.

first demographic transition The transition by a country or region from a pretransition period of high fertility and high mortality, to a mid-transition period of declining mortality followed by declining fertility, to a posttransition period in which both mortality and fertility are low.

first immigration era The period before 1875, in which immigration into the United States was essentially unregulated by the U.S. government.

foreign direct investment (FDI) A type of investment by a company in one country to produce goods or services in another. This could involve the purchase of an existing business in the second country or by building factories and/or offices in the second country and hiring workers.

foreign investment Investment of capital from one country into another.

foreign-born citizen An immigrant who has obtained citizenship in his or her new country.

formal sanction A form of punishment written into law or rules and followed according to those rules.

fossil fuel An energy source, such as coal, oil, or natural gas, that is made of fossils that decomposed over millions of years under high pressure.

fourth immigration era In the period since 1965 in the United States, allowable immigration has been subject to a series of restrictions on immigration from both the Eastern and Western Hemispheres but without specific national origins quotas.

framing The specific ways in which ideas and beliefs are presented to other people. Politicians, political activists, and social movements all engage in framing efforts when they try to persuade others that their way of thinking is correct. Scholars of social movements have also focused on how activists try to frame or present their cause or ideas for change so that they make sense to or resonate with the beliefs of potential recruits and supporters.

full employment A situation in which everyone who wants a paid job is able to find one.

fundamental-cause theory A theory stating that individuals of higher socioeconomic status have access to knowledge, money, power, and social connections that are deployed throughout the life course to avoid disease and death. These resources can be deployed in a range of situations. As a result, this theory predicts that no matter what the causes of bad health, socioeconomic inequalities will inevitably emerge.

garbage-can model A type of decisionmaking in organizations where problems and solutions are addressed unsystematically and haphazardly.

gender The ways that social forces create differences between men's and women's behavior, preferences, treatment, and opportunities, and the characteristics of men and women that reflect these forces.

generalization Forming conclusions about broader society from research on a subgroup or sample of the broader society.

generalized other The social control exercised by commonsense understandings of what is appropriate given a specific time and place.

Geneva Conventions A set of international agreements between countries about how prisoners of war are to be treated.

genocide The deliberate and systematic killing of a category of people.

ghetto A poor, isolated neighborhood, often formed as the result of residential segregation in which a poor or low-status racial, ethnic, or religious group is compelled to live in the same place.

glass ceiling A term used to describe the limitations on the advancement of women in corporations, suggesting that even as firms begin to hire large numbers of women they are failing to promote them into positions of power and authority.

global city A city that contains a disproportionate amount of global business activity, particularly when connected by international finance, trade, culture, and communication to other cities around the world. Because it acts as a node at the center of global economic activity, global cities are places in which trade and investment are facilitated.

global culture Cultural practices that are common to large parts of the world.

global neighborhood A diverse neighborhood made up of people from several different national and ethnic groups.

global value chain The full range of activities that businesses and workers provide at each stage of the production of a good or service that add to its value. While a value chain can be entirely within a single company, or contained with one country, increasingly global value chains (with production inputs from more than one country) are being found.

global warming Describes the rising of Earth's average temperature.

globalization The growing permeability of national borders and the increase in flows of goods, services, and people across national borders.

Great Migration The move of African Americans from the rural South to the industrial North in the first half of the twentieth century.

green card A term used to describe a visa status for an immigrant to the United States that allows its holder to live in the United States permanently but does not make that immigrant a citizen.

greenhouse effect The result of high levels of CO_2 in the atmosphere allowing the sun's heat to pass through to the Earth's surface while stopping it from spreading back into space.

gross domestic product (GDP) The total value of all goods and services, plus investment and government expenditures, that a country produces.

group style The set of norms and practices that distinguishes one group from another.

growth machine A coalition of business interests and city boosters who work together with local governments to attract residents and economic investment to a particular area.

guerilla warfare A type of warfare in which an outmanned army hides from its larger opponent and engages in attacks only in situations where it thinks it can gain an advantage.

habitus A concept introduced by sociologist Pierre Bourdieu to refer to the diverse ways in which individuals develop intuitive understandings and engrained habits reflecting their class background and upbringing.

Hawthorne studies An influential series of studies at the Hawthorne plant of the Western Electric company in the 1920s. Two major findings emerged from these studies: (1) the experiment effect, which is any change interpreted by workers as management's attempt to improve conditions, especially those that provide mental stimulation, improve workers' productivity; and (2) the social group effect, in which workers moved to separate spaces as a group develop bonds that increase their productivity.

health disparity A difference in health status linked to social, economic, or environmental conditions including socioeconomic status, race and ethnicity, gender, and geographic location.

healthy life expectancy The average number of healthy years one can expect to live if current patterns of death and illness remain the same.

hegemony Widely shared beliefs about what is right or wrong that legitimize and empower a society's elites.

heteronormativity A type of prejudice that claims that being heterosexual is the only normal option for an individuals' sexual orientation.

heterosexism Discrimination or bias against persons because they are not heterosexual.

hidden curriculum The often unstated standards of behavior that teachers and administrators expect from children within the education system. These often unstated expectations may reflect the middle-class biases and norms of school professionals.

historical research Research based on examining records and documents from the past to understand how people, places, or things worked in a previous time.

homelessness An extreme form of poverty defined by lack of permanent shelter to live in.

homophobia Discrimination or bias against homosexual persons that is based in fear.

hookup Sexual behavior (not always intercourse) that occurs in a situation that was not a prearranged date and between individuals who may or may not be interested in an exclusive romantic relationship.

hospice care The treatment of people with incurable diseases in the final stage of life. The goal of hospice care is to attempt to help patients live as pain-free as possible in their final days.

hypothesis A prediction researchers make that they will test in their research.

ideology A set of ideas that constitutes one's goals, expectations, and actions.

immigration A term that describes the movement of people across borders.

immobility A situation in which individuals are unable to move from one economic or social class into another. Usually immobility means that people remain in the same social and economic situation that they are born into (in other words, in the same class or income group as their parents).

import A good or service purchased in one country but manufactured in another.

import-substituting industrialization (ISI) Government policies that attempt to replace imported goods with similar goods produced by domestic companies. Examples of such policies include putting very high taxes on certain imported goods, or barring them altogether. ISI was a strategy used by many poor and moderate income developing countries in the twentieth century in attempt to foster domestic economic growth.

incarceration The holding of an individual in a jail or prison.

income The receipt of money or goods over a particular accounting period (such as hourly, weekly, monthly, or yearly). Income may include wages from a job, benefits from a pension or government program, or income from investments.

independent variable A factor that might help to explain some outcome of interest. An example might be the impact of educational level – in this case, the independent variable — on one's income as an adult.

individual discrimination Intentional action carried out by an individual or small group that is meant to harm, exclude, or disadvantage members of a certain group.

Industrial Revolution The period in which mass production in factories began to develop and fostered rapid economic growth. The timing of the industrial revolution varied from country to country, but is generally thought to have begun in the late eighteenth century and evolved throughout the nineteenth and early twentieth centuries.

industrialization A process of economic change characterized by the decline of farming and the growth of factories and large-scale goods production.

inequality The unequal distribution of valued goods and opportunities in society.

infectious disease A disease caused by the entrance, presence, or growth of a microorganism or other foreign agent inside the body.

informal sanction A form of punishment or expression of disapproval that is ad hoc and not systematically applied or written down.

informed consent The voluntary participation of someone in a research project based on the participant having a full understanding of possible risks and benefits involved.

institution A complex term used to stand for structured and enduring practices of human life that are built around well-established rules and norms or are centered in important organizations like the government, legal courts, churches, schools, or the military.

institutional (or structural) discrimination Occurs when the actions or policies of organizations or social institutions exclude, disadvantage, or harm members of particular groups. Such discrimination need not be intentional, and in practice it is often hard to discern whether or not discriminatory intentions lay behind a particular policy or practice.

institutional differences Differences in students' learning experiences based on the schools they attend or the educational track they are assigned to.

institutional review board (IRB) Required at all universities that receive federal funds for research, these boards review researchers' proposals before any work can begin in order to assess the potential harm of the research for participants being studied.

institutionalized The process by which a social practice or organization begins to become an institution; the introduction of formal roles and rules in an organized form.

interactionism The understanding that individuals (their personalities, their preferences, their ideas, etc.) are constructed and shaped by and through communication with other individuals, groups, and institutions.

interdisciplinary research A method of research that integrates ideas, theories, and data from different academic fields.

interest group An organization established to promote the interests of a group or corporation, especially in Congress or at the level of state governments.

intergenerational social mobility The movement of individuals from the social position, or stratification order, of their parents into a new social position as adults. Compares children's occupational achievements with those of their parents.

intermarriage Marriage between people in different social groups.

interpretivism A form of sociological analysis that focuses on understanding how people give meaning to social life, objects, and processes—and how they make sense of social reality and navigate social interaction.

interview A method of collecting data based on asking a person a set of questions and having a conversation with him or her focused on gathering information related to the research.

irreligion The absence of religion.

jail A place of detention where individuals are held either before trial or serve relatively minor sentences. *Prisons* generally hold offenders convicted of more serious crimes.

journalism The production and dissemination of information about contemporary affairs of general importance.

kin Other people that individuals have important social relationships with. These important others often include immediate (and sometimes extended) family members but also can include close friends and even other acquaintances who play an important (and sometimes supportive) role in one's life.

kinship system The social links and boundaries, defined by biology and social custom, that establish who is related to whom.

labeling theory A theory of deviance that stresses that many kinds of behaviors are deviant solely because they are labeled as such.

labor market The process through which employers identify and hire individuals to work under specified terms of employment.

labor process The organization of work, in terms of the relationship between workers and employers, the way specific work tasks are structured and performed, and the technologies and organizational environments in which the work is performed.

laissez-faire economics An economic system in which there is minimal government regulation of economic activity. In this environment, individuals and organizations are free to do whatever they choose in the pursuit of profit, as long as they abide by the terms of the contracts they agree to with one another.

language A comprehensive system of words or symbols representing concepts, which is often but not always spoken.

lean production A term used to describe the efforts of economic organizations in recent years to achieve more efficiency by constantly scrutinizing and reducing costs in every possible way.

legal permanent resident (LPR) One who is allowed to live permanently in a country even though he or she is not a citizen. In the United States, such a person would hold a green card.

legal temporary resident A person allowed to live in a country for a specified period of time.

liberation theology A strain of theology first associated with Latin American Catholicism that emphasizes god's concern for the poor and downtrodden and the rightness of social justice causes.

life-course perspective A model that highlights the effects that social contexts a person inhabits throughout life have on his or her health.

life expectancy (at age *x*) The average number of additional years (past age *x*) that the average person in a population can expect to live.

life chances An individual's long-term possibilities and potential, including future income and opportunities, given his or her current attributes such as level of education, social networks, and possession of marketable skills or assets. Members of the same class are generally said to have similar life chances.

life course The transitions individuals make as they age through their lives. A typical life course includes childhood, adolescence, the transition to adulthood and first job, perhaps becoming a parent, retiring, and death. The study of the life course by sociologists centers on the key transitions, or turning points, in individual lives and the larger social patterns they represent.

longitudinal research Research based on data collected over a long period of time.

looking-glass self A term coined by sociologist Charles Horton Cooley to emphasize the extent to which our own self-understandings are dependent on how others view us.

loose coupling An organizational environment in which those at the top do not have control over the activities and decisions underneath them. This often arises in complex organizations with multiple units.

lynching The killing of someone by a group, without a trial or due process, for some specified behavior.

mainstream culture The most widely shared systems of meaning in a society. Mainstream culture includes the most widely consumed cultural products (music, literature, films), foods, ways of speaking, and widely shared ideas about normal or appropriate behavior.

market Any setting in which buyers and sellers engage in exchange.

mass communication Communication within society as a whole through the mass media (television, Internet, newspapers, radio), as opposed to between individuals.

mass incarceration A term used to describe a situation in which a very high proportion of people are held in prisons. It has been used to describe developments in the American criminal justice system over the past 30 years.

median A statistical term that refers to the value that lies at the middle (or midpoint) of all the data, with an equal number of cases with either higher or lower values.

Medicare A government program in the United States that provides health insurance to all individuals over 65 years of age.

megacity A city with a population over 10 million.

megaregion A geographically continuous urban area containing at least two very large cities and their surrounding towns, which are connected through economic and transportation infrastructure.

meritocracy A system where rewards and positions are distributed by ability, not social background or personal connections.

middle class A group of people who occupy the middle positions in terms of income and status in an economic system.

migrant energy The special skills and determination brought to a country by migrants, who may be especially motivated to succeed.

migrant remittance The process by which a migrant sends money to family or friends in his or her home country.

migration The process by which individuals move from one location, region, country, or city to another.

mimetic isomorphism The tendency of similar organizations to adopt the same kinds of rules and procedures in the belief that what works for one organization should work for others.

minimum wage Established by law, minimum wage is the lowest hourly wage a worker can be paid.

moral behavior Behavior that is guided by a belief about what is right and proper to do.

moral shock An unexpected event that surprises, distresses, and outrages people, often to the point of motivating them to join or even start a movement to eliminate the source of their outrage.

mortality The process by which individuals in a population gradually die.

mover An individual who leaves a place to live in another.

multiculturalism Beliefs or policies promoting the equal accommodation of different ethnic or cultural groups within a society. It is sometimes also used to refer to the benefits of dialogue and interaction between different groups.

national culture The set of shared cultural practices and beliefs of people living within a nation-state.

nationalism A set of beliefs about the virtues of one's country. In the sociology of race and ethnicity, nationalism includes the assumption that people are inherently members of a specific nation, and that their identities are in large part defined by their national membership.

naturalization The process of becoming a citizen in a new country.

net financial assets (NFA) The total value of savings, investments, and other convertible assets a person has, minus any debts, and excluding one's primary home (if it is owned).

networked public An online public sphere.

new religious movement A religious group that emerges independently of existing religious traditions or makes significant revisions and additions to them.

niche A unique place or opportunity that can be profitably filled by someone or some group. Niches arise in a variety of ways, especially when existing organizations or government agencies fail to meet some underlying social need.

normalize To make or declare some action as normal or appropriate.

normative isomorphism The process of organizations becoming similar because of a widespread belief among their members and the members of similar organizations that they should adopt certain rules or procedures.

norm A basic rule of society that helps us know what is and is not appropriate to do in a situation. Norms evolve over time as social attitudes and expectations change, although those changes are typically very slow.

nuclear family A term used to describe a family consisting of a husband and wife and their children.

occupation A job that has been formally established and has some requirements (often formalized) for training or knowledge to perform it.

occupational sex segregation When women and men are distributed differently across occupations, such that some jobs are filled mostly by men and others mostly by women.

one-drop rule Enshrined in many state laws in the United States around the turn of the nineteenth century, this method of racial classification defined any individual with any African ancestry as black. From this viewpoint someone with one black great-grandparent and seven white great-grandparents is considered black because their "drop of black blood" means they have more in common with blacks than with whites.

operationalize When researchers define the methods and techniques to be used to assess and define the concepts that are being investigated.

organization A social group or social network that is unified by a common institutional structure, such as a government agency, a school, a business firm, the military, a religion, and many others.

organizational isomorphism The process by which similar organizations adopt similar rules and procedures.

outsourcing Common in globalization, outsourcing refers to the contracting of parts of the production process to another party, possibly located abroad. A common example in the United States is of credit-card companies hiring people in India to handle customer service calls.

palliative care All types of healthcare designed to reduce pain and suffering by helping patients get better. It is often contrasted with hospice care, where there is no hope of curing or improving a patient.

path dependency The process by which the historical legacies and outcomes of the past impact actors and organizations in the present, making some choices or outcomes appear logical and others illogical.

patriarchy A gender system in which men have substantially more power than women in politics, the economy, and the family.

patrilocal A family relationship in which a married couple resides with the husband's parents.

peasant A person who works in agriculture but does not own the land he or she farms.

physically and mentally unhealthy days The number of days people in a given population rated their physical or mental health as "not good."

pluralism A theory of how democracies work that argues that as long as competing groups (or interest groups) have sufficient power to participate, the final outcome of any policy or political controversy will reflect the general preferences of the society as a whole. The ability to influence outcomes reflects not just wealth or prestige (although these may be important) but also the ability to mobilize resources or citizens to support a cause.

pluralism (in religion) The coexistence of individuals and religious groups with significantly different beliefs and cultures in the same society.

political action committee (PAC) A term used in U.S. politics to describe an organization set up to collect political donations from individuals, corporations, or unions to influence political and electoral outcomes.

political-process perspective A theoretical perspective that emphasizes that movements are concerned with politics, not individual psychological states, and are a rational form of politics ("politics by other means") and a normal response, under certain circumstances, to routine institutional political processes. Movements emerge and may be successful if those political processes create political opportunities for certain kinds of collective protest.

polygamy The practice of marriage of one individual to two or more other individuals.

population aging A term used to describe a society where the average age of the population is increasing.

population dynamics The process by which a population changes in size over time.

population momentum The tendency of a population that has been changing in size to continue to change in size even if factors such as fertility and mortality have shifted to levels that would, in the long run, imply no change in population size.

positivism An approach to knowledge based on the claim that the only true way to gain knowledge about the world is to use the logic of the natural sciences—by distancing ourselves from what we study, using universal standards to advance truth claims, determining cause and effect, and generalizing from part to whole.

poverty line Established by the government, it is the minimum income necessary to afford basic necessities. Anyone below this threshold is considered to be in poverty.

power Power has three distinct dimensions in the sociological sense: (1) the power of an individual or group to get another individual or group to do something it wants, which sometimes may involve force; (2) the power to control the agenda of issues that are to be decided; and finally (3) the power to persuade others that their interests are the same as those of a powerholder. Power can be possessed by individuals or groups.

power elite An idea, associated with C. Wright Mills, who wrote a book by that title in 1956, arguing that a small group of people, drawn from similar backgrounds and sharing broadly similar worldviews, dominates the upper levels of U.S. institutions and shapes the policies of the federal government.

precapitalist economy All of the different types of economies that existed before the rise of capitalism, including those based on hunting or agriculture.

prejudice Negative beliefs or attitudes held about entire groups based on subjective, selective, or inaccurate information. They lead to "prejudgment" of the individuals associated with stigmatized groups.

preservationist One who believes that the environment has intrinsic value and should be maintained in as pristine a state as possible.

principal In the immigration process, the family member who is applying for the right to live in another country (with his or her family members as secondary applicants) is called the principal.

prison A place of detention where people convicted of felonies (serious crimes requiring at least one year of detention) are held.

privilege The ability or right to have special access to opportunities or claims on rewards.

probability sampling A technique for choosing participants for a research study (i.e., a probability sample) in which each person in the population is assigned a known and likely chance of being selected. Some groups of people can be assigned different probabilities of being selected when the probability sample is stratified based on group membership.

probation A criminal conviction that does not require a prison or jail sentence. During probation, a convicted offender is subject to regular supervision but is allowed to live in their community.

productivity The amount of output an individual is able to produce in a given period of time.

progressive tax system A tax system in which tax rates are higher on richer people than poorer people, with the idea being that it is fairer to ask those who can afford to pay more to do so. These systems can be based on a progressive income tax and can also differentially assess taxes on wealth transfers, such as inheritances.

Prohibition The period from 1920 to 1933 in which the consumption or sale of alcohol was barred by a Constitutional amendment (repealed in 1933).

proletariat Individuals in capitalist economies who work in exchange for pay. The term is usually reserved for people performing manual jobs and is synonymous with "working class."

proportional representation (PR) A system of elections in which seats in a legislature are divided up based on the percentage of the vote received. In many PR systems, there is a minimum threshold, such as 5 percent, for a party to cross before it receives seats.

protestant ethic The belief that hard work and thrift are signs of god's grace.

public opinion The views of citizens in the aggregate on social and political topics. Public opinion is usually measured through opinion polls and surveys, where modern sampling techniques allow researchers to estimate opinions by asking a smaller representative group of citizens.

public policy All of the policies adopted or implemented by the government. A distinction between foreign policy and domestic policy is important, with the former including all policies relating to foreign governments and national security issues, while the latter refers to all of the policies and programs that aim to address social problems or issues inside the country.

public sphere A social space—physical, virtual, or theoretical—where private citizens can come together as a public body to discuss and express opinions about matters of general interest.

pull factor In the immigration context, when an individual's motivation to move to another country is based on the perceived attractions of life in the new country.

push factor When an individual decides to leave a country because of something that is making her or him unhappy (such as low pay, lack of jobs, limited opportunities, or political or religious persecution).

qualitative research Research that relies on nonnumerical data, such as words, observations, or pictures.

quantitative research Research that relies on statistical analysis of numerical or categorical data.

race A system for classifying people who are believed to share common descent, based on perceived innate physical similarities.

racism Prejudice against individuals who are members or particular racial or ethnic groups, often drawing on negative stereotypes about the group. Institutional racism refers to rules and regulations that organizations adopt that significantly harm members of a racial or ethnic group.

random sampling A technique for choosing participants for a research study in which each person in the population of interest has an equal chance of being chosen so that the sample mirrors a larger population and reflects its characteristics or dynamics.

random-assignment experiment A study using a method of assigning participants or groups to receive different treatments that ensures that any posttreatment differences result from the different treatments they received.

rational-choice perspective A perspective in social and economic theory that emphasizes the centrality of individual decision making based on how individuals think about their well-being and how best to advance it. While there are a variety of different versions of the rational-choice perspective, all emphasize that individual action is the foundation of society and social order.

receiving country The country migrants move to.

redlining The determination by governments and banks that neighborhoods with high percentages of racial minorities were ineligible for mortgage loans. Redlining has been illegal since the 1970s.

reference group A set of individuals who share similar preferences or social positions and have influence on an individual or members of a group.

refugee status A form of protection that may be granted to people who have been persecuted or fear they will be persecuted on account of race, religion, nationality, political opinions, or membership in a particular social group.

rehabilitation The attempt to reform a convicted offender so that he or she will not commit crimes in the future. Rehabilitation often involves the use of therapies of various kinds, as well as helping an offender develop job and life skills that will help him or her desist from crime in the future.

relative poverty A term used to define people as poor not by assessing whether their resources are sufficient to obtain basic social necessities but rather by comparing their incomes relative to other people in society.

reliability The extent to which the same measurement technique in additional studies would end up producing similar results.

remittance Money sent from an individual in one country to an individual (often a family member) in another country.

renewable energy Sources of energy that are capable of being replaced by natural ecological cycles, such as wind, sunlight, and water.

replacement fertility A level of fertility in which individuals in a population, on average have a sufficient number of offspring that will imply, over the long run, no change in the size of the population.

representative sample A small group of people, ideally selected at random, who are similar to the entire population.

representative sampling A small group of a larger population is selected, ideally at random but in a way in which each member of the larger population has an equal chance of being chosen, to represent the entire population. A truly representative sample will have average characteristics that reflect those of the total population under study. This smaller group can be studied at much lower cost than the entire population, but the results of any study should be very similar to what would be found in the entire population.

research memo An extended version of research notes, usually organized analytically, that allows researchers to work through their findings and the evidence they have to support them.

research method The approach used for gathering data to answer a research question. Different research methods represent different approaches to gathering data; a major distinction is between qualitative and quantitative research methods.

resource-mobilization approach A theoretical perspective that emphasizes the importance of resources, like labor and money, for generating and sustaining social movements. The more resources a movement is able to employ or mobilize, the more successful it is likely to be.

respondent A person participating in a study who can be asked specific questions of interest to the investigator.

retribution Punishment that aims at making a criminal offender experience as much harm as he or she has caused others.

revolution A revolution consists, at minimum, of a change of government or political regime brought about, at least in part, by popular protest. Some define revolutions (or "social revolutions") more narrowly, as entailing not only a change of regime but also a fundamental change in a society's economic institutions and class structure.

revolutionary movement A social movement that seeks to overthrow a government or fundamentally change a society's economic institutions and class structure.

revolutionary situation A situation that occurs when two or more political institutions or groups claim to be the rightful or legitimate rulers of a certain territory or population. Such a situation is also called "dual power" or "multiple sovereignty."

riot A spontaneous, unplanned collective protest, loosely organized at best, involving attacks on property and (sometimes) persons.

role A position within an institution or organization that comes with specific social expectations for how to behave and be treated. Some roles may be ascribed, that is, assigned to us by birth (man, woman, white, black), and some may be achieved, that is, acquired through our actions (doctor, professor, class clown).

role conflict When two or more discordant demands are placed on individuals, rendering them unable to fulfill their own or others' expectations.

role model A specific individual who exhibits significant influence on others and acts as a reference for how to act.

role set The expected ways to act given a particular set of social relations.

sacred Holy; worthy of special reverence.

sampling A technique to define what or whom to include in a study.

sanction Any type of punishment, including both formal punishment (based on laws or written rules), or informal types of punishments.

scientific management A movement that arose in the late nineteenth and early twentieth centuries that attempted to improve productivity by ensuring that managers controlled all aspects of the labor process and would utilize the best practices available given existing technology and knowledge.

scientific method A step-by-step process of conducting research that begins with formulating a research hypotheses, then operationalizing variables, then collecting data, and finally drawing empirical and conceptual generalizations from the data.

second generation The children of immigrants.

second immigration era The period between 1875 and 1920, in which the United States made its first attempts to establish some restrictions on immigration. This era included restrictions on immigrants from China, those who were sick or impoverished, those lacking literacy, and other such restrictions.

second shift A term created and popularized by Arlie Hochschild to refer to housework, childcare, and elder care disproportionally done by women. The first shift refers to one's paid job, whereas the second shift refers to the labor needed to keep households going.

secularization A process of declining influence or marginalization of religion in society.

segmented assimilation The various pathways by which immigrant groups become part of the larger social fabric; instead of the pattern where the children of immigrants are economically upwardly mobile and their ethnic difference dissipates with future generations, new forms of assimilation include economic instability and continuing traditional ethnic practices.

segregation The spatial separation of the population based on race or ethnicity.

self The conscious being, personified in a human body, which is made and reformulated through social interaction.

self-fulfilling prophecy A term coined by Robert Merton to mean the process by which someone is defined in a particular way and then comes to fulfill the expectations of that definition.

self-selected When individuals have the opportunity to choose to be in some condition, those making that choice may be different than those who do not make that choice. The "selection effect" reflects the differences between those two groups.

sending country The country migrants were born in.

sensitive-period model (or latency model) A model focused on the idea that very early life exposures can affect adult outcomes but may remain latent for years.

serf Under feudalism, a person who is legally obligated to work for the landowner.

serial relationships A pattern of having repeated, short-term intimate relationships with other adults.

sex Whether a person is classified as male or female based on anatomical or chromosomal criteria.

sexual minority A group whose sexual behavior or attractions are unusual in a given society. Those who are homosexual, bisexual, or transgendered are sexual minorities.

sexual orientation Whether one's sexual attractions are to members of the same sex, the other sex, or both.

significant other A term coined by George Herbert Mead to mean individuals close enough to us to have a strong capacity to motivate our behavior.

skill-biased technical change (SBTC) The ways in which technological advancements create jobs that require high skill.

slavery A social system that denies some individuals all basic rights, allowing these individuals to be owned, controlled, and compelled to work for others.

smog A smoky air pollutant produced when tailpipe or smokestack emissions that linger in the atmosphere chemically react with the sunlight.

social background A person's family or the community where he or she lives and where he or she grew up.

social capital The resources available to a particular individual through his or her connections to others.

social closure The idea that education serves a credentialing function that limits entry into some professions and thus raises the rewards of people in them.

social construct A social phenomenon (for example a belief, discourse, or category) that was invented by individuals and is shaped by the social forces present in the time and place of its creation.

social construction (of the environment) The process by which people interpret the natural world and make it meaningful.

social construction (of gender) The social processes that create and sustain gender differences and gender inequality.

social construction (of reality) The interactive process by which knowledge is produced and codified, making it specific to a certain group or society.

social context The social environments, including economic and cultural conditions, that influence people's lives.

social control The institutions, norms, and rules through which societies attempt to shape and control individuals. Behavior that violates social rules is typically punished either formally or informally, reflecting the different ways in which social control is administered.

social democratic model A system of organizing production and the economy that combines features of socialism and capitalism. It also provides workers with far greater protections against mistreatment and arbitrary layoffs, and ensures access to health insurance, retirement benefits, vacation, and paid maternity and paternity leave.

social group A collection of individuals formed around some kind of social identity or for some specific purpose.

social hierarchy A set of important social relationships that provide individuals and groups with different kinds of status in which some are elevated above others.

social institution A structured and enduring practice of human life that is built around well-established rules and norms or is centered in important organizations.

social interaction The way people act together, including how they modify and alter their behavior in response to the presence of others. Social interaction is governed by norms.

social isolation When an individual has a relative lack of connections to others.

social mobility The movement of individuals from one social position into another. Intergenerational social mobility is a measure of the extent to which parents and their children have similar or different social and economic positions in adulthood. Upward mobility is said to occur when an individual's class is higher than that of his or her parents; downward mobility is the opposite.

social movement A conscious, concerted, and sustained effort by ordinary people to change (or preserve) some aspect of their society by using extrainstitutional means. "Extrainstitutional means" refers to collective actions undertaken outside existing institutions, like courts and legislatures, although movements may also work through such institutions, at least part of the time.

social movement organization (SMO) A formal organization that participates in, and may initiate or lead, a social movement. SMOs generally pool resources, like labor and money, which may be crucial for movements. Some movements encompass a number of SMOs that alternately cooperate and compete with one another.

social network The ties or connections between people, groups, and organizations.

social problem A term used to capture a wide range of individual, group, or societal behaviors or societal issues that are thought to have harmful consequences. Examples might include poverty, crime, drug abuse, homelessness, inequality, racism, sexism, and discrimination.

social science The fields of research on the social world of human beings. The social sciences began to emerge in the nineteenth century, as people turned from abstract ideas or debates (like "democracy is good") to thinking about how to study the way things work in the real world. Along with sociology, the social sciences are principally made up of economics, political science, anthropology, and psychology (with many smaller disciplines that have grown out of these disciplines).

social stratification A subfield of sociology that examines inequalities among individuals and groups.

social structure The external forces, most notably social hierarchies, norms, and institutions, that provide the context for individual and group action.

social theory An overarching framework that suggests certain assumptions and assertions about the way the world works. These frameworks are used for posing research questions and evaluating evidence related to those questions.

social ties The various types of connections individuals make with other people.

social-trajectory model An approach focused on the idea that early life experiences determine where a person ends up in the social pecking order, which in turn influences his or her health.

socialism An economic system where the government owns some or most of all productive enterprises, and makes decisions about the amount and type of goods and services to be produced.

socialization The process by which individuals come to understand the expectations and norms of their groups as well as the various roles they transition into over the life course and how to behave in society or in particular social settings.

socialization theory A theory regarding the impact of education that focuses on how education transmits knowledge, skills, and values that persist in adulthood and that employers believe increase productivity.

socialized The project of socialization, or the process by which individuals come to understand the expectations and norms of their groups.

socially deviant Behavior that violates the written or unwritten rules of society.

society A large group of people who live in the same area and participate in a common economy or culture.

socioeconomic gradient (in health) A term used to describe how those with the lowest status are less healthy than those in the middle, who are less healthy than those at the top.

socioeconomic status (SES) A broad definition of a person's social class based on components such as education, income, and occupation.

sociological imagination The capacity to think systematically about how many things we experience as personal problems—for example, debt from student loans, competing demands from divorced parents, or an inability to form a rewarding romantic relationship at college—are really social issues that are widely shared by others born in a similar time and social location as us. It involves taking into account how our individual lives are impacted by historical and social contexts.

sociology The study of societies and the social worlds that individuals inhabit within them.

spatial concentration When significant numbers of people from the same group, such as a racial or ethnic group, live in the same physical location, such as a neighborhood or city.

spurious relationship When two factors seem to move in the same direction but both are themselves caused by something else (i.e., a third factor), sociologists refer to the apparent relationship between the first two factors as a spurious relationship.

state All of the agencies and offices of governing institutions, including government bureaucracies, law and the legal system, and the military) constitute what sociologists call the state. It is a term that is meant to capture than just the current government in power by incorporating the idea that the there are permanent institutions that are independent of whomever is in power.

state deviance Deviant behavior by governments or government agencies.

statistically deviant Behavior that is different or unusual, but not necessarily in violation of social norms.

status A distinct social category that is set off from others and has associated with it a set of expected behaviors and roles for individuals to assume. The category can often involve prestige, such as that accorded to individuals and to important social or economic roles (like "priest," "lawyer," "truck driver"). An individual's status may reflect some accomplishment or position attained, one's membership in a particular group, or both.

stayer One who chooses not to leave.

stereotype A simplified and often negative generalization about a group (e.g., women or men) that is often false or exaggerated. Stereotypes are most often negative, although positive stereotypes can sometimes be found.

structural inertia The extent to which an organization's rules and routines are relatively fixed and difficult to change.

structuralism The view that social structures exert so much power that individuals are fundamentally limited in their agency or capacity to make free choices and exert their own will.

stylized facts A series of facts or empirical regularities that we think we know with great certainty.

subculture A relatively small group of people whose affiliation is based on shared beliefs, preferences, and practices that distinguish them from the mainstream or larger social group to which they also belong.

suburb Traditionally, a residential enclave within commuting distance of a city.

suburban sprawl The continuing geographic spread of sparse residential areas.

supernatural Attributed to a force or entity beyond scientific understanding and the laws of nature.

survey A type of research in which information is derived by asking people to answer standardized questions, which may collect information about any aspect of human life of interest to the investigator, including information about jobs, employment, family life, health, education, and policy or political attitudes and values.

sustainability Refers to a system of development and consumption that satisfies a society's current needs without imperiling the ability of future generations to do the same.

symbol Something that communicates an idea while being distinct from the idea itself.

symbolic boundary The distinctions people make between themselves and others on the basis of taste, socioeconomic status, morality, or other differences.

syncretic Combining religious ideas and practices drawn from more than one distinct tradition.

tariff A tax on goods being imported into a country.

taste A person's cultural preferences.

terrorism A type of warfare in which a weaker group challenges a more powerful group by attacking civilian targets of importance to the more powerful group. State terrorism occurs when a country's military attacks civilian populations.

theodicy A justification of the goodness and rightness of god, or more generally of a particular religious system, in the face of the evils of the world.

theology Discussions and systematic reasoning about god and other religious matters.

theoretical generalizability The application of conclusions from findings based on a sample or case to larger sociological processes and theories about the world.

theoretical tradition A conceptual framework or paradigm that sociologists use to imagine and make sense of the world.

thick description A rich, detailed description of the ways people make sense of their lives.

third immigration era The period from 1921 to 1965, in which the United States tightly controlled immigration into the United States using strict quotas on entry from different countries.

tool kit In the sociology of culture, the view that culture is a set of symbolic skills, devices, or strategies that people learn throughout their lives, and can deploy strategically in different situations. The tool kit also supplies a set of ideas to justify a course of action retrospectively.

total fertility rate A measure of fertility in a given calendar year reflecting the fertility of women at different childbearing ages. A total fertility rate of 3.2 in 2010 in a given population means that the average woman would have 3.2 children during her lifetime, *if* fertility rates in this population remained the same.

totemism A belief system in which clans adopt a plant or animal as their group emblem, and declare it sacred.

tracking A term used to describe how schools assign students to distinct groups based on ability or curriculum.

transfer A term used in immigration research to refer to the transfer of money from an immigrant back home, or to an immigrant from her or his family back home.

transgendered Individuals who were assigned one sex category at birth based on anatomical criteria but who come to believe they belong in the other gender category and take action to be in the other category.

transnational corporation (TNC) A company with business operations in multiple countries.

unauthorized migrant A person living in a country where he or she is not legally allowed to reside. In current political discussions, these individuals are often referred to as "illegal immigrants."

union An organized association of workers created in order to protect and fight for rights or resources for their members. Unions can be organized at a single workplace, across multiple workplaces of the same company or in the same industry.

unit of analysis The level of a topic that a researcher focuses on. It is the "what" or "who" that is being studied.

urban area A geographic area with a high population density (e.g., 1,000 individuals per square mile).

urban ecology An approach to the study of cities, social change, and urban life introduced into sociology by the Chicago School to explain how different social groups within cities compete over scarce resources. This competition was thought to promote efficiency and social equilibrium, as distinct sectors of the population adapted to their local environments.

urban ghetto A section of a city that is characterized by severe racial or ethnic segregation and deep poverty.

urban renewal The attempt to improve impoverished areas by tearing down existing structures and even whole neighborhoods. In the mid-twentieth century, at the height of the urban renewal movement, many working-class neighborhoods across America were destroyed, in many cases benefiting real estate developers and business interests who moved in and redeveloped the areas.

urbanization The growth of cities.

validity The extent to which the measurement a researcher uses accurately measures what it is intended to measure.

value A judgment about what is intrinsically important or meaningful. When it comes to research, values held by sociologists shape their views of and perspectives on the questions they ask.

visa A legal status specifying the terms and length under which someone may live (or visit) another country. It may range from permission to enter for a few days to being allowed to live there permanently (in the United States, the latter type of visa is known as a "green card").

war on drugs The United States' effort to reduce the sale and consumption of illegal drugs by increasing police surveillance and punishment of drug offenders.

war on terror The United States government's effort to combat terrorism, especially in the period since the attacks of September 11, 2001.

Washington Consensus The common prescriptions of Washington, D.C.–based organizations such as the International Monetary Fund, the World Bank, and the U.S. Treasury Department for how developing countries should respond to economic problems or crises. These prescriptions typically suggest that developing countries should engage in free trade, reduce the role and expense of government, and more generally encourage the growth of free markets.

wealth The wealth of an individual or family is the net value of all assets owned by an individual or family, including the value of their home.

welfare state The bundle of programs that provide social insurance and social assistance for people falling into one or another category of attributes (such as old age, disability, or poverty). The most important types of welfare-state programs are old-age pensions (known in the United States as Social Security), health insurance programs, unemployment insurance, job training programs, and general welfare assistance for the very poor. Some analysts also include education in the mix of programs considered part of the welfare state.

well-being The different dimensions of life that are essential to our everyday lives. Among the most important aspects of well-being are health, exposure to crime and violence, exposure to environmental risks like air or water pollution, and even one's general level of happiness.

white-collar crime Illegal activities undertaken by businesses or by individuals working for corporations.

white flight A term used to describe the large-scale migration of white families in the United States in the mid-20th century out of racially mixed cities and urban neighborhoods to racially homogeneous suburban areas.

working poor People who do not make enough income to be free from poverty, even if they work full time.

REFERENCES

CHAPTER 1

Abbott, Andrew. 2001. *The Chaos of the Disciplines*. Chicago: University of Chicago Press.

Arum, Richard and Josipa Roksa. 2011. *Academically Adrift*. Chicago: University of Chicago Press.

Chodorow, Nancy. 1978. *The Reproduction of Mothering*. Berkeley: University of California Press.

Comte, Auguste. [1839–1853] 2009. *The Positive Philosophy of Auguste Comte*. Ed. and trans. Harriet Martineau. New York: Cambridge University Press.

Duster, Troy. 1990. *Backdoor to Eugenics*. New York: Routledge.

Jerolmack, Colin. 2013. *The Global Pigeon*. Chicago: University of Chicago Press.

Mills, C. Wright. 1959. *The Sociological Imagination*. New York: Oxford University Press.

Molotch, Harvey and Laura Noren, eds. 2010. *Toilet: Public Restrooms and the Politics of Sharing*. New York: New York University Press.

Saperstein, Aliya and Andrew Penner. 2010. "The Race of a Criminal Record: How Incarceration Colors Racial Perceptions." *Social Problems* 57:92–113.

Sharkey, Patrick. 2010. "The Acute Effect of Local Homicides on Children's Cognitive Performance." *Proceedings of the National Academy of Sciences* 107:11733–11738.

CHAPTER 2

Burawoy, Michael. 1979. *Manufacturing Consent*. Chicago: University of Chicago Press.

Burawoy, Michael. 2009. *The Extended Case Method*. Berkeley: University of California Press.

Burawoy, Michael, Alice Burton, Anne Arnett Ferguson, and Kathryn J. Fox. 1991. *Ethnography Unbound: Power and Resistance in the Modern Metropolis*. Berkeley: University of California Press.

Burawoy, Michael, Joseph A. Blum, Sheba Mariam George, Zsuzsa Gille, Millie Thayer, Sheba George, Teresa Gowan, Lynne Haney, Marin Klawiter, Steve H. Lopez, and Sean Riain. 2000. *Global Ethnography: Forces, Connections, and Imaginations in a Postmodern World*. Berkeley: University of California Press.

Coleman, James, Robert H. Bremner, Burton R. Clark, John B. Davis, Dorothy H. Eichorn, Zvi Griliches, Joseph F. Kett, Norman B. Ryder, Zahava Blum Doering, and John M. Mays. [1966] 1974. *Youth: Transition to Adulthood. Report of the Panel on Youth of the President's Science Advisory Committee*. Chicago: University of Chicago Press.

Coleman, James and Thomas Hoffer. 1987. *Public and Private High Schools: The Impact of Communities*. New York:

Duneier, Mitchell. 1999. *Sidewalk*. New York: Farrer, Strauss, and Giroux.

Edin, Kathryn. 1997. *Making Ends Meet*. New York: Russell Sage Foundation Press.

Hochschild, Arlie. 1989. *The Second Shift*. New York: Viking.

Luker, Kristin. 2010. *Salsa Dancing in the Social Sciences*. Berkeley: University of California Press.

Skocpol, Theda. 1979. *States and Social Revolutions*. New York: Cambridge University Press.

Solinger, Rickie. 2002. *Beggars and Choosers: How the Politics of Choice Shapes Adoption, Abortion, and Welfare in the United States*. New York: Hill and Wang.

Weber, Max. [1904] 1976. *The Protestant Ethic and the Spirit of Capitalism*. New York: Scribner's.

CHAPTER 3

Asch, Solomon. 1955. "Opinions and Social Pressure." *Scientific American* 193:1–8.

Atkinson, Max. 1984. "Our Master's Voices: The Language and Body Language of Politics." London: Methuen.

Blass, Thomas. 1999. "The Milgram paradigm after 35 years: Some things we now know about obedience to authority." *Journal of Applied Social Psychology* 29(5):955–78.

Boden, Deirdre and Harvey Molotch. "Cyberspace Meets the Compulsion of Proximity" in *The Cybercities Reader*, edited by Stephen Graham. London: Routledge, 2004: 101–05.

Collins, Randall. 2008. *Violence: A Micro-Sociological Theory*. Princeton, NJ: Princeton University Press.

Comscore Media Matrix. 2011. "Average Time Spent Online per U.S. Visitor in 2010." Retrieved June 1, 2012 (http://www.comscoredatamine.com/2011/01/average-time-spent-online-per-u-s-visitor-in-2010/).

Davidson, Judy. 1984. "Subsequent Versions of Invitations, Offers, Requests, and Proposals Dealing with Potential or Actual Rejection." Pp. 102–28 in *Structures of Social Action: Studies in Conversation Analysis*, edited by John Heritage and J. Maxwell Atkinson. New York: Cambridge University Press.

Duneier, M. and H. Molotch. 1999. "Talking City Trouble: Interactional Vandalism, Social Inequality, and the 'Urban Interaction Problem.'" *American Journal of Sociology* 104:1263–95.

Garfinkel, Harold. 1967. *Studies in Ethnomethodology*. Englewood Cliffs, NJ: Prentice-Hall.

Goffman, Erving. 1959. *The Presentation of Self in Everyday Life*. Garden City, NY: Doubleday.

Goffman, Erving. 1978. "Response Cries." *Language* 54:787–815.

Haney, Craig. 2003. "Health Issues in Long-Term Solitary and 'Supermax' Confinement." *Crime & Delinquency* 49:124–56.

Katz, Jack. 1999. *How Emotions Work*. Chicago: University of Chicago Press.

Lewin, Tamar. 2011. "If Your Kids Are Awake, They're Probably Online." *The New York Times*. Retrieved June 1, 2012 (http://www.nytimes.com/2010/01/20/education/20wired.html).

McPherson, Miller, Lynne Smith-Lovin, and James M. Cook. 2001. "Birds of a Feather: Homophily in Social Networks." *Annual Review of Sociology* 27:415–44.

Menchik, Daniel A. and Xiaoli Tian. 2008. "Putting Social Context into Text: The Semiotics of Email Interaction." *American Journal of Sociology* 114:332–70.

Merton, Robert King. 1949. *Social Theory and Social Structure: Toward the Codification of Theory and Research*. Glencoe, IL: Free Press.

Milgram, Stanley. 1963. "Behavioral Study of Obedience." *Journal of Abnormal and Social Psychology* 67:371–78.

Nippert-Eng, Christena. 2010. *Islands of Privacy*. Chicago: University of Chicago Press.

Pew Research Center. 2011. "Social networking sites and our lives." Retrieved June 1, 2012 (http://pewinternet.org/~/media/Files/Reports/2011/PIP%20-%20Social%20networking%20sites%20and%20our%20lives.pdf).

Richardson, Pete. 2009. "Doing Things with Wood: Builders, Managers and Wittgenstein in an Idaho Sawmill." *Critique of Anthropology* 29:160–82.

Rosenhan, David L. 1973. "On Being Sane in Insane Places." *Science* 179:250–58.

Saurez, Nicole, "Smoking in the Girls' Room: Toilets and Female Gender Formation," senior project, Metropolitan Studies, Department of Social and Cultural Analysis, NYU, May 2008.

Scheff, Thomas J. 1999. *Being Mentally Ill: A Sociological Theory*. New York: Aldine de Gruyter.

Schegloff, Emanuel A. 1996. "Confirming Allusions: Toward an Empirical Account of Action." *American Journal of Sociology* 102:161–216.

Schegloff, Emanuel A. 2000. "Overlapping Talk and the Organization of Turn-Taking for Conversation." *Language in Society* 29:1–63.

Simmel, Georg. 1950. "The Metropolis and Mental Life." Pp. 11–20 in *The Blackwell City Reader*, edited by Gary Bridge and Sophie Watson. Oxford: Blackwell, 2002. *The Sociology of Georg Simmel*, edited by Kurt H. Wolf. New York: The Free Press.

Spitz, René A. 1945. "Hospitalism: An Inquiry into the Genesis of Psychiatric Conditions in Early Childhood." *Psychoanalytic Study of the Child* 1:53–74.

Sudnow, David. 1967. *Passing On: The Social Organization of Dying*. Englewood Cliffs, NJ: Prentice-Hall.

U.S. Bureau of Labor Statistics. 2010. "Table A-1. Time spent in detailed primary activities 1 and percent of the civilian population engaging in each detailed primary activity category, averages per day by sex, 2010 annual averages." Retrieved June 1, 2012 (http://www.bls.gov/tus/tables/a1_2010.pdf).

West, Candace. 1984. "When the Doctor Is a 'Lady': Power, Status and Gender in Physician-Patient Encounters." *Symbolic Interaction* 7:87–106.

West, Candace, and Don H. Zimmerman. 1977. "Women's Place in Everyday Talk: Reflection on Parent-Child Interaction." *Social Problems* 24:521–29.

Zimbardo, Philip. 2007. *The Lucifer Effect: How Good People Turn Evil*. New York: Random House.

Zimmerman, Don. 1970. "The Practicalities of Rule Use." Pp. 221–38 in *Understanding Everyday Life: Toward the Reconstruction of Sociological Knowledge*, edited by Jack D. Douglas. Chicago: Aldine.

CHAPTER 4

Blau, Peter and Otis D. Duncan. 1967. *The American Occupational Structure*. New York: Free Press.

Bourdieu, Pierre. 1990. *The Logic of Practice*. Cambridge: Polity Press. Electronic Information Bulletin Number 3, June 2005.

Deutschkron, Inge. 1989. *Outcast: A Jewish Girl in Wartime Berlin*. New York: Fromm International Publishing Group.

Dimitri, Carolyn, Anne Effland, and Neilson Conklin. 2005. "The 20th Century Transformation of U.S. Agriculture and Farm Policy". United States Department of Agriculture. Electronic Information Bulletin Number 3, June 2005.

DiPrete, Thomas. 2002. "Life Course Risks, Mobility Regimes, and Mobility Consequences: A Comparison of Sweden, Germany, and the U.S." *American Journal of Sociology* 108: 267–309.

Garfinkel, Irwin, Lee Rainwater, and Timothy Smeeding. 2010. *Wealth and Welfare States: Is the United States a Laggard or a Leader?* New York: Russell Sage Foundation Press.

Ignatiev, Noel. 1995. *How the Irish Became White*. New York: Routledge.

Jacobson, Matthew F. 1998. *Whiteness of a Different Color*. Cambridge, MA: Harvard University Press.

Kahneman, Daniel. 2011. *Thinking Slow and Fast*. New York: Farrar, Straus, and Giroux.

Klinenberg, Eric. 2012. Going Solo: The Extraordinary Rise and Surprising Appeal of Living Alone. New York: Penguin.

Molotch, Harvey and Laura Noren, eds. 2010. *Toilet: Public Restrooms and the Politics of Sharing*. New York: New York University Press.

Pierson, Paul. 2000. "Path Dependence, Increasing Returns, and the Study of Politics." *American Political Science Review* 94: 251–67.

Przeworski, Adam. 1985. *Capitalism and Social Democracy*. New York: Cambridge University Press.

Schumpeter, Joseph. 1955. *Imperialism and Social Class*. New York: Meridian.

Simmel, Georg. [1902] 1950. *The Sociology of Georg Simmel*. Edited and translated by Kurt Wolff. Glencoe, IL: The Free Press.

CHAPTER 5

Anderson, Benedict. 1991. *Imagined Communities: Reflections on the Origin and Spread of Nationalism*. Revised ed. London and New York: Verso.

Appadurai, Arjun. 1996. *Modernity at Large: Cultural Dimensions of Globalization*. Minneapolis: University of Minnesota Press.

Barnum, P.T. [1880] 1999. *Art of Money Getting*. Bedford, MA: Applewood Books. P. 68.

Blethen, Frank A. 2002. "American Democracy at Risk: Can American Democracy Survive the Loss of an Independent Press and a Diversity of Voices?" Speech delivered to the School of Journalism and Communications at the University of Oregon, The Ruhl Symposium on Ethics in Journalism, May 14.

Bourdieu, Pierre. 1984. *Distinction: A Social Critique of the Judgement of Taste*. Translated by Richard Nice. Cambridge, MA: Harvard University Press.

Bourdieu, Pierre. 1992. *The Logic of Practice*. Translated by Richard Nice. Cambridge: Polity Press.

Boyd, Danah. 2008. "Why Youth (Heart) Social Network Sites: The Role of Networked Publics in Teenage Social Life." Pp. 119–42 in *MacArthur Foundation Series on Digital Learning: Youth, Identity, and Digital Media Volume*, edited by David Buckingham. Cambridge, MA: MIT Press.

Burgess, Jean and Joshua Green. 2009. *YouTube: Online Video and Participatory Culture*. Cambridge, MA: Polity Press.

Castells, Manuel. 2009. *Communication Power*. Oxford, UK: Oxford University Press.

Clarke, John, Stuart Hall, Tony Jefferson, and Brian Roberts. 1975. "Subcultures, Cultures and Class: A Theoretical Overview." Pp. 9–74 in *Resistance through Rituals: Youth Subcultures in Post-War Britain*, edited by Stuart Hall and Tony Jefferson. New York and London: Routledge.

Cresswell, Tim. 1996. *In Place/Out of Place: Geography, Ideology, and Transgression*. Minneapolis: University of Minnesota Press.

Eliasoph, Nina and Paul Lichterman. 2003. "Culture in Interaction." *American Journal of Sociology* 108(4):735–94.

Elliot, Michael A. 2007. "Human Rights and the Triumph of the Individual in World Culture." *Cultural Sociology* 1(3):343–63.

Fischer, Claude S. 1975. "Toward a Subcultural Theory of Urbanism." *American Journal of Sociology* 80(6):1319–41.

Frank, Thomas. 2004. *What's the Matter with Kansas? How Conservatives Won the Heart of America*. New York: Metropolitan Books.

Fraser, Nancy. 1992. "Rethinking the Public Sphere: A Contribution to the Critique of Actually Existing Democracy." Pp. 109–42 in *Habermas and the Public Sphere*, edited by Craig Calhoun. Cambridge, MA, and London: MIT Press.

Gans, Herbert J. 1999. *Popular Culture and High Culture: An Analysis and Evaluation of Taste*, 2nd ed. New York: Basic Books.

Geertz, Clifford. 1972. "Deep Play: Notes on the Balinese Cockfight." *Daedalus* 101(1):1–37.

Gitlin, Todd. 1980. *The Whole World Is Watching: Mass Media in the Making and Unmaking of the New Left*. Berkeley: University of California Press.

Gitlin, Todd. 2007. *Media Unlimited: How the Torrent of Images and Sounds Overwhelms Our Lives*, Revised ed. New York: Metropolitan Books.

Graber, Doris. 2003. "The Media and Democracy: Beyond Myths and Stereotypes." *Annual Review of Political Science* 6:139–60.

Habermas, Jürgen. 1962. *The Structural Transformation of the Public Sphere: An Inquiry into a Category of Bourgeois Society*. Translated by Thomas Burger with Frederick Lawrence. Cambridge, MA: MIT Press.

Hall, Stuart and Tony Jefferson, eds. 1975. *Resistance through Rituals: Youth Subcultures in Post-War Britain*. New York and London: Routledge.

Herman, Edward S. and Noam Chomsky. 1988. *Manufacturing Consent: The Political Economy of the Mass Media*. New York: Pantheon.

Hindman, Matthew. 2008. *The Myth of Digital Democracy*. Princeton, NJ: Princeton University Press.

Hofstadter, Richard. 1960. *The Age of Reform*. New York: Vintage.

Holt, Douglas B. 1997. "Distinction in America? Recovering Bourdieu's Theory of Tastes from Its Critics." *Poetics* 25:93–120.

Holt, Douglas B. 1998. "Does Cultural Capital Structure American Consumption?" *The Journal of Consumer Research* 25(1):1–25.

Horkheimer, Max and Theodor W. Adorno. [1947] 2002. *Dialectic of Enlightenment: Philosophical Fragments*. Translated by Edmund Jephcott and edited by Gunzelin Schmid Noerr. Stanford, CT: Stanford University Press.

Hunter, James Davison. 1991. *Culture Wars: The Struggle to Define America*. New York: Basic Books.

Innis, Harold A. 1951. *The Bias of Communication*. Toronto: University of Toronto Press.

Jenkins, Henry. 2006. *Convergence Culture: Where Old and New Media Collide*. New York: NYU Press.

Johnson, Steven. 2005. *Everything Bad Is Good for You*. New York: Riverhead.

Klein, Naomi. 2000. *No Logo: Taking Aim at the Brand Bullies*. New York: Picador.

Klinenberg, Eric. 2007. *Fighting for Air: The Battle to Control America's Media*. New York: Metropolitan Books.

Klinenberg, Eric. 2012. *Going Solo: The Extraordinary Rise and Surprising Appeal of Living Alone*. New York: Penguin Press.

Lamont, Michèle. 1992. *Money, Morals, and Manners: The Culture of the French and the American Upper-Middle Class*. Chicago: University of Chicago Press.

Lareau, Annette. 2003. *Unequal Childhoods: Class, Race, and Family Life*. Berkeley: University of California Press.

Lippmann, Walter. 1922. *Public Opinion*. New York: Harcourt, Brace and Company.

Marx, Karl and Frederick Engels. [1845] 1972. "The German Ideology: Part 1." Pp. 146–200 in *The Marx-Engels Reader*, edited by Robert C. Tucker, translated by S. Ryazanskaya. New York: W.W. Norton & Company.

McChesney, Robert W. 1999. *Rich Media, Poor Democracy*. New York: New Press.

McLuhan, Marshall. 1964. *Understanding Media: The Extensions of Man*. Cambridge, MA: MIT Press.

Meyer, John W., John Boli, George M. Thomas, and Francisco O. Ramirez. 1997. "World Society and the Nation-State." *American Journal of Sociology* 103(1):144–81.

Nielsen. 2011. *Television Audience Report 2010-2011*. http://researchticker.com/wp-content/uploads/2011/12/2010-2011-nielsen-television-audience-report.pdf.

Norris, Pippa. 2001. *Digital Divide: Civic Engagement, Information Poverty, and the Internet Worldwide*. Cambridge, UK: Cambridge University Press.

Palfrey, John and Urs Gasser. 2008. *Born Digital: Understanding the First Generation of Digital Natives*. New York: Basic Books.

Park, Robert E. 1923. "The Natural History of the Newspaper." *American Journal of Sociology* 29(3):273–89.

Peterson, Richard A. and Roger M. Kern. 1996. "Changing Highbrow Taste: From Snob to Omnivore." *American Sociological Review* 61(5):900–07.

Pew Research Center. 2012. "State of the News Media 2011." http://stateofthemedia.org/2011/network-essay/data-page-5/.

Postman, Neil. 1985. *Amusing Ourselves to Death: Public Discourse in the Age of Show Business*. New York: Penguin.

Schudson, Michael. 2003. *The Sociology of News*. New York: Norton.

Sewell, William H., Jr. 2005. *Logics of History: Social Theory and Social Transformation*. Chicago: University of Chicago Press.

Swidler, Ann. 1986. "Culture in Action: Symbols and Strategies." *American Sociological Review* 51(2):273–86.

Swidler, Ann. 2003. *Talk of Love: How Culture Matters*. Chicago: University of Chicago Press.

Takhteyev, Yuri, Anatoliy Gruzd, and Barry Wellman. 2012. "Geography of Twitter Networks." *Social Networks* 34(1):73–81.

Tobin, Joseph J., David Y. H. Wu, and Dana H. Davidson. 1989. *Preschool in Three Cultures: Japan, China and the United States*. New Haven, CT: Yale University Press.

Van Der Bly, Martha C. E. 2007. "Globalization and the Rise of One Heterogeneous World Culture: A Microperspective of a Global Village." *International Journal of Comparative Sociology* 48(2–3):234–56.

Weber, Max. [1905] 2002. *The Protestant Ethic and the "Spirit" of Capitalism*. Edited and translated by Peter Baehr and Gordon C. Wells. London: Penguin.

Williams, Raymond. 1976. *Keywords: A Vocabulary of Culture and Society*. Oxford, UK: Oxford University Press.

Willis, Paul. 1977. *Learning to Labor: How Working Class Kids Get Working Class Jobs*. New York: Columbia University Press.

CHAPTER 6

Bartels, Larry M. 2008. *Unequal Democracy*. Princeton, NJ: Princeton University Press.

Block, Fred. 1987. *State Theory*. Philadelphia: Temple University Press.

Buffett, Warren. 2011. "Stop Coddling the Super Rich." *New York Times*, August 14, 2011. http://www.nytimes.com/2011/08/15/opinion/stop-coddling-the-super-rich.html.

Clawson, Dan, Richard Neustadtl, and Mark Weller. 1998. *Dollars and Votes: How Business Campaign Contributions Subvert Democracy*. Philadelphia: Temple University Press.

Dahl, Robert. 1958. "A Critique of the Ruling Elite Model," American Political Science Review 52: 463–69.

Dahl, Robert. 1961. *Who Governs?* New Haven, CT: Yale University Press.

Domhoff, G. William. 2006. *Who Rules America? Power, Politics, and Social Change*. New York: McGraw-Hill.

Goffman, Erving. 1971. *Relations in Public*. New York: Harper.

Graetz, Michael and Ian Shapiro. 2005. *Death by a Thousand Cuts*. New Haven, CT: Yale University Press.

Hacker, Jacob and Paul Pierson. 2010. *Winner-Take-All Politics*. New York: Simon and Shuster.

Johnson, Simon and James Kwak. 2010. *Thirteen Bankers*. New York: Pantheon.

Kocieniewski, David. 2011. "G.E.'s Strategies Let It Avoid Paying Taxes Altogether." *New York Times,* March 24, p. A1.

Krippner, Greta. 2011. *Capitalizing on Crisis: The Political Origins of the Rise of Finance*. Cambridge, MA: Harvard University Press.

Lemert, Charles. 1997. *Social Things*. Lanham, MD: Rowman and Littlefield.

Madrick, Jeff. 2011. *The Age of Greed: The Triumph of Finance and the Decline of America, 1970 to the Present*. New York: Knopf.

Manza, Jeff, Clem Brooks, and Michael Sauder. 2004. "Money, Participation, and Votes: Social Cleavages and Electoral Politics." Pp. 201–26 in *Handbook of Political Sociology*, edited by Thomas Janoski et al. New York: Cambridge University Press.

Mischel, Lawrence, Jared Bernstein, and Heidi Shierholz. 2009. *The State of Working America 2008–2009*. Ithaca, NY: Cornell University Press.

Page, Benjamin and Lawrence Jacobs. 2009. *Class War? What Americans Really Think about Economic Inequality*. Chicago: University of Chicago Press.

Piven, Frances Fox and Richard Cloward. 1997. *The Breaking of the American Social Compact*. New York: The New Press.

Quadagno, Jill. 2006. *One Nation, Uninsured: Why the U.S. Has No National Health Insurance*. New York: Oxford University Press.

Smeeding, Timothy, Karen Robson, Coady Wing, and Jonathan Gershuny. 2009. "Income Poverty and Income Support for Minority and Immigrant Children in Rich Countries." Working Paper No. 527, Luxemburg Income Study, retrieved February 15, 2012 (http://www.lisdatacenter.org/wps/liswps/527.pdf).

Starr, Paul. 2011. *Remedy and Reaction: The Peculiar American Struggle over Health Care Reform*. New Haven: Yale University Press.

Winters, Jeffrey. 2011. *Oligarchy*. New York: Cambridge University Press.

CHAPTER 7

Alberto Alesina, Edward Glaeser, and Bruce Sacerdote. 2005. "Work and Leisure in the United States and Europe: Why So Different?" *NBER Macroeconomics Annual* 20:1–64. Retrieved July 3, 2012 (http://www.nber.org/chapters/c0073.pdf).

Arum, Richard and Walter Müeller, 2004. *The Reemergence of Self-Employment: A Comparative Study of Self-Employment Dynamics and Social Inequality*. Princeton University Press.

Becker, Gary. 1976. *The Economic Approach to Human Life*. Chicago: University of Chicago Press.

Braverman, Harry. 1974. *Labor and Monopoly Capital*. New York: Monthly Review Press.

Castles, Francis. 2004. *The Future of the Welfare State: Crisis Myths and Crisis Realities*. New York: Oxford University Press.

Coen, Robert M. 1973. "Labor Force and Unemployment in the 1920s and 1930s: A Re-examination Based on Postwar Experience." *Review of Economics and Statistics* 55:46–55.

DiMaggio, Paul and Woodrow W. Powell. 1983. "The 'Iron Cage' Revisited: Institutional Isomorphism and Collective Rationality in Organizational Fields." *American Sociological Review* 48:147–60.

Gladwell, Malcolm. 2000. *The Tipping Point: How Little Things Can Make a Big Difference*. Boston: Little, Brown.

Goldin, Claudia and Lawrence Katz. 2010. *The Race between Education and Technology*. Cambridge, MA: Harvard University Press.

Granovetter, Mark S. 1973. "The Strength of Weak Ties." *American Journal of Sociology*, Vol. 78, No. 6 (May, 1973), pp. 1360-1380

Hacker, Jacob. 2006. *The Great Risk Shift*. New York: Oxford University Press.

Hagan, John. 1993. "The Social Embeddedness of Crime and Unemployment." *Criminology* 31:465–91.

Hannan, Michael and John Freeman. 1989. *Organizational Ecology*. Cambridge, MA: Harvard University Press.

Hochschild, Arlie. 2012. *The Outsourced Self: Intimate Life in Market Times*. New York: Metropolitan Books.

Kalleberg, Arne L. "Nonstandard Employment Relations: Part-Time, Temporary and Contract Work." *Annual Review of Sociology*, Vol. 26, (2000), pp. 341–365.

Lichtenstein, Nelson. 2009. *The Retail Revolution: How Wal-Mart Created a Brave New World of Business*. New York: Metropolitan Books.

Lovell, Philip and Julia Isaacs. 2010. *Families of the Recession: Unemployed Parents and Their Children*. Washington, D.C.: Brookings Institute.

Polanyi, Karl. [1944] 1957. *The Great Transformation: The Political and Economic Origins of Our Time*. Boston: Beacon Press.

Pontusson, Jonas. 2005. *Inequality and Prosperity: Social Europe v. Liberal America*. Ithaca, NY: Cornell University Press.

Romer, Christina. 1986. "Spurious Volatility in Historical Unemployment Data." *Journal of Political Economy* 94:1–37.

Rose, David. 2003. *The March of Dimes*. Charleston, SC: Arcadia Publishing.

Segal, David. 2012. "A Georgia Town Takes the People's Business Private." *New York Times,* June 23, 2012.

U.S. Department of Labor, Bureau of Labor Statistics. n.d. *Employment Status of the Civilian Noninstitutional Population, 1940 to Present*. (http://www.bls.gov).

Uzzi, Brian. 1999. "Embeddedness in the Making of Financial Capital: How Social Relations and Networks Benefit Firms Seeking Finance." *American Sociological Review* 64:481–505.

Vallas, Steven, William Finlay, and Amy S. Wharton, eds. 2009. *The Sociology of Work: Structures and Inequalities*. New York: Oxford University Press.

Weber, Max. [1922] 1978. *Economy and Society*. Berkeley: University of California Press.

Wright, Erik Olin and Rachel Dwyer. 2000. "The American Jobs Machine: Is the New Economy Creating Good Jobs?" *Boston Review* 25(6).

Zelizer, Vivian. 2011. "How I Became a Relational Economic Sociologist and What Does that Mean?" *Politics and Society* (forthcoming).

CHAPTER 8

Addams, Jane. 1910. *Twenty Years at Hull House*. New York: MacMillan Company.

Anderson, Elijah. 1999. *Code of the Street: Decency, Violence, and the Moral Life of the Inner City*. New York: W.W. Norton & Company.

Baldassare, Mark. 1992. "Suburban Communities." *Annual Review of Sociology* 18:475-94.

Banfield, Edward C. 1970. *The Unheavenly City: The Nature and the Future of Our Urban Crisis*. New York: Little Brown and Co.

Card, David. 2007. "How Immigration Affects U.S. Cities." Centre for Research and Analysis of Migration Discussion Paper Series, CDP No 11-07. London: University College London.

Castells, Manuel. 2000. *The Rise of Network Society*. 2nd ed. Cambridge, MA: Blackwell.

Cohen, Cathy and Michael Dawson. 1993. "Neighborhood Poverty and African-American Politics." *American Political Science Review* 87:286–302.

Coleman, James S. 1988. "Social Capital in the Creation of Human Capital." *American Journal of Sociology* 94:S95–120.

Davis, Kingsley. 1965. "The Urbanization of the Human Population." *Scientific American* 213:40–53.

Davis, Mike. 1990. *City of Quartz: Excavating the Future of Los Angeles*. London: Verso.

DeParle, Jason. 2007. "Migrant Money Flow: A $300 Billion Current." *New York Times,* November 18, 2007.

DeParle, Jason. 2010. "Global Migration: A World Ever More on the Move." *New York Times,* June 26, 2010.

Downs, Anthony. 1994. *New Visions for Metropolitan America*. Washington, DC: Brookings Institution Press.

Drake, St. Claire and Horace R. Cayton. 1945. *Black Metropolis: A Study of Negro Life in a Northern City*. New York: Harcourt.

Duany, Andres, Elizabeth Plater-Zyberk, and Jeff Speck. 2001. *Suburban Nation*. New York: North Point Press.

Ellison, Nicole B., Charles Steinfield, and Cliff Lampe. 2007. "The Benefits of Facebook 'Friends': Exploring the Relationship between College Students' Use of Online Social Networks and Social Capital." *Journal of Computer-Mediated Communication* 12(3):1143–68.

Engels, Frederick. [1845] 1972. "The Condition of the Working Class in England in 1844." In *The Marx-Engels Reader*, edited by Robert C. Tucker. New York: W.W. Norton & Co. Inc.

Farley, Reynolds, Sheldon Danziger, and Harry J. Holzer. 2000. *Detroit Divided*. New York: Russell Sage.

Fernandez, Manny. 2008. "Door to Door, Foreclosure Knocks Here." *New York Times,* October 18, 2008.

Fischer, Claude. 1975. "Toward a Subcultural Theory of Urbanism." *American Journal of Sociology* 80:1319–41.

Florida, Richard. 2003. "Cities and the Creative Class." *City and Community* 2(1):3–19.

Florida, Richard. 2008. *Who's Your City?: How the Creative Economy Is Making Where to Live the Most Important Decision of Your Life*. New York: Basic Books.

Gans, Herbert J. 1962. *The Urban Villagers: Group and Class in the Life of Italian-Americans*. New York: The Free Press.

Gans, Herbert J. 1968. "Urbanism and Suburbanism as a Way of Life: A Reevaluation of Definitions." In *People and Plans: Essays on Urban Problems and Solutions*. New York: Basic Books.

Garreau, Joel. 1991. *Edge City: Life on the New Frontier*. New York: Anchor Doubleday Books.

Glaeser, Edward. 2011. *Triumph of the City: How Our Greatest Invention Makes Us Richer, Smarter, Greener, Healthier, and Happier*. New York: Penguin Press.

Gottman, Jean. 1966. *Megalopolis: The Urbanized Northeastern Seaport of the United States*. Cambridge, MA: M.I.T. Press.

Granovetter, Mark S. 1974. "The Strength of Weak Ties." *American Journal of Sociology* 78(6):1360–80.

Holliday, Amy L. and Rachel E. Dwyer. 2009. "Suburban Neighborhood Poverty in U.S. Metropolitan Areas in 2000." *City & Community* 8(2):155–76.

Holzer, Harry. 1991. "The Spatial Mismatch Hypothesis: What Has the Evidence Shown?" *Urban Studies* 28:105–22.

Immergluck, Dan and Geoff Smith. 2006. "The Impact of Single-Family Mortgage Foreclosures on Neighborhood Crime." *Housing Studies* 21:851–66.

Jacobs, Jane. 1961. *The Death and Life of Great American Cities*. New York: Random House.

Jargowsky, Paul. 1997. *Poverty and Place: Ghettos, Barrios and the American City*. New York: Russell Sage.

Klinenberg, Eric. 2002. *Heat Wave: A Social Autopsy of Disaster in Chicago*. Chicago: University of Chicago Press.

Klinenberg, Eric. 2012. *Going Solo: The Extraordinary Rise and Surprising Appeal of Living Alone*. New York: Penguin Press.

Lemann, Nicholas. 1991. *The Promised Land: The Great Migration and How It Changed America*. New York: Knopf.

Logan, John and Harvey Molotch. 1987. *Urban Fortunes: The Political Economy of Place*. Berkeley: University of California Press.

Logan, John R. and Brian J. Stults. 2011. "The Persistence of Segregation in the Metropolis." Retrieved June 4, 2012. (http://www.s4.brown.edu/us2010/Data/Report/report2.pdf.)

Logan, John R. and Charles Zhang. 2010. "Global Neighborhoods: New Pathways to Diversity and Separation." *American Journal of Sociology* 115:1069–109.

Marcuse, Peter and Ronald van Kempen. 2002. *Of States and Cities: The Partitioning of Urban Space*. Oxford, UK: Oxford University Press.

Massey, Douglas and Nancy Denton. 1993. *American Apartheid: Segregation and the Making of the Underclass*. Cambridge, MA: Harvard University Press.

Montgomery, Mark, Richard Stren, and Barney Cohen. 2003. *Cities Transformed*. Washington, DC: National Academy Press.

Osofsky, Joy D. 1999. "The Impact of Violence on Children." *Future of Children* 9(3):33–49.

Park, Robert E. and Ernest Burgess. [1925] 1967. *The City: Suggestions for Investigation of Human Behavior in the Urban Environment*. Chicago: University of Chicago Press.

Peck, Jamie. 2005. "Struggling with the Creative Class." *International Journal of Urban and Regional Research* 29(4):740–70.

Portes, Alejandro and Min Zhou. 1993. "The New Second Generation: Segmented Assimilation and Its Variants." *Annals of the American Academy of Political and Social Sciences* 530:74–96.

Putnam, Robert D. 2000. *Bowling Alone: The Collapse and Revival of American Community*. New York: Simon and Schuster.

Ravallion, Martin, Shaohua Chen, and Prem Sangraula. 2007. "New Evidence on the Urbanization of Global Poverty." *Population and Development Review* 33(4):667–701. Retrieved October 27, 2011. (http://www.jstor.org/stable/25487618).

Sampson, Robert J., Stephen M. Raudenbush, and Felton Earls. 1997. "Neighborhoods and Violent Crime: A Multilevel Study of Collective Efficacy." *Science* 227(5328):918–24.

Sassen, Saskia. 1991. *The Global City: New York, London, Tokyo*. Princeton, NJ: Princeton University Press.

Sassen, Saskia. 1996. "Cities and Communities in the Global Economy: Rethinking Our Concepts." *American Behavioral Scientist* 39:629–39.

Sassen, Saskia. 2007. *A Sociology of Globalization*. New York: W.W. Norton & Company.

Sassen, Saskia. 2008. "New York City's Two Global Geographies of Talk." Pp. 10–16 in *New York Talk Exchange*. Cambridge, MA: SENSEable City Lab.

Sharkey, Patrick. 2010. "The Acute Effect of Local Homicides on Children's Cognitive Performance." *Proceedings of the National Academy of Sciences* 107:11733–38.

Short, John Rennie. 2007. *Liquid City: Megalopolis and the Contemporary Northeast*. RFF Press.

Simmel, Georg. [1902] 1972. "The Metropolis and Mental Life." In *Georg Simmel On Individuality and Social Forms*. Chicago: University of Chicago Press.

Stack, Carol B. 1974. *All Our Kin: Strategies for Survival in a Black Community*. New York: Basic Books.

Sulzberger, A. G. 2011. "As Rural Areas Lose People, Legislators' Power Ebbs." *New York Times*, June 2, 2011.

Tavernise, Sabrina and Robert Gebeloff. 2010. "Immigrants Make Paths to Suburbia, Not Cities." *New York Times,* December 14, 2010.

Tolnay, Stewart E. 2003. "The African American 'Great Migration' and Beyond." *Annual Review of Sociology* 29:209–32.

United Nations, Department of Economic and Social Affairs, Population Division. 2010. *World Urbanization Prospects, the 2009 Revision: Highlights*. New York.

U.S. Census Bureau, Geography Division. 2009. *Census 2000 Urban and Rural Classification*. Washington, DC: U.S. Census Bureau. Retrieved June 4, 2012. (http://www.census.gov/geo/www/ua/uac2k_90.html).

Venkatesh, Sudhir and Isil Celimli. 2004. "Tearing Down the Community." *Shelterforce: The Journal of Affordable Housing and Community Building* 138:29–35.

Wacquant, Loic J. D. 2009. *Urban Outcasts: A Comparative Sociology of Advanced Marginality*. Cambridge, MA: Polity Press.

Waters, Mary C., Reed Ueda, and Helen B. Marrow, eds. 2007. *The New Americans: A Guide to Immigration since 1965*. Cambridge, MA: Harvard University Press.

Webber, Melvin. 1968. "The Post-City Age." *Daedalus* 97:1106–7.

Wellman, Barry. 1979. "The Community Question: The Intimate Networks of East Yorkers." *American Journal of Sociology* 84(5):1201–31.

Wilson, William Julius. 1987. *The Truly Disadvantaged: The Inner City, the Underclass, and Public Policy*. Chicago: University of Chicago Press.

Wirth, Louis. 1938. "Urbanism as a Way of Life." *American Journal of Sociology* 44(1):1–24.

Zimring, Frank. 2007. *The Great American Crime Decline*. New York: Oxford University Press.

Zukin, Sharon. 1982. *Loft Living: Culture and Capital in Urban Change*. Baltimore, MD: Johns Hopkins University Press.

Zukin, Sharon. 1992. "The City as a Landscape of Power: London and New York as Global Financial Capitals." In *Global Finance and Urban Living: A Study of Metropolitan Change*, edited by Leslie Budd & Sam Whimster. New York: Routledge.

CHAPTER 9

Bussuk, Ellen L., Christina Murphy, Natalie T. Coupe, Rachael R. Kenney, and Corey A. Beach. 2011. *America's Youngest Outcasts 2010*. Needham, MA: The National Center on Family Homelessness. Retrieved April 24, 2012 (http://www.homelesschildrenamerica.org/media/NCFH_AmericaOutcast2010_web.pdf).

Davies, James, Susanna Sandström, Anthony Shorrocks, and Edward N. Wolff. 2007. "Estimating the Level and Distribution of Global Household Wealth." World Institute for Development Economics Research of the United Nations University, WIDER Research Paper, volume 2007/77. Retrieved April 6, 2012 (http://www.wider.unu.edu/publications/working-papers/research-papers/2007/en_GB/rp2007-77/).

Domhoff, G. William. 2010. *Who Rules America?* 6th ed. New York: McGraw-Hill.

Duhigg, Charles and David Barboza. 2012. "In China, Human Costs Are Built into the iPad." *New York Times*, January 25, 2012.

Duncan, Greg J., Kathleen M. Ziol-Guest and Ariel Kalil. 2010. "Early-Childhood Poverty and Adult Attainment, Behavior, and Health." *Child Development* 81(1): 306–325.

Edin, Kathryn and Laura Lein. 1997. *Making Ends Meet. How Single Mothers Survive Welfare and Low-Wage Work*. New York: Russell Sage Foundation.

Ericsson, K. Anders, Neil Charness, Paul J. Feltovich, and Robert R. Hoffman, eds. 2006. *The Cambridge Handbook of Expertise and Expert Performance*. New York: Cambridge University Press.

Erikson, Robert and John Goldthorpe. 1992. *The Constant Flux. A Study of Class Mobility in Industrial Nations*. Oxford: Clarendon Press.

Esping-Andersen, Gosta. 1990. *The Three Worlds of Welfare Capitalism*. Princeton: Princeton University Press.

Forbes. 2012. "The World's Richest Billionaires." Retrieved April 23, 2012 (http://www.forbes.com/billionaires/).

Frank, Robert. 1999. *Luxury Fever*. New York: The Free Press.

Friedman, Thomas. 2012. "Made in the World." *New York Times*. Retrieved January 28, 2012. (http://www.nytimes.com/2012/01/29/opinion/sunday/friedman-made-in-the-world.html).

Garfinkel, Irwin, Lee Rainwater and Timothy Smeeding. 2010. *Wealth and Welfare States. Is America Laggard or Leader?* Oxford: Oxford University Press.

Goldin, Claudia and Lawrence Katz. 2010. *The Race between Education and Technology*. Cambridge, MA: Harvard University Press.

Hacker, Jacob and Paul Pierson. 2010. *Winner Take All Politics*. New York: Simon and Shuster.

Jencks, Christopher. 1995. *The Homeless*. Cambridge, MA: Harvard University Press.

Link, Bruce, et al. 1994. "Life-Time and Five-Year Prevalence of Homelessness in the United States." *American Journal of Public Health* 84:1907–12.

Maddison, Angus. 1995. *Monitoring the World Economy, 1820–1992*. Paris: OECD.

Marx, Karl and Friedrich Engels. [1948] 1983. *Manifesto of the Communist Party*. New York: International Publishers.

Mayer, Susan. 1997. *What Money Can't Buy: Family Income and Children's Life Chances*. Cambridge MA: Harvard University Press.

Morris, Martina and Bruce Western. 1999. "Inequality in Earnings at the Close of the Twentieth Century" Annual Review of Sociology 25: 623–657.

Neckerman, Kathryn and Florencia Torche. 2007. "Inequality: Causes and Consequences" Annual Review of Sociology 33: 335–357.

Oishi, Kesebir S. and Diener, E. 2011. "Income Inequality and Happiness." *Psychological Science* 22:1095–1100.

Saez, Emmanuel and Thomas Piketty. 2003. "Income inequality in the United States 1913–1998" Quarterly Journal of Economics 118: 1–39. (Available online at: http://elsa.berkeley.edu/~saez/).

Smeeding, Timothy. 2006. "Poor People in Rich Nations: The United States in Comparative Perspective." *Journal of Economic Perspectives* 20(1):69–90.

Smith, Adam. [1776] 1976. *An Inquiry into the Nature and Causes of the Wealth of Nations*. London: MacMillan.

Sullivan, Theresa, Elizabeth Warren, and Jay Westbrook. 2001. *The Fragile Middle Class: Americans in Debt.* New Haven, CT: Yale University Press.

United States Department of Housing and Urban Development. 2010. *The Annual Homeless Assessment Report to Congress.* Washington: Government Printing Office. Retrieved April 24, 2012 (http://www.hudhre.info/documents/2010HomelessAssessmentReport.pdf).

Wilkinson, Richard. 2006. *The Impact of Inequality: How to Make Sick Societies Healthier.* New York: The New Press.

Wright, Erik Olin. 1986. "What is Middle About the Middle Class?" In *Analytical Marxism*, ed. John Roemer, pp. 114–40. New York: Cambridge University Press.

CHAPTER 10

"race, n.6". OED Online. March 2012. Oxford University Press.

Alba, Richard D. 2009. *Blurring the Color Line: The New Chance for a More Integrated America.* Cambridge, MA: Harvard University Press.

Allport, Gordon. 1954. *The Nature of Prejudice.* Cambridge, MA: Addison-Wesley Pub. Co.

American Sociological Association. 2003. "The Importance of Collecting Data and Doing Social Scientific Research on Race." Washington, DC: American Sociological Association.

Bertrand, Marianne and Sendhil Mullainathan. 2004. "Are Emily and Greg More Employable than Lakisha and Jamal: A Field Experiment on Labor Market Discrimination." *American Economic Review* 94: 991–1013.

Bonilla-Silva, Eduardo. 1996. "Rethinking Racism: Toward a Structural Interpretation." *American Sociological Review* 62(3):465–80.

Bonilla-Silva, Eduardo. 2002. "The Linguistics of Color Blind Racism: How to Talk Nasty about Blacks without Sounding 'Racist'." *Critical Sociology* 28(1–2):41–64.

Bonilla-Silva, Eduardo. 2006. *Racism without Racists: Color-Blind Racism and the Persistence of Racial Inequality in the United States.* Lanham, MD: Rowman & Littlefield, Inc.

Bourdieu, Pierre. 1986. "The Forms of Capital." Pp. 241–258 in *Handbook of theory of research for the sociology of education*, edited by J.E. Richardson. New York: Greenwood Press.

Brittingham, Angela, and G. Patricia de la Cruz. 2004. "Ancestry: 2000." *Census Brief* C2KBR-35 (June). Washington, DC: U.S. Census Bureau.

Brown, Michael K., Martin Carnoy, Elliott Currie, Troy Duster, David B. Oppenheimer, Marjorie M. Schultz, and David Wellman. 2003. *Whitewashing Race: The Myth of a Color-Blind Society.* Berkeley, CA: University of California Press.

Carnoy, Martin and Henry M. Levin. 1985. *Schooling and Work in the Democratic State.* Stanford: Stanford University Press.

Center for Disease Control and Prevention. 2011. "CDC Health Disparities and Inequalities Report—2011." *Morbidity and Mortality Weekly Report* Vol. 60 (Supplement): 1-113. Retrieved February 20, 2012 (http://www.cdc.gov/mmwr/pdf/other/su6001.pdf).

Conley, Dalton. 1999. *Being Black, Living in Red: Race, Wealth, and Social Policy in America.* Berkeley, CA: University of California Press.

Cornell, Stephen, and Douglas Hartmann. 2004. "Conceptual Confusions and Divides: Race, Ethnicity, and the Study of Immigration." Pp. 23–41 in *Not Just Black and White: Historical and Contemporary Perspectives on Immigration, Race, and Ethnicity in the United States*, edited by Nancy Foner and George M. Fredrickson. New York: Russell Sage Foundation.

—. 2007. *Ethnicity and Race: Making Identities in a Changing World.* Thousand Oaks, CA: Pine Forge Press.

DaCosta, Kimberly McClain. 2007. *Making Multiracials: State, Family, and Market in the Redrawing of the Color Line.* Stanford, CA: Stanford University Press.

Dikötter, Frank. 2008. "The Racialization of the Globe: An Interactive Interpretation." *Ethnic and Racial Studies* 31(8):1478–96.

Evett, Ian, Peter D. Gill, John K. Scranage, and B.S. Weir. 1996. "Establishing the Robustness of Short-Tandem-Repeat Statistics for Forensic Applications." *American Journal of Human Genetics* 58:398–407.

Fischer, Claude S., Michael Hout, Martín Sánchez Jankowski, Samuel R. Lucas, Ann Swidler and Kim Vos. 1996. *Inequality by Design: Cracking the Bell Curve Myth.* Princeton: Princeton University Press.

Frankenberg, Ruth. 1993. *White Women, Race Matters: The Social Construction of Whiteness.* Minneapolis, MN: University of Minnesota Press.

Fredrickson, George M. 2002. *Racism: A Short History.* Princeton, NJ: Princeton University Press.

Gans, Herbert J. 1999. "The Possibility of a New Racial Hierarchy in the 21st Century United States." Pp. 371–90 in *The Cultural Territories of Race: Black and White Boundaries*, edited by Michèle Lamont. Chicago and New York: University of Chicago Press and the Russell Sage Foundation.

Gould, Stephen Jay. 1996. *The Mismeasure of Man.* New York: W.W. Norton and Co.

Graham, Hugh Davis. 2002. "The Origins of Official Minority Designation." Pp. 288–99 in *The New Race Question: How the Census Counts Multiracial Individuals*, edited by Joel Perlmann and Mary C. Waters. New York and Annandale-on-Hudson, NY: Russell Sage Foundation and the Levy Economics Institute of Bard College.

Gullickson, Aaron, and Ann Morning. 2011. "Choosing Race: Multiracial Ancestry and Identification." *Social Science Research* 40:498–512.

Hall, Bruce S. 2011. *A History of Race in Muslim West Africa, 1600-1960.* Cambridge: Cambridge University Press.

Hannaford, Ivan. 1996. *Race: The History of an Idea in the West.* Washington, DC: The Woodrow Wilson Center Press.

Helgren, David M., and Robert J. Sager. 2000. *World Geography Today.* Austin, TX: Holt, Rinehart and Winston.

Herrnstein, Richard J. and Charles Murray. 1994. *The Bell Curve.* New York: The Free Press.

Humes, Karen R., Nicholas A. Jones, and Roberto R. Ramirez. 2011. "Overview of Race and Hispanic Origin: 2010." *Census 2010 Brief* C2010BR-02 (March). Washington, DC: U.S. Census Bureau.

Jackson Nakazawa, Donna. 2003. "A New Generation is Leading the Way: What Young People of Mixed Race Can Tell Us About the Future of Our Children." Pp. 4–5 in *Parade*: July 6.

Jacobson, Matthew Frye. 1998. *Whiteness of a Different Color: European Immigrants and the Alchemy of Race.* Cambridge, MA: Harvard University Press.

Jensen, Arthur R. 1969. "How much can we boost I.Q. and scholastic achievement?" *Harvard Educational Review* 33: 1–123.

Kim, Nadia Y. 2008. *Imperial Citizens: Koreans and Race from Seoul to LA.* Stanford, CA: Stanford University Press.

Kochlar, Rakesh, Richard Fry, and Paul Taylor. 2011. *Wealth Gap Rises to Record Highs Between Whites, Blacks and Latinos.* Washington DC: Pew Research Center.

Kritz, Mary M., and Douglas T. Gurak. 2004. *Immigration and a Changing America.* New York and Washington, DC: Russell Sage Foundation and Population Reference Bureau.

Landry, Bart and Krish Marsh. 2011. "The Evolution of the New Black Middle Class." *Annual Review of Sociology* 37: 373–394.

Lee, Jennifer, and Frank D. Bean. 2004. "America's Changing Color Lines: Immigration, Race/Ethnicity, and Multiracial Identification." *Annual Review of Sociology* 30:221–42.

Lee, Sharon M. 1993. "Racial Classifications in the U.S. Census: 1890–1990." *Ethnic and Racial Studies* 16(1):75–94.

Lewis, Bernard. 1990. *Race and Slavery in the Middle East.* New York: Oxford University Press.

Lewis, Oscar. 1966. *La Vida: A Puerto Rican Family in the Culture of Poverty—San Juan and New York.* New York: Random House.

Liebow, Elliott. [1967] 2003. *Tally's Corner: A Study of Negro Streetcorner Men.* 2nd ed. Lanham, MD: Rowman & Littlefield.

Lind, Michael. 1995. *The Next American Nation: The New Nationalism and the Fourth American Revolution.* New York: The Free Press.

Liptak, Adam. 2008. "U.S. Prison Population Dwarfs that of Other Nations." *New York Times*, April 23. Retrieved March 19, 2010 (http://www.nytimes.com/2008/04/23/world/americas/23iht-23prison.12253738.html).

Loewen, James. 2005. *Sundown Towns: A Hidden Dimension of American Racism.* New York: The New Press.

Manza, Jeff, and Christopher Uggen. 2008. *Locked Out: Felon Disenfranchisement and American Democracy.* New York: Oxford University Press.

Marger, Martin N. 2003. *Race and Ethnic Relations: American and Global Perspectives*, 6th Edition. Belmont, CA: Wadsworth.

Marks, Jonathan. 2002. *What it Means to be 98% Chimpanzee: Apes, People, and their Genes.* Berkeley: University of California Press.

Martin, Philip, and Elizabeth Midgley. 2010. *Immigration in America 2010.* Population Bulletin Update (June). Washington, DC: Population Reference Bureau.

Massey, Douglas S. 1995. "The New Immigration and Ethnicity in the United States." *Population and Development Review* 21(3):631–52.

Massey, Douglas S., and Nancy A. Denton. 1993. *American Apartheid: Segregation and the Making of the Underclass.* Cambridge, MA: Harvard University Press.

Morning, Ann. 2008. "Ethnic Classification in Global Perspective: A Cross-National Survey of the 2000 Census Round." *Population Research and Policy Review* 27(2):239–72.

—. 2011. *The Nature of Race: How Scientists Think and Teach about Human Difference.* Berkeley, CA: University of California Press.

National Center for Education Statistics. 2011a. "Table 8." *Digest of Educational Statistics: 2010.* Retrieved February 22, 2012 (http://nces.ed.gov/programs/digest/d10/tables/dt10_008.asp?referrer=list).

National Center for Education Statistics. 2011b. "Table 115." *Digest of Educational Statistics: 2010.* Retrieved Feburary 22, 2012 (http://nces.ed.gov/programs/digest/d10/tables/dt10_115.asp?referrer=list).

Nelkin, Dorothy, and M. Susan Lindee. 1995. *The DNA Mystique: The Gene as Cultural Icon.* New York: Freeman.

Nobles, Melissa. 2000. *Shades of Citizenship: Race and the Census in Modern Politics.* Stanford, CA: Stanford University Press.

Oliver, Melvin L., and Thomas M. Shapiro. 1997. *Black Wealth, White Wealth: A New Perspective on Racial Inequality.* New York and London: Routledge.

Omi, Michael and Howard Winant. 1994. *Racial Formation in the United States: From the 1960s to the 1990s.* New York: Routledge.

Pager, Devah. 2003. "The Mark of a Criminal Record." *American Journal of Sociology* 108(5):937–75.

Pager, Devah. 2007. *Marked: Race, Crime, and Finding Work in an Era of Mass Incarceration.* Chicago, IL: University of Chicago Press.

Pager, Devah, Bruce Western, and Bart Bonikowski. 2009. "Discrimination in a Low-Wage Labor Market: A Field Experiment." *American Sociological Review* 74(5): 777–779.

Portes, Alejandro and Jozsef Borocz. 1989. "Contemporary Immigration: Theoretical Perspectives on Its Determinants and Modes of Incorporation." *International Migration Review* 87(23): 606–630.

Puente, Maria and Martin Kasindorf. 1999. "The New Face of America: Blended Races Making a True Melting Pot." Pp. 1A, 13A in *USA Today:* September 7.

Rockquemore, Kerry Ann, and David L. Brunsma. 2002. *Beyond Black: Biracial Identity in America.* Thousand Oaks, CA: Sage.

Royster, Deirdre A. 2003. *Race and the Invisible Hand: How White Networks Exclude Black. Men from Blue-Collar Jobs.* Berkeley: University of California Press.

Sacks, Karen. 1994. "How Did Jews Become White Folks?" Pp. 78–102 in *Race*, edited by Steven Gregory and Roger Sanjek. New Brunswick, NJ: Rutgers University Press.

Schuman, Howard, Charlotte Steeh, Lawrence Bobo, and Maria Krysan. 1997. *Racial Attitudes in America: Trends and Interpretations.* Cambridge, MA: Harvard University Press.

Sharkey, Patrick. 2008. "The Intergenerational Transmission of Context." *American Journal of Sociology* 113(4):931–69.

Smedley, Audrey. 2007. *Race in North America: Origin and Evolution of a Worldview.* Boulder, CO: Westview Press.

Snowden, Frank M., Jr. 1983. *Before Color Prejudice: The Ancient View of Blacks.* Cambridge, MA: Harvard University Press.

Stevens, Jacqueline. 2003. "Racial Meanings and Scientific Methods: Changing Policies for NIH-Sponsored Publications Reporting Human Variation." *Journal of Health Politics, Policy and Law* 28(6):1033–87.

Streeter, Caroline A. 2003. "The Hazards of Visibility: 'Biracial' Women, Media Images, and Narratives of Identity." Pp. 301–22 in *New Faces in Changing America: Multiracial Identity in the 21st Century,* edited by Herman DeBose and Loretta Winters. Thousand Oaks, CA: Sage.

Steinberg, Stephan. [1989] 2001. *The Ethnic Myth: Race, Ethnicity, and Class in America,* 3rd Edition. Boston, MA: Beacon Press.

Swidler, Ann. 1986. "Culture in Action: Symbols and Strategies." *American Sociological Review* 51(2):273–286.

U.S. Bureau of Justice Statistics. 2011. "Prisoners in 2010." Washington D.C.: U.S. Government Printing Office. Retrieved February 18, 2012 (http://www.bjs.gov/content/pub/pdf/p10.pdf).

U.S. Bureau of Labor Statistics. 2011. "Labor Force Characteristics by Race and Ethnicity, 2010." Report 1032, Washington DC: U.S. Government Printing Office. Retrieved February 13, 2012 (http://www.bls.gov/cps/cpsrace2010.pdf).

U.S. Bureau of Labor Statistics. 2012. "Economic News Release: The Employment Situation-January 2012." Retrieved February 12, 2012 (http://www.bls.gov/news.release/pdf/empsit.pdf).

U.S. Census Bureau. 1918. "Negro Population 1790–1915." In *Census Bureau,* edited by U.S. Department of Commerce. Washington, DC: Government Printing Office.

U.S. Census Bureau. 2011. "Income, Poverty, and Health Insurance Coverage in the United States: 2010." Current Population Reports, P60-23., Washington, DC: U.S. Government Printing Office. Retrieved February 10, 2012 (http://www.census.gov/prod/2011pubs/p60-239.pdf).

U.S. Department of Health and Human Services. 2000. "Addressing Racial and Ethnic Disparities in Health Care Fact Sheet." AHRQ Publication No. 00-PO41, February 2000. Rockville, MD: Agency for Healthcare Research and Quality. (http://www.ahrq.gov/research/disparit.htm)

U.S. Kerner Commission. 1968. "Report of the National Advisory Commission on Civil Disorders." Washington: U.S. Government Printing Office.

Van Ausdale, Debra and Joe R. Feagin. 2001. *The First R: How Children Learn Race and Racism.* Lanham, MD: Rowman and Littlefield.

Walters, Nathan P., and Edward N. Trevelyan. 2011. "The Newly-Arrived Foreign-Born Population of the United States: 2010." *American Community Survey Brief* ACSBR/10-16. Washington, DC: U.S. Census Bureau.

Wang, Wendy. 2012. "The Rise of Intermarriage: Rates, Characteristics Vary by Race and Gender." *Social and Demographic Trends,* February 12. Washington, DC: Pew Research Center.

Waters, Mary C. 1990. *Ethnic Options: Choosing Identities in America.* Berkeley, CA: University of California Press.

Weber, Max. 1978. *Economy and Society.* Berkeley: University of California Press.

Western, Bruce. 2006. *Punishment and Inequality in America.* New York: Russell Sage Foundation.

Williams, Kim M. 2006. *Mark One or More: Civil Rights in Multiracial America.* Ann Arbor, MI: University of Michigan Press.

Williamson, Joel. 1980. *New People: Miscegenation and Mulattoes in the United States.* New York: The Free Press.

Wolfe, Patrick. 2001. "Land, Labor, and Difference: Elementary Structures of Race." *The American Historical Review* 106(3):866–905.

CHAPTER 11

Akerlof, George A., Janet. L. Yellen, and Michael L. Katz. 1996. "An Analysis of Out-of-Wedlock Childbearing in the United States." *Quarterly Journal of Economics* 111:277–317.

Armstrong, Elizabeth A. 2002. *Forging Gay Identities: Organizing Sexuality in San Francisco, 1950–1994.* Chicago: University of Chicago Press.

Armstrong, Elizabeth, Paula England, and Alison Fogarty. 2012. "Accounting for Women's Orgasm and Sexual Enjoyment in College Hookups and Relationships." *American Sociological Review.*

Autor, David H., Lawrence F. Katz, and Melissa Kearney. 2008. "Trends in U.S. Wage Inequality: Revising the Revisionists." 90(2):300–23.

Bailey, Martha. 2006. "More Power to the Pill: The Impact of Contraceptive Freedom on Women's Life Cycle Labor Supply." *Quarterly Journal of Economics* 121(1):289–320.

Bailey, J. Michael, Michael P. Dunne, Michael Nicholas, and Martin Nicholas. 2000. "Genetic and Environmental Influences on Sexual Orientation and Its Correlates in an Australian Twin Sample." *Journal of Personality and Social Psychology* 78(3):524–36.

Bailey, J. Michael and R. C. Pillard. 1991. "A Genetic Study of Male Sexual Orientation." *Archives of General Psychiatry* 48:1089–96.

Bailey, J. Michael, R. C. Pillard, M. C. Neale, and Y. Agyei. 1993. "Heritable Factors Influence Sexual Orientation in Women." *Archives of General Psychiatry* 50:217–23.

Bergmann, Barbara R. 1986. *The Economic Emergence of Women.* New York: Basic Books.

Bianchi, Suzanne M., John P. Robinson, and Melissa A. Milkie. 2006. Chapter 5 in *Changing Rhythms of American Family Life.* New York: Russell Sage Foundation.

Budig, Michelle J. 2002. "Male Advantage and the Gender Composition of Jobs: Who Rides the Glass Escalator?" *Social Problems* 49(2):258–77.

Buss, David M. 1994. *The Evolution of Desire: Strategies of Human Mating.* New York: Basic Books.

Charles, Maria and Karen Bradley. 2009. "Indulging Our Gendered Selves? Sex Segregation by Field of Study in 44 Countries." *American Journal of Sociology* 114(4):924–76.

Correll, Shelley. 2004. "Constraints into Preferences: Gender, Status, and Emerging Career Aspirations." *American Sociological Review* 69(1):93–113.

Correll, Shelley, Stephen Benard, and In Paik. 2007. "Getting a Job: Is There a Motherhood Penalty?" *American Journal of Sociology* 112:1297–338.

Cotter, David A., Joan M. Hermsen, and Reeve Vanneman. 2011. "The End of the Gender Revolution? Gender Role Attitudes from 1977 to 2008." *American Journal of Sociology* 117:259–89.

Crawford, Mary and Danielle Popp. 2003. "Sexual Double Standards: A Review and Methodological Critique of Two Decades of Research." *Journal of Sex Research* 40:13–26.

Dee, T. 2007. "Teachers and the Gender Gaps in Student Achievement." *Journal of Human Resources* 42(3):1–28.

Diamond, Lisa M. 2008. *Sexual Fluidity: Understanding Women's Love and Desire.* Cambridge, MA: Harvard University Press.

Digest of Education Statistics. 2001. Table 247. Retrieved November 4, 2011 (http://nces.ed.gov/programs/digest/d01/dt247.asp).

DiPrete, Thomas and Claudia Buchmann. Forthcoming. *The Rise of Women: The Female Advantage in Education and What It Means for American Schools.* New York: Russell Sage Foundation.

Eckstein, Zvi and Eva Nagypal. 2004. "The Evolution of U.S. Earnings Inequality: 1961-2002." *Federal Reserve Bank of Minneapolis Quarterly Review* 28(2):10–29.

Ellwood, David T. and Christopher Jencks. 2004. "The Spread of Single-Parent Families in the United States since 1960." Pp. 25–65 in *The Future of the Family,* edited by D. P. Moynihan, T. M. Smeeding, and L. Rainwater. New York: Russell Sage Foundation.

England, Paula. 1992. *Comparable Worth: Theories and Evidence.* New York: Aldine.

England, Paula. 2010. "The Gender Revolution: Uneven and Stalled." *Gender & Society* 24(2):149–66.

England, Paula. 2011. "Reassessing the Uneven Gender Revolution and Its Slowdown." *Gender & Society* 25(1):113–23.

England, Paula, Emily Fitzgibbons Shafer, and Alison C. K. Fogarty. 2008. "Hooking Up and Forming Romantic Relationships on Today's College Campuses." Pp. 531–47 in *The Gendered Society Reader* (3rd Ed.), edited by Michael Kimmel and Amy Aronson. New York: Oxford University Press.

England, Paula, Elizabeth McClintock, and Emily Shafer. 2011. "Birth Control Use and Early, Unintended Births: Evidence for a Class Gradient." Pp. 21–49 in *Social Class and Changing Families in an Unequal America* edited by Marcia Carlson and Paula England. Stanford, CA: Stanford University Press.

Finer, Lawrence B. 2007. "Trends in Premarital Sex in the United States, 1954–2003." *Public Health Reports* 122:7–78.

Gagnon, John H. and William Simon. 1973. *Sexual Conduct: The Social Sources of Human Sexuality.* Chicago: Aldine.

Gordon, Robert J. and Ian Dew-Becker. 2007. "Selected Issues in the Rise of Income Inequality." *Brookings Papers on Economic Activity* 2:169–90.

Holtzman, Linda. 2000. *Media Messages: What Film, Television, and Popular Music Teach Us about Race, Class, Gender and Sexual Orientation.* New York: M.E. Sharpe.

Hyde, Janet Shibley. 1984. "How Large Are Gender Differences in Aggression? A Developmental Meta-Analysis." *Developmental Psychology* 20(4):722–36.

Hyde, Janet Shibley. 2005. "The Gender Similarities Hypothesis." *American Psychologist* 60(6):581–92.

Hyde, Janet S., Sara M. Lindberg, Marcia C. Linn, Amy B. Ellis, and Caroline C. Williams. 2008. "Gender Similarities Characterize Math Performance." *Science* 321(5888):494–95.

Juhn, Chinhui and Kevin M. Murphy. 1997. "Wage Inequality and Family Labor Supply." *Journal of Labor Economics* 15:72–79.

Kinsey, Alfred C., Wardell H. Pomeroy, and Clyde E. Martin. 1948/1998. *Sexual Behavior in the Human Male*. Philadelphia: W.B. Saunders; Bloomington: Indiana U. Press.

Kinsey, Alfred C., Wardell H. Pomeroy, Clyde E. Martin, and Paul H. Gebhard. [1953] 1998. *Sexual Behavior in the Human Female*. Philadelphia: W.B. Saunders; Bloomington: Indiana University Press.

Kreager, Derek A. and Jeremy Staff. 2009. "The Sexual Double Standard and Adolescent Peer Acceptance." *Social Psychology Quarterly* 72:143–64.

Levanon, Asaf, Paula England, and Paul Allison. 2009. "Occupational Feminization and Pay: Assessing Causal Dynamics Using 1950-2000 Census Data." *Social Forces* 88(2):865–92.

Lightdale, Jenifer R. and Deborah A. Prentice. 1994. "Rethinking Sex Differences in Aggression: Aggressive Behavior in the Absence of Social Roles." *Personality and Social Psychology Bulletin* 20:34–44.

Mackie, Gerry. 1996. "Ending Footbinding and Infibulation: A Convention Account." *American Sociological Review* 61:999–1017.

Maccoby, Eleanor Emmons and Carol Nagy Jacklin. 1974. *The Psychology of Sex Differences*. Stanford, CA: Stanford University Press.

Martinez, G., C. E. Copen, and J. C. Abma. 2011. "Teenagers in the United States: Sexual Activity, Contraceptive Use, and Childbearing, 2006–2010 National Survey of Family Growth." National Center for Health Statistics. *Vital Health Statistics* 23(31).

Mazur, Allan and Alan Booth. 1998. "Testosterone and Dominance in Men." *Behavioral and Brain Sciences* 21:353–97.

McDaniel, Anne, Thomas A. DiPrete, Claudia Buchmann, and Uri Shwed. 2011. "The Black Gender Gap in Educational Attainment: Historical Trends and Racial Comparisons." *Demography* 48:889–914.

McKenna, Wendy and Suzanne Kessler. 2006. "Transgendering: Blurring the Boundaries of Gender," in *Handbook of Gender and Women's Studies*, edited by Mary S. Evans, Kathy David, and Judith Lorber. Thousand Oaks, CA: Sage Publications: 342–354.

Michael, Robert T., John H. Gagnon, Edward O. Laumann, and Gina Kolata. 1994. *Sex in America: A Definitive Survey*. Boston: Little, Brown and Company.

O'Brien, Jodi. 2000. "Heterosexism and Homophobia." Pp. 6672–76 in *International Encyclopedia of the Social & Behavioral Sciences*, Volume 10, edited by Neil J. Smelser and Paul B. Baltes. London: Elsevier.

Oppenheimer, Valerie. 1970. *The Female Labor Force in the United States: Demographic and Economic Factors Governing Its Growth and Changing Composition*. Berkeley: University of California Press.

Ottosson, Daniel. 2010. "State-Sponsored Homophobia: A World Survey of Laws Prohibiting Same Sex Behavior between Consenting Adults." Report from the International Lesbian, Gay, Bisexual, Trans, and Intersex Association.

Pascoe, C. J. 2007. *"Dude, You're a Fag": Masculinity and Sexuality in High School*. Berkeley: University of California Press.

Regnerus, Mark D. 2007. *Forbidden Fruit: Sex and Religion in the Lives of American Teenagers*. Oxford, UK: Oxford University Press.

Reskin, Barbara and Patricia Roos. 1990. *Job Queues, Gender Queues*. Philadelphia: Temple University Press.

Risman, Barbara J. 2004. "Gender as a Social Structure: Theory Wrestling with Social Change." *Gender & Society* 18(4):429–50.

Savin-Williams, Ritch C. 1998. *"And Then I Became Gay": Young Men's Stories*. New York: Routledge.

Sayer, Liana, Paula England, Paul Allison, and Nicole Kangas. 2011. "She Left, He Left: How Employment and Satisfaction Affect Women's and Men's Decisions to Leave Marriages." *American Journal of Sociology* 116(6):1982–2018.

Schalet, Amy T. 2011. *Not Under My Roof: Parents, Teens, and the Culture of Sex*. Chicago: University of Chicago Press.

Schmitt, David P. 2003. "Universal Sex Differences in the Desire for Sexual Variety." *Journal of Personality and Social Psychology* 85(1):85–104.

Sell, Randall L. 1997. "Defining and Measuring Sexual Orientation: A Review." *Archives of Sexual Behavior* 26(6):643–58.

Spencer, S. J., C. M. Steele, and D. M. Quinn. 1999. "Stereotype Threat and Women's Math Performance." *Journal of Experimental Social Psychology* 35:4–28.

Steffensmeier, Darrell and Emilie Allan. 1996. "Gender and Crime: Toward a Gendered Theory of Female Offending." *Annual Review of Sociology* 22:459–87.

Stein, Edward. 2001. "Sexual Orientation: Biological Influences." Pp. 13995–99 in *International Encyclopedia of the Social & Behavioral Sciences*, Vol. 21, edited by Neil J. Smelser and Paul B. Baltes. London: Elsevier.

Udry, J. Richard. 1988. "Biological Predispositions and Social Control in Adolescent Sexual Behavior." *American Sociological Review* 53(5):709–22.

Willer, Robb, Christabel Rogalin, Bridget Conlon, and Michael T. Wojnowicz. 2011. "Overdoing Gender: A Test of the Masculine Overcompensation Thesis." Working paper, Department of Sociology, University of California–Berkeley.

CHAPTER 12

Alba, Richard and Victor Nee. 2003. *Remaking the American Mainstream: Assimilation and Contemporary Immigration*. Cambridge, MA: Harvard University Press.

Barrionuevo, Alexei. 2012. "At over $90 Million, Sale of Midtown Penthouse Sets a New York Record." *New York Times*, May 17, 2012.

Bean, Frank D. and Gillian Stevens. 2003. *America's Newcomers and the Dynamics of Diversity*. New York: Russell Sage.

Calavita, Kitty. 1992. *Inside the State: The Bracero Program, Immigration, and the I.N.S.* New York: Routledge. Reissued in 2010 in the Classics in Law and Society Series.

Ignatiev, Noel. 1995. *How the Irish Became White*. New York: Routledge.

Jacobson, Matthew F. 1999. *Whiteness of a Different Color: European Immigrants and the Alchemy of Race*. Cambridge, MA: Harvard University Press.

Jasso, Guillermina. 1988. "Whom Shall We Welcome? Elite Judgments of the Criteria for the Selection of Immigrants." *American Sociological Review* 53:919–32.

Jasso, Guillermina. 2011. "Migration and Stratification." *Social Science Research* 40:1292-336.

Jasso, Guillermina. 2012. "Is It Remittances or Is It Tickets to America? A First Look at Transfers Behavior among New U.S. Legal Immigrants Born in Mexico." Pp. 203–41 in *Migration and Remittances from Mexico: Trends, Impacts, and New Challenges*, edited by Alfredo Cuecuecha and Carla Pederzini. Lanham, MD: Lexington.

Jasso, Guillermina, Douglas S. Massey, Mark R. Rosenzweig, and James P. Smith. 2000. "The New Immigrant Survey Pilot (NIS-P): Overview and New Findings about U.S. Legal Immigrants at Admission." *Demography* 37:127–38.

Jasso, Guillermina, Douglas S. Massey, Mark R. Rosenzweig, and James P. Smith. 2008. "From Illegal to Legal: Estimating Previous Illegal Experience among New Legal Immigrants to the United States." *International Migration Review* 42:803–43.

Jasso, Guillermina and Mark R. Rosenzweig. 2006. "Characteristics of Immigrants to the United States: 1820–2003." Pp. 328–58 in Reed Ueda (ed.), *A Companion to American Immigration*. Blackwell Companions to American History Series. Malden, MA: Blackwell Publishing.

Jasso, Guillermina and Mark R. Rosenzweig. 2012. "Remit or Reunify? US Immigrant Parents, Remittances, and the Sponsorship of Children." Presented at the Research Conference on Remittances and Immigration, Federal Reserve Bank of Atlanta, Atlanta, GA, November 2010.

Keyssar, Alexander. 2000. *The Right to Vote*. New York: Basic books.

Maimbo, Samuel Munzele and Dilip Ratha. 2005. "Remittances: An Overview." Pp. 1–16 in *Remittances: Development Impact and Future Prospects*, edited by Samuel Munzele Maimbo and Dilip Ratha. Washington, DC: World Bank.

Massey, Douglas S., Joaquin Arango, Graeme Hugo, Ali Kouaouci, Adela Pellegrino, and J. Edward Taylor. 1993. "Theories of International Migration: A Review and Appraisal." *Population and Development Review* 19:431–66.

Mincer, Jacob. 1978. "Family Migration Decisions." *Journal of Political Economy* 86:749–73.

Portes, Alejandro and Ruben Rumbaut. 2006. *Immigrant America: A Portrait*. 3rd ed. Berkeley: University of California Press.

Rapoport, Hillel and Frederic Docquier. 2006. "The Economics of Migrants' Remittances." Pp. 1135–200 in *Handbook of the Economics of Giving, Altruism and Reciprocity: Applications*, Volume 2, edited by Serge-Christophe Kolm and Jean Mercier Ythier. Amsterdam, Netherlands: North-Holland.

Smith, James P. and Barry Edmonston, eds. 1997. *The New Americans: Economic, Demographic, and Fiscal Effects of Immigration*. Report of the National Research Council. Washington, DC: National Academy Press.

Smith, Marian. 2002. "Race, Nationality, and Reality: INS Administration of Racial Provisions in U.S. Immigration and Nationality Law since 1898." *U.S. National Archives and Records Administration* 34:2. Available at http://www.archives.gov.

U.S. Department of Homeland Security, Office of Immigration Statistics. 2002–2011. *Yearbook of Immigration Statistics*. Washington, DC: Government Printing Office.

U.S. Department of State. n.d. *Visa Bulletin*.

U.S. Department of State. 2011. *Annual Report of Immigrant Visa Applicants in the Family-sponsored and Employment-based Preferences Registered at the National Visa Center as of November 1, 2011*.

U.S. Immigration Commission. 1911. *Reports of the Immigration Commission*. 42 vols. Washington, DC: U.S. Government Printing Office.

Valdés, Guadalupe. 2003. *Expanding Definitions of Giftedness: Young Interpreters of Immigrant Background*. Erlbaum.

World Bank. 2011a. *Migration and Remittances Factbook 2011*. Washington, DC: World Bank.

World Bank. 2011b. "News and Broadcast: Migration and Remittances." Retrieved July 16, 2012 (http://web.worldbank.org/WBSITE/EXTERNAL/NEWS/0,,contentMDK:20648762~pagePK:64257043~piPK:437376~theSitePK:4607,00.html).

CHAPTER 13

Acock, Alan C. and David H. Demo. 1994. *Family Diversity and Well-Being.* Thousand Oaks, CA: Sage.

Ahrons, Constance. 2006. "Family Ties after Divorce: Long-Term Implications for Children." *Family Issues* 46:53–65.

Amato, Paul R. and Alan Booth. 1997. *A Generation at Risk: Growing Up in an Era of Family Upheaval.* Cambridge, MA: Harvard University Press.

Banerjee, Neela. 2008. "Taking Their Faith, but Not Their Politics, to the People." *New York Times,* June 1.

Barnett, Rosalind C. and Caryl Rivers. 1996. *She Works/He Works: How Two-Income Families Are Happier, Healthier, and Better-Off.* San Francisco: Harper San Francisco.

Barnett, Rosalind C. and Caryl Rivers. 2004. *Same Difference: How Gender Myths Are Hurting Our Relationships, Our Children, and Our Jobs.* New York: Basic Books.

Belkin, Lisa. 2003. "The Opt-Out Revolution." *New York Times Magazine,* October 26.

Bellah, Robert N., Richard Madsen, William M. Sullivan, Ann Swidler, and Stephen M. Tipton. 1985. *Habits of the Heart: Individualism and Commitment in American Life.* Berkeley and Los Angeles: University of California Press.

Bengston, Vern L., Timothy J. Biblarz, and Robert E. L. Roberts. 2002. *How Families Still Matter: A Longitudinal Study of Youth in Two Generations.* New York: Cambridge University Press.

Bianchi, Suzanne M. 2000. "Maternal Employment and Time with Children: Dramatic Change or Surprising Continuity?" *Demography* 37(4):401–14.

Bianchi, Suzanne M., John P. Robinson, and Melissa A. Milkie. 2006. *Changing Rhythms of American Family Life.* New York: Russell Sage Foundation.

Blair-Loy, Mary. 2003. *Competing Devotions: Career and Family among Women Executives.* Cambridge, MA: Harvard University Press.

Blankenhorn, David. 1995. *Fatherless America: Confronting Our Most Urgent Social Problem.* New York: Basic Books.

Blankenhorn, David. 2009. *The Future of Marriage.* New York: Encounter Books.

Blow, Charles M. 2008. "Talking Down and Stepping Up." *New York Times,* July 12.

Boushey, Heather. 2008. "'Opting Out'? The Effect of Children on Women's Employment in the United States." *Feminist Economics* 14(1):1–36.

Burchinal, Margaret and Alison Clarke-Stewart. 2007. "Maternal Employment and Child Cognitive Outcomes: The Importance of an Analytic Approach." *Developmental Psychology* 43:1140–55.

Cahn, Naomi and June Carbone. 2010. *Red Families v. Blue Families: Legal Polarization and the Creation of Culture.* New York: Oxford University Press.

Cancian, Francesca M. 1987. *Love in America: Gender and Self-Development.* New York: Cambridge University Press.

Casper, Lynne M. and Suzanne Bianchi. 2002. *Continuity and Change in the American Family.* Thousand Oaks, CA: Sage.

Cherlin, Andrew J. 1992. *Marriage, Divorce, Remarriage.* Cambridge, MA: Harvard University Press.

Cherlin, Andrew J. 2009. *The Marriage-Go-Round: The State of Marriage and the Family in America Today.* New York: Alfred A. Knopf.

Cherlin, Andrew J., Frank F. Furstenberg, Jr., P. Lindsey Chase-Lansdale, K. E. Kiernan, P. K. Robins, D. R. Morrison, and J. O. Teitler. 1991. "Longitudinal Studies of the Effects of Divorce on Children in Great Britain and the United States." *Science* 252 (June):1386–89.

Cohany, Sharon R. and Emy Sok. 2007. "Trends in the Labor Force Participation of Married Mothers of Infants." *Monthly Labor Review,* February 2007, 9–16.

Coltrane, Scott. 2004. "Fathering: Paradoxes, Contradictions and Dilemmas." Pp. 224–43 in *Handbook of Contemporary Families: Considering the Past, Contemplating the Future,* edited by Marilyn Coleman and Lawrence Ganong. Thousand Oaks, CA: Sage.

Conley, Dalton. 2004. *The Pecking Order: Which Siblings Succeed and Why.* New York: Pantheon.

Cooke, Lynn P. 2006. "'Doing' Gender in Context: Household Bargaining and Risk of Divorce in Germany and the United States." *American Journal of Sociology* 112(2):442–72.

Coontz, Stephanie. 1992. *The Way We Never Were: American Families and the Nostalgia Trap.* New York: Basic Books.

Coontz, Stephanie. 2005. *Marriage, a History: From Obedience to Intimacy, or How Love Conquered Marriage.* New York: Viking.

Cotter, David A., Paula England, and Joan Hermsen. 2010. "Moms and Jobs: Trends in Mothers' Employment and Which Mothers Stay Home." Pp. 416–24 in *Families as They Really Are,* edited by Barbara J. Risman. New York: W.W. Norton.

Crouter, Ann C. and Susan M. McHale. 2005. "Work Time, Family Time, and Children's Time: Implications for Youth." Pp. 49–66 in *Work, Family, Health, and Well-Being,* edited by Suzanne Bianchi, Lynne Casper, and R. B. King. New York: Routledge.

Damaske, Sarah. 2011. *For the Family? How Class and Gender Shape Women's Work.* New York: Oxford University Press.

Deutsch, Francine. 1999. *Halving It All: How Equally Shared Parenting Works.* Cambridge, MA: Harvard University Press.

DiMaggio, Paul, John Evans, and Bethany Bryson. 1996. "Have Americans' Social Attitudes Become More Polarized?" *American Journal of Sociology* 102:690–755.

Edin, Kathryn and Maria Kefalas. 2005. *Promises I Can Keep: Why Poor Women Put Motherhood before Marriage.* Berkeley and Los Angeles: University of California Press.

Edlund, Lena and Rohini Pande. 2002. "Why Have Women Become Left-Wing? The Political Gender Gap and the Decline of Marriage." *Quarterly Journal of Economics* 117:917–61.

Epstein, Cynthia F., Carroll Seron, Bonnie Oglensky, and Robert Saute. 1999. *The Part-Time Paradox: Time Norms, Professional Lives, Family, and Gender.* New York: Routledge.

Esping-Andersen, Gosta. 2009. *The Incomplete Revolution: Adapting Welfare States to Women's New Roles.* Cambridge, UK: Polity Press.

Ferree, Myra Marx. 1990. "Beyond Separate Spheres: Feminism and Family Research." *Journal of Marriage and the Family* 52:866–84.

Folbre, Nancy. 2008. *Valuing Children: Rethinking the Economics of the Family.* Cambridge, MA: Harvard University Press.

Friedan, Betty. [2001] 1963. *The Feminine Mystique.* New York: W.W Norton & Company.

Furstenberg, Frank F. 2007. *Destinies of the Disadvantaged: The Politics of Teenage Childbearing.* New York: Russell Sage Foundation.

Furstenberg, Frank F. and Andrew J. Cherlin. 1991. *Divided Families: What Happens to Children When Parents Part.* Cambridge, MA: Harvard University Press.

Furstenberg, Frank F., Sheela Kennedy, Vonnie C. Mcloyd, Ruben Rumbaut, and Richard A. Settersten, Jr. 2004. "Growing Up Is Harder to Do." *Contexts* 3:33–41.

Furstenberg, Frank F., Ruben G. Rumbaut, and Richard A. Settersten Jr., eds. 2005. *On the Frontier of Adulthood: Emerging Themes and New Directions.* Chicago: University of Chicago Press.

Galinsky, Ellen. 1999. *Ask the Children: What America's Children Really Think about Working Parents.* New York: William Morrow.

Galinksy, Ellen, Kerstin Aumann, and James T. Bond. 2009. "Gender and Generation at Home and at Work." New York: Families and Work Institute.

Gerson, Kathleen. 2011. *The Unfinished Revolution: Coming of Age in a New Era of Gender, Work, and Family.* New York: Oxford University Press.

Giele, Janet Z. 1996. "Decline of the Family: Conservative, Liberal, and Feminist Views." Pp. 89–115 in *Promises to Keep: Decline and Renewal of Marriage in America,* edited by David Poponoe, Jean Bethke Elshtain, and David Blankenhorn. Lanham, MD: Rowman & Littlefield.

Goode, William J. 1963. *World Revolution and Family Patterns.* New York: Free Press.

Goode, William J. 1982. *The Family,* 2nd ed. Upper Saddle River: Pearson.

Gornick, Janet C. and Marcia K. Meyers. 2003. *Families That Work: Policies for Reconciling Parenthood and Employment.* New York: Russell Sage Foundation.

Gornick, Janet C. and Marcia K. Meyers. 2009. *Gender Equality: Transforming Family Divisions of Labor.* New York: Verso Books.

Harvey, Lisa. 1999. "Short-Term and Long-Term Effects of Early Parental Employment on Children of the National Longitudinal Survey of Youth." *Developmental Psychology* 35(2):445–59.

Hays, Sharon. 1996. *The Cultural Contradictions of Motherhood.* New Haven, CT: Yale University Press.

_____. 2003. *Flat Broke with Children: Women in the Age of Welfare Reform.* New York: Oxford University Press.

Hertz, Rosanna. 2006. *Single by Chance, Mothers by Choice: How Women Are Choosing Parenthood without Marriage and Creating the New American Family.* New York: Oxford University Press.

Hetherington, E. Mavis and John Kelly. 2002. *For Better or For Worse: Divorce Reconsidered.* New York: W.W. Norton.

Hill Collins, Patricia. 1991. *Black Feminist Thought: Knowledge, Consciousness, and the Politics of Empowerment.* London and New York: Routledge.

Hochschild, Arlie R., with Anne Machung. 1989. *The Second Shift: Working Parents and the Revolution at Home.* New York: Viking.

Hochschild, Arlie R. 1997. *The Time Bind: When Work Becomes Home and Home Becomes Work.* New York: Henry Holt.

Hoffman, Lois, Norma Wladis, and Lise M. Youngblade. 1999. *Mothers at Work: Effects on Children's Well-Being.* Cambridge, UK: Cambridge University Press.

Jacobs, Jerry A. and Kathleen Gerson. 2004. *The Time Divide: Work, Family, and Gender Inequality.* Cambridge, MA: Harvard University Press.

Jayson, Sharon. 2007. "Gen Y's Attitudes Differ from Parents.'" *USA Today,* January 9.

Kefalas, Maria J., Frank F. Furstenberg, Patrick J. Carr, and Laura Napolitano. 2011. "'Marriage Is More Than Being Together': The Meaning of Marriage for Young Adults." *Journal of Family Issues,* February 23.

Kimmel, Michael. 2008. *Guyland: The Perilous World Where Boys Become Men.* New York: HarperCollins Publishers.

Lareau, Annette. 2003. *Unequal Childhoods: Class, Race, and Family Life.* Berkeley and Los Angeles: University of California Press.

Levi-Strauss, Claude. 1964. "Reciprocity, the Essence of Social Life." Pp. 3–14 in *The Family: Its Structure and Functions,* edited by Rose Laub Coser. New York: St. Martins Press.

Li, Allen J. 2007. "The Kids Are OK: Divorce and Children's Behavior Problems." RAND Working Paper No. WR-489.

Lorber, Judith. 1994. *Paradoxes of Gender*. New Haven, CT: Yale University Press.

Luker, Kristin. 2007. *When Sex Goes to School: Warring Views on Sex—and Sex Education—Since the Sixties*. New York: W.W. Norton.

Malinowski, Bronislaw. [1913] 1964. "Parenthood, the Basis of Social Structure." Pp. 51-63 in *The Family: Its Structure and Functions*, edited by Rose Laub Coser. New York: St. Martins Press.

Marquardt, Elizabeth. 2005. *Between Two Worlds: The Inner Lives of Children of Divorce*. New York: Crown.

McLanahan, Sara and Gary D. Sandefur. 1994. *Growing Up with a Single Parent: What Hurts, What Helps*. Cambridge, MA: Harvard University Press.

Moen, Phyllis and Patricia Roehling. 2005. *The Career Mystique: Cracks in the American Dream*. Lanham, MD: Rowman & Littlefield.

Moore, Kristin A., Rosemary Chalk, Juliet Scarpa, and Sharon Vandiverre. 2002. "Family Strengths: Often Overlooked, But Real." Child Trends Research Brief. Washington, DC: Annie E. Casey Foundation.

Newman, Katherine S. 2009. "Ties That Bind: Cultural Interpretations of Delayed Adulthood in Western Europe and Japan." *Sociological Forum* Vol. 23 (4): 645–69.

Newman, Katherine S., and Victor Tan Chen. 2007. *The Missing Class: Portraits of the Near-Poor in America*. Boston: Beacon Press.

Parcel, Toby L. and Elizabeth G. Menaghan. 1994. *Parents' Jobs and Children's Lives*. New York: Aldine de Gruyter.

Parsons, Talcott and Robert F. Bales. 1954. *Family, Socialization, and Interaction Process*. Glencoe, IL: Free Press.

Percheski, Christine. 2008. "Opting Out? Cohort Differences in Professional Women's Employment from 1960 to 2005." *American Sociological Review* 73:497–517.

Pew Research Center. 2007a. "Generation Gap in Values, Behavior: As Marriage and Parenthood Drift Apart, Public Is Concerned about Social Impact." Pew Research Center Social and Demographic Trends Report, July 1.

Pew Research Center. 2007b. *How Young People View Their Lives, Futures and Politics: A Portrait of the 'Generation Next.'* New York: Pew Research Center.

Pew Research Center. 2010. "The Decline of Marriage and Rise of New Families." Pew Research Center, November 18.

Popenoe, David. 1988. *Disturbing the Nest: Family Change and Decline in Modern Societies*. New York: Aldine de Gruyter.

Popenoe, David, Jean B. Elshtain, and David Blankenhorn. 1996. *Promises to Keep: Decline and Renewal of Marriage in America*. Lanham, MD: Rowman & Littlefield.

Porter, Eduardo and Michelle O'Donnell. 2006. "Facing Middle Age with No Degree, and No Wife." *New York Times*, August 6.

Poulin, Colleen and Virginia Rutter. 2011. "How Color-Blind Is Love? Interracial Dating Facts and Puzzles." Council on Contemporary Families Briefing Paper (March).

Powell, Brian, Catherine Bolzendahl, Claudia Geist, and Lala Carr Steelman. 2010. *Counted Out: Same-Sex Relations and American's Definitions of Family*. New York: Russell Sage Foundation.

Presser, Harriet B. 2003. *Working in a 24/7 Economy: Challenges for American Families*. New York: Russell Sage Foundation.

Risman, Barbara J. 1998. *Gender Vertigo: American Families in Transition*. New Haven, CT: Yale University Press.

Risman, Barbara J., ed. 2010. *Families as They Really Are*. New York: W.W. Norton.

Rosenfeld, Michael J. 2009. *The Age of Independence: Interracial Unions, Same-Sex Unions, and Changing American Family*. Cambridge, MA: Harvard University Press.

Rubin, Lillian B. 1994. *Families on the Fault Line*. New York: HarperCollins.

Rutter, Virginia. 2010. "The Case for Divorce." Pp. 159–69 in *Families as They Really Are*, edited by Barbara J. Risman. New York: W.W. Norton.

Shorter, Edward. 1975. *The Making of the Modern Family*. New York: Basic Books.

Skolnick, Arlene. 2006. "Beyond the 'M' Word: The Tangled Web of Politics and Marriage." *Dissent* (Fall):81–87.

Smith, Christian with Kari Christofferson, Hilary Davidson, and Patricia Herzog. 2011. *Lost in Translation: The Dark Side of Emerging Adulthood*. New York: Oxford University Press.

Smock, Pamela. 2000. "Cohabitation in the United States: An Appraisal of Research Themes, Findings, and Implications." *Annual Review of Sociology* 26:1–20.

Smock, Pamela J. and Wendy Manning. 2010. "New Couples, New Families: The Cohabitation Revolution in the United States." In *Families as They Really Are*, edited by Barbara J. Risman. New York: W.W. Norton.

Stacey, Judith. 1996. *In the Name of the Family: Rethinking Family Values in the Postmodern Age*. Boston: Beacon Press.

Stack, Carol B. 1974. *All Our Kin: Strategies for Survival in a Black Community*. New York: Harper and Row.

Stone, Pamela. 2007. *Opting Out? Why Women Really Quit Careers and Head Home*. Berkeley and Los Angeles: University of California Press.

Struening, Karen. 2010. "Families 'In Law' and Families 'In Practice': Does the Law Recognize Families as They Really Are?" Pp. 75–90 in *Families as They Really Are*, edited by Barbara J. Risman. New York: W.W. Norton.

Sullivan, Oriel and Scott Coltrane. 2008. "Men's Changing Contribution to Housework and Child Care." Chicago, IL: Council on Contemporary Families Briefing Paper (April 25).

Swidler, Ann. 1980. "Love and Adulthood in American Culture." Pp. 120–47 in *Themes of Love and Work in Adulthood*, edited by Erik H. Erikson and Neil J. Smelser. Cambridge, MA: Harvard University Press.

Teixeira, Ruy. 2009. "The Coming End of the Culture Wars." Washington, DC: Center for American Progress.

U.S. Census Bureau. 2006. "Current Population Survey Annual Social and Economic Supplement: Families and Living Arrangements: 2005." Washington, DC.

U.S. Census Bureau. 2007. "Single-Parent Households Showed Little Variation since 1994." Washington, DC.

Waldfogel, Jane. 2006. *What Children Need*. Cambridge, MA: Harvard University Press.

Wallerstein, Judith S., Julia M. Lewis, and Sandra Blakeslee. 2000. *The Unexpected Legacy of Divorce: A 25-Year Landmark Study*. New York: Hyperion.

Warren, Elizabeth and Amelia W. Tyagi. 2003. *The Two-Income Trap: Why Middle-Class Mothers and Fathers Are Going Broke*. New York: Basic Books.

Weitzman, Lenore. 1985. *The Divorce Revolution: The Unexpected Consequences for Women and Children*. New York: Free Press.

Whitehead, Barbara D. 1997. *The Divorce Culture*. New York: Alfred A. Knopf.

Whyte, William H., Jr. 1956. *The Organization Man*. New York: Simon & Schuster.

Williams, Joan C. 2000. *Unbending Gender: Why Family and Work Conflict and What to Do about It*. New York: Oxford University Press.

Williams, Joan C. 2010. *Reshaping the Work-Family Debate: Why Men and Class Matter*. Cambridge, MA: Harvard University Press.

CHAPTER 14

Amont, Jonathan. 2005. *American Jewish Religious Denominations*. United Jewish Communities Report Series on the National Jewish Population Survey, 2000–2001.

Beit-Hallahmi, Benjamin and Michael Argyle. 1997. *The Psychology of Religious Behavior, Belief and Experience*. London: Routledge.

Bellah, Robert N., Richard Madsen, William M. Sullivan, Ann Swidler, and Steven M. Tipton. 1985. *Habits of the Heart: Individualism and Commitment in America Life*. Berkeley: University of California Press.

Chang, Chul Tim. 2006. "Korean Ethnic Church Growth Phenomenon in the United States." Presented at the American Academy of Religion, March 12, Claremont, CA (http://www.duke.edu/~myhan/kaf0603.pdf).

Chaves, Mark. 2004. *Congregations in America*. Cambridge, MA: Harvard University Press.

Chaves, Mark, C. Kirk Hadaway, and Penny Long Marler. 1993. "What the Polls Don't Show: A Closer Look at U.S. Church Attendance," *American Sociological Review*.

Demerath, N. J. 2003. *Crossing the Gods*. New Brunswick, NJ: Rutgers University Press.

Demerath, N. J. 2006. "Chapters and Verse for Preaching to the Choir of International Religion Researchers": Comparative Religion Research Conference, Copenhagen, Denmark, June 2–4.

Dillon, Michelle and Paul Wink. 2007. *In the Course of a Lifetime*. Berkeley: University of California Press.

Durkheim, Emile. [1898] 1951. *Suicide: A Study in Sociology*. Translated by John A. Spaulding and George Simpson. New York: The Free Press.

Durkheim, Emile. [1912] 2001. *The Elementary Forms of Religious Life*. Translated by Carol Cosman. New York: Oxford University Press.

European Commission. 2005. "Eurobarometer 225: Social Values, Science and Technology."

Geneva Declaration Secretariat. 2008. *Global Burden of Armed Violence Report*. Retrieved July 27, 2011 (http://www.genevadeclaration.org/fileadmin/docs/Global-Burden-of-Armed-Violence-full-report.pdf).

Greeley, Andrew and Michael Hout. 2006. *The Truth about Conservative Christians: What They Think and What They Believe*. Chicago: The University of Chicago Press.

Gross, Neil and Solon Simmons. 2009. "The Religiosity of American College and University Professors." *Sociology of Religion* 70(2):101–29.

Guttmacher Institute. 2011. "Contraceptive Use Is the Norm among Religious Women." April 13, 2011 (http://www.guttmacher.org/media/nr/2011/04/13/index.html).

Hout, Michael and Claude Fisher. 2002. "Why More Americans Have No Religious Preference: Politics and Generations." *American Sociological Review* 67(2):165–90.

Leonhardt, David. 2011. "Is Your Religion Your Financial Destiny?" *New York Times*, May 11. Retrieved July 26, 2011 (http://www.nytimes.com/2011/05/15/magazine/is-your-religion-your-financial-destiny.html?_r=1).

Marx, Karl. [1844] 2001. "Critique of Hegel's Philosophy of Right." In *Marx on Religion*, edited by J. Raines. Philadelphia: Temple University Press.

Moaddel, Mansoor. 2007. "The Saudi Public Speaks: Religion, Gender, and Politics." Pp. 209–48 in *Values and Perceptions of the Islamic and Middle East Publics*, edited by Mansoor Moaddel. New York: Palgrave Macmillan.

Nepstad, Sharon Erickson. 1996. "Popular Religion, Protest, and Revolt: The Emergence of Political Insurgency in the Nicaraguan and Salvadoran Churches of the 1960s–80s." Pp. 105–24 in *Disruptive Religion: The Force of Faith in Social Movement Activism*, edited by C. Smith. New York: Routledge.

Newport, Frank. 2006. "A Look at Religious Switching in America Today." Gallup, June 23. Retrieved July 27, 2011 (http://www.gallup.com/poll/23467/look-religious-switching-america-today.aspx).

Norris, Pippa and Ronald Inglehart. 2004. *Sacred and Secular.* New York: Cambridge University Press.

Osteen, Joel. 2004. *Your Best Life Now.* New York: Faith Word.

Pew Research Center's Forum on Religion and Public Life. 2006. *Spirit and Power: A 10-Country Survey of Pentecostals.* December. Retrieved July 27, 2011 (http://pewforum.org/Christian/Evangelical-Protestant-Churches/Spirit-and-Power-A-10-Country-Survey-of-Pentecostals%283%29.aspx).

Putnam, Robert and David Campbell. 2010. *American Grace: How Religion Divides and Unites Us.* New York: Simon and Schuster.

Sela, Avraham. 1994. "The 'Wailing Wall' Riots (1929) as a Watershed in the Palestine Conflict." *The Muslim World* 84(1–2):60–94.

Smith, Christian. 2009. *Soul Searching: The Religious and Spiritual Lives of American Teenagers.* New York: Oxford University Press.

Stark, Rodney. 1996. *The Rise of Christianity: How the Obscure, Marginal Jesus Movement Became the Dominant Religious Force.* Princeton, NJ: Princeton University Press.

Stark, Rodney and Roger Finke. 2000. *Acts of Faith: Explaining the Human Side of Religion.* Berkeley: University of California Press.

Sullins, D. Paul. 2006. "Gender and Religion: Deconstructing Universality, Constructing Complexity." *American Journal of Sociology,* 112 (3):838–880.

U.S. Census Bureau. 2010. "DP-1: Profile of General Population and Housing Characteristics: 2010. 2010 Demographic Profile Data." Retrieved June 19, 2012 (http://factfinder2.census.gov/faces/tableservices/jsf/pages/productview.xhtml?src=bkmk).

Weber, Max. [1904] 1958. *The Protestant Ethic and the Spirit of Capitalism.* New York: Charles Scribner's Sons.

Weber, Max. [1915] 1968. *The Religion of China: Confucianism and Taoism.* New York: The Free Press.

Weber, Max. [1916] 1958. *The Religion of India: The Sociology of Hinduism and Buddhism.* New York: The Free Press.

Weber, Max. [1917] 1952. *Ancient Judaism.* New York: The Free Press.

CHAPTER 15

100 Milestone Documents. "Servicemen's Readjustment Act (1944)." Retrieved May 15, 2012 (http://www.ourdocuments.gov/doc.php?flash=true&doc=76).

Alexander, Karl L., M. Cook, and Edward L. McDill. 1978. "Curriculum Tracking and Educational Stratification: Some Further Evidence." *American Sociological Review* 43:47–66.

Alexander, Karl L. and Edward L. McDill. 1976. "Selection and Allocation within Schools: Some Causes and Consequences of Curriculum Placement." *American Sociological Review* 41:963–80.

Arum, Richard. 1996. "Do Private Schools Force Public Schools to Compete?" *American Sociological Review* 61:29–46.

Arum, Richard and Josipa Roksa. 2010. *Academically Adrift: Limited Learning on College Campuses.* Chicago: University of Chicago Press.

Baker, David P. and Deborah Perkins Jones. 1993. "Creating Gender Equality: Cross-National Gender Stratification and Mathematical Performance," *Sociology of Education* 66 (April): 91–103.

Baraniuk, Richard G. 2008. "Challenges and Opportunities for the Open Education Movement: A Connexions Case Study." Pp. 229–46 in *Opening Up Education,* edited by Toru Iiyoshi and Vijay Kumar. Cambridge, MA: MIT Press.

Blossfeld, Hans-Peter and Yossi Shavit. 1993. "Persisting Barriers: Changes in Educational Opportunities in Thirteen Countries." Pp. 1–23 *Persistent Inequality: Changing Educational Attainment in Thirteen Countries,* edited by Yossi Shavit and Hans-Peter Blossfeld. Boulder, CO: Westview Press.

Booher-Jennings, Jennifer. 2005. "Below the Bubble: 'Educational Triage' and the Texas Accountability System." *American Educational Research Journal* 42:231–68.

Bowles, Samuel and Herbert Gintis. 1976. *Schooling in Capitalist America: Educational Reform and the Contradictions of Economic Life.* New York: Basic Books.

Braddock, Jomills H., II, and James McPartland. 1990. "Alternatives to Tracking." *Educational Leadership* 47(7): 76–79.

Brint, Steven and Jerome Karabel. 1989. *The Diverted Dream: Community Colleges and the Promise of Educational Opportunity in America, 1900–1980.* New York: Oxford University Press.

Brown, Ryan. 2011. "Community-College Students Perform Worse Online Than Face to Face," *Chronicle of Higher Education* (July 18). Retrieved July 19, 2011 (http://chronicle.com/article/Community-College-Students/128281/?sid=wc&utm_source=wc&utm_medium=en).

Buchmann Claudia and Thomas A. DiPrete. 2006. "The Growing Female Advantage in College Completion: the role of family background and academic achievement. *American Sociological. Review* 71(4):515–41.

Buchmann, Claudia, Thomas A. DiPrete, and Anne McDaniel. 2008. "Gender Inequalities in Education." *Annual Review of Sociology* 34:319–37.

Clifford, Stephanie. 2009. "Ads Follow Web Users, and Get Deeply Personal." *New York Times,* July 31, 2009.

Coleman, James S., Ernest Q. Campbell, Alexander M. Mood, Frederick D. Weinfeld, and Robert L. York. 1966. *Equality of Educational Opportunity.* Washington, DC: U.S. Government Printing Office.

Coleman, James S. and Thomas Hoffer. 1987. *Public and Private High Schools: The Impact of Communities.* New York: Basic Books.

Coleman, James S., Thomas Hoffer, and Sally Kilgore. 1982. *High School Achievement.* New York: Basic Books.

Collins, Randall. 1977. "Functional and Conflict Theories of Educational Stratification." Pp. 118–36 in *Power and Ideology in Education,* edited by J. Karabel and A. H. Halsey. New York: Oxford University Press.

Condron, Dennis J. 2010. "Affluence, Inequality, and Educational Achievement: A Structural Analysis of 97 Jurisdictions across the Globe." Unpublished paper. Atlanta, GA: Emory University.

Condron, Dennis J. and Vincent J. Roscigno. 2003. "Disparities Within: Unequal Spending and Achievement in an Urban School District." *Sociology of Education* 76:18–36.

Cookson, Peter W. Jr. and Caroline Hodges Persell. 1985. *Preparing for Power: America's Elite Boarding Schools.* New York: Basic Books.

Darling-Hammond, Linda. 2001. "Inequality and Access to Knowledge." Pp. 465–483 in *Handbook of Research on Multicultural Education,* edited by J. A. Banks and C. A. M. Banks. San Francisco: Jossey-Bass.

Downey, Douglas B., Paul T. von Hippel, and Melanie Hughes. 2008. "Are 'Failing' Schools Really Failing? Using Seasonal Comparison to Evaluate School Effectiveness." *Sociology of Education* 81:242–70.

Dreeben, Robert and Rebecca Barr. 1988. "Classroom Composition and the Design of Instruction." *Sociology of Education.* 61(3):129–42.

Dworkin, A. Gary. 2005. "The No Child Left Behind Act: Accountability, High-Stakes Testing, and Roles for Sociologists." *Sociology of Education* 78:170–74.

England, Paula and Su Li. 2006. "Desegregation Stalled: The Changing Gender Composition of College Majors, 1971–2002." *Gender and Society* 20(5):657–77.

Espenshade, Thomas J. and Alexandria Walton Radford. 2009. *No Longer Separate, Not Yet Equal: Race and Class in Elite College Admission and Campus Life.* Princeton, NJ: Princeton University Press.

Falsey, Barbara and Barbara Heyns. 1984. "The College Channel: Private and Public Schools Reconsidered." *Sociology of Education* 57:163–79.

Finkelstein, Amy, Sarah Taubman, Bill Wright, Mira Bernstein, Jonathan Gruber, Joseph P. Newhouse, Heidi Allen, and Katherine Baicker. 2011. "The Oregon Health Insurance Experiment: Evidence from the First Year." National Bureau of Economic Research, Working Paper 17190. Cambridge, MA: NBER.

Freiberg, Jerome. 1970. *The Effects of Ability Grouping on Interactions in the Classroom.* ERIC Document Reproduction Service. ED 053194.

Fryer, Roland G. Jr., and Steven D. Levitt. 2004a. "Understanding the Black-White Test Score Gap in the First Two Years of School." *Review of Economics and Statistics* 86:447–64.

Fryer, Roland G. Jr. and Steven D. Levitt. 2004b. "The Black-White Test Score Gap through Third Grade." *American Law and Economic Review* 8:249–81.

Gamoran, Adam. 1984. *Teaching, Grouping, and Learning: A study of the consequences of educational stratification.* Unpublished doctoral dissertation, University of Chicago.

Gamoran, Adam. 1986. "Instructional and Institutional Effects of Ability Grouping." *Sociology of Education* 59(4): 185–98.

Gamoran, Adam. 2001. "American Schooling and Educational Inequality: A Forecast for the 21st Century." *Sociology of Education* 74 Extra Issue:135–53.

Gaztambide-Fernández, Rubén. 2009. "What Is an Elite Boarding School?" *Review of Educational Research* 79:1090–1128.

Goldin, Claudia and Lawrence F. Katz. 2008. *The Race between Education and Technology.* Cambridge, MA: Harvard University Press.

Gracey, Harry. "Learning the Student Role: Kindergarten as Academic Boot Camp." Retrieved June 14, 2012 (http://www.sociology101.net/readings/Learning-the-Student-Role.pdf).

Granovetter, Mark S. 1974. *Getting a Job: A Study of Contacts and Careers.* Cambridge, MA Harvard University Press.

Haertel, E. H., T. James, and Henry M. Levin. 1987. "Introduction." In *Comparing Public and Private Schools: School Achievement,* vol. 2, edited by E. H. Haertel, T. James, and H. M. Levin. Philadelphia: Falmer Press.

Hallinan, Maureen T. 1987. "Ability Grouping and Student Learning." Pp. 41–69 in *The Social Organization of Schools: New Conceptualizations of the Learning Process,* edited by M. T. Hallinan. New York: Plenum.

Hallinan, Maureen T. 2001. "Sociological Perspectives on Black-White Inequalities in American Schooling." *Sociology of Education* 74 Extra Issue:50–70.

Hanson, S. L. 1994. "Lost Talent: Unrealized Educational Aspirations and Expectations among U.S. Youths." *Sociology of Education* 3:159–83.

Hargittai, Eszter. 2010. "Digital Na(t)ives? Variation in Internet Skills and Uses among Members of the Net Generation." *Sociological Inquiry* 80(1):92–113.

Hedges, Larry V. and Amy Nowell. 1998. "Black-White Test Score Convergence since 1965." Pp. 149-81 in *The Black-White Test Score Gap,* edited by Christopher Jencks and Meredith Phillips. Washington, DC: Brookings Institution Press.

Jacobs, Jerry. 1995. "Gender and Academic Specialties: Trends among Recipients of College Degrees in the 1980s," *Sociology of Education* 68(April):81–98.

Jaffe, Abraham J. and Walter Adams. 1970. *Academic and Socio-Economic Factors Related to Entrance and Retention at Two- and Four-Year Colleges in the Late 1960s.* New York: Bureau of Applied Social Research, Columbia University.

Lewis, L. S. and R. A. Wanner. 1979. "Private Schooling and the Status Attainment Process." *Sociology of Education* 52:99–112.

Lucas, Samuel R. and Mark Berends. 2002. "Sociodemographic Diversity, Correlated Achievement, and De Facto Tracking." *Sociology of Education* 75:328–48.

Mare, Robert D. 1981. "Change and Stability in Educational Stratification." *American Sociological Review* 46:72–87.

Marmot, Michael. 2004. *The Status Syndrome: How Social Standing Affects Our Health and Longevity.* New York: Owl Book, Henry Holt.

Martin, Steven P. 2006. "Trends in Marital Dissolution by Women's Education in the United States." *Demographic Research* 15, Article 20: 538-60. Accessed June 15, 2012 (http://www.demographic-research.org/Volumes/Vol15/20/15-20.pdf).

Mayer, Susan E. 2001. "How Did the Increase in Economic Inequality between 1970 and 1990 Affect Children's Educational Attainment?" *American Journal of Sociology* 107:1–32.

Meyer, John W. 1977. "Education as an Institution." *American Journal of Sociology* 83:55–77.

Montt, Guillermo. 2011. "Cross-national Differences in Educational Achievement Inequality." *Sociology of Education* 84:49–68.

Mulkey, Lynn M., Lala Carr Steelman, Sophia Catsambis, and Robert Crain. 2005. "The Long Term Effects of Ability Grouping on Mathematics Achievement." *Social Psychology of Education* 8:137–77.

Murnane, Richard J., John B. Willett, and Frank Levy. 1995. "The Growing Importance of Cognitive Skills in Wage Determination," *The Review of Economics and Statistics,* MIT Press, 77(2 May): 251-66.

National Research Council. 2011. *Incentives and Test-Based Accountability in Education.* Committee on Incentives and Test-Based Accountability in Public Education, M. Hout and S.W. Elliott, eds. Board on Testing and Assessment, Division of Behavioral and Social Sciences and Education. Washington, DC: The National Academies Press.

Nettles, Michael T. and Laura W. Perna. 1997. *The African American Education Data Book.* Vol. I: *Higher and Adult Education.* Fairfax, VA: Frederick D. Patterson Research Institute.

Oakes, Jeannie. 1985. *Keeping Track: How Schools Structure Inequality.* New Haven, CT: Yale University Press.

Oakes, Jeannie. 1992. "Can Tracking Research Inform Practice? Technical, Normative, and Political Considerations." *Educational Researcher* 21: 12–21.

Oakes, J., Wells, A. S., Jones, M., and Datnow, A. 1997. "Detracking: The Social Construction of Ability, Cultural Politics, and Resistance to Reform." *Teachers College Record,* 98(3): 482–510.

OECD. 2001. *Education at a Glance: OECD Indicators.* Paris: OECD.

OECD. 2010. *PISA 2009 Results: What Students Know and Can Do.* Vol. 1. Paris: Organisation for Economic Co-operation and Development (OECD).

Pallas, Aaron M. 2000. "The Effects of Schooling on Individual Lives." Pp. 499–525 in *Handbook of the Sociology of Education,* edited by M. T. Hallinan. New York: Kluwer Academic/Plenum.

Pallas, Aaron M., Doris R. Entwisle, Karl L. Alexander, and M. Francis Stulka. 1994. "Ability-Group Effects: Instructional, Social, or Institutional?" *Sociology of Education* 67:27-46.

Pascoe, C. J. 2007. *Dude You're a Fag: Masculinity and Sexuality in High School.* Berkeley: University of California Press.

Persell, Caroline Hodges. 1977. *Education and Inequality: The Roots and Results of Stratification in America's Schools.* New York: Free Press.

Persell, Caroline Hodges. 1990. *Understanding Society: An Introduction to Sociology.* Third Edition. New York: Harper and Row.

Persell, Caroline Hodges, Sophia Catsambis, and Cookson, Peter W. Jr. 1992. "Differential Asset Conversion: Class and Gendered Pathways to Selective Colleges." *Sociology of Education* 65:208–25.

Persell, Caroline Hodges and Giselle F. Hendrie. 2005. "Race, Education, and Inequality." Pp. 286–324 in *Blackwell Companion to Social Inequalities,* edited by M. Romero and E. Margolis. London: Basil Blackwell.

Persell, Caroline Hodges, Carrie James, Trivina Kang, and Karrie Snyder. 1999. "Gender and Education in Global Perspective." Pp. 407–40 in *Handbook on Gender Sociology,* edited by Janet S. Chafetz. New York: Plenum.

Reardon, Sean F. 2011. "The Widening Socioeconomic Status Achievement Gap: New Evidence and Possible Explanations." Pp. 91-116 in *Social Inequality and Economic Disadvantage,* edited by Richard Murname and Greg Duncan. Washington, DC: Brookings Institution.

Reuman, D. A. 1989. How Social Comparison Mediates the Relation between Ability-Grouping Practices and Students' Achievement Expectancies in Mathematics. *Journal of Educational Psychology,* 81(1): 78–89.

Rosenbaum, James E. 1976. *Making Inequality.* New York: Wiley-Interscience.

Rosenbaum, James E. 1980. "Track Misperceptions and Frustrated College Plans: An Analysis of the Effects of Tracks and Track Perceptions in the National Longitudinal Survey." *Sociology of Education* 53:74–88.

Ross, Catherine E. and John Mirowsky. 1989. "Explaining the Social Patterns of Depression: Control and Problem-solving or Support and Talking." *Journal of Health and Social Behavior* 30 (2 June): 206-19.

Ross, Catherine E. and Marieke M. Van Willigen. 1997. "Education and the Subjective Quality of Life." *Journal of Health and Social Behavior* 38 (September): 275-97.

Spence, Andrew Michael. 1974. *Market Signaling: Informational Transfer in Hiring and Related Screening Practices.* Cambridge: Harvard University Press.

Strickland, Jonathan. 2012. "How Web 3.0 Will Work." HowStuffWorks.com. Retrieved May 14, 2012 (http://computer.howstuffworks.com/web-30.htm).

Torche, Florencia. 2005. "Privatization Reform and Inequality of Educational Opportunity: The Case of Chile." *Sociology of Education* 78 (October): 316-43.

Tucker, M. S. 2011. *Standing on the Shoulders of Giants: An American Agenda for Education Reform.* Washington, DC: National Center on Education and the Economy.

Tyson, Karolyn. 2011. *Integration Interrupted: Tracking, Black Students, and Acting White after Brown.* New York: Oxford University Press.

Tyson, Karolyn. 2005. "It's Not 'a Black Thing': Understanding the Burden of Acting White and Other Dilemmas of High Achievement." *American Sociological Review* 70:582-605.

U.S. Department of Education, National Center for Education Statistics. 2009. *The Condition of Education 2009* (NCES 2009-081) Indicator 6.

Vanfossen, Beth E., James D. Jones and Joan Z. Spade. 1987. "Curriculum Tracking and Status Maintenance." *Sociology of Education.* 60(2): 104–22.

Weeden, Kim A. 2002. "Why Do Some Occupations Pay More than Others? Social Closure and Earnings Inequality in the U.S." *American Journal of Sociology* 108:55–101.

Wheelock, Anne. 1992. *Crossing the Tracks: How "Untracking'" Can Save America's Schools.* New York: New Press.

Whitehead, M., P. Townsend, and N. Davidsen. 1992. "Inequalities in Health: The Black Report/The Health Divide." London: Pelican.

Wilkinson, Roger G. 1996. *Unhealthy Societies: The Afflictions of Inequality.* London: Routledge.

Winter, Greg. 2003 (April 23). "New ammunition for backers of do-or-die exams." *New York Times,* p. B9.

World Bank. 2012. "School Enrollment (secondary), Private, Percent of Total Secondary School Enrollment in Private Education, 2002-2011, by Country." *World Development Indicators* (WDI). Accessed June 17, 2012.

Yeung, W. Jean, Caroline Hodges Persell, and Michael Chavez Reilly. 2010. "Intergenerational Racial Stratification and the Black-White Achievement Gap." Paper presented at the American Sociological Association annual meeting, Atlanta, Georgia, August.

Yeung, Wei-Jun Jean and Kathryn May Pfeiffer. 2009. "The Black-White Test Score Gap and Early Home Environment." *Social Science Research* 38:412–37.

Zernike, Kate. January 21, 2007. "Why Are There So Many Single Americans?" *New York Times.* Retrieved June 15, 2012 (http://www.nytimes.com/2007/01/21/weekinreview/21zernike.html?pagewanted=all).

CHAPTER 16

Alexander, Michelle. 2010. *The New Jim Crow: Mass Incarceration in the Age of Colorblindness.* New York: The New Press.

Associated Press. 2012. "NATO Restricts Air Strikes on Afghan Homes to Troop Self-Defense after Civilian Deaths." *Washington Post,* June 11. Retrieved June 19, 2012 (http://www.washingtonpost.com/world/asia_pacific/afghan-government-roadside-bomb-kills-pregnant-woman-and-family-en-route-to-hospital/2012/06/11/gJQABtW6TV_story.html).

Baker, Wayne. 2005. *America's Crisis of Values: Reality and Percpetion.* Princeton, NJ: Princeton University Press.

Becker, Howard. 1963. *Outsiders.* New York: Free Press.

Bergen, Peter and Katherine Tiedemann. 2010. "No Secrets in the Sky." *New York Times* (online edition, April 26:1-2). Retrieved April 26, 2010. (http://www.nytimes.com/2010/04/26/opinion/26bergen.html).

Beisel, Nicola. 1997. *Imperiled Innocents: Anthony Comstock and Family Reproduction.* Princeton, NJ: Princeton University Press.

Bittner, Egon. 1967. "The Police on Skid-Row: A 'study of peace-keeping.'" *American Sociological Review* 32:699–715.

Brooks, Clem and Jeff Manza. 2013. *Who is Us? Counterterrorism and the Dark Side of American Public Opinion.* New York: Russell Sage.

Cannon, Carl. 2005. "Petty Crime, Outrageous Punishment: Why the Three-Strikes Law Doesn't Work." *Reader's Digest,* October 2005. Retrieved Jun 24, 2012 (http://www.november.org/stayinfo/breaking3/Outrageous.html).

Cicourel, Aaron V. 1967. *The Social Organization of Juvenile Justice.* New York: Wiley.

Durkhieim, Emile. [1890] 1997. *The Division of Labor in Society.* New York: The Free Press.

Duster, Troy. 1970. *The Legislation of Morality: Law, Drugs, and Moral Judgment*. New York: The Free Press.

Entman, Robert and Andrew Rojeki. 2001. *The Black Image in the White Mind*. Chicago: University of Chicago Press.

Fox, Loren. 2003. *Enron: The Rise and Fall*. Hoboken, NJ: Wiley.

Garland, David. 2001. *Mass Imprisonment: Social Causes and Consequences*. Newbury Park, CA: Sage Publications.

Garland, David. 2010. *Peculiar Institution: America's Death Penalty in an Age of Abolition*. Cambridge, MA: Harvard University Press.

Goffman, Erving. 1959. *The Presentation of Self in Everday Life*. Glencoe, IL: The Free Press.

Goffman, Erving. 1963. *Behavior in Public Places: Notes on the Social Organization of Gatherings.*: Glence, IL: The Free Press.

Gordon-Reed, Annette. 2008. *The Hemingses of Monticello: An American Family*. New York: W. W. Norton.

Gusfield, Joseph R. 1963. *Symbolic Crusade: Status Politics and the American Temperance Movement*. Urbana: University of Illinois Press.

Hagan, John. 2010. *Who Are the Criminals? The Politics of Crime Policy from the Age of Roosevelt to the Age of Reagan*. Princeton, NJ: Princeton University Press.

Hagan, John and Holly Foster. 2009. "The Mass Incarceration of American Parents: Issues of Race/Ethnicity, Collateral Consequences, and Prisoner Re-Entry." *Annals of the American Academy of Political and Social Science* 623:195–213.

Hersh, Seymour. 2005. *Chain of Command: The Road from 9/11 to Abu Ghraib*. New York: Harper.

Klinkner, Philip and Rogers Smith. 1997. *The Unsteady March: The Rise and Decline of Racial Equality in America*. Chicago: University of Chicago Press.

Lamont, Michele and Virag Molnar. 2002. "The Study of Boundaries in the Social Sciences." *Annual Review of Sociology* 28:167–95.

Lichtblau, Eric. 2008. *Bush's Law: The Remaking of American Justice*. New York: Random House.

Manza, Jeff and Christopher Uggen. 2006. *Locked Out: Felon Disenfranchisment and American Democracy*. New York: Oxford University Press.

Mayer, Jane. 2008. *The Dark Side: The Inside Story of How the War on Terror Became a War on American Ideals*. New York: Doubleday.

Mendelberg, Tali. 2001. *The Race Card: Campaign Strategy, Implicit Messages, and the Norm of Equality*. Princeton, NJ: Princeton University Press.

New York Civil Liberties Union. 2011. *Stop and Frisk 2011 Report*. Retrieved June 24, 2012 (http://www.nyclu.org/files/publications/NYCLU_2011_Stop-and-Frisk_Report.pdf).

Okrent, David. 2010. *Last Call: The Rise and Fall of Prohibition*. New York: Scribner.

Pager, Devah. 2007. *Marked*. Chicago: University of Chicago Press.

Paul, Joel R. 2009. *Unlikely Allies: How a Merchant, a Playwright, and a Spy Saved the American Revolution*. New York: Riverhead Books.

Ranulf, Svend. 1938. *Moral Indignation and Middle Class Psychology*. Copenhagen: Munksgaard and Munksgaard.

Richards, Sarah. 2006. "Remembering the 'Naked Guy.'" *Salon*, May 22, 2006. Retrieved June 21, 2006 (http://www.salon.com/2006/05/22/naked_guy/)/

Rorabaugh, W. J. 1979. *The Alcoholic Republic: An American Tradition*. New York: Oxford University Press.

Sudnow, David. 1965. "Normal Crimes: Sociological Features of the Penal Code in a Public Defender Office," *Social Problems* 12: 255–76.

Sutherland, Edwin. 1949. *White Collar Crime*. New York: Dryden Press.

Terry, Charles E. and Mildred Pellens. 1970. *The Opium Problem*. Montclair, NJ: Patterson-Smith.

Tonry, Michael. 1995. *Malign Neglect: Race, Crime, and Punishment in America*. New York: Oxford University Press.

Wakefield, Sara and Christopher Uggen. 2010. "Incarceration and Stratification." *Annual Review of Sociology* 36:387–406.

Western, Bruce. 2006. *Punishment and Inequality in America*. New York: Russell Sage Foundation Press.

Williamson, Joel. 1984. *The Crucible of Race: Black-White Relations in the American South since Emancipation*. New York: Oxford University Press.

Zengerle, Jason. 2006. "The Naked Guy," New York Times (Dec. 31, 2006) (http://www.nytimes.com/2006/12/31/magazine/31naked.t.html).

CHAPTER 17

Alfano, Sean. 2009. "Poll: Women's Movement Worthwhile," CBS News (Feb. 11, 2009) (http://www.cbsnews.com/2100-500160_162-965224.html).

Alinsky, Saul. 1971. *Rules for Radicals: A Pragmatic Primer for Realistic Radicals*. New York: Vintage.

Amenta, Edwin, Neal Caren, Sheera Joy Olasky, and James E. Stobaugh. 2008. "All the SMOs Fit to Print." (http://www.socsci.uci.edu/~ea3/allthesmosfittoprint.pdf).

Brockett, Charles. 1993. "A Protest Cycle Resolution of the Repression/Protest Paradox." *Social Science History* 17(3):457–84.

Chenoweth, Erica and Maria J. Stephan. 2011. *Why Civil Resistance Works: The Strategic Logic of Nonviolent Conflict*. New York: Columbia University Press.

Cohen, Jean L. and Andrew Arato. 1992. *Civil Society and Political Theory*. Cambridge, MA: MIT Press.

Epstein, Barbara. 2001. "What Happened to the Women's Movement?" *Monthly Review* 53(1):1–13.

Gamson, Joshua. 1995. "Must Identity Movements Self-Destruct? A Queer Dilemma." *Social Problems* 42(3):390–407.

Gamson, William A. 1990. *The Strategy of Social Protest*. 2nd ed. Homewood, IL: Dorsey.

Inglehart, Ronald. 1977. *The Silent Revolution: Changing Values and Political Styles among Western Publics*. Princeton, NJ: Princeton University Press.

Jasper, James M. 1997. *The Art of Moral Protest: Culture, Biography, and Creativity in Social Movements*. Chicago: University of Chicago Press.

Jones, Jeffrey M. 2011. "New High of 55% of Americans Foresee Labor Unions Weakening," Gallup (Sept. 1, 2011) (http://www.gallup.com/poll/149300/New-High-Americans-Foresee-Labor-Unions-Weakening.aspx).

Kurzman, Charles. 1996. "Structural Opportunity and Perceived Opportunity in Social-Movement Theory: The Iranian Revolution of 1979." *American Sociological Review* 61(1):153–70.

Kurzman, Charles. 2002. "Bin Laden and Other Thoroughly Modern Muslims." *Contexts* 1(4):13–20.

Lenin, V. I. 1915. "The collapse of the Second International." *Lenin: Collected Works*, Vol. 21. Moscow: Progress Publishers.

Luker, Kristin. 1984. *Abortion and the Politics of Motherhood*. Berkeley and Los Angeles: University of California Press.

McAdam, Doug. 1982. *Political Process and the Development of Black Insurgency, 1930–1970*. Chicago: University of Chicago Press.

McAdam, Doug. 1988. *Freedom Summer*. New York: Oxford University Press.

McCarthy, John D. and Mayer N. Zald. 1977. "Resource Mobilization and Social Movements: A Partial Theory." *American Journal of Sociology* 82:1212–41.

Morin, Rich. 2012. "Rising Share of Americans See Conflict Between Rich and Poor," Pew Research Center (Jan. 11, 2012) (http://www.pewsocialtrends.org/2012/01/11/rising-share-of-americans-see-conflict-between-rich-and-poor).

Morris, Aldon D. 1984. *The Origins of the Civil Rights Movement: Black Communities Organizing for Change*. New York: Free Press.

Munson, Ziad W. 2008. *The Making of Pro-Life Activists: How Social Movement Mobilization Works*. Chicago: University of Chicago Press.

Newport, Frank. 2011. "Blacks, Whites Differ on Government's Role in Civil Rights," Gallup (Aug. 19, 2011) (http://www.gallup.com/poll/149087/Blacks-Whites-Differ-Government-Role-Civil-Rights.aspx)

Olson, Mancur. 1965. *The Logic of Collective Action: Public Goods and the Theory of Groups*. Cambridge, MA: Harvard University Press.

Pew Research Center. 2011a. "More Now Disagree with Tea Party—Even in Tea Party Districts" (Nov. 29, 2011) (http://www.people-press.org/2011/11/29/more-now-disagree-with-tea-party-even-in-tea-party-districts).

Pew Research Center. 2011b. "Frustration With Congress CouldHurt Republican Incumbents" (Dec. 15, 2011) (http://www.people-press.org/2011/12/15/section-2-occupy-wall-street-and-inequality).

Piven, Frances Fox and Richard A. Cloward. 1977. *Poor People's Movements: Why They Succeed, How They Fail*. New York: Vintage.

Roxborough, Ian. 2007. "Counterinsurgency." *Contexts* 6(2):15–21.

Saad, Lydia. 2010. "On 40th Earth Day, Image of Green Movement Still Positive," Gallup (April 22, 2010) (http://www.gallup.com/poll/127484/40th-Earth-Day-Image-Green-Movement-Positive.aspx).

Saad, Lydia. 2012. "'Pro-Choice' Americans at Record-Low 41%," Gallup (May 23, 2012) (http://www.gallup.com/poll/154838/pro-choice-americans-record-low.aspx).

Schwartz, Michael. 1976. *Radical Protest and Social Structure: The Southern Farmers' Alliance and Cotton Tenancy, 1880–1890*. Chicago: University of Chicago Press.

Schwartz, Michael. 2011. "The Egyptian Uprising: The Mass Strike in the Time of Neoliberal Globalization." *New Labor Forum* 20(3):32–43.

Silver, Nate. 2012. "Support for Gay Marriage Outweighs Opposition in Polls," The New York Times (May 9, 2012) (http://fivethirtyeight.blogs.nytimes.com/2012/05/09/support-for-gay-marriage-outweighs-opposition-in-polls).

Skocpol, Theda. 1979. *States and Social Revolutions: A Comparative Analysis of France, Russia, and China*. Cambridge: Cambridge University Press.

Snow, David A. and Robert D. Benford. 1988. "Ideology, Frame Resonance, and Participant Mobilization." *International Social Movement Research* 1:197–217.

Teixeira, Ruy. 2012. "Public Opinion Snapshot: Rich Drawing Away from the Poor and Middle Class," Center for American Progress (June 18, 2012) (http://www.americanprogress.org/issues/2012/06/snapshot_061812.html).

Tilly, Charles. 1986. *The Contentious French*. Cambridge, MA: Harvard University Press.

Walsh, Edward J. 1981. "Resource Mobilization and Citizen Protest in Communities around Three Mile Island." *Social Problems* 29:1–21.

CHAPTER 18

Auyero, Javier and Débora Swistun. 2009. *Flammable*. Oxford, UK: Oxford University Press.

Baskind, Chris. 2010. "5 Reasons Not to Drink Bottled Water." Mother Nature Network. Retrieved January 2011 (http://www.mnn.com/food/healthy-eating/stories/5-reasons-not-to-drink-bottled-water).

Bell, Michael Mayerfeld. 1994. *Childerley*. Chicago: University of Chicago Press.

Broughton, Edward. 2005. "The Bhopal Disaster and Its Aftermath: A Review." *Environmental Health: A Global Access Science Source* 4(6):1–6.

Brulle, Robert J. 1996. "Environmental Discourse and Social Movement Organizations: A Historical Perspective on the Development of U.S. Environmental Organizations." *Sociological Inquiry* 66(1):58–83.

Brulle, Robert J. and David Pellow. 2006. "Environmental Justice: Human Health and Environmental Inequalities." *Annual Review of Public Health* 27:103–24.

Bryskine, Sonya. 2010. "HK's 2010 Air Pollution Death Toll Nears 600." *Epoch Times*, October 14.

Bullard, Robert D. 1983. "Solid Waste Sites and the Houston Black Community." *Sociological Inquiry* 53:273–88.

Bullard, Robert D. 1990. *Dumping in Dixie*. Boulder, CO: Westview.

Californians Against Waste. 2011. "Plastic Bag Litter Pollution." Retrieved January 2011 (http://www.cawrecycles.org/issues/plastic_campaign/plastic_bags).

Carson, Rachel. 1962. *Silent Spring*. New York: Houghton Mifflin.

Catton, William R. Jr. and Riley E. Dunlap. 1980. "A New Ecological Paradigm for a Post-exuberant Sociology." *American Behavioral Scientist* 24:15–47.

Commission for Racial Justice. 1987. *Toxic Wastes and Race in the United States*. United Church of Christ. Public Data Access, Inc.

Cooperative for Assistance and Relief Everywhere. 2008. *In Search of Shelter: Mapping the Effects of Climate Change on Human Migration and Displacement*. Retrieved January 2011 (http://www.ciesin.columbia.edu/documents/ClimMigr-rpt-june09.pdf).

Cronon, William. 1992. *Nature's Metropolis*. New York: W.W. Norton & Company.

Department of Energy. 2011. "Coal." Retrieved January 2011 (http://www.energy.gov/energysources/coal.htm).

Diamond, Jared. 1995. "Easter Island's End." *Discover Magazine*, August, 63–9.

Diamond, Jared. 1997. *Guns, Germs, and Steel*. New York: W.W. Norton & Co.

Dollemore, Doug. 2008. "Newly Detected Air Pollutant Mimics Damaging Effects of Cigarette Smoke." American Chemical Society. Retrieved January 2011 (http://www.sciencedaily.com/releases/2008/08/080817223432.htm).

Duhigg, Charles. 2009. "Clean Waters Laws Are Neglected, at a Cost in Suffering." *New York Times*, September 13.

Dunlap, Riley E. and Aaron M. McCright. 2011. "Organized Climate Change Denial." Pp. 144–60 in *The Oxford Handbook of Climate Change*, edited by J. S. Dryzek, R. B. Norgaard, and D. Schlosberg. London: Oxford.

Durkheim, Emile. 1915. *Elementary Forms of Religious Life*. New York: Macmillan.

E Magazine. 2001. "A Run On the Banks." Retrieved January 2011 (http://www.emagazine.com/view/?507).

Ehrlich, Paul. 1968. *The Population Bomb*. New York: Ballantine Books.

Energy Information Administration. 2009. "Petroleum Statistics." Retrieved January 2011 (http://www.eia.doe.gov/energyexplained/index.cfm?page=oil_home#tab2).

Energy Information Administration. 2010a. "International Energy Outlook, 2010." Retrieved January 2011 (http://www.eia.doe.gov/oiaf/ieo/world.html).

Energy Information Administration. 2010b. "Renewable Energy Trends in Consumption and Electricity." Retrieved January 2011 (http://www.eia.doe.gov/cneaf/solar.renewables/page/trends/rentrends.html).

Environmental Protection Agency. 2011. "Non-hazardous Waste." Retrieved January 2011 (http://www.epa.gov/osw/nonhaz/index.htm).

Erikson, Kai. 1976. *Everything in Its Path*. New York: Simon & Schuster.

Fernandez, Manny. 2006. "A Study Links Trucks' Exhaust to Bronx Schoolchildren's Asthma." *New York Times*, October 29.

Freudenberg, William R. and Robert Gramling. 1989. "The Emergence of Environmental Sociology: Contributions of Riley E. Dunlap and William R. Catton, Jr." *Sociological Inquiry* 59(4):439–52.

Greenpeace. 2009. "Amazon Cattle Footprint." Retrieved January 2011 (http://www.greenpeace.org/international/en/publications/reports/amazon-cattle-footprint-mato/).

Greider, Thomas and Lorraine Garkovich. 1994. "Landscapes: The Social Construction of Nature and the Environment." *Rural Sociology* 59(1):1–24.

Hardin, Garrett. 1968. "The Tragedy of the Commons." *Science* 162(3859):1243–48.

Jones, P.D. and M.E. Mann (2004). "Climate over past millennia." *Reviews of Geophysics* 42: RG2002.

Jones, P.D., D.E. Parker, T.J. Osborn, and K.R. Briffa. 2005. "Global and hemispheric temperature anomalies—land and marine instrumental records." In *Trends: A Compendium of Data on Global Change*. Carbon Dioxide Information Analysis Center, Oak Ridge National Laboratory, U.S. Department of Energy, Oak Ridge, Tenn., U.S.A. (http://cdiac.esd.ornl.gov/trends/temp/jonescru/jones.html).

Klinenberg, Eric. 1999. "Denaturalizing Disaster: A Social Autopsy of the 1995 Chicago Heat Wave." *Theory and Society* 28(2):239–95.

Kolbert, Elizabeth. 2007. *Field Notes from a Catastrophe: Man, Nature, and Climate Change*. New York: Bloomsbury, USA.

Malinowksi, Bronislaw. 1948. *Magic, Science and Religion and Other Essays*. New York: The Free Press.

Marx, Karl and Friedrich Engels. 1977. *The German Ideology*. Pp. 159–91 in *Karl Marx: Selected Writings*, edited by David McLellan. Oxford: Oxford University Press.

Park, Robert E. and Ernest W. Burgess. 1925. *The City*. Chicago: University of Chicago Press.

Scarce, Rik. 2005. "More than Mere Wolves at the Door: Reconstructing Community amidst a Wildlife Controversy." Pp. 123–46 in *Mad about Wildlife*, edited by Ann Herda-Rapp and Theresa L. Goedeke. Boston: Brill.

Schnaiberg, Allan. 1980. *The Environment: From Surplus to Scarcity*. New York: Oxford University Press.

Sharkey, Patrick. 2007. "Survival and Death in New Orleans: An Empirical Look at the Human Impact of Katrina." *Journal of Black Studies* 37(4):482–501.

Social Science Research Council. 2006. "Understanding Katrina: Perspectives from the Social Sciences." Retrieved January 2011 (http://understandingkatrina.ssrc.org/).

Szasz, Andrew and Michael Meuser. 1997. "Environmental Inequalities: Literature Review and Proposals for New Directions in Research and Theory." *Current Sociology* 45(3):99–120.

Taylor, Alan. 1998. "'Wasty Ways': Stories of American Settlement." *Environmental History* 3(3):291–310.

Taylor, Peter J. and Frederick H. Buttel. 1992. "How Do We Know We Have Environmental Problems?' Science and the Globalization of Environmental Discourse." *Geoforum* 23(3):405–16.

UNDP. 2010. *Technology Needs Assessment for Climate Change*. New York: United Nations Development Programme.

Zalasiewicz, Jan, Mark Williams, Will Steffan, and Paul Crutzen. 2010. "The New World of the Anthropocene." *Environmental Science and Technology* 44(7):2228–31.

CHAPTER 19

Adler, Nancy E. and Joan Ostrove. 1999. "Socioeconomic Status and Health: What We Know and What We Don't." Pp. 3–15 in *Socioeconomic Status and Health in Industrial Nations: Social, Psychological, and Biological Pathways*, edited by Nancy E. Adler, Michael Marmot, Bruce S. McEwen, and Judith Stewart. New York: New York Academy of Sciences.

American Lung Association. 2012. "Key Facts about Smoking among Hispanics." Retrieved July 7, 2012 (http://www.lungusa.org/stop-smoking/about-smoking/facts-figures/hispanics-and-tobacco-use.html).

Arias, Elizabeth. 2011. "United States Life Tables, 2007." *National Vital Statistics Reports* 59(9):1–61.

Banks, James, Michael Marmot, Zoe Oldfield, and James P. Smith. 2006. "Disease and Disadvantaged in the United States and England." *Journal of the American Medical Association* 295(17):2037–45.

Barnato Amber E., F. Lee Luca, Douglas Staiger, David E. Wennberg, and Amitabh Chandra. 2005. "Hospital-Level Racial Disparities in Acute Myocardial Infarction Treatment and Outcomes." *Medical Care* 43(4):308–19.

Bulatao, Rudolfo A. and John B. Casterline, eds. 2001. *Global Fertility Transition*. New York: Population Council.

Case, Anne, Darren Lubotsky, and Christina Paxson. 2002. "Economic Status and Health in Childhood: The Origins of the Gradient." *American Economic Review* 92(5):1308–34.

Casper, Michele L., Elizabeth Barnett, G. Ishmael Williams, Joel A. Halverson, Valerie E. Braham, and Kurt J. Greenlund. 2003. *Atlas of Stroke Mortality: Racial, Ethnic, and Geographic Disparities in the United States*. Atlanta, GA: Department of Health and Human Services, Centers for Disease Control and Prevention.

Centers for Disease Control. 2011. *CDC Health Disparities and Inequalities Report" United States*. Atlanta, GA: Department of Health and Human Services, Centers for Disease Control and Prevention.

Chandra, Amitabh. 2009. "Who You Are and Where You Live: Race and the Geography of Health Care." *Medical Care* 47(2):135–37.

Christakis, Nicholas A. and James H. Fowler. 2007. "The Spread of Obesity in a Large Social Network over 32 years." *New England Journal of Medicine* 357(4):370–79.

Coale, Ansley J. 1973. "The Demographic Transition Reconsidered." Pp. 53–72 in *Proceedings: International Population Conference, Liege*. Liege: International Union for the Scientific Study of Populations.

Congressional Budget Office. 2011. *CBO's 2011 Long-Term Budget Outlook*. Pub. No. 4277. Washington, DC: CBO.

Cutler, David M., Adriana Lleras-Muney, and Tom Vogl. 2008. "Socioeconomic Status and Health: Dimensions and Mechanisms." NBER Working Papers 14333. Cambridge, MA: National Bureau of Economic Research.

Davis, Kingsley. 1963. "The Theory of Change and Response in Modern Demographic History." *Population Index* 29:145–66.

Durkheim, Emile. [1897] 2006. *On Suicide*. London: Penguin Classics.

Economist Intelligence Unit. 2010. *The Quality of Death: Ranking End-of-Life Care across the World*. London: The Economist.

Ehrlich, Paul. 1968. *The Population Time Bomb*. New York: Ballantine Books.

Elo, Irma, Cassio M. Turra, Burt Kestenbaum, and B. Renee Ferguson. 2004. "Mortality among Elderly Hispanics in the United States: Past Evidence and New Results." *Demography* 41:109–28.

Hirschman, Charles. 1994. "Why Fertility Changes." *Annual Review of Sociology* 20:203–33.

Hoefer, Michael, Nancy Rytina, and Bryan C. Baker. 2010. "Estimates of the Unauthorized Immigrant Population Residing in the United States, January 2010." Office of Immigration Statistics, Department of Homeland Security (http://www.dhs.gov/xlibrary/assets/statistics/publications/ois_ill_pe_2010.pdf).

Institute of Medicine. 2002. *Unequal Treatment: Confronting Racial and Ethnic Disparities in Health Care.* Washington, DC: National Academies Press.

Kohler, Hans-Peter, Francesco C. Billari, and Antonio Ortega. 2002. "The Emergence of Lowest-Low Fertility in Europe." *Population and Development Review* 28(4):641–80.

Krieger, Nancy. 1987. "Shades of Difference: Theoretical Underpinnings of the Medical Controversy on Black/White Differences in the United States, 1830–1870," *International Journal of Health Services* 17(2):259–78.

Lam, David. 2011. "How the World Survived the Population Bomb: Lessons from 50 Years of Extraordinary Demographic History." *Demography* 48(4):1231–62.

Link, Bruce G. and Jo C. Phelan. 1995. "Social Conditions and Fundamental Causes of Disease." *Journal of Health and Social Behavior* 80–94.

Lleras-Muney, Adriana. 2005. "The Relationship between Education and Adult Mortality in the United States." *Review of Economic Studies* 72:189–221.

Malthus, Thomas Robert. 1798. *An Essay on the Principle of Population.* London: J. Johnson.

Marmot, Michael. 2004. *The Status Syndrome: How Social Standing Affects Our Health and Longevity.* New York: Holt.

McNeil, Donald. 2011. "Broad Disparities Seen in Americans' Ills." *New York Times,* January 13.

National Center for Health Statistics. 2011. "National Vital Statistics Reports: United States Life Tables, 2007." Washington, DC: US Department of Health and Human Services.

National Institute on Aging, National Institutes of Health, U.S. Department of Health and Human Services, and the U.S. Department of State. 2007. *Why Population Aging Matters: A Global Perspective.*

National Hospice and Palliative Care Organization. 2011. *NHPCO Facts and Figures: Hospice Care in America* (http://www.nhpco.org/files/public/Statistics_Research/2011_Facts_Figures.pdf).

Nonnemaker, Lynn and Shelly Ann Sinclair. 2011. "Medicare Beneficiaries Out-of-Pocket Spending for Health Care." Washington, DC: American Association of Retired Persons Policy Institute.

Notestein, Frank Wallace. 1953. "Economic Problems of Population Change." Pp. 13–31 in *Proceedings of the Eighth International Conference of Agricultural Economists.*

Omran, Abdel R. 1971. "The Epidemiologic Transition: A Theory of the Epidemiology of Population Change." *Milbank Memorial Fund Quarterly* 49(4/1):509–38.

Pew Research Center. 2009. "Growing Old in America: Expectations vs. Reality." Philadelphia: Pew Foundation.

Read, Jen'nan Ghazal and Bridget K. Gorman. 2010. "Gender and Health Inequality." *Annual Review of Sociology* 36:371–86.

Rose, Geoffrey. 1985. "Sick Individuals and Sick Populations." *International Journal of Epidemiology* 14:32–38.

Roseboom, Tessa, Susanne de Rooij, and Rebecca Painter. 2006. "The Dutch Famine and Its Long-Term Consequences for Adult Health." *Early Human Development* 82:485–91.

Skinner, Jonathan, Douglas Staiger, Amitabh Chandra, Julie Lee, and Mark McClellan. 2005. "Mortality after Acute Myocardial Infarction in Hospitals that Disproportionately Treat Black Patients." *Circulation* 112:2634–41.

Smith, Kirsten P. and Nicholas Christakis. 2008. "Social Networks and Health." *Annual Review of Sociology* 34:405–29.

Springer, Kristen W. and Dawne W. Mouzon. 2011. "'Macho Men' and Preventative Health Care: Implications for Older Men in Different Social Classes." *Journal of Health and Social Behavior* 52: 212-227.

Stewart, Susan T., David M. Cutler and Allison B. Rosen. 2009. "Forecasting the Effects of Obesity and Smoking on U.S. Life Expectancy". *New England Journal of Medicine* (361) 23: 2252–2260.

U.S. Department of Health and Human Services. 2008. *Healthy People 2020 Framework.* Washington, DC: USDHHS.

World Bank. 2011. "World Development Indicators: Life Expectancy at Birth." (http://data.worldbank.org/indicator/SP.DYN.LE00.IN).

World Health Organization. 2011. "Preamble to the Constitution of the World Health Organization." Adopted by the International Health Conference, New York, June 19–July 22, 1946; signed on 22 July 1946 by the representatives of 61 states (Official Records of the World Health Organization, no. 2, p. 100) and entered into force on April 7, 1948. Retrieved March 28, 2011 (http://www.who.int/suggestions/faq/en).

World Health Organization. 2008. *Planning Human Resources Development to Achieve Priority Health Programme Goals.* Human Resources for Health Development, World Health Organization. Pp. 7.

CHAPTER 20

Abramowitz, Michael. 2008. "White House Defends NAFTA as Bush Meets With Heads of Mexico, Canada," *Washington Post,* April 22.

Audley, John J., Demetrios G. Papademetriou, Sandra Polaski and Scott Vaughan. 2003. *NAFTA's Promise and Reality: Lessons from Mexico for the Hemisphere.* Carnegie Endowment for International Peace.

Bacon, David. 2012. "How US Farm Policies Fuel Mexico's Great Migration." *The Nation* January 23.

Bernstein, Jared and Lawrence Mishel. 2007. "Economy's Gains Fail to Reach Most Workers' Paychecks." *Economic Policy Institute Briefing Papers* 195.

Bronfenbrenner, Kate. 2000. *Uneasy Terrain: The Impact of Capital Mobility on Workers, Wages and Union Organizing* [Electronic version]. Ithaca, NY: Author. http://digitalcommons.ilr.cornell.edu/reports/3/

Carrere, Celine and Maurice Schiff. 2004. "On the Geography of Trade: Distance Is Alive and Well." *World Bank Policy Research Working Papers* #3206, February.

Chang, Ha-joon. 2002. *Kicking Away the Ladder.* London: Anthem Press.

China Labor Watch. 2011. *Tragedies of Globalization: The Truth Behind Electronics Sweatshops.* http://www.chinalaborwatch.org/pro/proshow-149.html.

Clinton, William J. 1993. "Remarks at the Signing Ceremony for the Supplemental Agreements to the North American Free Trade Agreement." *Public Papers of the Presidents of the United States* Vol. 2. Washington, DC: US Government Printing Office.

DeLong, J. Bradford. 2006. "Neoliberalism has a Patchy Mexican Record." *Taipei Times* September 30.

Dicken, Peter. 2011. *Global Shift.* New York. Guilford.

Duhigg, Charles and David Barbosa. 2012. "In China, the Human Costs That Are Built Into an iPad." *New York Times* January 26.

Duhigg, Charles and Keith Bradsher. 2012. "How the U.S. Lost Out on iPhone Work." *New York Times* January 12. Retrieved May 18, 2012 (http://www.nytimes.com/2012/01/22/business/apple-america-and-a-squeezed-middle-class.html).

Feller, Gordon. 2008. "Focus: NAFTA: A Controversial Treaty," *Global Finance* April.

Franklin, Stephen. 1993. "Unions Urge Clinton To Renegotiate Trade Pact." *Chicago Tribune* February 18.

Friedman, Thomas. 2005. *The World Is Flat: A Brief History of the Twenty-first Century.* New York: Farrar, Straus and Giroux.

Gindin, Sam and Leo Panitch. 2012. *The Making of Global Capitalism.* London: Verso.

Henriques, Gisele and Raj Patel. 2004. "NAFTA, Corn, and Mexico's Agricultural Trade Liberalization." *Americas Program Special Report.*

Hirst, Paul, Grahame Thompson, and Simon Bromley. 2009. *Globalization in Question.* 3rd ed. London: Polity Press.

Hufbauer, Gary Clyde and Jeffrey J. Schott. 1993. *NAFTA: An Assessment.* Washington, D.C.: Institute for International Economics.

Hurd, John. 1975. "Railways and the Expansion of Markets in India." *Explorations in Economic History* 12:263–68.

Koopman, Robert, Zhi Wang and Shang-Jin Wei. 2008. "How much of Chinese exports is really made in China?" *VoxEU* August 8, 2008. Retrieved May 18, 2012 (http://www.voxeu.org/index.php?q=node/1524).

Office of the United States Trade Representative. 2008. "NAFTA: Myths versus Facts."

O'Rourke, Kevin and Jeffrey G. Williamson. 2000. *Globalization and History: The Evolution of a Nineteenth Century Atlantic Economy.* Cambridge, MA: MIT Press.

Public Citizen. 2008. "Debunking USTR Claims in Defense of NAFTA: The Real NAFTA Score 2008." Retrieved July 27, 2012. (http://www.citizen.org/documents/NAFTA_USTR_Debunk_web.pdf. Accessed July 27, 2012).

Rugman, Alan. 2005. *The Regional Multinationals: MNEs and "Global" Strategic Management.* Cambridge, UK: Cambridge University Press.

Scott, Robert E. 2011. "Heading South: US-Mexico Trade and Job Displacement After NAFTA." *Economic Policy Institute Briefing Papers* 308.

Sutcliffe, Bob and Andrew Glyn. 2010. "Measures of Globalization and Their Misinterpretation." Pp. 61-78 in *Handbook of Globalization,* edited by Jonathan Michie, 2nd ed. Cheltenham, UK: Edward Elgar.

United Nations Conference on Trade and Development (UNCTAD). 2007. *Trade and Development Report.*

United Nations Conference on Trade and Development (UNCTAD). 2011. *World Investment Report.*

United States Department of Commerce, Census Bureau, Foreign Trade Division. 2012. Retrieved May 18, 2012 (http://www.trade.gov/mas/ian/build/groups/public/@tg_ian/documents/webcontent/tg_ian_003364.pdf).

CREDITS

Text Credits

CHAPTER 1   **p. 18:** U.S. Census Bureau.

CHAPTER 2   **p. 40:** Gallup Poll: http://www.gallup.com/poll/28417/most-americans-approve-interracial-marriages.aspx.

CHAPTER 3   **p. 65:** Davidson, Judy. 1984. Structures of Social Action: Studies in Conversation Analysis, edited by John Heritage and J. Maxwell Atkinson. New York: Cambridge University Press.; **p. 77:** Reproduced with permission. Copyright © (1955) Scientific American, Inc. All rights reserved.; **p. 79:** Table 2, Distribution of Breakoff Points- Page 376 in Milgram, Stanley. 1963. "Behavioral Study of Obedience." *Journal of Abnormal and Social Psychology* 1963 Vol. 67:371–378.

CHAPTER 4   **p. 93:** Voyaging Through U.S. Jobs, September 7, 2009 by Donald Marron; **p. 94:** Business Insider, from http://economicdata.blogspot.com/.

CHAPTER 5   **p. 118:** *Talk of Love: How Culture Matters,* Ann Swidler is published by University of Chicago Press; **p. 119:** Appadurai, Arjun. 1993. *Modernity At Large: Cultural Dimensions of Globalization.* University of Minnesota Press.; **p. 123:** Appadurai, Arjun. 1993. *Modernity At Large: Cultural Dimensions of Globalization.* University of Minnesota Press.

CHAPTER 6   **p. 142:** Lemert, Charles. 1997. *Social Things.* Lanham, MD: Rowman and Littlefield.; **p. 148:** From *Power and Powerlessness: Quiescence and Rebellion in an Appalachian Valley* Copyright 1980 by John Gaventa. Used with permission of the University of Illinois Press.; **p. 166:** Bartels, Larry M; *Unequal Democracy.* © 2008 by Russell Sage Foundation. Published Princeton University Press. Reprinted by permission of Princeton University Press.; **p. 155:** Andrew Leigh, "How Closely Do top Income Shares Track Other Measures of Inequality?" *The Economic Journal* 117 (November 2007); **p. 158:** Adapted from Lawrence Mischel and Josh Bivens, Occupy Wall Streeters are right about skewed economic rewards in the United States, Economic Policy Institute Briefing Paper #331, 2011.; **p. 165:** 2006 International Social Survey Program, Role of Government Module (Author's Tabulations). www.issp.org.; **p. 165:** General Social Survey Cumulative File (www.norc.gss).

CHAPTER 7   **p. 186:** NBER Macroeconomics Annual 20 (2005).; **p. 188:** Erik Olin Wright and Rachel Dwyer, "The American Jobs Machine: Is the New Economy Creating Good Jobs?" Boston Review 25, no. 6, 2000; **p. 194:** U.S. Department of Labor.

CHAPTER 8   **p. 208:** Burgess' concentric zones map of Chicago from Park and Burgess "The City" 1925 Natural Areas and Urban Zones.; **p. 217:** http://www.socialexplorer.com/pub/maps/map3.aspx?g=0&mapi=se0006&themei=48548.0720707501.135.70 19&l=-88.05661393209377&r=-87.83384063269213&t=43.101578056812286&b=43.026788011193275&rndi=1&style=seq%20%2D%20Hipster; **p. 217:** http://www.socialexplorer.com/pub/maps/map3.aspx?g=0&mapi=se0007&themei=48682.7143368 036.6706.809&l=-88.05661393209377&r=-87.83384063269213&t=43.101578056812 286&b=43.026788011193275&rndi=1&style=seq%20%2D%20Hipster; **p. 217:** http://www.socialexplorer.com/pub/maps/map3.aspx?g=0&mapi=se0001&themei=48796.026 4846853.3921.068&l=-88.05661393209377&r=-87.83384063269213&t=43.1015780 56812286&b=43.026788011193275&rndi=1&style=seq%20%2D%20Hipster; **p. 217:** http://www.socialexplorer.com/pub/maps/map3.aspx?g=0&mapi=se0012&themei=767 701.499323037.889.5063&l=-88.05661393209377&r=-87.83384063269213&t=43.1 01578056812286&b=43.026788011193275&rndi=1&style=seq%20%2D%20Hipster; **p. 218:** Logan, John R. and Brian J. Stults. 2011. "The Persistence of Segregation in the Metropolis." (http://www.s4.brown.edu/us2010/Data/Report/report2.pdf.); **p. 219:** New Evidence on the Urbanization of Global Poverty, Martin Ravallion, Shaohua Chen, Prem Sangraula Reviewed work(s), Published by: Population Council Stable URL: http://www.jstor.org/stable/25487618.The World Bank.; **p. 220:** NYTE New York Talk Exchange; **p. 221:** NYTE New York Talk Exchange; **p. 222:** http://www.socialexplorer.com/pub/maps/map3.aspx?g=0&mapi=se0006&themei=48543.4854230817.6460.988&l=-80.50251592830037&r=-79.94576459258697&t=25.83729363977909&b=25.685099065 303802&rndi=1&style=seq%20%2D%20Hipster; **p. 222:** http://www.socialexplorer.com/pub/maps/map3.aspx?g=0&mapi=se0007&themei=48680.7061367748.5572.016&l=-80.50251592830037&r=-79.94576459258697&t=25.83729363977909&b=25.685099065 303802&rndi=1&style=seq%20%2D%20Hipster; **p. 222:** http://www.socialexplorer.com/pub/maps/map3.aspx?g=0&mapi=se0001&themei=48793.3401893868.6452.817&l=-80.50251592830037&r=-79.94576459258697&t=25.83729363977909&b=25.685099065 303802&rndi=1&style=seq%20%2D%20Hipster; **p. 222:** http://www.socialexplorer.com/pub/maps/map3.aspx?g=0&mapi=se0012&themei=767694.843113658.635.5143&l=-80.50251596260044&r=-79.9457645582869&t=25.837290287017822&b=25.685101747 512817&rndi=1&style=seq%20%2D%20Hipster.

CHAPTER 9   **p. 233:** Maddison, A. (2006),The World Economy: Volume 1: A Millennial Perspective, OECD Publishing. http://dx.doi.org/10.1787/9789264022621-en; **p. 233:** Volume 2: Historical Statistics, Development Centre Studies, OECD Publishing. http://dx.doi.org/10.1787/9789264022621-en; **p. 234:** U.S. Census Bureau; **p. 235:** Originally published in Edward N. Wolff, "Recent Trends in Household Wealth in the United States: Rising Debt and the Middle-Class Squeeze- An Update to 2007," Working Paper no. 589, Annandale-on-Hudson, N. Y.:Levy Economic Institute of Bard College, 2010. Reprinted by permission of the publisher.; **p. 236:** U.S. Bureau of the Census; **p. 236:** By Permission, Economagic.com; **p. 238:** *The Constant Flux: A Study of Class Mobility in Industrial Nations* by Erikson & Goldthorpe (1992) Table.2.1. By permission of Oxford University Press; **p. 245:** The State of Working America, Economic Policy Institute http://stateofworkingamerica.org/charts/hourly-wage-and-compensation-growth-for-productionnonsupervisory-workers-and-productivity-1947-2009/; **p. 246:** U.S. Department of Treasury; **p. 246:** Economic Policy Institute. Available: http://www.epi.org/publication/state_of_working_america_preview_the_declining_value_of_minimum_wage/; **p. 247:** Jeffrey Winters. 2011. *Oligarchy.* Reprinted with the permission of Cambridge University Press.; **p. 247:** Economic Policy Institute – The State of Working America http://stateofworkingamerica.org/charts/share-of-pre-tax-income-growth-1979-2007/ **p. 250:** Blanden, Jo (2009) "How much can we learn from international comparisons of social mobility?" Working Document, Centre for the Economics of Education, London School of Economics, ISSN 2045-6557, online http://cee.lse.ac.uk/ceedps/ceedp111.pdf; **p. 251:** Corak, Miles (2012) Inequality from generation to generation: The United States in Comparison. Forthcoming in "The Economics of Inequality, Poverty, and Discrimination in the 21st Century" edited by Robert Rycroft. ABC-CLIO, forthcoming; **p. 253:** US Census Bureau.

CHAPTER 10   **p. 268:** Weber, Max. 1978. Economy and Society. Berkeley: University of California Press.; **p. 277:** U.S. Census Bureau 2011; U.S Bureau of Labor Statistics 2012; **p. 277:** Kochlar, Rakesh, Richard Fry, and Paul Taylor. 2011. Wealth Gap Rises to Record Highs Between Whites, Blacks and Latinos. Washington DC: Pew Research Center. **p. 280:** Bureau of Labor Statistics (2011); **p. 280:** Bureau of Justice Statistics (2011); **p. 280:** Digest of Educational Statistics: 2010. (http://nces.ed.gov/programs/digest/d10/tables/dt10_008.asp?referrer=list). Accessed February 22, 2012, National Center for Education Statistics; **p. 280:** "Table 115." Digest of Educational Statistics: 2010. (http://nces.ed.gov/programs/digest/d10/tables/dt10_115.asp?referrer=list). Accessed February 22, 2012, National Center for Educational Statistics (2011a); **p. 281:** Center for Disease Control and Prevention (2011); **p. 287:** U.S. Census Bureau.

CHAPTER 11   **p. 300:** http://www.bsos.umd.edu/socy/vanneman/endofgr/cpsempsex.html; **p. 300:** National Center for Education Statistics (http://nces.ed.gov/programs/digest/d10/tables/dt10_279.asp; **p. 302:** The Institute for Women's Policy Research 2011; **p. 313:** Paula England's calculations from Online College Social Life Survey, 2010 version.; **p. 314:** Paula England's calculations from Online College Social Life Survey, 2010 version.

CHAPTER 12   **p. 323:** 2011. Migration and Remittances Factbook. ©World Bank. License: Creative Commons Attribution CC BY 3.0 (http://creativecommons.org/licenses/by/3.0).; **p. 326:** DHS Yearbooks; **p. 336:** Based on data from the New Immigrant Survey, NIS-2003; **p. 343:** 2011. Migration and Remittances Factbook. ©World Bank. License: Creative Commons Attribution CC BY 3.0 (http://creativecommons.org/licenses/by/3.0).

CHAPTER 13   **p. 356:** U.S. Census Bureau, Current Population Survey, 1970, 1980, 1990, 1995, 2000, 2005, 2011 Annual Social and Economic Supplements.; **p. 359:** The Pew Research Center for the People and the Press, http://pewresearch.org/pubs/1802/decline-marriage-rise-new-families; **p. 362:** *Hard Choices: How Women Decide About Work, Career, and Motherhood,* by Kathleen Gerson, © 1985 by the Regents of the University of California. Published by the University of California Press.; **p. 365:** The Pew Research Center, http://www.pewsocialtrends.org/2010/11/18/the-decline-of-marriage-and-rise-of-new-families/5/; **p. 367:** *The Unfinished Revolution: Coming of Age in a New Era of Gender, Work, and Family* by Kathleen Gerson (2011) Fig. 5.3 **p. 122.** By permission of Oxford University Press, Inc.; **p. 368:** The Pew Research Center, http://www.pewsocialtrends.org/2010/11/18/the-decline-of-marriage-and-rise-of-new-families/3/; **p. 371:** Rebecca Ray, Janet Gornick, and John Schmitt, 2009. "Parental Leave Policies in 21 Countries: Assessing Generosity and Gender Equality," Figure 1, page 6. (Center for Economic Policy Research, Washington, DC.

CHAPTER 14   **p. 385:** religionfacts.com; **p. 400:** Source: Pew Research Center's Forum on Religion & Public Life, "Religion Among the Millennials," (c) 2010, Pew Research Center, http://www.pewforum.org.; **p. 400:** Dillon, Michelle and Paul Wink. 2007. *In the Course of a Lifetime.* Berkeley: University of California Press.; **p. 406:** Based on data from Putnam and Campbell (2010).

CHAPTER 15   **p. 414:** UNESCO Institute for Statistics (USI) http://stats.usi.unesco.org; **p. 417:** Arum, Richard and Josipa Roksa. 2010. *Academically Adrift: Limited Learning on College Campuses.* Chicago: University of Chicago Press.; **p. 419:** US. Department of Commerce, Census Bureau, Current Population Survey (CPS), March 2009; **p. 424:** 2007 Census of Governments Survey of Local Government Finances – School Systems. U.S. Census Bureau.

CHAPTER 16   **p. 466:** Bureau of Justice Statistics (Sentencing Project); **p. 469:** Felony Sentences in State Courts series (Washington, D.C.: U.S. Government Printing Office, 1989, 2004).

CHAPTER 17   **p. 494:** Gamson, William A. 1990. *The Strategy of Social Protest*, 2nd edn. Homewood, IL: Dorsey, Wadsworth Publishing Company

CHAPTER 18   **p. 515:** Scripps Institution of Oceanography, UCSD, http://scrippsco2.ucsd.edu/program_history/keeling_curve_lessons.html; **p. 515:** Created using data from Jones & M.E. Mann. 2004. Climate over past millenia. Reviews of Geophysics, 42, article number RG2002 and Jones, P.D., D.E. Parker, T.J. Osborn & K.R. Briffa. 2005. Global and hemispheric temperature anomalies – land and marine instrumental records. In Trends: A Compendium of Data on Global Change. Carbon Dioxide Information Analysis Center, Oak Ridge National Laboratory, U.S. Department of Energy, Oak Ridge, Tenn., U.S.A. [http://cdiac.esd.ornl.gov/trends/temp/jonescru/jones.html]; **p. 528:** Energy Information Administration 2010a.

CHAPTER 19   **p. 540:** U.S. Census Bureau; **p. 543:** U.S. Census Bureau; **p. 547:** U. S. Census Bureau; **p. 557:** CDC.

CHAPTER 20   **p. 570:** Paul Hirst, Grahame Thompson and Simon Bromley, Globalization in Question, 3rd edition, (Cambridge: Polity, 2009)

Photo Credits

Cover: Jon Helgason / Alamy; **Design Elements:** CVI Textures / Alamy; CVI Textures / Alamy.

CHAPTER 1   **p. 2:** Pearson; **p. 3:** PUNIT PARANJPE/AFP/Getty Images/Newscom; **p. 5 (bl):** Dominic Harris / Alamy; **(br):** Ingolf Pompe/LOOK Die Bildagentur der Fotografen GmbH / Alamy; **(cr):** TIPS/Photoshot; **(tl):** age fotostock / SuperStock; **p. 6 (br):** Photo by Yaroslava/Nik Mills Studio; **(t):** age fotostock / SuperStock; **p. 7:** Oleksiy Maksymenko Photos/Alamy; **p. 10:** Myrleen Pearson/Alamy; **p. 12, (tr):** ZUMA Wire Service / Alamy; **(c):** TIPS/Photoshot; **p. 14 (bl):** Jim West / Alamy; **(c):** jon le-bon/Shutterstock; **p. 15:** A. Ramey / PhotoEdit; **p. 17:** Dominic Harris / Alamy; **p. 18:** Underwood & Underwood/Corbis; **p. 20:** AFP/Getty Images/Newscom; **p. 21:** SHOUT/Alamy; **p. 22:** Deco / Alamy; **p. 23 (t):** Ingolf Pompe/LOOK Die Bildagentur der Fotografen GmbH / Alamy; **p. 24 (tr):** ZUMA Wire Service / Alamy; **(br):** A. Ramey / PhotoEdit; **p. 25 (br):** Ingolf Pompe/LOOK Die Bildagentur der Fotografen GmbH / Alamy; **(cr):** Underwood & Underwood/Corbis.

CHAPTER 2   **p. 26:** Pearson; **p. 27:** Mark Allen Johnson/ZUMA Press/Newscom; **p. 28:** Sean Cayton / The Image Works; **p. 29 (br):** Ikon Images / Alamy; **(bl):** Jeff Greenberg / Alamy; **(tl):** Ian Lishman/Juice Images/Glow Images; **(cr):** Lichtmeister / Shutterstock; **p. 30:** Ian Lishman/Juice Images/Glow Images; **p. 31:** F1online digitale Bildagentur GmbH/Alamy; **p. 36:** Lichtmeister / Shutterstock; **p. 37:** RichardBakerHeathrow / Alamy; **p. 38:** Jeff Greenberg / Alamy; **p. 41:** Mauro Fermariello/Photo Researchers, Inc.; **p. 45 (cr):** David Grossman/Alamy; **(tr):** Tetra Images / Alamy; **p. 47:** Leila Cutler / Alamy; **p. 48:** Regina and Stanley. Marcy Houses. Brooklyn, NY, 1996. Photograph (c) Regina Monfort; **p. 49:** Jeremy Woodhouse/Getty Images; **p. 51:** Ikon Images / Alamy; **p. 54:** F1online digitale Bildagentur GmbH/ Alamy; **p. 55:** RichardBakerHeathrow / Alamy; **p. 56:** Mauro Fermariello/Photo Researchers, Inc.; **p. 57:** Ikon Images / Alamy.

CHAPTER 3   **p. 58:** Pearson; **p. 59:** Gideon Mendel/In Pictures/Corbis; **p. 61 (br):** Caro / Alamy; **(cl):** Corbis Flirt / Alamy; **(cr):** D. Hurst/Alamy; **(tl):** Ros Drinkwater/ Alamy; **p. 62:** Ros Drinkwater/Alamy; **p. 63:** PhotoAlto sas / Alamy; **p. 64:** D. Hurst/ Alamy; **p. 65:** Michael Newman / PhotoEdit; **p. 66:** KCNA KCNA/REUTERS; **p. 67 (tr):** JASON REED/Reuters /Landov; **(cr):** Everett Collection/Newscom; **(bl):** JOSHUA ROBERTS/UPI/Newscom; **(cl):** MANDEL NGAN/AFP/Getty Images/ Newscom; **p. 68:** Gary Conner/PhotoEdit; **p. 70:** Randy Duchaine / Alamy; **p. 71:** Dennis MacDonald / Alamy; **p. 72:** Corbis Flirt / Alamy; **p. 73 (tl):** © NetPics/ Alamy; **(tc):** ArtBabii / Alamy; **(cl):** CJG - Technology / Alamy; **p. 74:** Caro / Alamy; **p. 76:** Robin Nelson / PhotoEdit; **p. 78:** From the film Obedience (c) 1968 by Stanley Milgram, (c) renewed 1993 Alexandra Milgram; **p. 80:** Philip G. Zimbardo, Inc.; **p. 81:** PhotoAlto sas / Alamy; **p. 81 (bc):** Corbis Flirt / Alamy; **(tr):** KCNA KCNA/ REUTERS; **p. 83:** Robin Nelson / PhotoEdit.

CHAPTER 4   **p. 84:** Pearson; **p. 85:** Roger-Viollet / Topham / The Image Works; **p. 86:** AP Photo/Franka Bruns; **p. 87 (cr):** A. Astes/Alamy; **(br):** PCN Photography/ Alamy; **(tl):** Stephen Barnett/ImageState / Alamy; **(cl):** Tom Mackie/Alamy; **(bl):** Andersen Ross/Getty Images; **p. 88:** Stephen Barnett/ImageState / Alamy; **p. 89:** Magnum Distribution/Magnum Photos; **p. 90:** A. Astes/Alamy; **p. 91:** Bruce Roberts/ Photo Researchers, Inc.; **p. 96 (c):** Tom Mackie/Alamy; **(tr):** Topham/The Image Works; **p. 98:** PCN Photography/Alamy; **p. 99:** Steve Gorton/DK Images; **p. 100:** Phanie/ SuperStock; **p. 101 (cl):** David Grossman/Alamy; **(bl):** Jeff Greenberg/Alamy; **(cr):** Monkey Business/Fotolia LLC; **p. 104:** Andersen Ross/Getty Images; **p. 105:** Editorial Image, LLC/Alamy; **p. 107 (tr):** Magnum Distribution/Magnum Photos; **(br):** Bruce Roberts/Photo Researchers, Inc.; **p. 108 (cr):** Tom Mackie/Alamy; **(br):** Steve Gorton/ DK Images; **p. 109:** Andersen Ross/Getty Images.

CHAPTER 5   **p. 110:** Pearson; **p. 111:** Arnaud Chicurel/Hemis/Corbis; **p. 111:** Joson /Corbis; **p. 112:** Zhao Kang/Xinhua/Photoshot/Newscom; **p. 113 (bl):** JoeFox/ Alamy; **(tl):** National Geographic Image Collection / Alamy; **(br):** Songquan Deng/ Alamy; **(cr):** Frans Lemmens / SuperStock; **p. 114:** National Geographic Image Collection / Alamy; **p. 115:** Paparazzi by Appointment / Alamy; **p. 116 (tr):** David Edsam/Alamy; **(bl):** Science and Society / SuperStock; **p. 119:** Frans Lemmens / SuperStock; **p. 120:** Paul Carstairs/Alamy; **p. 122:** Jim West / Alamy; **p. 125 (tr):** Stuart Bay/Alamy; **(c):** Neil Emmerson/Robert Harding World Imagery; **p. 126:** Russell Gordon/Danita Delimont/Alamy; **p. 128:** Songquan Deng/Alamy; **p. 130:** ANNA ZIEMINSKI/AFP/Newscom; **p. 132:** JoeFox/Alamy; **p. 135:** AF archive / Alamy; **p. 136:** ZUMA Wire Service / Alamy; **p. 137:** Paparazzi by Appointment / Alamy; **p. 138 (tr):** Paul Carstairs/Alamy; **(cr):** Russell Gordon/Danita Delimont/Alamy; **(br):** Songquan Deng/Alamy; **p. 139:** ZUMA Wire Service / Alamy.

CHAPTER 6   **p. 140:** Pearson; **p. 141:** BEN STANSALL/AFP/Getty Images; **p. 142:** AP Photo; **p. 143 (tl):** Robert Munro/Alamy; **(cr):** MISHELLA/Shutterstock; **(bl):** SeanPavonePhoto/Shutterstock; **p. 144:** Robert Munro/Alamy; **p. 145:** Ali Bitar/Upi / Landov; **p. 146:** Kristoffer Tirpplaar / Pool/Epa/Newscom; **p. 147:** ZUMA Wire Service / Alamy; **p. 149 (bl):** David J. Green—lifestyle themes/Alamy; **(br):** Jack Sullivan / Alamy; **(tc):** Roger Viollet/Photoshot; **p. 150:** MISHELLA/Shutterstock; **p. 151:** AP Photo/J. Scott Applewhite; **p. 153:** Library of Congress Prints and Photographs Division [LC-DIG-ppmsca-03128]; **p. 154:** SeanPavonePhoto/Shutterstock; **p. 155 (tr):** ALEXIS C. GLENN/ UPI/Newscom; **p. 157 (tl):** Andrea Renault/ZUMAPRESS/Newscom; **p. 162 (tr):** Cheryl Ann Quigley / Alamy; **p. 163:** Bob Daemmrich/Alamy; **p. 168 (cr):** Ali Bitar/Upi /Landov; **(br):** Library of Congress Prints and Photographs Division [LC-DIG-ppmsca-03128]; **p. 169:** ALEXIS C. GLENN/UPI/Newscom.

CHAPTER 7   **p. 170:** Pearson; **p. 171:** ZUMA Wire Service/Alamy; **p. 173 (tl):** Alex Segre/Alamy; **(bl):** Randy Duchaine/Alamy; **(cr):** ZUMA Press, Inc. / Alamy; **(br):** Bloomberg/Getty Images; **(cl):** Jonathan Nourok/PhotoEdit; **p. 174:** Alex Segre/Alamy; **p. 175:** AP Photo/Brad Horn; **p. 177:** MARKA /Alamy; **p. 178:** ZUMA Press, Inc. / Alamy; **p. 179:** Rachel Epstein/PhotoEdit; **p. 181:** Andy Sacks/Getty Images; **p. 182:** Jonathan Nourok/PhotoEdit; **p. 184:** gyn9037/Shutterstock; **p. 185:** Bloomberg/Getty Images; **p. 187:** Allan Cash Picture Library / Alamy; **p. 189 (cr):** HUFTON + CROW/ View Pictures/Age Fotostock; **(cl):** Andy Sacks/Stone/Getty Images; **(tr):** Tim Boyle/ Getty Images; **p. 190:** Randy Duchaine/Alamy; **p. 191:** Michael Newman/PhotoEdit; **p. 195 (cr):** AP Photo/Brad Horn; **(br):** Rachel Epstein/PhotoEdit; **p. 196 (br):** Allan Cash Picture Library / Alamy; **(tr):** gyn9037/Shutterstock; **p. 197:** Michael Newman/PhotoEdit.

CHAPTER 8   **p. 198:** Pearson; **p. 199:** MARCELO SAYAO/epa/Corbis; **p. 201 (tl):** Ton Koene/Age Fotostock; **(cl):** Bob Pardue—Georgia / Alamy; **(br):** Eric Nathan / Alamy; **(bl):** s.s. / Alamy; **(cr):** Stock Connection Blue / Alamy; **p. 202:** Ton Koene/ Age Fotostock; **p. 205:** Joe Munroe/Archive Photos/Getty Images; **p. 206:** Stock Connection Blue / Alamy; **p. 207:** Stock Connection Blue / Alamy; **p. 209 (br):** David McNew/Getty Images; **(tr):** Ron Janoski; **p. 210:** Bob Pardue - Georgia / Alamy; **p. 211:** Lee Foster/Alamy; **p. 212 (cr):** ZUMA Wire Service/Alamy; **(tr):** Cultura/Frank and Helena/Getty Images; **p. 214 (r):** AP Photo/Carlos Osori , FILE; **(l):** AP Photo/Mark Duncan; **p. 215 (t):** Eric Nathan / Alamy; **(br):** Pictorial Press Ltd/Alamy; **p. 216:** chicagoview / Alamy; **p. 220 (t):** s.s. / Alamy; **p. 223:** Yadid Levy / Alamy; **p. 224:** Eddie Gerald / Alamy; **p. 225 (br):** Stock Connection Blue / Alamy; **(cr):** Joe Munroe/Archive Photos/Getty Images; **p. 226 (br):** Pictorial Press Ltd/Alamy; **(tr):** Cultura/Frank and Helena/Getty Images; **p. 227:** Yadid Levy / Alamy.

CHAPTER 9   **p. 228:** Pearson; **p. 229:** DPA/ZUMApress.com; **p. 230:** MATTRAVEL/ Alamy; **p. 231 (br):** Nathan Benn/Alamy; **(cr):** Tom Zuback / Alamy; **(cl):** Cathy

Melloan/PhotoEdit; **(tl):** Dhoxax/Shutterstock; **p. 232:** Dhoxax/Shutterstock; **p. 239:** Fancy Collection / SuperStock; **p. 240:** Tom Zuback / Alamy; **p. 241 (r):** World History Archive/Alamy; **(l):** Joe Raedle/Getty Images; **p. 244:** YM YIK/EPA/Newscom; **p. 248:** Cathy Melloan/PhotoEdit; **p. 249:** Everett Collection Inc / Alamy; **p. 252:** Nathan Benn/ Alamy; **p. 257:** Fancy Collection / SuperStock; **p. 258 (c):** YM YIK/EPA/Newscom; **(br):** Cathy Melloan/PhotoEdit; **p. 259:** Nathan Benn/Alamy.

CHAPTER 10 **p. 260:** Pearson; **p. 261:** Alix Minde/PhotoAlto/Age Fotostock; **p. 262:** photothek / ullstein bild / The Image Works; **p. 263 (cr):** Malcolm Fairman / Alamy; **(bl):** Peter Casolino/Alamy; **(cl):** AP Photo/Heather Coit; **(tl):** Gino Santa Maria/ Fotolia LLC; **(br):** Chuck Fishman / Getty Images; **p. 264:** Gino Santa Maria/Fotolia LLC; **p. 265:** OBAMA PRESS OFFICE/New/Newscom; **p. 266:** Julien McRoberts Danita Delimont Photography/Newscom; **p. 267:** Malcolm Fairman / Alamy; **p. 269:** Philip Date/Shutterstock; **p. 270:** Homer W Sykes / Alamy; **p. 271:** AP Photo/Heather Coit; **p. 273 (r):** Dimj/Shutterstock.com; **(l):** Kim Ruoff/Shutterstock; **p. 275:** AP Photo/Rogelio V. Solis; **p. 276:** Chuck Fishman / Getty Images; **p. 279:** Jim West / Alamy; **p. 283:** Jim West/Age Fotostock; **p. 284:** Peter Casolino/Alamy; **p. 285:** Daily Mail/Rex / Alamy; **p. 287:** Nik Taylor / Alamy; **p. 289 (br):** Homer W Sykes / Alamy; **(cr):** OBAMA PRESS OFFICE/New/Newscom; **p. 290 (br):** Jim West / Alamy; **(cr):** AP Photo/Heather Coit; **p. 291:** Nik Taylor / Alamy.

CHAPTER 11 **p. 292:** Pearson; **p. 293:** I love images/Alamy; **p. 293:** DK Images; **p. 294 (cr):** Enigma / Alamy; **(tl):** Marmaduke St. John / Alamy; **(br):** Old Visuals/ Glow Images; **(bl):** James Atoa/Everett Collection/Newscom; **p. 295:** Marmaduke St. John / Alamy; **p. 296:** David C Poole/Robert Harding World Imagery; **p. 297:** Radius Images/Getty Images; **p. 299:** Enigma / Alamy; **p. 301:** prism68/Shutterstock; **p. 303:** Kzenon/Shutterstock; **p. 304:** Parshotam/Gopal, PacificCoastNews/Newscom; **p. 305 (bl):** Chris Hammond Photography/Alamy; **(t):** James Atoa/Everett Collection/ Newscom; **p. 306 (b):** Janine Wiedel Photolibrary / Alamy; **(cl):** Jon Hicks/Alamy; **(cr):** Paul Gapper/Alamy; **p. 307:** Hemis/Alamy; **p. 309:** AP Photo/Natacha Pisarenko; **p. 310:** TERRY SCHMITT/UPI/Newscom; **p. 311:** Queerstock, Inc. / Alamy; **p. 312:** Old Visuals/Glow Images; **p. 313:** Gianni Muratore / Alamy; **p. 316 (cr):** David C Poole/Robert Harding World Imagery; **(br):** prism68/Shutterstock; **p. 317 (cr):** Chris Hammond Photography/Alamy; (br): Gianni Muratore / Alamy.

CHAPTER 12 **p. 318:** Pearson; **p. 319:** Jim West/Alamy; **p. 321 (br):** Bob Daemmrich/ Alamy; **(cl):** Inge Johnsson / Alamy; **(cr):** AP Photo/Nick Ut; **p. 322:** Library of Congress Prints and Photographs Division/LC-USZ62-20621; **p. 324:** Popperfoto/ Getty Images; **p. 325:** Everett Collection Inc / Alamy; **p. 327 (bl):** David R. Frazier Photolibrary, Inc. / Alamy; **(c):** AP Photo/Leslie Hoffman; **(br):** Tom Pennington/Fort Worth Star-Telegram/MCT via Getty Images; **p. 330:** AP Photo; **p. 317:** AP Photo/ Nick Ut; **p. 333:** Jeff Greenberg / The Image Works; **p. 334:** Inge Johnsson / Alamy; **p. 337:** Jim West/Alamy; **p. 338:** Bob Daemmrich/Alamy; **p. 340:** Pictorial Parade/ Getty Images; **p. 342:** David R. Frazier Photolibrary, Inc./Alamy; **p. 345:** Popperfoto/ Getty Images; **p. 346 (br):** Jim West/Alamy; **(cr):** Jeff Greenberg / The Image Works; **p. 347:** David R. Frazier Photolibrary, Inc./Alamy.

CHAPTER 13 **p. 348:** Kathleen Gerson; **p. 349:** Blend Images / Alamy; **p. 349:** Blue Lantern Studio/Corbis; **p. 350:** JuanSharma/Bruja, PacificCoastNews/Newscom; **p. 351 (cl):** Big Cheese Photo LLC/Alamy; **(b):** Jon Arnold Images Ltd / Alamy; **(br):** DK Images; **(bl):** Deborah Davis/PhotoEdit; **(cr):** Wolfgang Spunbarg / PhotoEdit; **(tl):** StockHouse/Shutterstock; **p. 352:** StockHouse/Shutterstock; **p. 353:** rSnapshotPhotos/ Shutterstock; **p. 354:** Ariel Skelley/Blend Images / Alamy; **p. 355:** Wolfgang Spunbarg / PhotoEdit; **p. 357:** imagebroker.net / SuperStock; **p. 358:** Big Cheese Photo LLC/ Alamy; **p. 359:** Glow Images, Inc/Getty Images; **p. 363:** Mary Steinbacher / PhotoEdit; **p. 364:** DK Images; **p. 367:** keith morris / Alamy; **p. 368:** Deborah Davis/PhotoEdit; **p. 369:** Exactostock/SuperStock; **p. 370:** Jon Arnold Images Ltd / Alamy; **p. 372 (cl):** Design Pics Inc. / Alamy; **(cr):** Tetra Images / Alamy; **(bl):** Richard Kalvar/Magnum Photos; **(tc):** Haruyoshi Yamaguchi/REUTERS; **p. 373:** OLIVIER HOSLET/ EPA/Newscom; **p. 375 (cr):** rSnapshotPhotos/Shutterstock; **(br):** imagebroker.net / SuperStock; **p. 376 (br):** keith morris / Alamy; **(cr):** Glow Images, Inc/Getty Images; **p. 377 (cr):** OLIVIER HOSLET/EPA/Newscom; **(tr):** Exactostock/SuperStock.

CHAPTER 14 **p. 378:** Pearson; **p. 379:** Dan Barba/SCPhotos / Alamy; **p. 380 (l):** Andrew Aitchison / Alamy; **(r):** Pascal Deloche/GODONG/picture-alliance/Godong/ Newscom; **p. 381 (cr):** FOTOSEARCH RM/Age Fotostock; **(c):** Robert Harding Picture Library Ltd/Alamy; **(b):** Rostislav Glinsky/Fotolia LLC; **(tl):** Sonu Mehta/Hindustan Times/Getty Images; **(br):** Michel SETBOUN/PhotoNonStop/Glow Images; **p. 382:** Sonu Mehta/Hindustan Times/Getty Images; **p. 383:** Grant Rooney / Alamy; **p. 384:** AP Photo/ Jalil BOUNHAR; **p. 389 (br):** PhotoEdit / Alamy; **(bl):** AP Photo/John Bazemore; **p. 390:** Paul Harris, BWP Media/atticusimages/Newscom; **p. 391 (cl):** David Grossman/Alamy; **(cr):** Angie Knost,llc/Alamy; **(bl):** Brian Harris / Alamy; **(cr):** Greg Ashman/Icon SMI CCJ/Greg Ashman/Icon SMI/Newscom; **p. 392:** FOTOSEARCH RM/Age Fotostock; **p. 393:** AP Photo/Richard Burkhart/The Savannah Morning News; **p. 395:** brianindia/Alamy; **p. 397:** AP Photo/John-Marshall Mantel; **p. 398:** Robert Harding Picture Library Ltd/Alamy; **p. 401:** Michel SETBOUN/PhotoNonStop/Glow Images; **p. 402:** Sunil Malhotra/REUTERS; **p. 403:** Rostislav Glinsky/Fotolia LLC; **p. 405:** Jim West/Alamy; **p. 409 (cr):** Grant Rooney / Alamy; **p. 410 (cr):** Robert Harding Picture Library Ltd/Alamy; **(tr):** AP Photo/Richard Burkhart/The Savannah Morning News; **(br):** Sunil Malhotra/REUTERS; **p. 411:** Jim West/Alamy.

CHAPTER 15 **p. 412:** Pearson; **p. 413:** RICHARD LEE KRT/Newscom; **p. 415 (bl):** Bob Daemmrich/Alamy; **(tr):** Rainier Ehrhardt/The Augusta Chronicle/ZUMA Wire Service/Alamy; **(tl):** Jeff Dunn/Photolibrary/Getty Images; **(br):** Sophia Paris/Handout/ UN Photo/REUTERS; **(cl):** Radius/SuperStock; **p. 416:** Jeff Dunn/Photolibrary/ Getty Images; **p. 417:** Robert Galbraith/REUTERS; **p. 418:** Rainier Ehrhardt/The Augusta Chronicle/ZUMA Wire Service/Alamy; **p. 421:** Jeff Greenberg / Alamy; **p. 422:** Radius/SuperStock; **p. 427:** PETER FOLEY/EPA/Newscom; **p. 429:** Sophia Paris/Handout/UN Photo/REUTERS; **p. 430 (br):** ZUMA Wire Service/Alamy; **(cl):** Michael Sofronski/The Image Works; **p. 431:** Steve Gorton/DK Images; **p. 433:** David Grossman/Alamy; **p. 434:** Bob Daemmrich/Alamy; **p. 435:** Lisa F. Young / Alamy; **p. 436:** ZUMA Press, Inc. / Alamy; **p. 439 (br):** Jeff Greenberg / Alamy; **(tr):** Robert Galbraith/REUTERS; **p. 440 (br):** Steve Gorton/DK Images; **(tr):** PETER FOLEY/ EPA/Newscom; **p. 441:** Lisa F. Young / Alamy.

CHAPTER 16 **p. 442:** Pearson; **p. 443:** ZUMA Press/Newscom; **p. 444:** Jason M. Grow/KRT/Newscom; **p. 445 (b):** Jim Pickerell/Stock Connection Blue/Alamy; **(cl):** SERGEY DOLZHENKO/EPA/Newscom; **(cr):** Will Rose/Starstock/Photoshot/ Newscom; **(t):** Marko Djurica/REUTERS; **p. 446:** Marko Djurica/REUTERS; **p. 447:** Terry Harris/Alamy; **p. 450:** Will Rose/Starstock/Photoshot/Newscom; **p. 451:** Everett Collection Inc / Alamy; **p. 452:** Bettmann/CORBIS; **p. 454:** Jason Merritt/ WireImage/Getty Images; **p. 455:** SERGEY DOLZHENKO/EPA/Newscom; **p. 458:** Kevin Lamarque/REUTERS; **p. 460:** akg-images/Newscom; **p. 461 (bl):** Beth Dixson / Alamy; **(br):**AP Photo/Yola Monakhov; **p. 462 (cl):** AP Photo; **(bc):** AP Photo; **(cr):** AP Photo/Tony Gutierrez; **p. 464:** Jim Pickerell/Stock Connection Blue/Alamy; **p. 469:** Pamela Price/ZUMA Press/Newscom; **p. 471:** Stacy Walsh Rosenstock/Alamy; **p. 472 (br):** Everett Collection Inc / Alamy; **(tr):** Marko Djurica/REUTERS; **p. 473 (br):** Pamela Price/ZUMA Press/Newscom; **(tr):** Kevin Lamarque/REUTERS.

CHAPTER 17 **p. 474:** Pearson; **p. 475:** Mario Tama/Getty Images News/Getty Images; **p. 476 (cl):** Richard Wareham Fotografie/Alamy; **(tl):** Vespasian / Alamy; **(cr):** akg-images/Newscom; **(br):** Barry Iverson Photography/Barry Iverson/Newscom; **p. 477:** Vespasian / Alamy; **p. 478:** Jim West/Age Fotostock; **p. 479:** JOHN G. MABANGLO/AFP/Newscom; **p. 480:** akg-images/Newscom; **p. 481:** Fred W. McDarrah/Premium Archive /Getty Images; **p. 482:** Richard Corkery/NY Daily News Archive/Getty Images; **p. 486:** ASHRAF AMRA / Demotix/Demotix/Corbis; **p. 487:** Richard Wareham Fotografie/Alamy; **p. 489:** Jim West/PhotoEdit; **p. 490:** Tom Williams/Roll Call/Getty Images; **p. 491 (bc):** Jim West / Alamy; **(cr):** Dennis Van Tine/LFI/Photoshot/Newscom; **(cl):** Rapport Press/Newscom; **p. 493:** AP Photo/ Bill Waugh; **p. 496:** Barry Iverson Photography/Barry Iverson/Newscom; **p. 497:** ZUMA Press, Inc/Alamy; **p. 499:** oubeir Souissi/Reuters/Landov; **p. 501:** Image Asset Management Ltd/Superstock; **p. 504 (cr):** Jim West/Age Fotostock; **(br):** Fred W. McDarrah/Premium Archive /Getty Images; **p. 505 (br):** ZUMA Press, Inc/Alamy; **(tr):** Jim West/PhotoEdit.

CHAPTER 18 **p. 506:** Pearson; **p. 507:** Gabriel Bouys/AFP/Getty Images/Newscom; **p. 508:** Accent Alaska.com/Alamy; **p. 509 (t):** Luciano Leon / Alamy; **(b):** esbobeldijk/ Shutterstock; **(cl):** Philip Lange/Shutterstock; **(cr):** Tyler Olson /Shutterstock; **p. 510:** Luciano Leon / Alamy; **p. 511:** Deco / Alamy; **p. 512:** DK Images; **p. 513:** Dennis Donohue / Fotolia LLC; **p. 514:** Tyler Olson /Shutterstock; **p. 516:** HO/AFP/ Getty Images/Newscom; **p. 517:** US Coast Guard Photo / Alamy; **p. 519:** Huguette Roe /Shutterstock; **p. 521:** John Nordell / The Image Works; **p. 522:** Philip Lange/ Shutterstock; **p. 523:** Library of Congress Prints and Photographs Division [LC-USZC4-4698]; **p. 524:** AP Photo; **p. 526:** DAVID J. PHILLIP/AFP/Getty Images/ Newscom; **p. 527:** esbobeldijk/Shutterstock; **p. 530 (c):** Andrew Rubtsov / Alamy; **(r):** Jim West / Alamy; **(l):** Roberto Jayme/REUTERS; **p. 531:** Jim West / PhotoEdit; **p. 532:** Robert Stainforth / Alamy; **p. 534 (tr):** Deco / Alamy; **(br):** HO/AFP/Getty Images/Newscom; **p. 535 (tr):** Library of Congress Prints and Photographs Division [LC-USZC4-4698]; **(br):** Jim West / PhotoEdit.

CHAPTER 19 **p. 536:** Pearson; **p. 537:** Antony Ratcliffe / Alamy; **p. 538:** Pearson; **p. 539 (tl):** frans lemmens/Alamy; **(cl):** Reimar 9/Alamy; **(br):** ANAT GIVON/AP Images; **(cr):** Gallo Images/ Getty Images News/ Getty Images; **p. 540:** frans lemmens/ Alamy; **p. 542:** SAYYID AZIM/AFP/Getty Images; **p. 545:** Shoko Yukitake/Taxi/Getty Images; **p. 546:** Gallo Images/ Getty Images News/ Getty Images; **p. 549:** Marmaduke St. John / Alamy; **p. 550:** Jerry Wolford/Polaris/Newscom; **p. 551:** Reimar 9/Alamy; **p. 552:** Dennis MacDonald/Alamy; **p. 555:** Gaetano Images Inc/Alamy; **p. 556 (cr):** Andrew Alvrez/AFP/Getty Images; **(tl):** Natasha Burley/Stringer/AFP/Getty Images; (bl): Glow Images; **p. 558:** ANAT GIVON/AP Images; **p. 559:** Dennis MacDonald/ Alamy; **p. 563 (br):** Dennis MacDonald/Alamy; **(cr):** Dennis MacDonald/Alamy.

CHAPTER 20 **p. 564:** Pearson; **p. 565:** Bill Bachmann / Alamy; **p. 566 (tl):** Thomas Marchessault / Alamy; **(cr):** Arctic-Images/ The Image Bank/Getty Images; **(cl):** ERIK DE CASTRO/Reuters /Landov; **(br):** Patrick Olear / PhotoEdit; **p. 567:** Thomas Marchessault / Alamy; **p. 568:** Courtesy: Everett Col/Age Fotostock; **p. 571:** Arctic-Images/ The Image Bank/Getty Images; **p. 573:** Superstock/Glow Images; **p. 575:** ERIK DE CASTRO/ Reuters /Landov; **p. 576:** AP Photo/Guillermo Arias; **p. 577:** Lou Linwei/Alamy; **p. 578:** Keith Czechanski/Zuma Press/Newscom; **p. 579 (t):** Patrick Olear / PhotoEdit; **p. 580 (l):** AF archive/Alamy; **(r):** imagebroker.net / SuperStock; **p. 581 (br):** AFP/Getty Images; **p. 582:** Jennifer Szymaszek/REUTERS; **p. 584:** Superstock/Glow Images; **p. 585 (tr):** AP Photo/Guillermo Arias; (br): AFP/Getty Images.

INDEX

Theories and theorists featured in *The Sociology Project* are highlighted in blue in the index.

A

AARP, 129
Abbott, Andrew, 17
Abercrombie and Fitch, 126
Abma, J. C., 313
Abolitionist movement, 479
Aboriginal Australians, 271, 511
Abortion, 48, 121
Abramowitz, Michael, 582
Absolute poverty, 253, 254–255
Abu Ghraib scandal, 462, 463
Academic departments, 22
Acceptance, social movements and, 493
Access, 40
Access to education, 429, 431
Accommodation, cultural, 121
Accomplishment of natural growth, 128
Achievement gap, 426
Achievement testing, 432–433
Acid rain, 521
Acock, Alan C., 365
Actors' Equity Association, 488
ADA (Americans with Disabilities Act), 184–185
Adams, John, 334, 471
Adams, Walter, 424
Addams, Jane, 215
Adelson, Sheldon, 234
Adler, Nancy E., 558
Adorno, Theodor, 129–130
Adult, becoming, 366–367
Adulthood commitments, changes in, 358–363
Advance directives, 550
Advance Placement (AP) courses, 433
Advertising, 135
Affirmative action, 283, 489
Afghanistan, 429, 461
AFL-CIO (American Federation of Labor-Congress of Industrial Organizations), 488
Africa, 331, 407, 582
African Americans. *See also* Race and ethnicity; Racism
  births outside marriage, 314–315
  black churches, 393–394, 483
  black isolation in U.S. metro areas, 218
  in Chicago, 208
  criminal justice supervision, 280
  Du Bois on, 103
  education and, 279–280, 300, 426
  employment and unemployment, 279
  family inequality and, 370
  Great Migration, 93, 203, 217
  growth coalitions and, 209
  health and, 280–281, 560–561
  ideas about race and, 271
  income and wealth, 276–277, 278

  mortgage lending crisis, 283
  political participation and representation, 281
  poverty and, 219, 253
  racial hierarchy, 105
  redlining, 205–206
  residential segregation, 279–280, 394
  as share of U.S. population, 284, 286
  single-parent families, 368
  suburbs and, 206
  suicide rates, 561
  urban ghettos, 216–217
  urban renewal and, 216
  voting rights, 159
  war on drugs, 454
African American Studies, 21
Age, religion and, 398–401
Agency, 103
Agenda setting, 146–147, 160–163
Agenda-setting organizations, 163
Age pyramids, 544, 547, 548
Agility and adaptability, 438
Aging population. *See also* Population
  Baby Boomers, 288, 543, 547
  death and dying around the world, 550
  epidemiological transition, 546–547
  health in, 548–550
  implications of, 546–550
  population dynamics, 548
Agricultural employment, 93
Agricultural revolution, 511
Agriculture, sustainable, 530
Agyei, Y., 307
Ahrons, Constance, 365
AI (artificial intelligence), 16
AIDS epidemic, 454, 547
AIG (American International Group), 155
Air pollution, 521–522
Aka tribe, 296
Akerlof, George A., 315
Akron, Ohio, 93
Alabama, 557
Aladura, 386
Alaska, 506, 508
Alaska Natives, 284, 286, 561
Al-Assad, Bashar, 145
Alba, Richard, 288
Albrecht, Karl, 234
Albright, Joseph, 318
Albright, Madeline, 318, 320
Alcohol consumption, 451, 453. *See also* Prohibition
Alesina, Alberto, 186
Alexander, Karl L., 424, 434
Alexander, Michelle, 470
Algeria, 497
Alinsky, Saul, 489
Allan, Emilie, 300
Allen, Heidi, 421
Allende, Salvador, 502

Allison, Paul, 301, 303
Allocation theory, 419–420, 421
Almodóvar, Pedro, 126
Al Qaeda, 461
Al Scripps Institute of Oceanography, 515
Alter-globalization movement, 479
Alternative forms of education, 430
Alternative workplaces, 189
Amato, Paul R., 365
Amazon rainforest, 513–514
Ambani, Mukesh, 234
Amenta, Edwin, 488
American Anthropological Association, 19
American Civil Liberties Organization, 488
American Dream, 248
American Economics Association, 19
American Enterprise Institute, 163
American exceptionalism, 404–405, 492
American families, contemporary, 355–358
American Federation of Labor-Congress of Industrial Organizations (AFL-CIO), 488
American International Group (AIG), 155
American Jewish Committee, 488
American Jewish Congress, 488
American Legion, 488
American Lung Association, 561
American Political Science Association, 19
American Psychological Association, 19
American Society for the Prevention of Cruelty to Animals, 488
American Sociological Association, 19, 22
American Sociological Association Code of Ethics, 35
Americans with Disabilities Act (ADA), 184–185
American Time Use Survey, 73
Amish, 394
Amont, Jonathan, 397
Anderson, Benedict, 123
Anderson, Elijah, 218
Anderson, James Craig, 275
Anglican Church, 389, 396
Angola, 497
Animal extinctions, 516, 518, 519
Animal protection movement, 482
Animism, 388
Anthropocentrism, 513
Anthropology, 510
Antiabortion movement, 479, 486, 494, 495
Antidiscrimination policies, 373
Anti-immigrant tensions, 329
Antipoverty policy and programs, 154, 158–160, 252

Anti-Saloon League, 488
Antitoxics movement, 525
AP (Advance Placement) courses, 433
Apartheid, 94, 96, 272
Appadurai, Arjun, 119, 123
Applause, 68–69
Apple Computers, 179–180, 244–245, 417, 435, 577
Aquifers, 518
Arab Spring
  Internet activism and, 135–136
  Morocco, 500
  political environments and, 501
  as political revolutions, 496
  revolutionary situations, 498–499
  social media and, 484
  strategies and tactics, 489
  use of force and, 145
Arango, Joaquin, 333
Arato, Andrew, 478
Arbitrary decisions in labeling deviance and crime, 456
Archival research, 41, 449
Arctic National Wildlife Refuge, 516
Arctic Sea, 515
Argentina, 251, 310, 527
Argyle, Michael, 398, 399
Arias, Elizabeth, 560
Arkansas, 557
Armstrong, Elizabeth A., 309, 314
Arnault, Bernard, 234
Arthur Andersen accounting firm, 457
Artificial intelligence (AI), 16
Arum, Richard, 2, 9, 170, 228, 417, 432
Asch, Solomon, 77–78
Asian Americans
  education and, 279–280
  family inequality and, 370
  health and healthcare coverage, 281
  income and wealth, 277
  in rural areas, 206
  as share of U.S. population, 284, 286
  single-parent families, 368
  suicide rates, 561
Assembly lines, 187–188, 189
Assets, 90
Assimilation, 268
Assimilation, cultural, 207, 268
Assimilation process
  ethnic enclaves, 337–338
  measures of, 334–335
  recent research on, 335–337
Associated Press, 463
Assumptions, 31–32
Aswan Dam, 518–519
Asylum status, 325
Atari, 417
Atkinson, Max, 68–69
Atlanta, 110, 218
Auditing industry, 177
Audley, John J., 582